Codification Series of
Extraterritorial
Notarization Law

域外公证法
汇编系列

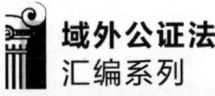

域外公证法汇编系列

厦门大学现代法律服务研究中心课题成果

美洲公证法汇编

COMPENDIUM OF
NOTARIZATION LAWS
IN THE AMERICAS

苏国强　汤庆发　刘志云 / 编

厦门大学出版社　国家一级出版社
XIAMEN UNIVERSITY PRESS　全国百佳图书出版单位

图书在版编目(CIP)数据

美洲公证法汇编/苏国强,汤庆发,刘志云编. —厦门:厦门大学出版社,2018.12
(域外公证法汇编系列)
ISBN 978-7-5615-6955-9

Ⅰ.①美… Ⅱ.①苏…②汤…③刘… Ⅲ.①公证法—汇编—美洲 Ⅳ.①D970.6

中国版本图书馆 CIP 数据核字(2018)第 217201 号

出版人	郑文礼
责任编辑	李 宁
装帧设计	李夏凌
技术编辑	许克华

出版发行	厦门大学出版社
社 址	厦门市软件园二期望海路 39 号
邮政编码	361008
总编办	0592-2182177 0592-2181406(传真)
营销中心	0592-2184458 0592-2181365
网 址	http://www.xmupress.com
邮 箱	xmupress@126.com
印 刷	厦门集大印刷厂

开本 787 mm×1 092 mm 1/16
印张 46.75
字数 1750 千字
版次 2018 年 12 月第 1 版
印次 2018 年 12 月第 1 次印刷
定价 358.00 元

本书如有印装质量问题请直接寄承印厂调换

厦门大学出版社
微信二维码

厦门大学出版社
微博二维码

苏国强

一级公证员,现任福建省厦门市鹭江公证处党总支书记、主任,厦门大学现代法律服务研究中心理事会理事。主要社会职务有:福建省人大代表、厦门市人大代表、厦门市人大内务司法委员会委员、厦门市政府立法咨询专家、中国公证协会常务理事、中国公证协会信息化建设委员会主任委员、厦门市公证协会会长、厦门市总商会副会长、厦门仲裁委员会仲裁员。发表专业论文数十篇,共同主编《域外公证法汇编》《欧洲公证法汇编》《公证信息化:理论前沿与技术规范》《"大家"之言——厦门市鹭江公证处成立十五周年名人传经讲座实录》《市场经济与公证立法》等。先后获得"全国优秀公证员""福建省十佳公证员""福建省公证行业文明公证员""厦门市优秀社会主义事业建设者""厦门市第四批、第五批、第九批拔尖人才""厦门市直机关优秀共产党员""2011—2015年厦门市法治宣传教育先进个人""厦门市非公企业和社会组织党建领军人才"等荣誉。

汤庆发

一级公证员,现任福建省厦门市鹭江公证处党总支副书记、执行主任,厦门大学现代法律服务研究中心理事会理事。主要社会职务有:中国公证协会业务指导委员会副主任委员、福建省公证协会业务指导委员会主任、福建省公证协会公证理论研究委员会委员、厦门仲裁委员会仲裁员。发表《商品房预售资金监管实验的报告》《论公证程序的价值》《公证审查程序的证据规则》《商事财产在继承公证实务中的认定》

《〈公证法〉第六条"公证机构不以营利为目的"探析》等专业论文十余篇；共同主编《域外公证法汇编》《欧洲公证法汇编》《"大家"之言——厦门市鹭江公证处成立十五周年名人传经讲座实录》等。先后获得"全国优秀公证员""厦门市劳动模范""厦门市创建全国文明城市先进个人""厦门市精神文明建设积极分子""厦门市司法行政系统先进工作者""厦门市直机关创先争优活动优秀党务工作者""厦门市直机关优秀共产党员"等荣誉。

刘志云

法学博士，现为两岸关系和平发展协同创新中心／厦门大学法学院教授、博士生导师，厦门大学现代法律服务研究中心执行主任，全国青联委员。至今已在《中国社会科学》等国内外杂志以中英文发表法学论文百余篇，出版个人专著 5 部、主著 4 部、合著／译著 10 余部。先后入选中组部"万人计划——首批青年拔尖人才支持计划""教育部新世纪优秀人才支持计划"。先后被评为"福建省优秀青年社会科学专家""福建省优秀青年法学人才""福建省法学英才"。

前言

随着社会经济、互联网技术,尤其是互联网金融的迅猛发展,公证业务,尤其是电子公证将有着广泛的应用空间。但对于这一新生事物,需要在法律、政策以及技术等问题上实现一系列的突破,并进行长期跟踪研究。由此,厦门大学、福建省厦门市鹭江公证处与法信公证云(厦门)科技有限公司在2014年6月达成共同发起成立"厦门大学公证法律与信息化研究中心"(以下简称"研究中心")的共识。研究中心在2014年7月正式成立。研究中心是致力于公证法以及相关法律政策、电子公证以及信息化等相关领域的跨学科研究基地。2018年11月,为了更好地适应全面依法治国、深化司法改革的新要求,积极应对科技革命给法律服务行业带来的机遇和挑战,合作各方在总结实践经验的基础上,以更开阔的视野、更高的格局、面向未来的目标,调整研究中心的定位和发展方向,并决定将其更名为"厦门大学现代法律服务研究中心"。研究中心将在今后工作中始终坚持"产学研"一体化发展道路,充分凝聚合作各方力量,广泛借助政府、社会、教学科研资源,建立多领域、多层次的良性互动合作机制,聚力打造"服务高校、服务行业、服务社会"三位一体的功能格局。

长期以来，国内对公证领域的研究较少，尤其是缺乏一部比较全面与最新的域外公证法律汇编，供理论研究者与实务人员参考。鉴于此，在福建省厦门市鹭江公证处、法信公证云（厦门）科技有限公司的支持下，研究中心理事会原理事长、现理事苏国强先生，理事汤庆发先生，以及研究中心执行主任刘志云教授牵头成立了专门的"域外公证法律汇编系列"项目组。在2015年，项目组组织翻译与编写了《域外公证法律汇编》一书，并于2015年10月由法律出版社出版。该书出版后，引起公证行业的轰动，填补了公证理论研究与实务部门的一个空缺。短短两个月，该书就脱销，产生良好的学术价值与社会意义。在此基础上，研究中心与项目组计划在未来的几年，投入更多的人力物力，将更专门化的《欧洲公证法汇编》《美洲公证法汇编》《亚洲公证法汇编》《非洲公证法汇编》等逐一编译出，为公证行业的发展贡献绵薄之力。呈现在读者面前的这本《美洲公证法汇编》正是研究中心与项目组在2017年主要投入与产出的成果之一。

苏国强、汤庆发、刘志云等承担了本书的策划、组织、分工、讨论、协调、统稿、校对等工作。其中，各个部分翻译或整理分工如下（排名不分先后）：厦门大学王素芬负责《美国示范公证法》《美国阿拉斯加州现行成文法》《美国肯塔基州经修订现行成文法》《美国宾夕法尼亚州公证人法》《美国新宾夕法尼亚州公证人法》《美国宾夕法尼亚州统一确认法》《美国宾夕法尼亚州公证人收费新旧对比》等翻译工作；厦门大学杨帆负责《美国加利福尼亚州公证行为法》《美国加利福尼亚州公证人收费条款》《美国加利福尼亚州公证人手册》《美国加利福尼亚州政府组织法》《美国路易斯安那州民法典》《美国路易斯安那州行政法典》《伯利兹公证人法》《开曼群岛公证人法》《圭亚那公证人法》《波多黎各公证人法》等翻译工作；厦门大学周晓桐负责《美国佛罗里达州公证法》《美国明尼苏达州公证人法》《加拿大萨斯喀彻温省公证人法》《牙买加公证人法》《牙买加公证费用法》《特立尼达和多巴哥公证人法》等翻译工作；厦门大学吴靖负责《美国伊利诺伊州公证法》（部分）、《美国内华达州公证人法》、《加拿大新斯科舍省公证人和公证专员法案》、《多米尼克公证人法》、《多米尼克公证人法修正案》、《格林达纳公证人法》等翻译工作；厦门大学余怡璇负责《美国伊利诺伊州公证法》（部分）、《美国路易斯安那州公证法》、《安提瓜和巴布达公证人法》、《巴哈马公证人法》、《巴巴多斯公证人法》、《加拿大育空地区公证法》等翻译工作；厦门大学杨皖宁负责《阿根廷公证人员专业执业法》《墨西哥联邦区公证法》《委内瑞拉公共登记和公证法》等翻译工作；厦门大学张璜负责《巴西公证费用条例》《巴西公证及登记法》等翻译工作；厦门大学任宇负责《加拿大大不列颠哥伦比亚省公证人法案》《加拿大安大略省公证人法案》等翻译工作；厦门大学栗胜男负责《智利法官组织法（节选公证部分）》《古巴国家公证法》《古巴国家公证法实施条例》《古巴公证离婚法》《哥伦比亚公证与登记机构管理章程》《巴拿马关于公证处的组织运作以及其他规定》等翻译整理工作；法国洛林大学欧洲大学中心王依晨负责《海地公证人考试规则》《海地公证人法》《海地公证人法修正案》等翻译工作。此外，厦门大学栗胜男在课题组成员的联系、协调以及本书格式编排、校对整理、统稿等方面做出重要贡献，厦门大学史欣媛、王潺亦参与了本书的校对工作。

  无疑，搜集、整理以及翻译域外公证法律制度是一项费时费力的工作。翻译域外公证法律，尤其是涉及很多小语种的公证法律制度，对项目组来说是一个巨大的挑战。其不仅要求项目组成员必须谙熟域外语言的文字表达，还要懂得与了解相关公证法律制度的立法语境，才能准确翻译出相关法律条文。尽管项目组成员是来自各个单位的公证法专家、学者，也熟悉相关域外语言，多数成员都有在国外留学或访学交流的背景，但我们深知，要真正做到精准翻译是极其困难的，也超出了我们的能力范围。鉴于此，本书采取了中外文对照的方式，方便读者随时对照中外文条款，尽量避免被本书的中文译本可能存在的错译或疏漏所误导。同时，本书对美洲公证法律制度的翻译纯粹是民间译本，并不是官方指定的标准译本，仅供公证领域理论研究者与实务人员参考使用。

此外，受人力、物力、智力的条件所限，本书所汇编的美洲公证法律还是有限的，只是选取了美洲的一些典型国家。在条件成熟时，我们将推出本书的增补本，将更多的乃至全部美洲公证法律制度汇编进去，以飨读者。

苏国强、汤庆发、刘志云
2017 年 11 月 11 日

目 录
CONTENTS

美 国
示范公证法 ... 1
阿拉斯加州现行成文法（韦斯特注解版）... 47
加利福尼亚州 ... 59
 加利福尼亚州公证行为法 ... 59
 加利福尼亚州公证人收费条款 ... 61
 加利福尼亚州公证人手册 ... 62
 加利福尼亚州政府组织法 ... 95
佛罗里达州公证法 ... 123
伊利诺伊州公证法 ... 138
肯塔基州经修订现行成文法（鲍德温注解版）... 157
路易斯安那州 ... 165
 路易斯安那州公证法 ... 165
 路易斯安那州民法典 ... 223
 路易斯安那州行政法典 ... 225
 明尼苏达州公证人法 ... 236
 内华达州公证人法 ... 244
宾夕法尼亚州 ... 287
 宾夕法尼亚州公证人法 ... 287
 新宾夕法尼亚州公证人法 ... 297
 宾夕法尼亚州统一确认法 ... 299
 宾夕法尼亚州公证人收费新旧对比 ... 304

安提瓜和巴布达
安提瓜和巴布达公证人法 ... 306

阿根廷
公证人员专业执业法 ... 309

巴哈马
巴哈马公证人法 ... 328

巴巴多斯
巴巴多斯公证人法 ... 331

伯利兹
伯利兹公证人法 ... 333

巴西
巴西公证费用条例 ... 336
巴西公证及登记法 ... 339

加拿大
大不列颠哥伦比亚省公证人法案 ... 351
新斯科舍省公证人和公证专员法案 ... 376
安大略省公证人法案 ... 379
萨斯喀彻温省公证人法 ... 383
育空地区公证法 ... 386

开曼群岛
开曼群岛公证人法 ... 390

智利
法官组织法（节选公证部分） ... 401

古巴
国家公证法 ... 426
国家公证法实施条例 ... 437
公证离婚法 ... 468

哥伦比亚
公证与登记机构管理章程 ... 474

多米尼克
多米尼克公证人法 ... 515
多米尼克公证人法修正案 ... 519

圭亚那
圭亚那公证人法 ... 520

格林达纳
格林达纳公证人法 ... 522

海地
- 海地公证人考试规则 ... 526
- 海地公证人法 ... 529
- 海地公证人法修正案 ... 539

牙买加
- 牙买加公证人法 ... 544
- 牙买加公证费用法 ... 547

墨西哥
- 联邦区公证法 ... 551

巴拿马
- 关于公证处的组织运作以及其他规定 ... 646

波多黎各
- 波多黎各公证人法 ... 675

特立尼达和多巴哥
- 特立尼达和多巴哥公证人法 ... 701

委内瑞拉
- 公共登记和公证法 ... 705

美 国

示范公证法

THE
MODEL NOTARY ACT
January 1, 2010

Published As A Public Service By The
National Notary Association A Non-Profit Educational Organization

示范公证法

2010 年 1 月 1 日

由国家公证协会（非营利性教育组织）作为公共服务发布

Article I
Implementation and Definitions

Chapter 1 - Implementation

§ 1-1 Short Title.

This [Act] may be cited as the [Model Notary Act of 2010].

§ 1-2 Purposes.

This [Act] shall be construed and applied to advance its underlying purposes, which are:

(1) to promote, serve, and protect the public interest;

(2) to simplify, clarify, and modernize the law governing notaries;

(3) to foster ethical conduct among notaries;

(4) to enhance cross-border recognition of notarial acts;

(5) to integrate procedures for traditional and electronic notarial acts; and

(6) to unify state notarial laws.

§ 1-3 Interpretation.

In this [Act], unless the context otherwise requires, words in the singular include the plural, and words in the plural include the singular.

第一编
实施与定义

第一章　实施

§1–1 简称

本法即指《2010 年示范公证法》。

§1–2 立法目的

本法可被解释和适用于促进以下目的：

（1）促进、服务和保障社会公共利益；

（2）提炼、阐明公证法，并促进公证法的现代化发展；

（3）提升公证人队伍的职业道德操守；

（4）加强公证行为的跨国承认；

（5）整合传统公证和电子公证行为之程序；以及

（6）统一各州公证立法。

§1–3 解释

在本法中，除非上下文另有要求，单数形式的名词包括复数，复数形式的名词包括单数。

§ 1-4 Prospective Effect.

The existing bond, seal, length of commission term, and liability of current notaries commissioned before the [Act's] effective date may not be invalidated, modified, or terminated by this [Act], but those notaries shall comply with this [Act] in performing notarizations and in applying for new commissions.

§ 1-5 Severability Clause.

If any provision of this [Act] or its application to any person or circumstance is held invalid, the invalidity does not affect other provisions or applications of this [Act] that can be given effect without the invalid provision or application, and to this end the provisions of this [Act] are severable.

§ 1-6 Repeals.

The following acts and parts of acts are hereby repealed:

[_____].

§ 1-7 Effective Date.

This [Act] shall take effect [_____].

Chapter 2 - Definitions Used in This [Act]

§ 2-1 Acknowledgment.

"Acknowledgment" means a notarial act in which an individual at a single time and place:

(1) appears in person before the notary and presents a document;

(2) is personally known to the notary or identified by the notary through satisfactory evidence; and

(3) indicates to the notary that the signature on the document was voluntarily affixed by the individual for the purposes stated within the document and, if applicable, that the individual had due authority to sign in a particular representative capacity.

§ 2-2 Affirmation.

"Affirmation" means a notarial act, or part thereof, which is legally equivalent to an oath and in which an individual at a single time and place:

(1) appears in person before the notary;

(2) is personally known to the notary or identified by the notary through satisfactory evidence; and

(3) makes a vow of truthfulness or fidelity on penalty of perjury, based on personal honor and without invoking a deity or using any form of the word "swear."

---

§1-4 将来之生效

在本法生效之前，现行有关保证金、印章、委任期限以及现任公证人责任的规定不会因本法而失效、被修改或终止，但公证人在进行公证行为以及申请新的任命时应当遵守本法规定。

§1-5 条款可分性

如果本法任一条款或其对某些人或情形的适用被判决为无效，该无效不影响本法中其他不依赖无效条款和条款适用而生效的条款或其适用，为此，本法条款可分开适用。

§1-6 废止

特此废止以下法律或法律之部分：[_____]

§1-7 生效日期

本法于 _____ 生效。

第二章 本法使用之定义

§2-1 确认

"确认"是指一项公证行为，当事人在某时间、某地点：

（1）亲自向公证人递交文件；

（2）为公证人所熟知或通过充分的证据向公证人证实身份；以及

（3）向公证人说明文件中的签名是其为文件所述之目的自愿签署，并且，如果适用，当事人有权以特定代理的身份签署文件。

§2-2 声明

"声明"是指一项公证行为或行为之部分，在法律效果上等同于宣誓。在声明中，当事人在某时间、某地点：

（1）亲临公证现场；

（2）为公证人所熟知或通过充分的证据向公证人证实身份；以及

（3）基于个人信誉，对真实性和准确性宣誓，而非向神起誓或使用"宣誓"一词的任何形式，否则，将被认定为作伪证而受到处罚。

§ 2-3 Commission.

"Commission" means both to empower to perform notarial acts and the written evidence of authority to perform those acts.

§ 2-4 Copy Certification.

"Copy certification" means a notarial act in which a notary:

(1) locates or is presented with a paper or an electronic document that is neither a vital record, a public record, nor a recorded document;

(2) compares the document with a second paper or electronic document that either is:

(i) presented to the notary;

(ii) located by the notary; or

(iii) copied from the first document by the notary; and

(3) confirms through a visual or electronic comparison that the second document is an identical, exact, and complete copy of the image or text and, if applicable, metadata of the first document.

§ 2-5 Credible Witness.

"Credible witness" means an honest, reliable, and impartial person who personally knows an individual appearing before a notary and takes an oath or affirmation from the notary to vouch for that individual's identity.

§ 2-6 Journal of Notarial Acts.

"Journal of notarial acts" and "journal" mean a book to create and preserve a chronological record of notarizations that is maintained by the notary public who performed the same notarizations.

§ 2-7 Jurat.

"Jurat" means a notarial act in which an individual at a single time and place:

(1) appears in person before the notary and presents a document;

(2) is personally known to the notary or identified by the notary through satisfactory evidence;

(3) signs the document in the presence of the notary; and

(4) takes an oath or affirmation from the notary vouching for the truthfulness or accuracy of the signed document.

§ 2-8 Notarial Act and Notarization.

"Notarial act" and "notarization" mean any official act of certification, attestation, or administration that a no-

§2-3 任命/委任状

"任命/委任状"意指授权从事公证行为及具备从事该行为的权限的书面证据。

§2-4 副本核实

"副本核实"是指下述公证行为，公证人：

（1）找到或接收一份纸质或电子文件，该文件既非重要记录，也非公共记录或记录文件；

（2）将文件与源自以下途径的第二份纸质或电子文件相比较：

（i）公证人亲自接收；

（ii）由公证人查找、确认；或

（iii）由公证人从第一份文档复印得来；以及

（3）运用视觉或电子手段对比，证实第二份文件作为副本与第一份文件在图像和文本上相同、准确、完整，在可行的前提下，也包括元数据相同、准确、完整。

§2-5 可信证人

"可信证人"是指熟悉当事人，亲自向公证人宣誓或声明以证实当事人身份的诚实、可靠、公正之人。

§2-6 公证人日志

"公证人日志"和"日志"是指按时间顺序创设和保存，由实施公证行为的公证员本人维护的公证记录。

§2-7 宣誓证明

"宣誓证明"是指对当事人在某时间某地点的下述行为进行的公证行为：

（1）亲自向公证人递交文件；

（2）为公证人所熟知或通过充分的证据向公证人证实身份；

（3）在公证人的见证下签署文件；以及

（4）向公证人宣誓或声明证明该签署的文件的真实性和准确性。

§2-8 公证行为和公证

"公证行为"和"公证"是指公证人在本法授权下进行的包含证明、见证、执行在内的官方行为。

tary public is empowered to perform under this [Act].

§ 2-9 Notarial Certificate and Certificate.

"Notarial certificate" and "certificate" mean the part of, or attachment to, a notarized document that, in the performance of the notarization, is completed by the notary, bears the notary's official signature and seal, and states the date, venue, and facts attested by the notary in the particular notarial act.

§ 2-10 Notary Public and Notary.

"Notary public" and "notary" mean any person commissioned to perform notarial acts under this [Act].

§ 2-11 Oath.

"Oath" means a notarial act, or part thereof, which is legally equivalent to an affirmation and in which an individual at a single time and place:

(1) appears in person before the notary;

(2) is personally known to the notary or identified by the notary through satisfactory evidence; and

(3) makes a vow of truthfulness or fidelity on penalty of perjury while invoking a deity or using any form of the word "swear."

§ 2-12 Official Misconduct.

"Official misconduct" means:

(1) a notary's performance of any act prohibited, or failure to perform any act or duty mandated, by this [Act] or by any other law in connection with a notarial act; or

(2) a notary's performance of an official act or duty in a manner that is negligent, contrary to established norms of sound notarial practice, or against the public interest.

§ 2-13 Official Seal.

"Official seal" means:

(1) a device authorized by the [commissioning official] for affixing on a paper notarial certificate an image containing a notary's name, title, jurisdiction, commission expiration date, and other information related to the notary's commission; or

(2) the affixed image itself.

§ 2-14 Official Signature.

"Official signature" means a handwritten signature made by a notary that uses the exact name appearing in the notary's commission and is signed with the intent to perform a notarial act.

§ 2-15 Personal Appearance.

"Personal appearance before the notary" and "appears

§2-9 公证书和证书

"公证书"和"证书"是指公证文件的部分或附件，其由公证人在公证过程中完成，包含公证人正式签名和盖章，记录特定公证行为中由公证人证实的时间、地点和事实。

§2-10 公证人

公证人是指被任命依据本法从事公证行为的人。

§2-11 宣誓

"宣誓"是指一项公证行为或行为之部分，在法律效果上等同于声明，在宣誓中，当事人在某时间、某地点：

（1）亲临公证现场；

（2）为公证人所熟知或通过充分的证据向公证人证实身份；以及

（3）向神起誓或使用"宣誓"一词的任何形式，对真实性和准确性宣誓，否则，将被认定为作伪证而受到处罚。

§2-12 职务不当行为

"职务不当行为"是指：

（1）从事本法或与公证相关的其他法律禁止的行为或未从事本法或与公证相关的其他法律规定的职责；或者

（2）公证人的职务行为存在过失、违反既定的稳健公证实践准则或公共利益。

§2-13 公章

"公章"是指：

（1）由任命官员授权使用的工具，用以在纸质公证书上加盖包含公证人姓名、头衔、辖区、任期终止日期以及有关公证人任命的其他信息的图像；或者

（2）加盖图像本身。

§2-14 正式签名

"正式签名"是指公证员为从事公证行为所作之手写签名，必须与其委任状中所用姓名完全一致。

§2-15 亲自出席

"亲自出现在公证人面前"是指公证员与当事人、

in person before the notary" mean that the notary is physically close enough to see, hear, communicate with, and receive identification documents from a principal and any required witness.

§ 2-16 Personal Knowledge of Identity.

"Personal knowledge of identity" and "personally knows" mean familiarity with an individual resulting from interactions with that individual over a period of time sufficient to dispel any reasonable uncertainty that the individual has the identity claimed.

§ 2-17 Principal.

"Principal" means:

(1) a person whose signature is notarized; or

(2) a person, other than a credible witness, taking an oath or affirmation from the notary.

§ 2-18 Regular Place of Work or Business.

"Regular place of work or business" means a stationary office or workspace where one spends all or some of one's working or business hours.

§ 2-19 Requester of Fact.

"Requester of fact" means a person who asks the notary public to perform:

(1) a copy certification; or

(2) a verification of fact.

§ 2-20 Satisfactory Evidence of Identity.

"Satisfactory evidence of identity" means identification of an individual based on:

(1) at least 1 current document issued by a federal, state, or tribal government in a language understood by the notary and bearing the photographic image of the individual's face and signature and a physical description of the individual, or a properly stamped passport without a physical description; or

(2) the oath or affirmation of 1 credible witness disinterested in the document or transaction who is personally known to the notary and who personally knows the individual, or of 2 credible witnesses disinterested in the document or transaction who each personally knows the individual and shows to the notary documentary identification as described in Subparagraph (1) of this Section.

§ 2-21 Signature Witnessing.

"Signature witnessing" means a notarial act in which an individual at a single time and place:

(1) appears in person before the notary and presents a

证人距离之近，足以看到、听到当事人、证人，能够与之交流并接收证明文件。

§2-16 个人熟悉其身份

"个人熟悉其身份"和"个人了解"是指因交往一段时间而与当事人熟悉，足以排除对当事人所持身份的任何合理怀疑。

§2-17 当事人

"当事人"是指：

（1）签名已被认证者；或者

（2）除可信证人外在公证人处已进行宣誓或声明者。

§2-18 经常工作地/主要营业场所

"经常工作地/主要营业场所"是指全部或部分工作或营业时间内，个体所处的固定的办公室或工作区域。

§2-19 事实请求者

"事实请求者"是指请求公证人进行以下公证活动的当事人：

（1）副本证明；或者

（2）事实证明。

§2-20 证实身份的充分证据

"证实身份的充分证据"是指对个人身份的识别，该识别基于：

（1）至少一份由联邦政府、州政府或部族政府签发的现行文件，所用语言应为公证人所理解，该文件须包含当事人面部照片、签名和体征描述，或者是不包含体征描述的加盖公章的护照；或者

（2）由一名公证人所熟悉且熟知当事人、与文件或业务无利害关系的可信证人所作之宣誓或声明；或者由两名均熟悉当事人、与文件或业务无利害关系的可信证人所作之宣誓或声明，此种情况下该两名当事人须向公证人出示本条第1项所述之书面证明。

§2-21 签名证明

"签名证明"是指对当事人在某时间、某地点的下述行为进行的公证行为：

（1）亲自向公证人递交文件；

document;

(2) is personally known to the notary or identified by the notary through satisfactory evidence; and

(3) signs the document in the presence of the notary

§ 2-22 Verification of Fact.

"Verification of fact" means a notarial act in which a notary reviews public or vital records, or other legally accessible data, to ascertain or confirm any of the following facts:

(1) date of birth, death, marriage, or divorce;

(2) name of parent, marital partner, offspring, or sibling;

(3) any matter authorized for verification by a notary by other law or rule of this [State].

Article II
Notary Public

Chapter 3 - Commissioning of Notary Public

§ 3-1 Qualifications.

(a) Except as provided in Subsection (c), the [commissioningofficial] shall issue a notary commission to any qualified personwho submits an application in accordance with this Article.

(b) A person qualified for a notary commission shall:

(1) be at least 18 years of age;

(2) reside or have a regular place of work or business in this [State], as defined in Section 2-18;

(3) reside legally in the United States;

(4) read and write English;

(5) pass a course of instruction requiring a written examination under Section 4-3; and

(6) submit fingerprints to allow a criminal background check.

(c) The [commissioning official] may deny an application based on:

(1) submission of an official application containing material misstatement or omission of fact;

(2) the applicant's conviction or plea of admission or nolo contendere for a felony or any crime involving dishonesty or moral turpitude, but in no case may a commission be issued to the applicant within 5 years after such conviction or plea;

(3) a finding or admission of liability against the applicant in a civil lawsuit based on the applicant's deceit;

(4) revocation, suspension, restriction, or denial of a

（2）为公证人所熟知或通过充分的证据向公证人证实身份；以及

（3）在公证人的见证下签署文件。

§2-22 事实证明

"事实证明"是指公证人审查公共或重要记录，或其他来源合法之资料以确认以下事实的公证行为：

（1）出生日期、死亡日期、结婚日期及离婚日期；

（2）父母、配偶、子女以及兄弟姐妹的姓名；

（3）由本州其他法律或规则授权公证人核查的任何事项。

第二编
公证人

第三章　公证人之任命

§3-1 资格

（a）除本条（c）款规定的情形外，任命官员须向任何根据本编内容提交申请的合格人员签发公证人任命书。

（b）符合公证人任职资格的人员应具备以下条件：

（1）年满18周岁以上；

（2）居住在本州或者在本州有第二章第18条规定的经常工作地或主要营业场所；

（3）合法居住在美国；

（4）能够阅读和书写英语；

（5）通过第四章第3条规定的有笔试要求的培训课程；且

（6）提交指纹以备刑事犯罪背景审查。

（c）任命官可根据以下情形驳回公证人任命申请：

（1）提交的正式申请包含重大虚假陈述或遗漏重大事实；

（2）申请人因重罪以及任何涉及不诚信、道德犯罪之缘故而定罪、供认或进行无罪申诉的，自该种情形出现之日起5年内不得向其签发公证人任命；

（3）在申请人涉嫌欺诈行为的民事诉讼中，存在不利于申请人的裁决或申请人自认责任的；

（4）其公证人任命或执业执照被本州/国或他州/

notarial commission or professional license by this or any other state or nation, but in no case may a commission be issued to the applicant within 5 years after such disciplinary action; or

(5) an official finding that the applicant had engaged in official misconduct as defined in Section 2-12, whether or not disciplinary action resulted.

(d) Denial of an application may be appealed by filing in proper form with the [administrative body hearing appeal] within [time limit] after denial, except that an applicant may not appeal when the [commissioning official] within 5 years prior to the application has:

(1) denied or revoked for disciplinary reasons any previous application, commission, or license of the applicant; or

(2) made a finding under Section 13-3(d) that grounds for revocation of the applicant's commission existed.

§ 3-2 Jurisdiction and Term.

A person commissioned as a notary may perform notarial acts in any part of this [State] for a term of [4] years, unless the commission is earlier revoked under Section 13-3 or resigned under Section 12-3.

§ 3-3 Bond.

(a) A notary commission shall not [become effective / be issued] until an oath of office and [25,000] dollar bond have been filed with the [designated office]. The bond shall be executed by a licensed surety, for a term of [4] years commencing on the commission's effective date and terminating on its expiration date, with payment of bond funds to any person conditioned upon the notary's misconduct as defined in Section 2-12.

(b) The surety for a notary bond shall report all claims against the bond to the [commissioning official].

(c) If a notary bond has been exhausted by claims paid out by the surety, the [commissioning official] shall suspend the notary's commission until:

(1) a new bond is obtained by the notary; and

(2) the notary's fitness to serve the remainder of the commission term is determined by the [commissioning official].

§ 3-4 Commissioning Documents.

Upon issuing a notary commission, the [commissioning official] shall provide to the notary:

(1) a commission document stating the commission

国撤销、暂停、限制或拒发的，自惩戒行为发生之日起 5 年内不得向其签发公证人任命书；或者

（5）申请人被正式判决实施了第二章第 12 条的职务不当行为，无论该行为是否受到纪律处罚。

（d）对被驳回的申请，申请人可以在驳回后于限定期限内以适格方式向申诉机构申诉，但申诉前 5 年中有下列情形的，该申请不得申诉：

（1）任命官员因纪律原因拒绝或撤销先前申请、任命或执业许可；或者

（2）任命官员依据第十三章第 3 条（d）款裁决撤销任命之事由属实。

§3-2 管辖和任期

被任命为公证人的个人可以在本州任何区域从事公证活动，任期 4 年，除非其任命依据第十三章第 3 条被提前撤销或依据第十二章第 3 条辞职。

§3-3 保证金

（a）在向指定机构进行职业宣誓及缴纳 25000 美元保证金后，公证任命方可生效/签发。保证金由被许可的保证人管理，自任命生效之日起至到期日为期 4 年，保证金基金在公证人发生第二章第 12 条规定的职务不当行为时用以赔偿他人。

（b）公证人保证金之保证人须向任命官员汇报所有针对保证金的索赔事项。

（c）如果公证人保证金已由保证人支付索赔用尽，任命官员应当暂停公证人任命，直至：

（1）公证人取得新的保证金；且
（2）任命官员认为公证人能够胜任剩余任期。

§3-4 委任文书

公证人任命书一经签发，任命官员须向公证人提供以下文件：

（1）写明任命序号和任职起止日期的委任文书；

serial number and starting and ending dates; and

(2) a Certificate of Authorization to Purchase a Notary Seal stating the commission serial number.

§ 3-5 Recommissioning.

A current or former notary applying for a new notary commission shall submit a new completed application and comply anew with all of the provisions of Chapters 3 and 4.

Chapter 4 - Application for Notary Public Commission

§ 4-1 Application Materials.

Every application for a notary commission shall be made in a paper or electronic format established by the [commissioning official] and include:

(1) a statement of the applicant's personal qualifications, as described in Section 4-2;

(2) a certificate evidencing successful completion of a course of instruction, as described in Section 4-3;

(3) a notarized declaration of the applicant, as described in Section 4-4;

(4) a full set of fingerprints of the applicant;

(5) such other information as the [commissioning official] may deem appropriate; and

(6) an application fee, as specified in Section 4-5.

§ 4-2 Statement of Personal Qualifications.

The application for a notary commission shall state or include, at least:

(1) the applicant's date of birth;

(2) the applicant's residence address and telephone number;

(3) the applicant's business address and telephone number, the business mailing address, if different, and the name of the applicant's employer, if any;

(4) a declaration that the applicant is a citizen of the United States or proof of the applicant's legal residency in the country;

(5) a declaration that the applicant can read and write English;

(6) all issuances, denials, revocations, suspensions, restrictions, and resignations of a notarial commission, professional license, or public office involving the applicant in this or any other jurisdiction;

(7) all criminal convictions of the applicant, including any pleas of admission or nolo contendere, in this or any other state or nation; [and]

(8) all claims pending or disposed against a notary

以及

（2）写明任命序号的授权购买公证人印章的证明。

§3-5 再委任

现任或先前的公证人在申请新的公证任命时应提交新的完整的申请并仍须满足第三章和第四章的要求。

第四章 公证人任命申请

§4-1 申请材料

公证人任命申请须按任命官员确定的纸质或电子方式制作，并须包含以下内容：

（1）本章第2条中关于申请人个人资格的陈述；

（2）已完成本章第3条规定的培训课程之证明；

（3）本章第4条规定的申请人公证宣言；

（4）申请人全套指纹；

（5）任命官员认为适当的其他信息；以及

（6）本章第5条规定的申请费用。

§4-2 个人资格陈述

公证人任命申请应至少陈述或包括以下内容：

（1）申请人出生日期；

（2）申请人住址及联系方式；

（3）申请人工作地址和联系方式，若另有工作邮寄地址，须同时提供工作邮寄地址，如果受雇的话，还须提供雇主姓名；

（4）申请人是美国公民的声明或申请人拥有在美国合法居留权的证明；

（5）申请人能够读写英语的声明；

（6）申请人在本辖区或其他任一辖区所有涉及公证人任命、执业许可或公职的签发、拒绝、撤销、暂停、限制、辞职的情形；

（7）申请人在本州/国、其他州/国的所有刑事犯罪记录，包括供认和无罪申诉；以及

（8）所有在本州/国、其他州/国，针对申请人

bond held by the applicant, and all civil findings or admissions of fault or liability regarding the applicant's activities as a notary, in this or any other state or nation [; and

(9) if the notary elects to keep an electronic journal, the password or access instructions required by Section 7-6].

§ 4-3 Course and Examination.

(a) Every applicant for a notary commission shall take, within the 3 months preceding application, a course of instruction of at least 4 hours approved by the [commissioning official], and pass a written examination of this course.

(b) The content of the course and the basis for the written examination shall be notarial laws, procedures, and ethics.

§ 4-4 Notarized Declaration.

Every applicant for a notary commission shall sign the following declaration in the presence of a notary of this [State]:

Declaration of Applicant

I, _____(name of applicant), solemnly swear or affirm underpenalty of perjury that the personal information in this application is true, complete, and correct; that I understand the official duties and responsibilities of a Notary Public in this [State], as explained in the course of instruction I have taken; and that I will perform, to the best of my ability, all notarial acts in accordance with the law.

_____(signature of applicant)

(notarial certificate for a jurat as specified in Section 9-5)

§ 4-5 Application Fee.

Every applicant for a notary commission shall pay to this [State] a non-refundable application fee of [dollars].

§ 4-6 Confidentiality.

Information required by Section 4-2(7) shall be used by the [commissioning official] and designated [State] employees only for the purpose of performing official duties under this [Act] and shall not be disclosed to any person other than:

(1) a government agent acting in an official capacity and duly authorized to obtain such information;

(2) a person authorized by court order; or

(3) the applicant or the applicant's duly authorized agent.

公证人保证金的未决及已决索赔，以及所有认定申请人公证行为有过错或责任的民事判决或供认；以及

（9）如果公证人选择保存电子日志，还须提交第七章第6条规定的密码或访问指令。

§4-3 课程和考试

（a）公证人任命申请人均须在申请前3个月内参加一项由任命官员批准的至少4个小时的培训课程，并须通过该课程笔试；

（b）培训课程内容及笔试依据为公证法律、程序规范及职业道德。

§4-4 公证声明

公证任命申请人须在本州公证人见证下签署以下声明：

申请声明

我，_____（申请人姓名），以神的名义郑重起誓或我郑重发誓，如所言不实甘受伪证罪之罚，我所提交的个人申请信息真实、完整、正确；我明白本州公证人的义务和责任，正如我参加的培训课程所述；我将全心全意依法从事公证行为。

_____（申请人签名）

（第九章第5条规定的宣誓证明公证书）

§4-5 申请费用

申请人须以美元向本州缴纳美元申请费用，一经缴纳不予退还。

§4-6 保密条款

本章第2条第7项要求填报的信息仅供任命官员及指定的州雇员为履行本法所规定的工作职责之目的使用，除以下情形外，不得向其他人员泄露：

（1）被授权获取此类信息的政府官方代理人；

（2）法院命令授权的个人；或者

（3）申请人本人或其授权代理人。

Chapter 5 - Powers and Limitations of Notary Public

§ 5-1 Powers of Notary.

A notary is empowered to perform the following notarial acts:

(1) acknowledgments;

(2) oaths and affirmation;

(3) jurats;

(4) signature witnessings;

(5) copy certifications;

(6) verifications of fact; and

(7) any other acts so authorized by the law of this [State].

§ 5-2 Requirements for Notarial Acts.

A notary shall perform a notarial act only if the principal:

(1) is in the presence of the notary at the time of notarization;

(2) is personally known to the notary or identified by the notary through satisfactory evidence;

(3) appears to understand the nature of the transaction requiring a notarial act;

(4) appears to be acting of his or her own free will;

(5) signs using letters or characters of a language that is understood by the notary; and

(6) communicates directly with the notary in a language both understand.

§ 5-3 Signature by Mark.

A notary may certify the affixation of a signature by mark by a principal on a document presented for notarization if:

(1) the mark is affixed in the presence of the notary and 2 witnesses disinterested in the document;

(2) both witnesses sign their own names beside the mark;

(3) the notary writes below the mark: "Mark affixed by (name of signer by mark) in the presence of (names and addresses of 2 witnesses) and the undersigned notary pursuant to Section 5-3 of [Act]"; and

(4) the notary notarizes the signature by mark through an acknowledgment, jurat, or signature witnessing.

§ 5-4 Signing for Principal Unable to Sign.

A notary may sign the name of a principal physically unable to sign or make a mark on a document presented for notarization if:

第五章 公证人权力及限制

§5-1 公证人权利

公证人被授权从事下列公证行为：

（1）确认；

（2）宣誓和声明；

（3）宣誓证明；

（4）签名见证；

（5）副本证明；

（6）事实证明；以及

（7）本州法律授权的其他行为。

§5-2 公证行为要求

只有在当事人符合下列情形时，公证人才能从事相关公证行为：

（1）公证时亲临现场；

（2）为公证人所熟知或通过充分的证据向公证人证实身份；

（3）理解要求进行公证的交易的性质；

（4）出于自身意愿；

（5）以能够为公证人所理解的文字签名；以及

（6）以双方均能理解的语言与公证人直接交流。

§5-3 标记签名

在满足以下条件时，公证人对当事人提交公证的文件上的标记签名可予以认可：

（1）该标记在公证人及两名与被提交文件无利害关系之证人见证下签署；

（2）两名证人均在标记旁签署姓名；

（3）公证人在标记下写明："依据本法第五章第3条之规定，标记由（标记签名者姓名）在（两名证人姓名和住址）和在其下签名的公证人见证下签署"；

（4）公证人通过确认、宣誓证明或签名证明对标记签名进行公证。

§5-4 当事人签名不能时代签

在满足以下条件时，对因身体原因不能在提交公证的文件上签名或标记的当事人，公证人可代其签名：

(1) the principal directs the notary to do so in the presence of 2 witnesses disinterested in the document;

(2) the notary signs the principal's name in the presence of the principal and the witnesses;

(3) both witnesses sign their own names beside the signature;

(4) the notary writes below the signature: "Signature affixed by the notary at the direction and in the presence of (name of principal unable to sign or make a mark) and also in the presence of (names and addresses of 2 witnesses) pursuant to Section 5-4 of [Act]"; and

(5) the notary notarizes the signature through an acknowledgment, jurat, or signature witnessing.

§ 5-5 Disqualifications.

(a) A notary is disqualified from performing a notarial act if the notary:

(1) is a party to or named in the document that is to be notarized;

(2) will receive as a direct or indirect result any commission, fee, advantage, right, title, interest, cash, property, or other consideration exceeding in value the fees specified in Section 6-2 of this [Act];

(3) is a spouse, domestic partner, ancestor, descendant, or sibling of the principal, including in-law, step, and half relatives; or

(4) is an attorney who has prepared, explained, or recommended to the principal the document that is to be notarized.

(b) Notwithstanding Subsection (a)(2), a notary may collect a non-notarial fee for services as a signing agent if payment of that fee is not contingent upon the signing, initialing, or notarization of any document.

§ 5-6 Refusal to Notarize.

(a) A notary shall not refuse to perform a notarial act based on a personas race, advanced age, gender, sexual orientation, religion, national origin, disability, or status as a non-client or non-customer of the notary^s employer.

(b) A notary shall perform any notarial act described in Section 5-1 of this Chapter for any person requesting such an act who tenders the appropriate fee specified in Section 6-2(a), unless:

(1) the notary knows or has a reasonable belief that the notarial act or the associated transaction is unlawful;

(2) the act is prohibited under Section 5-2 or 5-5;

(3) the number or timing of the requested notarial act or acts practicably precludes completion at the time of

（1）当事人在两名与被提交文件无利害关系之证人见证下指示公证人签署；

（2）公证人在当事人和证人见证下签署当事人姓名；

（3）两名证人均在签名旁签署姓名；

（4）公证人在签名下写明："依据本法第五章第4条之规定，签名由公证人在（无法签名或标记的当事人之姓名）指示和见证且在（两名证人姓名和住址）见证下签署"；以及

（5）公证人通过确认、宣誓证明或签名证明对签名进行公证。

§5-5 剥夺任职资格情形

（a）一旦出现下列情形，公证人将被剥夺公证任职资格：

（1）公证人是待公证文件的一方当事人或在待公证文件中被提及；

（2）公证人将以佣金、费用、好处、权利、头衔、利益、现金、财产或其他形式直接或间接获得超过本法第六章第2条规定收费标准的报酬；

（3）公证人是当事人的配偶、同居伴侣、长辈、晚辈或兄弟姐妹，包括姻亲、继亲或半亲关系；或者

（4）公证人是当事人的代理人，并已向其就拟公证文件进行过准备、解释或建议。

（b）尽管本条（a）款第2项作出规定，但若费用支付无关乎对任何文件的签署或公证，公证人可收取作为签名代理人的非公证费用。

§5-6 拒绝公证

（a）公证人不得因当事人种族、高龄、性别、性取向、宗教信仰、出生地、残疾或者并非公证人雇主的顾客或客户而拒绝向其提供公证。

（b）公证人应当为已缴纳第六章第2条（a）款所规定的费用的当事人办理本章第1条规定之公证事项，下列情形除外：

（1）公证人知悉或有理由相信该公证行为或涉及非法业务；

（2）该公证行为为本章第2条或第5条所禁止；

（3）申请公证行为数量之巨、时间之紧事实上排除了公证人在请求时限内完成公证的可能性，在此种

the request, in which case the notary shall arrange for later completion of the requested act or acts without unreasonable delay; or

(4) in the case of a request to perform an electronic notarial act, the notary is not registered to notarize electronically in accordance with Chapter 16.

(c) A notary may but is not required to perform a notarial act outside of the notary's regular workplace or business hours.

§ 5-7 Improper Influence.

(a) Unless Section 5-6(b)(1) applies, a notary shall not influence a person either to enter into or avoid a transaction involving a notarial act by the notary.

(b) A notary commission shall not authorize the notary to investigate, ascertain, or attest to the lawfulness, propriety, accuracy, or truthfulness of a document or transaction involving a notarial act.

§ 5-8 Improper Certificate.

(a) A notary shall not execute a notarial certificate containing information known or believed by the notary to be false.

(b) A notary shall not affix an official signature or seal on a notarial certificate that is incomplete.

(c) A notary shall not affix an official signature or seal on a notarial certificate other than at the time of notarization and in the presence of the principal.

(d) A notary shall not provide or send a signed or sealed notarial certificate to another person with the understanding that it will be completed or attached to a document outside of the notary's presence.

§ 5-9 Improper Documents.

(a) A notary shall not notarize a signature:

(1) on a blank or incomplete document; or

(2) on a document without notarial certificate wording.

(b) A notary shall neither certify nor authenticate a photograph.

§ 5-10 Intent to Deceive.

A notary shall not perform any official action with the intent to deceive or defraud.

§ 5-11 Testimonials.

A notary shall not use the official notary title or seal to endorse, promote, denounce, or oppose any product, service, contest, candidate, or other offering.

情况下，公证人在排除不合理拖延后，应请求延期完成公证；或者

（4）当事人请求电子公证，而公证人未根据第十六章的规定登记为电子公证人。

（c）规定办公地点或办公时间之外，公证人可自由选择是否从事公证行为。

§5-7 不当影响

（a）除本章第6条（b）款第1项规定的情形外，公证人不得促使或劝阻当事人参与与该公证人公证行为相关之交易；

（b）公证人任命不得授权公证人调查、查明或证实与公证行为相关的文件或交易的合法性、适当性、准确性或真实性。

§5-8 不当证明

（a）公证人不得签署包含其知道或相信为虚假信息的公证书；

（b）公证人不得在未完成的公证书上签名或盖章；

（c）公证人只有在公证活动中、当事人在场时方可签名或盖章；

（d）在公证人知悉公证书将在公证人不在场时被补充完整或附于某文件之后时，公证人不得向他人提供或寄送已签名或盖章的公证书。

§5-9 不当文书

（a）公证员不得公证以下签名：

（1）在空白处或未完成的文件上；或者

（2）在未附有公证字句的文件上。

（b）公证人不得证明或证实摄影照片。

§5-10 欺诈

公证人不得以欺诈或欺骗之目的从事任何职务行为。

§5-11 证明书

公证人不得使用职务头衔或公章支持、促进、公开指责或反对某些产品、服务、竞赛、候选人或其他邀约。

§ 5-12 Unauthorized Practice of Law.

(a) A non-attorney notary shall not assist another person in drafting, completing, selecting, or understanding a document or transaction requiring a notarial act.

(b) If notarial certificate wording is not provided or indicated for a document, a non-attorney notary shall not determine the type of notarial act or certificate to be used.

§ 5-13 Permissible Advice.

Section 5-12 does not preclude a notary who is duly qualified, trained, licensed, or experienced in a particular industry or professional field from selecting, drafting, completing, or advising on a document or certificate related to a matter within that industry or field.

§ 5-14 Misrepresentation and Improper Advertising.

(a) A notary shall not claim to have powers, qualifications, rights, or privileges that the office of notary does not provide, including the power to counsel on immigration issues.

(b) A non-attorney notary who advertises notarial services in a language other than English shall include in the advertisement, notice, letterhead, or sign the following, prominently displayed in the same language:

(1) the statement: "I am not an attorney and have no authority to give advice on immigration or other legal matters"; and

(2) the fees for notarial acts specified in Section 6-2(a).

(c) A notary may not use the term "notario publico" or any equivalent non-English term in any business card, advertisement, notice, or sign.

§ 5-15 Notarial Officers Other Than Notaries.

(a) Notarial officers, other than notaries public, who are given the power to perform notarial acts by other laws of this [State] shall comply with the following sections of this [Act], in the same manner as notaries public, in performing their authorized notarial acts:

(1) regarding prohibitions and restrictions, Sections 5-2 through 5-14;

(2) regarding maintenance of a journal of notarial acts, Sections 7-1 through 7-2; and

(3) regarding execution of notarial certificates, Sections 9-1 through 9-9.

(b) Notarial officers, other than notaries public, shall follow all pertinent laws of this [State], except those set down in this [Act] apart from this section, and the rules

§5-12 法无授权实施

（a）非律师公证人不得帮助他人起草、完成、选择或理解拟公证的文件或业务；

（b）如果某文件的公证书措辞未提供或表明其文件类型，非律师公证人不得决定所应采取的公证行为或公证书类型。

§5-13 可允许建议

本章第12条并不排除在某特殊行业或专业领域确有资格、经过培训、获得执照或经验丰富的公证人对有关该行业或领域的文件或证明的选择、起草、完成或建议。

§5-14 错误表述和不当宣传

（a）公证人不得宣称拥有公证人职位未授予的权力、资格、权利或特权，包括对移民事务提供专业咨询的权力。

（b）以非英语语言宣传其公证服务的非律师公证人须在广告、通知、抬头中用该种语言对以下内容予以显著显示或标明：

（1）声明："我不是律师，没有针对移民或其他法律事务提供咨询意见的权限"；以及

（2）第六章第2条（a）款规定的公证费用。

（c）公证人不得在任何名片、广告、通知或标记中使用诸如"涉信律师"一词或该词在其他语种中的同义词。

§5-15 非公证人公证办事人员

（a）非公证人公证办事人员是指在本州其他法律授权下拥有从事公证行为权限的人员，其在从事授权的公证活动中应同公证人一样遵守本法以下规定：

（1）本章第2条至第14条关于禁止和限制的规定；

（2）第七章第1条、第2条关于公证人日志维护的规定；

（3）第九章第1条至第9条关于公证书制作的规定。

（b）非公证人公证办事人员除遵循上述提及的本法规定外，还须遵守本州所有相关法律，以及其授权雇佣机构经正当程序颁布的下列有关规则：

duly issued by their authorized employers in regard to:

(1) use or non-use of a seal of office;

(2) performance of electronic notarial acts;

(3) disposition of a seal of office and a journal of notarial acts after termination of status as a notarial officer; and

(4) all other matters, including discipline, related to their status as a notarial officer.

Chapter 6 - Fees of Notary Public

§ 6-1 Imposition and Waiver of Fees.

(a) For performing a notarial act, a notary may charge the maximum fee specified in Section 6-2, charge less than the maximum fee, or waive the fee.

(b) A notary shall not discriminatorily condition the fee for a notarial act on the attributes of the principal or requester of fact as set forth in Subsection 5-6(a), though a notary may waive or reduce fees for humanitarian or charitable reasons.

§ 6-2 Fees for Notarial Acts.

(a) The maximum fees that may be charged by a notary for notarial acts are:

(1) for an acknowledgment, [dollars] per signature;

(2) for an oath or affirmation without a signature, [dollars] per person;

(3) for a jurat, [dollars] per signature;

(4) for a signature witnessing, [dollars] per signature;

(5) for a certified copy, [dollars] per page certified with a minimum total charge of [dollars];

(6) for a verification of fact, [dollars] per certificate; and

(7) for an electronic notarization, as specified in Section 21-2.

(b) A notary may charge a travel fee when traveling to perform anotarial act if:

(1) the notary and the person requesting the notarial act agree upon the travel fee in advance of the travel; and

(2) the notary explains to the person requesting the notarial act that the travel fee is both separate from the notarial fee prescribed in Subsection (a) and neither specified nor mandated by law.

§ 6-3 Payment Prior to Act.

(a) A notary may require payment of any fees specified in Section 6¬2 prior to performance of a notarial act.

(b) Any fees paid to a notary prior to performance of

（1）是否使用公章；

（2）如何进行电子公证；

（3）作为公证办事人员任期结束后公章和公证人日志的妥善安置；以及

（4）与公证办事人员身份相关的包含行为准则在内的其他所有事项。

第六章 公证人费用

§6–1 收取或免除费用

（a）从事公证活动，公证人可按本章第 2 条规定的最高标准收取费用，也可少于最高标准收费或免除收费。

（b）公证人可基于人道主义精神或慈善因素免除或减少费用，但不得因第五章第 6 条（a）款所列当事人／申请者情形歧视性收费。

§6–2 公证收费

（a）公证人就公证行为可收取的最高额费用为：

（1）确认，每签名（美元）；

（2）不签名的宣誓或声明，每人（美元）；

（3）宣誓证明，每签名（美元）；

（4）签名见证，每签名（美元）；

（5）经证明的副本，每页（美元）且总收费不低于（美元）；

（6）事实证明，每份证书（美元）；以及

（7）电子公证，详见第二十一章第 2 条。

（b）在满足以下条件时，公证人可因异地公证收取差旅费：

（1）在出差之前公证人和申请人就差旅费达成一致；以及

（2）公证人须向申请人说明差旅费与（a）款公证费用无关，且并非法律明确规定或强制要求。

§6–3 预付费

（a）公证人可要求在公证前收取本章第 2 条规定的任何费用。

（b）在以下情形中，公证前收取的任何费用不予

a notarial act are non-refundable if:

(1) the act was completed; or

(2) in the case of travel fees paid in compliance with Subsection 6-2(b), the act was not completed after the notary traveled to meet the principal because it was prohibited under Section 5-2, or because the notary knew or had a reasonable belief that the notarial act or the associated transaction was unlawful.

§ 6-4 Fees of Employee Notary.

(a) An employer may prohibit an employee who is a notary from charging for notarial acts performed on the employer's time, but shall not condition imposition of a fee on attributes of the principal as described in Section 5-6(a).

(b) A private employer shall not require an employee who is a notary to surrender or share fees charged for any notarial acts.

(c) A governmental employer who has absorbed an employee's costs in becoming or operating as a notary shall require any fees for notarial acts performed on the employer's time either to be waived or surrendered to the employer to support public programs.

§ 6-5 Notice of Fees.

Notaries who charge for their notarial services shall conspicuously display in their places of business, or present to each principal outside their places of business, an English-language schedule of fees for notarial acts, as specified in Section 6-2(a). No part of any notarial fee schedule shall be printed in smaller than 10-point type.

Chapter 7 - Journal of Notarial Acts

§ 7-1 Maintaining Journal of Notarial Acts.

(a) A notary shall keep, maintain, protect, and provide for lawful inspection a chronological journal of notarial acts that is either:

(1) a permanently bound book with numbered pages; or

(2) an electronic journal of notarial acts as described in Section 20-2 of this [Act].

(b) A notary shall keep a record of electronic and non-electronic notarial acts in the same journal.

(c) A notary shall maintain only 1 active journal at the same time, except that a backup of each active and inactive electronic journal shall be retained by the notary in accordance with Section 20-2(3) as long as each respective

返还：

（1）公证行为已履行完毕；

（2）在依照本章第2条（b）款的规定已支付差旅费后，公证人前往外地，经与当事人会见，认为公证行为为第五章第2条所禁止或因公证人知悉或有理由相信公证行为或相关业务违法，公证行为因此未予完成。

§6-4 受雇公证人收费

（a）雇主可禁止受雇公证人就受雇期间的公证行为收费，但不得因前述第五章第6条（a）款所列当事人情形歧视性收费。

（b）私人雇主不得要求受雇公证人上缴或分享就公证行为收取的费用。

（c）承担了雇员申请执业或正式执业期间费用的政府雇主，可以支持公共项目为由，要求雇员就其受雇期间的公证收费予以免除或上缴。

§6-5 收费公告

因其公证服务收费的公证人应将本章第2条（a）款规定的英文公证收费表格显著列示于其营业场所，在营业场所之外则应交呈每位当事人。公证收费表格的任何部分不得以小于10号字体印刷。

第七章 公证人日志

§7-1 公证人日志的维护

（a）公证人日志按时间顺序记录，公证人应妥善保管、维护、保护，遇依法查验时及时予以提供，该日志为：

（1）编页的永久装订本；或者

（2）本法第二十章第2条规定的电子公证人日志；

（b）公证人应将电子公证行为和非电子公证行为记录于同一本日志。

（c）同一时间，公证人只能保存一份有效日志，除非依照第二十章第2条第3项规定保存一份电子日志的备份以备原件丢失。

original journal is retained.

§ 7-2 Journal Entries.

(a) For every notarial act, the notary shall record in the journal at the time of notarization at least the following:

(1) the date and time of day of the notarial act;

(2) the type of notarial act;

(3) the type, title, or a description of the document or proceeding;

(4) the signature, printed name, and address of each principal;

(5) the printed name and address of each requester of fact;

(6) the evidence of identity of each principal in the form of either: a statement that the person is "personally known" to the notary; a notation of the type of identification document, its issuing agency, its serial or identification number, and its date of issuance or expiration; or the handwritten signature and the name and address of each credible witness swearing or affirming to the principal's identity, and for credible witnesses who are not personally known to the notary, a description of the identification documents relied on by the notary;

(7) the thumbprint of each principal and witness, or, in the case of an electronic journal, the thumbprint or other recognized biometric identifier, in accordance with Section 20-2(4) of this [Act];

(8) the fee, if any, charged for the notarial act;

(9) the address where the notarization was performed, if not the notary's business address;

(10) the sequential number of any adhesive label bearing a notary seal image on the notarized document, in accordance with Section 8-2(d) of this [Act]; and

(11) in the case of an electronic notarization, the name of any authority issuing or registering the means used to create the electronic signature that was notarized; the source of this authority's license, if any; and the expiration date of the electronic process.

(b) A notary shall not record a Social Security or credit card number in the journal.

(c) A notary shall record in the journal the circumstances for not performing or completing any requested notarial act.

(d) A notary shall record in the journal the circumstances of any request to inspect or copy an entry in the journal, including the requester's name, address, handwritten signature, [thumbprint or other recognized biometric

§7-2 日志记录事项

（a）对每一项公证行为，公证人应于公证时至少在日志中记录以下事项：

（1）公证当日的日期和时间。

（2）公证行为的类型。

（3）文件或程序的类型、标题或者描述。

（4）全体当事人的签名、印制姓名及住址。

（5）全体事实请求者的印制姓名及住址。

（6）全体当事人的身份证明，其形式可以为：公证人与其"个人相识"的声明；对身份证明文件相关信息的记录，包括其种类、签发机关、序列号或识别号及签发或到期日期；对当事人身份宣誓或声明的全体可信证人的手写签名及姓名住址，若可信证人不为公证人认识，须附上公证人据以判断其可信证人身份的文件的描述。

（7）当事人和证人的拇指指纹；如遇电子公证之情形，则依据本法第二十章第2条第（4）项在日志中记录拇指指纹或其他可识别的生物计量学标志。

（8）如为收费公证，则须记录收费额。

（9）如在公证人营业场所外公证，须记录公证行为发生地。

（10）根据第八章第2条（d）款规定，粘贴于已公证文书上、加盖公证人印章的标签的序列号。

（11）电子公证中，据以创建待公证电子签名的装置的签发或登记当局之名称；如该当局有执照的话，其执照来源；以及该电子程序的到期日。

（b）公证人不得在日志中记录社保号或信用卡号。

（c）公证人须在日志中记录应申请而未进行或未完成公证的情形。

（d）公证人须在日志中记录所有申请查阅或复制日志记录事项的申请人的姓名、住址、手写签名（拇指指纹或其他可识别的生物计量学标志）以及身份证明。如拒绝其查阅或复制日志记录事项，原因也应予

identifier,] and evidence of identity. The reasons for refusal to allow inspection or copying of a journal entry shall also be recorded.

(e) As required in Section 9-3(4), a notary shall append to the pertinent entry in the journal a notation of the nature and date of the notary's correction of a completed notarial certificate corresponding to the entry.

§ 7-3 Inspection and Copying of Journal.

(a) In the notary's presence, any person may inspect and request a copy of an entry or entries in the notary's official journal during regular business hours, but only if:

(1) the person's identity is personally known to the notary or proven through satisfactory evidence;

(2) the person affixes a signature [and thumbprint or other recognized biometric identifier] in the journal in a separate, dated entry;

(3) the person specifies the month, year, type of document, and name of the principal or requester of fact for the notarial act or acts sought;

(4) the person is shown or given a requested copy of only the entry or entries specified; and

(5) the other entries on the same journal page are covered to prevent disclosure.

(b) If the notary has a reasonable and explainable belief that a person bears a criminal or harmful intent in requesting information from the notary's journal, the notary may deny access to any entry or entries.

(c) The journal may be examined and copied without restriction by a law enforcement officer in the course of an official investigation, subpoenaed by court order, or surrendered at the direction of the [commissioning official].

(d) Upon complying with a request for copies under Subsection (a), the notary shall charge not more than [dollars] per copy; and if a certified copy is requested, the fee is as specified in Section 6-2.

§ 7-4 Security of Journal.

(a) A notary shall safeguard the journal and all other notarial records and surrender or destroy them only by rule of law, by court order, or at the direction of the [commissioning official].

(b) When not in use, the journal shall be kept in a secure area under the exclusive control of the notary, and shall not be used by any other notary, nor surrendered to an employer upon termination of employment.

(c) Within 10 days after the journal is discovered to be stolen, lost, destroyed, damaged, or otherwise rendered

以记录。

（e）依据第九章第3条第4项的规定，公证人对已完成公证书相关记录进行修正的，应将修正的实质内容和日期追加记录至日志相关条目下。

§7-3 日志的查阅和复制

（a）满足以下情形时，任何人可在公证人在场的情况下于工作时间查阅或请求复制日志中所载事项：

（1）其个人身份为公证人所熟知或通过充分的证据被证实的；

（2）在日志中单列条目、标注日期，载明该人签名（以及拇指指纹或其他可识别的生物计量学标志）的；

（3）该人明确提供了待查询公证行为的（发生）年月、文书类型、当事人姓名和请求事项的；

（4）该人只能查阅或复印其指明的记录；以及

（5）日志同一页面上的其他记录需加以覆盖以免泄露。

（b）如果公证人基于合理和可解释的理由相信该人怀着犯罪或有害的目的获取公证人日志信息，公证人可拒绝其接触任何记录。

（c）正式调查过程中，执法人员可不受限制地查阅和复制公证人日志；公证人日志亦可经由法庭传唤呈堂，或应任命官员指令上交。

（d）根据本条（a）款规定应予提供复印件的，公证人对其收费不得超过每复印件（美元）；如果需要经证明的副本，其费用规定详见第六章第2条。

§7-4 日志的保护

（a）公证人须确保日志和其他公证记录的安全，非依法律规定、法院命令或任命官员指令，不得上交或销毁。

（b）公证人日志不用时，应在公证人全权控制之下保存于安全地点，不得为任何其他公证人使用并不得在雇佣期结束时上交雇主。

（c）如果公证人日志被盗、丢失、销毁、损坏或因其他原因不能使用或阅读，公证人应自发现之日起

unusable or unreadable, the notary, after informing the appropriate law enforcement agency in the case of theft or vandalism, shall notify the [commissioning official] by any means providing a tangible receipt, including certified mail and electronic transmission, and also provide a copy or identification number of any pertinent police report.

§ 7-5 Disposal of Journal.

(a) Upon resignation, revocation, or expiration of a notary commission, or death of the notary, the journal and notarial records shall be delivered to the [office designated by the commissioning official] in accordance with Sections 12-4(a) or 12-5(3) by any means providing a tangible receipt, including certified mail and electronic transmission, allowing that an electronic journal may be delivered on disk, printed on paper, or transmitted electronically, in accordance with the requirements of the same office.

(b) In the case of an electronic journal and its back-up copy whose disks or other physical storage media are not required to be surrendered, no further entries shall be made in the journal and its backup, both of which shall be safeguarded until both shall be erased or expunged after [5] years from the date of the last entry by the notary or the notary's personal representative.

§ 7-6 Electronic Journal.

If a notary elects to keep an electronic journal pursuant to Section 7-1(a), the notary shall:

(1) provide to the [commissioning official] the access instructions that allow journal entries to be viewed, printed out, and copied; and

(2) notify the [commissioning official] of any subsequent change to the access instructions.

Chapter 8 - Signature and Seal of Notary

§ 8-1 Official Signature.

In notarizing a paper document, a notary public shall affix an official signature on the notarial certificate at the time the notarial act is performed.

§ 8-2 Official Seal.

(a) In notarizing a paper document, a notary public shall affix an official seal on the notarial certificate at the time the notarial act is performed.

(b) The official seal of a notary public shall not be used for any purpose other than performing lawful notarizations.

(c) The official seal shall:

10 日内，在报告适格执法机关之后（如涉及盗窃或故意损毁），通过可给予回执的任何方式（包括挂号信和电子传输）通知任命官员，并提供警方相关报告的复印件或标识号。

§7-5 日志的处置

（a）公证人辞职、公证任命被撤销或任期结束以及公证人死亡的情况下，公证人日志及公证记录应按照第十二章第 4 条（a）款及第 5 条第 3 项的规定以可给予回执的任何方式（包括挂号信和电子传输）被送至任命官员指定的机构，电子日志按该机构要求可以光盘、纸质稿、电子传输等方式寄达。

（b）如电子日志及其以光盘或其他物理存储媒介保存的备份未被要求上交，则不得再向其中添加新条目，而应自添加最后一条记录之日起 5 年内，予以妥善保管，再由公证人或其个人代表擦除、抹消。

§7-6 电子日志

如果公证人依据本章第 1 条（a）款的规定选择创建电子日志，应当：

（1）向任命官员提供允许对日志记录进行浏览、打印及复制的访问指令；以及

（2）通知任命官员关于访问指令的所有后续变更情况。

第八章 公证人签名和印章

§8–1 正式签名

公证纸质文件时，公证人须在公证行为完成时在公证书上签署正式签名。

§8–2 公章

（a）公证纸质文件时，公证人须在公证行为完成时在公证书上加盖公章。

（b）公证人公章不得用于除履行法定公证行为外之任何目的。

（c）公章应当：

(1) be the exclusive property of the notary;

(2) not be affixed by any other person;

(3) be kept secure and accessible only to the notary; and

(4) not be surrendered to an employer upon termination of employment.

(d) An official seal affixed by an adhesive label shall bear a preprinted sequential number which shall be recorded in the journal of notarial acts for its respective notarization.

(e) Within 10 days after the official seal of a notary is discovered to be stolen, lost, damaged, or otherwise rendered incapable of affixing a legible image, the notary, after informing the appropriate law enforcement agency in the case of theft or vandalism, shall notify the [commissioning official] by any means providing a tangible receipt, including certified mail and electronic transmission, and also provide a copy or number of any pertinent police report. Upon receipt of such notice, the [commissioning official] shall issue to the notary a new Certificate of Authorization to Purchase a Notary Seal, which shall be presented to a seal vendor in accordance with Section 8-4.

(f) As soon as reasonably practicable after resignation, revocation, or expiration of a notary commission, or death of the notary, the seal shall be destroyed or defaced so that it may not be misused.

§ 8-3 Image of Official Seal.

(a) Near the notary's official signature on each paper notarial certificate, the notary shall affix a sharp, legible, permanent, and photographically reproducible image of the official seal that shall include the following elements:

(1) the notary's name exactly as stated on the commission;

(2) the identification number of the notary's commission;

(3) the words "Notary Public" and "[State] of [name of jurisdiction]" and "My commission expires (commission expiration date)";

(4) the notary's business address; and

(5) a border in a [rectangular/circular] shape no larger than [dimensions], surrounding the required words.

(b) Illegible information within a seal impression may be typed or printed legibly by the notary adjacent to but not within the impression, or another impression may be legibly affixed nearby.

(c) An embossed seal impression that is not photo-

（1）由公证人独占使用；

（2）不得被其他任何人加盖使用；

（3）妥善保管并只能为公证人所接触；且

（4）雇佣期结束时不得上交雇主。

（d）附有粘贴标签的公章应当有事先印制的序列号，该序列号须载入公证人日志以对其自身进行公证。

（e）如果公章被盗、丢失、损坏或因其他原因不能加盖可读图案，公证人应自发现之日起10日内，在报告适格执法机关之后（如涉及盗窃或故意损毁），通过可给予回执的任何方式（包括挂号信和电子传输）通知任命官员，并提供警方相关报告的复印件或标识号。接到该类通知后，任命官员须向公证人签发新的授权购买公证人印章的证明，该证明在依照本章第4条的规定购买印章时应向销售商出示。

（f）公证人辞职、公证任命被撤销或任期结束以及公证人死亡的情况下，印章应在合理时限内及早销毁或破坏印面，以防其被不当使用。

§8-3 公章图像

（a）在每页公证书公证人的正式签名旁，公证人须加盖清晰、可读、永久性、可影印复制的公章图像，该图像须包含以下内容：

（1）委任状中所使用的公证人姓名；

（2）公证人委任状序号；

（3）"公证人"、"辖区所属州"以及"我的任期结束于（任期结束日）"的字样；

（4）公证人营业场所；以及

（5）在要求的字样周围有一个不大于（尺寸）的（矩形/圆形）边框。

（b）章印中字迹模糊的信息可由公证人清晰地键入或印制在章印边上，而非章印之中，或在原章印旁另行加盖清晰章印。

（c）不可影印复制的钢印可用于本条（a）款所

graphically reproducible may be used in addition to but not in place of the official seal described in Subsection (a).

(d) A seal as described in Subsection (a) shall not be affixed over printed or written matter.

§ 8-4 Obtaining and Providing Official Seal.

(a) In order to sell or manufacture notary seals, a vendor or manufacturer shall apply for a permit from the [commissioning official], who shall charge a fee of [dollars] for issuance of this permit and maintain a controlled-access telephone number or Internet site to allow vendors and manufacturers to confirm the business mailing address and current standing of any notary in the [State].

(b) A vendor or manufacturer shall not provide a notary seal to a purchaser claiming to be a notary, unless the purchaser presents a Certificate of Authorization to Purchase a Notary Seal from the [commissioning official] and a photocopy of the respective notary commission, and unless:

(1) in the case of a purchaser appearing in person, the vendor or manufacturer identifies this individual as the person named in the commission and the Certificate of Authorization, through either personal knowledge or satisfactory evidence of identity; or

(2) in the case of a purchaser ordering a seal by mail or delivery service, the vendor or manufacturer confirms the business mailing address and current standing through the controlled-access telephone number or Internet site.

(c) A vendor or manufacturer shall mail or ship a notary seal only to a mailing address confirmed through the controlled-access telephone number or Internet site.

(d) For each Certificate of Authorization to Purchase a Notary Seal, a vendor or manufacturer shall make or sell one and only one seal, plus, if requested by the person presenting the Certificate, one and only one embossing seal.

(e) After manufacturing or providing a notary seal or seals, the vendor shall affix an image of all seals on the Certificate of Authorization to Purchase a Notary Seal and send the completed Certificate to the [commissioning official], retaining a copy of the Certificate and the Commission for [period of time].

(f) A notary obtaining a seal or seals as a result of a name or business address change shall present a copy of the Confirmation of Notary's Name or Address Change from the [commissioning official] in accordance with Sections 12-1 and 12-2.

(g) A vendor or manufacturer who fails to comply

述公章的增补而非替代。

（d）（a）款所述公章不得加盖于印刷品或手写材料之上。

§8-4 公章的获取和提供

（a）出售和制造公证人印章，供应商或制造商须向任命官员申请许可，任命官员收取美元费用，以发放该许可，并向其提供受控访问的电话号码或互联网网站服务，以允许供应商或制造商确认本州任一公证人的营业邮寄地址及当前身份。

（b）供应商或制造商不得向自称为公证人的买主提供公证人印章，除非该买主出示任命官员提供的授权购买公证人印章的证明及委任状复印件，并且：

（1）在买主亲自到场的情况下，供应商或制造商因个人熟知或通过充分的证据证实该个人为委任状及授权证明中所指之人；或者

（2）在买主通过邮件或快递订购印章的情况下，供应商或制造商通过受控访问的电话号码或互联网网站确认买主营业邮寄地址及当前身份。

（c）供应商或制造商只能将公证人印章邮寄或运送至通过控制访问电话号码或互联网网站确认过的邮寄地址。

（d）对每一份授权购买公证人印章的证明，供应商或制造商只得制造或销售一枚印章，以及在应出示证明的买主要求的情形下，再制造或销售一枚对应钢印。

（e）制造或销售公证人印章或其他印章之后，供应商应在该授权购买公证人印章的证明上加盖所有印章的图像，并将盖章后的证明递交任命官员，并保留证明和委任状的副本一定时期。

（f）如因姓名或营业地址变更，公证人需另购印章的，应根据第十二章第1条、第2条的规定出示任命官员提供的公证人姓名及地址变更确认书副本。

（g）违反本章规定的供应商或制造商应被认定为

with this section shall be guilty of a [class of offense], punishable upon conviction by a fine not exceeding [dollars]. For multiple violations, a vendor's permission to sell or manufacture notary seals shall be withdrawn by the [commissioning official]. Such conviction shall not preclude the civil liability of the vendor to parties injured by the vendor's failure to comply with this section.

Chapter 9 - Certificates for Notarial Acts

§ 9-1 Notarial Certificate.

(a) For every notarial act involving a document, a notary public of this [State] shall properly complete a notarial certificate that contains or states:

(1) the official signature of the notary, in accordance with Section 8-1;

(2) an impression of the official seal of the notary, in accordance with Section 8-2;

(3) the venue of the notarial act, including the name of this [State] and of the pertinent [county] [parish] [district];

(4) the date of the notarial act; and

(5) the facts and particulars attested by the notary in performing the respective notarial act, as defined in Chapter 2.

(b) A notarial certificate shall be sufficient for a particular notarial act only if it meets the requirements of Subsection 9-1 (a) and is in a form that:

(1) is set forth for that act in this Chapter;

(2) is otherwise prescribed for that act by the law of this [State];

(3) is prescribed for that act by a law, regulation, or custom of another jurisdiction, provided it does not require actions by the notary that are unauthorized by this [State]; or

(4) describes the actions of the notary in such a manner as to meet the requirements of the particular notarial act, as defined in Chapter 2.

(c) A notarial certificate shall be worded and completed using only letters, characters, and a language that are read, written, and understood by the notary public.

§9-2 Attaching Notarial Certificate.

A paper notarial certificate that is attached to a document during the notarization of the signature of a principal shall:

(1) be attached by stapling or other method that leaves evidence of any subsequent detachment;

（犯罪类型），一经定罪可处以最高（美元）罚款。对于多次违规的，任命官员应撤回供应商出售或制造公证人印章的许可。该定罪并不妨碍供应商向因其违规行为而受害的相关方承担民事责任。

第九章 公证书

§9-1 公证书

（a）对每一项涉及文件的公证行为，本州公证人应恰当地制作公证书，公证书应包含或陈述以下内容：

（1）根据第八章第1条规定的公证人正式签名；

（2）加盖第八章第2条规定的公证人公章；

（3）公证地点，包括本州、郡、市、区的名称；

（4）公证日期；以及

（5）在实施具体公证行为时，本法第二章中要求公证人证实的事实和细节。

（b）一项特定公证行为的公证书应满足本章第1条（a）款之要求，并采取以下格式：

（1）本章所确定的该公证行为的对应文书格式；

（2）或本州法律中规定的该公证行为的对应文书格式；

（3）如其无须经本州认可的公证人操作，则可采取其他辖区法律、法规或惯例规定的格式；或者

（4）能完整描述第二章规定的特定公证行为必备要件的格式。

（c）公证书只能使用字母、字符以及公证人能够阅读、书写和理解的语言行文制作。

§9-2 公证书附页方式

在当事人签名公证中，如纸质公证书需附有相关文件，应遵循以下要求：

（1）用装订或其他一旦拆离后可留下痕迹的方式附上；

(2) be attached, signed, and sealed only by the notary and only at the time of notarization and in the presence of the principal;

(3) be attached immediately following the signature page if the certificate is the same size as that page, or to the front of the signature page if the certificate is smaller; and

(4) contain all of the elements described in Section 9-1 on the same sheet of paper.

§9-3 Correcting Notarial Certificate.

A notary public may correct an error or omission made by that notary in a notarial certificate if:

(1) the original certificate and document are returned to the notary;

(2) the notary verifies the error by reference to the pertinent journal entry, the document itself, or to other determinative written evidence;

(3) the notary legibly corrects the certificate and initials and dates the correction in ink, or replaces the original certificate with a correct certificate; and

(4) the notary appends to the pertinent journal entry a notation regarding the nature and date of the correction.

§ 9-4 General Acknowledgment Certificate.

A notary shall use a certificate in substantially the following form in notarizing the signature or mark of any person acknowledging on his or her own behalf of a partner, corporate officer, attorney in fact, or in any other representative capacity:

[State] of _____

[County] of _____

On this _____ day of _____,20___, before me, the undersigned notary, personally appeared _____ (name of document signer),

(personally known to me)

(proved to me through identification documents, which were

_____,)

(proved to me on the oath or affirmation of _____, who is personally known to me and stated to me that (he)(she) personally knows the document signer and is unaffected by the document,)

(proved to me on the oath or affirmation of _____ and _____, whose identities have been proven to me through identification documents and who have stated to me that they personally know the document signer and are unaffected by the document,)

（2）只能在当事人在场的情况下，在公证时由公证人附上、署名、盖章；

（3）若公证书与签名页尺寸相同应紧接签名页面附上，若公证书较小应附于签名页前；以及

（4）篇幅上以一张纸为限，包含本章第1条中提到的全部要素。

§9-3 修正公证书

公证人在满足以下条件时可修正由该公证人制作的公证书中的错误或疏忽：

（1）原始证书和文件已返还给公证人；

（2）公证人通过参考相关日志记录、文件本身或其他决定性书面证据确定确有错误；

（3）公证人用油墨字迹清晰地修正证书、首字母以及日期，或用修正证书替换原始证书；以及

（4）公证人将修正的实质内容和日期追加至相关日志记录。

§9-4 一般确认公证书

对于任何亲自来办理其合伙人、公司官员、代理人或其他代表身份公证事宜的人，公证人在公证其签名或标志的过程中，应大致遵循以下格式：

_____（州）

_____（郡）

于20___年___月___日，在我，署名其下的公证人，见证下，亲自到场的_____（文件签名人姓名），

（为我所熟知）

（通过身份证明文件，即_____向我证明）

（通过_____的宣誓或声明向我证实，该人为我所熟知并向我说明他/她本人认识文件签名人且与文件无利害关系）

（通过_____和_____的宣誓或声明向我证实，该两人的身份已通过身份证明文件向我证明，且已向我说明他们本人认识文件签名人且与文件无利害关系）

to be the person whose name is signed on the preceding or attached document,and acknowledged to me that (he)(she) signed it voluntarily for its statedpurpose(.)

(as partner for _____, a partnership.)
(as _____ for _____, a corporation.)
(as attorney in fact for _____, the principal.)
(as _____ for _____, (a)(the) _____.)

_____
(official signature and seal of notary)

§ 9-5 Jurat Certificate.

A notary shall use a jurat certificate in substantially the following form innotarizing a signature or mark on an affidavit or other sworn or affirmed writtendeclaration:

[State] of _____
[County] of _____
On this _____ day of _____, 20___, before me, the undersigned notary,personally appeared _____ (name of document signer),
(personally known to me)
(proved to me through identification documents, which were_____,)
(proved to me on the oath or affirmation of _____, who ispersonally known to me and stated to me that (he)(she)personally knows the document signer and is unaffected bythe document,)
(proved to me on the oath or affirmation of _____ and_____, whose identities have been proven to methrough identification documents and who have stated to methat they personally know the document signer and areunaffected by the document,)
to be the person who signed the preceding or attached document in mypresence and who swore or affirmed to me that the contents of the documentare truthful and accurate to the best of (his)(her) knowledge and belief.

_____
(official signature and seal of notary)

§ 9-6 Signature Witnessing Certificate.

A notary shall use a certificate in substantially the following form innotarizing a signature or mark to confirm that it was affixed in the notary'spresence without administration of an oath or affirmation:

[State] of _____
[County] of _____
On this _____ day of _____, 20___, before me, the undersigned notary,personally appeared

是在前述文件或附件上签名之人，此人向我确认他/她为文件所述之目的自愿签署。

（作为 _____ 的合伙人）
（作为 _____ 公司的 _____）
（作为本人 _____ 的代理人）
（作为 _____ 的 _____）

_____
（公证人正式签名和盖章）

§9-5 宣誓证明公证书

宣誓书或其他经宣誓或确认的书面声明上的签名或标记，如需公证，公证人应大致遵循以下格式出具宣誓证明公证书：

_____（州）
_____（郡）
于20____年____月____日，在我，署名其下的公证人，见证下，亲自到场的 _____（文件签名人姓名），

（为我所熟知）
（通过身份证明文件，即 _____ 向我证明）
（通过 _____ 的宣誓或声明向我作证，该人为我所熟知并向我说明他/她本人认识文件签名人且与文件无利害关系）
（通过 _____ 和 _____ 的宣誓或声明向我作证，该两人的身份已通过身份证明文件向我证实，且已向我说明他们本人认识文件签名人且与文件无利害关系）

是在我在场时于前述文件或附件上签名之人，此人以他/她的所见及信念为限向我宣誓或声明文件内容真实、准确。

_____
（公证人正式签名和盖章）

§9-6 签名证明公证书

公证人对签名或标记进行公证，以证明其是在公证人在场的情况下未经宣誓或声明而签署的，需大致遵循以下格式出具公证书：

_____（州）
_____（郡）
于20____年____月____日，在我，署名其下的公证人，见证下，亲自到场的 _____（文件签名人姓名），

_____ (name of document signer),

(personally known to me)

(proved to me through identification documents, which were_____,)

(proved to me on the oath or affirmation of _____, who ispersonally known to me and stated to me that (he)(she)personally knows the document signer and is unaffected by the document,)

(proved to me on the oath or affirmation of _____ and _____, whose identities have been proven to methrough identification documents and who have stated to methat they personally know the document signer and areunaffected by the document,)

to be the person who signed the preceding or attached document in my presence.

_____
(official signature and seal of notary)

§ 9-7 Certificates for Signer by Mark and Person Unable to Sign.

On paper documents, certificates in Sections 9-4, 9-5, and 9-6 may be used for signers by mark or persons physically unable to sign or make a mark if:

(1) for a signer by mark, the notary and 2 witnesses disinterested in the document observe the affixation of the mark, both witnesses sign their own names beside the mark, and the notary writes below the mark: "Mark affixed by (name of signer by mark) in the presence of (names and addresses of 2 witnesses) and the undersigned notary pursuant to Section 5-3 of [Act]"; or

(2) for a person physically unable to sign or make a mark, the person directs the notary to sign on his or her behalf in the presence of 2 witnesses disinterested in the document, both witnesses sign their own names beside the signature, and the notary writes below the signature: "Signature affixed by the notary at the direction and in the presence of (name of principal unable to sign or make a mark) and also in the presence of (names and addresses of 2 witnesses) pursuant to Section 5-4 of [Act]".

§ 9-8 Certified Copy Certificate.

A notary shall use a certificate in substantially the following form innotarizing a certified copy:

[State] of _____

[County] of _____

On this _____ day of _____, 20___, I certify that the

(attached or following paper document)

（为我所熟知）

（通过身份证明文件，即_____向我证明）

（通过_____的宣誓或声明向我证实，该人为我所熟知并向我说明他／她本人认识文件签名人且与文件无利害关系）

（通过_____和_____的宣誓或声明向我证实，该两人的身份已通过身份证明文件向我证明，且已向我说明他们本人认识文件签名人且与文件无利害关系）

是在我在场时于前述文件或附件上签名之人。

_____
（公证人正式签名和盖章）

§9-7 适用于标记签名者和签名不能者之公证书

对于纸质文件，满足以下条件时，本章第4条、第5条、第6条规定的公证书格式同样适用于标记签名者和签名不能者：

（1）对标记签名者，公证人及两名与被提交文件无利害关系之证人见证标记之签署，两名证人均在标记旁签署姓名，公证人在标记下写明："依据本法第五章第3条之规定，标记由（标记签名者姓名）在（两名证人姓名和住址）和署名其下的公证人见证下签署"；或者

（2）因身体原因不能签名或标记之人，该人在两名与被提交文件无利害关系之证人见证下指示公证人代表他或她签署，两名证人均在签名旁签署姓名，公证人在签名下写明："依据本法第五章第4条之规定，该签名由公证人经由（签名或标记不能当事人姓名）指示和见证且在（两名证人姓名和住址）见证下签署。"

§9-8 副本证明公证书

在对已证实（与原本相符的）副本公证时，公证人应大致遵循以下格式出具公证书：

_____（州）

_____（郡）

于20___年___月___日，我证明

（附加或下述的纸质文件）

(affixed, attached, or logically associated electronic document)

has been (visually) (electronically) confirmed by me to be a true, exact, and complete copy of the image (or text) (and metadata) of _____ (description of original document),

(presented/e-mailed to me by _____,)

(found by me (online) at _____,)
(held in my custody as a notarial record,)

and that, to the best of my knowledge, the copied document is neither a vital record, a public record, nor a publicly recordable document, certified copies of which may be available from an official source other than a notary public.

_____
(official signature and seal of notary)

§ 9-9 Verification of Fact Certificate.

A notary shall use a certificate in substantially the following form in verifying a fact or facts :

[State] of _____
[County] of _____
On this _____ day of _____, 20___, I certify that I have reviewed the following record(s) or data,

(a) _____,
(b) _____,
(c) _____,
(d) _____,

at the following office, Internet or electronic system locations, respectively,

(a) _____,
(b) _____,
(c) _____,
(d) _____,

or upon the record(s) being presented to me by _____,

and hereby verify the following respective fact(s) as stated in these records:

(a) _____,
(b) _____,
(c) _____,
(d) _____.

_____
(official signature and seal of notary)

（附加、附属或逻辑上相关的电子文件）

由我经（视觉）或（电子途径）对比证实是_____（原始文件描述）图像（或文本）（以及元数据）相同、准确和完整的副本，

（原件由_____递交或通过电子邮件向我提供）

[原件由我在_____（网上）发现]
（原件是由我保管的既往公证记录）

并且，就我所知，被复制的原文件既非重要记录，也非公共记录或公开可记录文件，以致无法从公证人以外的官方渠道获得经认证的副本。

_____
（公证人正式签名和盖章）

§9–9 事实证明公证书

在对事实进行公证时，公证人应大致遵循以下格式出具公证书：

_____（州）
_____（郡）
于20___年___月___日，我证明我已复查了下述记录或资料：

（a）_____,
（b）_____,
（c）_____,
（d）_____,

分别在以下办公室、互联网或电子系统中：

（a）_____,
（b）_____,
（c）_____,
（d）_____,

或据由_____向我递交的记录，

据此证实了记录中分别陈述的以下事实：

（a）_____,
（b）_____,
（c）_____,
（d）_____,

_____
（公证人正式签名和盖章）

Chapter 10 - Evidence of Authenticity of Notarial Act

§ 10-1 Forms of Evidence.

On a notarized document sent to another state or nation, evidence of the authenticity of the official seal and signature of a notary of this [State], if required, shall be in the form of:

(1) a certificate of authority from the [commissioning official] and/ or [designated local official], authenticated as necessary by additional certificates from United States and/or foreign government agencies; or

(2) in the case of a notarized document to be used in a nation that has signed and ratified the Hague Convention Abolishing the Requirement of Legalization for Foreign Public Documents of October 5, 1961, an Apostille from the [federally designated official] in the form prescribed by the Convention and described in Section 10-3, with no additional authenticating certificates required.

§ 10-2 Certificate of Authority.

A certificate of authority evidencing the authenticity of the official seal andsignature of a notary of this [State] shall be substantially in the following form:

Certificate of Authority for a Notarial Act

I, _____ (name, title, jurisdiction of authenticating official), certifythat _____ (name of notary), the person named in the seal andsignature on the attached document, was a Notary Public for the [State] of_____ [name of jurisdiction] and authorized to act as such at thetime of the document's notarization.

To verify this Certificate of Authority for a Notarial Act, I have affixed below my signature and seal of office this _____ day of_____, 20___.

(Signature and seal of commissioning official)

§ 10-3 Apostille.

An Apostille prescribed by the Hague Convention Abolishing theRequirement of Legalization for Foreign Public Documents of October 5,1961, shall be in the form of a square with sides at least 9 centimeters longand contain exactly the following wording:

APOSTILLE

(Convention de La Haye du 5 octobre 1961)

1. Country:_____

This public document

2. has been

第十章　公证行为真实性证据

§10-1 证据格式

对于送往其他州或国家的经公证文件，如需要提供证明本州公证人公章和签名真实性的证据，应按以下格式附于其上：

（1）来自任命官员和/或指定地方官员的授权证书，必要时通过美国和/或外国政府机构出具的其他证书对该授权证书予以验证；或者

（2）对于将送往已签署和批准1961年10月5日《海牙关于取消要求外国公文书认证的公约》的国家使用的公证文书，由联邦指定官员按照公约和本章第3条所规定的形式进行旁注即可，不需要其他真实性证明。

§10-2 授权证书

证明本州公证人公章和签名真实性的授权证书应大致遵循以下格式：

公证行为授权证书

我，_____（姓名，头衔，辖区），证明_____（公证人姓名），附件所载印章、签名上标注之人，是_____（辖区名称）州之公证人，经授权在文件公证之时行使公证人职权。

为证明此公证行为授权证书，下附本人签名、盖章，20____年____月____日。

（任命官员签名盖章）

§10-3 旁注

由1961年10月5日《海牙关于取消要求外国公文书认证的公约》规定的旁注，应当是边长至少9厘米的正方形，并确切包含以下措辞：

旁注

（1961年10月5日海牙公约）

1. 国家：_____

此公文书

2. 由_____签署

signed by_____
3. acting in
the capacity of_____
4. bears the seal/stamp of_____
CERTIFIED
5. at _____
6. The _____
7. by_____
8. No._____
9. Seal/Stamp
10. Signature_____

§ 10-4 Fees.

The [commissioning/federally designated official] may charge:

(1) for issuing a certificate of authority, [dollars]; and

(2) for issuing an Apostille, [dollars].

Chapter 11 - Recognition of Notarial Acts

§ 11-1 Notarial Acts by Officers of This [State].

(a) A notarial act may be performed within this [State] by the following persons:

(1) a notary public of this [State];

(2) a judge, clerk, or deputy clerk of any court of this [State]; [or]

(3) [designations] of other officer[s]; or

(4)]any other officer authorized to perform a specific notarialact by the law of this [State].

(b) The official signature, seal, and title of a person authorized by Subsection (a) to perform a notarial act are prima facie evidence that the signature and seal are genuine and that the person holds the indicated title.

§ 11-2 Notarial Acts by Officers of Other United States Jurisdictions.

(a) A notarial act has the same effect under the law of this [State] as if performed by a notarial officer of this [State] if performed in another state, commonwealth, territory, district, or possession of the United States by any of the following persons:

(1) a notary public of that jurisdiction;

(2) a judge, clerk, or deputy clerk of a court of that jurisdiction; or

(3) any other person authorized by the law of that jurisdiction to perform notarial acts.

(b) The official signature, title, and, if required by law, seal of a person whose authority to perform notarial

3. 以_____身份从事该行为

4. 印有_____的印章
已由以下途径证实

5. 在_____

6. 该_____

7. 由_____

8. 号码_____

9. 盖章

10. 签名：_____

§ 10-4 费用

任命官员/联邦指定官员可就下列事项收取费用：

（1）签发授权证书,（美元）；以及

（2）签发旁注,（美元）。

第十一章 公证行为的承认

§ 11-1 本州官员公证行为

（a）在本州范围内，以下人员可从事公证行为：

（1）本州公证人；

（2）本州任何法庭的法官、书记员或副书记员；或者

（3）指定的其他官员；或者

（4）由本州法律授权从事特定公证行为的任何其他官员。

（b）由(a)款授权从事公证行为的个人，其正式签名、印章和头衔，是证实签名和印章是真实的且此人拥有所示头衔的初步证据。

§ 11-2 美国其他辖区官员之公证行为

（a）若一项公证行为由下列任一人员在美国其他州、自治政区、准州、区或属地履行，该公证行为依照本州法律与本州公证官员从事拥有同等效力：

（1）该辖区公证人；

（2）该辖区法官、法庭书记员或副书记员；或者

（3）由该辖区法律授权从事公证行为的任何其他人员。

（b）由(a)款授权从事公证行为的个人，其正式签名、头衔，如果法律要求，也包括印章是证实签名

acts is recognized by Subsection (a) are prima facie evidence that the signature and seal are genuine and that the person holds the indicated title, and, except in the case of Subparagraph (a)(3), conclusively establishes the authority of a holder of that title to perform a notarial act.

§ 11-3 Notarial Acts by Federal Officers of United States.

(a) A notarial act has the same effect under the law of this [State] as if performed by a notarial officer of this [State] if performed anywhere by any of the following persons under authority granted by the law of the United States:

(1) a judge, clerk, or deputy clerk of a court;

(2) a commissioned United States military officer on active duty;

(3) a foreign service or consular officer of the United States; or

(4) any other person authorized by federal law to perform notarial acts.

(b) The official signature, title, and, if required by law, seal of a person whose authority to perform notarial acts is recognized by Subsection (a) are prima facie evidence that the signature and seal are genuine, that the person holds the indicated title, and, except in the case of Subsection (a)(4), conclusively establishes the authority of a holder of that title to perform a notarial act.

§11-4 Notarial Acts by Foreign Officers.

(a) A notarial act has the same effect under the law of this [State] as if performed by a notarial officer of this [State] if performed within the jurisdiction and under authority of a foreign nation or its constituent units or a multi-national or international organization by any of the following persons:

(1) a notary public or other notarial officer;

(2) a judge, clerk, or deputy clerk of a court of record; or

(3) any other person authorized by the law of that jurisdiction to perform notarial acts.

(b) The official seal or stamp of a person whose authority to perform notarial acts is recognized by Subsection (a) are prima facie evidence that the signature is genuine, that the person holds the indicated title, and, except in the case of Subsection (a)(3), conclusively establishes the authority of a holder of that title to perform a notarial act.

(c) The authority of an officer to perform notarial acts is conclusively established if the title of the office and

和印章是真实的且此人拥有所示头衔的初步证据，除（a）款第 3 项规定的情形外，足以证实头衔拥有者有权从事公证行为。

§11-3 美国联邦官员之公证行为

（a）若一项公证行为由下列任一人员在美国法律的授权下在任一地点履行，该公证行为依照本州法律与本州公证官员从事拥有同等效力：

（1）法官、法庭书记员或副书记员；

（2）美国现役军官；

（3）美国外交官或领事官；或者

（4）由联邦法律授权从事公证行为的任何其他人员。

（b）由(a)款授权从事公证行为的个人，其正式签名、头衔，如果法律要求，也包括印章是证实签名和印章是真实的且此人拥有所示头衔的初步证据，除（a）款第 4 项规定的情形外，足以证实头衔拥有者有权从事公证行为。

§11-4 外国官员之公证行为

（a）若一项公证行为由下列任一人员在外国或其组成单元、多边或国际组织管辖和授权范围内履行，该公证行为依照本州法律与本州公证官员从事拥有同等效力：

（1）公证人或其他公证官员；

（2）记录法庭的法官、法庭书记员或副书记员；或者

（3）由该管辖范围内法律授权从事公证行为的任何其他人员。

（b）由(a)款授权从事公证行为的个人，其公章是证实签名为真实的且此人拥有所示头衔的初步证据，除（a）款第 3 项规定的情形外，足以证实头衔拥有者有权从事公证行为。

（c）若官职头衔出现在外国法律汇编或作为信息来源渠道所惯常使用的清单中，并显示其有权实施公

indication of authority to perform notarial acts appears either in a digest of foreign law or a list customarily used as a source for that information.

(d) An Apostille in the form prescribed by Section 10-3 conclusively establishes that the signature and seal of the notarial officer referenced in the Apostille are genuine and that the person holds the indicated office.

(e) A certificate of a foreign service or consular officer of the United States stationed in the nation under whose jurisdiction the notarial act was performed, or a certificate of a foreign service or consular officer of that nation stationed in the United States, conclusively establishes any matter relating to the authenticity or validity of the notarial act referenced in the certificate.

Chapter 12 - Changes of Status of Notary Public

§ 12-1 Change of Address.

(a) Within 10 days after the change of a notary's residence, business, or mailing address, the notary shall send to the [commissioning official] by any means providing a tangible receipt, including certified mail and electronic transmission, a signed notice of the change, giving both old and new addresses.

(b) If the business address is changed, the notary shall not notarize until:

(1) the notice described in Subsection (a) has been delivered or transmitted;

(2) a Confirmation of Notary's Name or Address Change has been received from the [commissioning official];

(3) a new seal bearing the new business address has been obtained; and

(4) the surety for the notary's bond has been informed in writing.

§ 12-2 Change of Name.

(a) Within 10 days after the change of a notary's name by court order or marriage, the notary shall send to the [commissioning official] by any means providing a tangible receipt, including certified mail and electronic transmission, a signed notice of the change, giving both former and new names, with a copy of any official authorization for such change.

(b) A notary with a new name shall continue to use the former name in performing notarial acts until the following steps have been completed, at which point the notary shall use the new name:

证行为，则足以证实该官员有权从事公证行为。

（d）按照第十章第3条规定的形式制作的旁注足以证实旁注中涉及的公证官员的签名和印章是真实的且此人拥有所示头衔。

（e）驻守在某国的美国外交官或领事官在该国管辖范围内从事公证行为所作之公证书，或驻扎在美国的外国外交官或领事官所作之公证书，足以证实与公证书所涉公证行为真实性或有效性有关的任何事项。

第十二章　公证人身份之变更

§12-1 地址变更

（a）公证人应自其住址、执业地点、通信地址发生变更之日起10日内以可给予回执的任何方式（包括挂号信和电子传输）将已签名的包含新旧地址的变更通知送达任命官员。

（b）若执业地点发生变更，公证人直至下列情形发生后才可继续从事公证行为：

（1）（a）款所述的通知已被递交或发出；

（2）已收到由任命官员发出的公证人姓名或地址变更确认回函；

（3）已取得印有新的营业地址的新印章；以及

（4）已书面通知公证人保证金之保证人。

§12-2 姓名变更

（a）公证人应在因法院命令或婚姻导致其姓名发生变更之日起10日内以可给予回执的任何方式（包括挂号信和电子传输）将已签名的包含原姓名及新姓名的变更通知以及进行该变更的官方授权副本送达任命官员。

（b）申请变更姓名的公证人应继续使用原姓名从事公证行为，直至下列步骤完成后，公证人方可使用新姓名：

(1) the notice described in Subsection (a) has been delivered or transmitted;

(2) a Confirmation of Notary's Name or Address Change has been received from the [commissioning official];

(3) a new seal bearing the new name exactly as in the Confirmation has been obtained; and

(4) the surety for the notary's bond has been informed in writing.

§ 12-3 Resignation.

(a) A notary who resigns his or her commission shall send to the [commissioning official] by any means providing a tangible receipt, including certified mail and electronic transmission, a signed notice indicating the effective date of resignation.

(b) Notaries who cease to reside in or to maintain a regular place of work or business in this [State], or who become permanently unable to perform their notarial duties, shall resign their commissions.

§ 12-4 Disposition of Seal and Journal.

(a) Except as provided in Subsection (b), when a notary commission expires or is resigned or revoked, the notary shall:

(1) as soon as reasonably practicable, destroy or deface all notary seals so that they may not be misused; and

(2) within 30 days after the effective date of resignation, revocation, or expiration, dispose of the journal and notarial records in accordance with Section 7-5 of this [Act].

(b) A former notary who intends to apply for a new commission and whose previous commission or application was not revoked or denied by this [State], need not dispose of the journal and notarial records within 30 days after commission expiration, but must do so within 3 months after expiration unless recommissioned within that period.

§ 12-5 Death of Notary.

If a notary dies during the term of commission or before fulfilling the obligations stipulated in Section 124, the notary's personal representative shall:

(1) notify the [commissioning official] of the death in writing;

(2) as soon as reasonably practicable, destroy or deface all notary seals so that they may not be misused; and

(3) within 30 days after death, dispose of the journal

（1）（a）款所述的通知已被递交或发出；

（2）已收到由任命官员发出的公证人姓名或地址变更确认回函；

（3）已取得印有与确认回函中所载完全一致的新姓名的新印章；以及

（4）已书面通知公证人保证金之保证人。

§12-3 辞职

（a）辞去任命的公证人应以可给予回执的任何方式（包括挂号信和电子传输）将已签名的注明辞职生效日期的变更通知送达任命官员。

（b）停止在本州居住或维持经常工作地或主要营业场所的，以及永久性丧失履行公证职责能力的公证人应当辞去其任命。

§12-4 印章和日志的处置

（a）除（b）款规定的情形外，当公证人任期结束或辞职或被撤销任命时，公证人应当：

（1）应在合理时限内及早销毁印章或破坏印面，以防其被不当使用；以及

（2）辞职、任命被撤销或任期结束的，自上述情形生效之日起30日内，依照本法第七章第5条的规定对日志及公证记录予以处置。

（b）想要重新申请任命，且其原任命或申请不存在被本州撤销或拒绝情形的前公证人，无须自任期结束之日起30日内处置其日志和公证记录，但如其新任命申请未获批的，必须于任期结束之日3个月内处置其日志和公证记录。

§12-5 公证人死亡

若公证人在任期内或在完成本章第4条规定的义务前死亡的，其个人代表应当：

（1）书面通知任命官员死亡事实；

（2）应在合理时限内及早销毁印章或破坏印面，以防其被不当使用；以及

（3）在死亡事实发生后30日内，依照本法第七

and notarial records in accordance with Section 7-5 of this [Act].

Chapter 13 – Liability, Sanctions, and Remedies for Improper Acts

§ 13-1 Liability of Notary, Surety, and Employer.

(a) A notary is liable to any person for all damages proximately caused that person by the notary's negligence, intentional violation of law, or official misconduct in relation to a notarization.

(b) A surety for a notary's bond is liable to any person for damages proximately caused that person by the notary's negligence, intentional violation of law, or official misconduct in relation to a notarization during the bond term, but this liability may not exceed the dollar amount of the bond or of any remaining bond funds that have not been disbursed to other claimants. Regardless of the number of claimants against the bond or the number of notarial acts cited in the claims, a surety's aggregate liability shall not exceed the dollar amount of the bond.

(c) An employer of a notary is liable to any person for all damages proximately caused that person by the notary's negligence, intentional violation of law, or official misconduct in performing a notarization during the course of employment, if the employer directed, expected, encouraged, approved, or tolerated the notary's negligence, violation of law, or official misconduct either in the particular transaction or, impliedly, by the employer's previous action in at least one similar transaction involving any notary employed by the employer.

(d) An employer of a notary is liable to the notary for all damages recovered from the notary as a result of any violation of law by the notary that was coerced by threat of the employer, if the threat, such as of demotion or dismissal, was made in reference to the particular notarization or, impliedly, by the employer's previous action in at least one similar transaction involving any notary employed by the employer. In addition, the employer is liable to the notary for damages caused the notary by demotion, dismissal, or other action resulting from the notary^s refusal to engage in a violation of law or official misconduct.

(e) Notwithstanding any other provision in this Act, for the purposes of this section "negligence" shall not include any good-faith determination made by the notary pursuant to the obligations imposed by Subparagraph 5-2 (3) or (4).

章第 5 条的规定对日志及公证记录予以处置。

第十三章 不当行为的责任、惩罚及赔偿

§13-1 公证人、保证人及雇主责任

（a）对与公证过程相关的，依近因原则可归咎于公证人过失、故意违法或职务不当行为的他人所有损失，公证人应予承担责任。

（b）对保证期内，与公证过程相关的，依近因原则可归咎于公证人过失、故意违法或职务不当行为的他人所有损失，公证人保证金之保证人应予承担责任，但其责任以保证金总额或未分配给其他索赔者的剩余保证金总额为限。保证人的总责任不应超过保证金总额，无论索赔者有多少名、索赔所涉公证行为有多少起。

（c）对雇用期内，与公证过程相关的，依近因原则可归咎于公证人过失、故意违法或职务不当行为的他人所有损失，如公证人之雇主指示、期望、鼓励、赞同或容忍了该特定过失、故意违法或职务不当行为，或者通过对其所雇公证员此前至少一起类似业务采取的举措，隐含地表明了上述态度的，则雇主应予承担责任。

（d）在特定公证行为中，公证人面对雇主降职或解雇的威胁，或因雇主对其所雇公证员此前至少一起类似业务采取的举措，而隐含地感受到上述威胁态度，进而违法操作导致承担损害赔偿金的，有权向其雇主追偿。此外，公证人如因拒绝参与违法或职务不当行为被降职、解雇或采取其他措施的，雇主应向其承担损害赔偿责任。

（e）无论本法其他条款作何规定，从本部分立法目的出发，"过失"不应包括公证人为履行第五章第 2 条第 3 项及第 4 项规定的义务所作之任何善意决定。

§ 13-2 Proximate Cause.

Recovery of damages against a notary, surety, or employer does not require that the notary^s negligence, violation of law, or official misconduct be either the sole or principal proximate cause of the damages.

§ 13-3 Revocation.

(a) The [commissioning official] may revoke a notary commission for any ground on which an application for a commission may be denied under Section 3-1(c).

(b) The [commissioning official] shall revoke the commission of any notary who fails:

(1) to maintain a residence or a regular place of work or business in this [State]; and

(2) to maintain status as a legal resident of the United States.

(c) Prior to revocation of a notary commission, the [commissioning official] shall inform the notary of the basis for the revocation and that the revocation takes effect on a particular date unless a proper appeal is filed with the [administrative body hearing appeal] before that date.

(d) Resignation or expiration of a notary commission does not terminate or preclude an investigation into the notary's conduct by the [commissioning official], who may pursue the investigation to a conclusion, whereupon it shall be made a matter of public record whether or not the finding would have been grounds for revocation.

§13-4 Other Remedial Actions for Misconduct.

(a) The [commissioning official] may deliver a written Official Warning to Cease Misconduct to any notary whose actions are judged to be official misconduct.

(b) The [commissioning official] may seek a court injunction to prevent a person from violating any provision of this [Act].

§ 13-5 Publication of Sanctions and Remedial Actions.

The [commissioning official] shall regularly publish a list of persons whose notary commissions have been revoked by the [commissioning official] or whose actions as a notary were the subject of a court injunction or Official Warning to Cease Misconduct.

§ 13-6 Criminal Sanctions.

(a) In performing a notarial act, a notary is guilty of a [class of offense], punishable upon conviction by a fine not exceeding [dollars] or imprisonment for not more than [term of imprisonment], or both, for knowingly:

§13-2 近因

公证人、保证人及雇主损害赔偿责任的成立并不要求公证人的过失、违法或职务不当行为是导致损害结果的单独或主要近因。

§13-3 撤销

（a）任命官员可根据第三章第1条（c）款拒绝任命申请的任一情形撤销公证人的任命。

（b）任命官员在公证人不符下列要求时，应当撤销其任命：

（1）在本州维持一个住所或经常工作地或主要营业场所；以及

（2）维持美国合法居留者身份。

（c）在撤销公证人任命前，任命官员应当通知公证人撤销理由，以及，除非在生效日期前向申诉机构提交恰当的申诉，该撤销于指定日期生效。

（d）公证人辞职或任期结束并不终止或排除任命官员对公证人行为的调查，任命官员可继续调查直至得出结论，无论该结论是否作为撤销依据，均应作为公共记录保存。

§13-4 对不当行为的其他补救措施

（a）任命官员可向被裁定有职务不当行为的任一公证人发出书面的停止不当行为的正式警告。

（b）任命官员可寻求法院禁令以阻止任何人违反本法规定。

§13-5 惩罚及补救行为的公布

任命官员应当定期公开公证人任命被任命官员撤销、公证行为触犯法院禁令或被正式警告停止不当行为的人员名单。

§13-6 刑事责任

（a）公证人从事公证行为时有下列故意行为，应被认定为（犯罪类型），一经定罪处以最高（美元）罚款或最长（刑期）监禁，或并处：

(1) failing to require the presence of a principal at the time of the notarial act;

(2) failing to identify a principal through personal knowledge or satisfactory evidence; or

(3) executing a false notarial certificate under Subsection 5- 8(a).

(b) A notary who knowingly performs or fails to perform any other act prohibited or mandated respectively by this [Act] may be guilty of a [class of offense], punishable upon conviction by a fine not exceeding [dollars] or imprisonment for not more than [term of imprisonment], or both.

§ 13-7 Additional Remedies and Sanctions Not Precluded.

The remedies and sanctions of this chapter do not preclude other remedies and sanctions provided by law.

Chapter 14 - Violations by Non-Notary

§ 14-1 Impersonation.

Any person not a notary who knowingly acts as or otherwise impersonates a notary is guilty of a [class of offense], punishable upon conviction by a fine not exceeding [dollars] or imprisonment for not more than [term of imprisonment], or both.

§ 14-2 Wrongful Possession.

Any person who knowingly obtains, conceals, defaces, or destroys the seal, journal, or official records of a notary is guilty of a [class of offense], punishable upon conviction by a fine not exceeding [dollars] or imprisonment for not more than [term of imprisonment], or both.

§ 14-3 Improper Influence.

Any person who knowingly solicits, coerces, or in any way influences a notary to commit official misconduct is guilty of a [class of offense], punishable upon conviction by a fine not exceeding [dollars] or imprisonment for not more than [term of imprisonment], or both.

§ 14-4 Additional Sanctions Not Precluded.

The sanctions of this chapter do not preclude other sanctions and remedies provided by law.

Article III
Electronic Notary

Chapter 15 - Definitions Used in This Article

§ 15-1 Capable of Independent Verification.

"Capable of independent verification" means that any

（1）公证时未要求当事人到场；

（2）未通过个人熟知或充分证据证实当事人身份；或者

（3）制作第五章第8条（a）款所述虚假公证书。

（b）公证人故意从事本法其他任何禁止行为或未履行本法其他任何指令行为，可被认定为（犯罪类型），一经定罪处以最高（美元）罚款或最长（刑期）监禁，或并处。

§13-7 不排除其他赔偿和惩罚的适用

本章规定的赔偿和惩罚措施并不排除法律规定的其他赔偿和惩罚的适用。

第十四章 非公证人的违法行为

§14-1 假冒

任何人故意假冒公证人应被认定为（犯罪类型），一经定罪处以最高（美元）罚款或最长（刑期）监禁，或并处。

§14-2 非法持有

任何人故意占有、隐匿、损坏或销毁公证人印章、日志或公务记录应被认定为（犯罪类型），一经定罪处以最高（美元）罚款或最长（刑期）监禁，或并处。

§14-3 不当影响

任何人故意唆使、胁迫或通过任何方式影响公证人，致使其作出职务不当行为的，应被认定为（犯罪类型），一经定罪处以最高（美元）罚款或最长（刑期）监禁，或并处。

§14-4 不排除其他惩罚的适用

本章规定的惩罚措施并不排除法律规定的其他惩罚和赔偿的适用。

第三编
电子公证

第十五章 本编使用之定义

§15-1 可独立核查

"可独立核查"是指任何有利害关系之个人可通

interested person may confirm the validity of an electronic notarial act and an electronic notary public^s identity and authority through a publicly accessible system.

§ 15-2 Electronic.

"Electronic" means relating to technology having electrical, digital, magnetic, wireless, optical, electromagnetic, or similar capabilities.

§ 15-3 Electronic Document.

"Electronic document" means information that is created, generated, sent, communicated, received, or stored by electronic means.

§ 15-4 Electronic Journal of Notarial Acts.

"Electronic journal of notarial acts" and "electronic journal" mean a chronological electronic record of notarizations that is maintained by the notary public who performed the same notarizations.

§ 15-5 Electronic Notarial Act and Electronic Notarization.

"Electronic notarial act" and "electronic notarization" mean an official act involving an electronic document that is performed in compliance with this Article by an electronic notary public as a security procedure [as defined in the Uniform Electronic Transactions Act].

§ 15-6 Electronic Notarial Certificate.

"Electronic notarial certificate" means the part of, or attachment to, a notarized electronic document that, in the performance of an electronic notarization, is completed by the electronic notary public, bears the notary's registered electronic signature and seal, and states the date, venue, and facts attested to or certified by the notary in the particular electronic notarization.

§ 15-7 Electronic Notary Public and Electronic Notary.

"Electronic notary public" and "electronic notary" mean a notary public who has registered with the [commissioning official] the capability to perform electronic notarial acts.

§ 15-8 Electronic Notary Seal.

"Electronic notary seal" and "electronic seal" mean information within a notarized electronic document that includes the electronic notary's name, title, jurisdiction, and commission expiration date.

过公开访问的系统确认电子公证行为的有效性和电子公证人的身份和授权。

§15-2 电子的

"电子的"是指同具有电学、数字、磁、无线、光学、电磁或相似性能的相关技术。

§15-3 电子文件

"电子文件"是指通过电子手段创设、生成、发送、传播、接收或存储的信息。

§15-4 电子公证人日志

"电子公证人日志"和"电子日志"是指由公证人本人维护，按公证时间先后顺序记录的电子公证记录。

§15-5 电子公证行为和电子公证

"电子公证行为"和"电子公证"是指由电子公证人依照本编规定，按照《统一电子交易法》中规定的安全程序实施的，包含电子文件的职务行为。

§15-6 电子公证书

"电子公证书"是指经公证的电子文件的一部分或其附件，其由电子公证人在电子公证过程中出具，载有公证人的注册电子签名和印章，记录了特定电子公证行为中已向公证人证明或经由公证人核实过的日期、地点和事实。

§15-7 电子公证人

"电子公证人"是指已向任命官员登记具备从事电子公证行为之资格的公证人。

§15-8 电子公证人印章

"电子公证人印章"和"电子印章"是指电子公证文件中包括电子公证人姓名、头衔、辖区、任期终止日期在内的一系列信息。

§ 15-9 Electronic Signature.

"Electronic signature" means an electronic sound, symbol, or process attached to or logically associated with an electronic document and executed or adopted by a person with the intent to sign the document.

§ 15-10 Registered Electronic Notary Seal.

"Registered electronic notary seal" means an electronic notary seal produced by a notary in the performance of an electronic notarial act by a means that was registered with the [commissioning official].

§ 15-11 Registered Electronic Signature.

"Registered electronic signature" means an electronic signature produced by a notary in the performance of an electronic notarial act by a means that was registered with the [commissioning official].

§ 15-12 Security Procedure.

"Security procedure" means a procedure employed for the purpose of verifying that an electronic signature, document, or performance is that of a specific person or for detecting changes or errors in the information in an electronic document. The term includes a procedure that requires the use of algorithms or other codes, identifying words or numbers, encryption, or callback, or other acknowledgment procedures.

Chapter 16 - Registration as Electronic Notary

§16-1 Registration with [Commissioning Official].

(a) A notary public shall register the capability to perform electronic notarial acts with the [commissioning official] before notarizing electronically.

(b) Upon recommissioning, a notary public shall again register with the [commissioning official] before notarizing electronically.

(c) A person may apply or reapply for a notary commission and register or reregister to perform electronic notarial acts at the same time.

§16-2 Course of Instruction and Examination.

(a) Before initially registering the capability to perform electronic notarial acts, an electronic notary public shall complete a course of instruction of [4] hours approved by the [commissioning official], in addition to the course required for commissioning as a notary, and pass an examination based on the course.

(b) The content of the course shall be notarial laws,

§15-9 电子签名

"电子签名"是指附于电子文件上或与电子文件有逻辑关系的电子声音、符号或程序上，该电子签名是当事人为签署之目的而制作或采用。

§15-10 注册电子公证人印章

"注册电子公证人印章"是指公证人在电子公证行为中，通过已向任命官员登记的方式加盖之电子公证印章。

§15-11 注册电子签名

"注册电子签名"是指公证人在电子公证行为中，通过已向任命官员登记的方式签署之电子签名。

§15-12 安全程序

"安全程序"是指一项程序，该程序用于确认一项电子签名、电子文件或电子履行确属某一特定个人，或用于检测电子文件中的信息变动或信息错误，该术语也囊括了需要使用算法或其他代码、鉴别词句和数字、加密、回调或其他确认程序的程序。

第十六章 电子公证人之登记

§16-1 向任命官员进行登记

（a）公证人在进行电子公证前应向任命官员登记其从事电子公证行为之资格。

（b）重新任命后，公证人在进行电子公证前应重新向任命官员登记。

（c）个人可同时申请/重新申请公证人任命以及登记/重新登记从事电子公证行为。

§16-2 培训课程和考试

（a）在首次登记从事电子公证行为之资格前，电子公证人除完成公证人任命要求所需课程外，另须完成一项由任命官员批准的至少4个小时的培训课程，并须通过该课程考试。

（b）培训课程内容为与电子公证有关的公证法

procedures, and ethics pertaining to electronic notarization.

§ 16-3 Term of Registration of Electronic Notary.

The term of registration of an electronic notary public begins on the registration starting date set by the [commissioning official] and continues as long as the notary's commission remains in effect or until registration is terminated under Subsection 24-2(a).

§ 16-4 Electronic Registration Form.

To register the capability to perform electronic notarial acts, a notary public shall electronically sign and submit to the [commissioning official] an electronic form prescribed by the [commission official] which includes:

(1) proof of successful completion of the course and examination required by Section 16-2;

(2) the following information:

(i) a description of each separate means that will be used to produce electronic signatures [and electronic notary seals];

(ii) any keys, codes, software, decrypting instructions, or graphics that will allow the electronic signatures [and seals] produced by the means described in Subparagraph (i) to be verified;

(iii) the names of any licensed authorities issuing the means for producing the electronic signatures [and seals], the source of each license, and the starting and expiration dates of each pertinent certificate, software, or process;

(iv) an explanation of any revocation, annulment, or other premature termination of any certificate, software, or process ever issued or registered to the applicant to produce an electronic signature or seal;[and]

[(v) a declaration that the notary public will use the means issued or authorized for issuance by the [commissioning official] for producing an electronic notary seal; and]

(3) if the notary will use an electronic journal of notarial acts as described in Chapter 20, the access instructions that will allow the journal to be viewed, printed out, and copied.

§16-5 Registration of Multiple Means.

Under Section 16-4, a notary public may register at the same or different times 1 or more respective means for producing electronic signatures and electronic notary seals, or single elements combining the required features of both, consistent with the requirements cited elsewhere in this [Act].

律、程序规范及职业道德。

§16-3 电子公证人登记之期限

电子公证人登记之期限始于任命官员设定的登记起始日期，终于公证人任期期满之日，或依据第二十四章第2条（a）款规定的终止登记之日。

§16-4 电子登记表

登记从事电子公证行为之资格，公证人应向任命官员以电子形式签署和提交一份由任命官员指定的包含以下内容的电子表格：

（1）顺利完成本章第2条要求的培训课程和考试的证明；

（2）以下信息：

（i）用于创建电子签名和电子公证人印章的各独立装置之描述；

（ii）用于验证（i）中所述的装置创建之电子签名和印章所需的秘钥、密码、软件、解密说明或图像；

（iii）任何签发创建电子签名和印章用装置的有权当局之名称，每一执照来源，以及每项相关证明、软件或程序的开始和终止日期；

（iv）如签发或注册给申请人用于生成电子签名和印章的证书、软件或程序存在被撤销、废止或其他提前终止情形，应予说明；以及

（v）公证人将使用由任命官员签发或授权签发的装置创建电子公证人印章的声明；以及

（3）若公证人使用第二十章规定的电子公证人日志，则包括对日志进行浏览、打印及复制的访问指令。

§16-5 多重装置的登记

根据本章第4条登记时，公证人可一次性或分多次登记一项或多项装置，用以生成电子签名和电子公证人印章，或登记符合本法其他章节规定的结合两者所有特征的单项要素。

§ 16-6 Material Misstatement or Omission of Fact.

The [commissioning official] shall deny registration to any applicant submitting an electronic registration form that contains a material misstatement or omission of fact.

§ 16-7 Fee for Registration.

The fee payable to the [commissioning official] for registering or reregistering as an electronic notary public is [dollars].

§ 16-8 Confidentiality.

Information in the registration form of an electronic notary public shall be used by the [commissioning official] and designated [State] employees only for the purpose of performing official duties, and shall not be disclosed to any person other than to:

(1) a government agent acting in an official capacity and duly authorized to obtain such information;

(2) a person authorized by court order; or

(3) the registrant or the registrant's duly authorized agent.

Chapter 17 - Electronic Notarial Acts

§ 17-1 Authorized Electronic Notarial Acts.

The following notarial acts may be performed electronically:

(1) acknowledgment;

(2) jurat;

(3) signature witnessing;

(4) copy certification; and

(5) verification of fact.

§ 17-2 Requirements for Electronic Notarial Acts.

An electronic notary public shall perform an electronic notarization only if the principal:

(1) is in the presence of the notary at the time of notarization;

(2) is personally known to the notary or identified by the notary through satisfactory evidence;

(3) appears to understand the nature of the transaction;

(4) appears to be acting of his or her own free will;

(5) communicates directly with the notary in a language both understand; and

(6) reasonably establishes the electronic signature as his or her own.

§16-6 重大虚假陈述或遗漏事实

对提交包含重大虚假陈述或遗漏事实的电子登记表的任何申请人，任命官员应当拒绝登记。

§16-7 登记费用

向任命官员支付的登记或重新登记成为电子公证人的费用为（美元）。

§16-8 保密条款

电子公证人注册表之信息只能由任命官员及指定的州雇员为履行职责之目的使用，除以下情形外，不得向其他人员泄露：

（1）以官方身份，被授权获取此类信息的政府官方代理人；
（2）法院命令授权的个人；或者
（3）登记人本人或其授权代理人。

第十七章　电子公证行为

§17-1 授权电子公证行为

下列公证行为可通过电子方式进行：

（1）确认；
（2）宣誓证明；
（3）签名证明；
（4）副本证明；以及
（5）事实证明。

§17-2 电子公证行为要求

只有在当事人符合下列情形时，电子公证人才能从事相关电子公证行为：
（1）公证时亲临现场；

（2）为公证人所熟知或通过充分的证据向公证人证实身份；
（3）理解公证行为的业务性质；

（4）出于自身意愿；
（5）能够以双方均能理解的语言与公证人直接交流；以及
（6）合理创建本人电子签名。

§17-3 Notary May Sign for Principal Unable to Sign Electronically.

An electronic notary public may electronically sign the name of a principal physically unable to make an electronic signature on an electronic document presented for notarization if:

(1) the principal directs the electronic notary to do so in the presence of 2 witnesses disinterested in the document;

(2) the electronic notary electronically signs the principal's name in the presence of the principal and the 2 witnesses;

(3) both witnesses sign their own names in the electronic notary's journal;

(4) the electronic notary writes on the electronic notarial certificate: "Signature made by the electronic notary at the direction and in the presence of (name of principal unable to sign electronically) and in the presence of (names and addresses of 2 witnesses) pursuant to Section 17-3 of [Act]"; and

(5) the electronic notary notarizes the signature through an acknowledgment, jurat, or signature witnessing.

§ 17-4 All Notarial Rules Apply.

In performing electronic notarial acts, an electronic notary shall adhere to all applicable rules governing notarial acts provided in this [Act].

Chapter 18 – Electronic Notarial Certificate

§18-1 Completion of Electronic Notarial Certificate.

In performing an electronic notarial act, the notary shall properly complete an electronic notarial certificate.

§18-2 Components of Electronic Notarial Certificate.

A proper electronic notarial certificate shall contain:

(1) completed wording appropriate to the particular electronic notarial act, as prescribed in Section 18-3;

(2) a registered electronic signature; and

(3) a registered electronic notary seal, which shall include:

(i) the name of the electronic notary fully and exactly as it is spelled on the notary's commissioning document;

(ii) the jurisdiction that commissioned and registered the electronic notary;

(iii) the title "Electronic Notary Public";

(iv) the commission or registration number of the

§17-3 当事人电子签名不能时公证人可代签情形

在满足以下条件时，对于因身体原因不能在提交待公证电子文件上签名的当事人，电子公证人可替代其进行电子签名：

（1）当事人在两名与被提交文件无利害关系之证人见证下指示电子公证人签署；

（2）电子公证人在当事人和两名证人见证下电子签署当事人姓名；

（3）两名证人均在电子公证人日志中签署姓名；

（4）电子公证人在电子公证书中写明："依据本法第十七章第3条之规定，签名由电子公证人在（电子签名不能当事人姓名）指示和见证且在（两名证人姓名和住址）见证下签署"；以及

（5）电子公证人通过确认、宣誓证明或签名证明对签名进行公证。

§17-4 公证规则普遍适用

从事电子公证行为时，电子公证人应当遵守本法所有调整公证行为之规则。

第十八章 电子公证书

§18-1 电子公证书之完成

在从事电子公证行为中，公证人应恰当地完成电子公证书。

§18-2 电子公证书之构成

一份恰当的电子公证书应当包含以下内容：

（1）本章第3条所规定的，针对特定电子公证行为的完整、恰当措辞；

（2）注册电子签名；以及

（3）包含以下信息的注册电子公证人印章：

（i）与委任状所载完全一致的电子公证人姓名；

（ii）任命、登记电子公证人的辖区；

（iii）"电子公证人"头衔；

（iv）电子公证人委任状或登记序号；以及

electronic notary; and

(v) the commission expiration date of the electronic notary.

§ 18-3 Form of Electronic Notarial Certificate.

(a) The wording of an electronic notarial certificate shall be in a form that:

(1) is set forth in Chapter 9 of this [Act];

(2) is otherwise prescribed by the law of this [State];

(3) is prescribed by a law, regulation, or custom of another jurisdiction, provided it does not require actions by the electronic notary that are unauthorized by this [State]; or

(4) describes the actions of the electronic notary in such a manner as to meet the requirements of the particular notarial act, as defined in Chapter 2 of this [Act].

(b) A notarial certificate shall be worded and completed using only letters, characters, and a language that are read, written, and understood by the electronic notary.

Chapter 19 – Registered Electronic Signature and Seal

§ 19-1 Electronic Signature and Seal Attributed to Notary.

In notarizing an electronic document, the notary shall attach to, or logically associate with, the electronic notarial certificate a registered electronic signature and a registered electronic notary seal, or a registered single element in conformance with Section 16-5, in such a manner that the signature and the seal, or the single element, are attributed to the notary as named on the commission.

§19-2 Attributes of Registered Electronic Signature.

A registered electronic signature shall be:

(1) unique to the electronic notary public;

(2) capable of independent verification;

(3) attached to or logically associated with an electronic notarial certificate in such a manner that any subsequent alteration of the certificate or underlying electronic document prominently displays evidence of the alteration; and

(4) attached or logically associated by a means under the electronic notary's sole control.

§19-3 Security of Registered Electronic Notary Seal.

At all times the means for producing registered electronic notary seals, or registered single elements as described in Section 16-5, shall be kept under the sole con-

（v）电子公证人任期结束日期。

§18-3 电子公证书之格式

（a）电子公证书之措辞应当符合以下格式：

（1）本法第九章中规定的格式；

（2）或本州法律中另有规定的格式；

（3）如果其不需要未经本州授权的电子公证人操作，可采取在其他辖区法律、法规或惯例规定的格式；或者

（4）描述电子公证人行为时，描述方式满足本法第二章规定的、针对特定公证行为的要求。

（b）公证书只能使用电子公证人能够阅读、书写和理解的字母、字符以及语言措辞来完成。

第十九章　注册电子签名和印章

§19-1 电子签名及印章可溯源至公证人

公证电子文件时，公证人应当将注册电子签名以及注册电子公证人印章，或依据第十六章第5条已登记之单项要素，以可识别其出自委任状所载公证人之手的方式，附于电子公证书，或符合逻辑地与电子公证书相联系。

§19-2 注册电子签名之特性

注册电子签名应当：
（1）专属于电子公证人；
（2）可独立核查；
（3）以针对证书或基础电子文件的后续修改都能留下显著证据的方式，附于电子公证书，或符合逻辑地与电子公证书相联系；以及

（4）在电子公证人全权控制下，附于电子公证书，或符合逻辑地与电子公证书相联系。

§19-3 注册电子公证人印章之保护

无论何时，创建注册电子公证人印章或第十六章第5条所述已登记之单项要素的装置应当在电子公证人全权控制下保管。

trol of the electronic notary.

§ 19-4 Employer Shall Not Use or Control Means.

An employer of an electronic notary shall not use or control the means for producing registered electronic signatures and notary seals, or registered single elements combining the required features of both, nor upon termination of a notary's employment, retain any software, coding, disk, certificate, card, token, or program that is intended exclusively to produce a registered electronic signature, notary seal, or combined single element, whether or not the employer financially supported the employee's activities as a notary.

§ 19-5 Non-Notarial Use.

(a) A registered electronic signature may be used by the electronic notary for lawful purposes other than performing electronic notarizations, provided that neither the title "notary" nor any other indication of status as a notarial officer is part of the signature.

(b) Neither a registered electronic notary seal nor a combined single element containing the seal shall be used by the electronic notary for any purpose other than performing lawful electronic notarizations.

Chapter 20 – Record of Electronic Notarial Acts

§ 20-1 Maintaining Journal of Electronic Notarial Acts.

(a) An electronic notary public shall keep, maintain, protect, and provide for lawful inspection a chronological journal of notarial acts that is either:

(1) a permanently bound book with numbered pages; or

(2) an electronic journal of notarial acts as described in Section 20-2.

(b) An electronic notary shall keep a record of electronic and non-electronic notarial acts in the same journal.

(c) An electronic notary shall maintain only 1 active journal at the same time, except that a backup of each active and inactive electronic journal shall be retained by the notary in accordance with Subparagraph 20-2(3) as long as each respective original journal is retained.

§20-2 Attributes of Electronic Journal.

An electronic journal of notarial acts shall:

(1) allow journal entries to be made, viewed, printed out, and copied only after access is obtained by a procedure that uses two factors of authentication;

§19-4 雇主不得使用或控制装置

电子公证人雇主不得使用或控制用于创建注册电子签名和公证人印章，或结合两者所有特征的单项要素之装置，不得在公证人雇佣期结束时，保留任何专门旨在创建注册电子签名、公证人印章或结合两者的单项要素之软件、代码、磁盘、证书、卡、令牌或程序，无论雇主是否对雇员的公证活动给予经济支持。

§19-5 非公证使用

（a）注册电子签名可被电子公证人用于除履行电子公证行为外之合法目的，只要签名中不出现"公证人"头衔及其他任何作为公证职员的迹象。

（b）注册电子公证人印章及包含印章的单项要素集合不得被电子公证人用于除履行法定电子公证行为外之任何目的。

第二十章 电子公证行为记录

§20-1 电子公证人日志的保存

（a）公证人日志按时间顺序记录，公证人应妥善保管、维护、保护，遇依法查验时及时予以提供，该日志为：

（1）编页的永久装订本；或者

（2）本法第二十章第2条规定的电子公证人日志。

（b）公证人应将电子公证行为和非电子公证行为记录于同一本日志。

（c）同一时间，公证人只能保存一本有效日志，除非依照第二十章第2条第3项规定保存一份电子日志的备份以备原始日志丢失。

§20-2 电子日志之特性

电子公证人日志应当：

（1）只有通过两认证因素的程序获取访问权限后，日志记录才能被创建、浏览、打印及复制；

(2) not allow a journal entry to be deleted or altered in content or sequence by the notary or any other person after a record of the notarization is entered and stored;

(3) have a backup system in place to provide a duplicate record of notarial acts as a precaution in the event of loss of the original record;

(4) be capable of capturing and storing the image of a handwritten signature and the data related to 1 other type of recognized biometric identifier; and

(5) be capable of printing out and providing electronic copies of any entry, including images of handwritten signatures and the data related to the 1 other selected type of recognized biometric identifier.

§20-3 Rules for Electronic Journal.

In maintaining an electronic journal of notarial acts, a notary public shall comply with the applicable prescriptions and prohibitions regarding the contents, copying, security, surrender, and disposition of a journal as set forth in Chapters 7 and 12 of this [Act].

§ 20-4 [Commissioning Official's] Access to Electronic Journal.

If an electronic notary public elects to keep an electronic journal of notarial acts pursuant to Subsection 20-1(a), the notary shall:

(1) provide to the [commissioning official] on the registration form described in Section 16-4 the access instructions that allow journal entries to be viewed, printed out, and copied; and

(2) notify the [commissioning official] of any subsequent change to the access instructions.

Chapter 21 - Fees of Electronic Notary

§ 21-1 Imposition and Waiver of Fees.

(a) For performing an electronic notarial act, an electronic notary public may charge the maximum fee specified in Section 21-2, charge less than the maximum fee, or waive the fee.

(b) An electronic notary shall not discriminatorily condition the fee for an electronic notarial act on the attributes of the principal or requester of fact as set forth in Subsection 5-6(a) of this [Act], though an electronic notary may waive or reduce fees for humanitarian or charitable reasons.

§ 21-2 Maximum Fees.

(a) The maximum fees that may be charged by an

（2）公证记录一经输入并存储后，公证人或其他任何人即无法删改其内容或顺序；

（3）作为预防措施，应具备备份系统，用以当原记录丢失时提供公证行为副本记录；

（4）能够捕获和存储手写签名图像以及与另一种可辨识计量生物学标志相关的数据；以及

（5）能够打印出和提供任一记录的电子副本，包括手写签名图像以及另一种选定的与可辨识计量生物学标志相关的数据。

§20-3 电子日志规则

保存电子公证人日志，公证人应当遵守本法第七章和第十二章阐明的有关日志内容、复制、保护、提交和处置的适用规定和禁令。

§20-4 任命官员对电子日志的访问

如果电子公证人依据本章第1条（a）款的规定选择创建电子公证人日志，应当：

（1）在第十六章第4条所述登记表中向任命官员提供允许对日志记录进行浏览、打印及复制的访问指令；以及

（2）通知任命官员 关于访问指令的所有后续变更情况。

第二十一章 电子公证人费用

§21-1 收取或免除费用

（a）对从事电子公证活动，电子公证人可按本章第2条规定的最高额收费，也可以低于最高额收费或免收费用。

（b）电子公证人可基于人道主义精神或慈善因素免除或减少费用，但不得因第五章第6条（a）款所列当事人及申请者情形歧视性收费。

§21-2 最高收费

（a）电子公证人从事电子公证行为最高收费标准

electronic notarypublic for performing an electronic notarial act are:

(1) for an acknowledgment, [dollars] per signature;

(2) for a jurat, [dollars] per signature;

(3) for a signature witnessing, [dollars] per signature;

(4) for a copy certification, [dollars] per [500 characters] certified but in no event shall the fee be less than [dollars]; and

(5) for a verification of fact, [dollars] per certificate.

(b) An electronic notary may charge a travel fee when traveling toperform an electronic notarial act if:

(1) the notary and the person requesting the electronic notarial act agree upon the travel fee in advance of the travel; and

(2) the notary explains to the person requesting the notarial act that the travel fee is both separate from the notarial fee prescribed in Subsection (a) and neither specified nor mandated by law.

§ 21-3 Payment Prior to Electronic Act.

(a) An electronic notary public may require payment of any fees specified in Section 21-2 prior to performance of an electronic notarial act.

(b) Any fees paid to an electronic notary prior to performance of an electronic notarial act are non-refundable if:

(1) the act was completed; or

(2) in the case of travel fees paid in compliance with Subsection 21-2(b), the act was not completed after the notary traveled to meet the principal because it was prohibited under Section 17-2, or because the notary knew or had a reasonable belief that the notarial act or the associated transaction was unlawful.

§ 21-4 Fees of Employee Electronic Notary.

The rules relating to fees for an employee notary public that are prescribed in Section 6-4 of this [Act] also apply to an electronic notary public in the performance of an electronic notarial act.

§ 21-5 Notice of Fees.

An electronic notary public who charges for performing electronic notarial acts shall conspicuously display in all of the notary's places of business and Internet sites, or present to each principal or requester of fact when outside such places of business, an English-language schedule of maximum fees for electronic notarial acts, as specified in Subsection 21-2(a). No part of any such notarial fee sched-

为：

（1）确认，每签名（美元）；

（2）宣誓证明，每签名（美元）；

（3）签名证明，每签名（美元）；

（4）经证明的副本，每500字符（美元），但总收费不低于（美元）；以及

（5）事实证明，每份证书（美元）。

（b）在满足以下条件时，电子公证人可因异地电子公证收取差旅费：

（1）在出差之前公证人和申请人就差旅费达成一致；以及

（2）公证人须向申请人说明差旅费与（a）款公证费用互不涵盖，且并非法律明确规定或强制要求。

§21-3 预付费

（a）电子公证人可要求在电子公证前收取本章第2条规定的任何费用。

（b）在以下情形中，电子公证前收取的任何费用不予返还：

（1）公证行为已履行完毕；

（2）在依照本章第2条（b）款的规定已支付差旅费后，公证人前往外地，经与当事人会见，认为公证行为为第十七章第2条所禁止或因公证人知悉或有理由相信公证行为或相关业务违法，公证行为因此未予完成。

§21-4 受雇电子公证人收费

本法第六章第4条规定的受雇公证人收费规则同样适用于电子公证人从事电子公证行为。

§21-5 收费公告

因从事电子公证行为收费的电子公证人应将本章第2条（a）款规定的英文电子公证最高收费表格显著列示于公证人所有营业场所及网站，在营业场所之外则应交呈每位当事人或事实请求者。该公证收费表格的任何部分不得以小于10号字体显示或印刷。

ule shall appear or be printed in smaller than 10-point type.

Chapter 22 – Evidence of Authenticity of Electronic Notarial Act

§ 22-1 Form of Evidence of Authority of Electronic Notarial Act.

(a) On a notarized electronic document transmitted to another state or nation, electronic evidence of the authenticity of the registered electronic signature and seal of an electronic notary public of this [State], if required, shall be in the form of an electronic certificate of authority signed by the [commissioning official] in conformance with any current and pertinent international treaties, agreements, and conventions subscribed by the government of the United States.

(b) The electronic certificate of authority described in Subsection (a) shall be attached to or logically associated with the electronically notarized document in such a manner that any subsequent alteration of the notarized document, or removal or alteration of the electronic certificate of authority, produces evidence of the change.

§ 22-2 Certificate of Authority for Electronic Notarial Act.

An electronic certificate of authority evidencing the authenticity of the registered electronic signature and seal of an electronic notary public of this [State] shall be in substantially the following form:

Certificate of Authority for Electronic Notarial Act

I, _____(name and title of commissioning official), certifythat (name of electronic notary public), the person named asElectronic Notary Public in the attached, associated, or accompanyingelectronic document, was registered as an Electronic Notary Public for the[State] of [name of jurisdiction] and authorized to act as such at the time thedocument was electronically notarized. I also certify that the documentbears no evidence of illegal or fraudulent alteration.

To verify this Certificate of Authority for an Electronic Notarial Act, I haveincluded herewith my electronic seal and signature this _____ day of_____, 20____.

(Electronic seal and signature of [commissioning official])

§ 22-3 Fee for Electronic Certificate of Authority.

For issuing an electronic certificate of authority for an electronic notarial act, including an electronic form of

第二十二章 电子公证行为真实性证据

§22-1 电子公证行为授权证据之格式

（a）对于送往其他州或国家的经公证电子文件，如需要提供证明本州电子公证人注册电子签名和印章真实性的证据，应以任命官员签名的电子授权证书形式附于其上，且应符合美国政府签订的所有现行有效的国际条约、协议和协定。

（b）（a）款所述电子授权证书应以对经公证文件进行后续修改、对电子授权证书进行后续删改均能留下改动证据之方式，附于电子公证文件上或符合逻辑地与电子公证书相联系。

§22-2 电子公证行为授权证书

证明本州电子公证人注册电子签名和印章真实性的电子授权证书应大致遵循以下格式出具：

电子公证行为授权证书

我，_____（任命官员姓名和头衔），证明_____（电子公证人姓名），在附件或链接电子文件中被称为电子公证人之人，在公证该文件之时，已登记为（辖区名称）（州）电子公证人，有权实施公证行为。此外，我证明没有证据显示该文件进行了非法或欺诈性的修改。

为证明此电子公证行为授权证书，随函附上本人电子盖章及签名，20____年____月____日。

[（任命官员）电子签名盖章]

§22-3 电子授权证书收费

签发电子公证行为电子授权证书，包括以本法第十章第3条规定的电子旁注形式签发，任命官员可收

the Apostille set forth in Section 10-3 of this [Act], the [commissioning official] may charge a maximum of [dollars].

Chapter 23 – Changes of Status of Electronic Notary

§ 23-1 Change of E-Mail Address.

Within [5] business days after the change of an electronic notary public's e-mail address, the notary shall electronically transmit to the [commissioning official] a notice of the change secured by a registered electronic signature of the notary.

§ 23-2 Change of Registration Data.

Any change or addition to the data on the electronic registration form described in Section 16-4, including any change to an electronic journal's access instructions, shall be reported within 10 days to the [commissioning official].

§ 23-3 Change of Means of Production.

(a) Upon becoming aware that the status, functionality, or validity of the means for producing a registered electronic signature, notaryseal, or single element combining the signature and seal, has changed, expired, terminated, or become compromised, the notary shall:

(1) immediately notify the [commissioning official];

(2) cease producing seals or signatures in electronic notarizations using that means;

(3) perform electronic notarizations only with a currently registered means or another means that has been registered within 30 days; and

(4) dispose of any software, coding, disk, certificate, card, token, or program that has been rendered defunct, in the manner described in Subsection 23-5(a).

(b) Pursuant to Subsection (a), the [commissioning official] shall immediately suspend the electronic status of a notary who has no other currently registered means for producing electronic signatures or notary seals, and if such means is not registered within 30 days, electronic status shall be terminated.

§ 23-4 Termination of Electronic Notary Registration.

(a) Any revocation, resignation, expiration, or other termination of the commission of a notary public immediately terminates any existing registration as an electronic notary.

(b) A notary's decision to terminate registration as an electronic notary shall not automatically terminate the

取最高额为（美元）的费用。

第二十三章 电子公证人身份之变更

§23-1 电子邮箱地址变更

公证人应自其电子邮箱地址变更之日起 5 个工作日内以电子传输方式向任命官员发送附有公证人注册电子签名的可信变更通知。

§23-2 登记数据变更

针对第十六章第 4 条规定的电子登记表数据的任何变更或添加，包括对电子日志访问指令的任何变更，应在 10 日内向任命官员报告。

§23-3 制作装置变更

（a）公证人一旦知悉创建注册电子签名、公证人印章或结合签名和印章的单项要素的装置之状态、功能或有效性改变、过期、终止或减损的，应当：

（1）立即通知任命官员；

（2）停止在电子公证中使用该装置创建签名或印章；

（3）仅使用当前登记的或 30 日内登记的其他装置从事电子公证；以及

（4）按照本章第 5 条（a）款规定的方式处置已失效的任何软件、代码、磁盘、证书、卡、令牌或程序。

（b）依据（a）款规定，任命官员应当立即暂停无其他当前已登记的创建电子签名及公证人印章用装置的公证人之电子身份，若在 30 日内未登记此类装置，则终止其电子身份。

§23-4 电子公证人登记之终止

（a）撤销、辞职、期满或其他针对公证人任命的终止情形将立即终止电子公证人的现有登记。

（b）公证人终止其作为电子公证人登记之决定，并不自动导致作为（其执业）依据的公证人任命失效。

underlying commission of the notary.

(c) A notary who terminates registration as an electronic notary shall notify the [commissioning official] in writing and dispose of any pertinent software, coding, disk, certificate, card, token, or program as described in Section 23-5(a).

§ 23-5 Disposition of Software and Hardware.

(a) Except as provided in Subsection (b), when the commission of an electronic notary public expires or is resigned or revoked, when registration as an electronic notary terminates, or when an electronic notary dies, the notary or the notary's duly authorized representative within [30] business days shall permanently erase or expunge the software, coding, disk, certificate, card, token, or program that is intended exclusively to produce registered electronic notary seals, registered single elements combining the required features of an electronic signature and notary seal, or registered electronic signatures that indicate status as a notary.

(b) A former electronic notary public whose previous commission expired need not comply with Subsection (a) if this person, within 3 months after expiration, is recommissioned and reregistered as an electronic notary using the same registered means for producing electronic notary seals and signatures.

Chapter 24 – Liability, Sanctions, and Remedies for Improper Acts

§ 24-1 Penalties and Remedies for Improper Electronic Acts.

The liability, sanctions, and remedies for the improper performance of electronic notarial acts by an electronic notary public are the same as described and provided in Chapter 13 of this [Act] for the improper performance of non-electronic notarial acts.

§ 24-2 Causes for Termination of Registration.

(a) The [commissioning official] shall terminate an electronic notary public's registration for any of the following reasons:

(1) submission of an electronic registration form containing material misstatement or omission of fact;

(2) failure to maintain the capability to perform electronic notarial acts, except as allowed in Subparagraph 23-3(a)(3); or

(3) the electronic notary's performance of official

（c）决定终止电子公证人登记的公证人应当书面通知任命官员，并按照本章第5条（a）款的规定处置所有相关软件、代码、磁盘、证书、卡、令牌或程序。

§23-5 软件和硬件之处置

（a）除（b）款规定的情形外，当电子公证人任期结束或辞职或被撤销任命时，当作为电子公证人的登记终止时，或当电子公证人死亡时，公证人或其适当授权的代理人应当在30个工作日内彻底擦除、抹消专用于创建注册电子公证人印章、结合电子签名及公证人印章所需特性的注册单项要素或显示公证人身份的注册电子签名之软件、代码、磁盘、证书、卡、令牌或程序。

（b）前电子公证人自任期结束之日起3个月内被重新任命或重新登记为电子公证人，且使用相同的已登记装置创建电子公证人签名及印章，则无须遵从（a）款规定。

第二十四章　不当行为的责任、惩罚及赔偿

§24-1 不当电子行为的惩罚和赔偿

电子公证人不当履行电子公证行为的，其责任、惩罚和赔偿与本法第十三章所规定的不当履行非电子公证行为相同。

§24-2 登记终止事由

（a）任命官员应当依下列任一原由终止电子公证人登记：

（1）提交包含重大虚假陈述或遗漏事实的电子登记表；

（2）不能从事电子公证行为，第二十三章第3条（a）款第3项允许的情形除外；或者

（3）电子公证人实施了职务不当行为。

misconduct.

(b) Prior to terminating an electronic notary's registration, the [commissioning official] shall inform the notary of the basis for the termination and that the termination shall take place on a particular date unless a proper appeal is filed with the [administrative body hearing the appeal] before that date.

(c) Neither resignation nor expiration of a notary commission or of an electronic notary registration precludes or terminates an investigation by the [commissioning official] into the electronic notary's conduct. The investigation may be pursued to a conclusion, whereupon it shall be made a matter of public record whether or not the finding would have been grounds for termination of the commission or registration of the electronic notary.

Chapter 25 – Violations by Person Not an Electronic Notary

§ 25-1 Impersonation and Improper Influence.

The criminal sanctions for impersonating an electronic notary public and for soliciting, coercing, or improperly influencing an electronic notary to commit official misconduct in performing notarial acts are the same sanctions described in Chapter 14 of this [Act] in regard to performing non-electronic notarial acts.

§ 25-2 Wrongful Destruction or Possession of Software or Hardware.

Any person who knowingly obtains, conceals, damages, or destroys the coding, disk, certificate, card, token, program, software, or hardware that is intended exclusively to enable an electronic notary public to produce a registered electronic signature, notary seal, or single element combining the required features of an electronic signature and notary seal, is guilty of a [class of offense], punishable upon conviction by a fine not exceeding [dollars] or imprisonment for not more than [term of imprisonment], or both.

§ 25-3 Additional Sanctions Not Precluded.

The sanctions of this chapter do not preclude other sanctions and remedies provided by law.

Chapter 26 – Administration

§ 26-1 Policies and Procedures.

The [commissioning official] may promulgate and enforce any policies and procedures necessary for the administration of this Article.

（b）在终止电子公证人登记前，任命官员应当通知公证人终止理由，以及，除非恰当的申诉在生效日期前被提交到申诉机构，该终止于指定日期生效。

（c）电子公证人辞职或电子公证人任命期满并不终止或排除任命官员对电子公证人行为的调查，任命官员可继续调查直至得出结论。无论该结论是否作为终止电子公证人任命或登记之依据，均应作为公共记录保存。

第二十五章　电子公证人以外者的违法行为

§25-1 假冒和不当影响

对假冒电子公证人、唆使、胁迫或不当影响公证人致使其在从事电子公证行为中作出职务不当行为的，其刑事处罚与本法第十四章针对从事非电子公证行为规定的处罚相同。

§25-2 非法破坏或持有软件或硬件

任何人故意占有、隐匿、损坏或销毁电子公证人专用于创建注册电子签名、公证人印章或结合电子签名及公证人印章所需特性的注册单项要素集合之代码、磁盘、证书、卡、令牌、程序、软件或硬件的，应被认定为（犯罪类型），一经定罪处以最高（美元）罚款或最长（刑期）监禁，或并处。

§25-3 不排除其他惩罚的适用

本章规定的惩罚措施并不排除法律规定的其他惩罚和赔偿的适用。

第二十六章　执行

§26-1 政策和程序

任命官员可发布和实施任何本编执行所必需之政策和程序。

阿拉斯加州现行成文法(韦斯特注解版)

West's Alaska Statutes Annotated Currentness

Title 44. State Government

\>\>Chapter 50. Notaries Public

\>\>s44.50.010.Notary public commission; term

(a) The lieutenant governor may commission for the state

(1) notaries public without limitation, who are authorized to use the notary seal for all legal purposes ; and

(2) limited governmental notaries public, who are state, municipal, or federal employees authorized to use the notary seal only for official government business.

(b) The term of a notary public commission is four years, except that the term of a limited governmental notary public commission coincides with the term of government employment.

(c) A person who is a state, municipal, or federal employee commissioned as a limited governmental notary public may also be commissioned as a notarypublic without limitation.

\>\>s 44.50.020. Qualifications

To be commissioned as a notary public, a person

(1) shall submit an application under AS 44.50.032

(2) shall be at least 18 years of age

(3) shall have established residency in this state under AS 01.10.055

(4) shall reside legally in the United States;

(5) may not, within 10 years before the commission takes effect, have been convicted of a felony or incarcerated in a correctional facility for a felony conviction;

阿拉斯加州现行成文法(韦斯特注解版)

标题 44. 州政府

第 50 章 公证人

s 44.50.010. 公证人任命;任期

(a)副州长可以代表本州任命

(1)无限制公证人,其经授权可为了一切法律目的使用公证人印章;以及

(2)有限政府公证人,其作为州、市或联邦政府雇员,被授权仅可将公证人印章用于官方政府业务;

(b)除有限政府公证人任期须与政府就职时间保持一致外,公证人任命任期(一般)为 4 年。

(c)身为州、市、联邦雇员,被任命为有限政府公证人者,亦可同时被任命为无限制公证人。

s 44.50.020. 资格

欲被任命为公证人者,需满足以下条件:

(1)依据 AS 44.50.032 条款提交申请;

(2)年满 18 周岁;

(3)根据 AS 01.10.055 条款拥有本州居住权;

(4)须合法居留于美国;

(5)在任命生效前十年间未被判犯有重罪或因被定重罪监禁于矫正机构。

(6) may not, within 10 years before the commission takes effect

(A) have had the person's notary public commission revoked under AS44.50.068(a)(2) or (4) or under the notary public laws of another jurisdiction for a substantially similar reason

(B) have had the person's notary public commission revoked under AS 44.50.068(a)(3), unless the person has reestablished residency in this state under AS 01.10.055 before the person submits the application;

(C) have been disciplined under AS 44.50.068 if, at the time the person applies for a notary public commission under this chapter, the disciplinary action prohibits the person from holding a notary public commission; or

(D) have been disciplined under the notary public laws of anotherjurisdiction if, at the time the person applies for a notary public commission under this chapter, the disciplinary action prohibits the person from holding a notary public commission; and

(7) shall meet the other requirements in this chapter to be commissioned as notary public.

>>s 44.50.030. Repealed by SLA 2005, ch. 60, s 14, eff. July 1, 2005

>>s 44.50.032. Application

(a) A person applying for a commission as a notary public shall submit acompleted application as required by this section, using the forms or format required by the lieutenant governor

(b) A completed application for a commission under AS 44.50.010(a)(1) must include

(1) an affirmation that the applicant meets the qualifications set out in AS44.50.020(2)--(6);

(2) the applicant's mailing and physical addresses; the applicant's telephone number, if any; the applicant's employer or business; the physical address and telephone number of the applicant's employer or business at the location where the applicant works; and an electronic mailing address, if any, where the applicant can be contacted

(3) information concerning any denial, suspension, revocation, or restriction of the applicant's commission as a notary public in this state or another jurisdiction; that information must include

(A) identification of the jurisdiction;

(B) the date the jurisdiction issued the denial, suspension, revocation, or restriction;

(C) the reasons for the denial, suspension, revocation,

（6）在任命生效前十年间，不得出现以下情形：

A. 依照 AS44.50.068(a) 款第 2 项或第 4 项被撤销公证人任命，或因基本类似的原因依据其他辖区的法律被撤销公证人任命；

B. 依照 AS 44.50.068(a) 款第 3 项被撤销公证人任命，申请者在提交申请之前已根据 AS 01.10.055 条款重新获得本州居留权的除外；

C. 依照 AS 44.50.068 条款被予以处罚，而根据其申请公证人任命之时的本章规定，该处罚措施将导致其丧失公证人任命；或者

D. 依照其他辖区的公证法被予以处罚，而根据其申请公证人任命之时的本章规定，该处罚措施将导致其丧失公证人任命；以及

（7）满足本章中规定的被任命为公证人需满足的其他条件。

s 44.50.030. 条被 2005 年 SLA 法案第 60 章第 14 条废止，自 2005 年 7 月 1 日起生效

s 44.50.032. 申请

（a）申请公证人任命的申请者需依照本条要求，以副州长要求的形式或格式提交完整的申请表。

（b）根据 AS 44.50.010(a) 款第 1 项，完整的任命申请表需包括：

（1）一份关于申请者满足 AS 44.50.020 第 2 项至第 6 项设立的要求的确认；

（2）申请者邮寄地址和实体地址；申请者电话号码（若有）；申请者的雇主或公司；申请者雇主或公司在申请者工作所在地的实体地址和电话号码；申请者电子邮箱地址（若有）；

（3）所有有关申请者在本州或其他辖区被否决、暂停、撤销或限制公证人任命的信息；包括

A. 指明所涉辖区；

B. 辖区作出否决、暂停、撤销或限制决定之日期；

C. 否决、暂停、撤销或限制的原因；

or restriction; and

(D) information concerning final resolution of the matter

(4) the applicant's notarized signature on the portion of the application that contains the oath or affirmation required by AS 44.50.035;

(5) the fee required by AS 44.50.033; and

(6) the bond required by AS 44.50.034.

(c) A completed application for a commission under AS 44.50.010(a)(2) must include

(1) a signed statement by the applicant's government employer that the commission is needed for the purpose of conducting official governmentbusiness;

(2) the applicant's mailing and physical addresses; the applicant's telephone number, if any; the applicant's employer; the name, address, and telephone number for the employer where the applicant works; and anelectronic mailing address, if any, where the applicant can be contacted;

(3) the affirmation, information, and signature required by (b)(1), (3), and (4) of this section; and

(4) the fee required by AS 44.50.033

>>s 44.50.033. Application fee

A person applying for a commission as a notary public shall pay a nonrefundable application fee of $40. However, an applicant for a limited governmental notary public commission under AS 44.50.010(a)(2) who is employed by the state may not be required to pay an application fee.

>>s 44.50.034. Bond

(a) A person applying for a commission as a notary public without limitation under AS 44.50.010(a)(1) shall execute an official bond of $1,000 and submit the bond with the application under AS 44.50.032. The bond must be for a term of four years from the date of commission.

(b) The lieutenant governor shall keep a bond submitted under this section for two years after the end of the term of the commission for which the bond was issued. Disposition of the bond after the end of the commission does not affect the time for commencing an action on the bond.

>>s 44.50.035. Oath

The application required by the lieutenant governor under AS 44.50.032 must contain an oath or affirmation, in the form set out in AS 39.05.045, to be signed by the applicant. A signed oath or affirmation submitted in an application under AS 44.50.032 takes effect on the date of

D. 有关事件最终处理结果的信息

（4）申请者经公证之签名，需落款于申请表上含有 AS 44.50.035 条款规定的宣誓或声明的那部分；

（5）AS 44.50.033 条款要求的费用；

（6）AS 44.50.034 条款要求的保证金。

（c）根据 AS 44.50.010(a) 款第 2 项，一份完整的委任申请必须包括

（1）一份由申请人的政府雇主签署的为开展政府职务工作需要任命的声明；

（2）申请者邮寄地址和实体地址；申请者电话号码（若有）；申请者的雇主；申请者效力之雇主的姓名、地址和电话号码；申请者电子邮箱地址（若有）；

（3）本条(b)款第1项、第3项和第4项规定的确认、信息和签名；以及

（4）AS 44.50.033 条款要求的费用

s 44.50.033. 申请费

申请公证人任命者需支付 40 美元申请费用，一经缴纳不再退还。但根据 AS 44.50.010(a) 款第 2 项申请有限政府公证人任命的政府雇员，可免交申请费。

s 44.50.034. 保证金

（a）申请 AS 44.50.010(a) 款第 1 项规定的无限制公证人任命者，应准备价值 1000 美元的保证金，并将其与 AS 44.50.032 条规定的申请表一并提交。自任命之日起的 4 年任期内，必须一直保有保证金。

（b）公证人任期结束后两年内，副州长应继续保管依据本条规定提交的保证金。任期结束后对保证金的处置，不影响就保证金提起诉讼的时间。

s 44.50.035. 宣誓

副州长依据 AS 44.50.032 条要求提交的申请需包含申请者签名的，以 AS 39.05.045 条规定的形式出具宣誓或声明。依据 AS 44.50.032 条提交的申请中的签名宣誓或声明自任命申请者作为本章规定的公证人之日起生效。

the applicant's commission as a notary public under this chapter.

>>s 44.50.036. Denial of applications

The lieutenant governor shall deny an application for a notary public commission if the

(1) applicant does not meet the requirements of this chapter;

(2) application is not complete or contains a material misstatement or omission of fact relating to the requirements for a commission under this chapter;

(3) applicant has, within 10 years before the commission is to take effect, been convicted of a felony or incarcerated in a correctional facility for a felony conviction; or

(4) applicant's commission as a notary public has been revoked, within 10 years before the commission is to take effect, in (A) this state for a reason stated in

(i) AS 44.50.068(a)(2) or (4);

(ii) AS 44.50.068(a)(3), unless the person has reestablished residency in this state under AS 01.10.055 before the person submits the application; or (B) another jurisdiction for a reason substantially similar to AS 44.50.068(a)(2) or (4)

>>s 44.50.037. Certificate of commission

Upon commission of a notary public under this chapter, the lieutenant governor shall provide to the notary public a certificate of commission indicating the commission and the dates of the term of the commission.

>>s 44.50.038. Subsequent commissions

A notary public whose term of commission is ending may apply for a new notary public commission by submitting a new application under AS 44.50.032 and complying with the requirements of this chapter. The lieutenant governor's approval of a new application for a commission for a notary public without limitation under AS 44.50.010(a)(1) terminates an applicant's existing commission under that paragraph

>>s 44.50.039. Limited governmental notaries public

A state, municipal, or federal employee commissioned as a notary public under AS 44.50.010(a)(2)

(1) is designated a limited governmental notary public;

(2) may perform notarial acts only in the conduct of

s 44.50.036. 拒绝申请

如有以下情形，副州长应当拒绝公证人任命申请：

（1）申请人不满足本章要求；

（2）申请不完整或存在与本章规定的有关任命要求的重大虚假陈述或遗漏事实；

（3）申请人在委任生效前十年间被判犯有重罪或因被定重罪监禁于矫正机构；或

（4）申请人在委任生效前十年间（A）在本州因下列法律规定的事由被撤销公证人任命：

（i）AS 44.50.068(a) 款第 2 项或第 4 项；

（ii）AS 44.50.068(a) 款第 3 项，申请者在递交申请之前，已经依据 AS 01.10.055 条重新获得本州居留权的除外；或者（B）在其他辖区因基本类似于 AS 44.50.068(a) 款第 2 项或第 4 项之原因被撤销公证人任命。

s 44.50.037. 任命书

在依据本章规定任命公证人时，副州长应向其提供载有任命和任期起止日期的任命书。

s 44.50.038. 后续授权

任期行将结束的公证人可依照 AS 44.50.032 条，通过提交满足本章规定的新申请，申请新的公证人任命。副州长同意其成为 AS 44.50.010(a) 款第 1 项规定的无限制公证人的，将终止其据此享有的现有任命。

s 44.50.039. 有限政府公证人

州、市或联邦雇员被任命为 AS 44.50.010(a) 款第 2 项规定的公证人的：

（1）指定为有限政府公证人；

（2）只有履行政府公务时才可实施公证；

official government business; and

(3) may not charge or receive a fee or other consideration for notarial services provided under this chapter.

>>s 44.50.040. Repealed by SLA 2005, ch. 60, s 14, eff. July 1, 2005

>>s 44.50.050. Renumbered as s 44.50.180(d)

>>s 44.50.060. Duties
A notary public may

(1) administer oaths and affirmations;

(2) take the acknowledgment of or proof of execution of instruments in writing, and give a notarial certificate of the proof or acknowledgment, included in or attached to the instrument; the notarial certificate shall be signed by the notary public in the notary public's own handwriting or by electronic means as authorized by regulations adopted by the lieutenant governor

>>s 44.50.061. Unauthorized practice

(a) A notary public who is not an attorney may complete but may not select notarial certificates, and may not assist another person in drafting, completing, selecting, or understanding a document or transaction requiring a notarial act.

(b) This section does not prohibit a notary public who is qualified in and, if required, licensed to practice, a particular profession from giving advice relating to matters in that professional field.

(c) A notary public may not make representations to have powers,qualifications, rights, or privileges that the office of notary public does not have.

>>s 44.50.062. rohibited acts
A notary public may not

(1) violate state or federal law in the performance of acts authorized by this chapter;

(2) influence a person to enter into or avoid a transaction involving a notarial act by the notary public;

(3) affix the notary public's signature or seal on a notarial certificate that is incomplete;

(4) charge a fee for a notarial act unless a fee schedule has been provided to the signer before the performance of the notarial act;

(5) affix the notary public's official seal to a document unless the personwho is to sign the document

(A) appears and signs the document before the notary public or, for an acknowledgment, appears and indicates

（3）不可因提供本章规定的公证服务而索取或接受费用或其他报酬。

s 44.50.040. 条被 2005 年 SLA 法案第 60 章第 14 条废止，自 2005 年 7 月 1 日起生效

s 44.50.050. 条被重新编号为 s 44.50.180(d) 条

s 44.50.060. 职责
公证人可

（1）监督实施宣誓和确认；

（2）就文书之生效手续进行确认或检验，并就该检验或确认出具公证书，囊括于文书中，或附于文书上；公证证书应当由公证人本人亲笔签字，或以副州长采用法规中授权的电子方式签名。

s 44.50.061. 未授权行为

（a）非律师公证人有权填写公证证书，但不可挑选公证证书，不可协助他人起草、完成、挑选或理解需公证的文件或交易。

（b）本条规定并不禁止在特定领域有相应资质（如果需要的话，和相应执业执照）的公证人就该领域相关事务提供建议。

（c）公证人不可宣称其具有公证人职务所不具备的权力、资格、权利或特权。

s 44.50.062. 禁止行为
公证人不得

（1）在从事本章所授权的行为时触犯州或联邦法律；

（2）促成或劝阻他人参与与其公证行为相关之交易；

（3）为不完整的公证证书签署公证人签名或盖章；

（4）收取公证费用，除非在实施公证前已向签名者提供了收费表；

（5）向文件加盖公证人公章，除非：

A. 该文件签署者亲临现场签署文件；对于办理确认的，要求该文件签署者须亲临现场，向公证人表

to the notary public that the person voluntarily affixed the person's signature on the document for the purposes stated within the document;

(B) gives an oath or affirmation if required under law or if the notarial certificate states that the document was signed under oath or affirmation; and

(C) is personally known to the notary public, produces government-issued identification containing the photograph and signature of the person signing, or produces

(i) government-issued identification containing the signature of the person signing, but without a photograph; and

(ii) another valid identification containing the photograph and signature of the person signing;

(6) perform a notarial act if the notary public

(A) is a signer of or named in the document that is to be notarized; or

(B) will receive directly from a transaction connected with the notarial act a commission, fee, advantage, right, title, interest, cash, property, or other consideration exceeding in value the normal fee charged by the notary for the notarial act.

>>s 44.50.063. Official signature

(a) When performing a notarization, a notary public shall

(1) sign in the notary public's own handwriting, on the notarial certificate, exactly and only the name indicated on the notary public's commission certificate, or sign an electronic document by electronic means as authorized by regulations adopted by the lieutenant governor; and

(2) affix the official signature only at the time the notarial act is performed.

(b) A notary public shall comply in a timely manner with a request by the lieutenant governor to supply a current sample of the notary public's official handwritten signature and information regarding the notary public's electronic signature.

(c) Within 10 days after the security of a notary public's electronic signature has been compromised, the notary public shall provide the lieutenant governor with written notification that the signature has been compromised. After the notary public has provided the lieutenant governor with the notification, the notary public shall provide the lieutenant governor with any additional information that the lieutenant governor requests about the compromise of the signature.

示其是自愿为实现文件所载之目的而签名的。

B. 如果法律对此有要求，或公证书中表明文件是经宣誓或声明而签署的，则该文件签署者需作出宣誓或声明；以及

C. 该文件签署者为公证人所熟悉，且留下了政府出具的包含其照片或签名的身份证明，或留下了：

（ⅰ）政府出具的，仅含签署者签名而无照片的身份证明；以及

（ⅱ）另一有效的，同时包含签署者照片和签名的身份证明。

（6）在下列情形下实施公证行为：

A. 公证人是待公证文件的一方签署者，或在待公证文件中被提及；

B. 公证人将从与公证行为相关之交易中直接获得超过公证人对此公证行为正常收费的价值，包括任命、费用、好处、权利、头衔、利息、现金、财产或其他报酬。

s 44.50.063. 官方签名：

（a）在实施公证时，公证人应当：

（1）以本人笔迹在公证书上署上与本人任命书上完全一致之姓名；签署电子文件时，则需以副州长采用法规中授权的电子方式签署；

(2) 仅可在公证过程中签署其正式签名。

（b）应副州长要求，公证人应及时提供包含其正式手写签名的现时样本和与公证人电子签名相关之信息。

（c）公证人电子签名安全性如受损，应于10日内向副州长发出签名受损的书面通知。在通知副州长之后，公证人应向副州长提供其要求的有关签名受损情况的一切额外信息。

>>s 44.50.064. Official seal

(a) A notary public shall keep an official seal, which is the exclusive property of the notary public, and shall ensure that another person does not possess or use the official seal.

(b) A notary public's official seal

(1) must contain

(A) the notary public's name exactly as indicated on the notary public's commission certificate;

(B) the words "Notary Public" and "State of Alaska"; and

(2) may be a circular form not over two inches in diameter, may be a rectangular form not more than one inch in width by two and one-half inches in length, or may be an electronic form as authorized by regulations adopted by the lieutenant governor.

(c) When not in use, a notary public's official seal shall be kept secure and under the exclusive control of the notary public.

(d) Within 10 days after a notary public's official seal is stolen or lost, or the security of the notary public's official electronic seal is compromised, the notary public shall provide the lieutenant governor with written notification of the theft, loss, or compromised security. After the notary public has provided the lieutenant governor with the notification, the notary public shall provide the lieutenant governor with any additional information that the lieutenant governor requests about the compromise of the seal.

(e) In order to avoid misuse, a notary public's official seal shall be destroyed or defaced

(1) upon the notary public's resignation or death;

(2) upon the revocation or termination by the lieutenant governor of the notary public's commission; or

(3) when the notary public's term of commission ends if the notary public has not received a new commission under this chapter

>>s 44.50.065. Seal impression or depiction

(a) With regard to each paper document being notarized, a sharp, legible, photographically reproducible impression or depiction of a notary public's official seal shall be affixed

(1) on the notarial certificate near the notary public's official signature; and

(2) only at the time the notarial act is performed

(b) For a notarized paper document, illegible information within a seal impression or depiction may be typed

s 44.50.064. 公章

（a）公章作为公证人专有财产，由公证人保管，且公证人应确保其不被他人占有或使用。

（b）公证人的公章：

（1）应当包含：

A. 与公证人任命书所载完全一致之公证人姓名；

B. "公证人"和"阿拉斯加州"的字样；以及

（2）公章形式上可采用直径不超过2英寸之圆形，或宽不超过1英寸、长不超过2.5英寸之矩形；或经副州长采用之法规授权的电子格式。

（c）当不使用公章时，公证人公章应保存于安全地点，且处于公证人全权控制之下。

（d）公证人公章被盗或遗失，或公证人电子公章之安全受到威胁，公证人应于10日内向副州长提供关于被盗、遗失或安全受威胁的书面通知。通知副州长之后，公证人应向副州长提供其要求的有关公章受损情况的一切额外信息。

（e）为防止其滥用，当出现下列情形时应销毁公证人公章或破坏其印面：

（1）公证人辞职或死亡；

（2）副州长撤销或终止公证人任命；或者

（3）公证人任期届满，而未根据本章被再次任命。

s 44.50.065. 章印或刻画

（a）就每份需公证的文件，公证人公章之章印或刻画应边缘清晰、可辨读、能以图像方式复制，加盖时应：

（1）位于公证证书上公证人正式签名旁；以及

（2）仅限于公证行为发生时。

（b）替代对于已公证文书，章印或刻画中无法辨识的信息可由公证人在其旁清晰地打字或印刷以补

or printed legibly by the notary public adjacent to, but not within, the impression or depiction.

(c) An embossed seal impression that is not photographically reproducible may be used in addition to, but not in place of the seal impression or depiction required by (a) of this section.

(d) A notary public may use a seal in electronic form on electronic documents notarized by the notary public as authorized by regulations adopted by the lieutenant governor. The seal shall be affixed only at the time the notarial act is performed

>>s 44.50.066. Notary public's status notification

(a) Within 30 days after change of a notary public's name, mailing address, or physical address, the notary public shall, on a form provided by the lieutenant governor, submit written notification of the change, signed by the notary public.

(b) The lieutenant governor may require limited governmental notaries public commissioned under AS 44.50.010(a)(2) who change departmental or agency employers to submit written notification of the change on a form provided by the lieutenant governor.

(c) A notary public commissioned under AS 44.50.010(a)(1) reporting a name change shall submit to the lieutenant governor payment of the fee under AS 44.19.024 for the issuance of a replacement certificate of commission.

(d) A notary public reporting a name change under (a) and (c) of this section shall use the person's former name for the performance of notarial acts until the person has

(1) provided written notification of the name change to the surety for any bond required under AS 44.50.034;

(2) received a replacement certificate of commission reflecting the name change from the lieutenant governor; and

(3) obtained a new seal reflecting the name change.

(e) The lieutenant governor may require a notary public to update the information required under AS 44.50.032, including the notary public's current notarized signature and information regarding the notary public's electronic signature.

>>s 44.50.067. Resignation

(a) To resign a commission, a notary public shall notify the lieutenant governor in writing of the resignation and the date that it is effective. The notary public shall sign the notification.

正，但不能直接标注其上。

（c）不可影印复制的钢印可用于本条（a）款所述章印或刻画的增补而非替代。

（d）公证电子文件，公证人可依副州长采用之法规中授权的电子形式使用印章。印章仅能于实施公证行为之时加盖。

s 44.50.066. 公证人的状态通知

（a）公证人姓名、邮寄地址或实体地址发生变更之日起 30 日内，公证人应以副州长规定之形式提交其已署名的书面变更通知。

（b）根据 AS 44.50.010(a) 款第 2 项任命的有限政府公证人如变更其部门或机构雇主的，副州长可要求有限政府公证人以其规定的形式提交书面变更通知。

（c）根据 AS 44.50.010(a) 款第 1 项任命之公证人报告其变更姓名的，应按 AS 44.19.024 条向副州长支付换发任命书之费用。

（d）根据本条（a）款和（c）款规定报告姓名变更的公证人，应继续使用原姓名，直至其：

（1）向根据 AS 44.50.034 条要求缴纳之保证金的保证人提供了有关姓名变更的书面通知；

（2）从副州长处收到了体现姓名变更的替换任命书；并且

（3）取得了体现姓名变更的新印章。

（e）副州长可要求公证人更新 AS 44.50.032 条下所要求的信息，包括公证人现有的经公证签名和有关公证人电子签名的信息。

s 44.50.067. 辞职

（a）辞职时，公证人应通过包含辞职意图和生效日期的书面材料告知副州长，并署名。

(b) A notary public who does not any longer meet the requirements of this chapter to be a notary public shall immediately resign the commission.

>>s44.50.068. Disciplinary action; complaint; appeal; hearing; delegation

(a) The lieutenant governor may suspend or revoke a notary public's commission or reprimand a notary public for good cause shown, including

(1) a ground on which an application for a commission may be denied;

(2) failure to comply with this chapter;

(3) failure to maintain residency in this state under AS 01.10.055; and

(4) incompetence or malfeasance in carrying out the notary public's duties under this chapter.

(b) A person harmed by the actions of a notary public may file a complaint with the lieutenant governor. The complaint shall be filed on a form prescribed by the lieutenant governor and shall be signed and verified by the person alleging misconduct by the notary public

(c) If the lieutenant governor determines that the allegations in the complaint do not warrant formal disciplinary action, the lieutenant governor may decline to act on the complaint or may advise the notary public of the appropriate conduct and the applicable statutes and regulations governing the conduct. The lieutenant governor shall notify the notary public and the complainant of the determination in writing.

(d) If the lieutenant governor determines that the complaint alleges sufficient facts to constitute good cause for disciplinary action, the lieutenant governor shall serve the notary public with a copy of the complaint as provided in Rule 4, Alaska Rules of Civil Procedure. The notary public may file a written response to the complaint with the lieutenant governor within 20 days after receipt of the complaint. The lieutenant governor may extend the time for the notary public's response. The lieutenant governor shall provide a copy of the notary public's response to the complainant.

(e) The lieutenant governor shall review the complaint and the response to determine whether formal disciplinary action may be warranted. The lieutenant governor may determine that the allegations in the complaint do not warrant formal disciplinary action, in which case the lieutenant governor may determine not to take further action on the complaint or may determine to advise the

（b）不再满足本章所述公证人任职要求的公证人应当立即辞职。

s 44.50.068. 纪律处分；投诉；提出上诉；听证会；代表团

（a）副州长可以因下述正当理由暂停或撤销公证人任命或训诫公证人：

（1）可据以驳回任命申请的理由；

（2）违反本章规定；

（3）根据 AS 01.10.055 条规定，不再享有本州居留权；以及

（4）根据本章规定履行公证人职责时，能力不足或渎职。

（b）因公证人行为受损之个人可向副州长投诉。投诉应以副州长规定的形式提出，并应由指控公证人存在不当行为者签名、证实。

（c）如副州长判定，投诉所涉指控不足以引发正式纪律处分的，副州长可拒绝应投诉采取行动，或可提醒公证人注意言行得当，遵守规范其行为的法律法规。副州长应以书面形式将处理结果告知公证人和投诉人。

（d）如副州长判定投诉所涉事实足以引发正式纪律处分的，副州长应依《阿拉斯加州民事诉讼法》第4条之规定，向公证人送达诉状副本。公证人可于收到诉状副本20日内，就诉状向副州长提交书面回应。副州长可延长公证人回应的期限。副州长应向投诉人提供一份公证人回应的副本。

（e）副州长应审查投诉和回应，以判定是否有必要采取正式纪律处分。副州长可判定投诉所涉指控不足以引发正式纪律处分，此时副州长可决定不再就投诉采取进一步行动或可决定提醒公证人注意言行得当，遵守规范其行为的法律法规。如副州长决定无须采取正式纪律处分的，副州长应以书面形式将决定之依据告知公证人和投诉人。

notary public of the appropriate conduct and the applicable statutes and regulations governing the conduct. If the lieutenant governor determines that formal disciplinary action is not warranted, the lieutenant governor shall provide the complainant and the notary public with a written statement of the basis for the determination.

(f) If the lieutenant governor finds that formal disciplinary action may be warranted, the lieutenant governor may suspend or revoke a notary public's commission or reprimand a notary public. If the lieutenant governor suspends or revokes the commission or issues a reprimand, the lieutenant governor shall provide, by certified mail, the notary public with a written statement of the lieutenant governor's decision, including a written statement of the basis for the determination.

(g) A person who is issued a reprimand, suspension, or revocation under (f) of this section may appeal the reprimand, suspension, or revocation by requesting a hearing within 15 days after receiving the statement provided under (f) of this section. If a hearing is requested, the lieutenant governor shall deny or grant the request under AS 44.64.060(b) and refer the matter to the office of administrative hearings under AS 44.64.060(b)

(h) The lieutenant governor may delegate the powers under this section.

>>s 44.50.070. Repealed by SLA 2005, ch. 60, s 14, eff. July 1, 2005

>>s 44.50.071. Confidentiality

(a) An address, telephone number, and electronic mail address of a notary public or an applicant that is submitted under AS 44.50.032 or 44.50.038 and that is designated by the notary public or applicant as confidential shall be kept confidential. However, a notary public shall provide a nonconfidential address and telephone number at which the notary public can be contacted.

(b) Compilations and data bases of those addresses, telephone numbers, and electronic mail addresses of notaries public that are confidential under (a) of this section shall be kept confidential, except that the lieutenant governor may disclose compilations and data bases if the lieutenant governor determines that disclosure is in the public interest.

(c) A complaint filed under AS 44.50.068 shall be kept confidential unless the lieutenant governor determines under AS 44.50.068(d) that the complaint alleges sufficient facts to constitute good cause for disciplinary action.

（f）如副州长判定有必要采取正式纪律处分的，副州长应暂停或撤销公证人之任命或对其加以训诫。如副州长暂停、撤销公证人之任命或对其加以训诫的，应以挂号信形式向公证人提供包含决定依据在内的书面决定。

（g）根据本条（f）款受到训诫或公证人资质被暂停或撤销者，可自收到本条（f）款所规定的书面决定之日起15日内要求就其举行听证。如遇请求举行听证的，副州长应依据AS 44.64.060(b)款决定驳回或准予该请求，并根据AS 44.64.060(b)款将事务移交给行政听证署处理。

（h）副州长可将本条规定的权力授权（给他人）。

s 44.50.070条被SLA2005法案第60章第14条废止，自2005年7月1日起生效。

s 44.50.071. 保密

（a）公证人或申请者根据AS 44.50.032条和44.50.038条提交，并指定为秘密信息的地址、电话号码、电子邮箱地址应予以保密。然而，为了联系公证人的方便起见，公证人应当提供一个非保密地址和电话。

（b）包含本条（a）款所规定的公证人地址、电话号码、电子邮箱地址此类保密信息的汇编资料和数据库亦应保密，副州长认为将其公布有利于公共利益的除外。

（c）根据AS 44.50.068条提出的投诉应予保密，但副州长根据AS 44.50.068(d)款认定投诉所涉事实足以引发纪律处分的除外。

>>s 44.50.072. Regulations

The lieutenant governor may adopt regulations under AS 44.62 (Administrative Procedure Act) to carry out the purposes of this chapter.

>>s 44.50.073. Published summary

The lieutenant governor may publish by electronic means for commissioned notaries public a summary of the provisions of this chapter and the regulations adopted under this chapter. The lieutenant governor shall, upon request, distribute the summary to each person who is commissioned a notary public under this chapter.

>>ss 44.50.080 to 44.50.140. Repealed by SLA 2005, ch. 60, s 14, eff. July 1,2005

>>s 44.50.150. Copy of bond as evidence

A certified copy of the record of the official bond with all affidavits, acknowledgments, endorsements, and attachments may be read in evidence with the same effect as the original, without further proof.

>>s 44.50.160. Misconduct or neglect

A notary and the sureties on the official bond are liable to persons injured for the damages sustained on account of misconduct or neglect of the notary.

>>s 44.50.170. Repealed by SLA 2005, ch. 60, s 14, eff. July 1, 2005

>>s 44.50.180. Postmasters as notaries

(a) Each postmaster in the state may perform the functions of a notary public in the state.

(b) Each official act of a postmaster as a notary public shall be signed by the postmaster, with a designation of the person's title as postmaster, shall have the cancellation stamp of the post office affixed, and shall state the name of the post office and the date on which the act was done.

(c) Repealed by SLA 2005, ch. 60, s 14, eff. June 25, 2005.

(d) Nothing in this chapter requires a postmaster to post a bond or to have a commission.

>>s 44.50.190. Repealed by SLA 2005, ch. 60, s 14, eff. July 1, 2005

>>s 44.50.200. Definitions

In this chapter, unless the context otherwise requires,

(1) "convicted" or "conviction" means that the person has entered a plea of guilty, guilty but mentally ill, or

s 44.50.072. 法规

副州长可根据 AS 44.62 条（行政诉讼法）采用法规，以实现本章之目的。

s 44.50.073. 发布总结

副州长可就本章规定和依据本章规定采用的法规制作摘要，并以电子方式向已任命的公证人发布。副州长应请求应将摘要分发给每位根据本章规定被任命为公证人者。

ss 44.50.080 条至 44.50.140 条被 2005 年 SLA 法案中第 60 章第 14 条废止，自 2005 年 7 月 1 日起生效。

s 44.50.150. 作为证据的保证金复印件

若无进一步证据，包含全部宣誓书、确认、认可和附件的经认证的官方保证金记录复印件可视为具有和原件相同的证据效力。

s 44.50.160. 不当行为或疏忽

他人因公证人的不当行为或疏忽之故受伤的，公证人及官方保证金之保证人需承担责任。

s 44.50.170 条被 2005 年 SLA 法案第 60 章第 14 条废止，自 2005 年 7 月 1 日起生效。

s 44.50.180. 邮政局长之公证人职能

（a）本州所有邮政局长均可在本州范围内行使公证人职能。

（b）邮政局长行使公证人职能做出的官方行为均须经其以邮政局长之身份签名，加盖所属邮局之邮戳，并载明邮局名称和实施行为之日期。

（c）被由 SLA2005 法案第 60 章第 14 条废止，自 2005 年 6 月 25 日起生效。

（d）本章无要求邮政局长缴纳保证金或取得任命之内容。

s 44.50.190 条被 2005 年 SLA 法案第 60 章第 14 条废止，自 2005 年 7 月 1 日起生效。

s 44.50.200. 定义

在本章中，除非上下文另有所指

（1）"定罪"是指该人提出认罪答辩 / 有罪但有精神疾患答辩 / 无罪申诉，或该人被法庭 / 陪审团判

nolo contendere, or has been found guilty or guilty but mentally ill by a court or jury;

(2) "notarial act" means an act that is identified as a notarial act under AS 09.63.120 and an act that a notary public is directed to perform under AS 44.50.060;

(3) "notary public" means a person commissioned to perform notarial acts under this chapter

决有罪/有罪但有精神疾患；

（2）"公证行为"是指依据 AS 09.63.120 条被认定为公证行为的行为，以及公证人根据 AS 44.50.060 条指导实施之行为；

（3）"公证人"是指本章中被任命实施公证行为者。

加利福尼亚州

加利福尼亚州公证行为法

West's Annotated California Codes
Currentness
Civil Code (Refs & Annos)

Division 2. Property (Refs & Annos)
Part 4. Acquisition of Property
Title 4. Transfer
Chapter 4. Recording Transfers

Article 3. Proof and Acknowledgment of Instruments (Refs & Annos)

>>>> s 1183.5. Notarial acts

Any officer on active duty or performing inactive-duty training in the armed forces having the general powers of a notary public pursuant to Section 936 or 1044a of Title 10 of the United States Code (Public Law 90-632 and 101-510) and any successor statutes may perform all notarial acts for any person serving in the armed forces of the United States, wherever he or she may be, or for any spouse of a person serving in the armed forces, wherever he or she may be, or for any person eligible for legal assistance under laws and regulations of the United States, wherever he or she may be, for any person serving with, employed by, or accompanying such armed forces outside the United States and outside the Canal Zone, Puerto Rico, Guam and the Virgin Islands, and any person subject to the Uniform Code of Military Justice outside of the United States.

Any instrument acknowledged by any such officer or any oath or affirmation made before such officer shall not be rendered invalid by the failure to state therein the place of execution or acknowledgment. No seal or authentication of the officer's certificate of acknowledgment or

加利福尼亚州现行法
韦斯特注解版
民法典（原文及注释）

第二编　物权（原文及注释）
第四部分　物权之取得
标题四　转让
第四章　转让的记录

第 3 条　证明和确认文书（原文及注释）

s 1183.5. 公证行为

根据《美国法典》第 10 章第 936 条或第 1044a 条（公法 90-632 和 101-510）以及后继法规的授权，具有现役职务的武装部队官员或执行公证人一般权力的公职人员可以对在美国武装部队任职的任何人及其配偶，无论其身在何处；对根据美国法律法规有资格获得法律援助的任何人；对在美国境外以及运河区、波多黎各、关岛和维尔京群岛以外的武装部队从事或从事这类武装的任何人，以及在美国本土之外，任何遵守《军事统一守则》法域地区的人执行所有公证行为。

任何公证人员所认证的文书，或作出的任何宣誓证明或确认，不因未能在其中述明执行地址或确认地点执行而无效。不得要求公证人提交已由其签署的任何陪审员的印章或身份证明的确认证明书，而承认上述人员的官员应出示证书或附上按照本州法律或以下

of any jurat signed by him or her shall be required but the officer taking the acknowledgment shall endorse thereon or attach thereto a certificate substantially in a form authorized by the laws of this state or in the following form:

On this the _____ day of _____, 19___, before me _____, the undersigned officer, personally appeared _____ known to me (or satisfactorily proven) to be (a) serving in the armed forces of the United States, (b) a spouse of a person serving in the armed forces of the United States, or (c) a person serving with, employed by, or accompanying the armed forces of the United States outside the United States and outside the Canal Zone, Puerto Rico, Guam, and the Virgin Islands, and to be the person whose name is subscribed to the within instrument and acknowledged that he or she executed the same. And the undersigned does further certify that he or she is at the date of this certificate a commissioned officer of the armed forces of the United States having the general powers of a notary public under the provisions of Section 936 or 1044a of Title 10 of the United States Code (Public Law 90-632 and 101-510).

_____

Signature of officer, rank, branch of service and capacity in which signed.

To any affidavit subscribed and sworn to before such officer there shall be attached a jurat substantially in the following form:

Subscribed and sworn to before me on this _____ day of _____, 19___.

_____

Signature of officer, rank, branch of service and capacity in which signed.

The recitals contained in any such certificate or jurat shall be prima facie evidence of the truth thereof, and any certificate of acknowledgment, oath or affirmation purporting to have been made by any commissioned officer of the Army, Air Force, Navy, Marine Corps or Coast Guard shall, notwithstanding the omission of any specific recitals therein, constitute presumptive evidence of the existence of the facts necessary to authorize such acknowledgment, oath or affirmation to be taken by the certifying officer pursuant to this section.

形式规定的授权证书：

19____年____月____日，以下签署人员亲自向本人____充分证明其：（a）在美国武装部队任职，（b）为在美国武装部队任职的人的配偶，或（c）在美国境外以及运河区、波多黎各、关岛和维尔京群岛以外的美国武装部队任职，从事武装部队的人员，文件中提及的人名为实际执行人。下列签署人进一步证明，其在本证明之日，根据美国第10号第936节或第1044a条的规定，拥有美国法典（公法90-632和101-510）下的公证人一般权力。

_____

官员签名，职级，任职机构和签字能力。

对于在该人员之前提交和宣誓的任何誓章，应以下列形式附上一名司法人员的认证：

19____年____月____日，向本人____提交并宣誓

_____

官员签名，职级，任职机构和签字能力。

任何上述证明书或陪审团所载的独立资料，均须为表面证据，任何由陆军、空军、海军、海军陆战队或海岸的委任人员作出的承认、宣誓或确认证明书，尽管没有任何具体的独立声明，应构成推定的证据，以证明是否存在授权认证官根据本条作出的承认、宣誓或确认所必需的事实。

加利福尼亚州公证人收费条款

West's Ann.Cal.Gov.Code s 12182.1
Government Code (Refs & Annos)

Government of the State of California
Division 3. Executive Department (Refs & Annos)
Part 2. Constitutional Officers (Refs & Annos)
Chapter 3. Secretary of State (Refs & Annos)

Article 3. Business Programs (Refs & Annos)

>>>> **s 12182.1. Notary public fee**

The Secretary of State shall establish by regulation an application, examination, and commission fee that shall not exceed the amount necessary to cover the costs of commissioning notaries public and the enforcement of laws governing notaries public. The fee shall not exceed one hundred dollars ($100) per commission.

加利福尼亚州现行法 韦斯特注解版
政府组织法（原文及注释）

加利福尼亚州政府
第三编　执行机构（原文及注释）
第二部分　执行官员（原文及注释）
第三章　州务卿（原文及注释）

第 3 条 商业计划（原文及注释）

s 12182.1. 公证费用

州务卿应当规定，申请、审查和任命费用不得超过依照公证人法的规定委托公证人和执行公证的费用。每次任命的费用不得超过一百美元（$100）。

加利福尼亚州公证人手册

Notary Public Handbook
Published by Debra Bowen Secretary of State

Notary Public Section
2014

Amendments and New Laws Effective January 1, 2014

The following laws became effective January 1, 2014.

Statutes of 2013, Chapter 78, amends Civil Code section 1188 to require the use of the certificate of acknowledgment prescribed in Civil Code section 1189, not a certificate substantially in that form. The law also amends Civil Code section 1195 to require the specified form to be used as a certificate for proof of execution of an instrument and amends the wording in the form.

Statutes of 2013, Chapter 159, amends Civil Code section 1185 to provide that an inmate identification card is an allowable form of identification if the card has been issued by the California Department of Corrections and Rehabilitation, is current or has been issued within 5 years, and the inmate is in custody in California state prison, whether or not the identification card contains all the previously required specific additional identifying information (photograph, description of the person, signature, or serial number).

Statutes of 2013, Chapter 571, adds Section 22449 to the Business and Professions Code, prohibiting notaries public from participating in practices that amount to price gouging when providing services associated with filing an application for the deferred action for childhood arrivals program announced by the United States Secretary of Homeland Security. A violation of this section shall be cause for the Secretary of State to revoke or suspend a notary public commission.

Statutes of 2013, Chapter 618, amends the list of crimes in Government Code section

8214.1(q) to include conviction for theft of certain types of animals and livestock (Penal Code section 487a(a)) as disqualifying a person from becoming a notary

公证人手册
州务卿德波拉·鲍温

公证科
2014 年

修订案和新法自 2014 年 1 月 1 日起施行。

以下法律自 2014 年 1 月 1 日起施行。

2013 年第 78 号章程对《民法典》第 1188 号的规定进行修正，运用《民法典》第 1189 条规定的方式进行证书的确认，而不再以形式手段进行认证。修订案对《民法典》第 1195 条作出修改，要求使用指定的表格作为公证文书的执行证明，同时对该表格的措辞进行了修订。

2013 年第 159 号章程对《民法典》第 1185 条进行修订，规定如果囚犯在加利福尼亚州监狱被关押，无论其身份证件是否包含所有先前所需的具体附加身份信息（照片、人物描述、签名或序列号），只要该身份证件是由加利福尼亚惩教和康复局现在或在 5 年内发放的，则允许向其提供一张身份证件。

2013 年第 571 章的规定将增加第 22449 节《商业与职业守则》，禁止公证人在提供美国国土安全部实施的儿童移民计划延期申请相关的服务时作出相当于价格欺诈的行为。有违反该规定的，由州务卿撤销或者暂停公证员资格。

2013 年第 618 号章程，修改了《政府组织法》第 8214.1（q）条中的犯罪行为清单，包括盗窃特定种类的动物和牲畜［《刑法典》第 487a（a）条］在

public or making a notary public subject to discipline.

Appointment and Qualifications

To become a notary public you must meet all of the following requirements: (Government Code section 8201)

Be a legal resident of the State of California;

Be at least 18 years of age;

Satisfactorily complete a course of study approved by the Secretary of State;

Pass a written examination prescribed by the Secretary of State; and

Pass a background check.

To determine if a person meets the requirements to fulfill the responsibilities of the position, a completed application and a "2 x 2" color passport photograph of the applicant shall be submitted at the examination site, then forwarded to the Secretary of State's office and reviewed by Secretary of State staff for qualifying information. (Government Code section 8201.5)

To assist the Secretary of State in determining the identity of an applicant and whether the applicant has been convicted of a disqualifying crime, state law requires all applicants to be fingerprinted as part of a thorough background check prior to being granted an appointment as a notary public. (Government Code section 8201.1) Information concerning the fingerprinting requirements will be mailed to candidates who pass the examination.

Convictions

Applicants are required to disclose on their applications all arrests for which trials are pending and all convictions, including convictions that have been dismissed under Penal Code section 1203.4 or 1203.4a. If you have any questions concerning the disclosure of convictions or arrests, contact the Secretary of State's office prior to signing the application. If you do not recall the specifics about your arrest(s) and/or conviction(s), you can contact the California Department of Justice at (916) 227-3849.

The Secretary of State may deny an application for the following reasons:

Failure to disclose any conviction;

Conviction of a felony; or

Conviction of a disqualifying lesser offense when less than 5 years have passed since the completion of probation.

The applicant has the right to appeal the denial through the administrative hearing process. (Government Code section 8214.3) For a complete list of reasons the

内的行为将导致公证人丧失资格或受到纪律处罚。

公证人的任命及资格

成为公证人，必须符合以下要求：（《政府组织法》第 8201 条）

为加利福尼亚州的合法居民；

年满 18 周岁；

圆满完成州务卿规定的培训课程；

通过州务卿规定的书面审查；以及

通过背景调查。

为确定申请人是否符合履行职位责任的要求，申请人的完整申请和"2×2"彩色护照照片应在现场提交，并转交给州务卿办公室，由工作人员进行资格认证。（《政府组织法》第 8201.5 条）

为协助州务卿确定申请人的身份，以及申请人是否被裁定犯有不合公证人资格的罪行，国家法律要求所有申请人在被任命为公证人之前，将指纹采集作为背景调查的一部分。（《政府组织法》第 8201.1 条）有关指纹要求的资料将向通过审查的候选人邮寄。

罪行

申请人必须在申请时披露所有被审判、逮捕和所有定罪记录，包括根据《刑法典》第 1203.4 条或第 1203.4a 被驳回的定罪。如果对公开定罪或逮捕有任何疑问，请在签署申请前联系州务卿办公室。如果您不记得有关您的逮捕和／或定罪的具体细节，可以致电（916）227-3849 与加利福尼亚司法部联系。

州务卿可能因以下原因拒绝公证人申请：

未如实披露任何曾经所犯罪行；

犯有重罪；或者

自缓刑完成 5 年内，犯有轻罪。

申请人有权通过行政听证程序对拒绝申请提出上诉。（《政府组织法》第 8214.3 条）有关州务卿可能拒绝提出申请的完整清单，请参阅《政府组织法》第

Secretary of State may deny an application, please refer to Government Code section 8214.1. Refer to the Secretary of State's Notary Public Disciplinary Guidelines for a list of the most common disqualifying convictions. The disciplinary guidelines are available on the Secretary of State's website or can be mailed to you upon request.

Notary Public Education

All persons are required to take and satisfactorily complete a six-hour course of study approved by the Secretary of State prior to appointment as a notary public. Please note that all persons being appointed, no matter how many commission terms held in the past, are required to take the initial six-hour course of study. (Government Code section 8201(a)(3) and (b))

A notary public who holds a current California notary public commission and who has completed an approved six-hour course at least one time is required to take and satisfactorily complete an approved three-hour refresher course prior to reappointment as a notary public. The three-hour refresher course can only be used to satisfy the education requirement if the notary public is applying for a new commission before their current commission has expired. If the notary public's commission has expired, the individual must satisfactorily complete a six-hour notary public education course before being appointed for another term, even if the individual already once satisfactorily completed an approved six-hour course for a previous commission.

The Secretary of State reviews and approves courses of study. These approved courses include all the material that a person is expected to know to pass the written examination.

The Secretary of State compiles a list of all vendors offering an approved course of study. This list is available on the Secretary of State's website or can be mailed to you upon request. (Government Code section 8201.2)

Requirements and Time Limit for Qualifying

Once the commission has been issued, a person has 30 calendar days from the beginning of the term prescribed in the commission to take, subscribe, and file an oath of office and file a $15,000 surety bond with the county clerk's office. The commission does not take effect until the oath and bond are filed with the county clerk's office. The filing must take place in the county where the notary public maintains a principal place of business as shown in the application on file with the Secretary of State. If the

8214.1条。州务卿公证纪律指南列出了最常见的不适格情形。该纪律指南可以在州务卿的网站上查阅，或者依申请人请求进行邮寄。

公证人教育

公证人在被任命之前必须顺利完成由州务卿举办的6小时培训项目。需要注意的是，无论之前的任命条件如何，所有被任命的人员必须参加最初的六小时培训。[《政府组织法》第8201（a）（3）条和第8201（b）条]

现在加州公证处任职的且至少完成一次的6小时培训的公证人，在重新任命为公证人之前，还需圆满完成规定的3小时复习培训。即使公证人已经圆满完成了6小时培训，只要公证人的任命到期，在新的任期前还需要完成6个小时的培训。

州务卿审查并批准培训课程。课程应包括公证人通过书面考试的所有材料。

州务卿编制了允许提供经批准的培训课程的所有供应商清单。该清单可在州务卿网站上查询，或可根据请求进行邮寄。（《政府组织法》第8201.2条）

资格要求和时间限制

公证人委任状一旦发出，自委任状规定之日起30日内，申请人须宣誓并向郡书记处提交誓言，并向郡书记处提交15000美元的保证金。在向郡书记处提交誓言和保证金之前，任命不生效。申请必须在公证人所在的郡内进行，执业地点划分如州务卿提供的文书所示。如果誓言和保证金在30日内未提交，则任命失效，被任命者在获得新的任命且遵守30日限制前不得担任公证人。《政府组织法》第8213（a）条允许公证人通过认证邮件提交已完成的誓言和保证

oath and bond are not filed within the 30-calendarday time period, the commission will not be valid, and the person commissioned may not act as a notary public until a new appointment is obtained and the person has properly qualified within the 30-calendar-day time limit. Government Code section 8213(a) permits the filing of completed oaths and bonds by the applicable county clerk by certified mail. Exceptions are not made to the 30-day filing requirement due to mail service delays, county clerk mail processing delays, or for any other reason. If mailing an oath and bond to the county clerk, sufficient time must be allowed by the newly appointed notary public to ensure timely filing. (Government Code sections 8212 and 8213)

Notary Public Bond

California law requires every notary public to file an official bond in the amount of $15,000. The notary public bond is not an insurance policy for the notary public. The bond is designed only to provide a limited source of funds for paying claims against the notary public. The notary public remains personally liable to the full extent of any damages sustained and may be required to reimburse the bonding company for sums paid by the company because of misconduct or negligence of the notary public. (Government Code sections 8212 to 8214)

Geographic Jurisdiction

A notary public can provide notarial services throughout the State of California. A notary public is not limited to providing services only in the county where the oath and bond are on file. In virtually all of the certificates the notary public is called on to complete, there will be a venue heading such as "State of California, County of _____." The county named in the heading in the notarial certificate is the county where the signer personally appeared before the notary public. (Government Code section 8200)

Acts Constituting the Practice of Law

California notaries public are prohibited from performing any duties that may be construed as the practice of law. Among the acts which constitute the practice of law are the preparation, drafting, or selection or determination of the kind of any legal document, or giving advice in relation to any legal documents or matters. If asked to perform such tasks, a California notary public should decline and refer the requester to an attorney.

金。由于邮件服务延误，郡办事员邮件处理延迟或任何其他原因，不构成30日提交要求的例外。如果以邮寄方式将宣誓和保证金提交到郡书记处，新接到委任的公证人必须有足够的时间确保能够及时提交。（《政府组织法》第8212条和第8213条）

公证保证金

加利福尼亚州法律要求每位公证人提供15000美元的官方保证金。公证保证金不是公证人的保险。保证金的设计只是为公证人进行赔偿时提供有限的资金来源。由于公证人的不当行为或疏忽，公证人对过错仍然承担全部责任，且可能需要偿还由保证金公司支付的款项。（《政府组织法》第8212条至第8214条）

地域管辖

公证人可以在整个加利福尼亚州提供公证服务。公证人不仅仅在提交誓言和保证金的郡提供服务。在公证人被请求完成的几乎所有的公证文书中，将会有一个管辖标题，如"加利福尼亚州，_____郡"。在公证书标题中指定的郡是签名人当面签署时所在的郡。（《政府组织法》第8200条）

构成法律执业的行为

加州公证人被禁止实施任何可能被视为法律执业的任务。构成法律执业的行为是指编制、起草法律文书或选择、确定任何法律文件的种类，或就任何法律文件或事宜提供意见。如果被要求执行这样的任务，加州公证人应拒绝并将请求者转介给律师。

Notary Public Seal

Each notary public is required to have and to use a seal. The seal must be kept in a locked and secured area, under the direct and exclusive control of the notary public, and must not be surrendered to an employer upon termination of employment, whether or not the employer paid for the seal, or to any other person.

Because of the legal requirement that the seal be photographically reproducible, the rubber stamp seal is almost universal. However, notaries public may use an embosser seal in addition to the rubber stamp. The legal requirements for a seal are shown below. (Government Code section 8207) The seal must:

Be photographically reproducible when affixed to a document;

Contain the State Seal and the words "Notary Public";

Contain the name of the notary public as shown on the commission;

Contain the name of the county where the oath of office and notary public bond are on file;

Contain the expiration date of the notary public's commission;

Contain the sequential identification number (commission number) assigned to the notary public, as well as the identification number assigned to the seal manufacturer or vendor; and

Be circular not over two inches in diameter, or be a rectangular form of not more than one inch in width by two and one-half inches in length, with a serrated or milled edged border.

Many documents that are acknowledged may later be recorded. A document may not be accepted by the recorder if the notary public seal is illegible. Notaries public are cautioned to make sure that the notary public stamp leaves a clear impression. All the elements must be discernible. The seal should not be placed over signatures or over any printed matter on the document. An illegible or improperly placed seal may result in rejection of the document for recordation and result in inconveniences and extra expenses for all those involved.

The law allows a limited exception when a notary public may authenticate an official act without using an official notary public seal. Because subdivision maps usually are drawn on a material that will not accept standard stamp pad ink and other acceptable inks are not as readily available, acknowledgments for California subdivision

公证人公章

每个公证人都必须保管并正确使用公章。公证公章必须在公证人直接和排他控制的情况下保存在锁定和安全的区域。不得在职务终止后将其交给雇主，无论雇主是否对印章支付了价款。

由于法律要求印章必须具有可再现性，橡皮印章几乎是通用的。不过，公证人除了橡皮印章之外还可以使用压花印章。印章的法律规定如下所示。(《政府组织法》第8207条）印章必须：

在文件上盖章时可以影像复印；

包含国家印章图样和"公证人"一词；

包含公证人的姓名，姓名应与委任状上的一致；

包含提交宣誓、保证金所在郡的名称；

包含公证人任命的有效期限；

包含分配给公证人的身份号码（委任状编号）以及分配给印章制造商或供应商的识别号码；以及

形状为直径不超过2英寸的圆形，或不超过1英寸宽、2.5英寸长的矩形，具有锯齿状或磨边边缘。

许多确认的文件可能会被记录下来。如果公证人公章无法辨认，则文件可能无法被记录机构接受。在此提醒公证人确保公证公章应留下清晰的印记。所有印章的构成元素均必须是清晰可辨的。不得在签名或文件任何印刷字体上盖章。非法或不合规的盖章可能导致文件被拒绝记录，并对所有参与者造成不便和额外费用。

法律允许有限的例外，当公证人认证正式行为时，可以不使用印章。因为细分地图通常是在不可采用标准印台油的材料上绘制的，而其他可接受的印油不易获得，因此加利福尼亚细分地图证书的确认可以在未盖章的情况下公证。公证人的姓名、公证人的主要执业地点以及任职到期日必须在公证人于公证书的

map certificates may be notarized without the official seal. The notary public's name, the county of the notary public's principal place of business, and the commission expiration date must be typed or printed below or immediately adjacent to the notary public's signature on the acknowledgment. (Government Code section 66436(c))

A NOTARY PUBLIC SHALL NOT USE THE OFFICIAL SEAL OR THE TITLE NOTARY PUBLIC FOR ANY PURPOSE OTHER THAN THE RENDERING OF NOTARIAL SERVICE. (Government Code section 8207)

A notary public is guilty of a misdemeanor if the notary public willfully fails to keep his or her notary public seal under the notary public's direct and exclusive control or if the notary public willfully surrenders the notary public's seal to any person not authorized to possess it. (Government Code section 8228.1)

When the notary public commission is no longer valid, the notary public seal must be destroyed to protect the notary public from possible fraudulent use by another. (Government Code section 8207)

Identification

When completing a certificate of acknowledgment or a jurat, a notary public is required to certify to the identity of the signer of the document. (Civil Code sections 1185(a), 1189, Government Code section 8202) Identity is established if the notary public is presented with satisfactory evidence of the signer's identity. (Civil Code section 1185(a))

Satisfactory Evidence – "Satisfactory Evidence" means the absence of any information, evidence, or other circumstances which would lead a reasonable person to believe that the individual is not the individual he or she claims to be and (A) paper identification documents or (B) the oath of a single credible witness or (C) the oaths of two credible witnesses under penalty of perjury, as specified below:

A. Paper Identification Documents – Identity of the signer can be established by the notary public's reasonable reliance on the presentation of any one of the following documents, if the identification document is current or has been issued within five years (Civil Code section 1185(b)(3) and (4)):

An identification card or driver's license issued by the California Department of Motor Vehicles;

A United States passport;

An inmate identification card issued by the Califor-

签名下方或紧邻的地方打印或标注。[《政府组织法》第 66436（c）条］

公证人不得出于任何非公证的目的使用公证印章或公证文书标题。(《政府组织法》第 8027 条）。

如果公证人故意不对公证印章实施直接和排他性控制，或公证人故意将公证人的印章交给任何无权拥有公证印章的公民，即属违法行为。(《政府组织法》第 8228.1 条）

当公证人任期届满时，必须销毁公证人的公章，以保护公证人的公章免于不当使用。(《政府组织法》第 8207 条）

身份认定

在填写确认证书或者宣誓证书时，公证人需要证明文件签字人的身份。[《民法典》第 1185（a）条、第 1189 条,《政府组织法》第 8202 条］如果签字人向公证人出示了充分的证据，其身份则得以确认。[《民法典》第 1185（a）条］

充分的证据 —— "充分的证据"是指没有任何其他信息、证据或其他情况导致一个理性人相信证明人不是他或她声称的人，以及（A）纸质身份证件或（B）一名可信证人的誓言，或（C）两名可信证人在承担伪证罪责任下所做的誓言，具体如下：

A. 纸质身份证明文件 —— 签字人的身份可以由公证人合理依赖以下提交的文件之一来确认，如果身份证明文件是现在或 5 年内发出的［《民法典》第 1185（b）(3）条和第 1185（b）(4）条］：

由加州机动车管理局发出的身份认证或驾驶执照；

美国护照；

如果因犯在加利福尼亚州监狱被关押，则从加利

nia Department of Corrections and Rehabilitation, if the inmate is in custody in California state prison.

A type of identification listed below, provided that it contains a photograph, description of the person, signature of the person, and an identifying number:

(a) A passport issued by a foreign government, provided that it has been stamped by the U.S. Immigration and Naturalization Service or the U.S. Citizenship and Immigration Services;

(b) A driver's license issued by another state or by a Canadian or Mexican public agency authorized to issue driver's licenses;

(c) An identification card issued by another state;

(d) A United States military identification card with the required photograph, description of the person, signature of the person, and an identifying number. (Some military identification cards do not contain all the required information.); or

(e) An employee identification card issued by an agency or office of the State of California, or an agency or office of a city, county, or city and county in California.

Note: The notary public must include in his or her journal the type of identifying document, the governmental agency issuing the document, the serial or identifying number of the document, and the date of issue or expiration of the document that was used to establish the identity of the signer. (Government Code section 8206(a)(2)(D))

B. Oath of a Single Credible Witness – The identity of the signer can be established by the oath of a single credible witness whom the notary public personally knows. (Civil Code section 1185(b)(1)) The notary public must establish the identity of the credible witness by the presentation of paper identification documents as set forth above. Under oath, the credible witness must swear or affirm that each of the following is true (Civil Code section 1185(b)(1) (A)(i)-(v)):

The individual appearing before the notary public as the signer of the document is the person named in the document;

The credible witness personally knows the signer;

The credible witness reasonably believes that the circumstances of the signer are such that it would be very difficult or impossible for the signer to obtain another form of identification;

The signer does not possess any of the identification documents authorized by law to establish the signer's identity; and

福尼亚惩教和康复部颁发的囚犯身份证进行认证。

以下列出的身份证明中的一种，只要其中包含照片、人员描述、人员签名和身份识别编号：

（a）外国政府签发的护照，但须由美国移民归化局或美国公民及移民服务局盖章；

（b）其他州或加拿大或墨西哥公共机构授权发放的驾照；

（c）另一国发放的身份证；

（d）具有所需照片、人员描述、人员签名以及身份识别号码的美国军事身份证（一些军事身份证不包含所有必需的信息）；或者

（e）由加利福尼亚州的机构或办事处或加利福尼亚州的市或/和郡的代理机构或办公室发放的雇佣证。

注意：公证人员必须在其公证人日志中包含身份认证文件的类型、发布文件的政府机构、文件的序列号或识别号以及用于认证签名人身份所依据的文件的发布日期或到期日期。（《政府组织法》第8206(a)(2)(D)条）

B. 一名可信证人的誓言 —— 签名人的身份可以由公证人个人了解的一名可信证人的誓言确定。[《民法典》第1185（b）(1)条] 公证人必须通过提交上述纸质身份证件来确定可信证人的身份。宣誓中，可信证人必须发誓或确认以下各项表述是真实的[《民法典》第1185（b）(1)（A）(i)-(v)条]：

作为文件签字人出现在公证人面前的是文件中所指定的人；

该可信证人个人了解签名人；

可信证人合理地认为，签名人的情况使其获得其他种类的身份证明是非常困难或不可能的；

签名人没有法律授权的任何其他身份证件以确定其身份；以及

The credible witness does not have a financial interest and is not named in the document signed.

Note: The single credible witness must sign the notary public's journal or the notary public must indicate in his or her journal the type of identifying document, the identifying number of the document, and the date of issuance or expiration of the document presented by the witness to establish the identity of the witness. (Government Code section 8206(a)(2)(D))

C. Oaths of Two Credible Witnesses – The identity of the signer can be established by the oaths of two credible witnesses whom the notary public does not personally know. (Civil Code section 1185(b)(2)) The notary public first must establish the identities of the two credible witnesses by the presentation of paper identification documents as listed above. Under oath, the credible witnesses must swear or affirm under penalty of perjury to each of the things sworn to or affirmed by a single credible witness, as set forth above. (Civil Code sections 1185(b)(2) and 1185(b)(1)(A)(i)-(v))

Note: The credible witnesses must sign the notary public's journal and the notary public must indicate in his or her journal the type of identifying documents, the identifying numbers of the documents, and the dates of issuance or expiration of the documents presented by the witnesses to establish their identities. (Government Code section 8206(a)(2)(E))

Notary Public Journal

A notary public is required to keep one active sequential journal at a time of all acts performed as a notary public. The journal must be kept in a locked and secured area (such as a lock box or locked desk drawer), under the direct and exclusive control of the notary public. The journal shall include the items shown below. (Government Code section 8206(a))

Date, time and type of each official act (e.g., acknowledgment, jurat).

Character of every instrument sworn to, affirmed, acknowledged or proved before the notary public (e.g., deed of trust).

The signature of each person whose signature is being notarized.

A statement that the identity of a person making an acknowledgment or taking an oath or affirmation was based on "satisfactory evidence" pursuant to Civil Code section 1185. If satisfactory evidence was based on:

可信证人不是公证文书的利益相关者，也没有在签名的文件中被提及。

注意：该名可信证人必须在公证人日志上签名，或者公证人必须在其日志中注明身份证明文件的类型、文件的识别号以及证人提交的文件的发布或到期日期以确认证人的身份。[《政府组织法》第8206（a）（2）（D）条]

C. 两名可信证人的誓言——签名人的身份可以由公证人非认识的两名可信证人的誓言确定。[《民法典》第1185（b）（2）条] 公证人首先必须通过提交上述的纸质身份证件来确定两名可信证人的身份。在誓言中，如上所述，可信证人必须对每一件由可信证人宣誓或确认的事件作承担伪证罪责任宣誓。[《民法典》第1185（b）（2）条和第1185（b）（1）（A）（i）-（v）条]

注意：可信证人必须在公证人日志上签字，公证人必须在其日志中注明身份证件的类型、文件的识别号以及证人提交的文件的发布或到期日期以确认证人的身份。[《政府组织法》第8206（a）（2）（E）条]

公证人日志

公证人必须在作为公证人执行的一切执业行为的时候保留一份连续日志。在公证人的直接和排他控制下，该日志必须保存在上锁和安全的区域（如锁箱或锁定的书桌抽屉）中。公证人日志应包括下列项目：[《政府组织法》第8206（a）条]

每个官方行为的日期，时间和类型（例如，确认、宣誓）。

每个在公证人面前宣誓、确认、认证或证明的文件性质（例如，信托契约）。

签名被公证的每位当事人的签名。

根据《民法典》第1185条的"可信的证据"作出承认或宣誓或确认的人的身份认证声明。如果可信的证据是基于：

Paper identification, the journal shall contain the type of identifying document, the governmental agency issuing the document, the serial or identifying number of the document, and the date of issue or expiration of the document;

A single credible witness personally known to the notary public, the journal shall contain the signature of the credible witness or the type of identifying document, the governmental agency issuing the document, the serial or identifying number of the document, and the date of issue or expiration of the document establishing the identity of the credible witness; or

3. Two credible witnesses whose identities are proven upon the presentation of satisfactory evidence, the journal shall contain the signatures of the credible witnesses and the type of identifying document, the governmental agency issuing the document, the serial or identifying number of the document, and the date of issue or expiration of the document establishing the identity of the credible witnesses.

The fee charged for the notarial service.

If the document to be notarized is a deed, quitclaim deed, deed of trust, or other document affecting real property or a power of attorney document, the notary public shall require the party signing the document to place his or her right thumbprint in the journal. If the right thumbprint is not available, then the notary public shall have the party use his or her left thumb, or any available finger and shall so indicate in the journal. If the party signing the document is physically unable to provide a thumb or fingerprint, the notary public shall so indicate in the journal and shall also provide an explanation of that physical condition. If the sequential journal is stolen, lost, misplaced, destroyed, damaged, or otherwise rendered unusable, the notary public immediately must notify the Secretary of State by certified or registered mail. The notification must include the periods of journal entries, the notary public commission number, the commission expiration date, and, when applicable, a photocopy of the police report that lists the journal. (Government Code section 8206(b))

A notary public must respond within 15 business days after the receipt of a written request from any member of the public for a copy of a transaction in the notary public journal by supplying either a photostatic copy of a line item from the notary public's journal or an acknowledgment that no such line item exists. The written request shall include the name of the parties, the type of document, and the month and year in which the document was

文书鉴定，日志应包含所认定文件的类型、发布文件的政府机构、文件的序列号或识别号以及文件的发行日期或到期日；

公证人个人了解的一名可信证人，该日志应载有可信证人的签名或身份证明文件的类型、发放文件的政府机构、文件的序列号或识别号以及发行或到期日，以确认可信证人的身份；或

3. 有两名可信证人的身份在提供充分证据后得到证实，该日志应载有可信证人的签名和身份证明文件的类型，发放文件的政府机构，文件的序列号或识别号以及发布日期或到期日，以确认可信证人的身份。

公证服务收费

如果要公证的文件是契约、财产转让契约、信托契约或影响不动产或其他法律文书的文件，公证人应要求签署文件的一方以右手拇指在日志上画押。如果无法提供上述正确的指纹，公证人应要求该方使用其左手拇指或任何可用的手指，并在公证日志中注释。如果签署文件的一方事实上无法提供拇指或指纹，公证人应在公证日志中注明，并提供其身体状况的说明。如果按顺序编号的工作日志被盗、丢失、错放、被销毁、损坏或因其他原因无法使用，公证人应立即通过认证或挂号邮件通知州务卿。该通知必须包括日志分录、公证委任状号码、委任状截止日期、如果可以，还应列出对该公证日志的警方报告的复印件。[《政府组织法》第 8206（b）条]

公证人必须在收到任何书面请求获得公证人日志中的某个事项副本的要求之后的 15 个工作日内，向其提供公证人日志的副本或确认不存在其所请求的事项。书面请求应包括双方的名称、文件的类型以及文件公证的月份和年份。提供所需信息的费用不得超过每页三十美分（$0.30）。[《政府组织法》第 8206（c）条和第 8206.5 条]

notarized. The cost to provide the requested information must not exceed thirty cents ($0.30) per page. (Government Code sections 8206(c) and 8206.5)

The sequential journal is the exclusive property of the notary public and shall not be surrendered to an employer upon termination of employment, whether or not the employer paid for the journal, or at any other time. The circumstances in which the notary public must relinquish the journal or permit inspection and copying of journal transactions and the procedures the notary public must follow are specified in Government Code section 8206(d).

A notary public is guilty of a misdemeanor if the notary public willfully fails to properly maintain the notary public's journal. (Government Code section 8228.1)

Within 30 days from the date the notary public commission is no longer valid, the notary public must deliver all notarial journals, records and papers to the county clerk's office where the oath is on file. If the notary public willfully fails or refuses to do so, the notary public is guilty of a misdemeanor, and shall be personally liable for damages to any person injured by that action or inaction. (Government Code section 8209) Any notarial journals, records and papers delivered to the Secretary of State will be returned to the sender.

Conflict of Interest

A notary public may notarize documents for relatives or others, unless doing so would provide a direct financial or beneficial interest to the notary public. Given California's community property law, care should be exercised if notarizing for a spouse or a domestic partner. A notary public would have a direct financial or beneficial interest to a transaction in the following situations (Government Code section 8224):

If a notary public is named, individually, as a principal to a financial transaction.

If a notary public is named, individually, as any of the following to a real property transaction: beneficiary, grantor, grantee, mortgagor, mortgagee, trustor, trustee, vendor, vendee, lessor, or lessee.

A notary public would not have a direct financial or beneficial interest in a transaction if a notary public is acting in the capacity of an agent, employee, insurer, attorney, escrow holder, or lender for a person having a direct financial or beneficial interest in the transaction. If in doubt as to whether or not to notarize, the notary public should seek the advice of an attorney.

按顺序编写的公证人日志是公证人的专有财产，无论其雇主是否在任何时间为日志付款，在公证人委任到期后不得向雇主交出公证人日志。公证人必须交出公证人日志或允许他人检查和复制公证人日志的情形以及公证人必须遵守的程序，参见《政府组织法》第 8206（d）条的规定。

公证人如果故意不妥善保管公证人日志，即构成轻罪。(《政府组织法》第 8228.1 条)

在公证人不再任职起的 30 日内，公证人必须将所有公证证书、公证记录和文件递交宣誓书所在郡的郡书记官办公室。公证人如果故意不当为之或者拒绝为之，即构成轻罪，对由于作为或不作为对他人造成损害的，应当承担个人赔偿责任。(《政府组织法》第 8209 条) 递交给州务卿的公证人日志、公证记录和文件将退还给发件人。

利益冲突

公证人可以公证其亲属或其他人的文件，除非这样做将为公证人带来直接的财务或其他利益。根据加利福尼亚州的社区财产法，如果为配偶或国内合作伙伴公证，应谨慎行事。以下情况属于公证人对交易具有直接的财务或实际利益(《政府组织法》第 8224 条)：

如果公证人被单独指定为金融交易的委托人。

如果公证人被单独指定为不动产交易的受益人、设保人、受让人、抵押人、抵押权人、受托人、受托人、供应商、受托人、出租人或承租人。

如果公证人以代理人、雇员、保险人、律师、代管人或直接财务或实际利益的贷款人的身份行事，则不属于对事项产生直接财务或实际利益的情形。如果对公证人是否能够办理公证有疑问，应征询律师的意见。

Acknowledgment

The form most frequently completed by the notary public is the certificate of acknowledgment. The certificate of acknowledgment must be in the form set forth in Civil Code section 1189. In the certificate of acknowledgment, the notary public certifies:

That the signer personally appeared before the notary public on the date indicated in the county indicated;

To the identity of the signer; and

That the signer acknowledged executing the document.

The notary public sequential journal must contain a statement that the identity of a person making the acknowledgment or taking the oath or affirmation was based on satisfactory evidence. If identity was established based on the oath of a credible witness personally known to the notary public, then the journal must contain the signature of the credible witness or the type of identifying document used to establish the witness' identity, the governmental agency issuing the document, the serial or identifying number of the document, and the date of issue or expiration of the document. If the identity of the person making the acknowledgment or taking the oath or affirmation was established by the oaths or affirmations of two credible witnesses whose identities are proven to the notary public upon the presentation of satisfactory evidence, then the journal must contain the signatures of the credible witnesses and the type of identifying documents, the identifying numbers of the documents and the dates of issuance or expiration of the documents presented by the witnesses to establish their identities. The certificate of acknowledgment must be filled completely out at the time the notary public's signature and seal are affixed. The certificate of acknowledgment is executed under penalty of perjury. (Civil Code section 1189(a)(1))

The completion of a certificate of acknowledgment that contains statements that the notary public knows to be false not only may cause the notary public to be liable for civil penalties and administrative action, but is also a criminal offense. The notary public who willfully states as true any material fact known to be false is subject to a civil penalty not exceeding $10,000. (Civil Code section 1189(a)(2))

A notary public may complete a certificate of acknowledgment required in another state or jurisdiction of the United States on documents to be filed in that other state or jurisdiction, provided the form does not require the

公证确认

最常见的公证业务形式是确认证明。确认证明书必须符合《民法典》第1189条的规定。在确认证明书中，公证人应证明：

在郡指定的日期，签字人亲自在公证人面前出示文书；

签名人的身份；以及

签名人确认执行该文件。

公证人日志必须载有基于充分的证据作出承认或作出誓言或确认的人的身份声明。如果签名人的身份是根据公证人个人相识的可信证人的誓言确定的，则公证人日志必须包含可信证人的签名或用于确定证人身份的识别文件的类型、发放文件的政府机构、文件的序列号或识别号以及文件的发布或到期日期。如果作出承认或宣誓或确认的人的身份是通过两名可信证人的宣誓或确认确定的，证人须在提供令人信服的证据时向公证人证明其身份，则公证人日志必须包含可信证人的签名、身份证明文件的类型、文件的识别号码以及证人提交的确定其身份的文件的发布或到期日。确认证明书必须在公证人签名和盖章时填写完整。确认证明书受伪证处罚规则的规制。[《民法典》第1189（a）（1）条]

公证人作出其知道其中包含虚假陈述的确认证明书，不仅可能导致公证人受到民事处罚和对行政诉讼承担责任，并且可能构成刑事犯罪。公证人将虚假的重大事实故意陈述为真的，会面临不超过10000美元的民事处罚。[《民法典》第1189（a）（2）条]

公证人可以为来自美国的其他州或法域的申请人请求对在另一州或法域提交的文件办理确认证书，前提是该确认不要求公证人确定或证明签名人持有特定的代表资格或作出加利福尼亚法律不允许的其他裁定

notary public to determine or certify that the signer holds a particular representative capacity or to make other determinations and certifications not allowed by California law.

Any certificate of acknowledgment taken within this state shall be in the following form:

State of California　　　}
County of _____

On _____ before me, (here insert name and title of the officer), personally appeared _____ who proved to me on the basis of satisfactory evidence to be the person(s) whose name(s) is/are subscribed to the within instrument and acknowledged to me that he/she/they executed the same in his/her/their authorized capacity(ies), and that by his/her/their signature(s) on the instrument the person(s), or the entity upon behalf of which the person(s) acted, executed the instrument.

I certify under PENALTY OF PERJURY under the laws of the State of California that the foregoing paragraph is true and correct.

WITNESS my hand and official seal.

Notary Public Signature　Notary Public Seal

Note: An acknowledgment cannot be affixed to a document mailed or otherwise delivered to a notary public whereby the signer did not personally appear before the notary public, even if the signer is known by the notary public. Also, a notary public seal and signature cannot be affixed to a document without the correct notarial wording.

Jurat

The second form most frequently completed by a notary public is the jurat. (Government Code section 8202) The jurat is identified by the wording "Subscribed and sworn to (or affirmed)" contained in the form. In the jurat, the notary public certifies:

That the signer personally appeared before the notary public on the date indicated and in the county indicated;

That the signer signed the document in the presence of the notary public;

That the notary public administered the oath or affirmation*; and

To the identity of the signer.

Any jurat taken within this state shall be in the following form:

State of California
County of _____

Subscribed and sworn to (or affirmed) before me on this _____ day of _____, 20_____, by

和证书。

在此情形下进行的任何确认证书的格式如下：

加利福尼亚州
_____郡
_____（时间），基于充分的证据，_____亲自向本人（公证人的姓名和职称）证明，其是文书签署者本人，其在授权范围内行使了文书中职能，其本人或者其所代表的实体均行了该文书。

本人根据加利福尼亚州法律中的伪证处罚条款，证明上述内容是真实和准确的。

证人签字和公章
公证人签字　　公证公章

注意：即使公证人知道签字人，如果签字人没有当面出现在公证人面前，则不得以邮寄或其他方式送达给公证人予以确认。另外，没有正确的公证字样，公证公章和签名不能附在文件上。

宣誓证明

公证人第二经常办理的公证文书是宣誓证明。（《政府组织法》第8202条）宣誓证明由表格中所载的"同意并宣誓（或已确认）"字样确定。公证人在宣誓证明中应证明：

在指定的郡于指定的日期，签字人亲自出现在公证人面前；

签名人在公证人在场的情况下签署了该文件；

经公证人公开宣誓或确认*；以及

签名人的身份。

在本州境内采取的任何宣誓证明应采取以下格式：

加利福尼亚州
_____郡
20____年___月___日，_____向本人提交并宣誓（确认），并基于充分证据证明其身份。

_____, proved to me on the basis of satisfactory evidence to be the person(s) who appeared before me.

Notary Public Signature   Notary Public Seal

Note: A jurat cannot be affixed to a document mailed or otherwise delivered to a notary public whereby the signer did not personally appear, take an oath, and sign in the presence of the notary public, even if the signer is known by the notary public. Also, a notary public seal and signature cannot be affixed to a document without the correct notarial wording.

*There is no prescribed wording for the oath, but an acceptable oath would be "Do you swear or affirm that the statements in this document are true?" When administering the oath, the signer and notary public traditionally each raise their right hand but this is not a legal requirement.

Proof of Execution by a Subscribing Witness

If a person, called the principal, has signed a document but does not personally appear before a notary public, another person can appear on the principal's behalf to prove the principal signed (or "executed") the document. That person is called a subscribing witness. (Code of Civil Procedure section 1935)

A proof of execution by a subscribing witness cannot be used in conjunction with any power of attorney, quitclaim deed, grant deed (other than a trustee's deed resulting from a decree of foreclosure, or a nonjudicial foreclosure pursuant to Civil Code section 2924, or to a deed of reconveyance), mortgage, deed of trust, security agreement, any instrument affecting real property, or any instrument requiring a notary public to obtain a thumbprint from the party signing the document in the notary public's journal. (Government Code section 27287 and Civil Code section 1195(b)(1) and (2))

The requirements for proof of execution by a subscribing witness are as follows:

The subscribing witness must prove (say under oath) that the person who signed the document as a party, the principal, is the person described in the document, and the subscribing witness personally knows the principal (Civil Code section 1197); and

The subscribing witness must say, under oath, that the subscribing witness saw the principal sign the document or in the presence of the principal heard the principal acknowledge that the principal signed the document (Code

公证人签名   公证公章

注意：即使公证人知道签名人，如果签名人没有亲自出现在公证人面前，进行宣誓并签字，宣誓证明不得以邮寄或以其他方式交付给公证人予以认证。同样的，没有正确的公证字样，公证公章和签名不得附在文件上。

＊宣誓没有规定的措辞，但可接受的誓言是"你是否发誓或肯定本文中的陈述为真实的"。在宣誓时，签名人和公证人传统上都会举起右手，但这不是法定要求。

签署见证人作出的执行证明

如果委托人在未亲自出现在公证人面前的情况下签署了一份文件，另一人可以代为出面，以证明委托人在该文件的签名（或执行），则其被称作签署见证人。(《民事诉讼法》第 1935 条）

签署见证人的执行证明不得与任何授权委托书、撤销契约、授予契约（受托人根据止赎令产生的契约或根据《民法典》第 2924 条规定的非司法原因止赎或转让契约除外）、抵押契约、信托契约、担保协议、涉及不动产的任何法律文书，或者任何要求公证人获得在公证人日志上签署文件的一方的指纹的文件一起使用。(《政府组织法》第 27287 条、《民法典》第 1195（b）（1）-（2）条）

签署见证人作出执行证明的要求如下：

签署见证人必须（在宣誓下）证明（签署文件的人是委托人，即文件中描述的人，且签署见证人个人认识委托人（《民法典》第 1197 条）；以及

签署见证人必须宣誓其亲眼目睹该委托人在该书上签字，或在委托人在场的情况下听见委托人承认其本人签署了该文件（《民事诉讼法》第 1935 条和《民法典》第 1197 条）；以及

of Civil Procedure section 1935 and Civil Code section 1197); and

The subscribing witness must say, under oath, that the subscribing witness was requested by the principal to sign the document as a witness and that the subscribing witness did so (Code of Civil Procedure section 1935 and Civil Code section 1197); and

The notary public must establish the identity of the subscribing witness by the oath of a credible witness whom the notary public personally knows and who personally knows the subscribing witness. The credible witness must also present to the notary public any identification document satisfying the requirements for satisfactory evidence as described in Civil Code section 1185(b)(3) or (4) (Civil Code section 1196); and

The subscribing witness must sign the notary public's official journal. The credible witness must sign the notary public's official journal or the notary public must record in the notary public's official journal the type of identification document presented, the governmental agency issuing the document, the serial number of the document, and the date of issue or expiration of the document. (Government Code section 8206(a)(2)(C) and (D))

Note: The identity of the subscribing witness must be established by the oath of a credible witness who personally knows the subscribing witness and who is known personally by the notary public. In addition, the credible witness must present an identification document satisfying the requirements of Civil Code section 1185(b)(3) or (4).

Because proof of execution by a subscribing witness is not commonly used, the following scenario is provided as an example of how proof by a subscribing witness may be used.

The principal, Paul, wants to have his signature on a document notarized. Paul is in the hospital and cannot appear before a notary public. So Paul asks a longtime friend, Sue, to visit the hospital and act as a subscribing witness. When Sue comes to the hospital, Sue must watch Paul sign the document. If Paul has signed the document prior to Sue's arrival, Paul must say (acknowledge) to Sue that Paul signed the document. Then Paul should ask Sue to sign the document as a subscribing witness, and Sue must do so.

Next, Sue must take the document to a notary public. Sue chooses Nancy Notary as the notary public. Sue must bring a credible witness with her to see Nancy Notary. Sue chooses Carl, a longtime friend, as a credible witness

签署见证人必须宣誓其被委托人要求在签署文件时作为签署见证人且其已按照委托人的请求行事（《民事诉讼法》第1935条和《民法典》第1197条）；以及

公证人必须通过自己个人认识与签署见证人个人认识的可信证人的誓言确定签署见证人的身份。可信证人还必须向公证人出示符合《民法典》第1185（b）（3）条或第1185（b）（4）条所规定的充分证据所要求的身份证明文件（《民法典》第1196条）；以及

签署见证人必须在公证人日志上签字。可信证人必须在公证人日志上签字，公证人必须在公证人日志上记录当事人所提供的身份证明文件的类型、发放文件的政府机构、文件的序列号、文件的发行或到期日。[《政府组织法》第8206（a）（2）（C）条和第8206（a）（2）（D）条]

注意：签署见证人的身份必须由个人认识签署见证人且个人认识公证人的可信证人的宣誓确定。另外，可信证人必须出示符合《民法典》第1185（b）（3）条或第1185（b）（4）条要求的身份证明文件。

签署见证人作出的执行证明没有普遍使用的格式，以下情景为可以使用的签署见证人证明的示例。

委托人保罗希望在公证文件上签字。但保罗在医院里不能当面见到公证人。所以保罗请求一个已认识很长一段时间的朋友苏去医院与其会面并作为保罗的签署见证人。当苏来到医院时，苏必须亲眼目睹保罗签署文件。如果保罗在苏到达之前签署了这份文件，保罗就必须向保证部门表示（承认）保罗已签署了该文件。而保罗应该要求苏作为签署见证人签署该文件，苏必须这样做。

接下来，苏必须把这份文件交给公证人。苏选择了南希作为公证人。苏与一名可信证人共同与公证人会面。苏选择了认识很长的朋友卡尔作为一个可信证人，因为卡尔与南希已合作多年。因此，卡尔可以作为苏的可信证人。

because Carl has worked with Nancy Notary for several years. Therefore, Carl can act as Sue's credible witness.

Sue and Carl appear together before Nancy. Nancy determines Nancy personally knows Carl and also examines Carl's California driver's license to establish Carl's identity. Then Nancy puts Carl under oath. Under oath or affirmation, Carl swears or affirms that Carl personally knows Sue, that Sue is the person who signed the document as a subscribing witness, and Carl does not have a financial interest in the document signed by Paul and subscribed by Sue, and is not named in the document signed by Paul and subscribed by Sue. Then Nancy puts Sue under oath. Under oath or affirmation, Sue swears or affirms Sue personally knows Paul, that Paul is the person described as a party in the document, that Sue watched Paul sign the document or heard Paul acknowledge that Paul signed the document, that Paul requested Sue sign the document as subscribing witness and that Sue did so.

Sue signs Nancy's notary public journal as a subscribing witness. Carl must sign Nancy's notary public journal as a credible witness, or Nancy must record in the notary public journal that Carl presented a California Department of Motor Vehicles driver's license, the license number, and the date the license expires.

Nancy completes Nancy's notary public journal entry. Nancy then completes a proof of execution certificate and attaches the proof of execution certificate to the document. Sue takes the notarized document back to Paul.

A certificate for proof of execution by a subscribing witness shall be in the following form. (Civil Code section 1195)

State of California } ss.
County of _____
On _____ (date), before me, _____ (name and title of officer), personally appeared _____ (name of subscribing witness), proved to me to be the person whose name is subscribed to the within instrument, as a witness thereto, on the oath of _____ (name of credible witness), a credible witness who is known to me and provided a satisfactory identifying document. _____ (name of subscribing witness), being by me duly sworn, said that he/she was present and saw/heard _____ (name[s] of principal[s]), the same person(s) described in and whose name(s) is/are subscribed to the within or attached instrument in his/her/their authorized capacity(ies) as (a) party(ies) thereto, execute or acknowledge executing the

苏和卡尔一起当面会见南希。南希认定,南希个人认识卡尔,并检查了卡尔的加利福尼亚驾驶执照,以确认卡尔的身份。然后,南希要求卡尔宣誓。在宣誓或确认中,卡尔发誓或确认卡尔个人认识苏,苏以签署见证人的身份在文书上签字,且卡尔对保罗签署、由苏提交的文件没有经济利益,且在由保罗签署、由苏提交的文件中没有涉及卡尔的名字。然后,南希应让苏宣誓。在宣誓或确认中,苏应发誓或者确认其个人认识保罗,保罗是文件中的一方当事人,苏目睹了保罗签署该文件或听到保罗承认其签署了该文件,保罗要求苏作为签署见证人签署该文件,而苏则这样做了。

苏应在公证人南希的公证人日志上作为签署见证人签字。卡尔也须在南希的公证人日志上作为可信证人签字,或者由南希在公证日志上记录卡尔提交的由加利福尼亚汽车驾驶执照部门颁发的驾驶执照、驾照号码以及驾照的到期日。

南希完成了公证人日志后,须出具完成执行证书的证明,并将执行证书的证明附于公证文书中。苏则将公证文件带回交给保罗。

签署见证人执行证明的证明书应采用以下格式。(《民法典》第1195条)

加利福尼亚州
_____郡
__年__月__日,_____(签署见证人的名字)作为证人,在本人认识的可信证人_____(可信证人的姓名)的宣誓下,亲自向本人_____(公证人姓名和职务)证明在文件中签名的人的身份,并提供了充分的身份证明文件。(签署见证人的名字)宣誓,其在场并亲自目睹或听见了_____(委托人的姓名)宣誓并签署文件,且证明委托人的姓名及描述与文件中一致,委托人具有执行和确认文书的能力,在(委托人的姓名)的请求下作为证人。

same, and that said affiant subscribed his/her name to the within or attached instrument as a witness at the request of_____ (name[s] of principal[s]).

WITNESS my hand and official seal.

Signature   (Seal)

Note: It is not acceptable to affix a notary public seal and signature to a document without the notarial wording.

Signature by Mark

When the signer of an instrument cannot write (sign) his or her name, that person may sign the document by mark. (Civil Code section 14) The requirements for notarizing a signature by mark are as follows:

The person signing the document by mark must be identified by the notary public by satisfactory evidence. (Civil Code section 1185)

The signer's mark must be witnessed by two persons who must subscribe their own names as witnesses on the document. One witness should write the person's name next to the person's mark and then the witness should sign his or her name as a witness. The witnesses are only verifying that they witnessed the individual make his or her mark on the document. A notary public is not required to identify the two persons who witnessed the signing by mark or to have the two witnesses sign the notary public's journal.

Exception: If the witnesses were acting in the capacity of credible witnesses in establishing the identity of the person signing by mark, then the witnesses' signatures must be entered in the notary public's journal.

The signer by mark must include his or her mark in the notary public journal. To qualify as a signature, the making of the mark in the notary public journal, must be witnessed by an individual who must write the person's name next to the mark and then sign his or her own name as a witness.

Following is an example of a document executed by signature by mark:

证人签字及公章

公证人签名   公证公章

注意：未注明公证字样，禁止将文件公章和签名附于在文件上。

标记签名

当文书的签名者无法书写（签署）姓名时，可以用标记来签署文件。（《民法典》第 14 条）通过标记签署公证文书的要求如下：

以标记来签署文件的人必须已经由公证人通过充分证据确认身份。（《民法典》第 1185 条）

签名人的标记必须由两名已经在文书上作为证人签名的人亲眼见证。证人应在签署人的标记旁边写上其作为证人的姓名。证人只用于证实其亲眼见证了签署人在文件上做标记。公证人不必认证标记签名的证人的身份，也不必要求证人在公证人日志上签字。

例外：如果证人在确认以标记签名的方式签署文件的人的身份时，是作为可信证人的身份行事的，则该证人必须在公证人日志上签字。

标记签名人必须在公证人日志上附上其使用的标记。为了确立标记签名的效力，在公证文书上附上标记时，必须由在该标记旁署名的证人亲眼见证且证人应作为证人签署自己的姓名。

以下是通过标记签名执行的公证文书的示例：

I, Bob Smith, give my power of attorney to Jane Brown to act as my attorney-in-fact on all matters pertaining to the handling of my estate, finances, and investments. This power of attorney is to remain in effect until another document revoking this instrument has been filed of record thereby rendering this instrument null and void.

Date: _____ Name: _____
By: _____
Witness 1
_____
Witness 2

State of California }
County of

On February 5, 2013, before me, John Doe, a notary public, personally appeared Bob Smith, who proved to me on the basis of satisfactory evidence to be the person(s) whose name(s) is/are subscribed to the within instrument and acknowledged to me that he/she/they executed the same in his/her/their authorized capacity(ies), and that by his/her/their signature(s) on the instrument the person(s), or the entity upon behalf of which the person(s) acted, executed the instrument.

I certify under PENALTY OF PERJURY under the laws of the State of California that the foregoing paragraph is true and correct.

WITNESS my hand and official seal.
Notary Public Signature Notary Public Seal

Note: A notary public seal and signature cannot be affixed to a document without the correct notarial wording.

Powers of Attorney - Certifying

A notary public can certify copies of powers of attorney. A certified copy of a power of attorney that has been certified by a notary public has the same force and effect as the original power of attorney. (Probate Code section 4307)

A suggested format for the certification is shown below. Other formats with similar wording may also be acceptable.

State of California
County of _____
I _____ (name of notary public), Notary Public, certify that on _____ (date), I examined the original power of attorney and the copy of the power of attorney. I further certify that the copy is a true and correct copy of the original power of attorney.

Notary Public Signature Notary Public Seal

Note: A notary public seal and signature cannot be affixed to a document without the correct notarial wording.

Notarization of Incomplete Documents

A notary public may not notarize a document that is

我，鲍勃·史密斯，向简·布莱恩授权处理关于本人的房地产、财务和投资的所有事宜。本项授权持续有效，直到本人提交撤销授权的文件，该文书方始无效。

日期：_____ 姓名：_____
由：_____
证人一
_____
证人二

加利福尼亚州
_____郡

2013 年 2 月 5 日，鲍勃·史密斯依据充分证据亲自向本公证人约翰·多尔证明，他是文书签署者本人，他在授权范围内行使了文书中职能，他本人或者他所代表的实体执行了该文书。

本人根据加利福尼亚州法律规定的伪证处罚条款，证明上述内容真实准确。

证人签名及公章
公证人签名   公证公章

注意： 如果没有正确的公证字样，禁止将公证公章和公证人签名附在文件上。

授权委托书的认证

公证人可以认证授权委托书副本。获得公证人认证的授权委托书核证副本与授权委托书正本具有相同的效力。(《遗嘱检验法规》第 4307 条）

推荐使用的认证格式如下所示。法律同样允许具有类似措辞的其他格式。

加利福尼亚州
_____郡
本公证人_____（公证人姓名）于_____（日期）核查了授权委托书的原件和副本，并进一步证明本副本的内容是真实准确的。

公证人签名   公证公章

注意： 如果没有正确的公证字样，禁止将公证公章和公证人签名附在文件上。

不完整文件的公证

公证人不得公证不完整的文件。如果公证人凭经

incomplete. If presented with a document for notarization, which the notary public knows from his or her experience to be incomplete or is without doubt on its face incomplete, the notary public must refuse to notarize the document. (Government Code section 8205)

Certified Copies

A notary public may only certify copies of powers of attorney under Probate Code section 4307 and his or her notary public journal. (Government Code sections 8205(a)(4), 8205(b)(1), and 8206(e))

Certified copies of birth, fetal death, death, and marriage records may be made only by the State Registrar, by duly appointed and acting local registrars during their term of office, and by county recorders. (Health & Safety Code section 103545)

Illegal Advertising

California law requires any non-attorney notary public who advertises notarial services in a language other than English to post a prescribed notice, in English and the other language, that the notary public is not an attorney and cannot give legal advice about immigration or any other legal matters. The notary public also must list the fees set by statute that a notary public may charge for notarial services. In any event, a notary public may not translate into Spanish the term "Notary Public," defined as "notario publico" or "notario," even if the prescribed notice also is posted. A first offense for violation of this law is grounds for the suspension or revocation of a notary public's commission. A second offense is grounds for the permanent revocation of a notary public's commission. (Government Code section 8219.5)

A notary public legally is barred from advertising in any manner whatsoever that he or she is a notary public if the notary public promotes himself or herself as an immigration specialist or consultant. (Government Code section 8223)

Immigration Documents

Contrary to popular belief, there is no prohibition against notarizing immigration documents. However, several laws specifically outline what a notary public can and cannot do. Only an attorney, a representative accredited by the U.S. Department of Justice, or a person who is registered by the California Secretary of State and bonded as an immigration consultant under the Business and Professions Code may assist a client in completing immigration forms.

验认定收到的文书是不完整的或者该文书毫无疑问是不完整的，则公证人应当拒绝进行公证。（《政府组织法》第 8205 条）

认证副本

公证人只能认证《遗嘱检验法规》第 4307 条规定的及其公证人日志上核证委托书的副本。[《政府组织法》第 8205（a）（4）条、第 8205（b）（1）条和第 8206（e）条]

出生证明、胎儿死亡、死亡和结婚记录的复印件，只能由州书记官、在任期内被正式任命的当地书记官和郡书记官认证。（《健康和安全守则》第 103545 条）

非法广告

加利福尼亚州的法律要求任何以英语以外的其他语言宣传公证服务的非律师公证人须另行以英文和另一种语言发布规定的广告。非律师公证人，也不能就移民或任何其他法律事宜提供法律意见。公证人也必须列出对申请人收取的公证费用。在任何情形下，即使规定的广告已经被发布，也不得将"公证人"一词翻译为西班牙语的"notario publico"或"notario"。第一次违反本条即构成暂停或撤销公证人任职资格的理由。两次违反本条将被永久撤销公证人任职资格。（《政府组织法》第 8219.5 条）

如果公证人作为移民专家或顾问进行公开宣传，不得同时以任何方式宣传其公证人身份。（《政府组织法》第 8223 号）

移民文件

与普遍的看法相反，法律并不禁止对移民证件的公证。不过，有法律明确指出了公证人有权和禁止实施的行为。只有律师、美国司法部认证的代表或由加州州务卿注册并根据《商业和职业守则》确立为移民顾问的人员，才有权协助客户填写移民表格。（《商业和职业守则》第 22440 条）。公证人不得对每位申请人的每套表格收取超过十美元（$10）的费用，除非公证人是作为提供专业服务的律师行事。（《政府组织

(Business and Professions Code section 22440). A notary public may not charge any individual more than ten dollars ($10) for each set of forms, unless the notary public is also an attorney who is rendering professional services as an attorney. (Government Code section 8223)

Confidential Marriage Licenses

A notary public who is interested in obtaining authorization to issue confidential marriage licenses may apply for approval to the county clerk in the county in which the notary public resides. A notary public must not issue a confidential marriage license unless he or she is approved by the county clerk having jurisdiction. The county clerk offers a course of instruction, which a notary public must complete before authorization will be granted. Additionally, in order for a notary public to perform the marriage, he/she must be one of the persons authorized under Family Code sections 400 to 402 (e.g., priest, minister, or rabbi). The county clerk in the county where the notary public resides may or may not approve the authorization to issue confidential marriage licenses. The county clerk should be consulted if the notary public is interested in obtaining approval. (Family Code section 530)

Grounds for Denial, Revocation, or Suspension of Appointment and Commission

The Secretary of State may refuse to appoint any person as notary public or may revoke or suspend the commission of a notary public for specific reasons. These reasons include but are not limited to: a substantial misstatement or omission in the application; conviction of a felony or a disqualifying criminal conviction; failure to furnish the Secretary of State with certified copies of the notary public journal when requested to do so or to provide information relating to official acts performed by the notary public; charging more than the fee prescribed by law; failure to complete the acknowledgment at the time the notary public's seal and signature are attached to the document; executing a false certificate; failure to submit to the Secretary of State any court ordered money judgment, including restitution; failure to secure the sequential journal or the official seal; willful failure to report the theft or loss of the sequential journal; making a false certificate or writing containing statements known to be false; fraud relating to a deed of trust; improper notarial acts; unlawfully acting as a notary; filing false or forged documents; forgery; grand theft; falsely obtaining personal information; willful failure to provide access to a journal when request-

法》第8223号）

秘密结婚证

想要取得签发秘密结婚证授权的公证人，可以向公证人所在郡的郡书记官申请批准。在得到有管辖权的郡书记官的批准前，公证人不得签发秘密结婚证。公证人必须在完成郡书记官提供的培训课程之后才能获得授权。此外，公证人如果需要举行结婚仪式，则其必须是根据《家庭法》第400条至第402条授权的人员之一（如牧师、部长或犹太教教士）。公证人所在郡的书记官有权决定是否批准发放秘密结婚证。如果公证人希望批准，应先征求郡书记官的意见。(《家庭法》第530条）

拒绝、撤销、暂停任用和委任的理由

州务卿可以拒绝任命公证人，也可以由于具体原因撤销或暂停公证人的任命。这些原因包括但不限于：申请中的重大错误或遗漏；犯有重罪或足以使其被取消资格的刑事定罪；当州务卿要求提供批准公证或者有关公证人执行的职务行为的资料时无法提供；收费超过法律规定的标准；公证人未能及时完成对附于文件的印章和签名的确认；执行虚假的公证证书；未能向州务卿提交或归还任何法院下达的判决书；未能妥善保管公证人日志或公章；故意对公证人日志的盗窃或遗失不作报告；已知内容虚假仍然出具虚假的公证证书或书面陈述，内含已知为虚假的陈述；进行与信托契约有关的诈骗；公证行为不当；为公证人禁止的行为；提交虚假或伪造的文件；伪造；盗窃；不当获取个人信息；在治安官要求查阅公证人日志时故意不提供；非法广告。(《政府组织法》第8205条、第8214.1条、第8219.5条和第8223条）

ed by a peace officer; and illegal advertising. (Government Code sections 8205, 8214.1, 8219.5 and 8223)

In addition, the Secretary of State may deny the notary public application or suspend the notary public commission of a person who has not complied with child or family support obligations. (Family Code section 17520)

Disciplinary Guidelines

The Secretary of State's disciplinary guidelines facilitate due process and maintain consistency in reviewing applications, investigating alleged violations, and implementing administrative actions. (Government Code section 8220)

The disciplinary guidelines assist administrative law judges, attorneys, notaries public, notary public applicants, and others involved in the disciplinary process. The disciplinary guidelines are available on the Secretary of State's website or can be mailed to you upon request.

Fees

Government Code section 8211 specifies the maximum fees that may be charged for notary public services. However, a notary public may decide to charge no fee or an amount that is less than the maximum amount prescribed by law. The charging of a fee and the amount of the fee charged is at the discretion of the notary public or the notary public's employer, provided it does not exceed the maximum fees. The notary public is required to make an entry in the notary public journal even if no fee was charged, such as "no fee" or "0." (Government Code section 8206)

Exceptions: 1) Pursuant to Government Code section 8203.6, no fees shall be collected by notaries public appointed to military and naval reservations in accordance with 8203.1; 2) Pursuant to Elections Code section 8080, no fee shall be collected by notaries public for verifying any nomination document or circulator's affidavit; 3) Pursuant to Government Code section 6106, no fee shall be collected by a notary public working for a public entity for services rendered in an affidavit, application, or voucher in relation to the securing of a pension; 4) Pursuant to Government Code section 6107, no fee may be charged to a United States military veteran for notarization of an application or a claim for a pension, allotment, allowance, compensation, insurance, or any other veteran's benefit; and 5) Pursuant to Government Code section 8211(d) no fee can be charged to notarize signatures on vote by mail ballot identification envelopes or other voting materials.

此外，州务卿还可以对没有履行抚养儿童或家庭义务的人拒绝其公证人申请，或者暂停其公证人资格。（《家庭法》第17520条）

纪律守则

州务卿制定的纪律准则应促进维护正当程序，并在审查申请、调查指控的违规行为和实施行政诉讼方面保持程序一致。（《政府组织法》第8220条）

纪律守则有助于对行政法官、律师、公证人、公证人申请者，以及其他人员在参与纪律行为时提供帮助。纪律守则的内容可以在州务卿的网站上查阅，或者可以根据请求进行邮寄。

公证费用

《政府组织法》第8211条规定了公证服务可收取的最高费用。公证人可以决定不收取任何费用或收取低于法律规定的最高金额的费用。收费与否和收费金额由公证人或公证人的雇主酌情决定，但不得超过最高费用。即使不收取费用，公证人也必须在公证人日志上记录，例如"免费"或"0"。（《政府组织法》第8206条）

例外情形：1）根据《政府组织法》第8203.6条，由第8203.1条被指定为任何军事或海上保留职务的公证人，不得收取任何费用；2）根据《选举法》第8080条，公证人不得对任何核查提名文件或证人宣誓书收取任何费用；3）根据《政府组织法》第6106条，在为领取养老金提供宣誓书、申请书或传票公证服务的公证机构工作的公证人不得收取任何费用；4）根据《政府组织法》第6107条，为美国军方退伍军人申请退休金、分配、津贴、赔偿、保险或任何其他退伍军人的利益提供公证服务时不得收取任何费用；以及5）根据《政府组织法》第8211（d）条，公证邮寄选票标识信封或其他投票材料上的签名不得收取任何费用。

In addition, Government Code section 6100 requires any notary public who is appointed to act for and on behalf of certain public agencies, pursuant to Government Code section 8202.5, to charge for all services and remit the fees received to the employing agency. Each fee charged must be entered in the journal.

Change of Address

A notary public is required to notify the Secretary of State of any change of business or residence address in writing, by certified mail, within 30 days. (Government Code section 8213.5) Willful failure to notify the Secretary of State of a change of address is punishable as an infraction by a fine of not more than $500. (Government Code section 8213.5)

Upon the change of a business address to a new county, a notary public may elect to file a new oath of office and bond in the new county. However, filing a new oath and bond is optional. Once commissioned, a notary public may perform notary public services anywhere in the state. The original oath and bond must be filed in the county where the notary public's principal place of business is located as shown in the application filed with the Secretary of State. Whether or not a county transfer is filed with the new county after the original oath and bond have been filed in the original county is permissive should the notary public move. (Government Code section 8213) There is no fee for the processing of address change notifications with the Secretary of State.

Note: To ensure proper processing, please include the following information when submitting the written address change notification to the Secretary of State:

Name of the notary public exactly as it appears on the commission certificate;

Commission number and expiration date of the commission;

Whether the address change is for the business, residence, and/or for mailing purposes; and

New business, including business name, residence, and/or mailing address.

Be sure the address change notification is signed and dated by the notary public. The change of address can be submitted in letter form or, for convenience, an address change form is available on the Secretary of State's website or can be mailed to you upon request.

Foreign Language

A notary public can notarize a signature on a docu-

此外,《政府组织法》第6100条规定,被任命或指定代理某些公共机构的公证人,有权按《政府组织法》第8202.5条的规定收取服务费,并将收到的费用汇报给雇主。每一笔收取的费用都必须记录在公证人日志上。

执业地址的变更

公证人必须在执业地点或居住地变更的30日内通过挂号信的方式书面通知州务卿。(《政府组织法》第8213.5条)故意不通知州务卿变更执业地点的,将被处以不超过500美元的罚款。(《政府组织法》第8213.5条)

当公证人的执业地点变更为新的郡时,公证人可以选择在新的郡提交新的宣誓和保证金。但是,是否提交新的宣誓和保证金是可由公证人自由选择的。一旦收到委任状,公证人可以在该州的任何地方进行公证服务。原来的誓言和保证金必须在公证人的执业地点所在的郡提交,正如向州务卿提交申请时一样。在公证人的执业郡发生变更时,原始的宣誓和保证金已经向原郡提交后,是否还需要向新的郡提交,由公证人决定。(《政府组织法》第8213条)通知州务卿处理执业地点变更的不收费。

注意: 为确保正确地处理,公证人在向州务卿提交书面地址变更通知时,应当包括以下信息:

公证人的姓名,且该姓名应与委任状上的一致;

委任状编码和委任的截止日期;

更改地址是否用于商业、居住和/或邮寄目的;以及

新业务,包括业务的名称,住所和/或邮寄地址。

确保地址变更通知已由公证人签名并注明日期。地址变更可以以书面形式提交,或者为了方便起见,地址变更表可在州务卿网站上查询,或者可以根据请求进行邮寄。

外语文书的公证

公证人可以对其不熟悉的外文撰写的文件进行公

ment in a foreign language with which the notary public is not familiar, since a notary public's function only relates to the signature and not the contents of the document. The notary public should be able to identify the type of document being notarized for entry in the notary public's journal. If unable to identify the type of document, the notary public must make an entry to that effect in the journal (e.g., "a document in a foreign language"). The notary public should be mindful of the completeness of the document and must not notarize the signature on the document if the document appears to be incomplete. The notary public is responsible for completing the acknowledgment or jurat form. When notarizing a signature on a document, a notary public must be able to communicate with the customer in order for the signer either to swear to or affirm the contents of the affidavit or to acknowledge the execution of the document. An interpreter should not be used, as vital information could be lost in the translation. If a notary public is unable to communicate with a customer, the customer should be referred to a notary public who speaks the customer's language.

CIVIL CODE

§ 14. Words and phrases; construction; tense; gender; number

signature or subscription includes mark, when the person cannot write, his name being written near it, by a person who writes his own name as a witness; provided, that when a signature is by mark it must in order that the same may be acknowledged or may serve as the signature to any sworn statement be witnessed by two persons who must subscribe their own names as witnesses thereto.

§ 1181. Notaries public; officers before whom proof or acknowledgment may be made

The proof or acknowledgment of an instrument may be made before a notary public at any place within this state, or within the county or city and county in this state in which the officer specified below was elected or appointed, before either:

(a) A clerk of a superior court.

(b) A county clerk.

(c) A court commissioner.

(d) A retired judge of a municipal or justice court.

(e) A district attorney.

(f) A clerk of a board of supervisors.

(g) A city clerk.

证，因为公证人的职能只与文件的签名有关而非文件的内容。公证人应该能够确定公证文书的类型，才能将文书记录在公证人日志中。如果无法确定文件的类型，公证人必须在日志上记录（如，"外文文件"字样）。公证人应注意文件的完整性，如果文件明显不完整，则不得对文件的签名进行公证。公证人负责完成确认书或宣誓证明的表格。当进行文书公证时，公证人必须能够与客户进行沟通，以便签字人宣誓或确认誓章的内容或确认文件的执行。不应该借助翻译进行公证，因为翻译可能遗漏重要信息。如果公证人无法与客户沟通，则应将客户转交给以客户使用的语言服务的公证人。

《民法典》中有关规定

§ 14 词句；结构；情绪；性别；数量

当事人不能书写时，可以用标记的方式进行签名和确认，由见证人在文书上写下其姓名，并在姓名旁边签字；当通过标记的方式签名时，对任何宣誓、声明的签字必须由两名已认证自己姓名的人亲眼见证。

§ 1181 公证人；进行证明或确认的公职人员

文书的证明或确认可以在本州的任何地方，在下列任何人员当选或任职的州的郡、市、郡城内的公证人之前完成：

（a）上级法院书记

（b）郡书记官

（c）法庭专员

（d）退休的市政法官或司法法官

（e）地区检察官

（f）监事会的职员

（g）市书记官

(h) A county counsel.

(i) A city attorney.

(g) Secretary of the Senate.

(k) Chief Clerk of the Assembly.

§ 1185. Acknowledgments; requisites

(a) The acknowledgment of an instrument shall not be taken unless the officer taking it has satisfactory evidence that the person making the acknowledgment is the individual who is described in and who executed the instrument.

(b) For the purposes of this section "satisfactory evidence" means the absence of information, evidence, or other circumstances that would lead a reasonable person to believe that the person making the acknowledgment is not the individual he or she claims to be and any one of the following:

(1)(A) The oath or affirmation of a credible witness personally known to the officer, whose identity is proven to the officer upon presentation of a document satisfying the requirements of paragraph (3) or (4), that the person making the acknowledgment is personally known to the witness and that each of the following are true:

(i) The person making the acknowledgment is the person named in the document.

(ii) The person making the acknowledgment is personally known to the witness.

(iii) That it is the reasonable belief of the witness that the circumstances of the person making the acknowledgment are such that it would be very difficult or impossible for that person to obtain another form of identification.

(iv) The person making the acknowledgment does not possess any of the identification documents named in paragraphs (3) and (4).

(v) The witness does not have a financial interest in the document being acknowledged and is not named in the document.

(B) A notary public who violates this section by failing to obtain the satisfactory evidence required by subparagraph (A) shall be subject to a civil penalty not exceeding ten thousand dollars ($10,000). An action to impose this civil penalty may be brought by the Secretary of State in an administrative proceeding or a public prosecutor in superior court, and shall be enforced as a civil judgment. A public prosecutor shall inform the secretary of any civil penalty imposed under this subparagraph.

(2) The oath or affirmation under penalty of perjury

（h）郡执业律师

（i）市执业律师

（j）参议院议长

（k）议会首席书记官

§1185 确认；前提条件

（a）文书的确认必须有认证证人提供的充分证据，证明作出文书确认的人是文书中描述的人，且文书由其执行。

（b）本条中，"充分的证据"是指没有资料、证据或其他情况会导致理智的人认为作出确认的人不是其所声称的个人，以及下列情形：

（1）（A）公证人个人认识的可信证人的宣誓或确认，该证人必须向公证人提交符合第 3 项或第 4 项规定的文件以证明其身份，并确认其个人认识作出文书确认的人，且以下事项均为属实：

（i）作出文书确认的人是文件中所指定的人。

（ii）可信证人个人认识作出文书确认的人。

（iii）可信证人合理地认为，作出文书确认的人的情况导致其使用另一种身份证明形式是非常困难或不可能的。

（iv）作出文书确认的人不具有第 3 项和第 4 项规定的任何身份证明文件。

（v）可信的证人不是认证文书的利益相关者，也没有在文件中被提及。

（B）公证人违反本款（A）项，未能获得相应的证据的，将被处以不超过一万美元（$10000）的处罚。本条规定应受民事处罚的行为，可以由州务卿在行政诉讼中提起或由上级法院的检察机关提起，并以民事判决的方式执行。检察官应将根据本项实施的任何民事处罚通知州务卿。

（2）来自承诺接受伪证处罚的两名可信证人的宣

of two credible witnesses, whose identities are proven to the officer upon the presentation of a document satisfying the requirements of paragraph (3) or (4), that each statement in paragraph (1) is true.

(3) Reasonable reliance on the presentation to the officer of any one of the following, if the document is current or has been issued within five years:

(A) An identification card or driver's license issued by the Department of Motor Vehicles.

(B) A passport issued by the Department of State of the United States.

(C) An inmate identification card issued by the Department of Corrections and Rehabilitation, if the inmate is in custody in prison.

(4) Reasonable reliance on the presentation of any one of the following, provided that a document specified in subparagraphs (A) to (E), inclusive, shall either be current or have been issued within five years and shall contain a photograph and description of the person named on it, shall be signed by the person, shall bear a serial or other identifying number, and, in the event that the document is a passport, shall have been stamped by the United States Citizenship and Immigration Services of the Department of Homeland Security:

(A) A passport issued by a foreign government.

(B) A driver's license issued by a state other than California or by a Canadian or Mexican public agency authorized to issue driver's licenses.

(C) An identification card issued by a state other than California.

(D) An identification card issued by any branch of the Armed Forces of the United States.

(E) An employee identification card issued by an agency or office of the State of California, or by an agency or office of a city, county, or city and county in this state.

(c) An officer who has taken an acknowledgment pursuant to this section shall be presumed to have operated in accordance with the provisions of law.

(d) A party who files an action for damages based on the failure of the officer to establish the proper identity of the person making the acknowledgment shall have the burden of proof in establishing the negligence or misconduct of the officer.

(e) A person convicted of perjury under this section shall forfeit any financial interest in the document.

誓或确认，可信证人须提交满足第 3 款或第 4 款要求的文件，以证明关于第 1 款中规定的每项陈述都是真实的。

（3）文书确认人的身份可以由公证人合理依赖以下提交的文件之一来确定，如果身份证明文件是现在或五年内发出的：

（A）由加州机动车管理局发出的身份认证或驾驶执照。

（B）由美国国务院发出的护照。

（C）如果因犯在州监狱被关押，则由州惩教和康复部颁发的因犯身份证进行认证。

（4）合理依赖以下提交的任何一项：（A）至（E）项中规定的文件应为五年内签发的，且应包含照片和描述并由该人签名，包含序列号或其他识别号码；如该文件为护照，则须包含美国国土安全部移民服务局盖章：

（A）外国政府签发的护照；

（B）加拿大或墨西哥公共机构授权发放的驾照；

（C）加利福尼亚州之外的其他州发放的身份证；

（D）由美国武装部队分支机构签发的身份证明；

（E）由加利福尼亚州的机构或办事处或加利福尼亚州的市或/和郡的代理机构或办公室发放的雇佣证。

（c）根据本条办理文书确认的公职人员，应推定为按照法律规定的程序进行。

（d）对公职人员未能确定作出文书确认的人的身份而提出损害赔偿诉讼的当事人有证明公职人员存在疏忽或不当行为成立的举证义务。

（e）根据本条被定罪的人员，将丧失该文书中约定的任何经济利益。

§ 1188. Certificate of acknowledgment

An officer taking the acknowledgment of an instrument shall endorse thereon or attach thereto a certificate pursuant to Section

§1189. Certificate of acknowledgment; form; sufficiency of out of state acknowledgment; force and effect of acknowledgment under prior laws

(a)(1) Any certificate of acknowledgment taken within this state shall be in the following form:

State of California

County of _____

On ____ before me, (here insert name and title of the officer), personally appeared _____ , who proved to me on the basis of satisfactory evidence to be the person(s) whose name(s) is/are subscribed to the within instrument and acknowledged to me that he/she/they executed the same in his/her/ their authorized capacity(ies), and that by his/her/their signature(s) on the instrument the person(s), or the entity upon behalf of which the person(s) acted, executed the instrument. I certify under PENALTY OF PERJURY under the laws of the State of California that the foregoing paragraph is true and correct.

WITNESS my hand and official seal.

Signature _____

(Seal)

(2) A notary public who willfully states as true any material fact that he or she knows to be false shall be subject to a civil penalty not exceeding ten thousand dollars ($10,000). An action to impose a civil penalty under this subdivision may be brought by the Secretary of State in an administrative proceeding or any public prosecutor in superior court, and shall be enforced as a civil judgment. A public prosecutor shall inform the secretary of any civil penalty imposed under this section.

(b) Any certificate of acknowledgment taken in another place shall be sufficient in this state if it is taken in accordance with the laws of the place where the acknowledgment is made.

(c) On documents to be filed in another state or jurisdiction of the United States, a California notary public may complete any acknowledgment form as may be required in that other state or jurisdiction on a document, provided the form does not require the notary to determine or certify that the signer holds a particular representative capacity or to make other determinations and certifications not allowed by California law.

§1188 确认证明

作出文书确认的公职人员应根据第1189条的规定进行核准或附上确认证明书。

§ 1189 确认证书；形式；加利福尼亚州之外文件确认的充分性；根据先前法律确认的强制力和效力

(a)(1) 在此情形下进行的任何确认证书的格式如下：

加利福尼亚州

_____ 郡

_____（时间），基于充分的证据，_____亲自向本人（公证人的姓名和职称）证明，其是文书签署本人，其在授权范围内行使了文书中职能，其本人或者其所代表的实体执行了该文书。本人受加利福尼亚州的法律伪证处罚条款监督，愿证明上述内容是真实和准确的。

证人签名、公章

公证人签名_____（公证公章）

（2）公证人故意陈述其明知为虚假的重大事实，应当受到不超过一万美元（$10000）的民事处罚。依据本条将受到民事处罚的行为，可以由州务卿提起行政处罚程序或由上级法院的任何检察机关提起，并以民事判决的方式执行。检察官应通知州务卿公证人根据本条实施的任何民事处罚。

（b）在其他州按照该地的法律完成的文书认证在本州仍然有效。

（c）对于在美国另一州或法域提交的文件，加利福尼亚州公证人可以根据其他州或法域的要求办理文书确认，前提是该确认不要求公认人确定或证明签名人具有的特定的代表资格或作出加利福尼亚州法律不允许的其他裁定和证书。

(d) An acknowledgment provided prior to January 1, 1993, and conforming to applicable provisions of former Sections 1189, 1190, 1190a, 1190.1, 1191, and 1192, as repealed by Chapter 335 of the Statutes of 1990, shall have the same force and effect as if those sections had not been repealed.

§ 1190. Certificate of acknowledgment as prima facie evidence; duly authorized person

The certificate of acknowledgment of an instrument executed on behalf of an incorporated or unincorporated entity by a duly authorized person in the form specified in Section 1189 shall be prima facie evidence that the instrument is the duly authorized act of the entity named in the instrument and shall be conclusive evidence thereof in favor of any good faith purchaser, lessee, or encumbrancer. "Duly authorized person," with respect to a domestic or foreign corporation, includes the president, vice president, secretary, and assistant secretary of the corporation.

§ 1193. Certificate of acknowledgment; authentication

Officers taking and certifying acknowledgments or proof of instruments for record, must authenticate their certificates by affixing thereto their signatures, followed by the names of their offices: also, their seals of office, if by the laws of the State or country where the acknowledgment or proof is taken, or by authority of which they are acting, they are required to have official seals.

§ 1195. Proof of execution; methods; certificate form

(a) Proof of the execution of an instrument, when not acknowledged, may be made by any of the following:

(1) By the party executing it, or either of them.

(2) By a subscribing witness.

(3) By other witnesses, in cases mentioned in Section 1198.

(b) (1) Proof of the execution of a power of attorney, grant deed, mortgage, deed of trust, quitclaim deed, security agreement, or any instrument affecting real property is not permitted pursuant to Section 27287 of the Government Code, though proof of the execution of a trustee's deed or deed of reconveyance is permitted.

(2) Proof of the execution for any instrument requiring a notary public to obtain a thumbprint from the party signing the document in the notary public's journal is not permitted.

（d）根据1993年1月1日之前和1990年第335号章程的第1189条、第1190条、第1190a条、第1190.1条、第1191条和第1192条废止前作出的文书确认，具有和法条废止前相同的效力。

§1190 作为表面证据的确认证明；正式授权的人

由正式授权的人以第1189条规定的形式代表法人或非法人团体执行的文书的确认证明能够作为表面证据，只要该文书是文书中指定的实体的正式授权的行为，并且有确凿的证据证明有利于善意购买者、承租人或留置人。"正式授权的人"是指国内或国外公司的总裁、副总裁、秘书和助理秘书。

§1193 确认证明；认证

公职人员认证和出具文书证明文件，必须通过附上签名对其证书进行认证，签名后应附上任职机构的名称，如果认证或证明处的国家或州法律或该地当局有规定的，也应当附上机构的公章。

§1195 执行证明；方法；证书表格

（a）未经确认的文书的执行证明可以通过以下任何一种方式作出：

（1）由参与的当事人一方或双方执行。

（2）由签署见证人作出。

（3）第1198条所述的情形可由其他证人作出。

（b）（1）根据《政府组织法》第27287条，不得对执行授权委托书、抵押权契约、信托契约、担保契约、担保协议或影响不动产的文书进行认证，而对受托人的契约或财产转让契约的执行可以认证。

（2）任何要求公证人从公证人日志上获得签字的一方指纹的文书执行证明不被允许。

(c) Any certificate for proof of execution taken within this state shall be in the following form:

State of California } ss.
County of _____
On _____ (date), before me, _____ (name and title of officer), personally appeared _____ (name of subscribing witness), proved to me to be the person whose name is subscribed to the within instrument, as a witness thereto, on the oath of _____ (name of credible witness), a credible witness who is known to me and provided a satisfactory identifying document. _____ (name of subscribing witness), being by me duly sworn, said that he/she was present and saw/heard _____ (name[s] of principal[s]), the same person(s) described in and whose name(s) is/are subscribed to the within or attached instrument in his/her/their authorized capacity(ies) as (a) party (ies) thereto, execute or acknowledge executing the same, and that said affiant subscribed his/her name to the within or attached instrument as a witness at the request of _____ (name[s] of principal[s]).
WITNESS my hand and official seal.
Signature_____ (Seal)

§ 1196. Subscribing witness; establishment of identity

A witness shall be proved to be a subscribing witness by the oath of a credible witness who provides the officer with any document satisfying the requirements of paragraph (3) or (4) of subdivision (b) of Section 1185.

§ 1197. Subscribing witness; items to be proved

The subscribing witness must prove that the person whose name is subscribed to the instrument as a party is the person described in it, and that such person executed it, and that the witness subscribed his name thereto as a witness.

§ 1633.11. Notarization and signature under penalty of perjury requirements

(a) If a law requires that a signature be notarized, the requirement is satisfied with respect to an electronic signature if an electronic record includes, in addition to the electronic signature to be notarized, the electronic signature of a notary public together with all other information required to be included in a notarization by other applicable law.

§ 1633.12. Retaining records; electronic satisfaction

(a) If a law requires that a record be retained, the

（c）在此情形下进行的证明证书的格式如下：

加利福尼亚州
_____郡
_____（日期），_____（签署见证人的名字）作为证人，在本人认识的可信证人_____（可信证人的姓名）的宣誓下，亲自向本人_____（公证人姓名和职务）证明在文件中签名的人的身份，并提供了充分的身份证明文件。_____（签署见证人的名字）宣誓，其在场并目睹或听见了_____（委托人的姓名）宣誓并签署文件，并证明委托人的姓名及描述与文件中一致，委托人具有执行和确认文书的能力，在_____（委托人的姓名）的请求下作为证人。

证人签名及盖章
公证人签名_____（公证公章）

§ 1196 签署见证人、确立身份

通过可信证人的誓言认证作为签署见证人的，可信证人应提供符合第1185条（b）款第3项或第4项要求的文件。

§ 1197 签署见证人；待证实的项目

签署见证人必须证明，在文书中签名的人是文书中所描述的人且文件由该人执行，见证人应在文书中以证人的身份签名。

§1633.11 公证和签字受伪证处罚规则的规制

（a）如果法律要求对签名进行公证，电子记录在电子签名外还包括公证人的电子签名以及所有其他适用法律要求纳入公证的信息，则电子签名也是符合要求的。

§1633.12 保存记录；电子记录的合规要求

（a）如果法律要求保留记录，则如果电子记录准

requirement is satisfied by retaining an electronic record of the information in the record, if the electronic record reflects accurately the information set forth in the record at the time it was first generated in its final form as an electronic record or otherwise, and the electronic record remains accessible for later reference.

(b) A requirement to retain a record in accordance with subdivision (a) does not apply to any information the sole purpose of which is to enable the record to be sent, communicated, or received.

(c) A person may satisfy subdivision (a) by using the services of another person if the requirements of subdivision (a) are satisfied.

(d) If a law requires a record to be retained in its original form, or provides consequences if the record is not retained in its original form, that law is satisfied by an electronic record retained in accordance with subdivision (a).

(e) If a law requires retention of a check, that requirement is satisfied by retention of an electronic record of the information on the front and back of the check in accordance with subdivision (a).

(f) A record retained as an electronic record in accordance with subdivision (a) satisfies a law requiring a person to retain a record for evidentiary, audit, or like purposes, unless a law enacted after the effective date of this title specifically prohibits the use of an electronic record for a specified purpose.

(g) This section does not preclude a governmental agency from specifying additional requirements for the retention of a record subject to the agency's jurisdiction.

CODE OF CIVIL PROCEDURE

§ 12a. Computation of time; holidays; application of section

(a) If the last day for the performance of any act provided or required by law to be performed within a specified period of time is a holiday, then that period is hereby extended to and including the next day that is not a holiday. For purposes of this section, "holiday" means all day on Saturdays, all holidays specified in Section 135 and, to the extent provided in Section 12b, all days that by terms of Section 12b are required to be considered as holidays.

§ 1935. Subscribing witness defined

A subscribing witness is one who sees a writing executed or hears it acknowledged, and at the request of the party thereupon signs his name as a witness.

确地反映了首次以电子或其他形式记录生成时所显示的信息，且电子记录仍可查阅，供以后参考的，则该电子记录符合要求。

（b）（a）款关于保留记录的要求不适用于其唯一目的是使记录能够发送、传达或接收的信息。

（c）当事人可以通过使用符合（a）款要求的其他人的服务来达到（a）款中的要求。

（d）如果法律要求以原始形式保留记录，或者规定了如果记录不以原始形式保留可能导致的后果，则符合（a）款要求的电子记录也为合法。

（e）如果法律要求保留支票，则按照（a）款的要求保留支票前后信息的电子记录是符合要求的。

（f）按照（a）款保留的电子记录能够满足法律关于保留证据、审计或类似目的的要求，除非在本法生效之日后颁布的法律明确禁止使用该用于指定目的的电子记录。

（g）本条并不排除政府机构保留对该机构管辖的记录提出额外要求。

《民事诉讼法》中有关规定

§12a 时间的计算；假期；本条的适用

（a）如果执行法律规定或要求的任何行为时指定期间的最后一天是假期，那么该日期延长至假期结束后的第二天。在本条中，"假期"系指星期六、第135条所指明的所有节假日、第12b条所规定的所有日期，以及按照第12b条被视为假期的时日。

§1935 签署见证人的定义

签署见证人是指目击或听到文书被执行或确认，并应当事方的要求签名作为证人的人。

§ 2093. Officers authorized to administer oaths or affirmations

(a) Every court, every judge, or clerk of any court, every justice, and every notary public, and every officer or person authorized to take testimony in any action or proceeding, or to decide upon evidence, has the power to administer oaths or affirmations.

(b)(1) Every shorthand reporter certified pursuant to Article 3 (commencing with Section 8020) of Chapter 13 of Division 3 of the Business and Professions Code has the power to administer oaths or affirmations and may perform the duties of the deposition officer pursuant to Chapter 9 (commencing with Section 2025.010) of Title 4. The certified shorthand reporter shall be entitled to receive fees for services rendered during a deposition, including fees for deposition services, as specified in subdivision (c) of Section 8211 of the Government Code.

(2) This subdivision shall also apply to depositions taken by telephone or other remote electronic means as specified in Chapter 2 (commencing with Section 2017.010), Chapter 3 (commencing with Section 2017.710), and Chapter 9 (commencing with Section 2025.010) of Title 4.

(c) A former judge or justice of a court of record in this state who retired or resigned from office, other than a judge or justice who was retired by the Supreme Court for disability, shall have the power to administer oaths or affirmations, if the former judge or justice requests and receives a certification from the Commission on Judicial Performance that there was no formal disciplinary proceeding pending at the time of retirement or resignation. Where no formal disciplinary proceeding was pending at the time of retirement or resignation, the Commission on Judicial Performance shall issue the certification.

No law, rule, or regulation regarding the confidentiality of proceedings of the Commission on Judicial Performance shall be construed to prohibit the Commission on Judicial Performance from issuing a certificate as provided for in this section.

§ 2094. Oath to witness; form

(a) An oath, affirmation, or declaration in an action or a proceeding, may be administered by obtaining an affirmative response to one of the following questions:

(1)"Do you solemnly state that the evidence you shall give in this issue (or matter) shall be the truth, the whole truth, and nothing but the truth, so help you God?"

§2093 授权执行宣誓或确认的公职人员

（a）任何法院、法官、书记官、其他司法员、公证人以及被授权在任何诉讼或程序中作证或作出证据决定的公职人员或公民，均有权执行誓言或确认宣誓。

（b）（1）根据《商业及职业守则》第13章第3节第3条（从第8020条开始），每位法庭书记员有权执行宣誓或确认，并可按照第9章第4条（从第2025.010条开始）履行宣誓作证的义务。根据《政府组织法》第8211条（c）款的规定，经认证的法庭书记员有权在执行宣誓作证的过程中收取费用，包括宣誓作证的服务费用。

（2）本款也适用于第2章（从第2017.010条开始），第3章（从第2017.710条开始）和第9章（从第2025.010条开始）规定的使用电话或其他远程电子方式进行宣誓或确认的情形。

（c）在该州退休或辞职的法官或司法人员，除了由于残疾从最高法院退休的法官或司法人员外，均应具有执行宣誓或确认的权力，只要前法官或司法人员在退休或辞职时未受过任何正式的纪律处分，经其要求并获得司法执行局的认可。对退休或辞职时未受过正式纪律处分的司法人员，司法履行委员会应当出具证明。

司法执行局颁布的关于法律程序保密的法律、法规、规章不得被解释为禁止司法执行局根据本节规定出具证明。

§ 2094 宣誓；格式

（a）在诉讼或其他司法程序中宣誓、确认或声明可以通过对以下问题作出肯定的答复进行：

（1）你是否愿意庄严地声明，你在这个问题上所提供的证据（或事情）均为事实，不存在虚假和遗漏，上帝保佑？

(2)"Do you solemnly state, under penalty of perjury, that the evidence that you shall give in this issue (or matter) shall be the truth, the whole truth, and nothing but the truth?"

ELECTIONS CODE

§ 8080. Fee for verification

No fee or charge shall be made or collected by any officer for verifying any nomination document or circulator's affidavit.

COMMERCIAL CODE

§ 3505. Protest; Noting for Protest

(b) A protest is a certificate of dishonor made by a United States consul or vice consul, or a notary public during the course and scope of employment with a financial institution or other person authorized to administer oaths by the laws of any other state, government, or country in the place where dishonor occurs. It may be made upon information satisfactory to that person. The protest shall identify the instrument and certify either that presentment has been made or, if not made, the reason why it was not made, and that the instrument has been dishonored by nonacceptance or nonpayment. The protest may also certify that notice of dishonor has been given to some or all parties.

PROBATE CODE

§ 4307. Certified copies of power of attorney

(a)A copy of a power of attorney certified under this section has the same force and effect as the original power of attorney.

(b)A copy of a power of attorney may be certified by any of the following:

(1)An attorney authorized to practice law in this state.

(2)A notary public in this state.

(3)An official of a state or of a political subdivision who is authorized to make certifications.

(c)The certification shall state that the certifying person has examined the original power of attorney and the copy and that the copy is a true and correct copy of the original power of attorney.

(d)Nothing in this section is intended to create an implication that a third person may be liable for acting in good faith reliance on a copy of a power of attorney that has not been certified under this section.

（2）你是否愿意接受伪证处罚的规则规制，庄严地声明，你在这个问题上所提供的证据（或事情）均为事实，不存在虚假和遗漏，上帝保佑？

《选举法》中有关规定

§8080 验证费用

任何公职人员不得对核实提名文件或宣誓书收取任何费用。

商法

§3505 拒绝；拒绝的通知

（b）拒绝证书是由美国领事或副领事或公证人根据金融机构或其他人授权对发生失信行为的国家、政府或其他为做出的宣誓作出的拒绝承认或执行的证书。拒绝证书根据充分的信息作出。拒绝证明应当确认具体文书，并证明该陈述已经作出，如果没有作出，则证明没有作出陈述，且该文书因不被接受或不付款而不被承认。拒绝证书也可以证明已经向一方或多方当事人送达的关于失信行为导致不兑现的通知。

《遗嘱检验法规》中有关规定

§4307 授权书的认证副本

（a）根据本条认证的授权书副本与原授权书具有相同的效力。

（b）委托书的副本可以通过以下任何一种形式证明：

（1）经授权在此州执业的律师；

（2）本州的公证人；

（3）获得认证的州或政治部门的官员。

（c）证明书应说明证明人已经审查了原来的委托书和副本，并且该副本是原始授权书的真实准确的复制件。

（d）本条中的任何内容均不构成对第三人善意地依赖未经本章认证的授权书副本的暗示。

PENAL CODE

§ 17. Felony; misdemeanor; infraction; classification of offenses

(a) A felony is a crime that is punishable with death, by imprisonment in the state prison, or notwithstanding any other provision of law, by imprisonment in a county jail under the provisions of subdivision (h) of Section 1170. Every other crime or public offense is a misdemeanor except those offenses that are classified as infractions.

§ 115.5. Filing false or forged documents relating to single-family residences; punishment; false statement to notary public

(a) Every person who files any false or forged document or instrument with the county recorder which affects title to, places an encumbrance on, or places an interest secured by a mortgage or deed of trust on, real property consisting of a single-family residence containing not more than four dwelling units, with knowledge that the document is false or forged, is punishable, in addition to any other punishment, by a fine not exceeding seventy-five thousand dollars ($75,000).

(b) Every person who makes a false sworn statement to a notary public, with knowledge that the statement is false, to induce the notary public to perform an improper notarial act on an instrument or document affecting title to, or placing an encumbrance on, real property consisting of a single-family residence containing not more than four dwelling units is guilty of a felony.

§ 118. Perjury defined; evidence necessary to support conviction

(a) Every person who, having taken an oath that he or she will testify, declare, depose, or certify truly before any competent tribunal, officer, or person, in any of the cases in which the oath may by law of the State of California be administered, willfully and contrary to the oath, states as true any material matter which he or she knows to be false, and every person who testifies, declares, deposes, or certifies under penalty of perjury in any of the cases in which the testimony, declarations, depositions, or certification is permitted by law of the State of California under penalty of perjury and willfully states as true any material matter which he or she knows to be false, is guilty of perjury.

This subdivision is applicable whether the statement, or the testimony, declaration, deposition, or certification is made or subscribed within or without the State

《刑法》中有关规定

§17 重罪；违规；犯罪分类

（a）重罪是指被处以死刑或在州立监狱监禁的罪行，或者依据第1170条第（h）款规定被处以在国立监狱监禁的罪行。其他罪行或公共违法行为均属轻罪，被划分为犯罪的公共违法行为除外。

§115.5 出具与独立住宅相关的虚假或伪造文件；惩罚；向公证人虚假陈述

（a）任何明知文件为伪造仍向郡记录员提交对不超过四个住宅单位的不动产的所有权、抵押权、担保债权产生影响的文件的，除了接受相应处罚外，还应处以不超过七万五千美元（$75000）的罚款。

（b）任何明知其陈述为虚假却仍向公证人作出虚假声明，导致公证人对不超过四个住宅单位的不动产的所有权、产生负担的文书进行不正当的公证行为的行为，属于重罪。

§118 伪证的定义；定罪所需的证据

（a）任何宣誓的人，在法庭、公职人员或其他人面前进行作证、声明、确认、证明或进行任何加利福尼亚州法律规定的宣誓行为时，故意违反誓词，将其明知为虚假的重大事项表述为真，以及任何承诺在作证、声明、确认、证明等宣誓中接受伪证处罚的人，在加利福尼亚州法律规定适用伪证处罚规则的证词、声明、确认或证明中，故意将将其明知为虚假的重大事项表述为真，即构成作伪证。

本款适用于在加利福尼亚州境内、境外进行作证、声明、确认或证明的行为。

of California.

(b)No person shall be convicted of perjury where proof of falsity rests solely upon contradiction by testimony of a single person other than the defendant. Proof of falsity may be established by direct or indirect evidence.

§ 126. Punishment

Perjury is punishable by imprisonment pursuant to subdivision (h) of Section 1170 for two, three or four years.

§ 470. Forgery; signatures or seals; corruption of records

(b) Every person who, with the intent to defraud, counterfeits or forges the seal or handwriting of another is guilty of forgery.

(d) Every person who, with the intent to defraud, falsely makes, alters, forges, or counterfeits, utters, publishes, passes or attempts or offers to pass, as true and genuine, any of the following items, knowing the same to be false, altered, forged, or counterfeited, is guilty of forgery: … or falsifies the acknowledgment of any notary public, or any notary public who issues an acknowledgment knowing it to be false; or any matter described in subdivision (b).

§ 473. Forgery; punishment

Forgery is punishable by imprisonment in a county jail for not more than one year, or by imprisonment pursuant to subdivision (h) of Section 1170.

§ 830.3. Peace officers; employing agencies; authority

The following persons are peace officers whose authority extends to any place in the state for the purpose of performing their primary duty or when making an arrest pursuant to Section 836 as to any public offense with respect to which there is immediate danger to person or property, or of the escape of the perpetrator of that offense, or pursuant to Section 8597 or 8598 of the Government Code.

(o) Investigators of the office of the Secretary of State designated by the Secretary of State, provided that the primary duty of these peace officers shall be the enforcement of the law as prescribed in Chapter 3 (commencing with Section 8200) of Division 1 of Title 2 of, and Section 12172.5 of, the Government Code.

（b）任何人不得仅凭其证词与除被告人以外的单个证人的证词矛盾而被认定为伪证罪。伪证可以通过直接或间接证据进行确定。

§126 处罚

根据第1170条（h）款，伪证罪可判处2-4年监禁。

§470 伪造罪；签名或印章；腐败记录

（b）任何人以欺诈为目的，伪造或仿造他人的印章或笔迹即犯有伪造罪。

（d）任何以欺诈为目的，假冒、伪造、仿造、发布、发表、提供或传播下列其明知是虚假的、被伪造、仿造的文件：……或者伪造公证人出具的公证文书或公证人明知存在虚假陈述仍然对文件进行确认；或者为（b）款中规定的行为，均构成伪造罪。

§473 伪造罪；罚则

伪造罪可处一年以下监禁或第1170条（h）款规定的监禁期。

§ 830.3 治安官；雇用机构；职权

下列人员是治安官：在本州任何地方履行其主要职责，根据第836条对直接危及人身或财产的公共犯罪行为进行逮捕，或根据《政府组织法》第8597条或第8598条追捕犯有该罪行的肇事逃逸者的官员。

（o）州务卿指定的职务调查员，这些治安官的主要职责是执行第3章（第8200条开始）第1节第2条和《政府组织法》第12172.5条规定的法律。

BUSINESS AND PROFESSIONS CODE

§ 22449. Deferred Action for Childhood Arrivals program; price gouging; penalties

(a) Immigration consultants, attorneys, notaries public, and organizations accredited by the United States Board of Immigration Appeals shall be the only individuals authorized to charge clients or prospective clients fees for providing consultations, legal advice, or notary public services, respectively, associated with filing an application under the federal Deferred Action for Childhood Arrivals program announced by the United States Secretary of Homeland Security on June 15, 2012.

(b)(1) Immigration consultants, attorneys, notaries public, and organizations accredited by the United States Board of Immigration Appeals shall be prohibited from participating in practices that amount to price gouging when a client or prospective client solicits services associated with filing an application for deferred action for childhood arrivals as described in subdivision (a).

(2) For the purposes of this section, "price gouging" means any practice that has the effect of pressuring the client or prospective client to purchase services immediately because purchasing them at a later time will result in the client or prospective client paying a higher price for the same services.

(c)(1) In addition to the civil and criminal penalties described in Section 22445, a violation of this section by an attorney shall be cause for discipline by the State Bar pursuant to Chapter 4 (commencing with Section 6000) of Division 3.

(2) In addition to the civil and criminal penalties described in Section 22445, a violation of this section by a notary public shall be cause for the revocation or suspension of his or her commission as a notary public by the Secretary of State and the application of any other applicable penalties pursuant to Chapter 3 (commencing with Section 8200) of Division 1 of Title 2 of the Government Code.

《商业及职业守则》中有关规定

§22449 儿童移民延期计划；价格欺诈；处罚

（a）移民顾问、律师、公证人和美国移民上诉委员会认可的组织应是唯一被授权向客户或潜在客户提供咨询、法律咨询或公证服务并收取费用的组织和个人，并须分别根据美国国土安全部长2012年6月15日公布的儿童移民延期计划提出申请。

（b）（1）移民顾问、律师、公证人和美国移民上诉委员会认可的组织，当客户或潜在客户咨询或申请有关（a）款提及的儿童移民延期计划的服务时，不得进行价格欺诈。

（2）本条中的"价格欺诈"是指任何有效迫使客户或潜在客户立即购买服务，因为以后购买将导致客户或潜在客户为同样的服务支付更高的费用的做法。

（c）（1）律师违反本条的规定，除了第22445条所述的民事和刑事处罚外，还应由国家律师协会根据第4章第3节（第6000条开始）的规定进行纪律处分。

（2）公证人违反本条的规定，除第22445条规定的民事和刑事处罚外，还应由州务卿和申请人撤销或暂停公证人任职资格，并可处以《政府组织法》第3章（第8200条开始）第1节第2条规定的任何其他处罚。

加利福尼亚州政府组织法

GOVERNMENT CODE

Notaries Public

(Chapter 3, Division 1, Title 2)

§ 8200. Appointment and commission; number; jurisdiction

The Secretary of State may appoint and commission notaries public in such number as the Secretary of State deems necessary for the public convenience. Notaries public may act as such notaries in any part of this state.

§ 8201. Qualifications to be a notary public; proof of course completion; reappointment

(a) Every person appointed as notary public shall meet all of the following requirements:

(1) Be at the time of appointment a legal resident of this state, except as otherwise provided in Section 8203.1.

(2) Be not less than 18 years of age.

(3) For appointments made on or after July 1, 2005, have satisfactorily completed a six-hour course of study approved by the Secretary of State pursuant to Section 8201.2 concerning the functions and duties of a notary public.

(4) Have satisfactorily completed a written examination prescribed by the Secretary of State to determine the fitness of the person to exercise the functions and duties of the office of notary public. All questions shall be based on the law of this state as set forth in the booklet of the laws of California relating to notaries public distributed by the Secretary of State.

(b) (1) Commencing July 1, 2005, each applicant for notary public shall provide satisfactory proof that he or she has completed the course of study required pursuant to paragraph (3) of subdivision (a) prior to approval of his or her appointment as a notary public by the Secretary of State.

(2) Commencing July 1, 2005, an applicant for notary public who holds a California notary public commission, and who has satisfactorily completed the six-hour course of study required pursuant to paragraph (1) at least one

政府组织法

公证人

（第3章，第1节，第2部分）

§8200 公证人的任命和委托；人数；管辖权

州务卿在其认为必要或方便的时候委任公证人。公证人可以本州的任何地方执业。

§8201 公证人的任职资格；培训完成证明；连任

（a）成为公证人，必须符合以下要求：

（1）在任命时为本州的合法居民，第8203.1条另有的规定除外。

（2）年满18周岁；

（3）在2005年7月1日起被任命的公证人，必须已经圆满完成州务卿根据第8201.2条规定的有关公证人任职的6小时培训。

（4）圆满完成州务卿规定的关于担任公证人职务的适当性的书面测试。测试中的所有问题都应以加利福尼亚州州务卿颁布的法律手册中有关公证人的规定为依据。

（b）（1）从2005年7月1日起，每位公证人申请人应提供令人信服的证明，以证明其已经完成了前述（a）款第3项要求的培训课程之后，才能由州务卿任命为公证人。

（2）2005年7月1日起，已获准被任命的加州公证人，需要至少完成一次第1项规定的6小时培训项目。在申请连任为公证人时，其需要提供令人信服的证明，证明其在接受州务卿的重新任命前已经圆满

time, shall provide satisfactory proof when applying for reappointment as a notary public that he or she has satisfactorily completed a three-hour refresher course of study prior to reappointment as a notary public by the Secretary of State.

§ 8201.1. Additional qualifications; determination; identification; fingerprints

(a) Prior to granting an appointment as a notary public, the Secretary of State shall determine that the applicant possesses the required honesty, credibility, truthfulness, and integrity to fulfill the responsibilities of the position. To assist in determining the identity of the applicant and whether the applicant has been convicted of a disqualifying crime specified in subdivision (b) of Section 8214.1, the Secretary of State shall require that applicants be fingerprinted.

(b) Applicants shall submit to the Department of Justice fingerprint images and related information required by the department for the purpose of obtaining information as to the existence and content of a record of state and federal convictions and arrests and information as to the existence and content of a record of state and federal arrests for which the department establishes that the person is free on bail, or on his or her recognizance, pending trial or appeal.

(c) The department shall forward the fingerprint images and related information received pursuant to subdivision (a) to the Federal Bureau of Investigation and request a federal summary of criminal information.

(d) The department shall review the information returned from the Federal Bureau of Investigation and compile and disseminate a response to the Secretary of State pursuant to paragraph (1) of subdivision (p) of Section 11105 of the Penal Code.

(e) The Secretary of State shall request from the department subsequent arrest notification service, pursuant to Section 11105.2 of the Penal Code, for each person who submitted information pursuant to subdivision (a).

(f) The department shall charge a fee sufficient to cover the cost of processing the requests described in this section.

§ 8201.2. Review of course of study for notary public; approval of education course of study, violation of regulations; civil penalties

(a) The Secretary of State shall review the course of study proposed by any vendor to be offered pursuant to paragraph (3) of subdivision (a) and paragraph (2) of

完成了3小时的复习项目。

§8201.1 其他资格要求；决定；身份识别；指纹

（a）州务卿在任命公证人之前，应当确定申请人具有履行职务职责所必需的诚实信用。为了确定申请人的身份，以及申请人是否被裁定犯有第8214.1条（b）款所指定的丧失资格的罪名，州务卿应要求申请人提供指纹。

（b）申请人应向司法部提交指纹图像和司法部要求的相关信息，以知悉关于国家和联邦定罪和逮捕记录的是否存在及其内容，以及关于根据司法部规定被所在州逮捕但可以使用保证金或保证人进行保释、等待审判或上诉的情形。

（c）司法部应将根据前述（a）款收到的指纹图像和相关信息转交给联邦调查局，并要求获得联邦犯罪信息摘要。

（d）司法部应审查联邦调查局提交的资料，并根据《刑法典》第11105条（p）款第1项的要求进行汇编并向州务卿答复。

（e）州务卿应根据《刑法典》第11105.2条的规定，在接受前述（a）款提交的资料后，还应要求其提交之后的逮捕通知书。

（f）司法部为支付处理本条程序所需有权收取足够的费用。

§8201.2 公证人培训的审查；批准教育项目；违规行为；民事处罚

（a）州务卿应审查任何培训提供者根据第8201条（a）款第3项和（b）款第2项提供的培训课程。如果该培训课程包括能够使公证人圆满完成第8201

subdivision (b) of Section 8201. If the course of study includes all material that a person is expected to know to satisfactorily complete the written examination required pursuant to paragraph (4) of subdivision (a) of Section 8201, the Secretary of State shall approve the course of study.

(b)(1) The Secretary of State shall, by regulation, prescribe an application form and adopt a certificate of approval for the notary public education course of study proposed by a vendor.

(2) The Secretary of State may also provide a notary public education course of study.

(c) The Secretary of State shall compile a list of all persons offering an approved course of study pursuant to subdivision (a) and shall provide the list with every booklet of the laws of California relating to notaries public distributed by the Secretary of State.

(d) (1) A person who provides notary public education and violates any of the regulations adopted by the Secretary of State for approved vendors is subject to a civil penalty not to exceed one thousand dollars ($1,000) for each violation and shall be required to pay restitution where appropriate.

(2) The local district attorney, city attorney, or the Attorney General may bring a civil action to recover the civil penalty prescribed pursuant to this subdivision. A public prosecutor shall inform the Secretary of State of any civil penalty imposed under this section.

§ 8201.5. Application form; confidential nature; use of information

The Secretary of State shall require an applicant for appointment and commission as a notary public to complete an application form and submit a photograph of their person as prescribed by the Secretary of State. Information on this form filed by an applicant with the Secretary of State, except for his or her name and address, is confidential and no individual record shall be divulged by an official or employee having access to it to any person other than the applicant, his or her authorized representative, or an employee or officer of the federal government, the state government, or a local agency, as defined in subdivision (b) of Section 6252 of the Government Code, acting in his or her official capacity. That information shall be used by the Secretary of State for the sole purpose of carrying out the duties of this chapter.

条（a）款第4项书面审查要求的所有内容，则州务卿应批准该培训课程。

（b）（1）州务卿应以规章的形式，制定供应商申请提供培训课程的申请单和通过审核之后的公证培训课程批准证书。

（2）州务卿亦可以提供公证培训教育。

（c）州务卿应编制所有按照（a）款的规定提供培训项目的人员名单，并提供加利福尼亚州所有关于公证人的法律清单。

（d）（1）提供公证培训的供应商违反州务卿制定的任何规定的，对每一次违规行为将处以不超过一千美元（$1000）的民事处罚，并酌情支付赔偿款。

（2）地方检察官、市检察官或律政司可以对公证人提起民事诉讼，追究根据本款所规定的民事责任。检察官应将本款规定的民事处罚通知州务卿。

§8201.5 申请表格；保密性质；信息的使用

州务卿应要求公证人资格申请人填写申请表，并按照州务卿的规定提交照片。申请人向州务卿提交的该表格中的信息，除了其姓名和地址外，均为保密信息，任何个人记录不得被其他人员或其雇员透露给除申请人及其授权代表、联邦政府、州政府或按照《政府组织法》第6252条（b）款规定的当地机构的雇员或高级职员以外的任何人。该资料仅供州务卿为履行本章的职责使用。

§ 8202. Execution of jurat; administration of oath or affirmation to affiant; attachment to affidavit

(a) When executing a jurat, a notary shall administer an oath or affirmation to the affiant and shall determine, from satisfactory evidence as described in Section 1185 of the Civil Code, that the affiant is the person executing the document. The affiant shall sign the document in the presence of the notary.

(b) To any affidavit subscribed and sworn to before a notary, there shall be attached a jurat in the following form:

State of California
County of _____
Subscribed and sworn to (or affirmed) before me on this _____ day of _____, 20__, by _____, proved to me on the basis of satisfactory evidence to be the person(s) who appeared before me.
Seal _____
Signature _____

§ 8202.5. State, county and school district employees; certificates; expenses

The Secretary of State may appoint and commission the number of state, city, county, and public school district employees as notaries public to act for and on behalf of the governmental entity for which appointed which the Secretary of State deems proper. Whenever a notary is appointed and commissioned, a duly authorized representative of the employing governmental entity shall execute a certificate that the appointment is made for the purposes of the employing governmental entity, and whenever the certificate is filed with any state or county officer, no fees shall be charged by the officer for the filing or issuance of any document in connection with the appointment.

The state or any city, county, or school district for which the notary public is appointed and commissioned pursuant to this section may pay from any funds available for its support the premiums on any bond and the cost of any stamps, seals, or other supplies required in connection with the appointment, commission, or performance of the duties of the notary public. Any fees collected or obtained by any notary public whose documents have been filed without charge and for whom bond premiums have been paid by the employer of the notary public shall be remitted by the notary public to the employing agency which shall deposit the funds to the credit of the fund from which the salary of the notary public is paid.

§8202 宣誓证明的执行；宣誓的确认；誓章附件

（a）公证人在执行宣誓证明时，应当向公民进行宣誓确认，并以《民法典》第1185条规定的充分证据确定该人是执行文件的人。宣誓人应在公证人面前签署该文件。

（b）任何向公证人提交和宣誓的誓章，应附上以下格式的宣誓证明：

加利福尼亚州
_____郡
20____年____月____日，_____依据充分证据亲自向本人宣誓（或确认）其身份。

公章 _____
签名 _____

§8202.5 州、郡、学区职工；证书；花费

州务卿可以任命与州、郡、公立学区的员工数量一致的公证人，以代表州务卿认为适当的政府实体行事。每当公证人被委任时，政府实体的正式授权代表应当出示为政府实体目的而作出聘任的证明书，每当向州或郡官员提交证书时，不得收取任何与提交或签发该委任有关的费用。

根据本条任命公证人的州、郡或公立学区可以从任何用于支持公证的资金中提取部分用于支付任何与公证保证金、票据、印章或与公证人的任职、委托或履行职责有关的其他用品的费用。当文件免费提交公证或公证人的雇主已经支付了保证金的情况下，公证人收取的费用，应存入公证人的用人单位，而用人单位应将其存入用于支付公证人工资的基金。

§ 8202.7. Private employers; agreement to pay premium on bonds and costs of supplies; remission of fees to employer

A private employer, pursuant to an agreement with an employee who is a notary public, may pay the premiums on any bond and the cost of any stamps, seals, or other supplies required in connection with the appointment, commission, or performance of the duties of such notary public. Such agreement may also provide for the remission of fees collected by such notary public to the employer, in which case any fees collected or obtained by such notary public while such agreement is in effect shall be remitted by such notary public to the employer which shall deposit such funds to the credit of the fund from which the compensation of the notary public is paid.

§ 8202.8. Private employers; limitation on provision of notarial services

Notwithstanding any other provision of law, a private employer of a notary public who has entered into an agreement with his or her employee pursuant to Section 8202.7 may limit, during the employee's ordinary course of employment, the providing of notarial services by the employee solely to transactions directly associated with the business purposes of the employer.

§ 8203.1. Military and naval reservations; appointment and commission of notaries; qualifications

The Secretary of State may appoint and commission notaries public for the military and naval reservations of the Army, Navy, Coast Guard, Air Force, and Marine Corps of the United States, wherever located in the state; provided, however, that the appointee shall be a citizen of the United States, not less than 18 years of age, and must meet the requirements set forth in paragraphs (3) and (4) of subdivision (a) of Section 8201.

§ 8203.2. Military and naval reservations, recommendation of commanding officer; jurisdiction of notary

Such notaries public shall be appointed only upon the recommendation of the commanding officer of the reservation in which they are to act, and they shall be authorized to act only within the boundaries of this reservation.

§ 8203.3. Military and naval reservations, qualifications of notaries

In addition to the qualifications established in Section 8203.1, appointment will be made only from among those

§8202.7 私人雇主；支付保证金和公证用品成本费用的协议；向雇主收取费用

私人雇主依据与作为公证人的雇员之间的协议，可以支付任何公证保证金，以及与公证人的委任有关的票据、印章费用，以及其他为履行公证人职责相关的其他用品的费用。此类协议亦可规定公证人向雇主服务时，收取的费用可进行减免，在该情况下，公证人在该协议有效的情况下收取或取得的费用，由公证人汇回给雇主，将这笔资金存入用于支付公证人赔偿金的基金。

§8202.8 私人雇主；提供公证服务的限制

尽管有其他法律规定，根据第 8202.7 条与其公证人雇员订立协议的私人雇主可以在雇员的正常工作过程中限制雇员提供公证服务，但这仅限于公证与雇主的商业目的直接相关的交易。

§8203.1 军事和海上保留；公证人的任命和委托；资格

州务卿可以为军事和海事保留任命公证人，负责为美国任何地方的陆军、海军、海岸警卫队、空军和海军陆战队提供公证服务；但是，委任人应为年满 18 周岁的美国公民，并且必须符合 8201 条（a）款第 3 项、第 4 项的要求。

§8203.2 军事和海事保留，指挥官的推荐；公证管辖

只有根据指挥官对公证人作出的保留推荐，方能委任公证人，且公证人只能在本保留范围内行事。

§8203.3 军事和海事保留，公证人的资格

除了第 8203.1 条规定的资格要求外，公民只有在作为公职人员的期间，才能获得保留任命。

persons who are federal civil service employees at the reservation in which they will act as notaries public.

§ 8203.4. Military and naval reservations; term of office; termination; resignation

The term of office shall be as set forth in Section 8204, except that the appointment shall terminate if the person shall cease to be employed as a federal civil service employee at the reservation for which appointed. The commanding officer of the reservation shall notify the Secretary of State of termination of employment at the reservation for which appointed within 30 days of such termination. A notary public whose appointment terminates pursuant to this section will have such termination treated as a resignation.

§ 8203.5. Military and naval reservations, jurat

In addition to the name of the State, the jurat shall also contain the name of the reservation in which the instrument is executed.

§ 8203.6. Military and naval reservations, fees

No fees shall be collected by such notaries public for service rendered within the reservation in the capacity of a notary public.

§ 8204. Term of office

The term of office of a notary public is for four years commencing with the date specified in the commission.

§ 8204.1. Cancellation of Commission; failure to pay; notice

The Secretary of State may cancel the commission of a notary public if a check or other remittance accepted as payment for the examination, application, commission, and fingerprint fee is not paid upon presentation to the financial institution upon which the check or other remittance was drawn. Upon receiving written notification that the item presented for payment has not been honored for payment, the Secretary of State shall first give a written notice of the applicability of this section to the notary public or the person submitting the instrument. Thereafter, if the amount is not paid by a cashier's check or the equivalent, the Secretary of State shall give a second written notice of cancellation and the cancellation shall thereupon be effective. This second notice shall be given at least 20 days after the first notice, and no more than 90 days after the commencement date of the commission.

§ 8203.4 军事和海事保留；任期；终止；辞职

任职期限应符合第 8204 条的规定，除非该人在该指定的保留期间不再受聘为联邦公职人员。保留指挥官应在任职终止起的 30 日内通知州务卿，公证人在指定的保留期内终止工作。根据本条终止任职的公证人将被视为辞职。

§ 8203.5 军事和海事保留，宣誓证明

除州的名称外，宣誓证明还应包含执行文书的保留名称。

§ 8203.6 军事和海事保留；费用

公证人在保留期内办理公证服务不得收取费用。

§ 8204 任期

公证人的任期自收到委任状之日起为期四年。

§ 8204.1 委任状的取消；未支付费用；通知

如果公证人在向支票或其他汇款所在的金融机构汇款时未支付关于公证人考试、申请、委任和指纹费用的支票或其他款项，则州务卿可以取消公证人的任命。收到付款项目尚未支付的书面通知后，州务卿应先向公证人或提交文书的人员发出适用本条的书面通知。公证人在收到通知后仍未支付款项的，则州务卿应再次发出取消委任的书面通知，取消通知在发出后即生效。第二次通知与第一次通知之间至少间隔 20 日，但不超过委任状发出后的 90 日。

§ 8205. Duties

(a) It is the duty of a notary public, when requested:

(1) To demand acceptance and payment of foreign and inland bills of exchange, or promissory notes, to protest them for nonacceptance and nonpayment, and, with regard only to the nonacceptance or nonpayment of bills and notes, to exercise any other powers and duties that by the law of nations and according to commercial usages, or by the laws of any other state, government, or country, may be performed by a notary. This paragraph applies only to a notary public employed by a financial institution, during the course and scope of the notary's employment with the financial institution.

(2) To take the acknowledgment or proof of advance health care directives, powers of attorney, mortgages, deeds, grants, transfers, and other instruments of writing executed by any person, and to give a certificate of that proof or acknowledgment, endorsed on or attached to the instrument. The certificate shall be signed by the notary public in the notary public's own handwriting. A notary public may not accept any acknowledgment or proof of any instrument that is incomplete.

(3) To take depositions and affidavits, and administer oaths and affirmations, in all matters incident to the duties of the office, or to be used before any court, judge, officer, or board. Any deposition, affidavit, oath, or affirmation shall be signed by the notary public in the notary public's own handwriting.

(4) To certify copies of powers of attorney under Section 4307 of the Probate Code. The certification shall be signed by the notary public in the notary public's own handwriting.

(b) It shall further be the duty of a notary public, upon written request:

(1) To furnish to the Secretary of State certified copies of the notary's journal.

(2) To respond within 30 days of receiving written requests sent by certified mail from the Secretary of State's office for information relating to official acts performed by the notary.

§ 8206. Sequential journal; contents; thumbprint; loss of journal; copies of pages; exclusive property of notary public; limitations on surrender

(a) (1) A notary public shall keep one active sequential journal at a time, of all official acts performed as a notary public. The journal shall be kept in a locked and

§8205 公证人的职责

（a）在收到申请时，公证人有以下职责：

（1）对要求接受和支付外国和内陆汇票或承兑票据的，发出拒绝接受并承兑的拒绝文书。只有出具拒绝接受和承兑文书，才能行使国家法律、与商业用途相关的法律或任何其他州政府制定的可适用于公证人的法律规定的其他权力和义务。本段仅对由金融机构聘用的公证人在金融机构工作的过程中和范围内适用。

（2）取得任何人签发的预先医疗指导书、委托书、抵押、契约、赠款、转让书和其他书面文件的确认或证明，并提供证明或确认证书，并附于文件上。证书应由公证人亲笔签字。公证人不得接受任何不完整的文书确认或证明。

（3）对所有涉及公共职务或涉及任何法庭、法官、官员或委员会的事务，起草并执行宣誓及确认书。所有誓言、誓章、宣誓和确认都必须由公证人亲笔签字。

（4）认证根据《遗嘱检验法规》第4307条发出的授权委托书的副本作出。该认证证书应由公证人亲笔签字。

（b）在收到书面请求时，公证人应进一步履行以下职责：

（1）向州务卿提交公证书的副本。

（2）在收到由州务卿办公室发出的核证邮件的书面请求后30日内作出答复，提交有关公证人执行的职务行为的资料。

§8206 公证人日志；内容；指纹；日志的遗失；页面副本；公证人的专有财产；日志上交的限制

（a）（1）公证人应将所有以公证人身份执行的职务行为，记录保存在一份连续的公证人日志中。公证人日志应处于公证人的直接和排他控制之下，被保存

secured area, under the direct and exclusive control of the notary. Failure to secure the journal shall be cause for the Secretary of State to take administrative action against the commission held by the notary public pursuant to Section 8214.1.

(2) The journal shall be in addition to, and apart from, any copies of notarized documents that may be in the possession of the notary public and shall include all of the following:

(A) Date, time, and type of each official act.

(B) Character of every instrument sworn to, affirmed, acknowledged, or proved before the notary.

(C) The signature of each person whose signature is being notarized.

(D) A statement as to whether the identity of a person making an acknowledgment or taking an oath or affirmation was based on satisfactory evidence. If identity was established by satisfactory evidence pursuant to Section 1185 of the Civil Code, the journal shall contain the signature of the credible witness swearing or affirming to the identity of the individual or the type of identifying document, the governmental agency issuing the document, the serial or identifying number of the document, and the date of issue or expiration of the document.

(E) If the identity of the person making the acknowledgment or taking the oath or affirmation was established by the oaths or affirmations of two credible witnesses whose identities are proven to the notary public by presentation of any document satisfying the requirements of paragraph (3) or (4) of subdivision (b) of Section 1185 of the Civil Code, the notary public shall record in the journal the type of documents identifying the witnesses, the identifying numbers on the documents identifying the witnesses, and the dates of issuance or expiration of the documents identifying the witnesses.

(F) The fee charged for the notarial service.

(G) If the document to be notarized is a deed, quitclaim deed, deed of trust, or other document affecting real property, or a power of attorney document, the notary public shall require the party signing the document to place his or her right thumbprint in the journal. If the right thumbprint is not available, then the notary shall have the party use his or her left thumb, or any available finger and shall so indicate in the journal. If the party signing the document is physically unable to provide a thumbprint or fingerprint, the notary shall so indicate in the journal and shall also provide an explanation of that physical condition. This

在可上锁的安全区域。如果公证人未能尽到保管公证人日志的责任，应由州务卿根据第 8214.1 条作出关于公证人任职资格的行政处罚。

（2）公证人日志应包括除了属于公证人私人所有外的全部文件，并包括以下内容：

（A）每个职务行为的日期、时间和类型。

（B）每份宣誓、确认、认证或证明的文件性质。

（C）需被认证的每位当事人的签名。

（D）关于作出承认或宣誓或确认的人的身份是否基于充分证据的声明。如果其身份是根据《民法典》第 1185 条规定的充分证据确定，则公证人日志应包含可信证人的签名、誓言、用以确认个人身份的身份证件类型、发布文件的政府机构、文件的序列号或识别号以及文件的发行日期或到期日。

（E）如果确认人或宣誓人的身份是通过两名可信证人的宣誓或确认得以确定的，且可信证人的身份已经由公证人根据第 3 项或《民法典》第 1185 条（b）款第 4 项的可信文件加以确认，则公证人应在公证日志上记录用以识别证人身份的文件的类型、识别号码，以及文件发出或到期的时间。

（F）公证人有权对公证服务收费。

（G）如果要公证的文件是契约、产权转让契约、信托契约或影响不动产的其他文件或授权委托书，则公证人应要求签署文件的当事人在公证人日志上以右手拇指指纹画押。如果当事人无法提供右手的指纹，那公证人应要求当事人使用其左手拇指或任何可用的手指，并在公证人日志中指出。如果签署文件的当事人实际上无法提供任何指纹，公证人应在日志中注明，并提供对其身体状况的说明。本款不适用于根据《民法典》第 2924 条规定的止赎令或非司法止赎令所产生的受托人契约，也不适用于财产转让契约。

paragraph shall not apply to a trustee's deed resulting from a decree of foreclosure or a nonjudicial foreclosure pursuant to Section 2924 of the Civil Code, nor to a deed of reconveyance.

(b) If a sequential journal of official acts performed by a notary public is stolen, lost, misplaced, destroyed, damaged, or otherwise rendered unusable as a record of notarial acts and information, the notary public shall immediately notify the Secretary of State by certified or registered mail. The notification shall include the period of the journal entries, the notary public commission number, and the expiration date of the commission, and when applicable, a photocopy of any police report that specifies the theft of the sequential journal of official acts.

(c) Upon written request of any member of the public, which request shall include the name of the parties, the type of document, and the month and year in which notarized, the notary shall supply a photostatic copy of the line item representing the requested transaction at a cost of not more than thirty cents ($0.30) per page.

(d) The journal of notarial acts of a notary public is the exclusive property of that notary public, and shall not be surrendered to an employer upon termination of employment, whether or not the employer paid for the journal, or at any other time. The notary public shall not surrender the journal to any other person, except the county clerk, pursuant to Section 8209, or immediately, or if the journal is not present then as soon as possible, upon request to a peace officer investigating a criminal offense who has reasonable suspicion to believe the journal contains evidence of a criminal offense, as defined in Sections 830.1, 830.2, and 830.3 of the Penal Code, acting in his or her official capacity and within his or her authority. If the peace officer seizes the notary journal, he or she must have probable cause as required by the laws of this state and the United States. A peace officer or law enforcement agency that seizes a notary journal shall notify the Secretary of State by facsimile within 24 hours, or as soon as possible thereafter, of the name of the notary public whose journal has been seized. The notary public shall obtain a receipt for the journal, and shall notify the Secretary of State by certified mail within 10 days that the journal was relinquished to a peace officer. The notification shall include the period of the journal entries, the commission number of the notary public, the expiration date of the commission, and a photocopy of the receipt. The notary public shall obtain a new sequential journal. If the journal

（b）如果记录公证人官方行为的公证人连续日志被盗、丢失、错放、销毁、损坏或以其他方式使其无法作为公证行为和信息的记录使用，公证人应立即通过经认证或登记的邮件通知州务卿。该通知应包括公证人日志的记录期间、公证人的授权号码以及委任状的有效期间，如果存在的话，还应包括任何公证人日志失窃的警方报告的复印件。

（c）在收到任何公共主体的书面请求时，公证人应提供其所要求的事务文书的影印本，对此项服务每页可收取不超过三十美分（$0.30）的费用。向公证人请求复印文书的申请应包括当事人的名称、文件的类型以及公证的年月份。

（d）公证人的公证行为日志是公证人的专有财产，无论雇主是否在任何时刻为公证人日志支付了费用，雇主在终止雇佣后不得要求公证人交还公证人日志。公证人不得将公证人日志交给其他任何人，除非根据第8209条的规定交给郡书记官，或者经合理怀疑相信该日志包含《刑法典》第830.1条、第830.2条和第830.3条所界定的犯罪行为的证据时，应调查犯罪行为的治安官的请求，可向其提交公证人日志，治安官应依照其身份在权限内使用。治安官保留公证人日志，必须满足美国联邦法律或州法律要求的条件。治安官或执法机关保留公证人日志的，应在24小时内或尽快将被扣留公证人日志的公证人的姓名以传真的方式通知州务卿。公证人应当获得提交公证人日志的收据，并应在10日内将该日志移交给治安官的事宜通过认证邮件通知州务卿。该通知应包括公证人日志记录的期间、公证人委任状编号、委任截止日期以及收据复印件。公证人应获取新的顺序日志。如果治安官将公证人日志归还给公证人时，公证人已经获得了新的日志，则公证人不得在交还的日志中新增记录。作为雇员的公证人应允许由其雇主正式指定的审核员或代理人进行公证人日志的检查和复制，但应在公证人在场的情况下进行，且所复制的公证文书中的事项应与雇主的经营目的有直接关系。公证人应雇主的要求，可以定期提供与雇主商业目的直接相关的事项的文书副本，但雇主不得要求公证人提供与其业务无关的任何事项的文书副本。提供给雇主的任何公证人日志副本的保密和妥善保管由雇主负责。

relinquished to a peace officer is returned to the notary public and a new journal has been obtained, the notary public shall make no new entries in the returned journal. A notary public who is an employee shall permit inspection and copying of journal transactions by a duly designated auditor or agent of the notary public's employer, provided that the inspection and copying is done in the presence of the notary public and the transactions are directly associated with the business purposes of the employer. The notary public, upon the request of the employer, shall regularly provide copies of all transactions that are directly associated with the business purposes of the employer, but shall not be required to provide copies of any transaction that is unrelated to the employer's business. Confidentiality and safekeeping of any copies of the journal provided to the employer shall be the responsibility of that employer.

(e)The notary public shall provide the journal for examination and copying in the presence of the notary public upon receipt of a subpoena duces tecum or a court order, and shall certify those copies if requested.

(f)Any applicable requirements of, or exceptions to, state and federal law shall apply to a peace officer engaged in the search or seizure of a sequential journal.

§ 8206.5. Notaries; supplying photostatic copies on request; defending position in a disciplinary proceeding

Upon receiving a request for a copy of a transaction pursuant to subdivision (c) of Section 8206, the notary shall respond to the request within 15 business days after receipt of the request and either supply the photostatic copy requested or acknowledge that no such line item exists. In a disciplinary proceeding for noncompliance with subdivision (c) of Section 8206 or this section, a notary may defend his or her delayed action on the basis of unavoidable, exigent business or personal circumstances.

§ 8207. Seal

A notary public shall provide and keep an official seal, which shall clearly show, when embossed, stamped, impressed or affixed to a document, the name of the notary, the State Seal, the words "Notary Public," and the name of the county wherein the bond and oath of office are filed, and the date the notary public's commission expires. The seal of every notary public commissioned on or after January 1, 1992, shall contain the sequential identification number assigned to the notary and the sequential identification number assigned to the manufacturer or vendor. The

（e）公证人在收到传票或法庭命令后，应到场提供需审查和复制的公证人日志，并应要求对复印件进行认证。

（f）联邦法律和州法律的任何适用要求或例外情况均适用于搜寻或扣押公证人日志的治安官。

§8206.5 公证人；根据要求提供影印本；在纪律处分中自我辩护

公证人应在收到根据第8206条（c）款规定的提交文书副本的请求15个工作日内回复，并提供所要求的事务文书的影印本，或确认不存在此事务文书。在违反第8206条（c）款或本条而进行的纪律处分程序中，公证人可以以不可避免、紧急业务或个人情况的事由为自己的延迟行动抗辩。

§8207 公证公章

公证人应当提供并保留公章，在文件上盖章、贴花时应当清晰，公证公章上应包含公证人姓名、州印章、"公证人"字样、提交保证金和宣誓的郡名，以及公证人的任职到期日。1992年1月1日起任职的公证人，其公章应包含分配给公证人的顺序识别号码和分配给制造商或供应商的顺序识别号码。公证人在所有职务执业行为中都应当使用公章。

notary public shall authenticate with the official seal all official acts.

A notary public shall not use the official notarial seal except for the purpose of carrying out the duties and responsibilities as set forth in this chapter. A notary public shall not use the title "notary public" except for the purpose of rendering notarial service.

The seal of every notary public shall be affixed by a seal press or stamp that will print or emboss a seal which legibly reproduces under photographic methods the required elements of the seal. The seal may be circular not over two inches in diameter, or may be a rectangular form of not more than one inch in width by two and one-half inches in length, with a serrated or milled edged border, and shall contain the information required by this section.

The seal shall be kept in a locked and secured area, under the direct and exclusive control of the notary. Failure to secure the seal shall be cause for the Secretary of State to take administrative action against the commission held by the notary public pursuant to Section 8214.1.

The official seal of a notary public is the exclusive property of that notary public, and shall not be surrendered to an employer upon the termination of employment, whether or not the employer paid for the seal, or to any other person. The notary, or his or her representative, shall destroy or deface the seal upon termination, resignation, or revocation of the notary's commission.

This section shall become operative on January 1, 1992.

§ 8207.1. Identification number

The Secretary of State shall assign a sequential identification number to each notary which shall appear on the notary commission.

This section shall become operative on January 1, 1992.

§ 8207.2. Manufacture, duplication, and sale of seal or stamp; procedures and guidelines for issuance of seals; certificate of authorization

(a) No notary seal or press stamp shall be manufactured, duplicated, sold, or offered for sale unless authorized by the Secretary of State.

(b) The Secretary of State shall develop and implement procedures and guidelines for the issuance of notary seals on or before January 1, 1992.

(c) The Secretary of State shall issue a permit with a sequential identification number to each manufacturer

除了履行本章规定的职责外，公证人不得在其他场合使用正式的公证印章。公证人除了提供公证服务时，不得使用"公证人"称号。

每个公证人的印章都必须附有用以以打印或压印方式清晰印制印章所需元素的印章扭或图章贴花。印章的形状可以是直径不超过 2 英寸的圆形，或者长度不超过 1 英寸宽度为 2 英寸的矩形，并且具有锯齿状或铣边边缘，并且应包含本条所规定的所有信息。

印章应在公证人的直接和排他控制下保存在锁定和安全区域。公证人如果未能妥善保管印章，应由州务卿根据第 8214.1 条的规定对公证人采取与其任职资格相关的行政处罚。

公证人的公证公章是公证人的专有财产，无论雇主是否在任何时刻为公章支付了费用，雇主在终止雇佣后不得要求公证人交出公证公章。公证人或其代表在终止，辞职或撤销公证人的委任时，应销毁印章。

本条将于 1992 年 1 月 1 日起施行。

§8207.1 识别码

州务卿应向公证人分配连续的身份识别码，并标注在公证人的委任状中。

本条将于 1992 年 1 月 1 日起施行。

§8207.2 制造，复制和销售印章或印花票；签发印章的程序和指引；授权证书

（a）非经州务卿授权，不得制造、复制或出售公证印章。

（b）1992 年 1 月 1 日前，州务卿应制定并实施签发公证印章的程序和准则。

（c）州务卿应向授权制作公证公章的每个制造商或供应商发出带有序号的许可证。州务卿可以为签发

or vendor authorized to issue notary seals. The Secretary of State may establish a fee for the issuance of the permit which shall not exceed the actual costs of issuing the permit.

(d) The Secretary of State shall develop a certificate of authorization to purchase a notary stamp from an authorized vendor.

(e) The certificate of authorization shall be designed to prevent forgeries and shall contain a sequential identification number.

(f) This section shall become operative on January 1, 1992.

§ 8207.3. Certificates of authorization; authorization to provide seal; lost, misplaced, damaged or otherwise unworkable seal

(a) The Secretary of State shall issue certificates of authorization with which a notary public can obtain an official notary seal.

(b) A vendor or manufacturer is authorized to provide a notary with an official seal only upon presentation by the notary public of a certificate of authorization.

(c) A vendor of official seals shall note the receipt of certificates of authorization and sequential identification numbers of certificates presented by a notary public upon a certificate of authorization.

(d) A copy of a certificate of authorization shall be retained by a vendor and the original, which shall contain a sample impression of the seal issued to the notary public, shall be submitted to the Secretary of State for verification and recordkeeping. The Secretary of State shall develop guidelines for submitting certificates of authorization by vendors.

(e) Any notary whose official seal is lost, misplaced, destroyed, broken, damaged, or is rendered otherwise unworkable shall immediately mail or deliver written notice of that fact to the Secretary of State. The Secretary of State, within five working days after receipt of the notice, if requested by a notary, shall issue a certificate of authorization which a notary may use to obtain a replacement seal.

(f) This section shall become operative on January 1, 1992.

§ 8207.4. Violations; penalties

(a) Any person who willfully violates any part of Section 8207.1, 8207.2, 8207.3, or 8207.4 shall be subject to a civil penalty not to exceed one thousand five hundred

许可证要求支付费用，但不得超过发放许可证产生的实际费用。

（d）州务卿应制发向供应商购买公证印花票的授权证书。

（e）授权证书应包含防伪设计，并应包含序列号。

（f）本条将于1992年1月1日起施行。

§8207.3 授权证明书；授权提供印章；丢失、放错、损坏或因其他原因不能使用印章

（a）州务卿应向公证人签发以获得官方公证印章的授权证书。

（b）只有在公证人出示授权证书后，供应商或制造商才有权向公证人提供公证印章。

（c）印章的供应商须记录获得授权证书的收据和授权证书上标注的公证人的连续识别号码。

（d）授权证书副本应由供应商保留，原件（含有向公证人签发的印章的图样）应提交给州务卿进行核实和存档。州务卿应为供应商提交授权证明文件制定标准。

（e）任何公章损坏、错放、销毁、破损、损坏或因其他原因不能使用的公证人，应立即向州务卿发送或者提交该事实的书面通知。州务卿在收到通知后5个工作日内，经公证人要求，应向公证人签发授权证明书，以便其获得替代公章。

（f）本条将于1992年1月1日起施行。

§8207.4 违规行为；处罚

（a）任何人故意违反第8207.1条、第8207.2条、第8207.3条或第8207.4条的任何部分的，每一次违规行为将被处以不超过一千五百美元（$1500）的民

dollars ($1,500) for each violation, which may be recovered in a civil action brought by the Attorney General or the district attorney or city attorney, or by a city prosecutor in any city and county.

(b) The penalty provided by this section is not an exclusive remedy, and does not affect any other relief or remedy provided by law.

(c) This section shall become operative on January 1, 1992.

§ 8208. Protest of bill or note for nonacceptance or nonpayment

The protest of a notary public acting in the course and scope of employment by a financial institution, under his or her hand and official seal, of a bill of exchange or promissory note for nonacceptance or nonpayment, specifying any of the following is prima facie evidence of the facts recited therein:

(a) The time and place of presentment.

(b) The fact that presentment was made and the manner thereof.

(c) The cause or reason for protesting the bill.

(d) The demand made and the answer given, if any, or the fact that the drawee or acceptor could not be found.

§ 8209. Resignation, disqualification or removal of notary; records delivered to clerk; misdemeanor; death; destruction of records

(a) If any notary public resigns, is disqualified, removed from office, or allows his or her appointment to expire without obtaining reappointment within 30 days, all notarial records and papers shall be delivered within 30 days to the clerk of the county in which the notary public's current official oath of office is on file. If the notary public willfully fails or refuses to deliver all notarial records and papers to the county clerk within 30 days, the person is guilty of a misdemeanor and shall be personally liable for damages to any person injured by that action or inaction.

(b) In the case of the death of a notary public, the personal representative of the deceased shall promptly notify the Secretary of State of the death of the notary public and shall deliver all notarial records and papers of the deceased to the clerk of the county in which the notary public's official oath of office is on file.

After 10 years from the date of deposit with the county clerk, if no request for, or reference to such records has been made, they may be destroyed upon order of court.

事处罚，处罚可以由律政司或地区检察官或任何郡或市的城市检察官作出。

（b）本条所提供的罚则并不是排他性救济，不影响法律规定的任何其他救济的适用。

（c）本条将于1992年1月1日起施行。

§8208 制作或出具票据被拒绝接受或承兑的拒绝证书

在金融机构工作的公证人可对拒绝接受或承兑的票据以亲自盖章的方式出具拒绝证书，以下列举了可作为表面证据的事实：

（a）提出承兑的时间和地点。
（b）提出承兑的事实及其方式。

（c）拒绝承兑的原因或理由。
（d）所提出的要求和回答，或者（如果有的话），没有找到付款人或受理人的事实。

§8209 公证人辞职、资格取消或除名；向书记官交出记录；轻罪；死亡；销毁记录

（a）如果公证人辞职，被取消资格、免职，或者其任命期满后30日内不能再获得任命，则所有公证记录和文件应在30日内交付给公证人当前正式宣誓就职所在郡的郡书记官。如公证人故意不履行这一义务或者拒绝在30日内将所有公证记录和文件交给郡书记官，则构成轻罪，应对其作为或不作为造成的损害承担赔偿责任。

（b）公证人死亡的，其遗属代理人应及时通知州务卿公证人死亡，并将死者的公证记录和文件送交公证人正式宣誓就职所在郡的郡书记官处。

自郡书记官封存之日起10年后，如果没有要求，或提及这些记录，可以在法庭命令下进行销毁。

§ 8211. Fees

Fees charged by a notary public for the following services shall not exceed the fees prescribed by this section.

(a) For taking an acknowledgment or proof of a deed, or other instrument, to include the seal and the writing of the certificate, the sum of ten dollars ($10) for each signature taken.

(b) For administering an oath or affirmation to one person and executing the jurat, including the seal, the sum of ten dollars ($10).

(c) For all services rendered in connection with the taking of any deposition, the sum of twenty dollars ($20), and in addition thereto, the sum of five dollars ($5) for administering the oath to the witness and the sum of five dollars ($5) for the certificate to the deposition.

(d) No fee may be charged to notarize signatures on vote by mail ballot identification envelopes or other voting materials.

(e) For certifying a copy of a power of attorney under Section 4307 of the Probate Code the sum of ten dollars ($10).

(f) In accordance with Section 6107, no fee may be charged to a United States military veteran for notarization of an application or a claim for a pension, allotment, allowance, compensation, insurance, or any other veteran's benefit.

§ 8212. Bond; amount; form

Every person appointed a notary public shall execute an official bond in the sum of fifteen thousand dollars ($15,000). The bond shall be in the form of a bond executed by an admitted surety insurer and not a deposit in lieu of bond.

§ 8213. Bonds and oaths; filing; certificate; copy of oath as evidence; transfer to new county; name changes; fees

(a) No later than 30 days after the beginning of the term prescribed in the commission, every person appointed a notary public shall file an official bond and an oath of office in the office of the county clerk of the county within which the person maintains a principal place of business as shown in the application submitted to the Secretary of State, and the commission shall not take effect unless this is done within the 30-day period. A person appointed to be a notary public shall take and subscribe the oath of office either in the office of that county clerk or before another notary public in that county. If the oath of office is taken

§ 8211 公证费用

公证人为以下服务收取的费用不得超过本条的规定。

（a）为了认证或证明契约或其他文书，包括印章和证明书的写作，每笔费用为十美元（$10）。

（b）为执行或确认宣誓，出具宣誓证明，包括印章在内，一共十美元（$10）。

（c）对于与所有宣誓公证有关的服务，二十美元（$20），另外五美元（$5）用于对证人的所有誓言进行公证，以及五美元（$5）为证书作宣誓公证。

（d）对邮寄选票识别信封或其他投票材料上的公民签名进行公证，不得收取费用。

（e）根据《遗嘱检验法规》第4307条证明一份授权书的副本收费十美元（$10）。

（f）根据第6107条，为美国退伍军人申请退休金、分配、津贴、赔偿、保险或任何其他退伍军人福利办理公证，不收取费用。

§ 8212 保证金；数量；形式

每名被任命为公证人的人员，应提交一万五千美元（$15000）的任职保证金。保证金的形式应为由获准的保证人执行的债券，而不得以存款代替保证金。

§ 8213 保证金及宣誓；备案；证书；作为证据的誓言副本；向新郡转移；名称变更；费用

（a）在任命规定的期限开始后30日内，每个被任命为公证人的人员应当在其主要履职地的郡书记办公室内，按照提交给州务卿的申请中的内容，提交正式保证金并宣誓，上述程序须在30日内完成，否则任命不生效。被任命为公证人的人，应当在该郡书记官的办公室或在该郡的另一名公证人面前宣誓。如果宣誓是在公证人面前完成的，则可以通过认证邮件的方式向郡书记官邮寄宣誓书和保证金。在收到宣誓书和保证金后，郡书记官应立即向州务卿递交一份证明文件，以证明收到上述文件的事实，并附上载有公证人符合委任状上规定形式的个人签名的宣誓书副本，

and subscribed before a notary public, the oath and bond may be filed with the county clerk by certified mail. Upon the filing of the oath and bond, the county clerk shall immediately transmit to the Secretary of State a certificate setting forth the fact of the filing and containing a copy of the official oath, personally signed by the notary public in the form set forth in the commission and shall immediately deliver the bond to the county recorder for recording. The county clerk shall retain the oath of office for one year following the expiration of the term of the commission for which the oath was taken, after which the oath may be destroyed or otherwise disposed of. The copy of the oath, personally signed by the notary public, on file with the Secretary of State may at any time be read in evidence with like effect as the original oath, without further proof.

(b) If a notary public transfers the principal place of business from one county to another, the notary public may file a new oath of office and bond, or a duplicate of the original bond with the county clerk to which the principal place of business was transferred. If the notary public elects to make a new filing, the notary public shall, within 30 days of the filing, obtain an official seal which shall include the name of the county to which the notary public has transferred. In a case where the notary public elects to make a new filing, the same filing and recording fees are applicable as in the case of the original filing and recording of the bond.

(c) If a notary public submits an application for a name change to the Secretary of State, the notary public shall, within 30 days from the date an amended commission is issued, file a new oath of office and an amendment to the bond with the county clerk in which the principal place of business is located. The amended commission with the name change shall not take effect unless the filing is completed within the 30-day period. The amended commission with the name change takes effect the date the oath and amendment to the bond is filed with the county clerk. If the principal place of business address was changed in the application for name change, either a new or duplicate of the original bond shall be filed with the county clerk with the amendment to the bond. The notary public shall, within 30 days of the filing, obtain an official seal that includes the name of the notary public and the name of the county to which the notary public has transferred, if applicable.

(d) The recording fee specified in Section 27361 of the Government Code shall be paid by the person appoint-

并立即将保证金交付郡记录员进行记录。郡书记官在公证人宣誓的任期届满后，仍需将宣誓书保留1年，之后可以销毁或以其他方式处置宣誓书。由公证人亲自签署的宣誓书副本，可随时向州务卿提交，其证据效力等同于宣誓书原件，而不必作进一步证明。

（b）如果公证人将主要营业地点从一个郡转移到另一个郡，公证人可以提交新的宣誓书和保证金文件，或者提交转移前所在郡的郡书记官处的宣誓书和保证金文件副本。如公证人选择提交新的宣誓和保证金文件，公证人应当在提交之日起30日内取得公证人公章，公章应包含公证人转换后的郡名。在公证人选择提交新的宣誓书和保证金的情况下，备案和记录费用与原始提交的情况一致。

（c）公证人如果向州务卿递交更改名称的申请，公证人应当自修改后的委任状发出之日起30日内，向其主要营业地点所在的郡书记官提交新的宣誓书和修改过的保证金，否则修改名称后的任命不得生效。修改名称后的变更任命自郡书记官备案了宣誓书和修正过的保证金后生效。如果在申请改变名称前，公证人的主要营业地址也发生了变更，则公证人应向郡书记官提交原始保证金文件的副本和修正过的保证金文件。公证人应当在申报之日起30日内，获得公证人姓名、公证人营业地转移后的郡名（如可得）的公章。

（d）《政府组织法》第27361条规定的记录费用由公证人指定的人员支付。该费用可以交给郡书记官，

ed a notary public. The fee may be paid to the county clerk who shall transmit it to the county recorder.

(e) The county recorder shall record the bond and shall thereafter mail, unless specified to the contrary, it to the person named in the instrument and, if no person is named, to the party leaving it for recording.

§ 8213.5. Change in location or address of business or residence; notice

A notary public shall notify the Secretary of State by certified mail within 30 days as to any change in the location or address of the principal place of business or residence. A notary public shall not use a commercial mail receiving agency or post office box as his or her principal place of business or residence, unless the notary public also provides the Secretary of State with a physical street address as the principal place of residence. Willful failure to notify the Secretary of State of a change of address shall be punishable as an infraction by a fine of not more than five hundred dollars ($500).

§ 8213.6. Name changes; application; filing

If a notary public changes his or her name, the notary public shall complete an application for name change form and file that application with the Secretary of State. Information on this form shall be subject to the confidentiality provisions described in Section 8201.5. Upon approval of the name change form, the Secretary of State shall issue a commission that reflects the new name of the notary public. The term of the commission and commission number shall remain the same. Willful failure to notify the Secretary of State of a name change shall be punishable as an infraction by a fine of not more than five hundred dollars ($500).

§ 8214. Misconduct or neglect

For the official misconduct or neglect of a notary public, the notary public and the sureties on the notary public's official bond are liable in a civil action to the persons injured thereby for all the damages sustained.

§ 8214.1. Grounds for refusal, revocation or suspension of commission

The Secretary of State may refuse to appoint any person as notary public or may revoke or suspend the commission of any notary public upon any of the following grounds:

(a) Substantial and material misstatement or omission in the application submitted to the Secretary of State to

并由其转交给郡记录员。

（e）郡记录员应记录该保证金，且除非另有规定，须发邮件通知文件中指定的人，如果没有被提及，则向出席记录现场的一方发送邮件。

§8213.5 改变执业地点或居住地的位置或地址；通知

公证人应在 30 日内通过认证邮件通知州务卿主要执业地点或居住地的位置或地址发生变更。公证人不得使用商业邮件接收机构或邮政信箱作为其执业地点或居住地，除非公证人另行向州务卿提供实际街道地址作为主要居住地点。故意未将地址变更通知州务卿的，将被处以不超过五百美元（$500）的罚款。

§8213.6 名称变更；申请；提交

公证人变更姓名的，应当填写姓名变更申请书，并向州务卿递交。本表格上的信息须遵守第 8201.5 条的保密规定。州务卿应出具记录了公证人新名称的委任状。委任状的编号和期限应保持不变。故意未将姓名变更通知州务卿的，将被处以不超过五百美元（$500）的罚款。

§8214 不当行为或疏忽

对于公证人的官方不当行为或疏忽，公证人和公证人公职保证金的担保人对由此产生的一切损失承担民事赔偿责任。

§8214.1 拒绝、撤销或暂停任命的理由

州务卿可以拒绝任命公证人，也可以由于具体原因撤销或暂停公证人的任命。这些原因包括：

（a）提交给州务卿成为公证人的申请中存在重大错误或遗漏。

become a notary public.

(b) Conviction of a felony, a lesser offense involving moral turpitude, or a lesser offense of a nature incompatible with the duties of a notary public. A conviction after a plea of nolo contendere is deemed to be a conviction within the meaning of this subdivision.

(c) Revocation, suspension, restriction, or denial of a professional license, if the revocation, suspension, restriction, or denial was for misconduct based on dishonesty, or for any cause substantially relating to the duties or responsibilities of a notary public.

(d) Failure to discharge fully and faithfully any of the duties or responsibilities required of a notary public.

(e) When adjudicated liable for damages in any suit grounded in fraud, misrepresentation, or for a violation of the state regulatory laws, or in any suit based upon a failure to discharge fully and faithfully the duties as a notary public.

(f) The use of false or misleading advertising wherein the notary public has represented that the notary public has duties, rights, or privileges that he or she does not possess by law.

(g) The practice of law in violation of Section 6125 of the Business and Professions Code.

(h) Charging more than the fees prescribed by this chapter.

(i) Commission of any act involving dishonesty, fraud, or deceit with the intent to substantially benefit the notary public or another, or substantially injure another.

(j) Failure to complete the acknowledgment at the time the notary's signature and seal are affixed to the document.

(k) Failure to administer the oath or affirmation as required by paragraph (3) of subdivision (a) of Section 8205.

(l) Execution of any certificate as a notary public containing a statement known to the notary public to be false.

(m) Violation of Section 8223.

(n) Failure to submit any remittance payable upon demand by the Secretary of State under this chapter or failure to satisfy any court-ordered money judgment, including restitution.

(o) Failure to secure the sequential journal of official acts, pursuant to Section 8206, or the official seal, pursuant to Section 8207, or willful failure to report the theft or loss of the sequential journal, pursuant to subdivision (b) of Section 8206.

（b）被判犯有重罪，道德上的轻罪，或与公证人的职责不符的轻罪。经过辩护后被判犯有本条规定的罪行。

（c）被撤销、暂停、限制或拒绝专业执照，且该撤销、暂停、限制或拒绝是基于不诚实的不当行为，或与公证人的职责相关的任何原因。

（d）没有充分、忠实地履行公证人的义务或责任。

（e）在任何以欺诈、虚假陈述或违反国家管理法规为由的诉讼中被判处需要承担赔偿责任，或以未能充分、忠实地履行作为公证人职责的诉讼中被判处需承担赔偿责任。

（f）使用虚假或误导性的广告，展示公证人法律未授予的职责、权力或特权。

（g）违反《商业与职业守则》第6125条的习惯法。

（h）收费超过本章的规定。

（i）公证人的任命涉嫌不诚实、欺诈或欺骗的行为，任何明显有利于公证人或其他人，或严重伤害其他人。

（j）在公证人的签名和盖章附于文件时未能及时完成文书确认。

（k）未按照第8205条（a）款第3项要求进行宣誓或确认。

（l）为任何公证人明知包含虚假信息的声明出具公证证书。

（m）违反第8223条的规定。

（n）没有按照本章要求缴纳任何州务卿要求支付的款项，或未能执行法院关于金钱的任何判决，包括归还金钱。

（o）未能根据第8206条的规定妥善保管公证人日志，或未能根据第8207条的规定妥善保管公证人公章，或触犯第8206条（b）款，对公证人日志遗失故意不报告。

(p) Violation of Section 8219.5.

(q) Commission of an act in violation of Section 6203, 8214.2, 8225, or 8227.3 of the Government Code or of Section 115, 470, 487, subdivision (a) of Section 487a, or Section 530.5 of the Penal Code.

(r) Willful failure to provide access to the sequential journal of official acts upon request by a peace officer.

§ 8214.15. Civil penalties

(a) In addition to any commissioning or disciplinary sanction, a violation of subdivision (f), (i), (l), (m), or (p) of Section 8214.1 is punishable by a civil penalty not to exceed one thousand five hundred dollars ($1,500).

(b) In addition to any commissioning or disciplinary sanction, a violation of subdivision (h), (j), or (k) of Section 8214.1, or a negligent violation of subdivision (d) of Section 8214.1 is punishable by a civil penalty not to exceed seven hundred fifty dollars ($750).

(c) The civil penalty may be imposed by the Secretary of State if a hearing is not requested pursuant to Section 8214.3. If a hearing is requested, the hearing officer shall make the determination.

(d) Any civil penalties collected pursuant to this section shall be transferred to the General Fund. It is the intent of the Legislature that to the extent General Fund moneys are raised by penalties collected pursuant to this section, that money shall be made available to the Secretary of State's office to defray its costs of investigating and pursuing commissioning and monetary remedies for violations of the notary public law.

§ 8214.2. Fraud relating to deed of trust; single-family residence; felony

(a) A notary public who knowingly and willfully with intent to defraud performs any notarial act in relation to a deed of trust on real property consisting of a single-family residence containing not more than four dwelling units, with knowledge that the deed of trust contains any false statements or is forged, in whole or in part, is guilty of a felony.

(b) The penalty provided by this section is not an exclusive remedy and does not affect any other relief or remedy provided by law.

§ 8214.21. Failure to provide access to the sequential journal of notarial acts; civil penalties

A notary public who willfully fails to provide access to the sequential journal of notarial acts when requested

（p）违反第 8219.5 条规定的行为。

（q）委任行为违反《政府组织法》第 6203 条、第 8214.2 条、第 8225 条、第 8227.3 条或第 487a 条（a）款或《刑法典》第 115 条、第 470 条、第 487 条（a）款或第 530.5 条的行为。

（r）故意未按照治安官的要求提供连续的官方公证人日志。

§8214.15 民事处罚

（a）除了任何委任或纪律处分外，违反第 8214.1 条（f）款、（i）款、（l）款、（m）款或（p）款的规定可以处以不超过一千五百美元（$1500）的民事处罚。

（b）除了任命或纪律处分外，违反第 8214.1 条（h）款、（j）款或（k）款或因疏忽违反第 8214.1 条（d）款的规定，将被处以不超过七百五十美元（$750）的民事处罚。

（c）如果当事人没有按照第 8214.3 条要求举行听证会，州务卿可以直接作出民事处罚决定。如果当事人要求举行听证会，则由听证官作出决定。

（d）根据本条收取的任何民事处罚款将转入公证基金。立法机关的意图是，根据本条收取的罚款提高公证基金的收入，该款可提供给州务卿，以支付对违反公证法的行为进行调查、追究和采取货币补救措施所需的费用。

§8214.2 与信托契约有关的欺诈；独立住宅；重罪

（a）公证人在为包括不超过四个住宅单位的独立住宅不动产的信托契约办理公证时，明知信托契约中部分或全部为虚假陈述或伪造信息，仍故意以欺诈手段作出公证行为，属于犯有重罪。

（b）本条所提供的处罚并不是排他性救济，不影响法律规定的任何其他救济的适用。

§8214.21 未能提供连续公证人日志；民事处罚

公证人在治安官要求的情况下故意不提供连续公证人日志的，应处以不超过两千五百美元（$2500）

by a peace officer shall be subject to a civil penalty not exceeding two thousand five hundred dollars ($2,500). An action to impose a civil penalty under this subdivision may be brought by the Secretary of State in an administrative proceeding or any public prosecutor in superior court, and shall be enforced as a civil judgment. A public prosecutor shall inform the secretary of any civil penalty imposed under this section.

§ 8214.23. Failure to obtain thumbprint; civil penalties; limitations

(a) A notary public who fails to obtain a thumbprint, as required by Section 8206, from a party signing a document shall be subject to a civil penalty not exceeding two thousand five hundred dollars ($2,500). An action to impose a civil penalty under this subdivision may be brought by the Secretary of State in an administrative proceeding or any public prosecutor in superior court, and shall be enforced as a civil judgment. A public prosecutor shall inform the secretary of any civil penalty imposed under this section.

(b) Not withstanding any other limitation of time described in Section 802 of the Penal Code, or any other provision of law, prosecution for a violation of this offense shall be commenced within four years after discovery of the commission of the offense, or within four years after the completion of the offense, whichever is later.

§ 8214.3. Hearing prior to denial or revocation of commission or imposition of civil penalties; law governing; exceptions

Prior to a revocation or suspension pursuant to this chapter or after a denial of a commission, or prior to the imposition of a civil penalty, the person affected shall have a right to a hearing on the matter and the proceeding shall be conducted in accordance with Chapter 5 (commencing with Section 11500) of Part 1 of Division 3, except that a person shall not have a right to a hearing after a denial of an application for a notary public commission in either of the following cases:

(a) The Secretary of State has, within one year previous to the application, and after proceedings conducted in accordance with Chapter 5 (commencing with Section 11500) of Part 1 of Division 3, denied or revoked the applicant's application or commission.

(b) The Secretary of State has entered an order pursuant to Section 8214.4 finding that the applicant has committed or omitted acts constituting grounds for suspension

的民事处罚。本条规定应受民事处罚的行为，可以由州务卿在行政诉讼中提起或由上级法院的任何检察机关提起，并以民事判决的方式执行。检察官应将根据本条实施的任何民事处罚通知州务卿。

§8214.23 未能获得指纹；民事处罚；限制

（a）公证人未能根据第8206条要求，从签署文件的当事人处获得指纹的，将被处以不超过二千五百美元（$2500）的民事处罚。依据本条将受到民事处罚的行为，可以由州务卿提起行政处罚程序或由上级法院的任何检察机关提起，并以民事判决的方式执行。检察官应将根据本条实施的任何民事处罚通知州务卿。

（b）除了《刑法典》第802条和其他法律规定的期限限制外，违法犯罪行为应在犯罪行为发生之日或犯罪行为完成之日起四年内起诉，二者以较迟的时限为准。

§8214.3 在拒绝或撤销任命或实施民事处罚之前的听证；适用法律的例外

公证人在根据本章的规定被撤销或暂停执业之前，或者在被拒绝任命之后，或在被实施民事处罚之前，应有权就该事宜申请听证，听证程序应按照第5章（从第11500条开始）第3节第1部分的规定进行，但是有以下情况之一的，拒绝任命后，不得申请听证：

（a）州务卿在接到申请之日起一年内，拒绝申请人的申请或撤销公证人的任命，并且已完成了第五章（第11500条开始）第3节第1部分规定的诉讼程序。

（b）州务卿根据第8214.4条的规定发布指令，裁定申请人的作为或不作为已经构成被暂停或撤销公证人任命的理由。

or revocation of a notary public's commission.

§ 8214.4. Resignation or expiration of commission not a bar to investigation or disciplinary proceedings

Notwithstanding this chapter or Chapter 5 (commencing with Section 11500) of Part 1 of Division 3, if the Secretary of State determines, after proceedings conducted in accordance with Chapter 5 (commencing with Section 11500) of Part 1 of Division 3, that any notary public has committed or omitted acts constituting grounds for suspension or revocation of a notary public's commission, the resignation or expiration of the notary public's commission shall not bar the Secretary of State from instituting or continuing an investigation or instituting disciplinary proceedings. Upon completion of the disciplinary proceedings, the Secretary of State shall enter an order finding the facts and stating the conclusion that the facts would or would not have constituted grounds for suspension or revocation of the commission if the commission had still been in effect.

§ 8214.5. Revocation of commission; filing copy with county clerk

Whenever the Secretary of State revokes the commission of any notary public, the Secretary of State shall file with the county clerk of the county in which the notary public's principal place of business is located a copy of the revocation. The county clerk shall note such revocation and its date upon the original record of such certificate.

§ 8214.8. Revocation upon certain convictions

Upon conviction of any offense in this chapter, or of Section 6203, or of any felony, of a person commissioned as a notary public, in addition to any other penalty, the court shall revoke the commission of the notary public, and shall require the notary public to surrender to the court the seal of the notary public. The court shall forward the seal, together with a certified copy of the judgment of conviction, to the Secretary of State.

§ 8216. Release of surety

When a surety of a notary desires to be released from responsibility on account of future acts, the release shall be pursuant to Article 11 (commencing with Section 996.110), and not by cancellation or withdrawal pursuant to Article 13 (commencing with Section 996.310), of Chapter 2 of Title 14 of Part 2 of the Code of Civil Procedure. For this purpose the surety shall make application to the superior court of the county in which the notary public's principal place of business is located and the copy of the application

§8214.4 辞职或任命过期不是调查或纪律处分的条件

尽管本章或第5章（从第11500条开始）第3节第1部分有规定，但如果州务卿完成了第5章（从第11500条开始）第3节第1部分规定的程序之后，确定任何公证人的作为或不作为构成暂停或撤销公证人任命的理由，则公证人辞职或任职到期不能阻却州务卿对其进行调查或者进行纪律处分。在完成纪律处分程序后，州务卿应当下达指令公布查明的事实，并说明如果任命仍然有效，现查明的事实是否构成暂停或撤销任命的理由。

§8214.5 撤销任命；向郡书记官备案

当州务卿撤销公证人的任命时，州务卿应向公证人的主要营业地点所在郡的郡书记官提交撤销任命的文书副本。郡书记官应当根据该证书的原始记录注明任命被撤销的日期。

§8214.8 因特定罪行撤销任命

一旦公证人被判定犯有本章或第6203条的任何罪行或其他重罪，除了接受其他处罚外，法院应当撤销公证人的任命，并要求公证人向法庭递交公证人印章。法院应将该印章以及定罪判决的核证副本送交州务卿。

§8216 解除担保

当公证人的担保人希望不再为未来的行为承担责任时，其应依照第11条（从第996.110款开始）的规定进行，而不是根据《民事诉讼法》第2部分第14分部第2章第13条（从第996.310款开始）取消或撤销其担保。担保人应向公证人的主要营业地点所在郡的上级法院提出申请，并将作为受益人的申请书和听证通知书副本送达州务卿。

and notice of hearing shall be served on the Secretary of State as the beneficiary.

§ 8219.5. Advertising in language other than English; posting of notice relating to legal advice and fees; translation of notary public into Spanish; suspension

(a) Every notary public who is not an attorney who advertises the services of a notary public in a language other than English by signs or other means of written communication, with the exception of a single desk plaque, shall post with that advertisement a notice in English and in the other language which sets forth the following:

(1) This statement: I am not an attorney and, therefore, cannot give legal advice about immigration or any other legal matters.

(2) The fees set by statute which a notary public may charge.

(b) The notice required by subdivision (a) shall be printed and posted as prescribed by the Secretary of State.

(c) Literal translation of the phrase "notary public" into Spanish, hereby defined as "notario publico" or "notario," is prohibited. For purposes of this subdivision, "literal translation" of a word or phrase from one language to another means the translation of a word or phrase without regard to the true meaning of the word or phrase in the language which is being translated.

(d) The Secretary of State shall suspend for a period of not less than one year or revoke the commission of any notary public who fails to comply with subdivision (a) or (c). However, on the second offense the commission of such notary public shall be revoked permanently.

§ 8220. Rules and regulations

The Secretary of State may adopt rules and regulations to carry out the provisions of this chapter.

The regulations shall be adopted in accordance with the Administrative Procedure Act (Chapter 3.5 (commencing with Section 11340) of Part 1 of Division 3).

§ 8221. Destruction, defacement or concealment of records or papers; misdemeanor; liability for damages

(a) If any person shall knowingly destroy, deface, or conceal any records or papers belonging to the office of a notary public, such person shall be guilty of a misdemeanor and be liable in a civil action for damages to any person injured as a result of such destruction, defacing, or concealment.

(b) Notwithstanding any other limitation of time

§8219.5 以英语以外的其他语言发布的广告；发布关于法律咨询和费用的通知；公证人的西班牙译文；公示

（a）不是律师的公证人，除了桌铭牌以外，需要以标识或其他书面通知方式，用英文以外的其他语言宣传公证人的服务的，应以英文和另一种语言作出以下格式的说明：

（1）说明：我不是律师，因此不能就移民或其他法律事宜提供法律意见。

（2）公证人可以对公证服务收取法定费用。

（b）（a）款所要求的说明应按照州务卿的规定印制和张贴。

（c）禁止将"公证人"一词翻译成西班牙文"notario publico"或"notario"。出于本款目的进行的翻译，从一种语言到另一种语言的单词或短语的"字面直译"意味着该翻译不考虑正在翻译的语言中该单词或短语的真实含义。

（d）如果公证人不遵守（a）款或（c）款的规定，州务卿应暂停或撤销其任命不少于一年的时间。如果公证人第二次违反，则其任命将被永久撤销。

§8220 规章和条例
州务卿可以通过制定规章来执行本章的规定。

规章应按照《行政诉讼法》第3编第1部分第3.5章（自第11340条始）的规定制定。

§8221 破坏、污损或隐藏记录或文件；轻罪；赔偿责任

（a）如果任何人故意销毁、污损或隐藏关于公证人执业的记录或文件，则该人即犯有轻罪，并且其应在民事诉讼中对因此而造成的任何损失负责。

（b）除了《刑法典》第802条和其他法律规定的

described in Section 802 of the Penal Code, or any other provision of law, prosecution for a violation of this offense shall be commenced within four years after discovery of the commission of the offense, or within four years after the completion of the offense, whichever is later.

(c) The penalty provided by this section is not an exclusive remedy and does not affect any other relief or remedy provided by law.

§ 8222. Injunction; reimbursement for expenses

(a) Whenever it appears to the Secretary of State that any person has engaged or is about to engage in any acts or practices which constitute or will constitute a violation of any provision of this chapter or any rule or regulation prescribed under the authority thereof, the Secretary of State may apply for an injunction, and upon a proper showing, any court of competent jurisdiction has power to issue a permanent or temporary injunction or restraining order to enforce the provisions of this chapter, and any party to the action has the right to prosecute an appeal from the order or judgment of the court.

(b) The court may order a person subject to an injunction or restraining order provided for in this section to reimburse the Secretary of State for expenses incurred in the investigation related to the petition. The Secretary of State shall refund any amount received as reimbursement should the injunction or restraining order be dissolved by an appellate court.

§ 8223. Notary public with expertise in immigration matters; advertising status as notary public; entry of information on forms; fee limitations

(a) No notary public who holds himself or herself out as being an immigration specialist, immigration consultant or any other title or description reflecting an expertise in immigration matters shall advertise in any manner whatsoever that he or she is a notary public.

(b) A notary public qualified and bonded as an immigration consultant under Chapter 19.5 (commencing with Section 22440) of Division 8 of the Business and Professions Code may enter data, provided by the client, on immigration forms provided by a federal or state agency. The fee for this service shall not exceed ten dollars ($10) per individual for each set of forms. If notary services are performed in relation to the set of immigration forms, additional fees may be collected pursuant to Section 8211. This fee limitation shall not apply to an attorney, who is also a notary public, who is rendering professional servic-

期限限制外，违法犯罪行为应在犯罪行为发现之日或犯罪行为完成之日起四年内起诉，二者以较迟的时间为准。

（c）本条所提供的罚则并不是排他性救济，不影响法律规定的任何其他救济的适用。

§8222 禁令；费用补偿

（a）州务卿认为任何人已经或即将从事任何已构成或将构成违反本章规定的行为，或从事将构成违反其授权制定的规则或条例的行为，即有权向有管辖权的适当法院申请永久或暂时的禁令，以执行本章的规定，法院的裁定或判决的任何一方都有权提出上诉。

（b）法院可以裁定根据本条规定受到禁令或限制令的人向州务卿补偿与请愿有关的调查费用。如果上诉法院撤销禁令或限制令，州务卿应退还所有收到的补偿款项。

§8223 具有移民事务专长的公证人；在广告中宣传公证人身份；在表格中输入资料；费用限制

（a）作为移民专家，移民顾问或其他具备移民事务专业知识的公证人不得以头衔或描述的方式宣传其公证人身份。

（b）根据《商业和职业守则》第19.5章（从第22440条开始）第8节，经过认证作为移民顾问的公证人可以输入由客户提供的联邦或州政府机构移民表格的数据。每项表格的费用不得超过每人十美元（$10）。如果根据一套移民表格进行公证服务，则可以根据第8211条收取额外费用。此费用限制不适用于也是公证人的律师，且该律师正在就移民事务提供专业服务的情形。

es regarding immigration matters.

(c) Nothing in this section shall be construed to exempt a notary public who enters data on an immigration form at the direction of a client, or otherwise performs the services of an immigration consultant, as defined by Section 22441 of the Business and Professions Code, from the requirements of Chapter 19.5 (commencing with Section 22440) of Division 8 of the Business and Professions Code. A notary public who is not qualified and bonded as an immigration consultant under Chapter 19.5 (commencing with Section 22440) of Division 8 of the Business and Professions Code may not enter data provided by a client on immigration forms nor otherwise perform the services of an immigration consultant.

§ 8224. Conflict of interest; financial or beneficial interest in transaction; exceptions

A notary public who has a direct financial or beneficial interest in a transaction shall not perform any notarial act in connection with such transaction.

For purposes of this section, a notary public has a direct financial or beneficial interest in a transaction if the notary public:

(a) With respect to a financial transaction, is named, individually, as a principal to the transaction.

(b) With respect to real property, is named, individually, as a grantor, grantee, mortgagor, mortgagee, trustor, trustee, beneficiary, vendor, vendee, lessor, or lessee, to the transaction.

For purposes of this section, a notary public has no direct financial or beneficial interest in a transaction where the notary public acts in the capacity of an agent, employee, insurer, attorney, escrow, or lender for a person having a direct financial or beneficial interest in the transaction.

§ 8224.1. Writings, depositions or affidavits of notary public; prohibitions against proof or taking by that notary public

A notary public shall not take the acknowledgment or proof of instruments of writing executed by the notary public nor shall depositions or affidavits of the notary public be taken by the notary public.

§ 8225. Improper notarial acts, solicitation, coercion or influence of performance; misdemeanor

(a)Any person who solicits, coerces, or in any manner influences a notary public to perform an improper notarial act knowing that act to be an improper notarial act,

（c）本条不得解释为免除在客户指导下输入移民表格资料的公证人，或以其他方式履行《商业和职业守则》第22441条所定义的移民顾问服务的公证人，在《商业和职业守则》第19.5章（从第22440条开始）第8节下的义务。根据《商业和职业守则》第19.5章（从第22440条开始）第8节，不具备移民顾问资格的公证人不得输入客户提供的关于移民形式的数据，也不得提供移民服务咨询。

§8224 利益冲突；财务或交易中的利益；例外

在交易中具有直接财务或实际利益的公证人不得从事与该交易有关的公证行为。

为了实现本条的立法目的，有以下情形的，视为公证人与交易存在直接财务或实际利益：

（a）被单独指定为金融交易的委托人。

（b）在不动产交易中，单独被指定为交易的保证人、受让人、抵押人、抵押权人、受托人、受益人、供应商、出租人或承租人。

在本条中，公证人作为与交易有直接财务或其他利益的人的代理人、雇员、保险人、律师、代管人或放款人的，不认为在交易中有直接的财务或实际利益。

§8224.1 公证人办理的文书、确认或宣誓；公证人不得办理的证明

公证人不对其所执行的书面文件进行认证或证明，也不得执行其办理的证词确认或宣誓书。

§8225 不正当的公证行为，招揽，胁迫或行为的影响；轻罪

（a）任何人唆使、胁迫或以任何方式影响公证人进行被认定为属于不正当公证行为的行为，包括根据第8206条规定的属于公证人执业行为的任何行为，

including any act required of a notary public under Section 8206, shall be guilty of a misdemeanor.

(b) Notwithstanding any other limitation of time described in Section 802 of the Penal Code, or any other provision of law, prosecution for a violation of this offense shall be commenced within four years after discovery of the commission of the offense, or within four years after the completion of the offense, whichever is later.

(c) The penalty provided by this section is not an exclusive remedy, and does not affect any other relief or remedy provided by law.

§ 8227.1. Unlawful acts by one not a notary public; misdemeanor

It shall be a misdemeanor for any person who is not a duly commissioned, qualified, and acting notary public for the State of California to do any of the following:

(a) Represent or hold himself or herself out to the public or to any person as being entitled to act as a notary public.

(b) Assume, use or advertise the title of notary public in such a manner as to convey the impression that the person is a notary public.

(c) Purport to act as a notary public.

§ 8227.3. Unlawful acts by one not a notary public; deeds of trust on single-family residences; felony

Any person who is not a duly commissioned, qualified, and acting notary public who does any of the acts prohibited by Section 8227.1 in relation to any document or instrument affecting title to, placing an encumbrance on, or placing an interest secured by a mortgage or deed of trust on, real property consisting of a single-family residence containing not more than four dwelling units, is guilty of a felony.

§ 8228. Enforcement of chapter; examination of notarial books, records, etc.

The Secretary of State or a peace officer, as defined in Sections 830.1, 830.2, and 830.3 of the Penal Code, possessing reasonable suspicion and acting in his or her official capacity and within his or her authority, may enforce the provisions of this chapter through the examination of a notary public's books, records, letters, contracts, and other pertinent documents relating to the official acts of the notary public.

均属轻罪。

(b)除了《刑法典》第802条和其他法律规定的期限限制外，违法犯罪行为应在犯罪行为发生之日或犯罪行为完成之日起四年内起诉，二者以较迟的时间为准。

(c)本条所提供的罚则并不是排他性救济，不影响法律规定的任何其他救济的适用。

§8227.1 非公证人的非法行为；轻罪

未经加利福尼亚州正式委任和确认，任何人执行以下行为将构成轻罪：

(a)向公众或任何人表示或宣称自己有权从事公证事务。

(b)表现、使用或宣传其作为公证人的身份，向他人传达其是公证人的印象。

(c)声称自己担任公证人。

§8227.3 非公证人的非法行为；对独立住宅的信托契约；重罪

任何未经公证人任命、授权和代理的人，如果执行第8227.1条所禁止的对由不超过四个单位的独立住宅组成的不动产施加抵押或信托担保等权利负担，即属重罪。

§8228 执行书；公证书；记录簿等的检查

根据《刑法典》第830.1条、第830.2条和第830.3条的规定，州务卿或治安官具有合理怀疑的，以其官方身份并在其授权范围内，可以执行本章规定，审查公证人的公证书、记录、信件、合同等与公证人执业行为有关的文件。

§ 8228.1. Willful failure to perform duty or control notarial seal

(a) Any notary public who willfully fails to perform any duty required of a notary public under Section 8206, or who willfully fails to keep the seal of the notary public under the direct and exclusive control of the notary public, or who surrenders the seal of the notary public to any person not otherwise authorized by law to possess the seal of the notary, shall be guilty of a misdemeanor.

(b) Notwithstanding any other limitation of time described in Section 802 of the Penal Code or any other provision of law, prosecution for a violation of this offense shall be commenced within four years after discovery of the commission of the offense, or within four years after the completion of the offense, whichever is later.

(c) The penalty provided by this section is not an exclusive remedy, and does not affect any other relief or remedy provided by law.

§ 8230. Identification of affiant; verification

If a notary public executes a jurat and the statement sworn or subscribed to is contained in a document purporting to identify the affiant, and includes the birthdate or age of the person and a purported photograph or finger or thumbprint of the person so swearing or subscribing, the notary public shall require, as a condition to executing the jurat, that the person verify the birthdate or age contained in the statement by showing either:

(a) A certified copy of the person's birth certificate, or

(b) An identification card or driver's license issued by the Department of Motor Vehicles.

For the purposes of preparing for submission of forms required by the United States Immigration and Naturalization Service, and only for such purposes, a notary public may also accept for identification any documents or declarations acceptable to the United States Immigration and Naturalization Service.

§ 1360. Necessity of taking constitutional oath

Unless otherwise provided, before any officer enters on the duties of his office, he shall take and subscribe the oath or affirmation set forth in Section 3 of Article XX of the Constitution of California.

§ 1362. Administration by authorized officer

Unless otherwise provided, the oath may be taken before any officer authorized to administer oaths.

§8228.1 故意不履行义务或保管公证公章

（a）任何公证人故意不履行第 8206 条规定的义务，或者故意放弃直接和排他控制的公证公章，或者向任何未经法律许可的人员交出公证公章的，均构成轻罪。

（b）除了《刑法典》第 802 条和其他法律规定的期限限制外，违法犯罪行为应在犯罪行为发生之日或犯罪行为完成之日起四年内起诉，二者以较迟的时间为准。

（c）本条所提供的罚则并不是排他性救济，不影响法律规定的任何其他救济的适用。

§ 8230 宣誓人的认证；验证

如果公证人执行的宣誓证明，宣誓或确认的声明包含证明宣誓人身份、宣誓人的出生日期或年龄的文件以及宣誓或提交文书的照片或指纹，则公证人执行宣誓证明的条件是要求通过以下任一方式验证宣誓中包含的出生日期或年龄：

（a）该人的出生证明的核证副本，或

（b）由加州机动车管理局发出的身份认证或驾驶执照；

只有为准备提交美国移民归化局所要求的表格的目的，公证人才可以对美国移民归化局可接受的文件或声明进行认证。

§1360 宪法宣誓的必要性

除非另有规定，任何人员履职之前，应完成《加州宪法》第 20 条第 3 款所述的宣誓或确认程序。

§1362 经授权人员

除非另有规定，宣誓可以在获授权执行宣誓的人员之前进行。

§ 6100. Performance of services; officers; notaries public

Officers of the state, or of a county or judicial district, shall not perform any official services unless upon the payment of the fees prescribed by law for the performance of the services, except as provided in this chapter.

This section shall not be construed to prohibit any notary public, except a notary public whose fees are required by law to be remitted to the state or any other public agency, from performing notarial services without charging a fee.

§ 6106. Pensions

Neither the State, nor any county or city, nor any public officer or body acting in his official capacity on behalf of the State, any county, or city, including notaries public, shall receive any fee or compensation for services rendered in an affidavit, or application relating to the securing of a pension, or the payment of a pension voucher, or any matter relating thereto.

§ 6107. Veterans

(a) No public entity, including the state, a county, city, or other political subdivision, nor any officer or employee thereof, including notaries public, shall demand or receive any fee or compensation for doing any of the following:

(1) Recording, indexing, or issuing certified copies of any discharge, certificate of service, certificate of satisfactory service, notice of separation, or report of separation of any member of the Armed Forces of the United States.

(2) Furnishing a certified copy of, or searching for, any public record that is to be used in an application or claim for a pension, allotment, allowance, compensation, insurance (including automatic insurance), or any other benefits under any act of Congress for service in the Armed Forces of the United States or under any law of this state relating to veterans' benefits.

(3) Furnishing a certified copy of, or searching for, any public record that is required by the Veterans Administration to be used in determining the eligibility of any person to participate in benefits made available by the Veterans Administration.

(4) Rendering any other service in connection with an application or claim referred to in paragraph (2) or (3).

(b) A certified copy of any record referred to in subdivision (a) may be made available only to one of the following:

§6100 公证服务；官员；公证人

州或郡或司法管辖区内官员，必须按照本章规定的方式缴纳法律规定的费用，否则不得办理公证执业服务。

本条不得解释为：除法律规定的公证人向国家或其他公共机构汇出费用外，公证人不得收取公证费。

§6106 养老金

任何州、郡、市的公证人，包括以公证执业人员身份行事的公职人员或机构均不得对提供宣誓书或有关申请获得养老金、支付抚恤金凭证等服务收取任何费用或报酬。

§6107 退伍军人

（a）任何公共机构，包括州、郡、市、其他机构，其公职人员或其雇员，包括公证人，均不得对以下服务要求或收取任何费用或报酬：

（1）记录、索引或发出美国武装部队任何成员的任何解职、服务证明、良好服役证明、调离通知或调离报告的核证副本。

（2）申请或搜索要求领取养老金、拨款、津贴、补偿、保险（包括自动保险）的任何公共记录的核证副本，或根据美国国会或本州法律为退伍军人提供福利服务的任何其他福利的核证副本。

（3）提供或搜索退伍军人管理局要求的用于确定任何人参与退伍军人管理局所提供的资助项目的资格的公开记录的核证副本。

（4）提交与第2项或第3项所述的申请或索赔相关的任何其他服务。

（b）（a）款中任何记录的核证副本，只能提供以下之一：

(1) The person who is the subject of the record upon presentation of proper photo identification.

(2) A family member or legal representative of the person who is the subject of the record upon presentation of proper photo identification and certification of their relationship to the subject of the record.

(3) A county office that provides veteran's benefits services upon written request of that office.

(4) A United States official upon written request of that official. A public officer or employee is liable on his or her official bond for failure or refusal to render the services.

§ 6108. Oaths of office; claim against counties

No officer of a county or judicial district shall charge or receive any fee or compensation for administering or certifying the oath of office or for filing or swearing to any claim or demand against any county in the State.

§ 6109. Receipt of fees; written account; officer liability

Every officer of a county or judicial district, upon receiving any fees for official duty or service, may be required by the person paying the fees to make out in writing and to deliver to the person a particular account of the fees. The account shall specify for what the fees, respectively, accrued, and the officer shall receipt it. If the officer refuses or neglects to do so when required, he is liable to the person paying the fees in treble the amount so paid.

§ 6110. Performance of services following payment; officer liability

Upon payment of the fees required by law, the officer shall perform the services required. For every failure or refusal to do so, the officer is liable upon his official bond.

§ 6203. False certificate or writing by officer

(a) Every officer authorized by law to make or give any certificate or other writing is guilty of a misdemeanor if he or she makes and delivers as true any certificate or writing containing statements which he or she knows to be false.

(b) Notwithstanding any other limitation of time described in Section 802 of the Penal Code, or any other provision of law, prosecution for a violation of this offense shall be commenced within four years after discovery of the commission of the offense, or within four years after the completion of the offense, whichever is later.

(c) The penalty provided by this section is not an exclusive remedy, and does not affect any other relief or remedy provided by law.

（1）提交正确的照片身份证明的记录主体。

（2）作为记录主体的人的家庭成员或法定代表人，提交适当的照片和身份证明以证明其与记录主体的关系。

（3）根据书面请求提供退伍军人福利服务的郡办事处。

（4）经书面要求的美国官员。公职人员或雇员应对其未履行或拒绝提供服务负责。

§6108 就职宣誓；向郡提交宣誓

郡或司法管辖区的公职人员不得收取任何关于管理或证明就职宣誓或者向郡提交誓言或宣誓书的费用或报酬。

§6109 费用收据；书面账号；公职人员责任

郡或司法管辖区的每一名公职人员，在收到任何职务税收或服务费后，如缴纳人要求，应向其书面提供费用明细和缴费所进入的特定账户。该账户应分别列明应收取的费用和官员收到的费用。如果公证人在被要求提供账户明细时拒绝或者不予理会，则其应向缴费人支付三倍的赔偿。

§6110 付款后履行的服务；公职人员责任

在支付法定的费用后，公职人员应履行相应的服务。如果拒绝或未能履行的，公职人员应以其任职保证金承担责任。

§6203 公职人员出具的虚假证明或文件

（a）法律授权的每一名公职人员所作出或发出的证明书或其他书面材料中，如果包含其明知是虚假陈述的内容，却将其描述为真，即构成轻罪。

（b）除了《刑法典》第802条和其他法律规定的期限限制外，违法犯罪行为应在犯罪行为发生之日或犯罪行为完成之日起四年内起诉，二者以较迟的时间为准。

（c）本条所提供的罚则并不是排他性救济，不影响法律规定的任何其他救济的适用。

§ 6800. Computation of time in which act is to be done

The time in which any act provided by law is to be done is computed by excluding the first day, and including the last, unless the last day is a holiday, and then it is also excluded.

§ 27287. Acknowledgment of execution or proof by subscribing witness required before recording; exceptions

before an instrument can be recorded its execution shall be acknowledged by the person executing it, or if executed by a corporation, by its president or secretary or other person executing it on behalf of the corporation, or, except for any power of attorney, quitclaim deed, grant deed, mortgage, deed of trust, security agreement, or other document affecting real property, proved by subscribing witness or as provided in Sections 1198 and 1199 of the Civil Code, and the acknowledgment or proof certified as prescribed by law. This section shall not apply to a trustee's deed resulting from a decree of foreclosure, or a nonjudicial foreclosure pursuant to Section 2924 of the Civil Code, or to a deed of reconveyance.

§ 66433. Content and form; application of article

The content and form of final maps shall be governed by the provisions of this article.

§ 66436. Statement of consent; necessity; exceptions; nonliability for omission of signature; notary acknow-ledgment

(a) A statement, signed and acknowledged by all parties having any record title interest in the subdivided real property, consenting to the preparation and recordation of the final map is required,

(c) A notary acknowledgment shall be deemed complete for recording without the official seal of the notary, so long as the name of the notary, the county of the notary's principal place of business, and the notary's commission expiration date are typed or printed below or immediately adjacent to the notary's signature in the acknowledgment.

§ 6800 日期的计算

法律规定的日期均不含起始日，但包含最后日，除非最后日为假期。

§ 27287 要求记录前签署见证人确认执行或证明；例外

在文书被记录之前，其执行应由执行人认证，如果执行人是法人，则由其总裁或秘书或代表该法人执行的其他人认证，除了授权书、撤销契约、授权契约、抵押、信托契约、担保协议或其他影响不动产的文件外，可通过签署见证人认证，或者依照《民法典》第1198条和第1199条的规定和法律规定的认证或证明方式进行认证。本条不适用于根据《民法典》第2924条规定的止赎令或非司法止赎令所产生的受托人契约，也不适用于财产转让契约。

§ 66433 内容和形式；条款的适用

文件的最终内容和格式应受本条规定的约束。

§ 66436 同意声明；必要性；例外情况；对遗漏签名不负责；公证确认

（a）关于细分不动产记录所有权的声明，同意预备书声明和记录的最终地图，需要由所有各方签署并承认。

（c）在确认书中，公证人的姓名、主要营业地点，以及公证人的任期到期日均应在公证人签名的下方或紧邻处打印或标注。

佛罗里达州公证法

West's Florida Statutes Annotated Currentness

Title X.
Public Officers, Employees, and Records
(Chapters 110-123)

>> Chapter 117. Notaries Public (Refs & Annos)

>>117.01. Appointment, application, suspension, revocation, application fee, bond, and oath

(1) The Governor may appoint as many notaries public as he or she deems necessary, each of whom shall be at least 18 years of age and a legal resident of the state. A permanent resident alien may apply and be appointed and shall file with his or her application a recorded Declaration of Domicile. The residence required for appointment must be maintained throughout the term of appointment. Notaries public shall be appointed for 4 years and shall use and exercise the office of notary public within the boundaries of this state. An applicant must be able to read, write, and understand the English language.

(2) The application for appointment shall be signed and sworn to by the applicant and shall be accompanied by a fee of $25, together with the $10 commission fee required by s. 113.01, and a surcharge of $4, which $4 is appropriated to the Executive Office of the Governor to be used to educate and assist notaries public. The Executive Office of the Governor may contract with private vendors to provide the services set forth in this section.

However, no commission fee shall be required for the issuance of a commission as a notary public to a veteran who served during a period of wartime service, as defined

佛罗里达州现行成文法

（韦斯特注释版）

第十篇
公职人员、雇员和记录
（第110–123章）

第 117 章　公证人（法条和注释）

117.01 委任、申请、中止、撤销、申请费、保证金和宣誓

（1）州长可委任必要数量的公证人，公证人必须年满18岁，为本州的合法居民。永久居住的外国居民可以申请并被任命为公证人，但应提交其户籍声明的记录。在任用期间应持续满足任命的住所要求。公证人任期为4年，在本州境内运用和行使公证人职责。申请人必须能够阅读、书写和理解英语。

（2）任命申请须由申请人签字并宣誓，缴纳25美元的费用，以及根据第113.01条所需的10美元手续费和4美元附加费，附加费将拨给州长执行办公室，用于支持教育以及协助公证人执行职务。州长执行办公室可以与私人供应商签订合同，以提供本节规定的服务。

但是，根据第1.01（14）条的定义，向战时服役的退伍军人以及被美国政府或被美国退伍军人部或其前身残疾评级达到50%以上残疾的人发行公证人委

in s. 1.01(14), and who has been rated by the United States Government or the United States Department of Veterans Affairs or its predecessor to have a disability rating of 50 percent or more; such a disability is subject to verification by the Secretary of State, who has authority to adopt reasonable procedures to implement this act.

The oath of office and notary bond required by this section shall also accompany the application and shall be in a form prescribed by the Department of State which shall require, but not be limited to, the following information: full name, residence address and telephone number, business address and telephone number, date of birth, race, sex, social security number, citizenship status, driver license number or the number of other official state-issued identification, affidavit of good character from someone unrelated to the applicant who has known the applicant for 1 year or more, a list of all professional licenses and commissions issued by the state during the previous 10 years and a statement as to whether or not the applicant has had such license or commission revoked or suspended, and a statement as to whether or not the applicant has been convicted of a felony, and, if there has been a conviction, a statement of the nature of the felony and restoration of civil rights.

The applicant may not use a fictitious or assumed name other than a nickname on an application for commission. The application shall be maintained by the Department of State for the full term of a notary commission. A notary public shall notify, in writing, the Department of State of any change in his or her business address, home telephone number, business telephone number, home address, or criminal record within 60 days after such change. The Governor may require any other information he or she deems necessary for determining whether an applicant is eligible for a notary public commission. Each applicant must swear or affirm on the application that the information on the application is true and correct.

(3) As part of the oath, the applicant must swear that he or she has read this chapter and knows the duties, responsibilities, limitations, and powers of a notary public.

(4) The Governor may suspend a notary public for any of the grounds provided in s. 7, Art. IV of the State Constitution. Grounds constituting malfeasance, misfeasance, or neglect of duty include, but are not limited to, the following:

(a) A material false statement on the application.

(b) A complaint found to have merit by the Governor.

任书时，不收取手续费。残疾登记需要得到州务卿的核查，州务卿有权采取合理的程序进行核查。

本条所规定的就职宣誓书和公证人保证金也应随同申请一并附上，并应采用州务院规定的格式，包括但不限于以下信息：全名、居住地址和电话号码、办公地址和工作电话、出生日期、种族、性别、社会保障号码、公民身份证号码，驾驶执照号码或其他州颁发的正式身份证件的数量，以及了解申请人1年以上的与申请人无利益关联的人员的对申请人具备良好品格的宣誓；过去10年内收到的所有国家专业执照和任命的清单；申请人是否有过类似许可证或任命被撤销或暂停的声明，以及申请人是否有被判有重罪的声明，如果申请人曾经被定罪，需要提供有关犯罪性质和恢复民事权利的声明。

申请人不得使用虚构的姓名或别名、昵称进行任职的申请。申请书在整个任期内由州务院保管。公证人应当在办公地址、住宅电话号码、办公电话号码、住址或犯罪记录发生变更后60日内书面通知州务院。州长可要求提供其认为必要的其他信息来确定申请人是否有资格获得公证人任命。每个申请人必须在申请上发誓或确认申请信息真实正确。

（3）作为宣誓的一部分，申请人必须发誓其已阅读本章的规定，并了解公证人的职责、责任、限制和权力。

（4）州长有权以州宪法第4条第7款规定的任何理由暂停公证人职务。构成渎职、失职或忽视职责的理由包括但不限于：

（a）申请材料存在虚假陈述。

（b）州长认为重要的投诉。

(c) Failure to cooperate or respond to an investigation by the Governor's office or the Department of State regarding a complaint.

(d) Official misconduct as defined in s. 838.022.

(e) False or misleading advertising relating to notary public services.

(f) Unauthorized practice of law.

(g) Failure to report a change in business or home address or telephone number, or failure to submit documentation to request an amended commission after a lawful name change, within the specified period of time.

(h) Commission of fraud, misrepresentation, or any intentional violation of this chapter.

(i) Charging fees in excess of fees authorized by this chapter.

(j) Failure to maintain the bond required by this section.

(5)(a) If a notary public receives notice from the Department of State that his or her office has been declared vacant, the notary shall forthwith mail or deliver to the Secretary of State his or her notary commission.

(b) A notary public who wishes to resign his or her commission, or a notary public who does not maintain legal residence in this state during the entire term of appointment, or a notary public whose resignation is required by the Governor, shall send a signed letter of resignation to the Governor and shall return his or her certificate of notary public commission. The resigning notary public shall destroy his or her official notary public seal of office, unless the Governor requests its return.

(6) No person may be automatically reappointed as a notary public. The application process must be completed regardless of whether an applicant is requesting his or her first notary commission, a renewal of a commission, or any subsequent commission.

(7)(a) A notary public shall, prior to executing the duties of the office and throughout the term of office, give bond, payable to any individual harmed as a result of a breach of duty by the notary public acting in his or her official capacity, in the amount of $7,500, conditioned for the due discharge of the office and shall take an oath that he or she will honestly, diligently, and faithfully discharge the duties of the notary public. The bond shall be approved and filed with the Department of State and executed by a surety company for hire duly authorized to transact business in this state.

(b) Any notary public whose term of appointment

（c）未能配合州长办公室或州务院进行有关投诉的调查或做出回应。

（d）第 838.022 条规定的职务不当行为。

（e）与公证服务有关的虚假或误导性广告。

（f）未经授权的法律执业。

（g）未能报告营业地或家庭住址或电话的变更或在合法名称变更后未能在规定期限内提交文件要求修改委任状。

（h）任职欺诈、虚假陈述或任何故意违反这一章的规定的行为。

（i）超出本章授权的收费项目进行收费。

（j）未能维持本条所要求的保证金。

（5）（a）如公证人收到州务院其职务已经被取消的通知，公证人应立即向州务卿邮寄或者递交其公证人委任书。

（b）在整个任职期间，如果公证人想要辞职，或不再维持境内的法定居所，或者州长要求其辞职，其应当向州长提交附有公证人签字的辞职信，并退回公证人委任书。除非州长要求归还，否则辞职的公证人应销毁其职务公章。

（6）任何人不得自动被再次任命为公证人，必须经过申请过程，无论申请人是第一次申请公证人任命，还是委任续期，或是任何后续的委任。

（7）（a）公证人在执行整个任期的职务之前，需缴纳 7500 美元的保证金，以便向因违反公证人职责而受到损害的个人支付，在任职期间应宣誓，其将诚实、勤勉、忠实履行公证人的职责。该保证金应经州务院批准并支付给州务院，并由经正式授权在本州办理业务的担保公司执行。

（b）任何任期延长至1999年1月1日的公证人，

extends beyond January 1, 1999, is required to increase the amount of his or her bond to $7,500 only upon reappointment on or after January 1, 1999.

(c) Beginning July 1, 1996, surety companies for hire which process notary public applications, oaths, affidavits of character, and bonds for submission to the Department of State must properly submit these documents in a software and hard copy format approved by the Department of State.

(8) Upon payment to any individual harmed as a result of a breach of duty by the notary public, the entity who has issued the bond for the notary public shall notify the Governor of the payment and the circumstances which led to the claim.

>>117.02. Repealed by Laws 1991, c. 91-291, s 8, eff. Jan. 1, 1992

>>117.021. Electronic notarization

(1) Any document requiring notarization may be notarized electronically.

The provisions of ss. 117.01, 117.03, 117.04, 117.05(1)-(11), (13), and (14), 117.105, and 117.107 apply to all notarizations under this section.

(2) In performing an electronic notarial act, a notary public shall use an electronic signature that is:

(a) Unique to the notary public;

(b) Capable of independent verification;

(c) Retained under the notary public's sole control; and

(d) Attached to or logically associated with the electronic document in a manner that any subsequent alteration to the electronic document displays evidence of the alteration.

(3) When a signature is required to be accompanied by a notary public seal, the requirement is satisfied when the electronic signature of the notary public contains all of the following seal information:

(a) The full name of the notary public exactly as provided on the notary public's application for commission;

(b) The words "Notary Public State of Florida";

(c) The date of expiration of the commission of the notary public; and

(d) The notary public's commission number.

(4) Failure of a notary public to comply with any of the requirements of this section may constitute grounds for suspension of the notary public's commission by the Exec-

在1999年1月1日以后再次被任命时，应将其保证金的金额增加至7500美元．

（c）从1996年7月1日起，担保公司出具公证申请、宣誓、品格宣誓书以及提交给州务院的保证金，必须以州务院规定的软件和硬件的拷贝格式提交。

（8）为公证人发放保证金的机构应将其因公证人违反职责而导致索赔并向受损害的个人付款的情况及时通知州长。

>> 第117.02条被1991年法律第91-291章第8条废除，于1992年1月1日生效

>>117.021. 电子公证书

（1）任何需要公证的文件都可以通过电子方式公证。

第117.01条、第117.03条、第117.04条、第117.05条第（1）项至第（11）项以及第（13）项、第（14）项、第117.105条和第117.107条的规定适用于本节下的所有公证行为。

（2）在进行电子公证时，公证人应使用满足以下条件的电子签名：

（a）特殊的专属于公证人的；

（b）能够进行独立核查；

（c）在公证人的专属控制下保管；以及

（d）对电子公证书的后续修改都能以留下显著证据的方式附于电子公证书，或符合逻辑地与电子公证书相联系。

（3）当签字需要附有公证人公章时，公证人的电子签章应包含以下所有满足要求的信息：

（a）与公证人任职申请上一致的公证人全名；

（b）含有"弗罗里达州公证人"字样；

（c）公证人任期的截止时间；

（d）公证人的委任号。

（4）未能遵守该部分的要求将作为州长办公室对公证人停职的理由。

utive Office of the Governor.

(5) The Department of State may adopt rules to ensure the security, reliability, and uniformity of signatures and seals authorized in this section.

>>117.03. Administration of oath

A notary public may administer an oath and make a certificate thereof when it is necessary for the execution of any writing or document to be published under the seal of a notary public. The notary public may not take an acknowledgment of execution in lieu of an oath if an oath is required.

>>117.04. Acknowledgments

A notary public is authorized to take the acknowledgments of deeds and other instruments of writing for record, as fully as other officers of this state.

>>117.045. Marriages

A notary public is authorized to solemnize the rites of matrimony. For solemnizing the rites of matrimony, the fee of a notary public may not exceed those provided by law to the clerks of the circuit court for like services.

>>117.05. Use of notary commission; unlawful use; notary fee; seal; duties employer liability; name change; advertising; photocopies; penalties

(1) No person shall obtain or use a notary public commission in other than his or her legal name, and it is unlawful for a notary public to notarize his or her own signature. Any person applying for a notary public commission must submit proof of identity to the Department of State if so requested.

Any person who violates the provisions of this subsection is guilty of a felony of the third degree, punishable as provided in s. 775.082, s. 775.083, or s. 775.084.

(2)(a) The fee of a notary public may not exceed $10 for any one notarial act, except as provided in s. 117.045.

(b) A notary public may not charge a fee for witnessing an absentee ballot in an election, and must witness such a ballot upon the request of an elector, provided the notarial act is in accordance with the provisions of this chapter.

(3)(a) A notary public seal shall be affixed to all notarized paper documents and shall be of the rubber stamp type and shall include the words "Notary Public-State of Florida." The seal shall also include the name of the notary public, the date of expiration of the commission of the notary public, and the commission number. The rubber

（5）州务院有权制定规则以确保经本条授权的签名和印章的安全、可靠、一致。

>>117.03 宣誓

当公证人认为有必要时，为执行加盖有公证人印章的任何书面材料或文件，公证人可以出示誓言并作出证明。如果宣誓是必经程序，则公证人不得以承认执行来取代宣誓。

>>117.04 确认

公证人有权与本州其他官员一样，承认契约和其他书面确认书。

>>117.045 婚姻

公证人被授予举办婚礼的权利，为了举行婚礼仪式，公证人的收费不得超过法律规定的巡回法庭书记员提供类似服务的费用。

>>117.05 公证人任命的使用；非法使用；公证费；公证公章；职务；雇主责任；名称变更；广告；影印本；处罚

（1）任何人不得以其法定姓名之外的名字取得或使用公证人任命，公证人不得公证自己的签名。任何申请公证人任命的人，如果有要求，必须向州务院递交身份证件。

任何人违反本款的规定，均属犯第三级重罪，应按照第 775.082 条、第 775.083 条或第 775.084 条的规定予以处罚。

（2）（a）任何公证人收取的公证费不得超过 10 美元，除了第 117.045 条规定的情况。

（b）公证人在选举中不得收取缺席投票的费用，只要公证行为符合本章规定，应按照选民的要求进行投票。

（3）（a）所有经过公证的纸质文件上应盖有公证公章，印章应为橡皮戳类型，并包括"佛罗里达公证人"字样。印章还应包括公证人的名称、公证人任职的到期日以及任职编号。橡皮印章必须以逼真的可复写的炭黑墨水形式盖在经过公证的纸张文件中。每个公证人应在纸质文件上手签、印刷、输入或印上其与

stamp seal must be affixed to the notarized paper document in photographically reproducible black ink. Every notary public shall print, type, or stamp below his or her signature on a paper document his or her name exactly as commissioned. An impression-type seal may be used in addition to the rubber stamp seal, but the rubber stamp seal shall be the official seal for use on a paper document, and the impression-type seal may not be substituted therefor

(b) The notary public official seal and the certificate of notary public commission are the exclusive property of the notary public and must be kept under the direct and exclusive control of the notary public. The seal and certificate of commission must not be surrendered to an employer upon termination of employment, regardless of whether the employer paid for the seal or for the commission.

(c) A notary public whose official seal is lost, stolen, or believed to be in the possession of another person shall immediately notify the Department of State or the Governor in writing.

(d) Any person who unlawfully possesses a notary public official seal or any papers or copies relating to notarial acts is guilty of a misdemeanor of the second degree, punishable as provided in s. 775.082 or s. 775.083.

(4) When notarizing a signature, a notary public shall complete a jurat or notarial certificate in substantially the same form as those found in subsection (13). The jurat or certificate of acknowledgment shall contain the following elements:

(a) The venue stating the location of the notarization in the format, "State of Florida, County of _____."

(b) The type of notarial act performed, an oath or an acknowledgment, evidenced by the words "sworn" or "acknowledged."

(c) That the signer personally appeared before the notary public at the time of the notarization.

(d) The exact date of the notarial act.

(e) The name of the person whose signature is being notarized. It is presumed, absent such specific notation by the notary public, that notarization is to all signatures.

(f) The specific type of identification the notary public is relying upon in identifying the signer, either based on personal knowledge or satisfactory evidence specified in subsection (5).

(g) The notary's official signature.

(h) The notary's name, typed, printed, or stamped below the signature.

(i) The notary's official seal affixed below or to either

任职书上一致的签名。除橡皮印章外，还可以使用按压式印章，但是橡皮印章应为用于纸张文件的官方印章，而不得替换为按压式印章。

（b）公证人公章和公证人委任书是公证人的专有财产，必须由公证人直接、排他地控制。无论雇主是否为印章或委任书支付费用，印章和委任书不得在终止雇佣后交回雇主。

（c）公证人的公章丢失、被盗或认为已被他人占有的，应当立即以书面形式通知州务院或州长。

（d）任何非法持有公证人公章或与公证行为有关的文件或复印件的人，即属第二级轻罪，应当按照第775.082 条或第 775.083 条的规定予以处罚。

（4）当确认签名时，公证人应以第 13 款规定的格式填写宣誓证明书或公证书。宣誓证明书或确认书应包含以下内容：

（a）以"佛罗里达州，_____ 郡"的格式表示所描述的公证地点。

（b）公证行为的类型，宣誓或确认，由"已宣誓"或"已确认"一词证明。

（c）公证人在公证时，签名人应亲自出现在公证人面前。

（d）公证行为的准确日期。

（e）在公证文书上签名的人的姓名。如果公证人没有特别备注，公证适用于所有的签名。

（f）公证人依据个人知识或第 5 款规定的充分证据来确定签字者身份所依赖的具体身份识别类型。

（g）公证人的官方签名。

（h）公证人的名字，在签名下方键入、印制或盖章。

（i）公证人的公章应印在公证人签名的下方或任

side of the notary's signature.

(5) A notary public may not notarize a signature on a document unless he or she personally knows, or has satisfactory evidence, that the person whose signature is to be notarized is the individual who is described in and who is executing the instrument. A notary public shall certify in the certificate of acknowledgment or jurat the type of identification, either based on personal knowledge or other form of identification, upon which the notary public is relying.

(a) For purposes of this subsection, "personally knows" means having an acquaintance, derived from association with the individual, which establishes the individual's identity with at least a reasonable certainty.

(b) For the purposes of this subsection, "satisfactory evidence" means the absence of any information, evidence, or other circumstances which would lead a reasonable person to believe that the person whose signature is to be notarized is not the person he or she claims to be and any one of the following:

1. The sworn written statement of one credible witness personally known to the notary public or the sworn written statement of two credible witnesses whose identities are proven to the notary public upon the presentation of satisfactory evidence that each of the following is true:

a. That the person whose signature is to be notarized is the person named in the document;

b. That the person whose signature is to be notarized is personally known to the witnesses;

c. That it is the reasonable belief of the witnesses that the circumstances of the person whose signature is to be notarized are such that it would be very difficult or impossible for that person to obtain another acceptable form of identification;

d. That it is the reasonable belief of the witnesses that the person whose signature is to be notarized does not possess any of the identification documents specified in subparagraph 2.; and

e. That the witnesses do not have a financial interest in nor are parties to the underlying transaction; or

2. Reasonable reliance on the presentation to the notary public of any one of the following forms of identification, if the document is current or has been issued within the past 5 years and bears a serial or other identifying number:

a. A Florida identification card or driver license issued by the public agency authorized to issue driver li-

何一边。

（5）公证人不得对文件上的签名进行公证，除非其亲自知道或有充分证据表明被公证姓名的人是文件中提到的人，也是正在执行文书的人。公证人应依据个人知识或其他形式的身份证明对确认证书或宣誓证书中的身份识别类型进行认定。

（a）在本款中，"亲自知道"是指与个人有联系的熟人，其至少具有合理的确定性以确定个人的身份。

（b）本款中，"充分证据"是指没有任何信息、证据或其他情况会导致一个合理的人相信被公证签名的人不是他或她所声称的人或下列任何情形：

1. 公证人熟悉的一个可信证人宣誓的书面声明或者两名可信证人宣誓的书面声明，该证人的身份因符合下列事实而被公证人证明：

a. 文件中出现的人的签名被公证；

b. 被证人所熟知的人的签名被公证；

c. 证人合理地认为签名被公证的人员，其很难或不可能获得另一个可接受的身份识别形式；

d. 证人认为，经过公证的人员不具有第2项规定的任何身份证明文件；并且

e. 在本交易中，证人不享有经济利益，也不是交易的当事人；或者

2. 公证人基于以下任何一种身份证明文件作出的陈述具有合理信赖性，只要该文件是现行有效的，或者是在过去5年内发出的，并附有序列号或其他识别号码：

a. 获得有权发放驾驶执照的公共机构签发的佛罗里达州身份证或驾驶执照；

censes;

b. A passport issued by the Department of State of the United States;

c. A passport issued by a foreign government if the document is stamped by the United States Bureau of Citizenship and Immigration Services;

d. A driver license or an identification card issued by a public agency authorized to issue driver licenses in a state other than Florida, a territory of the United States, or Canada or Mexico;

e. An identification card issued by any branch of the armed forces of the United States;

f. An inmate identification card issued on or after January 1, 1991, by the Florida Department of Corrections for an inmate who is in the custody of the department;

g. An inmate identification card issued by the United States Department of Justice, Bureau of Prisons, for an inmate who is in the custody of the department;

h. A sworn, written statement from a sworn law enforcement officer that the forms of identification for an inmate in an institution of confinement were confiscated upon confinement and that the person named in the document is the person whose signature is to be notarized; or

i. An identification card issued by the United States Bureau of Citizenship and Immigration Services.

(6) The employer of a notary public shall be liable to the persons involved for all damages proximately caused by the notary's official misconduct, if the notary public was acting within the scope of his or her employment at the time the notary engaged in the official misconduct.

(7) Any person who acts as or otherwise willfully impersonates a notary public while not lawfully appointed and commissioned to perform notarial acts is guilty of a misdemeanor of the second degree, punishable as provided in s. 775.082 or s. 775.083.

(8) Any notary public who knowingly acts as a notary public after his or her commission has expired is guilty of a misdemeanor of the second degree, punishable as provided in s. 775.082 or s. 775.083.

(9) Any notary public who lawfully changes his or her name shall, within 60 days after such change, request an amended commission from the Secretary of State and shall send $25, his or her current commission, and a notice of change form, obtained from the Secretary of State, which shall include the new name and contain a specimen of his or her official signature. The Secretary of State shall issue an amended commission to the notary public

b 美国国务院颁发的护照；

c. 外国政府签发的护照，且该护照已由美国公民和移民服务局盖章；

d. 在除佛罗里达州外美国境内的其他州，或加拿大、墨西哥授权签发驾驶执照的公共机构签发的驾照或身份证；

e. 美国武装部队发行的身份证；

f. 1991年1月1日当日或之后由佛罗里达惩教部门签发给被该部门拘留的囚犯的身份证；

g. 由美国司法部监狱管理局发出的由该部门监护的囚犯的身份证；

h. 执法人员作出的宣誓、书面声明，证明监禁机构的囚犯身份证明文件已被没收，但文件中指定的人员是经过公证的人员；或者

i. 由美国公民和移民服务局颁发的身份证。

（6）如果公证人在其工作范围内从事职务行为时发生了不当行为，公证人的雇主应对公证人的职务违法行为所造成的损害承担赔偿责任。

（7）任何通过不合法指定和任命进行公证行为或以其他方式故意冒充公证人的人，均构成违反第775.082条或第775.083条规定的第二级轻罪，应承担刑事责任。

（8）公证人在其任职期满后故意继续作为公证人行事的，构成违反第775.082条或第775.083条规定的第二级轻罪，应承担刑事责任。

（9）合法更改其姓名的公证人应当在姓名变更后60日内向州务卿提出修改委任书的申请，并交付25美元和从州务卿获得当前委任书和变更通知书，其中应包括新名称，并载有其正式签名的样本。州务卿应以新姓名向公证人发布经修改的委任书。公证人保证金的附文必须附有变更通知单。在向州务卿提交变更通知书和附文后，公证人可以继续以原名从事公证行为60日或直到收到修改后的委任书为止，二者以较

in the new name. A rider to the notary public's bond must accompany the notice of change form. After submitting the required notice of change form and rider to the Secretary of State, the notary public may continue to perform notarial acts in his or her former name for 60 days or until receipt of the amended commission, whichever date is earlier.

(10) A notary public who is not an attorney who advertises the services of a notary public in a language other than English, whether by radio, television, signs, pamphlets, newspapers, or other written communication, with the exception of a single desk plaque, shall post or otherwise include with the advertisement a notice in English and in the language used for the advertisement. The notice shall be of a conspicuous size, if in writing, and shall state: "I AM NOT AN ATTORNEY LICENSED TO PRACTICE LAW IN THE STATE OF FLORIDA, AND I MAY NOT GIVE LEGAL ADVICE OR ACCEPT FEES FOR LEGAL ADVICE." If the advertisement is by radio or television, the statement may be modified but must include substantially the same message.

(11) Literal translation of the phrase "Notary Public" into a language other than English is prohibited in an advertisement for notarial services.

(12) (a) A notary public may supervise the making of a photocopy of an original document and attest to the trueness of the copy, provided the document is neither a vital record in this state, another state, a territory of the United States, or another country, nor a public record, if a copy can be made by the custodian of the public record.

(b) A notary public must use a certificate in substantially the following form in notarizing an attested copy:
　　　　STATE OF FLORIDA
　　　　COUNTY OF _____
　　On this ___ day of _____, (year), I attest that the preceding or attached document is a true, exact, complete, and unaltered photocopy made by me of (description of document) presented to me by the document's custodian, _____, and, to the best of my knowledge, that the photocopied document is neither a vital record nor a public record, certified copies of which are available from an official source other than a notary public.
　　(Official Notary Signature and Notary Seal)
　　(Name of Notary Typed, Printed or Stamped)

(13) The following notarial certificates are sufficient for the purposes indicated, if completed with the information required by this chapter. The specification of forms

早的时间为准。

（10）以英文以外的其他语言宣传公证人的服务的非律师公证人，无论是通过无线电、电视、标志、宣传册、报纸或其他书面通讯，除了单张桌牌外，应张贴或在广告中加入以英文和用于广告的其他语言进行的提示。提示应采用书面形式，声明："我不是在佛罗里达州被授权从事法律事务的律师，我不会对法律咨询业务提供法律建议或接受费用。"如果广告是通过广播或电视发布，则可以修改该声明的措辞，但必须包括基本相同的信息。

（11）在公证服务的广告中禁止将"公证人"一词字面直译成英文以外的语言。

（12）（a）公证人可以监督原件的副本的制作，并证明该副本的真实性，前提是该文件既不是本州、其他州、美国境内或另一个国家的重要记录，也不是公共记录，如果公共记录的保管人可以提供副本。

（b）公证人必须出具大致按照下列形式进行公证核证副本的证明文件：
　　弗罗里达州
　　_____郡
　　在____年____月___日，我证明上述或附带的文件是由我提供的真实、完整、未经修改的副本（由文件的保管人向我提供的文件）_____，且据我所知，该副本既不是重要记录，又不是可从公证人以外的官方来源获取的公共记录。

（官方公证人签名及公证公章）
（公证人姓名，打印或盖章）

（13）如果完成了本章要求的信息，以下格式的公证书足以表明其目的。本款规定的表格并不排除使用其他形式。

under this subsection does not preclude the use of other forms.

(a) For an oath or affirmation:
STATE OF FLORIDA
COUNTY OF _____
Sworn to (or affirmed) and subscribed before me this _____ day of ___, (year), by (name of person making statement) .

(Signature of Notary Public--State of Florida)

(Print, Type, or Stamp Commissioned Name of Notary Public)

Personally Known _____ OR Produced Identification _____

Type of Identification Produced _____

(b) For an acknowledgment in an individual capacity:
STATE OF FLORIDA
COUNTY OF _____
The foregoing instrument was acknowledged before me this ___ day of ___, (year) , by (name of person acknowledging) .

(Signature of Notary Public--State of Florida)

(Print, Type, or Stamp Commissioned Name of Notary Public)

Personally Known _____ OR Produced Identification _____

Type of Identification Produced _____

(c) For an acknowledgment in a representative capacity:
STATE OF FLORIDA
COUNTY OF _____
The foregoing instrument was acknowledged before me this _____ day of _____, (year), by (name of person) as (type of authority, e.g. officer, trustee, attorney in fact) for (name of party on behalf of whom instrument was executed) .

(Signature of Notary Public--State of Florida)

(Print, Type, or Stamp Commissioned Name of Notary Public)

Personally Known _____ OR Produced Identification _____

Type of Identification Produced _____

(14) A notary public must make reasonable accommodations to provide notarial services to persons with disabilities.

(a) A notary public may notarize the signature of a person who is blind after the notary public has read the entire instrument to that person.

(b) A notary public may notarize the signature of a

（a）对于宣誓或声明
佛罗里达州
_____郡
_____年___月___日在我面前宣誓（或确认）、签署，由（制作声明者的姓名）制作。

（公证人签名，佛罗里达州）
（公证人的任职姓名，打印或盖章）

被_____所熟知或由_____颁发的身份证明

所使用身份证明类型_____

（b）个人能力的承认
佛罗里达州
_____郡
上述文书在_____年___月_____日在我面前被（承认人姓名）承认。

（公证人签名，佛罗里达州）
（公证人的任职姓名，打印或盖章）

被_____所熟知或由_____颁发的身份证明

所使用身份证明类型_____

（c）相关能力的承认
佛罗里达州
_____郡
上述文书在_____年___月_____日在我面前被（承认人姓名）确认为（代理人的类型，例如官员、受托人、代理人）（代表执行文件的缔约方的名称）。

（公证人签名，佛罗里达州）
（公证人的任职姓名，打印或盖章）

被_____所熟知或由_____颁发的身份证明
所使用身份证明类型_____

（14）公证人必须采取适当的方式，为残疾人提供公证服务。

（a）公证人将全部文书内容向盲人朗读后，可以对盲人的签名进行公证。

（b）公证人可以公证记号签名，如果

person who signs with a mark if:

　　1. The document signing is witnessed by two disinterested persons;

　　2. The notary prints the person's first name at the beginning of the designated signature line and the person's last name at the end of the designated signature line; and

　　3. The notary prints the words "his (or her) mark" below the person's signature mark.

　　(c) The following notarial certificates are sufficient for the purpose of notarizing for a person who signs with a mark:

　　1. For an oath or affirmation:

(First Name) (Last Name)

His (or Her) Mark

STATE OF FLORIDA

COUNTY OF _____

　　Sworn to and subscribed before me this ___ day of _____, (year), by (name of person making statement), who signed with a mark in the presence of these witnesses:

(Signature of Notary Public--State of Florida)

(Print, Type, or Stamp Commissioned Name of Notary Public)

　　Personally Known _____ OR Produced Identification _____

Type of Identification Produced _____

　　2. For an acknowledgment in an individual capacity:

(First Name) (Last Name)

His (or Her) Mark

STATE OF FLORIDA

COUNTY OF _____

　　The foregoing instrument was acknowledged before me this ___ day of _____, (year), by (name of person acknowledging), who signed with a mark in the presence of these witnesses:

(Signature of Notary Public--State of Florida)

(Print, Type, or Stamp Commissioned Name of Notary Public

　　Personally Known _____ OR Produced Identification _____

Type of Identification Produced _____

　　(d) A notary public may sign the name of a person whose signature is to be notarized when that person is physically unable to sign or make a signature mark on a document if:

　　1. The person with a disability directs the notary to sign in his or her presence;

　　2. The document signing is witnessed by two disin-

1.文件签字由两个无利害关系的人见证；

2.公证人在指定签名行开头打印该人的名字，并在指定签名行末尾打印该人的姓氏；以及

3.公证人在该人的签名标记下方印上"他（或她）的标记"。

（c）以下公证证书足以为使用标记签名的人进行公证：

1.宣誓或声明

（名字）（姓氏）

他（或她）的标记

佛罗里达州

_____郡

_____年_____月___日，（声明人的姓名）在我面前发誓并签字，在下列证人面前以标记签名签署文件：

（公证人签名，佛罗里达州）

（公证人的任职姓名，打印或盖章）

被_____所熟知或由_____颁发的身份证明

所使用身份证明类型_____

2.个人能力的确认

（名字）（姓氏）

他（或她）的标记

佛罗里达州

_____郡

上述文书在_____年_____月___日在我面前被（确认人姓名）确认，在证人见证下用标记签名。

（公证人签名，佛罗里达州）

（公证人的任职姓名，打印或盖章）

被_____所熟知或由_____颁发的身份证明

所使用身份证明类型_____

（d）如果存在以下情况，当签名人的身体状况无法在文件上签字或签署标记时，公证人可以签署将被公证的人的签名：

1.残疾人指示公证人进行签名；

2.两个无利害关系的人见证了这份文件的签字；

terested persons;

3. The notary writes below the signature the following statement: "Signature affixed by notary, pursuant to s. 117.05(14), Florida Statutes," and states the circumstances of the signing in the notarial certificate.

(e) The following notarial certificates are sufficient for the purpose of notarizing for a person with a disability who directs the notary to sign his or her name:

1. For an oath or affirmation:
STATE OF FLORIDA
COUNTY OF _____

Sworn to (or affirmed) before me this ____ day of _____, (year), by (name of person making statement), and subscribed by (name of notary) at the direction of and in the presence of (name of person making statement), and in the presence of these witnesses:

(Signature of Notary Public--State of Florida)

(Print, Type, or Stamp Commissioned Name of Notary Public)

Personally Known _____ OR Produced Identification _____

Type of Identification Produced _____

2. For an acknowledgment in an individual capacity:
STATE OF FLORID
COUNTY OF _____

The foregoing instrument was acknowledged before me this ____ day of ____, (year), by (name of person acknowledging) and subscribed by (name of notary) at the direction of and in the presence of (name of person acknowledging), and in the presence of these witnesses:

(Signature of Notary Public--State of Florida)

(Print, Type, or Stamp Commissioned Name of Notary Public)

Personally Known _____ OR Produced Identification _____

Type of Identification Produced _____

>>117.06. Validity of acts prior to April 1, 1903

Any and all notarial acts that were done by any notary public in the state prior to April 1, 1903, which would have been valid had not the term of office of the notary public expired, are declared to be valid.

>>117.07. Repealed by Laws 1991, c. 91-291, s 8, eff. Jan. 1, 1992

>>117.08. Repealed by Laws 1991, c. 91-291, s 8, eff. Jan. 1, 1992

3. 公证人在签名下方写下如下声明:"公证人根据《佛罗里达州章程》第117.05(14)条签字,"并在公证书上说明签字的情况。

(e)以下公证证书足以证明残疾人指示公证人签署其姓名:

1. 宣誓或声明
佛罗里达州
_____郡

____年____月____日,_____(作出声明的人员的姓名)在我面前宣誓(或确认),在_____(公证人的姓名)的指示和出席下由(公证人的姓名)签署,并有见证人的参与。

(公证人签名,佛罗里达州)
(公证人的任职姓名,打印或盖章)

被_____所熟知或由_____颁发的身份证明

所使用身份证明类型_____

2. 个人能力的承认
佛罗里达州
_____郡

____年____月____日上述文件在我面前由(作出确认的人员的姓名)确认,并在(作出确认的人员的姓名)(公证人的姓名)的指示和见证下由(公证人的姓名)签署,并有见证人的参与。

(公证人签名,佛罗里达州)
(公证人的任职姓名,打印或盖章)

被_____所熟知或由_____颁发的身份证明

所使用身份证明类型_____

>>117.06 1903年4月1日前的行为的效力
任何公证人在1903年4月1日以前进行的公证行为在公证人任期未届满时均被宣告为有效。

>>117.07 本条被1991年法律第91-291章第8条废止,自1992年7月1日起生效

>> 117.08 本条被1991年法律第91-291章第8条废止,自1992年1月1日生效

>>117.09.Repealed by Laws 1991, c. 91-291, s 8, eff. Jan. 1, 1992

>>117.10. Law enforcement and correctional officers

Law enforcement officers, correctional officers, and correctional probation officers, as defined in s. 943.10, and traffic accident investigation officers and traffic infraction enforcement officers, as described in s. 316.640, are authorized to administer oaths when engaged in the performance of official duties. Sections 117.01, 117.04, 117.045, 117.05, and 117.103 do not apply to the provisions of this section. An officer may not notarize his or her own signature.

>>117.103. Certification of notary's authority by Secretary of State

A notary public is not required to record his or her notary public commission in an office of a clerk of the circuit court. If certification of the notary public's commission is required, it must be obtained from the Secretary of State. Upon the receipt of a written request and a fee of $10 payable to the Secretary of State, the Secretary of State shall issue a certificate of notarial authority, in a form prescribed by the Secretary of State, which shall include a statement explaining the legal qualifications and authority of a notary public in this state.

>>117.105. False or fraudulent acknowledgments; penalty

A notary public who falsely or fraudulently takes an acknowledgment of an instrument as a notary public or who falsely or fraudulently makes a certificate as a notary public or who falsely takes or receives an acknowledgment of the signature on a written instrument is guilty of a felony of the third degree, punishable as provided in s. 775.082, s. 775.083, or s.775.084.

>>117.107. Prohibited act

(1) A notary public may not use a name or initial in signing certificates other than that by which the notary public is commissioned.

(2) A notary public may not sign notarial certificates using a facsimile signature stamp unless the notary public has a physical disability that limits or prohibits his or her ability to make a written signature and unless the notary public has first submitted written notice to the Department of State with an exemplar of the facsimile signature stamp.

(3) A notary public may not affix his or her signature

>> 117.09 本条被 1991 年法律第 91-291 章第 8 条废止，自 1992 年 1 月 1 日生效

>>117.10 执法和惩教人员

根据第 943.10 条定义的执法人员、矫正人员和惩教缓刑官员，根据第 316.640 条定义的交通事故调查人员和交通违法执法人员，在执行公务时有权执行宣誓。第 117.01 条、第 117.04 条、第 117.045 条、第 117.05 条和第 117.103 条不适用于本条的规定。公证人不得公证自己的签名。

>>117.103 州务卿对公证人的职权证书

公证人不需要在巡回法庭书记员的办公室记录其公证人委任书。如果需要公证人委任书，必须从州务卿处获得。在向州务卿递交书面请求和 10 美元费用的情况下，州务卿应以规定的格式发放公证证书，其中应包括解释法定资格的声明以及公证人在本州的职权。

>>117.105 虚假或欺诈性承认；罚款

公证人虚假或欺诈地承认文书，或虚假或欺诈地制作公证人的证明书，或者虚假地接收或接受书面文书或承认文书上的签字的，即构成三级重罪，将按照第 775.082 条、第 775.083 条或第 775.084 条的规定予以处罚。

>>117.107 禁止的行为

（1）公证人不得在未经授权的认证书上使用姓名或者姓名的首字母缩写。

（2）公证人不得使用传真签字印章签署公证书，除非公证人有身体残障，限制或使其丧失了书面签字的能力，且公证人预先向州部门书面提交了传真签名的印鉴样本。

（3）公证人不得将其签名贴在空白形式的宣誓书

to a blank form of affidavit or certificate of acknowledgment and deliver that form to another person with the intent that it be used as an affidavit or acknowledgment.

(4) A notary public may not take the acknowledgment of or administer an oath to a person whom the notary public actually knows to have been adjudicated mentally incapacitated by a court of competent jurisdiction, where the acknowledgment or oath necessitates the exercise of a right that has been removed pursuant to s. 744.3215(2) or (3), and where the person has not been restored to capacity as a matter of record.

(5) A notary public may not notarize a signature on a document if it appears that the person is mentally incapable of understanding the nature and effect of the document at the time of notarization.

(6) A notary public may not take the acknowledgment of a person who does not speak or understand the English language, unless the nature and effect of the instrument to be notarized is translated into a language which the person does understand.

(7) A notary public may not change anything in a written instrument after it has been signed by anyone.

(8) A notary public may not amend a notarial certificate after the notarization is complete.

(9) A notary public may not notarize a signature on a document if the person whose signature is being notarized is not in the presence of the notary public at the time the signature is notarized. Any notary public who violates this subsection is guilty of a civil infraction, punishable by penalty not exceeding $5,000, and such violation constitutes malfeasance and misfeasance in the conduct of official duties. It is no defense to the civil infraction specified in this subsection that the notary public acted without intent to defraud. A notary public who violates this subsection with the intent to defraud is guilty of violating s. 117.105.

(10) A notary public may not notarize a signature on a document if the document is incomplete or blank. However, an endorsement or assignment in blank of a negotiable or nonnegotiable note and the assignment in blank of any instrument given as security for such note is not deemed incomplete.

(11) A notary public may not notarize a signature on a document if the person whose signature is to be notarized is the spouse, son, daughter, mother, or father of the notary public.

(12) A notary public may not notarize a signature on a document if the notary public has a financial interest

或确认书上,并将该表格交付给打算将其作为宣誓书或确认书使用的其他人。

(4)对公证人明知被具有管辖权的法院裁定为精神上无行为能力的人,根据第744.3215条第2项或第3项,其已不具备宣誓以获得行为能力的权利并且该人不存在已恢复行为能力的记录,则公证人不得承认或管理其宣誓、确认书。

(5)如果在公证时,该人员在精神上无法理解文件的性质和效果,则公证人不得在文件上对其进行公证。

(6)公证人不得对不会说英语、无法理解英语的人进行文书确认,除非经过公证的文书的性质和效果已被翻译成该人所了解的语言。

(7)公证人不得在所有人签字后对书面文书作出任何改变。

(8)公证完成后,任何人不得修改公证书。

(9)如果在公证时该人员未出现在公证人面前,公证人不得对文件上的签名进行公证。公证人违反本款规定构成民事违法行为的,可被处以不超过5000美元的罚款,该违法行为构成公务人员渎职行为。在公证人没有诈骗故意时,本款规定的民事违法行为不被认为是故意为之。故意违反本款的公证人构成违反第117.105条的刑事犯罪。

(10)如果文件不完整或存在空白,公证人不得对文件上的签名进行公证。但是,可转让或不可转让票据进行空白的背书或转让,以及作为该票据担保的任何文书的空白转让不被视为不完整。

(11)如果被公证人是公证人的配偶、儿子、女儿、母亲、父亲,公证人不得对其签名进行公证。

(12)如果公证人对基础交易有经济利益或者是基础交易的一方当事人时,公证人不得对文件上的签

in or is a party to the underlying transaction; however, a notary public who is an employee may notarize a signature for his or her employer, and this employment does not constitute a financial interest in the transaction nor make the notary a party to the transaction under this subsection as long as he or she does not receive a benefit other than his or her salary and the fee for services as a notary public authorized by law. For purposes of this subsection, a notary public who is an attorney does not have a financial interest in and is not a party to the underlying transaction evidenced by a notarized document if he or she notarizes a signature on that document for a client for whom he or she serves as an attorney of record and he or she has no interest in the document other than the fee paid to him or her for legal services and the fee authorized by law for services as a notary public.

>>117.108. Validity of acts, seals, and certificates prior to January 1, 1995

A notarial act performed, a notarial certificate signed, or a notarial seal used by any notary public before January 1, 1995, which would have been valid under the laws in effect in this state on January 1, 1991, is valid.

>>117.20. Repealed by Laws 1999, c. 99-251, s 165, eff. July 1, 1999

名进行公证。但是，作为雇员的公证人可以公证其雇主的签名，这项工作不构成在交易中存在经济利益，也不会使公证人成为本款规定的交易一方当事人，只要其并未得到工资和法律授权的公证人服务费以外的其他福利。在本款中，作为律师的公证人作为代理人为被代理人进行文书公证，不属于本款规定的具有经济利益或属于公证文件的一方当事人的情形，如果他或她为其以记录律师服务的雇主公证，只要其在提供法律服务的费用以及法律授权的公证人服务费以外，没有收取其他费用。

>>117.108 1995 年 1 月 1 日前的行为、印章和证书的有效性

1991 年 1 月 1 日前，公证人已完成的公证行为、已签署的公证书、已使用的公证公章根据该州 1995 年 1 月 1 日生效的法律仍为有效。

>> 117.20 本条被 1991 年法律第 99-251 章第 165 条废止，自 1999 年 7 月 1 日生效

伊利诺伊州公证法

ILLINOIS NOTARY PUBLIC ACT

ARTICLE I GENERAL PROVISIONS

1-101. Short Title.

This Act may be cited as the Illinois Notary Public Act.

1-102. Purposes and Rules of Construction.

(a) This Act shall be construed and applied to promote its underlying purposesand policies.

(b) The underlying purposes and policies of this Act are:

(1) to simplify, clarify, and modernize the law governing notaries public; and

(2) to promote, serve, and protect the public interest.

1-103 Prospective Effect of Act.

This Act applies prospectively. Nothing in this Act shall be construed to revoke any notary public commission existing on the effective date of this Act. All reappointments of notarial commissions shall be obtained in accordance with this Act.

1-104 Notary Public and Notarization Defined.

(a)The terms "notary public" and "notary" are used interchangeably to mean any individual appointed and commissioned to perform notarial acts.

(b) "Notarization" means the performance of a notarial act.

(c) "Accredited immigration representative" means a not-for-profit organization recognized by the Board of Immigration Appeals under 8 C.F.R. 292.2(a) and employees

伊利诺伊州公证法

第1条 一般条款

1–101 简称

本法简称为《伊利诺伊州公证法》。

1–102 立法目的与规范

（a）本法以促进其基本目的和政策为目标而设立和适用。

（b）本法的基本目的和政策目标是：

（1）简化、明晰现代化公证执法；和

（2）促进、服务和保护公共利益。

1–103 本法的效力

本法不具有溯及力。本法不得废除任何在本法生效之日前已完成的公证人任命。所有公证人的重新任命，均按照本法规定。

1–104 公证人和公证的定义

（a）"公证人"是指任何被指定和任命进行公证行为的个人。

（b）"公证"是指进行公证行为。

（c）"经认可的移民事务代表"是指根据 8 C.F.R. 292.2（a）由移民上诉局认可的非营利组织和根据 8 C.F.R.292.2（d）认证的组织的雇员。

of those organizations accredited under 8 C.F.R. 292.2(d) .

ARTICLE II APPOINTMENT PROVISIONS

2-101. Appointment.

The Secretary of State may appoint and commission as notaries public for a four-year term as many persons resident in a county in this State as he deems necessary. The Secretary of State may appoint and commission as notaries public for a one-year term as many persons who are residents of a state bordering Illinois whose place of work or business is within a county in this State as the Secretary deems necessary, but only if the laws of that state authorize residents of Illinois to be appointed and commissioned as notaries public in that state.

2-102. Application.

Every applicant for appointment and commission as a notary shall complete an application form furnished by the Secretary of State to be filed with the Secretary of State, stating:

(a) the applicant's official name, which contains his or her last name and at least the initial of the first name;

(b) the county in which the applicant resides or, if the applicant is a resident of a state bordering Illinois, the county in Illinois in which that person's principal place of work or principal place of business is located;

(c) the applicant's residence address and business address, if any, or any address at which an applicant will use a notary public commission to receive fees;

(d) that the applicant has resided in the State of Illinois for 30 days preceding the application or that the applicant who is a resident of a state bordering Illinois has worked or maintained a business in Illinois for 30 days preceding the application;

(e) that the applicant is a citizen of the United States or an alien lawfully admitted for permanent residence in the United States;

(f) that the applicant is at least 18 years of age;

(g) that the applicant is able to read and write the English language;

(h) that the applicant has never been the holder of a notary public appointment that was revoked or suspended during the past 10 years;

(i) that the applicant has not been convicted of a felony; and

(j) any other information the Secretary of State deems necessary.

第 2 条 任命条款

2-101 任命

州务卿可以在本州的居民中任命其认为必要数量的公证人，任期为 4 年。对于生活在与伊利诺伊州接壤的州内，或者其工作地点或业务地点在伊利诺伊州一个郡内且其居住州的法律授权伊利诺伊州居民在该州可任命为公证人的居民，则州务卿可以任命其为必要数量的非居民公证人，任期为 1 年。

2-102 申请人

任何申请成为公证人的申请人，应填写提交给州务卿的申请表，声明：

（a）申请人的正式姓名，其中包含姓氏，至少包括姓名的首字母；

（b）申请人所在的郡，或者如果申请人是伊利诺斯州接壤州的居民，则写明其在伊利诺伊州的主要工作地点或主要营业地点所在的郡；

（c）申请人的住所地和营业地址（如存在），或申请人将用作收取公证费用的任何地址；

（d）申请人在申请前居住在伊利诺伊州已满 30 日，如果申请人是伊利诺伊州接壤州的居民，应在申请前已在伊利诺伊州工作或营业超过 30 日；

（e）申请人是美国公民，或法律许可的在美国永久居留的外国人；

（f）申请人年满 18 周岁；

（g）申请人能够使用英文阅读和写作；

（h）申请人并非过去 10 年被吊销或暂停的公证人任命的公职人员；

（i）申请人没有被判有重罪；以及

（j）州务卿认为必要的任何其他资料。

2-103. Appointment Fee.

Every applicant for appointment and commission as a notary public shall pay to the Secretary of State a fee of $10.

2-104. Oath.

Every applicant for appointment and commission as a notary public shall take the following oath in the presence of a person qualified to administer an oath in this State:

"I, _____ (name of applicant), solemnly affirm, under the penalty of perjury, that the answers to all questions in this application are true, complete, and correct; that I have carefully read the notary law of this State; and that, if appointed and commissioned as a notary public, I will perform faithfully, to the best of my ability, all notarial acts in accordance with the law."

_____ (Signature of applicant)

Subscribed and affirmed before me on _____ _____, _____

_____

(Official signature and official seal of notary)"

2-105. Bond.

Every application for appointment and commission as a notary public shall be accompanied by an executed bond commencing on the date of the appointment with a term of four years, in the sum of $5,000, with, as surety thereon, a company qualified to write surety bonds in this State. The bond shall be conditioned upon the faithful performance of all notarial acts in accordance with this Act. The Secretary of State may prescribe an official bond form.

2-106. Appointment Recorded by County Clerk.

The appointment of the applicant as a notary public is complete when the commission is recorded with the county clerk.

The Secretary of State shall forward the applicant's commission to the county clerk of the county in which the applicant resides or, if the applicant is a resident of a state bordering Illinois, the county in Illinois in which the applicant's principal place of work or principal place of business is located. Upon receipt thereof, the county clerk shall notify the applicant of the action taken by the Secretary of State, and the applicant shall either appear at the county clerk's office to record the same and receive the commission or request by mail to have the commission sent to the applicant with a specimen signature of the applicant at-

2-103 任命费用

任何申请成为公证人的申请人应向州务卿缴纳10美元的费用。

2-104 宣誓

任何申请成为公证人的申请人应在有权在本州执行宣誓的人面前作出以下宣誓：

"我，_____（申请人的姓名），庄严地申明，根据伪证处罚条款，本申请中所有问题的答案都是真实、完整和正确的；我已仔细阅读了伊利诺伊州的公证法；如果被任命为公证人，我将依法尽全力忠实履行所有公证行为。"

_____（申请人签名）

我确认在本人面前成为 _____，_____

_____

（公证人的正式签名和公章）

2-105 保证金

任何公证人任命申请人，应提交从任命之日起四年的保证金，总额为5000美元，担保人应为本州内有资格担保的公司。该保证金的设立是为了公证人可以根据本法忠实履行所有公证行为。州务卿有权规定官方保证金的形式。

2-106 任命记录

当任命被郡书记官记录时，申请人作为公证人的任命完成。

州务卿应将申请人的任命转交给申请人居住郡的郡书记官，如果申请人是与伊利诺伊州接壤州的居民，则交于其主要工作地点或主要业务地点所在的伊利诺伊州的郡的郡书记官。郡书记官在收到通知后，应当向州务卿出具收据，申请人可到郡办事处出示记录接受任命，或请求通过邮件方式接受任命，请求邮件中应附有申请人的签名。申请人应当保存一份任命记录，并将任命期限的到期日记入郡办事处的记录中。如果申请人在郡书记官处办理任职，申请人应当支付5美元的费用，届时，郡书记官应当向申请人发出委任书。

tached to the request. The applicant shall have a record of the appointment, and the time when the commission will expire, entered in the records of the office of the county clerk. When the applicant appears before the county clerk, the applicant shall pay a fee of $5, at which time the county clerk shall then deliver the commission to the applicant.

If the appointment is completed by mail, the applicant shall pay the county clerk a fee of $10, which shall be submitted with the request to the county clerk. The county clerk shall then record the appointment and send the commission by mail to the applicant.

If an applicant does not respond to the notification by the county clerk within 30 days, the county clerk shall again notify the applicant that the county clerk has received the applicant's notary public commission issued by the Secretary of State. The second notice shall be in substantially the following form:

"The records of this office indicate that you have not picked up your notary public commission from the Office of the County Clerk.

The Illinois Notary Public Law requires you to appear in person in the clerk's office, record your commission, and pay a fee of $5 to the county clerk or request that your commission be mailed to you. This request must be accompanied by a specimen of your signature and $10 fee payable to the county clerk.

Your appointment as a notary is not complete until the commission is recorded with the county clerk. Furthermore, if you do not make arrangements with the clerk for recording and delivery of your commission within 30 days from the date of this letter, the county clerk will return your commission to the Secretary of State. Your commission will be cancelled and your name will be removed from the list of notaries in the State of Illinois.

I should also like to remind you that any person who attests to any document as a notary and is not a notary in good standing with the Office of the Secretary of State is guilty of official misconduct and may be subject to a fine or imprisonment."

The Secretary of State shall cancel the appointment of all notaries whose commissions are returned to his office by the county clerks. No application fee will be refunded and no bonding company is required to issue a refund when an appointment is cancelled.

如果通过邮寄方式完成任命程序，申请人应向郡书记官支付 10 美元的费用，并按照要求向郡书记官提交任命请求。随后郡书记官将将委任书邮寄给申请人。

如果申请人在 30 日内没有对郡书记官的通知进行回复，郡书记官应再次通知申请人，郡办事处已经收到了州务卿签发的公证人任命。第二个通知应基本按照如下格式：

"本办公室的记录表明您没有从郡书记官办公室领取您的公证人委任书。

《伊利诺伊州公证法》要求您亲自来到郡书记官办公室，记录您的任命，并向郡书记官支付 5 美元的费用，或根据您的请求将您的委任书邮寄给您。此项请求必须附有签名样本和提交给郡书记官的 10 美元费用。

您作为公证人的任命在郡书记官记录之前并未完成。此外，如果您在本函注明之日起 30 日内不与郡书记官处理本事宜，郡书记官将把您的委任书交还州务卿。您的任命将被取消，您的姓名将从伊利诺伊州公证人名册中删除。

我还希望提醒您，未经州务卿办公室认证公证人身份的人，擅自进行文件公证的行为，均属于职务违法行为，将被处以罚款或监禁。"

州务卿将取消所有由郡书记官将委任书退还给州办公室的公证人任命。取消任命时，不退还申请费用，也不需要担保公司退款。

ARTICLE III DUTIES – FEES – AUTHORITY

3-101. Official Seal and Signature.

(a) Each notary public shall, upon receiving the commission from the county clerk, obtain an official rubber stamp seal with which the notary shall authenticate his official acts. The rubber stamp seal shall contain the following information:

(1) the words "Official Seal;"

(2) the notary's official name;

(3) the words "Notary Public," "State of Illinois," and "My commission expires_____(commission expiration date);" and

(4) a serrated or milled edge border in a rectangular form not more than one inch in height by two and one-half inches in length surrounding the information.

(b) At the time of the notarial act, a notary public shall officially sign every notary certificate and affix the rubber stamp seal clearly and legibly using black ink, so that it is capable of photographic reproduction. The illegibility of any of the information required by this Section does not affect the validity of a transaction.

This subsection does not apply on or after July 1, 2013.

3-102. Notarial Record; Residential Real Property Transactions.

(a) This Section shall apply to every notarial act in Illinois involving a document of conveyance that transfers or purports to transfer title to residential real property located in Cook County.

(b) As used in this Section, the following terms shall have the meanings ascribed to them:

(1) "Document of Conveyance" shall mean a written instrument that transfers or purports to transfer title effecting a change in ownership to Residential Real Property, excluding:

(i) court-ordered and court-authorized conveyances of Residential Real Property, including without limitation, quit-claim deeds executed pursuant to a marital settlement agreement incorporated into a judgment of dissolution of marriage, and transfers in the administration of a probate estate;

(ii) judicial sale deeds relating to Residential Real Property, including without limitation, sale deeds issued pursuant to proceedings to foreclose a mortgage or execute on a levy to enforce a judgment;

(iii) deeds transferring ownership of Residential Real

第 3 条 义务、费用、职能

3-101 官方印章和签名

（a）公证人在收到郡书记官的委任书后，应当获得对其公证行为进行认证的正式橡皮图章。橡皮图章须包含以下信息：

（1）"官方印章"一词；

（2）公证人的正式名称；

（3）"公证人""伊利诺伊州"和"我的任命到期_____（任命到期日）"字样；以及

（4）具有锯齿状或铣削的边缘，环绕信息的矩形，长度不超过二又二分之一英寸，宽不超过一英寸。

（b）在进行公证行为时，公证人应在每个公证文件上正式签名，并用黑色墨水清晰地用橡皮图章盖章，使其能够被清楚地复印。盖章与本节要求的任何信息的不相符，不影响公证行为的有效性。

本款于 2013 年 7 月 1 日或之后不再适用。

3-102 公证记录；住宅房地产交易

（a）本条适用于伊利诺伊州每一个涉及转让或意图将位于库克郡的住宅不动产进行转让的文书的公证行为。

（b）在本条中，下列术语具有以下含义：

（1）"转让文书"指转让或者意图转让住宅房地产所有权的书面文书，但不包括：

（i）法院命令和法院授权的住宅不动产交易，包括但不限于根据婚姻纠纷解决协议中解除婚姻的决定，以及遗产动产转让；

（ii）涉及住宅房地产的司法拍卖事宜，包括但不限于诉讼引发的抵押权执行或执行征收判决；

（iii）将住宅不动产所有权转让给受托人，其中

Property to a trust where the beneficiary is also the grantor;

(iv) deeds from grantors to themselves that are intended to change the nature or type of tenancy by which they own Residential Real Property;

(v) deeds from a grantor to the grantor and another natural person that are intended to establish a tenancy by which the grantor and the other natural person own Residential Real Property;

(vi) deeds executed to the mortgagee in lieu of foreclosure of a mortgage; and

(vii) deeds transferring ownership to a revocable or irrevocable grantor trust where the beneficiary includes the grantor.

(2) "Financial Institution" shall mean a State or federally chartered bank, savings and loan association, savings bank, or credit union.

(3) "Notarial Record" shall mean the written document created in conformity with this Section by a notary in connection with Documents of Conveyance.

(4) "Residential Real Property" shall mean a building or buildings located in Cook County, Illinois and containing one to four dwelling units or an individual residential condominium unit.

(5) "Title Insurance Agent" shall have the meaning ascribed to it under the Title Insurance Act.

(6) "Title Insurance Company" shall have the meaning ascribed to it under the Title Insurance Act.

(c) A notary appointed and commissioned as a notary in Illinois shall, in addition to compliance with other provisions of this Act, create a Notarial Record of each notarial act performed in connection with a Document of Conveyance. The Notarial Record shall contain:

(1) The date of the notarial act;

(2) The type, title, or a description of the Document of Conveyance being notarized, and the property index number ("PIN") used to identify the Residential Real Property for assessment or taxation purposes and the common street address for the Residential Real Property that is the subject of the Document of Conveyance;

(3) The signature, printed name, and residence street address of each person whose signature is the subject of the notarial act and a certification by the person that the property is Residential Real Property as defined in this Section, which states "The undersigned grantor hereby certifies that the real property identified in this Notarial Record is Residential Real Property as defined in the Illi-

受益人依然为让与人的契约；

（iv）让与人旨在改变其拥有的住宅不动产的类型或性质的契约；

（v）让与人向其本人和另一自然人发出的旨在建立让与人和其他自然人租赁关系的契约。

（vi）向抵押权人发出的代替抵押物止赎的契约；以及

（vii）将所有权转让给可撤销或不可撤销的让与人信托，受益人包括让与人。

（2）"金融机构"是指国家或联邦特许银行、储蓄和贷款协会、储蓄银行或信用合作社。

（3）"公证记录"是指由公证人依照本条制作的与转让文件有关的书面文件。

（4）"住宅房地产"是指位于伊利诺伊州库克郡的一栋或多栋建筑物，其中包含一至四个住宅单位或个人住宅公寓单位。

（5）"保险代理人"具有《保险法》规定的含义。

（6）"产权保险公司"具有《财产保险法》规定的含义。

（c）在伊利诺伊州被任命为公证人的人除了遵守本法规定之外，还应制作一份公证记录，记录与转让文件相关的每个公证行为。公证记录应包含：

（1）公证行为的日期；

（2）转让文件的类型、标题或描述，以及可确定住宅房地产用于评估或税务的财产索引编号（"PIN"）和转让文件中住宅房地产的具体街区地址；

（3）在公证行为中签名的当事人的签名、印刷名称和居住街道地址，以及由本条规定的财产为住宅不动产的人员出具的证明，其中须声明："特此证明，下列让与人在本公证书中确定的不动产属于《伊利诺伊州公证法》中所界定的住宅不动产。"

nois Notary Public Act."

(4) A description of the satisfactory evidence reviewed by the notary to determine the identity of the person whose signature is the subject of the notarial act;

(5) The date of notarization, the fee charged for the notarial act, the Notary's home or business phone number, the Notary's residence street address, the Notary's commission expiration date, the correct legal name of the Notary's employer or principal, and the business street address of the Notary's employer or principal; and

(6) The notary public shall require the person signing the Document of Conveyance (including an agent acting on behalf of a principal under a duly executed power of attorney), whose signature is the subject of the notarial act, to place his or her right thumbprint on the Notarial Record. If the right thumbprint is not available, then the notary shall have the party use his or her left thumb, or any available finger, and shall so indicate on the Notarial Record. If the party signing the document is physically unable to provide a thumbprint or fingerprint, the notary shall so indicate on the Notarial Record and shall also provide an explanation of that physical condition. The notary may obtain the thumbprint by any means that reliably captures the image of the finger in a physical or electronic medium.

(d) If a notarial act under this Section is performed by a notary who is a principal, employee, or agent of a Title Insurance Company, Title Insurance Agent, Financial Institution, or attorney at law, the notary shall deliver the original Notarial Record to the notary's employer or principal within 14 days after the performance of the notarial act for retention for a period of seven years as part of the employer's or principal's business records. In the event of a sale or merger of any of the foregoing entities or persons, the successor or assignee of the entity or person shall assume the responsibility to maintain the Notarial Record for the balance of the seven-year business records retention period. Liquidation or other cessation of activities in the ordinary course of business by any of the foregoing entities or persons shall relieve the entity or person from the obligation to maintain Notarial Records after delivery of Notarial Records to the Recorder of Deeds of Cook County, Illinois.

(e) If a notarial act is performed by a notary who is not a principal, employee, oragent of a Title Insurance Company, Title Insurance Agent, Financial Institution, or attorney at law, the notary shall deliver the original Notarial Record within 14 days after the performance of the

（4）公证人应审查证据，确认公证行为签字人的身份；

（5）公证的日期、公证的费用、公证人的家庭或办公电话号码、公证人住所街道地址、公证人的任命到期日、公证人的雇主或委托人的正确法定名称，以及公证人的雇主或委托人的业务街道地址；以及

（6）公证人应对签署转让文件的人（包括获得正式授权委托书的代理人）的右手拇指的指纹进行公证记录。如果右手拇指指纹无法记录，则公证人应该使用其左拇指或任何可用的手指，并在公证记录上注明。如果签署该文件的一方由于身体原因无法提供指纹，则公证人应在公证记录上注明，并提供该身体状况的说明。公证人有权通过物理、电子介质以及能够可靠地捕获指纹的图像的任何方式获得指纹。

（d）如果根据本条进行的公证行为由作为产权保险公司、保险代理机构、金融机构的雇员或代理人或是律师的公证人履行，则公证人应在执行公证行为后14日内向公证人的雇主或委托人提交公证记录的原件，并作为雇主或委托人的商业记录保留7年。在任何上述机构或个人出让或合并的情况下，该机构或个人的继承人或受让人有义务妥善保管7年业务记录。任何上述机构或个人在正常业务过程中出现清算或其他经营活动停止的情形，应免除机构或个人履行向伊利诺伊州库克郡契约记录员提供公证记录的义务。

（e）如果公证行为不是由作为职业保险公司、保险代理机构、金融机构的雇员、代理人或是律师的公证人履行的，公证人应在公证行为完成后的14日内将原始公证记录，交由伊利诺伊州库克郡契约记录员保留7年，并交纳5美元的费用。

notarial act to the Recorder of Deeds of Cook County, Illinois for retention for a period of seven years, accompanied by a filing fee of $5.

(f) The Notarial Record required under subsection (c) of this Section shall be created and maintained for each person whose signature is the subject of a notarial act regarding a Document of Conveyance and shall be in substantially the following form:

NOTARIAL RECORD - RESIDENTIAL REAL PROPERTY TRANSACTIONS

Date Notarized:
Fee: $
The undersigned grantor hereby certifies that the real property identified in this Notarial Record is Residential Real Property as defined in the Illinois Notary Public Act.
Grantor's (Signer's) Printed Name:
Grantor's (Signer's) Signature:
Grantor's (Signer's) Residential Street Address, City, State, and Zip:
Type or Name of Document of Conveyance:
PIN No. of Residential Real Property:
Common Street Address of Residential Real Property:
Thumbprint or Fingerprint:
Description of Means of Identification:
Additional Comments:
Name of Notary Printed:
Notary Phone Number:
Commission Expiration Date:
Residential Street Address of Notary, City, State, and Zip:
Name of Notary's Employer or Principal:
Business Street Address of Notary's Employer or Principal, City, State, and Zip:

(g) No copies of the original Notarial Record may be made or retained by the Notary. The Notary's employer or principal may retain copies of the Notarial Records as part of its business records, subject to applicable privacy and confidentiality standards.

(h) The failure of a notary to comply with the procedure set forth in this Section shall not affect the validity of the Residential Real Property transaction in connection to which the Document of Conveyance is executed, in the absence of fraud.

(i) The Notarial Record or other medium containing

the thumbprint or fingerprint required by subsection (c) (6) shall be made available or disclosed only upon receipt of a subpoena duly authorized by a court of competent jurisdiction. Such Notarial Record or other medium shall not be subject to disclosure under the Freedom of Information Act and shall not be made available to any other party, other than a party in succession of interest to the party maintaining the Notarial Record or other medium pursuant to subsection (d) or (e).

(j) In the event there is a breach in the security of a Notarial Record maintained pursuant to subsections (d) and (e) by the Recorder of Deeds of Cook County, Illinois, the Recorder shall notify the person identified as the "signer" in the Notarial Record at the signer's residential street address set forth in the Notarial Record. "Breach" shall mean unauthorized acquisition of the fingerprint data contained in the Notarial Record that compromises the security, confidentiality, or integrity of the fingerprint data maintained by the Recorder. The notification shall be in writing and made in the most expedient time possible and without unreasonable delay, consistent with any measures necessary to determine the scope of the breach and restore the reasonable security, confidentiality, and integrity of the Recorder's data system.

(k) Subsections (a) through (i) shall not apply on and after July 1, 2013.

Beginning July 1, 2013, at the time of notarization, a notary public shall officially sign every notary certificate and affix the rubber stamp seal clearly and legibly using black ink, so that it is capable of photographic reproduction. The illegibility of any of the information required by this Section does not affect the validity of a transaction.

3-103. Notice.

(a) Every notary public who is not an attorney or an accredited immigration representative who advertises the services of a notary public in a language other than English, whether by radio, television, signs, pamphlets, newspapers, or other written communication, with the exception of a single desk plaque, shall include in the document, advertisement, stationery, letterhead, business card, or other comparable written material the following: notice in English and the language in which the written communication appears. This notice shall be of a conspicuous size, if in writing, and shall state: "I AM NOT AN ATTORNEY LICENSED TO PRACTICE LAW IN ILLINOIS AND MAY NOT GIVE LEGAL ADVICE OR ACCEPT FEES

它指纹的公证记录或其他媒介，只有在收到有管辖权的法院正式授权的传票后才能提供或披露。此类公证记录或其他媒介不得根据《信息自由法》的规定进行披露，不得向其他任何一方提供，除非根据（d）款或（e）款所述的公证记录或其他媒介记录的一方的关联利益方。

（j）如果根据（d）款或（e）款伊利诺斯州库克郡契约记录员就公证记录保存的安全性存在违规，记录员应根据公证记录中的居住街道通知被确定为"签字人"的人。在公证记录中，"违规"将意味着未经授权地获取公证记录中包含的指纹数据、损害维护指纹数据的记录仪的安全性、机密性或完整性。通知书应以最快的时间且无不合理延迟地送出，并根据违规范围确定所需的任何补救措施，以恢复记录仪数据系统的合理安全性、保密性和完整性。

（k）第（a）款至第（i）款于2013年7月1日之后失效。

2013年7月1日起，公证人在公证文书上必须有正式签名，并使用黑色墨水，清晰地用橡皮图章盖章，使其能够复印。本条要求的任何信息存在不符时不影响交易的有效性。

3-103 通知

（a）不具备律师或经认可的移民代表身份的公证人，在以英文以外的其他语言为其提供的公证人服务作宣传时，无论是通过电台、电视、标牌、宣传册、报纸还是其他除了单张桌牌外的书面形式，宣传时必须在文件、广告、文具、信笺、名片或其他类似的书面材料内作提示。提示通用英语和书面宣传中出现的语言来制作。本通知应采用显而易见的尺寸，如果采用书面形式，应作出以下声明："我并非伊利诺伊州的执业律师，不能提供法律意见也不接受法律咨询费用。"如果此类宣传是通过广播或电视进行的，该声明的措辞可以进行修改，但必须包含基本相同的信息。

FOR LEGAL ADVICE." If such advertisement is by radio or television, the statement may be modified but must include substantially the same message.

A notary public shall not, in any document, advertisement, stationery, letterhead, business card, or other comparable written material describing the role of the notary public, literally translate from English into another language terms or titles including, but not limited to, notary public, notary, licensed, attorney, lawyer, or any other term that implies the person is an attorney. To illustrate, the word "notario" is prohibited under this provision.

Failure to follow the procedures in this Section shall result in a fine of $1,000 for each written violation. The second violation shall result in suspension of notary authorization. The third violation shall result in permanent revocation of the commission of notary public. Violations shall not preempt or preclude additional appropriate civil or criminal penalties.

(b) All notaries public required to comply with the provisions of subsection (a) shall prominently post at their place of business as recorded with the Secretary of State pursuant to Section 2-102 of this Act a schedule of fees established by law which a notary public may charge. The fee schedule shall be written in English and in the non-English language in which notary services were solicited and shall contain the disavowal of legal representation required above in subsection (a), unless such notice of disavowal is already prominently posted.

(c) No notary public, agency or any other person who is not an attorney shall represent, hold themselves out or advertise that they are experts on immigration matters or provide any other assistance that requires legal analysis, legal judgment, or interpretation of the law unless they are a designated entity as defined pursuant to Section 245a.1 of Part 245a of the Code of Federal Regulations (8CFR 245a.1) or an entity accredited by the Board of Immigration Appeals.

(d) Any person who aids, abets or otherwise induces another person to give false information concerning immigration status shall be guilty of a Class A misdemeanor for a first offense and a Class 3 felony for a second or subsequent offense committed within five years of a previous conviction for the same offense.

Any notary public who violates the provisions of this Section shall be guilty of official misconduct and subject to fine or imprisonment.

Nothing in this Section shall preclude any consumer

公证人不得在任何文件、广告、文具、信笺、名片、或其他类似的书面材料上描述公证人的职能，不得将术语或头衔从英语字面直译成其他语言，包括但不限于"notary public" "notary" "licensed" "attorney" "lawyer"，或用任何其他术语来暗示该人是一名律师。为阐明这一规定，本条款禁止"notario"一词。

如不遵守本条规定的程序，每项书面违规行为将被罚款1000美元。第二次违规，将被暂停公证人任命。第三次违规，将永久吊销公证人的任命。对违规行为的处罚不排除附加适当的民事或刑事处罚。

（b）所有需要遵守（a）款规定的公证人，应按本法2-102条，在其与在州务卿的备案相一致的营业地显眼处张贴一份由法律规定的公证人收费表。收费表须以英文书写，如果被要求，则可以用非英文书写，表格应包含各项公证服务，并应载有（a）款所规定的否认法定代表权的声明，除非该否认声明已作显著提示。

（c）任何公证人、代理人或非律师的其他人不得代表、自称或宣传他们是移民事务方面的专家，或提供任何其他需要法律分析的协助、法律判断或法律解释，除非是根据《联邦条例》（8CFR 245 a.1）第245a部分第245a.1条所界定的指定实体或移民上诉委员会认可的实体。

（d）任何人协助、教唆或以其他方式诱使另一人提供有关移民身份的错误信息，初犯时将会被判A级轻罪，在前罪定罪后五年内第二次或多次触犯相同罪名的，将被判处三级重罪。

任何违反本条规定的公证人，构成渎职罪，将被处以罚款或监禁。

本条并不排除任何公证服务的接受者寻求法律提

of notary public services from pursuing other civil remedies available under the law.

(e) No notary public who is not an attorney or an accredited representative shall accept payment in exchange for providing legal advice or any other assistance that requires legal analysis, legal judgment, or interpretation of the law.

(f) Violation of subsection (e) is a business offense punishable by a fine of three times the amount received for services, or $1,001 minimum, and restitution of the amount paid to the consumer. Nothing in this Section shall be construed to preempt nor preclude additional appropriate civil remedies or criminal charges available under law.

(g) If a notary public of this State is convicted of two or more business offenses involving a violation of this Act within a 12-month period while commissioned, or of three or more business offenses involving a violation of this Act within a five-year period regardless of being commissioned, the Secretary shall automatically revoke the notary public commission of that person on the date that the person's most recent business offense conviction is entered as a final judgment.

3-104. Maximum Fee.

(a) Except as provided in subsection (b) of this Section, the maximum fee in this State is $1 for any notarial act performed and, until July 1, 2013, up to $25 for any notarial act performed pursuant to Section 3-102.

(b) Fees for a notary public, agency, or any other person who is not an attorney or an accredited representative filling out immigration forms shall be limited to the following:

(1) $10 per form completion；

(2) $10 per page for the translation of a non-English language into English where such translation is required for immigration forms;

(3) $1 for notarizing;

(4) $3 to execute any procedures necessary to obtain a document required to complete immigration forms; and

(5) A maximum of $75 for one complete application.

Fees authorized under this subsection shall not include application fees required to be submitted with immigration applications.

Any person who violates the provisions of this subsection shall be guilty of a Class A misdemeanor for a first offense and a Class 3 felony for a second or subsequent offense committed within 5 years of a previous conviction

供的其它民事法律救济。

（e）不具备律师或经认可的代表身份的公证人不可接受因提供法律咨询或任何其他需要法律分析、法律判断或法律解释的援助的付款。

（f）违反（e）款的任职规定，可处以三倍于服务费的罚金，罚金不低于1001美元，并将该款项归还给接受服务者。本条不得解释为预先排除依法可获得的额外适当的民事补救或刑事指控。

（g）如果本州的公证人，在受委任之日起12个月内违反本法被判犯有两次或两次以上的商业犯罪，或无论其是否受委托，在五年内违反本法被判三项或多项商业犯罪，州务卿应在该人最近的商业犯罪定罪的终审判决之日，主动撤销该人的公证人委任。

3-104 最高费用

（a）除本条（b）款另有规定外，直至2013年7月1日为止，任何公证行为在本州的最高收费为1美元，但根据第3-102条进行的任何公证行为收费可达25美元。

（b）公证人、代理人或任何其他非律师或经认可的代表，在填写移民表格时须限于以下各项：

（1）填写每张表格收取10美元；

（2）在移民表格需要翻译的地方，将非英语翻译成英文，每页10美元；

（3）公证费用1美元；

（4）执行任何必要的程序，以取得完成移民表格所需的文件，3美元；

（5）一份完整的申请书最高75美元。

根据本条授权收取的费用，不得包括需提交的移民申请费。

任何人初次违反本条的规定，可能被判处A级轻罪，在前罪定罪后五年内第二次或多次触犯相同罪名的，将被判处三级重罪。

for the same offense.

(c) Upon his own information or upon complaint of any person, the Attorney General or any State's Attorney, or their designee, may maintain an action for injunctive relief in the court against any notary public or any other person who violates the provisions of subsection (b) of this Section. These remedies are in addition to, and not in substitution for, other available remedies.

If the Attorney General or any State's Attorney fails to bring an action as provided pursuant to this subsection within 90 days of receipt of a complaint, any person may file a civil action to enforce the provisions of this subsection and maintain an action for injunctive relief.

(d) All notaries public must provide receipts and keep records for fees accepted for services provided. Failure to provide receipts and keep records that can be presented as evidence of no wrongdoing shall be construed as a presumptive admission of allegations raised in complaints against the notary for violations related to accepting prohibited fees.

3-105. Authority.

A notary public shall have authority to perform notarial acts throughout the State so long as the notary resides in the same county in which the notary was commissioned or, if the notary is a resident of a state bordering Illinois, so long as the notary's principal place of work or principal place of business is in the same county in Illinois in which the notary was commissioned.

3-106. Certificate of Authority.

Upon the receipt of a written request, the notarized document, and a fee of $2 payable to the Secretary of State or County Clerk, the Office of the Secretary of State or County Clerk shall provide a certificate of authority in substantially the following form :

I _____ (Secretary of State or _____ County Clerk) of the State of Illinois, which office is an office of record having a seal, certify that _____ (notary's name) by whom the foregoing or annexed document was notarized, was, on _____ (insert date) , appointed and commissioned a notary public in and for the State of Illinois and that as such, full faith and credit is and ought to be given to this notary's official attestations. In testimony whereof, I have affixed my signature and the seal of this office on _____ (insert date) .

（c）总检察长或任何州的律师或他们指派的人员，可根据其本人的资料或任何人的申诉，在法庭内，针对任何公证人或他人违反本条（b）款的规定的行为，采取禁令救济的措施。上述救济办法是附加的，而不是其他可用的救济措施的替代品。

如果总检察长或任何州的律师在收到投诉后90日内未能根据本条提起诉讼，则任何人可就此提起民事诉讼，以强制执行本条的规定和采取禁令救济的措施。

（d）所有公证人必须提供收据并记录提供服务所收取的费用。在对公证人提出的有关接受违禁费用的侵权指控中，若未提供可作为证明不存在不当行为证据的收据和记录，应解释为推定承认收取了不当费用。

3-105 权力

只要公证人居住的郡和受委任的郡相一致，或如果公证人是毗邻州的居民，只要公证人的受委任地与主要工作地或主要营业地在伊利诺斯州的同一郡，则公证人有权在全郡范围内执行公证行为。

3-106 授权证书

在收到书面请求、经公证的文件并支付给州务卿或郡书记官2美元的费用后，州务卿或郡书记官应提供一份授权证书，格式大致如下：

我_____是伊利诺伊州的_____（州务卿或郡书记官），本人的职责在于盖章确认记录，证明前述或附加文件是在_____（日期）由在伊利诺伊州被委任的公证人_____（公证人的名称）公证的，因此，应该给此公证人的官方认证以充分的信任。兹在证词中附上我的签名和职称的印章_____（插入日期）。_____

(Secretary of State) or (Lee County Clerk).

ARTICLE IV CHANGE OF NAME OR MOVE FROM COUNTY

4-101. Changes causing commission to cease to be in effect.

When any notary public legally changes his or her name or moves from the county in which he or she was commissioned or, if the notary public is a resident of a state bordering Illinois, no longer maintains a principal place of work or principal place of business in the same county in Illinois in which he or she was commissioned, the commission ceases to be in effect and should be returned to the Secretary of State. These individuals who desire to again become a notary public must file a new application, bond, and oath with the Secretary of State.

ARTICLE V REAPPOINTMENT AS A NOTARY PUBLIC

5-101. Reappointment.

No person is automatically reappointed as a notary public. At least 60 days prior to the expiration of a commission the Secretary of State shall mail notice of the expiration date to the holder of a commission. Every notary public who is an applicant for reappointment shall comply with the provisions of Article II of this Act.

5-102. Solicitation to Purchase Bond.

No person shall solicit any notary public and offer to provide a surety bond more than 60 days in advance of the expiration date of the notary public's commission.

Nor shall any person solicit any applicant for a commission or reappointment thereof and offer to provide a surety bond for the notary commission unless any such solicitation specifically sets forth in bold face type not less than 1/4 inch in height the following: "WE ARE NOT ASSOCIATED WITH ANY STATE OR LOCAL GOVERNMENTAL AGENCY."

Whenever it shall appear to the Secretary of State that any person is engaged or is about to engage in any acts or practices which constitute or will constitute a violation of the provisions of this Section, the Secretary of State may, in his discretion, through the Attorney General, apply for an injunction, and, upon a proper showing, any circuit court shall have power to issue a permanent or temporary injunction or restraining order without bond to enforce the provisions of this Act, and either party to such suit shall

（州务卿）或（郡书记官）。

第4条 名称变更或者从受委任的郡迁出

4–101 导致委任书失效的变动

任何公证人在法律上更改其姓名或从其受委任的郡中迁出，或公证人是毗邻州的居民，在伊利诺斯州内的受委任地与主要工作地或主要营业地不在同一郡，则其委任书将会失效，并应交还州务卿。那些希望再次成为公证人的人必须向州务卿提交新的申请、保证金和宣誓书。

第5条 公证人的连任

5–101 连任

任何公证人不得自动连任。在委任期届满前60日内，州务卿应将期满的通知邮寄给委任书的持有人。申请连任的公证人，应遵守本法第2条的规定。

5–102 提交保证金的要求

除距离公证人任期届满之日不足60日以外，任何人不得邀约公证人以及向其提供担保保证金。

任何人不得邀约申请委任或连任的申请人，或者向公证人的任命提供担保保证金，除非任何此类邀约明确地以不小于1/4英寸的粗体作出如下声明："我们与任何州或地方政府机构没有联系。"

当州务卿认为任何人参与或即将从事构成或即将构成违反本条规定的任何行为时，州务卿可主动向总检察长申请禁令，而在适当的情况下，任何巡回法院均有权发出永久或暂时禁制令或禁止令，以强制执行本法的有关规定，诉讼的任何一方均有权对法院的命令或判决提起上诉。

have the right to prosecute an appeal from the order or judgment of the court.

Any person, association, corporation, or others who violate the provisions of this Section shall be guilty of a business offense and punishable by a fine of not less than $500 for each offense.

ARTICLE VI NOTARIAL ACTS AND FORMS

6-101. Definitions.

(a) "Notarial act" means any act that a notary public of this State is authorized toperform and includes taking an acknowledgment, administering an oath or affirmation, taking a verification upon oath or affirmation, and witnessing or attesting a signature.

(b) "Acknowledgment" means a declaration by a person that the person has executed an instrument for the purposes stated therein and, if the instrument is executed in a representative capacity, that the person signed the instrument with proper authority and executed it as the act of the person or entity represented and identified therein.

(c) "Verification upon oath or affirmation" means a declaration that a statement is true made by a person upon oath or affirmation.

(d) "In a representative capacity" means:

(1) for and on behalf of a corporation, partnership, trust, or other entity, as an authorized officer, agent, partner, trustee, or other representative;

(2) as a public officer, personal representative, guardian, or other representative, in the capacity recited in the instrument;

(3) as an attorney in fact for a principal; or

(4) in any other capacity as an authorized representative of another.

6-102. Notarial Acts.

(a) In taking an acknowledgment, the notary public must determine, either from personal knowledge or from satisfactory evidence, that the person appearing before the notary and making the acknowledgment is the person whose true signature is on the instrument.

(b) In taking a verification upon oath or affirmation, the notary public must determine, either from personal knowledge or from satisfactory evidence, that the person appearing before the notary and making the verification is the person whose true signature is on the statement verified.

(c) In witnessing or attesting a signature, the notary

任何个人、团体、公司或其他违反本条规定的人，均属商业犯罪，每次的违规将被处以不少于500美元的罚款。

第6条 公证行为和形式

6-101 定义

（a）"公证行为"是指本州的公证人被授权履行的任何行为，包括作出确认书、执行宣誓或确认、在宣誓或确认时进行核查、见证或认证签名。

（b）"确认书"是指某人为其所述目的而执行文书的声明，如果该文书是由具有代表身份的人所执行的，且该人以适当的权限签署了文书，并以其中所代表和指明的个人或实体的名义加以执行。

（c）"经宣誓或确认后的核查"是指一种公告，表示该声明确实是由某人经宣誓或确认后作出的。

（d）"以代表身份"是指：

（1）代表公司、合伙企业、信托或其他实体，作为获得授权的签字人、代理人、合伙人、受托人或其他代表；

（2）以该文书所述的身份，作为公职人员、个人代表、监护人或其他代表；

（3）作为当事人的实际代理人；或

（4）作为授权代表的任何其他身份。

6-102 公证行为

（a）在作出确认书时，公证人必须依据个人知识或充分证据确定，出现在公证人面前并作出确认的人员都是在文书上真正签字的人。

（b）在进行宣誓或确认的核查时，公证人必须依据个人知识或从充分证据确认，以核实声明文件中出现的签名是亲自出席确认的人的真实签名。

（c）在见证或认证签字时，公证人必须依据个人

public must determine, either from personal knowledge or from satisfactory evidence, that the signature is that of the person appearing before the notary and named therein.

(d) A notary public has satisfactory evidence that a person is the person whose true signature is on a document if that person:

(1) is personally known to the notary;

(2) is identified upon the oath or affirmation of a credible witness personally known to the notary; or

(3) is identified on the basis of identification documents. Until July 1, 2013, identification documents are documents that are valid at the time of the notarial act, issued by a state or federal government agency, and bearing the photographic image of the individual's face and signature of the individual.

6-103. Certificate of Notarial Acts.

(a) A notarial act must be evidenced by a certificate signed and dated by the notary public. The certificate must include identification of the jurisdiction in which the notarial act is performed and the official seal of office.

(b) A certificate of a notarial act is sufficient if it meets the requirements of subsection (a) and it:

(1) is in the short form set forth in Section 6-105;

(2) is in a form otherwise prescribed by the law of this State; or

(3) sets forth the actions of the notary public and those are sufficient to meet the requirements of the designated notarial act.

6-104. Acts Prohibited.

(a) A notary public shall not use any name or initial in signing certificates other than that by which the notary was commissioned.

(b) A notary public shall not acknowledge any instrument in which the notary's name appears as a party to the transaction.

(c) A notary public shall not affix his signature to a blank form of affidavit or certificate of acknowledgment and deliver that form to another person with intent that it be used as an affidavit or acknowledgment.

(d) A notary public shall not take the acknowledgment of or administer an oath to any person whom the notary actually knows to have been adjudged mentally ill by a court of competent jurisdiction and who has not been restored to mental health as a matter of record.

(e) A notary public shall not take the acknowledgment of any person who is blind until the notary has read

知识或从充分证据确定，签署的签名是亲自出席见证的人的真实签名。

（d）满足下列情形的，认为公证人有充分证据证明某人是在文件上的真正署名人：

（1）为公证人个人所知悉；

（2）依据公证人知悉的可信证人的宣誓或确认后予以确定；或

（3）根据身份证明文件确定。直到2013年7月1日，在进行公证行为时，身份证明文件是州或联邦政府机构签发的有效证件，身份证明文件应附有面部照片图像和个人签名。

6-103 公证行为证书

（a）公证行为必须由公证人签署和注明日期的证书来证明。证书必须包含对公证行为管辖权和官方职称印章的确认。

（b）有效的公证行为证书应符合（a）款的要求，并且：

（1）以第6-105条所规定的简易形式；

（2）以本州法律另有规定的形式；或

（3）规定公证人的行为，确保行为足以满足特定的公证行为的要求。

6-104 禁止的行为

（a）除在公证人受委托的情形下，公证人不得使用任何名字或首字母签署证书。

（b）公证人不得对自己作为交易当事方的任何文书作出确认。

（c）公证人不得在誓词或确认书的空白处签名，并将该表格送交另一人，意图将其用作宣誓书或确认书。

（d）公证人不得对实际已知的被有管辖权的法院判定患有精神疾病且没有恢复健康记录的人作出确认书或执行宣誓。

（e）在公证人向盲人宣读文书前，公证人不得为盲人作确认书。

the instrument to such person.

(f) A notary public shall not take the acknowledgment of any person who does not speak or understand the English language, unless the nature and effect of the instrument to be notarized is translated into a language, which the person does understand.

(g) A notary public shall not change anything in a written instrument after it has been signed by anyone.

(h) No notary public shall be authorized to prepare any legal instrument, or fill in the blanks of an instrument, other than a notary certificate; however, this prohibition shall not prohibit an attorney, who is also a notary public, from performing notarial acts for any document prepared by that attorney.

(i) If a notary public accepts or receives any money from any one to whom an oath has been administered or on behalf of whom an acknowledgment has been taken for the purpose of transmitting or forwarding such money to another and willfully fails to transmit or forward such money promptly, the notary is personally liable for any loss sustained because of such failure. The person or persons damaged by such failure may bring an action to recover damages, together with interest and reasonable attorney fees, against such notary public or his bondsmen.

6-105. Short Forms.

The following short form certificates of notarial acts are sufficient for the purposes indicated.

(a) For an acknowledgment in an individual capacity:
State of _____
County of _____
This instrument was acknowledged before me on _____ (date) by _____
_____ (name/s of person/s.)

_____
(Signature of Notary Public)
(Seal) _____
_____

(b) For an acknowledgment in a representative capacity:
State of _____
County of _____
This instrument was acknowledged before me on _____ (date) by _____ (name/s of person/s) as _____ (type of authority, e.g., officer, trustee, etc.) of _____ (name of party on behalf of whom instrument was executed) .

（f）公证人不得为不会讲或不理解英文的人作确认书，除非公证文书的性质和效力已被翻译为该人理解的语言。

（g）经任何人签字后，公证人不得更改书面文书中的任何内容。

（h）不得授权公证人编写任何法律文书，或填写某份文书的空白处，除了公证证书；然而，此项禁止性规定不禁止律师公证人对其已编写的法律文书执行公证。

（i）如公证人接受或收受任何宣誓已受执行之人的金钱，或代表被作出确认书之人的金钱，意在将该款项转交或转往另一方却故意不及时转交该款项，公证人对此造成的任何损失负有个人责任。因该行为受到损害的人，可向该公证人或其保证人，提起损害赔偿诉讼，追讨款项、利息及合理的律师费。

6-105 简易形式

以下公证行为的简易形式证书足以说明其表明的目的。

（a）以个人身份承认
_____ 州
_____ 郡
这份文件于 _____（日期）由 _____（姓名）向本人进行了确认。

_____
（公证人签名）
（盖章）_____
_____

（b）以代表身份承认

_____ 州
_____ 郡
这份文件于 _____（日期）由 _____（人名）作为 _____（文书被执行一方代表的姓名）的 _____（授权类型，例如授权签字者、受托者等）向本人进行了确认。

_____
(Signature of Notary Public)
(Seal)

(c) For a verification upon oath or affirmation:
State of _____
County of _____
Signed and sworn (or affirmed) to before me on _____ (date) by _____ (name/s of person/s making statement) .

_____
(Signature of Notary Public)
(Seal)

(d) For witnessing or attesting a signature:
State of _____
County of _____
Signed and attested before me on _____ (date) by _____ (name/s of person/s) .

_____
(Signature of Notary Public)
(Seal)

ARTICLE VII LIABILITY AND REVOCATION

7-101. Liability of Notary and Surety.

A notary public and the surety on the notary's bond are liable to the persons involved for all damages caused by the notary's official misconduct.

7-102. Liability of Employer of Notary.

The employer of a notary public is also liable to the persons involved for all damages caused by the notary's official misconduct, if:

(a) the notary public was acting within the scope of the notary's employment at the time the notary engaged in the official misconduct; and

(b) the employer consented to the notary public's official misconduct.

7-103. Cause of Damages.

It is not essential to a recovery of damages that a notary's official misconduct be the only cause of the damages.

7-104. Official Misconduct Defined.

The term "official misconduct" generally means the wrongful exercise of a power or the wrongful performance of a duty and is fully defined in Section 33-3 of the Criminal Code of 1961. The term "wrongful" as used in

_____
（公证人签名）
（盖章）

（c）依据宣誓或确认的核查
_____州
_____郡
（作出声明人的姓名）_____已于_____（日期）在本人面前签署并宣誓（或确认）。

_____
（公证人签名）
（盖章）

（d）为见证或证明签名
_____州
_____郡
（姓名）_____于（日期）_____在本人面前签字并认证。

_____
（公证签名）
（盖章）

第7条 责任和撤销

7-101 公证人和担保人的责任

公证人及其担保人对由于公证人的不当职务行为造成的一切损害承担责任。

7-102 公证人雇主的责任

如果存在以下情形，公证人的雇主对由于公证人的不当职务行为所造成的一切损害承担责任：

（a）公证人所作出的不当职务行为是在受雇范围之内；以及

（b）雇主同意公证人的不当职务行为。

7-103 损害的原因

公证人并不是必须对损害做赔偿的，除非其不当职务行为是导致损害的唯一原因。

7-104 不当职务行为的定义

"不当职务行为"一词一般是指权力的不正当行使或义务的不正当履行，并在1961年《刑法典》第33-3条作了充分的界定。在不当职务行为的定义中使用的"不当"一词，是指未经授权、非法、滥用、疏忽、

the definition of official misconduct means unauthorized, unlawful, abusive, negligent, reckless, or injurious.

7-105. Official Misconduct.

(a) A notary public who knowingly and willfully commits any official misconductis guilty of a Class A misdemeanor.

(b) A notary public who recklessly or negligently commits any official misconductis guilty of a Class B misdemeanor.

7-106. Willful Impersonation.

Any person who acts as, or otherwise willfully impersonates, a notary public while not lawfully appointed and commissioned to perform notarial acts is guilty of a Class A misdemeanor.

7-107. Wrongful Possession.

Any person who unlawfully possesses a notary's official seal is guilty of a misdemeanor and punishable upon conviction by a fine not exceeding $1,000.

7-108. Revocation of Commission.

The Secretary of State may revoke the commission of any notary public who, during the current term of appointment:

(a) submits an application for commission and appointment as a notary public which contains substantial and material misstatement or omission of fact; or (b) is convicted of any felony, or official misconduct under this Act.

7-109. Action for Injunction, Unauthorized Practice of Law.

Upon his own information or upon complaint of any person, the Attorney General or any State's Attorney, or their designee, may maintain an action for injunctive relief in the circuit court against any notary public who renders, offers to render, or holds himself or herself out as rendering any service constituting the unauthorized practice of the law. Any organized bar association in this State may intervene in the action, at any stage of the proceeding, for good cause shown. The action may also be maintained by an organized bar association in this State. These remedies are in addition to, and not in substitution for, other available remedies.

鲁莽或有害地作出行为。

7-105 不当职务行为

（a）公证人明知而故意犯有构成A级轻罪的某类不当职务行为；

（b）公证人过失或疏忽大意而犯有构成B级轻罪的某类不当职务行为；

7-106 故意假冒

任何人假扮或以其他方式蓄意冒充公证人，非依任命和委托执行公证行为，即构成A级轻罪。

7-107 非法占有

任何人非法占有公证人的公证公章，即属轻罪，一经定罪，将被处以不超过1000美元的罚款。

7-108 撤销委任

对存在下列情形的公证人，州务卿有权撤销任何在其任期内的委任：

（a）提交的公证人委任和任命的申请书中载有重大实质的错报或事实遗漏；或（b）被判定犯有任何重罪或本法规定的不当职务行为。

7-109 行动禁令，未经授权的法律执业

依据自己的资料或任何他人的申诉，总检察长或任何州检察官或他们指派的人员，可在巡回法庭上针对任何公证人提供、要约提供或本人提供的任何未经法律授权的服务提起禁令救济。为了公益目的，任何在本州有组织的律师协会都可以在诉讼的任何阶段进行干预。该措施也可由在本州有组织的律师协会继续实行。上述救济办法是附加的，并不取代其他可行的救济途径。

ARTICLE VIII REPEALER AND EFFECTIVE DATE

Sec. 8-101. Section 2 of "An Act to increase the fee for issuing commissions to notaries public," approved June 3, 1897, as amended, is repealed.

Sec. 8-102. Section 28 of "An Act concerning fees and salaries, and to classify the several counties of this State with reference thereto," approved March 29, 1872, as amended, is repealed.

Sec. 8-103. "An Act to provide for the appointment, qualification and duties of notaries public and certifying their official acts and to provide for fines and penalties for the violation thereof," approved April 5, 1872, as amended, is repealed.

Sec. 8-104. This Act takes effect July 1, 1986.

第 8 条 废止和生效日期

Sec 8-101. 第 2 条中《增加对签发公证人委任状的收费的法令》，于 1897 年 6 月 3 日批准修正后，已被废止。

Sec 8-102. 第 28 条《关于以费用和薪金作为该州几个郡分级的参考的法令》，于 1872 年 3 月 29 日批准修正后，已被废止。

Sec 8-103.《对公证人的任命、资格和义务作出规定和审查其职务行为，并对其违反规定处以罚款和处罚的法令》，于 1872 年 4 月 5 日批准修正后，已被废止。

Sec 8-104. 本法于 1986 年 7 月 1 日生效。

肯塔基州经修订现行成文法（鲍德温注解版）

Baldwin's Kentucky Revised Statutes Annotated Currentness

肯塔基州经修订现行成文法
（鲍德温注解版）

Title XXXVIII.
Witnesses, Evidence, Notaries, Commissioners of ForeignDeeds, and Legal Notices

第 38 篇
证人、证据、公证人、涉外契约专员，以及法定通知

>> Chapter 423. Notaries Public and Commissioners of Foreign Deeds (Refs & Annos)

>> 第 423 章　公证人和涉外契约专员

>>423.010 Appointment, term, and qualifications of notaries; county clerk haspowers of notary when acting in capacity as clerk

>>423.010 公证人之任命、任期和资质；郡书记官行使其书记官职能时，享有公证人之权力

(1) The Secretary of State may appoint as many notaries public as he or she deems necessary, who shall hold office for four (4) years.

Any resident of the Commonwealth of Kentucky desiring to be appointed a notary public shallmake written application to the Secretary of State.

The application shall beapproved by the Circuit Judge, circuit clerk, county judge/executive, countyclerk, justice of the peace, or a member of the General Assembly of the county of the residence of the applicant or in the county in which the applicant's principal place of employment is located.

A person who is not a resident of Kentucky but who is employed in Kentucky may become a notary public by making an application to the Secretary of State which has been approved by an officer specified in this section from the county in which the applicant is principally employed in Kentucky.

（1）州务卿可根据需要任命相应数量的公证人，公证人任期为 4 年。

肯塔基州居民欲被任命为公证人者，须向州务卿提交书面申请。

申请书应当由巡回法官、巡回法庭书记员、郡法官 / 行政官、郡书记官、治安法官、或者申请者住所所在地 / 主要工作所在地郡大会批准。

虽非肯塔基州居民却就职于肯塔基州者，其申请经本条规定的主要工作所在郡官员批准后，可递交州务卿申请成为公证人。

No officer shall charge or accept any fee for approving the application.

A notary public shall be eighteen (18) years of age, a resident of the county from which he or she makes his or her application or be principally employed in the county from which he or she makes his or her application, of good moral character, and capable of discharging the duties imposed upon him or her by this chapter, and the endorsement of the officer approving the application shall so state.

The Secretary of State, in his or her certificate of appointment to the applicant, shall designate the limits within which the notary is to act.

Before a notary acts, he or she shall take an oath before any person authorized to administer an oath as set forth in KRS 62.020 that he or she will honestly and diligently discharge the duties of his or her office.

He or she shall in the same court give an obligation with good security, which shall be proven by a notarized statement from, and not the personal appearance of, the person providing the security, for the proper discharge of the duties of his or her office. Every certificate of a notary public shall state the date of the expiration of his or her commission.

The Secretary of State shall give to each notary appointed a certificate of his or her appointment under the seal of the Commonwealth of Kentucky in lieu of a commission heretofore required to be issued to the notary by the Governor of Kentucky, and receive a fee of ten dollars ($10) for the certificate.

(2) A county clerk shall have the powers of a notary public in the exercise of the official functions of the office of clerk within his or her county, and the official actions of the county clerk shall not require the witness or signature of a notary appointed pursuant to subsection (1) of this section.

>>423.020 Notary may act in any county; certification of notary's authority

(1) A notary public may exercise all the functions of his office in any county of the state, by filing in the county clerk's office in such county his written signature and a certificate of the county clerk of the county for which he was appointed, setting forth the fact of his appointment and qualification as a notary public, and paying a fee pursuant to KRS 64.012 to the county clerk.

(2) The county clerk of a county in whose office any notary public has so filed his signature and certificate

shall, when requested, subjoin to any certificate of proof or acknowledgment signed by the notary a certificate under his hand and seal, stating that such notary public has filed a certificate of his appointment and qualifications with his written signature in his office, and was at the time of taking such proof or acknowledgment duly authorized to take the same; that he is well acquainted with the handwriting of the notary public and believes that the signature to such proof or acknowledgment is genuine.

>>423.030 Protests to be recorded; copies as evidence

The notaries public shall record in a well bound and properly indexed book, kept by them for that purpose, all protests made by them for the nonacceptance or nonpayment of all bills of exchange, checks or promissory notes placed on the footing of bills of exchange, and on which a protest is required by law, or of which protest is evidence of dishonor.

A copy of such protest certified by the notary public under his notarial seal is prima facie evidence in all the courts of this state.

>>423.040 Notice of dishonor; to whom sent

Notaries public shall upon protesting any instrument mentioned in KRS 423.030 give notice of the dishonor to such parties thereto as are required by law to be notified to fix their liability on such paper.

When the residence of a party is unknown to the notary public, he shall send the notices to the holders of the paper, shall state in his protest the names of the parties to whom he gave notice, and the time and manner of giving the same and such statement in such protest shall be prima facie evidence that notices were given as therein stated.

>>423.050 Records of notary to be delivered to county clerk, when

Upon the resignation of a notary public or the expiration of his term of office if he is not reappointed, he shall place his record book in the office of the county clerk in the county in which he was appointed, and if a notary dies, his representative shall deposit the record book with the clerk aforesaid.

>>423.060 Foreign notary; when protest by is evidence

If any commercial paper is protested in any other state of the United States in which it is made payable, and by the laws of that state a notary public or other officer

附上其签章证明，声明公证人此前已向其办公室呈交了带有手写签名的任命和资质证明，在出具证据证明和确认证明之时已获得了相应授权；郡书记官熟悉公证人笔迹，相信证据证明和确认证明上签名的真实性。

>>423.030 待记录之拒绝证书；作为证据的副本

公证人就汇票、支票或本票之拒绝承兑或拒付出具拒绝证书的，应记录于妥善装订和编码索引的册子中，由公证人本人保管。拒绝证书应置于汇票页脚，是应法律要求而出具的，可作为证明拒绝的证据。

此类拒绝证书的副本加盖公证人公章，经其公证后，在本州所有法庭均可作为初步证据。

>>423.040 拒绝通知书；发送对象

遇 KRS 423.030 条款中提及的票据拒绝情形，公证人应立即根据法律要求向相关方发送拒绝通知书，以确认其责任。

如公证人不知道一方住址的，应将通知书交付给文件持有者，并在其拒绝证书中载明欲通知者的姓名、时间和通知送达方式，上述所载内容应作为通知书已按所载内容送达之初步证据。

>>423.050 逢下列情形，公证人之记录应送往郡书记官处

公证人辞职或其未获再次任命而任期届满时，应将其记录册交予其任命地郡书记官处；公证人身故的，其代表人应将记录册交存于前述书记官处。

>>423.060 他州公证人；他州拒绝证书之效力

如任何商业票据在其欲获支付的美国其他州被拒绝，而该州法律要求公证人或其他同样有权出具拒绝证书的官员须向相关方发送拒绝通知书的，或上述公

authorized to protest the same is required to give notice of dishonor to the parties or if the certificate of such notary or officer, or a copy thereof, stating that such notice was sent, is evidence, in the courts of that state, then such protest, certificate or copy is admissible as evidence and shall have the same effect in the courts of this state as is given to such evidence in the courts of the other state.

>>423.070 Commissioners of foreign deeds; appointment, term

The Governor may appoint and commission one (1) or more commissioners of deeds in each state of the United States for a term of two (2) years.

Before entering on the duties of his office, each commissioner shall make and subscribe an affidavit, before an officer authorized to administer an oath, to well and truly execute and perform all the duties of his office. The affidavit must be filed in the office of the Secretary of State of this state.

>>423.080 Powers of commissioners

Any commissioner of deeds appointed and qualified pursuant to KRS 423.070 maytake the acknowledgment of proof of any instrument of writing, except wills, which instrument is required by the laws of this state to be recorded.

The examination, acknowledgment or proof of any such instrument taken by a commissioner, and certified under his official seal, in the manner required by the laws of this state, shall authorize the instrument to be recorded in the proper office. A commissioner of deeds may administer any oath or take any affirmation necessary to discharge his official duties, and may take and certify depositions to be read on the trial of any action or proceeding in any of the courts of this state.

>>423.110 Recognition of notarial acts performed outside this state

For the purposes of KRS 423.110 to 423.190, "notarial acts" means acts which the laws and regulations of this state authorize notaries public of this state to perform, including the administering of oaths and affirmations, taking proof of execution and acknowledgments of instruments, and attesting documents.

Notarial acts may be performed outside this state for use in this state with the same effect as if performed by a notary public of this state by the following persons authorized pursuant to the laws and regulations of other governments in addition to any other person authorized by

证人／官员出具之证书／证书副本载明已发送上述通知书，并被该州法庭接受为证据的，则上述拒绝、拒绝证书及其副本在本州法庭可作为证据接受，并具有和在该州法庭上相同的效力。

>>423.070 涉外契约专员；任命和任期

州长可就美国每个州任命 1 名或多名契约专员，任期为 2 年。

履职之前，每位专员须在授权监督宣誓之官员面前，制作并签署宣誓书，保证充分履行其所有职责。宣誓书必须呈交本州州务卿办公室。

>>423.080 专员之权力

根据 KRS 423.070 条款任命和适格的专员均可对除遗嘱外的所有书面法律文件进行确认公证，遗嘱按照本州法律要求须进行记录。

专员就任何此类法律文件之检查、承认或证实，经其以本州法律规定的方式加盖公章认证，将授权该法律文件由适格部门记录。契约专员可采取任何必要之宣誓或声明以履行其职责，可录取或证实口供，以供在本州所有法庭诉讼时宣读使用。

>>423.110 州外实施的公证行为的认可

KRS 423.110 条至 423.190 条中，"公证行为"指的是本州法律法规授权本州公证人所为之行为，包括实施宣誓和声明，证实法律文件之执行和承认，以及证明文件。

除由本州法律法规授权者实施外，下列人士根据他州法律法规授权在本州之外实施之公证行为，用于本州时，具有与本州公证人实施之公证行为相同的效力：

the laws and regulations of this state:

(1) A notary public authorized to perform notarial acts in the place in which the act is performed;

(2) A judge, clerk, or deputy clerk of any court of record in the place in which the notarial act is performed;

(3) An officer of the foreign service of the United States, a consular agent, or any other person authorized by regulation of the United States Department of State to perform notarial acts in the place in which the act is performed;

(4) A commissioned officer in active service with the Armed Forces of the United States and any other person authorized by regulation of the Armed Forces to perform notarial acts if the notarial act is performed for one (1) of the following or his dependents: a merchant seaman of the United States, a member of the Armed Forces of the United States, or any other person serving with or accompanying the Armed Forces of the United States;

(5) Any other person authorized to perform notarial acts in the place in which the act is performed; or

(6) A person, either a resident or a nonresident of Kentucky, who is appointed by the Governor of Kentucky to perform notarial acts in or outside this state covering writings prepared for recordation in this state.

COMPLEMENTARY LEGISLATION:
Alaska-AS 09.63.050 to 09.63.130.
Arizona-A.R.S. ss 33-501 to 33-508.
Colorado-West's C.R.S.A. ss12-55-201 to 12-55-210.

Connecticut-C.G.S.A. ss 1-57 to 1-65.
Illinois-S.H.A. 765 ILCS 30/1 to 30/10.
Kentucky-KRS 423.110 to 423.190.
Maine-4 M.R.S.A. ss 1011 to 1019.
Michigan-M.C.L.A. ss 565.261 to 565.270.
Nebraska-R.R.S. 1943, ss 64-201 to 64-215.
North Dakota-NDCC 47-19-14.1 to 47-19-14.8.
Ohio-R.C. ss 147.51 to 147.58.
South Carolina-Code 1976, ss 26-3-10 to 26-3-90.
Virgin Islands-28 V.I.C. ss 81 to 89.
Virginia-Code 1950, ss 55-118.1 to 55-118.9.
West Virginia-Code, 39-1A-1 to 39-1A-9.

>>423.120 Authentication of authority of officer--Repealed

>>423.130 Certificate of person taking acknow-ledgment

（1）在公证行为地有权实施公证的公证人；

（2）公证行为地记录法庭的法官、书记员或副书记员；

（3）经美国国务院法规授权，有权在公证行为地实施公证的美国外交部门官员、领事代办或其他人；

（4）根据美国军方法规授权，有权为下列人员或其家属公证的现役美国军方官员或其他人：美国的商船水手、美国军方成员，或其他服务或陪同美国军方者；

（5）公证行为地其他有权实施公证者；或

（6）由肯塔基州州长任命，在本州内或本州之外就须记录于本州的文书实施公证者，无论其是否为肯塔基州居民。

补充立法：
阿拉斯加 -AS 09.63.050 至 09.63.130. 条
亚利桑那 --A.R.S. ss 33-501 至 33-508. 条
科罗拉多 - 西部 C.R.S.A. ss12-55-201 至 12-55-210 条
康涅狄格 -C.G.S.A. ss 1-57 至 1-65 条
伊利诺伊 -S.H.A. 765 ILCS 30/1 至 30/10 条
肯塔基 -KRS 423.110 至 423.190. 条
缅因 -4 M.R.S.A. ss 1011 至 1019. 条
密歇根 -M.C.L.A. ss 565.261 至 565.270. 条
内布拉斯加 -R.R.S. 1943, ss 64-201 至 64-215. 条
北达科他 -NDCC 47-19-14.1 至 47-19-14.8 条
俄亥俄 -R.C. ss 147.51 至 147.58. 条
南卡罗来纳 -Code 1976, ss 26-3-10 至 26-3-90. 条
英属维尔京群岛 -28 V.I.C. ss 81 至 89. 条
弗吉尼亚 -Code 1950, ss 55-118.1 至 55-118.9. 条
西弗吉尼亚 -Code, 39-1A-1 至 39-1A-9 条

>>423.120 官员授权之证实——已废止

>>423.130 实施确认者的证明

>>423.130 The person taking an acknowledgment shall certify that:

(1) The person acknowledging appeared before him and acknowledged he executed the instrument; and

(2) The person acknowledging was known to the person taking the acknowledgment or that the person taking the acknowledgment had satisfactory evidence that the person acknowledging was the person described in and who executed the instrument.

>>423.140 Recognition of certificate of acknow-ledgment

The form of a certificate of acknowledgment used by a person whose authority is recognized under KRS 423.110 shall be accepted in this state if:

(1) The certificate is in a form prescribed by the laws or regulations of this state;

(2) The certificate is in a form prescribed by the laws or regulations applicable in the place in which the acknowledgment is taken; or

(3) The certificate contains the words "acknowledged before me," or their substantial equivalent.

>>423.150 Certificate of acknowledgment

The words "acknowledged before me" mean:

(1) That the person acknowledging appeared before the person taking the acknowledgment;

(2) That he acknowledged he executed the instrument;

(3) That, in the case of:

(a) A natural person, he executed the instrument for the purposes therein stated;

(b) A corporation, the officer or agent acknowledged he held the position or title set forth in the instrument and certificate, he signed the instrument on behalf of the corporation by proper authority, and the instrument was the act of the corporation for the purpose therein stated;

(c) A partnership, the partner or agent acknowledged he signed the instrument on behalf of the partnership by proper authority and he executed the instrument as the act of the partnership for the purpose therein stated;

(d) A person acknowledging as principal by an attorney in fact, he executed the instrument by proper authority as the act of the principal for the purposes therein stated;

(e) A person acknowledging as a public officer, trustee, administrator, guardian, or other representative, he signed the instrument by proper authority and he executed the instrument in the capacity and for the purposes therein

>>423.130 实施确认者应证明：

（1）要求确认者亲临现场，确认其签署了法律文件；并且

（2）实施确认者与要求确认者相识，或有充分证据证明要求确认者是法律文件中所描述的人，或者是执行该法律文件者。

>>423.140 确认证书之认可

根据 KRS 423.110 条被授权者，在下列情况下应承认其出具的确认证书的效力：

（1）该证书以本州的法律或法规规定的形式出具；

（2）该证书以实施确认地的法律或法规规定的形式出具；或者

（3）该证书包含"在我面前确认"的字样，或其实质上的同义词。

>>423.150 确认证书

"在我面前确认"字样的含义是：

（1）要求确认者现身实施确认者面前；

（2）他确认他签署了法律文件；

（3）就以下情况而言：

（a）对自然人而言，其为文件所载之目的执行文件；

（b）对公司而言，官员或代理人确认其具有文件所载之职位或头衔，并证明，其经适当授权代表公司签署文件，文件是公司出于文件所载之目的的公司行为；

（c）对合伙企业而言，合伙人或代理人确认其经适当授权代表合伙企业签署文件，其以公司行为之名义出于文件所载之目的执行文件；

（d）要求确认者是当事人代理人的，其经适当授权以当事人名义出于文件所载之目的执行文件；

（e）要求确认者是公共官员、受托人、遗产管理人、监护人或其他代表人的，其经适当授权签署文件，出于文件所载之目的和权限执行文件；

stated; and

(4) That the person taking the acknowledgment either knew or had satisfactory evidence that the person acknowledging was the person named in the instrument or certificate.

>>423.160 Short forms of acknowledgment

The forms of acknowledgment set forth in this section may be used and are sufficient for their respective purposes under any law of this state.

The forms shall be known as "Statutory Short Forms of Acknowledgment" and may bereferred to by that name. The authorization of the forms in this section does not preclude the use of other forms.

(1) For an individual acting in his own right:

State of _____

County of _____

The foregoing instrument was acknowledged before me this (date) by (name ofperson acknowledged).

(Signature of person taking acknowledgment)

(Title or rank)

(Serial number, if any)

(2) For a corporation:

State of _____

County of _____

The foregoing instrument was acknowledged before me this (date) by (name ofofficer or agent, title of officer or agent) of (name ofcorporation acknowledging) a (state or place of incorporation) corporation, on behalf of the corporation.

(Signature of person taking acknowledgment)

(Title or rank)

(Serial number, if any)

(3) For a partnership:

State of _____

County of _____

The foregoing instrument was acknowledged before me this (date) by (name of acknowledging partner or agent), partner (or agent) on behalf of (name of partnership), a partnership.

(Signature of person taking acknowledgment)

(Title or rank)

(Serial number, if any)

(4) For an individual acting as principal by an attorney-in-fact:

State of _____

County of _____

（4）实施确认者知道或有充分证据证明要求确认者是文件或证书中指明的人。

>>423.160 确认的简易格式

本条所述确认之格式可用于实现本州各法律规定之目的，并足以实现上述目的。

下列格式名为"确认之法定简易格式"，援引时应用此名。本条对下列格式之授权并不排除其他格式的使用。

（1）对于行使本人权利之个人：

_____州

_____郡

前述文件于今日（日期）在我面前由（要求确认者之姓名）确认。

（执行确认者之签名）

（头衔或军衔）

（序列号，如有的话）

（2）对于公司：

_____州

_____郡

前述文件于今日（日期）在我面前由（公司所在州/地）（要求确认之公司名称）的（官员或代理人之姓名，官员或代理员之头衔）代表公司确认。

（执行确认者之签名）

（头衔或军衔）

（序列号，如有的话）

（3）对于合伙企业：

_____州

_____郡

前述文件于今日（日期）在我面前由合伙人/代理人（要求确认之合伙人或代理人姓名）代表（合伙企业名称）确认。

（执行确认者之签名）

（头衔或军衔）

（序列号，如有的话）

（4）对于当事人代理人：

_____州

_____郡

The foregoing instrument was acknowledged before me this (date) by (name of attorney-in-fact) as attorney-in-fact on behalf of (name of principal).

(Signature of person taking acknowledgment)

(Title or rank)

(Serial number, if any)

(5) By any public officer, trustee, or personal representative:

State of _____

County of _____

The foregoing instrument was acknowledged before me this (date) by (name and title of position).

(Signature of person taking acknowledgment)

(Title or rank)

(Serial number, if any)

>>423.170 Acknowledgments not affected by KRS 423.110 to 423.190

A notarial act performed prior to July 1, 1970, is not affected by KRS 423.110 to 423.190. KRS 423.110 to 423.190 provide an additional method of proving notarial acts. Nothing in KRS 423.110 to 423.190 diminishes or invalidates the recognition accorded to notarial acts by other laws or regulations of this state.

>>423.180 Uniformity of interpretation

KRS 423.110 to 423.190 shall be so interpreted as to make uniform the laws of those states which enact it.

>>423.190 Short title

KRS 423.110 to 423.190 may be cited as the "Uniform Recognition of Acknowledgments Act."

>>423.200 Admission of documents to the public record

Notwithstanding any other provision of law, any certificate of an acknowledgment given and certified as provided by KRS 423.110 to 423.190 or as provided by those sections and other provisions of law, together with the instrument acknowledged, may be admitted to the public record provided for the type of instrument so acknowledged, and any instrument required to be sworn to or affirmed in order to be recorded may be admitted to record upon a jurat recognized under the provisions of KRS 423.110 to 423.190.

>>423.990 Penalties

For each failure to record his protest as required by KRS 423.030, a notary public shall forfeit all his fees and shall be fined five dollars ($5).

前述文件于今日（日期）在我面前由（代理人姓名）作为代理人代表（当事人姓名）确认。

（执行确认者之签名）

（头衔或军衔）

（序列号，如有的话）

（5）对于公共官员、受托人或个人代表：

_____ 州

_____ 郡

前述文件于今日（日期）在我面前由（姓名以及职位头衔）确认。

（执行确认者之签名）

（头衔或军衔）

（序列号，如有的话）

>>423.170 不受 KRS 423.110 条至 423.190 条调整的确认

1970年7月1日前实施的公证行为不受KRS 423.110条至423.190条调整。KRS 423.110条至423.190条提供了证明公证行为的一条额外途径。根据本州其他法律法规授予之认可，不因KRS 423.110条至423.190条中的内容而撤销或无效。

>>423.180 解释之一致性

KRS 423.110条至423.190条应当以能统一各实施州法律的方式解释。

>>423.190 简称

KRS 423.110条至423.190条可引述为"确认行为之统一认可"。

>>423.200 确认文件之公开

无论其他法律条款如何规定，依据KRS 423.110条至423.190条或上述条款以及其他法律条款而出具、证明之确认证书，连同已确认的法律文件，可载入针对上述已确认法律文件的公共记录。任何须经宣誓或声明才能记录之法律文件，须附上为KRS 423.110条至423.190条所认可的宣誓证明，方可载入记录。

>>423.990 惩罚

公证人未按照KRS 423.030条记录其（出具的）拒绝证书的，没收其所有收费并每次罚款5美元。

路易斯安那州

路易斯安那州公证法

LOUISIANA REVISED STATUTES	**路易斯安那法规修正案**

TITLE 35. **NOTARIES PUBLIC AND COMMISSIONERS** **CHAPTER 1. GENERAL PROVISIONS** **§1. Appointment of notaries public** The governor may appoint, by and with the advice and consent of the Senate, and upon their meeting the qualifications for office provided for in this Title, notaries public in the different parishes. **§1.1. Commissions previously issued** A. Notwithstanding any other provision of law to the contrary, this Section shall apply to all acts, documents, or other instruments which were executed by or passed before a notary public who was duly appointed, and to each notarial commission which was issued, on or before January 1, 1999, without the applicant first obtaining a commission in the parish of residence of the applicant, and whose commission was based on the location of the office maintained by the applicant. B. All acts, documents, or other instruments which were executed by or passed before any notary public commissioned as set forth in Subsection A of this Section shall not be invalid based on the appointment of the notary public or the issuance of the notarial commission. **§2. General powers; administration of certain oaths in any parish** A.(1) Notaries public have power within their several parishes:	**第 35 编** **公证人及其任命** **第一章 一般规定** **§1. 公证人的任命** 州长经参议院的提议并同意，依照他们在会议中对公证人职位规定的要求，委任不同行政区的公证人。 **§1.1. 本法生效前的任命** A. 即使有相反规定，本条依然适用于经正当程序任命的公证人见证而订立或通过的所有行为、文件或其他文书，并适用于 1999 年 1 月 1 日当天及之前发布的所有公证人任命，但申请人首先在其住所行政区获得任命，且其任命是基于其所营运之公证处位置的除外。 B. 本条 A 款规定的公证人执行或通过的所有行为、文件或其他文书，不因新的公证人任命而无效。 **§2. 一般权力；管理任何行政区的特定誓言** A.（1）公证人在其管辖的行政区内有以下权力：

(a) To make inventories, appraisements, and partitions;

(b) To receive wills, make protests, matrimonial contracts, conveyances, and generally, all contracts and instruments of writing;

(c) To hold family meetings and meetings of creditors;

(d) To receive acknowledgements of instruments under private signature;

(e) To make affidavits of correction;

(f) To affix the seals upon the effects of deceased persons, and to raise the same.

(2) All acts executed by a notary public, in conformity with the provisions of Civil Code Art. 1833, shall be authentic acts.

(3) Notwithstanding any provision in the law to the contrary, a notary public shall have power, within the parish or parishes in which he is authorized, to exercise all of the functions of a notary public and to receive wills in which he is named as administrator, executor, trustee, attorney for the administrator, attorney for the executor, attorney for the trustee, attorney for a legatee, attorney for an heir, or attorney for the estate.

B. However, each notary public of this state shall have authority to administer oaths in any parish of the state, to swear in persons who appear to give testimony at a deposition before a general reporter or free-lance reporter certified under the provisions of R.S. 37:2551 et seq., and to verify interrogatories and other pleadings to be used in the courts of record of this state. Such oaths, and the certificates issued by such notaries shall be received in the courts of this state and shall have legal efficacy for purposes of the laws on perjury.

C. Every qualified notary public is authorized to certify true copies of any authentic act or any instrument under private signature hereafter or heretofore passed before him or acknowledged before him, and to make and certify copies, by any method, of any certificate, research, resolution, survey or other document annexed to the original of any authentic acts passed before him, and may certify such copies as true copies of the original document attached to the original passed before him.

§2.1. Affidavit of corrections

A. (1) A clerical error in a notarial act affecting movable or immovable property or any other rights, corporeal or incorporeal, may be corrected by an act of correction

（a）清查、评估和划分行政区；

（b）接受遗嘱、制作异议书、婚姻合同、交易合同以及总体上所有的合同和文书；

（c）举行家庭会议和债权人会议；

（d）接受私人签名的文书的确认；

（e）作出更正的誓章；

（f）在确认死者死亡影响的文件上盖上公章。

（2）公证人依照1833年《民法典》的规定执行的一切行为，应当是真实的行为。

（3）无论法律规定是否相反，公证人有权在其授权的行政区内行使公证人的所有职权，并接受他人遗嘱，作为管理人、执行人、受托人、管理人，并有权作为遗嘱或遗产执行人的律师、受托人的律师、合伙人的律师、继承人的律师。

B. 本州的公证人都有权在本州的任何行政区内执行宣誓，根据R.S. 37:2551条及项目的规定，在一般记者或自由撰稿记者证明的情况下，出庭作证宣誓，有权证明在本州记录的法庭中使用的询问单和其他书状。发出此类宣誓书或公证书，由本州法院接收，并受伪证法的规制。

C. 每个合格的公证人都有权证明，任何真实文书的副本或在其承认之前或之后进行了私人签名的文书，或在其面前递交或承认的任何文书，以及以任何方式向其递交的任何证明书、研究、解决方案、调查或其他真实文件的副本，公证人有权证明上述副本是与原件一致的真实副本。

§2.1. 错误的纠正

A.（1）公证行为中的文书错误，如果影响到动产或不动产或其他无论是物质的还是非物质的权利，都可以由以下任何一人进行纠正：

executed by any of the following:

(a) The person who was the notary or one of the notaries before whom the act was passed.

(b) The notary who actually prepared the act containing the error.

(c) In the event the person defined in Subparagraphs (a) or (b) of this Paragraph is deceased, incapacitated, or whose whereabouts are unknown, then by a Louisiana notary who has possession of the records of that person, which records contain information to support the correction.

(2) The act of correction shall be executed before two witnesses and a notary public.

B. The act of correction executed in compliance with this Section shall be given retroactive effect to the date of recordation of the original act. However, the act of correction shall not prejudice the rights acquired by any third person before the act of correction is recorded where the third person reasonably relied on the original act. The act of correction shall not alter the true agreement and intent of the parties.

C. A certified copy of the act of correction executed in compliance with this Section shall be deemed to be authentic for purposes of executory process.

D. This Section shall be in addition to other laws governing executory process.

§3. Oaths and acknowledgments

Oaths and acknowledgments, in all cases, may be taken or made by or before any notary public duly appointed and qualified in this state.

§4. Notaries connected with banks and other corporations; powers

It is lawful for any notary public who is a stockholder, director, officer, or employe of a bank or other corporation to take the acknowledgment of any party to any written instrument executed to or by such corporation, or to administer an oath to any other stockholder, director, officer, employe, or agent of such corporation, or to protest for non-acceptance or nonpayment bills of exchange, drafts, checks, notes, and other negotiable instruments which may be owned or held for collection by such corporation. It is unlawful for any notary public to take the acknowledgment of an instrument by or to a bank or other corporation of which he is a stockholder, director, officer, or employe, where the notary is a party to such instrument, either individually or as a representative of such corpo-

（a）作出该公证行为的公证人，或见证该公证行为完成的公证人。

（b）实际上为该包含错误的公证行为做准备的公证人。

（c）如果本款（a）项或（b）项所界定的人员死亡、丧失工作能力或下落不明，则由路易斯安那州保有该人的记录的公证人，将其相关信息更正。

（2）纠正应当在两名证人以及一名公证人面前执行。

B. 按照本条执行的纠正行为，其效力应当追溯到原始的公证之日。但是，纠正行为不得损害任何善意第三人在取消纠正行为之前所获得的权利。纠正行为不得改变双方的真实合同和意图。

C. 依照本条执行纠正行为的证明副本，应当被视为执行过程真实性的证明。

D. 本条是对其他关于执行程序的补充。

§3. 誓言和确认

在所有情况下，在本州正式任命的合格公证人有权作出宣誓和确认。

§4. 与银行和其他公司有联系的公证人；权力

作为银行或其他法人的股东、董事、高级书记官或雇用人员的公证人，有权对该公司作为任何一方当事人所执行的任何书面文书进行确认，或管理该公司任何股东、董事、高级书记官、雇员或代理人的宣誓，或拒绝承兑汇票、支票、票据和其他可能由该公司收取的票据。当银行或其他法人是该文书的一方当事人，而公证人是银行或其他法人的股东、董事、高级书记官、雇员，而公证人单独作为票据的一方当事人（无论代表公司还是自己）时，公证人为银行或其他法人所作出的或所拥有的票据进行承认的行为是非法的，对银行或法人持有或收取的任何可转让票据的拒绝承兑也是非法的。

ration, or to protest any negotiable instrument owned or held for collection by the corporation, where the notary is individually a party to the instrument.

§5. Foreign notaries; oaths, acts, and acknowledgments; effect

Oaths, acts, and acknowledgements taken, made, or executed by or before any person purporting to be a notary public, duly appointed and duly qualified in any other state, territory of the United States, or the District of Columbia shall have the same force and effect without further proof of the signatures as if taken, made, or executed by or before a notary public in Louisiana. This Section is remedial and shall be retroactive. All oaths, acts, and acknowledgements heretofore made in compliance with the provisions of this Section are hereby validated.

§6. Foreign notaries; acts and other instruments, effect

All acts passed before any notary public and two witnesses in the District of Columbia, or any state of the United States other than Louisiana shall be authentic acts and shall have the same force and effect as if passed before a notary public in Louisiana.

§7. Acts before authorized military personnel; force and effect

A. Every mortgage, sale, lease, transfer, assignment, power of attorney, or other instrument, heretofore or hereafter executed before any person authorized to act as a notary pursuant to 10 U.S.C. 1044a(b) , and bearing the signature of such person and the proper designation of his rank and branch of service or subdivision thereof, shall be admissible in evidence and eligible to record in this state, and shall have the same force and effect of an authentic act executed in Louisiana.

B. Any oath, affirmation, deposition, or affidavit executed before any person authorized to act as a notary pursuant to 10 U.S.C. 1044a(b) shall have the same force and effect as if made or executed before a notary in Louisiana.

C. Any testament, trust, or other legal instrument or act provided for in Subsections A and B executed before any person authorized to act as a notary pursuant to 10 U.S.C. 1044a(b) shall have the same force and effect as if made or executed before a notary in Louisiana.

D. The provisions of this Section apply to persons serving in or with the armed forces or the Coast Guard of the United States and other persons eligible for legal assis-

§5. 他州公证人；誓言，行为和承认；影响

在美国其他各州或是哥伦比亚特区任命的合格的公证人面前作出、执行的宣誓、行为、承认皆与路易斯安那州的公证行为效力一致。本条是补充立法，对之前的公证行为具有溯及力。所有根据本条规定进行的宣誓、行为和确认均有效。

§6. 他州公证人；行为和其他文书，效力

除路易斯安那以外的其他美国的州和哥伦比亚特区的任何公证人和两个见证人作出的行为均为真实的行为，并与路易斯安那州公证人执行的公证行为具有相同的效力。

§7. 被授权军事人员的行为；效力

A. 根据 10 U.S.C.1044（b）被授权作为公证人的个人，无论在任命之前还是之后执行的任何按揭、出售、租赁、转让、分配，委托书或其他文书，只要上面有该被授权人的签名、职称和服务部门，则这些行为应被接受为证据，并有资格在该州被记录，且具有与在路易斯安那州执行的其他真实行为相同的效力。

B. 根据 10U.S.C.1044a(b) 被授权作为公证人的人，在其面前完成的任何宣誓、确认、证词或宣誓书，都与在路易斯安那州公证人面前完成的具有相同的效力。

C. 根据 10 U.S.C.1044a(b) 被授权作为公证人的人，在其面前执行的 A 款和 B 款规定的任何遗嘱、信托或其他法律文书或行为，都与在路易斯安那州公证人面前完成的具有相同的效力。

D. 本条的规定适用于在美国海岸警卫队服役的以及根据 10 U.S.C. 或美国国防部的规定可获得法律援助的其他人员、受 10 U.S.C. 1044a(a) 指定的人员所

tance under the provisions of 10 U.S.C. 1044 or pursuant to regulations of the Department of Defense and all instruments and acts executed by persons designated in 10 U.S.C. 1044a(a) .

§8. Recorder's copies of instruments before military officers; effect

Whenever any original instrument executed pursuant to R.S. 35:7, has been deposited in the office of a parish recorder of this state, the recorder is authorized to make copies of the same which shall have the same force and effect of authentic acts executed in this state.

§9. Instruments, before ambassadors and consular officials

Every mortgage, sale, lease, transfer, assignment, power of attorney, or other instrument, and every oath or affirmation, made or taken in any foreign country, before any ambassador, minister, charge d'affaires, secretary of legation, consul general, consul, vice-consul, or commercial agent, or before one of the following officers commissioned or accredited to act at the place where the act is made or taken, and having an official seal, to wit: any officer of the United States, any notary public, or any commissioner or other agent of this state having power to take acknowledgements, and every acknowledgement, attestation or authentication of such instruments, oaths or affirmations made by any of these officers under their official seals and signatures, shall have the full force and effect of an authentic act executed in this state; and it shall not be necessary that the officer be assisted by two witnesses, as in the case of a notary executing an authentic act in this state, but the attestation, seal and signature of the officer shall of themselves be sufficient; nor shall it be necessary that the person appearing before the officer to execute any of these instruments, or to take any oath or affirmation, be a resident of the place where the officer is located. Whenever any such original instrument, oath, or affirmation has been deposited in the office of a notary in this state, the notary is authorized to make copies of the same, which shall have the same force and effect as copies of authentic acts executed in this state.

§10. Place of executing notarial acts

All notarial acts shall be made and executed at any place within the jurisdictional limits of the notary.

§11. Marital status of parties to be given

A. Whenever notaries pass any acts they shall give

执行的所有公证行为和文书。

§8. 在军官面前的记录副本；效力

根据 R.S.35:7 执行的任何原始文书，存放在本州行政区的记录办公室后，该记录可以被授权进行复制以形成具有与原件效力相同的复制品。

§9. 在大使和领事官员面前作出的文书

在任何大使、部长、临时代办、秘书长、总领事、副总领事、商业代理人或者在行为发生地被授权任命的官员面前办理按揭、出售、租赁、转让、分配委托书或其他文书，以及在任何外国所作的任何宣誓或确认书，其上具有官方盖章，并载有：任何美国官员，任何公证人，或该国有权力承认的任何专员或其他代理人，任何这些官员以公章和签名作出的誓言或确认，证明和认证这些文书，具有与在本州执行的真实行为的同等效力；公证人在本州作出真实的执行行为，则该官员无须两名证人的协助，但必须具有该人员的宣誓、印章和签名；也不要求任何在该官员面前执行该文书或作任何宣誓或确认的人是该官员所在地的居民。任何此类原始文书、誓言或确认书已经存放在本州公证处的，公证人可以复印，副本与正本具有相同的效力。

§10. 执行公证行为的地点

所有公证行为均应在公证人管辖范围内进行。

§11. 当事人婚姻状况

A. 公证人办理公证行为时，应当说明该行为所

the marital status of all parties to the act, viz: If either or any party or parties are men, they shall be described as single, married, or widower. If married or widower the christian and family name of wife shall be given. If either or any party or parties are women, they shall be described as single, married or widow. If married or widow, their christian and family name shall be given, adding that she is the wife of or widow of … the husband's name.

B. A declaration as to one's marital status in an acquisition of immovable property by the person acquiring the property creates a presumption that the marital status as declared in the act of acquisition is correct and, except as provided in Subsection C of this Section, any subsequent alienation, encumbrance, or lease of the immovable by onerous title shall not be attacked on the ground that the marital status was not as stated in the declaration.

C. Any person may file an action to attack the subsequent alienation, encumbrance, or lease on the ground that the marital status of the party as stated in the initial act of acquisition is false and incorrect; however, such action to attack the alienation, encumbrance, or lease shall not affect any right or rights acquired by a third person acting in good faith.

D. The presumption provided in Subsection B of this Section is hereby declared to be remedial and made retroactive to any alienation, encumbrance, or lease made prior to September 1, 1987. Any person who has a right as provided in Subsection C of this Section, which right has not prescribed or otherwise been extinguished or barred upon September 1, 1987 and who is adversely affected by the provisions of Subsection C of this Section shall have six months from September 1, 1987 to initiate an action to attack the transaction or otherwise be forever barred from exercising his right or cause of action.

§12. Names to be given in full, together with parties' permanent mailing addresses; identification numbers

A. (1) Notaries shall insert in their acts the Christian names and surnames of the parties in full and not their initial letters alone or the full names of the parties and not their initial letters alone, together with the permanent mailing addresses of the parties, and shall print or type the full names of the witnesses and of themselves under their respective signatures.

(2) For the purposes of this Section, a full name or a name in full shall include at least one given name and

涉及的各方的婚姻状况：任何一方或各方当事人为男性时，应被描述为单身、已婚或鳏夫。如果是已婚或鳏夫，则应当提供妻子的教名以及姓氏。如果当事人是女性，则应被描述为单身、已婚或寡妇。如果是已婚或寡妇，则应提供她们的教名和姓氏并补充说明，她是（丈夫的名字）的妻子或者遗孀。

B. 关于通过收购不动产获得该财产的人的个人婚姻状况的声明构成一种假设，即在收购行为中宣称的婚姻状况是正确的，除本条 C 款规定之外，任何随后的产权转让、产权负担或租赁，不得以婚姻状况未如实声明而受到异议。

C. 任何人可以用诉讼的方式，以在初步收购行为中一方的婚姻状况存在错误为理由，对抗产权转让、产权负担或租赁；然而，这种对产权转让、产权负担或租赁的异议，不得影响善意第三方善意取得的任何权利。

D. 本条 B 款是补充立法，对之前的公证行为具有溯及力，可追溯到 1987 年 9 月 1 日之前作出的任何转让、产权负担或租赁。任何具有本条 C 款规定的权利的人，而该权利从 1987 年 9 月 1 日起被禁止的，享有本条 C 款规定的权利，自 1987 年 9 月 1 日起其有六个月的时间提出异议，以诉讼或者其他方式对抗权利转移，否则该诉权将永久丧失。

§12. 全名，连同各方当事人永久邮寄地址；身份证号码

A.（1）公证人应当完整记录当事人的教名和姓氏，不得以缩写的方式记录。并且应同时记录当事人的永久邮寄地址，并在其各自的签名下印刷或输入证人的全名，由证人亲自签名。

（2）在本条中，除姓氏外，全名或姓名应至少包括名字或者其他首字母。它可以是名和中间名（如果

other initials in addition to the surname. It may be any combination of first name and middle initial or initials, if any, and the surname; or the first initial and at least one middle name and the surname; or the complete first and middle name or names and the surname. The notary shall type, print, or stamp his or her name as it appears on his or her commission.

B. Every document notarized in this state shall bear the notary identification number assigned by the secretary of state, except that if the notary is an attorney licensed to practice law in this state, he may use his Louisiana state bar roll number in lieu of his notary identification number. The number shall be typed or printed legibly and placed next to the typed, printed, or stamped name of the notary as required by Subsection A of this Section.

C. No person other than a regularly commissioned notary public shall use the title "Notary Public". Every person, other than a regularly commissioned notary, who is otherwise given notarial powers or authorized as a notary ex officio, shall clearly indicate his actual position or title from which his authority to notarize is derived, in addition to his notary identification number.

D.(1) Any document notarized in this state on or after January 1, 2005, submitted for filing or recording in the office of notarial records, register of conveyances, or recorder of mortgages in and for the parish of Orleans, or in the office of any clerk of court or recorder of mortgages or conveyances may be refused by the clerk or his employee if the document fails to contain the notary identification or attorney bar roll number and the typed, printed, or stamped name of the notary and the witnesses. However, documents filed in the civil or criminal suit records of any court shall not be subject to the provisions of this Subsection.

(2) Except as otherwise provided in this Section, no state office, agency, department, or political subdivision shall accept, file, or record any document notarized in this state on or after January 1, 2005, unless the document contains the notary identification or attorney bar roll number and the typed, printed, or stamped name of the notary and the witnesses.

(3) No office, agency, department, or political subdivision, or any officer or employee thereof, refusing to accept, file, or record any notarized document pursuant to the provisions of this Section shall be liable for any damages resulting from the refusal to accept, file, or record a notarized document for its failure to comply with the provisions of this Section.

有的话）和姓氏的任何组合，或第一首字母和至少一个中间名和姓氏，或完整的第一个和中间名或名字和姓氏。公证人应在其委托书上通过机打、印刷或盖上其姓名。

B. 在本州公证的每一份文件均应载有州务卿分配的公证人编号，但如果公证人是在本州执业的律师，则其可以使用路易斯安那州的律师编号代替其公证人编号。编号应清晰打印，附在本条 A 款要求的通过机打、印刷或盖章的公证人名字旁边。

C. 除长期被委任为公证人以外的任何人不得使用"公证人"头衔。除经常性被委任为公证人以外的其他任何人，虽然被授予公证人的权力，但应当清楚地在公证人编号旁注明其实际的身份或被授予的称号。

D.（1）在 2005 年 1 月 1 日当日或之后为了填写或者记录而交到公证记录办公室、移转登记处或者在奥尔良行政区的任何抵押登记员或者法院的任何办公室进行公证的任何文件，如果没有载有公证人编号或律师编号以及公证人和证人以机打、印刷或盖章的方式留有的名字，则这些抵押或者产权转让记录可能会被书记员或者其雇员拒绝。但是，任何法院民事或刑事诉讼记录中提交的文件均不受本条规定的约束。

（2）除本条另有规定外，任何州务院、机构、部门、政治部门不得接受、提交或者记录任何本州在 2005 年 1 月 1 日当日或以后公证的文件，除非该文件载有公证人编号或律师编号以及公证人和证人的以机打、印刷或盖章方式留有的名字。

（3）任何办公室、机构、部门或政治部门或其任何高级人员或雇员，不得拒绝接受、提出、记录符合本条规定的公证文件，如果上述人员违反此规定，则应当对因此造成的损失承担责任。

§13. Repealed by Acts 1976, No. 384, §1

§14. Disbarred or suspended attorney prohibited from exercising notarial functions

Any attorney at law, or person who was an attorney at law, who is disbarred or suspended from the practice of law due to charges filed by the Committee on Professional Responsibility of the Louisiana State Bar Association or who has consented to disbarment shall not be qualified or eligible nor shall he exercise any functions as a notary public in any parish of the state of Louisiana as long as he remains disbarred or suspended from the practice of law in Louisiana. Provided, however, that nothing in this Section shall apply to any action taken against an attorney at law for failure to pay annual dues.

§15. Revocation or suspension of notarial commission or authority to exercise notarial powers

A. A notary public who is not an attorney may have his notarial commission and powers revoked or suspended when it is demonstrated, by clear and convincing evidence after a rule to show cause, that the notary has engaged in any of the following:

(1) Dishonesty, fraud, deceit, or misrepresentation.

(2) A felony for which he has been convicted and no pardon has been issued.

(3) Gross misconduct or malfeasance in the exercise of his notarial powers.

(4) Certifying as true what he knew or should have known was false.

(5) Violation of any provision of this Title, or any other law governing the office of notary public or the exercise of any notarial power or duty.

(6) Ceasing to possess any qualification required for holding his commission as a notary public.

(7) Abandonment of his commission.

B. The rule to show cause shall be instituted by the district attorney or the attorney general in the district court of either the parish in which the notary is commissioned or the parish where the conduct complained of occurred. Such rule to show cause shall be tried in summary proceeding.

C. (1) If after a hearing the court finds that the notary public was convicted of a felony for which no pardon has been issued, or engaged in an act of gross misconduct or malfeasance in the exercise of his notarial powers, or ceased to possess any qualification required for holding

§13. 本条被1976年第384号法案第1条废止

§14. 被取消资格或暂停执业的律师禁止行使公证职能

因路易斯安那州律师协会专业责任委员会提出的指控而被解除或暂停执业的律师，或者自愿取消律师资格的律师，只要其仍然在路易斯安那州处于取消律师职业资格或停止执业的状态，便不符合公证人的资格，也不得在路易斯安那州的任何行政区内行使公证人的任何职能，但是，本条款不适用于未支付年费的律师。

§15. 撤销或暂停公证人的任命或行使公证的权力

A. 如果根据明确而充分的证据证明非律师的公证人从事以下任何行为，其公证人任命或权力会被撤销或暂停：

（1）不诚实、欺诈、欺骗或虚假陈述。

（2）已被判处重罪且尚未被赦免。

（3）行使公证权力的过程中存在严重不当行为或者渎职行为。

（4）事实证明，其明知内容虚假仍作出公证行为。

（5）违反本法规定的公证人条款，或违反涉及公证人职务以及公证人执行权和责任的其他法律。

（6）缺少履行公证人职务必须的资格。

（7）放弃任命。

B. 上诉应由地方检察官或总检察长在公证人任职的行政区或引发诉讼的行为发生地的行政区的地方法院提起。此案应当按简易程序审理。

C.（1）如果听审后，法院认定，公证人确实犯有不能被赦免的重罪，或者行使其公证权力时有严重不当行为或者渎职行为，或者缺少履行公证人职务所需的资格，法院应责令撤销公证人任命，并禁止公证人进一步行使公证权力。

his commission, the court shall order the revocation of the notary's commission and shall prohibit the notary from the further exercise of notarial powers.

(2) If after a hearing the court finds that the notary public committed any other act set forth in Subsection A of this Section, the court may revoke the notary's commission and prohibit the notary from further exercise of notarial powers, or may suspend his commission and authority to exercise notarial powers for a specific period of time, to be determined by the court.

D. A court ordering the revocation of a notary's commission or the suspension of his notarial powers shall further cast the notary in judgment for attorney fees and court costs. The court may additionally order restitution to be paid by the notary public to such persons as the court determines were damaged by the conduct giving rise to the suspension of notarial powers or the revocation of commission.

E. When the rule to show cause is instituted against a person for his actions as an ex-officio notary public, or for his performance of notarial powers on behalf of an employer as authorized by law, then the person appointing the ex-officio notary or the person's employer, as applicable, shall also be named as a defendant and required to show cause why the notarial powers or commission should not be revoked. Any additional defendant named pursuant to this Subsection shall not be cast in judgment for attorney fees, costs, or restitution.

F. The provisions of this Section shall not apply to an attorney licensed to practice law in this state who exercises notarial powers.

§15.1. Administrative revocation of notarial commission or authority

A. The secretary of state shall suspend the commission of a notary public who is not an attorney when the notary ceases to be a registered voter in the parish of that notary's commission, or is convicted of a felony. The secretary of state shall send a notice of suspension by certified mail, return receipt requested, to the notary public stating the reasons for his suspension.

B. If the suspension arises from failure of the notary to be registered as a voter in his parish of commission, the notice of suspension shall give the notary public ten days from the date of receipt to register as a voter in the parish of his commission. If the notary public fails to do so, the secretary of state shall notify the district attorney

（2）如果听审后，法院认定，公证人犯有本条A款中规定的其他行为，法院可以撤销公证人任命并且禁止公证人进一步行使公证权力，或者可以在一段特定的时间内暂停其任命和行使公证职务的权力，上述处罚由法院决定。

D. 法院裁定撤销公证人任命或暂停公证的权力，还应判处公证人支付律师费和法院费用。法院还可以向公证人追究赔偿责任，赔付给法院认为因取消公证人任命或者暂停行使公证人权力而受到损害的人。

E. 当向依职能行使公证人行为的人，或者向代表法律授权的雇主履行公证权力的人提起以上诉讼时，则授权其公证人职能的人或者雇主应当也以被告的身份参与诉讼，并举证证明不应撤销公证人的权力或任命。法庭不得判令附加的被告人承担律师费、诉讼费用以及其他赔偿。

F. 本条的规定不适用于在本州执行公证权力的执业律师。

§15.1. 公证人任命和权力的行政撤销

A. 如果非律师公证人在其任命的行政区内已不具备选民资格或者犯下重罪时，州务卿应暂停对该非律师公证人的任命。州务卿应通过认证邮件，向该公证人告知暂停的理由，并要求公证人送交回执。

B. 如果暂停职务的原因是由于公证人未在其行政区内注册为选民，则暂停通知应给予公证人自回复之日起10日内在其任命的行政区内注册为选民的机会。如果公证人不这样做，州务卿应通知公证人任命的行政区的地方检察官，按照规则R.S. 35:15撤销其任命。

of the parish in which the notary is commissioned for the purpose of instituting a rule to show cause to revoke the commission pursuant to R.S. 35:15.

C. If the suspension arises from conviction of a felony, the period of suspension shall continue until the conviction is final and all appellate review of the original trial court proceedings has been exhausted. If the conviction is reversed upon appeal, or if a pardon is issued for the conviction, the suspension shall terminate and the commission shall be reinstated. When the conviction is final and all appellate review of the original trial court proceedings is exhausted, and if no pardon has been issued, the secretary of state shall notify the district attorney of the parish in which the notary is commissioned for the purpose of instituting a rule to show cause to revoke the commission pursuant to R.S. 35:15.

§17. Acts affecting immovable property; municipal number or address of property; social security number or employer identification number of parties

NOTE: Repealed by Acts 2005, No. 169, §8, eff. Jan. 1, 2006. Acts 2005, 1st Ex. Sess., No. 13, §1, changed the effective date to July 1, 2006.

CHAPTER 2. BONDS OF NOTARIES PUBLIC GENERALLY

§71. Requirement of bond or insurance; suspension of notarial commissions; renewal of bonds or insurance; penalty

A.(1) Unless otherwise provided by law, the authority of a notary public to exercise any of the functions of a notary public within his jurisdictional limits shall remain in effect, provided that the notary posts and maintains bond, with good and solvent security, in the amount of ten thousand dollars conditioned on the faithful performance of all duties required by law toward all persons who may employ him in his official capacity as notary public, or that the notary maintains a minimum of ten thousand dollars in errors and omissions insurance coverage.

(2) The provisions of this Section shall not be applicable to notarial bonds which are currently valid and enforceable until such bonds expire and are required to be renewed.

B. All notaries required to post bond, or required to maintain insurance coverage in lieu of posting bond in accordance with this Section, shall file their bond or evi-

C. 如果公证人的任命因被判处重罪而暂停，则暂停任命应持续到法院作出最终裁判，且对原审法庭诉讼的所有上诉救济已经用尽。如果上诉中定罪被驳回，或者如果罪刑被赦免，则终止暂停任务，并恢复对公证人的任命。如果对原审法庭诉讼的所有上诉救济都被用尽时，公证人被最终裁定犯有重罪且没有被赦免，州务卿应通知公证人任命的行政区的地方检察官，按照规则 R.S. 35:15 撤销其任命。

§17. 影响不动产的行为；市级号码或财产地址；社会保障号码或当事人雇主编号

注：根据2005年第169号法案第8条废止2005年第13号法案第1条，生效日期更改为2006年7月1日。

第二章　普通公证保证金

§71. 保证金或担保要求；暂停公证任命；保证金或保险续期；罚款

A.（1）除法律另有规定外，公证人在其管辖范围内行使公证人职能的权力应当持续有效，前提是公证人提交并保持信誉以及安全度良好的一万美元保证金，并以此为基础对所有可能会聘任其作为公证人的人保证其将忠实履行法律所要求的所有义务，或者公证人可以选择持有至少一万美元的错误和遗漏保险。

（2）本条规定不适用于在该保证金到期并被要求更新之前有效且可执行的公证保证金。

B. 依据本条被要求交纳保证金或保持保险范围能够替代保证金的所有公证人，应当将其保证金或者当前保险范围的证据提交州务卿，并一直将其在州务

dence of current insurance coverage with the secretary of state, and shall maintain on file with the secretary of state their bond or evidence of current insurance coverage at all times.

C. Any court of competent jurisdiction may suspend the commission of any notary for failure to pay over money entrusted to him in his official capacity as a notary public, for failure to satisfy any final judgment rendered against him in such capacity, or for other just cause.

D. (1) All notaries shall renew their bonds every five years except those notaries who are bonded with a personal surety, as provided in R.S. 35:75. Notaries with a personal surety bond shall renew their bonds upon the death of the personal surety in accordance with the provisions of this Chapter.

(2) All notaries required to renew their bonds shall file the new or renewed bond or evidence of current insurance coverage with the secretary of state as provided in Subsection B of this Section.

E. The commission of any qualified notary, other than a licensed attorney at law, who fails to renew his notarial bond timely or who fails to timely file his new or renewed bond or evidence of insurance coverage, as provided in Paragraph (D) (2) of this Section, shall be automatically suspended, and the notary shall have no authority to exercise any of the functions of a notary public until the required bond or insurance is in force and effect, and the bond or evidence of insurance has been filed with the secretary of state.

F. The secretary of state shall be authorized to promulgate rules and regulations, where necessary, for implementation of this Section, in accordance with the Administrative Procedure Act.

§72. Bonds; elimination of requirement

Notwithstanding any provision of law to the contrary, after August 1, 1988, no notary, who is a licensed attorney at law, shall be required to post a bond of any kind.

§73. Bond not mortgage until suit filed and notice of lis pendens recorded

The official notarial bond, given by any notary public shall not, when recorded as provided by law, operate as a mortgage either against the property of the principal or of the surety or sureties thereon, unless and until a suit has been filed against the notary to recover on the bond, and a notice of lis pendens has been placed of record against the notary in connection with the suit in the parish where the

卿处存档。

C. 任何有管辖权的法院，可以对任何因为没有支付与公证人任职资格有关的款项或是没有执行因上述行为产生的最终判决的公证人，暂停公证人任命。

D.（1）所有公证人应每隔五年更新一次保证金，除非是根据 R.S. 35:75 可以例外的以个人担保的公证人。具有个人担保人的公证人应当按照本章的规定，在个人担保人去世后续缴保证金。

（2）所有被要求更新保证金的公证人，应当向本条 B 款规定的州务卿提交新的保证金凭据或续保现行担保的证据。

E. 除依法执业的律师外，所有任命合格的公证人，若未能及时更新其公证保证金，或未按照（D）款第（2）项的规定及时提交新的保证金或更新担保证据，则该公证人的公证任命自动暂停，公证人无权行使公证人的任何职能，直到所要求的保证金或担保有效或者公证人的保证金和担保凭据已提交与州务卿为止。

F. 根据《行政诉讼法》授权，州务卿为施行该条规范，有权在必要时颁布执行相应的法规。

§72. 保证金；要求的例外

无论是否有相反的法律规定，1988 年 8 月 1 日以后，依法是执业律师的公证人，不得被要求提交任何形式的保证金。

§73. 保证金直到诉讼被提起且未决判决的通知被记录才可抵押

任何公证人提交的官方公证保证金，不得在法律规定的情况下，为本人或担保人的财产作抵押，除非有针对公证人提起的给付债权的诉讼，并且针对公证人的未决判决被记录在保证金登记的行政区内，并已经对公证人作出通知，在这种情况下，该保证金将作为对本人或其他担保人财产的抵押。

bond is recorded, in which case the bond shall then operate as a mortgage against the property of both the principal and surety, or sureties, thereon

§74. Inclusion of bonds in mortgage certificates

The clerks of court in preparing mortgage certificates shall not include notarial bonds thereon unless an action has been commenced on the bond and a notice of lis pendens has been filed in connection therewith as provided in R.S. 35:73.

§75. Substituted notarial bond with personal surety

In all cases where notaries public throughout the state of Louisiana have filed or recorded, or may hereafter file and record, bonds in the offices of the several clerks of court and ex-officio recorder of conveyances and mortgages, and the register of conveyances and mortgages of the parish of Orleans, with any surety company authorized to do business in the state of Louisiana as surety, as permitted by existing laws, may, in lieu of such bonds of any surety company aforesaid, substitute a bond with personal surety acceptable to the presiding judge of the parish for which the notary is commissioned. The Secretary of State shall accept said substituted notarial bond with personal surety in lieu of notarial bond with surety company as surety.

§76. Release of surety company upon acceptance of personal surety bond

The Secretary of State for the state of Louisiana, upon filing and recordation of a notarial bond with the Secretary of State, with personal surety in lieu of a surety company, shall upon request execute a release of the surety company effective as of the date of the acceptance of the personal surety bond in lieu thereof.

§77. Cancellation of surety company bond

Upon presentation of such personal surety bond containing a certificate of its sufficiency by the presiding judge of the parish of the state for which the notary was commissioned, and certificate of approval by the Secretary of State to any clerk of court and ex-officio recorder of conveyances and mortgages, and the register of conveyances and mortgages of the parish of Orleans, the said clerk, register or recorder of mortgages, shall upon application by any interested party cancel and erase in full from the records of his office said notarial bond with surety company as surety now or hereafter recorded in the conveyance or mortgage records of his office.

§74. 将保证金纳入抵押证明

法院书记员在准备抵押证明时,不得包括公证保证金,除非已经开始对保证金进行诉讼,并且根据 R.S. 35:73 的规定已经提交了与该未决诉讼有关的通知。

§75. 由个人担保的替代公证保证金

根据现行法律许可,路易斯安纳州的公证员已经或者即将归档或记录,由路易斯安纳州授权经营的公司担保的法院多个书记员办公室内记录的保证金、依职权记录的转让证书和抵押契据,以及在奥尔良行政区登记的转让证书和抵押契据,只要公证员任命的行政区首席法官认可,则在任何情形下均可以个人担保替代前述公司担保。州务卿应当接受上述由个人担保的替代公证保证金,以代替由公司担保的公证保证金。

§76. 接受个人担保解除担保公司保证金

向路易斯安那州州务卿提交和记录个人担保而非公司担保的保证金,以个人担保人代替担保公司的,应当按照要求,自接受个人担保代替公司担保之日起解除公司担保义务,并于当日生效。

§77. 取消担保公司保证金

包含有公证人被任命的行政区内的主审法官给予的证书的个人担保保证金,经由州务卿确认的关于任何法院书记员或者依据职能记录的产权转让和抵押,以及在奥尔良行政区登记的转让证书和抵押契据,上述文员记录的抵押,经利害关系人提出申请后,应从其办公室的记录中全面清理公司担保的公证保证金以及现在或之后在其办公室中关于产权转让或抵押的担保记录。

CHAPTER 3. LEAVES OF ABSENCE

§131. Grant of leave of absence; designation of substitute notary; suspension of prescription

A. The secretary of state on behalf of the governor may grant leave of absence to notaries public for a period not exceeding thirty-six months, to date from the day the leave is granted.

B. Absence from the state suspends the running of prescription against the notary.

§132. Notaries in military service, leave of absence

A leave of absence may be granted by the governor to any notary public upon his application to the secretary of state in writing certifying that he is a member of the Army, Navy, Marine Corps or any other branch of the military service of the United States, or of the state of Louisiana, and stating the expiration date of his bond.

§133. Notaries in military service, period of leave

The period of the leaves of absence granted in accordance with R.S. 35:132 shall date from the day the leave is granted and shall terminate sixty days after the date of discharge of the notary from the military service of the United States or the state of Louisiana.

§134. Expiration of bond during military service; renewal

When the notarial bond of a notary public expires during his term of military service, the notary shall have sixty days from the date of his discharge from military service in which to apply for a new bond.

CHAPTER 4. APPOINTMENT QUALIFICATIONS, AND BONDS OF NOTARIES

§191. Appointment; qualifications and bond; examination; examiners

A. (1) Any person may be appointed a notary public in and for the parish in which he resides and in and for any one other parish in which he maintains an office, provided that he:

(a) Is a resident citizen or alien of this state.

(b) Is eighteen years of age or older.

(c) Reads, writes, speaks, and is sufficiently knowledgeable of the English language.

(d) Has received a high school diploma, has received a diploma for completion of a home study program approved by the State Board of Elementary and Secondary

第三章 休假

§131. 批准休假；指定代理公证人；暂停指示

A. 代表州长的州务卿有权批准公证人不超过36个月的休假，自批准之日起算。

B. 休假将暂停州对公证人的指示。

§132. 公证人服役，休假

公证人以书面方式证明其是陆军、海军、海军陆战队或美国其他兵役部门的成员，或路易斯安那州其他军区成员，并说明其保证金到期日的，向书记官员提出休假申请后，由州长批准休假。

§133. 公证人服役期间

根据 R.S. 35:132 批准的休假应自批准之日起算，并应在公证人从美国或路易斯安那州军队解职之日起60日内终止。

§134. 服役过程中保证金到期；更新

公证人在服役期间内公证保证金到期的，公证人应当自其从军队解职之日起60日内申请新的保证金。

第四章 任用，资格和公证保证金

§191. 任用；资格和保证金；考试；考官

A.（1）任何人都可能在他所居住的行政区及任何具有办公地点的行政区被任命为公证人，但须符合以下条件：

（a）是本州居民或本州侨民。

（b）18周岁以上（包含本数）。

（c）能够阅读、写作、说话，并且充分理解英语。

（d）已获得高中文凭，或已获得国家会计委员会批准的中小学家庭学习课程文凭，或者成功通过普通教育发展考试后获得高中毕业文凭。

Education, or has been issued a high school equivalency diploma after successfully completing the test of General Educational Development.

(e) Is not under interdiction or incapable of serving as a notary because of mental infirmity.

(f) Has not been convicted of a felony, or if convicted of a felony, has been pardoned.

(g) Meets the requirements established by law for each commission sought.

(2) Notwithstanding the provisions of Paragraph A(1) or Subsection C of this Section, a person validly appointed notary public in the parish of his residence may exercise any and all of the functions of a notary public in all adjacent parishes that have a population of less than forty thousand and in which he or his employer maintains an office, without additional bonding or further application or examination.

(3) (a) A valid notarial commission shall be one that has not been revoked or resigned, and that was issued to a person who, at the time of issuance in accordance with the provisions of this Section, possessed the qualifications for office set forth in Paragraph (A) (1) and Subsection B of this Section, and who is currently possessed of those qualifications.

(b) A validly appointed notary public is a person who currently holds a valid notarial commission.

(c) A notarial commission that has been or is currently suspended by a court of competent jurisdiction as provided by R.S. 35:71(C) , or otherwise by operation of law pursuant to R.S. 35:14 or for the failure of the notary to maintain the required bond or insurance, or for failure to timely file the annual report as provided by law, shall not, solely for the reason that it is a suspended commission, be deemed an invalid notarial commission.

B. A resident citizen seeking to be appointed notary public in the parish of his residence or possessing a valid notarial commission in and for a parish based on his residence must be a registered voter of that parish.

C. Each applicant, otherwise qualified, may be appointed a notary public in and for a parish upon meeting all of the following conditions:

(1) (a) Submitting an application to the office of the secretary of state together with a certificate establishing his age, residence, location of his office when the applicant seeks to be appointed a notary based on such office, and location of the office which was the basis for a current appointment as a notary in any other parish, if any.

（e）不存在由于精神虚弱而不能担任公证人的情况。

（f）没有被判有重罪，或犯有重罪但已被赦免。

（g）符合法律规定的所有任命要求。

（2）尽管存在有本条A款第（1）项或C款规定的情形，在其居住的行政区被有效任命的公证人，有权在所有与其居住地相临近的居住人口少于四万且其或者其雇主拥有办公地的行政区内行使全部的公证人职能，在其或其雇主办公地执业，无须额外的保证金或其他的申请或考试。

（3）（a）有效的公证任命是指没有被撤销或者放弃的、根据本条的规定任命并符合本条A款第（1）项和B款规定的资格的任命。

（b）有效的公证人是目前持有有效任命的公证人。

（c）因具有管辖权的法院依据R.S. 35:71(C)，或者根据R.S. 35:14或公证人未能持有要求的保证金或者保险或未能按法律规定及时提交年度报告，公证人任命被暂停的，不得仅因为被暂停就被视为无效任命。

B. 寻求在其居住地的行政区任职为公证人的居民，或在其居住行政区内拥有有效的公证人任命的居民，必须是该行政区的注册选民。

C. 每个申请人，在满足以下所有条件时，可以被任命为行政区公证人：

（1）（a）向州务卿提交申请书，并附上一份证明书，说明年龄、居住地点、办公地点，以及目前在其他行政区的办公地点（如果有），以寻求被任命为公证人。

(b) The application and qualifying process shall be administered by the office of the secretary of state.

(i) The application provided by the office of the secretary of state shall require the applicant to attest to his good moral character, integrity, and sober habits.

(ii) In the event that any of the applicant's answers or responses call into question the applicant's good moral character, integrity, or sober habits, the secretary of state shall submit such application to the district court in the parish for which the appointment is sought for judicial review and approval. If found competent as to character and fitness to serve as a notary public, the court shall issue to the secretary of state an appropriate certificate for the applicant signed by a judge of the court.

(iii) The application shall include the sworn statement of the applicant declaring the information provided therein is true and correct.

(c) The office of the secretary of state shall charge a fee of thirty-five dollars for filing and processing any application to be appointed a notary public provided for in Subparagraph (C) (1) (a) of this Section.

(d) The deadline for the application provided for in Subparagraph (C) (1) (a) of this Section and the application fee provided for in Subparagraph (C) (1) (c) or to register to take the exam as provided for in R.S. 35:191.1 shall be no later than sixty days prior to the date of the examination.

(2) (a) Taking a pre-assessment test, with no minimum score required, administered by the secretary of state to assess the probability of the applicant passing the examination as provided in R.S. 35:191.1.

(b) To qualify to take the pre-assessment test, the applicant shall have satisfied all requirements to be commissioned as a notary public in the parish, except for passing the examination as provided in R.S. 35:191.1.

(c) The pre-assessment test provided by this Paragraph shall be dispensed with if the applicant has been duly admitted to practice law in this state or holds a valid notarial commission in this state.

(3) (a) Taking and passing a written examination, as provided in R. S. 35:191.1, administered by the secretary of state.

(b) (i) The notary examination shall be given twice per year on the first Saturday of June and December. Should the scheduled Saturday be a state holiday, then the next non-holiday Saturday shall be the test date.

(ii) To qualify to be examined, the candidate shall

（b）申请和资格审核程序应由州务卿办公室负责管理。

（i）由州务卿办公室提出的申请要求，应当包含申请人证明其拥有良好的道德品格、诚信和良好的习惯的证明。

（ii）如果任何申请人的良好道德品格、诚信或良好习惯遭到质疑，州务卿应将此类申请提交给将任命公证人的行政区的地方法院寻求司法审查。如果法院发现该申请人具备作为公证人的能力以及合适的品格，应向州务卿颁发由法院法官签署的申请人合格的证明。

（iii）申请书应包括申请人的宣誓声明，声明其提供的信息是真实和正确的。

（c）州务卿办公室应当对根据本条第（C）(1)(a)申请被任命为公证人的提交和申请程序，收取35美元的费用。

（d）本条第（C）（1）（a）规定的申请截止日期和缴纳第（C）（1）（c）规定的申请费用，或者按照RS 35：191.1的规定登记参与考试均不得迟于考试之日前60日。

（2）（a）预评估测试没有最低分数要求，是由州务卿根据 R.S. 35:191.1 管理，以评估申请人通过考试的可能性。

（b）为获得参加预评估测试的资格，申请人应满足在该行政区对公证人除通过R.S. 35：191.1规定的考试外的所有要求。

（c）如果申请人在本州被许可执业，或在本州持有有效的公证任命，则本部分规定的预评估试验将免除。

（3）（a）按照 R. S. 35：191.1 的规定，参与并通过州务卿管理的书面考试。

（b）（i）公证人考试应于每年的六月和十二月的第一个星期六举行。如果预定的星期六是州假期，则下一个非假期的星期六应为测试日期。

（ii）为有资格接受考试，候选人应满足行政区公

have satisfied all requirements to be commissioned as a notary public in the parish, except for passing the examination.

(iii) The qualified candidate shall be permitted to register for any notary public examinations administered by the secretary of state within one year after the date the secretary of state notifies the candidate of his approval to take the examination. No further application fee shall be required during this period. The required examination fee, however, shall be paid for each examination.

(c) The examination provided for in this Paragraph shall be dispensed with if the applicant has been duly admitted to practice law in this state or holds a valid notarial commission in this state.

D. Notwithstanding any other provision of law to the contrary, any person who is validly appointed notary public in and for the parish of Orleans, the parish of St. Bernard, the parish of Plaquemines, or the parish of Jefferson is hereby authorized and deemed eligible and qualified to exercise any and all of the functions of a notary public in the parishes of Orleans, Plaquemines, St. Bernard, and Jefferson.

E. (1) Notwithstanding any other provision of law to the contrary, any person who has held a valid notarial commission in or for any parish either for a period of five years or who has taken and passed the written examination, as provided in R.S. 35:191.1 on or after June 13, 2005, and who changes his residence to another parish, and who complies with the laws governing application and qualifying for appointment to the office of notary public in the parish of his new residence , except taking and passing an examination, and who meets the prerequisites for commission issuance specified in R.S. 35:201, shall be issued a notarial commission for the parish of his new residence by the governor without advice and consent of the Senate and may exercise the functions of notary public in that parish.

(2) A notary who is establishing a residence in a parish other than the parish of his commission and who seeks a commission in the parish of the new residence shall be deemed to be validly commissioned in the parish of his former residence for a period of sixty days, during which time he shall meet all the qualifications for appointment in and for the parish of the new residence. Should such notary desire to remain commissioned in the original parish based on maintaining an office in that parish, he shall file an affidavit to that effect with the secretary of state designating the location of the office and shall otherwise

证人任命的除通过考试外的所有要求。

（iii）合格候选人在州务卿通知候选人批准其参加考试之日起 1 年内，允许参加由州务卿管理的任何公证人考试。在此期间不需要重新交纳申请费用。但是，每次考试应支付所需的考试费用。

（c）如果申请人在本州被许可执业，或在本州持有有效的公证任命，则本部分规定的考试将免除。

D. 尽管存在相反的法律规定，任何在奥尔良行政区、圣伯纳德行政区、普拉克明行政区或杰斐逊行政区被有效任命的公证人，均被授权并被视为符合条件且有资格在奥尔良、普拉克明、圣伯纳德和杰斐逊等行政区行使公证人的所有职能。

E.（1）尽管存在其他相反的法律规定，持有在任何行政区为期 5 年的有效公证人任命，或在 2005 年 6 月 13 日或以后已经通过了 R.S. 35：191.1 规定的笔试，将其居住地改为另一个行政区的及法律有关申请资格的规定及其新居住地行政区公证人除通过考试外所有条件的人，以及符合 R.S. 35:201RS 规定的任命先决条件的人，无须参议院建议和同意，其新居住地的州长应任命其为公证人，并可在该行政区行使公证人职能。

（2）公证人在其任命行政区以外的行政区设立住所，并在新居住的行政区寻求任命，应视作在其前居住地的行政区有效任命期为 60 日，在这段时间内，其应当满足新居住的行政区的任用条件。如果公证人希望在原行政区保留办公室而继续在原行政区任职，应向州务卿提出誓章，指明办公室的所在地，否则其应满足本条规定的双重任命要求。

comply with the requirements for maintaining a dual commission as provided for in this Section.

F. Notwithstanding any other provision of law to the contrary, any person who is validly appointed notary public in and for any of the parishes of Tangipahoa, Livingston or St. Helena is hereby authorized and deemed eligible and qualified to exercise any and all of the functions a notary public in the parishes of Tangipahoa, Livingston and St. Helena.

G. Notwithstanding any other provision of law to the contrary, any person who is validly appointed notary public in and for any of the parishes of Bienville, Caldwell, East Carroll, Franklin, Jackson, Lincoln, Madison, Morehouse, Ouachita, Richland, Union, or West Carroll is hereby authorized and deemed eligible and qualified to exercise any and all of the functions of a notary public in the parishes of Bienville, Caldwell, East Carroll, Franklin, Jackson, Lincoln, Madison, Morehouse, Ouachita, Richland, Union, or West Carroll.

H. Notwithstanding any other provision of law to the contrary, any person who is validly appointed notary public in and for any of the parishes of Caddo, Bossier, Bienville, DeSoto, Claiborne, or Webster is hereby authorized and deemed eligible and qualified to exercise any and all of the functions of a notary public in the parishes of Caddo, Bossier, Bienville, DeSoto, Claiborne, and Webster. No additional bonding or further application or examination shall be required due to the expanded jurisdictional limits authorized by this Subsection.

I. Notwithstanding any other provision of law to the contrary, any person who is validly appointed notary public in and for either of the parishes of Catahoula or Concordia is hereby authorized and deemed eligible and qualified to exercise any and all of the functions of a notary public in the parishes of Catahoula and Concordia.

J. Notwithstanding any other provision of law to the contrary, any person who is a validly appointed notary public in and for either of the parishes of Iberia or St. Mary is hereby authorized and deemed eligible and qualified to exercise any and all of the functions of a notary public in the parishes of Iberia and St. Mary.

K. Notwithstanding any other provision of law to the contrary, any person who is validly appointed notary public in and for any of the parishes of Allen, Beauregard, Calcasieu, Cameron, Vernon, or Jefferson Davis is hereby authorized and deemed eligible and qualified to exercise any and all functions of a notary public in the parishes of

F. 尽管存在相反的法律规定，任何在唐吉帕霍尔、利文斯顿、圣赫勒拿的任一行政区内被有效指定为公证人的人，均被授权并被视为合格且有资格在唐吉帕霍尔、利文斯顿和圣赫勒拿等行政区中行使所有的公证人职能。

G. 尽管存在相反的法律规定，任何在毕一维拉、考德威尔、东卡罗尔、富兰克林、杰克逊、林昆、麦迪逊、奥其它、里奇兰、尤宁、莫尔豪斯、西卡罗尔的任一行政区内，被有效指定为公证人的人，均被授权并被视为合格且有资格在毕一维拉、考德威尔、东卡罗尔、富兰克林、杰克逊、林昆、麦迪逊、奥其它、里奇兰、尤宁、莫尔豪斯、西卡罗尔等所有行政区中行使所有的公证人职能。

H. 尽管存在相反的法律规定，任何在卡杜、布舍尔、毕一维拉、德索托、克莱本、维斯特的任一行政区，被有效指定为公证人的人，均被授权并被视为合格且有资格在卡杜、布舍尔、毕一维拉、德索托、克莱本、维斯特等所有行政区中行使所有的公证人职能。依据本款授权的扩大管辖范围，不得要求额外的保证金、申请、考试。

I. 尽管存在相反的法律规定，任何在卡塔霍拉、迪亚任一行政区内，被有效指定为公证人的人，均被授权并被视为合格且有资格在卡塔霍拉、迪亚两个行政区中行使所有的公证人职能。

J. 尽管存在相反的法律规定，任何在伊比利亚和圣玛丽的任一行政区内，被有效指定为公证人的人，均被授权并被视为合格且有资格在伊比利亚和圣玛丽两个行政区中行使所有的公证人职能。

K. 尽管存在相反的法律规定，任何在艾伦、博若加尔、卡纳西耶、卡梅伦、弗农、杰斐逊·戴维斯的任一行政区内，被有效指定为公证人的人，均被授权并被视为合格且有资格在艾伦、博若加尔、卡纳西耶、卡梅伦、弗农、杰斐逊·戴维斯的所有行政区中行使所有的公证人职能。依据本款授权的扩大管辖范

Allen, Beauregard, Calcasieu, Cameron, Vernon, and Jefferson Davis. No additional bonding or further application or examination shall be required due to the expanded jurisdictional limits authorized by this Subsection.

L. Any notary public in and for the parish of Acadia, Lafayette, or Vermilion is hereby authorized and qualified to exercise all of the functions of a notary public in and for any of said parishes. No additional bonding or further application or examination shall be required due to the expanded jurisdictional limits authorized by this Subsection.

M. Any notary public appointed in and for the parish of Iberia or Vermilion is hereby authorized and qualified to exercise any and all functions of a notary public in both parishes. No additional bonding or further application or examination shall be required due to the expanded jurisdictional limits authorized by this Subsection.

N. Any notary public appointed in and for the parish of Ascension, East Baton Rouge, East Feliciana, Iberville, Livingston, Pointe Coupee, West Baton Rouge, or West Feliciana is hereby authorized and qualified to exercise all of the functions of a notary public in and for any of said parishes. No additional bonding or further application or examination shall be required due to the expanded jurisdictional limits authorized by this Subsection.

O. Notwithstanding any other provision of law to the contrary, any person who is validly appointed notary public in and for any of the parishes of Acadia, Evangeline, or St. Landry is hereby authorized and deemed eligible and qualified to exercise any and all of the functions of a notary public in the parishes of Acadia, Evangeline, and St. Landry. No additional bonding or further application or examination shall be required due to the expanded jurisdictional limits authorized by this Subsection.

P. (1) (a) Notwithstanding any other provision of law to the contrary including but not limited to the provisions of Subsection E of this Section and the duties imposed in that Subsection as a result of a change in residence, each person who is licensed to practice law in this state who is a notary public in and for any parish in this state may exercise the functions of a notary public in every parish in this state.

(b) Notwithstanding any other provision of law to the contrary, each person who is a validly appointed notary public in and for any parish in this state and who has taken and passed the written examination, as provided in R.S. 35:191.1 on or after June 13, 2005, may exercise the functions of a notary public in every parish in this state.

围，不得要求额外的保证金、申请、考试。

L. 任何在阿卡迪亚、拉斐特或弗米利恩行政区的公证人，特此授权有资格在上述行政区内行使公证人的所有职能。依据本款授权的扩大管辖范围，不得要求额外的保证金、申请、考试。

M. 任何在伊比利亚或弗米利恩行政区的公证人，有权在上述两个政区内行使公证人的所有职能。依据本款授权的扩大管辖范围，不得要求额外的保证金、申请、考试。

N. 在阿森松、东巴吞鲁日、东菲丽西那、伊贝维尔、利文斯顿、库毕、西巴吞鲁日、西菲丽西那的行政区内任职的公证人有资格在上述行政区行使公证人的所有职能。依据本款授权的扩大管辖范围，不得要求额外的保证金、申请、考试。

O. 尽管存在相反的法律规定，任何在阿卡迪亚、伊万杰琳或圣兰德里行政区内，被有效指定为公证人的人，均被视为合格且有资格在阿卡迪亚、伊万杰琳、圣兰德里的所有行政区的中行使所有的公证人职能。依据本款授权的扩大管辖范围，不得要求额外的保证金、申请、考试。

P.（1）（a）尽管存在相反的法律规定，包括但不限于本条 E 款的规定以及该款中由于居住地改变而产生的义务，在本州有法律执业执照且在本州的任一行政区中作为公证人的，也可以在本州的每个行政区行使公证人的所有职能。

（b）尽管存在相反的法律规定，每个在本州任一行政区中有效任命的公证人，并且在 2005 年 6 月 13 日或之后通过 R.S. 35:191.1 规定的笔试的人，可以在本州任一行政区行使公证人的职能。

(c) The expanded jurisdictional limits authorized by this Subsection are additional to other provisions of law. No additional bonding or further application or examination shall be required due to the expanded jurisdictional limits authorized by this Subsection.

(2) In order to qualify for the expanded jurisdictional limits authorized by this Subsection, any regularly commissioned notary public in and for any parish in this state who is not licensed to practice law in this state and who has not taken and passed the written examination as provided in R.S. 35:191.1 on or after June 13, 2005, may take the examination provided that he register directly with the secretary of state on a form provided for that purpose and pay the examination fee authorized by law no later than forty-five days before the date of a scheduled examination. Failure of such notary to pass the examination shall have no effect on the status of the commission of the notary.

Q. Notwithstanding any other provision of law to the contrary, any person who is validly appointed notary public in and for either of the parishes of Lafayette or St. Landry is hereby authorized and qualified to exercise all of the functions of a notary public in and for both parishes. No additional bonding or further application or examination shall be required due to the expanded jurisdictional limits authorized by this Subsection.

R. Notwithstanding any other provision of law to the contrary, any person who is a validly appointed notary public in and for any of the parishes of Iberia, St. Martin, or St. Mary is hereby authorized and deemed eligible and qualified to exercise any and all of the functions of a notary public in the parishes of Iberia, St. Martin, and St. Mary. No additional bonding or further application or examination shall be required due to the expanded jurisdictional limits authorized by this Subsection.

S. Notwithstanding any other provision of law to the contrary, any person who is a validly appointed notary public in and for either of the parishes of Sabine or Vernon is hereby authorized and deemed eligible and qualified to exercise any and all of the functions of a notary public in the parishes of Sabine and Vernon. No additional bonding or further application or examination shall be required due to the expanded jurisdictional limits authorized by this Subsection.

T. Notwithstanding any other provision of law to the contrary, any person who is a validly appointed notary public in and for any of the parishes of Avoyelles, Grant, or Rapides is hereby authorized and deemed eligible and

（c）本条规定的扩大的管辖范围是其他法律规定的补充。依据本条授权的扩大的管辖范围，不得要求额外的保证金、申请、考试。

（2）为符合本款授权的扩大的管辖范围，任何在本州得到长期任命的公证人，如果并未取得在本州进行法律执业的执照，且未于2005年6月13日或之后参加通过R.S. 35:191.1规定的笔试，可以直接在州务卿为此目的提供的表格上登记并参加考试，并在考试前45日支付考试费用。公证人未通过考试，对公证人的任命不会产生影响。

Q. 尽管存在相反的法律规定，任何在拉菲特或圣兰德里的任一行政区内，被有效指定为公证人的人，均被视为合格且有资格在拉菲特或圣兰德里两个行政区中行使所有的公证人职能。依据本款授权的扩大管辖范围，不得要求额外的保证金、申请、考试。

R. 尽管存在相反的法律规定，任何在伊比利亚、圣马丁或圣玛丽任一行政区内，被有效指定为公证人的人，均被视为合格且有资格在伊比利亚、圣马丁和圣玛丽的所有行政区中行使所有的公证人职能。依据本款授权的扩大管辖范围，不得要求额外的保证金、申请、考试。

S. 尽管存在相反的法律规定，任何在萨宾、弗农任一行政区内，被有效指定为公证人的人，均被视为合格且有资格在萨宾和弗农的所有行政区中行使所有的公证人职能。依据本款授权的扩大管辖范围，不得要求额外的保证金、申请、考试。

T. 尽管存在相反的法律规定，任何在阿耶拉斯、格兰特、拉皮德任一行政区内，被有效指定为公证人的人，均被授权并被视为合格且有资格在阿耶拉斯、格兰特、拉皮德的所有行政区中行使所有的公证人职

qualified to exercise any and all of the functions of a notary public in the parishes of Avoyelles, Grant, and Rapides. No additional bonding or further application or examination shall be required due to the expanded jurisdictional limits authorized by this Subsection.

U. Notwithstanding any other provision of law to the contrary, any person who is validly appointed notary public in and for the parish of St. Mary, the parish of Assumption, the parish of Lafourche, or the parish of Terrebonne is hereby authorized and deemed eligible and qualified to exercise any and all of the functions of notary in the parishes of St. Mary, Assumption, Lafourche, and Terrebonne.

V.(1) Any notary public appointed in and for the parishes of Allen, Beauregard, Calcasieu, Cameron, Jefferson, Jefferson Davis, Plaquemines, Orleans, St. Bernard, St. Tammany, Vermilion, and Washington who were displaced in the aftermath of Hurricane Katrina or Hurricane Rita may exercise any and all of the functions of a notary public in the parish of their temporary residence and in any other parish with which the parish of their temporary residence is grouped under the provisions of Subsections D, F through O, and Q through U of this Section, provided that such notary registers his temporary address with the secretary of state. No additional bonding requirement or examination shall be required under the authority granted by this Subsection.

(2) Any notary public qualified under Paragraph (V)(1) of this Section who complies with the laws governing application and qualifying for appointment to the office of notary public in said parish, except taking and passing an examination, and who meets the prerequisites for commission issuance specified in R.S. 35:201, shall be issued a notarial commission for the parish of his new residence by the governor without advice and consent of the Senate and may exercise the functions of notary public in that parish.

(3) The authority granted by this Section shall expire on January 1,2007.

W.(1) (a) Notwithstanding any provision of this Section or any other law to the contrary, any person who resides in a parish with a population of less than forty thousand, and who has passed the examination provided by R.S. 35:191.1, except for any performance assessment component, during examinations administered between December 1, 2009, and December 31, 2012, may be provisionally appointed to the office of notary public in and for that parish upon fulfillment of all requirements of this Subsection and upon meeting all other qualifications necessary

能。依据本款授权的扩大管辖范围，不得要求额外的保证金、申请、考试。

U. 尽管存在相反的法律规定，任何在圣玛丽、阿胜普宣、拉富什任一行政区内，被有效指定为公证人的人，均被授权并被视为合格且有资格在圣玛丽、阿胜普宣、拉富什的所有行政区中行使所有的公证人职能。

V.（1）在艾伦、柏拉达格、卡尔克苏、卡梅伦、杰佛逊、杰斐逊·戴维斯、普拉可迈、奥尔良、圣伯纳德、圣坦慕尼协会、卧迈兰和华盛顿的任一行政区内任职的公证人，如果在受到卡特里娜飓风或丽塔飓风后迁移，可以在其临时居住的行政区，以及其按照D、F至O和本部分的Q的规定关联的任何其他行政区行使公证人的职能，只要该公证人向州务卿登记了临时地址。根据本条的授权，不得要求额外的保证金和考试。

（2）符合本条（V）（1）项规定的公证人，如果其符合上述行政区内有关申请公证人除参与和通过考试外的所有要求，且符合R.S. 35:201规定的取得任命的前提条件，则无经参议院建议和同意，其新居住地的州长应任命其为公证人，并可在该行政区行使公证人职务。

（3）本条授予的权力将于2007年1月1日到期。

W.（1）（a）尽管存在与本条或其他法律相反的规定，任何居住在人口少于四万的行政区，并且通过了R.S. 35：191.1规定的考试的人，除了在2009年12月1日至2012年12月31日期间绩效评估的外，可以在满足本条规定的所有要求和其他必要条件后临时任命到该行政区的公证人办公室任职。

to be appointed to the office of notary public in this state.

(b) Notwithstanding any provision of this Section or any other law to the contrary, any person who resides in a parish with a population of less than forty thousand and who passes the examination provided by R.S. 35:191.1, except for any performance assessment component, during examinations administered after January 1, 2013, and before August 1, 2016, may be provisionally appointed to the office of notary public in and for that parish upon fulfillment of all requirements of this Subsection and upon meeting all other qualifications necessary to be appointed to the office of notary public in this state.

(2) (a) A notary commissioned pursuant to this Subsection shall have authority to exercise all the powers of a notary public commissioned in this state as enumerated in R.S. 35:2, but shall exercise notarial functions only within the course and scope of his employment and under the direction of a supervisor for the employer who is not a notary commissioned under this Subsection. The term "employer" as used in this Subsection shall include only businesses that are in existence on the effective date of this Act, but shall not include a business whose primary function is to provide notary services. The exercise of any notarial functions under this Subsection shall be deemed to be within the course and scope of employment if either of the following is applicable:

(i) The employer of the notary is a party to the act or other instrument being sworn to, acknowledged, or passed before the notary, or the act or other instrument is necessary to or incidental to the business activities or operations of the employer.

(ii) At least one of the persons appearing before the notary to execute an affidavit, acknowledgment, or other notarial act or instrument is a former, current, or prospective client or customer of the employer.

(b) A notary commissioned pursuant to this Subsection shall not do any of the following in the course and scope of his employment:

(i) Draft and prepare a last will and testament or donation mortis causa.

(ii) Draft and prepare a trust.

(iii) Draft and prepare any instrument that transfers title to immovable property including but not limited to an act of sale or act of donation.

(3) A notary commissioned pursuant to this Subsection shall have jurisdiction within the parish of commission, and in any adjacent parish with a population of

(b)尽管存在与本条或其他法律相反的规定,任何居住在人口少于四万的行政区,并且通过了 R.S. 35∶191.1 规定的考试的人,除了在 2013 年 1 月 1 日至 2016 年 8 月 1 日期间绩效评估的外,可以在满足本条规定的所有要求和其他必要条件后临时任命到该行政区的公证人办公室任职。

(2)(a)根据本条款规定任命的公证人有权根据 R.S. 35:2 在本州行使公证人的所有职能。但公证职能的行使应在其受雇的范围内,并根据本条款规定而非公证人的雇主的指导。本条款中使用的"雇主"一词仅包括本法生效之日起存续的企业,但不得包括以提供公证服务为主要业务的企业。根据本条款行使公证职能,如果存在以下任一情形,应当认为公证职能的行使在其受雇的范围内:

(i)公证人的雇主是公证人宣誓、承认或通过的行为或其他文书的一方当事人,或者该行为或文书对雇主的业务活动或操作是必要的或附带的。

(ii)公证人执行誓章、确认或其他公证行为或文书时至少其中一位当事人是雇主的前任、现任或潜在客户。

(b)根据本条款任命的公证人在其工作范围内不得从事以下事项:

(i)起草并准备遗嘱或遗赠文书。

(ii)起草和准备信托文书。

(iii)起草和准备不动产所有权的文书,包括但不限于出售或捐赠行为。

(3)根据本款任命的公证人在任命的行政区内,以及公证人的雇主具有办公地点人口不足四万的任何相邻行政区内均有管辖权。

less than forty thousand where the employer of the notary maintains an office.

(4) (a) All notaries commissioned pursuant to this Subsection shall post and maintain a bond, at the expense of the employer, with a commercial surety licensed in this state, in the amount of twenty thousand dollars conditioned on the faithful performance of all duties required by law toward all persons who receive his services in his official capacity as notary public. The minimum bond requirements described in this Paragraph shall be in lieu of those provided by R.S. 35:71.

(b) The employer shall hold the notary harmless for any claim made against his bond when the notary is acting in the course and scope of the employment or under the direction of the employer.

(c) All persons requesting a commission pursuant to this Subsection shall, in addition to all other documents required for issuance of a commission pursuant to this Title, submit a statement signed by the applicant and the employer of the applicant providing all of the following:

(i) The name and principal business address of the employer.

(ii) The primary address at which the applicant will exercise notarial functions.

(iii) An acknowledgment of the limits of the authority and jurisdiction of a commission issued pursuant to the provisions of this Subsection and the penalties that may be imposed for violations of the limitations and prohibitions imposed by this Subsection.

(d) All notaries commissioned pursuant to this Subsection shall be required to attend a notary orientation class approved by the secretary of state.

(5) (a) If the employer named in the statement required by Subparagraph (4) (c) of this Subsection terminates the employment of the notary commissioned pursuant to this Subsection, or if the employer no longer wishes to be bound by the provisions of this Subsection with respect to any person commissioned pursuant to its provisions, the employer shall immediately send written notice to the secretary of state, and the commission shall be automatically revoked unless the notary complies with the provisions of Item (b) (i) or (ii) of this Paragraph.

(b) If the notary commissioned pursuant to the provisions of this Subsection voluntarily terminates his employment with the employer named in the statement required by Subparagraph (4) (c) of this Subsection, the notary shall immediately send written notice to the secretary of state,

（4）（a）根据本条款委任的所有公证人应持有金额为 2000 美元的保证金，由在本州有商业担保资格的雇主支付，以保证公证人依照法律规定忠实地向所有接受其公证服务的人履行义务。本段所述的最低保证金要求应代替 R.S. 35:71 的要求。

（b）当公证人在工作的过程和范围内或在雇主的指导下行事时，面对针对公证人保证金的索赔，雇主应保证公证人不受影响。

（c）根据本款规定，要求任命的所有人员除依照公证人任命所需的所有文件外，还应提交申请人和申请人雇主签署的声明，其中包括以下所有内容：

（i）雇主的姓名及主营业地址。

（ii）申请人将履行公证职务的主要地址。

（iii）本条规定的任命权限和管辖权的范围的承认，以及违反本款规定的限制和禁止行为可能施加的处罚。

（d）依照本款规定委任的所有公证人均须参加州务卿要求的公证班。

（5）（a）如果本条（4）款（c）项要求的陈述中指定的雇主终止了根据本款任命的公证人的雇用，或者雇主不再希望受到条款的约束，雇主应立即向州务卿发送书面通知，公证人任命应自动撤销，除非公证人符合（b）（i）项或（ii）项规定。

（b）如果根据本条规定任命的公证人自愿终止与本条（4）款（c）项规定的雇主的雇佣关系，公证人应立即向州务卿通知，任命应以成文方式书写如下：

and the commission shall be assigned a status as follows:

(i) If the notary declares in writing his intention to remain qualified under this Subsection, the secretary of state shall assign the notary a provisional inactive status until the notary submits a new statement required by Subparagraph (4) (c) of this Subsection, and the notary shall exercise no notarial functions until the secretary of state notifies him and the new employer that the required statement has been received and that the commission registry reflects a provisional active status.

(ii) If the notary declares in writing his intention to pursue successful completion of the performance assessment component of the examination provided by R.S. 35:191.1, the secretary of state shall assign the notary a provisional inactive status until he passes the performance assessment component, and the notary shall exercise no notarial functions until he passes the performance assessment component and is notified by the secretary of state that his commission status is changed.

(6) (a) No notarial act executed by a notary commissioned pursuant to this Subsection shall be deemed invalid or unenforceable as a notarial act solely on the basis that the execution of the act exceeded the authority or jurisdiction limitations imposed by Paragraphs (2) and (3) of this Subsection.

(b) An employer shall have no liability to any person for any damages caused by the negligent or fraudulent errors or omissions by any notary commissioned pursuant to this Subsection when the exercise of the notarial functions giving rise to the damages was occasioned by the notary acting outside the course and scope of his employment as established by this Subsection.

(7) Any person receiving a notary commission pursuant to this Subsection may have his commission suspended or revoked by the court pursuant to R.S. 35:15. In addition, upon receipt of a sworn affidavit and a determination by the secretary of state that reasonable grounds exist requiring immediate action in order to protect the public from unauthorized notarial practice, the secretary of state may summarily suspend the commission of a notary commissioned pursuant to this Subsection prior to the rule to show cause hearing provided for in R.S. 35:15. Upon such a suspension, the secretary of state shall notify the notary whose commission was suspended by certified mail, return receipt requested, and include a copy of the order of immediate suspension informing the notary that he has thirty days from receipt of the notice to file a written appeal with

（i）如公证人以书面形式声明其根据本款保留资格的意图，则州务卿应将公证人的任命转为临时无效状态，直至公证人提交本条4款c项要求的新陈述，以及州务卿通知他和新雇主已经接受必要的陈述，再向任命登记处要求将临时无效状态改为活跃，在此之前公证人不得行使公证职能。

（ii）如果公证人以书面形式宣布其完成由R.S.35：191.1要求的考试的绩效评估部分的意图，州务卿应通过绩效评估通知公证人任命处于暂时无效状态，直到通过绩效评估并由州务卿通知其任命状态已更改，在此之前公证人不得行使公证职能。

（6）（a）公证人根据本款规定执行的公证行为，如果超过2款和3款规定的权限或管辖权范围，不得被视为当然无效或不可执行。

（b）雇主对根据本条款任命的公证人的疏忽或欺诈性的错误或遗漏以及在超出任命范围造成的任何损失不承担责任。

（7）根据本款接受公证任命的任何人其任命可能会由法院根据R.S.35:15.暂停或撤销。此外，州务卿经宣誓并决定，有合理理由要求立即采取行动，以保护公众免受未经授权的公证行为的侵害，可以在适用R.S. 35:15的听证会举行前就暂停公证人的任命。暂停执行后，州务卿应通过认证邮件通知被停职的公证人，并附上立即停止任命的命令副本，通知公证人在其已收到通知书的30日内向州务卿就停职决定提出书面上诉。在暂停期间，公证人无权行使公证人的任何职责。如果公证人没有在收到通知书的30日内提出书面上诉，或者在收到公证人的30日内提出了书面上诉，州务卿依然维持停职决定的，应通知公证人行政区的地方检察官，根据RS.35:15撤销公证人的任命。

the secretary of state contesting the decision to suspend the commission. During such a period of suspension, the notary shall have no authority to exercise any of the duties or functions of a notary public. If the notary fails to file a written appeal within thirty days of receipt of the notice or if no later than thirty days after receipt of the notary's written appeal the secretary of state determines that the suspension should be upheld, the secretary of state shall notify the district attorney of the parish in which the notary is commissioned for the purpose of institution of the rule to show cause proceeding to revoke the commission pursuant to R.S. 35:15.

(8) The secretary of state shall on or before March 1, 2014, and March 1, 2015, provide a written report to the House Civil Law and Procedure Committee and the Senate Committee on Judiciary A detailing the intervening progress in implementation of the acts which originated as House Bill No. 929 and House Bill No. 1192 of the 2012 Regular Session. The secretary of state shall include in his report a compilation of the results of the notary examinations administered, the number of non-attorney and provisional notaries commissioned in Louisiana, the parishes where such provisional notaries are authorized to practice as a notary, and the number of provisional notaries whose commission has been suspended by the secretary of state, or suspended and/or revoked by the court.

(9) The provisions of this Subsection shall expire on August 1, 2016, and any commission granted pursuant to this Subsection shall also expire on that date, except if the notary has, subsequent to issuance of a commission pursuant to this Subsection, passed all components of the examination provided by R.S. 35:191.1 on or before August 1, 2016.

§191.1. Secretary of state; uniform statewide standards, rules, and procedures for notarial examinations

A. The secretary of state shall, with the advice and assistance of the courts and such subject matter experts as the secretary of state may request, develop uniform statewide standards for notarial examinations required by R.S. 35:191(C), which shall be administered by at regional testing centers by the secretary of state. The standards developed shall include all of the following:

(1) The procedures and rules for administering and grading the examination for applicants required to take an examination.

（8）州务卿应在2014年3月1日至2015年3月1日前提交书面报告至民政诉讼委员会和参议院司法委员会，详细说明《第929号议会法案》和2012年例会通过的《第1192号议会法案》的执行进展情况。州务卿在其报告中应列出其管理的公证考试结果、在路易斯安那州任命的非律师和临时公证人的数量、临时公证人被授权作为公证人执业的行政区，以及州务卿决定暂停执行或由法院暂停或撤销的临时公证人的编号。

（9）本条规定将于2016年8月1日届满，根据本条款授予的公证任命也将于该日期届满，除非公证人在2016年8月1日或之前通过RS.35：191.1规定的所有考试，并且根据本条款获得下一期的任命。

§191.1. 州务卿；全州统一的标准，公证考试的规则和程序

A. 州务卿应在法院的建议和协助下，按照州务卿专家的要求，根据R.S.35：191（C）制定州统一的公证考试标准，由州务卿在区域检测中心管理。制定的标准应包括以下所有内容：

（1）对申请人进行考试的管理和分级的程序和规定。

(2) The format and content of the examination.

(3) The procedures for review by the secretary of state of any examination which was taken pursuant to R.S. 35:191(C) and which was failed by the examinee.

The secretary of state shall also:

(1) Charge a fee not to exceed seventy-five dollars for each examinee taking an examination.

(2) Publish and make available to the public a document containing the material and sources from which examination questions are devised for use as a study guide and charge a fee for the actual cost not to exceed one hundred dollars.

C. The secretary of state is authorized to develop, with the advice and assistance of academically credentialed education professionals, a notary education program for the formal education of candidates for a notary commission.

§191.2. Secretary of state; uniform statewide standards, rules, and procedures for notarial examinations

The secretary of state shall:

(1) Develop a system for compiling and maintaining a current and accurate database of all notaries in this state and assign to each notary a unique "notary identification number".

(2) Develop the annual report form and mail by United States Postal Service, or provide by electronic means, the annual report form:

(a) To all notaries required to submit an annual report pursuant to R.S. 35:202(A), at least sixty days prior to the anniversary of the date each notary received his commission, commencing with anniversaries occurring on January 1, 2004.

(b) To all offices, agencies, departments, and political subdivisions required to submit an annual report pursuant to R.S. 35:202(D) on May first of each year, commencing on May 1, 2004.

(3) Collect a fee for receiving and processing the annual report of each notary, not to exceed twenty-five dollars per report.

(4) Publish a list of all fees charged by the secretary of state pursuant to this Title in the State Register.

§191.3. Notary change of address; duty to register

A. It shall be the duty of every notary public or other person authorized to exercise notarial functions in the state to whom the secretary of state has issued a notary identification number to notify the office of the secretary of state

（2）考试的形式和内容。

（3）州务卿对根据 R.S.35：191（C）进行考试以及未通过考生采取的任何检查的程序。

州务卿还应：

（1）向每名考试人员收费不得超过 75 美元。

（2）向公众发布一份包含考试题目的材料和来源的文件，作为学习指南，并为实际成本收取不超过 100 美元的费用。

C. 州务卿在学历教育专业人员的建议和协助下，制定公证人员候选人正式公证教育方案。

§191.2. 州务卿；统一的全州公证考试的标准、规则和程序

州务卿应：

（1）建立准确地编制和维护当前所有公证人的数据库系统，并分配给每个公证人一个独特的公证人编号。

（2）制定通过美国邮政系统邮寄的年度报告表和信件，或以电子方式提供年度报告表：

（a）根据 R.S.35：202（A）要求所有公证人提交年度报告，提交时间为每年各个公证人接受任命的日期至少 60 日之前，自 2004 年 1 月 1 日开始。

（b）所有办事处、机构、部门和政治部门必须根据 R.S. 35：202（D）于每年 5 月 1 日提交年度报告，自 2004 年 5 月 1 日起。

（3）收取接受和处理每个公证人的年度报告的费用，每次报告不得收费超过 25 美元。

（4）发布州务卿根据在州登记处的所有费用清单。

§191.3. 公证人地址变更；登记义务

A. 具有州务卿签发公证身份证号的，公证人或其他被授权履行公证职能的人员有义务在住宅地址、邮寄地址或两者都有变化的情况下，在发生变化后 60 日内通知州务卿。

within sixty days after the date of any change in residential address, mailing address, or both.

B. The secretary of state shall include notice of this requirement on its notary annual report form.

§ 191.4. Secretary of state; procedures for registration and reporting of notary instructors

A. (1) The secretary of state shall develop and administer a program to provide for the registration and reporting of persons who provide notary examination preparatory education and instruction.

(2) As used in this Section, a "provider" shall mean any person who provides a course or courses of instruction or study for the training and instruction of persons preparing for the Louisiana notary public examination required for the office of notary public and who charges a fee to any consumer for such service.

B. Beginning February 28, 2015, each person who provides notary examination preparatory education and instruction shall be required to be a commissioned notary public with statewide notarial authority.

C. Each provider shall submit an annual registration statement to the secretary of state on or before January first of each year beginning January 1, 2010. The secretary of state shall provide the form to be used for registration with the secretary of state and all registrations shall be submitted on the form provided by the secretary of state.

D. Each provider, except an educational institution that operates under the oversight of the Board of Regents, Board of Supervisors for the University of Louisiana System, Board of Supervisors of Louisiana State University and Agricultural and Mechanical College, Board of Supervisors of Southern University and Agricultural and Mechanical College or Board of Supervisors of Community and Technical Colleges, shall annually post a bond guaranteed by a commercial surety licensed to do business in this state with the secretary of state in the amount of twenty-five thousand dollars. The bond shall be to ensure the performance of the provider's obligation to deliver any educational services contracted for and shall remain in effect for a period of one year.

E. Beginning in 2010, each provider shall submit a semiannual report to the secretary of state on or before June thirtieth and December thirty-first listing the name and address of each person who received a course or courses of instruction or study from the provider for the training and instruction for the Louisiana notary public

B. 州务卿应当在公证年度报告表上注明有该申请。

§191.4. 州务卿；公证人登记注册程序

A.（1）州务卿应制定和管理，一个用以提供公证考试预备教育和指导的人员的登记和报告方案。

（2）在本条中，"提供者"是指为公证人办公室所要求的路易斯安那公证考试准备的人员提供的培训和指导课程或学习课程的，并向上述服务消费者收取服务费用的人。

B. 从2015年2月28日起，每个提供公证考试的预备教育和指导的提供者必须是符合公证制度的获得任命的公证人。

C. 每个提供者应从2010年1月1日起在每年1月1日或之前向州务卿提交年度注册声明。州务卿应提供用于注册登记的所有表格且最终应以州务卿提供的表格提交。

D. 除了在路易斯安那州立大学监督委员会、路易斯安那州立大学农工机械学院监督委员会、南方大学监督委员会、农工机械学院或社区技术学院监事会监管下运行的教育机构外，提供者应每年保有25万美元的由持有经营许可证的商业担保人担保的保证金。保证金应确保提供者履行为期一年的合同，在期限内提供有效的教育服务。

E. 2010年开始，每个提供者应在6月30日和12月30日或之前向州务卿提交半年度报告，首先列出在报告所涉及期间内，从提供者那里为通过公证人考试，获得课程或学习课程的每个人的姓名和地址。州务卿应提供半年报告使用的表格，所有报告应以州务卿提供的表格或州务卿提供的报告所载相同信息的表

examination required for the office of notary public during the time period covered by the report. The secretary of state shall provide the form to be used for the semiannual report and all reports shall be submitted on the form provided by the secretary of state or on a form which contains the same information as required by the report provided by the secretary of state.

F. (1) The secretary of state may impose a penalty of not more than one thousand dollars per day against a provider who is not in compliance with the requirements of this Section.

(2) If a penalty imposed under the provisions of this Section is not timely paid by a provider within thirty days of imposition of the penalty by the secretary of state, the attorney general shall institute proceedings against the provider to collect such penalty.

G. Each provider shall be exempt from the licensing requirements of R.S. 17:3141.1 et seq., pertaining to such educational programs or instruction.

H. The secretary of state may establish and require an annual professional development and education program for providers.

I. The secretary of state may promulgate rules and regulations, where necessary, for implementation of the provisions of this Section, in accordance with the Administrative Procedure Act.

§192. Execution and recordation of bond; filing of certificate of competency

A. The bond required of notaries by R.S. 35:191 shall be submitted to the clerk of court and ex officio recorder of mortgages for the parish where the notary will exercise the functions of his office, and, together with the certificate of competency above provided for, shall be filed in the office of the secretary of state. The bond shall be subscribed in favor of the governor, approved by the clerk, and if secured by personal surety, recorded in the mortgage office of the parish.

B. The provisions of Subsection A of this Section shall not affect the validity of bonds given or recorded in the mortgage or conveyance office of any parish prior to September 9, 1977.

§193. Original surety company bond; necessity for recordation

In all cases where notaries public furnish bond for the faithful performance of their duties, signed by a surety company, authorized to do business in this state, it shall

格提交。

F.（1）州务卿对不符合本条规定的提供者可处以每日不超过1000美元的罚款。

（2）根据本条规定进行的罚款，若30日以内未及时向州务卿支付，由总检察长向提供者提起诉讼，收取罚金。

G. 提供者提供教育方案或课程可豁免R.S. 17：3141.1及项下条款的规定，不必提交许可证。

H. 州务卿可以为提供者制定和要求一年一度的专业发展和教育计划。

I. 州务卿根据《行政诉讼法》，可以在必要时颁布执行本条规定的规章制度。

§192. 执行和记录保证金；提交能力证书

A. R.S.35：191规定的公证人所需的保证金应当向公证人行使其职务的法院和行政区记录官提交，并连同上述规定的合格证书一并提交给州务卿。该保证金应当由州长通过，由书记官批准，如果由个人担保人担保，则记录在行政区的抵押办公室。

B. 本条A款的规定不得影响任何1977年9月9日之前建立的行政区的抵押或产权转让部门给予或记录的保证金的有效期。

§193. 原始担保公司保证金；记录的必要性

在公证人为忠实履行其职责而缴纳保证金的情况下，授权在本州营业的担保，无须将保证金记录在行政区抵押记录员办公室内。在公证人履行职责的情况

not be necessary to record the bond in the office of the recorder of mortgages of the parish where the notary performs his duties, and in all cases, when existing bonds or future bonds of this character are filed and recorded in the mortgage office, they shall not operate as mortgages upon the property of the principal.

§194. Substitution of personal surety bond or special mortgage

In all cases where notaries public throughout the state have filed or recorded bonds in the offices of the several clerks of court and ex officio recorders of mortgages, with personal or individual surety, or who have executed and recorded a special mortgage on immovable property, as permitted by existing law, may, in lieu of such bonds, and in lieu of such special mortgages, substitute a bond in the same sum with any surety company authorized to do business in the state as surety.

§195. Cancellation of personal surety bond or special mortgage

Upon presentation of the surety bond provided for in R.S. 35:194 to any clerk of court and ex-officio recorder of mortgages, the clerk shall file the bond, and upon application by any interested party, shall cancel and erase in full from the records of his office any bond with personal surety recorded in the mortgage records of his office, and likewise any special mortgage executed and recorded by any notary public, conditioned for the faithful performance of his duties as notary.

§196. Substituted surety company bond; necessity for recordation

The surety bond provided for in R.S. 35:194 shall not be recorded in the mortgage records of the clerks of court and ex-officio recorders of mortgages and shall not in any event be an encumbrance against the property of any notary making and executing such bond.

§197. Repealed by Acts 1977, No. 451, §3

§198. Liability of notary and surety; effect of surety company bond; cancellation of bond for nonpayment

A. Nothing contained in R.S. 35:193 shall in any way affect the liability of a notary for the failure to perform his duties, nor the liability of his surety for any neglect thereof, or in any way alter the requirements of the recording of bonds not signed by a surety company, or their legal effect when so recorded.

下，将现有保证金或者未来保证金提交并记录在抵押办公室内时，不得作为其本金的抵押。

§194. 替换个人担保保证金或特别抵押

现行法律允许，本州的公证人向多名法庭文职处和记录员办理抵押，由个人担保，或者为不动产执行和记录特别抵押的办公室提交或记录保证金。这种特殊抵押可以代替上述保证金，替代保证金由授权在该州经营的担保公司以相同的金额代替保证金作为担保。

§195. 取消个人担保保证金或特别抵押

在到任何法院书记员和抵押记录员提供R.S. 35：194规定的担保保证金后，书记员应上交保证金，并在任何利害关系方提出申请后，从其办公室的记录中全部取消和删除记录在册的个人保证金担保人的办公室的抵押记录，以及任何公证人执行和记录的任何特别抵押，前提是公证人忠实履行了其公证职责。

§196. 替代担保公司保证金；记录的必要性

R.S. 35：194规定的担保保证金不得记录在法院文职人员和记录员的抵押记录中，公证人作出上述担保不视为对公证人财产的负担。

§197. 本条由1977年第451号法令§3条废止

§198. 公证和担保责任；担保公司保证金的效力；取消未支付的保证金

A. R.S. 35：193的规定不包含在以任何方式影响公证人不履行职责的责任，也不影响担保人对其任何疏忽负有的责任，或以任何方式更改担保人公司未签署的保证金的记录要求，或其法律效力。

B. When the notary in Orleans Parish has given bond with a surety company, the surety has the right to cancel the bond for nonpayment of the premium by giving notice through registered mail to the custodian of notarial records for the parish of Orleans. This notice must be given thirty days prior to any anniversary date of the bond, after which anniversary date the liability of the surety company on the bond shall cease.

§199. Duty to file, register, or record notarial instruments

A. Notaries public shall record all acts of sale, exchange, donation, and mortgage of immovable property passed before them, together with all resolutions, powers of attorney, and other documents annexed to or made part of the acts, in their proper order, and after first making a careful record of the acts in record books to be kept for that purpose as follows:

(1) If the immovable is located in this state outside of the parish of Orleans, the notary shall record the instrument within fifteen days after they are passed, with the appropriate recorder of the parish or parishes in which the immovable property is situated.

(2) (a) If the immovable is situated within the parish of Orleans, the notary shall file the instrument in the office of the custodian of notarial records for the parish of Orleans and record the instrument with the register of conveyances or recorder of mortgages or both.

(b) If the instrument is an act of sale or any other act evidencing a transfer of immoveable property situated in the parish of Orleans, it shall be the duty of the notary to cause the act to be registered with the office of the clerk as the recorder for the parish of Orleans, within forty-eight hours after the passage of the act.

(c) The original of every authentic act, except chattel mortgages and acts relating to immovable property outside of Orleans Parish, passed before a notary public in Orleans Parish, and also every act, contract, and instrument except money judgments and chattel mortgages filed for record in the offices of either the recorder of mortgages or the registrar of conveyances for the parish of Orleans, shall, as a condition precedent to such filing in the office of the recorder of mortgages or the register of conveyances for the parish of Orleans, be first filed in the notarial archives of the parish of Orleans.

B. The provisions of Subsection A of this Section shall not be applicable to instruments affecting cemetery

B. 当奥尔良行政区的公证人经由担保公司支付保证金时，担保人有权通过挂号信邮寄通知奥尔良行政区的公证记录员该公证人因未及时支付保费而被取消保证金。该通知必须在保证金年度计算的终止日的前30日送出，在此年度之后，担保公司对保证金的责任将终止。

§199. 提交、登记或记录公证书的义务

A. 公证人应当按照适当的顺序，记录所有通过的不动产的销售、交换、捐赠和抵押的行为，连同所有决议、授权委托书、附带或部分行为的其他文件，并应首先在为此目的保存的记录簿中仔细记录以下行为：

（1）如果不动产位于本州在奥尔良行政区以外的地区，公证人应在交易通过后15日内，于不动产所在的行政区或行政区的适当记录设备记录文书。

（2）（a）如果不动产位于奥尔良行政区内，公证人应将文书提交给奥尔良行政区的公证记录保管人办公室，并将该文书记录在产权转让登记册或抵押记录簿上或两处皆记录。

（b）如果该文书是出售的行为或证明移交位于奥尔良行政区的不动产的任何其他行为，公证人有义务在行为通过后的48小时内将其登记在奥尔良行政区书记官办公室内的记录册中。

（c）除在奥尔良行政区外发生的动产抵押和与不动产相关的行为，每一个真实的行为，以及其他行为、合同、文件，均应在奥尔良行政区公证员面前通过。在奥尔良行政区抵押记录册或者产权转让登记簿记录或登记的金钱判决和动产抵押，作为前置条件，应在抵押记录册或者产权转让登记簿归档前首先在奥尔良行政区公证档案馆归档。

B. 本条A款的规定不适用于影响公墓地区的文书，不包括存货清单或财产分割类文书，或法律规定

plots and shall not be so construed as embracing inventories or partitions or any other act required by law to be performed by notaries or parish recorders under any order of court, but the original of all such acts, without being recorded, shall be returned to the court from which the order is issued.

C. All notaries who contravene the provisions of this Section shall be subject to a fine of two hundred dollars for each infraction of the same, to be recovered before any court of competent jurisdiction, one-half for the benefit of the informer, as well as all such damages as the parties may suffer thereby.

D. A notary public shall be relieved of his obligations under Paragraph (A) (1) and Subparagraph (A) (2) (a) of this Section when he has been expressly directed in writing by all parties to the instrument to defer or refrain from such recordation or to deliver the instruments to one of the parties or to another person.

§200. Limitation on actions

A. No action for damages against any notary public duly commissioned in any parish in this state, any partnership of such notaries public, or any professional corporation, company, organization, association, enterprise, or other commercial business or professional combination answerable for the damage occasioned by such notary public in the exercise of the functions of a notary public, whether based upon tort, or breach of contract, or otherwise, arising out of an engagement to provide notarial services shall be brought unless filed in a court of competent jurisdiction and proper venue within one year from the date of the alleged act, omission, or neglect, or within one year from the date that the alleged act, omission, or neglect is discovered or should have been discovered; however, even as to actions filed within one year from the date of such discovery, in all events such actions shall be filed at the latest within three years from the date of the alleged act, omission, or neglect.

B. The provisions of this Section are remedial and apply to all causes of action without regard to the date when the alleged act, omission, or neglect occurred. However, with respect to any alleged act, omission, or neglect occurring prior to July 1, 2004, actions shall, in all events, be filed in a court of competent jurisdiction and proper venue on or before July 1, 2007, without regard to the date of discovery of the alleged act, omission, or neglect. The one-year and three-year periods of limitation provided in

根据任何法院命令由公证人或行政区记录员执行的任何其他行为。但所有此类行为的原件未经记录，均须退回发出命令的法院。

C. 违反本条规定的公证人，对其每一次违法行为处以200美元的罚款，并由有管辖权的法院追讨，一半用于奖励举报者，另一半用于赔偿各方因此可能遭受的损害。

D. 若各方明确书面指示以推迟或禁止这种记录或将文书交付给一方或另一方，则公证人免于履行本条（A）（1）款和（A）（2）（a）款所规定的义务。

§200. 行动限制

A. 任何公证人、公司、组织、协会、企业或其他商业事业或专业组合的任何合作伙伴关系可能对损害负责由公证人行使公证人的职能，无论是基于侵权行为、违反合同，还是以其他方式引起的纠纷，均不得对本州任何行政区委任的公证人采取任何行动，除非提交法院审判。起诉时间应在违法行为、遗漏或疏忽行为之日起1年内，提交有管辖权和适当地点的法院提起诉讼；然而，即使从发现之日起1年内提起诉讼，一经发生，最迟也应在所称行为、遗漏或疏忽之日起3年内提出诉讼。

B. 本条的规定是救济性条款，适用于所有诉讼因由，而不考虑被诉行为、遗漏或疏忽的日期。但是，对于在2004年7月1日之前发生的任何违法行为、遗漏或疏忽行为，无论其具体发生的日期，必须在2007年7月1日前提交给具有管辖权和适当地点的法院。本条A款规定的1年和3年期限是《民法典》第3458条所规定的强制期限，根据《民法典》第3461条的规定，不得放弃、中断或暂停执行。

Subsection A of this Section are peremptive periods within the meaning of Civil Code Article 3458 and, in accordance with Civil Code Article 3461, may not be renounced, interrupted, or suspended.

C. Notwithstanding any other law to the contrary, in all actions brought in this state against any notary public duly commissioned in this state, any partnership of such notaries public, or any professional corporation, company, organization, association, enterprise, or other commercial business or professional combination answerable for the damage occasioned by such notary public in the exercise of the functions of a notary public, the prescriptive and peremptive period shall be governed exclusively by this Section.

D. The provisions of this Section shall apply to all persons whether or not infirm or under disability of any kind and including minors and interdicts.

E. The peremptive period provided in Subsection A of this Section shall not apply in cases of fraud, as defined in Civil Code Article 1953.

F. The provisions of this Section shall not apply to notaries who are attorneys, who shall be subject to the provisions of R.S. 9:5605.

§201. Granting of commission; prerequisites

A. Before the governor shall issue to the applicant a commission of notary public for any parish, he shall require of him the production of all of the following:

(1) The certificate provided by R.S. 35:191(C)(1)(b)(ii), if applicable.

(2) His oath of office.

(3) His bond, properly executed, approved, and registered as provided in R.S. 35:192, or evidence of current insurance coverage as required by R.S. 35:71.

(4) His official signature.

B. Upon the issuing of the commission, all of the above shall be deposited in the office of the secretary of state and annexed in the margin of a book to be kept for that purpose by the secretary of state.

C. Notwithstanding any other provision of law to the contrary, an appointment to the office of notary public that requires the advice and consent of the Senate shall be an interim appointment subject to Senate confirmation as follows:

(1) If the legislature is in regular session at the time the appointment is made, the secretary of state on behalf of the governor shall submit for Senate confirmation the

C. 尽管存在任何其他相反的法律规定，针对在本州正式任命的公证人的所有诉讼中，公证人或任何专业公司、公司、组织、协会、企业或其他商业的任何伙伴、专业组合对公证人行使公证人职能所造成的损害负责的行为，规定性和强制性期限仅由本条规定。

D. 本条的规定适用于所有人，无论是否属于智力低下者或残疾人，包括未成年人和违禁者。

E. 本条A款规定的强制期不适用于《民法典》1953年规定的欺诈案件。

F. 本条的规定不适用于律师公证人，其适用R.S. 9：5605的规定。

§201. 授予任命；先决条件

A. 在州长向申请人发出任何行政区公证人的任命时，应要求其提交以下所有内容：

（1）根据R.S.35（191）(C)（1）(b)（ii）的规定提供的证明。

（2）其誓言。

（3）按照R.S. 35：192的规定，准确移交、确认、登记的保证金，或根据R.S.35：71的要求提供担保的证据。

（4）其正式签名。

B. 签发任命后，全部由州务卿存放在州务卿办公室的登记簿中，由州务卿保存。

C. 尽管存在任何其他相反的法律规定，需要参议院建议并同意的公证人任命，属于参议院确认的临时任用程序，具体如下：

（1）如果立法机关对公证人的任命是在定期立法会上作出的，州务卿应代理人州长在公证人任命后48小时内，向参议院提交确认的合格人选姓名。在会议

name of a qualified appointee within forty-eight hours after the appointment is made. Failure of the Senate to confirm the appointment prior to the end of the session shall constitute a rejection of the appointment and the interim appointment shall terminate

(2) If the legislature is not in regular session at the time the appointment is made, the appointment shall expire at the end of the next regular session, unless the Senate confirms the appointment during that session.

(3) Any person whose appointment is not confirmed by the Senate shall not be appointed to the office of notary public in any parish during any recess of the legislature.

(4) (a) Notwithstanding any other provision of this Section to the contrary, if it is discovered prior to the time that the appointment is submitted to the Senate for confirmation that the interim appointee to hold the office for which a commission has been issued does not meet the qualifications for appointment, the secretary of state on behalf of the governor shall notify the appointee by certified mail that the appointee will not be submitted for Senate confirmation until the appointee meets the qualifications for appointment. The appointee shall thereafter exercise no notarial duties or functions until the appointee meets the qualifications for appointment. If the appointee fails to meet the qualifications for appointment and the appointment terminates or expires as provided in this Subsection, the commission shall be rescinded and the appointee shall surrender his commission to the secretary of state.

(b) Notwithstanding any other provision of this Section to the contrary, if it is discovered after the appointment has been submitted to the Senate for confirmation, that the interim appointee to hold the office for which a commission has been issued does not meet the qualifications for appointment, the secretary of state on behalf of the governor shall notify the appointee by certified mail that the appointee does not meet the qualifications for appointment. The appointee shall thereafter exercise no notarial duties or functions until the appointee meets the qualifications for appointment. If the appointee fails to meet the qualifications for appointment and the appointment terminates or expires as provided herein, the commission shall be rescinded and the appointee shall surrender his commission to the secretary of state.

§202. Annual report; filing fee; penalties; suspension

A. Except as provided in Subsection F of this Sec-

结束前参议院未对该任命进行确认，将构成对该任命的拒绝，临时任用将终止。

（2）如果立法机关在任命时不是在正式立法会期间，除非参议院在下届会议期间确认任命，否则任命将在下届会议结束时届满。

（3）任何任命未经参议院确认的人员，不得在任何行政区中被任命为公证人。

（4）（a）尽管本法存在其他相反的规定，如果在提交参议院确认任命之前发现临时被任命人的任命不符合标准的，州务卿应代理州长通过认证邮件的方式通知被任命人，被任命人的任命不会提交参议院确认，直到被任命人的任命符合标准为止。被任命人随后不得行使公证人的职责，直至被任命人符合任用资格为止。如果被任命人在任用终止或到期前不能符合本条规定的任用资格，则被任命人应向州务卿放弃其任命。

（b）尽管本法可能存在其他相反的规定，如果在任命被提交参议院确认之后，发现临时被任命人的任命不符合标准的，州务卿应代理人州长通过认证邮件的方式通知被任命人，被任命人的任命不会提交参议院确认，直到被任命人的任命符合标准为止。被任命人随后不得行使公证人的职责，直至被任命人符合任用资格为止。如果在任用终止或到期前被任命人不能符合本条规定的任用资格，则被任命人应向州务卿放弃其任命。

§202. 年度报告；申报费；停职

A. 除本节 F 款规定外，所有任命的长期性的非

tion, all regularly commissioned non-attorney notaries shall file an annual report with the secretary of state on or before the anniversary date of his commission on the form developed and mailed, or provided by electronic means, by the secretary of state pursuant to R.S. 35:191.2(2) (a) , together with payment of the filing fee established by the secretary of state pursuant to R.S. 35:191.2(3) . The annual report shall be completed in full and signed by the notary.

B. Except as provided in Subsection F of this Section, a notary who fails to timely file the required annual report and pay the filing fee pursuant to Subsection A of this Section shall be assessed a late fee not to exceed fifty dollars by the secretary of state.

C. The commission of any notary who fails to timely file his fully completed annual report within sixty days after its due date as provided in Subsection A of this Section shall be automatically suspended, and the notary shall have no authority to exercise any of the duties or functions of a notary public until a current required annual report has been filed, and the notary has paid all accrued fees and late charges for a period not to exceed three years in connection with the suspension of his commission.

D. All offices, agencies, and departments of the state and political subdivisions with authority to appoint certain persons as ex officio notaries or otherwise authorize persons to exercise any notarial powers pursuant to the revised statutes and codes of this state shall file an annual report on the form developed and mailed, or provided by electronic means, by the secretary of state pursuant to R.S. 35:191.2(2) (b) , not later than the first day of July of each year.

E. The secretary of state shall send by certified mail to any office, agency, department of the state, or political subdivision of the state which fails to timely file the required annual report within the delays provided by Subsection D of this Section a notice of such failure to timely file the required report. The authority of a person appointed as an ex officio notary or otherwise authorized by the revised statutes and codes of this state to exercise the function of a notary public and the authority of any office, agency, department of the state, or political subdivision of the state to appoint ex officio notaries or to otherwise authorize persons to exercise notarial functions shall be suspended if the annual report is not filed within sixty days as provided in this Section.

F. A notary granted a leave of absence by the governor pursuant to R.S. 35:131 or 132 shall not be subject

律师公证人应在其任命的周年日当天或之前，以邮寄或电子回执的形式，根据 R.S. 35：191.2（2）（a）向州务卿提交年度报告，并根据 R.S.35：191.2（3）向州务卿缴纳申请费。年度报告应全文完成并由公证人签字。

B. 除本条 F 款规定外，未能及时提交所需年度报告并按照本条 A 款缴纳申报费的公证人，由州务卿征收不超过 50 美元的延期费用。

C. 未按照本条 A 款的规定，在法定提交期后 60 日内未能提交完整年度报告的公证人，其任命将自动暂停，公证人无权行使任何公证人的职责，直到其提交当前所有的年度报告、应计费用和逾期费用为止，且逾期时间不可超过从其任命暂停之日起 3 年。

D. 所有州办公室、办理机构和行政部门，任命特定人为公证人或者以其他方式授权人员依照本州经修订的章程和法规行使公证职权，应于每年 7 月 1 日，根据 R.S. 35：191.2（2）（b）由邮寄或由电子方式向州务卿提交年度报告。

E. 州务卿应通过认证邮件的方式向，任何根据本条 D 款不能及时提交年度报告的州办公室、机构、部门或州政治部门，通知及时提交年度报告。被任命为当然公证人的人或依本条经修订的章程和法规被授权行使公证人职能的人，以及被任州办公室、机构、部门或州政治部门任命为当然公证人的或者以其他方式获授权行使公证职务的人，因未按本条规定 60 日内提交年度报告的，予以暂停行使公证资格。

F. 公证人根据 R.S.35:131 或 R.S.35:132 被准予休假的，在其休假期间不适用本条 A 款、B 款、C 款确

to the fees or penalties established by Subsection A, B, or C of this Section during the term of his leave of absence. However, a notary granted a leave of absence shall provide the secretary of state with a current address during such leave.

G. A regularly commissioned non-attorney notary who is seventy years of age or older shall be permitted to elect a special commission status upon retirement from active service as a notary public by filing with the secretary of state a written request for such status along with an affidavit attesting to such status and certifying that he will no longer exercise the duties and functions of a notary public during such time as such status is in effect. A notary with such inactive status shall not be required to maintain a bond or file an annual report. However, a notary granted inactive status shall notify the secretary of state of any change of address to ensure the accuracy of information contained in the notary database maintained by the secretary of state. A notary may resume active commission status by filing a current annual report with the required fees with the secretary of state and posting bond in the amount then required by law.

CHAPTER 5. NOTARIES IN ORLEANS PARISH

PART I. APPOINTMENT, BOND, AND OFFICE [REPEALED]

§251. §§251 to 257 Repealed by Acts 1977, No. 451, §3

PART II. POWERS AND DUTIES

§281. Change of address in Orleans Parish; filing with board of assessors

Whenever a taxpayer who owns property situated in the parish of Orleans changes his home or mailing address, notice of such change shall within thirty days be given to the Board of Assessors for the parish of Orleans. Such notice shall list each property situated in the parish of Orleans in which the taxpayer has an interest. Failure to give such notice shall cause the taxpayer to forfeit all claims for failure to timely receive a tax bill. Amended by Acts 1964, No. 43, §1; Acts 2004, No. 141, §1; Amended by Acts 2006, No. 730, §1.

§282. Repealed by Acts 2006, No. 730 §2

§283. Repealed by Acts 2006, No. 730 §2

定的费用或处罚规定。但是，公证人应向州务卿提供休假期间的现有地址。

G. 年龄在70周岁以上的非律师长期公证人，向州务卿提交书面请求书，允许其处于从活跃的公证人地位到退休的特殊的任命状态，并证明公证人在这种状态时不再行使公证人的职责。具有这种不活跃状态的公证人不需要保留保证金或者提交年度报告。但是，处于不活跃状态的公证人，更改任何地址都应当通知州务卿，以确保州务卿保留的公证人资料的准确性。公证人可以通过向州务卿提交所需的费用、年度报告，以及保证金以申请转为活跃公证人的状态。

第五章 奥尔良行政区公证人

第一部分 任命、保证金和办事处（经修订）

§251. §251至§257由1977年第451号法案第3条废止

第二部分 权力和职责

§281. 在奥尔良行政区内的地址变更；提交评审委员会

每当拥有位于奥尔良行政区的财产的纳税人改变家庭或邮寄地址时，应在30日内通知奥尔良行政区的评估委员会。该通知应列出与纳税人利益相关的位于奥尔良行政区的所有财产。如果纳税人没有通知，则纳税人将失去因未能及时收到税收账单的索赔资格。本条由1964年法第43号法案§1、2004年第141号法案§1、2006年第730号法案§1修正。

§282. 本条由2006年第730号法令§2废止。

§283. 本条由2006年第730号法令§2废止。

§284. Repealed by Acts 2006, No. 730 §2

§285. Repealed by Acts 2006, No. 730 §2

§286. Repealed by Acts 2006, No. 730 §2

§287. Deputies

Every notary public in the Parish of Orleans may appoint one or more deputies to assist him in the making of protests and delivery of notices of protests of bills of exchange and promissory notes. Each notary shall be personally responsible for the acts of each deputy employed by him. Each deputy shall take an oath faithfully to perform his duties as such. The certificate of notice of protest shall state by whom made or served.

PART III. OFFICE AND CUSTODIAN OF NOTARIAL RECORDS

§321. Terms defined

As used in this Part, the terms defined in this Section shall have the meanings here given to them, except when the context clearly indicates otherwise:

(1) "Notary" or "Notary Public" shall mean a "Notary Public in and for the Parish of Orleans".

(2) "Custodian" means "Custodian of Notarial Records in and for the Parish of Orleans".

(3) "New Orleans Notarial Archives" means "office of notarial records in and for the parish of Orleans".

§322. Appointment and qualifications; vacancies

A. The governor by and with the advice and consent of the Senate shall appoint a custodian of notarial records, whose term of office shall be for four years, and run concurrent with the governor. In the event of a vacancy in said office, the governor by and with the advice and consent of the Senate shall appoint a custodian for the unexpired term.

B. The custodian shall be a duly licensed and practicing attorney at law and notary public in the parish of Orleans, and shall be a member in good standing of the Louisiana State Bar Association.

§323. Central office; preservation of notarial records; permanent volumes

A. The custodian shall maintain a central office in the city of New Orleans in the Civil District Court Building in quarters presently provided by the city of New Orleans or other quarters in said courthouse to be provided in the city of New Orleans. The custodian shall demand, take possession of, collect, keep, and preserve in this office or in an

§284. 本条由 2006 年第 730 号法令 §2 废止。

§285. 本条由 2006 年第 730 号法令 §2 废止。

§286. 本条由 2006 年第 730 号法令 §2 废止。

§287. 代理人

奥尔良行政区的所有公证人都可以任命一名或多名代理人协助其进行汇票及期票的拒绝接受和承兑通知。每名公证人应对其所雇用的每一名雇员的行为负责。每个代理人都应该宣誓忠实履行他的职责。拒绝承兑书应当载明开具票据或被送达票据的人。

第三部分 公证记录管理人和办公室

§321. 术语定义

在本部分中所用的术语，具有本条所赋予的含义，除非上下文明确具有其他含义除外：

（1）"公证人"是指"奥尔良行政区公证人"。

（2）"管理人"是指"奥尔良行政区的公证记录管理人"。

（3）"新奥尔良公证档案室"是指"奥尔良行政区的公证记录办公室"。

§322. 任用和资格；空缺

A. 经参议院的建议和同意，州长有权任命一名任期为 4 年的公证记录管理人，与州长任期一致。在上述职位空缺的情况下，由州长经过参议院的建议和同意，任命一名管理人，任期为上述职位的未满期限。

B. 管理人应是在奥尔良行政区的正式执业的律师且为公证人，并且是路易斯安那州律师协会的良好成员。

§323. 中央办公室；保存公证记录；永久卷

A. 管理人应在新奥尔良市的民事法院大楼或者由新奥尔良市的其他建筑中设立一个中央办公室。管理人应在要求的该办公室或档案安全的环境中管理、收集和保存奥尔良行政区的公证记录。

archival-safe environment the notarial records of notaries in the parish of Orleans.

B.(1) (a) The original of every authentic act, except chattel mortgages and acts relating to real property outside of Orleans Parish, passed before a notary public in Orleans Parish, and also every act, contract, and instrument except money judgments and chattel mortgages filed for record in the office of either the recorder of mortgages or the register of conveyances for the parish of Orleans, shall, as a condition precedent to such filin g in the office of the recorder of mortgages or the register of conveyances for the parish of Orleans, be first filed in the office of the custodian of notarial records for the parish of Orleans.

(b) The custodian shall endorse on each act, contract, or instrument filed in his office the date of such filing and a serial number, and shall issue a receipt for such act, contract, or instrument, showing the date of its filing and the serial number. All acts, contracts, or instruments so endorsed, if required by law, shall be filed for record with the recorder of mortgages or the register of conveyances for the parish of Orleans, or both, and shall be registered and/or recorded with the serial number furnished by the custodian; however, nothing herein shall be deemed to impose upon the custodian any obligation to file any act, contract, or instrument with either the recorder of mortgages or the register of conveyances.

(c) The recorder of mortgages and register of conveyances for the parish of Orleans shall thereafter endorse said act, contract, or instrument to the custodian, showing the date and time of filing, and the book and folio or instrument number endorsed thereon by the recorder of mortgages or the registrar of conveyances, and shall return the act to the custodian who shall thereupon have permanent custody of the said act, contract, or instrument, and shall file same in his office in permanent, bound form according to the serial number endorsed thereon by the custodian.

(2) It shall be the duty of all notaries public filing acts for registration and/or recordation pursuant hereto to deposit with the custodian all attachments such as certificates, tax researches, surveys, and other documents pertaining to any act passed before them and this deposit must be made within sixty days of the date of registration and/or recordation of said act. It shall be the duty of the custodian to file these attachments in permanent, bound form, to the act to which they pertain. The bookbinding shall be done in accordance to standards that will ensure the indefinite survival of the records.

B.(1)(a)除在奥尔良行政区外发生的动产抵押和与不动产相关的行为，每一个真实的行为，以及其他行为、合同、文件，均应在奥尔良行政区公证员面前通过。在奥尔良行政区抵押记录册或者产权转让登记簿记录或登记的金钱判决和动产抵押，作为前置条件，应在抵押记录册或者产权转让登记簿归档前首先在奥尔良行政区公证档案保管处归档。

（b）管理人应在其办公室提交的每个行为记录、合同或文书上签发备案日期和序列号，并发出接受此类行为记录、合同或文书的收据，显示其提交日期、序列号。凡符合法律要求的所有行为记录、合同或文书，均须记录在奥尔良行政区抵押记录员处或者移转记录员处，或者二者同时记录，并须以连续序号方式记录。但是，不得视为对管理人施加任何将行为记录、合同或文书，提交给抵押记录员或移转登记员的义务。

（c）奥尔良行政区的抵押和移转记录员随后将所述行为记录、合同或文书，以显示提交的日期和时间的方式登记后，退回给管理人，由管理人永久性保管该等文件，并按照序列号在办公室中永久性归档。

（2）所有的公证人均有义务向管理人归档所有公证机关登记和/或记录的所有附件，如证件、税务研究、调查和其他与之前通过的行为有关的文件，存放必须在登记和/或记录的后 60 日内进行。管理人有责任永久性地保存这些附件。装订工作应按照确保记录可无限期保存的标准进行。

C.(1) The custodian of notarial records shall charge the sum of ten dollars for each act, contract, or other instrument thus filed and deposited in his office, and twenty dollars for each sketch, blueprint, or survey, with one-half of the fee collected to be dedicated to microfilm or other imaging projects, with the remainder to be used only for the expenses and maintenance of said office.

(2) Notwithstanding the provisions of this subsection, all veterans of the armed forces of the United States of America shall be exempt from paying any fee for the filing and depositing of their discharge certificates or other evidence of honorable separation from the armed forces with the custodian of notarial records.

(3) Notwithstanding the provisions of this Subsection, the city of New Orleans shall be exempt from payment of any filing fees.

D. Repealed by Acts 1997, No. 1102, §2.

E. Every living, qualified notary public is authorized to certify true copies of any authentic act or any instrument under private signature hereafter or heretofore passed before him or acknowledged before him, and to make and certify copies, by any method, of any certificate, research, resolution, survey or other document annexed to the original of any authentic acts passed before him, and may certify such copies as true copies of the original document attached to the original passed before him.

F. Whenever any notary public for the parish of Orleans shall fail to comply with the provisions of this section then it shall be the duty of the custodian of notarial records to institute proceedings by rule in the Civil District Court for the parish of Orleans to require said notary public to show cause why his notarial commission should not be forfeited and why he should not be ordered to turn over all his notarial archives and records to the custodian of notarial records and pay all costs of said proceedings.

G. Repealed by Acts 1997, No. 1102, §2.

§323.1. Microfilm records; use; separate location

A. Permission is hereby granted to the custodian to install and use microfilm or other modern technological machinery and apparatus in the recordation, filing, preservation, display, and reproduction of all records and documents filed or deposited with the custodian prior to July 29, 1970, and subsequent thereto.

B. The original master negative of such microfilm may be used for preparing digital images which can be utilized in lieu of the original document or record. Such

C.（1）公证记录的管理人应为每个行为记录、合同或其他存放在其办公室的文书收取 10 美元的费用，每个素描、蓝图或调查收取的费用为 20 美元，其中一半费用是用于微缩胶片或其他成像工作，剩余的费用仅可用于所述办公室的支出和维护费用。

（2）尽管有本款的规定，美利坚合众国武装部队的所有退伍军人均无须为其向公证管理人提交、记录离职证明或者其他证明其荣誉退伍的证据支付任何费用。

（3）尽管有本款的规定，新奥尔良市居民无须缴纳任何申请费。

D. 本条由 1997 年第 1102 号法令 §2 废止。

E. 任何健在的、有资格的公证人均有权证明行为副本或在其面前通过或承认的私人签名的任何文书的真实性，并以研究、解决、调查或其他附于原始文件的任何方式制作和证明副本，并且有权证明该副本与原始文件相一致。

F. 任何奥尔良行政区公证人不遵守本条规定的，公证人的管理人有义务在奥尔良行政区民事法院提起诉讼，要求公证人证明自己的公证人任命不得没收的原因，为何其不得被指令将所有公证档案和记录转交公证记录管理人，以及拒绝支付所有诉讼费用的原因。

G. 本条由 1997 年第 1102 号法案 §2 废止。

§323.1. 缩微胶片记录；使用；分开存放

A. 特此授权管理人对在 1970 年 7 月 29 日之前向管理人提交或交存的所有记录和文件，通过安装和使用缩微胶片或其他机器设备等现代技术进行记录、备份、保存。

B. 这种缩微胶卷的原底片可以用作代替原始文件或记录的数字图像。这种缩微胶片应与管理人管理的原始记录和文件分开放置。管理人可以拥有任何

microfilm shall be kept at a separate location from the original records and documents filed with the custodian. The custodian may have working copies made of any of the master negatives, and keep the working copies on the premises of the New Orleans Notarial Archives to be used at his discretion in connection with the preservation of fragile volumes. The custodian may substitute the working copies for daily use of original volumes, so long as the original volumes remain in the collection and are easily available for examination in cases where the working copies of the microfilms are difficult to decipher.

C. Such microfilm copy shall be deemed to be an original record for all purposes, and shall be admissible in evidence in all courts or administrative agencies. A facsimile, exemplification or certified copy thereof shall for all purposes be deemed to be a transcript, exemplification or certified copy of the original.

D. Nothing contained herein shall in any manner be construed to permit the destruction of any notarial records presently in the possession of, or which may hereafter come into the possession of, the custodian of notarial records.

§324. Bond of custodian

The custodian shall give bond, in addition to his notarial bond, in the amount of ten thousand dollars in favor of the governor, with one or more good and solvent sureties approved by the presiding judge of the Civil District Court of the Parish of Orleans, conditioned upon the faithful performance of his duties as custodian. This bond shall be filed in the office of the Secretary of State.

§335. Repealed by Acts 2007, No. 212, § 1.

§336. Deputy of custodian; appointment of archivist

A. The custodian may appoint one deputy, who shall be sworn according to law, and such deputy, when appointed and sworn, shall have power to certify copies of acts and records of all kinds in the office. The deputy appointed by the custodian shall devote full time to the duties of that office and not receive a salary that exceeds forty thousand dollars per annum.

B. (1) The custodian shall employ full-time professional archivist to assist the custodian with the responsibilities of the office and to ensure the adequate preservation of records and documents, whose salary shall not exceed thirty-five thousand dollars per annum.

(2) The archivist shall be certified by the Academy of

主要文件的工作副本，并将少量文件的副本保留在新奥尔良公证档案馆进行工作。管理人可以用工作副本替换原始卷来日常使用，只要原始卷仍被保存，以便在缩微胶片的工作副本难以破译的情况下进行查阅和校对。

C. 所有的缩微胶片副本应被视为原始记录，并应在所有法院或行政机构中被接受为证据。所有的传真、示例或认证副本应被视为原件的抄本、示例或认证副本。

D. 本条的任何内容均不得以任何方式解释为允许销毁目前由管理人机构管理的的公证文件。

§324. 管理人的保证金

管理人除了公证保证金外，还应交给州长1万美元的保证金，该保证金是由一名或多名由奥尔良行政区民事法院主审法官批准的担保保证金，以保证管理人忠实履行职责。该保证金应交给州务卿办公室。

§335. 本条由2007年第212号法案 §1废止

§336. 管理人代理人；档案工作者的任命

A. 管理人可以任命一名依法宣誓的代理人，该代理人在被任命和宣誓后，有权在办公室内核实各种行为和记录的副本。该管理人任命的代理人应当全职负责该职务，且不得领取年薪超过4万美元的工资。

B.（1）管理人应当聘请全职专业的档案工作者协助管理人负责办公室的事务，确保妥善保存所有的记录和文件，且档案工作者年薪不得超过3.5万美元。

（2）档案工作者须经档案工作者学院的认证。

Certified Archivists.

§337. Fees, salary, and excess funds of custodian

A. The custodian may charge and receive the same fees of office as are allowed by law to other notaries for the making and certifying of copies. The compensation of the custodian shall not exceed forty thousand dollars per annum and any remainder of fees shall be used solely to operate and maintain the functions of the office of notarial records.

B. Any unexpended or unencumbered funds remaining at the end of the fiscal year to the credit of the account of monies, fees, or sums collected by the custodian of notarial records shall be dedicated to microfilming or other imaging projects to ensure the indefinite survival of the records.

§337.1. City of New Orleans; exemption from fees

The city of New Orleans shall not be required to pay any of the fees charged for the services of the custodian of notarial records.

§338. Annual budget; submission to enumerated entities

A. The custodian of notarial records shall prepare a detailed annual budget at the end of his fiscal year and submit a copy of that budget to both the legislative auditor pursuant to R.S. 24:513 et seq. and the Joint Legislative Committee on the Budget, and shall publish a copy in the official journal of the parish of Orleans, at his own expense, commencing January 1, 1989.

B. The custodian shall include in the annual budget adequate provisions to ensure that there is systematic rebinding, page repair, and microfilming of notarial records created before July 29, 1970. The custodian shall be empowered to and shall make such reasonable rules and regulations relative to the use and preservation of documents and volumes in the New Orleans Notarial Archives as he judges necessary, except that nothing in this Section shall be construed to mean that the public shall not have free access to either original records or facsimiles thereof during all regular office hours, not including extended office hours.

CHAPTER 6. EX OFFICIO NOTARIES

§391. Ex officio notaries; qualifications

Any person may be appointed an ex officio notary as authorized in this Chapter, provided he:

§337. 费用，工资和管理人的超额资金

A. 管理人可以向其他公证人收取法律允许的办公费用，用于制作和证实副本。管理人据此获得的费用不得超过每年 4 万美元，其余费用仅可用于运转和维持公证记录办公室的功能。

B. 财政年度结束时，由公证记录管理人收取的款项、费用或总额，其中剩余的未花费或未支配资金，应用缩微胶片或其他影像保存，确保无限期保存记录。

§337.1. 新奥尔良市；费用免除

新奥尔良市无须为公证记录管理人的服务支付任何费用。

§338. 年度预算；提交给枚举实体

A. 公证记录的管理人应在其财政年度结束时编制详细的年度预算，并根据 R.S.24:513 等条款向立法审计员和联合预算案委员会提交该预算的副本，并自 1989 年 1 月 1 日起，自费将预算副本发布在奥尔良行政区的官方杂志上。

B. 管理人应在年度预算中加入适当的条款，以确保 1970 年 7 月 29 日之前制作的公证记录被系统地重新绑定、页面修复和以缩微胶卷的方式被记录。管理人在其认为必要时应有权制定合理的规则和条例，规定关于使用和保存新奥尔良公证记录档案、文件、卷本等内容。除此之外，本条中其他内容不得被解释为公众在正式办公时间不包括延长办公时间内，不得自由获得原始记录或传真。

第六章 当然公证人

§391. 当然公证人；资格

任何人可被任命为本章授权的当然公证人，前提是：

(1) Is a resident citizen or alien of the state.

(2) Is eighteen years of age or older.

(3) Is able to read, write, and speak the English language and be possessed of sufficient knowledge of the English language.

(4) Is not under interdiction or incapable of serving as an ex officio notary because of a mental infirmity.

(5) Is not under indictment for a felony and has not been convicted of a felony for which he has not been pardoned.

(6) Has given bond, with good and solvent security, in the sum of ten thousand dollars conditioned for the faithful performance of all duties required by law toward all persons who may employ him in his profession of ex officio notary, or he has maintained a minimum of ten thousand dollars in errors and omissions insurance coverage.

(7) In the case of a state employee who serves as an ex officio notary in the course and scope of his employment, records his oath of office with the secretary of state.

§392. Ex officio notaries; bond; oath

A. The bond required of all ex officio notaries, except those state employees who serve as ex officio notaries in the course and scope of their employment, shall be submitted to the clerk of court and ex officio recorder of mortgages for the parish where the ex officio notary will exercise the functions of his office, as well as filed in the office of the secretary of state. The bond shall be subscribed in favor of the governor; approved by the clerk, except in Orleans Parish; and if secured by personal surety, recorded in the mortgage office of the parish in a special book kept for bonds required of all notaries. In Orleans Parish, the bond shall be approved by the custodian of notarial records. The bond for state employees who serve as ex officio notaries shall be maintained in the division of administration, office of risk management.

B. The provisions governing the recordation of bonds issued by surety companies doing business in the state, the substitution and cancellation of personal surety bonds or special mortgages, the filing of substituted surety company bonds, the liability of notaries and sureties, and the limitation of actions against sureties, R.S. 35:193 through 200, shall apply to bonds issued for the faithful performance of the duties of ex officio notaries.

C. No ex officio notary who holds such office by virtue of duties affiliated with employment with a political

（1）在本州居住的公民或外地人。

（2）18周岁以上。

（3）能够用英文阅读、写作和说，掌握足够的英语知识。

（4）没有存在由于精神虚弱，而不能担任当然公证人的状态。

（5）没有因重罪而被起诉，没有犯不可赦免的重罪。

（6）具有良好且安全的1万美元的保证金，以确保其对所有聘请的当然公证人，依法忠实履行所有职务，或者维持至少1万美元的错误和遗漏保险。

（7）州工作人员在其工作任职期间担任当然公证人时，应将其对州务卿的就职宣誓记录在案。

§392. 当然公证人；保证金；誓言

A. 在除了工作任职期间担任当然公证人的州工作人员外，所有的当然公证人都应当有保证金，应当记录在当然公证人将会行使其职权的行政区的法院书记官和抵押记录员处，并在州务卿办公室备案。除奥尔良行政区外，该保证金应当缴纳给州长且经办事处批准。而且，如果保证金由个人担保人担保，应当被记录在行政区的抵押办公室的特别登记簿中，该登记薄载有所有公证人所需的保证金。在奥尔良行政区中，保证金应由公证记录管理人批准。作为当然公证人的州工作人员的保证金，应当被保存在在行政部门风险管理办公室。

B. 关于由在本州开展业务的担保公司担保的保证金记录、替代和取消个人担保保证金或特别抵押、提交替代担保公司保证金、公证人和担保人的责任，以及担保人诉讼的限制等事宜，依照RS 35：193至RS 35：200的规定，适用于所有为确保当然公证人忠实履行公证人职责而发放的保证金。

C. 具有与国家政治部门相关职务的当然公证人，无须向任一行政区法院书记员提交公证人的任

subdivision of the state shall be required to file his or her oath of office as notary with any parish clerk of court.

§392.1. Ex officio notaries

A. Any person, not a regularly commissioned notary, who is an ex officio notary, or who is otherwise authorized under the various revised statutes and codes of this state to administer oaths or exercise any or all of the functions, powers, and authority of a notary, is authorized to perform those functions, powers, and authority only as they are directly related to and required for the operation of the office, agency, or department under which the authority is granted. All acts which are performed beyond the specific authority granted in the various statutes and codes of this state to administer oaths and to perform the functions, powers, and authority of a notary and which are not directly related to or required for the operation of the office, agency, or department shall be null and void.

B. The provisions of this Section shall not be applicable to documents notarized by a clerk of court or any of the deputy clerks of court who are employees of the clerk of court when such documents are notarized within the course and scope of their employment with the office of clerk of court. However, nothing in this Section shall prohibit such clerks and deputy clerks from notarizing vehicle titles or acknowledging the signatures on authentic acts even if such authentic acts are not within the course and scope of their employment.

§393. Ex officio notaries public for the Department of Public Safety and Corrections; powers

A. Notwithstanding any provisions in the law relative to qualifications for and limitations on the number of notaries public, the governor is authorized to appoint, upon recommendation by the secretary of the Department of Public Safety and Corrections, the supervisors of each troop headquarters, any investigator of the internal affairs unit of the office of state police in the Department of Public Safety and Corrections, and the executive assistant to the general counsel of the Department of Public Safety and Corrections as ex officio notaries public who shall perform the duties provided hereunder without charge or other compensation. Any ex officio notary public appointed under the provisions of this Section shall possess those notarial powers as provided by law to administer oaths and take acknowledgments.

B. Additionally, specially designated commissioned Louisiana state police officers assigned to intelligence, de-

职宣誓。

§392.1. 当然公证人

A. 任何非长期任命的当然公证人，或非根据本州各种修订的法规和规范获得授权去管理誓言或行使公证人职权的人，只在涉及与授予其权力的办公室、机构或部门的运作直接相关的事宜时，才有权行使公证人的全部或者任一职能。所有超过在本州各种法规和规范中授予的特定权力行使的执行宣誓等行为，以及不直接与办公室、机构或部门的运作并与公证人的职能、权力相关的行为，皆是无效的。

B. 本条的规定不适用于法院书记员，或者受到法庭雇佣作为法院书记员代理人在其受法院雇佣所行使的职权范围内进行公证的文件。然而，即使法院书记员或书记员代理人公证的机动车登记或对公证行为的签名的承认超过了其职权范围，依然不受本条禁止。

§393. 当然公证人与公共安全部和惩戒部；权力

A. 尽管法律中有关于公证人资格和公证人人数限制的规定，州长仍有权根据公共安全部和惩戒部秘书的建议任命各部门的主管、公共安全部和惩戒部内部事务单位调查人员、公共安全部及惩戒部总顾问行政助理，要求履行本条规定的当然公证人职责，并不得收取费用或其他补偿。根据本条规定任用的当然公证人应具有履行法律规定的管理誓言和承认的职能。

B. 另外，专门指定为路易斯安那州情报、侦察、麻醉或内政的特警委员，国家消防部长办公室特别指

tectives, narcotics, or internal affairs, specially designated commissioned officers of the office of the state fire marshal, and commissioned agents of the office of alcohol and tobacco control shall have the power to administer oaths and receive sworn statements, in connection with their official duties.

§393.1. Ex officio notaries public for the Department of Public Safety and Corrections; appointment by secretary

A. Notwithstanding any provision in the law relative to qualifications for and limitations on the number of notaries public, the secretary of the Department of Public Safety and Corrections is authorized to designate officers in his office and appoint them as ex officio notaries public.

B. Each officer so appointed may exercise the functions of a notary public only to administer oaths, receive sworn statements, and shall otherwise be limited to matters within the official functions of the Department of Public Safety and Corrections.

C. All acts performed by such an ex officio notary public authorized by this Section shall be performed without charge or other compensation and without the necessity of giving bond.

D. The secretary may suspend or terminate any appointment made pursuant to this Section at any time, and separation from the employ of the Department of Public Safety and Corrections shall automatically terminate the powers of such an ex officio notary public.

§394. Ex officio notaries public for the Department of Justice

A. Notwithstanding any provisions of the law relative to qualifications for and limitations on the number of notaries public, the governor is authorized to appoint, upon recommendation by the attorney general, investigators in the Department of Justice as ex officio notaries public. Each ex officio notary public appointed under the provisions of this Section shall be submitted to the Senate for confirmation.

B. Such an ex officio notary public may exercise the functions of a notary public only to administer oaths and receive sworn statements and shall otherwise be limited to matters within the official functions of the Department of Justice.

C. All acts performed by such an ex officio notary public authorized by this Section shall be performed without charge or other compensation.

定的委托人员以及任命为酒类和烟草控制办公室的当然公证人，应当具有执行宣誓的权力，并有权接受与其公职有关的宣誓。

§393.1. 当然公证人与公共安全部和惩戒部；秘书任命

A. 尽管法律中有关于公证人资格和人数限制的规定，但公共安全部和惩戒部秘书有权指派其办公室的人员，任命为当然公证人。

B. 据此任命的公证人，只能履行执行宣誓、接受宣誓声明的职能，其他公证人职能的行使仅限于公共安全部和惩戒部的内部职能。

C. 本条授权的当然公证人行使的所有行为，应当是免费的且不得收取其他方式的补偿，此类当然公证人不需要交纳保证金。

D. 秘书可随时暂停或终止根据本条提出的任何任命，并且当然公证人在公共安全部和惩戒部的聘用结束时，其当然公证人职权自动终止。

§394. 司法部当然公证人

A. 尽管法律中有关于公证人资格和人数限制的规定，州长有权根据律政司的建议，任命司法部的调查人员为当然公证人。根据本条规定任命的每名当然公证人应经过参议院确认。

B. 据此任命的公证人，只能履行执行宣誓、接受宣誓声明的职能，其他的公证人职能仅限于司法部的内部职能。

C. 本条授权的当然公证人行使的所有行为，应当是免费且不得收取其他方式的补偿。

D. The attorney general may suspend or terminate any appointment made pursuant to this Section at any time, and separation from the employ of the Department of Justice shall automatically terminate the powers of such an ex officio notary public.

§395. Ex officio notaries public for the Department of State

A. Notwithstanding any provisions of the law relative to qualifications for notaries public, the secretary of state is authorized to appoint not more than six essential employees within the Department of State as ex officio notaries public.

B. Such ex officio notaries public may exercise the functions of a notary public only to administer oaths and receive sworn statements and shall be limited to matters within the official functions of the Department of State. They shall use the official seal of the department.

C. All acts performed by such ex officio notaries public authorized by this Section shall be performed without charge or other compensation.

§396. Ex officio notaries public for the Governor's Consumer Protection Division

A. Notwithstanding any provisions of the law relative to qualifications for and limitations on the number of notaries public, the governor is authorized to appoint, upon recommendation by the director of the Governor's Consumer Protection Division, investigative staff members in the Governor's Consumer Protection Division as ex officio notaries public. Each ex officio notary public appointed under the provisions of this Section shall be submitted to the Senate for confirmation.

B. Such ex officio notaries public may exercise the functions of a notary public only to administer oaths and receive sworn statements and shall otherwise be limited to matters within the official functions of the Governor's Consumer Protection Division as set forth in R.S. 51:1404.

C. All acts performed by such ex officio notary public authorized by this Section shall be performed without charge or other compensation.

D. The director of the Governor's Consumer Protection Division may suspend or terminate any appointment made pursuant to this Section at any time, and separation from the employ of the Governor's Consumer Protection Division shall automatically terminate the powers of such an ex officio notary public.

D. 律政司可随时暂停或终止根据本条提出的任何任命，并且当然公证人在律政司的聘用结束时，其当然公证人职权自动终止。

§395. 州务院当然公证人

A. 尽管存在关于公证人资格的法律规定，州务卿有权任命州务院内不超过6名骨干公务员为当然公证人。

B. 据此任命的当然公证人，只能履行执行宣誓、接受宣誓声明的公证人职能，且仅限于州务院的内部职能。其必须使用该部门的官方印章。

C. 本条授权的当然公证人行使的所有行为，应当是免费的且不得收取其他方式的补偿。

§396. 州消费者保护司的当然公证人

A. 尽管法律中有关于公证人资格和人数限制的规定，州长有权根据州消费者保护司司长的建议，任命州消费者保护司的调查人员为当然公证人。根据本条规定任命的每名当然公证人应经过参议院确认。

B. 据此任命的当然公证人，只能履行执行宣誓、接受宣誓声明的公证人职能，其他公证人职能仅限于消费者保护司根据R.S. 51:1404规定的内部职能。

C. 本条授权的当然公证人行使的所有行为，应当是免费的且不得收取其他方式的补偿。

D. 消费者保护司司长可随时暂停或终止根据本条提出的任何任命，并且当然公证人在消费者保护司的聘用结束时，其当然公证人职权自动终止。

§397. Ex officio notaries public for the Louisiana State Racing Commission

A. Notwithstanding any provisions of the law relative to qualifications for notaries public, the governor, upon the recommendation of the chairman of the Louisiana State Racing Commission, shall appoint not more than two of its employees at each racing commission office as ex officio notaries public.

B. Such ex officio notaries public may exercise the functions of a notary public only to administer oaths and receive sworn statements and shall be limited to matters within the official duties of R.S. 4:150(B) (11).

C. All acts performed by such ex officio notary public authorized by this Section shall be performed without charge or other compensation.

D. The provisions of this Section shall not cause any additional cost to the state.

§398. Ex officio notaries for district attorneys

A. Notwithstanding any provisions of the law relative to qualifications for and limitations on the number of notaries public, each district attorney may designate an investigator in his office as administrative assistant and appoint him as an ex officio notary public.

B. Such an ex officio notary public may exercise, in the judicial district which the district attorney serves, the functions of a notary public only to administer oaths and execute affidavits, acknowledgments, and other documents, all limited to matters within the official functions of the office of district attorney.

C. Such ex officio notary public shall fulfill the same bond requirements as provided by law in the parish or parishes comprising the district which the district attorney serves, provided the total amount of the bond shall not exceed the amount required to exercise the functions of notary public in a single parish.

D. All acts performed by such an ex officio notary public authorized by this Section shall be performed without charge or other compensation.

E. The district attorney may suspend or terminate an appointment made pursuant to this Section at any time, and separation from the employ of the district attorney shall automatically terminate the powers of such an ex officio notary public.

F. The district attorney shall pay as an expense of his office the costs of the notarial seal, the notarial bond, and any fees required for filing the bond.

§397. 路易斯安那州赛马委员会的当然公证人

A. 尽管存在有关公证人资格的法律规定，州长有权根据路易斯安那州赛马委员会主席的推荐，在每次赛马中任命不超过 2 名工作人员为当然公证人。

B. 据此任命的当然公证人，只能履行执行宣誓、接受宣誓声明的公证人职能，且仅限于 R.S. 4:150(B)(11) 规定的正式职能。

C. 本条授权的当然公证人行使的所有行为，应当是免费的且不得要求其他方式的补偿。

D. 本条规定不得对本州造成任何额外费用。

§398. 地方检察官的当然公证人

A. 尽管法律中有关于公证人资格和人数限制的规定，每个地区检察官，可以提名其办公室内的调查人员为行政助理并任命其为当然公证人。

B. 据此任命的当然公证人，有权在地区检察院的正式职能范围内履行执行宣誓、支持、承认文件的公证人职能。

C. 此类当然公证人应当交纳该行政区法律规定的地区检察官应当交纳的保证金，但保证金数额不得超过该行政区公证人的保证金。

D. 本条授权的当然公证人行使的所有行为，应当是免费的且不得获取其他方式的补偿。

E. 地区检察官可随时暂停或终止根据本条提出的任何任命，并且当然公证人在地区检察院的聘用结束时，其当然公证人职权自动终止。

F. 地方检察官应当以其办公室的费用支付公证印章的费用和公证保证金所需的任何费用。

§399. Repealed by Acts 2005, No. 55, §2

§400. Ex officio notaries public for the United States Forest Service

A. Notwithstanding any provisions of the law relative to qualification for and limitations on the number of notaries public, the governor is authorized to appoint, upon recommendation by the Forest Supervisor, realty specialists in the United States Forest Service as ex officio notaries public.

B. This ex officio notary public may exercise the functions of a notary public only to administer oaths and execute affidavits, acknowledgments, and other documents, all limited to matters within the official functions of his employment with the United States Forest Service.

C. All acts performed by an ex officio notary public authorized by this Section may be performed in any parish where national forest lands are administered, and shall be performed without charge or other compensation.

D. Separation from the employ of the United States Forest Service shall automatically terminate the powers of this ex officio notary public.

§401. Ex officio notary public for the Sabine River Authority

A. Notwithstanding any provisions of the law relative to qualification for notaries public, the director of the Sabine River Authority may appoint one employee of the Sabine River Authority as ex officio notary public

B. Such ex officio notary public may exercise the functions of a notary public only to administer oaths, receive sworn statements, and execute affidavits, acknowledgments, and other documents, and shall be limited to matters within the official functions of the Sabine River Authority.

C. All acts performed by such ex officio notary public authorized by this Section may be performed only in the parishes of Sabine, DeSoto, Beauregard, Calcasieu, Cameron, and Vernon and shall be performed without charge or other compensation.

D. The director of the Sabine River Authority may suspend or terminate any appointment made pursuant to this Section at any time and separation from the employ of the Sabine River Authority shall automatically terminate the powers of such ex officio notary public.

§402. Ex officio notaries public for the vital records registry

A. Notwithstanding any other provisions of the law

§399. 本条由 2005 年第 55 号法案 §2 废止

§400. 美国森林局当然公证人

A. 尽管法律中有关于公证人资格和人数限制的规定，州长有权根据森林局局长的建议，任命美国森林局中专家为当然公证人。

B. 据此任命的当然公证人，只能履行执行宣誓、支持、承认文件的公证人职能，且仅限于美国森林局的正式职能。

C. 本条授权的当然公证人在任何森林行政区内行使的所有行为，应当是免费的且不得收取其他方式的补偿。

D. 当美国森林局的雇佣终止时，则其当然公证人职权将自动终止。

§401. 萨宾河管理局当然公证人

A. 尽管存在关于公证人资格的法律规定，萨宾河管理局局长可以任命萨宾河管理局的 1 名雇员为当然公证人。

B. 据此任命的每名官员，只能履行执行宣誓、支持、承认文件的公证人职能，且仅限于萨宾河管理局的正式职能。

C. 本条授权的当然公证人只能在萨宾、德索图、博格瑞德、考卡希尔、卡曼罗、维曼行政区内行使，且所有行为应当是免费的且不得收取其他方式的补偿。

D. 萨宾河管理局局长可随时暂停或终止根据本条提出的任命，并且当然公证人在萨宾河管理局的聘用结束时，其当然公证人职权自动终止。

§402. 重要记录登记的当然公证人

A. 尽管存在关于公证人资格任用的法律规定，

to the contrary governing the qualifications and appointment of notaries public, the governor may appoint the state registrar of vital records to serve as ex officio notary public, and the state registrar of vital records may designate not more than three employees in the vital records registry to serve as ex officio notaries public.

B. Such ex officio notaries public may exercise the functions of a notary public only to execute affidavits as required under R.S. 9:224(B) to verify information contained in applications for a marriage license.

C. All acts performed by each ex officio notary public authorized by this Section shall be performed without charge or other compensation.

D. The state registrar of vital records may suspend or terminate any notary public he has appointed pursuant to this Section at any time, and separation from office or employment in the office of the state registrar of vital records of any ex officio notary public under this Section shall automatically terminate the powers of such an ex officio notary public.

§403. Ex officio notaries for hospital service district hospitals

A. Notwithstanding any provisions of the law relative to qualifications of notaries public, the director of a hospital service district hospital may appoint not more than two employees of the hospital as ex officio notaries public.

B. Such ex officio notaries may exercise the functions of a notary public only to administer oaths, receive sworn statements, execute affidavits, and acknowledgments and shall be limited to matters within the official business functions of the hospital.

C. Each ex officio notary public shall fulfill the same bond requirements as provided by law for notaries in the parish in which the hospital is located. The hospital shall pay as an expense of the hospital the costs of the notarial seal, the notarial bond, and any fees required for filing the bond.

D. All acts performed by each ex officio notary public authorized by this Section shall be performed without charge or other compensation.

E. The director of the hospital may suspend or terminate an appointment made pursuant to this Section at any time, and separation from the employ of the hospital shall automatically terminate the powers of the ex officio notary public.

但州长可以任命州重要记录的登记员担任当然公证人，且州重要记录登记员不得指定超过3名该部门的雇员担任当然公证人。

B. 据此任命的当然公证人仅可按R.S.9：224(B)的规定在申请结婚证时对相关信息进行确认，作出誓章。

C. 本条授权的每名当然公证人执行的所有行为，应当免费且不得收取其他方式的补偿。

D. 州重要记录登记局可随时暂停或终止根据本条提出的任何任命，并且当然公证人在重要记录登记局的聘用结束时，其当然公证人职权自动终止。

§403. 医院服务区医院的当然公证人

A. 尽管存在关于公证人资格的法律规定，医院服务区医院院长可以任命不超过2名医院职工为当然公证人。

B. 据此任命的当然公证人，只能履行执行誓言、接受宣誓声明、执行誓章和确认书的职能，且仅限于医院官方职能范围内的事项。

C. 每名当然公证人应交纳医院所在地区公证人依法规定的需交纳的相同保证金。医院应以医疗费用支付公证印章、公证保证金所需的费用。

D. 本条授权的当然公证人行使的所有行为，应当是免费的且不得获取其他方式的补偿。

E. 医院院长可随时暂停或终止根据本条提出的任何任命，并且当然公证人在医院的聘用结束时，其当然公证人职权自动终止。

§404. Ex officio notaries public of the office of financial institutions

A. Notwithstanding any provisions of law relative to qualifications for notaries public, except R.S. 35:391, the commissioner of financial institutions may appoint two investigators in his office as ex officio notaries public.

B. Such ex officio notaries public may exercise the functions of a notary public only to administer oaths and receive sworn statements and shall be limited to matters within the official functions of the office of financial institutions. They shall use the official seal of the department.

C. All acts performed by each ex officio notary public authorized by this Section shall be performed without charge or other compensation.

§405. Ex officio notary public for levee district police

A. Notwithstanding any provisions of law relative to qualifications for notaries public, except R.S. 35:391, the board of commissioners of a levee district created pursuant to the laws of this state may appoint three officers as ex officio notaries public. For purposes of this Section, "officer" means an employee who has attained the rank of lieutenant or a higher rank and who is a full-time commissioned police officer of the levee district.

B. Such ex officio notary public may exercise the functions of a notary public only to administer oaths, receive sworn statements, execute affidavits, acknowledgments, and other documents, and shall be limited to matters within the official functions of the law enforcement division of the levee district.

C. All acts performed by an ex officio notary public authorized by this Section may be performed only in the parishes in which the respective levee district has jurisdiction.

D. The board of commissioners of each levee district may suspend or terminate an appointment made pursuant to this Section at any time, and separation from the employ of a levee district shall automatically terminate the powers of such an ex officio notary public.

§406. Ex officio notaries public of the adult protection agency

A. Notwithstanding any provisions of law relative to qualifications for notaries public, except R.S. 35:391:

(1) The director of the office of elderly affairs may appoint two investigators in each region of the adult protection agency, office of elderly affairs, office of the governor, as ex officio notaries public.

§404. 金融机构办公室的当然公证人

A. 尽管存在除了 R.S. 35：391 有关公证人资格的规定，金融机构专员可以在其办公室任命 2 名调查员为当然公证人。

B. 据此任命的当然公证人，只能执行誓言、接受宣誓声明、执行誓章，且仅限于金融机构官方职能范围内的事项。进行公证行为时应使用部门的公章。

C. 本条授权的当然公证人行使的所有行为，应当是免费的且不得收取其他方式的补偿。

§405. 防洪警察的当然公证人

A. 尽管存在除了 R.S. 35：391 的有关公证人资格的规定，根据本州法律设立的堤防专员委员会可以任命 3 名官员为当然公证人。就在本条中，"官员"是指已达到中级或高级职级的职工，并且是该地区全职委托警务人员。

B. 据此任命的当然公证人只能执行誓言、接受宣誓声明、执行誓章和确认书等文件的职能，并仅限于防洪执法部门的正式职能范围内的事项。

C. 本条授权的当然公证人执行的所有行为，只能在相应防洪区的行政区内进行。

D. 防洪区委员会可随时暂停或终止根据本条提出的任何任命，并且当然公证人在防洪区的聘用结束时，其当然公证人职权自动终止。

§406. 成人保护机构的当然公证人

A. 尽管存在除了 R.S. 35：391 的有关公证人资格的规定：

（1）老年事务办公室主任可以在成人保护机构、老年事务办公室、州长办公室各任命 2 名调查员为当然公证人。

(2) The secretary of the Department of Health and Hospitals may appoint three investigators in the adult protection agency, Department of Health and Hospitals, as ex officio notaries public.

B. Such an ex officio notary public may exercise the functions of a notary public only to administer oaths, receive sworn statements, and execute affidavits and other documents, which shall be limited solely to matters within the official functions of the adult protection agency as provided in R.S. 14:403.2.

C. All acts performed by each ex officio notary public authorized by this Section shall be performed without charge or other compensation.

D. The director or secretary authorized to make such appointments may suspend or terminate any appointment made pursuant to this Section at any time. Separation from the employ of the adult protection agency shall automatically terminate the powers of such an ex officio notary public.

§407. Ex officio notaries for municipal police departments

A. Notwithstanding any provisions of the law relative to qualifications of notaries public, any chief of police of a municipal police department may designate officers in his office and any mayor in a municipality with a population of less than fifteen thousand may designate employees in his office, and appoint them as ex officio notaries public. Such designation by a mayor shall be for notarial service to the municipal police department and to the office of the mayor.

B. Each officer or employee so appointed as ex officio notary may exercise, within his respective jurisdictional limits, the functions of a notary public only to administer oaths and execute affidavits, acknowledgments, traffic tickets, and other documents, all limited to matters within the official functions of the office of the mayor or the municipal police department for the enforcement of the provisions of any statute which provides for criminal penalties and of the municipal ordinances which the police department is charged with enforcing, and any affidavit required for the enforcement of R.S. 32:661 through 669.

C. All acts performed by each ex officio notary public of a police department or office of the mayor authorized by this Section shall be performed without charge or other compensation and without the necessity of giving bond.

D. The chief of police of the police department or mayor may suspend or terminate an appointment made in

（2）卫生署和医院的秘书可以从成人保护机构任命3名调查人员担任当然公证人。

B. 据此任命的当然公证人只能行使执行宣誓、接受宣誓声明述和执行誓章和其他文件的公证职能，且仅限于根据 RS 14：403.2 规定的成人保护机构的正式职能范围内的事项。

C. 本条授权当然公证人行使的所有行为，应当是免费的且不得收取其他方式的补偿。

D. 授权任命的董事或秘书可随时暂停或终止根据本条提出的任何任命，并且当然公证人在成人保护机构的聘用结束时，其当然公证人职权自动终止。

§407. 市政警察局的当然公证人

A. 尽管存在有关公证人资格的法律规定，市警察局局长有权在其办公室内提名官员，任何人口少于15万的市长可以在办公室内提名员工，并任命他们为当然公证人。由市长指定的公证人应当为市警察局和市长办公室提供公证服务。

B. 任何据此被任命为当然公证人的官员或雇员，可以在其各自的管辖范围内行使公证人的职能，职能仅为执行宣誓并执行誓章和确认书、交通票据和其他文件，且限于市长办公室或市警察局执行任何关于刑事犯罪的规定以及警察局负责执行的市政条例的规定的官方职能，以及为执行 R.S. 32:661 至 669 条款所要求的誓章。

C. 本条授权的警察局或市长办公室的每名当然公证人行使的所有行为，应当是免费的且不得收取其他方式的补偿，且不需要提交保证金。

D. 警察局长或市长可随时暂停或终止根据本条提出的任何任命，并且当然公证人在警察局或市长办

his office pursuant to this Section at any time and separation from the employ of the police department or office of the mayor shall automatically terminate the powers of the ex officio notary public.

§408. Repealed by Acts 2012, No. 866, §3

§409. Ex officio notaries for university police departments

A. Notwithstanding any provisions of the law relative to qualifications for and limitations on the number of notaries public, the chief of police of a university police department, which employs peace officers who are certified pursuant to the Peace Officer Standards and Training Law and are duly authorized with the powers of arrest, may designate these officers in his office as ex officio notaries public.

B. Each officer appointed an ex officio notary public may exercise, within the jurisdictional limits of the university police department, the functions of a notary public only to administer oaths and execute affidavits, acknowledgments, traffic tickets, and other documents, all limited to matters within the official functions of the university police department.

C. Such ex officio notary public appointed pursuant to this Section, except for any state employee who serves as an ex officio notary public in the course and scope of his employment, shall fulfill the same bond requirements as provided by law for a notary in the parish in which the university is located. The university shall pay as an expense the costs of the notarial seal, the notarial bond, and any fees required for filing the bond.

D. All acts performed by such an ex officio notary public authorized by this Section shall be performed without charge or other compensation.

E. The chief of police of the university police department may suspend or terminate an appointment made pursuant to this Section at any time, and separation from the employ of the police department shall automatically terminate the powers of such an ex officio notary public.

§410. Ex officio notaries public for the Louisiana Agricultural Finance Authority or the Department of Agriculture and Forestry

A. Notwithstanding any provisions of the law relative to qualifications for and limitations on the number of notaries public, the commissioner of agriculture and forestry may appoint employees of the Louisiana Agricultural Finance Authority or the Department of Agriculture and

公室的聘用结束时，其当然公证人职权自动终止。

§408. 由2012年第866号法案§3废止

§409. 大学警察所的当然公证人

A. 尽管有关于公证人资格和人数量限制的法律规定，大学警察所的所长可以任命其雇佣的符合治安官标准且通过培训认证并且正式被授予逮捕权的治安官作为当然公证人。

B. 任何据此被任命为当然公证人的官员，可以在其管辖范围内行使公证人的职能，职能仅为执行誓言、誓章、确认书、交通票据和其他文件，且全部限于大学警察所的官方职能。

C. 根据本条任命的当然公证人，除在其工作和职业范围内担任当然公证人的州工作人员外，应按照法律规定与大学所在地的行政区的公证人交纳同样的保证金。大学应负担公证印章、公证保证金和其他要求的费用。

D. 本条授权的当然公证人行使的所有行为，应当是免费的且不得收取其他方式的补偿。

E. 大学警察所所长可随时暂停或终止根据本条提出的任何任命，并且当然公证人在大学警察所的聘用结束时，其当然公证人职权自动终止。

§410. 路易斯安那州农业金融局或农业和林业局的当然公证人

A. 尽管有关于公证人资格和数量限制的法律规定，农林局局长可以指定路易斯安那州农业金融局或农林业部的职员作为农业贷款计划的当然公证人。

Forestry as ex officio notaries public for the agriculture loan program.

B. Such ex officio notaries public may exercise the functions of a notary public only to administer oaths, receive sworn statements, and execute affidavits, acknowledgments, and other documents, and shall be limited to matters within the official functions for the agriculture loan program.

C. All acts performed by each ex officio notary public authorized by this Section shall be performed without charge or other compensation.

D. The commissioner of agriculture and forestry may suspend or terminate any appointment made pursuant to this Section at any time. Separation from the employ of the Louisiana Agricultural Finance Authority or the Department of Agriculture and Forestry shall automatically terminate the powers of such an ex officio notary public.

§411. Ex officio notaries public for the Office of Coastal Protection and Restoration

A. The executive director of the Office of Coastal Protection and Restoration may designate as ex officio notaries public up to five employees of the office.

B. Employees so designated may administer oaths, take acknowledgments, and attest on affidavits, and the authority granted under this Section is limited to acts and instruments to which the office, the executive director acting for the office, or the Coastal Protection and Restoration Authority, is a party, and other documents concerning any matter in which the office or the Coastal Protection and Restoration Authority has an official interest.

C. All acts performed by such ex officio notary public authorized by this Section shall be performed without charge or other compensation and without the necessity of giving bond.

D. The executive director may suspend or terminate any appointment made pursuant to this Section at any time, and separation from the employ of the office shall automatically terminate the powers of such an ex officio notary public.

E. The cost of each notarial seal shall be paid by the Office of Coastal Protection and Restoration.

§412. Ex officio notaries; nonresident persons licensed to practice law with offices in this state

A. A person licensed to practice law in this state who is not a resident of this state but who maintains an office for the practice of law in this state, shall be a notary public

B. 据此任命的公职人员只能履行执行誓言、接受宣誓声明、执行誓章和承认书等文件的职能，且仅限于农业贷款计划正式职能。

C. 本条授权的当然公证人行使的所有行为，应当是免费的且不得收取其他方式的补偿。

D. 农林专员可随时暂停或终止根据本条提出的任何任命，并且当然公证人在路易斯安那州农业金融局或农业和林业局的聘用结束时，其当然公证人职权自动终止。

§411 海岸保护和恢复办公室的当然公证人

A. 海岸保护和恢复办公室主任可以最多任命5名办公室雇员为当然公证人。

B. 据此成为当然公证人的员工有执行誓言、确认书和证明誓章的职能，以及与办公室有关的内部职能，或与海岸保护和恢复当局的利益有关的或是其为一方当事人的事务。

C. 本条授权的当然公证人行使的所有行为，应当是免费的且不得收取其他方式的补偿，且不需要交纳保证金。

D. 执行董事有权随时暂停或终止根据本条提出的任何任命，并且当然公证人在离职时，其当然公证人职权自动终止。

E. 公证印章的费用应由海岸保护和恢复办公室支付。

§412. 当然公证人；州非居民获准执法的办公室

A. 虽不具有本州居民身份，但在本州执法办公室担任法律执业职务的人员，应当有权被任命为当然公证人，并有权在任何其法律执业所在的办公室的行

ex officio and is authorized and empowered to exercise all the powers and functions of a regularly commissioned notary public in this state in any parish or parishes in which he maintains an office open to the public for the practice of law, upon filing a certificate of good standing from the Louisiana Supreme Court with the secretary of state.

B. No person qualified under this Section shall be required to otherwise qualify for, or hold, a regular commission as notary public to exercise such powers; however, the notary public ex officio shall furnish his current office address and residence address to the secretary of state as the registrar of notaries for the state.

C. Notwithstanding any provision of law to the contrary, any person exercising notarial functions pursuant to this Section is authorized to use the designation "notary public ex officio" with respect to the exercise of his powers, and shall be required to post bond or maintain insurance as required by the provisions of R.S. 35:71

D. A notary public ex officio exercising notarial functions as authorized by the provisions of this Section may charge fees for notary services commensurate with the reasonable and customary fees for notarial services in the parish or parishes where the notary public ex officio maintains his office.

E. Any exercise of notarial powers pursuant to the provisions of this Section shall be deemed the practice of law for purposes of regulation by the Louisiana Supreme Court.

F. A person authorized as a notary public ex officio pursuant to the provisions of this Section shall exercise his powers and functions as a notary public ex officio only within the parish or parishes in which he maintains an office open to the public for the practice of law in this state.

§413. Ex officio notaries public for municipal or parish fire departments and fire protection districts

A. Notwithstanding any provisions of the law relative to qualifications of notaries public, any fire chief of a municipal or parish fire department or fire protection district may designate no more than three employees in his office and appoint them as ex officio notaries public.

B. Each employee so appointed as ex officio notary public may exercise, within his respective jurisdictional limits, the functions of a notary public only to administer oaths and execute affidavits and acknowledgments, all limited to matters within the official functions of the office of the municipal or parish fire department or fire protection district.

政区内行使所有在该州长期任职的公证人的职能，并将由路易斯安那州最高法院提供的信誉证明提交给州务卿。

B. 符合本条规定的人员不得被要求满足其他资格或持有正式公证人任命以行使该等权力；但当然公证人当然地应当向州务卿提交现任办公地址和居住地址。

C. 尽管有相反的法律规定，根据本条行使公证职能的人员有权在行使其职权时使用"当然公证人"称谓，并按照 R.S.35:71 的规定保有保证金或者是保险。

D. 当当然公证人按本条规定行使公证职能时，可以按公证人办公室的所在地的公证人收费标准对公证服务收费。

E. 根据本条规定行使公证职权，应当被路易斯安那州最高法院视为出于法律实践的目的。

F. 据此被任命为当然公证人的人，仅有权在其维持公开职位的行政区内行使公证人职责。

§413. 市或区消防部门和防火部门的当然公证人

A. 尽管存在有关公证人资格的法律规定，市或区消防部门和防火部门的长官可以在其办公室内指定不超过 3 名的雇员，任命为当然公证人。

B. 任何据此任命为当然公证人的员工，可以在各自的管辖范围内行使公证人的职能，仅限于执行宣誓声明、执行誓章和承认书，且全部限于市、区的消防部门和防火部门的官方职能。

C. All acts performed by each ex officio notary public of a municipal or parish fire department or fire protection district authorized by this Section shall be performed without charge or other compensation and without the necessity of giving bond.

D. The fire chief of the municipal or parish fire department or fire protection district may suspend or terminate an appointment made in his office pursuant to this Section at any time, and separation from the employ of the municipal or parish fire department or fire protection district shall automatically terminate the powers of the ex officio notary public.

CHAPTER 7. COMMISSIONERS [REPEALED]

§451. §§451 to 460 Repealed by Acts 1977, No. 225, §1

CHAPTER 8. ACKNOWLEDGMENTS

PART I. ACKNOWLEDGMENTS WITHIN STATE

§511. Forms of acknowledgment

Either the forms of acknowledgment now in use in this State, or the following, may be used in the case of conveyances or other written instruments, whenever such acknowledgment is required or authorized by law for any purpose:

(Begin in all cases by a caption specifying the state and place where the acknowledgment is taken).

1. In the case of natural persons acting in their own right:

On this _____ day of _____, 20____, _____ before me personally appeared A B (or A B and C D), to me known to be the person (or persons) described in and who executed the foregoing instrument, and acknowledged that he (or they) executed it as his (or their) free act and deed.

2. In the case of natural persons acting by attorney:

On this _____ day of _____, 20__, before me personally appeared A B, to me known to be the person who executed the foregoing instrument in behalf of C D, and acknowledged that he executed it as the free act and deed of said C D.

3. In the case of corporations or joint stock associations:

On this _____ day of _____, 20__, before me

C. 本条授权的当然公证人行使的所有行为，应当是免费的且不得收取其他方式的补偿，且不需要提交保证金。

D. 市、区消防部门或防火部门的长官可随时暂停或终止根据本条提出的任何任命，并且当然公证人在市、区消防部门或防火部门的聘用结束时，其当然公证人职权自动终止。

第七章　任命 [已废止]

§451. §451 至 §460 由 1977 年法案，第 225 号 §1 废止

第八章　确认

第一部分　州内确认

§511. 确认的格式

任何现在在本州使用的确认格式，或以下内容，可在转让证书或其他书面文书使用，无论何时为任何目的被要求或授权：

（在所有情况下，都以说明确认所在的州和地点开始）

1. 自然人自己行事的情况：

在 20_____ 年 _____ 月 _____ 日，AB（或 AB 和 CD），亲自出现在本人面前，我知道他（他们）是执行上述文书的人，并承认他（或他们）执行它作为他（或他们）的自由的行为。

2. 以律师代理自然人的情况：

在 20_____ 年 _____ 月 _____ 日，AB 亲自在本人面前出现，我知道其是代表 CD 执行上述文书的人，并承认他以 CD 的自由行为和契据的方式执行文书。

3. 在公司或股份公司的情况下：

在 20_____ 年 _____ 月 _____ 日，AB 亲自在本人面

appeared A B, to me personally known, who, being by me duly sworn (or affirmed) did say that he is the president (or other officer or agent of the corporation or association), of (describing the corporation or association), and that the seal affixed to said instrument is the corporate seal of said corporation (or association) and that the instrument was signed and sealed in behalf of the corporation (or association) by authority of its Board of Directors (or trustees) and that A B acknowledged the instrument to be the free act and deed of the corporation (or association).

(In case the corporation or association has no corporate seal, omit the words "the seal affixed to said instrument is the corporate seal of the corporation (or association), and that" and add, at the end of the affidavit clause, the words "and that the corporation (or association) has no corporate seal").

(In all cases, acknowledgments taken in this state shall be signed in conformity with the provisions of R.S. 35:12 and either Article 1836 of the Louisiana Civil Code or R.S. 13:3720).

§512. Married women, acknowledgment by

The acknowledgment of a married woman when required by law may be taken in the same form as if she were sole and without any examination separate and apart from her husband.

§513. Officers before whom proof or acknowledgment taken in other states

The proof or acknowledgment of any deed or other written instrument required to be proved or acknowledged in order to enable the same to be recorded or read in evidence, when made by any person without this state and within any other state, territory, or district of the United States, may be made before any officer of such state, territory or district, authorized by the laws thereof to take the proof and acknowledgment of deeds, and when so taken and certified under his official seal, shall be entitled to be recorded in this state, and may be read in evidence in the same manner and with like effect as proofs and acknowledgments taken before any of the officers now authorized by law to take such proofs and acknowledgments, and whose authority so to do is not intended to be hereby affected.

PART II. FOREIGN ACKNOWLEDGMENTS

§551. Officers before whom made

All instruments requiring acknowledgment, if ac-

前出现，被本人正式宣誓（或确认）其是公司或协会的总裁（或其他官员或代理人）（描述公司或协会），并且公证文书上的印章是该公司（或协会）的法人印章，该文书是以其董事会授权董事（或受托人）代表公司（或协会）签署并盖章的。AB 认为该文书是公司（或协会）的自由行为和契据。

[如法人团体没有法人印章，则不得在附上"公证文书上的印章是该公司（或协会）的法人印章"的语句，并应在誓章条文末尾加上"并且公司（或协会）没有印章"]

[在所有情况下，在本州作出的确认应按照第 R.S.35:12 条和《路易斯安那州民法典》第 1836 条或第 R.S.13：3720 条的规定作出]

§512. 已婚妇女，确认

依据法律要求对已婚妇女进行确认，可以采取与确认女性单身相同的形式，且不需要其与丈夫分离的检查。

§513. 在其他州进行文书证明或确认的官员

为了使证明或确认能够成为被记录或阅读的证据，在本州和美国的任何其他州、领土或地区外做出的确认，可以在任何上述州、领土或地区的官员面前作出。经法律授权进行证明和确认，并由加盖公证公章证实的确认书，有权在本州记录，并可以以相同的方式作为证据。根据上述规定作出的确认与在法律授权的任何现任官员面前提出证明和确认的效果一致，并且该官员的权限不应受到特别的影响。

第二部分 外国确认书

§551. 作出确认的官员

所有要求确认的文书，如果没有美国的确认，应

knowledged without the United States, shall be acknowledged before an ambassador, minister, envoy or charge d'affaires of the United States, in the country to which he is accredited, or before one of the following officers commissioned or accredited to act at the place where the acknowledgment is taken, and having an official seal, viz.:--any officer of the United States; a notary public; or a commissioner or other agent of this state having power to take acknowledgments.

§552. Form of certificate of acknowledgment

Every certificate of acknowledgment, made without the United States, shall contain the name or names of the person or persons making the acknowledgment, the date when and the place where made, a statement of the fact that the person or persons making the acknowledgment knew the contents of the instrument, and acknowledged it to be his, her or their act; the certificate shall also contain the name of the person before whom made, his official title, and be sealed with his official seal and may be substantially in the following form:

_____ (name of country) .

_____ (name of city, province or other political subdivision)

Before the undersigned _____ (naming the officer and designating his official title) duly commissioned (or appointed) and qualified, this day personally appeared at the place above named _____ (naming the person or pesons acknowledging) who declared that he (she or they) knew the contents of the foregoing instrument, and acknowledged it to be his (her or their) act.

Witness my hand and official seal this _____ day of _____ 19.

_____ (name of officer) .

(seal)

_____ (official title)

When the seal affixed shall contain the names or the official style of the officer, any error in stating, or failure to state otherwise the name or the official style of the officer, shall not render the certificate defective.

§553. Acknowledgments in form used in state

A certificate of acknowledgment of a deed or other instrument acknowledged without the United States before any officer mentioned in R.S. 35:551 shall also be valid if in the same form as now is or hereafter may be required by law, for an acknowledgment within this state.

在美国大使、部长、特使或临时代办人认可的国家之前，或在下列其中一名拥有官方印章且被任命或授权的官员之前完成：美国的任何官员、公证人或该国有权力确认的专员或其他代理人。

§552. 确认证明书的形式

每个未经美国制作的确认证明书，应载明作出确认的人的姓名或名称，作出的日期和地点，作出确认的人知道的真实声明文书的内容，并确认是他或她的行为；该证明书亦须载有所作出的人的姓名及其正式名称，并以公章盖章，大致按照下列格式：

_____（州名称）

_____（市，省或其他行政区划的名称）

签字人_____在今天一天亲自出现在上述地点_____经合格委托（或任命）的公证人_____（公证人姓名和职称）确认，_____（他或她们）知道上述文书的内容，并确认（他或她）是行为的确认人。

本人亲笔签字和公章_____

19_____年_____月_____日

_____（公证人姓名）

（盖章）

_____（公证人职称）

盖上的印章包含公证人的姓名或官方格式时，除了公证人的姓名或官方格式，其他错误或声明上瑕疵的，均不影响证书的效力。

§553. 在本州使用的确认书的格式

如果遵照现在或以后法律要求的相同格式并在本州内确认，则在美国之外 R.S. 35：551 规定的公证人面前作出的承认契约或其他文书的证明书也应为有效。

§554. Interpretation and construction

This Part shall be so interpreted and construed as to effectuate its general purpose to make uniform the law of those states which enact it.

§555. Force and effect

Every acknowledgment or proof of any legal instrument and any oath or affirmation, taken or made before a commissioner, ambassador, minister, charge d'affaires, secretary of legation, consul general, consul, or vice consul, and every attestation or authentication made by them, when duly certified as above provided, shall have the force and effect of an authentic act executed in this state.

CHAPTER 9. UNAUTHORIZED EXERCISE OF NOTARIAL POWERS

§601. Unlawful exercise of notarial powers; penalties

A. A person, who has not first been duly authorized to exercise notarial powers in this state or whose authority to exercise notarial powers in this state has been judicially revoked, shall not perform any of the following actions:

(1) Exercise or purport to exercise any notarial function.

(2) Hold himself out to the public as being entitled to exercise notarial functions.

(3) Render or furnish notarial services.

(4) Take any acknowledgment, administer any oath, or execute any instrument purportedly as a notary public or as a person purportedly authorized to exercise notarial power and authority.

(5) Assume to be a notary public or to be authorized to exercise notarial functions.

(6) Assume, use, or advertise the title of notary public or ex officio notary or equivalent terms in any language, or any similar title in such a manner as to convey the impression that he is authorized to exercise notarial powers.

B. (1) Any person who violates any provision of this Section shall be fined not more than one thousand dollars or imprisoned for not more than two years, or both.

(2) In addition to the penalties provided by Paragraph (1) of this Subsection, the person shall be required to make full restitution for all costs required to authenticate, confirm, or ratify any instruments that fail to qualify as notarial acts due to the lack of proper authority of the notary or purported notary, including all costs of recordation and all damages each affected party may suffer.

§554. 解释与建设

本部分法条的解释应为实现其一般目的，并促进各州法律的统一。

§555. 效力

任何法律文书的确认或证明，以及在专员、大使、部长、临时代办、领事秘书、领事馆领事或副领事面前作出的任何宣誓或确认，具有在本州执行的真实公证行为的效力。

第九章　未经授权行使公证权力

§601. 非法行使公证权力；处罚

A. 未经本州正式授权在本州从事公证行为或者在本州行使公证权力的人被司法撤销职务的人，不得履行以下行为：

（1）行使或宣称行使公证职能。

（2）自行出面向公众行使公证职能。

（3）提供公证服务。

（4）作出任何确认、管理宣誓，或执行任何公证人或被视为获授权行使公证权力的人有权作出的行为。

（5）假装是公证人或被授权行使公证职能。

（6）以任何语言或任何类似标题假设、使用或宣传公证人或当然公证人或同等用语的标题，以表达他被授权行使公证权力的印象。

B.（1）违反本条规定的，处2年以下有期徒刑或1000美元以下的罚金，或两者并处。

（2）除了本款第（1）项规定的处罚外，该人必须全额支付认证、确认或批准任何不符合公证行为资格的文书的全部费用，以及全额赔偿因缺乏公证人资质或未经授权而被视为公证人而导致的信赖利益的损失，包括所有的记录费用和受影响的一方可能遭受的所有损失。

§602. Unlawful exercise of prior authorized or limited notarial powers; penalties

A. No person who has been duly appointed to the office of notary public or who has been otherwise authorized to exercise notarial functions in this state shall exercise any notarial function in this state during any period when:

(1) His commission or authority to exercise notarial functions is either:

(a) Statutorily or judicially suspended.

(b) Statutorily or administratively revoked.

(2) He is no longer validly commissioned in this state.

(3) He has elected to place his commission in retirement status under the provisions of R.S. 35:202(G).

(4) He is no longer validly possessed of the office or position from which his authority to exercise notarial functions was derived.

(5) He has been convicted of a felony and has not been pardoned.

(6) He is not authorized by law to exercise that particular notarial function.

B. (1) Any person who knowingly violates any provision of this Section shall be fined not more than one thousand dollars and shall be required to make full restitution for all costs required to authenticate, confirm, or ratify any instruments that fail to qualify as notarial acts due to the lack of proper authority of the notary or purported notary, including all costs of recordation and all damages each affected party may suffer.

(2) In addition to the penalties provided in Paragraph (1) of this Subsection, the person shall also be subject to a suspension or revocation of his commission and shall be subject to being permanently enjoined from exercising any notarial function in any capacity.

§603. Secretary of state; duties upon receipt of sworn complaint

A. The secretary of state, upon receipt of a sworn complaint alleging a violation of the provisions of R.S. 35:601 or 602, shall proceed as follows:

(1) If the records of the secretary of state indicate that the person who is the subject of the complaint has a valid active status, the secretary shall notify that person and the complainant of the findings.

(2) If the records of the secretary of state indicate that the person who is the subject of the complaint does not have a valid active status, the secretary of state shall send

§602. 非法行使先前授权的或有限的公证权力；处罚

A. 任何经正式委任为公证人或经本公司授权行使公证职务的人，出现下列情形时，不得在本州行使公证职能：

（1）其行使公证职能的任命或授权是以下之一情形：

（a）法定或司法上暂停执行。

（b）法定或行政决定撤销。

（2）其在这个州不再被有效委任。

（3）根据 R.S. 35：202（G）的规定将其任职处于休眠状态。

（4）其不再有效地拥有能够执行公证职能的职位。

（5）被判有重罪，并没有被赦免。

（6）未经法律授权行使该公证职能。

B.（1）任何人明知而故意违反本条规定的，将被处以不超过 1000 美元的罚款，并要求对由于缺乏公证人或被视为公证人的适当授权，认证、确认或批准任何不符合条件的文书所需的一切费用全额归还，以及全额赔偿因缺乏公证人资质或未经授权而被视为公证人而导致的信赖利益的损失，包括所有的记录费用和受影响的一方可能遭受的所有损失。

（2）除本款第（1）项规定的罚款外，该人还应暂停或撤销其佣金，并应永久不得以任何身份行使公证职能。

§603. 州务卿；收到宣誓的投诉后的职责

A. 州务卿在收到诉称违反 R.S. 35：601 或 R.S. 35：602 条款的投诉时，应按照以下程序处理：

（1）如果州务卿的记录表明作为投诉对象的人具有有效的活跃状态，州务卿应将调查结果通知该人和申诉人。

（2）州务卿的记录表明，申诉对象的人员不处于有效的活跃状态，州务卿应通过认证邮件向该人发送通知，告知其权力受到妨碍，并允许该人在收到通知

notice by certified mail, return receipt requested, to that person of the impediment to his authority and allow that person to remedy, if possible, the impediment within ten days of receipt of the notice.

(3) If the person who is the subject of the complaint fails to remedy the impediment to his authority within the time provided by Paragraph (2) of this Subsection, the secretary of state shall transmit a copy of the sworn complaint to the appropriate law enforcement or prosecutorial agency for further investigation or prosecution.

B. The secretary of state shall provide a form to be used to file a complaint alleging a violation of the provisions of R.S. 35:601 or 602. All complaints filed with the secretary of state shall be on the complaint form prepared by the secretary of state or on a form which contains the same information as required by the complaint form prepared by the secretary of state.

C. Nothing in this Section shall operate to limit any other legal methods of notice, service of process, or enforcement of any provision of R.S. 35:601 or 602.

§604. Applicability to licensed attorneys

Notwithstanding any provision of law to the contrary, the authority of the Louisiana Supreme Court to regulate the practice of law shall supersede the provision of this Chapter with respect to the enforcement of its provisions against an attorney licensed to practice law in this state.

TITLE 36.
ORGANIZATION OF THE EXECUTIVE BRANCH

§742. Powers and duties of secretary of state

In addition to the functions, powers, and duties otherwise vested in the secretary of state by law, he shall:

(1) Represent the public interest in the administration of this Chapter and shall be responsible to the legislature and the public therefor.

(2) Employ, appoint, remove, assign, and promote such personnel as is necessary for the efficient administration of the department.

(3) In accordance with the Administrative Procedure Act, make, alter, amend, and promulgate rules and regulations necessary for the administration and the functions of the department.

(4) Organize, plan, supervise, direct, administer, execute and be responsible for the functions and programs vested in the department.

后10日内补救（如有可能）障碍，该邮件应要求回执。

（3）如果被投诉人在本款第（2）项规定的期限内没有补救其职权的障碍，则州务卿应将宣誓申诉的副本转交给适当的法律执法或检察机关进一步调查或起诉。

B. 州务卿应提供一种表示违反R.S.35：601或R.S.35：602条的格式投诉书。向州务卿提出的所有投诉，应填写由州务卿编制的投诉表格或者包含与州务卿编制的投诉表所要求的相同资料的表格。

C. 本条中的任何内容均不得限制其他合法途径的通知，传票的送达，以及对R.S.35：601或R.S.35：602的执行。

§604. 对执业律师的适用性

尽管有相反的法律规定，路易斯安那最高法院管理习惯法的权力应取代本条针对执业律师的规定。

第三十六编
执行委员会的组织

§742. 州务卿的职权

除依法赋予州务卿的职能、权力和职责外，州务卿还有权：

（1）代表本章规定的公共利益，对立法机关和公众负责。

（2）聘请、委任、撤销、调拨、提拔该部门有效管理所需的人员。

（3）根据《行政诉讼法》，制定、修改和颁布管理和部门职能所需的规章制度。

（4）组织、规划、督导、指导、管理、执行、负责该部门职能和方案。

(5) Make reports and recommendations on his own initiative or upon the request of the legislature, or any committee or member thereof.

(6) Provide for the ongoing reorganization and consolidation of the department and submit a report thereon to the legislature, which report shall accompany the budget request which he submits under provisions of R.S. 39:33. Such report shall include a statement of the goals of the department and of the programs thereof and shall summarize the accomplishments of the department in meeting such goals and implementing such programs. The report shall also contain a specific statement of the reorganization and consolidation plan for the department for the next year and shall include a report on the implementation of such reorganization and consolidation plan for the previous year. The report concerning reorganization shall specifically detail the extent to which the department has achieved goals stated the previous year with respect to merger and consolidation of functions, consolidation of administrative and programmatic divisions of the department, elimination of job positions, and efficiency and economy in delivery of services. The report shall contain any recommendations with respect to reorganization which may require legislative action under the provisions of this Title. A copy of the report and recommended legislation shall also be submitted by the secretary of state to the presiding officer of each house of the legislature. The presiding officer shall refer the report to the appropriate committee having jurisdiction of the subject matter as provided in the rules of the respective house.

(7) Be responsible for accounting and budget control, procurement and contract management, management and program analysis, data processing, personnel management, and grants management for the department.

(8) Investigate allegations of election irregularities.

(9) Do such other things, not inconsistent with law, as are necessary to perform properly the functions vested in him.

（5）主动提出报告和建议，或应立法机关或任何委员会或其成员的要求提出报告和建议。

（6）筹划当局正在进行的重组和合并，并向立法机关提交报告，该报告应附有根据 R.S. 39:33 的规定提交的预算请求。该报告应包括部门目标和方案说明，并总结部门实现这些目标和实施这些方案的成就。报告还应载明下一年度部门重组和合并计划的具体说明，并附有上一年度重组和合并计划实施情况的报告。关于重组的报告应具体说明该部门在合并和重组职能方面达成目标的程度，行政部门和方案部门的合并，职位削减，提升效率和经济性的服务等情况。报告应载有关于重组的建议，可能需要根据本标题规定采取立法行动。报告和建议立法的副本也由州务卿提交给立法机关各院长的主持人。主审人员应将报告提交给具有相应管辖权的适当委员会。

（7）负责会计和预算控制、采购和合同管理、管理和程序分析、数据处理、人事管理和部门的赠款管理。

（8）调查选举违规行为的指控。

（9）不违反法律规定的其他履行职务的必要事宜。

路易斯安那州民法典

LOUISIANA CIVIL CODE
BOOK III OF THE DIFFERENT MODES
OF ACQUIRING THE OWNERSHIP OF THINGS

路易斯安那州民法典
新版第三册
获得所有权

TITLE VII —
PARENT AND CHILD

CHAPTER 5. PROOF OF OBLIGATIONS

Art. 1833. Authentic act

A. An authentic act is a writing executed before a notary public or other officer authorized to perform that function, in the presence of two witnesses, and signed by each party who executed it, by each witness, and by each notary public before whom it was executed. The typed or hand-printed name of each person shall be placed in a legible form immediately beneath the signature of each person signing the act.

B. To be an authentic act, the writing need not be executed at one time or place, or before the same notary public or in the presence of the same witnesses, provided that each party who executes it does so before a notary public or other officer authorized to perform that function, and in the presence of two witnesses and each party, each witness, and each notary public signs it. The failure to include the typed or hand-printed name of each person signing the act shall not affect the validity or authenticity of the act.

C. If a party is unable or does not know how to sign his name, the notary public must cause him to affix his mark to the writing.

Art. 1834. Act that fails to be authentic

An act that fails to be authentic because of the lack of competence or capacity of the notary public, or because of a defect of form, may still be valid as an act under private signature.

Art. 1835. Authentic act constitutes full proof between parties and heirs

An authentic act constitutes full proof of the agreement it contains, as against the parties, their heirs, and

第七编
父母和子女

第五章 义务证明

第 1833 条 认证行为

A. 认证行为是指在公证人或其他获得执行公证职能的官员面前，在两名证人在场的情况下执行，并由执行行为的每一方当事人、每名证人以及执行公证人书面签字。每个人应立即在签署执行书的每个人姓名下方清晰地手签或打印自己的姓名。

B. 进行认证行为时，执行行为不必在同一时间或地点，或同一公证人或同一证人在场的情况下执行，只要执行行为的每一方在公证人或其他授权的公职人员面前进行、在两名证人和每一方当事人出席的情况下进行，且每位证人和每位公证人均在文书上签字。未能在文件上手签或打印姓名不影响该行为的有效性或真实性。

C. 如果当事人不能或不知道如何签署姓名，公证人必须要求其在文书上加上标记。

第 1834 条 未能通过认证的文书

由于公证人缺乏行为能力，或由于形式上的缺陷，而未能通过认证的文书仍可根据私人签字而有效。

第 1835 条 认证文书构成各方和继承人之间的充分证据

认证文书构成对其所包含的协议，以及其中的当事人和通过普遍或特定方式获得继承权的继承人的充

successors by universal or particular title.

Art. 1836. Act under private signature duly acknowledged

An act under private signature is regarded prima facie as the true and genuine act of a party executing it when his signature has been acknowledged, and the act shall be admitted in evidence without further proof.

An act under private signature may be acknowledged by a party to that act by recognizing the signature as his own before a court, or before a notary public, or other officer authorized to perform that function, in the presence of two witnesses. An act under private signature may be acknowledged also in any other manner authorized by law.

Nevertheless, an act under private signature, though acknowledged, cannot substitute for an authentic act when the law prescribes such an act.

Art. 1837. Act under private signature

An act under private signature need not be written by the parties, but must be signed by them.

Art. 1838. Party must acknowledge or deny signature

A party against whom an act under private signature is asserted must acknowledge his signature or deny that it is his.

In case of denial, any means of proof may be used to establish that the signature belongs to that party.

Art. 1839. Transfer of immovable property

A transfer of immovable property must be made by authentic act or by act under private signature. Nevertheless, an oral transfer is valid between the parties when the property has been actually delivered and the transferor recognizes the transfer when interrogated on oath.

An instrument involving immovable property shall have effect against third persons only from the time it is filed for registry in the parish where the property is located.

Art. 1840. Copy of authentic act

When certified by the notary public or other officer before whom the act was passed, a copy of an authentic act constitutes proof of the contents of the original, unless the copy is proved to be incorrect.

Art. 1841. Copy of recorded writing

When an authentic act or an acknowledged act under private signature has been filed for registry with a public officer, a copy of the act thus filed, when certified by that officer, constitutes proof of the contents of the original.

分证据。

第1836条 私人签字的行为的法律适用

当私人签名被认可后，其下的行为被当然认为是认证签字一方当事人的真实行为，并且该行为应被接纳为证据，无须进一步证明。

私人签署姓名的行为可以通过在两名证人的见证下，在法庭上，或在公证人或被授权履行公证职能的其他人员面前进行认证。私人签字的行为也可以以法律授权的任何其他方式进行认证。

然而，私人签字的行为即使经过确认，在法律有规定时，也不能代替认证文书。

第1837条 私人签名的行为

私人签名的行为不必由双方亲自书写，但必须由其签署。

第1838条 缔约方必须承认或拒绝签字

以私人签名方式进行确认的当事人必须承认或否认文书上的签名是其本人的。

在拒绝的情况下，可以使用任何证明手段来确定签名属于该方。

第1839条 不动产转让

不动产转让必须以认证文书或私人签字的方式进行。然而，当财产实际交付时，双方之间的口头转让是有效的，转让人在宣誓讯问时应承认转让。

涉及不动产的文书，只有在财产所在的行政区进行登记时才对第三人有效。

第1840条 认证文书的副本

在公证人或其他官员面前作出的行为经过认证，认证文书的副本即构成对原件内容的证明，除非该副本被证明不正确。

第1841条 记录文书的副本

当私人签名的认证文书或已确认的文书已经提交给公职人员登记时，在由该人员证明的情况下提交的文书副本构成对原件内容的证明。

路易斯安那州行政法典

LOUISIANA ADMINISTRATIVE CODE

路易斯安那州行政法典

TITLE 46
PROFESSIONAL AND OCCUPATIONAL STANDARDS

第46编
专业和职业标准

PART XLVI. NOTARIES PUBLIC

第 XLVI 部分 公证人

CHAPTER 1. NOTARIES PUBLIC

第一章 公证人

46: XLVI.101. Qualifications

A. Any resident citizen or alien of the state, 18 years of age or older, may be appointed a notary public in and for the parish in which he resides provided that he/she meets the requirements established by R.S. 35:191(C).

B. The applicant is required to complete an application to qualify form requiring the applicant to:

1. be a citizen or resident alien of the state;

2. be 18 years of age or older;

3. be registered to vote in the parish in which he seeks commission;

4. attest to his good moral character, integrity and sober habits;

5. must not be under an order of interdiction or is incapable of serving because of mental infirmity; and

6. must not have been convicted of a felony or has been pardoned if convicted.

C. The applicant must be able to read, write, speak, and be sufficiently knowledgeable of the English language. In addition, he must have one of the following:

1. received a high school diploma;

2. received a diploma for completion of a home study program approved by the State Board of Elementary and Secondary Education; or

3. been issued a high school equivalency diploma after successfully completing the test of General Education Development (GED).

D. The qualifying application fee is shown in § 129.

46:XLVI.103. Applications

A. Notary applicant must be qualified by the notary

46：XLVI.101 资格

A. 符合 R.S.35：191（C）规定的要求的 18 周岁以上的任何居民公民或外地人可被任命为其居住的行政区的公证人。

B. 申请人必须填写资格表，要求申请人：

1. 为本州的公民或外籍居民；

2. 年满 18 周岁；

3. 在其申请的行政区是已登记的选民；

4. 证明其良好的道德品格、诚信和习惯；

5. 不得因为精神虚弱而被禁止或无能力服务；以及

6. 不得因重罪被定罪或被定罪但被赦免。

C. 申请人必须能够阅读、写作、表达并熟练掌握英语。此外，还必须满足以下条件之一：

1. 获得高中文凭；

2. 获得州中小学教育局批准的家庭学习课程文凭；或者

3. 成功完成通识教育发展考试后，获得高中毕业文凭证书。

D. 申请资格表的费用见第 129 条的规定。

46：XLVI.103 申请人

A. 公证人必须由州务卿办公室的公证部门授权，

division in the office of the secretary of state and must take and pass the Louisiana state notary examination (referred to as "notary exam"), unless the applicant is licensed to practice law in Louisiana.

B. The applicant must complete an application to qualify form and send it to the notary division in the secretary of state's office. Once the application to qualify form has been approved by the secretary of state's office, the applicant can register to take the notary exam by:

1. registering online at the secretary of state's website using a credit card; or 2. completing the examination registration form and:

a. attaching a check or money order made payable to the secretary of state and mailing the examination registration form to the notary division; or

b. completing a credit card cover sheet and faxing or emailing the sheet with the examination registration form to the notary division.

C. To file online, the applicant must contact the notary division to obtain his access code by emailing notaries@sos.la.gov or by calling (225) 922-0507.

D. The registration fee to take the notary exam is shown in § 129.

E. Deadlines for submitting application to qualify and examination registration form are listed on the secretary of state's website notary division.

F. The notary exam is given twice a year on the first Saturday in June and December. If the date falls on a state holiday, the notary exam will be given on the next nonholiday Saturday. The Office of Assessment and Evaluation within Louisiana State University conducts the notary exams regionally on behalf of the secretary of state's office.

G. Any notary public commissioned by passing a parish notary exam can take the notary exam to obtain statewide jurisdiction. Failure to pass the notary exam shall have no effect on the status of the commission of the notary.

46: XLVI.105. Study Guide

A. The official study guide for the notary exam is "The Fundamentals of Louisiana Notarial Law and Practice."

B. The cost to purchase the study guide is shown in § 129 and is non-refundable.

C. The study guide can be purchased by:

1. ordering online at the secretary of state's website using a credit card;

2. completing an order form, attaching a check or money order made payable to the secretary of state, and mailing to the notary division;

3. completing an order form and providing a credit card number and faxing or emailing to the notary division; or

4. visiting the notary division's customer service counter at the secretary of state's office at 8585 Archives Drive, Baton Rouge, LA during office hours of 8 a.m. to 4:30 p.m.

D. The study guide is sent via U.S. mail on the day of receipt of the order if received before 12:30 p.m. Orders received after 12:30 p.m. will be mailed the next business day.

46:XLVI.107. Courses

A. Applicants are not required by law to take a course or instruction class in order for an applicant to take the notary exam.

B. Although the secretary of state does not recommend particular courses or instructors, the department does maintain a list of registered and bonded notary exam preparatory course providers.

C. All course providers, except an educational institution listed in R.S. 35:191.4(D), shall annually post a bond guarantee by a commercial surety company licensed to do business in Louisiana with the secretary of state in the amount of $25,000.

D. Beginning February 8, 2015, all persons providing notary examination preparatory education and instruction must be a notary public with statewide notarial authority.

E. Each provider must submit an annual registration statement to the secretary of state on or before January 1 of each year on a form provided by the secretary of state. In addition, each provider shall submit a semiannual report to the secretary of state on or before June 30 and December 31 listing the name and address of each person who received a course or courses of instruction or study from the provider for the training and instruction for the notary exam required by the secretary of state during the time covered by the report.

F. Pursuant to R.S. 35:191.4(F), if a provider does not submit an annual report or the annual report is not submitted timely, penalties may be imposed up to $1,000 for each day the provider is not in compliance with this section.

2. 填写订单，附上支票或汇款单，并寄往公证处；

3. 完成订单并提供信用卡号码，并向公证部门发送传真或电子邮件；或者

4. 在上午 8 时到下午 4:30 的办公时间，在洛杉矶巴吞鲁日 8585 档案馆州务院办公室访问公证处的客服柜台。

D. 在 12:30 之前收到的学习指南订购申请，将在收到指令之日前通过美国邮件寄送，12:30 之后收到订单将在下一个工作日邮寄。

46：XLVI.107 课程

A. 法律不要求参加公证考试的申请人参加课程或指导班。

B. 虽然州务卿不推荐特定的课程或教员，但该部门确实保留了注册和保税公证考试预备课程提供者的名单。

C. 所有课程提供者，除了需满足 R.S. 35：191.4（D）的规定，还需通过路易斯安那州许可营业的商业担保公司每年向州务卿缴纳 25000 美元的保证金。

D. 自 2015 年 2 月 8 日起，所有提供公证考试预备教育和指导的人员必须是公证机关的公证人。

E. 每位课程提供者必须在每年 1 月 1 日当天或之前向州务卿提交以州务卿规定的格式作出的年度报告声明。另外，每位课程供应者应在 6 月 30 日至 12 月 31 日期间或之前向州务卿提交半年度报告，列出州务卿在报告所涉时间内举行的公证考试中，从提供者处接受培训和指导的课程或学习课程的每个人的姓名和地址。

F. 根据 R.S. 35：191.4（F），如果提供者未提交或未及时提交年度报告，可能会被处以每一天高达 1000 美元的罚款。

46:XLVI.109. Louisiana State Notary Public Examinations

A. The notary exams are given at regional testing centers throughout the state.

B. The examinee can elect to take the notary exam in a computer-testing format or a paper-and-pencil format.

C. The registration fee for the notary exam is shown in § 129.

D. Statewide standards for the notary exam are available on the secretary of state's website under the section notary division examinations. These standards include:

1. application procedures;

2. examination schedule;

3. examination format and content; and

4. procedures for review of any examination which was taken and was failed by the examinee.

E. The Office of Assessment and Evaluation for Louisiana State University is offering a notary exam pre-assessment test to show the likelihood of a candidate's ability to be successful on the notary exam. Please refer to the secretary of state's website notary division for more information regarding this pre-assessment test. See § 129 for the pre-assessment test fee.

46: XLVI.111. Notary Commission

A. Once an applicant has taken and passed the notary exam, the following documents must be filed with the secretary of state's office along with the commission filing fee (see §129), in order to receive his notary commission;

1. two oaths of office forms, properly executed (one copy filed with secretary of state and one copy filed with parish clerk of court)

2. official signature page;

3. either of the following (exempt if an attorney):

a. surety bond or personal surety bond that has been approved by the parish clerk of court in the amount of $10,000; or

b. errors and omissions policy in the amount of $10,000; or

4. if an attorney, a certificate of good standing from the Louisiana Supreme Court (in lieu of bond or errors and omissions policy); and

5. commission filing fee (see § 129) with a check or money order made payable to the secretary of state.

B. A notary is commissioned based upon the commission date indicated on the notary database. He does not have to wait until he receives the commission certificate

46：XLVI.109 路易斯安那州公证考试

A. 公证考试在全州各区域的测试中心进行。

B. 考生可以选择以电脑形式或纸笔形式参加公证考试。

C. 公证考试的报名费见第129条的规定。

D. 全州公证考试标准可以在州务卿网站上的公证部门考试栏目查阅。上述标准包括：

1. 申请程序；

2. 考试时间表；

3. 考试形式和内容；以及

4. 通过或未通过考试者的复核程序。

E. 路易斯安那州立大学测试和评估办公室为公证考试提供评估测试，以确定申请人在公证考试中通过的可能性。有关此预评估测试的更多信息，请参阅州务院网站公证部门。有关预评估测试的费用见第129条的规定。

46：XLVI.111 公证任命

A. 申请人一旦通过了公证考试，必须向州务卿提交以下文件以及任命申请费（见第129条），以便领取公证人任命：

1. 两份妥善执行的职务宣誓（一份副本提交给州务卿和一份副本提交给行政区法庭书记官）；

2. 官方签名页；

3. 以下任一项（如果是律师公证人，可免除）：

a. 经行政区法庭书记官核准的金额为1万美元的保证金或个人担保；或者

b. 金额1万美元的错误和遗漏保险；或者

4. 如果是律师，须提交高路易斯安那最高法院的良好证书（代替保证金或错误和遗漏担保）；以及

5. 任命申请费（见第129条），并附上支付给州务卿的支票或汇票。

B. 公证人根据公证人员数据库中的任命日期进行委任。公证人不必等到收到州务卿发送的委任书，即可履行公证职能。另外，公证人的任命为终身制。

from the secretary of state's office before performing notary functions. In addition, a notary is commissioned for life.

C. A notary may request an additional commission certificate or replace a certificate by logging into his file online or by contacting the notary division. The fees for a certificate of notary commission or a replacement notary certificate are shown in § 129.

46: XLVI.113. Attorneys

A. An attorney who is licensed to practice law in Louisiana can obtain a notary commission by filing a qualifying application and commission documents.

B. The notary commission for an attorney must be filed in the parish of their residence.

C. An attorney is exempt from taking the notary exam and from the surety bond or personal surety bond requirements.

D. An attorney has statewide jurisdiction.

46: XLVI.115. Parish Changes

A. If a notary moves to another parish, he must submit the following to the secretary of state:

1. completed qualifying application form with the qualifying fee which is separate from commission filing fee;

2. two oaths of office forms, properly executed (one copy filed with secretary of state and one copy filed with parish clerk of court);

3. official signature page;

4. either of the following (exempt if an attorney):

a. surety bond or personal surety bond that has been approved by the parish clerk of court in the amount of $10,000;

b. errors and omissions policy in the amount of $10,000; or

c. rider for an existing surety bond that has been approved by the parish clerk of court changing the parish; and

5. commission filing fee (see § 129) with a check or money order made payable to the secretary of state.

46: XLVI.117. Name Change

A. If a notary's name changes, the notary must submit the following to the secretary of state:

1. two oaths of office forms, properly executed (one copy filed with secretary of state and one copy filed with parish clerk of court);

2. name change form listing name on current commission, new name requested, and reason for change;

C. 公证人可以通过在线登录系统或联系公证部门来要求附加的任命证书或更换证书。第 129 条规定了为公证人颁发证书或替代证书的费用。

46：XLVI.113 律师

A. 在路易斯安那州获得法律执业许可的律师可以通过提交合格申请和委任文件来获得公证人任命。

B. 律师的公证人任命必须在其居住的行政区提交。

C. 对律师免除参加公证考试以及缴纳保证金或提供个人担保的要求。

D. 律师拥有全州管辖权。

46：XLVI.115 行政区变化

A. 如果公证人搬到另一个行政区，其必须将以下内容提交给州务卿：

1. 填写完整的合格申请表，提交获取资格的费用，该费用与任命申请费分开；

2. 两份妥善执行的职务宣誓（一份副本提交给州务卿，一份副本提交给行政区法庭书记官）；

3. 官方签名页；

4. 以下任一项（如果是律师公证人，可免除）：

a. 经行政区法庭书记官核准的金额为 1 万美元的保证金或个人担保；或者

b. 金额为 1 万美元的错误和遗漏保险；或者

c. 已缴纳保证金，由行政区法庭书记官批准改变行政区；以及

5. 任命申请费（见第 129 条），并附上支付给州务卿的支票或汇票。

46：XLVI.117 名称变更

A. 如果公证人姓名发生变更，其必须将以下内容提交给州务卿：

1. 两份妥善执行的职务宣誓（一份副本提交给州务卿，一份副本提交给行政区法庭书记官）；

2. 名称变更表，列明当前的任命情况，新姓名以及变更原因；

3. official signature page;

4. either of the following (exempt if an attorney):

a. original or certified true copy surety or personal surety bond that has been approved by the parish clerk of court in the amount of $10,000;

b. original errors and omissions policy in the amount of $10,000; or

c. rider for an existing surety bond that has been approved by the parish clerk of court changing the name on the bond; and

5. commission filing fee (see § 129) with a check or money order made payable to the secretary of state.

46: XLVI.119. Dual Commission

A. Dual commissions can only be obtained for one other parish in which the notary maintains an office and is not reciprocal with the existing commission (see reciprocal parish list.)

B. If a notary requests a dual commission, he must submit the following to the secretary of state:

1. two oaths of office forms, properly executed (one copy filed with secretary of state and one copy filed with parish clerk of court);

2. official signature page;

3. either of the following (exempt if an attorney):

a. surety bond or personal surety bond that has been approved by the parish clerk of court in the amount of $10,000; or

b. errors and omissions policy in the amount of $10,000; and

4. commission filing fee (see § 129) with a check or money order made payable to the secretary of state.

46: XLVI.121. Notary Bond Renewal

A. Surety bonds and errors and omissions policies are filed with the secretary of state every five years. Personal surety bonds expire at the death of the surety and must be renewed when such occurs.

B. Either of the following must be submitted to the secretary of state for bond renewal (exempt if an attorney):

1. surety bond or personal surety bond that has been approved by the parish clerk of court in the amount of $10,000; or

2. errors and omissions policy in the amount of $10,000.

C. A check or money order made payable to the secretary of state for the notary bond renewal filing fee (see § 129) must accompany the renewal for the notary bond.

3. 官方签名页；

4. 以下任一项（如果是律师公证人，可免除）：

a. 经行政区法庭书记官核准的金额为1万美元的保证金或个人担保的原件或认证副本；或者

b. 金额1万美元的错误和遗漏保险原件；或者

c. 已缴纳保证金，由行政区法庭书记官批准改变姓名；以及

5. 任命申请费（见第129条），并附上提交给州务卿的支票或汇票。

46：XLVI.119 双重任命

A. 双重任命只能在另一个行政区获得，在那拥有办公室，且与现有任命无关联（见互惠行政区名单）。

B. 如果公证人要求双重任命，其必须提交以下材料给州务卿：

1. 两份妥善执行的职务宣誓（一份副本提交给州务卿，一份副本提交给行政区法庭书记官）；

2. 官方签名页；

3. 以下任一项（如果是律师公证人，可免除）：

a. 经行政区法庭书记官核准的金额为1万美元的保证金或个人担保；或者

b. 金额1万美元的错误和遗漏保险；以及

4. 任命申请费（见第129条），并附上提交给州务卿的支票或汇票。

46：XLVI.121 公证保证金续期

A. 每五年向州务卿提交保证金和错误遗漏保险。个人担保在担保人死亡时到期，且在发生这种情况时必须更新。

B. 为更新保证金，必须向州务卿提交以下任何一项（如果是律师公证人，可免除）：

1. 经行政区法庭书记官核准的金额为1万美元的保证金或个人担保；或者

2. 金额1万美元的错误和遗漏保险；或者

C. 支付给州务卿的支票或汇票，以缴纳公证人续期申请费（见第129条），其中必须涵盖公证人保证金续期的费用。

D. A notary who fails to renew his notarial bond timely or fails to file his new or renewed bond of evidence of insurance coverage will be automatically suspended and will not have authority to perform the functions of a notary.

46: XLVI.123. Leave of Absence

A. The secretary of state, on behalf of the governor, may grant a leave of absence to any notary that is absent from the state for a period not to exceed 36 months. The notary must provide the secretary of state with a letter requesting the leave specifying the date the notary is to be absent and the date of return.

B. If a notary is in the military service, he should notify the secretary of state's office certifying that he is a member of the military service of the United States or state of Louisiana. Included on the notification letter, he should show the expiration date of his bond and the period of leave which begins when the leave is granted. The notary will then have 60 days after the date of discharge to give the notary time to apply for a new bond.

46: XLVI.125. Retirement Status

A. Any notary who is 70 years or older shall be permitted to retire his commission by filing a retirement status affidavit form attesting to the notary's age and certifying that he will no longer exercise the duties and functions of a notary while retirement status is in effect.

46: XLVI.127. Resignation

A. Any notary may resign his commission by signing a letter of resignation and forwarding it to the secretary of state's office. After resigning, the notary shall not exercise any duties or functions of a notary public and may become an active notary again only by completing the application process of his parish including taking the exam, if applicable.

46: XLVI.129. Notary Division Fee Schedule

A. The fee schedule for notaries public is as follows:

Item	Fee
Annual Report	$25
Certificate of Notary Commission	$20
Certified Copy of Notary Bond	$20
Commission Filing Fee	$35
Notary Bond Renewal	$20
Notary Exam Pre-Assessment Test	$30
Notary Exam Registration Fee	$75
Notary Filing Information Packet	$0
Notary Study Guide	$90
Qualifying Application Fee	$35
Replacement Identification Card	$3
Replacement Notary Certificate	$15

D. 未能及时更新公证保证金的公证人，或者未能提交新的或重新提供保证金的公证人将自动被暂停任命，不具有履行公证人职能的权力。

46：XLVI.123 休假

A. 州务卿可以代表州长向离开本州的公证人批注不超过36个月的休假。公证人必须向州务卿写信要求休假，并注明休假日期和返回日期。

B. 如果公证人在服兵役，其应通知州务卿，证明其是美国或路易斯安那州军队的成员。在通知信中，其应该注明其任职保证金到期日期以及休假的开始和结束的时间。公证人应在休假结束后60日内申请新的保证金。

46：XLVI.125 退休状况

A. 任何70周岁以上的公证人，可以通过提交公证人年龄的退休身份证明表，并且确认退休期间不再行使公证人的职责，而被批准退休。

46：XLVI.127 辞职

A. 任何公证人可以通过签名的辞职信进行辞职，并将其转交给州务卿办公室。辞职后，公证人不得行使公证人的义务或职能，只有在完成其行政区的申请程序（包括参加考试）（如适用）的情况下，才能再次成为有权执业的公证人。

46：XLVI.129 公证科费用表

A. 公证事宜的收费表如下：

项目	费
年度报告	$25
公证人任命书	$20
经认证的公证保证金副本	$20
任命申请费	$35
公证保证金续期	$20
预评估测试费	$30
公证考试报名费	$75
公证信息提交	$0
公证课程学习	$90
资格申请费	$5
更换公证人身份证	$3
更换公证证书	$15

46: XLVI.131. Notary Seal

A. A notary's signature is his seal. If he elects to have a seal to use when notarizing documents, he is not required to have a particular style of seal to give authenticity to his copies.

B. The name of the notary and the witnesses must be typed, printed legibly, or stamped.

C. Every document notarized in the state of Louisiana shall have the notary identification number assigned to him/her by the secretary of state and that number shall be typed or printed legibly and placed next to the notary's name. If the notary is an attorney who is licensed to practice law in the state of Louisiana, he may use his Louisiana state bar roll number in lieu of his notary identification number.

46: XLVI.133. Reciprocal Parishes

A. There are groups of reciprocal parishes created by the legislature (see R.S. 35:191). The reciprocal agreement allows a validly appointed notary in a parish authorization to exercise any and all functions of a notary in the reciprocal parishes without additional bonding or examination. For a list of reciprocal parishes, see the secretary of state's website notary division.

If a notary moves to a parish that is in his reciprocal grouping, he is still required to be commissioned in the parish he resides in.

46: XLVI.135. Fees to be Charged by a Notary Public

A. Louisiana does not have a statutory fee schedule which would determine or limit what a notary can charge for his services.

46: XLVI.137. Notary Database

A. The secretary of state's website contains current contact information on all notaries commissioned in the state of Louisiana.

B. If a notary is listed on the notary database as being suspended, the notary did not file his annual report or his bond has expired.

46: XLVI.139. Annual Report

A. Within 60 days prior to the anniversary date of the notary's commission, the notary division shall mail out an annual report notice to all notaries in the state of Louisiana.

B. The notary can file his report by:
1. registering online at the secretary of state's website

46：XLVI.113 公证公章

A. 公证人的签名是他的印章。如果公证人选择在公证文件时使用印章，不需要具有特殊格式的印章为文件副本提供真实性。

B. 公证人和证人的名字必须清晰打印、印刷或盖章。

C. 路易斯安那州经过公证的每一份文件均应具有州务卿分配给他／她的公证身份证件号码，并应清楚地打印或印刷在公证人的名字旁边。如果公证人是在路易斯安那州获准执业的律师，则可以使用其路易斯安那州律师执业证号码代替公证身份证号码。

46：XLVI.133 互惠行政区

A. 立法机关创建互惠行政区（见 R.S.35：191 条款）。互惠协议允许在某一行政区被有效任命的公证人在互惠教区行使公证人的所有职能，而无需额外的保证金或审查。互惠行政区列表，参见州务卿公证部门的公示。

如果一名公证人搬到互惠行政区，其仍然需要在其所在的行政区接受任命。

46：XLVI.135 公证人收费

A. 路易斯安那州没有法定收费表，用以确定或限制公证人为其服务收取的费用。

46：XLVI.117 公证数据库

A. 州务卿的网站包含路易斯安那州任命的所有公证人的当前联系信息。

B. 如果公证人在公证人资料库上被列为暂停公证人员，代表该公证人没有提交年度报告或保证金已过期。

46：XLVI.139 年度报告

A. 在公证任命每年期满之前的 60 日内，公证处应向路易斯安那州的所有公证人发出年报通知。

B. 公证人可以通过以下方式提交报告：
1. 使用信用卡在州务院网站上注册；或者

using a credit card; or

    2. completing the annual report form and:

    a. attaching a check or money order made payable to the secretary of state and mailing to the notary division; or

    b. completing the credit card cover sheet and faxing or emailing with the annual report to the notary division.

    C. The annual report filing fee is shown in § 129.

    D. To file online, the notary will be required to use his notary identification number and the unique access code which is printed on the front of the annual report renewal notice post card.

46: XLVI.141. Ex-Officio Notaries Public

    A. An ex-officio notary public must meet the same qualifications as a notary public listed in § 101 above.

    B. An ex-officio notary is required to file either of the following with the notary division of the secretary of state's office as a condition for the faithful performance of all duties required by law toward all persons who may employ him as an ex-officio notary:

    1. original or certified true copy surety or personal surety bond that has been approved by the parish clerk of court in the amount of $10,000; or

    2. original errors or omissions policy in the amount of $10,000.

    C. If the ex-officio notary is a state employee who serves as an ex-officio notary in the course and scope of his employment, he must file his oath of office with the secretary of state's office.

    D. An ex-officio notary is authorized to perform functions, powers, and authority only as directly related to and required for the operation of the office, agency, or department under which the authority is granted.

    E. Title 35 Chapter 6 of the Revised Statutes contains specific requirements for ex-officio notaries who will perform various functions of a notary public in their place of employment (i.e. administer oaths, take acknowledgments, attest on affidavits, etc.).

46: XLVI.143. Provisional Notary

    A. A notary applicant can be provisionally commissioned if he meets the following qualifications and requirements:

    1. the applicant resides and maintains a residence in a parish with a population of less than 40,000;

    2. the applicant has passed the multiple choice and research section of the notary exam on or after December 1, 2009;

    2. 填写年度报表，以及：

    a. 附上支付给州务卿的支票或汇票，并邮寄给公证部门；或者

    b. 将信用卡封面和年度报告通过传真或电子邮件发送给公证部门。

    C. 年度报告申报费用见第 129 条的规定。

    D. 如果使用在线提交方式，公证人需要使用其公证身份证号码和打印在年度报告续期通知单上的唯一访问代码。

46：XLVI.141 当然公证人

    A. 当然公证人必须符合上文第 101 条所列公证人的资格。

    B. 当然公证人必须满足州务院办公厅的公证部门提出的以下要求之一，作为忠实履行法律对所有可能聘请其作为当然公证人的条件：

    1. 经行政区法庭书记官核准的金额为 1 万美元的保证金或个人担保的原件或认证副本；或者

    2. 金额为 1 万美元的错误和遗漏保险。

    C. 如果当然公证人是在其职务行为中作为当然公证人，其必须向州务卿办公室宣誓就职。

    D. 仅授权当然公证人与授权机构所在的办公室、机构或部门的运作直接相关并且被要求的相关职权。

    E.《修订法案》第 35 编第 6 章载有对当然公证人的具体要求，其将在履职地点履行公证人的各种职能（例如：执行誓言、确认、证明誓章等）。

46：XLVI.143 临时公证人

    A. 如果符合以下资格和要求，可以临时委任公证人：

    1. 申请人在一个人口少于四万的行政区居住并拥有住所；

    2. 申请人于 2009 年 12 月 1 日或之后通过了公证考试的多项选择和研究部分；

3. the applicant's authority to exercise the powers of a notary public is only within the course and scope of the applicant's employment;

4. the applicant's notarial authority shall be under the direction of a supervisor for the employer

5. the applicant's supervisor shall not be a notary;

6. the applicant's employer must be a business that was in existence prior to January 1, 2013;

7. the applicant's employer shall not be a business whose primary function is to provide notary services;

8. the applicant's employer must be a party to the act or instrument being sworn to, acknowledged or passed before or the act or other instrument is necessary to or incidental to the business activity or operations of the employer;

9. at least one of the persons appearing before the applicant to execute an affidavit, acknowledgment, or other notarial act or instrument is a former, current, or prospective client or a customer of the employer;

10. applicant's jurisdiction is within the parish of commission and in any adjacent parish with a population of less than 40,000 where his employer maintains an office;

11. the applicant must post and maintain a bond, at the expense of employer, in the amount of $20,000;

12. the applicant's employer shall hold harmless any claim made against the notary bond when the applicant is acting in the course and scope of employment or under the direction of the employer;

13. the applicant must submit the completed and notarized application for provisional notarial appointment provided by the secretary of state to the notary division;

14. the applicant is required to attend the notary orientation class provided by the secretary of state;

15. if the employer terminates the employment or no longer wishes to be bound by these provisions, he shall immediately send written notice to the secretary of state and the commission shall be automatically revoked unless:

a. the applicant declares in writing his intention to remain a provisional notary with an inactive status until a new application for provisional notary form from another employer is submitted to the secretary of state; or

b. the applicant declares in writing the desire to remain a provisional notary with an inactive status while pursuing successful completion of the notary exam and shall exercise no notarial functions until notified by the secretary of state that his status has been changed;

3. 申请人行使公证人权力仅在申请人就业的范围内；

4. 申请人的公证机关由雇主直接领导

5. 申请人的主管人不得是公证人；

6. 申请人的任职单位必须是在 2013 年 1 月 1 日之前存在的企业；

7. 申请人的任职单位的主要职能不是提供公证服务；

8. 申请人的雇主必须是被宣誓、确认或通过的行为或文书的一方当事人，或者该行为或其他文书对雇主的业务活动或业务是必要的或附带的；

9. 申请人出席誓章，确认书或其他公证行为或文书的当事人中至少有一人是其之前、现任或潜在客户或是雇主的客户；

10. 申请人的管辖权范围在被任命的行政区内，以及在其雇主拥有办公室的人口少于四万的任何相邻行政区内；

11. 申请人必须缴纳雇主支付的 20000 美元用以缴纳和维持保证金；

12. 申请人在工作范围内或在雇主的指导下行事时，申请人的雇主不得要求使用公证人保证金支付任何损害赔偿；

13. 申请人必须向州公证部门提交州务卿提供的临时公证申请；

14. 申请人必须参加州务卿提供的公证课程；

15. 如果雇主终止雇用或不再希望受到上述规定的约束，应立即向州务卿发送书面通知，任命将自动撤销，除非：

a. 申请人以书面形式表示，打算继续担任无效状态的临时公证人，直至向另一位雇主提交新的临时公证人申请表；或者

b. 申请人以书面形式表示希望在成功完成公证考试的同时继续留任无效状态的临时公证人，在此期间，其不得履行公证职能，直至州务卿通知其身份已变更为止；

16. if the applicant voluntarily terminates employment with named employer, a written notification to the secretary of state must be submitted and:

a. the applicant declares in writing his intention to remain a provisional notary with an inactive status until a new application for provisional notary form from another employer is submitted to the secretary of state; or

b. declares in writing his intention to remain a provisional notary with an inactive status while pursuing successful completion of the notary exam and shall have no authority to exercise notarial functions until notified by the secretary of state that his status has been changed;

17. the applicant understands that the employer is not liable for any damages caused by negligent or fraudulent errors or omissions when notarizing outside the course and scope of employment;

18. the commission can be suspended or revoked by the court or suspended by the secretary of state pursuant to R.S. 35:15; and

19. the provisional notary commission shall expire on August 1, 2016 unless all sections of the notary exam have been successfully completed.

B. The provisional notary has no authority to:

1. draft and prepare a last will and testament or donation mortis causa;

2. draft and prepare a trust; or

draft and prepare any instrument that transfers title to immovable property including but not limited to an act of sale or act of donation.

16. 如果申请人自愿终止雇佣关系，则必须向州务卿提交书面通知，并且：

a. 申请人以书面形式表示，打算继续担任无效状态的临时公证人，直至向另一位雇主提交新的临时公证人申请表；或者

b. 以书面形式表示希望在成功完成公证考试的同时继续留任无效状态的临时公证人，在此期间，其不得履行公证职能，直至州务卿通知其身份已变更为止；

17. 申请人知悉在公司外进行公证时，雇主对因疏忽或欺诈性错误或遗漏造成的损害概不负责；

18. 该任命可以由法院暂停或撤销，或由州务卿依照 R.S.35:15 的规定暂停执行；以及

19. 临时公证任命将于 2016 年 8 月 1 日到期，除非临时公证人成功完成所有公证考试。

B. 临时公证人无权：

1. 起草并准备的遗嘱和临终遗赠文书；

2. 起草和准备信任；或者

起草和准备转让不动产所有权的任何文书，包括但不限于出售行为或捐赠行为。

明尼苏达州公证人法

Minnesota Statutes Annotated Currentness
Court and Filing Fees; Attestations
(Ch.357-359)

明尼苏达州现行法规及注释
法院和申请费；证词
（第 357 章至第 359 章）

>> **Chapter 359. Notaries Public**

第 359 章　公证人

>>**359.01. Commission**
Subdivision 1. Resident notaries.

The governor may appoint and commission as notaries public, by and with the advice and consent of the senate, as many citizens of this state or resident aliens, over the age of 18 years, as the governor considers necessary. The governor will appoint and commission notaries public and the secretary of state shall receive applications for appointments and commissions, shall keep a register of those persons appointed and commissioned as notaries public by the governor with the advice and consent of the senate, shall update that register when informed of a change in name and address by a notary public, shall process applications by a notary public for reappointment, shall receive fees for the performance of these functions to be deposited into the general fund, and shall perform those clerical and administrative duties associated with these functions. The governor may also receive such applications directly.

Subd. 2. Nonresident notaries.

(a) The governor, by and with the advice and consent of the senate, may appoint as notary public a person who is not a resident of this state if:

(1) the person is a resident of Wisconsin, Iowa, North Dakota, or South Dakota;

(2) the person designates the secretary of state as agent for the service of process for all purposes relating to notarial acts and for receipt of all correspondence relating to notarial acts; and

(3) the person designates the Minnesota county in which the person's notary commission will be recorded pursuant to section 359.061.

(b) The secretary of state shall receive applications for nonresident notary appointments and commissions, shall keep a register of those persons appointed and com-

>>359.01 公证人的委任
第 1 款　居民公证人

州长可以在公民中指定和委任公证人，州长可经参议院的提出意见并同意，委任其认为必要数量的 18 周岁以上的本州公民或外国居民作为公证人。州长任命公证人时，州务卿应接受指定和任命的申请，并经参议院的同意，备存州长委任公证人的登记册，并在得到公证人的姓名和地址变更通知时更新登记册。州务卿还应当处理公证人再次任命的申请，并收取履行上述职能所需的费用存入普通基金；履行与职能相关的文书和行政性职责。州长也可以直接受理这样的申请。

第 2 款　非居民公证人

（a）州长经参议院建议和同意后，可以指定符合以下要求的非本州居民作为公证人：

（1）该人是威斯康星州、爱荷华州、北达科他州或南达科他州的居民；

（2）该人指定州务卿作为代理人，进行一切与公证行为有关的程序服务并接收一切与公证行为有关的通知；以及

（3）根据第 359.061 条，该人员的公证人任命将被记录在明尼苏达州。

（b）州务卿应接受非居民公证人任命和委任的申请，并经征求参议院的意见和同意，保管由州长备存的公证人登记册，并在收到公证人姓名和地址的变更

missioned as notaries public by the governor with the advice and consent of the senate, shall update that register when informed of a change in name and address by a notary public, shall process applications by a notary public for reappointment, shall receive fees for the performance of these functions to be deposited into the general fund, and shall perform those clerical and administrative duties associated with these functions. The governor may also receive such applications directly.

Subd. 3. Fees.

(a) When making application for a commission the applicant must submit, along with the information required by the secretary of state, a nonrefundable fee of $120, which shall be forwarded by the secretary of state to the commissioner of management and budget to be deposited in the state treasury and credited to the general fund.

(b) Except as otherwise provided in paragraph (a), all fees shall be retained by the secretary of state and are nonreturnable, except for an overpayment of a fee.

Subd. 4. Application.

The secretary of state shall prepare the application form for a commission. The form may request personal information about the applicant, including, but not limited to, relevant civil litigation, occupational license history, and criminal background, if any. For the purposes of this section, "criminal background" includes, but is not limited to, criminal charges, arrests, indictments, pleas, and convictions.

Subd. 5. Registration to perform electronic notarizations.

Before performing electronic notarial acts, a notary public shall register the capability to notarize electronically with the secretary of state. Before performing electronic notarial acts after recommissioning, a notary public shall reregister with the secretary of state. The requirements of this chapter relating to electronic notarial acts do not apply to notarial acts performed under sections 358.15, paragraph (a), clause (4), and 358.43, paragraph (a), clause (2).

>>359.02. Term

A notary commissioned under section 359.01 holds office until January 31 of the fifth year following the year the commission was issued, unless sooner removed by the governor or the district court, or by action of the commissioner of commerce. Six months before the expiration of the commission, a notary may renew the notary's commission for a new term to commence and to be designated in the new commission as beginning upon the day immedi-

通知时更新该登记册；州务卿还应当处理公证人再次任命的申请，并将收取的履行上述职能所需的费用存入普通基金；履行与职能相关的文书和行政性职责。州长也可以直接受理这样的申请。

第 3 款 费用

（a）申请人在提出申请时，申请人必须连同州务卿所要求的资料一并提交 120 美元，该费用不可退还，由州务卿转交给管理层和预算委员，存入国库并归入普通基金。

（b）除（a）款另有规定外，所有费用均由州务卿保留，且不可退还，除非存在超额缴纳费用的情况。

第 4 款 申请

州务卿应准备任职申请表。表格可以要求申请人填写有关的个人信息，包括但不限于相关的民事诉讼、职业许可的历史和犯罪背景（如果有的话）。在本条中，"犯罪背景"包括但不限于刑事指控、逮捕、收到起诉书、入狱和被定罪。

第 5 款 电子公证的注册

在进行电子公证行为之前，公证人应当向州务卿登记其进行电子公证的行为能力。公证人获得再次任命后，在进行电子公证行为前，需要向州务卿再次登记。本章有关电子公证行为的要求不适用于根据第 358.15 条（a）款第 4 项和第 358.43 条（a）款第 2 项进行的公证行为。

>>359.02 任期

根据第 359.01 条委任的公证人任职期限到委任书颁发年度后第 5 年的 1 月 31 日，除非在此之前被州长或地方法院撤职，或被商业专员吊销资格。在任期届满前 6 个月，公证人可以续延公证人的任职期，新的任期从原任期到期日之后的第一天开始。任职到期的公证人可以在到期日后再申请延续任期。虽然进行任命的州长在任期内可能不再担任州长职务，但重新任命或延任任职期限仍是合法有效的。

ately following the date of the expiration. A notary whose commission expires may apply for reappointment after the expiration date. The reappointment or renewal takes effect and is valid although the appointing governor may not be in the Office of Governor on the effective day.

>>359.03. Stamp; register
Subdivision 1. Requirement.

Every notary, including an ex officio notary under section 358.15, shall obtain an official notarial stamp as specified in subdivision 3, with which to authenticate official acts. The official notarial stamp, and the notary's official journal, are the personal property of the notary and are exempt from execution.

Subd. 2. Validation and legalization of certain instruments.

(a) All instruments heretofore duly made and executed which have been acknowledged before a notary public as provided by law, but the seal or stamp used thereon has engraved on it "notary public," are hereby validated and legalized, and in case such instruments are recorded, the recording is hereby validated and legalized, and all such instruments are validated to the same extent as though properly sealed at the time of their acknowledgment. This subdivision shall not affect any action now pending in any of the courts of this state.

(b) The official notarial stamp required by this section, whether applied to the record physically or electronically, is deemed to be a "seal" for purposes of the admission of a document in court.

Subd. 3. Specifications.

The official notarial stamp consists of the seal of the state of Minnesota, the name of the notary as it appears on the commission or the name of the ex officio notary, the words "Notary Public," or "Notarial Officer" in the case of an ex officio notary, and the words "My commission expires _____ (or where applicable) My term is indeterminate," with the expiration date shown on it and must be able to be reproduced in any legibly reproducible manner. The official notarial stamp shall be a rectangular form of not more than three-fourths of an inch vertically by 2-1/2 inches horizontally, with a serrated or milled edge border, and shall contain the information required by this subdivision.

Subd. 4. Notarial stamp may be affixed electronically.

The information required by this section may be affixed electronically and shall be logically and securely

>>359.03 印章；登记
第1款 要求

根据第358.15条，包括当然公证人在内的每个公证人均应取得第3款所规定的公证公章，用于在职务行为中进行认证。公证公章和公证人的职务日志是公证人的个人财产，不可被执行。

第2款 文书的有效和合法化

（a）依法在公证人面前已经确认、制作并执行的所有文书，附上"公证人"字样的印章或标记则这些文书为有效、合法的，如果这些文书被记录在案，则记录也是有效和合法的，只要在确认时其被妥善密封，上述文书具有同等的效力。本项不影响本州任何法院现行的任何行动。

（b）本条所规定的官方公证印记，无论是以实物或电子方式记录，均被视为"盖章"，以便在法庭上接受文件。

第3款 规格

公证公章是明尼苏达州公章的组成部分，因包括委任状上的公证人姓名或当然公证人的姓名、"公证人"或"公证人员"等字样（就当然的公证人而言），任职到期日也必须体现在印章上，通过"任职到期日"（适用的话）"任期是不确定的"等方式标注，印章应能以任何可重现的方式复制。公证公章应为不超过3/4英寸的矩形，水平方向为1/2英寸，锯齿状或铣边边缘，并应包含本款规定的信息。

第4款 公证盖章可以电子方式进行

本条所要求的信息可以电子方式附加，应有逻辑和安全地附于文书上或与正在公证的电子记录相

affixed or associated with the electronic record being notarized.

>>359.04. Powers

Every notary public so appointed, commissioned, and qualified shall have power throughout this state to administer all oaths required or authorized to be administered in this state; to take and certify all depositions to be used in any of the courts of this state; to take and certify all acknowledgments of deeds, mortgages, liens, powers of attorney, and other instruments in writing or electronic records; and to receive, make out, and record notarial protests.

>>359.05. Repealed by Laws 2010, c. 380, s 18, eff. August 1, 2010

>>359.06. Repealed by Laws 1976, c. 2, s 128, eff. August 1, 2010

>>359.061. Record of commission

Subdivision 1. Resident notaries.

The commission of every notary commissioned under section 359.01, together with: (1) a signature that matches the first, middle, and last name as listed on the notary's commission and shown on the notarial stamp, and (2) a sample signature in the style in which the notary will actually execute notarial acts, shall be recorded in the office of the local registrar of the notary's county of residence or in the county department to which duties relating to notaries public have been assigned under section 485.27, in a record kept for that purpose.

Subd. 2. Nonresident notaries.

The commission of a nonresident notary must be recorded in the Minnesota county the notary designates pursuant to section 359.01, subdivision 2, clause (3), in the county department to which duties relating to notaries public have been assigned under section 485.27.

Subd. 3. Certificate of court administrator.

The court administrator, when requested, shall certify to official acts in the manner and for the fees prescribed by statute or court rule.

Subd. 4. County notary certificate.

The county department, to which duties relating to notaries public have been assigned under section 485.27, shall certify to official acts under this section for the fee of $5 and in the form of:

关联。

>>359.04 公证人的职权

所有被指定、委任和具备资质的公证人均有权管理本州的所有宣誓或被授权在本州管理所有宣誓；取得并证明在本州所有法院使用的口供；取得并证明对所有契约，抵押权，留置权，委托书和其他书面文书或电子记录的确认书；并有权接受，制造和记录拒绝承兑书。

>>359.05 第380章第18条被2010年法律废止，于2010年8月1日生效

>>359.06 第2章第128条，被2010年法律废止，于2010年8月1日生效

>>359.061 任命记录

第1款 居民公证人

根据第359.01条被任命的每个公证人的委任状应包含：（1）与公证人委任书上和公证公章上标注的与姓氏匹配的姓名、中间名的签名，以及（2）公证人实际执行公证行为的签章模板。以上信息应记录在公证人所在地登记官办公室或第485.27条规定的与公证人职务有关的郡部门办公室。

第2款 非居民公证人

非居民公证人依据第359.01条第2款第3项获得的任命必须记录在明尼苏达州内，登记在第485.27条规定的与公证人有关的郡部门办公室。

第3款 法院管理人证明书

法院管理人员接到请求时，应以法定或法院规定的方式和费用证明职务行为。

第4款 郡公证证书

根据第485.27条，职责与公证人有关的郡部门应根据本条对作出的职务行为进行证明，费用为5美元，证明格式为：

State of Minnesota

_____ County

"I the undersigned ._____, in and for said county and state, do hereby certify that _____, whose name is subscribed to on the attached document held the office of notary public in said county and state at the date of said subscription and was authorized under the laws of this state to take acknowledgments, to administer oaths, take depositions, acknowledgments of deeds, and other written instruments, and exercise all such powers and duties authorized by the laws of Minnesota as notary public. I further certify that I have compared the subscribed signature to the signature on file in this office and believe them to be the same.

Signed this date _____ in the county of _____, state of Minnesota."

Signature _____

Title _____

>>359.062. Notice; languages other than English

(a) A notary public who is not an attorney who advertises the services of a notary public in a language other than English, whether by radio, television, signs, pamphlets, newspapers, or other written communication, with the exception of a single desk plaque, shall post or otherwise include with the advertisement a notice in English and the language in which the advertisement appears. This notice must be of a conspicuous size, if in writing, and must state: "I AM NOT AN ATTORNEY LICENSED TO PRACTICE LAW IN MINNESOTA AND MAY NOT GIVE LEGAL ADVICE OR ACCEPT FEES FOR LEGAL ADVICE." If the advertisement is by radio or television, the statement may be modified but must include substantially the same message.

(b) A notary public who violates this section is guilty of a misdemeanor.

>>359.07. Notary in detached county

Subdivision 1. Powers.

In any county which has heretofore been detached from another county of this state, and which has been newly created and organized, any notary public residing in such newly created and organized county, who was a resident of the county from which the new county was detached and created, shall have the same powers during the unexpired term of appointment as such notary public was authorized by law to exercise under the commission issued to the notary as a resident of the county from which the

明尼苏达州

_____ 郡

"本人签名确认_____，向本州和本郡证明，_____，在上述签署日其在存放在上述郡和州公证人办公室的附件上签名，并根据本州法律授权，确认、管理誓言，获取口供，确认契约等书面文书，并行使法律授权作为明尼苏达州公证人的所有权力和义务。本人进一步证明，我已经将签名与该办公室的档案上的签名进行了比较，并相信他们是一致的。

日期 _____ 签名 _____ 郡，明尼苏达州。"

签名 _____

职务 _____

>>359.062 说明；英语以外的语言

（a）不是律师的公证人，无论是通过广播、电视、标志、宣传册、报纸或其他书面信息宣传时，除了使用单独的桌牌，如果需以英文以外的其他语言宣传公证人的服务，还须张贴或以其他方式刊登以英文和该宣传使用的语言表述的说明。如果是书面形式，公告须采用引人注目的字号，并声明："我不是在明尼苏达州执业的律师，不得提供法律建议或接受法律顾问的费用。"如果宣传是通过广播或电视作出，则可以修改该声明的措辞，但必须包括基本相同的信息。

（b）违反本条的公证人构成轻罪。

>> 359.07 独立郡的公证人

第1款 权力

对于之前从本州的另一个郡脱离并已经新建和组织的任何郡，居住在这个新建立和组织的郡的公证人，其与和新郡相独立的郡的居民公证人，在未到期的任命期间具有相同的权力，因为公证人被依法授权，有权在发给作为与新设郡相独立的郡的居民公证人委任书及公证人的原始委任书的范围内行使职权；且任何公证人所做的一切行为，尽管其居住在独立郡，但仍为合法有效，即使公证人最初被作为新设郡的居民受到委任，其公证行为也具有同等效力。

new county was detached and created and within which the original appointment as notary public was made; and all acts heretofore done by any such notary public, while residing in the newly created and organized county, otherwise in conformity of law, are hereby declared to be legal and valid and to the same effect as if the notary public had been originally commissioned as a resident of the newly created and organized county.

Subd. 2. Record of commission.

Such notary public so residing in the new created and organized county shall have the commission as such notary public recorded by the court administrator of the district court of the newly created and organized county of residence, or of the county to which the newly created county is attached for judicial purposes, as provided in section 359.061, and when so recorded shall be entitled to the same certificate of and from the court administrator of the district court as provided in section 359.061.

Subd. 3. Seal.

Such notary shall, immediately upon the adoption of this section, get an official seal, as provided in and in conformity with section 359.03.

>>359.071. Change of name or address

A notary shall notify the secretary of state of any name or address change within 30 days of the change.

>>359.08. Misconduct

Any notary who shall exercise the duties of office after the expiration of a term, or when otherwise disqualified, shall be guilty of a misdemeanor.

>>359.085. Standards of conduct for notarial acts

Subdivision 1. Acknowledgments.

In taking an acknowledgment, the notarial officer must determine, either from personal knowledge or from satisfactory evidence, that the person appearing before the officer and making the acknowledgment is the person whose true signature is on the instrument or electronic record.

Subd. 2. Verifications.

In taking a verification upon oath or affirmation, the notarial officer must determine, either from personal knowledge or from satisfactory evidence, that the person appearing before the officer and making the verification is the person whose true signature is made in the presence of the officer on the statement verified.

Subd. 3. Witnessing or attesting signatures.

In witnessing or attesting a signature, the notarial

第 2 款 任命记录

根据第 359.061 条的规定，居住在新独立的郡的公证人应当将委任书交由新独立的郡的郡级法院行政人员或者因司法目的与新独立的郡有关联的法院行政人员记录，当进行上述记录后，应同等获得按照第 359.061 条的规定，由地方法院出具的证书。

第 3 款 公证公章

上述公证人在符合本条规定后，应当按照第 359.03 条的规定及时获得公证公章。

>>359.071 更改名称或地址

公证人应在名称或地址发生变更后 30 日内通知州务卿。

>>359.08 轻罪

任何在任期到期后仍然进行职务行为的公证人或者有其他资格不符要求的公证人，均构成轻罪。

>> 359.085 公证行为标准

第 1 款 确认

公证人在作出确认时，必须依据个人知识或充分证据确定出席确认现场并对其作出确认的人是在文书或电子记录上真实签名的人。

第 2 款 认证

公证人在认证宣誓或宣誓书时，必须依据个人知识或充分证据确定出席认证现场并做出认证的人是在公证人面前就经验证的陈述的进行真实签名的人。

第 3 款 证人或见证签名

公证人在确认证人或见证签名时，必须依据个人

officer must determine, either from personal knowledge or from satisfactory evidence, that the signature is that of the person appearing before the officer and named in the document or electronic record. When witnessing or attesting a signature, the officer must be present when the signature is made.

Subd. 4. Certifying or attesting documents.

In certifying or attesting a copy of a document, electronic record, or other item, the notarial officer must determine that the proffered copy is a full, true, and accurate transcription or reproduction of that which was copied.

Subd. 5. Making or noting protests of negotiable instruments.

In making or noting a protest of a negotiable instrument or electronic record, the notarial officer must determine the matters set forth in section 336.3-505.

Subd. 6. Satisfactory evidence.

A notarial officer has satisfactory evidence that a person is the person whose true signature is on a document or electronic record if that person (i) is personally known to the notarial officer, (ii) is identified upon the oath or affirmation of a credible witness personally known to the notarial officer, or (iii) is identified on the basis of identification documents.

Subd. 7. Prohibited acts.

A notarial officer may not acknowledge, witness or attest to the officer's own signature, or take a verification of the officer's own oath or affirmation.

Subd. 8. Repealed by Laws 2007, c. 148, art. 2, s 84, eff. July 1, 2007.

>>359.09. Repealed by Laws 1965, c. 811, art. 10, s 336.10-102, eff. July 1,1966

>>359.091. Accommodation of physical limitations

(a) A notary public may certify as to the subscription or signature of an individual when it appears that the individual has a physical limitation that restricts the individual's ability to sign by writing or making a mark, pursuant to the following:

(1) the name of an individual may be signed, or attached electronically in the case of an electronic record, by another individual other than the notary public at the direction and in the presence of the individual whose name is to be signed and in the presence of the notary public. The signature may be made by a rubber stamp facsimile of the person's actual signature, mark, or a signature of the person's name or mark made by another and adopted

知识或充分证据确定该签名是出现在该公证人面前并且其名字在文件或电子记录中出现的人的签名。当证人或见证签字时，公证人必须在场。

第4款 证明或见证文件

在对文件，电子记录或其他项目的副本进行证明或见证时，公证人必须确定提供的副本是完整、真实、准确的转录品或复制品。

第5款 制作或签注可转让票据的拒绝承兑书

在作出或签注可转让票据或电子记录的拒绝承兑书时，公证人员必须确定第336.3-505条规定的事项。

第6款 充分证据

符合下列条件的，属于公证人员有充分证据表明，该人是在文件或电子记录上作出真实签名的人：（ⅰ）该人员被公证人员所熟知，（ⅱ）经宣誓确认或由公证人熟知的可靠的证人确定身份的人，或（ⅲ）根据身份证明文件确定的人。

第7款 禁止的行为

公证人不得确认、作证或见证该公证人员自己的签名，或对自己的誓言或宣誓书进行验证。

第8款 第148章第2条第84款被2007年法律废止，于2007年7月1日生效

>>359.09 第811章第10条第336.10-102款被1965年法律废止，于1966年7月1日生效

>>359.091 由于身体限制的调整

（a）公证人如果认为当事人存在无法书写或标记签名的身体限制，则可以通过下列方式验证其署名或签名：

（1）当事人的姓名可以由公证人以外的另一个人签写或在电子记录中以电子的形式附加，签名的人和公证人须同时在场参与。签名可以由标记了个人签名图样、标记签名图样或他人签名或标记的图样的橡皮图章进行，本款适用于所有身体有限制的人进行任何用途的签名；以及

for all purposes of signature by the person with a physical limitation; and

(2) the words "Signature written by" or "Signature attached by" in the case of an electronic record, "(name of individual directed to sign or directed to attach) at the direction and in the presence of (name as signed) on whose behalf the signature was written" or "attached electronically" in the case of an electronic record, or words of substantially similar effect must appear under or near the signature.

(b) A notary public may use signals or electronic or mechanical means to take an acknowledgment from, administer an oath or affirmation to, or otherwise communicate with any individual in the presence of such notary public when it appears that the individual is unable to communicate verbally or in writing.

>>359.10. Repealed by Laws 1965, c. 811, art. 10, s 336.10-102, eff. July 1, 1966

>>359.11. Taking depositions

In taking depositions, the notary shall have the power to compel the attendance of and to punish witnesses for refusing to testify as provided by statute or court rule. All sheriffs shall serve and return all process issued by any notary in taking depositions.

>>359.12. Administrative actions and penalties

Every notary who shall charge or receive a fee or reward for any act or service done or rendered as a notary greater than the amount allowed by law, or who dishonestly or unfaithfully discharges duties as notary, or who has pleaded guilty, with or without explicitly admitting guilt, plead nolo contendere, or been convicted of a felony, gross misdemeanor, or misdemeanor involving moral turpitude, is subject to the penalties imposed pursuant to section 45.027. A notary may be removed from office only by the governor, the district court, or the commissioner of commerce. The commissioner of commerce has all the powers provided by section 45.027 and shall proceed in the manner provided by that section in actions against notaries.

Notwithstanding section 359.03, subdivision 1, upon removal from office by the commissioner of commerce, a notary public shall deliver the notary's official notarial stamp to the commissioner of commerce.

（2）在电子记录的情况下，"（签名或附加签名）"（被指导签署或附加签名的人）在被指导和（签名的人）共同出席，以电子记录的形式，以"书面形式"或以"电子方式"签名，或者在签名下方或附近填写具有相似效果的词句。

（b）当出现个人无法进行语言或书面沟通的情况时，公证人可以现场使用信号、电子或机械手段进行确认、宣誓或认证或以其他方式与该人员沟通。

>>359.10 第811章第10条第336.10-102项，由1965年法律废止，于1966年7月1日生效

>>359.11 录取口供

公证人有权按法定规则或法院规则强制证人出庭作证和因证人拒绝作证而惩罚证人。所有治安官均应服从公证人录取口供的所有程序。

>> 359.12 行政行为和处罚

凡公证人就其职务行为或服务索要、收取超过法律许可范围的费用或酬金，或不诚信或不忠实地履行公证职责，或被判有罪的公证人，无论是否承认有罪、进行无罪申诉、被定罪为重罪或被认定为明显的行为失职或涉及道德败坏的轻罪，均应受到第45.027条规定的处罚。公证人只能由州长、地方法院或商务专员撤销职务。商务专员具有第45.027条规定的所有权力，并有权按照该条规定的方式，对公证人采取行动。

尽管有第359.03条第1款的规定，经商务专员撤职后，公证人应向商务专员交出公证人公章。

内华达州公证人法

Title 19.
Miscellaneous Matters Related to Government and Public Affairs (Chapters 234-242)

Chapter 240.
Notaries Public and Commissioned Abstracters (Refs & Annos)

+ **Notaries Public**
>> General Provisions

>>**240.001. Definitions**

As used in NRS 240.001 to 240.206, inclusive, unless the context otherwise requires, the words and terms defined in NRS 240.002 to 240.0067, inclusive, have the meanings ascribed to them in those sections.

>>**240.002. "Acknowledgment" defined**

"Acknowledgment" means a declaration by a person that he or she has executed an instrument for the purposes stated therein and, if the instrument is executed in a representative capacity, that the person signed the instrument with proper authority and executed it as the act of the person or entity represented and identified therein.

>>**240.0025. "Credible witness" defined**

"Credible witness" means a person who:

1. Swears or affirms that the signer of a document is the person whom he or she claims to be; and

2. Is known personally to the signer of the document and the notarial officer.

>>**240.0028. "Domestic partners" defined**

"Domestic partners" has the meaning ascribed to it in NRS 122A.030.

>>**240.003. "In a representativecapacity" defined**

"In a representative capacity" means:

1. For and on behalf of a corporation, partnership, trust or other entity, as an authorized officer, agent, partner, trustee or other representative;

2. As a public officer, personal representative, guardian or other representative, in the capacity recited in the

标题 19
与政府及公共事务相关的事项
（第 234-242 章）

第 240 章　公证人及概括委托人（原文及注释）

+ 公证人
>> 一般规定

>> 240.001 定义

如《内华达州修正法案》第 240.001 条至第 240.206 条所示，除非上下文另有定义，否则《内华达州修正法案》第 240.002 条至第 240.0067 条中所定义的词语和术语在本法具有一致的含义。

>> 240.002 "确认书"定义

"确认书"是指个人为其所述的目的而执行文书的声明，或者该文书是由具有代表身份的人所执行的，且该人以适当的权限签署该文书，并以其中所代表和指明的个人或实体的名义进行执行。

>> 240.0025 "可信证人"的定义

"可信证人"是指以下人士：

1. 发誓或证明文件的签署人是其所声称的个人；以及

2. 个人认识文件的签署人和公证人。

>> 240.0028 "家庭伴侣"的定义

"家庭伴侣"的定义参照《内华达州修正法案》122 a.030 中的规定。

>> 240.003 "以代表身份"的定义

"以代表身份"是指：

1. 代表公司、合伙企业、信托或其它实体，作为获得授权的签字人、代理人、合伙人、受托人或其它代表；

2. 作为公职人员、个人代表、监护人或其他在该文书中所列举的身份；

instrument;

    3. As an attorney-in-fact for a principal; or

    4. In any other capacity as an authorized representative of another.

>>240.0035. "Jurat" defined

"Jurat" means a declaration by a notarial officer that the signer of a document signed the document in the presence of the notarial officer and swore to or affirmed that the statements in the document are true.

>>240.004. "Notarial act" defined

"Notarial act" means an act that a notarial officer of this state is authorized to perform. The term includes:

    1. Taking an acknowledgment;

    2. Administering an oath or affirmation;

    3. Certifying a copy;

    4. Executing a jurat;

    5. Noting a protest of a negotiable instrument; and

    6. Performing such other duties as may be prescribed by a specific statute.

>>240.005. "Notarial officer" defined

"Notarial officer" means a notary public or an officer authorized to perform notarial acts.

>>240.0055. "Notarial record" defined

"Notarial record" means:

    1. The journal that a notary public is required to keep pursuant to NRS 240.120;

    2. The journal that an electronic notary public is required to keep pursuant to NRS 240.201; and

    3. A document or other evidence retained by a notary public or an electronic notary public to record the performance of a notarial act or an electronic notarial act.

>>240.006. Repealed

>>240.0063. "Notary public" defined

"Notary public" means a person appointed to perform a notarial act by the Secretary of State pursuant to NRS 240.010.

>>240.0065. "Person" defined

"Person" means a natural person.

>>240.0067. "State" defined

"State" means a state of the United States, the District of Columbia, Puerto Rico, the United States Virgin Islands or any territory or insular possession subject to the jurisdiction of the United States.

    3. 作为当事人的实际代理人；或者

    4. 作为授权代表的任何其他身份。

>> 240.0035"宣誓证明书"的定义

"宣誓证明书"是指公证人员声明，证明文件的签字人在公证人在场的情况下签署了该文件，并发誓或确认该文件中的陈述属实。

>> 240.004"公证行为"的定义

"公证行为"是指本州的公证人员经授权可实施的行为，包括：

    1. 作出确认书；

    2. 执行宣誓或确认；

    3. 证明文书副本；

    4. 执行宣誓证明书；

    5. 登记可转让票据的异议书；以及

    6. 执行某一特定法规规定的其他职责。

>> 240.005"公证办公人员"的定义

"公证办公人员"指公证人或被授权从事公证行为的官员。

>> 240.0055"公证记录"的定义

"公证记录"是指：

    1. 根据《内华达州修正法案》第240.120条规定，要求公证人做的日志；

    2. 根据《内华达州修正法案》第240.201条规定，要求电子公证人做的日志；

    3. 公证人或电子公证人为记录公证行为或执行电子公证行为而保留的文件或其他证据。

>> 240.006 已被废止

>> 240.0063"公证人"的定义

"公证人"是指由州务卿根据《内华达州修正法案》第240.010条的规定任命执行公证行为的人员。

>> 240.0065"人"的定义

"人"是指自然人。

>> 240.0067"州"的定义

"州"是指美国各州、哥伦比亚特区、波多黎各、美属维尔京群岛或任何受美国管辖的领域或岛屿。

>>240.007. Information and documents filed with or obtained by Secretary of State: Public examination; confidentiality; disclosure

1. Except as otherwise provided in subsections 2 and 3, information and documents filed with or obtained by the Secretary of State pursuant to NRS 240.001 to 240.206, inclusive, are public information and are available for public examination.

2. Information and documents filed with or obtained by the Secretary of State pursuant to or in accordance with subsection 3 of NRS 240.010 are not public information and are confidential.

3. Except as otherwise provided in subsections 4 and 5 and in NRS 239.0115, information and documents obtained by or filed with the Secretary of State in connection with an investigation concerning a possible violation of the provisions of NRS 240.001 to 240.206, inclusive, are not public information and are confidential.

4. The Secretary of State may submit any information or evidence obtained in connection with an investigation concerning a possible violation of the provisions of NRS 240.001 to 240.206, inclusive, to the appropriate district attorney for the purpose of prosecuting a criminal action.

5. The Secretary of State may disclose any information or documents obtained in connection with an investigation concerning a possible violation of the provisions of NRS 240.001 to 240.206, inclusive, to an agency of this State or a political subdivision of this State.

Appointment and Practice

>>240.010. Appointment by Secretary of State; cancellation of appointment; unlawful acts; injunctive relief

1. The Secretary of State may appoint notaries public in this State.

2. The Secretary of State shall not appoint as a notary public a person:

(a) Who submits an application containing a substantial and material misstatement or omission of fact.

(b) Whose previous appointment as a notary public in this State has been revoked.

(c) Who, except as otherwise provided in subsection 3, has been convicted of:

(1) A crime involving moral turpitude; or

(2) Burglary, conversion, embezzlement, extortion, forgery, fraud, identity theft, larceny, obtaining money under false pretenses, robbery or any other crime involving

>> 240.007 由州务卿存档或获取的资料和文件：公开审查；保密；披露

1. 除第 2 条和第 3 条另有规定外，州务卿根据《内华达州修正法案》第 240.001 条至第 240.206 条存档或取得的资料和文件均为公共信息，可供公众查阅。

2. 州务卿根据或按照《内华达州修正法案》第 240.010 条第 3 段提交或取得的资料和文件不是公共信息，应保密。

3. 除第 4 条、第 5 条和《内华达州修正法案》第 239.0115 条另有规定外，在调查可能违反《内华达州修正法案》第 240.001 条至第 240.206 条规定时，由州务卿获得或存档的资料和文件，都不是公共信息，应保密。

4. 州务卿可将任何涉嫌违反《内华达州修正法案》第 240.001 条至第 240.206 条的规定的调查资料或证据，送交适当的地方检察官，用于起诉犯罪行为。

5. 州务卿可披露任何涉嫌违反《内华达州修正法案》第 240.001 条至第 240.206 条的规定的调查资料或证据，送交该州的代理机构或该州的政治分部。

任命和执业

>> 240.010 州务卿任命；取消委任；不法行为；禁令救济

1. 州务卿有权任命本州的公证人。

2. 下列人员州务卿不得委任为公证人：

（a）提交含有重大实质性错报或遗漏事实的申请书的。

（b）曾经在本州被任命为公证人，但已被撤销的。

（c）除第 3 款另有规定外，已被裁定有以下犯罪的：

（1）涉及道德败坏的犯罪；或

（2）如果州务卿在作出任命之前知道其犯有：入室盗窃、兑换、盗用公款、勒索、伪造文书、诈骗、身份盗窃、盗窃、以虚假名义获取钱财、抢劫或其他

misappropriation of the identity or property of another person or entity, if the Secretary of State is aware of such a conviction before the Secretary of State makes the appointment.

(d) Against whom a complaint that alleges a violation of a provision of this chapter is pending.

(e) Who has not submitted to the Secretary of State proof satisfactory to the Secretary of State that the person has enrolled in and successfully completed a course of study provided pursuant to NRS 240.018.

3. A person who has been convicted of a crime involving moral turpitude may apply for appointment as a notary public if the person provides proof satisfactory to the Secretary of State that:

(a) More than 10 years have elapsed since the date of the person's release from confinement or the expiration of the period of his or her parole, probation or sentence, whichever is later;

(b) The person has made complete restitution for his or her crime involving moral turpitude, if applicable;

(c) The person possesses his or her civil rights; and

(d) The crime for which the person was convicted is not one of the crimes enumerated in subparagraph (2) of paragraph (c) of subsection 2.

4. A notary public may cancel his or her appointment by submitting a written notice to the Secretary of State.

5. It is unlawful for a person to:

(a) Represent himself or herself as a notary public appointed pursuant to this section if the person has not received a certificate of appointment from the Secretary of State pursuant to this chapter.

(b) Submit an application for appointment as a notary public that contains a substantial and material misstatement or omission of fact.

6. The Secretary of State may request that the Attorney General bring an action to enjoin any violation of paragraph (a) of subsection 5.

>>**240.015. General qualifications; expiration of appointment after termination of lawful admission for permanent residency in United States; conditions for appointment of resident of adjoining state**

1. Except as otherwise provided in this section, a person appointed as a notary public must:

(a) During the period of his or her appointment, be a citizen of the United States or lawfully admitted for permanent residency in the United States as verified by the

涉及盗用他人或机构的身份或财产的其他犯罪。

（d）存在违反本章规定的指控而未确定结果的。

（e）尚未向州务卿提交充分证据，证明该人已登记并顺利完成了根据《内华达州修正法案》第240.018条所规定的培训课程。

3. 被判定犯有道德败坏罪的人，如果该人提供了以下证据交州务卿采信，则可申请作为公证人的任命：

（a）自该人被释放或假释、缓刑或刑期届满之日起超过10年，以最晚者为准；

（b）如适用赔偿条款，该人已对其包括道德败坏在内的犯罪作出完全赔偿；

（c）该人拥有公民权利；以及

（d）该人被定罪的罪行不是第2款c项第2目所列举的罪行之一。

4. 公证人可向州务卿提交书面通知来取消其任命。

5. 以下行为是非法的：

（a）没有根据本章的规定从州务卿处获得任命证书，却按照本条的规定以公证人身份自居。

（b）提交的申请任命为公证人的申请书中存在实质重大的错报或遗漏事实。

6. 州务卿可要求总检察长提起诉讼，以禁止任何违反第5款a项的行为。

>> **240.015 一般资格；任期终止于在美国的合法永久居留权结束；毗邻州居民的任用条件**

1. 除本条另有规定外，获委任为公证人的人必须：

（a）在其任职期间，是美国公民或在美国拥有经美国公民和移民服务局核实的合法的永久居留权。

United States Citizenship and Immigration Services.

(b) Be a resident of this State.

(c) Be at least 18 years of age.

(d) Possess his or her civil rights.

2. If a person appointed as a notary public ceases to be lawfully admitted for permanent residency in the United States during his or her appointment, the person shall, within 90 days after his or her lawful admission has expired or is otherwise terminated, submit to the Secretary of State evidence that the person is lawfully readmitted for permanent residency as verified by the United States Citizenship and Immigration Services. If the person fails to submit such evidence within the prescribed time, the person's appointment expires by operation of law.

3. The Secretary of State may appoint a person who resides in an adjoining state as a notary public if the person:

(a) Maintains a place of business in the State of Nevada that is licensed pursuant to chapter 76 of NRS and any applicable business licensing requirements of the local government where the business is located; or

(b) Is regularly employed at an office, business or facility located within the State of Nevada by an employer licensed to do business in this State.

If such a person ceases to maintain a place of business in this State or regular employment at an office, business or facility located within this State, the Secretary of State may suspend the person's appointment. The Secretary of State may reinstate an appointment suspended pursuant to this subsection if the notary public submits to the Secretary of State, before his or her term of appointment as a notary public expires, the information required pursuant to subsection 2 of NRS 240.030.

>>240.017. Regulations of Secretary of State

The Secretary of State:

1. May adopt regulations:

(a) Prescribing the procedure for the appointment and mandatory training of a notary public.

(b) Establishing procedures for the notarization of digital or electronic signatures.

2. Shall adopt regulations prescribing the form of each affidavit required pursuant to subsection 2 of NRS 240.030.

>>240.018. Courses of study for mandatory training of notaries public; fees; persons required to enroll in and successfully complete course of study; Notary

（b）为该州居民。

（c）至少18周岁。

（d）享有公民权利。

2. 如果公证人的任期内，其在美国合法的永久居留权被终止，该人应在其合法居留期满或终止后90日内，向州务卿提交证据，证明其已经重新获得经美国公民资格和移民服务局核实的永久居留权。如该人未能在规定的时间内提交该证据，则该人的任命被依法终止。

3. 州务卿可任命居住在毗邻州的人为公证人，如果其满足下列条件：

（a）在内华达州内拥有营业地，即根据《内华达州修正法案》第76章获得营业许可，并符合该业务所在地政府对于任何营业执照的要求。

（b）长期受雇于内华达州的办事处、企业或机构中，且雇主拥有在该州的营业许可证。

如果该人停止在本州营业地的营业或停止在本州的办事处、企业或机构中的长期雇用，州务卿可暂停该人的任命。如果公证人在其任期届满前向州务卿提交了根据《内华达州修正法案》第240.030条第2款所要求的资料，则州务卿可恢复其被暂停的任命。

>> 240.017 州务卿规章

州务卿：

1. 有权制定规章：

（a）规定公证人的委任程序及强制培训。

（b）建立数字化公证或电子签名的程序。

2. 有权通过规章，规定根据《内华达州修正法案》第240.030条第2款所规定的每份誓章的格式。

>> 240.018 公证人强制性培训课程；费用；要求公证人注册并顺利完成培训；公证培训账户；超额收费的处置

Public Training Account; disposition of excess fees

1. The Secretary of State may:

(a) Provide courses of study for the mandatory training of notaries public. Such courses of study must include at least 4 hours of instruction relating to the functions and duties of notaries public.

(b) Charge a reasonable fee to each person who enrolls in a course of study for the mandatory training of notaries public.

2. A course of study provided pursuant to this section must comply with the regulations adopted pursuant to subsection 1 of NRS 240.017.

3. The following persons are required to enroll in and successfully complete a course of study provided pursuant to this section:

(a) A person applying for appointment as a notary public for the first time.

(b) A person renewing his or her appointment as a notary public, if the appointment has expired for a period greater than 1 year.

(c) A person renewing his or her appointment as a notary public, if during the immediately preceding 4 years the person has been fined for failing to comply with a statute or regulation of this State relating to notaries public.

A person who holds a current appointment as a notary public is not required to enroll in and successfully complete a course of study provided pursuant to this section if the person is in compliance with all of the statutes and regulations of this State relating to notaries public.

4. The Secretary of State shall deposit the fees collected pursuant to paragraph (b) of subsection 1 in the Notary Public Training Account which is hereby created in the State General Fund. The Account must be administered by the Secretary of State. Any interest and income earned on the money in the Account, after deducting any applicable charges, must be credited to the Account. Any money remaining in the Account at the end of a fiscal year does not revert to the State General Fund, and the balance in the Account must be carried forward. All claims against the Account must be paid as other claims against the State are paid. The money in the Account may be expended:

(a) To pay for expenses related to providing courses of study for the mandatory training of notaries public, including, without limitation, the rental of rooms and other facilities, advertising, travel and the printing and preparation of course materials; or

(b) For any other purpose authorized by the Legisla-

1. 州务卿有权：

（a）为公证人提供强制性培训的课程。此类培训课程必须包括至少 4 小时有关公证人的职能和职责的教导。

（b）向每名注册参与公证人强制性培训课程的人收取合理的费用。

2. 根据本条提供的培训课程，必须符合根据《内华达州修正法案》第 240.017 条第 1 款制定的规章。

3. 下列人员必须注册并顺利完成根据本条提供的培训课程：

（a）首次申请担任公证人的人。

（b）前项任命已届满超过 1 年而重新获得公证人任命的人；

（c）重新获得公证人任命的人，如果在随后的 4 年中因未遵守本州有关公证人的法规或规章而被处以罚金。

根据本条规定，如该人符合本条有关公证人的所有法律及条例，则其担任公证人无须注册和完成根据本节提供的培训课程。

4. 州务卿应将根据第 1 款 b 项所收取的费用存入由国家普通基金设立的公证培训账户。该帐户必须由州务卿管理。在扣除任何合理的费用后，在该账户上赚取的任何利息和收入必须记入帐户。在财政年度结算时，账户中剩余的任何款项都不会归还国家普通基金，账户余额必须结转。所有对该账户的索赔必须支付，因为其他针对州的索赔是有偿的。帐户中的钱可能会被支出用于：

（a）支付关于提供公证人强制性培训课程的费用，包括但不限于租用房间和其他设施、广告、差旅及印刷和准备课程材料等的费用；或

（b）为了立法机关授权的任何其他目的。

ture.

5. At the end of each fiscal year, the Secretary of State shall reconcile the amount of the fees collected pursuant to paragraph (b) of subsection 1 and the expenses related to administering the training of notaries public pursuant to this chapter and deposit any excess fees received with the State Treasurer for credit to the State General Fund.

>>240.020. Powers limited to areas within this State; term of office

A person appointed as a notary public pursuant to this chapter may perform notarial acts in any part of this state for a term of 4 years, unless sooner removed. Such an appointment does not authorize the person to perform notarial acts in another state.

>>240.030. Application for appointment; oath and bond; fingerprints; additional requirements for resident of adjoining state; commencement of term; fee for original, duplicate or amended certificate of appointment

1. Each person applying for appointment as a notary public must:

(a) At the time the applicant submits his or her application, pay to the Secretary of State $35.

(b) Take and subscribe to the oath set forth in Section 2 of Article 15 of the Constitution of the State of Nevada as if the applicant were a public officer.

(c) Submit to the Secretary of State proof satisfactory to the Secretary of State that the applicant has enrolled in and successfully completed a course of study provided pursuant to NRS 240.018.

(d) Enter into a bond to the State of Nevada in the sum of $10,000, to be filed with the clerk of the county in which the applicant resides or, if the applicant is a resident of an adjoining state, with the clerk of the county in this State in which the applicant maintains a place of business or is employed. The applicant must submit to the Secretary of State a certificate issued by the appropriate county clerk which indicates that the applicant filed the bond required pursuant to this paragraph.

(e) If required by the Secretary of State, submit:

(1) A complete set of the fingerprints of the applicant and written permission authorizing the Secretary of State to forward the fingerprints to the Central Repository for Nevada Records of Criminal History for submission to the Federal Bureau of Investigation for its report; and

5. 在每一个财政年度结算时，州务卿应保证根据第 1 款 b 项所收取的费用数额与根据本章规定的公证人培训的花费数额相一致，并将州司库收取的任何超额费用存入国家普通基金。

>> 240.020 限于本州范围内的权力；任职期限

依照本章规定被任命为公证人的人，除非被提前撤销，可以在本州的任何范围进行 4 年的公证行为。本任命不得授权其在另一州进行公证行为。

>> 240.030 申请任命；宣誓与保证金；指纹；对毗邻州居民的额外要求；任期的开始；正本、副本或经修订的委任证明书的费用

1. 申请公证人任命的人必须：

（a）在提交申请时，向州务卿支付 35 美元的费用。

（b）申请人应与公职人员一样接受并签署《内华达州宪法》第 15 条 2 款所载的宣誓。

（c）向州务卿提交充分证据，证明申请人已注册并顺利完成了根据《内华达州修正法案》第 240.018 条提供的培训课程。

（d）在内华达州，居民申请人需向所在郡的书记官提交 1 万美元的保证金，如果申请人是毗邻州的居民，则须向申请人营业地或被雇用地所在州的郡书记官提交。申请人必须向州务卿提交由适格的郡书记官出具的证明，表明申请人已根据本款的要求提交了保证金。

（e）根据州务卿的要求，需要提交；

（1）申请人的整套指纹和书面许可申请，州务卿有权将指纹提交中央存储库内的内华达犯罪史记录机构，由其提交给联邦调查局用于报告；以及

(2) A fee established by regulation of the Secretary of State which must not exceed the sum of the amounts charged by the Central Repository for Nevada Records of Criminal History and the Federal Bureau of Investigation for processing the fingerprints.

2. In addition to the requirements set forth in subsection 1, an applicant for appointment as a notary public who resides in an adjoining state must submit to the Secretary of State with the application:

(a) An affidavit setting forth the adjoining state in which the applicant resides, the applicant's mailing address and the address of the applicant's place of business or employment that is located within the State of Nevada;

(b) A copy of the applicant's state business license issued pursuant to chapter 76 of NRS and any business license required by the local government where the business is located, if the applicant is self-employed; and

(c) Unless the applicant is self-employed, a copy of the state business license of the applicant's employer, a copy of any business license of the applicant's employer that is required by the local government where the business is located and an affidavit from the applicant's employer setting forth the facts which show that the employer regularly employs the applicant at an office, business or facility which is located within the State of Nevada.

3. In completing an application, bond, oath or other document necessary to apply for appointment as a notary public, an applicant must not be required to disclose his or her residential address or telephone number on any such document which will become available to the public.

4. The bond, together with the oath, must be filed and recorded in the office of the county clerk of the county in which the applicant resides when the applicant applies for the appointment or, if the applicant is a resident of an adjoining state, with the clerk of the county in this State in which the applicant maintains a place of business or is employed. On a form provided by the Secretary of State, the county clerk shall immediately certify to the Secretary of State that the required bond and oath have been filed and recorded. Upon receipt of the application, fee and certification that the required bond and oath have been filed and recorded, the Secretary of State shall issue a certificate of appointment as a notary public to the applicant.

5. The term of a notary public commences on the effective date of the bond required pursuant to paragraph (d) of subsection 1. A notary public shall not perform a notarial act after the effective date of the bond unless the notary

（2）州务卿规定收取的费用，不得超过中央存储库的内华达犯罪史记录机构和联邦调查局处理指纹的费用的总和。

2. 除第 1 款规定的要求外，居住在毗邻州的申请公证人任命的申请人向州务卿提出申请时应附上下列材料：

（a）一份列明申请人所在的毗邻州、申请人的邮寄地址和申请人在内华达州境内的营业地或就业地址的宣誓书；

（b）如果申请人是自营职业者，需提交根据《内华达州修正法案》第 76 章签发的申请人居所州的营业执照副本以及该营业地的政府所要求的营业执照；

（c）申请人为非自营职业者时，需提交申请人雇主的州营业执照副本、申请人雇主的当地政府所要求的任何营业执照的复印件、申请人的雇主出具的宣誓书，阐明该人定期受雇于内华达州境内的公务或商业场所的事实。

3. 申请人在填写申请、保证金、宣誓书或其它申请任命公证人需要的文件时，无须在向公众公开的文件上披露其住址或电话号码。

4. 该保证金连同宣誓书，必须在申请人申请时的居所地的郡书记官的办公室中备案和记录，如果申请人是毗邻州的居民，则申请人须在其营业地或被雇用地的郡书记官处提交和登记。郡书记官应立即向州务卿证明所要求的保证金和宣誓书已被存档和记录在州务卿提供的表格中。在收到申请、费用和所要求的保证金和宣誓书已备案记录的证明后，州务卿应向申请人颁发公证人的委任证书。

5. 公证人的任期始于根据第 1 款 d 项所规定的保证金的生效日期。公证人不得在保证金生效之日起就执行公证行为，除非公证人已获得任职证书。

public has been issued a certificate of appointment.

6. Except as otherwise provided in this subsection, the Secretary of State shall charge a fee of $10 for each duplicate or amended certificate of appointment which is issued to a notary. If the notary public does not receive an original certificate of appointment, the Secretary of State shall provide a duplicate certificate of appointment without charge if the notary public requests such a duplicate within 60 days after the date on which the original certificate was issued.

>>240.031. Annual submission of copy of business license by resident of adjoining state

A notary public who is a resident of an adjoining state shall submit to the Secretary of State annually, within 30 days before the anniversary date of his or her appointment as a notary public, a copy of the state business license of the place of employment of the notary public in the State of Nevada issued pursuant to chapter 76 of NRS, a copy of any license required by the local government where the business is located and the information required pursuant to subsection 2 of NRS 240.030.

>>240.033. Requirements for bond; notification of exhaustion of penal sum; release of surety; suspension of appointment; reinstatement of appointment

1. The bond required to be filed pursuant to NRS 240.030 must be executed by the person applying to become a notary public as principal and by a surety company qualified and authorized to do business in this State. The bond must be made payable to the State of Nevada and be conditioned to provide indemnification to a person determined to have suffered damage as a result of an act by the notary public which violates a provision of NRS 240.001 to 240.169, inclusive. The surety company shall pay a final, nonappealable judgment of a court of this State that has jurisdiction, upon receipt of written notice of final judgment. The bond may be continuous but, regardless of the duration of the bond, the aggregate liability of the surety does not exceed the penal sum of the bond.

2. If the penal sum of the bond is exhausted, the surety company shall notify the Secretary of State in writing within 30 days after its exhaustion.

3. The surety bond must cover the period of the appointment of the notary public, except when a surety is released.

4. A surety on a bond filed pursuant to NRS 240.030 may be released after the surety gives 30 days' written

6. 除本款另有规定的外，州务卿在向公证人签发每份副本或经修订的任职证书时，应收取10美元的费用。如果公证人没有收到任职证书的原件，公证人可在签发证书原件之日起60日内提出给付副本的请求，州务卿应免费提供该任用证书的副本。

>> 240.031 毗邻州居民应每年提交营业执照副本

公证人为毗邻州居民的，每年应在任命的满周年日前30日内，向州务卿提交根据《内华达州修正法案》第76章颁发的内华达州公证人就业地州的营业执照副本和任何该营业地所在政府所要求的执照副本，以及根据《内华达州修正法案》第240.030条第2款所要求的资料。

>> 240.033 对保证金的要求；关于用尽罚金的通知；担保的免除；暂停任用；恢复任用

1. 根据《内华达州修正法案》第240.030条要求提交的保证金，必须由申请成为公证人的人作为当事人，并由有资质和被授权在本州营业的担保公司执行。该保证金必须支付给内华达州，并向被认定因公证人违反《内华达州修正法案》第240.001条至第240.169条的规定而遭受损害之人提供赔偿。担保公司在收到终审判决的书面通知后，应当向作出不可上诉的终审判决且具有管辖权的州法院支付赔偿金。保证金可以是连续的，但无论保证金的期限如何，担保人的总负债不得超过该保证金总额。

2. 如果保证金用尽，担保公司应在其用尽后30日内书面通知州务卿。

3. 保证金必须覆盖公证人的任命期限，除非担保机构不再进行担保。

4. 在担保人向州务卿和公证人发出30日的书面通知后，根据《内华达州修正法案》第240.030条提

notice to the Secretary of State and notary public, but the release does not discharge or otherwise affect a claim filed by a person for damage resulting from an act of the notary public which is alleged to have occurred while the bond was in effect.

5. The appointment of a notary public is suspended by operation of law when the notary public is no longer covered by a surety bond as required by this section and NRS 240.030 or the penal sum of the bond is exhausted. If the Secretary of State receives notice pursuant to subsection 4 that the bond will be released or pursuant to subsection 2 that the penal sum of the bond is exhausted, the Secretary of State shall immediately notify the notary public in writing that his or her appointment will be suspended by operation of law until another surety bond is filed in the same manner and amount as the bond being terminated.

6. The Secretary of State may reinstate the appointment of a notary public whose appointment has been suspended pursuant to subsection 5, if the notary public, before his or her current term of appointment expires:

(a) Submits to the Secretary of State:

(1) An application for an amended certificate of appointment as a notary public; and

(2) A certificate issued by the clerk of the county in which the applicant resides or, if the applicant is a resident of an adjoining state, the county in this State in which the applicant maintains a place of business or is employed, which indicates that the applicant filed a new surety bond with the clerk.

(b) Pays to the Secretary of State a fee of $10.

>>240.036. Amended certificate of appointment: Required for certain changes in information; suspension for failure to obtain; fee; issuance

1. If, at any time during his or her appointment, a notary public changes his or her mailing address, county of residence or signature or, if the notary public is a resident of an adjoining state, changes his or her place of business or employment, the notary public shall submit to the Secretary of State a request for an amended certificate of appointment on a form provided by the Secretary of State. The request must:

(a) Include the new information;

(b) Be submitted within 30 days after making that change; and

(c) Be accompanied by a fee of $10.

2. The Secretary of State may suspend the appoint-

交保证金的担保人不再进行担保，但并不解除或以其他方式影响受害人在该保证金生效期间因公证人的行为而受到损害的索赔。

5. 当公证人不在被本节和《内华达州修正法案》第 240.030 条要求的保证金担保或保证金用尽时，应依法暂停对公证人任命。如州务卿收到根据第 4 款发出的通知，则该担保机构解除担保，或根据第 2 款该保证金已经用尽，州务卿应立即以书面形式通知公证人，其任命已依法被暂停，直到其以相同的方式再次提交等额的保证金。

6. 如果公证人在其现任任期届满之前，根据第 5 款被暂停职务，存在下列情形的，州务卿可恢复其公证人的任命：

（a）向州务卿提交：

（1）要求获得公证人任命的修订证书的申请书；以及

（2）申请人居住地的郡书记官出具的证书，如果申请人是毗邻州的居民，则由申请人在该州营业地或工作地的郡书记官出具证书，表明申请人向书记官提交了新的保证金。

（b）向州务卿支付 10 美元的费用。

>> 240.036 修订的任命证书：对某些信息变化的请求；未取得而中止；费用；签发

1. 如果在任期的任何时间，本州公证人更改其邮寄地址、居住地址或签名，或公证人毗邻州的居民，更改其营业地或工作地点，公证人应向州务卿请求发出修订的任命证书。该请求必须满足以下条件：

（a）列入新的信息；

（b）在作出该项更改后 30 日内提交；以及

（c）提交 10 美元的费用。

2. 对不提供第 1 款所列任何信息的变更通知的公

ment of a notary public who fails to provide to the Secretary of State notice of a change in any of the information specified in subsection 1.

3. If a notary public changes his or her name during his or her appointment and the notary public intends to use his or her new name in the performance of notarial duties, the notary public shall submit to the Secretary of State a request for an amended certificate of appointment on a form provided by the Secretary of State. The request must:

(a) Include the new name and signature and the address of the notary public;

(b) Be submitted within 30 days after making the change; and

(c) Be accompanied by a fee of $10.

4. Upon receipt of a request for an amended certificate of appointment and the appropriate fee, the Secretary of State shall issue an amended certificate of appointment.

5. When the notary public receives the amended certificate of appointment, the notary public shall:

(a) Destroy his or her notary's stamp and obtain a new notary's stamp which includes the information on the amended certificate.

(b) Notify the surety company which issued his or her bond of the changes.

>>240.040. Use of stamp; embossed notarial seal not required; requirements of stamp; storage of stamp

1. The statement required by paragraph (d) of subsection 1 of NRS 240.1655 must:

(a) Be imprinted in indelible, photographically reproducible ink with a rubber or other mechanical stamp; and

(b) Set forth:

(1) The name of the notary public;

(2) The phrase "Notary Public, State of Nevada";

(3) The date on which the appointment of the notary public expires;

(4) The number of the certificate of appointment of the notary public;

(5) If the notary public so desires, the Great Seal of the State of Nevada; and

(6) If the notary public is a resident of an adjoining state, the word "nonresident."

2. After July 1, 1965, an embossed notarial seal is not required on notarized documents.

3. The stamp required pursuant to subsection 1 must:

(a) Be a rectangle, not larger than 1 inch by 2 1/2 inches, and may contain a border design; and

证人，州务卿可暂停其任命。

3. 如果公证人在其任用期间变更姓名，并希望履行公证职责时使用其新姓名，则公证人应向州务卿请求获得修订后的任用证书。该请求必须：

（a）包括新的名称和签名以及公证人的地址；

（b）在作出变更后30日内提交；以及

（c）提交10美元的费用。

4. 在收到对变更的任用证书的请求和适当费用后，州务卿应签发修订后的任用证书。

5. 公证人收到修订的任用证书后，应当：

（a）销毁该公证人公章，并取得公证人的新公章，其中包括修订的证书中的信息。

（b）将上述变更通知为该公证人提供保证金的担保公司。

>> 240.040 印章的使用；不需要浮雕公证印章；印章的要求；印章的保存

1.《内华达州修正法案》240.1655条第1款d项规定的印章必须符合以下要求：

（a）用橡胶或其他机械印章印上不可磨灭、逼真的可复制的印记；并且

（b）列明：

（1）公证人的名字；

（2）"内华达州公证人"一词；

（3）公证人的任期届满日；

（4）公证人的任用证书数量；

（5）内华达州的公章印（如果公证人想要）；以及

（6）如果公证人是毗邻州的居民，附上"非居民"一词。

2. 1965年7月1日以后，在公证文件上不需要加盖有浮雕的公证印章。

3. 第1款所要求的印章必须满足以下条件：

（a）宽、长分别不大于1英寸和2.5英寸的矩形，并可包含边缘设计；

(b) Produce a legible imprint.

4. A notary public shall not affix his or her stamp over printed material.

5. A notary public shall keep his or her stamp in a secure location during any period in which the notary public is not using the stamp to perform a notarial act.

6. As used in this section, "mechanical stamp" includes an imprint made by a computer or other similar technology.

>>**240.045. Replacement of lost or inoperable stamp; prerequisite to production of stamp**

1. If the stamp of a notary public is lost, the notary public shall, within 10 days after the stamp is lost, submit to the Secretary of State a request for an amended certificate of appointment, on a form provided by the Secretary of State, and obtain a new stamp in accordance with NRS 240.036. The request must be accompanied by a fee of $10.

2. If the stamp is destroyed, broken, damaged or otherwise rendered inoperable, the notary public shall immediately notify the Secretary of State of that fact and obtain a new stamp.

3. A person or governmental entity shall not make, manufacture or otherwise produce a notary's stamp unless the notary public presents his or her original or amended certificate of appointment or a certified copy of his or her original or amended certificate of appointment to that person or governmental entity.

>>**240.051. Actions required upon resignation or death of notary public**

1. If a notary public resigns or dies during his or her appointment, the notary public, or the executor of the estate of the notary public, as appropriate, shall:

(a) Notify the Secretary of State of the resignation or death; and

(b) Destroy the notary's stamp.

2. Upon the receipt of the notice required by subsection 1, the Secretary of State shall cancel the appointment of the notary public, effective on the date on which the notice was received.

>>**240.060. Powers of notary public**

A notary public may, during normal business hours, perform notarial acts in lawful transactions for a person who requests the act and tenders the appropriate fee.

>>**240.061. Performance of authorized notarial**

（b）可印制清晰的印记。

4. 公证人不得在印刷材料上加盖印章。

5. 公证人在其未使用印章执行公证行为的任何期间，应将其印章存放在安全地点。

6. 如本节所指，"机械印记"包括由计算机或其它类似技术制成的印记。

>> **240.045 更换遗失或不实用的印章；制造印章的首要条件**

1. 如果公证人的印章遗失，公证人应当在遗失后10日内，向州务卿提交请求，申请由州务卿提供修订版任命证书，并按照《内华达州修正法案》第240.036条的规定取得新的印章。这项请求必须附有10美元的费用。

2. 如果印章被毁坏、破损、损坏或因其他原因无法操作，公证人应立即将该事实通知州务卿并取得新的印章。

3. 个人或政府机构不得制作、制造或以其他方式生产公证人印章，除非公证人向个人或政府实体出示其任命证书的正本或修订本，或正本或修订本的副本。

>> **240.051 公证人辞职或死亡时所需采取的措施**

1. 如果公证人在其任职期间辞职或死亡，公证人或公证人遗产的执行者应：

（a）将辞职或死亡的情况通知州务卿；以及

（b）销毁公证人的印章。

2. 在收到第1款规定的通知后，州务卿应撤销公证人的任命，该撤销在接到通知之日起生效。

>> **240.060 公证人的权力**

公证人可以在正常的营业时间内，为请求人的个人合法交易进行公证，并收取适当的费用。

>> **240.061 授权公证行为的执行；限制性公证**

acts; restricted notarial acts

1. A notarial officer may perform a notarial act authorized by NRS 240.001 to 240.169, inclusive, or by law of this State other than NRS 240.001 to 240.169 , inclusive.

2. A notarial officer other than a notary public may not perform a notarial act with respect to a document to which the officer or the officer's spouse or domestic partner is a party, or in which either of them has a direct beneficial interest. A notary public may not perform a notarial act if the notarial act is prohibited by NRS 240.001 to 240.169, inclusive. A notarial act performed in violation of this subsection is voidable.

>>240.062. Personal knowledge of identity

For the purposes of NRS 240.001 to 240.169, inclusive, a notarial officer has personal knowledge of the identity of a person appearing before the officer if the person is personally known to the officer through dealings sufficient to provide reasonable certainty that the person has the identity claimed.

>>240.063. Evidentiary effect of signature; limitations on evidentiary effect of certification of documents

1. The signature of a notary public on a document shall be deemed to be evidence only that the notary public knows the contents of the document that constitute the signature, execution, acknowledgment, oath, affirmation or affidavit.

2. When a notary public certifies that a document is a certified or true copy of an original document, the certification shall not be deemed to be evidence that the notary public knows the contents of the document.

>>240.065. Restrictions on powers of notary public; exception

1. A notary public may not perform a notarial act if:

(a) The notary public executed or is named in the instrument acknowledged, sworn to or witnessed or attested;

(b) Except as otherwise provided in subsection 2, the notary public has or will receive directly from a transaction relating to the instrument or pleading a commission, fee, advantage, right, title, interest, property or other consideration in excess of the fee authorized pursuant to NRS 240.100 for the notarial act;

(c) The notary public and the person whose signature is to be acknowledged, sworn to or witnessed or attested are domestic partners; or

行为

1. 公证人可执行由《内华达州修正法案》第240.001条至第240.169条或由本州法律（除《内华达州修正法案》第240.001条至第240.169条）授权的公证行为。

2. 公证人以外的公证处官员不得对与自己或自己的配偶或家庭伴侣的一方有直接利益关系的文件进行公证。公证人不得执行《内华达州修正法案》第240.001条至第240.169条禁止的公证行为。违反本条执行的公证行为是无效的。

>> 240.062 以个人认识作为身份证明

在《内华达州修正法案》第240.001条至第240.169条中，如果该人通过交易个人认识公证人，则公证人可以认为其个人认识出现在其面前之人，就足以为该人所主张的身份提供合理的证据。

>> 240.063 签字的证据效力；文件认证的证据效力之局限

1. 公证人在文件上的签字应仅被视为公证人知悉文件内容的证据，文件内容包括签字、执行、确认书、宣誓书、证词或誓章。

2. 当公证人证明一份文件是已经过认证或是原件的真实副本时，该证明不得视为公证人知悉该文件内容的证据。

>> 240.065 对公证人权力的限制；例外

1. 公证人不得执行下列公证行为：

（a）由公证人执行或签署、宣誓、作证或认证的文书；

（b）除第2款另有规定外，公证人直接从与该文书有关的交易中收取的佣金、费用、利益、权利、所有权、利息、财产或其他费用超过了公证法《内华达州修正法案》第240.100条的规定；

（c）由公证人及其家庭伴侣签名的确认、宣誓、作证或认证的文书；或者

(d) The person whose signature is to be acknowledged, sworn to or witnessed or attested is a relative of the domestic partner of the notary public or a relative of the notary public by marriage or consanguinity.

2. A notary public who is an attorney licensed to practice law in this State may perform a notarial act on an instrument or pleading if the notary public has or will receive directly from a transaction relating to the instrument or pleading a fee for providing legal services in excess of the fee authorized pursuant to NRS 240.100 for the notarial act.

3. As used in this section, "relative" includes, without limitation:

(a) A spouse or domestic partner, parent, grandparent or stepparent;

(b) A natural born child, stepchild or adopted child;

(c) A grandchild, brother, sister, half brother, half sister, stepbrother or stepsister;

(d) A grandparent, parent, brother, sister, half brother, half sister, stepbrother or stepsister of the spouse or domestic partner of the notary public; and

(e) A natural born child, stepchild or adopted child of a sibling or half sibling of the notary public or of a sibling or half sibling of the spouse or domestic partner of the notary public.

\>\>240.069. Repealed

\>\>240.075. Prohibited acts

A notary public shall not:

1. Influence a person to enter or not enter into a lawful transaction involving a notarial act performed by the notary public.

2. Certify an instrument containing a statement known by the notary public to be false.

3. Perform any act as a notary public with intent to deceive or defraud, including, without limitation, altering the journal that the notary public is required to keep pursuant to NRS 240.120.

4. Endorse or promote any product, service or offering if his or her appointment as a notary public is used in the endorsement or promotional statement.

5. Certify photocopies of a certificate of birth, death or marriage or a divorce decree.

6. Allow any other person to use his or her notary's stamp.

7. Allow any other person to sign the notary's name in a notarial capacity.

（d）与公证人有姻亲或血缘关系的亲属签名的确认、宣誓、作证或认证的文书。

2. 如果公证人是在本州执业的律师，对文书或诉状进行公证时，有权在直接从与该文书有关的交易或提供法律服务的公证行为中收取超过《内华达州修正法案》第240.100条规定的费用。

3. 本条中，"亲属"的含义包括但不限于：

（a）配偶或家庭伴侣、父母、祖父母或继父母；

（b）亲生子女、继子女或养子女；

（c）孙子、兄弟、姐妹、同父异母或同母异父的兄弟姐妹、继兄弟姐妹；

（d）公证人及其配偶或家庭伴侣的祖父母、父母、兄弟、姐妹、同父异母或同母异父的兄弟姐妹、继兄弟姊妹；以及

（e）公证人或其配偶或其家庭伴侣的同父异母或同母异父的姊妹的亲生子女、继子女或养子女。

\>\> 240.069 已废止

\>\> 240.075 禁止的行为

公证人不得：

1. 影响任何人参与或不参与与公证人所执行的公证行为有关的合法交易。

2. 认证公证人明知包含虚假声明的文书。

3. 执行任何包括但不限于意图欺骗或诈骗的行为，对根据《内华达州修正法案》第240.120条要求公证人保存的日志进行修改。

4. 在代言或促销声明中以公证人身份出现，进行认可或推广任何产品、服务或要约。

5. 公证出生证、死亡证或结婚证、离婚判决书的影印本。

6. 允许他人使用公证人的公章。

7. 允许他人以公证人身份签署其姓名。

8. Perform a notarial act on a document that contains only a signature.

9. Perform a notarial act on a document, including a form that requires the signer to provide information within blank spaces, unless the document has been filled out completely and has been signed.

10. Make or note a protest of a negotiable instrument unless the notary public is employed by a depository institution and the protest is made or noted within the scope of that employment. As used in this subsection, "depository institution" has the meaning ascribed to it in NRS 657.037.

>>240.085. Advertisements in language other than English to contain notice if notary public is not an attorney; penalties

1. Every notary public who is not an attorney licensed to practice law in this State and who advertises his or her services as a notary public in a language other than English by any form of communication, except a single plaque on his or her desk, shall post or otherwise include with the advertisement a notice in the language in which the advertisement appears. The notice must be of a conspicuous size, if in writing, and must appear in substantially the following form:

I AM NOT AN ATTORNEY IN THE STATE OF NEVADA. I AM NOT LICENSED TO GIVE LEGAL ADVICE. I MAY NOT ACCEPT FEES FOR GIVING LEGAL ADVICE.

2. A notary public who is not an attorney licensed to practice law in this State shall not use the term "notario," "notario publico" or any other equivalent non-English term in any form of communication that advertises his or her services as a notary public, including, without limitation, a business card, stationery, notice and sign.

3. If the Secretary of State finds a notary public guilty of violating the provisions of subsection 1 or 2, the Secretary of State shall:

(a) Suspend the appointment of the notary public for not less than 1 year.

(b) Revoke the appointment of the notary public for a third or subsequent offense.

4. A notary public who is found guilty in a criminal prosecution of violating subsection 1 or 2 shall be punished by a fine of not more than $2,000.

>>240.100. Fees for services; additional fees for travel expenses; notarial acts performed within and outside scope of employment

8. 对仅包含签名的文件进行公证。

9. 对要求签名人在空白处填写信息的文件（包括表格）执行公证，除非该文件已填写完整并署名。

10. 制作或登记可转让票据的异议，除非公证人受雇于某一储蓄机构，并在其雇佣范围内提出或登记异议。在本条中的"储蓄机构"，与《内华达州修正法案》第657.037条中所的含义一致。

>> 240.085 非律师公证人在以英文以外的其他语言进行宣传时应包含提示；处罚

1. 每一位不是本州执业律师的公证人，在以英语以外的语言通过任何除单张桌牌外的方式宣传其作为公证人的服务时应作出提示，还应以该语言进行公告或在宣传广告中进行提示。如果是书面形式，公告须采用引人注目的字号，并基本遵循以下格式：

我不是内华达州的律师，无权提供法律意见，也不接受提供法律咨询的费用。

2. 非本州执业律师的公证人，不得在任何通讯方式中，包括但不限于商业名片、信纸、提示和标志中使用"notario""notario publico"或任何其他类似的非英语词汇，来宣传其作为公证人的服务。

3. 如果州务卿认为公证人违反第1款或第2款的规定，州务卿应：

（a）暂停公证人的任命不少于1年。

（b）三次或三次以上违反规定应撤销公证人的任命。

4. 对违反第1款或第2款的规定而受到刑事指控的公证人，将被处以2000美元以下的罚款。

>> 240.100 服务费；差旅支出的附加费用；在受雇范围内外进行的公证行为

1. Except as otherwise provided in subsection 3, a notary public may charge the following fees and no more: ($)

For taking an acknowledgment, for the first signature of each signer (5.00)

For each additional signature of each signer (2.50)

For administering an oath or affirmation without a signature (2.50)

For a certified copy (2.50)

For a jurat, for each signature on the affidavit (5.00)

For performing a marriage ceremony (75.00)

2. All fees prescribed in this section are payable in advance, if demanded.

3. A notary public may charge an additional fee for traveling to perform a notarial act if:

(a) The person requesting the notarial act asks the notary public to travel;

(b) The notary public explains to the person requesting the notarial act that the fee is in addition to the fee authorized in subsection 1 and is not required by law;

(c) The person requesting the notarial act agrees in advance upon the hourly rate that the notary public will charge for the additional fee; and

(d) The additional fee does not exceed:

(1) If the person requesting the notarial act asks the notary public to travel between the hours of 6 a.m. and 7 p.m., $10 per hour.

(2) If the person requesting the notarial act asks the notary public to travel between the hours of 7 p.m. and 6 a.m., $25 per hour.

The notary public may charge a minimum of 2 hours for such travel and shall charge on a pro rata basis after the first 2 hours.

4. A notary public is entitled to charge the amount of the additional fee agreed to in advance by the person requesting the notarial act pursuant to subsection 3 if:

(a) The person requesting the notarial act cancels the request after the notary public begins his or her travel to perform the requested notarial act.

(b) The notary public is unable to perform the requested notarial act as a result of the actions of the person who requested the notarial act or any other person who is necessary for the performance of the notarial act.

5. For each additional fee that a notary public charges for traveling to perform a notarial act pursuant to subsec-

1. 除第 3 款另有规定外，公证人有权在规定的范围内收取以下费用：（单位：美元）

为每个签名者的首次签名作出确认书（5.00）

为每个签名者附加签字（2.50）

在没有签名的情况下进行宣誓（2.50）

认证副本（2.50）

在每份宣誓证明书、誓章上签字（5.00）

为婚庆典礼进行公证（75.00）

2. 如有需要，本节所规定的所有费用均须预先缴付。

3. 公证人可以收取为执行公证行为产生的额外差旅费用，如果：

（a）公证请求人要求公证人出差；

（b）公证人向公证请求人阐明，该费用是第 1 条授权的费用之外的附加费用，法律并无强制要求。

（c）公证请求人事先同意公证人收取额外的计时费用；以及

（d）额外费用不超过：

（1）如果公证请求人要求公证人在早上 6 点至下午 7 点之间出差，每小时 10 美元。

（2）如果公证请求人要求公证人在下午 7 点至凌晨 6 点之间出差，每小时 25 美元。

公证人可收取最少 2 小时的差旅费，并须在首个 2 小时后按比例收取费用。

4. 在下列情形下，得到公证请求人的事先同意后，公证人有权收取根据第 3 款规定的额外费用：

（a）公证请求人在公证人开始为执行公证行为出差后取消了请求。

（b）由于公证请求人或执行公证行为所必需的任何其他人的行为导致公证人无法执行所要求的公证行为。

5. 公证人根据第 3 款规定，为执行公证行为出差而收取的额外费用，应依据《内华达州修正法案》第

tion 3, the notary public shall enter in the journal that he or she keeps pursuant to NRS 240.120:

(a) The amount of the fee; and

(b) The date and time that the notary public began and ended such travel.

6. A person who employs a notary public may prohibit the notary public from charging a fee for a notarial act that the notary public performs within the scope of the employment. Such a person shall not require the notary public whom the person employs to surrender to the person all or part of a fee charged by the notary public for a notarial act performed outside the scope of the employment of the notary public.

>>240.110. Posting of table of fees

If a notary public charges fees for performing notarial acts, the notary public shall publish and set up in some conspicuous place in his or her office a table of those fees, according to this chapter, for the inspection of all persons who have business in his or her office. The schedule must not be printed in smaller than 1/2-inch type. A notary public shall not charge fees unless the notary public has published and set up a table of fees in accordance with this subsection.

>>240.120. Journal of notarial acts: Duty to maintain; contents; verification based upon credible witness; copy of entry; storage; period of retention; report of loss or theft; exceptions

1. Except as otherwise provided in subsection 2, each notary public shall keep a journal in his or her office in which the notary public shall enter for each notarial act performed, at the time the act is performed:

(a) The fees charged, if any;

(b) The title of the document;

(c) The date on which the notary public performed the act;

(d) Except as otherwise provided in subsection 3, the name and signature of the person whose signature is being notarized;

(e) Subject to the provisions of subsection 4, a description of the evidence used by the notary public to verify the identification of the person whose signature is being notarized;

(f) An indication of whether the notary public administered an oath; and

(g) The type of certificate used to evidence the notarial act, as required pursuant to NRS 240.1655.

240.120 条的要求在其保管的日志中记录以下内容：

（a）费用的数额；以及

（b）公证人开始和结束出差的日期和时间。

6. 雇用公证人的人可禁止公证人在其受雇范围内收取执行公证行为的费用。该人不得要求该被雇佣的公证人向其交出全部或部分在受雇范围外执行公证行为收取的费用。

>> 240.110 费用表的公示

公证人对执行公证行为收取费用的，应当按照本章的规定，在其办公室的显眼处公布、张贴费用表，供所有在其办公室办理业务的人员查阅。该表不得以小于 1/2 英寸的尺寸打印。在未根据本款公布并设置收费表的情形下，公证人不得收取费用。

>> 240.120 公证行为日志；保管义务；内容；基于可信证人的确认；入境副本；存储；保留期；丢失或盗窃的汇报；例外

1. 除第 2 款另有规定外，每位公证人将要或正在执行公证行为时，须在其办公室内备存一份日志并记录以下信息：

（a）收取的费用（如果有）；

（b）该文件的标题；

（c）公证人执行公证行为的日期；

（d）除第 3 款另有规定外，其被公证之人的姓名和签名；

（e）在符合第 4 款规定的情况下，对公证人使用的证据进行说明，以核实其签名正在被公证之人的身份；

（f）公证人是否履行了宣誓的程序；以及

（g）根据《内华达州修正法案》第 240.1655 条的要求，用于证明公证行为的证书类型。

2. A notary public may make one entry in the journal which documents more than one notarial act if the notarial acts documented are performed:

(a) For the same person and at the same time; and

(b) On one document or on similar documents.

3. When performing a notarial act for a person, a notary public need not require the person to sign the journal if:

(a) The notary public has performed a notarial act for the person within the previous 6 months;

(b) The notary public has personal knowledge of the identity of the person; and

(c) The person is an employer or coworker of the notary public and the notarial act relates to a transaction performed in the ordinary course of the person's business.

4. If, pursuant to subsection 3, a notary public does not require a person to sign the journal, the notary public shall enter "known personally" as the description required to be entered into the journal pursuant to paragraph (e) of subsection 1.

5. If the notary verifies the identification of the person whose signature is being notarized on the basis of a credible witness, the notary public shall:

(a) Require the witness to sign the journal in the space provided for the description of the evidence used; and

(b) Make a notation in the journal that the witness is a credible witness.

6. The journal must:

(a) Be open to public inspection.

(b) Be in a bound volume with preprinted page numbers.

7. A notary public shall, upon request and payment of the fee set forth in NRS 240.100, provide a certified copy of an entry in his or her journal.

8. A notary public shall keep his or her journal in a secure location during any period in which the notary public is not making an entry or notation in the journal pursuant to this section.

9. A notary public shall retain each journal that the notary public has kept pursuant to this section until 7 years after the date on which he or she ceases to be a notary public.

10. A notary public shall file a report with the Secretary of State and the appropriate law enforcement agency if the journal of the notary public is lost or stolen.

11. The provisions of this section do not apply to a

2. 公证人可将多个公证行为在日志中作一项记载，如果该公证行为满足以下要求：

（a）为同一人在同一时间作出；以及

（b）同一文件或类似文件。

3. 在为某人执行公证行为时，公证人无须要求该人签署该日志，如果：

（a）公证人在过去6个月内为该人执行了公证行为；

（b）公证人个人了解该人的身份；以及

（c）该人是公证人的雇主或同事，而公证行为涉及该人在正常业务过程中进行的交易。

4. 如果根据第3款的规定，公证人不要求任何人签署该公证人日志，则公证人须按照第1款e项的规定，在日志中以"个人了解"的描述记载有关人员。

5. 如果公证人在可信证人的基础上对其签名正在进行公证的人员进行身份核实，公证人应：

（a）要求证人在公证人日志中的证据说明处签名；以及

（b）在日志中标记该证人是可信证人。

6. 公证人日志必须：

（a）接受公众查阅；

（b）装订成册并预先打印页码。

7. 对要求提供公证人日志中的部分条目的核证副本的请求，公证人有权要求其支付《内华达州修正法案》第240.100条所列明的费用。

8. 根据本条的规定，公证人在不做登记和记录的期间内，应将其日志保存在安全地点。

9. 根据本条的规定，公证人须保留其备存的每份日志，直至不再担任公证人之日起7年为止。

10. 如果公证人的日志遗失或被盗，公证人应向州务卿和适格的执法机构提交报告。

11. 本条不适用于根据《内华达州修正法案》第

person who is authorized to perform a notarial act pursuant to paragraph (b), (c), (d) or (e) of subsection 1 of NRS 240.1635.

>>240.130. Only authorized fees to be charged

A notary public shall not charge a fee to perform a service unless the notary public is authorized to charge a fee for such a service pursuant to this chapter.

>>240.143. Unlawful possession of certain personal property of notary public

1. The following items are the personal property of a notary public:

(a) His or her official stamp;

(b) His or her journal; and

(c) His or her certificate of appointment.

2. It is unlawful for a person who comes into possession of the official stamp, journal or certificate of appointment of a notary public to withhold such an item from the notary public, whether or not the person provided the notary public with the money to acquire the item.

>>240.145. Unlawful reproduction or use of completed notarial certificate; penalty

1. It is unlawful for any person to:

(a) Photocopy or otherwise reproduce a completed notarial certificate with a notary's statement and signature if that certificate is reproduced for use in a mailing to endorse, promote or sell any product, service or offering; or

(b) Include a photocopy or other reproduction of a completed notarial certificate with a notary's statement and signature in a mailing to endorse, promote or sell any product, service or offering.

2. Any person who violates any of the provisions of subsection 1 is guilty of a gross misdemeanor.

>>240.147. Unlawful destruction, defacement or concealment of notarial record

It is unlawful for a person to knowingly destroy, deface or conceal a notarial record.

>>240.150. Liability for misconduct or neglect; liability of employer; penalties for willful violation or neglect of duty; procedure upon revocation or suspension

1. For misconduct or neglect in a case in which a notary public appointed pursuant to the authority of this State may act, either by the law of this State or of another state, territory or country, or by the law of nations, or by commercial usage, the notary public is liable on his or her

240.1635 条第 1 款 b 项、c 项、d 项或 e 项获授权执行公证行为的人。

>> 240.130 只收取授权的费用

公证人提供服务不得收取本章授权收取的服务费之外的费用。

>> 240.143 非法持有公证人的私人财产

1.下列项目是公证人的个人财产：

（a）他或她的公证公章；

（b）他或她的公证人日志；以及

（c）他或她的委任证书。

2.任何人如果从公证人处获得公证人的公证公章、日志或委任证书等物品，无论是否向公证人支付金钱以取得该物品，均属违法行为。

>> 240.145 非法复制或使用已完成的公证证书；处罚

1.下列行为属于非法行为：

（a）复印或以其他方式复制已完成的附公证人声明和签名的公证文书，如果该证书被复制后，在邮件中用于宣传、推广或销售任何产品、服务或要约的；或者

（b）将已完成的附有公证人声明和签名的公证书的影印件或其他复制品，在邮件中用于宣传、推广或销售任何产品、服务或要约的。

2.任何人违反第 1 款的规定，即构成轻罪。

>> 240.147 非法破坏、污损或隐瞒公证记录

任何人明知而毁坏、污损或隐瞒公证记录，即属违行为法。

>> 240.150 不当行为或疏忽的责任；雇主责任；故意违反或玩忽职守的处罚；撤销或中止任命的程序

1.依据本州授权任命的公证人存在不当行为或疏忽，公证人应根据本州或另一州、某一地区或国家的法律，或根据商业惯例，通过其职务保证金对受损害的当事人承担赔偿责任。

official bond to the parties injured thereby, for all the damages sustained.

2. The employer of a notary public may be assessed a civil penalty by the Secretary of State of not more than $2,000 for each violation specified in subsection 4 committed by the notary public, and the employer is liable for any damages proximately caused by the misconduct of the notary public, if:

(a) The notary public was acting within the scope of his or her employment at the time the notary public engaged in the misconduct; and

(b) The employer of the notary public consented to the misconduct of the notary public.

3. The Secretary of State may refuse to appoint or may suspend or revoke the appointment of a notary public who fails to provide to the Secretary of State, within a reasonable time, information that the Secretary of State requests from the notary public in connection with a complaint which alleges a violation of this chapter.

4. Except as otherwise provided in this chapter, for any willful violation or neglect of duty or other violation of this chapter, or upon proof that a notary public has been convicted of a crime described in paragraph (c) of subsection 2 of NRS 240.010:

(a) The appointment of the notary public may be suspended for a period determined by the Secretary of State, but not exceeding the time remaining on the appointment;

(b) The appointment of the notary public may be revoked after a hearing; or

(c) The notary public may be assessed a civil penalty of not more than $2,000 for each violation.

5. If the Secretary of State revokes or suspends the appointment of a notary public pursuant to this section, the Secretary of State shall:

(a) Notify the notary public in writing of the revocation or suspension;

(b) Cause notice of the revocation or suspension to be published on the website of the Secretary of State; and

(c) If a county clerk has issued a certificate of permission to perform marriages to the notary public pursuant to NRS 122.064, notify the county clerk of the revocation or suspension.

6. Except as otherwise provided by law, the Secretary of State may assess the civil penalty that is authorized pursuant to this section upon a notary public whose appointment has expired if the notary public committed the violation that justifies the civil penalty before his or her

2. 如果公证人的行为违反第4款的规定，由州务卿对公证人的雇主处以不超过2000美元的民事处罚，并且如果存在以下情形，雇主对公证人的不当行为造成的任何损害直接负责：

（a）公证人在其受雇范围内从事不当行为；以及

（b）雇主认同公证人的不当行为。

3. 如果公证人在合理时间内未向州务卿提供其要求的有关公证人违反本章规定的投诉的有关资料，州务卿可拒绝、中止或撤销公证人任命。

4. 除本章另有规定外，对任何故意违反、玩忽职守或其他违反本章的行为，或公证人已被裁定犯有《内华达州修正法案》第240.010条第2款c项所述罪行的情况下：

（a）可由州务卿决定暂停公证人任命的期间，但不得超过剩余的任用时间；

（b）公证人的任命可在听证后撤销；或

（c）对每项违规行为，可对公证人处以不超过2000美元的民事处罚。

5. 如果州务卿根据本条撤销或暂停公证人的任命，州务卿应：

（a）书面通知公证人撤销或中止的决定；

（b）撤销或暂停的决定应在州务卿的网站上公布，以进行公示；以及

（c）如果郡书记官根据《内华达州修正法案》第122.064条已向公证人签发了公证婚姻事宜的许可证书，则通知郡书记官撤销或暂停上述许可证。

6. 除法律另有规定外，如果公证人在其任命期满前因违规被判处民事处罚，则州务卿可按照根据本条规定的对任命期已届满的公证人的该民事处罚进行评估。

appointment expired.

7. The appointment of a notary public may be suspended or revoked by the Secretary of State pending a hearing if the Secretary of State believes it is in the public interest or is necessary to protect the public.

>>240.155. Notarization of signature of person not in presence of notary public unlawful; penalty

1. A notary public who is appointed pursuant to this chapter shall not willfully notarize the signature of a person unless the person is in the presence of the notary public and:

(a) Is known to the notary public; or

(b) If unknown to the notary public, provides a credible witness or documentary evidence of identification to the notary public.

2. A person who:

(a) Violates the provisions of subsection 1; or

(b) Aids and abets a notary public to commit a violation of subsection 1, is guilty of a gross misdemeanor.

Uniform Law on Notarial Acts
(Refs & Annos)

>>240.161. Short title; uniformity of application and construction

1. NRS 240.161 to 240.169, inclusive, may be cited as the Uniform Law on Notarial Acts.

2. These sections must be applied and construed to effectuate their general purpose to make uniform the law with respect to the subject of these sections among states enacting them.

>>240.163. Repealed

>>240.1635. Notarial acts in this State

1. A notarial act may be performed within this State by the following persons:

(a) A notary public of this State;

(b) A judge, clerk or deputy clerk of any court of this State;

(c) A justice of the peace;

(d) Any other person authorized to perform the specific act by the law of this State; or

(e) A person authorized to perform the specific act by the law of a federally recognized Indian tribe or nation.

2. Notarial acts performed within this State under federal authority as provided in NRS 240.1645 have the same effect as if performed by a notarial officer of this State.

7. 州务卿为了公众利益或为保护公众的必要，在听证期间，有权暂停或撤销对公证人的任命。

>> 240.155 公证人不在场的签名公证违法；处罚

1. 根据本章任命的公证人不得随意公证某人的签字，除非该人亲自出现在公证人面前，并且：

（a）为公证人所知；或者

（b）如果公证人不了解，则需向公证人提供可信证人的证言或证明文件。

2. 以下人员：
（a）违反第 1 款的规定的；或者
（b）协助和教唆公证人违反第 1 款的，构成轻罪。

统一公证行为法
（引用和注释）

>> 240.161 简称：适用与解释的统一性

1.《内华达州修正法案》第 240.161 条至第 240.169 条所包含的法条可简称为《统一公证行为法》。

2. 出于实现法律统一的一般目的，本法必须得到妥善的实施和解释。

>> 240.163 已废止

>> 240.1635 在本州内的公证行为

1. 下列人士可在本州境内执行公证行为：

（a）本州的公证人；

（b）本州任何法院的法官、书记官或副书记官；

（c）治安法官；

（d）任何被授权根据本州法律执行具体公证行为的其他人；或者

（e）根据联邦承认的印第安人部落或民族的法律，被授权执行具体公证行为的人。

2.《内华达州修正法案》第 240.1645 条所规定的联邦当局在本州境内进行的公证行为，其效力与本州公证人进行的公证行为相同。

3. The signature and title of a person performing a notarial act are prima facie evidence that the signature is genuine and that the person holds the designated title.

>>240.164. Notarial acts in other jurisdictions of United States

1. A notarial act has the same effect under the law of this State as if performed by a notarial officer of this State, if performed in another state, commonwealth, territory, district or possession of the United States by any of the following persons:

(a) A notary public of that jurisdiction;

(b) A judge, clerk or deputy clerk of a court of that jurisdiction; or

(c) Any other person authorized by the law of that jurisdiction to perform notarial acts.

2. Notarial acts performed in other jurisdictions of the United States under federal authority as provided in NRS 240.1645 have the same effect as if performed by a notarial officer of this State.

3. The signature and title of a person performing a notarial act are prima facie evidence that the signature is genuine and that the person holds the designated title.

4. The signature and indicated title of an officer listed in paragraph (a) or (b) of subsection 1 conclusively establish the authority of a holder of that title to perform a notarial act.

>>240.1645. Notarial acts under federal authority

1. A notarial act has the same effect under the law of this State as if performed by a notarial officer of this State if performed anywhere by any of the following persons under authority granted by the law of the United States:

(a) A judge, clerk or deputy clerk of a court;

(b) A commissioned officer on active duty in the military service of the United States;

(c) An officer of the foreign service or consular officer of the United States; or

(d) Any other person authorized by federal law to perform notarial acts.

2. The signature and title of a person performing a notarial act are prima facie evidence that the signature is genuine and that the person holds the designated title.

3. The signature and indicated title of an officer listed in paragraph (a), (b) or (c) of subsection 1 conclusively establish the authority of a holder of that title to perform a notarial act.

3. 执行公证行为之人的签字和头衔可作为证明签字是真实的且此人拥有特定的权力的表面证据。

>> 240.164 美国其他司法管辖区的公证行为

1. 根据本州法律，下列人员在其他州、联邦、美国的领土、地区或领地执行的公证行为，与本州的公证人员执行的公证行为具有相同的效力：

（a）该司法管辖区的公证人；

（b）该司法管辖区法院的法官、书记官或副书记官；或者

（c）在该司法管辖区由法律授权从事公证行为的任何其他人。

2. 根据《内华达州修正法案》第240.1645条的规定，在联邦授权下，在美国其他司法管辖区内执行的公证行为，与本州的公证人员执行的公证行为具有相同的效力。

3. 执行公证行为之人的签字和头衔可作为证明签字是真实的且此人拥有指定的权力的表面证据。

4. 根据第1款a项或b项所列人员的签字和标明的头衔，最终确定该头衔的持有人进行公证行为的权力。

>> 240.1645 联邦授权的公证行为

1. 根据本州法律，下列人员根据美国联邦法律的授权在任何地方执行的公证行为，与本州的公证人员执行的公证行为具有相同的效力：

（a）法院的法官、书记官或副书记官；

（b）在美国服兵役的现役军官；

（c）美国外交人员或领事官员；或者

（d）由联邦法律授权执行公证行为的任何其他人。

2. 执行公证行为之人的签字和头衔是证明签字是真实的且此人拥有指定的权力的表面证据。

3. 根据第1款a项、b项或c项所列人员的签字和标明的头衔，最终确定该头衔的持有人进行公证行为的权力。

>>240.165. Foreign notarial acts

1. A notarial act has the same effect under the law of this State as if performed by a notarial officer of this State if performed within the jurisdiction of and under authority of a foreign nation or its constituent units or a multinational or international organization by the following persons:

(a) A notary public;

(b) A judge, clerk or deputy clerk of a court of record;

(c) A person authorized by the law of that jurisdiction to perform notarial acts;

(d) A person authorized by federal law to perform notarial acts; or

(e) A person authorized by the law of a federally recognized Indian tribe or nation to perform notarial acts.

2. A certificate by an officer of the foreign service or consular officer of the United States stationed in the nation under the jurisdiction of which the notarial act was performed, or a certificate by an officer of the foreign service or consular officer of that nation stationed in the United States, conclusively establishes a matter relating to the authenticity or validity of the notarial act set forth in the certificate.

3. An official stamp or seal of the person performing the notarial act is prima facie evidence that the signature is genuine and that the person holds the indicated title.

4. An official stamp or seal of an officer listed in paragraph (a) or (b) of subsection 1 is prima facie evidence that a person with the indicated title has authority to perform notarial acts.

5. If the title of office and indication of authority to perform notarial acts appears either in a digest of foreign law or in a list customarily used as a source for that information, the authority of an officer with that title to perform notarial acts is conclusively established.

>>240.1655. Notarial acts

1. A notarial act must be evidenced by a certificate that:

(a) Identifies the county, including, without limitation, Carson City, in this State in which the notarial act was performed in substantially the following form:

State of Nevada

County of _____

(b) Except as otherwise provided in this paragraph, includes the name of the person whose signature is being notarized. If the certificate is for certifying a copy of a document, the certificate must include the name of the

>> 240.165 涉外公证行为

1. 根据本州法律，下列人员在外国或其组成单位或跨国公司或国际组织的司法管辖范围内执行的公证行为，与本州的公证人员执行的公证行为具有相同的效力：

（a）公证人；

（b）法官、法庭书记官或副书记官；

（c）由该司法管辖区的法律授权执行公证行为的人；

（d）由联邦法律授权执行公证行为的人；或者

（e）经联邦承认的印第安部落或民族的法律授权从事公证行为的人。

2. 由执行公证行为的管辖国驻美国办事处或领事馆官员出具的证明证书，或美国驻外办事处或领事馆的高级人员出具的证明证书最终确定证明书所列公证行为的真实性或有效性。

3. 执行公证行为之人的公证公章是证明签字是真实的且此人拥有所表明的权力的表面证据。

4. 第1款a项或b项所列人员的官方印章为表面证据，表明具有该头衔的人有权执行公证行为。

5. 如果职务的头衔和执行公证行为的权力表征出现在外国法律摘要或存在于通常用作该信息来源的列表中，则可最终确定具有该头衔的人员执行公证行为的权力。

>> 240.1655 公证行为

1. 公证行为必须通过证书证明：

（a）各郡，包括但不限于卡森市，在内华达州内执行公证行为大体采用以下格式：

内华达州

_____ 郡

（b）除本条另有规定外，证书应包括其签名正在被公证之人的姓名。如果证书是为了证明某一文件的副本，则证书必须包括提交该文件之人的姓名。如果证书用于签署见证人的宣誓证明书，则证书必须包含

person presenting the document. If the certificate is for the jurat of a subscribing witness, the certificate must include the name of the subscribing witness.

(c) Is signed and dated in ink by the notarial officer performing the notarial act. The certificate must be signed in the same manner as the signature of the notarial officer that is on file with the Secretary of State.

(d) If the notarial officer performing the notarial act is a notary public, includes the statement imprinted with the stamp of the notary public, as described in NRS 240.040.

(e) If the notarial officer performing the notarial act is not a notary public, includes the title of the office of the notarial officer and may include the official stamp or seal of that office. If the officer is a commissioned officer on active duty in the military service of the United States, the certificate must also include the officer's rank.

2. Except as otherwise provided in subsection 8, a notarial officer shall:

(a) In taking an acknowledgment, determine, from personal knowledge or satisfactory evidence, that the person making the acknowledgment is the person whose signature is on the document. The person who signed the document shall present the document to the notarial officer in person.

(b) In administering an oath or affirmation, determine, from personal knowledge or satisfactory evidence, the identity of the person taking the oath or affirmation.

(c) In certifying a copy of a document, photocopy the entire document and certify that the photocopy is a true and correct copy of the document that was presented to the notarial officer.

(d) In making or noting a protest of a negotiable instrument, verify compliance with the provisions of subsection 2 of NRS 104.3505.

(e) In executing a jurat, administer an oath or affirmation to the affiant and determine, from personal knowledge or satisfactory evidence, that the affiant is the person named in the document. The affiant shall sign the document in the presence of the notarial officer. The notarial officer shall administer the oath or affirmation required pursuant to this paragraph in substantially the following form:

Do you (solemnly swear, or affirm) that the statements in this document are true, (so help you God)?

3. A certificate of a notarial act is sufficient if it meets the requirements of subsections 1 and 2 and it:

(a) Is in the short form set forth in NRS 240.166 to

该签署见证人的姓名。

（c）执行公证行为的公证人应用墨水笔签字并注明日期。证明证书的签字必须与州务卿存档的签字方式相同。

（d）按照《内华达州修正法案》第240.040条的规定，如果执行公证行为的公证官员是公证人，公证证书还应包括印有公证人的印章。

（e）如果执行公证行为的公证人员不是公证人，应包括公证人员办事处的名称，还可包括该办事处的正式印章。如果该人员是美国军队中的现役军官，该证书还必须包括该军官的军衔。

2. 除第8款另有规定外，公证人应：

（a）在作出确认书时，根据个人知识或充分证据确定作出确认的人正是签署文件的人。签署文件的人应当亲自向公证人提交文件。

（b）在执行宣誓或誓词时，根据个人知识或充分证据确定作出该宣誓或誓词之人的身份。

（c）在核证一份文件的副本时，影印整份文件并确认该影印本是真实的，以及提交公证人的副本是正确的。

（d）在作出或登记可转让票据的异议时，核查是否符合《内华达州修正法案》第104.3505条第2款的规定。

（e）在执行宣誓者的宣誓证明书、誓章或誓词时，根据个人知识或充分证据确定宣誓人是文件中所指的人。宣誓人应在公证人在场的情况下签署该文件。公证人执行宣誓或誓词时应按照本款所要求的规定格式，大体上如下：

你是否（郑重宣誓，或肯定），这份文件中的声明是真实的，（上帝保佑）？

3. 满足下列条件的公证行为证书视为符合第1款、第2款的要求：

（a）采用《内华达州修正法案》第240.166条至

240.169, inclusive;

(b) Is in a form otherwise prescribed by the law of this State;

(c) Is in a form prescribed by the laws or regulations applicable in the place in which the notarial act was performed; or

(d) Sets forth the actions of the notarial officer and those are sufficient to meet the requirements of the designated notarial act.

4. For the purposes of paragraphs (a), (b) and (e) of subsection 2, a notarial officer has satisfactory evidence that a person is the person whose signature is on a document if the person:

(a) Is personally known to the notarial officer;

(b) Is identified upon the oath or affirmation of a credible witness who personally appears before the notarial officer;

(c) Is identified on the basis of an identifying document which contains a signature and a photograph;

(d) Is identified on the basis of a consular identification card;

(e) Is identified upon an oath or affirmation of a subscribing witness who is personally known to the notarial officer; or

(f) In the case of a person who is 65 years of age or older and cannot satisfy the requirements of paragraphs (a) to (e), inclusive, is identified upon the basis of an identification card issued by a governmental agency or a senior citizen center.

5. An oath or affirmation administered pursuant to paragraph (b) of subsection 4 must be in substantially the following form:

Do you (solemnly swear, or affirm) that you personally know _____(name of person who signed the document)_____, (so help you God)?

6. A notarial officer shall not affix his or her signature overprinted material.

7. By executing a certificate of a notarial act, the notarial officer certifies that the notarial officer has complied with all the requirements of this section.

8. If a person is physically unable to sign a document that is presented to a notarial officer pursuant to this section, the person may direct a person other than the notarial officer to sign the person's name on the document. The notarial officer shall insert "Signature affixed by (insert name of other person) at the direction of (insert name of person)" or words of similar import.

第240.169条所规定的简易格式；

（b）以本州法律另有规定的格式；

（c）采用公证行为所适用的法律或条例所规定的格式；或

（d）规定公证官员的行为，这些行为将充分满足所指定的公证行为的要求。

4. 第2款a项、b项和e项中，满足下列条件的，视为公证人有充分证据证明某人是在文件上签字的人：

（a）是公证人个人认识的；

（b）依据出现在公证人面前的可信证人的宣誓或确认来确定的；

（c）是根据载有签名和照片的鉴定文件确定的；

（d）是根据领事身份证件确定的；

（e）依据公证人本人认识的签署见证人的宣誓或确认确定的；或

（f）65岁及其以上的人，在不能满足a项至e项包含的要求的情况下，应根据政府机构或老年人中心签发的身份证来确定。

5. 根据第4款b项执行宣誓或确认的格式必须大致如下：

你是否（郑重宣誓，或肯定），你本人知道_____（签署该文件的人的姓名）_____，（上帝保佑）？

6. 公证人不得在套印的材料上签名。

7. 通过执行公证行为的证书，证明该公证人已遵守本条的所有规定。

8. 如某人不能亲自签署根据本条提交公证人的文件，则该人可指示除公证人以外的人在该文件上签名。公证人应当在（代签人姓名）的地方写下"签字署名（他人姓名）"或类似含义的字样。

9. As used in this section, unless the context otherwise requires, "consular identification card" means an identification card issued by a consulate of a foreign government, which consulate is located within the State of Nevada.

>>240.1657. Authentication of signature of notarial officer by Secretary of State

1. Except as otherwise provided in subsection 2, the Secretary of State shall, upon request and payment of a fee of $20, issue an authentication to verify that the signature of the notarial officer on a document is genuine and that the notarial officer holds the office indicated on the document. If the document:

(a) Is intended for use in a foreign country that is a participant in the Hague Convention of October 5, 1961, the Secretary of State must issue an apostille in the form prescribed by the Hague Convention of October 5, 1961.

(b) Is intended for use in the United States or in a foreign country that is not a participant in the Hague Convention of October 5, 1961, the Secretary of State must issue a certification.

2. The Secretary of State shall not issue an authentication pursuant to subsection 1 if:

(a) The document has not been notarized in accordance with the provisions of this chapter; or

(b) The Secretary of State has reasonable cause to believe that the document may be used to accomplish any fraudulent, criminal or unlawful purpose.

>>240.166. Short form for acknowledgment in individual capacity

Upon compliance with the requirements of NRS 240.1655, the following certificate is sufficient for an acknowledgment in an individual capacity:

State of Nevada
County of _____
This instrument was acknowledged before me on _____(date)_____ (name(s) of person(s))_____
(Signature of notarial officer)
(Seal, if any)
(Title and rank (optional))

>>240.1663. Short form for administering oath or affirmation of office

Upon compliance with the requirements of NRS 240.1655, the following certificate is sufficient for administering an oath or affirmation of office:

9. 除上下文另有规定外，本条所称"领事身份证"是一种由外国政府领事馆签发的身份证，该领事馆须位于内华达州境内。

>> 240.1657 州务卿认证公证人签名

1. 除第 2 款另有规定外，州务卿一经请求并被支付 20 美元的费用后应出具认证书，以核实公证官员在文件上的签字是否真实，且公证官员拥有在文件中标明的职务。如果该文件：

（a）拟供 1961 年 10 月 5 日《海牙公约》参与国（非本国）使用，州务卿必须以 1961 年 10 月 5 日《海牙公约》规定的格式加注旁注。

（b）拟供美国或非 1961 年 10 月 5 日《海牙公约》的参与国家使用，州务卿必须出具证书。

2. 在下列情况下，州务卿不得根据第 1 款的规定签发证明：

（a）该文件没有按照本章的规定进行公证；或

（b）州务卿有合理理由相信该文件可能用于实现任何欺诈、犯罪或非法目的。

>> 240.166 私人身份确认的简易格式

在符合《内华达州修正法案》第 240.1655 条要求的情况下，以下证书足以用于私人身份的确认：

内华达州
_____郡
在本人面前的这份文件已得到确认 _____（日期）_____（人名）_____
（公证官员签字）
（盖章，如有）
［头衔和等级（可选择）］

>> 240.1663 执行宣誓或确认的简易格式

在符合《内华达州修正法案》第 240.1655 条规定的条件下，以下证书足以用于执行官方的宣誓或确认：

State of Nevada

County of _____

I, _____(name of person taking oath or affirmation of office) _____, do solemnly swear (or affirm) that I will support, protect and defend the Constitution and Government of the United States and the Constitution and Government of the State of Nevada against all enemies, whether domestic or foreign, and that I will bear true faith, allegiance and loyalty to the same, any ordinance, resolution or law of any state notwithstanding, and that I will well and faithfully perform all the duties of the office of _____ (title of office) _____, on which I am about to enter; (if an oath) so help me God; (if an affirmation) under the pains and penalties of perjury.

(Signature of person taking oath or affirmation of office)

Signed and sworn to (or affirmed) before me on _____(date)by _____(name of person taking oath or affirmation of office)

(Signature of notarial officer)

(Seal, if any)

(Title and rank (optional))

>>240.1665. Short form for acknowledgment in representative capacity

Upon compliance with the requirements of NRS 240.1655, the following certificate is sufficient for an acknowledgment in a representative capacity:

State of Nevada

County of _____

This instrument was acknowledged before me on _____(date) by _____(name(s) of person(s))_____ as _____(type of authority, e.g., officer, trustee, etc.) _____ of _____ (name of party on behalf of whom instrument was executed)_____

(Signature of notarial officer)

(Seal, if any)

(Title and rank (optional))

>>240.1667. Short form for acknowledgment containing power of attorney

Upon compliance with the requirements of NRS 240.1655, the following certificate is sufficient for an acknowledgment that contains a power of attorney:

State of Nevada

County of _____

This instrument was acknowledged before me on _____(date) _____ by(name of person holding pow-

内华达州

_____郡

我_____（宣誓或确认就职的人之姓名）庄严宣誓（或确认）_____、我将支持、保护和捍卫美国宪法和政府及内华达州的宪法和政府并反对所有的敌人，无论在国内或国外，我将秉承信仰，效忠于任何州的统一条例、决议及法律，并且我将充分和忠实地履行我即将就职的_____（职务）_____的职责；（如果是宣誓书）上帝保佑；（如果是确认书）我愿承受伪证的痛苦和惩罚。

（宣誓人或确认人签名）

_____（日期）由_____（宣誓或确认就职的人的姓名）_____在我面前签署并宣誓（或确认）

（公证人签字）

（盖章，如有）

[头衔和等级（可选择）]

>> 240.1665 代表身份确认的简易格式

在符合《内华达州修正法案》第240.1655条要求的情况下，以下证书足以用于代表身份的确认：

内华达州

_____郡

_____（日期）在我面前的这份文件已得到确认_____由（人名）作为_____（代表执行文书的当事方名称）的_____（职权类别，如官职、受托人等）_____

（公证官员签字）

（盖章，如有）

[头衔和等级（可选）]

>> 240.1667 包含授权书的确认书的简易格式

在符合《内华达州修正法案》第240.1655条要求的情况下，以下证书足以用于授权委托书的确认书：

内华达州

_____郡

_____（日期）在我面前的这份文件已得到确认由_____（持有委托书的人的姓名）为_____（委托人/

er of attorney)_____ as attorney-in-fact for _____ (name of principal/person whose name is in the document)_____

 (Signature of notarial officer)
 (Seal, if any)
 (Title and rank (optional))

≫240.167. Short form for execution of jurat

Upon compliance with the requirements of NRS 240.1655, the following certificate is sufficient for executing a jurat:

 State of Nevada
 County of_____

Signed and sworn to (or affirmed) before me on___ (date)_____ by_____ (name(s) of person(s) making statement)_____

 (Signature of notarial officer)
 (Seal, if any)
 (Title and rank (optional))

≫240.168. Short form for certifying copy of document

Upon compliance with the requirements of NRS 240.1655, the following certificate is sufficient for certifying a copy of a document:

 State of Nevada
 County of _____

I certify that this is a true and correct copy of a document in the possession of _____ (name of person who presents the document) _____

 Dated_____
 (Signature of notarial officer)
 (Seal, if any)
 (Title and rank (optional))

≫240.1685. Short form for jurat of subscribing witness

 Upon compliance with the requirements of NRS 240.1655, the following certificate is sufficient for a jurat of a subscribing witness:

 State of Nevada
 County of _____

On_____ (date)_____, _____ (subscribing witness)_____ personally appeared before me, whom I know to be the person who signed this jurat of a subscribing witness while under oath, and swears that he or she was present and witnessed _____ (signer of the document) sign his or her name to the above document.

文件中的人名）代理

（公证人签字）
（盖章，如有）
[头衔和等级（可选）]

≫ 240.167 宣誓证明书执行的简易格式

在符合《内华达州修正法案》第 240.1655 条要求的情况下，以下证书足以用于执行宣誓证明书：

内华达州
_____郡
_____（日期）由 _____（发表声明的人姓名）在我面前的这份文件已得到签署和宣誓（或确认）

（公证人签字）
（盖章，如有）
[头衔和等级（可选）]

≫ 240.168 证明文件副本的简易格式

在符合《内华达州修正法案》第 240.1655 条要求的情况下，以下证书足以证明文件的副本：

内华达州
_____郡
我证明，本文件是真实的和正确的文件副本，由 _____（提交文档的人员姓名）拥有

日期 _____
（公证人签字）
（盖章，如有）
（头衔和等级（可选））

≫ 240.1685. 宣誓证明书的签署见证人的简易格式

在符合《内华达州修正法案》第 240.1655 条要求的情况下，下列证书足以用于确认宣誓证明书的签署见证人：

内华达州
_____郡
在 _____（日期），_____（签署见证人）亲自我面前作为宣誓证明书的签署见证人签名，并发誓他或她在现场见证了 _____（文件的签名者）在该文件上签署了他或她的名字。

(Signature of subscribing witness)

Signed and sworn before me on _____ (date)_____ by_____(subscribing witness) _____

(Signature of notarial officer)

(Seal, if any)

(Title and rank (optional))

>>240.169. Short form for acknowledgment of credible witness

Upon compliance with the requirements of NRS 240.1655, the following certificate is sufficient for an acknowledgment of a credible witness:

State of Nevada

County of _____

This instrument was acknowledged before me on _____(date)_____ by _____(name of person)_____ who personally appeared before me and whose identity I verified upon the oath of _____ (name of credible witness) _____, a credible witness personally known to me and to the person who acknowledged this instrument before me.

(Signature of notarial officer)

(Seal, if any)

(Title and rank (optional))

Electronic Notary Public Authorization Act

>>240.181. Short title

NRS 240.181 to 240.206, inclusive, [FN1] may be cited as the Electronic Notary Public Authorization Act.

[FN1] The Electronic Notary Public Authorization Act was codified within the same range of statutes as former NRS 240.170 to 240.230, relating to commissioners of deeds, repealed by laws 2001, c. 120, s 20, eff. Oct. 1, 2001. See repealed NRS 240.170 to 240.230, infra.

>>240.182. Definitions

As used in NRS 240.181 to 240.206, inclusive, unless the context otherwise requires, the words and terms defined in NRS 240.183 to 240.188, inclusive, have the meanings ascribed to them in those sections.

>>240.183. "Electronic" defined

"Electronic" means of or relating to technology having electrical, digital, magnetic, wireless, optical, electromagnetic or similar capabilities.

（签署证人的签字）

_____（日期）（签署见证人）_____已在我面前签署并宣誓（签署见证人签字）

（公证人签字）

（盖章，如有）

[头衔和等级（可选）]

>> 240.169 确认可信证人的简易格式

在符合《内华达州修正法案》第240.1655条要求的条件下，以下证书足以证明可信证人的确认：

内华达州

_____郡

_____（日期）在我面前的这份文件已得到确认由_____（人的名字）宣誓并亲自核实了在我面前的可信证人的身份_____（可信证人的姓名），可信证人亲自了解本人以及在本人面前确认了这一文书。

（公证人签字）

（盖章，如有）

[头衔和等级（可选）]

电子公证人授权法

>> 240.181 简称

《内华达州修正法案》第240.181条至第240.206条所包含的法条，[FN1] 可简称为《电子公证人授权法》。

[FN1]《电子公证人授权法》在与之前的法规《内华达州修正法案》第240.170条至第240.230条相同的范围内编纂，涉及委托人行为的法律已在2001年10月1日被c. 120、s 20法规废止。在下文可见废止《内华达州修正法案》第240.170条至第240.230条的条款。

>> 240.182 定义

如《内华达州修正法案》第240.181条至第240.206条所示，除非上下文另有规定，否则在《内华达州修正法案》第240.183条至第240.188条中定义的词语和术语具有一致的含义。

>> 240.183 "电子"的定义

"电子"是指有关电、数字、磁性、无线、光学、电磁或类似功能的技术。

>>240.184. "Electronic document" defined

"Electronic document" means a document that is created, generated, sent, communicated, received or stored by electronic means.

>>240.185. "Electronic notarial act" defined

"Electronic notarial act" means an act that an electronic notary public of this State is authorized to perform. The term includes:

1. Taking an acknowledgment;
2. Administering an oath or affirmation;
3. Executing a jurat; and
4. Performing such other duties as may be prescribed by a specific statute.

>>240.186. "Electronic notary public" defined

"Electronic notary public" means a person appointed by the Secretary of State pursuant to NRS 240.181 to 240.206, inclusive, to perform electronic notarial acts.

>>240.187. "Electronic seal" defined

"Electronic seal" means information within a notarized electronic document that includes the name, jurisdiction and expiration date of the appointment of an electronic notary public and generally includes the information required to be set forth in a mechanical stamp pursuant to NRS 240.040.

>>240.188. "Electronic signature" defined

"Electronic signature" means an electronic symbol or process attached to or logically associated with an electronic document and executed or adopted by a person with the intent to sign the electronic document.

>>240.189. Applicability

An electronic notary public shall comply with those provisions of NRS 240.001 to 240.169, inclusive, which are not inconsistent with NRS 240.181 to 240.206 , inclusive. To the extent that the provisions of NRS 240.001 to 240.169, inclusive, conflict with the provisions of NRS 240.181 to 240.206, inclusive, the provisions of NRS 240.181 to 240.206, inclusive, control.

>>240.191. Appointment by Secretary of State; cancellation of appointment; unlawful acts; injunctive relief

1. The Secretary of State may appoint electronic notaries public in this State.
2. The Secretary of State shall not appoint as an electronic notary public a person who submits an applica-

>> 240.184 "电子文件"的定义

"电子文件"是指以电子方式创建、生成、发送、传递、接收或储存的文件。

>> 240.185 "电子公证行为"定义

"电子公证行为"是指本州电子公证人经授权执行的行为。该术语包括：

1. 作出承认；
2. 执行宣誓或确认；
3. 执行宣誓证明书；以及
4. 执行某一特定法规规定的其他职责。

>> 240.186 "电子公证人"定义

"电子公证人"是指由州务卿根据《内华达州修正法案》第240.181条至第240.206条任命的执行电子公证行为的人员。

>> 240.187 "电子印章"的定义

"电子印章"是指包含在经公证的电子文件内的资料，其中包括任命的电子公证人的名称、管辖权及有效期，并包括根据《内华达州修正法案》第240.040条所规定的机械印章所载的一般资料。

>> 240.188 "电子签名"的定义

"电子签名"是指与单据相连或与之逻辑关联的电子符号或程序，并由意图签署电子文件的人执行或采用。

>> 240.189 适用性

电子公证人应当遵守《内华达州修正法案》第240.001条至第240.169条的规定，这些规定不与《内华达州修正法案》第240.181条至第240.206条的规定相抵触。如果在某些情形下，《内华达州修正法案》第240.001条至第240.169条的规定与《内华达州修正法案》第240.181条至第240.206条的规定相抵触，则遵循《内华达州修正法案》第240.181条至第240.206条的规定。

>> 240.191 州务卿的任命；委任的取消；不法行为；禁令救济

1. 州务卿可任命本州的电子公证人。

2. 州务卿不应任命提交申请书中含有重大实质错报或遗漏事实的电子公证人。

tion containing a substantial and material misstatement or omission of fact.

3. An electronic notary public may cancel his or her appointment by submitting a written notice to the Secretary of State.

4. It is unlawful for a person to:

(a) Represent himself or herself as an electronic notary public appointed pursuant to this section if the person has not received a certificate of appointment from the Secretary of State pursuant to NRS 240.192.

(b) Submit an application for appointment as an electronic notary public that contains a substantial and material misstatement or omission of fact.

5. The Secretary of State may request that the Attorney General bring an action to enjoin any violation of paragraph (a) of subsection 4.

>>240.192. Application for appointment; oath and bond; additional requirements for resident of adjoining state; commencement of term; fee for original, duplicate or amended certificate of appointment

1. Each person applying for appointment as an electronic notary public must:

(a) At the time of application, be a notarial officer in this State and have been a notarial officer in this State for not less than 4 years;

(b) Submit to the Secretary of State an electronic application pursuant to subsection 2;

(c) Pay to the Secretary of State an application fee of $50;

(d) Take and subscribe to the oath set forth in Section 2 of Article 15 of the Constitution of the State of Nevada as if the applicant were a public officer;

(e) Submit to the Secretary of State proof satisfactory to the Secretary of State that the applicant has successfully completed a course of study provided pursuant to NRS 240.195; and

(f) Enter into a bond to the State of Nevada in the sum of $10,000, to be filed with the clerk of the county in which the applicant resides or, if the applicant is a resident of an adjoining state, with the clerk of the county in this State in which the applicant maintains a place of business or is employed. The applicant must submit to the Secretary of State a certificate issued by the appropriate county clerk which indicates that the applicant filed the bond required pursuant to this paragraph.

2. The application for an appointment as an electron-

3. 电子公证人可向州务卿提交书面申请，取消其任命。

4. 下列行为为非法行为：

（a）如果此人没有根据《内华达州修正法案》第240.192 条的规定，获得到州务卿的任命证书，却根据本款的规定就以电子公证人自居。

（b）提交的任命申请书中含有重大实质错误或遗漏事实。

5. 州务卿可请求总检察长提起诉讼，以禁止任何违反第 4 款 a 项的行为。

>> 240.192 申请任命；誓言和保证金；对于毗邻州居民的附加要求；生效日期；任命证书的原件、复印件或修订本的费用

1. 申请任命为电子公证人的人士，必须：

（a）在申请时，是本州的公证官员，并在本州担任公证官员不少于 4 年；

（b）根据第 2 款向州务卿提交电子申请；

（c）向州务卿支付 50 美元的申请费；

（d）申请人须像公职人员一样作出并签署《内华达州宪法》第 15 章第 2 节所述的宣誓；

（e）向州务卿提出充分证据，证明申请人已顺利地完成《内华达州修正法案》第 240.195 条规定的培训课程；

（f）在内达华州，如果申请人是本州居民，应向所在郡的书记官提交 10000 美元的保证金，如果申请人是毗邻州的居民，则须向申请人营业地或被雇佣地所在州的郡书记官提交。申请人必须向州务卿提交一份由合适的郡书记官出具的证明，表明申请人已根据本款提交了所要求的保证金。

2. 申请电子公证人的任命申请书必须以电子文件

ic notary public must be submitted as an electronic document and must contain, without limitation, the following information:

(a) The applicant's full legal name, and the name to be used for appointment, if different.

(b) The county in which the applicant resides.

(c) The electronic mail address of the applicant.

(d) A description of the technology or device, approved by the Secretary of State, that the applicant intends to use to create his or her electronic signature in performing electronic notarial acts.

(e) The electronic signature of the applicant.

(f) Any other information requested by the Secretary of State.

3. An applicant for appointment as an electronic notary public who resides in an adjoining state, in addition to the requirements set forth in subsections 1 and 2, must submit to the Secretary of State with the application:

(a) An affidavit setting forth the adjoining state in which the applicant resides, the applicant's mailing address and the address of the applicant's place of business or employment that is located within the State of Nevada;

(b) A copy of the applicant's state business license issued pursuant to chapter 76 of NRS and any business license required by the local government where the applicant's business is located, if the applicant is self-employed; and

(c) Unless the applicant is self-employed, a copy of the state business license of the applicant's employer issued pursuant to chapter 76 of NRS, a copy of any business license of the applicant's employer that is required by the local government where the business is located and an affidavit from the applicant's employer setting forth the facts which show that the employer regularly employs the applicant at an office, business or facility which is located within the State of Nevada.

4. In completing an application, bond, oath or other document necessary to apply for appointment as an electronic notary public, an applicant must not be required to disclose his or her residential address or telephone number on any such document which will become available to the public.

5. The bond, together with the oath, must be filed and recorded in the office of the county clerk of the county in which the applicant resides when the applicant applies for appointment or, if the applicant is a resident of an adjoining state, with the clerk of the county in this State in

提交，并且必须包括但不限于下列资料：

（a）申请人的全名，以及用于任命的名字，如果二者存在不同。

（b）申请人所在的郡。

（c）申请人的电子邮件地址。

（d）为执行电子公证行为，申请人将用于创建电子签名的技术或装置，需由州务卿批准。

（e）申请人的电子签名。

（f）州务卿要求提供的任何其他资料。

3. 除了第1款和第2款所规定的要求外，居住在毗邻州的电子公证人的任命申请人，还须向州务卿提交以下材料：

（a）一份宣誓书，列明申请人所在的毗邻州、申请人的邮寄地址和申请人在内华达州境内的营业地或就业地点的地址；

（b）如果申请人是自营职业者，则依据《内华达州修正法案》第76章和申请人企业所在地的政府要求，需要提交申请者的州营业执照副本；

（c）除非申请人是自营职业者，否则还需提交该州政府要求的根据《内华达州修正法案》第76章签发的申请人雇主的州营业执照副本、申请人雇主的任何营业执照的副本、申请人雇主出具的宣誓书，表明雇主长期雇佣该申请人于内华达州境内的办公室或商业设施内。

4. 申请人在填写申请、提交保证金、宣誓书或其它作为电子公证人的任命所需的文件时，无须在向公众公开的任何该类文件上披露其住址或电话号码。

5. 保证金连同宣誓书，必须在申请人申请任命时所在郡的郡书记官办公室中存档和记录。如申请人是毗邻州的居民，则申请人应将保证金和宣誓书交由长期营业地或被雇佣地的郡书记官备案和记录。郡书记官应立即按照州务卿规定的格式证明其所要求的保证

which the applicant maintains a place of business or is employed. On a form provided by the Secretary of State, the county clerk shall immediately certify to the Secretary of State that the required bond and oath have been filed and recorded. Upon receipt of the application, fee and certification that the required bond and oath have been filed and recorded, the Secretary of State shall issue a certificate of appointment as an electronic notary public to the applicant.

6. The term of an electronic notary public commences on the effective date of the bond required pursuant to paragraph (f) of subsection 1. An electronic notary public shall not perform an electronic notarial act after the effective date of the bond unless the electronic notary public has been issued a certificate of appointment pursuant to subsection 5.

7. Except as otherwise provided in this subsection, the Secretary of State shall charge a fee of $10 for each duplicate or amended certificate of appointment which is issued to an electronic notary public. If the electronic notary public does not receive an original certificate of appointment, the Secretary of State shall provide a duplicate certificate of appointment without charge if the electronic notary public requests such a duplicate within 60 days after the date on which the original certificate was issued.

>>240.193. Requirements for bond; notification of exhaustion of penal sum; release of surety; suspension of appointment; reinstatement of appointment

1. The bond required to be filed pursuant to NRS 240.192 must be executed by the person applying to become an electronic notary public as principal and by a surety company qualified and authorized to do business in this State. The bond must be made payable to the State of Nevada and be conditioned to provide indemnification to a person determined to have suffered damage as a result of an act by the electronic notary public which violates a provision of NRS 240.001 to 240.206, inclusive. The surety company shall pay a final, nonappealable judgment of a court of this State that has jurisdiction, upon receipt of written notice of final judgment. The bond may be continuous, but regardless of the duration of the bond, the aggregate liability of the surety does not exceed the penal sum of the bond.

2. If the penal sum of the bond is exhausted, the surety company shall notify the Secretary of State in writing within 30 days after its exhaustion.

3. The surety bond must cover the period of the ap-

金和宣誓书已被存档和记录。在收到申请书、费用和所要求的保证金和宣誓书已被存档和记录的证明后，州务卿应向申请人出具电子公证人的任命证书。

6. 电子公证人的任期开始于根据第 1 款 f 项规定的保证金生效之日。电子公证人不得在保证金有效日期外执行电子公证行为，除非电子公证人已根据第 5 款获得了签发的任命证书。

7. 除本款另有规定外，对于发给电子公证人的每份副本或修订的任命证书，州务卿应收取 10 美元的费用。如果电子公证人没有收到任用证书的原件，且电子公证人任命证书原件被发出之日起 60 日内要求提供任命证书的副本，州务卿应免费向其提供。

>> 240.193 对保证金的要求；关于用尽保证金的通知；担保的解除；暂停任命；恢复任命

1. 根据《内华达州修正法案》第 240.192 条要求提交的保证金，必须由申请成为电子公证人的人作为当事人，并由有资质和被授权在本州营业的担保公司执行。该保证金必须支付给内华达州，并向由于电子公证人违反了《内华达州修正法案》第 240.001 条至第 240.206 条的规定而遭受损害的个人提供赔偿。担保公司在收到终局判决的书面通知后，应当向作出不可上诉的终审判决并且具有管辖权的州法院支付赔偿金。保证金可以是连续的，但无论保证金的期限如何，担保人的总负债不得超过该罚金总额。

2. 如果保证金用尽，担保公司应在其用尽后 30 日内书面通知州务卿。

3. 保证金必须担保电子公证人的整个任期，除非

pointment of the electronic notary public, except when a surety is released.

4. A surety on a bond filed pursuant to NRS 240.192 may be released after the surety gives 30 days' written notice to the Secretary of State and the electronic notary public, but the release does not discharge or otherwise affect a claim filed by a person for damage resulting from an act of the electronic notary public which is alleged to have occurred while the bond was in effect.

5. The appointment of an electronic notary public is suspended by operation of law when the electronic notary public is no longer covered by a surety bond as required by this section and NRS 240.192 or the penal sum of the bond is exhausted. If the Secretary of State receives notice pursuant to subsection 4 that the bond will be released or pursuant to subsection 2 that the penal sum of the bond is exhausted, the Secretary of State shall immediately notify the electronic notary public in writing that his or her appointment will be suspended by operation of law until another surety bond is filed in the same manner and amount as the bond being terminated.

6. The Secretary of State may reinstate the appointment of an electronic notary public whose appointment has been suspended pursuant to subsection 5 if the electronic notary public, before his or her current term of appointment expires:

(a) Submits to the Secretary of State:

(1) An application for an amended certificate of appointment as an electronic notary public; and

(2) A certificate issued by the clerk of the county in which the applicant resides or, if the applicant is a resident of an adjoining state, the county in this State in which the applicant maintains a place of business or is employed, which indicates that the applicant filed a new surety bond with the clerk; and

(b) Pays to the Secretary of State a fee of $10.

>>240.194. Term of office; suspension of appointment by operation of law; changes of information

1. The initial term of appointment as an electronic notary public is 2 years. Each term of appointment as an electronic notary public subsequent to the initial term is 4 years.

2. The appointment of an electronic notary public is suspended by operation of law when the electronic notary public is no longer appointed as a notary public in this State. If the appointment of an electronic notary public has expired or been revoked or suspended, the Secretary of

担保人已解除担保。

4. 在担保人向州务卿和电子公证人发出书面通知30日之后，根据《内华达州修正法案》第240.192条提交保证金的担保人可以解除担保，但并不解除或以其他方式影响在该保证金生效期间，因电子公证人的行为引发的索赔。

5. 当电子公证人不再被本条和《内华达州修正法案》第240.192条要求的保证金担保或保证金用尽时，应依法暂停对公证人的任命。如州务卿收到通知担保将根据第4款被解除，或根据第2款保证金已被用尽，州务卿应立即以书面形式通知电子公证人，其任命将被依法暂停，直至以其相同的方式再次提交等额的保证金。

6. 如果电子公证人在其任期届满之前，根据第5款被停职时，满足下列情形的，州务卿可恢复其公证人的任命：

（a）向州务卿提交下列材料：

（1）要求获得电子公证人任命的修订证书的申请书；

（2）申请人居住地郡书记官出具的证书，如果申请人是毗邻州的居民，则由申请人在该州营业地或工作地的郡书记官出具证书，表明申请人向书记官处提交了新的保证金；以及

（b）向州务卿支付10美元的费用。

>> 240.194 任职期限；依法中止任命；信息变更

1. 电子公证人的最初任命期限为2年。在最初任期后，每位电子公证人的任期为4年。

2. 当公证人不再被任命为本州的公证人时，电子公证人的任命也会被暂停。如果电子公证人的任命已过期或被撤销或中止，州务卿应立即以书面形式通知电子公证人，书面通知的内容为：其作为电子公证人

State shall immediately notify the electronic notary public in writing that his or her appointment as an electronic notary public will be suspended by operation of law until he or she is appointed as a notary public in this State.

3. If, at any time during his or her appointment, an electronic notary public changes his or her electronic mail address, county of residence, name, electronic signature or the technology or device used to create his or her electronic signature, the electronic notary public shall, within 10 days after making the change, submit to the Secretary of State:

(a) An electronic document, signed with the electronic signature submitted by the electronic notary public pursuant to subsection 2 of NRS 240.192, that includes the change of information; and

(b) A fee of $10.

>>240.195. Courses of study required; persons required to successfully complete course of study; fees

1. Except as otherwise provided in subsection 2, an applicant for appointment as an electronic notary public must successfully:

(a) Complete a course of study that is in accordance with the requirements of subsection 5; and

(b) Pass an examination at the completion of the course.

2. The following persons must successfully complete a course of study as required pursuant to subsection 1:

(a) A person applying for his or her first appointment as an electronic notary public;

(b) A person renewing his or her appointment as an electronic notary public if the appointment as an electronic notary public has been expired for a period of more than 1 year; and

(c) A person renewing his or her appointment as an electronic notary public if, during the 4 years immediately preceding the application for renewal, the Secretary of State took action against the person pursuant to NRS 240.150 for failing to comply with any provision of this chapter or any regulations adopted pursuant thereto.

A person renewing his or her appointment as an electronic notary public need not successfully complete a course of study as required pursuant to subsection 1 if the appointment as an electronic notary public has been expired for a period of 1 year or less.

3. A course of study required to be completed pursuant to subsection 1 must:

的任命将依法中止，直到他或她再次被任命为本州的公证人为止。

3. 如果在电子公证人被任命期间的任何时段内，电子公证人更改其电子邮件地址、居住地、姓名、电子签名或用于制作其电子签名的技术或装置，电子公证人应在做出更改后 10 日内向州务卿提交：

（a）电子文档，其中包括电子公证人根据《内华达州修正法案》第 240.192 条第 2 款提交的电子签名，以及变更的信息；以及

（b）10 美元的费用。

>> 240.195 需要培训的课程；需要顺利完成培训课程的人；费用

1. 除第 2 款另有规定外，申请任命为电子公证人的申请人必须顺利：

（a）完成符合第 5 款规定的培训课程；

（b）课程完成时通过考试。

2. 下列人员必须按照第 1 款的规定完成该项培训课程：

（a）首次申请担任电子公证人的个人；

（b）前项任命已届满超过 1 年而重新获得电子公证人任命的人；

（c）重新获得公证人任命的人，如果在随后 4 年中因未遵守本州有关公证人的法规或条例而被州务卿根据《内华达州修正法案》第 240.150 条采取措施。

电子公证人的任命已届满 1 年或 1 年以内，在重新恢复电子公证人的任命时，无须按照第 1 款的规定完成该项培训课程。

3. 根据第 1 款完成的培训课程必须：

(a) Include at least 3 hours of instruction;

(b) Provide instruction in electronic notarization, including, without limitation, notarial law and ethics, technology and procedures;

(c) Include an examination of the course content;

(d) Comply with the regulations adopted pursuant to NRS 240.206; and

(e) Be approved by the Secretary of State.

4. The Secretary of State may, with respect to a course of study required to be completed pursuant to subsection 1:

(a) Provide such a course of study; and

(b) Charge a reasonable fee to each person who enrolls in such a course of study.

5. A course of study provided pursuant to this section must satisfy the criteria set forth in subsection 3 and comply with the requirements set forth in the regulations adopted pursuant to NRS 240.206.

6. The Secretary of State shall deposit the fees collected pursuant to paragraph (b) of subsection 4 in the Notary Public Training Account created pursuant to NRS 240.018.

>>240.196. Powers of electronic notary public

A person appointed as an electronic notary public pursuant to NRS 240.181 to 240.206, inclusive, may, during normal business hours, perform the following electronic notarial acts for a person who requests the electronic notarial act and tenders the appropriate fee:

1. Taking an acknowledgment;

2. Executing a jurat; and

3. Administering an oath or affirmation.

>>240.197. Fees for services; additional fees for travel expenses; notarial acts performed within and outside scope of employment

1. An electronic notary public may charge the following fees and no more:

(a) For taking an acknowledgment, for each signature ($10)

(b) For executing a jurat, for each signature ($10)

(c) For administering an oath or affirmation without a signature ($10)

2. An electronic notary public shall not charge a fee to perform a service unless he or she is authorized to charge a fee for such a service pursuant to this section.

3. All fees prescribed in this section are payable in

（a）至少包括 3 小时的授课；

（b）提供电子公证的指导，包括但不限于公证法律和道德、技术和程序；

（c）包括对课程内容的审查；

（d）遵守根据《内华达州修正法案》第 240.206 条所通过的条例；

（e）由州务卿批准。

4. 对于需要根据第 1 款完成的研究课程，州务卿有权：

（a）提供此种培训课程；

（b）向在每一位参与培训的个人收取合理的费用。

5. 根据本条提供的培训课程必须符合第 3 款所列的标准，并符合根据《内华达州修正法案》第 240.206 条所通过的规章的要求。

6. 州务卿应根据《内华达州修正法案》第 240.018 条设立公证人培训公共帐户，将按照第 4 款 b 项所收取的费用存入其中。

>> 240.196 电子公证人的权力

根据《内华达州修正法案》第 240.181 条至第 240.206 条中的规定，在正常营业时间内，电子公证人可以向需要电子公证并愿意支付适当费用的人提供下列电子公证服务：

1. 作出确认书；

2. 执行宣誓证明书；

3. 执行宣誓或确认。

>> 240.197 服务费；差旅费用的附加费用；在受雇范围内外执行的公证行为

1. 电子公证人只能收取下列费用：

（a）作出确认书，每个签名（10 美元）

（b）执行宣誓证明书，每个签名（10 美元）

（c）在没有签名的情况下进行宣誓或确认（10 美元）

2. 电子公证人除非获授权根据本条收取该项服务的费用，否则不得收取服务费。

3. 如有需要，本条所规定的费用均须预先缴付。

advance, if demanded.

4. An electronic notary public may charge an additional fee for traveling to perform an electronic notarial act if:

(a) The person requesting the electronic notarial act asks the electronic notary public to travel;

(b) The electronic notary public explains to the person requesting the electronic notarial act that the fee for travel is in addition to the fee authorized in subsection 1 and is not required by law;

(c) The person requesting the electronic notarial act agrees in advance upon the hourly rate that the electronic notary public will charge for the additional fee for travel; and

(d) The additional fee for travel does not exceed:

(1) If the person requesting the electronic notarial act asks the electronic notary public to travel between the hours of 6 a.m. and 7 p.m., $10 per hour.

(2) If the person requesting the electronic notarial act asks the electronic notary public to travel between the hours of 7 p.m. and 6 a.m., $25 per hour.

The electronic notary public may charge a minimum of 2 hours for such travel and shall charge on a pro rata basis after the first 2 hours.

5. An electronic notary public is entitled to charge the amount of the additional fee for travel agreed to in advance by the person requesting the electronic notarial act pursuant to subsection 4 if:

(a) The person requesting the electronic notarial act cancels the request after the electronic notary public begins traveling to perform the requested electronic notarial act.

(b) The electronic notary public is unable to perform the requested electronic notarial act as a result of the actions of the person who requested the electronic notarial act or any other person who is necessary for the performance of the electronic notarial act.

6. For each additional fee for travel that an electronic notary public charges pursuant to subsection 4, the electronic notary public shall enter in the journal that he or she keeps pursuant to NRS 240.201:

(a) The amount of the fee; and

(b) The date and time that the electronic notary public began and ended such travel.

7. A person who employs an electronic notary public may prohibit the electronic notary public from charging a fee for an electronic notarial act that the electronic notary public performs within the scope of the employment. Such

4. 电子公证人可以收取执行公证行为的额外差旅费用，如果：

（a）公证请求人要求电子公证人员出差；

（b）电子公证人向公证请求人阐明，该费用是第1款授权费用之外的附加费用，法律并无强制要求；

（c）公证请求人事先同意电子公证人收取额外的计时差旅费用；

（d）额外的差旅费用不超过：

（1）如果公证请求人要求电子公证人在早晨6点至下午7点之间出差，每小时10美元。

（2）如果公证请求人要求电子公证人在下午7点至早晨6点之间出差，每小时25美元。

电子公证人可收取最少2小时的差旅费，并且须在第一个2小时后按比例收取费用。

5. 在得到公证请求人的事先同意之下，如果出现以下情形，电子公证人有权根据第4款的规定，收取额外的差旅费用：

（a）公证请求人在电子公证人开始为执行电子公证行为而出差后取消了请求。

（b）电子公证人无法执行所要求的电子公证行为，是因为请求人或执行电子公证行为所必需的任何其他人的行为所导致。

6. 对于电子公证人根据第4款规定收取的额外差旅费，应在根据《内华达州修正法案》第240.201条备存的公证人日志上记录：

（a）该费用的总额；以及

（b）电子公证人开始和结束此差旅的日期和时间。

7. 雇用电子公证人的人可禁止电子公证人在其受雇范围内收取执行公证行为的费用。但雇主不得要求该被雇用的电子公证人向其交出全部或部分在受雇范围外收取的执行费用。

a person shall not require the electronic notary public whom the person employs to surrender to the person all or part of a fee charged by the electronic notary public for an electronic notarial act performed outside the scope of the employment of the electronic notary public.

>>240.198. Notarization of signature of person not in presence of notary public unlawful; penalty; notarization of certain electronic documents prohibited; powers limited to areas within this State

1. An electronic notary public shall not willfully electronically notarize the signature or electronic signature of a person unless the person is in the presence of the electronic notary public at the time of notarization and:

(a) Is known to the electronic notary public; or

(b) If unknown to the electronic notary public, provides a credible witness or documentary evidence of identification to the electronic notary public.

2. A person who:

(a) Violates the provisions of subsection 1; or

(b) Aids and abets an electronic notary public to commit a violation of subsection 1, is guilty of a gross misdemeanor.

3. An electronic notary public shall not electronically notarize any electronic document related to the following:

(a) A will, codicil or testamentary trust; and

(b) Any transaction governed by the Uniform Commercial Code other than NRS 104.1306, 104.2101 to 104.2725, inclusive, and 104A.2101 to 104A.2532, inclusive.

4. An appointment as an electronic notary public pursuant to NRS 240.181 to 240.206, inclusive, does not authorize the electronic notary public to perform notarial acts in another state.

>>240.199. Evidence of electronic notarial act

An electronic notarial act must be evidenced by the following, which must be attached to or logically associated with the electronic document that is the subject of the electronic notarial act and which must be immediately perceptible and reproducible:

1. The electronic signature of the electronic notary public;

2. The electronic seal of the electronic notary public; and

3. The wording of a notarial certificate pursuant to NRS 240.1655, 240.166 to 240.167, inclusive, 240.1685 or 240.169.

>> 240.198 公证人不在场的签名公证违法；处罚；特定电子文件公证的禁止；限于本州范围内的权力

1. 电子公证人不得故意以电子方式公证某人的签名或电子签名，除非电子公证人在公证时该人在场，并且：

（a）电子公证人个人认识此人；或者

（b）如果电子公证人不了解该人，则向电子公证人提供可信证人的证词或证明文件。

2. 以下人员：

（a）违反第1款的规定；或者

（b）协助及教唆电子公证人触犯第1款的规定，构成轻罪。

3. 电子公证人不得以电子方式公证任何下列与之相关的文件：

（a）遗嘱、遗嘱附录或遗嘱信托；以及

（b）除《内华达州修正法案》第104.1306条、第104.2101条至第104.2725条和第104 A. 2101条至第104 A. 2532条之外的统一商法典所规定的任何交易。

4. 根据《内华达州修正法案》第240.181条至第240.206条的规定，对电子公证人的任命，不得授权电子公证人在另一州从事公证行为。

>> 240.199 电子公证行为的证据

电子公证行为必须通过下列方式证明，以下证明材料必须依附于或合乎逻辑地与电子公证行为相关的电子文件相联系，而且必须可被直接察觉和可重复：

1. 电子公证人的电子签名；

2. 电子公证人的电子公章；以及

3. 公证书的措词符合《内华达州修正法案》第240.1655条、第240.166条至第240.167条、第240.1685条或第240.169条所包含的规定。

>>**240.201. Duty to keep journal of electronic notarial acts; suspension of appointment for failure to produce journal entry; delivery of notarial records to Secretary of State upon resignation, revocation or expiration of appointment**

1. An electronic notary public shall keep a journal of each electronic notarial act which includes, without limitation, the requirements of subsections 1 and 5 of NRS 240.120.

2. The Secretary of State may suspend the appointment of an electronic notary public who fails to produce any journal entry within 10 days after receipt of a request from the Secretary of State.

3. Upon resignation, revocation or expiration of an appointment as an electronic notary public, all notarial records required pursuant to NRS 240.001 to 240.206, inclusive, must be delivered to the Secretary of State.

>>**240.202. Use of electronic signature and electronic seal; safeguarding of electronic signature, electronic seal and notarial records; maintenance of technology or device used to create electronic signature**

1. The electronic signature and electronic seal of an electronic notary public must be used only for the purposes of performing electronic notarial acts.

2. An electronic notary public shall safeguard his or her electronic signature, the electronic seal and all notarial records maintained by the electronic notary public as follows:

(a) When not in use, the electronic notary public shall keep the electronic signature, electronic seal and all notarial records secure, under the exclusive control of the electronic notary public and protected by a password where applicable.

(b) An electronic notary public shall not permit his or her electronic signature or electronic seal to be used by any other person.

(c) An electronic notary public shall not surrender or destroy his or her notarial records except as otherwise required by the order of a court or as allowed pursuant to NRS 240.001 to 240.206, inclusive, or any regulations adopted pursuant thereto.

(d) Except as otherwise provided in subsection 3, an electronic notary public, within 10 days after discovering that his or her electronic signature or electronic seal has been stolen, lost, damaged or otherwise rendered incapable of affixing a legible image, shall:

>> 240.201 电子公证行为日志的保管职责；未制作日志记录的暂停任用；在辞职、撤销或任用期满时向州务卿交付公证记录

1. 电子公证人应备存每份电子公证行为的日志，遵守包括但不限于《内华达州修正法案》第240.120条第1款和第5款的要求。

2. 电子公证人在收到州务卿的要求后10日内，未制作任何日志记录的，州务卿可暂停对电子公证人的任命。

3. 在电子公证人辞职、任命被撤销或期满后，所有根据《内华达州修正法案》第240.001条至第240.206条所要求的公证记录必须送交州务卿。

>> 240.202 电子签名和电子印章的使用；电子签名、电子印章、公证记录的维护；用于创建电子签名的技术或设备的维护

1. 电子公证人的电子签名和电子印章必须仅用于执行电子公证行为的目的。

2. 电子公证人应按照以下规则保护其电子签名、电子印章和电子公证人维护的所有公证记录：

（a）在不使用的情况下，电子公证人应保证电子签名、电子印章和所有公证记录安全地处于电子公证人的专属控制下，并在适当的情况下使用密码加以保护。

（b）电子公证人不得允许他人使用其电子签名或电子印章。

（c）电子公证人不得交出或销毁其公证记录，除非法院命令或根据《内华达州修正法案》第240.001条至第240.206条或根据其他规章要求销毁记录。

（d）除第3款另有规定外，电子公证人在发现其电子签名或电子印章已被盗、遗失、损坏或因其他原因无法印制清晰的图像后，应在10日内：

(1) Inform the appropriate law enforcement agency in the case of theft or vandalism; and

(2) Notify the Secretary of State in writing, including, without limitation, a signature using the name on the certificate of appointment issued pursuant to subsection 5 of NRS 240.192.

3. An electronic notary public shall take reasonable steps to maintain the technology or device used to create his or her electronic signature, and to ensure that the technology or device has not been recalled, revoked, terminated or otherwise rendered ineffective or unsecure by the entity that created the technology or device. Upon learning that the technology or device used to create his or her electronic signature has been rendered ineffective or unsecure, an electronic notary public shall cease performing electronic notarial acts until:

(a) A new technology or device is acquired; and

(b) The electronic notary public sends an electronic notice to the Secretary of State that includes, without limitation, the information required pursuant to paragraphs (d) and (e) of subsection 2 of NRS 240.192 relating to the new technology or device.

>>240.203. Notice to Secretary of State of resignation or death of notary public or revocation or expiration of appointment; duty to erase, delete, destroy or otherwise render ineffective the notary's electronic signature technology or device

1. Except as otherwise provided in subsection 3, if an electronic notary public dies or resigns during his or her appointment, or if the appointment of the electronic notary public is revoked or expires, the electronic notary public, the executor of his or her estate or an authorized representative of the electronic notary public, as appropriate, shall:

(a) Notify the Secretary of State of the resignation or death; and

(b) Erase, delete, destroy or otherwise render ineffective the technology or device used to create his or her electronic signature.

2. Upon receipt of the notice required by subsection 1, the Secretary of State shall cancel the appointment of the electronic notary public, effective on the date on which the notice was received.

3. A former electronic notary public whose previous appointment as an electronic notary public was not revoked and whose previous application for appointment as an electronic notary public was not denied is not required

（1）在被盗或故意破坏的情况下，通知有关执法机构；以及

（2）以书面形式通知州务卿，包括但不限于使用根据《内华达州修正法案》第240.192条第5款签发的任命证书上的姓名签字。

3. 电子公证人应采取合理步骤，维护用于制作其电子签名的技术或装置，并确保技术或设备未被由创建该技术或装置的实体召回、撤销、终止或以其他方式使其失效或不安全。在得知用于制造其电子签名的技术或设备已无效或不安全时，电子公证人应停止执行电子公证行为，直至：

（a）购置新的技术或装置；并且

（b）电子公证人向州务卿发送一份电子通知，其中包含但不限于按照《内华达州修正法案》第240.192条第2款d项和e项规定的关于新技术或装置的所需的资料。

>> 240.203 通知州务卿公证人的辞职或死亡或撤销或任期届满；消除、删除、销毁或以其他方式使公证人的电子签名技术或设备失效的责任

1. 除第3款另有规定外，如果电子公证人在其任职期间死亡或辞职，或电子公证人的任命被吊销或任期届满，电子公证人、其遗产的执行人或电子公证人的授权代表人应：

（a）将辞职或死亡通知州务卿；以及

（b）擦除、删除、销毁用于制造其电子签名的技术或装置，或以其他方式使其失效。

2. 在收到第1款规定的通知后，州务卿应撤销对电子公证人的任用，并在接到通知之日起生效。

3. 前电子公证人先前的任命未被撤销且未被拒绝的，如果该电子公证人在其先前的任期届满后3个月内重新得到的任命且使用同一电子签名，则不必擦除、删去、销毁或以其他方式使制作其电子签名的技

to erase, delete, destroy or otherwise render ineffective the technology or device used to create his or her electronic signature if the former electronic notary public renews his or her appointment, using the same electronic signature, within 3 months after the expiration of his or her previous appointment as an electronic notary public.

>>240.204. Unlawful acts

1. A person who knowingly creates, manufactures or distributes software or hardware for the purpose of allowing a person to act as an electronic notary public without being appointed in accordance with NRS 240.181 to 240.206, inclusive, is guilty of a gross misdemeanor.

2. A person who wrongfully obtains, conceals, damages or destroys the technology or device used to create the electronic signature of an electronic notary public is guilty of a gross misdemeanor.

>>240.205. Authentication of signature of electronic notary public by Secretary of State

1. Except as otherwise provided in subsection 2, the Secretary of State shall, upon request, issue an authentication to verify that the electronic signature of the electronic notary public on an electronic document is genuine and that the electronic notary public holds the office indicated on the electronic document. The authentication must be:

(a) Signed by the Secretary of State; and

(b) In conformance with any relevant international treaties, agreements and conventions subscribed to by the Government of the United States, including, without limitation, The Hague Convention of October 5, 1961.

2. The Secretary of State shall not issue an authentication pursuant to subsection 1 if:

(a) The electronic document has not been electronically notarized in accordance with the provisions of NRS 240.001 to 240.206, inclusive; or

(b) The Secretary of State has reasonable cause to believe that the electronic document may be used to accomplish any fraudulent, criminal or unlawful purpose.

>>240.206. Regulations

The Secretary of State may adopt regulations to carry out the provisions of NRS 240.181 to 240.206, inclusive.

Commissioners of Deeds
>>240.170 to 240.230. Repealed [FN1]
>>240.170 to 240.230. Repealed [FN1]
>>240.170 to 240.230. Repealed [FN1]

术或装置无效。

>> 240.204 不法行为

1. 任何人明知却故意制造、制作或散布软件或硬件，试图达到未按照《内华达州修正法案》第240.181条至第240.206条的规定被任命的某人充当电子公证人的目的，构成严重的轻罪。

2. 任何人不正当地获取、隐瞒、损害或毁坏用于制作电子公证人电子签名的技术或装置，构成严重的轻罪。

>> 240.205 州务卿对电子公证人签名认证

1. 除第2款另有规定外，州务卿应根据请求发出认证，以核实电子公证人在电子文件上的电子签名是真实的，以及电子公证人拥有在电子文件中表明的职权。该认证必须：

（a）由州务卿签署；以及

（b）遵守美国政府签署的任何有关国际条约、协定和公约，包括但不限于1961年10月5日的《海牙公约》。

2. 在下列情况下，州务卿不得根据第1款发出身份验证：

（a）电子文件未按照《内华达州修正法案》第240.001条至第240.206条的规定以电子方式公证；或者

（b）州务卿有合理理由相信电子文件可能用于完成任何欺诈、犯罪或非法目的。

>> 240.206 条例

州务卿可采用条例来执行《内华达州修正法案》第240.181条至第240.206条包括的规定。

行动专员
第240.170条至第240.230条被废止 [FN1]
第240.170条至第240.230条被废止 [FN1]
第240.170条至第240.230条被废止 [FN1]

>>240.170 to 240.230. Repealed [FN1]
>>240.170 to 240.230. Repealed [FN1]
>>240.170 to 240.230. Repealed [FN1]
>>240.170 to 240.230. Repealed [FN1]

Commissioned Abstracters

>>**240.240. Creation of office**

The office of commissioned abstracter, in and for the several counties of this State, is hereby created.

>>**240.250. Appointment and commission**

The Secretary of State is empowered to appoint and commission commissioned abstracters in and for the several counties of this State, in any number in which applications may be made to the Secretary of State, as in his or her judgment may be deemed advisable.

>>**240.260. Term of office**

The term of office of a commissioned abstracter shall be for 4 years.

>>**240.270. Fee for commission; oath and bond**

1. Each commissioned abstracter, before entering upon the acts authorized in NRS 240.240 to 240.330, inclusive, and at the time the commissioned abstracter receives his or her commission, shall:

(a) Pay to the Secretary of State the sum of $10.

(b) Take the official oath as prescribed by law, which oath shall be endorsed on his or her commission.

(c) Enter into a bond to the State of Nevada in the sum of $2,000, to be approved by the district judge of the county for which the commissioned abstracter may be appointed.

2. Each commissioned abstracter shall have his or her commission, together with the bond, recorded in the office of the clerk of the county for which the commissioned abstracter has been appointed.

>>**240.280. Seal**

1. Each commissioned abstracter shall provide an official seal with which the commissioned abstracter shall authenticate all his or her official acts. There shall be engraved on the official seal:

(a) The name of the county for which the commissioned abstracter has been commissioned.

(b) The name of the State.

(c) The name of the commissioned abstracter.

(d) The words "Commissioned Abstracter."

2. An impression of the official seal shall be made on

第 240.170 条至第 240.230 条被废止 [FN1]
第 240.170 条至第 240.230 条被废止 [FN1]
第 240.170 条至第 240.230 条被废止 [FN1]
第 240.170 条至第 240.230 条被废止 [FN1]

概括委托人

>> 240.240 职务的设立

特此为本州的某些郡设立概括委托人职称。

>> 240.250 任命和委托

州务卿有权为本州的某些郡任命和指定概括委托人，任何认为自己具备明智的判断力的人均可以向州务卿提出申请。

>> 240.260 任职期限

概括委托人的任期为4年。

>> 240.270 委任费用；宣誓与保证金

1. 概括委托人在收到委任状或在执行根据《内华达州修正法案》第 240.240 条至第 240.330 条授权的行为之前，应：

（a）向州务卿支付 10 美元。

（b）依法正式宣誓，宣誓应在其委任状上背书。

（c）向内华达州提供 2000 美元的保证金，在得到该郡的地方法官批准后，该概括委托人的任命成立。

2. 每个概括委托人应将其委任状连同保证金在作出任命的郡书记官办公室记录存档。

>> 240.280 印章

1. 每位概括委托人应提供正式印章，用于概括委托人可对其所有的职务行为进行认证。公章上应刻有：

（a）被委托时所在郡的名称。

（b）州的名称。

（c）概括委托人的姓名。

（d）"概括委托人"一词。

2. 在记录保证金之前，应在每个概括委托人的官

the official bond of each commissioned abstracter before recording the bond.

>>240.290. Acts may be performed anywhere in State

All acts of any commissioned abstracter performed anywhere within this State shall be of the same force and validity as if performed within the county for which the commissioned abstracter was appointed and in which he or she resides.

>>240.300. Powers

A commissioned abstracter shall have authority:

1. To make search and examination of all public records and compile abstracts of title to real property or other property therefrom.

2. To make abstracts or copies of any and all instruments of record in any public office within this state, and certify the same in the official name and title of the commissioned abstracter, and under his or her official seal.

>>240.310. Fees

Each commissioned abstracter shall be entitled to charge and receive, from a person or persons by whom the commissioned abstracter is employed, for services rendered, such fees as would be considered just and reasonable.

>>240.320. Revocation of commission

The Secretary of State may at any time, for cause, revoke the commission of a commissioned abstracter.

>>240.330. Penalties

1. For any misconduct or neglect in any of the matters in which any commissioned abstracter appointed under the authority of NRS 240.240 to 240.330, inclusive, is authorized to act, the commissioned abstracter shall be liable on his or her official bond to the person or persons injured thereby for all damages sustained.

2. For any willful violation or neglect any commissioned abstracter shall be subject to criminal prosecution, and may be punished by fine not exceeding $2,000 and removal from office.

方保证金上印公章。

>> 240.290 可在州的任何地方执行职务

概括委托人在本州任何地方执行的所有职务行为，与概括委托人在被委任郡内进行的行为具有相同的效力。

>> 240.300 权力

概括委托人有权：

1. 对所有公共记录进行搜索和审查，编纂不动产或其他财产的所有权摘要。

2. 制作本州的公职部门中所有记录文书的摘要或副本并以概括委托人的职称、头衔和公章证实文书的摘要或副本与原件一致。

>> 240.310 费用

每名概括委托人，均有权从雇主处收取为其提供服务的费用，此项费用应被视为是公正合理的。

>> 240.320 委任的撤销

州务卿可在任何时候，有理由地撤销概括委托人的委任。

>> 240.330 处罚

1. 概括委托人根据《内华达州修正法案》第240.240 条至第 240.330 条被委任和授权，因履行职务中的任何不当行为或疏忽造成持续损害的，须使用职务保证金向受到损害的人承担责任。

2. 作出任何故意违反或疏忽行为的概括委托人应受到刑事起诉，并将被处以不超过 2000 美元的罚款和免职处罚。

宾夕法尼亚州

宾夕法尼亚州公证人法

The Notary Public Law
(Act No. 373 of 1953, as amended by Act 151 of 2002, effective July 1, 2003)

公证人法
（1953年第373号法案，经2002年第151号法案修改，2003年7月1日生效）

Section1 1. Short Title

This act shall be known and may be cited as "The Notary Public Law."

Section 2. Appointment of Notaries

The Secretary of the Commonwealth is hereby authorized to appoint and commission, for a term of four years from the date of appointment, as many notaries public as, in the Secretary's judgment, the interest of the public may require, whose jurisdiction shall be co-extensive with the boundaries of the Commonwealth.

Section 3. Eligibility

(a) Any person who is eighteen (18) years of age or over, who resides or is employed within this Commonwealth and who is of good character, integrity and ability shall be eligible for the office of notary public.

(b) Any person who is a notary public and who resides outside this Commonwealth shall be deemed to have irrevocably appointed the Secretary of the Commonwealth as the person's agent upon whom may be served any summons, subpoena, order or other process.

Section 4. Disqualification; Exception

The following persons shall be ineligible to hold the office of notary public:

(1) Any person holding any judicial office in this Commonwealth, except the office of justice of the peace, magistrate, or alderman.

(2) Every member of Congress, and any person,

第1条 简称

本法案应称为并可引用为《公证人法》。

第2条 公证人之任命

本法授权州务卿在本州范围内依据其判断，任命、委任维护本州利益所必需数量的公证人，公证人任期自任命之日起计4年。

第3条 任职资格

（a）年满18周岁，居住或就职于本州，品行良好、正直有为者可担任公证人一职。

（b）居住于本州之外的公证人视为其已不可撤销地授权州务卿为其代理，可代为接收传唤、传票、法院命令或处理其他程序。

第4条 无任职资格情形及其例外

下列人无公证人任职资格：

（1）承担司法职务者，治安法官、治安官、市议员除外；

（2）美国国会成员，以及任何基于利益或信任供

whether an officer, a subordinate officer, or agent, holding any office or appointment of profit or trust under the legislative, executive, or judiciary departments of the government of the United States, to which a salary, fees or perquisites are attached.

Section 5. Application to Become a Notary Public

(a) Applications for appointment to the office of notary public shall be made to the Secretary of the Commonwealth, on forms prescribed and furnished by the secretary, and shall be accompanied by a nonrefundable filing fee as set forth in section 618-A of the act of April 9, 1929 (P.L. 177, No. 175), known as "The Administrative Code of 1929," payable to the order of the "Commonwealth of Pennsylvania." Each application shall bear the endorsement of the Senator of the district in which the applicant resides or, if the applicant does not reside in this Commonwealth, the endorsement of the Senator of the district in which the applicant is employed. In the case of a vacancy in that senatorial district, the application shall be endorsed by the Senator of an adjacent district.

(b) Before issuing to any applicant a commission as notary public, the Secretary of the Commonwealth shall be satisfied that the applicant is of good moral character, and is familiar with the duties and responsibilities of a notary public. The application must contain no material misstatement or omission of fact, and the applicant shall not:

(1) have been convicted of or pled guilty or nolo contendere to a felony or a lesser offense incompatible with the duties of a notary public during the five (5) year period preceding the date of the application; or

(2) have had a prior notary public commission revoked by the Commonwealth or any other state during the five (5) year period preceding the date of the application. The Secretary of the Commonwealth may, for good cause, reject any application of any notary public subject to the right of notice, hearing and adjudication and the right of appeal therefrom in accordance with 2 Pa.C.S. Chs. 5 Subch. A (relating to practice and procedure of Commonwealth agencies) and 7 Subch. A (relating to judicial review of Commonwealth agency action), known as the Administrative Agency Law.

(c) As a condition for the Secretary of the Commonwealth's issuance of a notary commission to an applicant not appointed to the office of notary public as of the effective date of this subsection, a notary applicant must complete at least three (3) hours of approved notary education

职于美国政府立法、行政、司法部门或受其任命，享有工资、费用或补贴者，无论其是官员、下级官员还是代理人。

第 5 条　成为公证人之申请

（a）成为公证人之申请应以州务卿指定并提供之格式向其提交，随申请需附上 1929 年 4 月 9 日法案（即《1929 年行政法典》）618-A 条规定的申请费，申请费凭宾夕法尼亚联盟指定付款，一经缴纳不予退还。申请材料需经申请者居住地所在区参议员背书，如申请者非本州居民，则由供职地所在区参议员背书。该选区参议员空缺时，申请材料应由毗邻选区参议员背书。

（b）在发给申请者公证人委任状前，州务卿应确定申请者品行良好，熟悉公证人职责。申请材料中不得包含重大虚假陈述或事实遗漏，且申请者：

（1）自申请之日起回溯 5 年内，不得就重罪或与公证人职责冲突之较轻罪行被判或自认有罪。

（2）自申请之日起回溯 5 年内，不得有被本州或他州撤销此前公证人任命之情形。州务卿可依据正当理由拒绝受理公证人申请，对此，申请者依据 2 Pa.C.S. Chs. 5 Subch. A（关于州机构的实践与程序）和 7 Subch. A（关于州机构行为的司法审查），即《行政机构法》，享有告知权、听证权、终裁权和上诉权。

（c）对于截至本款规定生效前尚未被任命为公证人的申请者，州务卿向其发放公证人委任状的一项条件是，该申请人在申请前 6 个月内必须完成至少 3 小时的经认证公证人教育课程。

within the six (6) month period immediately preceding their application.

(d) Notary education may either be interactive or classroom instruction. All education programs shall be preapproved by the Secretary of the Commonwealth with a core curriculum that includes the duties and responsibilities of the notary office and electronic notarization. Compiler's Note: Section 15 of Act 67 of 1990 provided that section 5 is repealed insofar as it relates to fee payments.

Section 6. Application for Reappointment

Applications for reappointment to the office of notary public shall be filed at least two months prior to the expiration of the commission under which the notary is acting. Persons seeking reappointment must continue to meet the requirements set forth in section 5 in order to be reappointed

Section 7. Vacation of Office; Change of Residence

(a) In the event of any change of address within the Commonwealth, notice in writing or electronically shall be given to the Secretary of the Commonwealth and the recorder of deeds of the county of original appointment by a notary public within five (5) days of such change. For the purpose of this subsection, "address" means office address. A notary public vacates his office by removing the notary's residence and business address from the Commonwealth, and such removal shall constitute a resignation from the office of notary public as of the date of removal.

(b) If a notary public neither resides nor works in the Commonwealth, that notary public shall be deemed to have resigned from the office of notary public as of the date the residency ceases or employment within the Commonwealth terminates. A notary public who resigns that notary's commission in accordance with this subsection shall notify the Secretary of the Commonwealth in writing of the effective date of the resignation.

Section 8. Oath of Office; Bond; Recording

Every notary, upon appointment and prior to entering upon the duties of the office of notary public, shall take and subscribe the constitutional oath of office, and shall give a surety bond, payable to the Commonwealth of Pennsylvania, in the amount of ten thousand dollars ($ 10,000), which bond shall, after being recorded, be approved by and filed with the Secretary of the Commonwealth. Every such bond shall have as surety a duly authorized surety company or two sufficient individual sureties, to be approved by the Secretary of the Common-

（d）公证人教育课程既可以是互动教学，也可以是课堂教学。所有的教育项目须事先经州务卿批准，并包含阐述公证人职责和电子公证的核心课程。

编纂者批注：根据1990年第67号法案第15条，第5条有关费用支付之规定已被废止。

第6条 连任之申请

寻求连任之公证人应在其现有任期期满前，至少提前2个月提交申请。寻求连任者须确保持续满足第5条所列明的要求，以获得连任。

第7条 辞职及变更居住地

（a）如公证人在本州范围内变更其地址的，公证人应自变更之日起5日内，以书面或电子形式通知州务卿和原任命郡的契约记录人。就本款而言，"地址"是指办公地址。公证人通过将其住所地和营业地转移出本州辞职，此类转移自转移之日起构成辞职。

（b）如公证人不居住且不供职于本州的，则自其不再居住或不再供职于本州之日起，视为其已辞去公证人一职。公证人根据本款规定辞去公证人一职的，应以书面形式通知州务卿辞职生效日期。

第8条 就职宣誓；保证金；记录

所有公证人，一经任命，在履职前应进行就职宣誓并签名，并应向宾夕法尼亚联盟缴纳数额为10000美元的保证金，该保证金在登记后，应交由州务卿批准并向其提交。所有该类保证金应由一个经正式授权的公司或两个足可胜任的个人充当保证人，并须经州务卿批准，以保证公证人诚信履职，保证如遇公证人死亡、辞职或被剥夺公证人资格的，自发生之日起30日内，其登记簿和印章将及时送达适格郡的契约记录人处。此类保证金，连同任命和就职宣誓，应一并由公证人获任命或连任时，公证人营业地所在郡的契约

wealth, conditioned for the faithful performance of the duties of the office of notary public and for the delivery of the notary's register and seal to the office of the recorder of deeds of the proper county in case of the death, resignation or disqualification of the notary within thirty (30) days of such event. Such bond, as well as the commission and oath of office, shall be recorded in the office of the recorder of deeds of the county in which the notary maintains an office at the time of appointment or reappointment. The commission of any notary hereafter appointed who shall, for forty-five (45) days after the beginning of the term, neglect to give bond and cause the bond and the commission and oath to be recorded, as above directed, shall be null and void.

Section 9. Registration of Notary's Signature; Fee

(a) The official signature of each notary public shall be registered, in the "Notary Register" provided for such purpose in the prothonotary's office of the county wherein the notary maintains an office, within forty-five (45) days after appointment or reappointment, and in any county to which the notary may sub-sequently move the notary's office, within thirty (30) days thereafter. In counties of the second class, such signature shall also be registered in the clerk of courts' office within said period.

(b) The fee to be charged by the prothonotary for recording a notary's signature shall be fifty ($ .50) cents.

(c) In acting as a notary public, a notary shall sign the notary's name exactly and only as it appears on the commission or otherwise execute the notary's electronic signature in a manner that attributes such signature to the notary public identified on the commission.

(d) A county may permit notaries to register their electronic signatures

Section 10. Change of Name

Whenever the name of any notary is changed by decree of court, or otherwise, such notary may continue to perform official acts, in the name in which he or she was commissioned, until the expiration of his or her term, but he or she shall, within thirty (30) days after entry of such decree, or after such name change, if not by decree of court, notify the Secretary of the Commonwealth and the recorder of deeds of the county in which he or she maintains an office of such change of name. The Secretary of the Commonwealth shall mark the public records relating to the notary accordingly and the recorder of deeds shall record the notification. Application for reappointment of

记录人记录。此后任命之公证人，在其任期开始后45日内未按上述要求缴纳保证金或记录保证金、任命和宣誓的，其任命失效。

第九条 公证人签名之登记及收费

（a）自任命或连任之日起45日内，各公证人的正式签名应登记于公证人营业地所在郡首席书记官办公室的公证人登记簿上；公证人此后将营业地迁移至他郡的，应在迁移后30日内向当地登记签名。在第二类郡中，此类签名还应在上述期限内向法庭书记官办公室登记。

（b）首席书记官就记录公证人签名收取的费用为50美分。

（c）公证人执业过程中，仅可用与委任状所载完全一致的姓名签名；使用电子签名时，签名方式应确保可识别出签名出自委任状上所指的公证人。

（d）各郡应允许公证人登记其电子签名。

第10条 姓名之变更

无论何时，公证人姓名因法院裁决或其他原因变更的，公证人在其任期期满前，可继续以其受任命之姓名实施职务行为，但他／她应自接到此类裁决后30日内，或自变更之日起30日内（如果是因法院裁决以外的原因变更姓名的），告知州务卿和其营业地所在郡契约记录人姓名变更情况。州务卿应相应标记与公证人相关之公共记录，而契约记录人则应记录该告知。此类公证人申请连任时应使用新的姓名。

such notary shall be made in the new name.

Section 11. Refund of Fee. – (Repealed June 30, 1988, P.L. 462, No. 78)

Section 12. Notarial Seal

(a) A notary public shall provide and keep an official seal which shall be used to authenticate all the acts, instruments and attestations of the notary. The seal shall be a rubber stamp and shall show clearly in the following order: the words "Notarial Seal"; the name and surname of the notary and the words "Notary Public"; the name of the municipality and county in which the notary maintains an office; and the date the notary's commission expires.

(b) The seal shall have a maximum height of one (1) inch and width of three and one-half (3 1/2) inches, with a plain border. It shall be stamped in a prominent place on the official notarial certificate near the notary's signature in such a manner as to be capable of photographic reproduction.

(c) (Deleted by Act 151 of 2002, effective July 1, 2003)

(d) The notary public seal is the exclusive property of the notary to whom it is issued, and a notary shall be responsible at all times for maintaining custody and control of the seal. No notary public shall permit the use of the seal by another person

(e) The use of a notary public seal by a person who is not the notary public named on the seal shall be deemed an impersonation of a notary public under and shall be subject to the penalties set forth in 18 Pa.C.S. § 4913 (relating to impersonating a notary public).

(f) Notwithstanding other provisions of this section, in accordance with the act of December 16, 1999 (P.L. 971, No. 69), known as the "Electronic Transactions Act," a notary public is not required to use an electronic seal for the notarization, acknowledgment or verification of electronic records and electronic signatures, provided that, in any event, the following information is attached to or logically associated with the electronic signature or electronic record being notarized, acknowledged or verified

(1) The full name of the notary along with the words "Notary Public."

(2) The name of the municipality and the county in which the notary maintains an office.

(3) The date the notary's commission is due to expire.

第 11 条 款项之退还（1988 年 6 月 30 日由 P.L. 462, No. 78 法案废止）

第 12 条 公证印章

（a）公证人应当配备并保有一枚公章，以用于证实公证人的所有行动、法律文件和证词。公章应采用橡皮章，并按下列顺序清晰显示图样："公证印章"字样；公证人的名和姓氏以及"公证人"字样；公证人执业地市、郡名称；公证人任期期满之日。

（b）印章应高不过 1 英寸，宽不过 3.5 英寸，边缘清晰。印章应当以可影印复制的方式，显著加盖于公证证书上公证人签名旁。

（c）由 2002 年第 151 号法案删除，自 2003 年 7 月 1 日起生效。

（d）公证印章是领受该印章的公证人的专有财产，公证人应确保印章时刻处于其保管和掌控下。公证人不得允许他人使用印章。

（e）非印章上指明之公证人者，使用公证人印章的，视为 18 Pa.C.S. § 4913 条款（关于假冒公证人）规定之假冒公证人情形，并应根据该条款惩处。

（f）无论本条其他款项如何规定，依照 1999 年 12 月 16 日法案（P.L. 971, No. 69），即《电子交易法》之规定，公证人在公证、确认或证明电子记录、电子签名时，如待公证、确认或证明之电子记录、电子签名中包含下列信息，或下列信息能与待公证、确认或证明之电子记录、电子签名符合逻辑地相联系，则可无须使用电子印章：

（1）公证人全名和"公证人"字样。

（2）公证人执业地市、郡名称。

（3）公证人任期期满之日。

Section 12.1. Determining Identity of Person Appearing

(a) The officer notarizing the instrument shall know through personal knowledge or have satisfactory evidence that the person appearing before the notary is the person described in and who is executing the instrument. For the purposes of this act and section 5 of the act of July 24, 1941 (P.L.490, No.188), known as the "Uniform Acknowledgment Act," "personal knowledge" means having an acquaintance, derived from association with the individual in relation to other people and based upon a chain of cir-cum-stances surrounding the individual, which establishes the individual's identity, and "satisfactory evidence" means the reliance on the presentation of a current, government-issued identification card bearing a photograph, signature or physical description and serial or identification number, or the oath or affirmation of a credible witness who is personally known to the notary and who personally knows the individual.

(b) In certifying a copy of a document or other item, a notary public shall determine that the proffered copy is a full, true and accurate transcription or reproduction of that which was copied.

Section 13. Date of Expiration of Commission. – (Repealed June 30, 1988, P.L. 462, No. 78)

Section 14. Position of Seal and Date of Expiration of Commission. – (Repealed June 30, 1988, P.L. 462, No. 78)

Section 15. Register; Copies of Records

(a) Every notary public shall keep and maintain custody and control of an accurate chronological register of all official acts by that notary done by virtue of that notary's office, and shall, when thereunto required, give a certified copy of the register in the notary's office to any person applying for same. Each register shall contain the date of the act, the character of the act, and the date and parties to the instrument, and the amount of fee collected for the service. Each notarization shall be indicated separately.

(b) The register and other public records of such notary shall not in any case be liable to be seized, attached or taken in execution for debt or for any demand whatsoever.

(c) A notary public register is the exclusive property of the notary public, may not be used by any other person and may not be surrendered to any employer of the notary upon termination of employment

第12.1条 现身者身份之确定

（a）公证文书之官员应当个人认识或有充分证据证明现身者是文件所载的、执行文件之人。就本法和1941年7月24日法案（即P.L.490, No.188,《统一确认法》）第5条而言，"个人认识"意指通过他人与现身者有所联系，并基于可确立现身者身份的有关事实链条而对其有所了解，"充分证据"则意指依据以下证据之出示：载有照片、签名或体貌描述以及序列号或识别号的现行有效的政府印发之身份证；或公证人个人认识且与现身者个人认识之可信证人的宣誓或声明。

（b）在证实文件或其他物件的副本时，公证人应确定副本是其原件完整、真实且准确的抄本或复制品。

第13条 任期到期日（1988年6月30日由P.L. 462, No. 78法案废止）

第14条 印章之安置与任期到期日（1988年6月30日由P.L. 462, No. 78法案废止）

第15条 登记簿；记录副本

（a）所有公证人应时刻维持其对登记簿的保管和掌控，登记簿按日期排序，准确记录公证人凭借公证人职务所为之所有职务行为，应申请时，公证人应于其办公室给予申请者其要求的经证明的登记簿副本。登记簿中须记载行为日期、行为特征、法律文件之日期和相关当事方，以及所收取之服务费数额。每项公证行为应单独记录。

（b）无论何种情况下，登记簿以及公证人的其他公共记录不可因强制执行债务或其他原因而被没收、扣押或取走。

（c）公证人登记簿是公证人的专属财产，他人不可使用，公证人离职时也不可交付给其雇主。

(d) Upon a notary public's resignation, death or disqualification or upon the revocation or expiration of a commission, unless the notary public applies for a commission within thirty (30) days of the expiration of the prior commission, the notary public's register shall be delivered to the office of the recorder of deeds of the proper county within thirty (30) days of such event.

Section 16. Power to Administer Oaths and Affirmations

(a) Notaries shall have power to administer oaths and affirmations, certify copies and take depositions, affidavits, verifications, upon oath or affirmation and acknowledgments according to law, in all matters belonging or incident to the exercise of their notarial office.

(b) Any person who shall be convicted of having wilfully and knowingly made or taken a false oath, affirmation, deposition, affidavit, certification or acknowledgment before any notary in any matters within their official duties shall be guilty of perjury under and shall be subject to the penalties set forth in 18 Pa.C.S. § 4902 (relating to perjury).

Section 17. Power to take Acknowledgment of Instruments of Writing Relating to Commerce or Navigation and to Make Declarations. – Repealed by 2002, Dec. 9, P.L. 1269, No. 151, effective July 1, 2003

Section 18. Power to Take Depositions, Affidavits and Acknowledgment of Writings Relative to Lands. – Repealed by 2002, Dec. 9, P.L. 1269, No. 151, effective July 1, 2003

Section 19. Limitation on Powers; Fees

(a)to (c)　(Deleted by Act 151 of 2002, effective July 1, 2003.)

(d) No district justice, holding at the same time the office of notary public, shall have jurisdiction in cases arising on papers or documents containing acts by him done in the office of notary public.

(e) No notary public may act as such in any transaction in which he is a party directly or pecuniarily interested. For the purpose of this section, none of the following shall constitute a direct or pecuniary interest:

(1) being a shareholder in a publicly traded company that is a party to the notarized transaction;

(2) being an officer, director or employee of a company that is a party to the notarized transaction, unless the director, officer or employe personally benefits from the transaction other than as provided in clause (3); or

（d）公证人辞职、死亡、失去任职资格或其任命被撤销或到期的，除非该公证人在前一任命到期30日内申请任命，否则公证人登记簿应于上述情形发生30日内交付给适格郡的契约记录人办公室。

第16条　实施宣誓和声明之权力

（a）公证人根据法律实施宣誓、声明和确认时，就其公证职务范围内事项或相关事项，有权实施宣誓和声明，证明副本，提取口供、宣誓证明和证明。

（b）任何人就其职务范围内事项向公证人出具或进行虚假宣誓、声明、证词、宣誓书、证明或确认的，应根据18 Pa.C.S. § 4902条以伪证罪并受到相应惩处。

第17条　就与贸易或航海相关之书面文件进行确认、发表声明之权力（已由2002年12月9日P.L. 1269, No. 151法案废止，自2003年7月1日起生效）

第18条　就与土地相关之书面文件提取口供、出具宣誓书和进行确认之权力（已由2002年12月9日P.L. 1269, No. 151法案废止，自2003年7月1日起生效）

第19条　权力限制；费用

（a）至（c）（由2001年第151号法案删除，自2003年7月1日起生效）

（d）任何地区法官，如同时担任公证人的，遇案件涉及包含其公证行为的文书或文件的，不得管辖。

（e）就与其直接利害相关或经济利益相关之交易，公证人不得进行公证。就本条而言，以下情形不构成与其直接利害相关或经济利益相关：

（1）公证业务一方为公开交易公司，而公证人为其股东的；

（2）公证业务一方为公司，而公证人担任其官员、董事或雇员的。该官员、董事或雇员以第3款以外的方式从业务中个人获利的除外；

(3) receiving a fee that is not contingent upon the completion of the notarized transaction.

Section 20. Admissibility in Evidence

Repealed April 28, 1978, P.L. 202, No. 53, effective June 27, 1978

Section 21. Fees of Notaries Public

(a) The fees of notaries public shall be fixed by the Secretary of the Commonwealth with the approval of the Attorney General.

(b) A notary public shall not charge, attempt to charge or receive a notary public fee that is in excess of the fees fixed by the Secretary of the Commonwealth.

(c) The fees of notaries public shall be displayed in a conspicuous location in the notary's place of business or be provided upon request to any person utilizing the services of the notary. The fees of the notary shall be separately stated. A notary public may waive the right to charge a fee, in which case the requirements of this subsection regarding the display or provision of fees shall not apply.

(d) The fee for any notary public employed by a bank, banking institution or trust company shall be the property of the notary and in no case belong to or be received by the corporation for whom the notary is employed.

Section 22. Rejection of Application; Removal

(a) The Secretary of the Commonwealth may, for good cause, reject any application, issue a written reprimand, suspend or revoke the commission of any notary public.

(b) The Secretary of the Commonwealth may, for good cause, impose a civil penalty not to exceed five hundred dollars ($ 500) for each act or omission which constitutes a violation of this act.

(c) The Secretary of the Commonwealth may, for good cause, order a notary to attend education courses for an act or omission which constitutes a violation of this act.

(d) Any action taken under this section shall be subject to the right of notice, hearing and adjudication, and the right of appeal therefrom, in accordance with 2 Pa.C.S. Chs. 5 Subch. A (relating to practice and procedure of Commonwealth agencies) and 7 Subch. A (relating to judicial review of Commonwealth agency action), known as the Administrative Agency Law.

Section 22.1. Surrender of Seal

(a) Should an application or renewal be rejected,

第 20 条　证据可采性

由 1978 年 4 月 28 日 P.L. 202, No. 53 法案废止，自 1978 年 6 月 27 日起生效。

第 21 条　公证人收费标准

（a）公证人收费标准应经检察总长批准后由州务卿确定。

（b）公证人不得收取、试图收取或接受超出州务卿所定收费标准之公证人费用。

（c）公证人收费标准应列示于其营业地显著位置，或应利用公证服务者要求向其提供。公证人收费标准应分条列明。公证人可放弃其收费之权利，此种情形下，本款有关列示或提供收费标准之要求不再适用。

（d）受银行、金融机构或信托公司雇佣之公证人，其收费为其个人财产，任何情况下不归其雇佣单位所有，不由其雇佣单位收取。

第 22 条　申请之拒绝；免职

（a）依据正当理由，州务卿可拒绝公证人之申请，向其发布书面训诫，暂停或撤销其任命。

（b）依据正当理由，州务卿就每项触犯本法之行为或过失，可处以不超过 500 美元的民事罚款。

（c）依据正当理由，州务卿可命令公证人就其触犯本法之行为或过失，参加教育课程。

（d）就依据本法采取之任何行动，公证人依据 2 Pa.C.S. Chs. 5 Subch. A（关于州机构的实践与程序）和 7 Subch. A（关于州机构行为的司法审查），即《行政机构法》，享有告知权、听证权、终裁权和上诉权。

第 22.1 条　印章之上交

（a）任命申请或连任申请被拒绝的，或因任何原

or should a commission be revoked or recalled for any reason, or should a notary public resign, the applicant or notary shall deliver the seal of office to the Department of State within ten (10) days after notice from the department or from the date of resignation, as the case may be. Any person who violates the provisions of this subsection shall be guilty of a summary offense and upon conviction thereof shall be sentenced to pay a fine not exceeding three hundred dollars ($ 300) or to imprisonment not exceeding ninety (90) days, or both.

(b) Upon the death of a notary public, the notary's personal representative shall deliver the seal of office to the Department of State within ninety (90) days of the date of the notary's death.

Section 22.2. Revocation of Commission for Certain Personal Checks

(a) The Secretary of the Commonwealth may revoke the notary public commission of a notary public who issues to the order of any State agency or the Commonwealth a personal check without sufficient funds on deposit.

(b) Any action taken by the Secretary of the Commonwealth under this section shall be subject to the right of notice, hearing and adjudication and right of appeal therefrom in accordance with 2 Pa.C.S. Chs. 5 Subch. A relating to practice and procedure of Commonwealth agencies) and 7 Subch. A (relating to judicial review of Commonwealth agency action), known as the Administrative Agency Law.

Section 22.3. Regulations. – The Secretary of the Commonwealth shall have the authority to promulgate such rules and regulations as are necessary to administer and enforce this act

Section 23. Specific Repeal

The act, approved the eighteenth day of May, one thousand nine hundred forty-nine (Pamphlet Laws 1440), entitled "An act concerning notaries public and amending, revising, consolidating and changing the law relating thereto," is hereby repealed absolutely.

Section 24. Repeals

(a) The following acts and parts of acts are repealed:

The act of April 14, 1828 (P.L.447, No.188), entitled "An act to authorizes the appointment of commissioners to take the acknowledgement of deeds and instruments of writing under seal."

因被撤销或收回任命的，或公证人辞职的，公证人应自接到通知之日或辞职之日起10日内，将公章上交州务院。任何违反本款规定者，将被判处即决犯罪，并据此除以最高300美元的罚款或最长90天的监禁或两者并处。

（b）公证人死亡的，其个人代表应自其去世之日起90日内将公章上交州务院。

第22.2条　因个人支票原因撤销任命

（a）公证人开立空头支票以应对国家机关或本州要求的，州务卿可撤销其任命。

（b）就州务卿依据本条规定采取的任何行动，公证人依据2 Pa.C.S. Chs. 5 Subch. A（关于州机构的实践与程序）和7 Subch. A（关于州机构行为的司法审查），即《行政机构法》，享有告知权、听证权、终裁权和上诉权。

第22.3条　法规（为实施、执行本法，州务卿应有权颁布必要之规则、法规）

第23条　明确废止

兹彻底废止1949年5月18日通过的《关于公证人和有关法律修正、修订、统一、变更之法案》（法律汇编1440）。

第24条　废止

（a）以下法案全部或部分废止：

1828年4月14日法案（P.L.447, No.188），题为《授权任命专员以确认盖章契约和书面文件之法案》。

The act of March 13, 1839 (P.L.92, No.44), entitled "A supplement to an act entitled 'An act to authorize the appointment of commissioners to take the acknowledgment of deeds and instruments of writing under seal,' approved on the fourteenth day of April, one thousand eight hundred and twenty- eight."

The act of April 6, 1843 (P.L.175, No.83), entitled "A supplement to an act entitled 'An Act to authorize the appointment of Commissioners to take the acknowledgment of deeds and instruments of writing under seal.'"

Section 15 of the act of April 9, 1849 (P.L.524, No.354), entitled "A supplement to an act relative to the venders of mineral waters; and an act relative to the Washington coal company; to sheriffs' sales of real estate; to the substitution of executors and trustees when plaintiffs; to partition in the courts of common pleas, and for other purposes."

(b) All other acts and parts of acts are repealed insofar as they are inconsistent with this act.

1839年3月13日法案（P.L.92, No.44），题为《〈授权任命专员以确认盖章契约和书面文件之法案〉之补充法案》（1828年4月14日通过）。

1843年4月6日法案（P.L.175, No.83），题为《〈授权任命专员以确认盖章契约和书面文件之法案〉之补充法案》。

1849年4月9日法案（P.L.524, No.354）第15条，该法案题为《有关矿泉水供应商、华盛顿煤炭公司、不动产司法拍卖、原告方变更执行人和受托人、普通法院之财产分割及其他目的之法案的补充法案》。

（b）所有其他法案，全部或部分与本法不一致的，相应废止。

新宾夕法尼亚州公证人法

NEW PENNSYLVANIA NOTARY PUBLIC LAW

House Bill 25 was signed into law on October 9, 2013 and became Act 73 of 2013. Act 73 adopts the Revised Uniform Law on Notarial Acts (RULONA) and completely replaces the former Notary Public Law and Uniform Acknowledgment Act with modern language and best practices.

Act 73 will be implemented in several phases

Effective immediately on October 9, 2013 is the Department's authority to make regulations to implement the new law; the Department's authority to approve basic and continuing notary education courses; and section 329.1(a) of the Act (relating to the authority of the Department of fix the fees of notaries public by regulation).

The remainder of RULONA impacting Pennsylvania notary public practice and procedure will most likely not take effect until 2015. Prior to approving new education courses and implementing RULONA in full, the Department of State plans to adopt comprehensive regulations to implement the new law. Until the regulations are finalized and the Department has approved new notary education courses that include the content of the new regulations, the remainder of RULONA will not go into effect.

After the Department has approved basic and continuing notary education courses, which will prepare notaries public for the requirements of the new law, it will issue public notice that the remainder of RULONA will take effect in 180 days from the date of the notice.

Notaries who hold or have held commissions on the date of the notice will have six months to comply with the revised education requirement if they are seeking reappointment after the 180 days has passed. New applicants for appointment and commission who apply 180 days after the date of the notice will be required to comply with the new law, including a new requirement to pass an examination covering the statutes, regulations, procedures and ethics relevant to notarial acts.

Important changes included in Act 73/RULONA which will take effect 180 days from the date of the notice that the Department has approved new notary education

新宾夕法尼亚州公证人法

众议院第 25 号法案于 2013 年 10 月 9 日签署通过立法，成为 2013 年第 73 号法案。第 73 号法案采纳经修订的《公证行为统一法》（RULONA）并用现代的语言和最佳实践完全取代了原公证人法律和统一确认法。

第 73 号法案将分成几阶段实施

自 2013 年 10 月 9 日起立即生效的：州务院制定法规以贯彻新法的权力；州务院批准公证人基础教育和继续教育课程的权力；法案第 329.1(a) 条（有关州务院通过法规确定公证人收费标准之权力）。

RULONA 中影响宾夕法尼亚州公证人实践和程序的剩余部分在 2015 年前不大可能生效。在批准新的教育课程和完全实施 RULONA 之前，州务院计划先采取一系列法规以落实新法。在所有法规最终得以确定，并且州务院批准包含新法规内容的新公证教育课程前，RULONA 剩余部分不会生效。

在州务院批准旨在帮助公证人适应新法要求的公证人基础教育和继续教育课程后，州务院应发布公告，宣布 RULONA 剩余部分自公告之日起 180 日后生效。

截至公告之日持有或曾持有公证人任命的公证人，如寻求 180 日后再次任命的，有 6 个月时间达到修订后的教育要求。自公告之日起 180 日后申请任命的新申请人，将要求其满足新法规定，包括通过一场旨在考查与公证行为相关的法律、法规、程序和职业道德的考试。

第 73 号法案/RULONA 自州务院批准新公证人教育课程之公告发布之日起 180 日后生效，其中的重要变化包括：

courses include:

New notaries will be required to pass an examination to obtain their first commission;

All notaries seeking reappointment must complete continuing education (even those previously exempt) but will have the option of more varied continuing education courses to ensure the maintenance and enhancement of skill, knowledge and competency.

Application fee will be $42

A new notarial act of witnessing or attesting a signature is defined in the law

Basic forms of certificates for most notarial acts are set forth in the law

Specific prohibitions on use of the term "notario publico" and practicing law and related new advertising requirements

Increased enforcement and administrative penalties available to the Department for violation of the Act

What remains the same:

The appointment and commissioning process, including:

Notary commission is four years in length

Senatorial endorsement of applicant is required

$10,000 bond is required (unless changed by regulation of the Department)

A notary must record bond, oath and commission with the county Recorder of Deeds prior to entering into duties as notary public

A notary must register his official signature with the county Prothonotary (Clerk of Courts in counties of the second class)

The Department will maintain a public searchable notary database (includes notaries authorized for electronic notarization)

A notary must maintain a register of all notarial acts (now called a journal)

A notary must require the personal appearance of a document signer before the notary

A notary must have personal knowledge or satisfactory evidence of identity of the individual appearing before the notary

A notary must use a notary seal (now called official stamp) on all official acts of the notary

The regulations promulgated by the Department will provide more detail on both new and unchanged statutory requirements. Please look for more information on this webpage as the Department implements Act 73 of 2013.

December 5, 2013

将要求新公证人通过考试以获取其首次任命；

所有寻求再次任命的公证人必须完成继续教育（包括之前被豁免者），但亦可选择完成可确保技能、知识和能力得以保持和提升的其他更为多样化的继续教育课程。

申请费变更为42美元。

法律中新规定了一种见证或证实签名的公证行为。

法律中规定了大多数公证行为对应的证书基本格式。

有关术语"涉信律师"（notario publico）之使用和法律执业的特殊禁止性规定，以及相关的新宣传要求。

就违反本法行为，赋予州务院更强的执行权和行政处罚权。

相同的是：

在任命和委任环节包括：

公证人任期均为四年；

均要求申请人获得参议员背书；

均要求缴纳10000美元保证金（除非州务院法规另有规定）；

公证人在履职前，必须至郡契约记录人处记录其保证金、宣誓和任命。

公证人必须在郡首席书记官（第二类郡的法院书记官）处登记其正式签名。

州务院必须建有公用的能进行搜索的公证人数据库（包含授权进行电子公证的公证人信息）。

公证人必须保有一本记录所有公证行为的登记簿（现称之为日志）。

公证人必须要求文件签署者亲临现场。

公证人必须与亲临现场者个人认识，或有充分证据证明其身份。

公证人进行所有公证行为时，必须使用公证人印章（现称之为公章）。

就新出台的和保持不变的法定要求，州务院发布的法规将提供更多细节。想要寻求更多信息的，请于州务院实施2013年第73号法案期间，登录本网页查看。

2013年12月5日

宾夕法尼亚州统一确认法

Uniform Acknowledgment Act

(Act No. 188, approved July 24, 1941, as amended by Acts 353 and 354 of 1947, Act 3 of 1951, Act 58 of 1957, Act 61 of 1961 and Act 71 of 1981)

AN ACT

Relating to acknowledgments of written instruments, and to make uniform the law with relation thereto.

The General Assembly of the Commonwealth of Pennsylvania hereby enacts as follows:

Section 1. Acknowledgment of Instruments

Any instruments may be acknowledged in the manner and form now provided by the laws of this State or as provided by this act

Section 2. Acknowledgment within this State

The acknowledgment of any instrument may be made in this State before

A judge of a court of record;

A clerk, prothonotary or deputy prothonotary or deputy clerk of a court having a seal;

A recorder of deeds or deputy recorder of deeds;

A notary public;

A justice of the peace, magistrate or alderman.

Section 3. Acknowledgment within the United States

The acknowledgmentof any instrument may be made without the State, but within the United States, orterritory or insular possession of the United States, or in the District of Columbia, and within the jurisdiction of the officer before

A clerk or deputy of any federal court;

clerk, prothonotary or deputy prothonotary or deputy clerk of anycourt of record of any state or other jurisdiction;

A notary public;

A recorder of deeds.

Section 4. Acknowledgment without the United States

Theacknowledgment of any instrument may be made

统一确认法

（第 188 号法案，1941 年 7 月 24 日通过，由 1947 年第 353 号、第 354 号法案，1957 年第 3 号法案，1957 年第 58 号法案，1961 年第 61 号法案和 1981 年第 71 号法案修正）

本法案
关乎书面法律文件之确认和相关法律之统一。

宾夕法尼亚联盟大会现颁布法律如下：

第 1 条　法律文件之确认

所有法律文件均可以本州法律或本法案规定的方式和形式进行确认。

第 2 条　本州境内之确认

本州境内，任何法律文件可由下列人士确认：

记录法庭的法官；
持有印章的法庭书记官、法庭首席书记官、法庭代理首席书记官、法庭代理书记官；
契约记录人或代理契约记录人；
公证人；
治安法官、安官或市议员。

第 3 条　美国国境内之确认

身处本州州境外，而位于美国国内，或美国管辖之领土和岛屿上，或哥伦比亚特区内，任何法律文件可由该辖区的下列人士确认：

联邦法庭之书记官或代理书记官；
任何州或其他辖区的记录法庭的书记官、首席书记官或代理首席书记官或代理书记官；
公证人；
契约记录人。

第 4 条　美国境外的确认

于美国境外，任何法律文件可由下列人士确认：

without the United States before:

An ambassador, minister, charge d' affaires, counselor to or secretaryof a legation, consul general, consul, vice-consul, commercial attache orconsular agent of the Untied States accredited to the country whereacknowledgment is made;

A notary public of the country where acknowledgment is made;

A judge or clerk of a court of record of the country where acknowledgment is made.

Section 5. Requisites of Acknowledgment

The officer taking the acknowledgment shall know or have satisfactory evidence that the person making the acknowledgment is the person described in and who executed the instrument

Section 6. Acknowledgment by a Married Women

An acknowledgment of amarried woman may be made in the same form as though she were unmarried

Section 7. Forms of Certificates

An officer taking the acknowledgment shallendorse thereon or attach thereto a certificate substantially in one of the following forms:

(1)By individuals –
State of _____
County of _____
On this, the _____ day of _____, 19____, before me _____,
the undersigned officer, personally appeared _____, known to me (orsatisfactorily proven) to be the person(s) whose name(s) is/are subscribed to thewithin instrument, and acknowledged that _____ executed the same forthe purposes therein contained.

In witness whereof, I hereunto set my hand and official seals.

(2)By a Corporation
State of _____
County of _____
On this, the _____ day of _____, 19____, before me _____,
the undersigned officer, personally appeared _____, known to me (orsatisfactorily proven) to be the person(s) whose name(s) is/are subscribed to thewithin instrument, and acknowledged that _____ executed the same forthe purposes therein contained.

In witness whereof, I hereunto set my hand and offi-

美国派驻确认实施地所在国的大使、公使、代办、参赞或公使馆的秘书、总领事、领事、副领事、商务专员或领事代理人；

确认实施地所在国公证人；

确认实施地所在国记录法庭的法官或书记员。

第5条 认证要件

实施确认的官员应认识，或有充分证据证明要求确认者是法律文件中所述之人和签署法律文件之人：

第6条 已婚女性之确认

已婚女性在实施公证时，所采取之格式和未婚女性无异。

第7条 证明之格式

实施确认的官员应大致按照以下格式在证书上背书或给证书粘贴附件：

（1）个人进行确认的：
_____ 州
_____ 郡
于此，19____ 年 ____ 月 ____ 日，
署名其下的官员 ____ 亲临
本人 ____ 面前，
我知悉（或有充分证据证明）其为签署文件者，且该官员确认其为文件所载之目的签署了文件。

为证明以上内容，我特此签名并盖章。

（2）公司进行确认的：
_____ 州
_____ 郡
于此，19____ 年 ____ 月 ____ 日，
署名其下的官员 ____ 亲临
本人 ____ 面前，
我知悉（或有充分证据证明）其为签署文件者，且该官员确认其为文件所载之目的签署了文件。

为证明以上内容，我特此签名并盖章。

cial seals.

Any deed, conveyance, mortgage or other instrument in writing, made andexecuted by a corporation, may be acknowledged by any officer of saidcorporation whose signature appears on such deed, conveyance, mortgage or otherinstrument in writing, in execution or in attestation of the execution thereof.

(3) By an attorney in fact
State of _____
County of _____
On this, the _____ day of _____, 19____, before me _____,
he undersigned officer, personally appeared ___ _____, known to me (orsatisfactorily proven) to be the person(s) whose name(s) is/are subscribed to thewithin instrument, and acknowledged that _____ executed the same forthe purposes therein contained.

In witness whereof, I hereunto set my hand and official seals.

(4)By any public official or deputy thereof or by any trustee, administrator, guardian, or executor
State of _____
County of _____
On this, the _____ day of _____, 19____, before me _____,
he undersigned officer, personally appeared _____, known to me (or satisfactorily proven) to be the person(s) whose name(s) is/are subscribed to the within instrument, and acknowledged that _____ executed the same for the purposes therein contained.

In witness whereof, I hereunto set my hand and official seals.

(5) By any attorney-at-law --
State of _____
County of _____
On this, the _____ day of _____, 19____, before me _____,
the undersigned officer, personally appeared ____ _____, known to me (or satisfactorily proven) to be a member of the bar of the highest court of said state and a subscribing witness to the within instrument and certified that he was personally present when _____, whose name(s) is/are subscribed to the within instrument executed the same, and that said persons acknowledge that _____ executed the same for the purposes therein contained.

In witness whereof, I hereunto set my hand and offi-

任何由公司出具并签署之契约、产权转让证书、抵押单据或其他书面法律文件，上述公司之官员在起草、签署或证实签署时在上述文件上署名的，可对上述文件进行确认。

（3）代理人进行确认的：
_____ 州
_____ 郡
于此，19____ 年 ____ 月 ____ 日，
署名其下的官员 _____ 亲临
本人 ____ 面前，
我知悉（或有充分证据证明）其为签署文件者，
且该官员确认其为文件所载之目的签署了文件。

为证明以上内容，我特此签名并盖章。

（4）公职人员或其副手或受托人、管理人监护人或遗嘱执行人进行确认的
_____ 州
_____ 郡
于此，19____ 年 ____ 月 ____ 日，
署名其下的官员 _____ 亲临
本人 _____ 面前，
我知悉（或有充分证据证明）其为签署文件者，且该官员确认其为文件所载之目的签署了文件。

为证明以上内容，我特此签名并盖章。

（5）律师进行确认的：
_____ 州
_____ 郡
于此，19____ 年 ____ 月 ____ 日，
署名其下的官员 _____ 亲临
本人 ____ 面前，
我知悉（或有充分证据证明）其为上述州的最高法院律师协会会员且是文件的签名见证人，该官员证明当签署文件者 ____ 签名时，他正在现场，且签署者 ____ 确认其为文件所载之目的签署了文件。

为证明以上内容，我特此签名并盖章。

cial seals.

Section 8. Execution of Certificate

The certificate of the acknowledging officer shall be completed by his signature, his official seal, if he has one, the title of his office, and, if he is a notary public, the date his commission expires.

Section 9. Authentication of Acknowledgments

(1) If the acknowledgment is taken within this State, or if taken without this State by an officer of this State, or is made without the United States by an officer of the Untied States, no authentication shall be necessary.

(2) If the acknowledgment is taken without this State, but in the United States, a territory or insular possession of the United States, or the District of Columbia, no authentication shall be necessary if the official before whom the acknowledgment is taken affixes his official seal to the instrument so acknowledged; otherwise the certificate shall be authenticated by a certificate as to the official character of such officer, executed(1) if the acknowledgment is taken by a clerk or deputy clerk of court, by the presiding judge of the court, or (2) if the acknowledgment is taken by some other authorized officer, by the official having custody of the official record of the election, appointment or commission of the officer taking such acknowledgment.

Section 10. Acknowledgments under Laws of other States

Notwithstanding any provision in this act contained, the acknowledgment of any instrument without this State in compliance with the manner and form prescribed by the laws of the place of its execution, if in a state, territory or insular possession of the United States, or in the District of Columbia, verified by the official seal of the officer before whom it is acknowledged or authenticated, in the manner provided by section 9, subsection 2 hereof, shall have the same effect as an acknowledgment in the manner and form prescribed by the laws of this State for instruments executed within the State

Section 10.1. Acknowledgment by persons Serving in or with the Armed Forces of the Untied States

In addition to the acknowledgment of instruments in the manner and form and as otherwise now and hereafter authorized by the laws of this State or by this Act, persons serving in or with the Armed Forces of the United States or their dependents wherever located may acknowledge the same before any commissioned officer in active ser-

第 8 条　证书之生效

实施公证的官员的证明应包含其签名、公章、职务头衔（若有的话）和其任命到期日（若其为公证人的话）。

第 9 条　确认之证实

（1）如确认是在本州内实施的，或是由本州官员在本州之外实施的，或是由美国官员在美国境外实施的，则无须加以证实。

（2）如果确认实施地位于本州外，但在美国国内，在美国领土或美国管辖的岛屿上，或在哥伦比亚特区的，则对于实施公证之官员已在经确认文件上加盖公章的，无须证实；否则的话，该确认证书须经有关实施者职务角色的证书证实，①如实施确认者是法院书记员或代理书记员的，证书由首席法官签署，②如实施确认者是其他经授权的官员的，证书由掌握实施确认者选举、任命、委任官方记录的官员签署。

第 10 条　根据他州法律实施之确认

无论本法如何规定，在本州之外，遵照实施地法律规定的方式和格式对任何法律文件进行确认的，如发生在美国其他州、美国管辖领土或岛屿、哥伦比亚特区，并经由实施确认和证明的官员依据第 9 条第 2 款规定之方式加盖公章证明的，效力上应与在本州依本法规定之方式、格式实施的确认相同。

10.1 条　在美国军中服役者 / 服务美国军方者进行确认的

作为本州法律 / 本法有关现有及今后确认法律文件之方式、格式的规定的补充，在美国军中服役者 / 服务美国军方者及其家属无论身处何处，均可在特定现役官员面前进行确认，前提是该官员正效力于美国军方，并在陆军、空军、海军陆战队、海军或海岸警卫队中享有少尉及以上军衔。

vice of the armed forces of the United States with the rank of Second Lieutenant or higher in the Army, Air Force, or Marine Corps or Ensign or higher in the Navy or Coast Guard. The instrument shall not be rendered invalid by the failure to state therein the place of execution or acknowledgment. No authentication of the officer's certificate of acknowledgment shall be required but the officer taking the acknowledgment shall endorse thereon or attach thereto a certificate substantially in the following form

On this the _____ day of _____, 19____ before me_____ the undersigned officer personally appeared _____(Serial No.)(if any) known to me (or satisfactorily proven) to be (serving in or withthe armed forces of the United States) [a dependent of _____ (Serial No.) (if any) a person serving in or with the armed forces of the Untied States] and to be the person whose name is subscribed to the within instrument and acknowledged that he executed the same for the purposes therein contained. And theundersigned does further certify that he is at the date of this certificate a commissioned officer of the rank stated below and is in the active service of the armed forces of the United States.

_____
Signature of the Officer

_____
Rank and Serial No. of Officer and Command to which attached

Section 11. Acknowledgments not Affected by this Act

No acknowledgment heretofore taken shall be affected by anything contained herein.

Section 12. Uniformity of Interpretation

This act shall be so interpreted as to make uniform the laws of those States which enact it.

Section 13. Name of Act

This act may be cited as the UniformAcknowledgment Act.

Section 14. Time of Taking Effect

This act shall take effect immediately uponfinal enactment.

法律文件不因未记载签署地或实施确认地而失效该官员出具的确认证书无需进行证实，但实施确认之官员应以下列格式对其背书或附上证明。

于此，19__ 年 __ 月 ___ 日，
署名其下的官员 ____（序列号，如有的话）
亲临本人 _____ 面前，
　我知悉（或有充分证据证明）其在美国军中服役或服务于美国军方 [我知悉（或有充分证据证明）其乃在美国军中服役或服务美国军方者 _____（序列号，如有的话）之家属]，其乃文件签署者，为文件所载之目的签署了文件。署名其下者更进一步证明，在出具本证明之日，其身为具有下面列明之军衔的现役官员，正效力于美国军方。

_____
官员之签名

_____
官员之军衔和序列号，以及由其统率之部队

第 11 条　不受此法案影响的确认

此前实施之确认不受本法内容调整。

第 12 条　解释之一致性
本法案应从统一各实施州的法律的角度解释。

第 13 条　法案名称
本法案可引述为《统一确认法》。

第 14 条　生效时间
该法案将在最终颁布后立即生效。

宾夕法尼亚州公证人收费新旧对比

With the enactment of Act 73 of 2013 (the Revised Law on Notarial Acts or RULONA) on October 9, 2013, Section 329.1 (relating to fees of notaries public) of the Act is immediately effective.

Following is a side-by-side comparison of the new law and the former law relating to the fees charged by notaries and what this change means for notaries public in Pennsylvania.

随着 2013 年 11 月 9 日 2013 年 73 号法案颁布（对公证法案或 RULONA 的修订法），第 329.1 号法案（有关公证人费用）立即生效。

接下来是关于公证收费和该变化如何影响宾夕法尼亚州公证员的新旧法的并排比较。

New Law - RULONA
新法《公证行为统一法》

57 P.S. § 329.1. Fees of notaries public.

(a) Department.--The fees of notaries public shall be fixed by the department by regulation.

(b) Prohibition.--A notary public may not charge or receive a notary public fee in excess of the fee fixed by the department.

(c) Operation.--

(1) The fees of the notary shall be separately stated.

(2) A notary public may waive the right to charge a fee.

(3) Unless paragraph (2) applies, a notary public shall:

(i) display fees in a conspicuous location in the place of business of the notary public; or

(ii) provide fees, upon request, to a person utilizing the services of the notary public.

(d) Presumption.--The fee for a notary public:

(1) shall be the property of the notary public; and

(2) unless mutually agreed by the notary public and the employer, shall not belong to or be received by the entity that employs the notary public.

57 P.S. § 329.1. 公证费用

（a）部门：公证人的收费数额应由该部门通过规则来规定。

Old Law – Section 21 of Notary Public Act
旧法 –《公证人法》第 21 条

57 P.S. §167. Fees of Notaries Public.

(a) The fees of notaries public shall be fixed by the Secretary of the Commonwealth with the approval of the Attorney General.

(b) A notary public shall not charge, attempt to charge or receive a notary public fee that is in excess of the fees fixed by the Secretary of the Commonwealth.

(c) The fees of notaries public shall be displayed in a conspicuous location in the notary's place of business or be provided upon request to any person utilizing the services of the notary. The fees of the notary shall be separately stated. A notary public may waive the right to charge a fee, in which case the requirements of this subsection regarding the display or provision of fees shall not apply.

(d) The fee for any notary public employed by a bank, banking institution or trust company shall.

be the property of the notary and in no case belong to or be received by the corporation for whom the notary is employed.

57 P.S. § 167. 公证费用

（a）公证人的费用须由联邦秘书在接到总检察长批准后规定。

（b）禁令：公证人不得收取或接收超过部门规定的公证人费用。
（c）经营：
（1）公证的费用应当单独列示。
（2）公证人可放弃除收取费用的权利。
（3）除非第二段实施，公证人应当：
（i）在公证人在经营场所的醒目位置陈列费用清单；
（ii）根据要求对利用公证服务的人提供费用。
（d）推定：对于公证费
（1）应当是公证人的财产；
（2）除非公证人和雇主双方同意，不应归属于雇用者或由雇用者收取。

The notary public fee schedule, as last revised by the Secretary of the Commonwealth on December 31, 2009, remains the same under the new law (RULONA), unless changed by regulation of the Department. The current fees which may be charged by notaries public for notarial acts can be found in regulation at 4 Pa. Code §161.1. They are:

Executing affidavits (no matter how many signatures) $5.00

Executing acknowledgments 5.00

In executing acknowledgments each additional name 2.00

Executing certificates (per certified copy) 5.00

Administering oaths (per individual taking an oath) 5.00

Taking depositions, per page 3.00
Executing verifications 5.00
Executing protests, per page 3.00

This comparison of the new and old law shows that the requirements as to fees are identical, except for the presumption (now codified) that the fees of the notary belong to the notary and not the notary's employer unless mutually agreed by the notary public and the employer. The presumption that the notary fees belong to the notary (like the notary commission and the powers and duties therefrom) now clearly applies to all employers and not only banks, banking institutions or trust companies. The new law also makes clear that this presumption may be varied by an employment contract, wherein the notary public employee and the employer agree to another arrangement. Thus, the notary public is free to waive this rule and arrange a suitable compensation arrangement with her employer which may take the notary fees into account.

（b）公证机构不得收取、试图收取或接收超过联邦秘书规定的公证费。
（c）公证人在经营场所的醒目位置陈列费用清单或根据请求对利用公证服务的人提供费用。公证费用应当分别列明。公证人可放弃收取一定的费用的权利，在此情况下有关费用列明或提供的规定不予适用。

（d）受雇于银行、金融机构或信托公司的公证人之收费归属于公证人财产，在任何情况下不应归属于雇用者或由雇用者收取。

公证费清单，正如 2009 年 12 月 31 日经联邦秘书修订的，和 *RULONA* 保持一致，除非部门规则改变。现存关于公证行为收费的法案可以在 4 Pa. Code § 161.1 找到，分别是：

执行宣誓书（无论多少签名）$5.00

执行确认 $5.00
在执行确认上每个额外的名字 $2.00

执行证书（每份核证副本）$5.00
誓言（每个个体宣誓）$5.00

每页证言 $3.00
执行验证 $5.00
每页执行抗议 $3.00

新老法这一比较表明除了推定（现编）属于公证人而非雇主（除非双方同意）的费用外，其他费用是相同的。属于公证人的公证费（如由此引申的公证委托和权力和职责）现在显然适用于所有雇主，而不是只有银行、金融机构或信托公司。新法律还明确指出，这种推定可以通过劳动合同来改变，这是公证人雇员和雇主同意的另一种安排。因此，公证机构可以自由地放弃这一规则，并安排与他的将公证费考虑在内的雇主适当的补偿安排。

安提瓜和巴布达

安提瓜和巴布达公证人法

LAWS OF ANTIGUA AND BARBUDA
NOTARIES PUBLIC

1. This Act may be cited as the Notaries Public

2.(1) The Chief Justice of the Supreme Court may, from time to time, appoint any person, whom he shall con-sider a fit and proper person, to be a notary public for Antigua and Barbuda to discharge the duties assigned to such office by the laws of Great Britain and Northern Ireland and of Antigua and Barbuda, or by the practice of commerce.

A. No person shall be appointed a notary public without being previously examined, by or under the direction of the Chief Justice, as to his competency to discharge the duties of the office, unless he is a barrister or solicitor of the Supreme Court, or unless the Chief Justice, on special grounds, dispenses with the examination.

B. Every person so appointed shall, on his appoint-ment, pay into the Treasury the sum of twenty-four dollars.

3. Every person so appointed shall, before entering upon the duties of his office, be sworn before the Goveror any person authorized by him to administer oaths, well and faithfully to discharge the duties of such his office.

4. Every person appointed to the office of a notary public shall cause his name to be enrolled in a book to be kept for the purpose in the office of the Registrar, and to be called the roll of notaries public, and he shall be entitled to a certificate of enrolment under the seal of the court, and no person whose name shall not be enrolled as aforesaid shall be entitled to perform the duties of a notary public within Antigua and Barbuda.

5. Every person discharging the duties of a notary public shall be deemed to be an officer of the Supreme

安提瓜和巴布达公证人法

1. 本法简称为《公证人法》。

2.（1）最高法院的首席法官可以不定时地根据大不列颠和北爱尔兰及安提瓜及巴布达的法案，或参考商业惯例委任任何其认为适当的人，担任安提瓜和巴布达的公证人，履行赋予该职务的法定职责。

A. 任何人不得在未通过终审法院首席法官考核的情况下被委任为公证人、获得其履行职务的职权，除非其是最高法院的大律师或首席大法官根据特别理由免除其考试。

B. 获得任命的公证人，均须向库务署缴付24美元。

3. 任何获得任命的公证人，在履行职务之前，须在授权的官员面前宣誓，承诺其将善意忠实地履行其职务的职责。

4. 被任命为公证处职员的人，均应将其名字登记在书记官处的簿册内，该簿册被称为公证人名册，公证人有权获得有法院印章的注册证书，任何未经登记的人员，均不得在安提瓜和巴布达境内履行公证人的职务。

5. 履行公证人职责的每个人均被视为最高法院的工作人员，如果法院任何法官证明，公证人在履行职

Court, and, upon a certificate from any Judge of the said Court that any notary public has been guilty of misconduct in the discharge of the duties of his office, such notary public shall be forthwith discharged by the Chief Justice from the duties of the said office.

6. Any person who discharges the duties of a notary public, not being duly qualified so to do, shall be liable, on summary conviction to a penalty not exceeding three thousand dollars.

7. In all cases where the circumstances shall appear to the notary suspicious, and not warranting the protest or other notarial act demanded, the notary shall refuse to act:

Provided that any person who considers himself aggrieved by the refusal of the notary to note the protest or do any other notarial act demanded, may apply to the High Court, or any Judge thereof, for an order calling upon the notary to act in the execution of his office, and, before applying for such order, notice of the application shall be given to the notary refusing to act, and to such persons, if any, in Antigua and Barbuda, as are interested in the subject of the protest.

8. When any protest or other notarial act shall be noted or done, the notary so refusing shall mark in the log book, bill of exchange, or other document, his refusal, with his signature and the date of refusal subscribed thereon.

9. Any notary public or other person who willfully certifies or propounds any false statement or document, or fraudulently, with intent to deceive, conceals, withholds, or perverts any fact or document pertinent to the subject of protest, or other notarial act, shall be guilty of a misdemeanour shall be liable to be imprisoned for any term not exceeding two years.

10. All fees for discharging the duties of a notary public shall be as specified in the Schedule.

SCHEDULE
Notarial' Fee of Office

	$	c.
Noting protest on bill or note	1	20
Extending protests on bills of exchange and promissory notes	3	60
Should the acceptor or drawer of a bill or note reside out of town, and the Notary has to present the bill or note, a further charge for the first mile	1	20
and, for every additional mile beyond the first mile	0	24
Minuting or noting ship's protest	1	92
Extending ship's protest	15	36

务时犯有不当行为，应立即由终审法院首席法官解除该公证人的职务。

6. 任何履行公证人职责的人员，如果不符合任职资格，经简易程序定罪，将处以不超过3000元的罚款。

7. 在任何情况下，只要公证人心存疑虑，且作出票据拒绝承兑书或其他公证行为并非必须，则公证人应拒绝公证：

任何认为自己因公证人拒绝出具票据拒绝承兑书或拒绝履行任何其他公证行为而感到不满的人，可以向高等法院或其任何法官申请，要求公证人办理公证事务。但在申请此类命令之前，应向拒绝做出公证的公证人发出通知，并通知安提瓜和巴布达内对该出具异议文书有相关利益的人（如有的话）。

8. 当公证人拒绝作出或记录任何票据拒绝承兑书或其他公证行为时，应在公证人日志、票据或其他文件中注明拒绝办理，并附上签名和拒绝的日期。

9. 公证人或其他人故意证明或提出任何虚假陈述或文件，或欺诈性地欺骗、隐瞒、扣留、或违反与拒绝承兑书或其他公证行为有关的任何事实或文件，均属违法行为，将被处以不超过两年的监禁。

10. 履行公证人职务的所有费用均应按照附表规定收取。

附表
公证收费

计价单位：	东加勒比元	分
标注拒绝承兑票据	1	20
续展汇票和期票的拒绝承兑书	3	60
如果票据的出票人或承兑人居住在城外，而公证人必须提示票据承兑，则公证人将对第一英里内的服务收取	1	20
第一英里之后的每增加一英里额外收取	0	24
记录或标注海损报告	1	92
送达海损报告书	15	36

Furnishing copy of extended protest.	7	68
Attestation to any document, if in town.	3	84
if out of town, additional for the first mile	1	20
and, for every additional mile beyond the first mile	0	24
Declaration thereto for the master, and for each additional declarant	0	24
Attendances, each	1	44

TRANSLATIONS

	$	c.
From Danish, German or Swedish per folio of 72 words	0	48
From French	0	48
From Latin	0	60
From Russian	1	80
Attestation to translation	2	28
Translation of common attestation to power for stocks	2	52

提供续展的拒绝承兑书副本	7	68
在城内证明任何文件	3	84
如果在城外，第一英里	1	20
第一英里之后每增加的一英里	0	24
为船长出具的声明和为其它每个人附加的声明	0	24
每次出席	1	44

翻 译

计价单位：	东加勒比元	分
来自丹麦语、德语或瑞典语，每页72个单词	0	48
法语	0	48
拉丁语	0	60
俄语	1	80
翻译认证	2	28
将普通认证翻译转化为具有股权效力的认证	2	52

阿根廷

公证人员专业执业法

LEY 12.990
Ejercicio Profesional de Escribanos
Buenos Aires, 19 de Junio de 1947
EL SENADO Y LA CAMARA DE DIPUTADOS DE LA NACION ARGENTINA, REUNIDOS EN CONGRESO, ETC.,
SANCIONAN CON FUERZA DE LEY:
Ver Antecedentes Normativos

SECCION PRIMERA
DE LOS ESCRIBANOS EN GENERAL

CAPITULO I
Condiciones para ejercer el notariado

ARTICULO 1º – Para ejercer el notariado se requiere:

a) Ser argentino, nativo o naturalizado, debiendo en este último caso, tener diez (10) años de naturalización;

b) Ser mayor de edad;

c) Tener título de escribano expedido por universidad nacional, provincial o privada, debidamente habilitado en el caso de estos dos últimos, con tal que su otorgamiento requiera estudios completos de la enseñanza media previos a los de carácter universitario, los que deberán abarcar la totalidad de las materias y disciplinas análogas a las que se cursen para la carrera de abogacía;

d) Haber cumplido dos (2) años de práctica notarial en la forma que determine la reglamentación;

e) Tener conducta, antecedentes y moral intachables;

f) Hallarse inscripto en la matrícula profesional.

(Artículo sustituido por art. 1º de la Ley Nº 22.171 B.O. 29/2/1980).

ARTICULO 2º – Los extremos pertinentes del artículo anterior deberán ser justificados ante el juez civil en

法律 12.990
公证人员专业执业
布宜诺斯艾利斯，1947 年 6 月 19 日
阿根廷参议院与众议院等，于国会会议上，

以法律效力批准：
见规范背景

第一部分
全体公证人员

第一章
公证员执业条件

第 1 条 担任公证员，应当具备下列条件：

a）阿根廷人，出生或规划入籍的阿根廷人，若为后一种情况，入籍需满 10 年；

b）成年；

c）具有国家、省或私立大学签发的公证员执业证书，持有省或私立大学签发的执业证书的公证人员，必须对从中学预科教育至大学教育进行全面的学习，且必须涵盖与法律专业相关的所有科目和学科；

d）按照规定的方式实习公证工作满二年；

e）公道正派，遵纪守法，品行良好；

f）在专业名录上登记在册。

（相关条款替换为发布在 1980 年 2 月 29 日《官方公报》上的第 22171 号法案第 1 条）

第 2 条 前款所述的相关条文应通过联邦首都时任民事法官或本国相关辖区的主管法官证明，且由公

turno de la Capital Federal o juez letrado de la respectiva jurisdicción en los territorios nacionales con intervención fiscal del Colegio de Escribanos, siendo las resoluciones apelables ante el Tribunal de Superintendencia.

ARTICULO 3º – (Artículo derogado por art. 5º de la Ley Nº 22.171 B.O. 29/2/1980).

ARTICULO 4º – No pueden ejercer funciones notariales:

a) Los ciegos, los sordos, los mudos y quienes adolezcan de defectos físicos y mentales que les inhabiliten para el ejercicio profesional;

b) Los incapaces;

c) Los encausados por cualquier delito, desde que se hubiera decretado la prisión preventiva y mientras ésta dure, siempre que no fuera motivada por hechos involuntarios o culposos;

d) Los condenados dentro o fuera del país por delitos que den lugar a la acción pública o por contravención a leyes nacionales de carácter penal, con excepción de las sentencias por actos culposos o involuntarios;

e) Los fallidos y concursados no rehabilitados;

f) Los que por inconducta o graves motivos de orden personal o profesional fueran descalificados para el ejercicio del notariado;

g) Los escribanos suspendidos en el ejercicio de su cargo en cualquier jurisdicción de la República, por el término de la suspensión.

CAPITULO II
De la matrícula profesional y domicilio

ARTICULO 5º – El Colegio de Escribanos llevará la matrícula profesional e inscribirá en ella a los que acrediten hallarse en las condiciones requeridas en los artículos anteriores y registren su firma y sello profesional. La matriculación en el Colegio de Escribanos de la Capital Federal es compatible con la matrícula de cualquier otro colegio notarial. Se cancelará la inscripción:

a) A pedido del propio escribano inscripto;

b) Por disposición del Tribunal de Superintendencia.

(Artículo sustituido por art. 9º de la Ley Nº 21.212 B.O. 29/10/1975).

ARTICULO 6º – Los escribanos deberán residir en el lugar en que ejerzan sus funciones o en un radio no mayor de cuarenta kilómetros del mismo, constituyendo ante el Tribunal de superintendencia y el colegio de Escribanos, un domicilio especial a todos los efectos previstos por esta ley. Salvo el caso de instrumentos autorizados por deleg-

证员协会监督，做出决议可以在最高法院上诉。

第3条 （相关条款替换为发布在1980年2月29日《官方公报》上的第22171号法案第5条）

第4条 （有下列情形之一的）不得担任公证员：

a）盲、聋、哑人，以及身体和精神上有缺陷者，不具备执业资格；

b）无执业资质；

c）因任何罪行被指控获审前羁押的，羁押期间不得从事公证工作，非主观或过失犯罪的情况除外；

d）在国内外犯罪引起公共诉讼或受到刑事处罚的，经判定为非主观或过失犯罪的情况除外；

e）信誉受损或破产且无法恢复的；

f）由于品行不端或严重的个人（专业）原因，导致丧失公证员执业资格的；

g）共和国任一辖区内，在其任职期间内被暂停公职的公证人员，停职期间不得从事公证工作。

第二章
专业注册登记及地址

第5条 公证员协会应当根据前款所述的必要条件进行专业注册登记，并注册其签字和专业印章。联邦首都公证员协会的登记不妨碍在任何其他公证员协会的登记。以下情况取消注册：

a）注册公证员自身原因；

b）最高法院法令。

（相关条款替换为发布在1975年10月29日《官方公报》上的第21212号法案第9条）

第6条 公证人员应在其行使公职的地方，或者不超过该地40公里的半径范围内居住，按照最高法院和公证员协会规定建立一个特别的办公场所，以便实现本法案规定的公证目的，除司法办事处授权的公证书外，只能在本国的领土管辖范围内开展业务。

ación judicial, sólo pueden actuar dentro de la jurisdicción territorial en que hubieren establecido su domicilio.

(Artículo sustituido por art. 1º del Decreto-Ley Nº 12.599/56 B.O. 20/7/1956).

CAPITULO III
De las incompatibilidades

ARTICULO 7º – El ejercicio del notariado es incompatible:

a) Con el desempeño de cualquier función o empleo público o privado, retribuido en cualquier forma.

b) Con el ejercicio del comercio, por cuenta propia o ajena.

c) Con el ejercicio de cualquier función o empleo, no incompatible, que le obligue a residir fuera del lugar en que ejerza sus funciones notariales.

d) Con el ejercicio de la abogacía, de la procuración o cualquier otra profesión liberal.

e) Con el ejercicio del notariado en otra jurisdicción.

(Artículo sustituido por art. 1º de la Ley Nº 14.054 B.O. 16/10/1951).

ARTICULO 8º – Exceptúase de las disposiciones del art. anterior, los cargos o empleos que impliquen el desempeño de funciones notariales; los de carácter electivo; los docentes; los de índole puramente científica o artística, dependientes de academias, bibliotecas, museos u otras instituciones científicas o artísticas; los cargos de directores o síndicos de sociedades anónimas y el carácter de accionistas de las mismas.

(Artículo sustituido por art. 1º de la Ley Nº 14.054 B.O. 16/10/1951).

ARTICULO 9º – Las incompatibilidades que expresa el artículo 7º han de entenderse para el ejercicio simultáneo del notariado con las funciones y cargos declarados incompatibles; pero el Colegio de Escribanos podrá, en casos especiales, conceder licencias no menores de tres meses, para que los escribanos puedan desempeñar tales cargos, siempre que durante su transcurso no se ejerzan funciones notariales de ningún género.

SECCION SEGUNDA
DE LOS REGISTROS

CAPITULO I
De los escribanos de registro

ARTICULO 10. – El escribano de registro es el

（相关条款替换为发布在1956年7月20日《官方公报》上的第12599/56号法案第1条）

第三章
违规行为

第7条 公证员不得有以下行为：

a）利用自身职能、公共或私人职务，以任何方式索要报酬；

b）从事为自己或他人牟利的交易；

c）从事任何需要其居住在其行使公证职能地点外的兼职工作或职务；

d）从事律师、检察官或任何其他自由职业；

e）在非所在管辖区开展公证业务。

（相关条款替换为发布在1951年10月16日《官方公报》上的第14054号法案第1条）

第8条 除前款规定外，公证员不得从事下列工作或担任职务：带有选举特性的工作；教育类工作；依托于学院、图书馆、博物馆或其他科学艺术机构的纯科学或艺术性质的工作；股份公司董事、理事及股东。

（相关条款替换为发布在1951年10月16日《官方公报》上的第14054号法案第1条）

第9条 第7条中所表述的违规行为即公证员不可同时从事公证业务与职务之外的任何职业；但在特殊情况下，公证员协会可以签发不少于3个月的许可证，以便公证人员可以执行相关工作，而该过程中不应存在任何公证职能。

第二部分
登记注册

第一章
公证登记

第10条 登记处公证员是根据法律以及在法律

funcionario público instituido para recibir y redactar y dar autenticidad, conforme a las leyes y en los casos que ellas autorizan, los actos y contratos que le fueran encomendados. Sólo a él compete el ejercicio del notariado.

(Artículo sustituido por art. 1º de la Ley Nº 14.054 B.O. 16/10/1951).

ARTICULO 11. – Son deberes esenciales de los escribanos de registro:

a) La conservación y custodia en perfecto estado de los actos y contratos que autorice, así como de los protocolos respectivos, mientras se hallen en su poder.

b) Expedir a las partes interesadas testimonios, copias, certificados y extractos de las escrituras otorgadas en su registro.

c) Mantener el secreto profesional sobre los actos en que intervenga en ejercicio de su función. La exhibición de los protocolos sólo podrá hacerla a requerimiento de los otorgantes o sus sucesores respecto de los actos en que hubieran intervenido y por otros escribanos en los casos y formas que establezca el reglamento, o por orden judicial.

d) Intervenir profesionalmente en los casos en que fuera requerido, cuando su intervención está autorizada por las leyes o no se encuentra impedido por otras obligaciones profesionales de igual o mayor urgencia.

(Artículo sustituido por art. 1º de la Ley Nº 14.054 B.O. 16/10/1951).

ARTICULO 12. – Las escrituras públicas y demás actos podrán ser autorizados por los escribanos de registro. A ellos compete también la realización de los siguientes actos:

a) Certificar la autenticidad de las firmas o impresiones digitales puestas en documentos privados y en su presencia;

b) Certificar la autenticidad de firmas puestas en documentos privados y en su presencia por personas en representación de terceros;

c) Practicar inventarios, sea por requerimiento privado o delegación judicial;

d) Desempeñar las funciones de secretario de tribunal arbitral;

e) Redactar actas de asambleas, reuniones de comisiones y actos análogos;

f) Labrar actas de notoriedad o protesta para comprobar hechos y reservar derechos;

g) Redactar toda constancia de actos o contratos civiles y comerciales;

h) Expedir testimonios sobre asientos de contabilidad

允许范围内接受、撰写和证明其受委托的文书及合同的真实性的公职人员，其职权范围仅限于公证。

（相关条款替换为发布在1951年10月16日《官方公报》上的第14054号法案第1条）

第11条　登记处公证员的基本义务为：

a）在其任职期间保存授权文书及合同以及相应的协议，并保管完好。

b）向有关方面发放其登记册中授予公证的证词、副本、证明和摘录。

c）对其参与执业的文件进行专业保密。议定书的公开只能由委托人或该相关文件中涉及的继承人，经由其他涉案公证人员，在法律规定的形式下，或通过司法手段强制进行。

d）在需要的情况下专业干预，在由法律授权的，或者不受其他同等或更紧迫的职业义务的阻碍的情况下进行。

（相关条款替换为发布在1951年10月16日《官方公报》上的第14054号法案第1条）

第12条　公职行为和其他事项可由登记处公证员授权行使。登记处公证员还负责执行以下事务：

a）核实私人文件中的签名或数字印章的真实性，及在场见证事实存在；

b）核实私人文件中签名的真实性，及代表第三方的人员在场见证事实存在；

c）应私人要求或司法授权处理库存资产；

d）履行仲裁庭秘书的各项职能；

e）负责编写集会、委员会会议记录和类似事项；

f）准备证据或抗辩依据，核实事实和保留权利；

g）提供有关民事和商业行为或合同的所有书面证据；

h）为法人团体、民间协会、私人公司或个人的

y actas de libros de sociedades anónimas, asociaciones civiles o sociedades o simples particulares;

i) Certificar sobre el envío de correspondencia, tomando a su cargo la entrega de la misma al correo;

j) Intervenir en todos los actos, documentos y contratos en que sea requerida su intervención profesional como asesores o peritos notariales;

k) Recopilar antecedentes de títulos;

l) Solicitar certificaciones ante reparticiones públicas nacionales, provinciales o municipales.

(Artículo sustituido por art. 1º de la Ley Nº 22.171 B.O. 29/2/1980).

ARTICULO 13. – Los escribanos de registros son civilmente responsables de los daños y perjuicios ocasionados a terceros por incumplimiento de las disposiciones del artículo 11, sin perjuicio de su responsabilidad penal o disciplinaria, si correspondiere.

ARTICULO 14. – Los escribanos de registro están obligados a concurrir asiduamente a su oficina y no podrán ausentarse del lugar de su domicilio por más de ocho días sin autorización del Colegio de Escribanos. En caso de enfermedad, ausencia u otro impedimento transitorio, el escribano de registro que no tuviere adscripto podrá proponer al Tribunal de Superintendencia el nombramiento de un suplente, que actuará en su reemplazo bajo la responsabilidad del proponente, en los supuestos previstos por el art. 23, último párrafo.

(Artículo sustituido por art. 1º de la Ley Nº 14.054 B.O. 16/10/1951).

ARTICULO 15. – Créase un fondo de garantía subsidiario de responsabilidad por el ejercicio de la función notarial constituido por el aporte de los escribanos de registro, titulares, adscriptos e interinos, y por las rentas que produzca su inversión en los sistemas financieros redituables del Estado. (Nota Infoleg: Por art. 1º del Decreto Nº 1909/1980 B.O. 19/9/1980, se dispone que el fondo de garantía que se menciona en el presente párrafo, se denominará "fondo de garantía subsidiario de responsabilidad por el ejercicio de la función notarial").

Dicho fondo responderá por las obligaciones de los escribanos en forma subsidiaria y después de haberse hecho excusión de los bienes del deudor principal, en los siguientes casos:

a) Por los daños y perjuicios causados con motivo de actos realizados en el ejercicio de la función notarial, siempre que existiere sentencia firme condenatoria y que el organismo administrador del fondo de garantía haya sido

会计记录和簿记记录出具证明；

ｉ）核实发信通知方式、信件邮寄的交付方式；

ｊ）以顾问或公证专家身份对一切法案、文件和合同提供所需的专业支持；

ｋ）编制授权文件的历史记录；

ｌ）向国家、省级或市级警察机关提交认证申请。

（相关条款替换为发布在 1980 年 2 月 29 日《官方公报》上的第 22171 号法案第 1 条）

第 13 条　登记处公证员对因违反第 11 条的规定而对第三方造成的损害负有民事责任，且不影响履行其刑事责任或纪律职责（如适用）。

第 14 条　登记处公证员有义务常驻办公地点，未经公证协会许可，不得擅自离开其主管片区超过 8 日。在病假、缺勤或有其他临时不便时，尚未指定的登记处公证员可向监督审裁处提议任命一名候补人员。该位候补人员将在提交人的职责范围内代其行使责任，以此处理第 23 条最后一段描述之情形。

（相关条款替换为发布在 1951 年 10 月 16 日《官方公报》上的第 14054 号法案第 1 条）

第 15 条　设立公证责任担保基金，由登记处公证员、任职人员、助理人员和临时人员出资，以及由其在国家盈利性财务制度中投资产生的收益所构成。(Infoleg 立法信息注释：依据发布在 1980 年 9 月 19 日《官方公报》上的第 1909/1980 号法案第 1 条，该条规定本款提及的担保基金应视为"履行公证职能的附属担保基金"）

上述基金在债务人不能负担债务时承担补充责任，主要包括以下情况：

ａ）对于履行公证职能的行为所造成的损害和损失，只要构成担保责任保险基金的管理人被视为第三方的结论，则该基金组织有义务做出偿付；

citado como tercero; dicho organismo estará autorizado para transigir;

b) Por el incumplimiento de las leyes fiscales en los casos en que actuaren como agentes de retención.

En los casos de los incisos precedentes se subrogará en los derechos del acreedor y reclamará el reintegro correspondiente.

El fondo de garantía no responderá por toda suma que exceda el total de los fondos que lo integren.

Excepto en los casos previstos en este artículo, el fondo de garantía será inembargable.

(Artículo sustituido por art. 1º de la Ley Nº 22.171 B.O. 29/2/1980).

ARTICULO 15 bis. – La reglamentación establecerá el organismo administrativo del fondo de garantía, el monto de los aportes, que será proporcional al desenvolvimiento profesional del escribano, y las sanciones que originen la demora o el incumplimiento en su pago. El organismo administrador determinará la forma y fecha de pago del aporte. Este será anual y en ningún caso susceptible de reintegro.

Las sanciones previstas en este artículo serán resarcitorias del capital, con sus actualizaciones e intereses, pudiendo, además, aplicarse las previstas en los incisos a) y c) del artículo 52.

(Artículo incorporado por art. 2º de la Ley Nº 22.171 B.O. 29/2/1980).

(Nota Infoleg: Por art. 4º del Decreto Nº 1909/1980 B.O. 19/9/1980, se dispone que el monto de los aportes que hace referencia el presente artículo será de $100 por foja de protocolo que adquieren los escribanos por año calendario).

ARTICULO 16. – Los escribanos titulares de registro no podrán ser separados de su cargo mientras dure su buena conducta. La suspensión, remoción o pérdida del cargo de escribano sólo podrá ser declarada por las causas y en la forma previstas por esta ley.

CAPITULO II
De los registros

ARTICULO 17. – Compete al Poder Ejecutivo la creación y cancelación de los registros y la designación y remoción de sus titulares y adscritos en el modo y forma establecidos por la presente ley. Los registros y protocolos notariales son de propiedad del Estado.

ARTICULO 18. – (Artículo derogado por art. 1º del Decreto Nº 240/99 B.O. 23/3/1999).

b）在担任存留代理人情况下不遵守税法。

在上述各款情况下，基金可以作为债权人要求获得偿还的相应退款。

担保基金不对超出损失总额以外的任何金额偿付。

除本条规定的情形之外，担保基金为不可附加使用。

（相关条款替换为发布在 1980 年 2 月 29 日《官方公报》上的第 22171 号法案第 1 条）

第 15 条之二　此类规定将确定该项担保基金的监管机构，担保基金缴款金额与公证员的业绩表现密切相关，延期或不付款行为应当采取处罚措施。监管机构将确定缴款的形式和日期。缴款每年一次，且任何情况下均不可退还。本条规定的处罚金额应当作为资本及其更新数额和利息之补偿，且同样适用于第 52 条 a 项和 c 项的规定。

（相关条款纳入发布在 1980 年 2 月 29 日《官方公报》上的第 22171 号法案第 2 条）

（InfoLEG 立法信息注释：依据 1980 年 9 月 19 日《官方公报》上的第 1909/1980 号法案第 4 条，本条所述的出资数额拟按每个日历年度公证员所获得的每份议定书 100 美元）

第 16 条　登记处任职公证员在其工作期间不可离开办公室。登记处办公室如遇暂停使用、迁移或者毁损，仅可采取本法规定之方式宣告具体缘由。

第二章
登记处

第 17 条　行政部门负责依据本法规定的方式和形式，设立和注销登记机构，任命和解雇其任职人员和助理人员。登记处和公证议定书属于国有财产。

第 18 条　（相关条款为 1999 年 3 月 23 日《官方公报》上的第 240/99 号法案第 1 条）

ARTICULO 19. – (Artículo derogado por art. Iº del Decreto Nº 240/99 B.O. 23/3/1999).

ARTICULO 20. – Los registros llevarán una numeración que será correlativa del 1 en adelante, manteniéndose para los existentes la numeración actual.

CAPITULO III
De las adscripciones

ARTICULO 21. – Cada escribano regente de registro podrá tener hasta dos escribanos adscriptos, que serán nombrados por el Poder Ejecutivo a propuesta del titular, previo informe del Colegio de Escribanos sobre los antecedentes de moralidad profesional del aspirante.

(Artículo sustituido por art. 1º de la Ley Nº 14.054 B.O. 16/10/1951).

ARTICULO 22. – Para ser designado adscrito deberá cumplirse con los requisitos y llenar las condiciones exigidas por la presente ley para el ejercicio del notariado.

(Artículo sustituido por art. 1º de la Ley Nº 14.054 B.O. 16/10/1951).

ARTICULO 23. – Los escribanos adscriptos, mientras conserven ese carácter, actuarán dentro del respectivo registro, con la misma extensión de facultades que el titular y simultánea e indistintamente con el mismo, pero bajo su total dependencia y responsabilidad, y reemplazarán a su regente en los casos de ausencia, enfermedad o cualquier otro impedimento transitorio.

El escribano titular es el responsable directo del trámite y conservación del protocolo y responderá de los actos de sus adscriptos en cuanto sean susceptibles de su apreciación y cuidado.

ARTICULO 24. – Los adscriptos sólo sucederán al titular, por renuncia, incapacidad total o fallecimiento de éste, en la forma que establece el artículo 19. Hasta tanto se provea la vacante, se desempeñará como regente el adscrito de mayor antigüedad.

(Artículo sustituido por art. 1º de la Ley Nº 14.054 B.O. 16/10/1951).

ARTICULO 25. – Los escribanos titulares podrán celebrar con sus adscriptos toda clase de convenciones para reglar sus derechos en el ejercicio en común de la actividad profesional, su participación en el producido de la misma y en los gastos de oficina, obligaciones recíprocas y aún sus previsiones para el caso de fallecimiento, siempre que tales compromisos no excedieran el plazo de cinco años de la muerte de cualquiera de ellos; pero quedan terminantemente prohibidas y se tendrán por inexistentes las

第19条 （相关条款为1999年3月23日《官方公报》上的第240/99号法案第1条）

第20条 登记机构应统一从"1"开始编号，现有记录维持现有编号方式。

第三章
助理任职

第21条 每位登记处公证员最多可以有两名助理公证员，他们应由行政部门根据任职人员的提议任命，并参考公证协会基于申请人职业道德背景资料提交的一份相关报告。

（相关条款替换为发布在1951年10月16日《官方公报》上的第14054号法案第1条）

第22条 职位任命必须满足相关要求，以及本法对公证业务所需之条件。

（相关条款替换为发布在1951年10月16日《官方公报》上的第14054号法案第1条）

第23条 助理公证员在履职期间，可在相应的登记机构内开展业务，与登记处公证员享有同样的权力范围，可同时且在大致与此相同情形下，受其完全信赖和责任所托，在缺席、疾病或任何有其他临时不便时替代其行使职责。

公证员直接负责议定书的拟定和保管工作，应对助理人员出自尽职操守的行为做出积极回应。

第24条 助理公证员仅当公证员提出辞呈、完全丧失工作能力或死亡的情况下按照第19条规定的形式接替其职位。在补充空缺职位之前，他是最有资历的主管人员。

（相关条款替换为发布在1951年10月16日《官方公报》上的第14054号法案第1条）

第25条 公证员可与助理公证员可订立各种合约，规范其在联合行使专业活动中的权力，包括文件制作和办公费用，以及相互承担的义务，甚至关于死亡事例的规定，但此类承诺不得超过任何一方死亡后5年期限。若助理系有偿行为，被禁止的规定无论是否导致支付该笔费用，或者规定助理公证员认可公证员自己支付部分费用，该合约均应当严格禁止并视为无效。此无效性一经确定，将不影响协约方接受因违反本法案应当受到的处罚。任职人员与助理人员之间

convenciones por las que resulte que se ha abonado o deba abonarse un precio por la adscripción, o se estipule que el adscripto reconozca a su titular una participación sobre sus propios honorarios o autoricen la presunción de que se ha traficado en alguna forma con la adscripción, nulidad que se establece sin perjuicio de las penalidades a que se hagan acreedores los contratantes por transgresión a esta ley. Todas las convenciones entre el titular y el adscripto deben considerarse hechas sin perjuicio de las disposiciones de esta ley.

ARTICULO 26. – El Colegio de Escribanos actuará como árbitro en todas las cuestiones que se susciten entre titular y adscrito, y sus fallos, pronunciados por mayoría de votos, serán inapelables.

(Artículo sustituido por art. 1º de la Ley Nº 14.054 B.O. 16/10/1951).

CAPITULO IV
De las designaciones de escribanos

ARTICULO 27. – Desde la promulgación de esta ley, las designaciones de escribanos para las reparticiones del Estado, autónomas, autárquicas o dependientes del Poder Ejecutivo, bancos oficiales, municipalidades y dependencias de los mismos, sean esas designaciones de carácter definitivo o transitorio, sólo podrán ser hechas por concurso en las condiciones que cada una de esas reparticiones o instituciones establezcan. Desde igual fecha, las designaciones de escribanos hechas de oficio por los jueces de la Capital Federal o territorios nacionales se realizarán por sorteo de una lista que formarán anualmente las Cámaras Federales, Civiles, Comercial y Criminal, o Tribunales de Superintendencia, respectivamente, siguiendo para la formación de estas listas el procedimiento que cada una de ellas establezca.

SECCION TERCERA
GOBIERNO Y DISCIPLINA DEL NOTARIADO

CAPITULO I
Responsabilidad de los escribanos

ARTICULO 28. – La responsabilidad de los escribanos, por mal desempeño de sus funciones profesionales, es de cuatro clases:
a) Administrativa;
b) Civil;

的所有公约必须在不违背本法规定的前提下考虑签订。

第 26 条　公证协会应当在公证员和助理公证员之间产生的一切事务中担任仲裁员角色，其以多数票通过的决定，当事方不得提起上诉。

（相关条款替换为发布在 1951 年 10 月 16 日《官方公报》上的第 14054 号法案第 1 条）

第四章
公证员的任命

第 27 条　自本法颁布起，国家机关、自治、自主或行政部门、官方银行、市政当局及其附属机构的公证员，均明确为暂时性质的任命，须依据这些部门或机构各自制定的条件通过竞争方式确定人选。自同日起，联邦首都或国家领土部门的法官根据职权范围作出的任命将编成一份名单，并遵循这些各自制定的程序，每年将分别组建联邦、民事、商业和刑事分庭或监督审裁处。

第三部分
公证人员的监管和纪律

第一章
公证员承担的责任

第 28 条　公证员履职不力的责任有四种：

a）行政责任；
b）民事责任；

c) Penal;

d) Profesional.

ARTICULO 29. – La responsabilidad administrativa deriva del incumplimiento de las leyes fiscales y de ella entenderán directamente los tribunales que determinen las leyes respectivas.

ARTICULO 30. – La responsabilidad civil de los escribanos resulta de los daños y perjuicios ocasionados a terceros por incumplimiento de la presente ley, o por mal desempeño de sus funciones, de acuerdo con lo establecido en las leyes generales.

ARTICULO 31. – La responsabilidad penal emana de la actuación del escribano en cuanto pueda considerarse delictuosa, y de ella entenderán los tribunales competentes conforme con lo establecido por las leyes penales.

ARTICULO 32. – La responsabilidad profesional emerge del incumplimiento, por parte de los escribanos, de la presente ley o del reglamento notarial o de las disposiciones que se dictaren para la mejor observancia de éstos o de los principios de ética profesional, en cuanto esas transgresiones afecten la institución notarial, los servicios que le son propios o el decoro del cuerpo, y su conocimiento compete al Tribunal de Superintendencia y Colegio de Escribanos.

ARTICULO 33. – Ninguna de las responsabilidades enunciadas debe considerarse excluyente de las demás, pudiendo el escribano ser llamado a responder de todas y cada una de ellas simultánea o sucesivamente.

ARTICULO 34. – En toda acción que se suscite contra un escribano, sea en el orden personal o por razón de sus funciones profesionales, deberá darse conocimiento al Colegio de Escribanos, para que éste, a su vez, adopte o aconseje las medidas que considere oportunas. A tal efecto, los jueces, de oficio o a pedido de partes, deberán notificar a dicho colegio toda acción intentada contra un escribano, dentro de los diez días de iniciada.

CAPITULO II
Del Tribunal de Superintendencia

ARTICULO 35. – El gobierno y disciplina del notariado corresponde al Tribunal de Superintendencia y al Colegio de Escribanos.

ARTICULO 36. – El Tribunal de Superintendencia estará integrado por un presidente, que lo será el presidente en turno de las cámaras de apelaciones en lo civil de la Capital Federal en superintendencia; dos vocales titulares, que dichas cámaras, reunidas en pleno, designarán

c）刑事责任；

d）专业责任。

第29条 行政责任源于违反税法，由订立各自法律的审裁处直接裁决。

第30条 公证员的民事责任在于违反本法规定的对第三方造成的损害赔偿责任，或依照一般法律规定履行职责不力的情况。

第31条 刑事责任源于公证员的职责履行不力，一旦被认定为犯罪行为，将由主管审裁处根据刑法规定裁决。

第32条 专业责任源于公证员未遵守本法或为确保遵守本法及职业道德原则而制定的公证条例或规定，因为这些违法行为会影响到公证机构本身的服务或自身形象，监督审裁处和公证协会负有责任监管责任。

第33条 列出的任何责任均不应视为排除其他应当承担的责任。为此，可要求公证员同时或相继对其中的每项职责作出回应。

第34条 在对公证员提起的任何诉讼中，无论是针对个人守则或是其专业职责，均须通知公证协会，以便后者采取或建议认为适当的措施来处理。于此，法官根据职权或应各方之要求，应当在起诉开始前10日之内通知上述协会对公证员可能采取的处理行为。

第二章
监督审裁处

第35条 公证人员的纪律监管归属监督审裁处和公证协会。

第36条 监督审裁处由一名主席组成，他担任联邦首府民事上诉委员会轮值主席；另有两位任职会员，每年应安排一次简单的全体投票；另有两名替补会员，在需要时可替代任职会员，并以前者同样方式任命。

anualmente a simple pluralidad de votos; y dos vocales suplentes, que reemplazarán a los titulares en caso necesario, y serán designados de igual modo que aquéllos.

En los territorios nacionales el expresado tribunal estará formado por el juez letrado de la jurisdicción y el secretario del juzgado respectivo, de mayor antigüedad.

ARTICULO 37. – Corresponde al Tribunal de Superintendencia ejercer la dirección y vigilancia sobre los escribanos, Colegio de Escribanos, archivos y todo cuanto tenga relación con el notariado y con el cumplimiento de la presente ley; a cuyo efecto ejercerá su acción por intermedio del Colegio de Escribanos, sin perjuicio de su intervención directa toda vez que lo estimare conveniente.

ARTICULO 38. – Conocerá en única instancia, previo sumario y dictamen del Colegio de Escribanos, los asuntos relativos a la responsabilidad profesional de los escribanos, cuando el mínimo de la pena aplicable consiste en suspensión por más de un mes.

ARTICULO 39. – Conocerá, en general, como tribunal de apelación y a pedido de parte, de todas las resoluciones del Colegio de Escribanos y especialmente de los fallos que éste pronunciara en los asuntos relativos a la responsabilidad profesional de los escribanos cuando la pena aplicada sea de suspensión por un mes o término menor.

ARTICULO 40. – El Tribunal de Superintendencia tomará sus decisiones por simple mayoría de votos, inclusive el del presidente, y sus miembros podrán excusarse o ser recusados por iguales motivos que los de la Cámara de Apelaciones en lo Civil.

ARTICULO 41. – Elevado el sumario, en los casos del artículo 38, en el expediente condenatorio, en los del artículo 39, el tribunal ordenará de inmediato las medidas de prueba y de descargo si las considerare convenientes y pronunciará su fallo en el término de 30 días contados de la fecha de entrada del asunto al tribunal.

ARTICULO 42. – La intervención fiscal en los asuntos que se tramiten en el Tribunal de Superintendencia estará a cargo del Colegio de Escribanos.

CAPITULO III
Del Colegio de Escribanos

ARTICULO 43. – Sin perjuicio de la jurisdicción concedida al Tribunal de Superintendencia, la dirección y vigilancia inmediata de los escribanos de la Capital Federal y territorios nacionales, así como todo lo relativo a la aplicación de la presente ley, le corresponderá al Colegio de Escribanos.

在处理国家领土的公证事务方面，监督审裁处由具有管辖权的法定法官和各自法院具有较高资历的秘书组成。

第37条 监督审裁处有责任对公证员、公证协会、档案馆以及与公证人员有关且符合现行法律的所有人员行使指示和监督职责。为此，监督审裁处将通过公证协会行使其职责，且可在不影响直接干预的情况下履行职责。

第38条 在特定情况下，除了公证协会的事先简易审和意见外，监督审裁处还将审理与公证员专业责任相关的事项，其适用的最低处罚包括停职1个月以上。

第39条 一般的，监督审裁处作为上诉法院，须应当事一方的要求，对公证协会的所有决定，特别是在处罚时与公证员的专业责任相关的事宜作出裁决，其适用处罚可为停职1个月或更短期限。

第40条 监督审裁处以简单多数票，包括主席的票数作出决定，其会员投票可能因与民事上诉庭相同的理由而被免除或拒绝。

第41条 提交至简易审程序，在第38条所述情形下判罚时，监督审裁处需兼顾第39条之规定，应当立即下令取证并采取解雇措施，并自案件提交法院之日起30日内适当时作出决定。

第42条 提交监督审裁处审理的案件所涉及的财政支出将由公证协会承担。

第三章
公证协会

第43条 在不妨碍监督审裁处管辖权情况下，对联邦首都和国家领土内公证员的直接指导和监督以及与本法适用有关的一切规定均适用于公证协会。

ARTICULO 44. – Son atribuciones y deberes esenciales del Colegio de Escribanos:

a) Vigilar el cumplimiento por parte de los escribanos de la presente ley, así como de toda disposición emergente de las leyes, decretos, reglamentos o resoluciones del colegio mismo que tengan atinencia con el notariado;

b) Inspeccionar periódicamente los registros y oficinas de los escribanos matriculados, a los efectos de comprobar el cumplimiento estricto de todas las obligaciones notariales;

c) Velar por el decoro profesional, por la mayor eficacia de los servicios notariales y por el cumplimiento de los principios de ética profesional;

d) Someter a la aprobación del Poder Ejecutivo, el reglamento notarial y la reforma de los mismos; (Nota Infoleg: Por art. 1º del Decreto Nº 240/99 B.O. 23/3/1999, se deroga la expresión "los aranceles notariales" del presente inciso).

el reglamento notarial y la reforma de los mismos;

e) Dictar resoluciones de carácter general tendientes a unificar los procedimientos notariales y mantener la disciplina y buena correspondencia entre los escribanos;

f) Llevar permanentemente depurado el registro de matrícula y publicar periódicamente los inscriptos en el mismo; sellar los cuadernos de protocolos, llevar el registro de rúbrica y legalizar los documentos notariales;

g) Organizar y mantener al día el registro profesional y el de estadística de los actos notariales;

h) Tomar conocimiento en todo juicio o sumario promovido contra un escribano a efectos de determinar sus antecedentes y responsabilidad;

i) Instruir sumario, de oficio o por denuncia de terceros, sobre los procedimientos de los escribanos matriculados, sea para juzgarlos directamente o para elevar a tal efecto las actuaciones al Tribunal de Superintendencia si así procediere, de acuerdo con los artículos 38 y 39;

j) Organizar los concursos para la provisión de registros a que se refiere el artículo 19 e informar al Poder Ejecutivo sobre los antecedentes y méritos de los escribanos aspirantes a titulares o adscriptos a los mismos.

(Artículo sustituido por art. 1º de la Ley Nº 14.054 B.O. 16/10/1951).

ARTICULO 45. – El Colegio de Escribanos tiene la representación gremial de los escribanos y además de los deberes y atribuciones que con carácter obligatorio se le asignan en el artículo anterior, y de las facultades que emanen del reglamento notarial y de su propio estatuto,

第 44 条　公证协会的基本职责如下：

a）监督公证员对本法的遵守情况，以及与公证人员有关的该协会的法律、法令、条例或者决议出现的任何突发情况；

b）定期检查登记公证员的登记记录和办公室，以核实所有公证职责是否得到严格遵守；

c）确保公证员的专业适当性、公证服务效率和遵守职业操守；

d）提交行政部门审核公证规定及其更新事项；（Infoleg 注释：依据1999年3月23日《官方公报》上的第240/99号法案第1条，本段所述"公证费"一词现予废除）

公证规定及其更新事项；

e）确定统一公证程序的一般性决议，维护公证员之间的良好纪律和相互沟通关系；

f）永久清理注册登记册，并定期公布其中已登记之事项；密封议定书日志，保留标准的登记事项并使公证文件合法化；

g）编排和维护公证事务最新的专业和统计记录；

h）针对公证员提起的任何审理或简易审案件，均应当确定其前因所在和责任归属；

i）在根据职权范围或第三方申诉情况适用注册公证员的简易审程序时，可直接作出裁决或者根据第38条和第39条酌情提交至监督审裁处审理；

j）依据第19条有关登记处的规定组织选拔活动，并向行政部门通报有志担当任职人员或助理人员的公证员背景资料和专业优势。

（相关条款替换为发布在1951年10月16日《官方公报》上的第14054号法案第1条）

第 45 条　公证协会可担任公证员的工会代表。同时，除上一条规定的责任和归属以及公证条例及其本身法规赋予的权力外，还适用于：

corresponde también al mismo:

a) Colaborar con las autoridades cuando fuere requerido para ello, en el estudio de los proyectos de leyes, decretos, reglamentaciones u ordenanzas; presentarse en demanda de cualquier resolución que tenga atinencia con el notariado o con los escribanos en general y evacuar las consultas que estas mismas autoridades, los escribanos individualmente o las instituciones análogas creyeran oportuno formularles sobre asuntos notariales.

b) Resolver arbitralmente las cuestiones que se suscitaren entre los escribanos.

c) Elevar al Poder Ejecutivo el presupuesto y balances anuales, y todo otro antecedente necesario para justificar la inversión de los fondos recaudados.

(Artículo sustituido por art. 1º de la Ley Nº 14.054 B.O. 16/10/1951).

ARTICULO 46. – El Colegio de Escribanos actuará por representación de su consejo directivo, que funcionará en la forma y condiciones que determine esta ley, el reglamento notarial y sus propios estatutos.

ARTICULO 47. – En ejercicio de su función de disciplina profesional, el Colegio de Escribanos podrá imponer a los escribanos las penas de prevención, apercibimiento, multa de pesos argentinos trescientos ($a 300) a pesos argentinos tres mil ($a 3000) y suspensión hasta un (1) mes. En caso que la gravedad de la infracción hiciera, a su juicio, pasible al escribano de una pena mayor, elevará las actuaciones al Tribunal de Superintendencia para que éste proceda conforme corresponda.

(Artículo sustituido por art. 1º de la Ley Nº 22.896 B.O. 9/9/1983).

CAPITULO IV
Organización y funcionamiento del Colegio de Escribanos

ARTICULO 48. – Para todos los efectos previstos en la presente ley, reconócese a la institución civil denominada Colegio de Escribanos, el cual ejercerá la representación colegiada de los escribanos de la Capital Federal y territorios nacionales y funcionará con el carácter, derechos y obligaciones de las personas jurídicas.

ARTICULO 49. – Se consideran colegiados los escribanos de registro, los autorizados y los matriculados con anterioridad al 1º de octubre de 1975. La colegiación se regirá por el estatuto del Colegio de Escribanos de acuerdo con lo establecido por esta ley y su reglamentación. En las asambleas del Colegio de Escribanos podrán participar con voz y voto solamente los escribanos colegiados.

a）必要时，在法律、法令、条例或法案的调研中与主管部门合作，应邀出席任何关于公证人员或一般公证员的决议审核，并在必要时就公证事宜甄别与这些主管部门、公证员个人或类似机构协商后得出结论。

b）随时对公证员之间出现的争议作出裁决。

c）向行政部门提交预算和年度资产负债表，以及为筹集资金投资所必需的任何其他前期资料。

（相关条款替换为发布在1951年10月16日《官方公报》上的第14054号法案第1条）

第46条　公证协会代表其董事会，依照本法、公证条例和本身章程规定的方式和条件行使职责。

第47条　公证协会行使职责时，可以向公证员处以三百至三千阿根廷比索的预防性和警告性罚款，并执行最长为期1个月的停职处理。如果协会认定公证员侵权的严重性理当受到更高一等判罚，可将该诉讼提交至监督审裁处，以便作出相应处置。

（相关条款替换为发布在1983年9月9日《官方公报》上的第22896号法案第1条）

第四章
公证协会的组织和运作

第48条　根据本法规定，公证协会为民间组织机构。该机构应当行使联邦首都和国家领土内公证员的合法代表权，并履行法人的性质、权利和义务。

第49条　1975年10月1日以前获得授权及注册的登记处公证员均视为大学学历。该公证员由公证协会依照本法规定及相关法规管辖。在公证协会选拔大会上，只有具备大学学历的公证员才允许以口头和投票方式参加选拔。

(Artículo sustituido por art. 10 de la Ley Nº 21.212 B.O. 29/10/1975).

ARTICULO 50. – El Colegio de Escribanos será dirigido por un consejo directivo, constituido de acuerdo con las siguientes bases:

a) Estará compuesto por un (1) presidente, un (1) vicepresidente, un (1) secretario, un (1) secretario de actas, dos (2) prosecretarios, un (1) tesorero, un (1) protesorero, diez (10) vocales titulares y cinco (5) suplentes;

b) Para ser electo presidente o vicepresidente se requerirá una antigüedad en la colegiación no menor de diez años, y de cinco años para los demás cargos del Consejo Directivo. (Inciso sustituido por art. 11 de la Ley Nº 21.212 B.O. 29/10/1975).

c) Serán elegidos por votación directa, secreta y obligatoria, salvo impedimento debidamente justificado, por los escribanos colegiados, a simple pluralidad de votos, designándose autoridades por dos (2) años y renovándose el consejo directivo por mitades cada año, pudiendo sus miembros ser reelectos por un período consecutivo;

d) Los cargos del consejo directivo serán "ad honorem" y obligatorios para todos los escribanos, salvo impedimento debidamente justificado o en el caso de reelección.

(Artículo sustituido por art. 1º de la Ley Nº 22.171 B.O. 29/2/1980).

ARTICULO 51. – El Colegio de Escribanos se mantendrá:

a) Con la cuota que abonará por una sola vez cada escribano al inscribirse o reinscribirse en la matrícula.

b) Con la cuota que abonará cada escribano como derecho de inscripción a cada concurso de oposición o antecedentes.

c) Con la cuota mensual que abonará cada escribano colegiado o matriculado y con una cuota mensual adicional que abonará cada escribano titular o adscripto de registro.

d) Con el aporte que abonarán los escribanos de registro por cada escritura que autoricen.

e) Con los fondos provenientes de los servicios específicos que prestare a sus asociados.

El monto de las cuotas y aportes que establece el presente artículo será fijado anualmente por el Colegio de Escribanos.

(Artículo sustituido por art. 1º de la Ley Nº 14.054 B.O. 16/10/1951).

（相关条款替换为发布在1975年10月29日《官方公报》上的第21212号法案第10条）

第50条　公证协会由符合以下基本条件的董事会负责管理：

a）由一名主席，一名副主席，一名秘书，两名副秘书，一名财务，一名上诉人，十名会员和五名候补会员组成；

b）当选主席或副主席者，其资历须具备不少于10年的会员资格，董事会其他职位则需具备5年的会员资格。（相关细则替换为发布在1975年10月29日《官方公报》上的第21212号法案第11条）

c）通过直接投票、秘密和具有约束力的选举方式，除非有正当理由的障碍，以简单多数投票，任期为2年，每年更换一半董事会成员，会员能够连选连任；

d）除非有正当理由的不便或连选连任，否则董事会的职务对所有公证员而言视为一份荣誉和义务。

（相关条款替换为发布在1980年2月29日《官方公报》上的第22171号法案第1条）

第51条　公证协会将执行以下收费政策：

a）通过注册或重新注册，每位公证员将支付一次费用；

b）每位公证员支付的费用作为每次选举或资质的登记权参考；

c）由每位协会或注册公证员的每月费用、额外的月费由登记处每位任职公证员或助理人员支付；

d）登记处公证员依据每份授权契约支付出资额；

e）其向联营公司提供具体服务获得的资金；

本条规定的费用和缴款金额由公证协会每年确定。

（相关条款替换为发布在1951年10月16日《官方公报》上的第14054号法案第1条）

SECCION CUARTA
DE LAS MEDIDAS DISCIPLINARIAS

CAPITULO UNICO

ARTICULO 52. – Las sanciones disciplinarias a que pueden ser sometidos los escribanos inscriptos en la matrícula, son las siguientes:

a) Apercibimiento;

b) Multa de pesos argentinos trescientos ($a 300) hasta pesos argentinos tres mil ($a 3000);

c) Suspensión desde tres (3) días hasta un (1) año;

d) Suspensión por tiempo indeterminado;

e) Privación del ejercicio de la profesión;

f) Destitución del cargo.

(Artículo sustituido por art. 1º de la Ley Nº 22.896 B.O. 9/9/1983).

ARTICULO 53. – Denunciada o establecida la irregularidad, el Colegio de Escribanos procederá a instruir un sumario, con intervención del inculpado, adoptando al efecto todas las medidas que estimen necesarias, debiendo concluir el mismo en el término de treinta días, pudiendo ampliar este plazo hasta dos períodos más cuando las circunstancias del caso lo exigieren.

(Artículo sustituido por art. 1º de la Ley Nº 14.054 B.O. 16/10/1951).

ARTICULO 54. – Terminado el sumario, el Colegio de Escribanos deberá expedirse dentro de los quince días subsiguientes; si la pena aplicable, a su juicio, es de apercibimiento, multa o suspensión hasta un mes, dictará la correspondiente sentencia, de la que se dará inmediato conocimiento al interesado a los efectos de la apelación. No produciéndose ésta o desestimándose el cargo, se ordenará el archivo de las actuaciones. Si el escribano castigado apelara dentro de los cinco días de notificado, se elevarán aquéllas al Tribunal de Superintendencia, a sus efectos.

ARTICULO 55. – Si, terminado el sumario, la pena aplicable a juicio del Colegio de Escribanos fuera superior a un mes de suspensión, elevará las actuaciones al Tribunal de Superintendencia, el cual deberá dictar su fallo dentro de los treinta días de notificada. En caso que la suspensión excediera del plazo de tres meses, el Colegio de Escribanos podrá solicitar la suspensión preventiva del escribano inculpado.

ARTICULO 56. – Las sanciones disciplinarias se aplicarán con arreglo a las siguientes normas:

第四部分
纪律措施

独立章节

第 52 条　公证协会可以依据如下政策对注册人予以纪律处分：

a）警告；

b）罚款三百至三千阿根廷比索；

c）停职 3 日至 1 年；

d）无限期停职；

e）取消专业资格；

f）解雇。

（相关条款替换为 1983 年 9 月 9 日《官方公报》上的第 22896 号法案第 1 条）

第 53 条　公证协会当谴责违规违纪行为，在当事人介入下适用简易审程序，并采取所有认为必要的措施，在 30 日内达成一致结果。必要时，可以延长处罚期限至两倍。

（相关条款替换为发布在 1951 年 10 月 16 日《官方公报》上的第 14054 号法案第 1 条）

第 54 条　简易审结束后，公证协会将在 15 日内发布审理结果；如果适用判决的处罚为一次警告、罚款或最多 1 个月的停职，相应处罚作出之后，将立即通知有关方以便其提出上诉。若非如此，或指控被驳回，诉讼将被强令提交。若被处罚公证员在接到通知后 5 日内提出上诉，则交由监督审裁处处理。

第 55 条　简易审结束后，若适用于公证协会处罚意见为超过 1 个月的停职处罚，该诉讼案件应提交给上诉法院——监督审裁处，该法院应在接到上诉通知后 30 日内作出决定。如果停职期限超过 3 个月，公证协会可以要求被起诉的公证员预防性停职。

第 56 条　纪律处分依照下列规定执行：

a) El pago de las multas deberá efectuarse en el plazo de diez días a partir de la notificación, respondiendo por las mismas la fianza otorgada por el escribano;

b) Las suspensiones se harán efectivas fijando el término durante el cual el escribano no podrá actuar profesionalmente;

c) La suspensión por tiempo indeterminado, privación del ejercicio de la profesión o destitución del cargo, importará la cancelación de la matrícula y la vacante del registro y secuestro de los protocolos, si se tratara de un escribano regente.

ARTICULO 57. – El escribano suspendido por tiempo indeterminado no podrá ser reintegrado a la profesión en un plazo menor de cinco años desde la fecha en que se pronunció el fallo.

ARTICULO 58. – De las suspensiones por tiempo indeterminado, destitución y privación del ejercicio de la profesión, deberá darse conocimiento al Poder Ejecutivo Nacional.

SECCION QUINTA
DISPOSICIONES COMPLEMENTARIAS Y TRANSITORIAS

CAPITULO I

ARTICULO 59. – Dentro de los ciento ochenta días de la fecha de la promulgación de esta ley, todos los escribanos de registro, titulares y adscriptos, procederán a renovar su inscripción en el registro de matrículas, requisito que podrán cumplir con la sola justificación de su carácter de escribano de registro, sin la formalidad del juramento.

ARTICULO 60. – Dentro de igual plazo del artículo anterior, los escribanos que, hallándose ya inscriptos en la matrícula a cargo de las cámaras civiles de la Capital Federal, desearen seguir actuando como tales, deberán proceder a renovar su inscripción, lo que podrán hacer mediante la justificación de encontrarse ya inscriptos, sin la formalidad del juramento.

ARTICULO 61. – Vencido el plazo establecido en los dos artículos anteriores, ningún escribano podrá matricularse ni renovar su inscripción sin previo cumplimiento de todos los requisitos exigidos.

ARTICULO 62. – A los efectos de las reinscripciones previstas en los artículos 59 y 60, las cámaras civiles expedirán a los escribanos que lo soliciten los certificados

a）罚款必须在接到通知之日起10日期限内支付，并对是否缴纳保释金给予书面回复；

b）停职处罚一经生效，即起算该职员不可从事专业工作的期限；

c）若为主管公证员，其无限期停职、取消职业资格或解雇等处罚决定将导致注册取消、注册处职位空缺以及议定书失效。

第57条 执行无限期停职的公证员，自作出决定之日起5年期限内不得复职。

第58条 无限期停职、解雇和取消职业资格等处罚结果必须向国家行政机关报告。

第五部分
附加条款和过渡条款

第一章

第59条 自本法颁布之日起180日内，所有登记处公证员、任职人员和助理人员应在注册登记处完成续期登记。此项要求可以通过注册状态作为履行的唯一理由，无须正式宣誓。

第60条 在上条所述同一期间，已经在联邦首府民政部门注册入职的公证员，如希望继续担任本职工作，必须更新其注册状态。他们可以通过已注册状态直接更新，无须正式宣誓。

第61条 一旦前两条所述期限已经过期，公证员不可在未达到所有要求的情况下完成注册或更新其注册状态。

第62条 为完成第59条和第60条规定的重新注册请求，民政部门应向公证员发放所需的资质证书。

necesarios.

ARTICULO 63. – El Colegio de Escribanos podrá, previo sumario, solicitar del Tribunal de Superintendencia la cancelación del registro de la matrícula de los escribanos que se hallen inscriptos o reinscriptos en contravención con las disposiciones de esta ley.

ARTICULO 64. – Una comisión compuesta por seis miembros, que deberán ser escribanos matriculados, designados por mitades por el Poder Ejecutivo Nacional y por el Colegio de Escribanos, bajo la presidencia del miembro que la misma comisión designe, se encargará de la inscripción en la matrícula prevista por el artículo 5 y procederá a formar una vez terminada aquélla, en el plazo que fija el artículo 59, un padrón de escribanos inscriptos, a efectos de constituir íntegramente el nuevo consejo directivo del Colegio de Escribanos, el que será designado en acto eleccionario a realizarse dentro de los treinta días subsiguientes de acuerdo con el actual estatuto de dicha entidad.

CAPITULO ADICIONAL

A) De la creación de nuevos registros

ARTICULO 65. – El Poder Ejecutivo Nacional podrá, por una sola vez, crear nuevos registros en la Capital Federal, de modo que con los ya existentes alcancen el número de 500 como máximo, los que serán provistos de acuerdo con las disposiciones de los artículos siguientes.

Las vacantes que se produzcan en estos registros, así como las ya existentes y los que se crearen fuera de los señalados en el párrafo precedente, serán provistos de conformidad con lo dispuesto en el artículo 19 Autorízase al Poder Ejecutivo Nacional para rever las autorizaciones de registros otorgadas con anterioridad a la presente ley y proceder a la adjudicación de las vacantes de conformidad con el artículo 19.

(Artículo sustituido por art. 1º de la Ley Nº 14.054 B.O. 16/10/1951).

ARTICULO 66. – Una cuarta parte de los nuevos registros será concedida a los escribanos que, siendo actualmente adscriptos a un registro de la Capital Federal, no hubieran estado asociados a su titular hasta el 1º de enero de 1945 para el ejercicio en común de su actividad profesional, participando cada uno de ellos de los beneficios y gastos de la oficina, cualquiera sea la proporción en que esa participación se haya establecido.

Se consideran comprendidos en este artículo a los

第 63 条 公证协会可在简易审之前，向监督审裁处请求取消违反本法规定的已注册或更新注册的公证员登记。

第 64 条 委员会由六名成员组成，均须为注册公证员，其中一半由国家行政部门和公证协会任命，并接受该委员会任命的主席成员领导，将负责第 5 条规定的入职登记工作，并在第 59 条规定的期限内完成一次登记处公证员的审查，以组建新的公证协会的董事会，并将根据现有实体的当前状态在未来 30 日内举行一次选举任命。

附章

A）创建新登记机构

第 65 条 国家行政部门可以一次性在联邦首府组建多个新的登记机构，以便现有的登记机构达到最大数量 500 个，这些机构将按照以下条款的规定组建。

这些登记处中存在的职位空缺和现有职位以及前款规定的职位空缺应按照第 19 条"授权国家行政权力"的规定补充，以核查在本法之颁布之前认可的注册授权，并据此根据第 19 条对空缺职位作出人选裁定。

（相关条款替换为发布在 1951 年 10 月 16 日《官方公报》上的第 14054 号法案第 1 条）

第 66 条 新登记机构的 1/4 将分配给当前归属联邦首都一家登记处的公证员。他们直到 1945 年 1 月 1 日为止，尚未与任职公证员共同参与相关的专业活动。无论其参与程度如何，均将影响公证处的福利分配和费用分担。

本条所涵盖之内容视为助理公证员已计入公证员

adscriptos que concedan una participación en los honorarios de las escrituras a su titular sin hallarse en iguales condiciones respecto de las que éste autorice, siempre que no se encuentren vinculados con el mismo por parentesco de consanguinidad dentro del cuarto grado.

ARTICULO 67. – Las otras tres cuartas partes deberán ser concedidas, a medida que se vayan creando los registros, a los escribanos diplomados en la universidad nacional, que se hallen domiciliados en la Capital Federal, siempre que reúnan las siguientes condiciones:

a) No encontrarse comprendidos en las incompatibilidades de los incisos c), e) y g) del artículo 7º;

b) Estar inscriptos en la matrícula de escribano de la Capital Federal;

c) Haber efectuado práctica de escribanía durante un plazo no menor de dos años posteriores a la obtención del título;

d) Tener una residencia inmediata en la Capital Federal, anterior al 1º de enero de 1945, no inferior a dos años;

e) No haber renunciado a la condición de titular o adscripto de registro con posterioridad al 1º de enero de 1945.

Para el caso son de aplicación las excepciones establecidas en el artículo 8.

ARTICULO 68. – La provisión de los nuevos registros a que se refiere el artículo 65 se efectuará de acuerdo con el orden de preferencia que, previo el correspondiente llamado a inscripción, efectuará un tribunal calificador designado por el Poder Ejecutivo en la forma que lo establezca la reglamentación.

ARTICULO 69. – La preferencia a que se refiere el artículo anterior será establecida, exclusivamente, en mérito a los siguientes antecedentes:

I. Antigüedad en el ejercicio activo de la profesión, que se determinará:

a) Por la fecha de inscripción en la matrícula profesional;

b) Por el ejercicio de la función notarial, sea como adscripto o como escribano adjunto a escribanías de la Capital Federal, o como empleado de las mismas.

II. Actuación institucional relacionada con la profesión, vinculación a instituciones notariales y publicación de trabajos.

III. Informes sobre capacidad, moralidad y conducta, expedidos por escribanos de la Capital Federal en base a la actuación del interesado.

ARTICULO 70. – La designación de titular de un

工作开支，前提是他们之间不属于四代内血亲关系，否则，将不考虑在此条件下是否给予他们授权。

第67条 其他3/4的名额必须在机构组建时分配给国立大学毕业并在联邦首都居住的公证员，应符合以下条件：

a）不包括在第7条c款、e款和g款小节的不适合条件中；

b）被列入联邦首都公证员登记注册；

c）在获得公证专业职称后参加过2年以上的任职公证员实践；

d）1945年1月1日之前居住在联邦首都，时间不少于2年；

e）1945年1月1日以后未放弃登记处任职公证员或助理身份。

在这种情况下，适用第8条规定的例外情形。

第68条 第65条提到的新登记机构，应按照优先顺序进行，在相应的登记申请之前，由行政部门以相关条例规定的方式指定的适格法院提供。

第69条 上一条中提到的选择倾向仅取决于下列前提条件：

I. 有效专业职能的资历获得条件：

a）专业注册登记之日；

b）行使公证职责时，在联邦首都机构任职或担任助理公证员，或作为其雇员。

II. 与专业有关或关系到公证机构和出版作品的机构行为。

III. 联邦首都的公证员根据有关表现发表的关于能力、道德和行为的报告。

第70条 登记处任职人员根据第65条规定予以

registro, de los creados de acuerdo con el artículo 65, se hará sin perjuicio de las disposiciones de los artículos 1º, 2º, 3º, 4º, 5º, 7º y 15 a cuyas exigencias deberá conformarse y satisfacer previamente el candidato.

ARTICULO 71. – Los registros creados de acuerdo con el artículo 65 de esta ley, funcionarán y estarán sometidos a todas las disposiciones de la misma.

ARTICULO 72. – (Artículo derogado por art. 2º de la Ley Nº 14.054 B.O. 16/10/1951).

ARTICULO 73. – (Artículo derogado por art. 2º de la Ley Nº 14.054 B.O. 16/10/1951).

ARTICULO 74. – Desde la promulgación de la presente ley el Poder Ejecutivo no creará nuevos registros que no se ajusten a las disposiciones de los artículos 18, 65 y siguientes.

ARTICULO 75. – Dentro de los treinta días de promulgada esta ley, el Poder Ejecutivo llamará, por quince días, a inscripción para la provisión de los registros a que se refiere el artículo 65.

ARTICULO 76. – Dentro de igual plazo se constituirá la comisión calificadora, la que deberá expedirse en el término de treinta días de finalizada la inscripción y elevar las actuaciones al Poder Ejecutivo Nacional, en mérito a las cuales éste dispondrá la creación de los registros necesarios y proveerá los mismos dentro de los treinta días.

B) De la Caja Nacional de Jubilaciones y Pensiones del Notariado

ARTICULO 77. – (Artículo sustituido por art. 65 de la Ley Nº 18.038 B.O. 10/1/1969. Vigencia: a partir del 1º de enero de 1969).

ARTICULO 78. – Quedan derogadas las disposiciones pertinentes de las Leyes números 1893, 1532, 2662, sus modificatorias y todas cuantas se opongan a la presente.

ARTICULO 79. – Comuníquese al Poder Ejecutivo. J. Hortensio Quijano – Ricardo C. Guardo – Alberto H. Reales – L. Zavalla Carbó.

Antecedentes Normativos

– Artículo 77, sustituido por art. 1º de la Ley Nº 16.594 B.O. 4/12/1964;

– Artículo 12, sustituido por art. 1º del Decreto-Ley Nº 12.454/57 B.O. 17/10/1957;

任命，不得妨碍履行第1条、第2条、第3条、第4条、第5条、第7条和第15条的规定，其规定必须符合并满足此前的候选人要求。

第71条 根据本法第65条创建的登记机构，将按照同样的规定运营。

第72条 （相关条款依据发布在1951年10月16日《官方公报》上的第14054号法案第2条已废止）

第73条 （相关条款依据发布在1951年10月16日《官方公报》上的第14054号法案第2条已废止）

第74条 自本法颁布以后，行政部门将不会创建不符合第18条、第65条及项下条款的新登记机构。

第75条 在本法颁布之日起30日内，行政部门应在15日内提出登记，以便提供第65条所述登记机构信息。

第76条 在同一期限内，组建资格委员会且必须在注册结束后30日内发布，并将此行动提交给国家行政部门，以便安排创建必要的登记机构，并在30日内提供详情。

B）国民年金和公证人员基金

第77条 （相关条款替换为1969年1月10日《官方公报》上的第18038号法案第65条。有效期：截至1969年1月1日）

第78条 第1893号、第1532号及第2662号法律的有关规定及其修正案及其他相关规定现予废止。

第79条 联系行政部门。霍特森西奥·夸亚诺（J. Hortensio Quijano）- 里卡多·瓜尔多（Ricardo C. Guardo）- 阿尔贝托·雷阿勒斯（Alberto H. Reales）- 扎瓦拉·卡博（L. Zavalla Carbó）。

适用规范说明

第77条替换为1964年12月4日《官方公报》上的第16594号法案第1条；

第12条替换为1957年10月17日《官方公报》上的第12454/57号法案第1条；

– Artículo 3º, sustituido por art. 1º de la Ley Nº 14.054 B.O. 16/10/1951;

– Artículo 5º, sustituido por art. 1º de la Ley Nº 14.054 B.O. 16/10/1951;

– Artículo 6º, sustituido por art. 1º de la Ley Nº 14.054 B.O. 16/10/1951;

– Artículo 12, sustituido por art. 1º de la Ley Nº 14.054 B.O. 16/10/1951;

– Artículo 18, sustituido por art. 1º de la Ley Nº 14.054 B.O. 16/10/1951;

– Artículo 19, sustituido por art. 1º de la Ley Nº 14.054 B.O. 16/10/1951;

第 3 条替换为发布在 1951 年 10 月 16 日《官方公报》上的第 14054 号法案第 1 条；

第 5 条替换为发布在 1951 年 10 月 16 日《官方公报》上的第 14054 号法案第 1 条；

第 6 条替换为发布在 1951 年 10 月 16 日《官方公报》上的第 14054 号法案第 1 条；

第 12 条替换为发布在 1951 年 10 月 16 日《官方公报》上的第 14054 号法案第 1 条；

第 18 条替换为发布在 1951 年 10 月 16 日《官方公报》上的第 14054 号法案第 1 条；

第 19 条替换为发布在 1951 年 10 月 16 日《官方公报》上的第 14054 号法案第 1 条。

巴哈马

巴哈马公证人法

CHAPTER 57 Notaries Public
An Act relating to Notaries Public.

1. This Act may be cited as the Notaries Public Act.

2. (1) In this Act, unless the context otherwise requires, the expression — "functions" includes powers and duties; "licence" means a licence as a notary public under section 5, and grammatical variations of that expression shall be construed accordingly; "Minister" means the Minister responsible for notaries public.

(2) Unless the contrary intention appears, references in this Act to a section are references to a section of this Act, and references in a section to a subsection are references to a subsection of that section.

3. Subject to the provisions of this Act, any of the following persons may be licensed as a notary public —

(a) any counsel and attorney of the Supreme Court;

(b) any person who immediately before the commencement of this Act was the holder of a licence as a notary public under section 3 of the Notaries Public Act (now repealed).

4. Any person holding or acting in a public office specified in the First Schedule shall be ex officio a notary public for The Bahamas and shall be entitled to exercise generally within The Bahamas all the functions of a notary public licensed under this Act:

Provided that all fees taken by such persons in the exercise of such functions shall be paid by them into the Consolidated Fund.

5. (1) Any person desiring to be licensed under this Act shall make application for the purpose to the Minister in such form accompanied by such information as the Minister may require.

(2) The Minister may, upon payment of the fee pre-

第57章 公证人
与公证人有关的法案

1. 本法简称为《公证人法》。

2.（1）在本法中，除文义另有所指外，"职能"包括权力和义务；"许可证"是指根据第5条的规定作为公证人的许可证，并且该表述的语法变化应具体解释；"部长"是指负责管理公证人的部长。

（2）除非出现相反的意图，否则本法中对某条的引用指的是本法中的某一条，对某条中某款的引用是对本法中该条该款的引用。

3. 在符合本法规定的情况下，任何以下人员均可被任命为公证人：

（a）最高法院的律师和检察官；

（b）本法生效之前已经根据《公证人法》第3条（现已废止），持有公证人许可证的任何人。

4. 任何持有许可证或在附表1中被指明为公职人员的人，均当然作为巴哈马的公证人，并有权在巴哈马境内行使本法规定的公证人的所有职能：

上述执行这种行为的人员取得的费用应该由其向统一基金缴纳。

5.（1）任何希望根据本法获得任命的人，应提交部长规定的资料，并向部长提出申请。

（2）在缴纳附表2所规定的费用后，部长可以将

scribed in the Second Schedule, grant to any person qualified in accordance with section 3 and making application as mentioned in subsection (1), a licence authorising such person to exercise either generally within The Bahamas, or within any Out Island district specified in the licence, the functions exercised by notaries public in The Bahamas immediately before the commencement of this Act.

6. (1) Every licence shall take effect on the date specified in the licence as the date on which it is to take effect and shall expire on the 31st day of December next following that date, unless renewed.

(2) Every licence may, if the Minister approves, be renewed by endorsement thereon, upon the application of the holder thereof and on payment of the fee prescribed in the Second Schedule.

(3) Where a licence has been lost, destroyed or mutilated, it may be replaced by the Minister by the issue of a copy thereof upon the application of the person entitled thereto and on the payment of the fee prescribed in the Second Schedule.

7. (1) It shall be the duty of the Permanent Secretary to the Minister to keep, and to amend from time to time as circumstances require, an alphabetical roll or book of all notaries public licensed under this Act, which roll or book shall be called the roll of notaries public, and to enter therein the names and particulars of every such notary public.

(2) Where the signature or seal of a notary public appears or is impressed upon any document issued by him in the exercise of the functions of a notary public, the Permanent Secretary may, on payment of the fee prescribed in the Second Schedule, authenticate or legalise the signature or seal:

Provided that no fee is payable in respect of the authentication or legalisation of a signature or seal appearing or impressed upon a document connected with or relating to the Crown or a department of the public service of The Bahamas and issued by a person who is, by virtue of the provisions of section 4, a notary public.

(3) In the performance of his functions under this section and under section 8 the Permanent Secretary shall be assisted by such other public officer or officers as the Minister may from time to time in writing designate for the purpose.

8. Before practising as a notary public or performing any notarial act every person licensed as a notary public shall take and subscribe an oath in the form set out in the

许可证授予任何符合第3条的资格规定并按第1条的规定提交申请的人，被授权人有权在巴哈马境内或在许可证中指定的任何外岛地区内行使公证人在本法生效前在巴哈马行使的职能。

6.（1）每个许可证均自许可证中所载明的日期起生效，并于该年的十二月三十一日届满，除非许可证得到更新。

（2）如经部长批准，任何许可证可根据持有人的申请并在缴纳附表2所列的费用后予以更新。

（3）凡许可证已被遗失、破坏或损毁的，根据许可证权利人的申请并在缴纳附表2所列费用后，可以由部长颁发副本。

7.（1）部长常务秘书有义务根据情况的需要，保管并不时修订按照本法规定的以公证人姓名字母排列的公证人名册，并在其中输入每一名公证人的姓名和资料。

（2）公证人行使其职能时在出具的文件中签名或盖章的，在缴纳附表2规定的费用后，常务秘书长可以对签名或印章进行认证或将其合法化：

但对于与官方或与巴哈马公共服务部门有关的文书，或根据第4条的规定由公证人签发的文件，公证人在其中签名或盖章的认证或合法化，无须支付任何费用。

（3）常务秘书长根据本条和第8条履行其职能时，应由部长不时以书面形式指定其他公职人员或官员予以协助。

8. 在作为公证人执业或作出公证行为之前，每位获得公证人任命的人，应以附表3所示的格式在部长常务秘书长或第7条第2款指定的人员面前签署誓

Third Schedule before the Permanent Secretary to the Minister or an officer designated pursuant to subsection (2) of section 7, who shall thereupon cause the name of such person to be enrolled in the roll of notaries public.

9. (1) No person duly licensed under this Act shall be deprived of his licence or suspended from the performance of any act whatsoever appertaining or belonging to his office unless he is found guilty of some crime, gross misconduct, negligence or unskilfulness by a judge of the Supreme Court, who shall be competent, upon a complaint made by any person appearing to him to have a sufficient interest, to hear and determine such complaint in a summary manner and to exercise in relation to such complaint the powers mentioned in subsection (2).

(2) Where any person is found guilty upon a complaint made pursuant to subsection (1) the judge hearing the complaint may, if in his judgment the circumstances so warrant, order that the name of such and, where such an order is made, the licence of such person shall be deemed to be withdrawn, and he shall be disqualified from performing any notarial act whatsoever, while such order is in force.

(3) Any order made by a judge under subsection (2) shall be final and conclusive, and shall not be subject to any appeal.

10. Every notary public shall have a seal which he shall impress upon all documents issued by him in the exercise of the functions of a notary public, and such seal shall be approved by the Minister.

11. (1) Subject to the provisions of section 4, any person who —

(a) practises as a notary public or performs any notarial act without having taken and subscribed an oath as required by section 8; or

(b) holds himself out to be a notary public or receives any fee or reward as a notary public when he is not a person duly licensed and enrolled under this Act, shall be guilty of an offence and liable on summary conviction thereof to a fine not exceeding one hundred and fifty dollars.

(2) This section shall not be construed to exempt any person from any prosecution under the provisions of any other Act to which he would otherwise be liable.

12. The Minister may, from time to time by order —

(a) amend the First Schedule by deleting therefrom any public office or including therein any other public office;

(b) add to or vary the fees prescribed in the Second Schedule.

言，宣誓之后其姓名才能被登记在公证人名册中。

9.（1）任何根据本法被授予许可证的人，除非被最高院的法官认定犯有某项罪行、严重的轻罪，疏忽或不正当的行为，否则不得被吊销许可证或暂停执行任何属于其自身或其职务的行为。对于任何可能与其有足够利益关联的人提出的投诉，最高院的法官须以简易方式听证并裁定，并就该投诉行使第2款所述的权力。

（2）任何公证人因根据第1款作出的投诉而被裁定为犯罪，如果在法官认为情势必要，在作出该裁决时，公证人的许可证应被视为撤销，而在该判决生效时，其将被取消公证人资格，不得再进行任何公证行为。

（3）法官根据第2款作出的任何命令，是终局性的，不得上诉。

10. 在行使公证人职务时，公证人应对他所发出的所有文件盖章，公证公章由部长批准。

11.（1）除第4条另有规定外，任何人：

（a）未按照第8条的规定宣誓并提交誓言，担任公证人或履行任何公证行为的；或者

（b）不担任公证人，或者当公证人不是根据本法正式许可和登记的人，接受作为公证人专属的费用或报酬的，构成犯罪，通过简易程序定罪，将被处以不超过150美元的处罚。

（2）本条不得解释为根据其他法律另有规定而免除起诉。

12. 部长可不时发布命令：

（a）通过废除任何公职或其中任何公证职务来修订附表1；

（b）增加或更改附表2所规定的费用。

巴巴多斯

巴巴多斯公证人法

NOTARIES PUBLIC ACT,2017-09
BARBADOS

Short title

1. This Act may be cited as the Notaries Public Act,2017.

Interpretation

2. In this Act ,"Minister" means the Minister responsible for notaries public.

Certain officers to be notaries public

3. Any person holding or acting in a public office specified in the First Schedule, shall be ex-officio a notary public for Barbados and shall be entitled to exercise generally all the functions of a notary public

Notarial duties

4. A person authorised under this Act to be a notary public

(a) shall have the rights and discharge the duties appertaining to the office of Notary Public; and

(b) may perform any notarial services specified in the Second Schedule.

Duty to affix seal

5. Every notary public entitled to practise under this Act shall have a seal which he shall impress upon all documents issued by him in the exercise of the functions of a notary public.

Fees for notarial services

6.(1) A notary public shall charge the applicable fee prescribed in the Second Schedule for the performance of the duties of his office.

(2) All fees collected by a notary public in the ex-

公证人法 2017-09
巴巴多斯

简称

1. 本法简称为《2017年公证人法》。

释义

2. 在本法中,"部长"特指负责管理公证人的部长。

某些官员公证人

3. 在附表1所指定的任何人员,依职权当然作为巴巴多斯的公证人,并有权行使公证人的所有职能。

公证人的职责

4. 根据本法授权为公证人的人员

(a)应对公证人职务享有相应的权利并履行相应的职务;

(b)可执行附表2所载明的公证服务。

印章的义务

5. 根据本法有权执业的所有公证人均应有持有公证公章,在其履行公证人职能的所有文件上盖章。

公证服务费用

6.(1)公证人应按照附表2所列的规定费用收取公证人服务费。

(2)公证人行使公证职务所收取的所有费用,均

ercise of notarial functions shall be paid by him into the Consolidated Fund.

(3) No fee is payable to a notary public in respect of matter relating to the Crown or to any Ministry or Department of Government.

Duty to record

7. Every notary public shall keep and maintain a book called a "Notarial Act Book" which shall be in the form set out in the Third Schedule an in which shall be recorded the details of every notarial act performed by him.

Power to amend Schedules

8. The Minister may amend any of the Schedules to this Act.

应缴纳入普通基金。

（3）对与政府部门或相关官员有关的公证事务，公证人不得收取公证费用。

记录的职责

7. 公证人应持有并保存一本名为"公证行为手册"的书，其格式应符合附表3的要求，内容应记录其履行的每一个公证行为的具体细节。

修改附表的权力

8. 部长可以修改本法规定的任何附表。

伯利兹

伯利兹公证人法

BELIZE NOTARIES PUBLIC ACT CHAPTER 129
REVISED EDITION 2000

ARRANGEMENT OF SECTIONS

1. Short title.
2. Commission, how to be obtained.
3. Penalty, unauthorised practitioner.
4. Commission to be enrolled.
5. May be struck off roll.
6. Fees which may be demanded by a notary public for his own use.

NOTARIES PUBLIC

1. This Act may be cited as the Notaries Public Act.

2. The Prime Minister may grant to any fit and proper person whose legal qualification to be appointed and enrolled as a notary public is certified to him in writing by the Chief Justice, a commission or licence under his hand, authorising that person to practise as a notary public within Belize, and upon every such commission there shall be paid to the Accountant General a fee of one hundred dollars.

3.-(1) Every person who, not being a person appointed under this Act and sworn as a notary public in the manner provided by section 4 (3), practises as a notary public, or does any notarial act is guilty of an offence and is liable on summary conviction to a fine not exceeding two hundred and fifty dollars.

(2) If the Supreme Court is satisfied that any notary public has permitted his name to be used for or on account of any person not being a notary public, on complaint thereof made in a summary way, then and in such case the said court shall order the notary public to be struck off from the roll of notaries public and he shall be for ever

伯利兹公证人法
2000 年修订版

章节安排
1. 简称
2. 公证人身份的取得
3. 未经授权的从业人员及处罚
4. 委员会注册
5. 公证人资格的剥夺
6. 公证人收取的费用

公证法全文

1. 本法可称为《公证人法》。

2. 总理可以授予被委任和登记为公证人的法定资格,由终审法院首席法官,以授权或执照的方式,以书面证明,授权其在伯利兹作为公证人行事。在每次授权时,均须向会计总监支付 100 伯利兹元的费用。

3.(1)凡未经本法令以第 4(3)条款规定的方式宣誓被任命为公证人的人以公证人的身份行事或从事公证行为均属犯罪,一经简易程序定罪,可处以不超过 250 伯利兹元的罚款。

(2)如果最高法院在简易程序中认定,公证人存在允许非公证人的人冒用其姓名从事公证活动的,应判处该公证人从公证人体系内被除名,且终身不得被授予公证人资格或从事公证活动。

disabled from practising as a notary public, or doing any notarial act in Belize.

4.-(1) Before practising as a notary public or doing any notarial act, every person already appointed or hereafter to be appointed a notary public shall cause his commission, licence or faculty to be enrolled in the office of the Registrar General.

(2) The Registrar General is hereby required to enrol such commission, licence or faculty upon the payment of a fee of three dollars.

(3) The notary public shall before practising as aforesaid make and sub-scribe in a book to be kept in the office of the Registrar General the oath set out in the First Schedule, or when the circumstances allow thereof, an affirmation or declaration to the like effect, which the Chief Justice or any judge of the Supreme Court or any Commissioner appointed to take affidavits to be used in the Supreme Court is hereby authorised to administer or receive.

(4) The Registrar General shall keep an alphabetical list of all persons so appointed and sworn as notaries public, which shall be called and be the Roll of Notaries Public.

5.-(1) No notary public appointed and sworn as aforesaid shall be deprived of his commission, licence or faculty or be suspended from the performance of any act whatever appertaining or belonging to his office, unless he is guilty of some crime, misdemeanour, gross misconduct, negligence or unskilfulness, complaint in respect of which shall be made to and heard and determined by the Supreme Court in a summary way.

(2) If any notary public is found guilty upon any such complaint his name shall be struck off the Roll by Order of the Supreme Court, and such person shall be for ever disabled from performing any notarial act whatever.

6. The fees in the Second Schedule shall be payable to and recoverable by notaries public to their own use for and in respect of the services therein enumerated.

FIRST SCHEDULE
Oath to be Subscribed by a Notary Public

"I, A.B., do swear that I will faithfully make contracts or instruments for or between any party or parties requiring the same, and I will not add or diminish anything without the knowledge and consent of such party or parties, that may alter the substance of the fact. I will not make or attest any act, contract or instrument in which

4.（1）在执业或办理公证之前，已经被任命或将被任命的公证人须将其授权文书、公证执业执照或注册书登记在长官办公室。

（2）特此规定注册总局有权对上述授权、执照或注册书的颁布行为收取3伯利兹元的费用。

（3）公证人应在上述授权和注册登记前，根据附表一的誓词宣誓，或在情况允许的情况下，由终审法院首席法官或最高法院的任何法官或任何专员，在最高法院作出誓章的确认或声明特此授权对公证人的管理或接纳。

（4）注册总局应保存所有被指定和宣誓作为公证人的以字母顺序排列的名单，该名册即为公证人名册卷。

5.-（1）除公职人员有违法犯罪行为之外，以上述方式被任命或宣誓作为公证人的人，不得随意被剥夺授权、执业执照或被取消注册。若公证人存在严重不当行为、疏忽或不忠实的情况，最高法院应对其提出指控，并以简易程序审理。

（2）如果在上述程序中，公证人被认定为有罪，法院应判处该公证人从公证人体系内除名，且终身不得被授予公证人资格或从事公证活动。

6. 公证人有权收取附表二列明的费用，以供其本人及其所提供的服务使用。

附表一
公证人宣誓誓词

我，姓名，发誓，我将忠实地为任何一方或双方或有任何相同要求的缔约方或之间作出合同或文书，如果没有该缔约方的知情和同意，我不会增加或减少或在任何方面对该事务作出实质性的改变。我不会作出或证明任何我知道有暴力或欺诈的行为、合约或文书；在所有公证事务上，我会根据我的技术和知识，正义公正地行事。上帝保佑。

I shall know there is violence or fraud; and in all things I will act uprightly and justly in the business of a notary public, according to the best of my skill and knowledge. So help me God."

SECOND SCHEDULE
Fees to be paid to Notary Public

	$	c.
Noting a protest	3.00	
Extending a protest, with one affidavit if not exceeding three folios	9.00	
Exceeding three folios, or with more than one affidavit	12.00	
Other notarial papers or accounts, per folio, each figure counting as a word	2.00	
Notarial certificates to any papers, with seal of office	8.00	
And for recording documents per folio	0.37 1/2	

Note. -A folio shall contain 160 words.

附表二
公证收费

计价单位：伯利兹元　分

制作证书	3.00
不超过三页的誓章延展证书	9.00
出具超过三页的文书或两个以上的誓章	12.00
其他公证文书，每个数字记作一个字，每一页	2.00
附带公证公章的公证证书	8.00
记录文件，每页	0.37 1/2

注：每页文书至少包含160字。

巴西

巴西公证费用条例

LEI No 10.169, DE 29 DE DEZEMBRO DE 2000.

O PRESIDENTE DA REPÚBLICA Faço saber que o Congresso Nacional decreta e eu sanciono a seguinte Lei:

Art. 1o Os Estados e o Distrito Federal fixarão o valor dos emolumentos relativos aos atos praticados pelos respectivos serviços notariais e de registro, observadas as normas desta Lei.

Parágrafo único. O valor fixado para os emolumentos deverá corresponder ao efetivo custo e à adequada e suficiente remuneração dos serviços prestados.

Art. 2o Para a fixação do valor dos emolumentos, a Lei dos Estados e do Distrito Federal levará em conta a natureza pública e o caráter social dos serviços notariais e de registro, atendidas ainda as seguintes regras:

I – os valores dos emolumentos constarão de tabelas e serão expressos em moeda corrente do País;

II – os atos comuns aos vários tipos de serviços notariais e de registro serão remunerados por emolumentos específicos, fixados para cada espécie de ato;

III – os atos específicos de cada serviço serão classificados em:

a) atos relativos a situações jurídicas, sem conteúdo financeiro, cujos emolumentos atenderão às peculiaridades socioeconômicas de cada região;

b) atos relativos a situações jurídicas, com conteúdo financeiro, cujos emolumentos serão fixados mediante a observância de faixas que estabeleçam valores mínimos e máximos, nas quais enquadrar-se-á o valor constante do documento apresentado aos serviços notariais e de registro.

Parágrafo único. Nos casos em que, por força de lei, devam ser utilizados valores decorrentes de avaliação ju-

2000年12月29日第10.169法令

共和国总统：我批准经国会颁布的本法令并使其知晓于公众。

第1条 国家及联邦地区应根据本法令之条款确定公证及登记服务的收费标准。

收费标准应根据实际产生的费用及服务履行应产生的相应报酬来确定。

第2条 在确定收费价格的过程中，国家及联邦地区的法律应考虑公证及登记服务的公众性及社会性，并应参照以下规定来确定：

（1）收费价格应以价目表的形式列出，并以国家通用货币作为计价单位；

（2）若公证及登记服务中涉及相同的法律行为，应根据这些行为性质对其进行分类并分别确定相应的收费价格；

（3）若公证及登记服务中涉及不同的法律行为，不同的法律行为间应按以下标准进行分类：

a）若是服务对象不涉及财产性的内容，其收费应根据每个地区的社会及经济状况来进行定价；

b）若是服务对象涉及财产性的内容，其收费应在法定的最高及最低价格区间确定。同时，定价时应考虑所要公证及登记的文件本身的价值。

在某些情形中，若需要根据司法估价或财政估价来确定价格，则应根据本条第三项b）目的相关规定

dicial ou fiscal, estes serão os valores considerados para os fins do disposto na alínea b do inciso III deste artigo.

Art. 3o É vedado:
I – (VETADO)

II – fixar emolumentos em percentual incidente sobre o valor do negócio jurídico objeto dos serviços notariais e de registro;

III – cobrar das partes interessadas quaisquer outras quantias não expressamente previstas nas tabelas de emolumentos;

IV – cobrar emolumentos em decorrência da prática de ato de retificação ou que teve de ser refeito ou renovado em razão de erro imputável aos respectivos serviços notariais e de registro;

V – (VETADO)

Art. 4o As tabelas de emolumentos serão publicadas nos órgãos oficiais das respectivas unidades da Federação, cabendo às autoridades competentes determinar a fiscalização do seu cumprimento e sua afixação obrigatória em local visível em cada serviço notarial e de registro.

Art. 5o Quando for o caso, o valor dos emolumentos poderá sofrer reajuste, publicando-se as respectivas tabelas, até o último dia do ano, observado o princípio da anterioridade.

Art. 6o Os notários e os registradores darão recibo dos emolumentos percebidos, sem prejuízo da indicação definitiva e obrigatória dos respectivos valores à margem do documento entregue ao interessado, em conformidade com a tabela vigente ao tempo da prática do ato.

Art. 7o O descumprimento, pelos notários e registradores, do disposto nesta Lei sujeitá-los-á às penalidades previstas na Lei no 8.935, de 18 de novembro de 1994, sem prejuízo da aplicação de outras sanções legais.

Art. 8o Os Estados e o Distrito Federal, no âmbito de sua competência, respeitado o prazo estabelecido no art. 9o desta Lei, estabelecerão forma de compensação aos registradores civis das pessoas naturais pelos atos gratuitos, por eles praticados, conforme estabelecido em lei federal.

Parágrafo único. O disposto no caput não poderá gerar ônus para o Poder Público.

Art. 9o Os Estados e o Distrito Federal deverão proceder à revisão das tabelas de emolumentos atualmente em vigor, a fim de adaptá-las ao disposto nesta Lei, no prazo

来确定。

第3条　应当禁止以下行为：
（1）（已废止）

（2）按所要公证或登记的交易或标的本身价值的百分之几作为其服务的定价；

（3）对当事人收取价目表未明确规定的其他费用；

（4）收取因公证或登记工作中产生的错误而需进一步地更正所为的法律行为、或其行为应当被他方所更正而产生的费用；

（5）（已废止）

第4条　相关的价目表应公布在各个联邦的官方刊物上，使得有管辖权的部门可以对其是否得到执行进行监督。同时，也应在公证处及登记处显眼的位置放置该价目表。

第5条　在必要的情形下，可对公证及登记的服务费用进行调整并公布新的价目表，但在每年的年末之前仍应执行旧的价目标准。

第6条　公证员及登记员应为当事人开具相关服务收据，并有义务在开具的收据中根据服务时所应执行的价目表的标准标明每项具体服务的费用。

第7条　当公证员及登记员未履行相应的服务义务时，应根据1994年11月18日第8935号法令中有关规定对其进行处罚，该处罚不影响其他法律制裁的适用。

第8条　在遵守本法第9条所规定的期限的情形下，各州或联邦特区可在其权力范围内根据巴西联邦法律的规定来制定对自然人民事登记员所从事的免费的法律服务项目的补偿办法。

上诉规定不应给相关公权机关造成财政上的负担。

第9条　在本法颁布后90日之内，各州或联邦特区应对现行有效的价目表进行修订使其符合本法的规定。

de noventa dias contado da data de sua vigência.

Parágrafo único. Até a publicação das novas tabelas de emolumentos, revistas e adaptadas conforme estabelece este artigo, os atos praticados pelos serviços notariais e de registro continuarão a ser remunerados na forma da legislação em vigor nos Estados e no Distrito Federal, observadas, desde logo, as vedações estabelecidas no art. 3o desta Lei.

Art. 10. Esta Lei entra em vigor na data de sua publicação.

Brasília, 29 de dezembro de 2000; 179o da Independência e 112o da República.

在根据本条规定修订的新价目表公布之前，相关的公证及登记服务仍应按各州及联邦特区原有的标准进行收费，但是第 3 条所规定的禁止性事项应立即生效。

第 10 条 本法令自公布之日起生效。

巴西利亚，2000 年 12 月 29 日，独立纪元 179 年，共和国纪元 112 年。

巴西公证及登记法

LEI Nº 8.935, DE 18 DE NOVEMBRO DE 1994.

O PRESIDENTE DA REPÚBLICA Faço saber que o Congresso Nacional decreta e eu sanciono a seguinte lei:

TÍTULO I
Dos Serviços Notariais e de Registros

CAPÍTULO I Natureza e Fins

Art. 1º Serviços notariais e de registro são os de organização técnica e administrativa destinados a garantir a publicidade, autenticidade, segurança e eficácia dos atos jurídicos.

Art. 2º (Vetado).

Art. 3º Notário, ou tabelião, e oficial de registro, ou registrador, são profissionais do direito, dotados de fé pública, a quem é delegado o exercício da atividade notarial e de registro.

Art. 4º Os serviços notariais e de registro serão prestados, de modo eficiente e adequado, em dias e horários estabelecidos pelo juízo competente, atendidas as peculiaridades locais, em local de fácil acesso ao público e que ofereça segurança para o arquivamento de livros e documentos.

§1º O serviço de registro civil das pessoas naturais será prestado, também, nos sábados, domingos e feriados pelo sistema de plantão.

§ 2º O atendimento ao público será, no mínimo, de seis horas diárias.

CAPÍTULO II Dos Notários e Registradores

SEÇÃO I Dos Titulares

Art. 5º Os titulares de serviços notariais e de registro são os:

I - tabeliães de notas;

1994 年 11 月 18 日第 8.935 法令

共和国总统：我批准经国会颁布的本法令并使其知晓于公众。

第一编
公证及登记服务

第一章 本质与目的

第 1 条 公证和登记服务是专门的公权力组织为了保证法律行为的公开性、真实性、安全性及有效性所从事的服务。

第 2 条 （已废止）

第 3 条 公证员或登记员为具有公信力的能从事公证或登记活动的法律专业人员。

第 4 条 公证或登记服务应以有效、足够的方式提供予公众。服务的具体时间及日期由有管辖权的法院根据各地区的特殊性加以确定。应保证公众能较为容易地获取该服务，并保证与服务有关的总簿及相关文件的安全。

对自然人的民事登记服务应以值班制的方式在周六、周日及节假日都开放予公众。

提供公众服务时间每天应保证至少六小时。

第二章 公证员及登记员

第一部分 具有从业资格的人

第 5 条 享有公证或登记资格的包括以下人员：

（1）一般文书公证员；

II - tabeliães e oficiais de registro de contratos marítimos;

III - tabeliães de protesto de títulos;

IV - oficiais de registro de imóveis;

V - oficiais de registro de títulos e documentos e civis das pessoas jurídicas;

VI - oficiais de registro civis das pessoas naturais e de interdições e tutelas;

VII - oficiais de registro de distribuição.

SEÇÃO II Das Atribuições e Competências dos Notários

Art. 6º Aos notários compete:

I - formalizar juridicamente a vontade das partes;

II - intervir nos atos e negócios jurídicos a que as partes devam ou queiram dar forma legal ou autenticidade, autorizando a redação ou redigindo os instrumentos adequados, conservando os originais e expedindo cópias fidedignas de seu conteúdo;

III - autenticar fatos.

Art. 7º Aos tabeliães de notas compete com exclusividade:

I - lavrar escrituras e procurações, públicas;

II - lavrar testamentos públicos e aprovar os cerrados;

III - lavrar atas notariais;

IV - reconhecer firmas;

V - autenticar cópias.

Parágrafo único. É facultado aos tabeliães de notas realizar todas as gestões e diligências necessárias ou convenientes ao preparo dos atos notariais, requerendo o que couber, sem ônus maiores que os emolumentos devidos pelo ato.

Art. 8º É livre a escolha do tabelião de notas, qualquer que seja o domicílio das partes ou o lugar de situação dos bens objeto do ato ou negócio.

Art. 9º O tabelião de notas não poderá praticar atos de seu ofício fora do Município para o qual recebeu delegação.

Art. 10. Aos tabeliães e oficiais de registro de contratos marítimos compete:

I - lavrar os atos, contratos e instrumentos relativos a transações de embarcações a que as partes devam ou queiram dar forma legal de escritura pública;

II - registrar os documentos da mesma natureza;

（2）海事合同公证员及登记员；

（3）票据拒绝公证员；

（4）不动产登记员；

（5）法人资格证书、与法人相关的文件及其它民事类登记之登记员；

（6）自然人民事登记员、自然人被剥夺权利或自然人监护之民事登记员；

（7）司法事务分配及登记员。

第二部分 公证人的责任和义务

第6条 公证员从事以下工作：

（1）以法定形式来证明当事人的意愿；

（2）在当事人应该或者有意愿为他们的法律及商业行为通过法定形式确保其真实性时，公证员可介入并有权制作相应的公证书，保存其原件并就原件内容颁发可信的副本；

（3）对事实行为提供证明。

第7条 一般文书公证员就以下公证事务享有专有的权力：

（1）制作公开性的（反映当事人意愿并能发生相应法律效力的）公证书或委托书；

（2）制作公开性的遗嘱或为密封遗嘱提供证明；

（3）制作（对事实进行客观描述的）公证书；

（4）对签名的有效性进行认证；

（5）对文件副本提供证明。

为保证公证服务质量，一般文书公证员应履行必要及合理的管理及勤勉义务，可收取必要及合理的费用。

第8条 当事人可在一方住所地或在标的所在地自由挑选一般文书公证员。

第9条 一般文书公证员不可在其所从事服务的市之外提供公证服务。

第10条 海事合同公证员及登记员从事以下工作：

（1）在双方当事人应当或者有意愿以公证的形式为其船舶交易提供法律依据时，制作相关的合同或其他法律文书；

（2）对此类文件进行登记；

III - reconhecer firmas em documentos destinados a fins de direito marítimo;

IV - expedir traslados e certidões.

Art. 11. Aos tabeliães de protesto de título compete privativamente:

I - protocolar de imediato os documentos de dívida, para prova do descumprimento da obrigação;

II - intimar os devedores dos títulos para aceitá-los, devolvê-los ou pagá-los, sob pena de protesto;

III - receber o pagamento dos títulos protocolizados, dando quitação;

IV - lavrar o protesto, registrando o ato em livro próprio, em microfilme ou sob outra forma de documentação;

V - acatar o pedido de desistência do protesto formulado pelo apresentante;

VI - averbar:

a) o cancelamento do protesto;

b) as alterações necessárias para atualização dos registros efetuados;

VII - expedir certidões de atos e documentos que constem de seus registros e papéis.

Parágrafo único. Havendo mais de um tabelião de protestos na mesma localidade, será obrigatória a prévia distribuição dos títulos.

SEÇÃO III Das Atribuições e Competências dos Oficiais de Registros

Art. 12. Aos oficiais de registro de imóveis, de títulos e documentos e civis das pessoas jurídicas, civis das pessoas naturais e de interdições e tutelas compete a prática dos atos relacionados na legislação pertinente aos registros públicos, de que são incumbidos, independentemente de prévia distribuição, mas sujeitos os oficiais de registro de imóveis e civis das pessoas naturais às normas que definirem as circunscrições geográficas.

Art. 13. Aos oficiais de registro de distribuição compete privativamente:

I - quando previamente exigida, proceder à distribuição eqüitativa pelos serviços da mesma natureza, registrando os atos praticados; em caso contrário, registrar as comunicações recebidas dos órgãos e serviços competentes;

II - efetuar as averbações e os cancelamentos de sua competência;

（3）对相关记载海事权利文件上的签名进行认证；

（4）颁发相应的副本及证书。

第11条　票据拒绝公证员就以下公证事务享有专有的权力：

（1）不加延迟地将债务性文件列档，以此证明债权性义务的存在；

（2）通知票据的债务人接受该票据，并要求其付款，否则将进行票据拒绝公证；

（3）接受该票据下的付款并出具相应的证明；

（4）制作票据拒绝公证并对该公证行为以登记簿、微缩胶卷拍摄技术或以其他形式进行登记；

（5）根据权利人的申请，接受其对因票据拒绝产生的权利的放弃；

（6）应对以下事项进行标注：
a）对票据之拒绝进行撤销；
b）因登记产生的必要性变动。

（7）颁发相应的公证书、登记性文件及其他文件。

若同一地区有一个以上的票据拒绝公证员，公证员的从业资格范围应按具体地区进行划分。

第三部分　登记员的职权和职能

第12条　不动产登记员、法人资格证书、与法人相关的文件及其他民事类登记之登记员、自然人民事登记员、自然人被剥夺权利或自然人监护之民事登记员应根据相关法律法规从事公共登记之法律行为。登记行为由上述登记员负责，并且无须以事先分配从业范围的方式来进行。但是不动产登记员及自然人民事登记员的职能确定应考虑其所在的地域状态。

第13条　司法事务分配及登记员就以下事务享有专有的权力：

（1）在事先有要求的情形下，根据服务的性质来公平地分配并登记记录相关法律事务；若无需事先要求，则对相关职能部门的公告进行登记记录；

（2）依职权进行相关的登记或撤销；

III - expedir certidões de atos e documentos que constem de seus registros e papéis.

TÍTULO II
Das Normas Comuns

CAPÍTULO I Do Ingresso na Atividade Notarial e de Registro

Art. 14. A delegação para o exercício da atividade notarial e de registro depende dos seguintes requisitos:
I - habilitação em concurso público de provas e títulos;
II - nacionalidade brasileira;
III - capacidade civil;
IV - quitação com as obrigações eleitorais e militares;
V - diploma de bacharel em direito;
VI - verificação de conduta condigna para o exercício da profissão.

Art. 15. Os concursos serão realizados pelo Poder Judiciário, com a participação, em todas as suas fases, da Ordem dos Advogados do Brasil, do Ministério Público, de um notário e de um registrador.

§ 1º O concurso será aberto com a publicação de edital, dele constando os critérios de desempate.

§ 2º Ao concurso público poderão concorrer candidatos não bacharéis em direito que tenham completado, até a data da primeira publicação do edital do concurso de provas e títulos, dez anos de exercício em serviço notarial ou de registro.

§ 3º (Vetado).

Art. 16. As vagas serão preenchidas alternadamente, duas terças partes por concurso público de provas e títulos e uma terça parte por concurso de remoção, de provas e títulos, não se permitindo que qualquer serventia notarial ou de registro fique vaga, sem abertura de concurso de provimento ou de remoção, por mais de seis meses. (Redação dada pela Lei nº 10.506, de 9.7.2002)

Parágrafo único. Para estabelecer o critério do preenchimento, tomar-se-á por base a data de vacância da titularidade ou, quando vagas na mesma data, aquela da criação do serviço.

Art. 17. Ao concurso de remoção somente serão admitidos titulares que exerçam a atividade por mais de dois anos.

Art. 18. A legislação estadual disporá sobre as normas e os critérios para o concurso de remoção.

（3）颁发相应的公证书、登记性文件及其他文件。

第二编
通则

第一章　进入公证及登记领域的条件

第 14 条　从事公证或登记工作必须具备以下条件：
（1）通过相关的考试并获得相应文凭；
（2）具有巴西国籍；
（3）具有民事行为能力；
（4）完成相应的选举义务和兵役义务；
（5）法学本科学位；
（6）能证明其具有履行该职业的能力。

第 15 条　相关考试应当由相应的司法机关组织举行，并在整个过程中应由巴西律师协会、公共部、一位公证员和一位登记员参加。

考试应以发布公告的形式告知社会大众并开放注册，并应说明详细标准。

未取得法学本科学位的人若在发布第一次考试通知前已有 10 年的公证或登记从业经验的，也可报名参加考试。

（这里尚存一段，但是已废止）

第 16 条　职位的空缺应以交替轮流的方式来填补。2/3 的职位空缺应通过组织公开考试挑选人才的方式来填补，另外 1/3 的职位空缺应通过组织职位调动考试的方式来填补。公证员或登记员职位空缺的状态在未组织公开考试或职业调动考试的情况下不得持续 6 个月以上。（由 2002 年 7 月 9 日第 10560 法令修订）

建立填补职位空缺的标准应考虑空缺开始的日期。当空缺开始之日与岗位设立之日为同一天时，也可以后者为基础。

第 17 条　职位调动考试只录取已经具有 2 年以上相关从业经验的人员。

第 18 条　各州立法制定职业调动考试的相关准则与标准。

Art. 19. Os candidatos serão declarados habilitados na rigorosa ordem de classificação no concurso.

CAPÍTULO II Dos Prepostos

Art. 20. Os notários e os oficiais de registro poderão, para o desempenho de suas funções, contratar escreventes, dentre eles escolhendo os substitutos, e auxiliares como empregados, com remuneração livremente ajustada e sob o regime da legislação do trabalho.

§ 1º Em cada serviço notarial ou de registro haverá tantos substitutos, escreventes e auxiliares quantos forem necessários, a critério de cada notário ou oficial de registro.

§ 2º Os notários e os oficiais de registro encaminharão ao juízo competente os nomes dos substitutos.

§ 3º Os escreventes poderão praticar somente os atos que o notário ou o oficial de registro autorizar.

§ 4º Os substitutos poderão, simultaneamente com o notário ou o oficial de registro, praticar todos os atos que lhe sejam próprios exceto, nos tabelionatos de notas, lavrar testamentos.

§ 5º Dentre os substitutos, um deles será designado pelo notário ou oficial de registro para responder pelo respectivo serviço nas ausências e nos impedimentos do titular.

Art. 21. O gerenciamento administrativo e financeiro dos serviços notariais e de registro é da responsabilidade exclusiva do respectivo titular, inclusive no que diz respeito às despesas de custeio, investimento e pessoal, cabendo-lhe estabelecer normas, condições e obrigações relativas à atribuição de funções e de remuneração de seus prepostos de modo a obter a melhor qualidade na prestação dos serviços.

CAPÍTULO III Da Responsabilidade Civil e Criminal

Art. 22. Os notários e oficiais de registro responderão pelos danos que eles e seus prepostos causem a terceiros, na prática de atos próprios da serventia, assegurado aos primeiros direito de regresso no caso de dolo ou culpa dos prepostos.

Art. 23. A responsabilidade civil independe da criminal.

Art. 24. A responsabilidade criminal será individualizada, aplicando-se, no que couber, a legislação relativa aos crimes contra a administração pública.

第 19 条 应试人员应在公开考试中经过严格的选拔程序及排名之后方能通过考试。

第二章 代理人

第 20 条 为了完成相关工作，公证员及登记员可雇佣书记员并从中挑选可作为替代性或辅助性的雇员，并应根据相应的劳动法律法规给予报酬。

每个公证员及登记员可依其需要决定替代性人员、书记员及辅助性人员的数量。

公证员及登记员应向有相应管辖权的法院报送替代性人员的名单。

书记员只能从事公证员或登记员授权从事的工作。

除了在一般公证中不能制作遗嘱，替代性人员可以与公证员或登记员从事一样的工作。

公证员或登记员可在所有的替代性人员中挑选一名作为其在缺勤或不能执行公务时的代理人。

第 21 条 公证员及登记员对自身的行政或财政事务负责，这些事务包括日常支出、投资或人员费用等。同时，为了使其能提供更高质量的服务，公证员或登记员可对其履行职权的报酬及其代理人的报酬制定相应的准则、条件或义务。

第三章 民事及刑事责任

第 22 条 公证员及登记员应对其或其代理人在履行相应的职权时给第三人所造成的损害承担责任。在其代表造成损害的情形下公证员或登记员可向前者追索赔偿。

第 23 条 民事责任不依附于刑事责任。

第 24 条 刑事责任应具有独立性，并且根据利用公职犯罪相应的法律规范加以确定。

Parágrafo único. A individualização prevista no caput não exime os notários e os oficiais de registro de sua responsabilidade civil.

CAPÍTULO IV Das Incompatibilidades e dos Impedimentos

Art. 25. O exercício da atividade notarial e de registro é incompatível com o da advocacia, o da intermediação de seus serviços ou o de qualquer cargo, emprego ou função públicos, ainda que em comissão.

§ 1º (Vetado).

§ 2º A diplomação, na hipótese de mandato eletivo, e a posse, nos demais casos, implicará no afastamento da atividade.

Art. 26. Não são acumuláveis os serviços enumerados no art. 5º.

Parágrafo único. Poderão, contudo, ser acumulados nos Municípios que não comportarem, em razão do volume dos serviços ou da receita, a instalação de mais de um dos serviços.

Art. 27. No serviço de que é titular, o notário e o registrador não poderão praticar, pessoalmente, qualquer ato de seu interesse, ou de interesse de seu cônjuge ou de parentes, na linha reta, ou na colateral, consangüíneos ou afins, até o terceiro grau.

CAPÍTULO V Dos Direitos e Deveres

Art. 28. Os notários e oficiais de registro gozam de independência no exercício de suas atribuições, têm direito à percepção dos emolumentos integrais pelos atos praticados na serventia e só perderão a delegação nas hipóteses previstas em lei.

Art. 29. São direitos do notário e do registrador:

I - exercer opção, nos casos de desmembramento ou desdobramento de sua serventia;

II - organizar associações ou sindicatos de classe e deles participar.

Art. 30. São deveres dos notários e dos oficiais de registro:

I - manter em ordem os livros, papéis e documentos de sua serventia, guardando-os em locais seguros;

II - atender as partes com eficiência, urbanidade e presteza;

上述情形中，公证员及登记员承担刑事责任的独立性并不意味着其民事责任被免除。

第四章 不兼容或禁止性事项

第25条 公证员及登记员不可兼任律师、调解员、其他公职或私职，即使是暂时性的兼职。

（这里尚存一段，但是已废止）

若因参选，或在其他因选举而产生任职的情形，则应暂停其岗位。

第26条 本法第5条中列举的职位不可兼任。

但是若由于服务数量不足、登记处或公证处收入不足的原因，公证员及登记员可在非本市兼任另一个职位。

第27条 公证员及登记员在履行职务时不可为自己或其配偶、父母、三代以内的直系或旁系的血亲或姻亲谋求利益。

第五章 权利和义务

第28条 公证员及登记员依法独立地从事其职权，并享有依其服务获得报酬的权利。只有在法律规定的情形下才丧失其从业资格。

第29条 公证员及登记员的权利如下：

（1）当业务范围分离成数个时，可行使选择权；

（2）组织协会或工会并参加其活动。

第30条 公证员及登记员的义务如下：

（1）妥善保管相应的总簿和文件，将其放置在安全区域内；

（2）有效、迅速、有礼地接待当事人；

III - atender prioritariamente as requisições de papéis, documentos, informações ou providências que lhes forem solicitadas pelas autoridades judiciárias ou administrativas para a defesa das pessoas jurídicas de direito público em juízo;

IV - manter em arquivo as leis, regulamentos, resoluções, provimentos, regimentos, ordens de serviço e quaisquer outros atos que digam respeito à sua atividade;

V - proceder de forma a dignificar a função exercida, tanto nas atividades profissionais como na vida privada;

VI - guardar sigilo sobre a documentação e os assuntos de natureza reservada de que tenham conhecimento em razão do exercício de sua profissão;

VII - afixar em local visível, de fácil leitura e acesso ao público, as tabelas de emolumentos em vigor;

VIII - observar os emolumentos fixados para a prática dos atos do seu ofício;

IX - dar recibo dos emolumentos percebidos;

X - observar os prazos legais fixados para a prática dos atos do seu ofício;

XI - fiscalizar o recolhimento dos impostos incidentes sobre os atos que devem praticar;

XII - facilitar, por todos os meios, o acesso à documentação existente às pessoas legalmente habilitadas;

XIII - encaminhar ao juízo competente as dúvidas levantadas pelos interessados, obedecida a sistemática processual fixada pela legislação respectiva;

XIV - observar as normas técnicas estabelecidas pelo juízo competente.

CAPÍTULO VI
Das Infrações Disciplinares e das Penalidades

Art. 31. São infrações disciplinares que sujeitam os notários e os oficiais de registro às penalidades previstas nesta lei:

I - a inobservância das prescrições legais ou normativas;

II - a conduta atentatória às instituições notariais e de registro;

III - a cobrança indevida ou excessiva de emolumentos, ainda que sob a alegação de urgência;

IV - a violação do sigilo profissional;

V - o descumprimento de quaisquer dos deveres descritos no art. 30.

Art. 32. Os notários e os oficiais de registro estão sujeitos, pelas infrações que praticarem, assegurado amplo

（3）优先为行政或司法机关提供所要求的相关文件、信息或决定，使后者能够在法庭上维护其公法上的法人地位；

（4）应妥善保管相关的法律、法规、决议、判决、规定、服务纪律及其他与其职务相关的法令；

（5）履行公职行为和私人生活作风应与身份相匹配；

（6）对履行职务时所接触的文件和事件的内容保密；

（7）应在公众容易接触到的显眼位置放置现行的服务费用价目表；

（8）应按相关服务价目表所规定的金额收取费用；

（9）提供收取相关费用的收据；

（10）应在法律规定的服务期限内提供服务；

（11）缴纳相应的税费；

（12）通过各种方式使法律规定的相关人员能接触到相关文件；

（13）根据相关的法定程序对当事人依法提起的诉讼进行应诉；

（14）遵守有管辖权的法院制定的行为准则。

第六章 违反纪律及处罚

第31条 依据本法，若公证员或登记员有如下行为则构成对职业纪律的违反并应受相应处罚：

（1）未遵守相应的法律规范；

（2）从事与公证或登记制度不相符的行为；

（3）收取了不应收取或超额收取了服务费用，即使是因加急所致；

（4）违反了保密义务；

（5）未履行根据本法第30条所确定的义务。

第32条 公证员或登记员因违反职业纪律应受以下处罚，但是其享有抗辩的权利：

direito de defesa, às seguintes penas:

I - repreensão;

II - multa;

III - suspensão por noventa dias, prorrogável por mais trinta;

IV - perda da delegação.

Art. 33. As penas serão aplicadas:

I - a de repreensão, no caso de falta leve;

II - a de multa, em caso de reincidência ou de infração que não configure falta mais grave;

III - a de suspensão, em caso de reiterado descumprimento dos deveres ou de falta grave.

Art. 34. As penas serão impostas pelo juízo competente, independentemente da ordem de gradação, conforme a gravidade do fato.

Art. 35. A perda da delegação dependerá:

I - de sentença judicial transitada em julgado; ou

II - de decisão decorrente de processo administrativo instaurado pelo juízo competente, assegurado amplo direito de defesa.

§ 1º Quando o caso configurar a perda da delegação, o juízo competente suspenderá o notário ou oficial de registro, até a decisão final, e designará interventor, observando-se o disposto no art. 36.

§ 2º (Vetado).

Art. 36. Quando, para a apuração de faltas imputadas a notários ou a oficiais de registro, for necessário o afastamento do titular do serviço, poderá ele ser suspenso, preventivamente, pelo prazo de noventa dias, prorrogável por mais trinta.

§ 1º Na hipótese do caput, o juízo competente designará interventor para responder pela serventia, quando o substituto também for acusado das faltas ou quando a medida se revelar conveniente para os serviços.

§ 2º Durante o período de afastamento, o titular perceberá metade da renda líquida da serventia; outra metade será depositada em conta bancária especial, com correção monetária.

§ 3º Absolvido o titular, receberá ele o montante dessa conta; condenado, caberá esse montante ao interventor.

CAPÍTULO VII Da Fiscalização pelo Poder Judiciário

Art. 37. A fiscalização judiciária dos atos notariais e de registro, mencionados nos artes. 6º a 13, será exercida

（1）谴责；

（2）罚金；

（3）90日的停职处分，处分可继续延长30日；

（4）被剥夺资格。

第33条　处罚适用于：

（1）轻微情形下，适用谴责；

（2）不是非常严重的情形的违反或再犯，适用罚金；

（3）重复性地未履行职责或在非常严重的情形下，适用停职。

第34条　有管辖权的法院可不依次适用处罚，而是根据纪律违反程度的严重性直接作出相应的处罚。

第35条　被剥夺资格的决定经以下程序作出：

（1）通过法官依法作出裁决；

（2）由有管辖权的法院经法定程序作出决定，相关公证员或登记员保留抗辩的权利。

当决定剥夺相关公证员或登记员资格时，有管辖权的法院应在决定作出之前暂停其职务并指派监察员根据本法第36条的规定代替其履行职务。

（这里尚存一段，但是已废止）

第36条　在需要消除相关公证员或登记员所犯错误的情形下，相关部门可预先对其作出暂停职务并离开岗位的决定，暂停职务及离开岗位的期限为90日并可延长30日。

在上述情形下，若替代性的人员也因与公证员或登记员同样的过错而被追究责任时，或因希望公证或登记服务能够更好地得到履行时，有管辖权的法院可指派监察员代替其履行职务。

在相关的公证员或登记员暂停职务离开岗位之时，其可从公证处及登记处所获得的收入中获得一半的报酬，剩下的另一半则应存入指定的银行账户中（并综合通货膨胀会计的方式加以计算）。

若是相关的公证员或登记员得到赦免，则其可从上述的银行账户中取回相应的金额；若其被剥夺从业资格，则该笔收入归监察员所有。

第七章　司法机关的审查

第37条　相关公证员及登记员是否根据本法第6条至第13条履行职务应由有管辖权的法院依法进

pelo juízo competente, assim definido na órbita estadual e do Distrito Federal, sempre que necessário, ou mediante representação de qualquer interessado, quando da inobservância de obrigação legal por parte de notário ou de oficial de registro, ou de seus prepostos.

Parágrafo único. Quando, em autos ou papéis de que conhecer, o Juiz verificar a existência de crime de ação pública, remeterá ao Ministério Público as cópias e os documentos necessários ao oferecimento da denúncia.

Art. 38. O juízo competente zelará para que os serviços notariais e de registro sejam prestados com rapidez, qualidade satisfatória e de modo eficiente, podendo sugerir à autoridade competente a elaboração de planos de adequada e melhor prestação desses serviços, observados, também, critérios populacionais e sócio-econômicos, publicados regularmente pela Fundação Instituto Brasileiro de Geografia e Estatística.

CAPÍTULO VIII Da Extinção da Delegação

Art. 39. Extinguir-se-á a delegação a notário ou a oficial de registro por:

I - morte;
II - aposentadoria facultativa;
III - invalidez;
IV - renúncia;
V - perda, nos termos do art. 35.
VI - descumprimento, comprovado, da gratuidade estabelecida na Lei no 9.534, de 10 de dezembro de 1997. (Incluído pela Lei nº 9.812, de 1999)

§ 1º Dar-se-á aposentadoria facultativa ou por invalidez nos termos da legislação previdenciária federal.

§ 2º Extinta a delegação a notário ou a oficial de registro, a autoridade competente declarará vago o respectivo serviço, designará o substituto mais antigo para responder pelo expediente e abrirá concurso.

CAPÍTULO IX Da Seguridade Social

Art. 40. Os notários, oficiais de registro, escreventes e auxiliares são vinculados à previdência social, de âmbito federal, e têm assegurada a contagem recíproca de tempo de serviço em sistemas diversos.

Parágrafo único. Ficam assegurados, aos notários, oficiais de registro, escreventes e auxiliares os direitos e vantagens previdenciários adquiridos até a data da publi-

行司法审查。必要时，有管辖权的法院的名单可由各州或联邦特区自行确定。同时，当公证员及登记员或其代理人未履行相关法律法规规定的义务时，也可由相关当事人的代表进行审查。

在诉讼审理中，若法官确定利用公职犯罪的情形存在，法官应向公共部报告此不法行为并提交相关的文件及副本以提供证明。

第38条 有管辖权的法院应保证公证及登记服务能以准确迅速、富有成效、令人满意的方式被履行。为使公证及登记服务能够更好地履行，有管辖权的法院应建议相关部门制定相应的计划和对策。服务履行的标准应与巴西地理统计研究所颁布的人口和经济社会标准相协调。

第八章 从业资格的消灭

第39条 公证员或登记员因以下情形导致从业资格的消灭：
（1）死亡；
（2）自愿退休；
（3）丧失行为能力；
（4）辞职；
（5）依本法第35条被剥夺从业资格；
（6）未完成1997年12月10日第9534号法令（已归入1999年第9812号法令）所规定的义务。

应根据巴西联邦社会保障法律法规中的条款对相关公证员或登记员自愿退休及丧失行为能力的事实进行确认。

当相应的公证员或登记员的资格消灭时，相关部门应宣告此服务位置的空缺，指派最资深的代理人代替其处理职务，并组织相关考试招聘新人。

第九章 社会保障

第40条 公证员、登记员、书记员及其他辅助性人员享有联邦级别的社会保障。服务时间的计算应以倒数计算的方式，并保证其在不同服务系统内服务的时间都被计算在内。

在本法颁布之前公证员、登记员、书记员及其他辅助性人员已取得的社会保障性权利和福利继续得到保证。

cação desta lei.

TÍTULO III
Das Disposições Gerais

Art. 41. Incumbe aos notários e aos oficiais de registro praticar, independentemente de autorização, todos os atos previstos em lei necessários à organização e execução dos serviços, podendo, ainda, adotar sistemas de computação, microfilmagem, disco ótico e outros meios de reprodução.

Art. 42. Os papéis referentes aos serviços dos notários e dos oficiais de registro serão arquivados mediante utilização de processos que facilitem as buscas.

Art. 43. Cada serviço notarial ou de registro funcionará em um só local, vedada a instalação de sucursal.

Art. 44. Verificada a absoluta impossibilidade de se prover, através de concurso público, a titularidade de serviço notarial ou de registro, por desinteresse ou inexistência de candidatos, o juízo competente proporá à autoridade competente a extinção do serviço e a anexação de suas atribuições ao serviço da mesma natureza mais próximo ou àquele localizado na sede do respectivo Município ou de Município contíguo.

§ 1º (Vetado).

§ 2º Em cada sede municipal haverá no mínimo um registrador civil das pessoas naturais.

§ 3º Nos municípios de significativa extensão territorial, a juízo do respectivo Estado, cada sede distrital disporá no mínimo de um registrador civil das pessoas naturais.

Art. 45. São gratuitos para os reconhecidamente pobres os assentos do registro civil de nascimento e o de óbito, bem como as respectivas certidões.

Art. 45. São gratuitos os assentos do registro civil de nascimento e o de óbito, bem como a primeira certidão respectiva. (Redação dada pela Lei nº 9.534, de 10.12.1997)

Parágrafo único. Para os reconhecidamente pobres não serão cobrados emolumentos pelas certidões a que se refere este artigo. (Parágrafo incluído pela Lei nº 9.534, de 10.12.1997)

§ 1º Para os reconhecidamente pobres não serão cobrados emolumentos pelas certidões a que se refere este artigo. (Incluído pela Lei nº 11.789, de 2008)

§ 2º É proibida a inserção nas certidões de que trata o § 1º deste artigo de expressões que indiquem condição

第三编
一般性措施

第 41 条 公证员及登记员应依据相关法律规定独立地组织并开展业务，其在履行服务中可采用计算机系统、微缩胶卷拍摄技术、可视光盘及其他可复制的系统及渠道。

第 42 条 公证员及登记员应根据使用习惯对相关文件进行分类并归档，以便需要时能准确迅速地取得。

第 43 条 每个公证处及登记处只能设在一个地方，并且不能设立分支机构。

第 44 条 若是相关公证员或登记员已完全不可能继续从事该职业的情形被证实，而且通过公开考试也无法招录到合适的人员，有管辖权的法院应向有关当局申请取消该服务岗位，或将该服务岗位合并到与之性质最为相近的服务中，或合并到本市或其他临近市的相关服务岗位中。

（这里尚存一段，但是已废止）
每个市应至少有一名自然人民事登记员。

若是在地域面积较大的市，可根据该州的规定在该市的每个地区安排至少一名自然人民事登记员。

第 45 条 出生和死亡登记服务是免费的，登记处出具的第一份证明也是免费的（根据 1997 年 12 月 10 日第 9534 号法令修改）。

登记员不可向家庭困难户收取根据本条应出具的证明而产生的费用。

登记员不可在根据本条应出示的证明中载入贫困等字眼（根据 2008 年第 11789 号法令修改）。

de pobreza ou semelhantes. (Incluído pela Lei nº 11.789, de 2008)

Art. 46. Os livros, fichas, documentos, papéis, microfilmes e sistemas de computação deverão permanecer sempre sob a guarda e responsabilidade do titular de serviço notarial ou de registro, que zelará por sua ordem, segurança e conservação.

Parágrafo único. Se houver necessidade de serem periciados, o exame deverá ocorrer na própria sede do serviço, em dia e hora adrede designados, com ciência do titular e autorização do juízo competente.

TÍTULO IV
Das Disposições Transitórias

Art. 47. O notário e o oficial de registro, legalmente nomeados até 5 de outubro de 1988, detêm a delegação constitucional de que trata o art. 2º.

Art. 48. Os notários e os oficiais de registro poderão contratar, segundo a legislação trabalhista, seus atuais escreventes e auxiliares de investidura estatutária ou em regime especial desde que estes aceitem a transformação de seu regime jurídico, em opção expressa, no prazo improrrogável de trinta dias, contados da publicação desta lei.

§ 1º Ocorrendo opção, o tempo de serviço prestado será integralmente considerado, para todos os efeitos de direito.

§ 2º Não ocorrendo opção, os escreventes e auxiliares de investidura estatutária ou em regime especial continuarão regidos pelas normas aplicáveis aos funcionários públicos ou pelas editadas pelo Tribunal de Justiça respectivo, vedadas novas admissões por qualquer desses regimes, a partir da publicação desta lei.

Art. 49. Quando da primeira vacância da titularidade de serviço notarial ou de registro, será procedida a desacumulação, nos termos do art. 26.

Art. 50. Em caso de vacância, os serviços notariais e de registro estatizados passarão automaticamente ao regime desta lei.

Art. 51. Aos atuais notários e oficiais de registro, quando da aposentadoria, fica assegurado o direito de percepção de proventos de acordo com a legislação que anteriormente os regia, desde que tenham mantido as con-

第 46 条 相关公证员或登记员对其公证处及登记处的总簿、文件、微缩胶卷、计算机系统负有妥善保管的责任。应保证其排列的有序性，对其合理收存并保证其安全。

若需要进行相关的专业技能训练，应获得有管辖权的法院的许可，并使相关的公证员或登记员知晓，并在指定的日期和时间在相关的公证处及登记处进行。

第四编
过渡性措施

第 47 条 在 1988 年 10 月 5 日前经法定程序获得任命的公证员及登记员，根据本法第 2 条依法享有宪法赋予的资格。

第 48 条 在本法颁布后的三十日（不可延长）的期限内，若是书记员及其它辅助性人员以明示的方式选择同意接受依据本法产生的法律制度的改变，则公证员及登记员可继续聘用现有的享有公务员资格或受特别程序管理的书记员及其他辅助性人员。聘用应符合相关的劳动法律法规。

若书记员及其他辅助性人员选择同意接受，则之前履行的服务期可被计算在内并继续产生相应的法律效力。

若享有公务员资格或受特别程序管理的书记员及其他辅助性人员选择拒绝接受，则其应继续受公务员法律规范或有管辖权的法院整理编辑的相应法规调整。同时，从本法颁布之日起，不再以这些程序录用新人。

第 49 条 若公证员或登记员职位出现首个空缺时，应根据第二十六条采用不兼任的方式填补。

第 50 条 若公证员及登记员职位出现空缺时，这些将被国有化的新填补职位将自动受本法调整。

第 51 条 现有的公证员或登记员退休时，根据之前颁行的法律法规应该获得的养老金待遇不变，其应根据之前的法律法规依法缴税直至丧失或让与此职位。

tribuições nela estipuladas até a data do deferimento do pedido ou de sua concessão.

§ 1º O disposto neste artigo aplica-se aos escreventes e auxiliares de investidura estatutária ou em regime especial que vierem a ser contratados em virtude da opção de que trata o art. 48.

§ 2º Os proventos de que trata este artigo serão os fixados pela legislação previdenciária aludida no caput.

§ 3º O disposto neste artigo aplica-se também às pensões deixadas, por morte, pelos notários, oficiais de registro, escreventes e auxiliares.

Art. 52. Nas unidades federativas onde já existia lei estadual específica, em vigor na data de publicação desta lei, são competentes para a lavratura de instrumentos traslatícios de direitos reais, procurações, reconhecimento de firmas e autenticação de cópia reprográfica os serviços de Registro Civil das Pessoas Naturais.

Art. 53. Nos Estados cujas organizações judiciárias, vigentes à época da publicação desta lei, assim preverem, continuam em vigor as determinações relativas à fixação da área territorial de atuação dos tabeliães de protesto de títulos, a quem os títulos serão distribuídos em obediência às respectivas zonas.

Parágrafo único. Quando da primeira vacância, aplicar-se-á à espécie o disposto no parágrafo único do art. 11.

Art. 54. Esta Lei entra em vigor na data da sua publicação.

Art. 55. Revogam-se as disposições em contrário.

Brasília, 18 de novembro de 1994; 173º da Independência e 106º da República.

本条规定也适用于依照第48条的规定已同意接受改变的享有公务员资格或受特别程序管理的书记员及其他辅助性人员。

本条所提到的养老金应根据上述的社会保障法律法规加以确定。

本条规定也适用于公证员、登记员、书记员及其他辅助性人员因死亡所获得的抚恤金。

第52条　在本法颁布之日，若在某些州或联邦区境内已经存在特别的尚在生效的法律，各州的自然人民事登记处有权制定对物权、委托授权、签名的认证、复印件的认证等的过渡性措施。

第53条　在本法颁布之日，若在某些州境内，有决定权的司法机关对票据拒绝公证员根据地区划分，并按照地区颁发给其从业资格从而使其在该地区内履行职务，该地区划分的决定仍然有效。

若首次出现该种类的公证员职位空缺时，新填补的职位应适用第11条第二段的规定。

第54条　本法自颁布之日起生效。

第55条　与本法相抵触的措施自动无效。

巴西利亚，1994年11月18日，独立纪元173年，共和国纪元106年。

加拿大

大不列颠哥伦比亚省公证人法案

This Act is Current to April 22, 2014

NOTARIES ACT
[RSBC 1996] CHAPTER 334

Contents
1 Definitions
2 Society continued
3 Approval of bylaws by Attorney General
4 Repealed
5 Application for enrollment
6 Enrollment
7-8 Repealed
9 Substitution for absent notary
10 Board of examiners
11 Enrollment after examination
12 Resignation must be approved by the directors
13 Duties of registrar
14 Authentication and certificate of good standing
15 Appointments by Lieutenant Governor in Council
16 Use of title "Notary Public"
17 Persons to be considered to act as a notary public
18 Rights and powers of members
19 Member not in good standing
20 Special fund
21 Repealed
22 Liability insurance fees held in trust
23 Accounts
24 Audit
25 Suspension by directors
26 Powers of discipline committee in relation to an inquiry
27 Inquiry by discipline committee

本法案直至 2014 年 4 月 22 日仍有效

公证人法案
[RSBC 1996] 第 334 章

目录
1 定义
2 协会得以延续
3 司法部长之章程批准权
4 废止
5 入会申请
6 入会
7-8 废止
9 缺席公证人的代职
10 主考委员会
11 经考试后入会
12 辞职须经理事批准
13 登记官职责
14 资格完备之证实和证明
15 议会副总督之任命权
16 "公证人"头衔的使用
17 视同公证人的人员
18 会员的权利与权力
19 资格不完备的会员
20 专项基金
21 废止
22 由信托机构保管的责任保险费用
23 账目
24 审计
25 理事的停职权
26 纪律委员会与调查相关之权力
27 纪律委员会的调查

28 Discipline inquiries	28 纪律调查
29 Notice of inquiry by discipline committee	29 纪律委员会的调查通知
30 Appearance before discipline committee	30 接受纪律委员会的调查
31 Nonappearance	31 缺席
32 Legal assistance to discipline committee	32 纪律委员会寻求法律援助
33 Report of discipline committee	33 纪律委员会的报告
34 Action by directors on report of discipline committee	34 依据纪律委员会的报告，理事采取的行动
35 Decision by directors	35 理事的决定
36 Participation by member of discipline committee	36 纪律委员会成员的参与权
37 Action on conviction of indictable offences	37 可起诉罪行定罪后的措施
38 Discipline by court	38 法院下达的处分
39 Status of suspended member	39 被停职会员的状态
40 Action by secretary	40 秘书的行动
41 Appeals	41 上诉
42 Definitions	42 定义
43 Custodianship of member's property	43 会员财产的保管
44 Notice of liens	44 留置权的通知
45 Dispensation and protection	45 豁免与保护
46 Action	46 措施
47 Validity of certain Acts	47 具体行为的有效性
48 Penalties	48 惩罚
49 Cost and fines	49 费用与罚款
50 Notary Foundation	50 公证人基金会
51 Board of governors	51 董事会
52 Application of fund	52 基金用途
53 Bylaws	53 章程
54 Interest on trust accounts	54 信托账户的利息
54.1 Power to make regulations — Lieutenant Governor in Council	54.1 副总督会同行政局的规章制定权
55 Power to make regulations — directors	55 理事的规章制定权
56 Spent	56 花费
57 Right to practise through a corporation	57 通过公司执业的权利
58 Corporate registration	58 公司注册
59 Prohibition against carrying on business	59 营业禁止
60 Voting agreements prohibited	60 禁止表决权协议
61 Responsibility of members	61 会员责任
62 Revocation of permits	62 许可的撤销
63 Rules	63 细则
64 Bylaws apply to corporations	64 适用于公司的章程
65 Appeals and other matters	65 上诉与其他事宜
Schedule	进度表

Definitions

1 In this Act:

"court" means the Supreme Court;

"director" means a director of the society;

定义

1 在此条例中：

"法院"指最高法院。

"理事"指协会理事。

"foundation" means the Notary Foundation established under section 50;

"limited liability partnership" means a partnership registered as a limited liability partnership under Part 6 of the Partnership Act;

"member" means a member of the society;

"notary corporation" means a corporation for which a permit has been issued;

"permit" means a permit issued under section 58 and includes a renewal of that permit;

"registrar" means the registrar of the court;

"secretary" means the secretary or acting secretary appointed by the directors;

"society" means the Society of Notaries Public of British Columbia;

"suspension" means temporary disqualification from the practice of a notary public under this Act but does not include the resignation by a member of membership in the society;

"termination" means permanent disqualification from the practice of a notary public under this Act but does not include the resignation by a member of membership in the society.

Society continued

2 The Society of Notaries Public of British Columbia is continued.

Approval of bylaws by Attorney General

3 (1) Bylaws of the society must be submitted to and approved by the Attorney General and no bylaw has force or effect until approved.

(2) The Society Act does not apply to the bylaws of the society.

Repealed

4 [Repealed 2008-39-59.]

Application for enrollment

5 (1) A Canadian citizen or permanent resident of Canada may, on payment of the prescribed fee, apply to the court under the Supreme Court Civil Rules for enrollment as a member.

(2) An application for enrollment as a member must be filed in the Vancouver registry and heard at Vancouver.

(3) At least 30 days before the hearing of an application for enrollment as a member a copy of the application must be served on the secretary of the society and on the executive director of the Law Society of British Columbia.

"基金会"指根据第 50 条建立之公证人基金会。

"有限责任合伙企业"指依照《合伙企业法案》第六部分的规定，注册为有限责任合伙企业的合伙企业。

"会员"指协会成员。

"公证人公司"指已获取许可的公证公司。

"许可"指根据第 58 条颁发的许可，及该许可到期后新发的。

"登记官"指法院的登记官。

"秘书"指理事任命的秘书或者执行秘书。

"协会"指不列颠哥伦比亚省公证人协会。

"停职"指根据本法暂时剥夺公证人的执业资格，不包括公证人协会成员辞职的情形。

"终止"指根据本法永久性地剥夺公证人的执业资格，不包括公证人协会成员辞职的情形。

协会得以延续

2 保留不列颠哥伦比亚省公证人协会。

司法部长之章程批准权

3（1）协会章程应当提交给司法部长并经其批准，否则无效。

（2）《社团法》不适用于协会章程。

废止

4［由 2008-39-59 号法令废止］

入会申请

5（1）在支付法定费用后，依照《最高法院民事规则》的规定，加拿大公民或永久居民可以向法院申请入会为会员。

（2）申请人应当向温哥华登记处提出申请并在温哥华接受听证。

（3）申请材料副本必须于举办入会申请听证会前，至少提前 30 日，送达至协会秘书及不列颠哥伦比亚省律师协会执行理事处。

(4) At least 30 days before the hearing of an application for enrollment as a member, a notice of the application and the date of the hearing must be published in a manner determined by the society.

(5) A person may oppose the application at the hearing, if the person serves notice of the person's opposition on the applicant and files a copy of the notice with the registrar.

Enrollment

6 (1) If the court is satisfied that an applicant is a fit person for enrollment as a member, it may order that the applicant be examined in the duties of a notary public and, if found qualified on the examination, be enrolled as a member.

(2) [Repealed 2008-39-59.]

Repealed

7-8 [Repealed 2008-39-59.]

Substitution for absent notary

9 (1) A member may conduct another member's practice for a period not longer than 4 months if the other member

(a) cannot conduct the practice because of illness or vacation, and

(b) obtains the prior consent of the directors to this substitution.

(2) The directors may extend the period referred to in subsection (1) for a further period not longer than 4 months.

Board of examiners

10 The Attorney General must appoint a board of examiners consisting of 3 persons to conduct the examinations of applicants for enrollment.

Enrollment after examination

11 If an applicant

(a) files proof with the registrar that the applicant has satisfactorily passed the required examination and has taken an oath of office in the prescribed form before a judge of the court, and

(b) pays the prescribed fee,

the registrar must enroll the applicant as a member.

Resignation must be approved by the directors

12 (1) A member may not resign from membership in the society without the consent of the directors.

(2) The directors may attach conditions to the grant-

（4）有关入会申请及听证会日期的公告，应当于举办入会申请听证会前，至少提前30日，以协会确定的方式进行发布。

（5）个人将异议通知送达申请人，并将该异议通知副本提交至登记官后，可在听证会中就该申请提出异议。

入会

6(1)如法院确信申请人是适宜入会的合适人选，可命令申请人就公证人职责进行考试，如其考试合格，可入会成为会员。

（2）[由2008-39-59号法令废止]

废止

7-8[由2008-39-59号法令废止]

缺席公证人的代职

9(1)会员可代其他会员执业，但时间不超过4个月，且被替代会员须：

（a）因病或因假无法执业；且

（b）事先就代替执业已获理事们的批准。

理事可延长第1款中提及的期间，延长的期间不超过4个月。

主考委员会

10 司法部长须任命由三人组成的主考委员会，主持申请入会者的考试事宜。

经考试后入会

11 若申请人

（a）向登记官提交证据表明已成功通过相关测试，并在法官见证下按照规定的形式进行了宣誓；且

（b）支付了法定费用；

则登记官必须将申请人登记为会员。

辞职须经理事批准

12(1)非经理事批准，会员不得辞去其会员资格。

（2）理事可规定同意辞职的前提条件。

ing of their consent to a resignation.

Duties of registrar

13 (1) The registrar must keep a roll called the Roll of Notaries Public.

(2) If the court orders or if the registrar is notified by the secretary of the termination of membership of a member, the registrar must strike the member from the roll.

(3) If a member is struck off the roll, the vacancy may be filled by a person enrolled under section 6.

(4) On request and on payment of the prescribed fee, the registrar must issue to a person empowered to act as a notary public by this Act a commission in the prescribed form.

Authentication and certificate of good standing

14 (1) On the request of a person and on payment of the fee set by the directors the secretary must authenticate the signature and seal of a member if satisfied that it is proper.

(2) On the request of a member and if the secretary is satisfied that the member is in good standing, the secretary must issue a certificate of good standing.

Appointments by Lieutenant Governor in Council

15 (1) On payment of the prescribed fee and, if required by the Attorney General, after the person provides security by way of a bond or by way of deposit of cash or securities in an amount determined by the Attorney General, the Lieutenant Governor in Council may, by commission under the Great Seal of British Columbia, appoint to be a notary public during pleasure

(a) any person if there is a need in a place for performance of the functions described in subsection (2),

(b) a permanent employee of the government of British Columbia or of the government of Canada, or

(c) a registrar, or person performing the functions of registrar, of a university under the Thompson Rivers University Act or the University Act.

(2) An appointment and commission under this section confers on the person named in the commission power only to administer oaths, to take affidavits, declarations and acknowledgements, to attest instruments by the person's seal and to give notarial certificates of the person's acts.

(3) An appointment and commission under this section may define and limit the geographic area in which the person appointed may practise and may contain directions

登记官职责

13（1）登记官必须保有称为《公证人名册》的名册。

（2）经法院命令，或经秘书告知某会员的会员资格已终止的，登记官须将其从名册上除名。

（3）遇会员被除名的，其空缺可由根据第6条规定入会者填补。

（4）应申请并确认其缴纳规定费用后，登记官须以规定形式向依据本法授权担任公证人者颁发委任状。

资格完备之证实和证明

14（1）应会员要求，并缴纳理事规定的费用后，秘书确信其要求合理的，应证实会员之签名、印章。

（2）应会员要求，秘书确信该会员资格完备的，须为其出具资格完备之证明。

议会副总督之任命权

15（1）经支付法定费用，如检察总长要求，在下列人员按总检察长确定之数额支付保证金或存入现金/证券作保后，议会副总督可依据不列颠哥伦比亚省玺之授权，在其任职期间任命为公证人：

（a）因在某地行使第2款规定的职权而有需求者；

（b）不列颠哥伦比亚省政府或加拿大政府的终身雇员；或者

（c）《汤普森河大学条例》或《高校条例》规定的大学登记注册人员，或承担登记注册职能者。

（2）依据本条规定获得的任命和委任仅赋予委任状上载明的人下列权力：实施宣誓，获取宣誓书、声明和确认，以盖印方式公证法律文件，就个人之行为出具公证证明。

（3）根据本条授予的任命和委任可阐明并限制受任命者执业的地理范围，并可以包含受任命者行使其公证人职权限度的指示。

as to the limits within which the person may exercise the person's functions as a notary public.

(4) A person appointed under this section is not a member of the society.

Use of title "Notary Public"

16 (1) A person who is a member of the society may use the style and title of Notary Public in and for the Province of British Columbia and is a notary public.

(2) A person appointed under section 15 may use the style and title of Notary Public in and for the Province of British Columbia.

(3) This section does not apply to a notary corporation.

Persons to be considered to act as a notary public

17 (1) A person acts as a notary public if the person, for or in expectation of a fee, gain or reward, direct or indirect,

(a) draws, prepares, issues or revises a document that is intended, permitted or required to be registered, recorded or filed in a registry or other public office or that is a will or testamentary instrument, or

(b) holds himself or herself out as qualified to draw, prepare, issue or revise a document referred to in paragraph (a).

(2) Subsection (1) does not apply

(a) if, by the provisions of a statute, the document in question is required or permitted to be drawn, prepared, issued or revised by that person or the class of persons or profession of which the person is a member, or

(b) if the person is an employee acting in the course of the person's employment, and the employer may lawfully do the act.

Rights and powers of members

18 A member enrolled and in good standing may do the following:

(a) draw instruments relating to property which are intended, permitted or required to be registered, recorded or filed in a registry or other public office, contracts, charter parties and other mercantile instruments in British Columbia;

(b) draw and supervise the execution of wills

(i) by which the will-maker directs the will-maker's estate to be distributed immediately on death,

(ii) that provide that if the beneficiaries named in the will predecease the will-maker, there is a gift over to alter-

（4）根据本条规定获得任命者不是协会会员。

"公证人"头衔的使用

16（1）协会会员是公证人，可在不列颠哥伦比亚省范围内代表该省使用"公证人"的称号和头衔。

（2）依据第15条获得任命者可在不列颠哥伦比亚省的范围内代表该省使用"公证人"的称号和头衔。

（3）本条规定不适用于公证人公司。

视同公证人的人员

17（1）个人以直接或间接获得费用、收益或者回报为目的，实施下列行为的，视同公证人：

（a）对文件、遗嘱或遗嘱性文书进行起草、准备、发布或修改，而该文件、遗嘱或遗嘱性文书是意图、获批或被要求送至登记处或其他公共部门进行登记、记录或提交的；或

（b）具备资质者，对a项中提及的文件进行起草、准备、发布或修改。

（2）下列情形，第1款之规定不适用：

（a）如果按照法律规定，所涉之文件必须或可以由该人／与该人同一等级者／与该人同一职业者起草、准备、发布或修改的；或

（b）如果该人是作为雇员在受雇期间实施该行为，且其雇主可合法实施该行为。

会员的权利与权力

18 已登记的资格完备的会员可以：

（a）在大不列颠哥伦比亚省内，就意图、获批或被要求送至登记处或其他公共部门进行登记、记录或提交的，与财产相关的法律文件、合同、租船合同及其他商业文件进行起草；

（b）可就下列遗嘱进行起草，并监督其执行：

（i）遗嘱中遗嘱人指示在其死后，立即分配其财产的；

（ii）遗嘱规定所载之受益人在遗嘱人之前死亡，则遗嘱人死后，财产立即转赠给替代受益人；或者

native beneficiaries vesting immediately on the death of the will-maker, or

 (iii) that provide for the assets of the deceased to vest in the beneficiary or beneficiaries as members of a class not later than the date when the beneficiary or beneficiaries or the youngest of the class attains majority;

 (c) attest or protest all commercial or other instruments brought before the member for attestation or public protestation;

 (d) draw affidavits, affirmations or statutory declarations that may or are required to be administered, sworn, affirmed or made by the law of British Columbia, another province of Canada, Canada or another country;

 (e) administer oaths;

 (e.1) draw instruments for the purposes of the Representation Agreement Act;

 (e.2) draw instruments relating to health care for the purposes of making advance directives, as defined in the Health Care (Consent) and Care Facility (Admission) Act;

 (e.3) draw instruments for the purposes of the Power of Attorney Act;

 (f) perform the duties authorized by an Act.

Member not in good standing

19 A member who is not in good standing must not

 (a) act or hold himself or herself out as entitled to act as a notary public, or

 (b) act in any other capacity that derives from the member's status as a notary public.

Special fund

20 (1) The directors must continue the special fund for the purpose of reimbursing, in the cases and to the extent in each case, as they think advisable, of pecuniary losses sustained by a person because of the misappropriation or wrongful conversion by a member or former member of money or other property that was entrusted to or received by that person in the person's capacity as a member.

(2) If the special fund falls below the prescribed amount, every member, on receipt of notice in writing from the secretary, must pay to the special fund in each practice year a sum set by the directors and the payments must be continued for each practice year until and including the practice year in which the special fund again reaches the prescribed amount.

(3) An amount set by the directors under subsection (2) may be increased by members of the society at a meet-

（iii）遗嘱规定受益人为一类人中的一人或数人，在全体受益人或其中最年幼者成年之际，授予其死者之财产。

（c）对会员亲证的要求进行签署见证或异议声明的所有商业或其他法律文件，出具证明或拒绝证明；

（d）起草宣誓书、宣言或法定声明，而上述宣誓口供、宣言或法定声明是根据不列颠哥伦比亚省、加拿大其他省、加拿大或其他国家的法律，允许或要求执行、宣誓、确认或制定的；

（e）执行宣誓；

（e.1）为《代表协议法案》所载之目的起草法律文件；

（e.2）起草《医疗保健（同意）与医疗设施（准入）法案》中规定的，旨在就医疗保健提前做出安排的法律文件；

（e.3）为《代理人权限法案》所载之目的起草法律文件；

（f）履行法律所授权的职责。

资格不完备的会员

19 资格不完备的会员不得：

（a）以授权公证人身份开展业务或自居；或者

（b）开展任何从该会员的公证人身份衍生而来的其他活动。

专项基金

20（1）理事必须持续运营用于偿付当事人经济损失的专项基金，具体个案是否偿付、偿付限度多少由理事判定。偿付范围限于因以下原因给当事人造成的经济损失：会员或前会员挪用或非法侵占了其以会员资格受托或收到的金钱或其他财产。

（2）若专项基金数额低于规定数额，每位协会成员在接到秘书的书面通知后，应当以理事规定的标准，按执业年度缴纳款项至专项基金。此后，会员应继续按执业年度缴纳款项，直至专项基金数额再次达到规定数额（包括达到规定数额当年）。

（3）在向全体会员送达增加专项基金数额的书面通知后，协会会员可召开协会会议，增加第 2 款中理

ing of the society if written notice of the proposed increase has been given to all members.

(4) The special fund is the property of the society and must be kept in a special account apart from the other funds or property of the society.

(5) The special fund is not subject to any process of seizure or attachment by any creditor of the society.

(6) The directors may invest or cause the special fund and the proceeds of it to be invested in the securities and in the manner they think fit.

(7) If the special fund exceeds the prescribed amount, the directors may invest and use the excess for the purposes of the society.

(8) The special fund is not subject to a trust in favour of a person claiming compensation under subsections (9) and (10).

(9) If a complaint in writing is made to the society, alleging that a person has sustained pecuniary loss for the reasons described in subsection (1), the directors may cause an inquiry to be made into the complaint.

(10) If as a result of an inquiry the directors are satisfied that the person has sustained the pecuniary loss because of the action of a member or former member, they may

(a) with or without terms, pay out of the special fund to the person entitled the whole or a part of the loss, or

(b) decide that in the circumstances no payment is to be made.

(11) Nothing in this section affects or impairs the powers of the directors or a committee of them under the disciplinary provisions of this Act.

(12) A person appointed under section 15 is excluded from participation in or contribution to the special fund.

(13) The special fund does not apply to a complaint respecting the action of a person who was appointed a notary public under section 19 (1) of the Notaries Act, R.S.B.C. 1979, c. 299, or under a former Act and who, until August 21, 1981, was required to be a member of the society.

Repealed

21 [Repealed 2008-39-59.]

Liability insurance fees held in trust

22 Money paid to the society consisting of the professional liability insurance fees

(a) must be accounted for separately from other funds, and

事所规定的专项基金数额。

（4）专项基金是协会财产，应当保存在独立于协会其他基金和财产的专项账户中。

（5）专项基金不受协会债权人任何没收扣押措施的影响。

（6）理事可以以其认为合适的方式，将专项基金及其收益投资于证券，或发起上述投资。

（7）若专项基金超过规定数额，理事以协会利益为宗旨可投资和使用多余部分。

（8）不能仅基于对根据第9款和第10款索赔的个人的信任，运用专项基金赔付。

（9）协会收到书面投诉，声称当事人因本条第1款所述原因遭受金钱损失的，理事可就该投诉发起调查。

（10）若经过调查，理事确信当事人是由于会员或前会员的行为遭受经济损失的，他们可

（a）无条件或有条件地，从专项基金中向当事人赔付全部或部分损失；或者

（b）基于给定情况，决定不予赔付。

（11）理事及理事委员会根据本法纪律条款可行使的权力，不受本条内容影响或损害。

（12）依据第15条任命者被排除参与或缴纳专项基金。

（13）专项基金不适用于有关下列人员的投诉：根据《公证人法案》（R.S.B.C. 1979, c. 299）第19条第1款或此前法案所任命的公证人，以及直至1981年8月21日应要求成为协会会员者。

废止

21[由2008-39-59号法令废止］

由信托机构保管的责任保险费用

22 向协会支付的包括职业责任保险费用在内的款项：

（a）应当独立于其他基金单独记账；且

(b) is not subject to any process of seizure or attachment by any creditor of the society.

Accounts

23 (1) In connection with a member's practice, the member must keep up to date records showing and readily distinguishing

(a) all money received and paid for or on behalf of others and the amount of money held on behalf of each other person, and

(b) money received and paid on the member's own behalf.

(2) Money received for or on behalf of a client

(a) is trust money,

(b) must be deposited in a savings institution in a trust account, and

(c) must be identified as a trust account in the records of the member and of the savings institution.

(3) Money must not be drawn from a trust account unless it is

(a) money paid to or on behalf of a client from funds that have been deposited in a trust account to the client's credit,

(b) money required for payment to the notary public for or on account of services rendered to or disbursements made on behalf of a client from money belonging to a client, or

(c) money paid into the trust account by mistake.

Audit

24 (1) The directors may at any time order and provide for the audit of the books and accounts of a member or former member.

(2) If the audit shows that the books and accounts are not in proper order and not kept up to date, the directors may require that the cost of the audit be paid to the society by the member or former member.

Suspension by directors

25 If an audit discloses that there has been a contravention of this Act or the regulations or rules relating to accounts, the directors may immediately suspend the member from practising and direct an inquiry under section 28.

Powers of discipline committee in relation to an inquiry

26 (1) The directors must appoint from among their number a discipline committee whose quorum is not less

（b）不受协会债权人任何没收扣押措施的影响。

账目

23（1）会员在制作与执业相关之记录时，应做到实时更新，列明以下内容且便于条目分辨：

（a）所有收、付款项，以及当代表他人时，代表每人所持有款项数额；以及

（b）以本人身份所收、付的款项。

（2）为客户或代表客户收取的款项：
（a）是信托款项；
（b）必须存入储蓄机构的信托账户；以及

（c）在协会成员及储蓄机构的记录中必须被标示为信托账户。

（3）不得从信托账号支取款项，但下列款项除外：

（a）从存入客户名下信托账户的款项中开支，支付给客户或代客户支付；

（b）鉴于所提供的服务而支付给公证人的款项，或代表客户垫付的款项，上述款项需从客户名下款项中支出；或者

（c）因误操作而汇入信托账户的款项。

审计

24（1）理事可随时要求就会员或前会员的簿册和账目进行审计，并为其进行准备。

（2）若审计显示簿册和账目所载记录顺序混乱或没有实时更新，理事可要求由该成员或前成员向协会支付审计费用。

理事的停职权

25 若审计表明存在触犯本法或其他与账目相关法规、规则的违法行为，理事可立即暂停成员的执业活动，并根据第 28 条展开调查。

纪律委员会与调查相关之权力

26（1）纪律委员会法定人数不低于 3 人，其成员从理事中任命产生。

than 3.

(2) In the case of a vacancy, the committee may appoint a director to fill the vacancy until the directors do so.

Inquiry by discipline committee

27 (1) A panel of 3 or more members of the discipline committee may inquire into the conduct of members or former members.

(1.1) For the purposes of an inquiry under this section, sections 34 (3) and (4), 48 and 49 of the Administrative Tribunals Act apply to the panel.

(1.2) If a member of a panel is unable for any reason to complete the member's duties, the remaining members of that panel, with the consent of the discipline committee, may continue the inquiry, and

(a) the vacancy does not invalidate the inquiry, and

(b) the provisions of this section concerning the panel apply to the remaining panel members.

(2) The committee or the panel may provide for preliminary inquiries by a member of the committee or by the secretary.

(3) The committee may order the suspension of the member until the consideration of its report by the directors.

(4) The committee or the panel may, at any time after a decision to inquire into the conduct of a member has been made, suspend the member until the conclusion of the hearing.

(5) Notice of a suspension under subsection (4) must be served on the member promptly.

Discipline inquiries

28 (1) At the request of the directors or on the application of a person, or of its own motion, the discipline committee may, whether a complaint is made or not, inquire whether a member or former member has been guilty of any of the following:

(a) misappropriation or wrongful conversion by the person of money or other property entrusted to or received by the person in the person's capacity as a member of the society;

(b) incompetence;

(c) other professional misconduct;

(d) a breach of a provision of this Act or a regulation or rule made under it, or of a bylaw of the society.

(2) In the same manner as in subsection (1), the discipline committee may inquire whether a member or former member has engaged in conduct that in the opinion of the

（2）一旦出现空缺，在理事任命委员前，委员会可先行任命一名理事以填补空缺。

纪律委员会的调查

27（1）纪律委员会成员中选出至少3人，组成专门小组，就会员或前会员的行为展开调查。

（1.1）根据本条展开调查时，专门小组应遵守《行政法庭法》第34条第3款和第4款，第48条和第49条之规定。

（1.2）如专门小组成员因任何原因不能履行其职责的，小组其他成员在获得纪律委员会同意后，可以继续进行调查；以及

（a）该空缺不会导致调查无效；以及

（b）本条中关于专门小组的规定适用于其余的小组成员。

（2）纪律委员会或小组可以派出一名纪律委员会成员或秘书为初步调查进行准备。

（3）纪律委员会可责令会员暂停工作直至理事完成报告审议。

（4）在做出对会员行为进行调查的决定后，纪律委员会或专门小组可随时暂停该成员工作，直至听证会得出结论。

（5）本条第4款中的停职通知应当及时送达至会员。

纪律调查

28（1）纪律委员会可以在无论是否存在投诉的情形下，应理事要求、依据相关人员的申请或自发就会员或前会员是否犯有以下行为开展调查：

（a）挪用或非法侵占其以会员资格受托或收到的金钱或其他财产；

（b）不能胜任工作的；

（c）其他违反职业操守的行为；

（d）违反本法案或本法案的下位法，或违反协会章程的。

（2）以本条第1款中规定的相同方式，纪律委员会可以调查会员或前会员是否参与了在委员会看来违背公众利益、违背公证行业利益或可能伤害公证行业

committee, ought to be reviewed by the directors to determine if it is conduct that in the opinion of the directors, is contrary to the best interest of the public or the notarial profession or tends to harm the standing of the notarial profession.

Notice of inquiry by discipline committee

29 (1) At least 7 days before an inquiry under section 27 is held, notice of the inquiry must be served on the member or former member in person or by registered mail sent to the last address shown on the records of the society.

(2) The notice must set out the time and place of the inquiry and give particulars of the complaint or of the matters to be inquired into.

(3) A notice sent by registered mail is conclusively deemed to have been given by the committee and to have been received by the member or former member on the 14th day after deposit of the notice in the Canada Post Office at any place in Canada.

Appearance before discipline committee

30 A member or former member may appear personally or with counsel before the discipline committee, and before the directors, on an inquiry or hearing into the person's conduct or competence and may cross examine witnesses and present evidence.

Nonappearance

31 If the member or former member fails to appear and on proof of service of notice, the discipline committee may proceed with the inquiry without further notice to the member or former member and may make a report of its findings, with or without a recommendation of action to be taken, or take other action it is authorized to take under this Act.

Legal assistance to discipline committee

32 The discipline committee or the directors may, for an inquiry or hearing, employ legal or other assistance they think necessary.

Report of discipline committee

33 The discipline committee must submit a written report of its findings to the directors.

Action by directors on report of discipline committee

34 On receipt of the report and on giving reasonable notice to the member or former member, the directors may

(a) accept and adopt a finding of fact reported by the discipline committee,

声誉的行为，同时委员会意见还需经理事复审。

纪律委员会的调查通知

29（1）在根据第27条发起调查前，应至少提前7日将调查通知送达会员或前会员本人，或以挂号信方式将调查通知邮寄至协会记录上显示的会员或前会员最新地址。

（2）通知必须列明调查的时间地点，并详细描述投诉内容或待调查事项。

（3）通知以挂号信方式发送的，自信件被投递于加拿大境内任何地点的邮局之日起第14日，应明确视为委员会已完成通知义务，且会员或前会员已收到通知。

接受纪律委员会的调查

30 在就会员或前会员之品行或能力进行调查或听证时，该会员或前会员可独自或偕同律师现身纪律委员会和理事面前，盘问证人，出示证据。

缺席

31 若会员或前会员未能出席，而证据表明通知已送达的，纪律委员会可不再通知，径行继续调查，并做出调查结果报告（不要求必须就待采取措施提出建议），或采取本法授权其实施的其他措施。

纪律委员会寻求法律援助

32 纪律委员会或理事可以聘请其认为必需的法律人士或其他人员，以协助进行调查或听证。

纪律委员会的报告

33 纪律委员会必须向理事提交书面调查结果报告。

依据纪律委员会的报告，理事采取的行动

34 在收到报告，并履行了其对会员或前会员的合理告知义务后，理事可以：

（a）接受并采纳纪律委员会报告的事实调查结果；

(b) review the proceedings and evidence taken by the committee,

(c) hear further evidence, and may make further findings of fact on the evidence, or

(d) refer the matter to the committee for further inquiry as to the whole or a specific part of it, in which case the provisions of section 29 apply.

Decision by directors

35 (1) On the conclusion of the inquiry the directors must decide whether or not the member or former member

(a) has committed any of the infractions which may be inquired into under section 28 (1), or

(b) engaged in conduct that in the opinion of the directors, is contrary to the best interests of the public or the notarial profession or tends to harm the standing of the notarial profession.

(2) By resolution passed by a majority of the directors present, the directors may

(a) if they decide that a member or former member has not committed any of those infractions or engaged in that conduct, exonerate the member or former member and dismiss the complaint,

(b) if they find that a member has committed any of those infractions or engaged in that conduct,

(i) reprimand the member and, in addition, fine the member an amount of not more than $5 000,

(ii) suspend the member for the period and subject to the conditions of practice they think fit and, in addition, fine the member an amount of not more than $5 000, or

(iii) order that the membership of the member be terminated, or

(c) if they find that a former member has committed any of those infractions or engaged in that conduct, fine the former member an amount of not more than $5 000.

(3) In any case, the directors may impose costs and set the amount of costs.

Participation by member of discipline committee

36 A director who is a member of the discipline committee may participate as a director on the consideration of the committee's report.

Action on conviction of indictable offences

37 On proof that a member of the society has been convicted of an indictable offence, the directors may, without following the procedure in sections 26 to 36, summarily order the suspension or termination of the person's

（b）审查调查记录和委员会采纳的证据；

（c）听取进一步证据，并可根据证据得出进一步的事实调查结果；或者

（d）将全部事项或部分特定事项提交委员会展开进一步调查，此时须遵守第29条之规定。

理事的决定

35（1）理事应根据调查结论判定会员或前会员是否：

（a）实施了依据第28条第1款应当加以调查的违法行为；或者

（b）参与了在委员会看来违背公众利益、违背公证行业利益或可能伤害公证行业声誉的行为。

（2）经出席的过半数理事通过决议，理事可：

（a）若他们认为会员或前会员并未实施任何前述违法行为或参与引发不良后果的行为，则可宣布该会员或前会员无罪，并驳回投诉；

（b）若他们认为会员实施了任何前述违法行为或参与了引发不良后果的行为，则可

（i）对该会员加以训诫，并加处最多5000加元的罚款；

（ii）对该会员处以其认为适宜期限的停职，对该会员执业附加其认为适宜的限制条件，并加处最多5000加元的罚款；或者

（iii）命令终止该会员的协会成员资格；或者

（c）若他们发现前会员实施了任何前述违法行为或参与了引发不良后果的行为，则可对该前协会成员处以最高5000加元的罚款。

（3）无论结果如何，理事均可征收成本费用，并设定成本费用数额。

纪律委员会成员的参与权

36 身为纪律委员会成员的理事，在审议委员会报告时，可作为理事参加。

可起诉罪行定罪后的措施

37 若有证据证明协会会员已被判犯有可起诉罪行，理事可无须遵守第26条至第36条规定之程序，即刻责令暂停或终止该会员的会员资格。

membership.

Discipline by court

38 (1) On petition by the Attorney General, the society or a person aggrieved, the court may inquire into alleged breaches of this Act or the regulations or rules by a member or into the professional conduct or alleged incompetence, negligence or fraud of a member.

(2) On the conclusion of an inquiry under subsection (1), the court may order that

(a) the member be suspended from practising for a period named in the order, or

(b) the member's membership be terminated.

Status of suspended member

39 A member of the society who is suspended must pay the membership dues, but no other fees or assessments, and the member is not in good standing.

Action by secretary

40 In every case of suspension or termination of membership, the secretary must

(a) publish notice of the suspension or termination of membership at the earliest reasonable opportunity, in the manner set out in the regulations, and

(b) notify all the following persons of the action taken:

(i) the Attorney General;

(ii) the registrar;

(iii) the district registrars of the Supreme Court;

(iv) the registrars of the land title offices;

(i) the members of the society.

Appeals

41 (1) If it is alleged by a member or former member that the directors have erred in a disciplinary action taken against the person, an appeal lies to the court.

(2) The member or former member must, within 14 days after the decision or order complained of, give written notice of the appeal to the directors.

(3) The appeal is a new hearing and the member or former member and the directors or their respective counsel are entitled to appear, present evidence and be heard.

(4) The court may affirm the decision or order and dismiss the appeal or make another order, as may seem just.

Definitions

42 In sections 43 to 45:

"member" includes a former member of the society;

"property" or "property of a member" means any-

法院下达的处分

38（1）由司法部长、协会或受到侵害的个人提请，法院可就其主张的会员违反本法案或规章条例的行为，或执业行为，或其主张的会员无能力胜任、疏忽大意或欺诈行为展开调查。

（2）根据第1款中规定的调查之结论，法院可责令：

（a）会员在令状所载期限内暂停执业；或

（b）终止该会员的会员资格。

被停职会员的状态

39 被停职的会员应当支付会费，但无须支付其他收费或分摊费用，且该会员处于资格不完备状态。

秘书的行动

40 凡遇暂停或终止会员资格情形的，秘书应当：

（a）以规章所载之方式，及早发布暂停或终止会员资格之通知；以及

（b）就采取的行动通知以下人员：

（i）司法部长；

（ii）登记官；

（iii）最高法院的地区登记官；

（iv）土地所有权办公室的登记官；

（v）协会成员。

上诉

41（1）若会员或前会员主张理事对其采取的处分行为存在错误的，可向法院上诉。

（2）该会员或前会员必须自收到其不服之决定或命令后14日内，将书面的上诉通知送达理事。

（3）上诉以听证会形式进行，会员或前会员及理事或他们各自的律师有权出席、提交证据并接受审理。

（4）法院可判令维持原决定/命令并驳回上诉，或作出其认为公正的新命令。

定义

42 在第43条至第45条中：

"会员"包括协会的前会员；

"财产"或"会员财产"指的是由会员自客户或

thing, wherever located, kept by, acquired by or given to a member by or for a client or other person if the property in any way relates to the member's practice or former practice as a notary public or to the business or affairs of the member's clients or former clients, and whether or not the property was kept, acquired or given before or after the member ceased to practise as a notary public, and includes ledgers, records, securities, trust money in cash or on deposit and chattels.

Custodianship of member's property

43 (1) The court may, on application by the society either without notice to anyone or on notice that the court requires, or, if the court has made an order under section 38, without such an application, appoint a person to be custodian of the property of a member and to manage, to arrange for the conduct of or to wind up the notarial practice of the member if

(a) the membership of the member is terminated,

(b) the member has been suspended,

(c) the member has died,

(d) because of physical or mental illness or for any other reason, the member is unable to practise as a notary public,

(e) the member has absconded or is otherwise improperly absent from the member's place of business,

(f) the member's practice has been neglected for an unduly extended period,

(g) there is reason to believe that trust money held by the member is not sufficient to meet the member's trust liabilities, or

(h) other sufficient grounds exist.

(2) An order under subsection (1) may

(a) direct the sheriff to seize and place in the custody of the custodian all property of the member, and

(b) authorize the sheriff to enter on the premises or open a safety deposit box or other receptacle where, at any of those places, the court considers there are grounds to believe that property of the member may be found.

(3) Unless otherwise directed by the court, the order must be served on the member.

(4) Subject to subsection (2), if a person receives notice that an order has been made under this section, the person must retain all property of a member that is in the person's possession or control until directed otherwise by the custodian or by order of the court.

(5) The court may, in an order under subsection (1) or

他人处 / 以客户或他人名义保管、获得或交付的，与会员执业活动或此前执业活动相关，或与客户或前客户之营业或事务相关的所有物品，无论其保管、获得或交付于会员停止以公证人身份执业之前或之后，无论其位于何地。包括账簿、记录、证券、现金或存款形式的信托资金，以及动产。

会员财产的保管

43（1）遇下列情形的，法院可依据未通知他人的或已按法院要求进行通知的协会申请，任命会员财产的管理人，以应对会员的行为，或结束会员的公证执业活动；法院此前已根据第38条作出命令的，可无须申请，直接任命上述管理人。

（a）该会员的会员资格被终止；

（b）该会员已停职；

（c）该会员已死亡；

（d）由于罹患身体或精神疾病或因其他原因，会员无法作为公证人执业；

（e）该成员已潜逃或有其他不当脱离营业地行为；

（f）该成员在过长期限内玩忽职守；

（g）有理由相信该成员持有的信托资金不足以覆盖该成员的信托债务；或者

（h）存在其他充分理由。

（2）本条第1款中所载命令可用于：

（a）指令治安官没收会员的所有财产，并将其置于管理人管理之下；

（b）授权治安官进入场所或开启保险箱及其他容器，只要法院认为有理由相信上述场所或容器可能藏有会员财产。

（3）除非法院另有指示，命令必须送达成员。

（4）依据本条第2款，若相关人员收到依据本条作出的命令，则该人员必须继续保有或控制手中的全部会员财产，直至管理人或法院以命令形式作出其他指示。

（5）法院可不经通知，或在送达法院要求的通知

on any later application by the custodian, the executor of a deceased member or any other interested person, either without notice to anyone or on notice the court requires,

(a) direct a person who holds the member's property on deposit to deal with, hold, pay over or dispose of the property to the custodian, or otherwise as directed by the court,

(b) remove any custodian appointed by the order and appoint another custodian,

(c) give directions to the custodian respecting the disposition of property in the custodian's hands or any part of it, and

(d) give directions or make orders that the nature of the situation requires.

Notice of liens

44 (1) If property of a member has been placed in the custody of a custodian, the secretary or other persons designated by the discipline committee must examine the property for the purposes of subsection (2).

(2) After the examination under subsection (1), the custodian must, by notice the custodian thinks proper, inform clients of the member and other persons the custodian considers necessary

(a) that the property of the member is in the custody of the custodian and that an examination of it indicates that the client or other person appears to have an interest in it, and

(b) that the client or other person may apply to the custodian, subject to any notary's lien of the member on the property,

(i) for the delivery to that person of the property in which the person appears to have an interest, or

(ii) for leave to make copies of documents and papers among the property that the person may require in respect of the transactions or dealings the person had with the member.

(3) If the custodian is satisfied that a person is entitled to property in the custodian's custody and that no notary's lien exists or appears to exist, the custodian may deliver the property to the person claiming it.

(4) If a member whose property has been placed in the custody of a custodian under section 43 claims to be entitled to a notary's lien on the property or any part of it, the member may, within 30 days from the service of the order on the member, file notice of the member's claim for lien with the custodian giving full particulars of it.

后，在本条第 1 款规定的法院命令中，或依据其后保管人、已故会员遗嘱执行人或其他利益相关者的申请：

（a）指令持有该成员定期储蓄财产者将该财产交由管理人处置、持有，或按法院指示的其他方式处理；

（b）开除依照命令任命的管理人，重新任命管理人；

（c）就管理人持有的全部或部分财产给予处置指示；且

（d）给予当前必须之指示或命令。

留置权通知

44（1）如会员财产已置于管理人保管下，为实施第 2 款，秘书或纪律委员会指派的其他人应对财产进行查验。

（2）在完成第 1 款所规定的查验后，管理人必须以其认为适宜之方式，就下列事项通知该会员之客户或其他管理人认为有必要通知者：

（a）该会员的财产处于管理人管理之下，对其进行的查验显示该财产涉及客户或其他人的利益；且

（b）就会员就该财产享有的公证人留置权，客户或他人可向管理人提出下列申请：

（i）请求将该财产交付给与该财产利益相关的申请人；

（ii）请求保留财产，以备申请人就财产中涉及其与会员业务或交易的文件和资料进行复制。

（3）如管理人确信某人就其管理之下的财产享有权利，且就该财产公证人不享有留置权，或没有证据显示公证人享有优先权的，管理人可将该财产交付给索要者。

（4）如会员财产已根据第 43 条置于管理人管理下，而该会员主张就该财产之全部或部分享有公证人留置权的，该会员应自命令送达后 30 日内，向管理人提交包含留置权所有细节的主张留置权通知。

(5) On receiving notice under subsection (4), the custodian must immediately give notice of the claim for lien to the apparent owner of the property on which a lien is claimed, and the rights of the parties must then be determined according to law.

(6) If a member fails to file a claim for lien under this section within the 30 day period referred to in subsection (4), a lien that the member might otherwise be entitled to is extinguished, and the custodian is entitled to deliver the property to the claimant if otherwise satisfied that it is proper to do so.

(7) The court may summarily determine the validity of a claim to a notary's lien.

Dispensation and protection

45 (1) Despite anything in section 43 or 44, the court may at any time extend or shorten the time within which anything is required to be done or dispense with any of the requirements of those sections.

(2) The provisions of section 46 apply to the protection of the custodian, society and any person designated by the discipline committee, or acting for any of them, in respect of a proceeding taken under section 43 or 44.

(3) The court may set and award the costs and fees allowed and paid by the member or other person, in respect of a proceeding under this section or section 43 or 44, including the costs and fees payable to a custodian, but no costs are to be awarded against the society, its officers, the directors or anyone designated by the directors in respect of a proceeding under this section and taken in good faith.

(4) Proceedings under this section or section 43 or 44 must be commenced by petition.

(5) A sheriff and any sheriff's officer executing an order under section 43 have the same powers as in the execution of a writ of seizure and sale.

Action

46 No action lies against a director or a member of the discipline committee or other committee appointed by the directors, or the secretary or an official or employee of the society, for anything done by the person in good faith while acting or purporting to act under this Act.

Validity of certain Acts

47 (1) An act done by a notary public must not be considered invalid or ineffectual only because it is done outside the geographic area to which the notary's practice

（5）接到第 4 款规定的通知后，管理人应立即将该留置权主张告知所涉财产的表面所有权人，双方的权利应随后依据法律确定。

（6）如会员未能在第 4 款规定的 30 日内主张本条规定的留置权，其可能享有的留置权将消灭，管理人在其确信适宜的情况下，有权将财产交付给索要者。

（7）主张享有公证人设置的优先权的，法院可即刻判定该主张的有效性。

豁免与保护

45（1）无论第 43 条和第 44 条如何规定，法院可随时延长或缩短上述条款中要求完成或实施某事的时限。

（2）管理人、协会、纪律委员会任命的任何人，或代上述人员行动者，在根据第 43 条或第 44 条采取行动时，受到第 46 条保护。

（3）就依据本条或第 43 条、第 44 条采取之程序，法院可设置并判决由会员或他人承担成本和费用，包括支付给管理人的成本和费用，但协会、其官员、理事或理事任命者不得因其善意地执行本条所载程序而承担成本。

（4）本条或第 43 条、第 44 条规定之程序必须应申请而发起。

（5）治安官和治安官助手在执行第 43 条所载命令时，有与执行没收拍卖令时相同的权力。

措施

46 当理事、纪律委员会成员、理事任命的其他委员会成员、秘书、协会官员或雇员依据或试图依据本法善意地行动时，不得对其采取任何对抗措施。

具体行为的有效性

47（1）公证人实施的行为，不得仅因其发生在公证人授权执业地域范围外，或与公证人入会或任命的限制条件或前提条件相悖而被认定无效。

is limited, or is done contrary to a limitation or condition to which the person's enrollment or commission is subject.

(2) Nothing in this Act relieves a person acting as a notary public from liability for loss, damages or costs caused to or incurred by another person by reason of anything done or omitted while so acting.

Penalties

48 (1) A person must not

(a) act as a notary public without being authorized to do so under this Act,

(b) hold himself or herself out as authorized to act as a notary public without being authorized to do so under this Act, or

(c) if the person is a notary public, practise outside the geographic area to which the person's practice is limited or practise in any way contrary to a limitation or condition to which the person's enrollment or commission is subject.

(2) A person who contravenes subsection (1) commits an offence, and is liable on conviction to a fine of not more than $2 000.

Cost and fines

49 Costs and fines imposed under section 35 or under the rules may be recovered as a debt owing to the society.

Notary Foundation

50 (1) The Notary Foundation is established as a corporation consisting of the members of the board of governors under section 51 (1).

(2) The foundation may acquire, dispose of and otherwise deal with its property for the purposes of the foundation.

(3) The foundation must be operated without purpose of gain for its members and any right or other accretions to the foundation must be used for the purposes for which the foundation is established.

Board of governors

51 (1) The foundation must be administered by a board of governors consisting of 11 members as follows:

(a) the Attorney General or the appointee of the Attorney General;

(b) 2 persons, not members of the society, appointed to the board of governors by the Attorney General;

(c) 8 persons appointed by the directors from among themselves.

（2）充当公证人角色者，因其充当期间的作为或不作为给他人造成损失、损害、费用的，本法不免除其相关责任。

惩罚

48（1）禁止实施以下行为：

（a）未经本法授权而充当公证人；

（b）未经本法授权而以授权公证人自居；或者

（c）身为公证人者，在授权执业地域范围外执业，或以与入会或任命的限制条件或前提条件相悖的方式执业。

（2）违反本条第 1 款者构成犯罪，一经定罪，将处以最高 2000 加元罚款。

费用与罚款

49 根据第 35 条或细则征收之费用和罚款，协会可视为自己享有之债权进行追讨。

公证人基金会

50（1）公证人基金会以法人形式建立，由第 51 条第 1 款规定的董事会成员组成。

（2）该基金会应当依据其宗旨，获取、处置或以其他方式处理其财产。

（3）基金会之运营，不得以帮助其成员获取利益为目的。在运用基金会所有之权利和其他附属物时，应秉承基金建立之宗旨。

董事会

51（1）基金会应当由以下 11 位成员组成的董事会管理：

（a）司法部长或由司法部长任命者；

（b）由司法部长任命为董事会成员的 2 名非会员人士；

（c）由理事从其内部任命产生的 8 名成员。

(2) Members of the board of governors, other than the Attorney General, hold office for a term of 3 years or until their successors are appointed, and they may be reappointed.

(3) The Attorney General or the directors may revoke the appointment of a member of the board of governors whom they appointed during that member's term of office.

(4) The members of the board of governors must elect one of their members to be chair of the board of governors.

(5) If a vacancy occurs, the Attorney General or the directors, as the case may be, may appoint a person eligible to be appointed to that office, and the person appointed holds office for the balance of the term for which the person is appointed, or until the person's successor is appointed.

(6) The continuing members of the board of governors may act even if there is a vacancy in the board of governors.

(7) An act of the board of governors is not invalid by reason only of a defect that is later discovered in the appointment of one or more of its members.

(8) An appointed member of the board of governors may resign from office on giving to the board of governors one month's notice in writing of the member's intention to do so, and the resignation takes effect on the expiration of the notice or on its earlier acceptance by the board of governors.

(9) A member of the board of governors ceases to hold office if

(a) the member ceases to hold the qualifications necessary for appointment,

(b) the member becomes a mentally disordered person,

(c) the member becomes bankrupt, or

(d) the member contravenes a provision of this Act or the rules made under this Act and a majority of the other members of the board of governors consider that the contravention is sufficiently serious to justify the member's removal from the board of governors.

(10) A quorum of the board of governors is 5 members.

Application of fund

52 (1) The purpose of the foundation is to establish and maintain a fund to be used for the following purposes:

(a) legal education;

（2）与司法部长不同，董事会成员任期3年，或任职直至其继任者获得任命，并可连任。

（3）司法部长或理事在其任命的董事任期内，可撤销对该董事的任命。

（4）董事会成员应当选出其中一员担任董事会主席。

（5）若出现空缺，可视情况由司法部长或董事任命有能力胜任者担任该空缺职位，受任命者将工作至该职位的剩余任期结束，或选出继任者。

（6）即使董事会中存在空缺，董事会中的剩余成员仍可继续履行职责。

（7）不可因董事会成员的任命稍后被发现存在瑕疵，而将董事会此前作出的行为归于无效。

（8）受任命的董事会成员在以书面形式提前一个月向董事会通知其辞职意图后，可辞职。其辞职自通知到期日，或在此之前自董事会同意该通知之日起生效。

（9）以下情况下，董事会成员不再任职：

（a）该成员不再具备任职所必需的资质；

（b）该成员罹患精神疾病；

（c）该成员破产；或者

（d）该成员违反了本法案的条款或者依据本法案制定的细则，且过半数董事会其他成员认为该违反行为的严重程度足以将该成员自董事会除名。

（10）董事会的法定人数为5人。

基金用途

52（1）基金会的目的在于建立并维持用于以下目的之基金：

（a）法律教育；

(b) legal research;

(c) legal aid;

(d) education and continuing education for notaries and applicants for enrollment as notaries;

(e) establishing, operating and maintaining law libraries in British Columbia;

(f) contributions to the special fund established under this Act.

(2) The foundation may employ members of the society in order to advance the purposes of the foundation.

(3) The funds of the foundation consist of

(a) all money remitted to the foundation by or on behalf of members under section 54 (3),

(b) interest accruing from investment of the funds of the foundation, and

(c) other money received by the foundation.

(4) The board of governors may pay out of the funds of the foundation the costs, charges and expenses

(a) involved in the administration of the foundation, or

(b) incurred by the board of governors in carrying out the purposes of the foundation.

(5) Until invested or applied in accordance with this section, all money of the foundation must be paid into a savings institution referred to in section 23 (2) and must be used for the purposes of the foundation.

(6) Any money that is not immediately required for the purposes of the foundation may be invested in the name of the foundation by the board of governors in any manner in which trustees are authorized to invest trust funds.

(7) The accounts of the foundation must be audited annually by a chartered accountant or certified general accountant appointed for that purpose by the directors.

(8) Money received by the foundation under subsection (3) (a) and (b) must be disbursed as follows:

(a) 55% to be paid to the Legal Services Society for legal aid;

(b) Repealed RS1996-334-56.

(c) 10% to be used for legal education, legal research and the establishing, operating and maintaining of law libraries in British Columbia;

(d) 35% to be used for

(i) salary and administrative expenses, and

(ii) education and continuing education for notaries and applicants for enrollment as notaries.

(9) Money received by the foundation under subsec-

（b）法律研究；

（c）法律援助；

（d）公证人和申请成为公证人者的教育与继续教育；

（e）在不列颠哥伦比亚省建立、运作并维护法律图书馆；

（f）为依据本法案设立的特别基金提供捐款。

（2）基金会可聘请协会成员以推进基金会实现其目的。

（3）基金会的基金包括：

（a）依据第 54 条第 3 款由成员或代表成员汇至基金会的所有钱款；

（b）运用基金会的基金投资所获收益；以及

（c）基金会收到的其他钱款。

（4）董事会可以从基金会的基金中列支下列成本、收费和开支：

（a）涉及基金会的管理；或者

（b）董事会为实现基金会的目的而作出的支出。

（5）在根据本条规定进行投资或运用之前，基金会的所有款项必须存入第 23 条第 2 款中提及的储蓄机构，并且必须用于达成基金会的目标。

（6）凡无须立即用于基金会目的的款项，均可由董事会以基金会名义进行投资，投资方式可采取授权受托人投资信托基金的各种方式。

（7）基金会的账目必须每年交由理事专门为此任命的特许会计师或注册会计师进行审计。

（8）基金会依据本条第 3 款 a 项与 b 项收到的钱款应当按照如下规则支出：

（a）55% 支付给法律服务协会用于法律援助；

（b）由第 RS1996-334-56 号法令废止；

（c）10% 用于法律教育、法律研究与在不列颠哥伦比亚省建立、运作并维护法律图书馆；

（d）35% 用作支付：

（i）工资与管理费用；与

（ii）公证人和申请成为公证人者的教育与继续教育。

（9）依据本条第 3 款 c 项收到的钱款应当依据钱

tion (3) (c) must be disbursed for one or more of the purposes specified in subsection (1) as directed in writing by the person from whom the money was received or, if there is no direction, in the same manner as money received under subsection (3) (a) and (b).

(10) [Repealed RS1996-334-56.]

Bylaws

53 The board of governors may make bylaws for purposes relating to the affairs, business, property and objects of the foundation, including bylaws respecting one or more of the following:

(a) the number and designation of officers of the foundation;

(b) the appointment and terms of office of officers of the foundation and all matters relating to their offices;

(c) the establishment of an executive committee and the delegation of powers to it;

(d) the resignation or removal from office of officers of the foundation;

(e) the number and designations of employees of the foundation, other than officers, and their conditions of employment;

(f) the remuneration, if any, of officers of the foundation;

(g) the operation of the notary foundation account.

Interest on trust accounts

54 (1) A member must deposit money received from or held for or on behalf of the member's clients generally in an interest bearing trust account at a savings institution referred to in section 23 (2).

(2) A member is not liable, because of the trust relationship between the notary as trustee and the beneficiary of the trust, to account to a client or beneficiary for interest received by the member on money received or held in an account established under subsection (1).

(3) A member who is credited by a savings institution with interest on money received or held on behalf of clients generally, holds the interest in trust for the foundation, and must remit the interest to the foundation in accordance with the rules of the society.

(4) Nothing in this section or in the rules made under this section applies to money deposited in a separate account for a client, and interest paid on money in a separate account is the property of the client.

款来源者的书面指示支出，以实现本条第 1 款规定的单个或多个目的，若无指示，则按照与依据本条第 3 款 a 项与 b 项收到的钱款的相同方式使用。

（10）[由 RS1996-334-56 号法令废止]

章程

53 为达成各项与基金会事务、业务、财产和物品相关之目的，董事会可制定规章，包括涉及以下一点或多点的规章：

（a）基金会高级职员的数量及职位；

（b）基金会高级职员的任命和任期，以及所有与其职位相关的事务；

（c）执行委员会的建立与对其的授权；

（d）基金会高级职员的辞职事宜和被免职事宜；

（e）除高级职员外，基金会其他工作人员的数量与职位及他们的雇佣条件；

（f）基金会管理人员可能需要的酬劳；

（g）公证人基金会账户的运作。

信托账户的利息

54（1）通常情况下，会员自其客户处收到，或为客户/代表客户持有的款项，必须存入第 23 条第 2 款中规定的储蓄机构的有息信托账户。

（2）基于公证人作为受托人与信托受益人之间的信任关系，会员将其收到或持有的款项存入依据第 1 款开立的账户，因而收到利息的，会员不负有就该利息向客户或受益人进行详细报告的义务。

（3）通常情况下，储蓄机构就会员收到或代客户持有的款项向会员发放利息的，会员应将该利息作为受托财产替基金会代持，并且必须根据协会细则将该利息汇至基金会。

（4）本条规定或依据本条制定的规则不适用于为客户开立的单独账户中的存款，单独账户中的存款所生利息属于客户财产。

Power to make regulations — Lieutenant Governor in Council

54.1 (1) The Lieutenant Governor in Council may make regulations referred to in section 41 of the Interpretation Act.

(2) Without limiting subsection (1), the Lieutenant Governor in Council may make regulations as follows:

(a) for the purposes of section 40 (a), setting out the manner of publication;

(b) prescribing an amount for the purposes of section 20 (2) and (7);

(c) for the purposes of section 15 (1) (a), setting out considerations or circumstances that may be taken into account by the Lieutenant Governor in Council in determining whether there is a need for performance of the functions described in section 15 (2).

Power to make regulations — directors

55 (1) The directors may make regulations referred to in section 41 of the Interpretation Act.

(2) Without limiting subsection (1), the directors may make regulations as follows:

(a) setting fees including fees for applications, examinations and enrollment and directing to whom they must be paid;

(b) respecting examinations of candidates for enrollment;

(c) prescribing forms of oaths;

(d) prescribing forms, including forms of commissions;

(e) authorizing members and notary corporations to carry on the business of providing notary services to the public through limited liability partnerships;

(f) establishing prerequisites, conditions, limitations and requirements for members and notary corporations to carry on the business of providing notary services to the public through limited liability partnerships.

(3) A regulation made under subsection (1) or (2) does not come into force until it is approved by the Lieutenant Governor in Council.

(4) The directors may make rules as follows:

(a) specifying the books, accounts and records to be kept by members, and providing for their inspection by the directors or their representatives and for their audit;

(b) specifying assessments and setting dues and fees to be paid to the society;

(c) providing for the filing with the society of au-

副总督会同行政局的规章制定权

54.1（1）副总督会同行政局可制定《解释法》第41条中提到的规章。

（2）在不限制本条第1款的情况下，副总督会同行政局可就下列事项制定规章：

（a）就第40条a项，规定（通知）发布方式；

（b）就第20条第2款与第7款，设定（专项基金的）规定数额；

（c）就第15条第1款a项，规定可供副总督会同行政局考虑的情况和因素，以判定是否有必要实施第15条第2款所述职能。

理事的规章制定权

55（1）理事可制定《解释法》第41条提到的规章。

（2）在不限制本条第1款的情况下，理事可就下列事项制定规章：

（a）设定包括申请、考试、注册费用在内的收费标准，并明确应向谁缴费；

（b）应试者注册考试相关事宜；

（c）规定宣誓的格式；

（d）规定包括任命状格式在内的各种格式；

（e）授权会员或公证人公司以有限责任合伙形式进行经营，以向公众提供公证服务；

（f）会员或公证人公司以有限责任合伙形式进行经营，以向公众提供公证服务的，确立其前提、条件、限制与要求。

（3）依据本条第1款与第2款制定的规章非经副总督会同行政局批准不产生效力。

（4）理事可就下列事项制定细则：

（a）规定会员须保存的簿册、账目和记录，规定理事或其代表对上述材料的审查权，以及对上述材料的审计；

（b）规定评估流程，设定付给协会的会费和费用标准；

（c）规定向协会就会员的簿册和账目申请审计证

ditors' certificates in the form specified by the directors respecting the books and accounts of members;

(d) providing for the imposition of fines on, and the suspension or termination of membership of a member for nonpayment of dues, fees, assessments or other money payable under this Act.

Spent

56 [Amendments to section 52. Spent. RS1996-334-56.]

Right to practise through a corporation

57 Subject to this Act, the regulations and the by-laws, a notary corporation may carry on the business of providing notary services to the public through one or more persons each of whom is

(a) a member of the society in good standing, or

(b) an employee of the notary corporation under the direct supervision of a member of the society in good standing.

Corporate registration

58 (1) The secretary must issue a notary corporation permit to a company within the meaning of the Business Corporations Act that is in good standing under that Act if the secretary is satisfied that

(a) the name of the corporation includes the words "notary" or "notaries",

(b) all the voting shares are legally and beneficially owned by a member or members in good standing,

(c) all the non-voting shares are legally and beneficially owned by

(i) members,

(ii) the spouse of a member who is a shareholder,

(iii) [Repealed 2000-24-27.]

(iv) a child, as defined in the Family Law Act, of a member who is a shareholder, or

(v) any other relative of a share holding member if the relative resides with that member,

(d) all the directors of the corporation are members in good standing, and

(e) all the persons who will be practising as notaries public on behalf of the corporation are members in good standing or are under the direct supervision of a member in good standing.

(1.1) In subsection (1), "spouse" means a person who

(a) is married to another person, or

(b) is living with another person in a marriage-like

明，该申请需以理事规定的格式提出；

（d）规定当会员未支付会费、费用或其他根据本法需支付款项时，对其施加的罚款和暂停、终止会员资格措施。

花费

56 [由 RS1996-334-56 号法案对已废止的第 52 条予以修正]

通过公司执业的权利

57 依据本法案、规则和章程，公证人公司可通过一个或多个下列人员经营面向公众的公证服务：

（a）资格完备的协会会员；或者

（b）受到资格完备的协会会员直接监管的公证人公司职员。

公司注册

58（1）如协会秘书确信下列各点，则应向符合《商业企业法》中"资格完备"之含义的公司颁发公证人公司许可：

（a）该公司的名称中包含"公证人"或"公证人（复数）"字样；

（b）所有有表决权的股份由一名或多名资格完备的会员合法及实益拥有；

（c）所有无表决权的股份由下列人员合法及实益拥有：

（i）会员；

（ii）持股会员的配偶；

（iii）[由第 2000-24-27 号法令废止]

（iv）持股会员的子女，"子女"一词的定义参见《家庭法法案》；或者

（v）与持股会员共同居住的持股会员其他亲属；

（d）该公司的所有董事均为资格完备的成员；以及

（e）将代表该公司以公证人身份执业的所有人均为资格完备的会员，或受资格完备的会员的直接监管。

(1.1) 在本条第 1 款中，"配偶"指：

（a）与对方结婚；或者

（b）与对方生活在一段类似婚姻的关系中，且该

relationship, and has been living in that relationship for a period of at least 2 years.

(2) The secretary may refuse to issue a permit under subsection (1) if

(a) the notary corporation has previously had its permit revoked, or

(b) a shareholder of the notary corporation was a shareholder of a notary corporation that previously had its permit revoked.

Prohibition against carrying on business

59 (1) A corporation that has the words "notary public" or "notaries public" as part of its name must not carry on any business unless it holds a permit or a permit under section 82 of the Legal Profession Act.

(2) A notary corporation that holds a permit must not carry on any activities that would, for the purposes of the Income Tax Act (Canada), give rise to income from business, except the provision of notary services or services that are directly associated with the provision of notary services.

(3) Subsection (2) does not prohibit a notary corporation from investing its funds in real estate, personal property, mortgages, stocks, bonds, insurance or any other type of investments.

(4) No act of a notary corporation, including a transfer of property to or by the corporation, is invalid only because the corporation contravenes subsection (1) or (2).

Voting agreements prohibited

60 A shareholder of a notary corporation must not enter into a voting trust agreement, proxy or any other type of agreement that vests in another person who is not a member of the society in good standing the authority to exercise the voting rights attached to any or all the shares.

Responsibility of members

61 (1) The liability for professional negligence of a member carrying on the notarial practice is not affected by the fact that the member is carrying on that practice

(a) as an employee of a notary corporation, or

(b) through a limited liability partnership.

(2) The application of the provisions of this Act, the regulations and the bylaws to a member is not affected by the member's relationship to

(a) a notary corporation as a shareholder, director, officer or employee, or

(b) a limited liability partnership as a partner or em-

关系已经持续至少两年。

（2）在下列情况下，协会秘书可以拒绝颁发本条第 1 款中的许可证：

（a）该公证人公司曾被撤销许可证；或者

（b）该公证人公司的股东曾参股此前被撤销许可证的公证人公司。

营业禁止

59（1）名称中包含有"公证人"或者"公证人（复数）"字样的公司，未获（相应）许可证或《法律职业法》第 82 条规定的许可证，不得营业。

（2）为实施《所得税法（加拿大）》，除提供公证服务或与之直接相关的服务外，持有许可证的公证人公司不得从事营利性活动。

（3）本条第 2 款不禁止公证人公司将其基金投资于房地产、动产、抵押贷款、股票、债券、保险或任何其他类型的投资项目。

（4）公证人公司的行为，包括公司受让财产或公司转让财产，不因公司仅违反本条第 1 款或者第 2 款而失效。

禁止表决权协议

60 公证人公司的股东不得签订表决信托协议、代理协议或其他类型的协议，授权并非资格完备会员者代为行使其部分或全部股份表决权。

会员责任

61（1）有关会员执业的下列事实不影响其承担公证执业过程中的专业过失责任：

（a）作为公证人公司的雇员执业；或者

（b）通过有限责任合伙形式执业。

（2）本法案、相关规章与章程之规定适用于会员，且不受会员下列关系影响：

（a）会员身为公证人公司之股东、董事、管理人员或雇员；或者

（b）会员身为有限责任合伙企业之合伙人或雇员。

ployee.

(3) Nothing in this Act affects, modifies or limits any law applicable to the fiduciary, confidential or ethical relationships between a member and a person receiving the professional services of that member.

(4) The relationship between a notary corporation carrying on business as permitted under this Act and a person receiving notary services provided by the corporation is subject to all applicable law relating to the fiduciary, confidential and ethical relationships that exist between a member and the member's client.

(5) All rights and obligations pertaining to professional communications made to or information received by a member, or in respect of any advice given by a member, apply to a notary corporation and its shareholders, directors, officers, employees and contractors.

(6) An undertaking given by or on behalf of a notary corporation that would constitute a notary's undertaking if given by a member is deemed to be given by the member who gives, signs or authorizes the undertaking.

Revocation of permits

62 (1) The directors may, after a hearing, revoke the permit issued to a notary corporation if

(a) in the course of providing notary services the corporation does anything that, if done by a member, would be professional misconduct or conduct unbecoming a member,

(b) the corporation contravenes section 59, or

(c) the corporation ceases to comply with a condition of qualification for a permit referred to in section 58 or a condition under section 63 (1) (c) or (2).

(2) The directors may, rather than revoking a permit under subsection (1),

(a) reprimand one or more of the shareholders of the notary corporation, or

(b) impose a fine on the notary corporation in an amount of not more than $10 000.

(3) If a permit is revoked under this section, the secretary must inform the Registrar of Companies.

(4) All shareholders, directors, officers and employees of a notary corporation may be

(a) compelled to give evidence at a proceeding under this Act, or

(b) required to produce all files and records that are in their possession or power and that are relevant to matters raised in the proceeding referred to in paragraph (a).

（3）用于调整会员与接受其专业服务者之间信托、保密或伦理关系的法律，不受本法内容影响、改变或限制。

（4）所有用于调整会员与其客户间信托、保密或伦理关系的法律，也适用于调整根据本法获许经营的公证人公司与接受该公司服务者之间的关系。

（5）与会员接受专业通讯／信息或给予建议相关的所有权利与义务，均适用于公证人公司及其股东、董事、管理人员、雇员和承揽人。

（6）由会员实施的，公证人公司给予或代表公证人公司给予的承诺，如满足公证人承诺的条件，则视为给予、签署或授权承诺的会员作出的承诺。

许可的撤销

62（1）下列情况下，经听证后，理事可撤销已颁发给公证人公司的许可证：

（a）在提供公证服务期间，公司实施了以会员标准看来，构成违反职业操守或与会员身份不符的行为；

（b）公司违反第 59 条；或者

（c）公司不再符合第 58 条规定的颁发许可证的资质条件或者第 63 条第 1 款 c 项或者第 2 款中规定的条件。

（2）除本条第 1 款中规定的撤销许可证外，理事还可采取以下（惩罚措施）：

（a）对公证人公司的一名或多名股东予以训诫；或者

（b）对公证人公司处以最高 10000 加元的罚款。

（3）若依据本条撤销了许可证，秘书必须通知公司注册处处长。

（4）公证人公司的股东、理事、管理人员及雇员可能：

（a）被强令在本法规定的程序中作证；或者

（b）被要求提交归其所有或在其职权范围内，与 a 项提及的程序中提出的事项相关的所有文件和记录。

Rules

63 (1) The directors may make rules that they consider necessary or advisable for the purposes of sections 57 to 62 including rules

(a) respecting the issue and renewal of permits, including

(i) the establishment of a procedure to obtain a permit and a renewal of a permit, and

(ii) setting fees for obtain a permit or a renewal of a permit,

(b) respecting procedures for revocation of permits, including the adaptation, in a manner that the directors consider necessary or advisable, of rules respecting proceedings before the directors,

(c) setting conditions that may be attached to permits that are issued or renewed under this Act,

(d) respecting names and the approval of names including the types of names by which a notary corporation may be known, and

(e) respecting the disposition of shares of a shareholder of a notary corporation who

(i) ceases to be a member, or

(ii) remains a member but is not qualified to practise as a notary public.

(2) The directors may, as a condition of issuing or renewing a permit, set an amount of insurance that the holder of the permit must carry, or must provide to each of its employees, for the purpose of providing indemnity against professional liability claims.

(3) The rules under subsection (1) or the amount set under subsection (2) may be different for different permit holders, at the discretion of the directors.

Bylaws apply to corporations

64 The rules under section 55 (4) and bylaws made under this Act respecting members and former members apply to notary corporations and the directors may exercise the powers given under this Act to enforce those rules and bylaws.

Appeals and other matters

65 Section 41 applies to a notary corporation as though it was a member.

Schedule

[Schedule repealed 2008-39-59.]

细则

63（1）为实施第57条至第62条，理事可制定其认为必需或可取的细则，包括：

（a）有关许可证发放和续期的细则，包括：

（i）制定获得许可证和许可证续期的程序；与

（ii）设定获得许可证和许可证续期的收费标准。

（b）关于撤销许可证程序的细则，包括以理事认为必需或可取的方式，改变与有理事参与的程序相关之细则。

（c）设定可附加于根据本法发放或续期的许可证之上的条件的细则。

（d）有关名称和名称之批准的细则，上述名称包括公证人公司（对外使用）为人所知的名称。

（e）有关公证人公司股东在下列情况下处分其股份的细则：

（i）股东丧失其会员身份；或者

（ii）仍具有会员身份，但已无公证人执业资质。

（2）作为发放许可证或许可证续期的条件，理事可以设定许可证持有者必须投保或向其所有雇员提供的保险的数额，以便当有人主张专业责任时，可提供赔偿。

（3）本条第1款中的规则或者本条第2款中的数量可因不同的许可持有人而不同，理事享有自由裁量权。

适用于公司的章程

64 第55条第4款中的规则与依据本法案制定的章程中，有关会员与前会员的部分，适用于公证公司。理事可以行使本法案所授予的权力以实施前述规则与章程。

上诉与其他事宜

65 公证人公司视同会员适用第41条。

进度表

[度表由2008-39-59号法令废止]

新斯科舍省公证人和公证专员法案

s 1. Short title

This Act may be cited as the Notaries and Commissioners Act.

s 2. Notary public

The Governor in Council may, by commission under his hand and seal, from time to time appoint such persons as he thinks fit to be notaries public for the Province.

s 3. Powers of notary public

Every such notary public shall have the power of drawing, passing, keeping and issuing all deeds and contracts, charter-parties and other mercantile transactions in this Province, and also of attesting all commercial instruments brought before him for public protestation, and otherwise of acting as is usual in the office of notary, and may demand, receive and have all the rights, profits and emoluments rightfully appertaining and belonging to the said calling of notary during pleasure.

s 4. Fee

Every person so appointed shall pay a fee of ten dollars to the Minister of Finance upon receipt of the commission appointing him.

s 5. Oath

Every notary public upon receiving his commission as such shall take and subscribe in writing an oath for the faithful performance of his duty, which oath may be administered by the Attorney General or Deputy Attorney General, a judge of the Supreme Court or a judge of a county court, or a notary public, and shall be filed in the office of the Attorney General.

s 6.

6(1) Commissioner of oaths for within Province

The Governor in Council may by commission from time to time empower such persons as he thinks fit to administer oaths and take and receive affidavits, declarations and affirmations within the Province in and concerning any cause, matter or thing depending or to be had in the Supreme Court or any other court in the Province.

6(2) Deemed officer of Supreme Court

Every person so empowered shall be deemed to be

s 1. 简称

本法简称为《公证人和公证专员法案》。

s 2. 公证人

在地方议会，省长有权不定期通过其签名盖章的委任状为该省任命某个其认为适当的人作为公证人。

s 3. 公证人的职权

每一个公证人都有权起草、通过、备存和签发该省所有的契据及合同，租船契约以及其他的商业交易文件，还有权为向其递交的商业文书作出认证以应对公众异议，有权履行其它通常的职务行为，能够要求、获得并享有所有相关的权利、利益，在休假期间执行职务或与职务相关行为有权获得正当收入。

s 4. 费用

每一个被任命的人在收到委任状后，均需要向财政部长支付十加元的费用。

s 5. 宣誓

在接受任命时，每一位公证人都应当为其忠实履行职责进行宣誓并签署一份誓词，该宣誓由司法部长或副部长、最高法院或县法院的法官、公证人执行，并应当在司法部长的办公室中存档。

s 6.

6（1）省内的监誓专员

在地方议会上，省长有权不定期授权其认为适合执行宣誓的人去获取和接收省内的誓词、声明和确认书，以及涉及最高法院或省内其他法院的任何事项的宣誓。

6（2）被视作最高法院的官员

每一个被授权的人都应被视为最高法院的一名

an officer of the Supreme Court.

s 7. Commissioner of oaths for without Province

The Governor in Council may by commission from time to time empower such persons as he thinks fit to administer oaths and take and receive affidavits, declarations and affirmations without the Province in and concerning any cause, matter or thing depending or to be had in the Supreme Court or any other court in the Province.

s 8. Oath or affidavit taken by interested person

An oath, affidavit, declaration or affirmation hereafter administered, taken or received by or before a person appointed under Section 6 or authorized under Section 12 of this Act who is a party to the transaction or matter in respect of which it is to be used or who is employed by such a party in connection with such transaction or matter shall not be evidence on behalf of the person or his employer in any proceedings in respect of such transaction or matter except with the consent of all other parties to the proceedings or on the order of the judge or other person presiding over the proceedings.

s 9. Revocation of commission

The Governor in Council may revoke the commission of any person appointed a commissioner to administer oaths, whether within or without the Province, whether such person was so appointed before or after the coming into force of this Act and such revocation shall operate as a revocation for all purposes.

s 10. Existing powers continued

The powers of every person at the coming into force of this Act, holding a commission to take affidavits to hold to bail or to administer oaths within or without the Province, shall be continued, and every such person shall be deemed to have been duly appointed such commissioner, and shall have the powers conferred by this Act.

s 11. Authority of barrister

Every barrister of the Supreme Court of Nova Scotia shall, by virtue of his office, and without any appointment by the Governor in Council, be, and he is hereby, authorized to administer oaths and take and receive affidavits, declarations and affirmations within the Province in and concerning any cause, matter or thing, depending or to be had in the Supreme Court, or any other court in the Province.

s 12. Authority of commissioned officer

Every commissioned officer of the Canadian Armed

官员。

s 7. 省外的监誓专员

在地方议会上，省长有权不定期地授权其认为适合执行宣誓的人去获取和接收省外的誓词、声明和确认书，以及涉及最高法院或省内其他法院的任何事项的宣誓。

s 8. 由利益相关人作出的宣誓或誓章

根据本法第6条任用的人员或根据本法第12条授权的人员，如果以前或现在是将要对交易发出宣誓、誓章、声明或确认的一方当事人或者受雇于与该交易或事宜而有关的人员，则在任何关于该交易或事宜的法律程序中，除非经法律程序的所有其他当事人的同意或法官或其他主持法律程序的人的命令，否则其宣誓、誓章、声明或确认不得作为其自己或其雇主的证据。

s 9. 委任的撤销

在地方议会上，省长有权撤销通过委任状任命的执行宣誓的专员，无论是在省内还是省外，无论该任命的作出是在该法案生效之前还是之后。任命的撤销为所有职能的撤销。

s 10. 现有权力的维持

在本法生效之时，持有委任状有权获取宣誓书、进行保释或执行省内或省外宣誓的人，其权力继续维持，其应被视为已正式任命的专员，并拥有本法授予的权力。

s 11. 大律师的权力

加拿大新斯科舍省最高法院的每一个律师，无须经省长在地方议会上的任命，可凭借其所处的职位，被授权执行省内的宣誓、获取、接收宣誓书、声明和确认书以及涉及最高法院或省内其他法院判决的任何事项的宣誓。

s 12. 现役军官的权力

每个现役的加拿大武装部队的军官，无论是在加

Forces being on active service, whether in Canada or outside of Canada, shall by virtue of his office, and without any appointment by the Governor in Council, be and is hereby authorized to administer oaths and take and receive affidavits, declarations and affirmations within or without the Province for use within the Province.

s 13. Authority of member of Assembly

Every member of the Assembly, while he is a member, is authorized to administer oaths and take and receive affidavits, declarations and affirmations within or without the Province for use within the Province.

s 13A.

Every chief officer of a municipal police department, every commissioned officer of the Royal Canadian Mounted Police being on active service and every non-commissioned officer of the Royal Canadian Mounted Police who is the head of a detachment being on active service in the Province is, by virtue of that person's office and without appointment by the Governor in Council, authorized to administer oaths and take and receive affidavits, declarations and affirmations within or without the Province for use within the Province.

s 13B.

Every funeral director holding a valid funeral director's licence, issued in accordance with the Embalmers and Funeral Directors Act, is authorized to administer oaths and take and receive affidavits, declarations and affirmations within the Province for use within the Province.

s 14. Duty to print name

A person before whom an oath, affidavit, declaration or affirmation is administered, taken or received shall cause his name to be typewritten or printed below or adjacent to his signature.

s 13. 议会的权力

议会的每一位成员，当作为议员时，可被授权执行宣誓，获取、接收省内的或为省内使用的省外宣誓书、声明和确认书。

s 13A.

市政警察部门的每一位首席官员，加拿大皇家骑警的每一位现役官员，或者并非加拿大皇家骑警的官员而是省内分队的现役长官，无须经省长在地方议会上的任命，可凭借其个人官职，被授权执行宣誓和获取、接收省内的或为省内使用的省外宣誓书、声明和确认书。

s 13B.

每个葬礼主持都有一个根据《防腐和丧葬法》颁发的葬礼主持有效执照，可被授权执行宣誓和获取、接收省内的或为省内使用的省外宣誓书、声明和确认书。

s 14. 印制姓名的义务

在某人的宣誓、誓词、声明或确认书被执行、获取或接收之前，应当将其姓名打印出来或印刷在其签名下方或相邻的地方。

安大略省公证人法案

Notaries Act
R.S.O. 1990, Chapter N.6
Last amendment: 2006, c. 35, Sched. C, s. 91.

Appointments

1. (1) Subject to section 2, the Attorney General may appoint such persons as he or she thinks fit as notaries public for Ontario. 2001, c. 9, Sched. B, s. 10 (1).

Delegation

(2) The Attorney General may, in writing, delegate the power conferred by subsection (1) to a public servant employed under Part III of the Public Service of Ontario Act, 2006. 2001, c. 9, Sched. B, s. 10 (1); 2006, c. 35, Sched. C, s. 91 (1).

Examination

2. (1) Any person, other than a barrister and solicitor, being a Canadian citizen, who is desirous of being appointed or reappointed a notary public, is subject to examination or re-examination, as the case may be, in regard to his or her qualification for the office by a judge of the Superior Court of Justice in the area in which he or she resides, or by a public servant employed for the purpose under Part III of the Public Service of Ontario Act, 2006, and no such person shall be appointed or reappointed a notary public without a certificate from the judge or public servant that he or she has examined or re-examined the applicant and finds him or her qualified for the office, and that in his or her opinion a notary public is needed for the public convenience in the place where the applicant resides and intends to carry on business. R.S.O. 1990, c. N.6, s. 2 (1); 2001, c. 9, Sched. B, s. 10 (2, 3); 2006, c. 35, Sched. C, s. 91 (2).

Restriction

(2) Where a person, other than a barrister and solicitor, is appointed or reappointed a notary public, restrictions may be imposed in the appointment limiting the territory and cases in which such person may use and exercise his or her powers. R.S.O. 1990, c. N.6, s. 2 (2); 2001, c. 9, Sched. B, s. 10 (4, 5).

公证人法案
R.S.O.1990，第N.6章
最新修正案：2006，c. 35，Sched. C，s. 91.

任命

1.（1）根据第2条，司法部长可任命他或她认为合适的人担任安大略省公证人。2001，c. 9，Sched. B，s. 10（1）。

授权

（2）司法部长可以以书面形式将依据本条第（1）款获得的权力授予依据《2006年安大略公共服务法案》第三部分聘任的公务员。2001，c. 9，Sched. B，s. 10（1）；2006，c. 35，Sched. C，s. 91（1）。

考试

2.（1）除出庭律师和初级律师外，所有有意愿被任命为或被再次任命为公证人的加拿大公民，应当参加考试或再次参加考试。考试视具体情况，由该申请人居住地的高级法院法官或者由依据《2006年安大略公共服务法案》第三部分聘任的公务员主考，以确定其是否具备任职资质。申请人不得被任命或再次任命为公证人，除非其具备法官或公务员出具的证明，表明申请人经考试或再次考试显示其具备任职资质，且主考者认为出于该申请人居住地或意图执业地之公共便利考虑，存在任命公证人的需求。R.S.O. 1990，c. N.6，s. 2（1）；2001，c. 9，Sched. B，s. 10（2，3）；2006，c. 35，Sched. C，s. 91（2）。

限制

（2）除出庭律师、初级律师以外者被任命或再次任命为公证人的，其任命可附加条件，限制其运用或行使其权力的地域和案件范围。

Powers

3. Subject to subsection 2 (2), a notary public has and may use and exercise the power of drawing, passing, keeping and issuing all deeds and contracts, charter-parties and other mercantile transactions in Ontario, and also of attesting all commercial instruments that may be brought before him or her for public protestation, and otherwise of acting as is usual in the office of notary public, and may demand, receive and have all the rights, profits and emoluments rightfully appertaining and belonging to the calling of notary public. R.S.O. 1990, c. N.6, s. 3.

Power to take affidavits

4. (1) A notary public has and may exercise the powers of a commissioner for taking affidavits in Ontario. R.S.O. 1990, c. N.6, s. 4 (1).

Need not affix seal on affidavits, etc.

(2) Where a notary public is authorized by any Act of the Legislature to administer oaths or to take affidavits or declarations in Ontario, it is not necessary to the validity of any such oath, affidavit or declaration that he or she affix his or her seal thereto. R.S.O. 1990, c. N.6, s. 4 (2).

Expiry of future appointments

5. (1) The appointment of every notary public, other than a barrister and solicitor, who is appointed on or after July 1, 1963, expires three years after the day on which he or she was appointed. 2001, c. 9, Sched. B, s. 10 (6).

Reappointment

(2) Any person whose appointment expires under subsection (1) may be reappointed from time to time for a period of three years on producing a fresh certificate under section 2. 2001, c. 9, Sched. B, s. 10 (6).

Indication of expiry of appointments

(3) Every notary public to whom this section applies shall indicate, by means of a stamp approved by the Attorney General or by his or her delegate under subsection 1 (2) and affixed under the notary's signature, the date on which his or her appointment expires and any limitations as to territory and purposes that are contained in the appointment. 2001, c. 9, Sched. B, s. 10 (6).

Offences, notaries

6. (1) Every notary public who as such exercises any power, performs any function or acts in any way that is not authorized by this Act or that he or she is not otherwise by law entitled to exercise, perform or do is guilty of an of-

权力

3. 就第 2 条第 2 款而言，公证人具备且可运用、行使的权力包括：在安大略省境内起草、通过、保管、发放所有契据、合同、租船合同与其他商业交易（记录），证实所有向其递交以实施公共声明的商业文书，以及公证人职位通常所具备的其他种种职权，和索取、接受及占有与公证人职业相关或附属于公证人执业的所有正当权利、收益和报酬的权力。R.S.O. 1990，c. N.6，s. 3。

提取宣誓证词的权力

4.（1）公证人在安大略省境内拥有并可行使专员的权力以提取宣誓证词。R.S.O. 1990, c. N.6, s. 4 (1)。

就宣誓证词等事项无需盖章

（2）公证人得到议会法案授权，在安大略省境内监督宣誓或提取宣誓证词或提取声明的，此类宣誓、宣誓证词或声明无须加盖公证人印章以生效。

日后任命期满

5.（1）除出庭律师和初级律师外，凡公证人在 1963 年 7 月 1 日当日或之后被任命的，自任命之日起三年后任期期满。2001，c. 9，Sched. B，s. 10（6）。

再任命

（2）依据本条第（1）款任期期满者，在取得第 2 条规定的新证明后，可以 3 年为任期随时获得重新任命。

任命期满日之标示

（3）受本条调整的所有公证人均应标示出其任命期满日以及任命的地域和宗旨限制，标示采用经司法部长或司法部长在第 1 条第 2 款中授权者批准的印章形式，并附于公证人签名之下。

公证人的违法行为

6.（1）凡公证人以其身份行使权力、履行职能或者从事其他活动，而未经本法或其他法律授权的，构成违法行为，一经定罪，处以最高 2000 加元罚款。R.S.O. 1990，c. N.6，s. 6（1）。

fence and on conviction is liable to a fine of not more than $2,000. R.S.O. 1990, c. N.6, s. 6 (1).

Idem

(2) Every notary public who fails to comply with any restriction imposed in his or her appointment under subsection 2 (2) or who fails to comply with subsection 5 (3) is guilty of an offence and on conviction is liable to a fine of not more than $1,000. R.S.O. 1990, c. N.6, s. 6 (2); 2001, c. 9, Sched. B, s. 10 (7).

Idem, other persons

(3) Every person who carries on business as a notary public or who holds himself or herself out as such or who, not being otherwise authorized by law, performs any function of a notary public without a subsisting appointment under this Act or any predecessor of this Act is guilty of an offence and on conviction is liable to a fine of not more than $10,000. R.S.O. 1990, c. N.6, s. 6 (3); 2001, c. 9, Sched. B, s. 10 (8).

Suspension

7. (1) If a notary public who is licensed under the Law Society Act to practise law in Ontario as a barrister and solicitor ceases for any reason to be so licensed or if his or her licence is under suspension or in abeyance, his or her appointment as a notary public is suspended until such time as he or she is relicensed under the Law Society Act to practise law in Ontario as a barrister and solicitor or until such time as his or her licence is no longer under suspension or in abeyance. 2006, c. 21, Sched. C, s. 120.

Revocation of appointment on conviction for offence

(2) The Attorney General may revoke the appointment of a notary public on his or her conviction for an offence against this Act or for any other conduct that in the Attorney General's opinion renders the person unfit to hold the office of notary public. 2001, c. 9, Sched. B, s. 10 (9).

Application

(3) Subsection (2) applies whether the appointment was made by the Attorney General on or after the date on which section 10 of Schedule B to the Government Efficiency Act, 2001 comes into force or by the Lieutenant Governor before that date. 2001, c. 9, Sched. B, s. 10 (9).

Regulations

8. The Lieutenant Governor in Council may make regulations,

同上

（2）凡公证人未能遵守依第2条第2款附加于其任命的限制条件的，或未能遵守第5条第3款的，构成违法行为，一经定罪，处以最高1000加元罚款。R.S.O. 1990，c. N.6，s. 6（2）；2001，c. 9，Sched. B，s. 10（7）。

同上，其他人员

（3）凡以公证人身份营业，或以公证人自居，而未依据本法获得现存有效任命，亦未经其他法律授权而行使公证人职能的，均构成违法行为，一经定罪，处以最高10000加元罚款。R.S.O. 1990，c. N.6，s. 6（3）；2001，c. 9，Sched. B，s. 10（8）。

停职

7.（1）对根据《律师协会法》获许以出庭律师或初级律师身份在安大略省进行法律执业的公证人，如其因任何原因不再获得许可，或其许可处于中止或搁置状态的，其公证人任命亦暂处停职状态，直至其依据《律师协会法》再次获许以出庭律师或初级律师身份在安大略省进行法律执业，或直至其许可不再处于中止或搁置状态。2006，c. 21，Sched. C，s. 120。

定罪后撤销任命

（2）公证人有触犯本法行为或司法部长认为的其他令其不宜担任公证人职位的行为，并因此被定罪的，司法部长可撤销该公证人之任命。2001，c. 9，Sched. B，s. 10（9）。

适用

（3）无论任命是由司法部长在《2001年政府效率法》所附B表第10条生效之日当日或其后做出的，或是由副总督在此前做出的，本条第2款均适用。2001，c. 9，Sched. B，s. 10（9）。

规章

8. 副总督会同行政局可制定如下规章：

(a) prescribing the fee to be paid upon appointment or reappointment as a notary public or any class thereof;

(b) prescribing the fee that the judge or other person examining is entitled to receive from a person examined or re-examined under section 2;

(c) respecting any matter necessary or advisable to carry out effectively the intent and purpose of this Act. R.S.O. 1990, c. N.6, s. 8; 2001, c. 9, Sched. B, s. 10 (10).

（a）规定任命或再任命公证人或其任何团体时需要支付的费用；

（b）规定第 2 条中主考法官或其他主考人员有权自参考或再次参考考生处收取的费用；

（c）为有效执行本法意图或目的，可就任何必需或可取的事项作出规定。R.S.O. 1990，c. N.6，s. 8；2001，c. 9，Sched. B，s. 10（10）。

萨斯喀彻温省公证人法

Saskatchewan Statutes
The Notaries Public Act
R.S.S. 1978, c. N-8
An Act respecting Notaries Public

s 1. Short title

This Act may be cited as The Notaries Public Act.

s 2. Appointments

The Minister of Justice may appoint any persons of the age of eighteen years or more who are Canadian citizens or other British subjects actually residing within Saskatchewan as notaries public for Saskatchewan.

s 2.1 Application

Any person who wishes to be appointed as a notary public shall apply to the Minister of Justice in the form that the minister may prescribe and shall provide any information or material that the minister may require in support of the application.

s 2.2 Solicitors are notaries

Every person who is a duly enrolled solicitor of Saskatchewan and holds a subsisting annual certificate issued pursuant to The Legal Profession Act, 1990 shall be a notary public for Saskatchewan.

s 3. Powers

Every notary public shall during pleasure have, use and exercise the power of drawing, passing, keeping and issuing all deeds and contracts, charter-parties and other mercantile documents in Saskatchewan, and also of attesting all commercial instruments that may be brought before him for public protestation and otherwise acting as usual in the office of notary, and may demand, receive and have all the rights, profits and emoluments rightfully appertaining and belonging to the calling of notary public.

s 4. Fees

The Lieutenant Governor in Council may prescribe by regulation the fees payable for appointment as a notary public.

萨斯喀彻温法规
公证人法
R.S.S. 1978 年，c。N–8
一个有关公证人的法案

s 1. 简称

该法简称为《公证人法》。

s 2. 任命

司法部长可以任命 18 周岁以上的加拿大公民或实际居住在萨斯喀彻温省的其他英国公民为萨斯喀彻温省的公证人。

s 2.1 申请

任何希望被任命为公证人的人员应以部长规定的形式向司法部长提出申请，并提供部长为支持申请而需要的任何信息或材料。

s 2.2 律师公证人

凡是在萨斯喀彻温省正式登记的律师，并持有根据《1990 年法律专业法》颁发的存续年度证书，均为萨斯喀彻温省的公证人。

s 3. 权力

公证人应享有、使用和行使在萨斯喀彻温省起草、通过、保存和发放的所有契约和合同、租船合同及其他商业文件的权力，并且还可以对所有为了公开抗议而可能提交给他的商业文书进行证实的权力，否则按照惯例在公证处办理，可以要求、收受所有属于公证人职业的正当权利的利润和报酬。

s 4. 费用

副州长可以通过规则的形式规定公证人任命所需支付的费用。

s 5. Duration of appointment

5(1) An appointment pursuant to section 2 made after the coming into force of this section expires five years from the last day of the month in which the appointment is made, unless it is sooner revoked.

5(2) The expiry date of an appointment of a person as a notary public made on the expiration of an appointment made prior to the coming into force of this section and expiring on December 31 in 1985, 1986, 1987, 1988, 1989 or 1990 is the last day of the month in which his birthday occurs in 1990, 1991, 1992, 1993, 1994 or 1995, respectively.

s 6. Date of expiration of appointment to be noted on certificate, etc.

6(1) A notary public whose appointment expires pursuant to section 5 shall write or stamp on every affidavit, declaration or other certificate made before or given by him the date on which the appointment expires.

6(2) A notary public who fails to comply with this section is guilty of an offence and liable on summary conviction to a fine not exceeding $50.

s 7. Revocation of appointment in certain cases

Where, pursuant to The Legal Profession Act, 1990, a solicitor is disbarred or suspended from practising:

(a) he thereupon ceases to be a notary public; and

(b) his appointment is thereupon automatically revoked.

(c) [Repealed 1984-85-86, c. 33, s. 7.]

s 8. Certificate of appointment

8(1) An appointment of a notary public shall be evidenced by a certificate in a form prescribed by the Attorney General which certificate:

(a) shall be issued under the signature of the Deputy Minister of Justice or the Acting Deputy Minister of Justice, which signature may be engraved, lithographed, printed or otherwise mechanically produced or affixed by a rubber or metal stamp; and

(b) if it is an appointment that expires, shall set out the date upon which the appointment expires.

8(2) Where the name of a notary public is changed, the Minister of Justice may direct the Deputy Minister of Justice or Acting Deputy Minister of Justice to issue to the notary public in his new name a certificate described in subsection (1).

s 5 任职期限

5（1）在该条生效后，根据第 2 条作出的委任，从任命的月份的最后一天起，为期 5 年，除非其在此之前被撤销。

5（2）在本条生效之前，任命一名人士为公证人的任期届满日期在 1985 年、1986 年、1987 年、1988 年、1989 年或 1990 年的最后一天，12 月 31 日，其生日分别为 1990 年、1991 年、1992 年、1993 年、1994 年或 1995 年的最后一天。

s 6. 在证书等上注明任用期满日期

6（1）根据第 5 条规定到期的公证人应在委任期满之日或之前由其提供的每份誓章、声明或其他证明书写上或盖章注明任用期满日期。

6（2）公证人不遵守本条，即属犯罪，一经简易程序定罪，可处罚款不超过 50 加元。

s 7. 在某些情况下撤销任用

凡根据《1990 年法律专业法》，律师被解除或暂停执业：

（a）他不再是公证人了；以及

（b）他的任命自动被撤销。

（c）[1984-85-86 废止，第 33 章第 7 条]

s 8. 委任证书

8（1）公证人的委任应由律政司规定的格式的证明书证明：

（a）应由司法部副部长或代理司法部副部长的签字印发，签字可以用橡胶或金属印章雕刻，平版印刷，印刷或以其他方式机械制造或贴上；以及

（b）如果是任命到期，应列出约定到期的日期。

8（2）如公证人姓名发生变更，律政司司长可指示司法部副部长或代理司法部副部长以新名称向公证人发出第 1 款所述的证明。

s 8.1 Prohibition re notarizing incomplete documents

8.1(1) No notary public shall subscribe his signature or affix his seal, where a seal is necessary, to a document until it has been fully completed with respect to the particulars required for the purposes of the document.

8.1(2) Any person who contravenes subsection (1) is guilty of an offence and liable on summary conviction to a fine of not more than $50.

s 8.2 Revocation of appointment

8.2(1) The Minister of Justice may revoke an appointment made pursuant to section 2 where a notary public:

(a) has been found guilty of an offence against this Act;

(b) has made a material misstatement in the material submitted in support of his application for appointment as a notary public pursuant to section 2.1; or

(c) is guilty of misrepresentation or fraud.

8.2(2) Any person whose appointment as a notary public is revoked pursuant to this Act shall immediately on the revocation forward his certificate of appointment to the Minister of Justice.

8.2(3) Any person who contravenes subsection (2) is guilty of an offence and liable on summary conviction to a fine of not more than $150.

s 8.3 Offence and penalty

Any person whose appointment as a notary public is revoked or has expired and who, after the revocation or expiration of his appointment, knowingly uses or exercises any of the powers conferred by this Act on a notary public is guilty of an offence and liable on summary conviction to a fine of not more than $500.

s 8.1 禁止对不完整的文件进行公证

8.1（1）公证人不得在必须盖章的文件上签名或盖章，直至实施文件的目的所需的详细资料完整为止。

8.1（2）任何人违反第 1 款，即属犯罪，一经简易程序定罪，可处不超过 50 加元的罚款。

s 8.2 撤销任用

8.2（1）存在下列情形的，司法部长可撤销根据第 2 条作出的公证人任命：

（a）已被裁定犯有违反本法罪行的；

（b）在根据第 2.1 条提交的委任公证人申请材料中发生重大错报的；或者

（c）犯有虚假陈述或欺诈罪的。

8.2（2）任何根据本法被撤销公证人委任的人，应立即将其任用证书转交给司法部长。

8.2（3）任何人违反第 2 款，即属犯罪，一经简易程序定罪，可处不超过 150 加元的罚款。

s 8.3 犯罪和罚款

任何人被任命为公证人的委任被撤销或已经过期，并且在其任命被撤销或到期之后，故意使用或行使本法赋予公证人的任何权力即属犯罪，一经简易程序定罪，可处不超过 500 加元的罚款。

育空地区公证法

Notaries Act	公证法
s 1. Registrar of notaries 1.Registrar of notaries 1(1) The Minister of Justice shall appoint from among the members of the public service a registrar of notaries who may designate one or more persons on the staff of the registrar's office to act on the registrar's behalf. 1(2) The registrar shall prepare and keep in the registrar's office a roll called the roll of notaries public.	**s 1. 公证登记员** 1. 公证登记员 1（1）司法部长应从公职人员中指定公证登记员，该公证登记员可以指定一名或多名登记机构的工作人员代为登记。 1（2）登记员须在登记机构准备并保存公证员名册。
s 2. Application for enrolment 2(1) Every person who seeks enrolment as a notary public shall make application in the prescribed form to the registrar and shall pay the prescribed fee. 2(2) No application shall be accepted unless the applicant is a citizen of Canada or a person who has the status of a permanent resident of Canada.	**s 2. 入职申请** 2（1）拟申请成为公证人的自然人，均须按照标准格式向登记员提出申请，并缴纳规定的费用。 2（2）申请人必须是加拿大公民或具有加拿大永久居民身份的人。
s 3. Order for and enrolment The registrar, if satisfied that the applicant is of good character, and that there is need for a notary public in the place where the applicant desires to practise, shall order that the applicant be examined in the duties of a notary public and that, if found qualified after that examination, the applicant be enrolled as a notary public.	**s 3. 任职要求** 如果登记员确信申请人具有良好的品格，并且在申请人申请执业的地方需要公证人，则登记员应当要求申请人参与公证人职责考试，如果考试结果合格，申请人将被任命为公证人。
s 4. Power of registrar to provide for examinations The registrar shall from time to time appoint a person or persons to conduct the examination of applicants, and shall prescribe the subjects in which they shall be examined, and shall set the fees to be paid to the examiners by the applicants, and, generally, may make rules in respect of examinations.	**s 4. 登记员有权举行考试** 登记员应不定时地指派一人或多人对申请人进行测试，并预先对申请人测验的内容进行规定，明确申请人需要向考试审查员交纳的费用，且一般情况下，登记员有权制定考试规则。
s 5. Enrolment after examination On the applicant filing proof in the prescribed form with the registrar that they have passed the examination, and taken the oath of office in the prescribed form before a judge of the Supreme Court or the Territorial Court or a justice, the registrar shall enroll the applicant as a notary public and shall record on the roll a memorandum of the	**s 5. 考试后入职** 在申请人以书面方式通知登记员、提交证明文件表明申请人已经通过考试，并以规定的形式向最高法院法官或管辖地法院法官或司法机关宣誓就职后，登记员应当将申请人注册登记为公证人，并将公证人记录在被授权执业的地区的公证人名册中。

area in which the notary public is authorized to practise.

s 6. Terms of office

Every person enrolled pursuant to section 5 may hold office for a period not exceeding five years but their enrolment may be renewed on application to the registrar and payment of the prescribed fee.

s 7. Strike-off and suspension

The Supreme Court has full power and authority on application by the registrar or any person aggrieved, in a summary manner, to inquire into the professional conduct or any alleged incompetence, negligence, or fraud of a notary public, and may, for cause shown order that a notary public be struck off the roll of notaries public, or be suspended from practising for a period named in the order or make any order that is just.

s 8. Offence and penalty

Any person who acts as a notary public or holds themselves out as qualified to act as a notary public without being qualified and authorized to do so in accordance with the provisions of this Act or in any way contrary to any limitation or condition to which their enrolment or commission is subject, commits an offence, and is liable, on summary conviction, to a fine not exceeding $500 or one year's imprisonment or to both fine and imprisonment.

s 9. Validity of certain acts

No act done by a notary public shall be deemed invalid or ineffectual only because of the fact that it is done contrary to any limitation or condition to which their enrolment or commission is subject and nothing in this Act relieves any person acting as a notary public from liability for any loss, damages, or costs caused to or incurred by any other person because of any act done while so acting.

s 10. Application of preceding sections

The preceding sections of this Act, except subsections 2(1) and (2), do not apply to lawyers.

s 11. Right to use title and exercise power of notary public

11(1) Every lawyer enrolled under the Legal Profession Act and every notary public qualified under this Act has and may use while so enrolled or qualified the style and title of "notary public in and for the Yukon" and, except as in this Act provided, has and may exercise while so enrolled or qualified the right and power to

(a) give notarial certificates of their acts;

s 6. 任职期限

根据第 5 条登记入职的公证人任职期限不得超过 5 年，但可以向登记员提出申请并缴纳费用后延长任职期限。

s 7. 除名和停职

最高法院有充分的权力，依据登记员或任何对公证程序中感到不满的人以简易程序提出的申请，对公证人的执业行为或公证人被指控的失职、疏忽或欺诈的行为进行审查，将公证人从公证人名册中除名，或者命令公证人在指定的期间内暂停执业。

s 8. 犯罪和罚款

任何公证人或者任何未依据本法被授予公证人身份或不符合公证人资格的人，以公证人身份行事，或者在任何程度上违反限制条件的人以公证人身份行事，其行为均构成犯罪，应当承担刑事责任，将被处以不超过 500 加元的罚款或监禁一年或二者并处。

s 9. 行为的有效性

不得以公证人作出的行为违反本法规定的任何入职、执行的限制或条件为由，而主张该行为无效，但本法并不免除公证人对因上述行为而造成的任何损失，或因引起他人支出的费用所应承担的责任。

s 10. 前述条款的适用

除第 2 条第 1 款和第 2 款外，本法前述条款不适用于律师。

s 11. 公证人使用公证人头衔和执行公证人行为的权力

11（1）根据《法律职业人员法》注册的所有律师和根据本法授予公证资格的所有公证人均可以使用"育空公证人"的头衔，除本法另有授权外，其可以同时行使以下的所有权力：

（a）提供证明公证行为的公证证书；

(b) attest or protest all commercial instruments brought before them for attestation or public protestation;

(c) administer oaths, affidavits, affirmations or statutory declarations that may or are required to be administered, sworn, affirmed, or made by the law of the Yukon, or of any province, or of Canada, or of any country other than Canada; and

(d) perform any duties authorized or prescribed by any Act.

11(2) No lawyer who is disbarred, disqualified or suspended from practice under any of the provisions of the Legal Profession Act shall, so long as the disbarment, disqualification or suspension continues, act as or use the style and title of a notary public, or have or exercise any of the powers, rights, duties, privileges, or fees referred to above.

11(3) A notary public is entitled to receive the fees pertaining to the office of notary public prescribed by the Commissioner in Executive Council.

s 11.1 Duty to print or stamp name

11.1(1) If, in the exercise of any power under section 11, a notary public is required to sign an instrument, they must, below or adjacent to that signature, legibly print or stamp

(a) their first and last name; and

(b) if not a lawyer enrolled under the Legal Profession Act, the expiry date of their term of enrolment.

11.1(2) The Commissioner in Executive Council may exempt the members of a class of notaries public from the application of subsection (1).

s 12. Commission

The registrar shall on request, and on payment of the prescribed fee, issue to every person empowered to act as a notary public under this Act, a commission in the prescribed form, and shall at any time, on request of any person so commissioned who has not been struck off the roll and is not suspended from practising, and on payment of the prescribed fee, give to that person a certificate stating that they are duly commissioned or entitled to act as a notary public under this Act.

s 13. Appeal

An appeal lies to the Court of Appeal from any order or decision of the Supreme Court under this Act.

s 14. Rules

The registrar may make rules not inconsistent with

（b）对向其提交的商业票据，出具证明或拒绝承兑书；

（c）根据育空地区及任何加拿大的其他省份，加拿大或加拿大以外任何国家法律可能或要求管理、确认的，行政官员的宣誓；

（d）执行法律授权或规定的其他职责。

11（2）律师根据《法律职业人员法》的规定被取消律师资格或暂停执业的，只要取消律师资格或不符合公证人资格或者暂停职业的状态存在，就不能继续以公证人身份自居，也不再享有或行使上述任何权力、权利、义务、特权，不得再收取公证费用。

11（3）公证人有权收取行政会议专员规定的公证费用。

s 11.1 打印或印记名称的义务

11.1（1）如在根据第11条行使任何权力时，公证人必须签署文书，签名应在该文件的签章下方或附近，清楚印刷或记录以下信息：

（a）公证人的姓氏；

（b）如果公证人不是根据《法律职业人员法》注册的律师，则应载明其任期的终止时间。

11.1（2）行政会议专员可免除某一类公证人员第1款规定的申请要求。

s 12. 任命

登记员应根据申请和缴纳的费用，向每个执行公证行为的人发布符合规定的委任状，并在任何时候，授权依据公证人名册对没有被除名、没有停止执业、并持续缴纳费用的公证人有权以公证人身份行事，并提供证书证明其任职权利。

s 13. 上诉

上诉法院应根据最高法院依据本法作出的命令或决定接受上诉。

s 14. 规则

注册服务机构可以制定与本法不一致的规则，制

this Act and establish forms and set fees for all proceedings under this Act not fully provided for herein, and may alter, add to, amend, or repeal those rules, forms, and fees as and when it may seem necessary or desirable.

s 15. Government employees

The Commissioner in Executive Council, if satisfied that the appointment of a notary public under this section is necessary in the public interest, may, by a commission, appoint any employee of the Government of the Yukon or the Government of Canada to be a notary public; and an appointment so made may be during pleasure or for any period the Commissioner in Executive Council may think fit, and the Commissioner in Executive Council may define and limit the area in which a person appointed under this section may practise as a notary public.

s 16. Powers of government notary

16(1) An appointment under section 15 shall confer on the person named, power only in connection with their employment, and without fee, to administer oaths, to take affidavits, declarations, and acknowledgements, to attest instruments by their seal and to give notarial certificates of their acts.

16(2) Every person appointed under this section shall be enrolled by the registrar after the person has filed proof with the registrar that they have taken the oath of office in the prescribed form before a judge of the Supreme Court or the Territorial Court or a justice.

s 17. Commissioners for oaths in the Yukon

A notary public is ex officio a commissioner for taking oaths in the Yukon, and when the notary public administers oaths or takes affidavits, affirmations, or declarations in the Yukon, it is not necessary to their validity that they affix their seal thereto.

s 18. Regulations

The Commissioner in Executive Council may make regulation:

(a) prescribing a class of notaries public the members of which are exempt from the application of section 11.1; or

(b) respecting any matter that the Commissioner in Executive Council considers necessary or advisable to carry out the purposes of this Act.

定表格并明确本法案中未充分规定的所有公证程序费用，并且在必要时可以随时更改、增加、修改或废除这些规则、表格和费用。

s 15. 政府雇员

如果行政会议专员确信为了公共利益而需要，根据本条任命公证人是必要的，可以由委员会任命育空政府或加拿大政府的任何雇员为公证人；上述任命可以在行政专员认为合适的任何期间，或处长在行政会议认为合适的期间内进行，同时行政会议专员可界定及限制根据本条获任命的人作为公证人履职的地域范围。

s 16. 政府公证人的权力

16（1）根据第15条作出的任命，应当授予被任命人与其职责有关的权力，在不收费的情况下，执行誓词、作出宣誓书和确认书，以盖章证明文件，并发放公证书。

16（2）每个根据本条获得任命的人，在向登记员证明其已在最高法院的法官或领土法院的法官或者大法官面前宣誓后，将被记入公证员名册。

s 17. 育空地区誓词管理官

公证人是在育空执行誓词的当然成员，当公证人在育空中执行宣誓或者作出誓章时，不必根据其盖章确定誓词的有效性。

s 18. 规则

行政会议专员有权制定以下规则：

（a）规定可免除适用第11.1条的公证人；或者

（b）关于执行局局长认为为执行本法令的目的所必需的事宜。

开曼群岛

开曼群岛公证人法

CAYMAN ISLANDS

Supplement No. 10 published with Extraordinary Gazette No. 75 of 10th October, 2014.

NOTARIES PUBLIC LAW
(2014 Revision)

Law 11 of 2013 consolidated with Law 26 of 2013.
Revised under the authority of the Law Revision Law (1999 Revision).

Originally enacted-
Law 11 of 2013-25th March, 2013
Law 26 of 2013-13th December, 2013
Consolidated and revised this 31st day of July, 2014.

NOTARIES PUBLIC LAW
(2014 Revision)

ARRANGEMENT OF SECTIONS

1. Short title
2. Definitions
3. Eligibility for appointment as notary public
4. Authorization and application for appointment
5. Appointment of notaries public
6. Register of notaries public
7. Certificate
8. Payment of annual fees
9. Notarial acts
10. Fees
11. Proceedings for misconduct
12. Offences
13. Notarial Acts Book
14. Duty to inform Clerk
15. Regulations
16. Repeal of Notaries Public Law (2006 Revision)

开曼群岛
2014年10月10日第75号特别公告第10号立法补充

公证人法
（2014年修订版）
2013年第11号法与2013年第26号法合并。
根据《法律修订法》（1999年修订）的授权进行修订。
原2013年3月25日第11号法案和2013年12月26日第26号法案在2014年7月31日被合并和修订。

公证人法
2014年修订版

章节安排

1. 简称
2. 概念
3. 公证人的资格
4. 公证人的申请和授权
5. 公证人的任命
6. 公证人注册
7. 公证证书
8. 缴纳年费
9. 公证行为
10. 公证费用
11. 不当行为诉讼
12. 罪行
13. 公证行为手册
14. 告知书记官的义务
15. 条例
16. 2006年版公证人法的废止

17. Transitional provisions
18. Validation

Schedule 1–Form of Application for Appointment as Notary Public

Schedule 2–Form of Oath

Schedule 3–Example of Notarial Seal

Schedule 4–Certificate of Notary Public

Schedule 5–Notarial acts and the Fee Schedule

Schedule 6–Notarial Acts Book

NOTARIES PUBLIC LAW
(2014 Revision)

1. This Law may be cited as the Notaries Public Law (2014 Revision).

2. In this Law- "Caymanian" has the same meaning as in the Immigration Law (2014 Revision);

"Clerk" means the Clerk of the Grand Court;

"permanent resident" has the same meaning as in the Immigration Law (2014 Revision);

"register" means the register of notaries public established pursuant to section 6; and

"the Convention" means the Convention Abolishing the Requirement of Legalisation for Foreign Public Documents done at the Hague, October 5, 1961.

3. A Caymanian or a permanent resident of the Islands who -

(a) has been employed in a management position in a company or in a public office for a period of three or more years;

(b) has been employed as, or has practised as, an attorney-at-law for a period of three or more years in the Islands or any other jurisdiction;

(c) has been employed as, or has practised as, a certified public or chartered accountant for a period of three years or more;

(d) has been employed in or has practised any other profession specified from time to time by the Cabinet by notice in the Gazette and government websites for such period of time as may be specified; or

(e) is of good character, and is considered by the Cabinet to be qualified, by virtue of his professional or business experience, to carry out the duties of a notary public, and is ordinarily resident in the Islands, has never been convicted of a crime punishable with imprisonment nor been found guilty of any act that constitutes misconduct in a professional respect or misconduct under this Law, is eligible to apply for appointment as a notary public.

17. 过渡性条款
18. 身份验证

附表1 任命公证员的申请表格

附表2 宣誓誓词

附表3 公证印章示例

附表4 公证人证明书

附表5 公证行为和收费表

附表6 公证行为手册

公证人法
（2014年修订版）

1. 本法应称为《公证人法（2014年修订版）》。

2. 在本法中，"开曼人"的含义与其在2014年修订版移民法中的概念一致；

"书记官"指大法院书记官；

在本法中，"永久住民"的含义与其在2014年修订版移民法中的概念一致；

"登记册"指根据第6条设立的公证人名册；以及

"公约"是指1961年10月5日在海牙签订的《关于取消要求外国公证文书的公约》。

3. 开曼群岛公民或群岛的永久居民指：

（a）已在公司或公职人员中担任管理职位，任期3年以上；

（b）在群岛或任何群岛的其他司法管辖区已作为律师被雇用或已执业3年以上；

（c）在群岛或任何群岛的其他司法管辖区已作为认证的公共或特许会计师被雇用或已执业3年以上；

（d）在内阁通过宪报和政府网站不定期的指定被雇佣或执业于任何其他特定职业并已从事或执业满特定时间的；或者

（e）具有良好的品格，被内阁认为凭借其专业或业务经验具备履行公证人职责的资格，以及，通常居住在群岛且从未被判定犯有可判处监禁的罪行，也没有被认定犯有本法规定违背职业道德或不当行为的人，有资格申请担任公证人。

4. (1) An applicant shall submit his application in writing to the Attorney

General in the form set out in Schedule 1 with the following documents attached -

(a) proof of his Caymanian status or permanent residency;

(b) two character references provided by an employer or former employer, a justice of the peace, a notary public, a minister of religion, a police officer in a gazetted rank, a medical doctor, a certified public or chartered accountant, a member of the Legislative Assembly or an attorney-at-law;

(c) a police clearance certificate;

(d) a photograph of the applicant certified by a justice of the peace, a notary public, a minster of religion, a police officer in a gazetted rank, a medical doctor, a certified public or chartered accountant, a member of the Legislative Assembly or an attorney-at-law, to be a true likeness of the applicant;

(e) any additional information that is proof of qualifications or experience relevant to appointment as a notary public; and

(f) any additional information that the Cabinet may require in considering an application under this section.

(2) The Attorney General, upon receipt of the completed application, shall submit either -

(a) his recommendation for authorization;

(b) a request for further information; or

(c) his recommendation for refusal,

to the Cabinet.

(3) On receipt of the recommendation under subsection (2) (a), the Cabinet may authorize the appointment of an eligible applicant as a notary public either on the basis that -

(a) the applicant participates in the prescribed training programme prior to being sworn in; or

(b) the applicant has relevant qualifications or work experience and is not required to participate in the prescribed training programme prior to being sworn in.

5. (1) A person in respect of whom the Cabinet has given an authorization public under section 4 shall, upon -

(a) participating in the prescribed training programme, where required, and providing proof of such participation or the exemption therefrom to the Clerk;

(b) depositing with the Clerk an impression of the embossed notarial Schedule 3 seal, substantially in the form set out in Schedule 3, to be used by him in his capacity as a notary public;

4.（1）申请人应以书面形式向律师提出申请。

附表1列出了通常需要提交的文件：

（a）证明其开曼人的公民身份或享有永久居留权的证据；

（b）雇主或前雇主、治安法官、公证人、宗教部长、司法公职人员、医生、认证公众或特许会计师、立法议会的成员或律师提供的两份品格证明；

（c）清关证明书；

（d）经治安法官、公证人、宗教部长、司法公职人员、医生、认证公众或特许会计师或立法议员或律师认证的申请人照片；

（e）作为公证人任命资格的证明或经验证明的任何额外资料；以及

（f）内阁在考虑根据本条提出的申请时可能需要的任何额外资料。

（2）律政司在收到已填妥的申请后，须向内阁提交以下材料：

（a）其授权建议；

（b）请求进一步资料；或者

（c）拒绝建议。

（3）内阁收到根据本条第（2）（a）款提出的建议后，可授权委任以下符合资格的申请人为公证人：

（a）申请人在宣誓就职前参加规定的培训计划；或者

（b）申请人有相关资质或工作经验，而无须在宣誓就职前参加规定的培训计划。

5.（1）内阁已根据第4条给予公证授权的人，

（a）如有需要，应参加规定的培训计划，并向秘书提供参与或豁免的证明；

（b）向书记官存放大致以附表3所列格式印制的压纹公证印章，供其作为公证人执业时使用；

(c) paying to the Treasury the sum of five hundred dollars and producing the receipt for such payment to the Clerk; and

(d) giving an undertaking signed by the applicant in which he agrees to file with the Clerk a notice setting out any of the following eventualities that may occur subsequent to his appointment as a notary public -

(i) change to his name;

(ii) change to his ordinary residence;

(iii) change to his status as a Caymanian or a permanent resident;

(iv) change to his profession or occupation;

(v) criminal conviction or determination of professional misconduct; or

(vi) adjudication as a bankrupt, then take before the Clerk the form of oath in Schedule 2 and be appointed a notary public.

(2) A person described at section 3(b) or at section 3(1) of the Legal Practitioners Law (2012 Revision) is exempt from participating in the training programme under subsection (1) .

(3) Cabinet may, by Order, declare that members of specified professional groups are exempt from participating in the training programme under subsection (1) (a) .

6. (1) The Clerk shall establish a register and shall enter the name of every person who has been appointed as a notary public and the date of his appointment.

(2) The Clerk shall endorse the register with an appropriate notation where a notary public's appointment -

(a) lapses under section 8;

(b) lapses by virtue of the notary public's residency outside of the Islands for more than twelve months; or

(c) is suspended under section 11 or section 14.

(3) The Clerk shall remove from the register the name of any person whose appointment is revoked under sections 8, 11 or 14.

7. (1) Upon appointment of a person as a notary public, the Clerk shall issue a certificate to the person in the form set out in Schedule 4.

(2) On appointment as a notary public, the certificate shall be valid until the thirty-first day of January in the year following the appointment.

(3) Where the notary public complies with the requirements under section 8, the Clerk shall endorse the certificate to the effect that the person named therein is authorized to act as a notary public until the thirty-first day of January in the following year.

（c）向库务署支付500美元的款项，并向书记官出示付款的收据；以及

（d）申请人同意向书记官提交一份通知，其中列明其被任命为公证人后可能发生的以下事项：

（i）姓名的变更；

（ii）住所的变更；

（iii）改变其作为开曼群岛公民或群岛的永久居民的身份；

（iv）专业或职业的变更；

（v）刑事犯罪或被裁定为职业违法行为；或者

（vi）作为破产人的裁定，且该裁定应根据附表2在书记官面前宣誓并在委任为公证人的程序之前提交。

（2）《法律执业者法（2012年修订）》第3（b）条或第3（1）条所述的人，根据第1款豁免参加培训计划。

（3）内阁有权发布指令，宣布指定的专业团体的成员可豁免参与根据第（1）（a）款进行的培训计划。

6.（1）最高法院书记官应建立公证人登记册，并在其中记载所有被委任为公证人的人的姓名及其任命日期。

（2）当公证人的任命出现以下情形时，书记官应以适当方式登记在册：

（a）根据第8条失效；

（b）公证人在群岛以外居住的时间超过12个月；或者

（c）根据第11条或第14条暂停执行。

（3）书记官须将任何根据第8条、第11条或第14条被撤销的人的姓名从公证人登记册中除名。

7.（1）公证人任命后，书记官须以附表4所列格式向该公证人发出证明书。

（2）在公证人被任命后，其任职证明书有效期至委任后一年的1月31日。

（3）公证人符合本法第8条规定的，书记官须核准该证明书，授权其中所指明的人截至到次年1月31日前有权作为公证人执业。

8. (1) Every notary public shall pay to the Treasury on or before the thirtyfirst day of January in each year subsequent to his first appointment as a notary public the following sums -

(a) in the case of a notary public resident in Cayman Brac or Little Cayman, the sum of two hundred and fifty dollars; or

(b) in the case of a notary public resident in Grand Cayman, the sum of five hundred dollars,

and where the notary public has not paid the sum within the time specified, his appointment as a notary public lapses and he shall not be authorized to perform any notarial act.

(2) Subject to subsection (3), upon payment of the annual fees, and the penalty of two hundred and fifty dollars, the lapsed appointment of a notary public shall be reinstated by the Clerk but such reinstatement shall take effect from the date of the payment of the prescribed fees and not from an earlier date.

(3) Where a notary public's appointment lapses for a period in excess of six months his appointment shall be revoked by the Clerk.

(4) The Clerk shall publish and update quarterly a list of all current notaries on the relevant Government websites.

9. A notary public may perform -

(a) any of the notarial acts listed in the second column of Schedule 5; or

(b) any act that is required to be performed by a notary public under any Law of the Islands including the provisions of any treaty or convention and any protocol to such treaty or convention that is applicable to the Islands.

10. (1) A notary public shall not charge for the performance of any notarial act a sum in excess of the fees listed in Schedule 5, and where he provides a service or carries out an act for which fees are not provided, the notary public's fees shall be as provided for under any rules of court or any other written law.

(2) Where the provisions of subsection (1) are contravened, the notary public's conduct shall be considered as misconduct in his capacity as a notary public.

11. (1) The appointment of a notary public may be revoked or suspended by the Cabinet where -

(a) he is convicted of an offence punishable with imprisonment or is found guilty of any act that constitutes misconduct, whether in his capacity as a notary public or otherwise;

8.（1）每名公证人在首次被委任为公证人后，每年 3 月 31 日或之前，应向财政部支付以下款项：

（a）如在公证人在开曼布拉克或小开曼执业，则总额为 250 美元；

（b）如在公证人在开曼全国执业，则总额为 500 美元；

公证人在规定的时间内尚未支付款项的，公证人的任命失效，不得开展公证执业行为。

（2）除第 3 款另有规定外，上述犯罪或违法的公证人在缴付年费并罚款 250 美元后，被暂停职务的公证人可由书记官复职，但该项复职不得早于缴纳年费和罚金之日生效。

（3）公证人自任用起超过 6 个月未履行职务的，由书记官撤销其公证人资格。

（4）书记官应每季度公布和更新相关政府网站上目前所有公证人的名单。

9. 公证人可以执行以下事务：

（a）附表 5 第 2 栏所列的任何公证行为；或者

（b）任何根据《群岛法》，包括任何条约或公约规定以及适用于该岛屿的条约或公约等任何议定书规定由公证人执行的行为。

10.（1）公证人不得为履行公证行为征收超过附表 5 所列费用的款项，附表中没有列明的提供服务或者执行公证事务的情形，公证费用应参照法院规则或其他成文法的规定。

（2）违反第 1 款的规定的行为应视为公证人履职不当行为。

11.（1）当出现以下情形时，公证人的任命可由内阁撤销或暂时中止：

（a）无论以公证人还是其他身份被认定犯有将被处以监禁以上的罪行，或被裁定构成违法行为；

(b) he contravenes the provisions in section 10; or

(c) he has failed to file with the Clerk a notice in accordance with section 14.

(2) Where the appointment of a notary public is revoked or suspended, the Attorney General shall direct the Clerk to endorse a notation of such suspension in the register or remove the name of the notary public from the register, as the case may be.

(3) Any court before which a notary public is convicted of an offence punishable with imprisonment or before which he is found guilty under subsection (1) shall make a report of such conviction or finding to the Attorney General who shall in turn advise the Cabinet.

(4) Where any person makes a complaint on oath charging a notary public with misconduct in his capacity as notary public, the Attorney General shall enquire into the facts and report his findings to the Cabinet, and where the Cabinet is of the opinion that the notary public's acts constitute misconduct, it may suspend or revoke the notary public's appointment and direct the Clerk to endorse a notation of such suspension or to remove his name from the register, as the case may be.

(5) Every complaint charging a notary public with misconduct shall be made to the Attorney General and shall contain a statement of the material facts on which the person complaining relies.

(6) Notwithstanding subsections (l) to (4), the Cabinet may revoke the appointment of any notary public where it is of the opinion that the notary public is unfit, incapable or incompetent to carry out the duties of the office.

(7) Where a notary public's appointment has been suspended or revoked, the Clerk shall cause notice of such fact to be published in the Gazette and by official notice on the relevant Government websites.

(8) A notary public who is aggrieved by a decision of the Cabinet made under this section may appeal therefrom to a Judge in Chambers in the manner and within the time prescribed by law or by the rules made, from time to time, by the Court relating to appeals in civil matters.

12. (1) Any person who falsely represents himself to be a notary public or, not being a notary public, purports to carry out any notarial act commits an offence and is liable on summary conviction to a fine of five thousand dollars or to imprisonment for a term of twelve months, or to both.

(2) A notary public who performs any notarial act while his appointment has lapsed, has been suspended or has been revoked commits an offence and is liable on

（b）存在违反第 10 条规定的行为；或者

（c）公证人没有按照第 14 条向书记官提交通知。

（2）若公证人的委任被撤销或暂停，律政司司长应指示书记官在注册中批注暂停执业的情况，或将该公证人的名称从公证人名册中除名（视属何情况而定）。

（3）任何法庭在对公证人判处犯有可被判监禁以上刑罚的罪行或根据第 1 款被裁定有罪的罪行前，须向律政司报告该定罪或裁定，并通知内阁。

（4）律政司应调查事实情况并向内阁报告调查结果，如果内阁认为公证人的行为构成不当行为，可以暂停或撤销公证人的任命，并指示书记官批准中止其执业资格或将其从公证人名册中除名（视属何情况而定）。

（5）每份投诉公证人存在不法行为的投诉书，均应载有投诉依赖的重大事实的陈述。

（6）除了第 1 款至第 4 款的规定，如果公证人不合格或无能力履行职责，内阁仍可以撤销公证人的任命。

（7）公证人的任命被暂停或者撤销的，书记官应在政府公报上公示，并在政府网站公布。

（8）对内阁根据本条作出的决定不服的公证人可以以法律规定的方式在规定的时间内向主管民事诉讼的法院提出上诉。

12.（1）任何人冒充公证人进行执业或以非公证人身份，从事视为公证的行为，即属犯罪，一经简易程序定罪，可处罚款 5000 美元或监禁 12 个月的处罚，或两者兼处。

（2）公证人在被起诉失职、暂停执业或已被吊销执业资格的情况下进行公证行为，即属犯罪，一经简易程序定罪，可处 5000 美元以下罚款或监禁 12 个月

summary conviction to a fine of five thousand dollars or to imprisonment for a term of twelve months, or to both.

13. (1) Every notary public shall maintain a book, called a "Notarial Acts Book" which shall be in the form set out in Schedule 6 in which he shall record the details of each notarial act carried out by him and shall preserve the record of each such notarial act for a period of not less than ten years from the making thereof and shall, after the expiration of that period, deliver the book to the Clerk for retention by him in the archives of the Grand Court.

(2) Any person whose appointment as a notary public has lapsed, has been suspended or has been revoked under this Law shall, within seven days from the date of such lapse, suspension or revocation, as the case may be, deliver all Notarial Acts Books in his possession to the Clerk for retention as part of the archives of the Grand Court.

(3) Any person who, not being a notary public, comes into possession of a Notarial Acts Book shall forthwith deliver such book to the Clerk.

(4) Any person who contravenes this section commits an offence and is liable on summary conviction to a fine of one thousand dollars or to imprisonment for a term of six months, or to both.

14. (1) A notary public whose name, residence or status under the Immigration Law (2014 Revision) changes, shall, within thirty days of such change, notify the Clerk in writing of that fact, providing the Clerk with the details on his new name, residence or status under that Law.

(2) A notary public who has been convicted, has been found by a professional body to have carried out acts that constitute professional misconduct, such body being set up to inquire into acts of professional misconduct within the respective profession, or has been adjudged a bankrupt, shall within seven days of any such decision, notify the Clerk in writing of the conviction, finding or judgment.

(3) Failure to inform the Clerk under this section within the stated time periods may result in the immediate suspension of the appointment of the notary public and he shall be liable under the provisions of section 12(2) of this Law should he purport to carry out any notarial acts.

(4) The Cabinet shall take such steps to uphold, suspend or revoke the appointment of a notary public pursuant to any determinations he may make under this section.

15. (1) Without prejudice to the powers of the Rules Committee under section 19(3) (g) of the Grand Court Law (2008 Revision), the Cabinet may make Regulations for the better carrying out of this Law and, without dero-

的处罚，或两者兼处。

13.（1）每名公证人应持有一本"公证手册"，公证人应以附表6所列的格式记录其所进行的每一项公证执业的细节，且手册记录自制作以来应妥善保存不少于10年，在该期限届满后，将该手册交给书记官保存在大法院的档案中。

（2）根据本法规定，任何公证人被暂停执行业务或者已被吊销执业资格的，应当自上述暂停执业或吊销执业资格的决定作出之日起7日内提供其作为公证人时保存的公证手册作为大法院档案的一部分交由大法院保存。

（3）任何非公证人持有公证手册的，应立即将该手册送交给书记官。

（4）任何人违反本条的行为即属犯罪，一经简易程序定罪，可处罚款1000美元或监禁6个月的处罚，或两者兼处。

14.（1）根据《移民法（2014年修订）》，姓名、居住地或身份发生变更的公证人应在发生上述变更的事实后30日内以书面形式通知书记官，并向书记官提供其新的姓名，居所或身份。

（2）若公证人已被定罪或由于了调查职业不端行为设立的专业机构查明其行为构成职业不端行为，或已被裁定为破产人的机构，在作出该决定的7日内，须将定罪、裁定或判决的结果书面通知书记官。

（3）在规定的期限内未能根据本条的规定通知书记官，可能会直接导致公证人的任命中止，如果其从事任何公证行为，即构成对本法第12条第2款的违反。

（4）根据本条的不同情形，内阁相应作出维持、暂停或撤销公证人任命的决定。

15.（1）在不影响规则委员会根据《大法院法（2008年修订）》第19（3）（g）条规定的权力的情况下，内阁可以制定条例，以便更好地执行本法，但不得减损上述一般性原则，此类条例可规定以下事项：

gating from the generality of the foregoing, such Regulations may provide for -

(a) the fees which may be charged for the carrying out of any notarial act;

(b) the annual fees or the fees payable upon the application for appointment as a notary public;

(c) the conduct of notaries public, including the manner in which the records are to be kept;

(d) the manner in which the Clerk shall preserve or dispose of seals or certificates surrendered to him;

(e) the programme of training under section 5, any handbook, or directions applicable to notaries public;

(f) the accreditation of any person, agency or educational institution for the delivery of the programme of training under section 5;

(g) the establishment of a body that will design and evaluate the programme of training under section 5 and advise generally on the standards of conduct for notaries public;

(h) the designation of a department of Government as the competent authority to carry out acts of certification by virtue of the Convention and the regulation of the competent authority; or

(i) any other matter related to the discharge of the duties or the functions of notaries public.

(2) The Cabinet may by Order amend any fees or penalties under this Law.

16. The Notaries Public Law (2006 Revision) is repealed.

17. (1) Notwithstanding the provisions of sections 3 and 5 of this Law, every valid appointment of a notary public under the Notaries Public Law (2006 Revision) shall be valid under this Law.

(2) A reference to the Notaries Public Law (2006 Revision) in any enactment, instrument or other document made by virtue of the Notaries Public Law (2006 Revision) shall, after the repeal of that Law, unless the context requires otherwise be construed as a reference to this Law.

(3) A reference to a notary public appointed under the Notaries Public Law (2006 Revision) in any enactment, instrument or other document passed or made before the repeal of that Law shall be construed, unless the context requires otherwise, as a reference to a notary public appointed under this Law.

18. Any act carried out between 6 November, 2013 and the coming into force of this Law by a person -

(a) whose appointment as a notary public lapsed by

（a）进行公证行为可能收取的费用；

（b）申请公证人资格时需缴纳的年费或费用；

（c）公证人的行为，包括记录的保存方式；

（d）书记官对向其交付的印章或证明书进行保存或处置的方式；

（e）根据第 5 条进行的培训计划，任何手册或适用于公证人的指示；

（f）任何个人、机构或教育机构根据第 5 条提交培训计划的认证；

（g）设立机构，以根据第 5 条设计和评估培训项目，并对公证人的行为标准提供一般性的建议；

（h）指定政府部门作为主管机关，依照公约和主管机关的规定进行认证行为；或者

（i）与履行职责或公证人职能有关的任何其他事宜。

（2）内阁可以依照本法规定修改任何关于费用或处罚的规定。

16.《公证人法（2006 年版）》已废止

17.（1）尽管有本法第 3 条和第 5 条的规定，根据《公证法（2006 年版）》对公证人的任用均仍为有效。

（2）根据《公证法（2006 年版）》提出的任何成文法则，文书或其他文件中提及《公证法（2006 年版）》，在该法律废止后，除文义另有所指外，可作为本法的参考。

（3）在《公证法（2006 年版）》废止之前，根据该法律通过或提出的任何成文法则、文书或其他文件中委任的公证人，除非另有要求，否则应解释为根据本法所指的公证人。

18. 个人在 2013 年 11 月 6 日至本法生效之间的行为：

（a）由于没有在 2013 年 11 月 5 日之前提供规定

reason of his not having provided proof of completion of the prescribed training programme by 5 November, 2013; and

(b) who was acting in purported exercise of the powers conferred by the Notaries Public Law, 2013, is validated.

SCHEDULE 1
Form of Application for Appointment as Notary Public

To: The Honourable Attorney General Attorney General's Chambers Grand Cayman

I, of apply, in accordance with the Notaries Public Law (2014 Revision), to be appointed as a Notary Public. I certify that the following information set out below and concerning myself is true-

1. Date of birth
2. Place of birth
3. Status under the Immigration Law (2014 Revision)
4. Place of business
5. Ordinary residence
6. Profession or occupation
7. Professional or other qualifications held
8. Work experience

and that I have not been convicted of any crime punishable with imprisonment nor have I been found guilty of any act that constitutes misconduct in a professional respect or misconduct under this Law.

Dated this day of, 20.
Signed
Applicant
Instructions to applicant

This application form shall be accompanied by the following documents –

(a) two character references provided by an employer or former employer, a justice of the peace, a notary public, a minister of religion, a police officer of the rank of Inspector or above, a medical doctor, a certified public or chartered accountant, a member of the Legislative Assembly or an attorney-at-law;

(b) police clearance certificate;

(c) a photograph of the applicant certified by a justice of the peace, a notary public, a minister of religion, a police officer of the rank of Inspector or above, a medical doctor, a certified public or chartered accountant, a member of the Legislative Assembly or an attorney at-law to be a true likeness of the applicant;

(d) proof of Caymanian or permanent residency status; and

(e) such other documents as the Cabinet may require.

SCHEDULE 2
Form of Oath

I, A. B., do swear that I will faithfully exercise the office of a notary public. I will faithfully carry out such notarial duties as may be required for any party or between any parties requiring

的培训计划的完成证明,因此被认定公证人的委任失效;以及

(b)行使2013年公证人法赋予的职权的,均为有效。

附表1
任命公证员的申请表格

致:大开曼律政司总办公室

我根据《公证法(2014年修订)》申请被任命为公证人。我证明下面列出的关于我的信息是真实的:

1. 出生日期;
2. 出生地点;
3. 《移民法(2014年修订)》下的身份;
4. 执业地点;
5. 经常住所地;
6. 专业或职业;
7. 专业或其他资格;
8. 工作经验。

以及,我从未被判定犯有可判处监禁刑的罪行,也没有被认定犯有本法规定的违背职业道德或不当行为。

当天日期,20xx年。
签名
申请人
申请文件

本申请表须附有以下文件:

(a)雇主或前雇主、治安法官、公证人、宗教部长、司法公职人员、医生、认证公众或特许会计师、立法会议员或律师提供的两份品格证明;

(b)清关证明书;

(c)经治安法官、公证人、宗教部长、司法公职人员、医生、认证公众或特许会计师、立法议员或律师认证的本人的照片;

(d)对其开曼人的公民身份或永久居留权的证明;以及

(e)内阁可能要求的其他文件。

附表2
宣誓誓词

我,A.B.发誓,我将忠实地履行公证人的职责。我将忠实地为任何一方或有相同要求的双方执行公证责任,如果没有该缔约方的知情和同意,我不会增加或减少或在任何方

the same, and I will not add or diminish anything without the knowledge and consent of such party or parties that may alter the substance of the facts. I will not make or attest any act, contract or instrument in which I shall know there is violence or fraud or is contrary to law; and in all things I will act uprightly and justly in the business of a notary public according to the best of my skill and ability. So help me God.

SCHEDULE 3
Example of Notarial Seal

SCHEDULE 4
Certificate of Notary Public

IT IS HEREBY CERTIFIED that whose signature and seal of office are appended hereto is admitted and sworn a notary public for the Cayman Islands and is authorized to act as such until the 31st day of January, 20_____.

_____
Signature of holder
Dated this day of, 20_____.

_____
Clerk of the Court
(Renewed until the 31st day of January, 20_____.
Dated this day of, 20_____.

_____
(Clerk of the Court)
(Renewed until the 31st day of January, 20_____.
Dated this day of , 20_____.

_____
(Clerk of the Court)
(Renewed until the 31st day of January, 20_____.
Dated this day of , 20_____.

_____
(Clerk of the Court)
(Renewed until the 31st day of January , 20_____.
Dated this day of , 20_____.

_____
(Clerk of the Court)

SCHEDULE 5
Notarial Acts and Fee Schedule Item Fee ($)

Bills of Exchange
1. Noting protest for non-acceptance and recording the

面对该事务作出实质性的改变。我不会作出或证明任何我知道有暴力或欺诈的行为;在所有公证事务上,我会根据我的技术和知识,正义公正地行事。上帝保佑。

附表 3
公证印章示例

附表 4
公证人证明书

现在证明,公证处的签名盖章已被附上,接纳并授权 ×× 作为开曼群岛的公证人,该授权至 20×× 年 1 月 31 日为止有效。

_____
持有人签名
当天日期, 20×× 年。

_____
书记官签名
(续订至 20×× 年 1 月 31 日为止)
当天日期, 20×× 年。

_____
书记官签名
(续订至 20×× 年 1 月 31 日为止)
当天日期, 20×× 年。

_____
书记官签名
(续订至 20×× 年 1 月 31 日为止)
当天日期, 20×× 年。

_____
书记官签名
(续订至 20×× 年 1 月 31 日为止)
当天日期, 20×× 年。

_____
书记官签名

附表 5
公证行为和收费表(计价单位:美元)

汇票承兑
1. 拒绝承兑汇票的证书 ················ 15

same ··· 15
   2. Noting protest for non-payment and recording the same ··· 15

Ship's Protests
   3. Noting protest and recording the same. ···············15
   4. Drawing, engrossing and recording an extended marine protest together with confirmation of the same. ···············65

Survey of ships
   5. Warrant of Survey (under seal) and recording the same ··· 25
   6. Return of Survey (under seal) and recording the same ··· 25
   7. Certificate of character attached to the Report of Survey (under seal) ··· 25

Bottomry and Respondentia Bonds
   8. Drawing and engrossing of bottomry and respondentia bonds in triplicate and recording the same ··········65
   9. Acknowledgement of master to bond ·······15
   10. Confirmation of bond together with certificate attached thereto (under seal) ··· 35
   11. Acknowledgement of assignment of bond and certificate (under seal) attached in triplicate ································· 35

Miscellaneous
   12. Administering an oath ··········· 15
   13. Verification (under seal) of auctioneer's or agent's signature to accounts ································ 25
   14. Declaration before a notary public with a certificate (under seal) ··· 25
   15. Certificate (under seal) attached to a power of attorney ··· 25
   16. Identification of an interpreter ················ 15
   17. Any notarial copy of a document.················ one half of the fee charged for the original
   18. Certificate (under seal) attached to any notarial copy of a document ··· 25
   19. Recording any document for which no fee is fixed therein, per folio of seventy-two words ································· 15
   20. Any certificate of record ················ 25
   21. Witnessing of any document not hereinbefore mentioned ··· 15

SCHEDULE 6
Notarial Acts Book

1	2	3	4	5	6
Date of Notarial act	Nature of notarial act	Title and date of document (if applicable)	Names of party of parties to document	Name of person whose signature has been verified or to whom oath administered	Fee Charged

Publication in consolidated and revised form authorised by the Cabinet this 16th day of September, 2014.

附表 6
公证行为手册

1	2	3	4	5	6
公证时间	公证行为的性质	若可得，公证文书标题和时间	文件当事人姓名	签名人或宣誓人姓名	收费

出版于 2014 年 9 月 16 日，经内阁授权整理和修订。

2. 制作与记录拒绝支付汇票的证书 ···············15

海事报告
3. 制作并记录拒绝出具报告的证明 ···············15
4. 绘制、整理和记录扩展的海域并进行同样的确认 ··· 65

海事调查
5. 保密书（密封）并记录 ··········· 25
6. 返还保密书（密封）并记录 ··········· 25
7. 已盖章并附有认证证明的调查报告 ··········· 25

海损规则
8. 制作海损规则并将其抄录一式三份，并做相应记录 ··· 65
9. 船长对海损规则的确认 ··········· 15
10. 附盖章证明书的海损规则确认书 ··········· 35
11. 确认海损的分配和已盖章的证明书一式三份 ··· 35

其他事项
12. 管理誓词 ··········· 15
13. 拍卖人或代理人在账户上的签名的已盖章的证明 ··· 25
14. 向公证机关提交的申报证明（已盖章）······25
15. 附有授权书的证明（已盖章）··········· 25
16. 口译员的身份证明 ··········· 15
17. 文件的公证副本··········制作原件的一半费用
18. 对公证文书副本的证明（已盖章）···25
19. 记录没有固定费用的文件，每张含72个字的对开页 ··· 15
20. 任何记录的认证证书 ··········· 25
21. 为上文未提及的其他文件办理公证 ··········· 15

智利

法官组织法(节选公证部分)

REPUBLICA DE CHILE **LEY NOTARIAL**	**智利共和国** **公证法**

6. De los Procuradores y especialmente de los Procuradores del Número

Art. 394°- Los procuradores del número, son oficiales de la administración de justicia encargados de representar en juicio a las partes.

Habrá para cada comuna o agrupación de comunas los procuradores del número que el Presidente de la República determine, previo informe de la Corte de Apelaciones respectiva.

Concordancias: Código de Procedimiento Civil: artículos 7° y 553. Código de Procedimientos Penal: artículos 250, 635 y 659.

Art. 395°- El acto por el cual una parte encomienda a un procurador la representación de sus derechos en juicio, es un mandato que se regirá por las reglas establecidas en el Código Civil, para los contratos de esta clase, salvas las modificaciones contenidas en los artículos siguientes.

Concordancias: Código Orgánico de Tribunales: artículos 395 y 528. Código de Procedimiento Civil: artículos 6° y 7°. Código de Procedimiento Penal: artículo 64. Ley N°18.120 de 18 de mayo de 1982.

Art. 396°- No termina por la muerte del mandante el mandato para negocios judiciales.

Concordancias: Código de Procedimiento Civil: artículo 7°.

Art. N°397- Además de la recta ejecución del mandato, son obligaciones de los procuradores del número:

1) Dar los avisos convenientes sobre el estado de los

6. 代诉人

第394条 代诉人是指在法庭上代表诉讼双方的司法行政专职人员。各城镇或各地区均有由总统根据相应上诉法院规定而任命的代诉人。

参见:《民事诉讼法》第7条和第553条;《刑事诉讼法》第250、第635条和第659条。

第395条 根据《民法典》规定,在法庭上,诉讼方的权利须由代诉人代表,除非下列条款发生变更。

参见:《法院组织法》第395条和第528条;《民事诉讼法》第6条和第7条;《刑事诉讼法》第64条;1982年5月18日颁布的第18120号法律。

第396条 司法事务中委托权不因委托人的死亡而终止。

参见:《民事诉讼法》第7条。

第397条 除依法行使委托权外,代诉人的义务还包括:

1)及时告知双方律师代诉案件的进程和裁决结

asuntos que tuvieren a su cargo, o sobre las providencias y resoluciones que en ellos se libraren, a los abogados a quienes estuviere encomendada la defensa de los mismos asuntos, y

2) Servir gratuitamente a los pobres con arreglo a lo dispuesto por el artículo 595.

Concordancias: Código de Procedimiento Civil: artículo 7°.

Art. N°398- Ante la Corte Suprema sólo se podrá comparecer por abogado habilitado o por procurador del número y ante las Cortes de Apelaciones las partes podrán comparecer personalmente o representadas por abogado o por procurador del número.

El litigante rebelde sólo podrá comparecer ante estos últimos tribunales representando por abogado habilitado o por procurador del número.

Concordancias: Código de Procedimiento Civil: artículos 4°, 7°, 202 y 308. Código de Procedimiento Penal: artículos 67, 278, 429, 526 y 659.

7. Los Notarios

Concordancias: Decreto N° 172 Reglamento Consular, D.O. 29.07.1977: Capítulos XXXII y XXXIII sobre funciones notariales de los Cónsules chilenos en el extranjero.

1) Su Organizacin

Artículo 399. Los notarios son ministros de fe pública encargados de autorizar y guardar en su archivo los instrumentos que ante ellos se otorgaren, de dar a las partes interesadas los testimonios que pidieren, y de practicar las demás diligencias que la ley les encomiende.

Concordancias: Código de Procedimiento Civil: artículo 648.

Artículo 400. En cada comuna o agrupación de comunas que constituya territorio jurisdiccional de jueces de letras, habrá a lo menos un notario.

En aquellos territorios jurisdiccionales formados por una agrupación de comunas, el Presidente de la República, previo informe favorable de la Corte de Apelaciones respectiva, podrá crear nuevas notarias disponiendo que los titulares restablezcan sus oficios dentro del territorio de una comuna determinada. Estos notarios podrá ejercer sus funciones dentro de todo el territorio del juzgado de letras en lo civil que corresponda.

En aquellas comunas en que exista más de una no-

果。

2）依第 595 条之规定，为穷人提供无偿辩护。

参见：《民事诉讼法》第 7 条。

第 398 条　最高法院中诉讼双方仅可由授权律师或代诉人代理出庭，上诉法院中除上述两者外，诉讼方可亲自出庭。

在上述两院中，若诉讼方缺席，则由授权律师或代诉人代理出庭。

参见：《民事诉讼法》第 4 条、第 7 条、第 202 条和第 308 条。《刑事诉讼法》第 67 条、第 278 条、第 429 条、第 526 条和第 659 条。

7. 公证员

参见：1977 年 7 月 29 日官方公报上发布的第 172 号关于领事条例的法令，第三十二章和第三十三章关于智利驻外使馆领事公证职责的相关规定。

1）组织

第 399 条　公证员是经法律授权，负责对他人所需的各种文件进行授权、记录、保管以及对其他行为进行公证、出具公证书的公职人员。

参见：《民事诉讼法》第 648 条。

第 400 条　同一司法管辖范围内的各城镇或各地区至少配有一名公证员。

如某司法辖区由多个城镇组成，总统有权在相应上诉法院同意的前提下，设立面向特定单独城镇的公证处。该公证处的公证员同时兼有处理同一司法管辖范围内民事事务的权力。

如同一司法辖区有多个公证员，总统须对其进行

taria, el Presidente de la República asignará a cada una de ellas una numeración correlativa, independientemente del nombre de quienes las sirvan.

Ningún notario podrá ejercer sus funciones fuera de su respectivo territorio.

Artículo 401. Son funciones de los notarios:

1°- Entender los instrumentos públicos con arreglo a las instrucciones que, de palabra o escrito, les dieren las partes otorgantes;

2°- Levantar inventarios solemnes;

3°- Efectuar protestos de letras de cambio y demás documentos mercantiles;

4°- Notificar los traspasos de acciones y constituciones y notificaciones de prenda que se les solicitaren;

5°- Asistir a las juntas generales de accionistas de sociedades anónimas, para los efectos que la ley o reglamento de ellas exigieren;

6°- En general, dar fe de los hechos para que fueren requeridos y que no estuvieren encomendados a otros funcionarios;

7°- Guardar y conservar en riguroso orden cronológico los instrumentos que ante ellos se otorguen, en forma de precaver todo extravío y hacer fácil y expedito su examen;

8°- Otorgar certificados o testimonios de los actos celebrados ante ellos o protocolizados en sus registros;

9°-Facilitar, a cualquiera persona que lo solicite, el examen de los instrumentos públicos que ante ellos se otorguen y documentos que protocolicen;

10. Autorizar las firmas que se estampen en documentos privados, sea en su presencia o cuya autenticidad les conste

11. Las demás que les encomienden las leyes.

Artículo 402. Cando un notario se ausentare o inhabilitare para el ejercicio de sus funciones, el juez de letras respectivo de turno, designará al abogado que haya de reemplazarle, mientras dure el impedimento o estuviere sin proveerse el cargo.

En los lugares de asiento de Corte de Apelaciones la designación de reemplazante corresponderá al Presidente de ella.

En ambos casos y siempre que no se trate de la aplicación de medidas disciplinarias que provoquen la inhabilidad del notario, éste podrá proponer al juez, el abogado que deba reemplazarlo bajo su responsabilidad.

Durante el tiempo que durare la ausencia o inhabilidad del notario, el reemplazante designado podrá autorizar

编号，编号与公证员姓名无关。

公证员仅能在其所属辖区范围内行使职权。

第401条 公证员的职权：

1. 按照公证当事人的口头或书面指令，知晓公证办理目的，以办理公证；

2. 进行盘点并加以证明；

3. 执行汇票等商务文件的拒付；

4. 按要求对股票转让、抵押和质押事项进行通知；

5. 依据相关法律法规规定，参加股份有限公司的股东大会；

6. 通常，公证员有权对其他公务人员无权代理的事件进行审查和公证；

7. 对签发的公证书进行妥善保管，并按时间排序，以便查阅；

8. 对在公证员亲自见证下订立的文书或者在其公证登记簿中登记的事项出具证明或经核证副本；

9. 协助任一申请人核查在公证员的见证下出具的公共文书或者由公证员存档登记的文件；

10. 确认私署文书签名的有效性；

11. 法律赋予公证员的其他职权；

第402条 当公证员缺席或者无法行使其法定职权时，时任的主管法官应临时指派一名律师在此期间代为履行其职权。

在上诉法院所在地，对公证员接替人选的任命权应由上诉法院院长行使。

上述两种情形中，除公证员因违纪被剥夺职权外，公证员均可向地区法官推荐其替补人选，并为此负责。

在公证员缺任或者无法行使其法定职权期间，接替人员有权批准或完成之前公证员已开始处理但尚未

las escrituras públicas y dar término a aquellas actuaciones iniciadas por el titular que hayan quedado pendientes, debiendo dejar constancia de tal circunstancia en el respectivo instrumento. Del mismo modo podrá proceder el titular respecto de las escrituras públicas y actuaciones iniciadas por el reemplazante.

2) De las escrituras públicas

Artículo 403. Escritura pública es el instrumento público o auténtico otorgado con las solemnidades que fija esta ley, por el competente notario, e incorporado en su protocolo o registro público.

Artículo 404. Las escrituras públicas deben escribirse en idioma castellano y estilo claro y preciso, y en ellas no podrán emplearse abreviaturas, cifras ni otros signos que los caracteres de uso corriente, ni contener espacios en blanco.

Podrán emplearse también palabras de otro idioma que sean generalmente usadas o como término de una determinada ciencia o arte.

El notario deberá inutilizar, con su firma y sello, el reverso no escrito de las hojas en que se contenga una escritura pública o de sus copias.

Artículo 405. Las escrituras públicas deberán otorgarse ante notario y podrán ser extendidas manuscritas, mecanografiadas o en otra forma que leyes especiales autoricen. Deberán indicar el lugar y fecha de su otorgamiento; la individualización del notario autorizante y el nombre de los comparecientes, con expresión de su nacionalidad, estado civil, profesión, domicilio y cédula de identidad, salvo en el caso de extranjeros y chilenos radicados en el extranjero, quienes podrán acreditar su identidad con el pasaporte o con el documento de identificación con que se les permitió su ingreso al país.

Además, el notario al autorizar la escritura indicará el número de anotación que tenga en el repertorio, la que se hará el día en que sea firmada por el primero de los otorgantes.

El reglamento fijará la forma y demás características que deben tener lo originales de escritura pública y sus copias.

Artículo 406. Las escrituras serán rubricadas y selladas en todas sus fojas por el notario.

Carecerá de valor el retiro unilateral de la firma estampada en el instrumento, si éste ya lo hubiere suscrito otro de los otorgantes.

完成的各种文件，并在公证书中注明。同样，公证员回归其岗位后也可继续处理由其临时接替人员受理的公证事项。

2）公证书

第 403 条　公证书是由有履职能力的公证员依法制作并收录于其公证登记簿立卷归档的权威性文件。

第 404 条　公证书必须用西班牙语书写，语言简明准确，不可使用文字或数字的缩写，或其他符号。只可使用常见文字，文本中不可留空。

公证书在使用科学或艺术专业词汇时也可用其他常用语言书写。

对于公证纸背面没有内容的，公证员应在公证书及其副本的背面签名盖章，以兹证明。

第 405 条　公证书应由公证员当面签发给公证申请人，公证书可为手写、机打或其他法律所允许的形式。公证书中必须写明签发时间和地点，承办公证员的独立自主性，申请人的姓名、国籍、婚姻状况、职业、住址和身份证号码。外国公民和长居国外的智利公民可提供护照或任何允许其进入智利的证件作为其身份证明。

此外，公证员在签发公证书时应告知申请人公证书编号，此编号自申请人签收公证书时生成。

公证书及其副本的格式和其他特征由法律规定。

第 406 条　公证书的每一页均须由公证员盖章画押，并由公证当事人共同签字。单方签字公证书视为无效。

Artículo 407. Cualquiera de las partes podrá exigir al notario que antes de firmarla, lea la escritura en alta voz, pero si todos los otorgantes están de acuerdo en omitir esta formalidad, leyéndola ellos mismos, podrá procederse así.

Artículo 408. Si alguno de los comparecientes o todos ellos no supieren o no pudieran firmar, lo hará a su ruego uno de los otorgantes que no tenga interés contrario, según el texto de la escritura, o una tercera persona, debiendo los que no firmen poner junto a la del que la hubiere firmado a su ruego, la impresión del pulgar de la mano derecha o, en su defecto, el de la izquierda. El notario dejará constancia de este hecho o de la imposibilidad absoluta de efectuarlo.

Artículo 409. Siempre que alguno de los otorgantes o el notario lo exijan, los firmantes dejarán su impresión digital en la forma indicada en el artículo anterior.

Artículo 410. No será obligatorio insertar en la escritura documentos de ninguna especie, a menos que alguno de los otorgantes lo requiera.

Si en virtud de una ley debe insertarse en la escritura determinado documento, se entenderá cumplida esta obligación con su exhibición al notario, quien dejará constancia de este hecho antes o después de la firma de los otorgantes indicando la fecha y número del documento, si los tuviere y la autoridad que lo expidió; y el documento será entregado al final del protocolo.

Artículo 411. Se tendrán por no escritas las adiciones, apostillas, entrerenglonaduras, raspaduras o enmendaduras u otra alteración en las escrituras originales que no aparezcan salvadas al final y antes de las firmas de los que la suscriban.

Corresponderá al notario, salvar las adiciones, apostillas, entrerenglonaduras, raspaduras o enmendaduras u otra alteración en las escrituras originales.

Artículo 412. Serán nulas las escrituras públicas:

1°. Que contengan disposiciones o estipulaciones a favor del notario que las autorice, de su cónyuge, ascendientes, descendientes o hermanos, y

2°. Aquellas en que los otorgantes no hayan acreditado su identidad en alguna de las formas establecidas en el artículo 405 o en que no aparezcan las firmas de las partes y el notario.

Artículo 413. Las escrituras de constitución, modificación, resciliación o liquidación de sociedades, de liquidación de sociedades conyugales, de partición de bienes, escrituras constitutivas de personalidad jurídica, de asociaciones de canalistas, cooperativas, contratos de transacciones y contratos de emisión de bonos de sociedades

第 407 条　公证当事人可在签字前要求公证员高声朗读公证书，如所有公证申请人均表示同意，可省略此步骤，由当事人自行阅读公证书。

第 408 条　如果某个或所有公证当事人不会或不能签署公证书，可以由与之没有利益冲突的其他当事人或者第三方代为签署，具体视公证书内容而定，代签时申请人要位于签字人身旁，画押时申请人需用右手大拇指，如有不便则用左手大拇指。进行代签的，公证员应当在公证书中予以说明；如果仍未能签署，公证员应当说明无法签字确认的理由。

第 409 条　如果任一公证申请人或公证员提出画押要求，签字人应遵循上条原则进行画押。

第 410 条　公证书中无须附带任何其他附件，但公证申请人有要求的除外。

如法律要求公证书须附带某类文件，申请人向公证员进行展示即可被认作有效。同时公证员要在申请人签署文件之前或之后书面证明自己已经看到过所说的这些附件，并且要写清公证书的编号和日期，上述的这些要求都是在有关单位对附件有要求的情况下才需进行的。公证文件会在公证流程最后递交给申请方。

第 411 条　凡是未在公证结尾出现、未在公证当事人签署前发现的添加、尾注、行间文字、删减、划除或者对原文的任何修改均被视为无效。

公证员负责对原文进行添加、尾注、插入行间文字、删减、划除或其他修改。

第 412 条　出现下列情形的，公证书无效：
1. 公证书中包含有利于公证员或其配偶、父母、子女或兄弟姐妹等近亲属的内容或条款；

2. 申请人未提供第 405 条规定的任何身份认定证件，或申请人或公证员未签名。

第 413 条　公司的注册、变动、解散、清算，夫妻共有公司的清算，财产分割，法人契约，运河公司，合资公司，贸易协议，发放企业债券等事项的文书，只有具备由执业律师签署的副本方可出具公证书并记入公证登记簿。

anónimas, sólo podrán ser extendidas en los protocolos notariales sobre la base de minutas firmadas por algún abogado.

Asimismo, el notario dejará constancia en las escrituras del nombre del abogado redactor de la minuta. La omisión de esa exigencia no afectará la validez de la escritura.

Las obligaciones establecidas en los incisos anteriores no regirán en los lugares donde no hubiere abogados en un número superior a tres.

El notario autorizará las escrituras una vez que éstas estén completas y hayan sido firmadas por todos los comparecientes.

Artículo 414. En cuanto al otorgamiento de testamento, se estará a lo establecido al respecto en el Código Civil, debiendo el notario dejar constancia de la hora y lugar en que se otorgue. La identidad del testador deberá ser acreditada en la forma establecida en el artículo 405. No regirá esta exigencia cuando, a juicio del notario, circunstancias calificadas así lo aconsejen.

Concordancias: Código Civil: 999, 1014 y 1016. D. F. L. N° 298 sobre testamentos otorgados en Término Antártico Chileno, D. O. 3.10.1956.

3) De las protocolizaciones

Artículo 415. Protocolización es el hecho de agregar un documento al final del registro de un notario, a pedido de quien lo solicita.

Para que la protocolización surta efecto legal deberá dejarse constancia de ella en el libro repertorio el día en que se presente el documento, en la forma establecida en el artículo 430.

Concordancias: Código de Procedimiento Civil: Artículo 863.

Artículo 416. No pueden protocolizarse, ni su protocolización producirá efecto alguno, los documentos en que se consignen actos o contratos con causa u objeto ilícitos, salvo que lo pidan personas distintas de los otorgantes o beneficiarios de ellos.

Artículo 417. La protocolización de testamentos cerrados, orales o privilegiados, ordenada por los jueces y la de los otorgados fuera del registro del notario, deberán hacerse agregando su original al protocolo con los antecedentes que lo acompañen.

Para protocolizar los testamentos será suficiente la sola firma del notario en el libro repertorio.

同时，公证员可将经办律师的姓名写入公证书。未写入的，不影响公证书的法律效力。

执业律师人数不足三人的地区，不适用上述规定。

一旦上述文件备齐并由所有当事人签字，公证员便可签发公证书。

第414条　遗嘱公证以《民法典》规定为准，公证员应标明公证的时间和地点。立嘱人应根据第405条规定的形式证明身份。如公证员依情所判，立嘱人身份明确，可不适用上述规定。

参见:《民法典》第999条、第1014条和第1016条；1956年10月3日官方公报上发布的第298号法令有关智利安达迪克省遗嘱公证的规定。

3）公证登记

第415条　公证登记是指在申请人的要求下将公证书记录在公证员的档案中。

公证登记只有在公证书签发当天、并以第403条规定的形式进行登记的情况下才具有法律效力。

参见:《民事诉讼法》第863条。

第416条　对于目的或缘由非法的文书或合同，不得办理公证登记，即使登记也不具有法律效力，但当事人或受益人以外的人员提出要求的除外。

第417条　法官要求的并未由公证员备录的遗嘱人已逝的、口述的或特殊情况的遗嘱公证，应附上之前所有相关文件的原件才可登记。

遗嘱公证登记仅需公证员在公证备案录上签字即可。

Artículo 418. El documento protocolizado sólo podrá ser desglosado del protocolo en virtud de decreto judicial.

Artículo 419. Sin perjuicio de lo dispuesto en el artículo 1703 del Código Civil la fecha de un instrumento privado se contará respecto de terceros desde su anotación en el repertorio con arreglo al presente Código.

Artículo 420. Una vez protocolizados, valdrán como instrumentos públicos:

1°- Los testamentos cerrados y abiertos en forma legal;

2°- Los testamentos solemnes abiertos que se otorguen en hojas sueltas, siempre que su protocolización se haya efectuado a más tardar, dentro del primer día siguiente hábil al de su otorgamiento;

3°- Los testamentos menos solemnes o privilegiados que no hayan sido autorizados por notario, previo decreto del juez competente;

4°- Las actas de oferta de pago; y

5°- Los instrumentos otorgados en el extranjero, las transcripciones y las traducciones efectuadas por el interprete oficial o los peritos nombrados al efecto por el juez competente y debidamente legalizadas, que sirvan para otorgar escrituras en Chile.

Concordancias: Código Civil: artículo 1014.

4) De las copias de escrituras públicas y documentos

Protocolizados y de los documentos privados

Artículo 421. Sólo podrán dar copias autorizadas de escrituras públicas o documentos protocolizados el notario autorizante, el que lo subroga o suceda legalmente al archivero a cuyo cargo esté el protocolo respectivo.

Artículo 422. Las copias podrán ser manuscritas, dactilografiadas, impresas, fotocopiadas, litografiadas o fotograbadas. En ellas deberá expresarse que son testimonio fiel de su original y llevarán la fecha, la firma y sello del funcionario autorizante. El notario deberá otorgar tantas copias cuantas se soliciten.

Artículo 423. Los notarios no podrán otorgar copia de una escritura pública mientras no se hayan pagado los impuestos que correspondan.

Esta misma norma se aplicará a los documentos protocolizados.

Artículo 424. Derogado.1

Artículo 425. Los notarios podrán autorizar las firmas que se estampen en documentos privados, siempre que den fe del conocimiento o de la identidad de los firmantes y

第418条 只有司法判令才可以抽除入档后的公证书。

第419条 依据《民法典》第1703条规定以及现行法律，私署文书对第三方的生效日期应当从被列入公证备案录之日起算。

第420条 一旦登记，下列公证书将被视为公共文书：

1. 符合法律规定、遗嘱人健在或已逝的遗嘱；

2. 公证签发后第一个工作日内登记的、遗嘱人健在的散页的正式遗嘱；

3. 在有行事能力法官判令下、非正式或特殊情况下未被公证员签署的遗嘱；

4. 付款通知书；

5. 在国外签发的，或由法官委任的翻译员或专家进行翻译或记录的被公证过的公证文书，且这些公证文书的目的是在智利境内进行公证使用。

参见：《民法典》第1014条。

4）公证书、公证登记文件和私署文书的副本

第421条 只有被授权的公证员才可签发各类公证书的副本。依法替代或继任的公证书备案公证员也可对其前任负责的公证书进行拷贝复制。

第422条 副本可以由手写、打印、印刷、影印、平版印刷或拍照等方式制作。所有副本均应与原文内容一致，并由授权官员签字盖章。公证员应根据申请人要求的份数进行复印。

第423条 公证员不能对没有上缴相应税费的公证书进行复印。

公证登记文件同样适用本规定。

第424条 本条已废止。

第425条 在确认签署人身份的前提下，公证员可对个人文件上的签名进行公证。公证时要注明签署日期。第409条规定也适用于此。

dejen constancia de la fecha en que se firman. Se aplicará también en este caso la regla del artículo 409.

Los testimonios autorizados por el notario, como copias, fotocopias o reproducciones fieles de documentos públicos o privados, tendrán valor en conformidad a las reglas generales.

5) De la falta de fuerza legal de las escrituras, Coplas testimonios notariales

Artículo 426. No se considerará pública o auténtica la escritura:

1°- Que no fuere autorizada por persona que no sea notario o por notario incompetente, suspendido o inhabilitado en forma legal;

2°- Que no esté incorporada en el protocolo o que éste no pertenezca al notario autorizante o al de quien esté subrogando ilegalmente;

3°- En que no conste la firma de los comparecientes o no se hubiere salvado este requisito en la forma prescrita en el artículo 408;

4°- Que no esté escrita en idioma castellano;

5°- Que en las firmas de las partes o del notario o en las escrituras manuscritas, no se haya usado tinta fija, o de pasta indeleble, y

6°- Que no se firme dentro de los sesenta días siguientes de su fecha de anotación en el repertorio.

Artículo 427. Los notarios sólo podrán dar copias íntegras de las escrituras o documentos protocolizados, salvo los casos en que la ley ordene otra cosa, o que por decreto judicial se le ordene certificar sobre parte de ellos.

Concordancias: Código de Procedimiento Penal: Artículos 169 y 170.

Artículo 428. Las palabras que en cualquier documento notarial aparezcan interlineadas, enmendadas o sobrepasadas, para tener valor deberán ser salvadas antes de las firmas del documento respectivo, y en caso de que no lo sean, se tendrán por no escritas.

Concordancias: Código de Procedimiento Penal: Artículos 169 y 170.

6) De los libros que deben llevar los notarlos

Artículo 429. Todo notario deberá llevar un protocolo, el que se formará Insertando las escrituras en el orden numérico que les haya correspondido en el repertorio.

A continuación de las escrituras se agregarán los documentos a que se refiere el artículo 415, también conforme

公证员公证过的证据，包括公共或个人材料的各种副本，依据相关法规应具有法律效力。

5）无效公证书，经核证副本

第 426 条　下列公证书不具有公共性或可信性：

1. 由非公证员或需回避、停职或被剥夺法律资格的公证员公证的；

2. 未登记或未由相应授权公证员或其合法代理进行公证的；

3. 公证当事人未签字，且未按第 408 条规定在公证书中予以说明的；

4. 未用西班牙语书写的；

5. 未用不可擦除的墨水笔或书写工具进行签字或手写文字的；

6. 公证书备案后 60 日内未签署的。

第 427 条　公证员仅可对公证书进行整体复印，但法律另有规定，或者根据司法令之规定对其中一部分进行证明的情况除外。

参见：《刑事诉讼法》第 169 条、第 170 条。

第 428 条　如公证书中含有隐含、修订、覆盖等引申内容，应在双方签署前进行解释，如未解释则视为无引申内容。

参见：《刑事诉讼法》第 169 条、第 170 条。

6）公证员应开立的各类工作簿

第 429 条　所有公证员须配有公证登记簿，其中应放有与备案录编号一致的公证书。

除公证书外，公证登记簿中也应添加第 415 条规定的文件，其编号也应与备案录编号一致。

al orden numérico asignado en el repertorio.

 Los protocolos deberán empastarse, a lo menos, cada dos meses no pudiendo formarse cada libro con más de quinientas fojas, incluidos los documentos protocolizados, que se agregarán al final en el mismo orden del repertorio. Cada foja, se numerará en su parte superior con letras y números.

 En casos calificados, los notarios podrán solicitar de la Corte de Apelaciones respectivas autorización para efectuar los empastes pro períodos superiores, siempre que no excedan de un año.

 Cada protocolo llevará, además, un índice de las escrituras y documentos protocolizados que contenga, y en su confección se observará lo dispuesto en el inciso tercero del artículo 431. Se iniciará con un certificado del notario en que exprese la fecha en que lo inicie, enunciación del respectivo contrato o escritura y nombre de los otorgantes de la escritura con que principia.

 Transcurridos dos meses, desde la fecha de cierre del protocolo, el notario certificará las escrituras que hubieren quedado sin efecto por no haberse suscrito por todos los otorgantes. Este certificado se pondrá al final del protocolo indicando el número de escrituras y documentos que contiene y la enunciación de las que hayan quedado sin efecto.

 Artículo 430. Todo notario llevará un libro repertorio de escrituras públicas y de documentos protocolizados en el que se dará un número a cada uno de estos instrumentos por riguroso orden de presentación.

 Cuando se tratare de escrituras, se dejará constancia en este libro de la fecha en que se efectúa la anotación; de las partes que la otorgan, a menos que sean más de dos, pues en este caso se indicarán los nombres de los dos primeros comparecientes seguidos de la expresión "y otros", del nombre del abogado o abogados si la hubieren redactado y de la denominación del acto o contrato.

 Tratándose de documentos protocolizados, se dejará constancia de la fecha en que se presenten, de las indicaciones necesarias para individualizarlos, del número de páginas de que consten y de la identidad de la persona que pida su protocolización.

 Sin embargo, si la protocolización se indicare en una escritura pública, bastará la anotación ordenada en el inciso segundo.

 El libro repertorio se cerrará diariamente, indicándose el número de la última anotación, la fecha y firma del notario. Si no hubiere efectuado anotaciones, se expresará esta circunstancia.

公证登记簿每册不得超过500页，应至少每两个月进行重新装订，每页页眉处应用数字和字母编码，登记簿最后要含括公证文件，与备案录编号顺序一致。

特殊情形下，公证员可向当地上诉法院申请许可，延长更新装订公证登记簿的时间，但更新频率不得超过一年。

每册公证登记簿配有公证书目录，制作方式参见第431条规定。公证登记簿开篇需由公证员撰写公证书，阐明本册记录的开始日期和首篇公证书的申请人姓名或公证事宜。

公证登记簿成册2个月后，公证员会取消其中申请人未签字接收的公证书效力，并对此进行公证。此公证书将附在公证登记簿的最后，标明失效公证书的编号，并对失效公证的内容予以说明。

第430条　所有公证员须配有备案录，其中对所有处理的公证书严格按照接收日期进行排序和标号。

如为公共公证书，备案录应记载公证书记录日期、申请方（如超过两人则记录前两人姓名，后加"其他"）、律师姓名（如有参与）以及公证名称。

如为个人公证登记，备案录将记载申请日期、登记缘由、页数、申请人身份。

如为公共公证书登记，则在上述第2款内容后加注即可。

备案录每日清点，须标明最后一份公证书的记录、日期和公证员的签名。如当日未有任何公证书记录，也应写明情况。

La falta de las anotaciones señaladas en el inciso segundo, no afectará la validez de una escritura pública otorgada, sin perjuicio de la responsabilidad del notario.

Artículo 431. El notario llevará un libro público, en el que anotará las escrituras por orden alfabético de los otorgantes; y otro privado en el que anotará, en la misma forma, los testamentos cerrados con indicación del lugar de su otorgamiento y del nombre y domicilio de sus testigos.

El primero estará a disposición del público, debiendo exhibirlo a quien lo solicite y el segundo deberá mantenerlo reservado, no teniendo obligación de exhibirlo, sino por decreto de juez competente o ante una solicitud de un particular que acompañe el certificado de defunción que corresponda al otorgante del testamento.

Los índices de escrituras deberán ser hechos con el nombre de los otorgantes y si se tratare de personas jurídicas, sucesiones u otra clase de comunidades bastará con anotar el nombre de éstas.

Artículo 432. El notario es responsable de las faltas, defectos o deterioros de los protocolos, mientras los conserven en su poder.

Artículo 433. El notario entregará al archivero judicial que corresponda, los protocolos a su cargo, que tengan mas de un año desde la fecha de cierre, y los índices de escrituras públicas que tengan más de diez años.

Artículo 434. Los protocolos y documentos protocolizados o agregados a los mismos, deberán guardarse en cajas de seguridad o bóvedas contra incendio.

Concordancias: Código de Procedimiento Penal: Artículo 152.

Artículo 435. Los protocolos y cualquier documento que se hubiere entregado al notario bajo custodia en razón de su oficio, sólo podrán sacarse de sus oficinas por decreto judicial o en casos de fuerza mayor. Si se tratare de decreto judicial, el notario personalmente deberá ejecutarlo.

Artículo 436. En los caso de pérdida, robo o inutilización de los protocolos o documentos pertenecientes a la notaria, el notario dará cuenta inmediatamente al ministerio público para que inicie la correspondiente investigación.

Artículo 437. Los protocolos o documentos perdidos o inutilizados deberán reponerse por orden del visitador de la notaría, con citación de los interesados.

Artículo 438. La reposición, en cuanto sea posible, se efectuará con las copias autorizadas expedidas por el notario, declaraciones de testigos y demás pruebas que el

记录时，本条第2款所示备案录格式如有缺漏，并不影响公共公证书的法律效力，也不能追究公证员的责任。

第431条 所有公证员须配有一本公证书公开记录。这本记录中应把所有公证申请人的姓名按字母顺序排列。还须配有一本不公开记录，同样按字母顺序排列所有去世后生效遗嘱的公证地点以及证人的姓名和住址。

公开记录面向大众，可申请查看。不公开记录应保密，无义务向他人展示，只有当收到法院法令或遗嘱人死亡证明时才被允许公开。

公证书目录应由申请人姓名组成。对于法人、继承人或其他类型，只写明其姓名或名称。

第432条 公证登记簿由公证员保管，对其丢失、损坏或破损负责。

第433条 公证员须将其处理的、自成册之日起超过1年的公证登记簿，以及超过10年的公共公证书目录交给法院档案馆保存。

第434条 公证登记簿和其他公证书均应放置在保险柜或防火的建筑物中保存。

参见：《刑事诉讼法》第152条。

第435条 公证登记簿或其他交由公证员保管的文件，只能因法院传令或其他不可抗力因素带出其办公室。公证员需亲自执行法院对其保管文件的传令。

第436条 如公证处发生失窃、偷盗或破坏，公证员需立即通知检察机关，以便其开展调查。

第437条 丢失或被破坏的公证登记簿或文件，应在公证处督察员的要求下进行恢复工作，并对相关人员进行传讯。

第438条 恢复工作应以公证员之前签发的文本副本为基础，同时配合证人的证词以及法院要求的其他必要证据。

tribunal estime convenientes.

Las personas que tengan copias autorizadas de las originales estarán obligadas a presentarlas al tribunal, y en caso de negarse a ello, se aplicará el procedimiento de apremio establecido en el artículo 276 del Código de Procedimiento Civil.

Artículo 439. Los testamentos abiertos o cerrados que se otorguen ante notario u otros funcionarios públicos que hagan sus veces, deberán figura, sin perjuicio de su inserción en los índices a que se refiere el artículo 431, en un registro índice general de disposiciones de última voluntad, que estará a cargo y bajo la responsabilidad del archivero judicial de Santiago. Este registro tendrá dos índices, uno para los testamentos abiertos y otro para los testamentos cerrados, los que se regirán por lo dispuesto en el inciso final del artículo 431 y deberán indicar, además, el funcionario ante quien se haya otorgado.

Estos registros serán reservados sin que ellos puedan ser exhibidos o se informe respecto de ellos, salvo por orden judicial o ante una petición de un particular que acompañe el certificado de defunción que corresponda al otorgante del testamento.

Los notarios de las tres primeras categorías del Escalafón deberán remitir al archivero judicial de Santiago, dentro de los diez primeros días de cada mes, por carta certificada, las nóminas de los testamentos abiertos y de los testamentos cerrados que se hubieren otorgado en sus oficios durante el mes anterior, con los datos indicados en el inciso tercero del artículo 431. Los notarios de la cuarta categoría del Escalafón y los funcionarios públicos que hagan las veces de notario, deberán hacer igual remisión por períodos bimestrales dentro de los diez primeros días siguientes al vencimiento del respectivo bimestre.

7) De las infracciones y sanciones

Artículo 440. El notario que faltare a sus obligaciones podrá ser sancionado disciplinariamente con amonestación, censura o suspensión, según sea la gravedad del hecho.

Sin embargo, podrá aplicarse la sanción de exoneración del cargo al notario que fuere reincidente en el período de dos años en los hechos siguientes:

a) Si se insertare en el protocolo escrituras o instrumentos sin haberse dado fiel cumplimiento a las exigencias de los artículos 405 y 430;

b) Si por su culpa o negligencia deja de tener la

丢失公证书副本的持有者须向法院提交该副本；如不配合，将依据《民事诉讼法》第276条规定对其采取强制措施。

第439条 在不与第431条创建目录发生冲突的前提下，遗嘱人已逝或健在的遗嘱在提交给公证人后，应在由圣地亚哥司法档案馆负责的遗嘱总条约下进行备案登记。该登记分为遗嘱人已逝和健在两类。第431条最后一款中涉及的情形应同时登记公务员的姓名。

该登记不对外公开，除司法命令、持有遗嘱人死亡证明的个人要求的情况外。

公证员分级前三类的须在每月前10日以挂号信的方式向圣地亚哥司法档案馆寄发一份上个月各类遗嘱的公证情况，其中要注明第431条第三款中规定的信息。第四类及临时公证员须每两个月一寄。

7）违反与处罚

第440条 未尽其职的公证员将会根据情节的严重程度，受到警告、谴责或停职的纪律处分。

公证员在2年内，再次触犯下列条款的，可被免职：

a）未依据第405条、第430条之规定在公证登记簿和备案录中录入公证书的；

b）由于公证员的过错或疏忽造成公证书失效或

calidad de pública o auténtica una escritura en virtud de cualquiera de las circunstancias previstas en el artículo 426;

c) Si no cumpliere con lo dispuesto en el artículo 421 o no cumpliere la obligación de salvar las palabras interlineadas, enmendadas o sobrepasadas establecidas en el artículo 411;

d) Si se perdiere un protocolo del notario por culpa o negligencia de éste, y

e) Si faltare a las obligaciones señaladas en los N° 7 y 8 del artículo 401 y en el 423.

Artículo 441. Si en alguno de los hechos descritos en las letras a), b), c) y e) del artículo 440 mediare malicia del notario, éste será castigado con la pena que señala el artículo 193 del Código Penal.

Artículo 442. El notario que ejerciere funciones de tal fuera del territorio para el que hubiere sido nombrado, sufrirá la pena de reclusión menor en cualquiera de sus grados.

Artículo 443. El notario que incurriere en falsedad autentificando una firma en conformidad con el artículo 425, que no corresponda a la persona que haya suscrito el instrumento respectivo, incurrirá en las penas del artículo 193 del Código Penal.

Cuando por negligencia o ignorancia inexcusables, autentificare una firma que no corresponda a la persona que aparece suscribiéndola, sufrirá la pena de presidio menor en su grado mínimo o multa de cinco a diez ingresos mínimos mensuales.

Concordancias: Código de Procedimiento Penal: Artículos 169 y 170.

Artículo 444. Derogado.

Artículo 445. Toda sanción penal impuesta a un notario en virtud de este párrafo, lleva consigo la inhabilitación especial perpetua para el ejercicio del cargo, sin perjuicio de las otras penas accesorias que procedan en conformidad al Código Penal.

8) Los Conservadores

Artículo 446. Son conservadores los ministros de fe encargados de los registros conservatorios de bienes raíces, de comercio, de minas, de accionistas de sociedades propiamente mineras, de asociaciones de canalistas, de prenda agraria, de prenda industrial, de especial de prenda y demás que les encomienden las leyes.

Artículo 447. Habrá un conservador en cada comuna

第 426 条中规定的任何情形的；

c）未履行第 421 条规定，或未依照第 411 条规定对公证书中的隐含、修正、覆盖等内容做出注解的；

d）由于公证员的过错或疏忽，造成公证书丢失的；

e）未履行第 401 条第 7 项和第 8 项以及第 423 条规定的义务的。

第 441 条 如果第 440 条第 2 款第 a 项、第 b 项、第 c 项和第 e 项中所列的任一情形，是出于公证员的主观故意，应当依据《刑法典》第 193 条予以处分。

第 442 条 公证员在其所属辖区外进行公证的，无论情节严重，均应处以短期监禁徒刑。

第 443 条 对第 425 条规定中的签名进行虚假公证、签字人与申请人不符的，构成对《刑法典》第 193 条的违反。

由于公证人的疏忽或过失，对不实签名进行公证的，情节轻微的将处以短期监禁徒刑，或 5 倍至 10 倍最低月工资水平的罚金。

参见：《刑事诉讼法》第 169 条、第 170 条。

第 444 条 本条已废止。

第 445 条 此章规定的所有对公证员的处罚措施，都配合实施永久取消公证员行业资格，并与刑法规定的其他附加判决保持一致。

8）保管人

第 446 条 保管人是指负责保管房地产、贸易、矿业、矿业股东、运河公司、农业抵押品、工业抵押品、特别抵押品及其他法律规定的备案记录的核证人。

第 447 条 同一司法管辖范围内的各城镇或各

o agrupación de comunas que constituya el territorio jurisdiccional de juzgado de letras.

En Valparaíso habrá un conservador para las comunas de Valparaíso y Juan Fernández y un conservador para la comuna de Viña del Mar.

En aquellos territorios jurisdiccionales en que sólo hubiere un notario, el Presidente de la República podrá disponer que éste también ejerza el cargo de conservador de los registros indicados en el artículo precedente. En tal caso, se entenderá el cargo de notario conservador como un solo oficio judicial para todos los efectos legales.

Artículo 448. En las comunas o agrupaciones de comunas en que hubiere dos o más notarios, uno de ellos llevará el registro de comercio y otro el registro de bienes raíces.

Al Presidente de la República toca en el caso del inciso anterior hacer entre los notarios la distribución de éstos registros.

Le corresponde igualmente designar de entre los notarios que existan en la comuna o agrupaciones de comunas, el que deberá tener a su cargo el registro de minas y el de accionistas de las sociedades propiamente mineras.

La distribución del Presidente de la República hiciere regirá también respecto de los sucesores en el oficio de los dichos notarios.

El notario que deba llevar el registro de bienes raíces llevará, además, los registros de asociaciones de canalistas, de prenda agraria, de prenda industrial y especial de prenda.

Artículo 449. Habrá un registro conservatorio con asiento en la comuna de Santiago para el servicio del territorio jurisdiccional de la Corte de Apelaciones de Santiago, el que constituirá un solo oficio desempeñado por tres funcionarios.

Uno, el Conservador del Registro de Propiedad, que tendrá a su cargo el registro del mismo nombre y el correspondiente repertorio; y los registros de comercio, de prenda industrial, de prenda agraria y de asociaciones de canalistas; otro, el Conservador de Hipotecas, que tendrá a su cargo el Registro de Hipotecas y Gravámenes; y el último, el Conservador de Registro de Interdicciones y Prohibiciones de Enajenar, que llevará el registro de ese nombre y además, el registro especial de prenda.

Cada uno de estos funcionarios intervendrán en las inscripciones, subinscripciones, certificaciones, dación de copias y demás actos o diligencias que competan a sus respectivos registros.

地区须配有一名保管人。

在瓦尔帕莱索，须配有一名保管人负责瓦尔帕莱索和胡安·费尔南德斯地区，一名保管人负责比尼亚德尔马地区。

在仅有一名公证员的司法管辖区，总统可赋予其保管上述文件的权力。此情况下，公证员和保管人二职合一。

第448条 在有两名以上的公证员的城镇，贸易登记与房地产登记分人负责。

总统对具体登记保管人的分工有决定权。

同时，总统也须任命各个城镇和地区的矿业和矿业股东登记保管人。

总统也对各个公证员的继任者有任命权。

负责房地产登记的公证员也将负责运河公司、农业抵押品、工业抵押品、特别抵押品的登记。

第449条 圣地亚哥专设圣地亚哥上诉法院管辖区登记保管处，由三名公务员专门负责。

其一负责财产登记及备案管理、贸易登记、工业抵押品登记、农业抵押品登记及运河公司登记；其二负责管理抵押贷款，对贷款和税收进行记录；其三负责管理禁止转让登记以及特殊抵押登记。

三位公务员各司其职，对其管辖范围内的注册、次级注册、公证书、公证副本、其他公证文书等事务负责。

Los interesados que ocurran a esta oficina no requerirán directamente la intervención del conservador que corresponda, sino la del conservador encargado del repertorio, quien repartirá sin tardanza los trabajos que competan a las otras secciones del registro conservatorio. El mismo conservador encargado del repertorio entregará al público los mencionados trabajos después de anotar en el registro la correspondiente inscripción que se hubiere efectuado.

La guarda y custodia de los libros corresponde conjuntamente a los tres conservadores, quienes a la vez, podrán servirse de todos ellos y de los índices y documentos de las otras secciones en cuanto les sean necesarios para la atención de la propia.

No obstante, para los efectos de las visitas judiciales, cada registro o sección considerará como oficio separado.

Las funciones y guarda de los libros y documentos que otras leyes encomienden a los conservadores de bienes raíces, corresponderán en Santiago, al conservador del registro de hipotecas.

En el caso de los conservadores a que se refiere este artículo, si faltare o se inhabilitare alguno para el ejercicio de sus funciones, será reemplazado por los otros conservadores conforme al orden de su antigüedad.

Artículo 450. El Presidente de la República, previo informe favorable de la Corte de Apelaciones, podrá determinar la separación de los cargos de notario y conservador, servidos por una misma persona, la que podrá optar a uno u otro cargo.

De igual manera, el Presidente de la República podrá disponer, previo informe favorable de la Corte de Apelaciones, la división del territorio Jurisdiccional servido por un conservador, cuando él esté constituido por una agrupación de comunas, creando al efecto los oficios conservatorios que estimare convenientes para el mejor servicio público.

Artículo 451. Derogado.

Artículo 452. Se extiende a los conservadores, en cuanto es adaptable a ellos, todo lo dicho en este Código respecto de los notarios.

9) Los Archiveros

Artículo 453. Los archiveros son ministros de fe pública encargados de la custodia de los documentos expresados en el artículo 455 de este Código y de dar a las partes interesadas los testimonios que de ellos pidieren.

Concordancias: Código de Procedimiento Penal:

前来办理登记的当事人不与办事公务员直接对接，而是向负责登记备案记录的公务员申请办理事宜，登记完成后也由相同的公务员向申请人通知登记结果。

三位登记公务员可因工作需要共享彼此之间的公证登记簿、备忘录、目录及其他文件。

但在进行司法检查时，三者需分开。

圣地亚哥抵押贷款登记保管人，负责管理法规规定的其他地区房地产登记管理人的职责分配和文件保管工作。

本章所述保管人如需回避行使职能，则由其他保管人接替，按资历排序。

第 450 条　总统在上诉法院的许可下，可以对身兼公证员、保管人二职的公务员的职务进行拆分。

总统在上诉法院的许可下，还可以对单人管理多个城镇区域的保管人的管辖范围进行重新规划，以便改善工作效率。

第 451 条　本条已废止。
第 452 条　本法有关公证员的条款，同样适用于保管人。

9）档案管理员

第 453 条　档案管理员是指负责管理本法第 455 条规定的各种文件的核证人，同时也为申请人提供公证。

参见：《刑事诉讼法》第 350 条之二。

artículo 350 bis.

Artículo 454. Habrá archivero en las comunas asiento de Corte de Apelaciones y en las demás comunas que determine el Presidente de la República, con previo informe de la Corte de Apelaciones.

Los archiveros judiciales tendrán por territorio jurisdiccional el que corresponda a los juzgados de letras de la respectiva comuna.

Cuando el archivero estuviere implicado o e imposibilitare por cualquier causa para el ejercicio de sus funciones, será reemplazado por los notarios del acomuna de su asiento, conforme al orden de su antigüedad.

Artículo 455. Son funciones de los archiveros:

1. La custodia de los documentos que en seguida se expresan:

a) Los procesos afinados que se hubieren iniciado ante los jueces de letras que existan en la comuna o agrupación de comunas, o ante la Corte de Apelaciones o ante la Corte Suprema, si el archivero lo fuere del territorio jurisdiccional en que estos tribunales tienen su asiento.

Todo expediente criminal que se ordene archivar será remitido al archivero dentro de tres meses a contar desde la fecha en que se disponga su archivo;

b) Los procesos afinados que se hubieren seguido dentro del territorio jurisdiccional respectivo ante jueces árbitros;

c) Los libros copiadores de sentencias de los tribunales expresados en la letra a), y

d) Los protocolos de escrituras públicas otorgadas en el territorio jurisdiccional respectivo.

2. Guardar con el conveniente arreglo los procesos, libros de sentencias, protocolos y demás papeles de su oficina, sujetándose a las órdenes e instrucciones que la Corte o juzgado respectivo les difiere sobre el particular.

3. Facilitar, a cualquiera persona que lo solicite, el examen de los procesos, libros o protocolos de su archivo.

4. Dar a las partes interesadas, con arreglo a la ley, los testimonios que pidieren de los documentos que existieren en su archivo.

5. Formar y publicar, dentro del término que el Presidente de la República señale en cada caso, los índices de los procesos y escrituras con que se instale la oficina; y en los meses de marzo y abril, después de instalada, los correspondientes al último año.

Estos índices serán formados con arreglo a las instrucciones que den las respectivas Cortes de Apelaciones.

6. Ejercer las mismas funciones señaladas preceden-

第454条 每个城镇或区域的上诉法院都应有档案管理员。其他档案管理员在上诉法院通过的前提下由总统任命。

司法档案管理员的管辖范围与其所属的地区法院一致。

档案管理员如需回避行使职能，则由其城镇或区域的公证员代替，按资历排序。

第455条 档案管理员职责如下：
1. 保管下列文件：

a）保管所属城镇或地区的地区法院、上诉法院、最高法院法官受理案件的最终记录；

责令存档的犯罪记录，应在管理员收到记录后3个月内记入档案；

b）在所属管辖范围内，对法官的最终判决进行更新、记录；

c）a）条中所规定的法院的判决书副本；以及

d）所属管辖范围内签发的公证书。

2. 根据法院或法官针对各个案件的不同要求，保存并整理相应的案卷、判决书、公证书及其他文件。

3. 向申请人提供其负责的案卷、公证登记簿及公证书等文件，以便其查阅。

4. 依照法律，向申请人开具在其档案簿中存档文件的正式副本。

5. 依照总统下达的具体指示，总结并公布其辖区内的案卷和公证书办理目录；每年三月至四月期间，公布上一年的办理目录。

此目录应按照其所在辖区上诉法院的指令编制。

6. 如前文所示，对担保法官和刑事口头判决法庭

temente respecto de los registros de las actuaciones efectuadas ante los jueces de garantía y los tribunales de juicio oral en lo penal.

Concordancias: Código de Procedimiento Penal: artículos 171 y 350 bis.

Art. 456°- Las funciones de los archiveros, en cuanto ministros de fe, se limitan a dar conforme a derecho, los testimonios y certificados que se les pidan; y a poner, a petición de todos las respectivas notas marginales en las estructuras públicas.

Los archiveros judiciales podrán dar copia autorizada de las escrituras contenidas en los protocolos de su archivo, en todos aquellos casos en que el notario que haya intervenido en su otorgamiento habría podido darlas.

Concordancias: Código de Procedimiento Penal: artículo 350 bis.

10) Los Bibliotecarios Sociales Judiciales

Art. 457° - Los asistentes sociales judiciales son auxiliares de la administración de justicia cuya función es la de informar al tribunal acerca de los aspectos sociales, económicos, ambientales, educacionales y demás que se les requiera, con respecto a las partes o a los hechos y situaciones que han provocado el conflicto o la conducta irregular del individuo.

En cada juzgado especial de menores habrá, a lo menos, un asistente social judicial.

Cuando por implicancia o recusación el asistente social judicial no pudiere intervenir en determinadas causas, o se imposibilitare para el ejercicio de su cargo, será subrogado por los demás asistentes sociales del tribunal a que pertenece, según el orden de sus nombramientos; en subsidio por el asistente social de cualquier servicio público que el juez designe, el que estará obligado a desempeñar el encargo.

11) Los Bibliotecarios Judiciales

Art. 457° bis- Los bibliotecarios judiciales son auxiliares de la Administración de Justicia cuya función es la custodia, mantenimiento y atención de la Biblioteca de la Corte en que desempeñen sus funciones, así como las que el tribunal o su Presidente le encomienden en relación a las estadísticas del tribunal.

El bibliotecario de la Corte Suprema tendrá a cargo la custodia de todos los documentos originales de calificación de los funcionarios y empleados del Poder Judicial,

进行记录。

参考：《刑事诉讼法》第 171 条和第 350 条之二。

第 456 条　档案管理员作为核证人，其职能仅限于为申请人提供法律、证据和公证方面的，以及公证书中附加条款所规定的信息。

司法档案管理员可以对其保管的公证书内容进行复制，参与该公证书撰写的公证员也具有这一权限。

参见：《刑事诉讼法》第 350 条之二。

10）社会司法助理

第 457 条　社会司法助理是司法行政助理人员，其职责是向法院提供有关当事各方的社会、经济、环境、教育背景、产生冲突的事实及背景，个人反常行为以及其他被要求的信息。

未成年人法庭至少需配一名社会司法助理。

社会司法助理由于利益关联、回避或无法行使职能等情况下不能在某些案件履行其职权的，其所属法院将按提名顺序安排另外一位助理。法官安排的替补助理必须执行其代理任务。

11）司法图书管理员

第 457 条之二　司法图书管理员是司法行政助理人员，其职责是保护、管理和维护所在法院图书馆的运行，以及执行法院或院长依据法院数据委派给他们的任务。

最高法院图书管理员保管所有司法系统公务员及工作人员的考核文件原件，年度考核完成后进行收录；也可向申请人提供有关公证书。

los que le deberán ser remitidos una vez ejecutoriado el proceso anual de calificación. Estará facultado para dar a las partes interesadas los testimonios que de ellos pidieren.

Este bibliotecario desempeñará, además, las funciones que la Corte Suprema le encomiende respecto a la formación del Escalafón Judicial.

Habrá un bibliotecario en la Corte Suprema y en aquellas Cortes de Apelaciones que determine el Presidente de la República, con previo informe de la misma.

TITULO XII
Disposiciones Generales Aplicables a Los Auxiliares de la Administración de Justicia

1. Nombramiento, requisitos, inhabilidades e incompatibilidades

Art. N° 458- Es aplicable a los auxiliares de la Administración de Justicia lo dispuesto en los artículos 244 y 245. Igualmente, regirán los requisitos establecidos por los incisos cuarto y quinto del artículo 294 para el nombramiento de dichos auxiliares, sin perjuicio de las exigencias especiales que para las mismas designaciones se contengan en este título y en otras leyes.

Ningún cargo de fiscal judicial, de defensor público o de relator podrá permanecer vacante, ni aún en el caso de estar servido interinamente, por más de cuatro meses si se trata d ellos dos primeros y de tres meses, si del último. Vencidos estos términos, el funcionario interino cesará de hecho en el ejercicio de sus funciones, y el Presidente de la República proveerá la plaza en propiedad.2

Art. N°459- Los fiscales judiciales, los defensores, los relatores y los demás auxiliares de la Administración de Justicia serán nombrados por el Presidente de la República previa Propuesta de la Corte Suprema o de la Corte de Apelaciones respectivas, en conformidad a las disposiciones contenidas en el párrafo tercero del Título X del presente Código.3

Para la designación de los funcionarios a que se refiere el inciso anterior deberán cumplirse, además los requisitos que se indican en los artículos siguientes.

Art. N°460- Las Cortes examinarán las aptitudes de los opositores que no sean abogados mediante un examen de competencia cuando se trate de proveer algún cargo para el cual no se requiera esa calidad. Podrán, asimismo, si lo estiman conveniente, abrir concurso y recibir ex-

本管理员也可依据最高法院的规定负责法律梯队建设的工作。

最高法院及上诉法院的图书管理员，由法院提出申请，共和国总统任命。

第十二篇
适用于司法行政助理人员的一般规定

1. 任命、资格要求、撤职及职务的不兼容性

第458条　第244条和第245条适用于司法行政助理人员。任命时须遵守第294条第4款和第5款的规定，以及本条和其他法律中的相关特殊规定。

司法检察官、公设辩护人以及报告员均不得长期空缺。对于临时任命人选的，司法检察官、公设辩护人的临时接替时间不得超过4个月，报告员的临时接替时间不得超过3个月。临时任期已满则须卸任，由总统任命正式接替人选。

第459条　司法检察官、公设辩护人、报告员和其他司法行政助理人员依照本法第十章第三段的规定，由相应的最高法院或上诉法院提名，总统最终任命。

上段所述公务员的任命须同时满足下列条款的要求。

第460条　选拔时，法院对参加公务员考试的候选人进行能力测试。候选人不应是通过与所需能力无关的测试的律师。选拔报告员时可视情况开设竞赛或考试。

ámenes cuando se trata de proveer el cargo de relator.

Art. N°461- Para ser fiscal judicial de la Corte Suprema o de una Corte de Apelaciones se requieren las mismas condiciones que para ser miembro del respectivo tribunal.

Art. N°462- Pueden ser defensores públicos los que pueden ser jueces de letras del respectivo territorio jurisdiccional.

Art. N°463- Para ser relator, secretario de la Corte Suprema o de las cortes de Apelaciones y notario se requieren las mismas condiciones que para ser juez de letras de comuna o agrupación de comunas.

Art. N°464- No pueden ser fiscales judiciales, defensores ni relatores los que no pueden ser jueces de letras.

Art. N°465- No pueden ser notarios:

1°Los que se hallaren en interdicción por causa de demencia o prodigalidad;

2°Los sordos, los ciegos y los mudos;

3°Los que se hallaren procesados por crimen o simple delito, y

4°Los que estuvieren sufriendo la pena de inhabilitación para cargos y oficios públicos.

Art. N°466- Para ser secretario de un juzgado de letras, archivero y conservador se requiere ser abogado.

Art. N°467- Para ser receptor ante los juzgados de letras y procurador del número es menester tener las cualidades requeridas para poder ejercer el derecho de sufragio en las elecciones populares y acreditar la aptitud necesaria para desempeñar el cargo. Siempre será necesaria la edad de veinticinco años a lo menos para desempeñar el cargo de procurador y de receptor.

Para ser asistente social judicial se requiere tener más de veintiún años de edad, encontrarse en posesión del título de asistente social otorgado pro alguna Universidad del Estado o reconocida por éste.

Art. N°468- Derogado.

Art. N°469- Las incapacidades en razón de parentesco establecidas en el artículo 258, rigen para todos los funcionarios del Escalafón Primario dependientes de una Corte de Apelaciones en su respectivo territorio jurisdiccional.

No podrán ser fiscales judiciales, administradores, subadministradores, jefes de unidades de tribunales con competencia en lo criminal o asistentes sociales judiciales en un tribunal las personas que tengan con uno o más jueces de él alguno de los parentescos indicados en el citado artículo.

第461条 最高法院或上诉法院的司法检察官必须同时满足成为相应法院工作人员的基本要求。

第462条 同一管辖区的地方律师可以成为相应管辖区的公设辩护人。

第463条 报告员、最高法院或上诉法院秘书及公务员的选拔条件与地区法院法官的任命条件一致。

第464条 不满足成为地区法官任命条件的候选人同样不能竞选成为司法检察官、公设辩护人或报告员。

第465条 下列人员不能成为公证员：

1. 智力残障人士或无法律行为能力的人；

2. 盲人和聋哑人；

3. 刑事或民事犯；

4. 被剥夺行使公职权利的。

第466条 地区法官的秘书、档案管理员、保管人必须有律师资格。

第467条 地区法院受理人和代诉人应当年满25周岁，满足享有选举权的条件，并通过相应职位的能力测试。

社会司法助理应当年满21周岁，并获得国家大专院校颁发的专业文凭或同等学历。

第468条 本条已废止。

第469条 所有第一梯队的公务员，须根据其司法管辖区内上诉法院的规定，履行第258条"亲属无资格履职"的规定。

任司法检察官、行政人员、副级行政人员、法院刑事案件部门主任或法院社会司法助理均须回避亲属任职。

No pueden ser defensores públicos los que tengan con alguno de los jueces de letras de propietarios del respectivo territorio jurisdiccional cualquiera de los parentescos indicados en dicho artículo.

Tampoco podrán desempeñar ante ningún juez funciones accidentales de defensores los que tengan con él cualquiera d ellos indicados parentescos.

Art. N°470- Las funciones de los auxiliares de la Administración de Justicia son incompatibles con toda otra remunerada con fondos fiscales o municipales, con excepción de los cargos docentes hasta un límite de doce semanales.

No obstante, los cargos de secretario, receptor y notario podrán ser desempeñados por una misma persona en aquellas comunas o agrupaciones de comunas en que, a juicio del Presidente de la República, no sea posible o conveniente hacerlos recaer en personas distintas por no permitirlo la exigüidad de los emolumentos correspondientes a cada uno de dichos cargos.

Las funciones de los fiscales judiciales son , además, incompatibles con las eclesiásticas y las de los defensores públicos con las eclesiásticas que tengan cura de almas.7-8

2. Juramento e Instalación

Art. N°471- Los auxiliares de la Administración de Justicia antes de desempeñar sus cargos prestarán juramento al tenor de la fórmula siguiente "¿Juráis por Dios Nuestro Señor y por estos Santos Evangelios que guardaréis la Constitución y las leyes de la República y que desempeñaréis fielmente las funciones de vuestro cargo?".

El interrogado responderá: "Sí juro", y el magistrado que le tome el juramento añadirá: "Si así lo hiciereis Dios os ayude; y si no, os lo demande".

Los fiscales judiciales, relatores y secretarios de Corte, prestarán juramento ante el presidente del tribunal del que formen parte.

Los otros funcionarios auxiliares lo harán ante el juez respectivo. Si el tribunal estuviere acéfalo lo prestarán ante el intendente o gobernador. La autoridad administrativa que haya recibido el juramento dará lo más pronto posible el respectivo aviso a la que le habría correspondido intervenir en la diligencia, remitiéndole lo obrado.

Art. N°472- Cuando algún fiscal judicial de las Cortes de Apelaciones que hubiere prestado el juramento correspondiente fuere nombrado para un puesto análogo al que desempeñaba, no será obligado a prestar nuevo jura-

公设辩护人与同管辖区地方法院法官不能有任何规定中的亲属关系。

其他性质的辩护人也不可和法官有任何亲属关系。

第470条 司法行政助理的职位不能与其他靠市政或国家财务拨款发放工资的职位重合，但每周教学安排不超过12课时的教师职位除外。

总统可在无能力发放工资的城镇和区域委任同一人身兼秘书、受理人、公证员三职。

司法检察职位也不可与神职人员或者具有神职人员身份的公设辩护人的职位兼容。

2. 宣誓和就职

第471条 司法行政助理人员在就职前须按以下方式宣誓："你是否向上帝和神灵宣誓，遵守国家宪法和法律，忠实履行本职工作？"

须回答："是的，我发誓"。法官接受宣誓并宣布："顺誓而为，天助人也；背誓而驰，必得惩戒。"

司法检察官、报告员和法院秘书须在其所在法院院长前宣誓。

其他助理人员在相应法官前宣誓。如法院无院长则在市长或省长前宣誓。宣誓后，行政部门应尽快向入职人员派分工作。

第472条 如上诉法院司法检察官被委任至类似的新职位，则无须重新宣誓。

mento.

Art. N°473- Los notarios, conservadores, archiveros, secretarios y receptores, que no sean los especiales a que se refiere el inciso segundo del artículo 391, así como los administradores de tribunales con competencia en lo criminal, deberán rendir una fianza para responder de las multas, costas e indemnizaciones de perjuicios a que puedan ser condenados en razón de los actos concernientes al desempeño de su ministerio, dentro de 30 días después de haber asumido el cargo.

Esta fianza será para los secretarios y administradores de tribunales el equivalente a un año de sueldo base asignado al cargo y para los demás funcionarios igual al monto del sueldo anual que la ley le fije para los efectos de su jubilación.

La fianza será calificada y aprobada por el funcionario a quien corresponda recibir el juramento.

3. Obligaciones y prohibiciones

Art. N° 474- Los auxiliares de la Administración de Justicia, salvo los relatores, estarán obligados a residir constantemente en la ciudad o población donde tenga asiento el tribunal en que deban prestar sus servicios.

No obstante, las Cortes de Apelaciones podrán, en casos calificados, autorizar transitoriamente a los auxiliares de su territorio jurisdiccional para que residan en un lugar diverso.

Concordancias: Constitución Política: artículo 19 N° 7.

Art. N°475- Los secretarios estarán obligados a asistir todos los días a la sala de su despacho durante las horas de funcionamiento de los tribunales.

Los secretarios deberán mantener abierta su oficina al público desde una hora antes de la designada para que tenga principio el despacho y hasta una hora después de terminado.

Los receptores deberán permanecer diariamente en sus oficinas durante las dos primeras horas de audiencia de los tribunales, a disposición de éstos y de los litigantes, especialmente para los efectos de lo dispuesto en el inciso segundo del artículo 390.

Sin embargo, el juez de la causa podrá autorizar su ausencia para el cumplimiento de diligencias urgentes.

Los notarios, los conservadores y los archiveros deberán mantener abierta su oficina al público en las horas que señalen las leyes y los reglamentos respectivos.

Los asistentes sociales judiciales en cumplimiento de

第473条 除第391条第2款所列特殊人员及刑事法院行政人员以外的公证员、保管人、档案管理员、秘书和受理人应在宣誓入职后30日内递交保证金。这笔资金是其今后工作中出现罚款、花销或损害赔偿时的保证金。

对秘书和法院行政人员，此笔保证金的金额为一年的基本工资，其他职位人员为法律规定的一年的养老金。

保证金须由接受宣誓的官员确认并同意。

3. 职责和禁限

第474条 除报告员以外的司法行政助理人员应长期居住于其所在管辖区域。

在特定情形下，上诉法院可批准司法助理人员暂时到另一管辖区域居住。

参见：《宪法》第19条第7项。

第475条 秘书在法院每日工作时段须在办公室坐班。

秘书应在对外开放前一小时到岗，并在结束工作一小时后离岗。

受理人每日在法院审理案件前两小时务必在岗，以便服务法院、诉讼人以及第390条第2款中规定的内容。

法官可因突发事件批准受理人缺席。

公证员、保管人和档案管理员依据法律法规规定的时间到岗工作。

社会司法助理的工作时间依据相应法官的指示

sus funciones, deberán atender en el recinto del tribunal los días y horas que señale el juez respectivo.

Art. N°476- Los relatores deberán asistir a la Corte diariamente con la anticipación necesaria para instruirse de los negocios de que deban dar cuenta.

Los procuradores deberán asistir a la secretaría de los tribunales a instruirse de lo que les concierne en el despacho de los negocios.

Art. N°477- Las obligaciones de residencia y asistencia cesan durante los días feriados.

Esta disposición no regirá en el feriado de vacaciones con los notarios, conservadores y archiveros, con los juzgados que queden de turno, ni con los auxiliares que determinen los tribunales colegiados para el funcionamiento de sus respectivas salas de verano.

Art. N°478- Ningún notario, conservador, archivero, secretario, administrador de tribunal, procurador o receptor podrá ausentarse del lugar de su residencia ni dejar de asistir diariamente a su oficina sin permiso del Presidente de la Corte si ejerciere sus funciones en el lugar de asiento de este tribunal, o del juez de letras respectivo o de turno, en los demás casos.

Este permiso podrá otorgarse como máximo, en cada año calendario, por una sola vez o fraccionado, por ocho días a los secretarios y administradores de tribunales, dos meses a los notarios, conservadores y archiveros y un mes a los otros funcionarios. Si el permiso solicitado excediere a los aludidos plazos y no pasare de un año, deberá pedirse por escrito ante el Presidente de la República. Si transcurrido un año no se presentare el funcionario a servir su destino, se tendrá esta inasistencia como causal bastante para que la autoridad competente, siguiendo los trámites legales, pueda declarar vacante el empelo.

En los permisos hasta por dos meses el notario, conservador y archivero podrá proponer al juez el abogado que deba subrogarlo bajo su responsabilidad, propuesta que en el caso de los notarios y conservadores de cuarta categoría podrá recaer en el oficial 1° de la oficina respectiva.

Art. N°479- Es prohibido a los auxiliares de la administración de justicia ejercer la abogacía y sólo podrán defender causas personales o de sus cónyuges, ascendientes, descendientes, hermanos o pupilos.

Les es igualmente prohibido representar en juicio a otras personas que las mencionadas en el precedente inciso.

No rige lo dispuesto en los incisos anteriores con los

而定。

第476条 报告员每日须对法院将要审理的案件有所预判。

代诉人应前往法院秘书处了解与其有关的案件。

第477条 到岗及考勤在节假日期间不作规定。

节假日期间，对公证员、保管人和档案管理员、值班法官、暑期法院助理的考勤，本法均不作规定。

第478条 所有公证员、保管人、档案管理员、秘书、法院行政人员、代诉人、受理人，都不得在未经法院主席或地方法院法官许可的情况下离开居住地，或不按时到岗。

每年许可的假期可一次或分次休完。秘书和法院行政人员为8日，公证员、保管人和档案管理员为两个月，其他公务员为一个月。如所需假期超过允许范围但短于一年，须向总统书面请示。如未履职满一年，则有关部门可依据相关法律的规定对外宣布职位空缺。

在公证员、保管人和档案管理员长达两个月的休假期间，他们可向法官提出此期间的代班律师人选。公证员和保管人的代班人选不受等级限制。

第479条 司法行政助理人员不得作为律师执业，仅能在涉及本人、配偶、直系亲属、兄弟姐妹或养子女的案件中进行辩护。

不得为上述群体以外的人员进行法庭辩护。
公设辩护人和公证员不受此限制。

但两者不可在所属的上诉法院提供律师服务。

defensores públicos y los procuradores del número. No obstante, estos últimos no podrán ejercer la profesión de abogado ante las Cortes de Apelaciones en que actúan.

Art. N°480- Los fiscales judiciales no podrán aceptar compromisos, excepto cuando el nombrado tuviere con alguna de las partes originariamente interesadas en el litigio, algún vínculo de parentesco que autorice su implicancia o recusación.

Es prohibido a los notarios la aceptación y desempeño de arbitrajes y particiones.

Art. N°481- La prohibición del articulo 321 regirá también con los fiscales judiciales, defensores, relatores, secretarios, receptores y asistentes sociales judiciales.

Los notarios y los procuradores del número no podrán comprar los bienes en cuyo litigio han intervenido y que se vendan a consecuencia del litigio, aunque la venta se haga en pública subasta.

La prohibición del artículo 322 rige respecto de los secretarios de los juzgados de letras en lo civil y de los conservadores de minas.

Art. N°482- Es aplicable a los auxiliares de la Administración de justicia lo dispuesto en el artículo 323.

4. De las implicancias y recusaciones

Art. N°483- Se prohibe a los fiscales judiciales, ya sean propietarios, interinos o suplentes, intervenir como tales funcionarios en los negocios en que sean parte o tengan interés personal ellos mismos o alguna de las personas expresadas en el artículo 195, o en que, antes de entrar en el ejercicio de sus funciones, hayan ellos intervenido como abogados o representantes de cualquiera de las partes; a menos que su interés o el interés de las personas a quienes el precipitado artículo se refiere a quienes dichos funcionarios hubieren defendido o representado no esté en oposición con el que le corresponde defender en razón de su ministerio.

Concordancias: Código de Procedimiento Civil: artículo 117.

Art. N°484- En los negocios en que los fiscales judiciales intervienen como terceros coadyuvantes, pueden ser recusados con expresión de causa por las personas naturales o jurídicas cuyos intereses y derechos son llamados a proteger y defender.

Las causas de recusación de estos funcionarios son las que designadas para la recusación de los jueces por el artículo 196, con exclusión de las comprendidas en los

第480条 司法检察官不应做出任何承诺，除当其与诉讼方有利益、亲属关系时，应放弃行事资格。

公证员不得接受或充当仲裁或参与遗产分配。

第481条 第321条规定的禁止事项同样适用于司法检察官、辩护人、报告人、秘书、受理人和社会司法助理。

公证员及代诉人不能购买其参与的财产纠纷中的物品，即使该物品进行公众拍卖也不可。

第322条 规定的禁止事项适用于民事法官秘书和矿业登记保管人。

第482条 第323条规定适用于司法行政助理人员。

4. 回避与行事资格无效

第483条 禁止正式、临时或替补的司法检察官在其参与、有个人利益关系或有第195条规定中出现的人群的案件中行使其司法权力，应当回避。也包括之前其作为律师所代理过的案件，但其之前代理的与本案无利益关系的案件不在此列。

参见：《民事诉讼法》第117条。

第484条 司法检察官应回避其作为第三方调停的案件，因为可能会被自然人或法人以保护自身权益的理由，拒绝其行使司法权。

上述人群的回避原因与规定法官回避的第196条规定一致，除该条第2项和第10项外。

números 2 y 10.

Y no podrá entablarse la recusación sino cuando según la presunción de la ley, la falta de imparcialidad que se supone en el recusado pueda perjudicar al recusante.

Art. N°485- Se prohibe, igualmente, a los defensores públicos intervenir en calidad de tales en los negocios en que sean parte o tengan interés personal ellos mismos o alguna de las personas expresados en el artículo 195 o en que, antes de entrar en el ejercicio de sus funciones, hayan ellos intervenido como abogados o representantes de cualquiera de las partes.

Concordancias: Código de Procedimiento Civil: artículo 117

Art. N°486- Los defensores públicos pueden ser recusados en los casos y por las personas por que pueden serlo los fiscales judiciales.

Art. N°487- Las causas de implicancia señaladas respecto de los jueces por el artículo 195 rigen también respecto de los relatores, secretarios, receptores y asistentes sociales judiciales.

En consecuencia, les es prohibido intervenir como tales en los negocios a que este artículo se refiere.

Concordancias: Código de Procedimiento Civil: artículo 117.

Art. N°488- Para recusar a los relatores, secretarios y asistentes sociales judiciales es menester expresar y probar causa legal.

Las causas de recusación de los secretarios y asistentes sociales judiciales son, en cuanto puedan ser aplicables a ellos, las determinadas para la recusación de los jueces por el artículo 196.

Son causas legales para los relatores las señaladas en los números 1, 2, 4, 5, 6, 7, 8, 11, 12, 13 y 16 del preciado artículo.

Sólo puede recusar la parte a quien, según la presunción de la ley, perjudique la falta de imparcialidad que estas causas inducen.

Concordancias: Código de Procedimiento Civil: artículo 117.

Art. N°489- Los receptores y los funcionarios llamados a subrogarlos podrán ser inhabilitados sin expresión de causa por una vez, por cada parte, en un mismo juicio. Pasado este número se deberá expresar y probar alguna de las causas de implicancia o recusación determinadas para los jueces en cuanto les sean aplicables.

Art. N°490- Regirá para los auxiliares de la Administración de Justicia lo dispuesto en el inciso primero del

只有当在法律范围内，不进行回避会影响到公正性时才可进行回避。

第485条 公设辩护人应回避其参与的与其个人或与第195条规定的人群有利益关系的或在之前作为律师或代表向其提供过法律服务的案件。

参见：《民事诉讼法》第117条。

第486条 公设辩护人可能会在某些案件中被司法检察官替换，被迫回避。

第487条 第195条规定的法官回避情形同样适用于报告人、秘书、受理人和社会司法助理。

因此，上述人群应回避本条规定的各类案件。

参见：《民事诉讼法》第117条。

第488条 当报告人、秘书和社会司法助理进行回避时，须提出法律依据。

秘书与社会司法助理的回避原因与第196条规定的法官回避原因一致。

报告人的回避原因是上条中第1项、第2项、第4项、第5项、第6项、第7项、第8项、第11项、第12项、第13项和第16项。

只有当在法律范围内，不进行回避会影响到公正性时才可进行回避。

参见：《民事诉讼法》第117条。

第489条 同一审判中，诉讼双方可分别无条件申请受理人和公务员回避一次。一次以上的则须援引相应法官回避事由进行解释。

第490条 第199条第1款的规定同样适用于司法行政助理人员。

artículo 199.

No obstante, se necesitará de solicitud previa para declarar la inhabilidad de cualquier funcionario auxiliar, producida por el hecho de ser parte o tener interés en el pleito una sociedad anónima de que aquél sea accionista, sin perjuicio de que dicho funcionario haga constar en el proceso la existencia de la causal.

Art. N°491- La implicancia y la recusación de los auxiliares de la Administración de Justicia se reclamarán ante el tribunal que conozca del negocio en que aquellos deban intervenir, y se admitirán sin más trámite cuando no necesiten fundarse en causa legal.

5. De su remuneración y de su prevision

Art. N°492- Los auxiliares de la Administración de Justicia tendrán los sueldos que les fijen las leyes, pero los defensores públicos que no sean de Santiago y Valparaíso, los notarios, archiveros, conservadores, receptores y procuradores del número gozarán de los emolumentos que les correspondan con arreglo al respectivo arancel.

Los secretarios de juzgados, en su carácter de tales, no podrán cobrar emolumentos de ninguna clase, salvo los que puedan corresponderles cuando desempeñen los cargos de actuarios en juicios arbitrales o de ministros de fe en la facción de inventarios.

Los auxiliares de la Administración de Justicia estarán, además, sometidos al régimen de previsión que determinen las leyes.

Concordancias: D. L. N° 2.876, contiene normas sobre aranceles, control y fiscalización de receptores judiciales, D. O. 23.11.1979

6. Suspensión y expiración de funciones. De las licencias.

Art. N°493- Los funcionarios que no gocen de inamovilidad, serán removidos por el Presidente con solo acuerdo de la mayoría de los miembros en ejercicio de la Corte respectiva.

El funcionario que figure el Lista Deficiente o, por segundo año consecutivo en Lista Condicional, una vez firma la calificación

Art. N° 494°- Los cargos de los auxiliares de la Administración de Justicia expiran por incurrir éstos en alguna de las incapacidades establecidas por la ley para ejercerlos o por las causas indicadas en los números 3, 4, 5, 6, 7, 8 y 11 del artículo 332 en cuanto les puedan ser aplicables. Expiran, asimismo, por la aceptación de todo cargo

如公务员助理因其在诉讼案件涉事企业中的股东身份或利益关系而需要回避，则须提前申请并进行证明。

第 491 条　司法行政助理人员的回避应向办案法院提出。如法院可无须任何法律依据做出判定，则直接批准回避。

5. 工资和预算

第 492 条　司法行政助理人员的工资固定，由法律规定。圣地亚哥和瓦尔帕莱索地区以外的公设辩护人、公证员、档案管理员、保管人、受理人、代诉人依据各地区税率不同工资不同。

法官秘书不应享有工资，但他们履行仲裁判决书记员或公信部门清点的工作的时候，便可以享有工资。

司法行政助理人员也应遵守法律规定的相应预算。

参见：在 1979 年 11 月 23 日的官方公报上发布的第 2876 号法令中关于司法受理人的关税、管理与审计的规定。

6. 停职察看、撤职，休假

第 493 条　不具不可罢免性的公务员职位，可在相应法院成员多数票表决同意的情况下，由总统进行撤换。

如被列入业绩不良名单或连续 2 年列入观察名单，则应立即被撤换。

第 494 条　司法行政助理人员，出现法律规定的任何无能力继续履职，或出现第 332 条第 3 项、第 4 项、第 5 项、第 6 项、第 7 项、第 8 项、第 11 项所述情形的，应予撤职。接任任何国家财政、半财政或市政开支工资的职位，或出现第 256 条第 1 项至第 4 项规定的失去任职资格的情形的，同样应予撤职。

o empleo remunerado con fondos fiscales, semifiscales o municipales, y cuando sobrevienen a los funcionarios algunas de las inhabilidades indicadas en los cuatro primeros números del articulo 256.

Es aplicable a los fiscales judiciales ya los relatores lo prescrito en el N° 9 del artículo 332.

Los fiscales judiciales y los defensores públicos cesarán, además, en sus cargos si se produce la situación prevista en el inciso final del artículo 470.

Los secretarios, notarios, conservadores, archiveros, receptores y procuradores cesarán también en sus funciones si fueren condenados a la pena de inhabilitación para cargos y oficios públicos.

Art. N° 495°- Si un auxiliar de la Administración de Justicia de los indicados en el artículo 469 y un ministro de la Corte de Apelaciones de que aquellos dependan contrajeren, después que hayan sido nombrados tales, alguno de los parentescos designados en el artículo 258, aquel por cuyo matrimonio se haya contraído el parentesco, cesará inmediatamente en el ejercicio de sus funciones y deberá ser separado de su destino.

Lo dispuesto en el inciso anterior es aplicable al fiscal judicial de la Corte Suprema con respecto a los miembros de dicho tribunal.

Art. N° 495° bis- Los auxiliares de la Administración de Justicia permanecerán en sus cargos hasta cumplir los setenta y cinco años de edad.

Art. N° 496°- Regirán con los auxiliares de la Administración de Justicia las causas de suspensión del cargo de juez señaladas en el artículo 335 en cuanto puedan ser aplicables a ellos.

Las funciones de los secretarios, receptores, procuradores, notarios, conservadores y archiveros, se suspenderán, además, por sentencia judicial que les imponga la pena de suspensión.

Art. N° 497°- Son igualmente aplicables a los auxiliares de la Administración de justicia las disposiciones relativas a las licencias, permisos y feriados de los jueces en el párrafo 9 del Título X del presente Código .

La disposición del artículo 343 regirá con los secretarios de los tribunales que no tienen derecho al feriado indicado en el artículo 313.

Los presidentes de las Cortes de Apelaciones fijarán un turno entre sus secretarios en forma que el feriado a que dicho artículo se refiere, no perjudique las labores del tribunal.

第 332 条第 9 项规定同样对司法检察官和报告员适用。

如出现第 470 条最后一款规定的情形，则司法检察官和公设辩护人须放弃任职。

秘书、公证员、保管人、档案馆管理员、受理人、代诉人被处以撤销职务或公职处罚的，均视为履职期结束。

第 495 条 第 469 条规定中的司法行政助理人员，一旦与其所属上诉法院的法官缔结婚姻，则构成第 258 条规定的亲缘关系。双方婚姻关系确定后，其中一方应立即停职，调任其他岗位。

前款内容同样适用于最高法院的司法检察官和该法院的其他成员。

第 495 条之二 司法行政助理人员的退休年龄为 75 周岁。

第 496 条 第 335 条中有关法官停职的规定同样适用于司法行政助理人员。

秘书、受理人、代诉人、公证员、保管人和档案管理员如被处以停职处分，则不能继续履职。

第 497 条 本法第十篇第 9 段中有关法官的假期、休假和节假日安排的规定，同时适用于司法行政助理人员。

第 343 条的规定，同样适用于第 313 条规定中提及的无休假法院秘书。

上诉法院院长应对其秘书的休假进行合理安排，以避免影响法院工作。

古巴

国家公证法

REPUBLICA DE CUBA
LEY N° 80
DE LAS NOTARIAS ESTATALES
GACETA OFICIAL DE LA REPUBLICA DE CUBA
EDICION ORDINARIA LA HABANA, VIERNES 1° DE MARZO DE 1985
Imprenta: Zanja N° 352, esq. a Escobar. - Habana 2
Número 3
Pagina 49

ASAMBLEA NACIONAL DEL PODER POPULAR POPULAR

FLAVIO BRAVO PARDO, presidente de la Asamblea Nacional del Poder Popular de la República de Cuba.

HAGO SABER-. Que la Asamblea Nacional del Poder Popular. en sesión ordinaria celebrada el día veintiocho de diciembre de 1984, correspondiente al séptimo periodo ordinario de sesiones de la segunda legislatura, aprobó lo siguiente:

POR CUANTO. El Estado socialista reconoce la existencia del Notario como funcionario público que realiza importantes funciones relacionadas con el cumplimiento de la legalidad socialista en la actividad extrajudicial de las personas naturales y jurídicas.

POR CUANTO. El proceso reorganizativo del notariado cubano permitió la eliminación del ejercicio privado de la función notarial y la integración de un notariado estatal unificado, de acuerdo con los requerimientos de nuestra sociedad, a fin de otorgar mayor estabilidad y seguridad jurídica a las personas en sus relaciones extrajudiciales.

POR CUANTO: Es necesario concretar en un solo cuerpo legal los principios generales de organización y funcionamiento de la actividad notarial que agrupa las nor-

古巴共和国
第 80 号法律
国家公证法
古巴共和国官方公报
常规版，1985 年 3 月 1 日星期五于哈瓦那

印刷：哈瓦那 2 区 Zanja 大街 352 号 Escobar 拐角处
第 3 号
第 49 页

古巴全国人民政权代表大会

本人，弗拉维奥·布拉沃·帕尔多，古巴共和国全国人民政权代表大会主席。

告知如下，全国人民政权代表大会于 1984 年 12 月 28 日召开常务会议，即第二届人民代表大会第七次会议，通过如下内容：

鉴于社会主义国家制度承认公证员为公务人员，在自然人和法人的各项行为，即司法外管辖的行为中，公证员为维护社会主义法制发挥重要作用。

鉴于古巴公证人职务有着影响社会结构的特性，因此取消了私人执业，而是统一纳入国家公证员编制，这符合我们的社会要求，从而为处在司法外管辖关系中的人们提供最大限度的稳定性和安全性。

鉴于有必要颁布一部法律文件来明确公证行为的一般组织结构和职责，总结该领域的现行法律规定，替代那些已经不适用的且不符合我们的社会、经济和

mas jurídicas vigentes en la materia y sustituye aquellas que resultan inoperantes y que no se correspondan con la realidad de nuestro desarrollo económico, social y político.

POR TANTO. La Asamblea Nacional del Poder Popular, en uso de las facultades que le están conferidas, ha adoptado la siguiente:

LEY N° 80 - DE LAS NOTARIAS ESTATALES

CAPITULO I Disposiciones Generales

Art. 1-El Notario es el funcionario público facultado para dar fe de los actos jurídicos extrajudiciales en los que por razón de su cargo interviene, de conformidad con lo establecido en la ley.

Art. 2-Los funcionarios consulares o diplomáticos cubanos en cl extranjero autorizados para ello, ejercen, para surtir efectos en Cuba, la función notarial en el país en que estén acreditados de conformidad con lo establecido en esta Ley y su Reglamento.

Art. 3-El Notario ejerce sus funciones dentro de la demarcación territorial que determine su nombramiento.

Art. 4-El Notario, en e] ejercicio de sus funciones, debe obediencia a la ley y cumple en sus actuaciones con la legalidad socialista.

Art. 5-Las autoridades del orden público y sus agentes auxilian al Notario en el ejercicio de sus funciones cuando éstas lo requieran.

Los dirigentes y funcionarios de los órganos y organismos del Estado, sus empresas y demás entidades estatales, de las cooperativas, y de las organizaciones sociales y de masa contribuirán con el Notario en el desempeño de sus funciones, en caso necesario.

CAPITULO II Del nombramiento y competencia de los Notarios

Art. 6- Sólo puede ejercer como Notario el funcionario nombrado de conformidad con esta Ley.

Art. 7-El Notario tiene competencia provincial o municipal. En casos especiales, el Ministro de Justicia puede nombrar notarios con competencia nacional o extender la misma a los demás notarios.

Art. 8-Para ser nombrado Notario se exige el cumplimiento de los requisitos siguientes:

a) ser ciudadano cubano:

b) ser doctor o licenciado en Derecho;

c) poseer buenas condiciones morales y gozar de

政治发展的法律条款。

因此，全国人民政权代表大会行使其被赋予的权力，通过如下内容：

第80号法律 国家公证法

第一章 总则

第1条 公证员是公职人员，其职责是根据法律规定，在其职责范围内对非司法范围内的各种法律行为进行公证。

第2条 领事官员或者其他受权在国外进行公证的古巴外交官的职责，就是根据本法及其实施条例，在派驻国家进行公证工作，从而使被公证事项在古巴产生效力。

第3条 公证员在其被任命的辖区范围内行使职权。

第4条 公证员在行使其职权的过程中，应当遵循法律规定并且符合社会主义法制规定。

第5条 如果在公证过程中有需要，执法机关及其工作人员应协助公证员履行其职责。

如有需要，国家各机构和各单位的领导和公职人员，国家企业和其他国家机关、合作社企业机构、其他社会机构和集体单位都应协助公证员履行其职责。

第二章 公证员的任命和职权

第6条 只有根据法律规定任命的公职人员才可担任公证员。

第7条 公证员的职权分为省级和市级。在特殊情况下，司法部长可以任命国家级职权的公证员，或将公证员的职权级别扩大到国家级。

第8条 任命的公证员必须符合以下要求：

a）是古巴公民；

b）是法律学学士或硕士；

c）有良好的道德品质并享有良好的声誉；

buen concepto público;

  ch) estar habilitado por el Ministerio de Justicia.

  Art. 9-Los notarios no pueden desempeñar otro cargo o empleo, bien sea electivo o, de nombramiento. que lleve aparejada autoridad, potestad administrativa o función ejecutiva, excepto que se trate de cargos en el Ministerio de Justicia, docentes o científicos, o de Delegado o Diputado a los órganos del Poder Popular, en estos dos últimos casos, si ocuparen cargos ejecutivos en dichos órganos no podrán ejercer como notarios.

CAPITULO II Del nombramiento y competencia de los Notarios

  Art. 10- EL Notario tiene las funciones y obligaciones siguientes:

  a) dar fe de los actos jurídicos en que la ley exige la formalización o autorización notarial y de aquéllos en que las partes así lo soliciten;

  b) dar fe de hechos, actos o circunstancias de relevancia jurídica de los que se deriven o declaren derechos o intereses legítimos para las personas o de cualquier otro acto de declaración licita;

  c) conocer, tramitar y resolver los expedientes de jurisdicción voluntaria y sucesorios de declaratoria de herederos, de conformidad con esta Ley y su Reglamento;

  ch) calificar la legalidad del acto jurídico, así como de los hechos, actos o circunstancias contenidos en el documento notarial de que se trate, cerciorándose de que éstos se ajusten a los requisitos exigidos para su autorización;

  d) emitir juicios sobre el conocimiento y capacidad de los comparecientes en el documento notarial de que se trate:

  e) dar fe de los protestos, requerimientos, notificaciones y legalizaciones;

  f) protocolizar toda clase de documentos públicos o privados;

  g) recibir en depósito documento mercantiles u otros, objetos, valores o bienes muebles, como prenda de contrato o para su custodia;

  h) dar fe de la vigencia de leyes nacionales para que surtan efecto en el extranjero y de traducciones del idioma español a cualquier otro idioma extranjero y viceversa; o de las que hiciere si conociere el idioma extranjero; dar fe de la existencia de personas u objetos;

  j) expedir copias literales o parciales de los instrumentos que obren en los protocolos y archivos de la no-

ch）取得司法部颁发的相关资质证明。

第9条 无论是经选举还是任命，公证员都不得在其他行政管理机关或执法部门任职，但在司法部任职、担任教育工作者、科学家或者人民政权机构代表或议员的情况除外。针对在人民政权机构担任代表或议员的情况，如果是在人民政权机构担任行政职务的，也不得担任公证员。

第三章 公证员的职责和义务

  第10条 公证员的职责和义务如下：

  a）针对法律要求合法化和公证的法律行为进行公证，另外对有关当事人要求进行证明的行为进行公证；

  b）针对涉及或者说明某人法律权利或利益的事实、文件或其他情况进行公证，或者证明其他任何法律声明文件；

  c）根据本法及其规定，公证、办理并出具属于自愿管辖范围内的文件以及继承权声明文件；

  ch）认证司法文件的合法性，证明公证书中说明的事实、文件和情况的合法性，同时确保这些文件和内容符合公证要求。

  d）针对公证书中涉及的公证当事人的认知和能力给出意见；

  e）公证付款票据、拒付票据、通知以及各种认证文件；

  f）将所有公共文件或者私有文件列入在案；

  g）留存商品或其它物品、证券、不动产的相关文件，留存原件或者作为签订相关合同的抵押；

  h）证明国内法的有效性，从而使其在国外产生效力，证明西班牙语翻译成其它语言的文件，或者证明其他语言翻译成西班牙语的文件；如果掌握其它语言，也可证明其他语言的文件；证明某人或某物的存在；

  j）出具需要公证的原始文件的全部内容或部分内容的副本以及该公证处其他文件的副本；

taría a su cargo;

k) autorizar actos de testimonio, literal o en relación, por exhibición de documentos que se le presenten a ese objeto o que se encuentren en archivos a los que se autorice su acceso;

l) autorizar la formalización de matrimonios;

ll) asesorar a las personas naturales o jurídicas que requieran sus servicios, a quienes instruye sus derechos y los medios jurídicos para el logro de sus fines, esclarece las dudas y advierte del alcance jurídico de las manifestaciones que formulen en el documento notarial de que se trate;

m) subsanar, de conformidad con el Reglamento de esta Ley, los errores u omisiones en los documentos notariales siempre que éstos no constituyan causa de nulidad o alteren substancialmente la identidad de los comparecientes en el documento de que se trate;

n) mantener la discreción necesaria en la tramitación de los asuntos de que conozca, excepto en los que, por su carácter publico pueden ser objeto de información y exhibición de conformidad con lo dispuesto en la ley;

ñ) hacer las advertencias previstas en la ley al momento de autorizar el documento notarial de que se trate;

o) organizar, dirigir, administrar y controlar técnicamente la actividad de la notaria a su cargo;

p) aplicar el arancel notarial vigente;

q) informar de su gestión a la autoridad superior competente;

r) cumplir las demás atribuciones que legalmente correspondan.

Art. 11-Se prohibe al Notario:

a) autorizar instrumentos notariales fuera de los límites de su competencia territorial, excepto en los casos del inciso c) de este Art.;

b) ejercer la función de abogado, excepto para asumir la dirección legal de los asuntos relacionados con sus propios derechos e intereses, los de su cónyuge o los de sus parientes hasta el cuarto grado de consanguinidad o segundo de afinidad;

c) negarse a prestar sus servicios cuando sea requerida su intervención, aún fuera de su horario de trabajo si el requirente o interesado se hallare en eminente peligro de muerte o en circunstancias excepcionales.

ch) constituirse en fiador de los contratos que autorice o autorizar documentos notariales que tenga interés o en que las partes o testigos sean parientes suyos dentro del cuarto grado de consanguinidad o segundo de afinidad;

k）接受公证书材料，证明公证书原件或相关文件的效力，或者证明存档的公证书的效力；

l）确认婚姻合法；

ll）帮助有需要的自然人或者法人达成目的，使其了解其权利和可采用的法律手段，澄清疑惑，并说明涉及的公证书中的内容的法律范畴。

m）根据本法相关规定，更正公证书中的错误和遗漏，但前提是这些错误或者遗漏不会导致文件失效并且也不会改变文件公证当事人的实际身份；

n）在办理手续的过程中，注意进行必要的保密工作；如果根据法律规定，经办事宜是可以公开告知或者公示的除外；

ñ）在认证公证书时，应当预先说明法律的相关规定。

o）从技术角度组织、管理并控制职责范围内的公证活动；

p）采用现行公证收费标准；

q）向其有关上级通报公证管理情况；

r）履行其他相应的法定职能。

第11条 公证员不得有以下行为：

a）公证非职权管辖范围内的文件，但本条c项列出的情况除外；

b）行使律师职能，除非是涉及自己本人、配偶或者近亲属权益的事件，这种情况下，可为自己的四代以内直系血亲或者二代内旁系血亲行使律师职能；

c）拒绝按要求提供公证服务，尤其是当需要服务的人或者公证当事人处在生命危急关头或者处在非常情况下的时候，即使已经超出公证员的工作时间，公证员也不得拒绝。

ch）担任合同文件的担保人，或者对涉及自己利益的文件进行公证，或者自己的四代以内直系血亲或者二代以内旁系血亲是公证当事人或者见证人时也不得公证该文件；在最后这种情况，如果这些亲属是代

en este último caso, podrá autorizarlos cuando los mencionados parientes corran en representación de persona natural o jurídica.

Se consideran prohibiciones, además, los actos o conductas que integran infracciones de las legislaciones sobre la disciplina de los dirigentes y funcionarios administrativos estatales.

Art. 12- El incumplimiento por los notarios de las funciones, obligaciones ó prohibiciones que se establecen en esta Ley y su Reglamento, dará lugar a la aplicación de las medidas disciplinarias previstas en la legislación sobre la disciplina de los dirigentes y funcionarios administrativos estatales de conformidad con el procedimiento que se regule en ésta, sin perjuicio de la responsabilidad penal o civil en que puedan haber incurrido.

CAPITULO IV De Los Documento Notariales

Art. 13- Los documento públicos que redacta y autoriza el Notario son los siguientes :

a) Las escrituras cuyo contenido es un acto jurídico;

b) las actas, en las que se hacen constar hechos, actos o circunstancias que, por su naturaleza, no constituyen acto jurídico;

c) cualquier otro que se establezca en la ley .-

Art. 14- En ningún documento notarial se podrán consignar cláusulas, manifestaciones de voluntad, hechos, actos o circunstancias contrarias a derecho o a la moral de nuestra sociedad y si se consignaren serán nulos.-

Art. 15- Las copias de los documentos originales que autoriza el Notario tienen la misma eficacia de éstos. Dichas copias podrán ser confeccionadas por medios manuales, mecánicos y automatizados.-

Art. 16- Son nulos los documento notariales :

a) autorizados por el Notario en las circunstancias a que se refiere el inciso a) del artículo 11 de esta Ley;

b) en que no conste la identidad y firma del Notario o la identidad, el juicio sobre el conocimiento o la capacidad y firma de los comparecientes y de los testigos, en su caso;

c) en los que el juicio que emite el Notario se basa en la declaraciones de testigos obligatorios y éstos sean inhábiles;

d) cuando concurran otras causas previstas en la ley.

La nulidad e invalidez de los documentos notariales sólo puede efectuarse mediante resolución de tribunal competente.

表其他自然人或法人，那么可以公证相关文件。

公证员还不得出现涉嫌构成违反国家公务员和领导纪律的行为。

第 12 条　如果根据本法和相关规定，公证员未能完成职责、未能履行自己的义务或者有明令禁止的行为出现，那么应当根据本法及其实施条例的规定，以及对国家公职人员要求的相关法律规定，对其进行纪律处分；另外追究其可能要承担的民事和刑事责任。

第四章　公证文书

第 13 条　公证员起草并公证的公共文件如下：

a）记载了法律行为的文书；

b）那些记录了事实、行为、情况，但实质上又不构成法律行为的会议记录；

c）法律规定的其他文件。

第 14 条　在任何公证书中都不得写入违反社会主义法律和道德的条款、意愿表达、事实、行为或者任何类似情况，如果有这些内容，则该公证书视为无效。

第 15 条　经公证员公证的原件副本具有与原件同等的效力。该副本可以是手写、机打或者自动生成的。

第 16 条　下列公证书无效：

a）在本法律第 11 条 a 项列出的情形下，公证员作出的公证；

b）在文件中没有写明公证员的身份或者没有公证员签名，或者没有公证员对公证对象的判断，或者根据具体情况没有写明公证当事人或者证明人的资格或者签名；

c）公证员作出的判断是建立在必要的证人证言的基础上，但是该证人无行为能力；

d）法律规定的其他情况。

只有相关法院才能判决公证书无效。

Art. 17- Son nulas las adiciones, enmiendas, textos entrelíneas, sobre raspados o testados, en los documentos notariales que no se salven al final de éstos, con aprobación expresa de los que deban suscribir el instrumento.

Art. 18- El Notario autoriza los documentos originales y las copias de éstos con su firma y el sello oficial de la notaría.

Art. 19- Para que los documentos notariales o certificaciones expedidas por Notario o funcionario extranjero surtan efecto en el territorio nacional, deben protocolizarse ante el Notario en cuba, previo el cumplimiento de las formalidades establecidas en el Reglamento de esta Ley, excepto lo dispuesto en tratados o convenios internacionales suscritos por nuestro país.

Art. 20- Los documentos notariales que autoricen actos de jurisdicción voluntaria, incluyendo el proceso sucesorio de declaratoria de herederos, podrán ser impugnados en la vía judicial, por los que tengan interés legítimo, de conformidad con la legislación civil.

CAPITULO V Del Protocolo Notarial

Art. 21- El protocolo se forma con los documentos originales y otros agregados por el Notario durante cada año natural.

Art. 22- El protocolo y los documentos que lo integran, no pueden ser extraídos del local que ocupa la notaría, oficina notarial o archivo provincial de protocolos notariales en que se custodian, excepto en las circunstancias siguientes :

a) para su traslado al archivo correspondiente;

b) por disposición del Ministerio de Justicia o de los tribunales;

c) en caso de fuerza mayor.

El protocolo y los documentos que lo integran no podrán ser destruidos, aún cuando se encuentren en mal estado. Se exceptúan los casos en que, habiendo sido reconstruidos total o parcialmente, su notoria inutilidad justifique su destrucción, previa aprobación del Ministerio de Justicia.

Art. 23- La reconstrucción de los documentos notariales compete al Notario y se ajustará a los requisitos y formalidades que se establecen en el Reglamento de la presente Ley. El documento reconstruido tiene la misma eficacia jurídica que el original.

Art. 24- Constituyen la base legal para la reconstrucción total o parcial del documento notarial :

第17条　如果在公证书中有刮擦或者删除的痕迹，且在这些删除处写有补充内容、修改内容或者行间批注文字，但是这些内容并未经过签字各方同意，那么这些批改内容无效。

第18条　公证员以签名并加盖公证处的公章来承认文件原件和副本的有效性。

第19条　除和古巴有国际协定或者国际约定的情况外，为使外国公证员或者公职人员签发的公证书或者证明书在古巴国境内有效，应当遵循本法之规定，在古巴公证处对该文件进行备案。

第20条　如果公证书涉及的是自愿管辖权内的行为，包括关于对继承人的继承权公证事项，可以由法定的利益相关方根据民法的规定，通过司法途径提出申诉。

第五章　公证存档

第21条　存档文件是每个自然年收存的文件原件和公证员添加的其他文件。

第22条　存档和其中的每一份文件都不得被带出公证处所在地，不得被带出公证处办公室或者省级的公证书档案馆，但下列情况除外：

a）为将文件迁入相应的档案馆；

b）司法部或者法院要求使用；

c）出现不可抗力。

存档和其中的每一份文件都不得损毁，即便是文件破损，也不得损毁。除非该文件无效可以销毁，或者对该文件进行全部或者部分重建，这些情况也都要通过司法部的事先批准。

第23条　应当根据本法规定各项要求，由公证员对公证文件进行重建。重建后的文件和原件具有同等的法律效力。

第24条　下列内容为重建公证文件的合法依据：

a) las copias autorizadas de éstos;

b) los que obren en el protocolo y su estado lo permita;

c) los antecedentes que obren en archivo y registros oficiales.

CAPITULO VI De Los Comparecientes En El Documento Notarial

Art. 25- Los comparecientes son los sujetos del documento notarial y su presencia por sí o por representación es obligatoria en el acto de autorización.

Art. 26- En todo documento notarial se consigna el o los nombres y apellidos de los comparecientes, el carácter con que concurren, el número de identidad permanente, ciudadanía, lugar de nacimiento, edad, ocupación, vecindad y cualquier otra circunstancia del estado civil que para el acto se requiera.

Art. 27-El Notario, para consignar los datos señalados en el artículo anterior, exige de los comparecientes el documento oficial de identidad, salvo en los casos siguientes:

a) que al momento de autorizar el acto y por circunstancias excepcionales, no lo pueda exhibir y siempre que sean conocidos por el Notario, en cuyo caso éste emite indicio de conocimiento.

b) cuando por circunstancias excepcionales la postergación de la autorización del documento notarial pudiera causar perjuicios irreparables en los interesados. En este caso el Notario autoriza el documento y exige la presencia de dos testigos de conocimiento.

En los casos de comparecientes extranjeros, el Notario exige además, el documento oficial que autoriza: su estancia en el territorio nacional.

Art. 28-Son incapaces para comparecer en los actos que autoriza el Notario, los que autorice expresamente; los incapaces para el acto de que se trate y que la ley determina en relación con un acto en particular.

Art. 29-Los testigos intervienen en el documento notarial de que se trate para acreditar, en su caso:

a) el conocimiento de los comparecientes;

b) la veracidad de la actuación notarial y su solemnidad cuando así se requiera;

c) La veracidad de las manifestaciones de los comparecientes.

Art. 30- No pueden ser testigos en el documento notarial :

a）该文件的公证副本；

b）组成该存档的其他可用文件；

c）存档文件中的相关背景资料和官方注册信息。

第六章　公证书中的公证当事人

第25条　公证当事人是公证书的主体，在公证过程中，公证当事人必须亲自或者派代表到场。

第26条　在所有公证书中都应写明公证当事人的姓名、关系、长效身份证件号码、市民身份、出生地、年龄、职业、居住地和婚姻状况等办理公证的必要信息。

第27条　为了写明上述信息，公证员要求公证当事人出示身份证件，但是下列情况除外：

a）在进行公证时，因为特殊情况无法出示身份证件，而公证员对该情况表示了解的，且公证员要出具情况说明；

b）在特殊情况下，如果延期进行公证的话，将会对公证当事人的利益造成无法挽回的损害。在这种情况下，公证员应当对文件进行公证，同时要求两名证人在场作证。

如果公证当事人为外国籍，公证员还应要求出具能证明其在古巴国内合法居留的文件。

第28条　公证员明确说明无出席公证行为能力的人员，以及法律规定不得出席某项公证事宜的人员不得出席公证过程。

第29条　下列情况需要证人出席公证过程来证明：

a）确认公证当事人；

b）如有需要，证明公证过程的真实性和严肃性；

c）公证当事人表述的真实性。

第30条　下列人员不得担任公证证人：

a) los menores de dieciocho años de edad;

b) los incapacitados judicialmente para el acto de que se trate;

c) los ciegos o sordos, para declarar sobre hechos cuyo conocimiento les está impedido, en razón de su limitación;

ch) los parientes del Notario interviniente dentro del cuarto grado de consanguinidad o segundo de afinidad;

d) los que hayan sido sancionados por delitos contra la fe pública o perjurio;

e) los herederos o legatarios, ni sus parientes dentro del cuarto grado de consanguinidad o segundo de afinidad;

f) los parientes del compareciente, dentro del cuarto grado de consanguinidad o segundo de afinidad;

g) los que no entienden el idioma del compareciente o en el que está redactado el documento.

CAPITULO VII De Las Notarias, Oficinas Notariales Y Archivos De Protocolos Notariales

Art. 31- La notaría está a cargo de un Notario. En un mismo municipio pueden tener su sede una o varias notarias.

Art. 32-Cuando un Notario tiene competencia en otros municipios además de aquél en que tiene la sede de su notaria, podrán habilitarse en aquéllos, oficinas notariales adscriptas a dicha notaria.

Art. 33-En las notarias y oficinas notariales consulares se archivan y custodian sus respectivos protocolos y los documentos notariales autorizados durante los últimos veinte años.

Art. 34- En cada provincia radica un archivo de protocolos notariales a cargo de un Notario. En los archivos se encuentran depositados los protocolos de veinte y hasta cuarenta años de antigüedad formados en las notarias y oficinas notariales de la provincia; en las oficinas consulares; transcurrido dicho término son remitidos a la sección correspondiente del Archivo Histórico de la Academia de Ciencias de Cuba.

El Notario a cargo del archivo provincial de protocolos notariales ejerce las funciones establecidas en los arts. 10 y 23 de esta Ley.

CAPITULO VIII De La Direccion Tecnica Y Administrativa De La Actividad Y Funcion Notariales

Art. 35- El Ministerio de Justicia ejerce la Dirección técnica, normativa y metodológica relacionada con la actividad y función notariales, y a tales efectos tiene las

a）不满18周岁的未成年人；

b）法律规定无相应行为能力的人员；

c）失明或失聪人士，因其身体因素限制，对所声明事件的认知有限；

ch）进行公证行为的公证员的四代以内直系血亲或者两代以内旁系血亲。

d）曾因违背社会公信被处罚，或因作伪证而被处罚的人员；

e）继承人或受遗赠人，以及其四代以内直系血亲或两代以内旁系血亲；

f）公证当事人的亲属，包括四代以内直系血亲或两代以内旁系血亲；

g）不懂公证当事人使用语言或者不懂公证文件使用语言的人。

第七章 公证处、公证办公室和公证档案馆

第31条 一名公证员负责一处公证处。在同一个城市可以有一处或多处公证处。

第32条 如果公证员除了在公证处总部所在城市外，在其他城市也有职权，那么可以在这些城市设立公证办公室，隶属于该公证处。

第33条 在公证处和各领事处公证办公室归档并留存相应的公证档案以及最近二十年来这些地方公证的文件。

第34条 在各省都有公证档案馆，由一名公证员负责。其中存档的包括在各公证处、各省公证办公室以及各领事处办公室的公证书，这些文件为近二十年乃至四十年来的公证书；一旦超过这一时间期限，这些文件将被存入古巴科学院历史档案馆。

负责省级公证档案馆的公证员，其职责在本法律第10条和第23条中都有规定。

第八章 公证工作和职责的技术与行政管理

第35条 司法部长对公证业务和职责进行技术、规范和方法上的管理，因此具有以下职权：

atribuciones siguientes:

a) asesorar, inspeccionar y controlar el trabajo de direcciones de justicia en la actividad y función notariales;

b) realizar o disponer que se efectúen inspecciones técnicas a las notarias, oficinas notariales y archivos provinciales de protocolos notariales para comprobar el, cumplimiento de las disposiciones y normas jurídicas relacionadas con esta actividad;

c) establecer normas metodológicas que regulen la proyección de la red de unidades notariales, así como los requisitos para la creación, traslado, fusión y cierre de dichas unidades;

ch) elaborar, promover, desarrollar y, en su caso, ejecutar planes y cursos regulares y especiales de capacitación y formación técnico notarial;

d) convocar a reuniones metodológicas, seminarios: otros eventos de carácter técnico en la actividad y función notariales;

e) brindar asesoramiento técnico en todas aquellas cuestiones que aseguren el adecuado cumplimiento de las normas y disposiciones establecidas y para el mejor funcionamiento y desarrollo de dichas actividades;

f) establecer la plantilla tipo para las unidades notariales, archivos de protocolos notariales y oficinas notariales;

g) establecer los modelos, formularios y demás documentos para el uso de los notarios en su actividad técnica;

h) las demás que se establecen en la ley.

Art. 36- Las direcciones de Justicia de los órganos provinciales del Poder Popular y la del Municipio Especial Isla de la Juventud ejercen el control de las actividades administrativas y de prestación de servicios relacionadas con las unidades notariales, incluyendo el nombramiento del Notario, de su personal administrativo y de servicio; y contribuyen, además, en la inspección, asesoramiento, capacitación y superación técnica del personal de esas unidades.

Disposiciones Especiales

PRIMERA : A partir de la vigencia de esta Ley los tribunales se abstendrán de conocer y resolver los expedientes de administración de bienes de ausentes, de consignación y de información para perpetua memoria correspondientes a la jurisdicción voluntaria, incluyendo el proceso sucesorio de declaratoria de herederos, que se transfieren a la función notarial, excepto en los casos

a）在公证业务和职责方面，进行法律方面的指导、监督和管控；

b）对公证处、公证办公室和省级档案馆进行监督，从而保证遵守公证业务相关的法律条款和规定；

c）制定管理方法，以便规范公证机构的分布，同时便于规范公证机构的创立、搬迁、合并和关闭；

ch）制定、推广并开展公证业务培训课程，根据具体情况制定一般或特殊公证业务培训计划和课程。

d）举办工作方法会议和讲座，开展其他与公证业务或职责有关的技术性活动；

e）为了遵守法律规定以及更好地开展公证工作，针对各种问题提供技术性支持；

f）为各级公证机构、公证档案馆和公证办公室制定规划样板；

g）为公证员制定开展技术性工作所需的编制模板、表格和其他文件；

h）法律规定的其他职权。

第36条 省级人民司法机关和青年岛特别市司法机关负责管控公证机构的行政管理工作，管控公证机构的其他有关工作，包括公证员的任命以及行政人员和服务人员的任命；另外，这些司法机关还要进行监督、咨询工作，以及对这些单位人员的技术培训和提高工作。

特别条例

一、自本法律生效之日起，对自愿管辖范围内的下列手续办理，即下落不明人员的财产的管理、分配和永久备忘，包括继承声明这些都划为公证职责范畴；如果各方意见不一、对他人造成侵害或者检察官给出不同意见，在这种情况下不属于公证范畴。

en que sea manifiesta la contradicción entre partes, resulten perjuicios a otras personas o se emita por el Fiscal dictamen en contrario.

Se exceptúan de lo dispuesto anteriormente los casos de incapacidad y las diligencias preventivas del proceso sucesorio a que se refiere la Ley de Procedimiento Civil, Administrativo y Laboral.

SEGUNDA : Para la substanciación de los asuntos a que se refiere la disposición anterior el Notario se regirá por lo que regule el Reglamento de esta Ley y en su defecto por el procedimiento establecido para éstos en la Ley de Procedimiento Civil, Administrativo y Laboral.

TERCERA : Los Notarios nombrados con anterioridad a la puesta en vigor de la presente Ley, siempre que al momento de su vigencia estén ejerciendo como tales, continuarán en esas funciones.

CUARTA : Los Notarios que se nombren por el Ministro de Justicia de conformidad con lo dispuesto en el decreto Ley 77, de 20 de enero de 1984, se regirán por la presente Ley en lo que al ejercicio de sus funciones, obligaciones y prohibiciones se establece, excepto lo estipulado en sus artículos 35, incisos a), c) y f), y 36.

Disposiciones Transitorias

PRIMERA : Los expedientes de jurisdicción voluntaria y de declaratoria de herederos a que se refiere la Primera de las Disposiciones Especiales y que al momento de entrada en vigor de la presente Ley están sustanciándose en los tribunales, se continuarán tramitando por estos, amparados en la legislación por la que se promovieron hasta su resolución definitiva.

SEGUNDA: Los protocolos con menos de cuarenta años que se encuentren a cargo de la sección correspondiente del Archivo Histórico de la Academia de Ciencias do Cuba se transferirán, en un término de ciento veinte días posteriores a la publicación de esta Ley, a los archivos provinciales de protocolos notariales correspondientes.

TERCERA: Los Notarios qué tengan en su poder protocolos con más de cuarenta años, los remitirán a la sección correspondiente del Archivo Histórico de la Academia de Ciencias de Cuba de la provincia de que se trate, en igual término establecido en la disposición anterior.:

Disposiciones Finales

PRIMERA: El Ministro de Justicia queda encargado, de dictar el Reglamento de la presente Ley dentro del

无资格的情况不包括在上述情况内，涉及民法、行政管理法和劳动法的财产继承前期手续也不包括在内。

二、针对上述条款列出的需要公证案件，公证员根据本法律规定进行办理；如有本法律未涉及部分，应根据民法、行政管理法和劳动法的相关规定办理。

三、在本法律生效前任命的公证员应继续履行其职能直到任期结束。

四、如果是司法部长根据1984年1月20日颁布的第77号法令任命的公证员，将根据本法规定行使公证员的职权、履行职责并遵守相关禁令，第35条第a项、c项和f项的内容除外。

过渡性条款

一、在本法生效之日，仍在由法院审理的自愿管辖范围内的案件和遗产继承声明，继续按照立案审理当时有效的法律规定执行，直至案件办结。

二、在本法颁布后的120日内，将在古巴科学院历史档案馆的相应部门存放的年限在40年以下的公证存档文件转移至相应的省级公证档案馆。

三、如果公证员留存有40年以上历史的公证存档文件，寄送到所在省的古巴科学院历史档案馆的相应部门，移交期限同上文规定。

最终条款

一、自本法颁布之日起，司法部长应在90日内颁布本法的实施条例，以及其他与本法的实施有关的

término de noventa días siguientes contados a partir de su vigencia y cuantas otras disposiciones se requieran para su cumplimento.

SEGUNDA: Se derogan el Código Notarial del 20 de febrero de l920; la Ley del 3 de junio de 1933; la Ley del 22 de agosto de 1936; el Decreto 2965 del 23 de noviembre de I969; la Ley 3 del 14 de noviembre del946; el Decreto 4678 del 21 de octubre de 1949, el artículo 23 de la Ley 714 del 22 de enero de l9 0; los artículos 3 y 4 de la Ley 118 del 25 de abril de 1965; y cuantas mas disposiciones legales, y reglamentarias se opongan al cumplimiento de la presente ley.

TERCERA: Esta Ley comenzará a regir a partir del día primero de junio de 1985.

DADA en la sala de sesiones de la Asamblea Nacional del Poder Popular, en la Ciudad de La Habana, a los veintiocho días del mes de diciembre de mil novecientos ochenta y cuatro.

Flavio Bravo Pardo

规定。

二、废止以下法律：1920年2月20日颁布的《公证法》；1933年6月3日颁布的法律；1936年8月22日颁布的法律；1969年11月23日颁布的第2965号法令；1946年11月14日颁布的第3号法令；1949年10月21日颁布的第4678号法令，1950年1月22日颁布的第714号法令第23条；1965年4月25日颁布的第118号法令第3条和第4条；以及其他和本法相悖的法律条款和规定。

三、本法自1985年6月1日起生效。

1984年12月28日，于哈瓦那市全国人民政权代表大会会议厅颁布。

弗拉维奥•布拉沃•帕尔多

国家公证法实施条例

GACETA OFICIAL de la REPUBLICA DE CUBA EDICION EXTRAORDINARIA LA HABANA, MARTES 9 DE JUNIO DE 1992 - AÑO XC

Distribución: Calle 43 N° 1157 e/36 y Lindero, Nuevo Vedado - Habana 4

Número 4 - Precio $ 0,05

Pag. 9

MINISTERIOS
JUSTICIA
RESOLUCION N° 70

POR CUANTO: La Ley N° 50, de 28 de diciembre de 1984. "Ley de las Notarias Estatales"; reguladora del ordenamiento técnico - administrativo de la actividad y función notariales, en su Disposición Final Primera, facultó al Ministro de Justicia para dictar el Reglamento de la misma, lo que se verificó mediante la Resolución 101 de 28 de junio de 1985.

POR CUANTO. La experiencia acumulada en estos años de aplicaci6n del referido Reglamento: ha permitido valorar la necesidad de atemperar: sus preceptivas a las exigencias del perfeccionamiento que requiere la actuaci6n notarial en el país.

POR TANTO. En uso de las facultades que me están conferidas,

: Resuelvo:

PRIMERO- Aprobar el nuevo Reglatmento de la Ley No. 50 de 28 de diciembre de 1984, "Ley de las Notarias, Estatales" que se anexa a la presente resolución, formando parte integrante de la misma y que comenzará a regir transcurridos sesenta días de su fecha.

SEGUNDO: Los servicios notariales que se encuentren en trámites a la entrada en vigor de este Reglamento, se continuarán tramitando de conformidad con la legislación notarial por la cual se promovieron:

TERCERO: Se deroga la Resolución 101 de 28 de Junio de l985, dictada por el Ministro de Justicia y cuantas otras disposiciones reglamentarias se opongan al cumplimiento de lo que establece este Reglamento.

CUARTO : Se faculta al Director de Registros y Notarías del Ministerio de Justicia para dictar cuantas disposiciones complementarias sean necesarias para la mejor

古巴共和国官方公报

特别版，1992年6月9日周二于哈瓦那

发行地址：哈瓦那4号，Nuevo Vedado 区第43号大街1137号和36号拐角处

第4号公报，定价0.05比索

第9页

司法部

第70号决议

鉴于1984年12月28日颁布的第50号法律《国家公证法》是规范公证活动和职责的技术行政管理规定，而在其最终条款中授权司法部长来颁布该法律的实施条例，该条例根据1985年6月28日的第101号决议获准通过。

鉴于根据该条例实施以来积累的多年经验，有必要结合目前国家公证业务的现状来调整相关要求，完善公证工作。

鉴于通过行使赋予我的法定职权，

我部决定：

一、批准1984年12月28日颁布的第50号法律《国家公证法》（该法律文本附在本决议后）的新实施条例，该条例是该法律的组成部分，自通过该决议之日起60日内生效。

二、在本条例生效之日，针对那些已在办理过程中的公证业务，仍按照既有公证法律规定继续办理。

三、废止司法部长于1985年6月28日颁布的第101号决议，同时废止和本条例相悖的其他管理规定。

四、授予司法部公证与登记处处长制定相应补充条款的权力，从而更好地落实和完善本条例内容。

aplicación y cumplimiento de lo que se establece en este Reglamento.

COMUNIQUESE a la Asamblea Nacional dei Poder Popular y al Comité Ejecutivo de! Consejo de Ministros.

NOTIFIQUESEa los Viceministros de Justicia, al Director de Registros y Notarías de este Organismo, a los Directores Provinciales de Justicia y del Municipio Especial Isla de la Juventud y a cuantas más personas naturales o jurídicas deban conocerla.

PUBLIQUESEen la Gaceta Oficial de la República para general conocimiento.

DADA en la ciudad de La Habana, Ministerio de Justicia, a los nueve días del mes de junio de mil novecientos noventa y dos.

Carlos Amat Forés - Ministro de Justicia

REGLAMENTO DE LA LEY DE LAS NOTARIAS ESTATALES

CAPITULO I
Disposiciones Generales

Sección Primera De los objetivos y alcance

Art. 1- Este Reglamento es complementario de la Ley No. 50, de 28 de diciembre de 1984, "Ley de las Notarías Estatales", a la que en el presente texto se aludirá abreviadamente como la "Ley", y establece las normas para su ejecución.

Art. 2- A los efectos de este Reglamento se entenderá como:

a) "Notario": al Notario, Notario - archivero de protocolos notariales y al Cónsul o funcionario diplomático en lo que corresponda;

b) "Unidad Notarial": a las notarías, archivos provinciales de protocolos notariales y oficinas notariales;

c) "Documento notarial": al documento público que autoriza el Notario, bien sea escritura, acta o cualquier otro previsto en la ley; y

Ch) "Matriz": al original del documento público que obra en el protocolo del Notario.

Art. 3- Cuando el Notario tuviere dudas sobre la correcta interpretación de la legislación, se dirigirá mediante escrito, en consulta, al Ministerio de Justicia por conducto de las Direcciones Provinciales de Justicia.

Las consultas serán evacuadas a través de los

请通报全国人民政权代表大会以及部长会议执行委员会。

请通知司法部部长、司法部公证与登记处处长、各省级司法局长、青年岛特别市司法局长，以及其他应知悉的自然人和法人。

请在共和国官方公报上公开本决议。

1992年6月9日在哈瓦那市司法部颁布

司法部长：卡洛斯·阿玛特·弗雷斯

国家公证法实施条例

第一章
总则

第一节　目的与范围

第1条　本条例是1984年12月28日颁布的第50号法律《国家公证法》（本文中简称为"法律"）的补充旨在落实该法律。

第2条　在本条例中各定义如下：

a）"公证员"：公证书存档管理人员、领事或者是从事相应工作的外交公务员；

b）"公证机构"：公证处、省级公证档案馆，以及公证办公室；

c）"公证书"：公证员出具的公共文书——可以是公证状、公证记录或者其他任何法律规定的形式；以及

Ch）"母本"：公证员存档的公共文件的原件。

第3条　如果公证员对法律的理解是否正确有疑问，可通过省级司法局向司法部进行书面咨询。

为了解决咨询事项，司法部应当根据咨询内容出

dictámenes correspondientes, los que serán de obligatoria observancia para la resolución de los asuntos sometidos a consulta.

Cuando a juicio de la Dirección de Registros y Notarías la respuesta de una consulta pudiera ser de aplicación para la generalidad de la actividad notarial, ésta se dará a conocer a los notarios y será de obligatorio cumplimiento.

Sección Segunda De la Habilitación

Art. 4-La habilitación es el proceso mediante el cual se determina la capacidad profesional para el ejercicio; de la función notarial.

Art. 5- El proceso de habilitación constará de:
a) convocatoria;
b) confección del expediente del interesado;
c) constitución del tribunal examinador;
ch) examen de capacidad;
d) evaluación de los resultados del examen y del expediente;
e) expedición del título de habilitación.

Art. 6- EL proceso de habilitación comenzará a partir de la convocatoria que al efecto libre el Ministerio de Justicia o las direcciones Provinciales de Justicia, en su caso. las convocatorias podrán ser ordinarias o extraordinarias.

Art. 7- Las solicitudes de los interesados se presentarán ante las direcciones provinciales de Justicia o el Ministerio de Justicia, en su caso, dentro del término que se establezca a partir de la publicación de la convocatoria.

Art. 8- Podrán solicitar la habilitación las personas que cumplan los requisitos siguientes :
a) ser ciudadano cubano;
b) ser doctor o licenciado en derecho; y
c) poseer buenas condiciones morales y gozar de buen concepto público.

Los requisitos anteriormente relacionados se acreditarán documentalmente por el interesado y se formará un expediente cuya confección estará a cargo de la oficina que reciba la solicitud de conformidad con el artículo 7 de este Reglamento.

Art. 9- Las direcciones provinciales de Justicia o el Ministerio de Justicie, en su caso, analizarán el resultado del expediente a que se refiere el artículo anterior y determinarán la continuación del proceso, lo que se comunicará oportunamente al aspirante seleccionado.

Art. 10- Cumplido el trámite a que se refiere el

具相关意见。

如果公证和注册登记处处长认为某一咨询的答复广泛适用于所有公证活动，应使所有的公证员都知悉并且都必须遵循这一答复内容。

第二节　资质认定

第4条　资质认定即确认其是否具有行使公证职权的资质。

第5条　资质评定程序为：
a）发出招考通知；
b）编制报考人员的档案；
c）成立评审委员会；
ch）资质考核；
d）对考核结果和相关文件进行评定；
e）颁发资质证书。

第6条　自司法部长或省级司法局发起招考工作之日起，便开始进行资质评定工作。可以是常规性招考也可以是特殊招考。

第7条　资质申请人应当向司法部或者省级司法局提交申请，应当在发出招考通知之日起的一定时间内提交该申请，该时间在招考文件中列明。

第8条　满足下列条件的人员可以申请资质：

a）是古巴公民；
b）是法学硕士或学士；
c）有良好的道德品质并享有良好的声誉。

应由申请人在文件中写明以上要求，该要求为评估文件的一部分；该评估文件由接受申请的公证办公室出具，文件内容应符合本条例第7条的规定。

第9条　根据具体情况，省级司法局或者司法部长将评估上文提到的文件并决定是否进行下一步评估，并以合适的方式将该文件评估结果告知申请人。

第10条　完成上文的手续后，经过筛选的候选

artículo anterior, los aspirantes seleccionados rendirán el examen de capacidad ante el tribunal correspondiente.

Art. 11- La constitución, integración y mandato de dichos tribunales se hará por Resolución del Ministro de Justicia.

Los tribunales estarán integrados por cinco juristas de reconocidos prestigio profesional y social. En el caso de las direcciones provinciales de Justicia, tres serán notarios y los restantes juristas, uno de éstos en representación de las mencionadas direcciones.

Art. 12- Constituido el tribunal, éste señalará día y hora de realización del examen. Dicho examen se efectuará en un término no superior a los sesenta días a partir del momento que se dé respuesta al aspirante seleccionado de conformidad con el artículo 9 de este Reglamento.

Si por causa injustificadas el aspirante seleccionado no se presentare al examen en el día y hora señalados, no se constituirá el proceso de habilitación.

Art. 13- Los tribunales realizarán los exámenes de conformidad con las temáticas y normas que establezcan de conjunto los Departamentos de Capacitación y Notarías, ambos del Ministerio de Justicia.

Art. 14- El Director Provincial de Justicia, por conducto de la Dirección de Registros y Notarías del Ministerio de Justicia, elevará al Ministro la propuesta de habilitación, a la cual acompañará su opinión respecto a las características personales del aspirante seleccionado y la valoración que el tribunal examinador realizó sobre los resultados obtenidos en el examen de habilitación. Copia del mencionado escrito se unirá al expediente, que quedará en la Dirección Provincial de Justicia.

Art. 15- Si el Ministro de Justicia aprobare la propuesta a que se refiere el artículo anterior, dictará resolución de habilitación y expedirá el título correspondiente.

Art. 16- En el título de habilitación se harán constar los datos siguientes :

a) nombres y apellidos del habilitado;
b) aptitud del habilitado para el ejercicio de la función notarial;
c) fecha de expedición y número del título; y
ch) firma del Ministro de Justicia.

El título de habilitación se hará en ejemplar único para el interesado, dejándose copia certificada en el expediente que a esos efectos se encuentra formado en la Dirección de Registros y Notarías del Ministerio de Justicia, la que podrá expedir cuantas certificaciones sean necesarias de dicho título a las personas naturales o jurídicas que

人将参加相应的评审委员会组织的考核。

第 11 条　由司法部成立、组成并授权相应的委员会。

评审委员会由五位具有一定职业和社会威望的法学专家组成。如果是省级司法局考核，委员会中将有三名公证员和两名法学家，其中一名法学家是省级司法局派出的代表。

第 12 条　评审委员会成立后，将说明考试日期和具体时间。在根据本条例第 9 条向入选人通知结果后，将在不超过 60 日的时间内举行考核。

如果入选人在考核当天未能按时参加考试，且没有正当理由，即视为未参加资格评定。

第 13 条　司法部下属培训处和公证处共同出台考核规定，委员会将根据该规定进行考核。

第 14 条　省级司法局局长应当通过司法部登记和公证处向司法部长提交考核结果，包括省级司法局长对入选人员的个人评价以及评审委员会给出的考核结果。这些书面内容副本将和评定文件一起留存在省级司法局。

第 15 条　如果司法部通过上文所说的考核结果，应当发布资质授予决议，并颁布资质证书。

第 16 条　资质证书上将写明下列内容：

a）资质获得者的姓名；
b）资质获得者的公证职权范围；
c）证书颁发日期和时间；以及
ch）司法局长签名。

应授予资质获得者资质证书的唯一正本，司法部登记和公证处留存副本；司法部登记和公证处可向需要知情的自然人或者法人出具关于该证书的各种证明，包括向司法部律师注册处出具证明。

deban conocerlo, incluyendo al Registro de Abogados del Ministerio de Justicia.

Art. 17- La habilitación se extinguirá por las causas siguientes :

a) fallecimiento,

b) renuncia a la habilitación,

c) renuncia al cargo de Notario salvo en los dos últimos casos contemplados en el artículo 9 de la Ley;

ch) revocación del cargo de Notario;

d) jubilación;

e) incapacidad física o intelectual;

f) transcurrido cinco años sin que en ese término el habilitado haya sido nombrado Notario;

g) otras causas justificadas.

Art. 18- Los aspirantes seleccionados que no resulten habilitados podrán repetir la solicitud en posteriores convocatorias.

Sección Tercera Del nombramiento

Art. 19- El jurista habilitado podrá ser nombrado Notario por el Director Provincial de Justicia o el Ministro de Justicia, en su caso, de conformidad con los intereses locales o nacionales para garantizar la prestación del servicio notarial.

Art. 20- El nombramiento se realizará mediante resolución, donde se hará constar que el interesado ha sido previamente habilitado por el Ministro de Justicia y se consignará el número del título de habilitación, la competencia territorial donde el nombrado ejercerá la función notarial, la sede de su notaría y las oficinas notariales que atenderá.

Art. 21- Copia de la resolución del nombramiento se entregará el interesado y otra será remitida al Ministerio de Justicia dentro de los cinco días hábiles siguientes al nombramiento, unido a las tarjetas de control de firma del Notario y cualquier otro documento que se solicite.

Art. 22- Del cargo de Notario se tomará posesión en el transcurso de los treinta días hábiles siguientes a partir de la notificación de la resolución de nombramiento. Transcurrido dicho término sin que se haya tomado posesión del cargo, quedará sin efectos el nombramiento, excepto en los casos de fuerza mayor.

Art. 23- El Notario al tomar posesión del cargo presta el juramento siguiente :

Yo Notario con competencia en y con sede en de la provincia de tomo posesión del cargo para el

第17条　如出现下列情况，将取消资质：

a）死亡；

b）放弃资质；

c）辞去公证员职务，但《公证法》第9条规定的情况除外；

ch）被撤销公证员职务。

d）退休；

e）身体或智力残疾；

f）资质获得者在5年时间内一直未被任命为公证员；

g）其他正当理由。

第18条　筛选出的候选人中未获得资质的，可再次参加之后的公证员招考活动。

第三节　任命

第19条　司法部长或者省级司法局长可以在保障公证工作的前提下，根据国家或地方的具体情况任命获得资质的法律人士为公证员。

第20条　任命要通过正式决议。在决议中要写明被任命人员是预先经过司法部资质评定的，还要写明资质证书号、被任命人行使公证职权的地理范围、被任命人的公证处以及下属公证办公室。

第21条　任命决议副本一份交付被任命人，一份在任命决议下达后5日内交付给司法部，一同交付给司法部的还有公证员签名样本卡以及其他需要的文件。

第22条　自通知任命决议之日起的30日内，公证员应当到任。如果超过30日，公证员未能到任，则该任命无效，不可抗力情况除外。

第23条　公证员就职时应作如下宣誓：

本人＿＿＿＿，系公证员，职权范围是＿＿＿＿，办公地点位于＿＿＿＿省，在＿＿＿＿的见证下就任职

cual he sido designado y en

presencia de

JURO

-Observar y hacer cumplir la Constitución, las leyes y demás normas jurídicas; y

-cumplir de manera cabal, las obligaciones que vienen impuestas por el cargo para el cual he sido nombrado.

DADO en la ciudad de a los días del mes de de 19..

Firma :

El juramento se hará por escrito en original con dos copias, el original será conservado por el Notario y las copias serán remitidas al Ministerio de Justicia y a la Dirección Provincial de Justicia correspondiente a los efectos procedentes.

Sección Cuarta De las Sustituciones

Art. 24- En caso de enfermedad, ausencia temporal o cualquier otra imposibilidad transitoria del Notario para ejercer sus funciones se encargará del protocolo a su cargo y lo sustituirá provisionalmente el Notario designado para ello mediante resolución, del Director Provincial de Justicia que corresponda o del Ministro de Justicia, en su caso.

Art. 25- En la resolución a que hace referencia el artículo anterior, se expresarán las razones que han motivado dicha sustitución provisional.

Art. 26- Previa a la sustitución, si esta fuera por un período mayor de 45 días, la Dirección Provincial de Justicia o el Ministerio de Justicia, en su caso, realizará una inspección técnica que permita conocer el estado en que se encuentra el protocolo notarial y otros particulares y una auditoría a los efectos de evaluar el control económico y financiero de la unidad.

Art. 27- En caso de muerte, jubilación, renuncia o revocación del cargo de Notario o cualquier otra causa que imposibilite definitivamente al Notario ejercer sus funciones, previo al nombramiento de otro Notario, se realizará la inspección técnica y la auditoria a que se refiere el artículo precedente.

Sección Quinta De la competencia

Art. 28- El Notario realizará sus funciones dentro de la demarcación territorial que se fije en su nombramiento.

Art. 29- En aquellos casos en que por razones de prestación de los servicios, sea necesario extender temporalmente la competencia de un Notario a otra provincia

务,

我宣誓

遵守并执行宪法、法律和其他法律规定；

严格履行我所就任职务的有关职责。

19×× 年 ×× 月 ×× 日于 ×××× 市。

签字：_____

宣誓书为书面形式，一份正本，两份副本。正本由公证员留存，而副本将寄送至司法部和相应的省级司法局。

第四节 替补

第 24 条   如果公证员因生病、短期离职或者其他任何临时性原因无法行使职责，将根据具体情况由司法部长或省级司法局局长通过颁布决议临时任命公证员来替补该职位，并负责原公证员管辖权下的公证书存档。

第 25 条   在上文提及的决议中，应说明该临时性替补的原因。

第 26 条   如果公证员离职时间超过 45 日，在任命替补之前，省级司法局或者司法部长应根据具体情况进行技术检查，了解公证存档文件和其他私人文件的情况；还要进行审计工作，评估该公证机构的经济和财务状况。

第 27 条   如果因为死亡、退休、辞职、职务撤销或者其他任何原因导致公证员永久性地无法行使职权，那么在任命新公证员之前，应当按上文所述进行技术检查和审计工作。

第五节 职权

第 28 条   公证员在其被任命的公证辖区范围内行使职权。

第 29 条   出于公务需要，有必要将公证员的职权暂时延伸到不属于其所在地省份的，涉及的省级司法局长应事先进行协调；一旦达成协议，这些省级司

distitna a la de su sede, los directores provinciales de Justicia interesados deberán coordinar previamente y una vez logrado el acuerdo, solicitarán al Ministro de Justicia dicha extensión y el término que durará la misma.

Art. 30- Los notarios comprendidos en el artículo anterior abrirán protocolos en los lugares donde se designe.

Art. 31- En el caso de los notarios con competencia nacional las matrices de los documentos que autoricen, serán incorporadas al protocolo de la notaria a su cargo.

CAPITULO II
Del Documento Notarial

Sección Primera Disposiciones generals

Art. 32- El documento o notarial se redactará en idioma español, con letra clara, sin abreviaturas, iniciales, ni dejar espacios en blanco y en él podrán utilizarse.

Art. 33- Los espacios en blanco en el documento notarial se inutilizará y lo escrito sobre ellos será nulo. En igual forma se procederá cuando los comparecientes firmen dejando espacios en blanco entre la firma y la conclusión del texto.

Art. 34- El documento notarial podrá hacerse en forma manuscrita, mecanografiada o por cualquier otro medio de reproducción y se ajustará a los requisitos siguientes :

a) el papel que se utilice será de la mejor calidad posible;

b) el anverso de cada hoja de las matrices tendrá al lado izquierdo un margen de 2 cm. Para la encuadernación, mas 6 cms. En blanco a lo largo de la plana para las notas y firmas y al lado derecho un margen de 1,5 cms; y

c) el reverso de la matriz tendrá también al lado izquierdo un margen en blanco de 6 cms. a lo largo del papel y al lado derecho otro margen de 2 cms. para la encuadernación.

Art. 35- El notario leerá el documento notarial a todos los comparecientes, testigos y cualquier otro interviniente, previa advertencia del derecho que le asiste a cada uno de leer aquel por sí. En el caso de que renunciaren a ese derecho, el Notario procederá a su lectura en voz alta lo cual hará de inmediato, salvo en aquellos actos que tengan diligencias sucesivas, en cuyo caso se hará al final de cada una de éstas.

El Notario hará mención de los demás documentos agregados sin necesidad de leerlos.

Cuando el compareciente no pudiere leer, podrá des-

法局长应当向司法部长申请职权延伸，同时申请延伸职权的期限。

第30条　上文提到的公证员将在被指派的其他区域进行文件存档。

第31条　如果是国家级职权的公证员，那么公证员公证的文件的母本应当存入其辖下的公证处档案中。

第二章
公证书

第一节　一般规定

第32条　公证书应用西班牙语撰写，字体清晰，不得有缩写、首字母缩写，也不能留有空格留白，以防止被利用。

第33条　公证书的空格留白处不得使用，该空白处的文字也无效。同样，如果公证当事人在签字时在文字末尾和签名处留有空白，这些留白也不得使用，留白处文字也无效。

第34条　公证书可以是以手写、机打或者其他任何形式生成，但须满足下列要求：

a）应尽可能使用最好质量的纸张；

b）每页原件的左侧都要有2厘米的留白，如果需要装订，则需要再加宽6厘米作留白。留白处可用作签字或注释，而在右侧要有1.5厘米宽的留白；以及

c）在原件的背面左侧要有6厘米的留白，而在右侧要有2厘米的留白，留作装订使用。

第35条　公证员应向所有公证当事人、证人和其他所有涉及人员宣读公证书，前提是要事先告知所有有关人员他们有权自行阅读该文件。如果相关人员拒绝行使自己的阅读权利，那么公证员就应当即自行大声宣读公证书。如果是继承公证，公证员应在所有相关人都阅读过公证书后再宣读该文件。

公证员还要列明其他附加文件，但不需要读出这些文件。

如果公证当事人无法阅读，可以委派一个人来阅

ignar a otra persona para ello, lo cual se hará constar en el documento.

Concluida la lectura, el Notario preguntará a los comparecientes, testigos y demás intervinientes, si están conformes con el contenido del documento notarial y si lo estuvieren, se procederá en el acto a su firma.

Art. 36- Los comparecientes y testigos firmarán al margen de cada pliego y al final de la matriz del documento notarial. Los demás intervinientes sólo firmarán al final de la matriz. El notario estampará su firma al margen de cada pliego u hoja que conforme la matriz y al final de ésta, así como en los demás documentos agregados.-

Art. 37- Si el compareciente no pudiera firmar, estampará en el documento notarial las huellas dactilares de los dedos pulgares de ambas manos y a falta de éstos, de los que tuviere y solicitará que otra persona de su elección firme, lo que se hará constar en el referido documento.

De no ser posible al compareciente estampar las impresiones dactilares en el documento notarial, el Notario requerirá del compareciente la presencia de dos testigos, de los cuales uno, a elección del interesado, firmará a su ruego. El Notario hará constar en el citado documento las razones que impiden la toma de dichas impresiones.

Art. 38- Cuando el compareciente sea sordo, ciego o mudo o esté privado de mas de uno de dichos sentidos, el Notario exigirá además de los testigos que por este Reglamento se requieren para proceder a la autorización del documento notarial de que se trate la presencia de un testigo idóneo designado libremente por el compareciente para que lo asista en la referida autorización y firme, todo lo cual se hará constar por el Notario en el referido documento.

Sección Segunda De la redacción del Documento Notarial

Art. 39- En la redacción del documento notarial el Notario se atendrá a las intenciones de los comparecientes, indagando, hasta donde sea posible, el alcance de sus manifestaciones y en todo caso, le informará a dicho compareciente el contenido de las cláusulas obligatorias que conformarán el contrato o acto que se autorizará.

Art. 40- El Notario redactará la matriz del documento notarial, encabezándola con el número que le corresponda en su protocolo por orden de su autorización; el nombre que en derecho le corresponda al acto jurídico; hecho; acto o circunstancia; seguido del lugar; fecha de autorización; nombres y apellidos del Notario con expresión e la notaría

读，但需要在公证书中说明这一情况。

阅读完毕，公证员要询问公证当事人、证人和其他当事人是否同意公证书内容，如果同意，各有关人员可着手准备签字。

第36条 公证当事人和证人应在公证书原件的每页留白处和文章末尾签字。其他相关人员只在原文末尾签字。公证员要在原件的每页留白处和文章末尾加盖签名章，还要在其他附加文件的相同位置加盖签名章。

第37条 如果公证当事人无法签字，可以在公证书上印上自己双手拇指的手印；如果不能加盖手印，可申请由自己委派的人选代为签字，但应在公证书中要说明这一情况。

如果公证当事人无法在公证书上加盖手印，那么公证员应要求公证当事人提供两名证人出席，并且公证当事人要选择其中一人代为签字。公证员应在公证书中说明无法加盖手印的原因。

第38条 如果公证当事人为盲人或者是聋哑人，只要患有以上任何一项残障，那么除了本条例要求的两名证人，公证员还应要求公证当事人指定一名合适的证人出席来协助其完成相应授权并签字；而公证员在公证书中对以上情况加以说明。

第二节 公证书的编写

第39条 在公证书的撰写过程中，公证人应听取公证当事人的意愿，尽可能清楚地了解公证当事人表达的意愿；在任何情形下，公证员都要向公证当事人说明公证内容或者需要公证的合同中必要条款的内容。

第40条 公证员在撰写公证书原件时，应在抬头写明文件存档编号，该法律行为相应的法律名称，事实、行为或者情况，公证的地点和日期，公证员的姓名以及公证员辖下公证处名称和所在地。

a su cargo y lugar donde se constituya, en su caso.

Art. 41- Si no fuere posible titular el documento notarial con un nombre conocido en derecho, el Notario consignará el que más se ajuste a los derechos y obligaciones que estipulan los interesados y demás circunstancias jurídicamente relevante que declaren.

Art. 42- Los comparecientes podrán ofrecer al Notario minuta donde consten sus instrucciones, en este caso el Notario se atiene a dichas instrucciones, adaptándolas a las normas que regulan el contrato o acto de que se trate.

Art. 43- Si las minutas a que se refiere el artículo anterior son ambiguas, confusas o les falta claridad, el Notario advertirá a los comparecientes de los defectos u omisiones de que adolecen y adoptará la redacción que legalmente corresponda.

Art. 44- Cuando se requiera la presentación de documentos complementarios para la realización del acto, el Notario comprobará su legalidad y consignará en la matriz los datos que los tipifican y los elementos que acreditan el derecho o acción que se pretende ejercitar.

Art. 45- Cuando un documento escrito en idioma extranjero deba adjuntarse al documento notarial para formar parte de la matriz, es requisito indispensable realizar su traducción oficial, salvo que el Notario la realice.

Art. 46- Las salvedades se consignarán al final del documento notarial con excepción de aquellos que tengan diligencias sucesivas, en cuyo caso las salvedades se harán al final de cada una de éstas. En las matrices se consignará que las salvedades se hacen con aprobación de los comparecientes.

Art. 47- Las notas se consignarán al margen del documento notarial de que se trate o en cualquier espacio en blanco al final del texto o en diligencia a continuación del mismo y sin que produzcan confusión.

Las notas tendrán carácter accesorio con respecto al documento notarial que se autoriza y contendrán declaraciones oficiales del Notario que las realice en virtud del cumplimiento de disposiciones legales, reglamentarias o complementarias.

Sección Tercera De la subsanación de errores en el documento notarial

Art. 48- La subsanación de errores u omisiones en la matriz del documento notarial que no sean constitutivos de causales de nulidad previstos en el artículo 16 de la Ley o afecten derechos de terceros, podrán enmendarse

第 41 条　如果无法用已知法律词汇作为公证书标题，那么公证员要使用最符合相关人员权利、责任和相关法律背景的词汇作为标题。

第 42 条　公证当事人可以向公证员提交备忘录写明自己的指令，在这种情况下公证员要遵从该指令，并根据相关规定调整当事人的指令。

第 43 条　如果上文所说的备忘录内容模棱两可或者含糊不清，公证员要提醒公证当事人内容中有误或者遗漏之处，并选择相应的合法方式撰写。

第 44 条　如果公证需要出示补充文件，公证员将核实该文件合法性，并在原件中写明补充文件的规范化信息，同时还要写明相关要素以证实即将公证的内容。

第 45 条　如果需要在公证书中加入外语文件作为公证原件的一部分，那么必须附有正式翻译文本，但公证员亲自翻译的情况除外。

第 46 条　公证员应在公证书的末尾做出文件改动有效性的说明；除非是继承公证，在这种情况下要在每项改动后注明改动有效性。在原件中还要说明是在公证当事人的同意下做出的文件改动有效性说明。

第 47 条　公证员应在相应的公证书留白处进行备注，在文章末尾空白处进行备注，或者在文章后面的批示处进行备注，而且这些备注不能产生歧义。

备注是公证书的附加部分，是公证员为符合法律法规或者补充条款的要求而做出的官方声明。

第三节　对公证书中错误的修正

第 48 条　如果公证书原件的错误和遗漏内容并不属于《国家公证法》第 16 条规定的导致文件无效的因素，或者这些内容并不影响第三方的权利，那么可以通过修正文件进行修改：在由有关方面提交符合

mediante acta de subsanación: en la forma a que se refiere el inciso g) del artículo 85 de este Reglamento, previa presentación por la parte interesada de las pruebas admitidas en derecho.

Art. 49- Cuando los errores u omisiones en la matriz sean imputables al Notario la tarifa correspondiente al acta será a su cargo o de la notaría, lo que se determinará por la Dirección de Registros y Notarías del Ministerio de Justicia o la Dirección Provincial de Justicia, en su caso.

Art. 5O- Se considerarán partes interesadas para solicitar la subsanación de. los errores u omisiones, las que, de conformidad con lo dispuesto en este Reglamento, tengan derecho a obtener copias del documento notarial.

Sección Cuarta De los comparecientes y testigos en el documento Notarial

Art. 51-Los comparecientes son las personas que intervienen en el documento notarial, por si o por representación, ya sea como otorgantes o requirentes.

Art. 52- Los testigos intervienen en el documento notarial a los efectos de acreditar, en su caso, el conocimiento de los comparecientes, la veracidad de la actuación notarial o su solemnidad, así como las manifestaciones de los comparecientes.

Art. 53- Cuando la legislación no exija edad determinada para comparecer en el acto de que se trate, el Notario se limitará a consignar que el otorgante o requirente, es mayor de edad.

Art. 54- El Notario podrá solicitar dictamen pericial cuando tenga dudas sobre la capacidad mental o volitiva de un compareciente.

Si la declaración o certificación pericial confirmare la incapacidad; mental o volitiva, el Notario se abstendrá de autorizar el documento notarial.

Art. 55- Cuando el compareciente esté recluido en un establecimiento penitenciario el Director de la unidad o la persona en quien éste delegue, tendrá la obligación de identificar al recluso.

Art. 56- El Director del establecimiento penal, bien por declaración o certificación, acreditará la interdicción civil a que está sujeto el recluso si la tuviere. La declaración o certificación se hará constar o se unirá, en su caso, al documento notarial de que se trate.

Igual procedimiento se seguirá cuando el recluso, con la autorización de la dirección del establecimiento penal concurra por sí ante el Notario.

法律要求的证明后，根据本条例第85条a项的规定进行修改。

第49条 如果是公证员的责任导致原文中出现错误或遗漏，那么应由公证员或公证处承担相应的修改文件的费用，根据具体情况，该费用标准由司法部登记公证处或者省级司法局制定。

第50条 根据本条例，有权留存公证书副本的各方为可申请修改错误或遗漏的利益相关各方。

第四节 公证文件的当事人和证人

第51条 公证文件的当事人是代表自己或者他人进行文件公证的人，既可以是公证申请人也可以是公证文件授予人。

第52条 证人是参与文件公证的人，根据具体情况证明当事人的身份、公证工作的真实性严肃性，以及证明当事人的表述。

第53条 如对于公证当事人的年龄没有特殊要求，那么公证员只需说明公证申请人或公证文件授予人已经成年。

第54条 如果公证员对于公证当事人的智力和意识状态存疑，应当申请专家给出鉴定意见。

如果专业声明或者证明否定了其智力或意识状态，那么公证员不能公证该文件。

第55条 如果公证当事人被监狱机关羁押，那么该监狱机关负责人或者负责人的代表有义务说明。

第56条 如果当事人在被关押期间还被剥夺公民权利，那么该监狱机关负责人应当通过声明或者证明文件说明或者证实该情况。根据具体情况，公证员应在相应公证书中做出说明，或者在公证书上附上该证明文件。

如果被羁押人员经监狱机关管理层批准，可以办理公证的，也应亲自在公证人的见证下，循上述同样程序进行。

Art. 57- Si el compareciente es extranjero y habla y lee el idioma español, el Notario lo hará constar en el documento notarial y en caso contrario, un intérprete realizará la traducción y firmará conjuntamente con el compareciente y el Notario.

Art. 58-La capacidad legal de los extranjeros que comparezcan ante Notario se regirá por su ley personal acreditada, si el Notario no la conociere.

Seccion Quinta De la Representación en el Documento Notarial

Art. 59- La representación podrá ser legal o voluntaria. EL Notarlo exigirá que se acredite la representación legal de los comparecientes, lo que hará constar en el documento notarial.

La representación voluntaria: se acreditará con la copia del poder que dé representación o del contrato de servicios jurídicos suscrito a favor de abogados de bufetes colectivos. EL Notario, en estos casos, dará fe de haberlos tenido a la vista y se asegurará de las facultades que en dicho poder o contrato se confieren para realizar el acto, sin necesidad de transcribirlas en el documento notarial.

Art. 60- Si el compareciente es representante de una sociedad mercantil o civil o de otra persona jurídica no prevista en el Art. siguiente, exhibirá los documentos que acrediten la constitución de ésta y su estatuto legal. De no constar en estos su condición de representante, deberá presentar la certificación que así lo justifique.

Art. 61- La representación de los órganos, organismos, empresas y demás entidades estatales, las cooperativas, así como de las organizaciones políticas, sociales o de masas, se acreditará mediante certificación que expida el funcionario competente, para hacerlo, de acuerdo con las normas que rigen su organización interna.

Art. 62- Los capitanes de naves o aeronaves extranjeras acreditarán la representación de las misma con la presentación del documento donde se justifique tal condición.

Seccion Sexta De las Escrituras

Art. 63- EL Notario, redactará la escritura observando un orden de prelación, que comenzará con el encabezamiento en la forma dispuesta en el artículo 40 de este Reglamento y continuará con la comparecencia la parte expositiva, la dispositiva, el otorgamiento y la autorización. En todos los casos la matriz de la escritura se incorporará al protocolo a cargo del Notario.

第57条　如果公证当事人是外国人，但是可以说和读西班牙语，那么公证员应在文件中说明该情况；否则，将由翻译人员进行翻译，并和当事人以及公证员一起在文件上签字。

第58条　如果公证员不了解外国的公证当事人的资格合法性，则应由该人员本国法律证明。

第五节　公证文件代理

第59条　公证文件代理应是合法的或自愿的。如果是法定代表，公证员应要求做出证明，并在公证文件上写明。

自愿公证代理：应附上代理授权文件副本，或者附上为律师事务所提供相应服务的合同副本。在这些情况下，公证员应证明看过这些文件并确认授权或者合同上写明的公证代理授权，但无须将这些内容写入公证文件中。

第60条　如果公证当事人代表的是一家商务机构、民间机构或者其他未在下文中说明的法人，那么该公证当事人应当提交有关文件，证明所代理方的合法组建和存续情况。如果在这些文件中未说明其代理情况，还应提交相应证明，来证明自己的代理人身份。

第61条　如果代表的是国家企业、机关或者其他国家单位，或者代表的是合作社、政治社会机构或者集体性质的单位，那么应由相关的公职人员，根据内部有关规定来出具代理证明。

第62条　外籍船长或者机长应当通过提交文件说明代理情况，以证明其代理身份。

第六节　公证书

第63条　公证员应当按照一定顺序撰写公证书：首先根据本条例第40条规定的格式写抬头，其次是公证当事人信息，再次是事实陈述部分、决议部分、授权部分和公证部分，最后文件原件都要由公证员存档。

Art. 64-La parte de la escritura correspondiente a la comparecencia contendrá :

a) la identificación de los comparecientes;

b) concepto, carácter o forma en que intervienen, y

c) el juicio de identidad y capacidad que hace el Notario de aquellos.

Art. 65- En la parte expositiva de la escritura se harán constar los antecedentes del acto o contrato de que se trate, identificando; el bien objeto del mismo, los derechos de su titular, su disponibilidad, así como el precio o valor, si lo tuviere.

Los particulares a que se refiere el párrafo anterior se harán constar de conformidad con los títulos documentos presentados o de las manifestaciones de los interesados si para el acto o contrato ello fuere permitido, consignando, en su caso, los datos del registro correspondiente al folio, tomo y número de la inscripción.

Art. 66- En la parte dispositiva de la escritura se hará constar la voluntad de los otorgantes en forma de estipulaciones o cláusulas que el Notario redactará con claridad, precisión y propiedad de estilo ordenándolas relativamente a los efectos jurídicos del acto o contrato, que se autoriza, procurando incluir. en cada una, aquellas circunstancias que tengan entre si alguna relación.

Art. 67- La parte de la escritura correspondiente al otorgamiento contiene el consentimiento y aprobación de los comparecientes y las advertencias legales procedentes.

Art. 68- La autorización es la aprobación o acreditación que, con su firma hará el Notario de la formalización, legalidad y veracidad del acto, contrato o circunstancia que contenga la escritura. Previo a la autorización el Notario hará constar los nombres, apellidos y demás generales que se requieran de los testigos y otros intervinientes, según el documento de que se trate.

Art. 69- En los poderes no será necesario consignar antecedentes del acto, bastando que en su redacción consten las facultades que el poderdante confiere a sus apoderados, los nombres y apellidos de éstos y demás generales, si el Notario las conociere.

Cuando se autorice la revocación totAl o parcial del poder, el Notario advertirá al otorgante;que mientras no llegue al conocimiento del representante la extinción de sus facultades, los actos realizados por éste obligan al representado o a sus causahabientes.

La revocación total o parcial del poder se consignará de oficio o a instancia del poderdante, en nota al margen de la matriz del poder.

第64条 公证书中的当事人信息部分包括：

a）当事人身份信息；

b）以什么名义、性质或方式参与公证；以及

c）公证员对其身份和资格的判定。

第65条 在公证书的事实陈述部分要说明相应合同或者文件的背景，包括该文件或者合同的目的、合同或文件持有者的权利、该文件的适用性以及相应的文件的价值。

公证书中应写明上文提及的内容，写明提交文件的标题；如果涉及人员对该文件或者合同有任何表述，也应写明；还应在公证书中写明文件的卷册登记信息以及登记编号。

第66条 在决议部分应以条款形式写明授权者的意愿：公证员应准确清晰地写出该内容，文体得当，并且内容应结合授权的文件或合同；还应尽量在每条条款中写明互相有联系的各情节内容。

第67条 公证书的授权部分包括各当事人的同意许可以及相应的法律说明。

第68条 公证部分即公证员通过签名来批准并证明公证书中的文件、合同或其他情节的有效性、合法性和真实性。公证员批准前，应根据文件的具体内容，写明证人或参与者的姓名以及其他信息。

第69条 在授权书中不需要写明文件背景，只需要写明授权人授予被授权人的权利，以及被授权人的姓名和公证员掌握的其他信息。

如果公证内容是部分或者全部撤销授权，那么公证员应通知授权人。在代理人对自己权利被撤销尚不知情的这段时间，该代理人办理的文件对于被代理人或者其权利的受让人都具有强制性。

应授权人的要求，或者以官方文件的形式部分或者全部撤销授权，要在授权书原件的留白处做备注。

Si el Notario no tuviere a su cargo el protocolo donde obre la matriz del poder que se revoca, remitirá de oficio comunicación al respecto haciéndoselo saber al Notario que posea dicho protocolo.

Art. 70- En las escrituras de los contratos en que medie precio cosa o cantidad,, el Notario así lo consignará, al igual que la forma de pago que las partes acordaren. Si el pago se efectuare en presencia del Notario, este dará fe y lo consignará en la escritura y si las partes manifestaren que el pago se realizó con anterioridad al acto, advertirá a los comparecientes que, confesado como ha sido el pago. de dicho precio o la entrega de la cosa o cantidad, queda libre el bien o derecho de toda reclamación por razón del mismo, aunque se justificare en lo sucesivo no ser cierta su entrega en todo o en parte.

Art. 71- Cuando el objeto del acto o contrato sea un bien inmueble, éste se describirá, de conformidad con la legislación especial que lo regula.

Cuando se trate, de fincas rústicas se hará constar, en su caso, el plan económico o agrícola a que las mismas se encuentran vinculadas.

Los bienes muebles y semovientes se describirán, atendiendo a su naturaleza, identificándolos respectivamente por su marca registral de fábrica, tipo, modelo y numeración de fábrica si los tuviere o por su color y raza.

Art. 72- Al describir los derechos del titular del bien, se harán constar en la escritura los datos que permitan identificar el documento acreditativo de la titularidad.

Art. 73- EL Notario que autorice mediante escritura la partición y, adjudicación de bienes adquiridos por herencia testada o intestada exigirá, además de la comparecencia de todos los llamados a heredar, los documentos que acrediten esa condición, . los títulos de que hacen mérito y las certificaciones de actos de última voluntad y declaratoria de herederos.

El Notario podrá prescindir de la certificación positiva de declaratoria de herederos, cuando por otros medios pueda dar fe del conocimiento de su inscripción.

En los casos en que resulte beneficiada alguna persona jurídica u organización política, social o de masas, el Notario dará cuenta de ello a sus representantes a los efectos procedentes.

Art. 74- El Notario se abstendrá de autorizar escrituras sobre transmisión, modificación o: extinci6n de derechos sobre bienes inmuebles sujetos, a ,regulaciones especiales, sin la previa autorización de las autoridades encargadas por la ley para concederla, en todo caso dicha

如果公证处辖下的档案中并没有需要撤销的授权的原件，那么公证员应发送官方文件，向保有该授权书原件的公证员通报该情况。

第70条 如公证的合同中涉及价格、物品或者数量等内容，公证员应根据各方协商一致的内容写明上述信息以及相应的支付方式。如果各方是在公证员面前完成的支付，那么公证员应予以证实，并在公证书中写明；如果各方表示已经在公证前支付了款项，那么公证员应向当事人求证。关于合同中涉及的价格、物品或者数量等内容，公证当事各方完全有权提出异议，但这需要在后续公证书中写明。

第71条 如果公证的文件或者合同的内容涉及不动产，那么公证员应根据相应的特殊法律法规作出描述。

如果涉及农庄，那么公证员应说明涉及该农庄的经济或农业规划。

应根据各动产的特性写明其信息，如果有的话，应写明厂家注册商标、生产类别、型号和数量；如果没有这些信息，则应写明颜色和种类。

第72条 在说明财产所有者的权利时，应在公证书中写明证明其所有权的文件信息。

第73条 如果公证员公证的内容是遗产继承，无论是否有书面遗嘱，除相关继承人员须到场外，还须书面说明该情况，提供相关证明以及最终遗嘱的证明文件。

如果公证员有其他可以证明遗嘱的方式，就不需要提供遗嘱证明文件。

如果法人、政治机构、社会机构或者集体机构是遗产受益人，那么公证员可以告知这些机构的代表人该事实以及相应结果。

第74条 如果没有法定有资格授权的机构的批准，公证员不得作如下公证：针对特殊法律规定下的不动产的权利进行转让、变更或废除。

autorización se unirá a la matriz de la escritura.

Art. 75- Cuando el Notario autorice actos o contratos sujetos a inscripción en registro públicos, así lo advertirá los interesados, consignando en la escritura los requisitos que de acuerdo con la legislación sobre la materia se exijan para su inscripción.

El Notario se abstendrá de actuar cuando la ley exija la registracion publica del documento acreditativo de la titularidad y ello no se hubiere verificado.

Art. 76- El Notario autorizará las escrituras de testamento de conformidad con lo establecido en el Código Civil y leyes especiales.

Art. 77- En los testamentos o revocación de estos el Notario podrá refundir los antecedentes expositivos con las manifestaciones de voluntad del testador siempre que con ello no afecte la claridad del documento.

La revocación total o parcial se consignará en nota al margen de la escritura de testamento, de oficio o a instancia del testador

Art. 78- El Notario, respecto las escrituras a que se refiere el Art. anterior y dentro de los tres días hábiles siguientes. a su autorización, remitirá comunicación al Registro de Actos de Ultirna Voluntad y de Declaratoria de Herederos del Ministerio de Justicia OO:I los datos siguientes:

a) nombres y apellidos del testador;
b) lugar de nacimiento y ciudadanía;
c) domicilio;
ch) nombres de sus padres;
d) estado conyugal;
e) nombres y apellidos del Notario autorizante y su sede;
f) número de orden del documento; y
g) fecha y hora de la autorización.

Esta comunicación deberá ser firmada y fechada por el notario que la expida.

El Notario hará constar, mediante nota en la matriz de la escritura de testamento o de revocación, que ha remitido la comunicación a que se. refiere el artículo anterior con expresión de la fecha, el tomo y el folio de la inscripción en el citado Registro.

Art. 79- EL Notario autorizará las escrituras de matrimonio ,de conformidad con lo establecido en la legislación para su formalización.

El Notario que autorice la escritura de matrimonio remitirá, dentro de los tres días hábiles siguientes, copia de la escritura y el expediente confeccionado al efecto al

第 75 条　如果公证员公证的文件或者合同是需要进行公共登记的，那么应在公证书中写明登记依法所需要的材料，并告知有关人员。

如果依法需要对所有权证明书进行公共登记，在未登记情况下，公证员不能公证该证明书。

第 76 条　公证员应按照民法和其他相关法律进行遗嘱公证。

第 77 条　在遗嘱或者遗嘱的撤销文件中，公证员可以根据立遗嘱人的意志，重新组织语言写出前情说明，但前提是不得影响文章内容的清晰表达。

在遗嘱公证书的留白处可写明对遗嘱的部分或全部撤销，写明这一撤销是应官方要求还是立遗嘱人要求而做的。

第 78 条　公证员在完成上文提及的公证内容之后，应在三个工作日内向司法部遗产继承和遗嘱公文登记处提交通报，通报包括下列信息：

a）立遗嘱人姓名；
b）出生地和公民身份信息；
c）住址；
ch）父母姓名。
d）婚姻状况；
e）公证员姓名和总部名称；
f）文件序列号；以及
g）公证日期和时间。

发布该通报的公证员应在文件上签名并注明日期。

公证员应在遗产公证或者撤销遗产的公证书原件上注明上文提及的通报已经发出，并写明日期，以及在该登记处登记的页码和卷宗号码。

第 79 条　公证员应当根据相关法律的规定进行婚姻公证。

公证员在进行婚姻公证后的 3 个工作日内向婚姻登记处提交公证书副本以及相应证明文件，并在公证书留白处注明寄送这些材料的日期以及在婚姻登记处

Registro del Estado Civil que corresponda y consignará al margen de dicha escritura nota con expresión de la fecha del referido envío y del tomo y folio al, que quedó inscripto el matrimonio.

Sección Séptima De las Actas

Art. 80- El Notario redactará las actas observando un orden de prelación que comenzará con el encabezamiento en la forma dispuesta en el Art. 40 de este Reglamento y continuará con la comparecencia la parte expositiva, la parte dispositiva y por último la autorización. En todos los casos la matriz del acta se incorporará al protocolo a cargo del Notario.

Art. 81- La parte del acta correspondiente a la comparecencia contendrá:

a) la identificación de los comparecientes;

b) concepto, carácter o forma en que intervienen; y

c) el juicio de identidad y capacidad que base el Notario de aquellos.

Art. 82- En la parte expositiva se consignará la narración del hecho, acto, circunstancia o manifestación de voluntad, así como las advertencias legales procedentes.

Art. 83- La parte dispositiva del acta. contiene el objeto o finalidad del documento.

Art. 84- La autorización se realizará en la forma dispuesta en el Art. 68 de este Reglamento.

Art. 85- Las actas se clasifican en:

a) de Protesto que se ajustan a las formalidades establecidas en la legislación especial sobre la materia, sin perjuicio de lo regulado en este Reglamento para el requerimiento;

b) de presencia, que acreditan la realidad o veracidad del hecho, acto o circunstancia cuya certeza le, consta al Notario por su comprobación personal. Esta acta incluye toda clase de requerimientos efectuados por una persona a otra, ofrecimientos de pago, entrega de dinero, documentos y objetos y de existencia de personas o cosas;

c) de referencia, relativas a un hecho, acto o circunstancia acaecido y que le consta al manifestante;

incluye la declaración jurada;

ch) de protocolización, que acredita que el Notario ha incorporado a su protocolo un documento cualquiera, sin más efectos que el de asegurar la identidad del mismo y su existencia en la fecha de su protocolización;

d) de depósito, que aseveran que el Notario ha recibido en tal concepto objetos, valores, documentos o canti-

存档的卷宗号和页码。

第七节 公证文件

第80条 公证员按照一定顺序撰写公证书：首先根据本条例第40条规定的格式写抬头，其次是公证当事人信息，再次是事实陈述部分、决议部分、公证部分，最后文件原件都要由公证员存档。

第81条 公证文件中的当事人部分包括下列内容：

a）当事人身份；

b）参与公证的身份、特征和方式；

c）公证员对当事人身份和资格的判定。

第82条 在陈述部分应说明事实、前情和相关的法律说明。

第83条 文件的决议部分包括本文件的意图和目标。

第84条 公证应根据本条例第68条规定的形式来进行。

第85条 公证文件包括：

a）根据相应法律条款和本条例内容而做出的拒付证明；

b）当面公证，即通过本人核实的方式来证明事实、文件或背景情况的真实性。这种公证文件包括对每个人的各项要求、付款、款项交接，文件以及其他物品的提交，人员或者事物的存在；

c）说明，即说明已发生的事实、已出具的文件情况的证明，包括声明公证；

ch）存档公证，即证明公证员已将文件归档，该公证只证明该文件的存在以及在某一日期归档。

d）抵押公证，即证明公证员收到物品、证券、文件等内容作为合同抵押或者代为保管；

dades corno prenda de contrato o para custodia;

e) de notoriedad, que acreditan: la comprobación o filiación de hechos notorios sobre los cuales podrán ser fundados, declarados o. reconocidos derechos o se legitimen hechos, situaciones o circunstancias personales o patrimoniales, con trascendencia jurídica;

f) de requerimiento, que acreditan que el requirente, bajo su responsabilidad, ejercitará sin fuerza coactiva cualquier acción lícita o derecho o para que el requerido diga, haga o deje de hacer algo;

g) de subsanación de errores u omisiones que acreditan la existencia de los errores u omisiones de que adolece el documento notarial y la forma en que éstos se han subsanado

h) de jurisdicción voluntaria, que tienen por objeto hacer constar hechos o actos que han producido o deban producir efectos jurídicos, esta acta .incluye la administración de bienes de ausentes, de consignación, y de informaci6n para perpetua memoria

i) de declaratoria 'de herederos, dirigidas a establecer la declaración del fallecimiento intestado del causante y la determinación de sus herederos; y

j) las demás que se establezcan.

Art. 86- Las actas podrán ser expedidas en unidad de acto y si no lo fueren, se distinguirá cada parte como diligencia diferente con expresión de la fecha, hora y lugar en que se redacten, las que serán suscritas por el Notario y los comparecientes.

Art. 87- En el acta de presencia relacionada con la fe de existencia de personas y objetos no será necesaria la intervención de testigos.

La copia del acta de fe de existencia se expedirá en la misma fecha de su autorización y en caso contrario se consignara en dicha copia que la existencia se acredita con referencia al día en que el acta fue autorizada.

Art. 88- En las actas de presencia el Notario podrá ser requerido a instancia de parte interesada, para que se constituya en cualquier lugar de su demarcación territorial a fin de comprobar la existencia y estado de un objeto determinado, así como para que presencie el acaecimiento de hechos o actos de cualquier índole que tengan relevancia jurídica y de los que puedan derivarse algún derecho a favor del requeriente o de persona que legítimamente represente.

Art. 89- Las actas que comporten una solicitud de requerimiento contendrán además.

a) el termino en que ha de practicarse el requerimien-

e）重大事项公证，即证明重大事项及其相互关联，可能基于这些事项产生相应权利，或者发生权利声明或认定，或者这些事项会从法律角度影响个人或者财产的情况，产生法律影响；

f）指令公证，即证明指令方有责任行使强制力或者采取任何合法行动，来要求被要求人说、做某事，或者要求其停止做某事；

g）修补错漏公证，即证明在公证文件中存在哪些错误或者遗漏，同时说明修补这些问题的方式；

h）自愿管辖范围公证，即证明那些产生法律后果的事实或者文件，包括下落不明人员的财产的管理、寄存公证和永久备忘公证；

i）遗产继承公证，包括确认立遗嘱人死亡的声明，继承人的确认；以及

j）其他规定需要公证的内容。

第86条　以上这些公证内容可以在一份文件中公证完毕。如果不在一份文件中，那么每份公证都应作为独立的公证文件，都应写明公证的日期、时间和地点，公证员和公证当事人也要根据每份公证文件的内容进行签字。

第87条　如果是证明人员或者物品存在性的当面公证，不需要证人参与。

公证文件的副本应在公证当天出具，否则需要在公证件副本中写明是在出具公证原件的当天证明其存在性的。

第88条　在当面公证过程中，公证人可应当事人要求在管辖地理范围内的任何区域进行当面公证，证明某一物品的存在和状态，同时证明某些事实的发生或者行为的落实。这些都是有法律效力的，而且公证申请人或者其法定代表也因该事件或者行为而产生相应权利。

第89条　指令公证申请还应包括下面内容：

a）完成指令的时间；

to;

b) persona a que se ha de notificar o requerir;

c) lugar en que habrá de practicarse la notificación o requerimiento;

ch) objeto de la notificación o requerimiento;

d) plazo que se fija al requerido o notificado para la diligencia de respuesta; y

e) obligación del Notario de hacer entrega de copia del documento al requerido.

Art. 90- El Notario practicara las diligencias de notificación a la persona designada por el requirente y en su defecto, a su apoderado, familiar o cualquier otra persona relacionada con el requerido en cuanto sea factible y en la forma y dentro del termino acordado.

La diligencia de notificación se extenderá en el mismo pliego en que termina el acta y si no fuere posible o faltare espacio, podrá hacerse al margen o en documento anexo.

Art. 91- En todo acto de requerimiento o de notificación, la persona requerida o notificada o quien legalmente la represente, tendrá derecho a contestar el requirimiento o la notificación en el acto lo que el Notario hará constar en la propia acta o mediante diligencia de respuesta, cuya copia entregará al requerido o notificado.

Art. 92- En el acta de notificación se expresarán, además, los datos y circunstancias necesarias para que el notificado queda debidamente instruido del contenido de la notificación.

Art. 93- Cuando el Notario es requerido para que notifique a otra persona en su domicilio y ésta no se encontrare en el lugar indicado, la notificación se practicara en la forma dispuesta en el Art. 90 de este Reglamento y en su defecto, por el procedimiento civil.

Art. 94- Sólo podrá practicarse el requerimiento o notificación en un centro de trabajo, cuando dicho acto este relacionado con la actividad laboral del requerido.

Art. 95- El Notario no podrá autorizar copia del acta de requerimiento sin que conste en ella la respuesta que diere el requerido, si hiciere uso de ese derecho o sin que haya transcurrido el plazo indicado para que este responsa.

Se exceptúa de lo regulado en el párrafo anterior, las copias que sean reclamadas por el requirente bajo su responsabilidad, aunque no haya concluido dicho plazo para ejercitar cualquier acción o derecho. El Notario hará constar este extremo en la autorización de la copia y en la nota de expedición que ha de consignar en la matriz.

Art. 96- La protocolización de todo documento que

b）需要通知或者传达指令的人员；

c）完成通知或者指令的地点；

ch）通知或者指令的内容。

d）被通知人或者被发出指令人应在多长时间内给出答复；以及

e）公证员有义务向被传达人提供文件副本；

第90条　公证员应当通知公证申请人要求通知的人员，如果要求通知的人员不能出席，应当通知其代理人、家人或者其他任何与被通知人有关系并可能出席的人员，还要按照规定方式和双方协定的内容进行通传。

通知文件应和公证文件写在同一页，如果不行或者页面篇幅不够，可在文件留白处注明或者以附件形式写明。

第91条　在所有的通知或者传达指令的行为中，被通传人或者其合法代表有权在公证员给出的公证文件上针对通知或指令进行回复，或者以公文的方式进行回复，被通传人留存回复文件的副本。

第92条　在通知文件中，还应写明必要的信息，确保被通传人了解通知内容。

第93条　如果需要公证员根据指定住址通知某人，而被通知人并不在该地址，那么应根据本条例第90条的规定进行通知，如果还无法完成通知，则遵循民法规定。

第94条　只有当公证文件涉及被通知人的工作时，才可以在其工作场所完成通知送达。

第95条　如果被通知人有权作出答复，但是还没有作出答复，且并未超过规定期限，那么公证员不得公证文件副本。

前款规定不包括下列情况：如果公证申请人有责任提供副本，那么即便在规定期限内被通知人未行使任何权利或者有任何动作，也应公证副本。公证员应在公证文件副本以及文件原件的备注处说明这种特殊情况。

第96条　为进行该公证而需要提交的所有文件，

se presentare al Notario con ese objeto se hará por medio de acta a requerimiento de cualquier persona interesada en su conservación o por mandamiento judicial o de la ley.

Art. 97- La protocolización de los documentos otorgados o expedidos por funcionarios extranjeros se llevara a efecto siempre que :

a) hayan sido autorizados o expedidos conforme a las leyes del país donde se otorgaron o expidieron; y

b) el funcionario autorizante estuviere plenamente facultado para ello.

Art. 98- Los particulares señalados en los incisos del Art. anterior se acreditaran mediante certificación expedida por el funcionario consular o diplomático cubano autorizado para ello en el país de que se trate, lo que hará a su juicio o basado en los documentos que al efecto exija y que podrá agregar a dicha certificación.

La firma del cónsul o funcionario consular cubano deberá estar legalizada por el Ministerio de Relaciones Exteriores de Cuba. Si los documentos estuvieren redactados en otro idioma, se procederá de acuerdo a lo que establece el Art. 45 de este Reglamento.

Art. 99- En el acta de protocolización se observarán además, los requisitos siguientes:

a) se hará constar que el documento ha sido examinado por el Notario;

b) que se actúa a instancia del requirente o en cumplimiento de mandamiento judicial :

c) que el documento cumple los requisitos establecidos en los artículos anteriores, cuando proceda;

ch) se consignara que el documento protocolizable queda unido al acta con indicación del total de folios que contiene y los demás documentos agregados; y

d) se hará constar la declaración del interesado en el sentido de que el documento que se protocoliza es fidedigno y que el contrato, manifestación de voluntad, acto o circunstancia que contiene es cierto, así como su obligación de responder a terceros si resultare falso.

Art. 100- En las actas de deposito se observaran, además los requisitos siguientes :

a) se consignaran las condiciones impuestas por el Notario para la constitución y devolución del deposito, pudiendo este fijar plazos o limites para la custodia;

b) se consignara todo cuanto fuere necesario para la identificación del objeto depositado; y

c) la devolución del objeto depositado se consignara al margen de la matriz del acta de deposito, firmada por el Notario, el depositante o por quien ostente su representac-

都应按照当事人申请的指令公证文件来进行归档，或者根据司法要求的公证文件来进行归档。

第97条 只有在下列情况下，外国公职人员颁布或者出具的文件才有效力：

a）遵循出具文件当地的法律而进行公证或者出具的文件；以及

b）公职人员有全权进行公证。

第98条 上一条所说的文件由派驻当地国家的古巴外交官或者领事基于相应文件和其他补充文件，结合自己的判断，出具证明予以认证。

领事或者领事处公职人员的签名应在古巴外交部进行认证。如果需要认证的文件是以外语写成，那么应按本条例第45条之规定执行。

第99条 存档公证还应满足下列要求：

a）证明公证员已审查过该文件；

b）是根据申请人要求或者为满足法律强制要求而进行的；

c）文件满足上述各条的相应要求；

ch）确保被公证的文件和存档公证文件在一起，且在存档公证中写明被公证文件的页数以及其他附加文件；以及

d）证明相关人员的声明：即被公证文件是真实的，而文件中写明的合同内容、意愿的表达以及文中的其他内容和情节属实，如果文件内容存在虚假，该人员有义务向相应的第三方承担责任。

第100条 抵押公证还应满足下列要求：

a）写明公证员为寄存以及退还行为列出的条件，公证员还要确定寄存的期限；

b）写明为了抵押公证而需要的物品数量；以及

c）在抵押公证原件的留白处写明寄存物的归还情况，并由公证员、保管员及其法定或者自愿代理人、寄存物权利承受人以及两名证人签字。

ión legal o voluntaria, sus causahabientes y por dos testigos.

Siempre que el Notario lo considere conveniente para su seguridad, podrá conservar los depósitos en una agencia bancaria advirtiéndoselo así a la persona que le confía la custodia, lo que consignara en el acta de deposito.

Art. 101- Si el Notario cesare como tal o la notaria fuere trasladada o extinguida, la devolución del deposito se ajustara a lo previsto en el acta.

Art. 102- El Notario redactará el acta de referencia de acuerdo con las manifestaciones que bajo juramento hacen las partes, usando, en lo que fuere posible, las mismas palabras y una vez hechas las advertencias legales pertinentes.

Art. 103- En las actas de notoriedad se observaran además, los requisitos siguientes :

a) la solicitud se hará por la persona que demuestre interés en el hecho, acto o circunstancia cuya notoriedad se pretenda acreditar, quien deberá aseverarlos bajo su responsabilidad y hechas previamente las advertencias legales por el Notario;

b) el Notario practicara o exigirá cuantas pruebas estime necesarias para comprobar la notoriedad pretendida; y

c) se hará constar el resultado de todas las pruebas así como cualquier otra incidencia.

Art. 104- El Notario se abstendrá de autorizar el acta de notoriedad en los casos siguientes :

a) si se acredita haberse entablado demanda en juicio declarativo con respecto al hecho, acto o circunstancia cuya notoriedad se interesa;

b) por tramitación ante los tribunales o porque haya recaído sentencia firme con respecto al hecho, acto o circunstancia cuya notoriedad se interesa;

c) cuando sea manifiesta la contradicción entre las partes o se deriven perjuicios a terceros; o

ch) cuando se acrediten que el hecho, acto o circunstancia ha sido declarado notorio con anterioridad; y

d) cuando del examen y calificación de las pruebas, no se justificare la notoriedad pretendida.

Art. 105- El acta de subsanación de errores u omisiones se autorizara con la intervención de los mismos comparecientes o sus representantes o causahabientes, salvo que lo que se subsane interese solamente a uno de los comparecientes y siempre que no cause perjuicio a los demás interesados.

Cuando el Notario no tuviere a su cargo el Protocolo donde obre la matriz del acta que se subsane, remitirá de oficio, comunicación al respecto, haciéndoselo saber al

公证员只有在出于安全考虑的情况下，才可以在银行机构保存该寄存物，并且通知当事人将物品交由银行保存，这些内容将在抵押公证中写明。

第101条　如果公证员离职、公证处搬迁或者关闭，应根据公证文件中规定的内容来进行寄存偿还。

第102条　公证员应根据各方的宣誓声明内容来进行说明公证，尽可能使用声明原文内容，同时进行相关法律说明。

第103条　重大事件公证还应满足下列要求：

a）应由希望证明该重大事件的有关人员来提交申请，说明事实和背景，承担相关责任；在这之前公证员应进行相关法律说明；

b）公证员应取证，或者要求提供必要的证明，来证实该事实的重大性；以及

c）应写明所有证据是否属实，以及其他相关内容。

第104条　如有下列情况，公证员将不予进行重大事件公证：

a）证实待公证的事实或者情况已经涉及需要法院裁决的相关诉讼；

b）针对待公证的事实或者情况已有法院的最终判决，待法院执行；

c）各方之间出现分歧或将损害到第三方；或者

ch）证实该事实或者情况已经在之前进行过公证；以及

d）经核实或者评估各项证据，证明不符合重大事件要求。

第105条　针对文件的错误和疏漏，在公证相应的修改文件时，当事人或其代表、当事人权利受让人都应出席；除非修改部分内容仅涉及当事人的其中一人，且不侵害其他相关人员的利益。

如果公证员辖下档案并未保留修改文件的对应原件，那么应发公文通知拥有相应原件的公证员，告知其修改文件。

Notario que posea dicho Protocolo.

Sección Octava De las actas de declaratoria de herederos y otras de jurisdicción voluntaria

Art.106- El Notario para la autorización de las actas de declaratoria de herederos requerirá :

a) escrito de solicitud del interesado;

b) los documentos que acrediten lo manifestado en el escrito de solicitud;

c) los documentos contentivos de las declaraciones de los testigos y el dictamen del fiscal, en su caso.

d) La tramitación del acta de declaratoria de herederos se hará mediante representación letrada.

Art. 107- El escrito de solicitud a que se refiere el inciso a) del Art. anterior contendrá los particulares siguientes :

a) identificación del solicitante;

b) expresión de la solicitud y relación de los hechos que fundamentan la misma;

c) declaración de existencia o no de padres del causante no aptos para el trabajo y que dependían económicamente de aquel;

c) declaración bajo juramento sobre la existencia o no de personas incapaces para heredar; y

d) declaración de existencia o no de diligencias preventivas.

e) Si existieren las diligencias a que se refiere el inciso c) el notario advertirá al interesado que debe comunicar al tribunal que las tramita, que se ha solicitado en la Notaria la autorización del acta de declaratoria de herederos.

Art. 108- La representación letrada deberá acompañar al escrito de solicitud del acta de declaratoria de herederos los documentos que se relacionan a continuación :

a) la certificación de defunción del causante;

b) las certificaciones que acrediten el parentesco de los presuntos herederos;

c) las certificaciones del Registro de Actos de Ultima Voluntad y de declaratoria de herederos; y

d) la ley personal del causante, si este fuere extranjero y el Notario no la conociere.

Art. 109- El Notario, una vez examinado los documentos presentados, podrá determinar :

a) si se requiere la realización de la prueba testifical para el esclarecimiento de algún particular; o/y

b) si dichos documentos deben ser remitidos al fiscal

第八节 遗产继承公证和其他自愿管辖范围内的公证

第 106 条 为进行继承公证，公证员要求当事人提交以下文件：

a）有关人员的书面申请；

b）证实书面申请内容的其他文件；

c）写有证人证言以及检察官意见的文件；

d）律师代为出席遗产继承公证的授权文件。

第 107 条 第 106 条 a 项提及的书面申请应包括以下内容：

a）申请人信息；

b）说明申请内容，陈述与继承公证有关的事实；

c）说明被继承人父母是否健在，是否工作，在经济上是否依赖被继承人；

c）声明是否有无权继承人员；以及

d）说明是否事先留有其他法律文件；

e）如果存在 c 项中提及的文件批示，公证员应告知有关人员，他将通知事先受理该案件的法院，告知该法院在其辖内公证处申请进行继承公证。

第 108 条 除了继承公证申请书，代理律师还应提交以下文件：

a）被继承人死亡证明；

b）待继承人的亲属关系证明；

c）遗嘱和继承文件登记处证明；以及

d）如果被继承人是外国人，且公证员对被继承人所在国家法律不了解，还须提交被继承人所在国家的法律内容。

第 109 条 公证员在审阅完所有提交的文件后，将决定：

a）是否需要认证来澄清某些问题；或者 / 以及

b）是否应将这些文件寄给检察官，让检察官来

a los efectos del dictamen correspondiente.

Art. 110- Si el dictamen del fiscal fuere condicionado, el Notario advertirá al interesado para que cumpla la condición impuesta en un termino de 90 días hábiles, y una vez cumplimentada esta se continuara el tramite sin tener que dar cuenta nuevamente al fiscal.

Si en el término señalado no se cumplimentara la condición el notario se ajustara a lo dispuesto en el Art. 115 de este Reglamento.

Art. 111- El acta de declaratoria de herederos contendrá las declaraciones siguientes :

a) el fallecimiento intestado del causante con expresión de sus nombres y apellidos, fecha del fallecimiento, lugar de su nacimiento, nombre de sus padres y estado conyugal;

b) nombre y apellidos de los herederos;

c) nombres y apellidos del o de los padres no aptos para el trabajo y que dependían económicamente del causante;

d) nombres y apellidos de las personas que resulten incapaces para heredarar de conformidad con lo establecido en la legislación civil; y

e) nombres y apellidos de los descendientes que resulten herederos en virtud de la aplicación del derecho de representación.

Art. 112- Para la autorización del acta de declaratoria de herederos el Notario tomara razón y dará fe del contenido de los documentos presentados a ese fin, los cuales devolverá al interesado al momento de la firma excepto las certificaciones expedidas por el Registro de Actos de Ultima Voluntad y de Declaratoria de Herederos, las que quedaran unidas a la matriz.

Art. 113- Una vez autorizada el acta de declaratoria de herederos el Notario, en un término de tres idas hábiles siguientes a su autorización remitirá copia de aquella al Registro de Actos de Ultima Voluntad y de Declaratoria de Herederos, a los efectos de su inscripción en el mismo, poniendo nota al margen de la matriz con expresión de la fecha de su envío, así como del tomo y folio al que quedo inscripta dicha acta en el citado Registro.

Art. 114- Las actas de declaratoria de herederos no se autorizaran :

a) cuando no se presentaren los documentos probatorios requeridos;

b) cuando el Notario compruebe la existencia de errores u omisiones en los documentos o pruebas presentados que a su juicio imposibiliten la autorización del acta;

做相应的决断。

第110条 如果检察官作出的判决包含一定要求，那么公证员应当告知当事人在九十个工作日内满足这些要求；符合这些要求后，将继续完成公证手续，无须再通告检察官。

如果未按照要求满足检察官提出的要求，那么公证员将遵循本条例第115条的规定。

第111条 继承公证应包含下列内容：

a）被继承人未立遗嘱死亡的，其姓名、死亡日期、出生日期、父母姓名和婚姻状况；

b）继承人姓名；

c）丧失劳动能力、在经济上依靠被继承人的父母双方或其中一方的姓名；

d）根据民法的规定，无权继承人员的姓名；

e）律师代理的有继承权的后代的姓名。

第112条 为进行继承公证，公证员应当登记并核实提交的有关文件，在公证书签字时将这些文件再退还给当事人；除遗嘱文件和遗产继承公证登记处出具的证明外，这些文件将和公证原件一并留存。

第113条 公证员在进行继承公证后，应当在三个工作日内将该公证书的副本寄至遗嘱文件和遗产继承公证登记处，以便在该处登记；公证员还要在公证原件的留白处写明副本寄送日期，以及该公证在登记处登记的卷宗号和文件号。

第114条 如有下列情况，不予进行继承公证：

a）未提交需要的证明文件；

b）公证员在证明文件或者其他证明材料中发现有错误或者遗漏之处，且公证员认为这些错误导致无法进行公证；

c) si el fiscal emite dictamen en contrario; y

ch) en los casos previstos en el Art. 104 de este Reglamento.

Art. 115- Si no procediera la autorización del acta por existir alguna de las causas señaladas en el Art. anterior, el Notario se pronunciara por escrito al respecto y devolverá los documentos presentados al interesado, instruyéndole sobre los medios para el logro de sus fines lo que hará constar en el Libro de Radicación de Asuntos.

Art. 116- El escrito de solicitud de las actas de administración de bienes del ausente se presentará por cualquiera de las personas llamadas a la sucesión intestada y se acompañara el auto firme del tribunal que declaro la ausencia el que quedara unido a la matriz.

El Notario en la autorización del acta se ajustara a lo establecido en la legislación sobre la materia.

Art. 117- En el escrito de solicitud de las actas de información para perpetua memoria, si estas trataran sobre hechos, actos o circunstancias relativos al estado civil de las personas se requerirá la certificación correspondiente del estado civil de aquellas sobre las cuales se pretende realizar el acto.

Art. 118- Para la solicitud del acta de consignación se exigirá la presentación del acta de deposito de la suma de dinero o cosa debida; el requerimiento del Notario al acreedor y la conformidad de este. Si el acreedor no mostrare su conformidad el Notario se abstendrá de autorizar el acta.

Art. 119- El Notario en el momento de autorizar el acta de consignación entregara, al acreedor la suma de dinero o cosa debida, lo que hará constar en el documento.

Art. 120- El Notario para la autorización de las actas de jurisdicción voluntaria a que se refieren los artículos 116, 117, 118 y 119 de este Reglamento, se ajustará, en lo posible, a las formalidades y requisitos generales regulados para la autorización de las actas.

Seccion Novena De otros documentos notariales

Art. 121- Se consideran otros documentos notariales:

a) la transcripción fiel que realice el Notario de los documentos que se exhiban o presenten a ese objeto o consten en archivos a los que se autorice su acceso;

b) la identificación o legitimación de firmas, libros o documentos que autorice el notario;

c) la traducción que hace el Notario de un documento en idioma español a otro idioma o viceversa;

c）检察官给出不同意进行公证的判决；

ch）本条例第 104 条列出的其他情况。

第 115 条　如果因为上文中的任何原因而导致继承公证无法进行，公证员应退还当事人提交的材料，并且在事项决议书中书面写明相关情况，同时写明如何才能完成继承公证。

第 116 条　任何一个有继承权的人都可以申请对下落不明人员财产的管理进行公证，和申请书一起提交的还有法院作出的人员下落不明的判定书，该文件最终将和公证原件一起留存。

在进行该类公证时，公证员应遵循法律相关规定。

第 117 条　在永久备忘公证申请中，如果涉及人员的婚姻状况、事实等信息，需要申请公证的有关人员提交婚姻状况证明。

第 118 条　如果申请寄存公证，申请人需要提交相应数额的金钱或者物品的存单，债权方则应符合公证员提出的要求。如果债权方不符合要求，那么公证员将不予公证。

第 119 条　公证员在进行寄存公证时，应将一定数额的金钱或者物品交付给债权方，这一点应在公证书中写明。

第 120 条　本条例第 116 条、第 117 条、第 118 条、第 119 条中提及的自愿管辖范围内的公证都应尽量符合公证的一般要求和规范。

第九节　其他公证文件

第 121 条　其他公证文件包括：

a）针对为公证而提交给公证员的文件、公证员有权查看的存档文件，以及公证员做出的副本；

b）公证员对签名、卷宗或者文件进行验证和合法化形成的文件；

c）公证员将西班牙语文件翻译成其他语言，或者将其他语言文件翻译成西班牙语的翻译件；

ch) la acreditación que realice el Notario de que una ley o norma jurídica nacional esta en vigor;

d) los referidos a actos migratorios que autorice el Notario incluyendo los de adquisición y perdida de la ciudadanía que la ley así lo disponga; y

e) los demás que se establezcan en la ley o este Reglamento.

Art. 122- En los documentos a que se refiere el Art. anterior no será necesario :

a) afirmar la capacidad de los comparecientes;

b) la intervención de testigos; ni

c) incorporarlos al protocolo.

Art. 123- El Notario encabezara estos documentos con su nombre, unidad notarial a su cargo y lugar donde se constituye y los finalizara consignando el lugar, fecha, su firma y sello que identifique la notaria.

Art. 124- En los documentos de identificación o legitimación de firmas o documentos, el Notario procederá a dar fe de la legitimidad de la firma de quien se trate o del documento, en su caso.-

La firma que se legitime se estampara ante Notario, y si no fuere así, este deberá cerciorarse de que es la misma que la persona acostumbra a usar en todos sus actos.

Art. 125- El Notario no asumirá responsabilidad alguna por el contenido del documento cuya firma legitima, no obstante se abstendrá de legalizar la firma si dicho contenido fuere contrario a derecho.

Art. 126- El Notario autorizara los documentos de legitimación de libros en la hoja inicial del mismo, dejando constancia del numero de folios que este contiene y la función para la cual se habilita.- En cada folio se estampara el sello de la notaria.

Art. 127- En los documentos sobre la vigencia de leyes nacionales se transcribirá el precepto de ley de que se trate.

Sección Décima De las copias

Art. 128- Las copias es la reproducción literal o parcial del documento notarial original que obra en el protocolo a cargo del Notario.

Art. 129- Solo el Notario a cuyo cargo este el protocolo, podrá expedir copias de los documentos notariales obrantes en el mismo.

Art. 130- Tendrán derecho a obtener copias de los documentos notariales;

a) las personas naturales o jurídicas a cuyo favor

ch）公证员证实某条国家法律或者法律规定有效的文件。

d）公证员公证的相关移民文件，包括根据法律获得或者放弃国籍的文件；以及

e）法律或者本条例包括的其他文件。

第 122 条　在第 121 条提到的文件中，不需要下列手续：

a）确认当事人的资格；

b）证人参与；

c）留存为存档文件。

第 123 条　在这些公证文件中，公证员要在开头写明自己的姓名、公证机构名称以及所在地址，在结尾处写明地点、时间、签名并加盖公证处公章。

第 124 条　在核实签名或者文件的公证过程中，公证员应根据具体情况证明相关人员的签名或者文件的合法性。

签字应在公证员面前进行，以便对其进行公证；如果未当面留下签名字迹，公证员也应确认待公证的签名是该人员在所有文件中惯用的签名。

第 125 条　公证员对需要公证签名的文件的内容不承担任何责任，如果该文件内容需要公证员承担责任，那么公证员可以不予公证。

第 126 条　公证员在需要证明文件合法性的卷宗首页进行公证，写明该卷宗的总页数以及公证的作用。在每页都应加盖公证处公章。

第 127 条　在证明国家法律有效性的公证书中应写明相应法律的具体内容。

第十节　副本

第 128 条　副本是指公证员存档的公证原件的全部或部分复制品。

第 129 条　只有负责文件存档的公证员才能根据存档文件原件出具副本。

第 130 条　公证书副本可以给下列人员：

a）涉及自身直接或间接权利的自然人或者法人；

resulte algún derecho, ya sea directo o adquirido por otro acto;

b) los que acrediten tener interés legitimo en el documento;

c) los representantes de las personas a que se refieren los incisos anteriores, previa la acreditación de la representación legal o voluntaria que ostenten.

Art. 131- En vida del testador, solo este o su representante para ello, podrán obtener copias de su testamento que en todo caso serán literales.

Fallecido el testador además de los herederos instituidos o sus representantes, tendrán derecho a obtener copias los legatarios, albaceas, contadores y demás personas a quienes se les reconozca algún derecho o facultad, previa acreditación, en su caso, de alguna de las condiciones anteriormente señaladas.

Art. 132- Las copias en que se observen errores u omisiones, no obrantes en la matriz, podrán ser subsanadas mediante nota o diligencia al final o a continuación del texto que será firmada por el Notario donde se hará constar el error u omisión y la forma correcta en que queda la copia.

Art. 133- Al margen de la matriz se anotará la expedición de la copia, la persona para quien se ha expedido, fecha, numero de hojas y tarifa cobrada.

Art. 134- Al final del texto de las copias se hará constar:

a) su concordancia con el documento original de que se trate;

b) el número de hojas, lugar y fecha de expedición y tarifa cobrada;

c) que en la escritura original existen fijados e inutilizados, los sellos del timbre correspondiente; y

ch) la copia se autorizará con el cuño oficial de la notaria y la firma del Notario que la expide.

Art. 135- En las copias, se podrán excepcionalmente, relacionar o producir los documentos agregados a la matriz cuando el fin para el para el que serán utilizadas así lo requiera.

Art. 136- Solo al momento de la autorización del documento notarial se expedirán copias literales de este a los comparecientes y en lo sucesivo, las copias para el que han de ser utilizadas así lo requiera o por mandamiento judicial a instancia del Ministerio de Justicia o de las direcciones provinciales de Justicia.

Art. 137- Las copias literales se encabezaran con el numero que en el protocolo tenga el documento matriz y

b）证明文件涉及自己合法权益的人；

c）在事先证实是法定代表或者自愿代表的身份的情况下，前文提及的这些人员的代表。

第131条　在立遗嘱人生前，只有其本人或者其代表可以得到遗嘱副本，且该副本是遗嘱的全文副本。

在立遗嘱人去世后，除了法定继承人和继承人代表，接受遗赠人、遗嘱执行人和会计以及其他有相应权利和职权的人可以获得遗嘱副本，对于这些人员，应事先核实其身份。

第132条　如果在副本中发现错误或者疏漏，而在原件中没有这些错漏，公证员应在文件正文后面或者文件末尾以备注方式写明，副本的错漏之处以及相应的正确的内容并签名。

第133条　公证员应当在文件原件留白处注明副本出具的时间、副本获得人的姓名、副本的页数以及收费金额。

第134条　公证员应当在副本结尾处写明：

a）副本和原件内容一致；

b）副本页数、出具副本的地点和时间以及所收费用；

c）在原件中有相应的盖章，但在副本中无效；以及

ch）在副本中另有公证处官方印章和出具副本的公证员的签名。

第135条　如果在开具文件副本的过程中还有其他需要，可以破例在副本中列出或者写明公证原件的其他附加文件。

第136条　副本只有在原件公证过程中才会被分发给当事人，这之后只有在有需要或者司法部、各省级司法局下达司法命令的时候，才能被出具。

第137条　全文副本的开头是原件存档的文件号，该副本应是原件的精确复制，包括原件的修改内

han de ser reproducción exacta de este, tal y como aparezca después de las subsanaciones hechas, sin consignar las salvedades realizadas, bastando que se inserte que las mismas han sido aprobadas por los comparecientes y que se agregue, entre paréntesis, según los casos una de estas frases : "Sigue una enmienda" o "Sigue relación de enmiendas". En las copias literales no se consignara el contenido de las notas, salvo por mandamiento judicial o por disposición del Ministerio de Justicia o de las direcciones provinciales de Justicia.

Art. 138- Las copias parciales constituyen la forma general de reproducción del documento notarial original y solo repetirán de este, aquellos extremos que resulten necesario e imprescindibles o que se requieran por las autoridades judiciales o administrativas para el acto que con dicha copia se persigue.

Art. 139- Las copias a que se refiere el artículo anterior, se encabezarán con la denominación "COPIA PARCIAL" y a continuación, por su orden, lo siguiente :

a) lugar y fecha de expedición de la copia;

b) nombres y apellidos del Notario que la expide y la notaria a su cargo;

c) nombres y apellidos y numero de identidad del solicitante de la copia;

ch) identificación de la matriz con expresión de su titulo, numero, fecha, Notario autorizante y su sede;

d) expresión de la fe notarial sobre los extremos de la matriz que se requiere hacer constar; y

e) los demás datos comunes a las copias previstos en el Art. 134.

CAPITULO III
De Los Protocolos

Art. 140- Los Notarios serán los responsables de la integridad de los protocolos a su cargo.

Art. 141- Los protocolos se formaran en uno o varios tomos, con las matrices de las escrituras, actas y demás documentos agregados a los mismos, autorizados por el Notario en cada año natural, aunque en el transcurso del mismo le sustituyera otro Notario. El Protocolo podrá llevarse en carpetas o tomos encuadernados.

Art. 142- Los protocolos y los documentos que lo integran solo podrán ser examinados, en función de su cargo, por las autoridades correspondientes del Ministerio de Justicia y de las direcciones provinciales de Justicia de los órganos locales del Poder Popular; por mandamiento

容，但不需要在副本中写出修改部分有效性的说明，只需要写入当事人同意修改即可。根据具体情况可在修改内容前用双引号写明"修改如下"或者"修改内容如下"。全文副本上无须写出原件的备注内容，除非司法部或者省级司法局下达司法要求表示需要。

第138条 部分副本的基本格式和公证原件相同，但只是复制了必要的、必不可少的部分内容，或者只复制了为达成某目的，司法或者行政当局需要的某些内容。

第139条 第139条提及的副本开头要写明"部分副本"，下面要依次写明如下内容：

a）出具副本的地点和日期；

b）出具副本的公证员的姓名以及其负责的公证处的名称；

c）副本申请者的姓名和身份证号码；

ch）公证原件的名称、文件号、公证日期、公证员姓名和公证所在地。

d）证明副本内容和原件相应内容一致；以及

e）本条例第134条中要求的副本上应有的其他信息。

第三章
存档文件

第140条 公证员应对其管辖内的存档文件的完整性负责。

第141条 存档文件可为一卷或者多卷，每份档案包括公证员在每个自然年公证的公证书、公证文件和其他相应附件。如果在一个自然年内中途有公证员的替换，也应继续存档。存档可以用文件夹或者装订卷宗方式来进行。

第142条 只有司法部或者省级司法局可以根据其职责，在有正当的司法命令或者其他理由的情况下，审阅档案和其内部所有文件。

judicial o interés histórico debidamente acreditado.

Art. 143- El Notario iniciara su Protocolo mediante diligencia de apertura que consignara en el margen superior del anverso de la primera hoja del primer documento que autoricen con el siguiente texto :

"Protocolo de los documentos notariales correspondientes al (año); y a continuación consignará la fecha sus nombres y apellidos, unidad notarial su firma y el sello de la notaria"

Si la diligencia no es posible consignarla en la forma prevista en el primer párrafo, ésta se extenderá en hoja aparte.

Art. 144- Una vez extendida la diligencia de apertura se colocaran los documentos sucesivamente por orden ascendente de numeración, comenzando por el numero uno y fecha de autorización.

Al iniciar un nuevo tomo se hará otra diligencia de apertura.

Art. 145-Todas las hojas del protocolo se foliarán con el número que les corresponda por su orden. Dicha foliatura podrá hacerse en letras, en guarismos o en forma impresa.

Art. 146- Si al foliar las matrices se cometiere error, el Notarlo lo salvara mediante diligencia que consignará a continuación del último folio enumerado, en la forma siguiente:

"Lic. (Dr.) ( ) Notario a cargo de este protocolo, doy fe, que en la foliación correspondiente al número ( ) se consignó erróneamente el numero ( ), por lo que procedí a tacharlo, consignando al lado el correcto.".

Al final de la diligencia se señalará el lugar, fecha, firma del Notario y sello que identifique a la notaria.

Art. 147- EL Notario cerrará el protocolo extendiendo diligencia al final del texto del último documento que ha autorizado hasta el 31 de diciembre de cada año.

Si no fuere posible extender la diligencia en la forma señalada en el párrafo anterior, ésta se hará en hoja adicional que se incorporará al protocolo.

La diligencia de cierre contendrá el texto siguiente:

"Concluye el protocolo del año ( ): que contiene ( ) tomos, ( ) documentos notariales y ( ) folios autorizados por mi el infrascripto Notario de (lugar). y doy fe de no haber autorizado otros."

Igual texto se utilizara para la diligencia de cierre de cada tomo, así como cuando el Notario cese definitivamente en su cargo.

Art. 148- Si el Notarlo, por fuerza mayor, no pudi-

第143条 公证员应当在每份档案的第一份公证书的第一页正面上方写下如下内容：

"本档案为（年份）的公证书档案；下面为该存档的日期、公证员姓名、公证机构名称、公证员签名以及公证处盖章。"

如果不能在第一页的第一段写出上述内容，那么可以单独在一页上写明上述内容。

第144条 公证员在写明档案建档批文后，就根据由小到大的数字牌号顺序收纳文件，第一份文件为1号，后面根据公证日期依次往后排。

如果重新开一个新的档案卷宗，则需要重新写建档批文。

第145条 所有的存档文件都应当根据其数字号码顺序装订。文件页码可以是文字、数字或者是印刷体文字。

第146条 如果在给原件编码时出现错误，公证员应当在装订的最后一页文件后面加写一段文字来进行改动，格式如下：

"（ ）学士（博士）是本档案负责人，特证明（ ）号编号的文件号码错编为（ ），因此将该错误号码划掉，在旁边再注明正确号码。"

在该批注的最后写明地点、日期、公证员签名以及公证处所在地。

第147条 公证员在存档的最后一份文件后写明闭档批文，存档的最后一份文件最晚可以是每年的12月31日公证的文件。

如果无法按照上段描述写明闭档批文，可以在存档的最后再加入一页空白页写明该内容。

闭档批文内容如下：

"（ ）年存档结束：包括（ ）卷、（ ）公证文件和（ ）页，这些内容由我，（地点）的公证员签名公证，我证明没有公证过其他文件。"

在每卷文件的最后都应写明相同批文，在公证员离职时也应写明这一批文。

第148条 如果公证员因为不可抗力无法进行

era practicar la diligencia de cierre, ésta la hará quien lo sustituya, o el Notario designado para ello por el Director Provincial de Justicia o el Ministro de Justicia, en su caso, lo que se consignará en la propia diligencia.

Art. 149- Cuando en el protocolo o en alguno de sus tomos, existieren documentos notariales autorizados por otro Notario, el que proceda al cierre lo hará constar asi en la diligencia a que se refiere el Art. 147 del Reglamento.

Igual procedimiento se seguirá si en el protocolo existieren documentos reconstruidos.

Art. 150- AI final de cada protocolo se colocará un índice alfabético de los comparecientes en los documentos obrantes en el mismo.

En el lomo de cada tomo que integre el protocolo, se rotulará el nombre de la notaria, oficina notarial o consular de que se trate, el nombre o los nombres de los notarios o funcionarios autorizantes, el año y el numero de documentos que comprende.

Art. 151- Si se acreditara ante el Notario, la desaparición o pérdida total de un protocolo, aquel podrá reconstruir los documentos que debieron obrar en el mismo.

Art. 152- El Notario reconstruirá, a instancia de parte interesada, las matrices de los protocolos que obren a su cargo, previo el cumplimiento de los requisitos que se establecen en el Art. 24 de la Ley. La reconstrucción puede ser total o parcial.

Art. 153-Se considerarán parte interesada para solicitar la reconstrucción de un documento notarial las personas a que se refiere el Art. 130 de este Reglamento.

Art. 154- Si la persona interesada presentare copia del documento original, se procederá a cotejar la firma del Notario autorizante con las que obren en protocolo del referido Notario o en cualquier registro oficial donde conste dicha firma.

Art. 155- Cuando la firma cotejada resultare coincidente con la del Notario autorizante, La copia del documento se protocolizará en la forma dispuesta en los artículos 96 y 99 de este Reglamento.

Art. 156-El Notario a cuyo cargo esté el protocolo donde obre el documento objeto de la reconstrucción hará constar en la matriz del mismo si ello fuere posible, los particulares relacionados con el acta de protocolización.

Art. 157- El Notario, dentro de los tres primeros meses de cada año, dirigirá comunicaci6n al Archivo Provincial de Protocolos, con la relaci6n de los tomos de su notarla que deberá remitir a dicho archivo en la que solicitará fijación de día y hora para su traslado.

闭档工作，应由其接替者完成，或者司法部或省级司法局委派公证员来完成这一工作，而这一情况也应在闭档批文中写明。

第149条 如存档文件或者其中任何一卷卷宗中有其他公证员公证的文件，那么进行闭档工作的公证员应根据本条例第147条的规定，在闭档批文中写明。

如果在档案中有重建文件，也应采取同样的方式处理。

第150条 在每份档案的最后，应当根据存档文件当事人姓名的字母顺序列出公证当事人姓名目录。

每份卷宗的书脊处应标明相应的公证处、公证办公室或领事处名称，一位或多位公证员公务员的姓名，年份以及文件数。

第151条 如果经公证员核实遗失一整卷档案，那么该公证员应当重建遗失存档中的所有文件。

第152条 根据《公证法》第24条的规定，公证员应当根据有关方面的需要重建其管理的档案中的文件原件，可以是完全重建，也可以是部分重建。

第153条 本条例第130条中提及的人员为可申请公证书重建的有关人员。

第154条 如果有关人员提供的是原件副本，那么公证员应当将副本中公证员的签名和该公证员在存档文件中的签名进行对比，或者和公证员在任何官方登记文件中留下的签名相比对。

第155条 如果待比对签名和公证员的签名相同，那么将根据本条例第96条、第99条的规定来对该副本进行存档。

第156条 如果可以，负责原件存档的公证员应在原件中写明存档文件的有关内容，以备日后对该文件重建使用。

第157条 在每年的头三个月，公证员应和省级文件档案馆联系，说明需要移交的卷宗有哪些，并请文件档案馆确定移送文件的日期和时间。

En igual término los funcionarios consulares o diplomáticos facultados para ello, por conducto del Ministerio de Relaciones Exteriores, y los responsables de las notarias no adscriptas a los órganos locales del Poder popular a través de la Dirección de Registros y Notarias del Ministerio de Justicia, remitirán la relación anteriormente señalada al Archivo Provincial de Protocolos Notariales de Ciudad de La Habana y proceder; asimismo' en caso de cierre definitivo del consulado y de la notaria.

La remisi6n de los protocolos de los consulados se ajustará a lo dispuesto conjuntamente por el Ministerio de Justicia y el Ministerio de Relaciones Exteriores.

Art. 158- Recibida la comunicación a que s refiere el Art. anterior, el Notario a cargo del Archivo Provincial, fijara día y hora para el traslado procederá a efectuar el mismo con la presencia del Notario de que se trate, o del representante del Ministerio de Relaciones Exteriores, en su caso, extendiéndose por el encargado del archivo, acta de dicha entrega donde se hará constar los tomos, cantidad de documentos y folios de los respectivos protocolos, adjuntándose una copia del índice anual y firmándose por ambos la diligencia de entrega, copia de la cual será remitida al Ministerio de Justicia.

Art. 159- La remisión de los protocolos correspondientes al archivo Histórico de la Academia de Ciencias de Cuba en la provincia de que se trate, se ajustara a lo dispuesto en los artículos anteriores según corresponda.

CAPITULO IV
De Las Notarias, Oficinas Notariales Y Archivos De Protocolos Notariales

Art. 160- La notaría estará integrada por un Notario, su protocolo y el personal auxiliar, con independencia de que en un mismo local radiquen una o más notarías. En este ultimo caso se considerará que existen tantas notarias como notarios haya.

Cuando un Notario tenga competencia en otro u otros municipios, además del municipio sede de su notarla podrán habilitarse, adscriptas a la sede, oficinas notariales con personal auxiliar para dar servicio y atención al público,. de conformidad con lo establecido en el inciso;) del Art. 167 de este Reglamento.

Art. 161- En cada provincia radicará un archivo de protocolos notariales que estará integrado por los protocolos a que hace referencia el Art. 34 de la Ley.

EL archivo provincial de protocolos notariales estará

同样，领事处官员或者有相关职权的外交官应当通过外交部移交上述存档文件，而非人民地方政府辖下的公证处负责人应当通过司法部登记和公证处移交该存档文件。这些存档文件都将被移送至哈瓦那市文件档案馆。如果领事处或者公证处关闭，存档同样程序进行。

移送领事处的存档文件应当根据司法部和外交部共同制定的规定进行。

第158条 在收到上文提及的通知后，省级文件档案馆应当确定移送文件的日期和时间，并在相关公证员或者外交部代表人在场的情况下进行文件移交。文件存档负责人应出具文件写明相应档案的卷宗、文件数和页数，同时附上该年度文件目录，并由文件移交的双方签名。该移交文件的副本将被送至司法部。

第159条 各省应存至古巴科学院历史档案馆的存档文件，应根据上文的相应规定进行移交。

第四章
公证处、公证办公室和公证书档案馆

第160条 公证处应由一名公证员，以及文件存档和相应的助理人员组成，在同一个地区可以有一家或多家公证处。如果在同一个地区有多家公证处，那么有多少公证处，就有多少相应的公证员。

如果公证员除了其公证处总部所在城市外，还在其他或者多个城市履行职权，那么应在总部辖下建公证办公室。公证办公室可以由助理人员根据本条例第167条规的定来提供服务以及进行对外接待工作。

第161条 每个省都应设有一处公证书档案馆，档案馆内的存档文件为本法第34条规定的文件。

省级公证书档案馆应由一名公证员来负责。

a cargo de un Notario.

Art. 162- En la propia unidad notarial se contrataran los servicios que deba prestar el Notario.

Art. 163- En las unidades notariales cada Notario llevará los siguientes libros, documentos y controles :

a) protocolo;

b) libro único de control de asuntos;

c) control económico y solicitud de servicios;

ch) copias de los depósitos bancarios;

d) controles estadísticos de los servicios prestados;

e) informaciones remitidas a las oficinas públicas que correspondan;

f) copias de las remisiones de los protocolos al archivo correspondiente;

g) índice alfabético, de cada protocolo; y

h) cualquier otro que se disponga por las direcciones provinciales de Justicia para el control de las actividades administrativas y de prestación de los servicios o por el Ministerio de Justicia, relacionados con la dirección normativa, metodológica y técnica.

Art. 164- Los locales de las unidades notariales tendrán la debida seguridad y el acondicionamiento que garanticen la actividad notarial, la privacidad de la función y la adecuada conservación de los protocolos y demás documentos.

Las unidades notariales tendrán un sello oficial que las identifique.

Art. 165- En los casos de cierre o extinción de una unidad notarial, sus protocolos, libros, documentos y controles se remitirán al Archivo Provincial de Protocolos que corresponda; y si fuere fusión o traslado, pasaran a la unidad que se cree o se traslade.

CAPITULO V
De La Direccion Tecnica Administrativa De La Actividad Y Funcion Notariales

Art. 166- El ministerio de Justicia, de conformidad con la Ley, ejerce la dirección técnica, normative y metodológica de la actividad y función notariales, y a estos efectos tendrá las atribuciones siguientes:

a) habilitar a los juristas para ser nombrados notarios;

b) nombrar notarios en casos especiales, con competencia nacional o extender la misma a otros notarios;

c) designar los sustitutos de los notarios comprendidos en el inciso b);

第162条　在每家公证机构，公证员都应提供相应的服务。

第163条　在公证机构，每位公证员都应备有下列文件簿、文件和管控措施：

a）文件存档；

b）唯一工作日志管理；

c）经济管理和服务申请记录；

ch）银行存单复印件。

d）提供服务的数据记录；

e）给相关公共机构发送的通报；

f）向相应档案馆进行存档文件移交的移交文件副本；

g）每份存档文件的字母索引表；以及

h）其他任何可供省级司法局进行行政管理和业务管控的文件，以及其他任何可供司法部进行行政管控、方法和技术管理的文件。

第164条　设有公证机构的各地方应有相应的安全措施和条件来保证公证工作的进行、确保公证的私密性，以及确保妥善保管存档文件和其他文件。

公证机构应当有用于身份识别的公章。

第165条　如果关闭或者撤销某公证机构，应将其存档文件、文件簿、其他文件和相关管控措施的材料寄送至相应的省级档案馆；如果公证机构合并或搬迁，应将这些文件移送至合并后或者新搬迁的公证机构。

第五章
公证工作和职责的技术和行政管理

第166条　根据法律规定，司法部长对公证工作和职责进行技术、行政和方法上的管理，因此具有以下职权：

a）向具有法学专业学位的人员授予资质来担任公证员；

b）在特殊情况下任命国家级公证员，或将其他公证员的职权提升至国家级；

c）任命b项中涉及的公证员的替补人员；

ch) aplicar a los notarios que nombre las medidas disciplinarias establecidas en la legislación especial y laboral vigentes;

d) asesorar, inspeccionar y controlar el trabajo de las direcciones Provinciales Justicia respecto a la actividad notarial;

e) realizar y disponer que se efectúen las inspecciones técnicas de las notarias y los archivos provinciales de protocolos notariales para comprobar el cumplimiento de las disposiciones y normas jurídicas vigentes;

f) comunicar a los notarios la existencia de contradicciones, perjuicios a terceros o violaciones de la legalidad que condicionan la abstención de la actuación notarial;

g) establecer las normas metodológicas que regulan la proyección de la red de unidades notariales en las respectivas provincias, así como los requisitos para la creación, traslado, fusión y cierre de dichas unidades;

h) elaborar y desarrollar planes de capacitación y cursos especiales para la formación y superación notarial;

i) establecer los tipos de modelos, formularios y demás documentos para el uso de los notarios en su actividad técnica;

j) asesorar y evacuar consultas técnicas en todas aquellas cuestiones que aseguren el adecuado cumplimiento de las normas y disposiciones establecidas en relación con la actividad notarial y el mejor funcionamiento y desarrollo de esta;

k) convocar a reuniones metodológicas, seminarios y otros eventos de carácter técnico;

m) establecer las plantillas tipo de las unidades notariales;

n) evaluar en su caso, a los notarios señalados en el apartado b), en su calificación técnica, conforme a las indicaciones metodológicas que establece el Comité Estatal de Trabajo y Seguridad Social.;

l) mantener un control nacional actualizado de los notarios en ejercicio y de las personas habilitadas como notarios; y

ll) realizar las demás funciones establecidas en este Reglamento y la Ley.

Art. 167- Las direcciones provinciales de justicia de los órganos locales del poder popular y la del municipio especial Isla de la Juventud, en sus correspondientes territorios tendrán de acuerdo con las facultades dadas por la Ley, en relación con la actividad y función notariales, las atribuciones siguientes:

a) librar las convocatorias para la habilitación de no-

ch）对任命的公证员，适用现行有关法律规定以及现行劳动法有关规定。

d）针对省级司法局的公证工作，提供顾问服务，监督并管控其相关工作；

e）对各公证处以及省级档案馆的工作进行技术监管和督促，从而保证履行现行法律规定；

f）就存在相互矛盾情形、存在对第三方的侵害，或者存在违法情况，通知公证员不能办理公证；

g）制定指导办法，从而规定在各省份的公证机构分布网，以及制定各公证机构的建立、搬迁、合并和关闭的相关要求；

h）制定并完善培训计划，制定供公证员培训和提高培训的特殊培训课程；

i）为公证员制定各类模板表格以及其他文件；

j）解答并澄清所有和公证活动相关的法律法规的疑问，从而更好地完成公证工作，提高公证水平；

k）召开指导会议、研讨会以及其他技术性活动；

m）为公证机构制定编制模式；

n）根据国家劳动和社会保险委员会的相关指导规定，评定b项中任命的公证员的技术水平；

l）实时更新管控制度，从而管理公证员和有公证员资格人员的工作；以及

ll）本条例和法律规定的其他职权。

第167条 根据法律规定的职权范围，各地方人民政府的省级司法局和青年岛特别市司法局在公证工作中，有下列职权：

a）召开公证员资质评定会议并向申请者出具资

tarios y confeccionar los expedientes de habilitación de los solicitantes;

b) proponer al Ministerio de Justicia, los tribunales ante los cuales se rendirán los exámenes de capacidad;

c) nombrar al notario y al personal auxiliar de las unidades notariales; así como designar los notarios sustitutos;

ch) aplicar al notario y personal auxiliar de las unidades notariales las medidas disciplinarias establecidas en la legislación especial y laboral vigentes;

d) supervisar, inspeccionar y dirigir el trabajo de servicios que prestan las unidades notariales, ejercer para esto el control administrativo y financiero de dichas unidades y del personal de las mismas e informar al Ministerio de Justicia de sus resultados

e) coadyuvar con el Ministerio de Justicia en la ejecución de las inspecciones técnicas de las unidades notariales;

f) ejecutar planes de capacitación, superación y formación técnica relacionados con la actividad y función notariales, aprobadas por el Ministerio de Justicia;

g) realizar la evaluación a los notarios en su calificación técnica, conforme a las indicaciones metodológicas que establece el Comité Estatal de Trabajo y Seguridad Social.

h) remitir al ministerio de Justicia la información oficial establecida y cualquier otra que este le solicite referidas a la actividad y función notariales;

i) remitir al ministerio de Justicia las tarjetas de firmas de los notarios e informar sus altas y bajas en un termino no superior a los quince idas de haberse producido las mismas.

j) crear, trasladar, fusionar o cerrar unidades notariales, de conformidad con las normas metodológicas que establece el Ministerio de Justicia, e informar a este en un termino no superior a los quince idas, las decisiones que al efecto se adopten; y

k) controlar y fiscalizar la aplicación de la tarifa de precios por los servicios que prestan las unidades notariales.

质评定文件；

b）向司法部长提议由哪些评委来进行资质评审；

c）任命各公证机构的公证员和助理人员，以及任命替补公证员；

ch）针对各公证机构的公证员和助理人员，适用现行相关法律和劳动法的规定。

d）监督和指导公证机构所提供的服务，为此对公证机构和其工作人员进行行政和财政管控，同时向司法部汇报管理情况；

e）协助司法部长对公证机构进行技术监督；

f）落实司法部长批准的、与公证工作相关的业务培训和提高培训；

g）根据国家劳动和社会保障协会制定的标准，对公证员进行技术水平评定；

h）向司法部长寄送规定的官方信息以及其他任何司法部长需要的和公证工作有关的信息；

i）自公证员注册任命或解除其任命15日内，向司法部报告，并提交签名样本卡；

j）根据司法部长制定的指导规范，成立、搬迁、合并以及关闭公证机构，并在作出该决定后的15日内向司法部长通报这一情况；以及

k）管控并监督各公证机构的服务收费价目表执行情况。

公证离婚法

GACETA OFICIAL DE LA REPUBLICA DE CUBA
EDICION ORDINARIA LA HABANA, LUNES 19 DE SEPTIEMBRE DE 1994
Numero 13 - Precio $ 0,10
Pág. 193

CONSEJO DE ESTADO

Fidel CASTRO CRUZ, Presidente del Consejo de Estado de la República de Cuba.

HAGO SABER: Que el Consejo de Estado ha acordado lo siguiente:

POR CUANTO. En la actualidad los tribunales municipales populares conocen y resuelven los procesos de divorcio en los cuales los cónyuges están de acuerdo en disolver el vínculo matrimonial y no existen contradicciones sobre los efectos jurídicos del acto ni perjuicios a terceros, lo cual ocasiona un alto numero de expedientes a tramitar en los tribunales, sin que efectivamente la actuación de estos sean necesaria y en consecuencia, se dificulte la agilidad y celeridad de otros tramites legales que por su carácter contencioso, trascendencia jurídica e importancia social requieren de la actuación judicial.

POR CUANTO. A partir de la vigencia de la Ley numero 50 de 28 de diciembre de 1984, "Ley de las Notarias Estatales" se transfirió a la actividad notarial el conocimiento de los expedientes de jurisdicción voluntaria referentes a administración de bienes de ausentes, consignación, información para perpetua memoria y declaratoria de herederos que anteriormente se resolvían por los tribunales municipales, lo que ha permitido a los notarios acumular una experiencia valiosa en la autorización de dichos actos jurídicos.

POR CUANTO. Los actuales requerimientos para el perfeccionamiento de los tribunales y la necesidad de disminución y agilización de trámites jurídicos que realiza la población, aconsejan extraer de la competencia de los tribunales populares y transferir a la función notarial el conocimiento y tramitación del divorcio, siempre que no existiere contradicción en los cónyuges en cuanto a las condiciones y efectos jurídicos del mismo ni perjuicios a terceros, por considerar que el Notario a través del ejer-

古巴共和国官方公报
常规版　1994年9月19日星期一于哈瓦那

13号 - 价格：$0.10
第193页

古巴国务委员会

菲德尔·卡斯特罗·克鲁斯，古巴共和国国务委员会主席。

告知如下：国务委员会商议如下：

鉴于如今市里法院处理了很多离婚案件，这些案件中的配偶同意解除婚姻关系，对于离婚判决无异议，且不损害第三方利益。这些离婚案件导致法院要处理大量文件，而这些文件并不全是必要的，并且还影响了其他法律案件的审理速度，这些其他案件因其争议性、法律影响力和社会重要性更需要司法程序。

鉴于自1984年12月28日第50号法律《国家公证法》生效以来，自愿管辖范围内的文件认定被定义为公证内容，这些内容包括下落不明人员财产的管理、寄存、永久备忘以及继承声明，这些之前都是由市级法院受理，而这些也使得公证员积累了丰富的公证经验。

鉴于基于优化法院职能，以及简化人民司法程序的要求，建议将离婚判决和离婚程序从人民法院职权中剥离，纳入公证职权，前提是只要配偶双方对于离婚的司法效力和条件没有异议，另外该离婚也不会侵犯第三方利益。另外，鉴于公证员通过公证行为这种非法律程序同样可以确保这些行为的合法性和法律效力，并不会弱化这些行为的司法影响力和社会重要性。

cicio de la fe publica, realiza actividades extrajudiciales, que garantizan igualmente la eficacia jurídica y legalidad de estos actos, sin que disminuya por ello la trascendencia jurídica e importancia social de estos.

POR TANTO. El Consejo de Estado, en uso de las atribuciones que le están conferidas por el Art. 90, inciso c) de la Constitución de la República, resuelve dictar el siguiente.

DECRETO-LEY NUMERO 154
DEL DIVORCIO NOTARIAL

Art. 1- El divorcio procederá por escritura notarial, cuando exista mutuo acuerdo entre los cónyuges sobre la disolución del vinculo matrimonial y sus efectos inmediatos y no se emita por el Fiscal dictamen en contrario, en su caso.

A falta del acuerdo a que se refiere el párrafo anterior o mediando dictamen en contrario del Fiscal sin que sus objeciones sean salvadas, el divorcio se tramitara por la vía judicial.

Art. 2- Los cónyuges solicitarán conjuntamente, por si o por representación, la disolución del vinculo matrimonial. En caso de representación letrada, un solo abogado podrá representar a ambos cónyuges.

Si los cónyuges no pudieran comparecer conjuntamente ante un mismo notario uno de ellos podrá declarar bajo juramento ante el notario que elija, su conformidad con la disolución del vinculo matrimonial y demás convenciones sobre los efectos inmediatos de dicha disolución.

El cónyuge o su representante que presente la solicitud de divorcio ante Notario, entregará a este copia de la declaración jurada del otro cónyuge.

Art. 3- El Notario, para la tramitación del divorcio, se regirá por los principios y normas del Código de Familia y lo establecido en la Ley de las Notarias Estatales y su Reglamento.

Art. 4- El Notario, al analizar las convenciones de los cónyuges y, en: especial, las referidas a las relaciones paterno filiales sobre patria potestad, guarda y cuidado de los hijos comunes menores, régimen de comunicación con éstos y pensiones, observará que las mismas no atenten contra:

a) el normal. desarrollo y educación de los hijos comunes menores ;

b) la adecuada interrelación y comunicación entre

因此，国务委员会，根据《共和国宪法》第90条c项赋予的职权，决定颁布下列法令。

第154号法令
公证离婚

第1条 如果夫妻双方协商同意解除婚姻关系并立即生效，且检察官也未给出相左的意见，那么可以通过公证书离婚。

如果没有前款所说的协议，或者和检察官判决意见不同，且分歧并未解决，那么应当通过法律途径离婚。

第2条 夫妻双方可以本人或者由律师代理申请解除婚姻关系。如果是由律师代理，一名律师即可代表夫妻双方。

如果夫妻双方不能同时出现在同一公证处，其中一方可以自行选择公证处进行宣誓声明，说明同意解除婚姻关系，并且同意针对离婚的法律后果所订立的其他协议。

申请公证离婚的夫妻任何一方或者代理律师还要向公证员递交夫妻另一方的声明文件副本。

第3条 在办理离婚过程中，公证员应遵守《家庭法》和《国家公证法》的相关规定。

第4条 公证员在审核夫妻离婚协议的过程中，尤其是在关系到共同的未成年子女的父母监护权和抚养问题、探视子女问题以及赡养问题时，应注意确保：

a）共同的未成年子女的正常成长和教育；

b）父母和子女间的正常沟通和互动；

padres e hijos ;

c) la satisfacción de las necesidades económicas de los hijos comunes menores,

ch) la salvaguarda de los intereses de los hijos comunes menores y

d) el cumplimiento de los deberes que corresponden a los padres.

Art. 5- El Notario dará traslado de la solicitud de divorcio al Fiscal cuando a su juicio los acuerdos de los cónyuges atenten contra cualquiera de los aspectos señalados en el Art. anterior o cuando pretendan deferir la patria potestad, sobre los hijos comunes menores a favor de uno solo de los padres.

Art. 6- El Fiscal al recibir una solicitud de divorcio de las referidas en el Art. anterior, analizara la procedencia o no de los acuerdos en relación con los intereses de los hijos comunes menores y emitirá un dictamen al respecto, que enviara al Notario encargado de tramitar la solicitud de disolución del vinculo matrimonial.

Art. 7- Si el dictamen del Fiscal fuera favorable a las convenciones propuestas por los cónyuges, el Notario continuara la tramitación del divorcio.

Art. 8- Si el Fiscal emite dictamen contrario a alguna de las convenciones propuestas por los cónyuges, el Notario lo hará saber a los interesados por si, en atención a lo señalado por el Fiscal, aceptan modificar sus acuerdos.

Si los cónyuges modificaren sus acuerdos en correspondencia a lo señalado por el Fiscal, el Notario continuara la tramitación del divorcio. En caso contrario interrumpirá su substanciación dejando expedita la vía judicial, lo que certificara a los interesados.

Art. 9- La escritura notarial que declare el divorcio tendrá fuerza ejecutiva directa e inmediata, a todos los efectos legales a partir de su fecha y contendrá los acuerdos de los exconyuges sobre los aspectos siguientes:

a) la disolución del vinculo matrimonial,

b) la determinación en relación con la conservación de la patria potestad sobre los hijos comunes menores, salvo que existiere fallo judicial en contrario, acreditado por alguno de los cónyuges.

c) el discernimiento de la guarda y cuidado de los hijos comunes menores.

ch) la determinación de la cuantía de la pensión que corresponda conceder a los hijos comunes menores y al excónyuge, en su caso,

d) el régimen de comunicación de aquel de los padres al que no se le confiera la guarda y cuidado de los hijos

c）未成年子女的经济需求得到满足；

ch）共同的未成年子女的利益得到维护；以及

d）父母履行应尽的责任。

第5条 如果公证员认为夫妻离婚协议内容违背了上文列出的内容，或者公证员认为离婚协议仅对夫妻中一方的监护权有利，那么公证员应将该离婚申请提交给检察官。

第6条 检察官在收到上文提及的离婚申请后，将分析该离婚协议是否以共同的未成年子女的利益为出发点，并作出相应判决；检察官会将该判决寄送给受理该离婚申请的公证员。

第7条 如果检察官同意夫妻达成的离婚协议，公证员就继续办理离婚手续。

第8条 如果检察官给出的判决和夫妻离婚协议中的任何一条有所不同，公证员应通知当事人，询问他们是否根据检察官给出的判决修改协议内容。

如果夫妻双方根据检察官的判决对协议进行修改，那么公证员将继续办理离婚手续。如果未对离婚协议进行修改，公证员将中止办理离婚手续，并通知当事人选择司法程序进行离婚。

第9条 自离婚声明公证书生效之日起，该公证书即可对所有可能的法律后果产生直接的效力，该公证书包括下列内容：

a）解除婚姻关系；

b）对于共同的未成年子女监护权的分配，如果夫妻任何一方证明存在与其相悖的司法判决，那么该协定无效；

c）对共同的未成年子女的抚养和照看的规定；

ch）根据具体情况，确认给共同的未成年子女和前配偶的赡养费金额。

d）父母中负责共同未成年抚养的一方给另一方探视子女的权利；

comunes menores con estos,

e) las convenciones de los cónyuges sobre el destino de la vivienda, si procediere,

f) las advertencias legales correspondientes en cuanto a la liquidación de la comunidad matrimonial de bienes, en caso de que expresamente declinaran su derecho a realizarla en el propio acto.

Art. 10- Las modificaciones de las convenciones sobre las relaciones paternofiliales referidas a la patria potestad, guarda y cuidado de los hijos comunes menores, régimen de comunicación o pensiones, que surjan con posterioridad a la fecha de la escritura de divorcio, se resolverán ante Notario, siempre que no exista contradicción entre los excónyuges.

Art. 11- 1.El Notario, dará traslado de la solicitud al Fiscal cuando a su juicio la pretensión atente contra cualquiera de los aspectos recogidos en el Art. 4 de este Decreto-Ley. Si se emitiere por el Fiscal dictamen en contrario, el Notario se abstendrá y el asunto se sustanciará por los tramites de los incidentes en el tribunal municipal popular correspondiente, ante el cual se presentará copia de la escritura de divorcio. 2. De lo resuelto por el Tribunal Municipal Popular, se remitirá certificación a la Notaria correspondiente donde obra la escritura de divorcio.

Art. 12- El incumplimiento por cualquiera de los excónyuges da algunos de los pronunciamientos contenidos en la escritura de divorcio, se resolverá en proceso de ejecución ante el tribunal municipal popular correspondiente.

La resolución judicial que recaiga en el asunto, sólo podrá modificarse por los trámites de incidentes. ante el tribunal competente.

Disposiciones Transitorias

PRIMERA: Los procesos de divorcios a que se refiere el presente Decreto-Ley que al momento de su entrada en vigor estén sustanciandose en los tribunales, se continuaran tramitando hasta su resolución definitiva por dichos tribunales, amparados en la legislación por la que se promovieron.

SEGUNDA: Los divorcios que hayan sido contratados por los abogados de los bufetes colectivos antes de la entrada en vigor de este Decreto-Ley, se presentarán para su resolución ante el tribunal correspondiente, dentro del término de 60 idas, a partir de su vigencia.

e）如果涉及房产问题，夫妻双方对房产分配达成的协议；

f）针对夫妻双方共有财产的分割问题，如果夫妻双方表示放弃该权利，将会有哪些相应的法律后果。

第10条 如果在出具离婚公证书之后，希望修改子女关系条款中涉及共同未成年子女监护权、抚养权、探视权以及赡养费的内容，则要到公证处进行修改，但前提是夫妻双方对这一修改内容没有分歧。

第11条 如果公证员认为该修改申请违背了本法令第4条中的任何一项内容，那么应将该申请递交至检察官。如果检察官给出不同意见，那公证员应中止手续的办理，由当地的市级人民法院作为附带事项进行受理，公证员应向法院递交离婚公证书。市级人民法院会以证明文件形式将判决结果寄送给出具相应离婚公证书的公证员。

第12条 如果夫妻中的任何一方未能履行离婚公证书中的协议内容，应当在相应的市级人民法院通过法律途径解决。

该判决只有通过附带事项程序才能在相应法院进行修改。

过渡性条款

一、截至本法令生效之日，仍在法院进行审理的离婚案件，继续由相应法院按照立案审理当时有效的法律规定执行，直至案件办结。

二、针对那些在本法令生效前就已经聘请公立律师事务所的律师来代理离婚的案件，要在该法令生效后的60日内将该离婚申请提交至相应的法院。

Disposiciones Finales

PRIMERA: El Ministro de Justicia, el Fiscal General de la República y el Consejo de Gobierno del Tribunal Supremo Popular quedan encargados de dictar, respectivamente y en lo que les corresponda, cuantas disposiciones complementarias se requieran para el cumplimiento del presente Decreto-Ley.

SEGUNDA: Se modifican al apartado 4) del Art. 43, el artículo 50 y el apartado 2) del Art. 93, todos del Código de Familia, los que quedarán redactados de la manera siguiente:

Art. 43- 4) por sentencia firme de divorcio o escritura de divorcio otorgada ante Notario.

Art. 50- el divorcio puede obtenerse por sentencia judicial o escritura notarial.

Art. 93- 2) cuando se atribuya a uno de' ellos por escritura notarial de divorcio o por sentencia firme dictada en proceso de divorcio o de nulidad de matrimonio o se prive a ambos por resolución judicial.

TERCERA: Se modifica el inciso c) del Art. 10 de la Ley numero 50 "Ley de las Notarias Estatales" de 28 de diciembre de 1984 el que quedara redactado de la forma siguiente: a) conocer, tramitar y resolver los asuntos de jurisdicción voluntaria, sucesorios de declaratoria de herederos y de divorcio de conformidad con la ley.

CUARTA: Se modifica el primer párrafo del Art. 372 y el Art. 380 ambos de la Ley de Procedimiento Civil, Administrativo y Laboral, los que quedaran redactados de la manera siguiente:

Art. 372 - El proceso de divorcio para la disolución de una matrimonio celebrado en Cuba podrá promoverse ante el tribunal competente cualquiera que sea la nacionalidad de los cónyuges. Cuando exista mutuo acuerdo entre estos sobre la disolución del vinculo matrimonial y sus efectos jurídicos y no se emita por el Fiscal dictamen en contrario, procederá tramitar el divorcio por la vía notarial,

Art. 380- Cuando el divorcio por mutuo acuerdo no proceda ante Notario quedará expedita la vía para tramitarlo ante el tribunal competente. En este caso el proceso se iniciara mediante escrito firmado por los cónyuges en el que solicitaran la disolución del vinculo matrimonial y harán constar las convenciones a que hayan llegado respecto a las relaciones paterno filiales referidas a la patria potestad, guarda y cuidado de los hijos comunes menores, régimen de comunicación con estos, pensiones que correspondan y separación de bienes comunes.

最终条款

一、司法部长、共和国总检察长和最高人民法院管理委员会负责在相应的职权范围内，制定落实本法令必需的补充条款。

二、修改《家庭法》中的第43条第4项、第50条和第93条第2项，修改后内容如下：

第43条 4）根据离婚判决或者公证员出具的离婚公证书。

第50条 可以通过法律判决或者公证书来完成离婚。

第93条 2）属于公证离婚、法院判决离婚或者法院判决婚姻无效中的任何一种情况，或者不属于以上任何一种情况，但通过法律途径解除婚姻关系的。

三、修改1984年12月28日颁布的第50号法律《国家公证法》第10条c项，修改后内容如下：

a）根据法律了解、受理并解决自愿管辖范围内的事项、遗产继承声明以及离婚事宜。

四、修改《民事、行政和劳动诉讼法》第372条第1款和第380条，修改后内容如下：

第372条 无论夫妻国籍如何，在古巴缔结的婚姻关系都可以在相应的法院解除。如果夫妻双方针对离婚及其相应的法律后果达成协议，且检察官未给出不同意见，那么可以通过公证途径来办理离婚。

第380条 如未在公证处完成离婚协议，那么可以在相应的法院完成。如果是这种情况，应提交夫妻双方签字的文件，写明申请解除婚姻关系，并写明关于子女关系方面达成的协议，包括共同的未成年子女的监护权、抚养权、探视权以及相应的赡养费，还有共同财产的分割。

La presentación de este escrito podrá hacerse indistintamente por cualquiera de los cónyuges, por ambos o por el letrado director y al mismo se acompañara la certificación expedida por el Notario absteniéndose de actuar en el caso.

QUINTA: Se derogan cuantas disposiciones legales y reglamentarias se opongan a lo dispuesto en el presente Decreto-Ley.

SEXTA: Este Decreto-Ley comenzara a regir a los sesenta idas de su publicación en la Gaceta Oficial de la República.

Dado en el Palacio de la Revolución, ciudad de La Habana, a 6 de septiembre de 1994.

Fidel Castro Ruz

夫妻双方或者任何一方都可以提交该文件，或者由代理律师提交该文件，同时还应提交公证员开具的证明，说明不予进行公证离婚办理。

五、废止所有与本法令内容相悖的法律规定。

六、本法令自在共和国官方公报上发布后第60个自然日起生效。

1994年9月6日于哈瓦那革命宫

菲德尔·卡斯特罗·鲁斯

哥伦比亚

公证与登记机构管理章程

| COLOMBIA
ESTATUTO DE NOTARIADO Y REGISTRO | 哥伦比亚
公证与登记机构管理章程 |

TITULO I
DE LA FUNCION NOTARIAL

CAPITULO UNICO Normas generals

Art. 1°- Derogado. Decr. 2163 de 1970, art. 46.

Art. 2°- La función notarial es incompatible con el ejercicio de autoridad o jurisdicción y no puede ejercerse sino dentro de los limites territoriales del respectivo Círculo de Notaría.

Conc.: Decr. 2148 de 1983, arts. 5°, 6°.

Art. 3°- Compete a los Notarios:

1. Recibir, extender y autorizar las declaraciones que conforme a las leyes requieran escritura pública y aquellas a las cuales los interesados quieran revestir de esta solemnidad.

2. Autorizar el reconocimiento espontáneo de documentos privados.

3. Dar testimonio de la autenticidad de firmas de funcionarios o particulares y de otros Notarios que las tengan registradas ante ellos.

4. Dar fe de la correspondencia o identidad que exista entre un documento que tenga a la vista y su copia mecánica o literal.

5. Acreditar la existencia de las personas naturales y expedir la correspondiente fe de vida.

6. Recibir y guardar dentro del protocolo los documentos o actuaciones que la ley o el juez ordenen pro-

第一篇
公证职能

独章　总则

第1条　已废止。1970年第2163号法令，第46条。

第2条　承担公证职能的人员不得兼任行政或司法职务，且仅能在相应的公证辖区范围内行使公证职能。

并行法规：1983年第2148号法令，第5条、第6条。

第3条　公证员的职责为：

1. 对于法律要求办理公证或者当事人要求公证的事项，按照要求受理、拟稿并授权。

2. 认可私署文书的效力。

3. 办理签名认证，证明公职人员、个人以及其他公证员签名的真实性和效力。

4. 对向其出示的文件原件及其影印件或抄录副本进行比对，证明副本与原件的相符性或同一性。

5. 证明自然人仍然健在并出具相应的健在证明。

6. 对法律或司法机关要求公证或者当事人希望以公证方式获得保障的文件或行为进行公证和存档

tocolizar o que los interesados quieran proteger de esta manera.

7. Expedir copias o certificaciones, según el caso, de los documentos que reposen en sus archivos.

8. Dar testimonio escrito con fines jurídico-probatorios de los hechos percibidos por ellos dentro del ejercicio de sus funciones y de que no haya quedado dato formal en sus archivos.

9. Intervenir en el otorgamiento, extensión y autorización de los testamentos solemnes que conforme a la ley civil deban otorgarse ante ellos.

10. Practicar apertura y publicación de los testamentos cerrados.

11. y 12. Derogados. Decr. 2163 de 1970, art. 46.

13. Llevar el registro del estado civil de las personas en los casos, por los sistemas y con las formalidades prescritos en la ley.

14. Las demás funciones que les señalen las leyes.

Conc.: Decrs. 902, 999 y 2668 de 1988; 1557 y 1712 de 1989.

Art. 4°- Los Notarios sólo procederán a ejercer sus funciones a solicitud de los interesados, quienes tienen el derecho a elegir libremente el Notario ante quien deseen acudir.

Conc.: Decr. 2148 de 1983, art. 2e.

Art. 5°- En general, los servicios notariales serán retribuidos por las partes según la tarifa oficial y el Notario no podrá negarse a prestarlos sino en los casos expresamente previstos en la ley.

Conc.: Decr. 172 de 1992.

Art. 6°- Corresponde al Notario la redacción de los instrumentos en que se consignen las declaraciones emitidas ante él, sin perjuicio de que los interesados las presenten redactadas por ellos a sus asesores. En todo caso, el Notario velará por la legalidad de tales declaraciones y pondrá de presente las irregularidades que advierta, sin negar la autorización del instrumento en caso de inasistencia de los interesados, salvo lo prevenido para la nulidad absoluta, dejando siempre en él constancia de lo ocurrido.

Art. 7°- El Notario está al servicio del derecho y no de ninguna de las partes; prestará su asesoría y consejo a todos los otorgantes en actitud conciliatoria.

Art. 8°- Los Notarios son autónomos en el ejercicio de sus funciones, y responsables conforme a la ley.

Art. 9°- Los Notarios responden de la regularidad formal de los instrumentos que autorizan, pero no de la veracidad de las declaraciones de los interesados; tampoco

保管。

7. 根据情况对其存档的文件出具经核证副本或证明书。

8. 为履行公证职能，对委托其证明且在档案中并没有正式资料的事项进行证明，出具文件的正式副本，作为合法证明材料。

9. 对民法要求应在公证员见证下认可的正式遗嘱的认可、拟稿、授权等事宜进行介入。

10. 对密封遗嘱执行开封和公示。

11-12. 已废止。1970 年第 2163 号法令，第 46 条。

13. 按照法律规定的形式，按不同的婚姻制度对个人婚姻状况进行登记。

14. 法律规定的其他职能。

并行法规：1988 年第 902 号、第 999 号和第 2668 号法令，1989 年第 1557 号和第 1712 号法令。

第 4 条 公证员仅在当事人申请的情况下才可行使职能，当事人有权自由选择公证员。

并行法规：1983 年第 2148 号法令，第 2e 条。

第 5 条 总体上讲，公证服务报酬应根据法律规定收取，除法律明文规定的情形外，公证员不得拒绝提供服务。

并行法规：1992 年第 172 号法令。

第 6 条 公证员应负责出具在其见证下声明事项的相关证明文件，当事人有权将该文件交与其顾问进行咨询。在任何情况下，公证员均应保证声明事项合法有效，并指出其中的不合规之处，但无需因当事人缺席而拒绝批准该文件，除非可预见该文件绝对无效，公证员应随时保留事件发生的证据。

第 7 条 公证员必须依法行事，不得偏向任何一方；公证员应当以中立态度为所有公证当事人提供咨询和建议。

第 8 条 公证员在行使职能时具备自主性，并依法承担责任。

第 9 条 公证员仅对文件在形式上的合规性负责，而不对当事人声明事项的真实性负责；对于当事人是否具有法定资格或能力实施相关行为或签署相应

responden de la capacidad o aptitud legal de estos para celebrar el acto o contrato respectivo.

Conc.: Decr. 2148 de 1983, art. 3°.

Art.10- Modificado. Ley 29 de 1973, art. 21. El ejercicio de la función notarial es incompatible con el de todo empleo o cargo publico; con la gestión particular u oficial de negocios ajenos; con el ejercicio de la profesión de abogado; con el de cargos de representación política; con la condición de Ministro de cualquier culto; con el de los cargos de albacea, curador dativo, auxiliar de la justicia, con toda intervención en política, distinta del ejercicio del sufragio y en general, con toda la actividad que perjudique el ejercicio de su cargo.

Conc.: Decr. 2148 de 1983, art. 5°.

Art. 11- Modificado. Decr. 2163 de 1970, art. 34. No obstante, el Notario podrá ejercer cargos docentes hasta un límite de ocho horas semanales, y académicos o de beneficencia en establecimientos públicos o privados.

Conc.: Decr. 2148 de 1983, art. 6°.

TITULO II
DEL EJERCICIO DE LAS FUNCIONES DEL N0TAR10

CAPITULO I De las escrituras públicas

Art.12- Deberán celebrarse por escritura pública todos los actos y contratos de disposición o gravamen de bienes inmuebles, y en general aquellos para los cuales la ley exige esta solemnidad.

Conc.: Decr. 2148 de 1983, arts. 8°, 9°.

Art.13- La escritura pública es el instrumento que contiene declaraciones en actos jurídicos, emitidas ente el Notario, con los requisitos previstos en la ley y que se incorpora al protocolo. El proceso de su perfeccionamiento consta de la recepción, la extensión, el otorgamiento y la autorización.

Art.14- La recepción consiste en percibir las declaraciones que hacen ante el Notario los interesados; la extensión, es la versión escrita de lo declarado; el otorgamiento es el asentimiento expreso que aquellos prestan al instrumento extendido y la autorización es la fe que imprime el Notario a este, en vista de que se han llenado los requisitos pertinentes, y de que las declaraciones han sido realmente emitidas por los interesados.

Art. 15- Cuando el Notario redacte el instrumento,

合同，公证人也不承担责任。

并行法规：1983年第2148号法令，第3条。

第10条　已修订。1973年第29号法律第21条。公证员不得同时兼任其他职业或公共职务；不得兼任其他商业管理人员或官员；不得兼任律师职业；不得兼任政治代表职位；不得兼任部委或宗教职位；不得兼任遗嘱执行人、监护人、助理司法人员；不得参与除选举以外的其他政治活动，以及任何可能影响其履行公证职能的活动。

并行法规：1983年第2148号法令，第5条。

第11条　已修订。1970年第2163号法令，第34条。公证员有权在公立或私营机构中担任教学、学术职务或从事慈善工作，但工作时间每周不得超过八小时。

并行法规：1983年第2148号法令，第6条。

第二篇
公证员职能的行使

第一章　公证书

第12条　涉及不动产的处置或留置权的文书与合同，以及法律要求这种正式手续的所有文书与合同，均应采用公证书的形式。

并行法规：1983年第2148号法令，第8条、第9条。

第13条　公证书是指按照法律规定的要求，在公证员的见证下出具并在公证登记簿中归档登记的包含法律协议相关声明事项的文书。全部流程包括受理、拟稿、认可和授权。

第14条　受理指公证员收到当事人希望公证的声明事项；拟稿，指为声明事项拟定书面版本；认可，指对公证书的明确认可；授权，指公证员认定声明事项已经符合相关要求，并的确由当事人所提出。

第15条　当公证员拟定文本时，应调查当事人

deberá averiguar los fines prácticos y jurídicos que los otorgantes se proponen alcanzar con sus declaraciones, para que queden fielmente expresados en el instrumentos; indicará el acto o contrato con su denominación legal si la tuviere; y al extender el instrumento velará por que contenga sus elementos esenciales y naturales propios de aquel, y las estipulaciones especiales que los interesados acuerden o indique el declarante único, redactado todo en el lenguaje sencillo, jurídico y preciso.

Art.16- Los instrumentos notariales se redactarán en idioma castellano. Cuando los otorgantes no lo conozcan suficientemente, serán asesorados por un intérprete que firmará con ellos, y de cuya intervención dejará constancia el Notario.

Art. 17- El Notario revisará las declaraciones que le presenten las partes, redactadas por ellas a su nombre, para establecer si se acomodan a la finalidad de los comparecientes, a las normas legales, a la clara expresión idiomática; en consecuencia, podrá sugerir las correcciones que juzgue necesarias.

Art.18- Las escrituras se extenderán por medios manuales o mecánicos, en caracteres claros y procurando su mayor seguridad y perduración; podrán ser impresas de antemano para llenar los claros con los datos propios del acto o contrato que se extiende, cuidando de ocupar los espacios sobrante con líneas u otros trazos que impidan su posterior utilización. No se dejarán claros o espacios vacíos ni aún para separar las distintas partes o cláusulas del instrumento, ni se usarán en los nombres abreviaturas o iniciales que puedan dar lugar a confusión.

Art.19- Las cantidades y referencias numéricas, se expresarán en letras, y entre paréntesis, se anotarán las cifras correspondientes. En caso de disparidad prevalecerá lo escrito en letras.

Art.20- Las escrituras originales o matrices se escribirán en papel autorizado por el Estado y al final de cada instrumento, antes de firmarse, se indicarán los números distintivos de las hojas empleadas, si los tuvieren.

Art. 21- Modificado. Decr. 2163 de 1970, art. 35. El Notario no autorizará el instrumento cuando quiera que el contenido de las declaraciones de los otorgantes o con apoyo en pruebas fehacientes o en hechos percibidos directamente por él, llegue a la convicción de que el acto sería absolutamente nulo por razón de lo dispuesto en el artículo 1504 del Código Civil.

Conc.: Decr 2148 de 1983, art.3°.

Art.22- La escritura autorizada por el Notario se

提出声明事项的实际目的和法律目的，以保证文本忠实反映其意图；若存在法律行为或合同的法定名称，应予以指出；在拟定文件文本时，公证员应保证文本内容包含声明事项核心内容及本身属性，包含当事人同意或唯一声明人指明的特殊规定，并保证使用法律语言简明、准确表达含义。

第 16 条　公证文件应使用西班牙语书写。若当事人不懂西班牙语，应配翻译，并由翻译人员同当事人一并签名。有翻译介入的，公证员应予写明。

第 17 条　公证员应审核当事人提交的以其名义撰写的声明事项，以验证该文件是否符合公证对象目的、是否符合法律规定、语言表述是否明确。若认为有必要，可建议进行修改。

第 18 条　公证书可以手写或打印，字体必须清晰，且要保证文件安全并得到良好保存。可预先将文本打印，之后再将相关法律行为或合同信息填入，有空白区域的，应划线或做其他标记以免后期增添内容。文本中不可留有空白或空行，包括不同章节或不同条款之间也不得留有空行，不得使用可能造成混淆的简称或首字母缩写。

第 19 条　有关数量和数字应使用大写表示，紧随其后可在括号中注明阿拉伯数字。若存在数字表述不一致的情况，以大写数字为准。

第 20 条　所有公证书正本均应使用由国家授权的专用纸张，在签名之前，若文件为多页，则每页页尾应标注页码。

第 21 条　已修订。1970 年第 2163 号法令，第 35 条。公证员根据当事人声明事项的内容判断，或有可靠证据证明，或根据公证员直接了解到的相关事实，认为属于《民法典》第 1504 条规定的无效行为的，公证员将不对公证事项授权。

并行法规：1983 年第 2148 号法令，第 3 条。

第 22 条　公证员授权的公证书将记录在公证登

anotará en el Libro de Relación, con lo cual se considerará incorporada en el protocolo, aunque materialmente no se haya formado aún el tomo correspondiente.

Art. 23- La escritura se distinguirá con el número de orden que le corresponde expresado en letras y cifras numerales. Se anotarán en el Municipio, Departamento y República, el nombre y apellidos del Notario o de quien haga sus veces y el Círculo que delimita su función.

Las escrituras se numerarán ininterrumpidamente en orden sucesivo durante cada año calendario. Con ellas se formará el protocolo con el número de tomos que sea consejable para seguridad y comodidad de la consulta.

Sección Primera Comparecencia

Art. 24- La identificación de los comparecientes se hará con los documentos legales pertinentes dejando testimonio de cuáles son estos. Sin embargo, en caso de urgencia, a falta del documento especial de identificación, podrá el Notario identificarlo con otros documentos auténticos, o mediante la fe de conocimiento por parte suya. Y cuando fuere cl caso, exigirá también la tarjeta militar.

Conc.: Decr. 2148 de 1983, art.11 .

Art. 25- En la escritura se consignarán cl nombre, apellidos, estado civil, edad y domicilio de los comparecientes. En caso de representación se expresará, además, la clase de ésta y los datos de las personas naturales representadas como si comparecieran directamente, o de las personas jurídicas tal como corresponde según la Ley o los estatutos, indicando su domicilio y naturaleza.

Art. 26- Cuando se trate de personas mayores no será necesario indicar sino esta circunstancia sin expresar la edad. El número de años cumplidos se anotará solo cuando se trate de menores adultos, o de adoptantes y adoptados en las escrituras de adopción.

Conc.: Decr. 2148 de 1983 art. 24.

Art.27- Quien disponga de un inmueble o constituya gravamen sobre él, deberá indicar la situación jurídica del bien respecto de la sociedad conyugal, caso de ser o haber sido casado.

Art. 28- Modificado. Decr. 2163 de 1970, art. 36. En caso de representación, el representante dirá la clase de representación que ejerce y presentará para su protocolización los documentos que la acrediten.

Si se trata de funcionarios públicos que representen al Estado, los Departamentos, Intendencias, Comisarías o Municipios se indicará el cargo, y cuando sean necesarios

记册中，一旦登记，该文件则被认定为加入归档登记簿，即使实际上尚未添加。

第 23 条　公证书将使用字母和阿拉伯数字序号标注排序。其中应写明国家、省、市，承办公证员或者代行公证职能的人员的姓名，以及所供职的公证机构的名称。

每一年的公证书均按次序不间断排列。所有文件装订成册，以安全和便于检索为原则，分为不同卷。

第一节　公证当事人

第 24 条　应根据合法身份证件验证公证当事人的身份。然而，若处于紧急情况，无法获得其专用身份证件，公证员可通过其他真实身份证件或通过个人了解的情况确认其身份。如果当事人为军人，也可要求出示军官证。

并行法规：1983 年第 2148 号法令，第 11 条。

第 25 条　公证书中应注明公证当事人的姓名、婚姻状况、年龄以及住址。另外，委托他人代理的，还应说明委托类型以及委托人的身份信息。委托人为自然人的，身份信息应按与本人直接办理的相同要求提供；委托人为法人的，应按照法律或章程要求提供，并指出地址和性质。

第 26 条　若公证对象为成年人，除非情况需要，否则不必特别标注其年龄。只有当事人是未成年人，或涉及领养相关文件中提到收养人和被收养人内容时，才需要写明年龄。

并行法规：1983 年第 2148 号法令，第 24 条。

第 27 条　拥有不动产或对不动产进行了抵押的人员，若为已婚或结过婚，应说明与婚姻财产法相关的财产法律情况。

第 28 条　已修订。1970 年第 2163 号法令，第 36 条。若委托他人代理，被委托人应说明该委托的性质，并提交相关证明文件，并收录到公证案卷中。

如果当事人是代表国家、省、州、地方、市的公职人员，应说明其职位，若有必要应登记备案。

se protocolizarán los documentos de autorización.

Conc.: Decr. 2148 de 1983 arts. 12 a 16; C. de P.C., 65, 259.

Nota: El articulo 309 de la Constitución Política de 1991, erigió en departamentos a las antiguas intendencias y comisarias.

Art.29- No habrá lugar a la intervención de testigos instrumentales en las escrituras. Respecto de los testamentos se estará a lo previsto en el Título 3°. del Libro III del Código Civil.

Sección Segunda De las estipulaciones

Art.30- Las declaraciones de los otorgantes se redactarán con toda claridad y precisión de manera que se acomoden lo más exactamente posible a sus propósitos y a la esencia y naturaleza del acto o contrato que se celebra y contendrán explícitamente las estipulaciones relativas a los derechos constituidos, transmitido, modificados o extinguidos, y al alcance de ellos y de las obligaciones que los otorgantes asuman.

Conc.: Decr 2148 de 1983 arts. 17, 20.

Art.31- Los inmuebles que sean objeto de enajenación, gravamen o limitación se identificarán por su cédula o registro catastral si lo tuvieren; por su nomenclatura, por el paraje o localidad donde están ubicados, y por sus linderos. Siempre que se exprese la cabida se empleará el sistema métrico decimal.

Conc.: Decr: 2148 de 1983 arts. 18, 19, 20.

Art.32- Será necesario indicar precisamente el titulo de adquisición del declarante del inmueble o que lo grava o afecta, con los datos de su registro. Si el disponente careciere de título inscrito, así lo expresará indicando la fuente de donde pretende derivar su derecho.

Conc.: Decr. 2148 de 1983 arts. 20, 21.

Art. 33- El disponente está en el deber de manifestar la existencia de gravámenes, derechos de usufructo, uso y habitación, servidumbres, limitaciones o condiciones y embargos o litigios pendientes, y en general, toda situación que pueda afectar al inmueble objeto de su declaración o los derechos constituidos sobre él, y si lo posee materialmente.

Conc.: Decr: 2148 de /983, art. 21.

Art. 34- El precio o la estimación del valor de los

并行法规：1983 年第 2148 号法令，第 12 条至第 16 条；《刑法典》第 65259 条。

注：根据 1991 年《政治宪法》第 309 条，在过去的州和地区基础上建立省行政单位。

第 29 条 文件相关证人不得参与公证书撰写。关于遗嘱部分，见《民法典》第三卷第三篇的规定。

第二节 相关规定

第 30 条 当事人声明事项应清晰明确地撰写，以保证其能准确反映其意图，并符合法律行为或合同本质和特性，且应明确包含已成立、转移、修改或废除的相关权利的规定以及相关权利范围，同时也应规定当事人承担的义务。

并行法规：1983 年第 2148 号法令，第 17 条、第 20 条。

第 31 条 涉及转让、留置权或使用限制的不动产，应按地籍注册信息或房产证件进行区分；或根据命名、所在地址或辖区进行区分；或根据其地产边界进行区分。无论使用何种方式统计均应使用十进制记数法。

并行法规：1983 年第 2148 号法令，第 18 条、第 19 条、第 20 条。

第 32 条 当事人必须通过登记资料，准确指明购买、抵押或者处置不动产的名目。若当事人无法提供相关证明，则必须说明该财产来源。

并行法规：1983 年第 2148 号法令，第 20 条、第 21 条。

第 33 条 当事人应提供其房屋缴税、房屋用益权、房屋的实际使用和居住、房屋地役权、使用限制或条件以及未决抵押或诉讼情况信息。总体来讲，若可能，应提供所有可能影响作为声明对象的不动产或当事人本身权益的相关证明。

并行法规：1983 年第 2148 号法令，第 21 条。

第 34 条 作为声明事项的财产或相关权利的价

bienes o derechos objeto de las declaraciones se expresarán en moneda colombiana, y si el acto o contrato estuviere referido a monedas extranjeras, se establecerá su equivalencia en moneda nacional según las normas vigentes sobre el particular.

Sección Tercera Del otorgamiento y de la autorización.

Art.35- Extendida la escritura será leída en su totalidad por el Notario, o por los otorgantes, o por la persona designada por éstos, quienes podrán aclarar, modificar o corregir lo que les pareciere y al estar conformes, expresarán su asentimiento. De lo ocurrido se dejará testimonio escrito en el propio instrumento y la firma de los otorgantes demuestra su aprobación.

Conc.: Decr. 2148 de 1983 arts. 22. 23.

Art.36- Si se tratare de personas sordas, la lectura será hecha por ellas mismas, y si de ciegas, únicamente por el Notario.

Conc.: Decr. 2148 de 1983 Art. 22.

Art.37- El Notario hará a los otorgantes las advertencias pertinentes según el acto o contrato celebrado, principalmente la relacionada con la necesidad de inscribir la copia en el competente registro dentro del término legal.

Art.38- La escritura concluirá con las firmas autógrafas de los otorgantes y de las demás personas que hayan intervenido en el instrumento. Si alguna firma no fuere completa o fácilmente legible se escribirá, a continuación, la denominación completa del firmante.

Art.39- Si alguno de los otorgantes no supiere o no pudiere firmar, el instrumento será suscrito por la persona a quien le ruegue, cuyo nombre, edad, domicilio e identificación se anotará en la escritura. El otorgante imprimirá a continuación su huella dactilar de lo cual se dejará testimonio escrito con indicación de cual huella ha sido impresa.

Conc.: Decr. 2 l48 de, 1983, art. 24.

Art.40- El Notario autorizará el instrumento una vez cumplidos los requisitos formales del caso, y presentados los comprobantes pertinentes, suscribiéndolo con firma autógrafa en último lugar.

Conc.: Decr. 2148 de 1983, arts. 25, 26.

Art.41- Cuando algún instrumento ya extendido dejare de ser firmado por alguno o algunos de los declarantes y no llegare a perfeccionarse por esta causa, el Notario, sin

格或估计价值，应使用哥伦比亚官方货币表示，若法律行为或合同涉及外币，则应按相关规定换算成本国货币。

第三节 认可和授权

第35条 已完成的书面公证文件应由公证员或当事人或当事人指定的人员通篇阅读，这些人员可对其认为必要的部分进行说明、变更或修改，若双方达成一致，则可声明对文本认可。相关变更应在原文件中保留书面证据，并由当事人签名表示同意。

并行法规：1983年第2148号法令，第22条、第23条。

第36条 若当事人为聋人，则可自行阅读公证文件；若为盲人，则仅可由公证员阅读公证文件。

并行法规：1983年第2148号法令，第22条。

第37条 公证员应就相关法律行为或合同对当事人发出提醒，该提醒主要与根据法律条款将文本复印件存档注册相关。

第38条 文本应包含当事人及文件相关人员的签名。若签名不完整或字迹不易辨识，应在旁边注明签名人全名。

第39条 若某一当事人不会签名或不能签名，文件将由其委托他人签署，并标明代签人的姓名、年龄、住址及身份信息。之后当事人应在文件上按指纹，并应做出书面证明，说明该指纹为哪个手指的指纹。

并行法规：1983年第2148号法令，第24条。

第40条 若已满足公证要求，并已提交全部证明，公证员可对文件进行授权，并在文件底部署名。

并行法规：1983年第2148号法令，第25条、第26条。

第41条 若已撰写的文本缺少某个或某些当事人签名，因此无法完全符合要求，公证员对此不予授权，但应在文件中写明情况。

autorizarlo anotará en él lo acaecido.

Art. 42- Derogado. Decr. 2163 de 1970, art. 46.

Sección Cuarta De los comprobantes fiscales

Art. 43- Modificado. Decr. 2163 de 1970, art. 37. Los comprobantes fiscales serán presentados por los interesados en el momento de solicitar el servicio notarial. Prohíbese a los Notarios extender instrumentos sin que previamente se hayan presentado los certificados y comprobantes fiscales exigidos por la ley para la prestación de servicios notariales. Aunque dichos instrumentos no sean numerados, fechados ni autorizados inmediatamente con la firma del Notario.

Conc.: Decr. 2148 de 1983, arts. 20, 21.

Art.44- Los comprobantes fiscales se agregarán a las escritura a que correspondan en forma original o en fotocopia autenticada por un Notario siempre que el original de donde provengan se halle protocolizado y se indique en ella la escritura con la cual lo está. En el original de la escritura se anotarán las especificaciones de todos los comprobantes allegados, por su numeración, lugar, fecha y oficina de expedición, personas a cuyo favor se hayan expedido, con su identificación, cuantía si la tuvieren y fecha límite de su vigencia.

Todos estos datos serán reproducidos en las copias que del instrumento llegaren a expedirse.

Conc.: Decr: 2148 de 1983, arts. 20, 21.

CAPITULO II De las cancelaciones

Art.45- La cancelación de una escritura, puede hacerse por declaración de los interesados o por decisión judicial en los casos de ley.

Art. 46- El otorgante o los otorgantes de una escritura pueden declararla cancelada o sin efecto por decisión individual o por mutuo acuerdo según el caso, en una nueva escritura, con todos los requisitos legales, siempre que la retractación o revocación no esté prohibida.

Art. 47- La cancelación decretada judicialmente se comunicará al Notario que conserva el original de la escritura cancelada mediante exhorto, que ha de contener la transcripción textual del encabezamiento, fecha y parte resolutiva pertinente de]a providencia, y que será protocolizado directamente por el interesado.

第 42 条　已废止。1970 年第 2163 号法令，第 46 条。

第四节　税务证明票据

第 43 条　已修订。1970 年第 2163 号法令，第 37 条。相关税务证明票据应由当事人在提出公证申请时提交。严禁公证员在未收到法律规定办理公证所需的税务证书或票据时撰写公证书文本。即使文件尚未编号、注明日期且即使公证员尚未签字，也属违规。

并行法规：1983 年第 2148 号法令，第 20 条、第 21 条。

第 44 条　税务证明票据原件应增添到公证书中，若原件已经被收录存档，则应提供公证员授权的复印件，并在公证书中说明情况。公证书原件中应注明所有票据详情，包括编号、开具地点、开具日期和办事处、为谁开具、此人身份、数目（若有）以及有效期限。

所有相关信息均应在公证书出具时留存副本。

并行法规：1983 年第 2148 号法令，第 20 条、第 21 条。

第二章　公证书的取消

第 45 条　公证书可由当事人发起声明取消，或在涉及法律情况下由司法部门裁决取消。

第 46 条　只要公证书未被禁止撤销或撤回，公证书一名或多名当事人可发起声明取消公证书或无效，并在符合法律规定的情形下，根据情况依个人决定或共同协商重拟公证书。

第 47 条　公证书取消的司法决定应告知公证员，公证员应保留被取消公证书的原件、公证书抬头、日期及当事各方，并将当事各方面直接记录在案。

Art. 48- La extinción de las obligaciones que consten en escritura pública se producirá por los medios extintivos contemplados en la ley, la cancelación de los instrumentos en que consten las obligaciones, se hará de la manera estatuida en el presente capítulo

Art.49- La cancelación de gravámenes o limitaciones o condiciones que aparezcan en una escritura pública, se hará por el titular del derecho, en otra escritura.

Art. 50- Cuando se trate de cancelación de hipoteca, bastará la declaración del acreedor de ser él el actual titular del crédito.

Inc.2°. Modificado. Decr. 2148 de 1983, art. 27. El causahabiente del crédito o el representante del acreedor deberá protocolizar con la escritura de cancelación de la hipoteca, copia de los documentos pertinentes con los cuales compruebe su calidad.

Art.51- Modificado. Decr. 2163 de 1970, art. 38. Cuando fallecido el acreedor no se hubiere aún liquidado su sucesión o el crédito no hubiere sido adjudicado, podrán hacer la cancelación de todos los herederos que hayan aceptado la herencia, y el cónyuge sobreviviente, quienes probarán su calidad de tales con copia de los autos de reconocimiento y certificación de que no existen otros interesados reconocidos.

Si se tratare de sucesión testada y hubiere albacea con tenencia de bienes, podrá éste, conjuntamente con el cónyuge hacer las cancelaciones. En tal caso, deberá probarse la extensión y vigencia del albaceazgo y la calidad del cónyuge.

En estos casos, tratándose de sucesiones en curso, el valor del crédito será depositado en el juzgado del conocimiento, y el Notario no expedirá certificado de cancelación mientras no se acredite ante él que el depósito ha sido constituido con destino a la sucesión.

Art.52- En todo caso de cancelación el Notario pondrá en el original de la escritura cancelada una nota que exprese el hecho, con indicación del número y fecha del instrumento por medio del cual se ha consignado la cancelación o del que contiene la protocolización de la orden judicial o del certificado de otro Notario, caso de que la cancelación no se haga ante el mismo que custodia el original. Dicha nota se escribirá en sentido diagonal, en tinta de color diferente al de la escritura del original, y se pondrá igualmente en todas las copias de la escritura canceladas previamente extendidas que le sean presentadas al Notario.

Art. 53- El Notario ante quien se cancele una escrit-

第48条 公证书中证明相关义务取消应按法律规定的流程进行，带有相关义务的文件在取消时应遵守本章的要求。

第49条 公证书中出现的留置权或限制条件的取消，应由权利享有人通过另一份公证书取消。

第50条 若涉及抵押贷款取消，仅需债权人声明目前贷款所有者为其本人即可。

第50条之二 已修订。1983年第2148号法令，第27条。贷款继承人或债权人代表应将抵押贷款取消公证书以及证明其真实性的相关文件存档保存。

第51条 已修订。1970年第2163号法令，第38条。若债权人去世且尚未指定贷款继承人或该债权未被授予给他人，任何接受其遗产的继承人均可对公证书执行取消，债权人在世配偶可提供判决书副本以及其他材料，以证明不存在其他利益相关人员。

若涉及遗嘱继承且存在暂时保管财产的遗嘱执行人，该执行人可与配偶共同取消公证书。在此情况下，必须验明遗嘱执行人身份的有效期限和配偶的身份。

若已经开始继承流程，信用单据应当交与法院保管，若未向公证员证明该笔款项用于继承，公证员应不予出具公证书。

第52条 任何公证书取消情况下，公证员均应在已取消的公证书中注明已取消，并标明宣布该公证书取消的文件序号和日期。若办理公证书取消手续的公证员并非保管原件的公证员，则应标明包含法令登记文件或其他公证员公证书的序号和日期的注释。该注释将按对角线形式书写，并使用与原件不同颜色的墨水，且所有向公证员提交的已取消公证书副本均应包含该注释。

第53条 通过受理当事人声明或依司法指令见

ura por declaración de los interesados o por mandato judicial comunicado, a él, expedirá certificación al respecto con destino al Registrador de Instrumentos Públicos a fin de que éste proceda a cancelar la inscripción. Si la cancelación fuere hecha ante un Notario distinto del que conserva el original, el primero expedirá, además, certificado con destino al segundo para que ante este se protocolice y con base en él se produzca la nota de cancelación.

Conc.: Decr. 2148 de 1983, art. 28.

Art. 54- En las certificaciones de cancelación se determinará precisamente el instrumento que contiene la cancelación o la protocolización en su caso, la autoridad que la haya decretado, con indicación de la fecha de la providencia y la denominación del proceso donde fue decretada, y además se precisará por su número, fecha y Notaría, la escritura que contiene el acto, la cuantía de las obligaciones y los datos pertinentes al registro.

Art. 55- El Notario no podrá expedir copias de las escrituras canceladas, sin transcripción inicial y destaca de la nota de cancelación.

CAPITULO III De las protocolizaciones

Art.56- La protocolización consiste en incorporar en el protocolo por medio de escritura pública las actuaciones, expediente o documentos que la ley o el juez ordenen insertar en él para su guarda y conservación, o que cualquiera persona le presenta al Notario con los mismos fines.

Art.57- Por la protocolización no adquiere el documento protocolizado mayor fuerza o firmeza de la que originalmente tenga.

Art.58- Cuando las actuaciones o documentos que deban protocolizarse estén sujetos al registro, esta formalidad se cumplirá previamente a la protocolización.

CAPITULO IV De la guarda, apertura y publicación del testamento cerrado

Art. 59- El testamento cerrado se dejará al Notario o cónsul colombiano que lo haya autorizado, para su custodia. en la forma y condiciones que determine el Reglamento.

Conc.: Decr. 2148 de 1983, art. 31.

Art. 60- El testamento cerrado será abierto y publicado por el Notario o cónsul que lo haya autorizado.

Conc.: Decr. 2148 cie 1983, art. 30.

Art. 61- Cualquier interesado presunto en la sucesión, podrá solicitar la apertura y publicación del testamento,

证公证书取消的公证员，应向公共文档登记员提交相关证明，以便登记员执行注销。若见证取消的公证员与保管原件的公证员并非同一人，前者应向后者出具证明，以便后者进行归档处理并添加注释。

并行法规：1983年第2148号法令，第28条。

第54条　取消证明中应准确说明包含取消信息的文件或归档情况、颁布法令的官方部门，并注明日期、处理流程代号，另外还应标明序号、日期和公证处名称、包含相关法律行为的公证书、债务金额以及相关登记信息。

第55条　公证员若无初步材料或公证书取消说明，不得提供已取消公证书副本。

第三章　归档

第56条　归档处理指以公证书的形式，根据法律或法官的要求，将事项、档案或文件汇编起来以便保存，或任何人为了相同目的向公证员提出归档要求。

第57条　归档处理后的文件并不比归档前具有更高效力或可信度。

第58条　若应归档的事项或文件需要登记，则登记应在归档前执行。

第四章　密封遗嘱的保存、开封和公示

第59条　密封遗嘱应由公证员或被授权的哥伦比亚领事按相关规定要求的形式和条件保管。

并行法规：1983年第2148号法令，第31条。

第60条　密封遗嘱将由公证员或被授权的领事开封。

并行法规：1983年第2148号法令，第30条。

第61条　任何与继承有利益关系的当事人，若能提供立遗嘱人已经死亡的法律证明，以及1931年

presentando prueba legal de la defunción del testador, copia de la escritura exigida por la Ley 36 de 1931, y cuando fuere el caso, el sobre que lo contenga, o petición de requerimiento de entrega a quien lo conserve.

Art. 62- Modificado. Decr. 2163 de 1970, art. 39. Presentada la solicitud y el sobre, el Notario hará constar el estado de éste, con expresión de las marcas, sellos y demás circunstancias distintivas, señalará el día y la hora en que deban comparecer ante él los testigos que intervinieron en la autorización del testamento y dispondrá que se les cite.

Conc.: Decr. 2148 de 1983, art. 32.

Art. 63- Llegados el día y la hora señalados, se procederá al reconocimiento del sobre y de las firmas puestas en él por el testador, los testigos y el Notario, teniendo a la vista el sobre y la escritura original que se haya otorgado en cumplimiento de los ordenado en la Ley 36 de 1931. Acto seguido el Notario, en presencia de los testigos e interesados concurrentes, extraerá el pliego contenido en la cubierta y lo leerá de viva voz; terminada la lectura, lo firmará con los testigos a continuación de la firma del testador o en las márgenes y en todas las hojas de que conste.

Art. 64- De lo ocurrido se sentará un acta con mención de los presentes y constancia de su identificación correspondiente, y transcripción del texto íntegro del testamento.

Conc: Decr 2148 de 1983, art. 33.

Art.65- Modificado Decr.2163 de 1970 Art.40. Cuando alguno o algunos de los testigos no concurrieren, el Notario ante quien se otorgó el testamento, abonará sus firmas mediante su confrontación con las del original de la escritura de protocolización. Si aquel Notario faltare, abonará su firma quien desempeñare actualmente sus funciones, mediante la misma confrontación, y aún con su firma en otros instrumentos de protocolo.

Art.66- El testamento así abierto y publicado, se protocolizará con lo actuado por el mismo Notario, quien expedirá las copias a que diere lugar. El registro se efectuará sobre copia enviada directamente por aquél y no sobre el original.

Conc.: Decr.208 de 1975, art. 1º, Decr. 2148 de 1983, art. 29.

Art.67- Si alguna persona que acredite interés en ello exponga las razones que tenga, se opusiere a la apertura, el Notario se abstendrá de practicar la apertura y publicación y entregará el sobre y copia de lo actuado al Juez competente para conocer del proceso de sucesión para que ante él se tramite y decida la oposición a la apertura como un

第36号法律规定的遗嘱复印件，均可申请遗嘱开封和公示，若有必要还可索要遗嘱信封，或要求遗嘱看管人交出遗嘱。

第62条 已修订。1970年第2163号法令，第39条。提交申请和遗嘱信封之后，公证员应检验该信封的状态，包括标记、印章和其他相关情况，并给出涉及遗嘱授权的相关证人出面公证的日期和时间，并在该日期传唤证人。

并行法规：1983年第2148号法令，第32条。

第63条 到规定的日期和时间，证人和公证员将遵循1931年第36号法律规定，拿出遗嘱信封和公证书原件，对信封及立遗嘱者、证人和公证员的签名进行验证。之后公证员在证人和相关当事人见证下，从信封中取出遗嘱，并朗读；朗读完毕后，公证员将与证人一同在立遗嘱人签名后面签名，并在遗嘱每一页签名。

第64条 上述事件将被记载到纪要中，该纪要将记录在场人员及其身份以及遗嘱全文。

并行法规：1983年第2148号法令，第33条。

第65条 已修订。1970年第2163号法令，第40条。若一名或多名证人缺席，公证员将通过与归档原件字迹比对的方式验证其签名；若之前的公证员离任，则由现在担任公证员职务的人员通过与其他归档文件字迹比对验证签名。

第66条 遗嘱一旦开封并公示，将由同一公证员归档，该公证员将出具遗嘱复印件。登记文件是公证员直接发送的复印件，而不是原件。

并行法规：1975年第208号法令，第1条；1983年第2148号法令，第29条。

第67条 若某一利益相关人员出于某种原因反对遗嘱开封，公证员应停止开封和公示手续并将信封和情况说明副本递送法官处，由法官了解继承流程的情况，并由法官见证手续办理，并将反对开封裁定为偶然事件。

incidente.

Si las firmas del Notario o los testigos no fueren reconocidas o abonadas, o la cubierta no apareciere cerrada, marcada y sellada como cuando se presentó para el otorgamiento, el Notario, dejando constancia de ello, practicará la apertura y publicación del testamento y enviará sobre, pliego y copia de su actuación al Juez competente. En este caso, el testamento no prestará mérito mientras no se declare su validez en proceso ordinario, con citación de quienes tengan interés en la sucesión por ley o por razón de un testamento anterior. Declarada la validez del testamento, el Juez ordenará su protocolización y posterior registro.

Conc.: Decr. 2148 de 1983, art. 29.

CAPITULO V Del reconocimiento de documentos privados

Art.68- Quienes suscrito un documento privado podrán acudir ante el Notario para que éste autorice el reconocimiento que hagan de sus firmas y del contenido de aquél. En este caso se procederá a extender una diligencia en el mismo documento o en hoja adicional, en que se exprese el nombre y descripción del cargo de Notario ante quien comparece; el nombre e identificación de los comparecientes; la declaración de éstos de que las formas son suyas y el contenido de documento es cierto, y el lugar y fecha de la diligencia, que terminará con las firmas de los declarantes y del Notario, quien además, estampará el sello de la Notaría.

Conc.: Decr.2148 de 1983, art.34.

Art.69- Cuando se trate de personas que no sepan o no puedan firmar, en la diligencia de reconocimiento, se leerá de viva voz el documento, de todo lo cual dejará constancia en el acta, que será suscrita por un testigo rogado por el compareciente, quien además, imprimirá su huella dactilar, circunstancia que también se consignará en la diligencia indicando cuál fue la impresa.

Art.70- Si se tratare de personas ciegas, el Notario leerá de viva voz el documento y si fuera consentido por el declarante, anotará esta circunstancia. Di entre los comparecientes hubiere sordos, ellos mismos leerán el documento y expresarán su conformidad, y si no supieran leer, manifestarán al Notario su intención para que establezca su concordancia con lo escrito y se cerciore del asentimiento de ellos tanto para obligarse en los términos del documento como para reconocer su contenido y rogar su firma. De

若在当事人提出公证申请时，密封遗嘱公证员签名或证人签名无法被识别或验证，或信封未闭合、标记或密封，公证员应记录并证明该情况后执行开封和公示，之后将信封、遗嘱内容和副本提交至相关法官。在此情况下，若不按常规规定声明其有效性，并依法或依之前遗嘱各利益相关方要求传唤遗产继承利益相关方人员，遗嘱将被宣布无效。若遗嘱有效性得到声明，法官将裁定后期对遗嘱归档登记。

并行法规：1983 年第 2148 号法令，第 29 条。

第五章 私署文书的公证

第 68 条 任何签署私署文书的人员均可向公证员申请对该文件署名及内容进行公证。在此情况下公证员应在原文件中增添注释或另附一页说明，其中应标明负责此案件的公证员姓名及职位，当事人姓名及身份信息，当事人声明保证签名文件所述内容真实并签名，添加注释的地点和日期，最终由当事人和公证员共同签名，盖公证处章。

并行法规：1983 年第 2148 号法令，第 34 条。

第 69 条 若当事人不会或无法在注释中签名，公证员应朗读文件，在纪要中记录其全部过程，并由当事人指定的证人作证，该证人应按指纹，公证员在注释中应说明所采集的是哪个手指的指纹。

第 70 条 若当事人为盲人，公证员应亲自朗读文件，若当事人同意，可将此事记录。若出席公证的人员为聋人，应由其自行阅读文件内容。若该人员不识字，则应将其意图告知公证员，由公证员调整文本，并与其沟通确认，以便用文件条款限定其义务，使其了解文本内容并要求其签名。否则，公证员不应添加注释。

otra manera el Notario no practicará la diligencia.

Art. 71- El Notario no prestará sus servicios si el compareciente fuere absolutamente incapaz y la incapacidad fuere percibida por aquel o constará en pruebas fehacientes.

Art.72- El reconocimiento practicado en la forma dispuesta en este Capítulo da plena autenticidad y fecha cierta al documento y procede respecto de lo otorgado para pactar expresamente obligaciones.

CAPITULO VI De las autenticaciones

Art.73- El Notario podrá dar testimonio escrito de que la firma puesta en un documento corresponde a la de la persona que la haya registrado ante él, previa confrontación de las dos. También podrá dar testimonio de que las firmas fueron puestas en su presencia, estableciendo la identidad de los firmantes.

Conc._Decr-2148 de 1983, art.35.

Art.74- Podrá autenticarse una copia mecánica o una literal de un documento, siempre que aquélla corresponda exactamente al original que se tenga a la vista o que ésta comprenda la integridad del documento exhibido y lo reproduzca con entera fidelidad.

Conc._Decr-2148 de 1983, art.35, 36.

Art.75- La autenticación se anotará en todas las hojas de que conste el documento autenticado, con expresión de la correspondencia de la firma puesta allí con la registrada, o de su contenido con el original; cuando éste reposare en el Archivo Notarial, se indicará esta circunstancia, con cita del instrumento que lo contiene o al cual se halla anexado. El acto terminará con mención de su fecha y la firma del Notario.

Conc._Decr-2148 de 1983, art.35.

Art.76- El Notario dará testimonio y autenticidad de una fotografía de persona si establece por sus sentidos que corresponde a ella y está agregada a un escrito asevere ser suya y en que reconozca la firma con que autorice dicha afirmación.

Art.77- La autenticación sólo procede respecto de documentos de que no emanen directamente obligaciones, no equivale al reconocimiento, tiene el valor de un testimonio fidedigno y no confiere al documento mayor guerza de la que por sí tenga.

第 71 条　若公证员发现或有相关证据表明当事人完全无行为能力，公证员应不予提供服务。

第 72 条　按本章规定执行的公证可证明相关文件的完全真实有效，且签署日期无误，并可依据已公证内容对义务进行明确商定。

第六章　授权

第 73 条　公证员可出具书面证明，表明通过字迹比对，可证明某一文件中的签名属于曾在其见证下注册签名的人员本人。同样也可证明签名是在其见证下进行，可确认签署者身份。

并行法规：1983 年第 2148 号法令，第 35 条。

第 74 条　若某文件复印件或手抄件与所出示原件完全吻合或包含原文件全部信息，且完全忠实地反映其内容，则可对该副本授权。

并行法规：1983 年第 2148 号法令，第 35 条、第 36 条。

第 75 条　授权信息应标注在被授权文件的每一页，并表明其中的签名与之前注册签名一致，或该文件与原文一致；若相关内容在公证处档案中，应说明该情况，在文件中注明或添加附件说明。该文件结尾处应注明日期并由公证员签名。

并行法规：1983 年第 2148 号法令，第 35 条。

第 76 条　对于人物照片，若公证员认为照片属于其本人，或者随照片附有文字，声明该照片系本人照片，且公证员可辨识该字迹并认定该声明有效，则可证明该照片的真实性。

第 77 条　授权仅在文件不涉及直接责任时进行，与认可不同，可以当作可信证据使用，但不赋予文件超出其本身的效力。

CAPITULO VII De la fe de la vida

Art.78- Modificado Decr.2148 de 1983, art.37. En el testimonio escrito de la supervivencia de una persona, el notario anotará el documento con que la hubiere identificado, los nombres y apellidos completos y el día y hora de la diligencia y hará estampar la huella dactilar del compareciente.

CAPITULO VIII De las copias

Art.79- El Notario puede expedir copia total o parcial de las escrituras públicas y de los documentos que reposan en su Archivo, por medio de la transcripción literal de unas y otros, o de su reproducción mecánica. La copia autorizada hace plena fe de su correspondencia en el original.

Si el Archivo Notarial no se hallare bajo la guarda del Notario, el funcionario encargado de su custodia estará investido de las mismas facultades para expedir copias.

Conc.:Decr-2148 de 1983, art.38, 40; Decr.1365 de 1986,art.11.

Art.80- Modificado. Decr.2163 de 1970, art.42. Toda persona tiene derecho a obtener copias auténticas de las escrituras públicas. Pero si se tratare de un instrumento en contra del cual pudiera exigirse el cumplimiento de una obligación, una vez que fuere presentado, el Notario señalará la copia que presta ese mérito, que será necesariamente la primera que del instrumento se expida, expresándolo así en caracteres destacados, junto con el nombre del acreedor a cuyo favor lo expide.

En las demás copias que del instrumento se compulsen en cualquier momento, y salvo lo prevenido en el articulo 81, se pondrá por el Notario una nota explicativa del ningún valor de dichas copias para exigir el pago o cumplimiento de la obligación o para su endoso.

Conc._Decr-2148 de 1983, art.38,39.

Art.81- En caso de pérdida o destrucción de la copia, con mérito para exigir el cumplimiento de la obligación, el Notario sólo podrá compulsar una sustitutiva a solicitud de ambas partes expresada en escritura pública o por orden judicial proferida con el lleno de los siguientes requisitos.

Que quien solicite la copia afirme ante el juez competente, bajo Juramento:

1. Ser el actual titular del derecho y que sin culpa o malicia de su parte se destruyó o perdió la copia que tenía en su poder.

2. Que la obligación no se ha extinguido en todo o en

第七章 健在证明

第 78 条 已修订。1983 年第 2148 号法令，第 37 条。在有关某人健在的书面证明中，公证员应标注此人身份证件、姓名全称、该注释添加的日期和时间并由当事人按指纹。

第八章 副本

第 79 条 公证员应出具公证书以及存档相关文件的全部或部分副本，副本可为手抄本或复印件。经授权的副本与原件具有同等效力。

若公证处档案并非由公证员保管，那么负责官员则具有与公证员相同的出具副本的权力。

并行法规：1983 年第 2148 号法令，第 38 条、第 40 条；1986 年第 1365 号法令，第 11 条。

第 80 条 已修订。1970 年第 2163 号法令，第 42 条。所有人均有权获取公证书真实副本。一旦出具某文件副本，此副本将涉及相关义务的履行，公证员应在副本中标注这一特性。该标注应放置在文件开头处，使用醒目字体，并注明申请该副本的债权人姓名。

在任何时间出具的该文件其他副本中，除第 81 条规定的情况外，均应由公证员添加解释性说明，表明所有副本均不可用于要求付款或履行义务或背书。

并行法规：1983 年第 2148 号法令，第 38 条、第 39 条。

第 81 条 若副本遗失或损毁，为保证义务履行，公证员应在公证书提到的双方提出申请情况下或得到司法命令时出具替代副本，并应满足以下条件：

申请索要副本的人员应在法官面前宣誓保证：

1. 其本人为权益所有人，且并非故意损毁或遗失所持有的副本。

2. 相关义务尚未全部履行完毕。

parte, según fuere el caso.

3. Que si la copia perdida apareciere, se obliga a no usarla y entregarla al Notario que la expidió para que este la inutilice.

La solicitud se tramitará como incidente, con notificación personal de la parte contraria, que solo podrá formular oposición fundada en el hecho de estar extinguida la obligación.

No habiendo oposición o desestimada ésta, el juez ordenará que se expida copia y el Notario procederá de conformidad, indicando que lo hace en virtud de orden judicial, mencionando su fecha y el juez que la profirió.

Conc._Decr-2148 de 1983, art.39.

Art. 82- La cesión de un crédito constituido por escritura pública se hará mediante nota suscrita por el actual titular puesta al pie de la copia con mérito para exigir el cumplimiento y la entrega de la misma al cesionario.

Art. 83- Modificado. Decr.2148 de 1983, art. 41. Toda copia se expedirá en papel común por medios manuales o mecánicos. Al final se dejará constancia del número y fecha de la escritura a la cual corresponda. 8i se tratare de copia parcial así se expresará.

Art. 84- La copia comprenderá la integridad del instrumento y los documentos anexos, pero podrá limitarse a uno solo de los varios actos o contratos que pueda contener aquel, caso de no existir correlación directa entre ellos, o a piezas separadas de un expediente protocolizado o a uno o varios documentos independientes que formen parte del protocolo. El Notario al expedir copia parcial expresará esta circunstancia y que lo omitido no guarda relación directa con lo copiado, o que se trata de piezas independientes o de documentos varios que se insertaron en el protocolo. La transcripción se hará en forma continua y sin dejar blancos o espacios libres, escribiendo en todos los renglones o llenando partes con rayas y otros trazos que impidan su posterior utilización; se iniciará con el número que tenga el original en el protocolo y su texto será el que aparezca una vez debidamente salvadas las enmendaduras y correcciones, si fuere del caso.

Art. 85- Completa la copia, a renglón seguido se pondrá la nota de su expedición que indicará el número ordinal correspondiente a ella, los números de las hojas del papel competente en que ha sido reproducida, la cantidad de estas y el lugar y la fecha en que se compulsa. Terminará con la firma autógrafa del notario y la imposición de su sello, con indicación del nombre y denominación del cargo. Todas las hojas serán rubricadas y selladas.

3. 若重新找回遗失副本，不得继续使用并应将其交于公证员处取消效力。

相关申请将按偶然事件办理手续，有反对意见的，将通知本人，仅可提出基于义务履行完毕这一事实的反对意见。

若无反对意见或反对意见被驳回，法官将下令出具副本，公证员将按规定执行，并说明此行为是按司法命令进行，注明日期和发布命令的法官。

并行法规：1983年第2148号法令，第39条。

第82条 通过公证书转让贷款，需要贷款现持有人在副本下方添加注释，以便保证履约及贷款转让。

第83条 已修订。1983年第2148号法令，第41条。所有副本均应抄录或复印到纸上。在副本底部应标注文件撰写编号和日期。若为节选副本，应注明情况。

第84条 副本应体现文件及相关附录完整性，但若众多协议与合同之间毫无联系，也可仅选取其中的一部分，或归档文本中分开的几部分，或构成归档文件的一个或几个文件。公证员在出具节选副本时应说明情况，并保证被省略的部分与保留部分无直接联系，或自成独立的部分或为构成归档文件的多个文件。文本应连续，不可留有空白或空行，每一行均要写字，或在空白处用线条或笔画占上位置以免后期添加内容；开头应标注归档序号，文本应保存修订和修改痕迹。

第85条 副本正文之后下一行应放置注释，标明页码、副本总页数、副本数量以及出具副本的地点和日期。副本底部应由公证员签名并盖章，并标明姓名和职务。所有页面均应签字盖章。

Conc.: Decr-2148 de 1983, art.42.

Art. 86- Si se cometieren errores en las copias, se corregirán en la forma prevenida para los originales y lo corregido o enmendado se salvará al final y antes de la firma del notario; pero si se advirtieren después de firmada la copia, la corrección se salvará a continuación y volverá a firmarse por el Notario, sin lo cual ésta no tendrá ningún valor; en tal caso, si la copia hubiere sido registrada se expedirá, además, un certificado para que en el Registro se haga la corrección a que hubiere lugar.

Conc.: Decr. 2148 de 1983, art. 42.

Art. 87- Modificado. Decr. 2163 de 1970, art. 43. Las primeras copias serán expedidas tan pronto quede autorizado el instrumento por el Notario, en el menor tiempo posible, que en ningún caso excederá de ocho (8) días hábiles. La demora hará al Notario responsable de los perjuicios que con ella se causen a los otorgantes.

Art. 88- Expedida la primera copia pondrá el notario en el original una constancia escrita sobre su expedición y la fecha de la compulsa. Esta nota se escribirá al margen del original, al final del mismo o en hoja adicional adosada a aquel.

CAPITULO IX De los certificados

Art. 89- Los Notarios están facultados para expedir certificaciones sobre aspectos especiales y concretos que consten en el protocolo, con fuerza probatoria de instrumentos públicos, solo en los casos autorizados por la ley.

Pertenecen a esta categoría los extractos de las escrituras de constitución, reforma, disolución o liquidación de sociedades, conforme a las normas pertinentes de los Códigos Civil y de Comercio.

Conc.: Decr. 2148 de 1983, art. 43.

Art. 90- Los Notarios podrán certificar también sobre aspectos concretos de un determinado instrumento o de un documentos protocolizado, tales como el hecho de haberse formalizado una compraventa con indicación del precio pactado o de haberse constituido un gravamen. Dichas certificaciones tendrán el mérito señalado en la ley.

Art. 91- Los certificados de cancelación de hipotecas o condiciones resolutorias se expedirán con destino al Registrador correspondiente y al Notario que custodia el original a que se refiere la cancelación cuando no sea el mismo ante quien se otorgó el instrumento que contenga el acto de cuya cancelación se trate.

并行法规：1983 年第 2148 号法令，第 42 条。

第 86 条 在公证员签名之前，若发现副本中有错误，应在原件中进行修改，对修改或修订记录应作有效说明；若在副本签名后发现错误，则应进行修改并作有效说明，之后由公证员重新签名，否则副本将不具备效力。另外，若副本已经登记注册，则应出具证明以便登记处进行修改。

并行法规：1983 年第 2148 号法令，第 42 条。

第 87 条 已修订。1970 年第 2163 号法令，第 43 条。一旦公证员对文件进行授权，第一批副本应尽快开具，在任何情况下均不得超过 8 个工作日。若发生延误，公证员应对当事人遭受的损失承担责任。

第 88 条 第一份副本开具完毕后，公证员应在原件中添加注释说明副本已开具以及开具日期。该注释应书写在原件边缘、底部或另附一页。

第九章 证明

第 89 条 公证员有权为归档文件中记录的特定和具体事项开具证明，该类证明具有证据效力，但仅在法律允许的情况下才可开具。

依据《民法典》和《商法典》相关规定，公司建立、改组、解散或清算相关文件节选属于此类。

并行法规：1983 年第 2148 号法令，第 43 条。

第 90 条 公证员还可为某一特定文件或已归档文件中的特定具体事项开具证明，例如已开始正式交易并已约定价格或已开始缴税。此类证明将具备法律规定的特性。

第 91 条 抵押贷款取消证明或决定性条件证明将发给对应的公证员，若最初负责现将被取消的包含协议文件的公证员与负责保管该原件的公证员并非同一人，则还应将证明发给负责保管的公证员。

CAPITULO X De las notas de referencia

Art.92- Siempre que una escritura contenga declaraciones que modifiquen, adicionen, aclaren o afecten en cualquier sentido el contenido de otra escritura otorgada por las mismas partes o por antecesores o causahabientes en los derechos de los otorgantes, se tomará nota de referencia en la escritura afectada, indicando el número, fecha y Notaría de la escritura en que se contiene la afectación. También habrá lugar a la anotación en los casos de corrección de errores, de conformidad con lo dispuesto en el presente estatuto.

Conc.: Decr. 2148 de 1983, art. 44.

Art. 93- Si la escritura a la cual deba imponerse la nota de referencia no se hallare bajo la custodia del Notario ante quien se otorga la que produce la afectación, éste expedirá un certificado con destino al funcionario que guarda el original que deba ser anotado, con todos los datos necesarios.

Art. 94- Las notas de referencia que deban ser puestas cuando se cancele una escritura. se sujetarán a las normas contenidas en el Capitulo 2°, del presente título.

CAPITULO XI De los testimonios especiales

Art. 95- El Notario podrá dar testimonio escrito de hechos ocurridos en su presencia de que no quede dato en el archivo, pero que tengan relación con el ejercicio de sus funciones.

Art. 96- Cuando fuere requerido para presenciar un hecho o situación perceptible por los sentidos en forma directa, relacionados con el ejercicio de sus funciones, podrá dar testimonio escrito de lo percibido por él, siempre que con ello se procure un efecto jurídico. De lo ocurrido se sentará acta que firmará el Nolamo y entregará al peticionario.

Conc.:Decr-2148 de 1983, art.45.

CAPITUL() XII De los dep ó sitos

Arts. 97 y 98-Derogados. Decr. 2163 de 1970, art. 46.

TITULO III
INVALIDACION Y SUBSANACION DE LOS ACTOS NOTARIALES

CAPITULO I De los actos notariales inválidos

Art. 99- Desde el punto de vista formal, son nulas las

第十章 参考注释

第 92 条 若一公证书包含的相关声明，对相同当事人或前任者或继任者发起的其他公证书产生修改、增添、澄清或其他任何影响，均应在受影响的公证书中对此进行标注。另外，若需要纠错，根据本章程要求，同样应添加注释。

并行法规：1983 年第 2148 号法令，第 44 条。

第 93 条 若负责保管加注释公证书的公证员并非受理公证书变更的公证员，后者应向前者出具证明，并在证明中附上全部必要信息。

第 94 条 当公证书取消时，添加的参考注释应符合本篇第二章相关规定。

第十一章 特别证明

第 95 条 公证员可就其见证的，未登记存档却与其职能相关的事项开具书面证明。

第 96 条 若被要求见证与其职能相关的事实或可以直接感知的情况，公证员可就其了解到的事项开具书面证明，只要通过该证明可达到法律效果即可。过程将编入纪要，并由公证员签名并转交申请人。

并行法规：1983 年第 2148 号法令，第 45 条。

第十二章 公证存档

第 97 条和第 98 条 已废止。1970 年第 2163 号法令，第 46 条。

第三篇
无效公证书修改

第一章 无效公证书

第 99 条 从正式性角度看，若发生以下情况，

escritura en que se omita el cumplimiento de los requisitos esenciales en los siguientes casos:

1. Cuando el Notario actúe fuera de los límites territoriales del respectivo círculo notarial.

2. Cuando faltare la comparecencia ante el Notario de cualquiera de los otorgantes, bien sea directamente o por representación.

3. Cuando los comparecientes no hayan prestado aprobación al texto del instrumento extendido.

4. Cuando no aparezca la fecha y el lugar de la autorización, la denominación legal del Notario, los comprobantes de la representación, o los necesarios para autorizar la cancelación.

5. Cuando no aparezca debidamente establecida la identificación de los otorgantes o de sus representantes, o la firma de aquellos o de cualquier compareciente.

6. Cuando no se hayan consignado los datos y circunstancias necesarios para determinar los bienes objeto de las declaraciones.

Art. 100- El instrumento que no haya sido autorizado por el Notario no adquiere la calidad de escritura pública y es inexistente como tal. Empero, si faltare solamente la firma del Notario, y la omisión se debiere a causas diferentes de las que justifican la negativa de la autorización, podrá la Superintendencia de Notariado y Registro, con conocimiento de causa, disponer que el instrumento se suscriba por quien se halle ejerciendo el cargo.

Conc.:Decr-2148 de 1983, art.47.

CAPITULO II De la corrección de errores y de la reconstrucción de escrituras

Art. 101- Los errores en que se haya incurrido al extender un instrumento advertidos antes de su firma, se corregirán subrayando y encerrando entre paréntesis las palabras o frases que deban suprimirse o insertando en el sitio pertinente y entre líneas las que deban agregarse y salvando al final lo corregido, reproduciéndolo entre comillas e indicando si vale o no vale lo suprimido o agregado. Podrá hacerse la corrección enmendando lo escrito o borrándolo y sustituyéndolo y así se indicará en la salvedad que se haga. Las salvedades serán autorizadas por todas las firmas que deba llevar el instrumento, pero si éste ya se hallare escrito, sin haberse autorizado aún, se salvarán las correcciones y se volverá a firmar por todos los comparecientes.

Sin dichos requisitos no valdrán las correcciones y se tendrán por verdaderas las expresiones originales.

公证书将被视作无效：

1. 若公证员不在其对应公证辖区内执行公证。

2. 若任何当事人缺席参加公证员见证，无论是本人直接缺席或是代表缺席。

3. 若当事人不认可撰写的公证书文本。

4. 若公证员授权中未标明日期和地点、公证员合法名称、代表证明文件或其他用于批准取消的必要信息。

5. 若未按要求标明当事人或其代表身份信息，或缺少任何一名相关当事人签名。

6. 若因缺乏必要数据和条件无法将某一财产作为声明事项。

第100条 未经公证员授权的文件不具备正式公证书效力，可视作不存在。然而，若仅缺少公证员签名，且缺少该签名的原因并非拒绝授权，公证单位及档案监督局可在了解案情的情况下，规定相关文件应由目前在任的负责人记录。

并行法规：1983年第2148号法令，第47条。

第二章 修改错误并重新出具公证书

第101条 若签名前在撰写的文本中发现错误，应用括号将用于替代的单词或句子加以强调，或在原位置文字空行处添加缺少的文本，并对修改记录作有效说明，使用引号并指明是否需要用新词汇替换或增加内容。可以在原文本上进行修改或者划掉并替换文本，并对改动作有效说明。相关改动将由文本中所有签名授权，若文件已书写完毕但未授权，则应对改动作有效说明，并由所有出席见证人重新签名。

若不满足上述要求，相关改动无效，原文件内容将被认定为正确内容。

Conc.: Decr. 2148 de 1983, art. 48.

Art. 102- Una vez autorizada la escritura, cualquier corrección que quisieren hacer los otorgantes deberá consignarse en instrumentos separados con todas las formalidades necesarias y por todas las personas que intervinieron en el instrumento, corregido, debiéndose tomar nota en éste de la escritura de corrección.

Art. 103- Sin embargo, los errores puramente aritméticos podrán ser corregidos en cualquier tiempo si los factores que los determinan se hallaren claramente establecidos en el propio instrumento. La cifra aritméticamente verdadera se pondrá en sustitución de la errónea, de la manera y por los trámites indicados en el artículo 101.

Si se cometiere error en la nomenclatura, denominación 0 descripción de un inmueble o en la cita de su cédula o registro catastral, podrá corregirse mediante el otorgamiento de escritura aclaratoria suscrita por el actual titular del derecho, si de los comprobantes allegados a la escritura en que se cometió el error y de los títulos antecedentes apareciere él de manifiesto. De igual modo se procederá si el error se cometiere en relación con los nombres o apellidos de alguno de los otorgantes, considerando los documentos de identificación anotados en el mismo instrumento.

Conc.: Decr. 2148 de 1983, art. 49, 50.

Art. 104- De la misma manera prevista en el artículo precedente podrá corregirse el error en la cita de los títulos antecedentes y sus inscripciones en el Registro, si fuere posible establecerlo con precisión mediante certificado actual del Registrador y éste se protocoliza.

Conc.: Decr: 2I48 de 1983, art. 49.

Art. 105- Una escritura perdida o destruida en todo o en parte, podrá ser reconstruida con su copia auténtica, de preferencia con la que repose en archivo oficial, mediante reproducción total y auténtica de ésta. El Notario colocará en el sitio correspondiente del protocolo la reproducción mencionada, indicando bajo su firma que reemplaza al original.

Si la pérdida o destrucción fuere de un tomo completo del protocolo, se procederá en igual forma y en testimonio de la reconstrucción se sentará por el Notario en acta que enumere todas las escritura que lo formaban. según el libro de relación. Esta acta

并行法规：1983 年第 2148 号法令，第 48 条。

第 102 条　一旦公证书得到授权，当事人无论希望作任何改动都应起草一份单独的新文件，并满足所有必要要求，且由所有与文件相关的当事人共同参与，并在新文本中说明修改情况。

第 103 条　然而，纯算术错误只要其表示的数据可在文件中明确即可随时修改。可根据第 101 条的相关规定使用正确数字代替错误数字。

当某一不动产名称、命名或描述或相关地籍登记或档案发生错误时，若与错误文本相关的证据和前期文件可证明业主身份，则该业主可出具澄清声明书加以修改。同样，若某一当事人姓名发生错误，则参考附在同一文件中的身份证件信息。

并行法规：1983 年第 2148 号法令，第 49 条、第 50 条。

第 104 条　前期文件及其在档案中的登记发生错误的，若登记员出具的证明中能明确说明，且该证明已归档，也可按前一条规定进行修改。

并行法规：1983 年第 2148 号法令，第 49 条。

第 105 条　若公证书遗失或部分或全部损毁，可根据官方归档的正式复印件重新草拟原件，但应完整、如实体现原内容。公证员应在归档记录对应的位置保存该重制原件，并在其签名下注明以此文件替代原件。

若归档文件整卷遗失或损毁，将按同样方式重制原件，公证员应在纪要中按案情摘要记录列举该卷包含的所有公证书。

TITULO IV
DE LOS LIBROS QUE DEBEN LLEVAR LOS NOTARIOS Y DE LOS ARCHIVOS

CAPITULO I De los libros

Art. 106- Corresponde al Notario llevar los siguientes libros que constituyen el archivo de la Notarla: el Libro de Protocolo; el Libro de Relación; el Indice Anual; y el Libro de Actas de Visita.

Conc.: Decr. 2148 de 1983, art. 55.

Art. 107- El protocolo es el archivo fundamental del Notario y se forma con todas las escrituras que se otorgan en él y con las actuaciones y documentos que se insertan en el mismo.

Tendrá vigencia desde el primero de enero hasta el treinta y uno de diciembre de cada año y constará del número de tomos que sea necesario formar, procurando que no exceda de mil el número de hojas de cada tomo. Las escrituras se colocarán en el orden numérico sucesivo que les corresponda y se numerarán las hojas que las compongan y las de los documentos agregados.

Art. 108- Los tomos del Protocolo se coserán y encuadernarán debidamente para que presten las mayores seguridades de integridad y conservación. al final de cada uno de ellos, el Notario pondrá la correspondiente nota de clausura con su firma entera y la fecha.

Art. 109- Como complementario del Protocolo, el Notario llevará el libro de relación en el cual se anotarán las escrituras que vaya enumerando, en el orden que lo sean. en cinco columnas que se destinarán a la consignación de los siguientes datos, en su orden:

1. Fecha del instrumento;

2. número de la escritura;

3. apellidos y nombres de los otorgantes; vendedores, permutantes que comparezcan en primer término, donantes, constituyentes de gravámenes, arrendadores, cancelantes, enajenantes, poderdantes' testadores, mutuantes, protocolizantes, declarantes, etc.;

4. nombres y apellidos de los comparecientes de la otra parte, cuando se trate de relaciones bilaterales, y

5. naturaleza del acto o contrato.

Art. 110- Cuando en la columna 3a deban anotarse los apellidos y nombres de varios comparecientes, se escribirán los del primero y se agregará la expresión "y otro" u "otros". Lo mismo se hará para el caso de pluralidad de contratantes que deban inscribirse en la columna 4a. Al

第四篇
公证员应保管的登记册及文档

第一章 登记册

第 106 条   公证员应保管公证处档案库中的以下登记册：归档登记册、案情摘要册、年度索引以及访问纪要登记册。

并行法规：1983 年第 2148 号法令，第 55 条

第 107 条   归档登记册是公证员最基本的文档，其中包含了所有其负责的公证书以及相关事项记录和文件。

有效期从每年 1 月 1 日起到 12 月 31 日止，其中包含卷的数量有一定规定，每卷最多不超过一千页。公证书按连续数字排序，每一份公证书包含的页面及附加文件包含的页面均应带有页码。

第 108 条   归档登记册中各卷应认真装订成册，最大限度以保证文档保存完整安全。在每卷最后，公证员应标注结束，签署全名并标注日期。

第 109 条   作为对归档登记册的补充，公证员还应保管案情摘要册，记录所有公证书，并按照其顺序分为五栏，记录以下信息：

1. 文件开具日期；
2. 公证书编号；
3. 当事人姓名、卖家、首次出面的交易员、捐赠者、纳税人、租赁人、取消人、转让人、委托人、立遗嘱人、借贷人、归档人、声明人等人员姓名；

4. 若为双边关系，另一方出面见证人姓名；

5. 法律行为或合同性质。

第 110 条   若第 3 栏中需要登记多名出面见证人姓名，只需记录第一个人名，之后标注"其他一名"或"其他多名"。若第 4 栏中需要登记多名签约人，也同样处理。若涉及法案归档，应标明流程属性以及各方姓名。法人的成立、合并、重组、解散或清算将

tratarse de protocolización de expedientes se indicará la naturaleza del proceso y el nombre de las partes. La constitución, incorporación, reforma, disolución o liquidación de personas jurídicas se anotará por la razón social o la denominación estatutaria.

Art. 111- A medida que se vayan anotando los instrumentos en el Libro de Relación, se irá formando el índice alfabético por los apellidos y nombres que figuren en la columna 3a de aquel, el cual contendrá, además, los datos de las columnas 1, 2, 4, y 5a. Este índice será también cronológico dentro de cada letra del alfabeto.

Art. 112- Las actas de las visitas ordinarias o extraordinarias que practiquen los funcionarios encargados de la vigilancia notarial, formarán el libro de actas de visita que mantendrá y guardará el Notario.

CAPITULO II De la guarda y conservación de los archivos

Art. 113- Los Protocolos y libros de Relación e Indice serán custodiados con la mayor vigilancia por los Notarios de cuyas oficinas no podrán sacarse. Si hubiere de practicarse inspección judicial sobre alguno de estos libros, el funcionario se trasladará con su Secretario a la Oficina del Notario respectivo para la práctica de la diligencia.

Art. 114- Cualquier persona podrá consultar los archivos notariales, con el permiso y bajo la vigilancia del notario o de personas autorizadas por éste.

Conc.: Decr. 2148 de 1983, art. 53, 54.

Art. 115- El Protocolo y los Libros de Relación e Indice se mantendrán en las Notarías hasta su envío al archivo oficial, según la reglamentación que sobre el particular se expida.

Conc.: Decr. 2148 de 1983, art. 55.

CAPITULO III De la entrega y recibo de los archivos

Art. 116- Tanto en el caso de traslado de los libros al archivo oficial como en el de reemplazo del Notario, habrá lugar a entrega del archivo a quien deba continuar en el ejercicio del cargo o asuma su guarda, mediante inventario que estará intervenido por funcionario de la vigilancia notarial o delegado de la misma. El inventario se consignará en acta de visita.

Conc.: Decr. 2148 de 1983, arl. 56.

Art. 117- La entrega comprenderá todo el archivo a cargo del Notario que la hace, con arreglo al inventario con que lo haya recibido e inclusión del que haya formado

登记公司名称或法定名称。

第111条 在案情摘要册记录文件的同时，还应按字母表顺序制作索引记录第3栏中涉及人员的姓名，另外，还应记录第1栏、第2栏、第4栏、第5栏的信息。该索引每个字母类别下应按时间顺序进行记录。

第112条 针对负责公证监督官员的日常访问和特别访问的相关纪要，应汇编为访问登记册，由公证员维护保管。

第二章 文档的保管和保存

第113条 归档登记册和案情摘要册以及索引应由公证员严格管控，不得带出办公室。若需对某一登记册进行司法调查，相关人员应与秘书一同进入公证员办公室进行尽职调查。

第114条 任何人均可检索公证档案，但须公证员或其授权人员许可并监督。

并行法规：1983年第2148号法令，第53条、第54条。

第115条 归档登记册和案情摘要册以及索引在转交公文档案处前均应由公证处维护保管，并应遵循相关规章制度。

并行法规：1983年第2148号法令，第55条。

第三章 文档的转交与接收

第116条 无论是将登记册转交公文档案处还是在公证员之间交接，均应将文档交与继续承担该职责或负责保管的人员，公证处监督官员或其代表应根据清单进行管控。清单应登记在访问纪要中。

并行法规：1983年第2148号法令，第56条。

第117条 文档转交时应涵盖负责转交的公证员掌管的全部文档，并应把所有其接收的文档和自行负责的文档加入清单。

en su propio ejercicio.

Art. 118- El Notario saliente hará entrega personal del archivo al sucesor, a menos que haya imposibilidad para ello, caso en el cual podrá hacerla su apoderado, curador, heredero, cónyuge o albacea. Si hubiere urgencia lo recibirá otro Notario o el Alcalde.

Art. 119- No habrá lugar a entrega en los casos de retiro temporal del Notario por licencia, cuando se haya encargado de las funciones a persona insinuada por el notario y bajo la responsabilidad de éste.

Art. 120- Cuando se trate de suspensión en el ejercicio del cargo, el Notario suspendido hará entrega al designado para sustituirlo, quien, cuando cese la suspensión, hará otro tanto.

TITULO V
DE LA ORGANIZACIONDEL NOTARIADO

CAPITULO I De los círculos notariales

Art. 121- Para la prestación del servicio notarial el territorio de la República se dividirá en Círculos de Notaría que corresponderán al territorio de uno o más Municipios del mismo Departamento, uno de los cuales será su cabecera y la sede del Notario.

Art. 122- En cada Círculo de Notaría podrá haber más de un Notario y en este caso los varios que existen se distinguirán por orden numérico.

Art. 123- El promedio anual de escrituras otorgadas en los últimos cinco años de cada Círculo de notaría determinará el número de notarios que deban prestar en él sus servicios durante el período siguiente. Cuando el promedio dicho sea superior a tres mil escrituras por cada notario, podrá crearse uno más por cada tres mil escrituras o fracción de exceso, si el círculo fuese de primera categoría y de dos mil o fracción, si el círculo fuese de segunda o tercera categoría.

Art. 124- Cuando en un determinado círculo haya tres o más notarías no podrá crearse para cada período, un desarrollo de lo dispuesto en el artículo 123 precedente, un número que exceda el cincuenta por ciento de las existentes. En los sucesivos períodos se procederá de igual manera hasta completar el número total que deba crearse de acuerdo con el articulo citado.

Art. 125- Cuando hubiere lugar al aumento del número de notarios de un círculo de notaría, el gobierno hará la declaración para que se proceda a hacer los nombrami-

第118条　转交文档的公证员应亲自将文档交与交接人，除非有特殊情况无法实现。若发生此情况，可通过其代理人、监护人、继承人、配偶或代执行人转交；若情况紧急，则由其他公证员或市政长官接收。

第119条　若公证员因休假暂时离岗，则不能进行文档转交；若该公证员指定某人承担相应职能，则由该人员负责转交。

第120条　若公证员停职，则被停职公证员应将文档转交给被指定替代他的人员，当原公证员复职时，此人应将文档交还。

第五篇
公证处组织结构

第一章　公证业务网络

第121条　为方便在哥伦比亚共和国领土范围内提供公证服务，应在同一省内一个或多个城市设置公证业务网络，其中一个网络将起主导作用，作为公证员办事处总部。

第122条　每个公证业务网络可拥有不止一名公证员，若有多名公证员，则应按编号区分。

第123条　近五年各公证业务网络平均受理的公证书数量决定下一周期该网络中所需的公证员数量。对于一级公证业务网络而言，若平均每名公证员受理公证书数量超过三千份，可按超出情况增派公证员或规定每三千份公证书增派一名公证员；若为二级或三级公证业务网络，则按超出情况增派或规定每两千份公证书增派一名公证员。

第124条　若某一特定公证业务网络中有三家或更多公证处，则基于对以上第123条的扩展，在下一个周期增派的公证员数量不能超过现有数量的50%。在之后的周期中，应按同等方式处理，直至公证员总数满足上一条的要求。

第125条　若某一公证业务网络中需要增加公证员数量，政府应发布声明，依照本章程制定的体系提名公证员。

entos requeridos por el sistema establecido en el presente estatuto.

Art. 126- Si el promedio anual de escritura otorgadas en los cinco años anteriores en un círculo de notaría resultare inferior a tres mil por cada notario, en los de primera categoría o de dos mil por cada notario, en los de segunda y tercera, podrán suprimirse oficinas sobrantes según el orden numérico y mediante decreto del Gobierno Nacional.

Art. 127- Para la creación de un nuevo círculo de notaría se requiere que el Municipio o Municipios que han de formarlo tengan en conjunto no menos de 300.000 habitantes y que el círculo 0 círculos de los cuales se segregan que den por lo menos con igual población. Además, se consultarán las necesidades del servicio, las facilidades de las comunicaciones y otras circunstancias que puedan tener influencia determinante.

Art. 128- No podrán agruparse en un mismo circulo de notaría municipios que pertenezcan a distintos departamentos. Cuando se constituya un nuevo municipio, el gobierno dispondrá a qué círculo de notaría habrá de pertenecer y a falta de declaración al respecto continuará adscrito a aquel a que pertenecía el municipio de donde se desprendió, y si se formare de varios, al que pertenecía la cabecera.

Conc.: Decr. 2148 de 1983, art. 57.

Art. 129- Sustituido. Ley 29 de 1973, art. 16. Los círculos de notaría se clasificarán en tres categorías de acuerdo con la división que, teniendo en cuenta el número de escritura otorgadas en cada uno de ellos en los últimos cinco años y los factores socio-económicos haga la Superintendencia de Notariado y Registro, Con aprobación del gobierno nacional.

Los círculos de notaría que tengan por cabecera la capital de la República y las capitales de departamento con más de trescientos mil habitantes, de acuerdo con los estimativos que haga al efecto el departamento Administrativo Nacional de Estadística a petición de la Superintendencia de Notariado y Registro, serán clasificados en la primera categoría.

Parágrafo: Mientras la clasificación a que se refiere el presente artículo se lleva a cabo, continuará vigente la actual.

Art. 130- Cuando por modificación de las condiciones previstas según censo legalmente aprobado, un círculo de notaría deba considerarse dentro de Una Categoría distinta, el gobierno nacional hará la declaración con

第126条 若近五年某一公证业务网络年度平均受理公证书数量，对于一级公证业务网络而言，若低于每名公证员三千份，对于二级和三级公证业务网络而言，若低于每名公证员两千份，依据政府法令，可根据各公证处受理数量排序，减少多余的办事处数量。

第127条 建立新的公证业务网络，要求相关的一个或多个城市拥有不少于300000居民，且相关一个或多个公证业务网络至少应覆盖相同人口。另外，还应参考服务需求、沟通便利性以及其他有决定性影响的因素。

第128条 属于不同省的城市不能加入同一个公证业务网络。若成立新城，政府应决定该城市属于哪个公证业务网络；没有明确说明的，则新成立的城市仍属于其分离出来的原城市的公证业务网络；若新城市由多个城市的区域组成，则归属于首府城市的公证业务网络。

并行法规：1983年第2148号法令，第57条。

第129条 已替换。1973年第29号法律，第16条。公证业务网络分为三个类别，由国家公证及注册监督局在中央政府批准下，依据在过去五年中各公证处受理的公证书数量以及相关社会经济指数分级。

共和国首都以及人口超过30万的首府城市所属的公证业务网络，根据国家统计局应公证及注册监督局要求所作的估计，将被分为第一级。

段落：本条涉及的分类方法执行前，现有分类保持有效。

第130条 若根据已被法律批准的调研结果对相关条件进行修改后，某一公证业务网络需要被归入另一类别的，中央政府应对相关变动发表声明，之后依据法律，决定在下一个周期把该网络分为更高一级

fundamento en los cambios operados y se tendrá en cuenta la nueva Categoría inferior o superior en el período subsiguiente para los efectos légales pertinentes.

Art. 131- El promedio anual de escrituras se obtendrá en el primer semestre del último año de cada periodo y dentro del mismo término se declarara el numero de notarios que aumentan o disminuyen en cada círculo, para el periodo siguiente.

CAPITULO II De los notarios

Art. 132- Para ser notario, a cualquier título, se requiere ser nacional colombiano, ciudadano en ejercicio, persona de excelente reputación y tener más de treinta anos de edad.

Conc.: Decr. 2148 de 1983, arts. 58, 59.

Art. 133- No podrán ser designados como notarios, a cualquier título:

1. Quienes se hallen en interdicción judicial.

2. Los sordos, los mudos, los ciegos y quienes padezcan cualquier afección física o mental que comprometa la capacidad necesaria para el debido desempeño del Cargo.

3. Quienes se encuentren bajo detención preventiva, aunque gocen del beneficio de excarcelación, y quienes hayan sido llamados a juicio por infracción penal, mientras se define su responsabilidad por providencia firme.

4. Quienes hayan sido condenados a pena de presidio, de presión o de relegación a colonia por delito intencional, salvo que se les haya cancelado la condena condicional.

5. Quienes se encuentren suspendidos en el ejercicio de la profesión de abogado, o hayan sido suspendidos por faltas graves contra la ética, o hayan sido excluidos de aquella.

6. Quienes como funcionarios o empleados de la Rama Jurisdiccional o del Ministerio Público, y por falta disciplinaria, hayan sido destituidos, o suspendidos por segunda vez por falta grave, o sancionados tres veces, cualquiera que hayan sido las faltas o las sanciones.

7. Quienes hayan sido destituidos de cualquier cargo público por faltas graves.

8. Las personas respecto de las cuales exista la convicción moral de que no observan una vida pública o privada compatible con la dignidad del cargo.

Art. 134-No podrán ser nombrados notarios quienes en el año inmediatamente anterior hayan desempeñado el cargo de ministro del despacho, magistrado de la Corte

或是更低一级。

第 131 条　年度平均受理公证书数量应在每一周期最后一年的上半年生成，与此同时，将决定在下一个周期增添或减少每个公证业务网络的公证员数量。

第二章　公证员

第 132 条　无论何种类型的公证员，均须是哥伦比亚国籍，依法享有公民权利，信誉良好且年龄在 30 周岁以上。

并行法规：1983 年第 2148 号法令，第 58 条、第 59 条。

第 133 条　若发现以下情况，则不可担任任何类型的公证员：

1. 被剥夺公民权利的。

2. 聋哑人、盲人以及任何身体或精神条件可能影响其承担职务的。

3. 被采取预防性拘禁措施的，包括刑满释放的以及因刑事犯罪被传唤，并最终被判定应被追究责任的。

4. 曾因故意犯罪被判处有期徒刑、拘役或流放的，但刑罚被取消者除外。

5. 曾任律师但被停职的，或曾因严重违反职业道德被停职或曾被禁止从事此类职业的。

6. 曾在司法机关或检察机关任职，但因违纪被撤职、因严重失职被第二次停职或被处分达三次的，无论何种失职及何种处分类型。

7. 因严重失职被从公共事业部门撤职的。

8. 从道德角度看其公共生活或私生活不适宜担任公证员职务的。

第 134 条　在过去一年中曾担任部委长官、最高法院法官或高级法院法官或检察官的人员不得被提名为公证员。

Suprema de Justicia o magistrado o fiscal de tribunal superior.

Art. 135-En ninguna designación de notario podrá postularse o designarse que sea cónyuge o pariente dentro del cuarto grado de consanguinidad, segundo de afinidad o primero civil, de alguno de los funcionarios que intervienen en la postulación o nombramiento, o de los que hayan participado en la elección o nombramiento de ellos.

Art. 136-No podrán ser designados para un mismo círculo notarial personas que sean entre sí cónyuges o parientes dentro del cuarto grado de consanguinidad, segundo de afinidad o primero civil.

Art. 137- No podrán ser designados notarios en propiedad quienes se hallen en condiciones de retiro forzoso, sea en la administración pública, sea en la de justicia o en el ministerio público, y quienes estén devengando pensión de jubilación.

Conc.: Dcr. 3047 de 1989, art. 1°.

Art. 138- La designación queda insubsistente:

1. Por la no aceptación.

2. Por la falta de confirmación del nombramiento, en los casos en que ella se exige.

3. Por la demora de diez días en tomar posesión del cargo, contados desde la fecha en que se reciba la confirmación del nombramiento, si ya está corriendo el período legal, salvo caso fortuito debidamente comprobado o prórroga hasta de treinta días, concedida justificadamente por quien hizo la designación.

Conc.: Decr.2148 de 1983, art.S8.

Art. 139- Los cargos pueden ser libremente aceptados o rehusados.

Quien reciba el nombramiento en propiedad, deberá comprobar ante quien lo hizo, que reúne los requisitos exigidos para el cargo, para los fines de la confirmación. Sin esta no podrá tomar posesión, ni ejercer el cargo.

El término que tiene el nombrado para presentar su documentación es de un mes contado desde el día en que reciba el nombramiento, si reside en cl país, y de tres meses si está en el extranjero.

Conc.: Decr.2148 de 1983,art.60.

Art. 140- La calidad de abogado se probará con copia del acta de grado o del título y certificación sobre su reconocimiento oficial o con la tarjeta de inscripción profesional.

El ejercicio de la abogacía se podrá acreditar con el desempeño habitual de cualesquiera actividades jurídicas, tanto independientes, como subordinadas, en cargo público

第135条 负责公证员提名或任命，或者参与公证员选拔或任命工作的官员，其配偶、四代以内直系血亲、两代以内旁系血亲和近姻亲关系在任何情况下均不得被提名或任命为公证员。

第136条 处于配偶关系、四代以内直系血亲、两代以内旁系血亲和近姻亲关系的人员不得被指派到同一公证业务网络。

第137条 已经从公共行政管理部门、司法部门或国家部委强制退休的人员，或领取养老金的人员不得被指派为公证员。

并行法规：1989年第3047号法令，第1条。

第138条 若发生以下情况，指派无效：

1. 当事人不接受的。

2. 任命在应确认时未得到确认。

3. 若法律期间已开始起算，但从确认任命当日计起超过10日仍未就任，被证明属偶然情况或指派人允许延期30日的情况除外。

并行法规：1983年第2148号法令，第58条。

第139条 相关人员可以自由选择接受或拒绝任命。

收到任命的人员应与提出任命人员进行核实，并提交所有职务要求的相关材料以便最终确认。若无此步骤，不得就任及行使职能。

若被任命人员居住在本国内，提交材料的期限为收到任命之日起计1个月，若居住在国外，该期限为3个月。

并行法规：1983年第2148号法令，第60条。

第140条 律师资质由学历或学位证以及官方认可书证明，或由职业登记卡证明。

律师事务所业务可通过从事任何常规法务活动证明，无论是以独立还是附属形式，也无论是公立还是私立。

o privado.

Art. 141- Para la confirmación de cargo y para la posesión cuando no haya lugar a aquella, deberán acreditarse los correspondientes requisitos legales con certificación de autoridades competentes y presentar certificación sobre conducta y antecedentes (carné judicial), en la que deberá constar la situación o definición de los procesos penales en que el designado hubiere sido sindicado, enjuiciado o condenado, y declaración juramentada de ausencia de todo impedimento. Sin el cumplimiento de tales formalidades no podrá procederse a la posesión, salvo el caso de encargo.

Copia del acta de posesión será enviara junto con los documentos originales al Consejo Superior de la Administración de Justicia.

Art. 142- Las funciones del cargo se asumen por la designación seguida de la posesión, pero las anomalías 4ue se hayan presentado en el nombramiento, confirmación o posesión de quien esté ejerciendo el cargo, no afectan la validez de la actuación oficial de él.

Art. 143- Sin perjuicio de la investigación penal a que hubiere lugar, el funcionario que haya hecho la designación podrá en cualquier tiempo, de oficio o a solicitud del Ministerio Público, de la vigilancia notarial 0 de cualquier persona, separar del cargo, de plano, hasta que se pronuncie la decisión disciplinaria, a quien haya entrado a ejercerlo con fundamento en certificación o declaración manifiestamente apócrifa.

Art. 144- El cargo se pierde:

1. Por aceptación de la renuncia.

2. Por ejercer otro cargo público. Sin embargo, quienes ejerzan Notaría en propiedad no la perderán cuando fueren designado interinamente o por encargo para alguno en la Rama Jurisdiccional o en el Ministerio Público, o en otra notaria o en la oficina de Registro.

3. Por no presentarse el Notario a desempeñarlo, vencido el término de la licencia 4ue se le haya concedido.

4. Por destitución decretada en providencia firme.

Art. 145- Los notarios pueden ser de carrera 0 de servicio, y desempeñar el cargo en propiedad, en interinidad o por encargo.

Conc.: Decr.2148 de 1983, art.65.

Art. 146- Para ser notario en propiedad, se requiere el lleno de los requisitos legales expedido para la correspondiente categoría, y además, haber sido seleccionado mediante concurso. Sin embargo, la postulación y la designación podrán hacerse prescindiendo de la selección de candidatos mediante concurso, cuando este no se haya

第141条 为了确认任命及就任，被任命人应先提交所有法律要求的材料以及有关部门提供的证明，并提供行为和前科记录（司法证件），以说明被任命人是否曾被检举、控告或审判，并宣誓声明对于就任无任何阻碍条件。若无上述材料，该人员不得就任，受委托就任的情况除外。

就任书副本将与材料原件一同交与国家司法最高理事会。

第142条 一旦指派后就任，相关人员即将开始行使职能，在任命、确认或就任中发生的异常情况不影响该人员的正式行政行为。

第143条 在不影响相关刑事调查的情况下，指派人可在任何时间，以例行公事或受公共事务部委托的形式对任何人进行公证监督，对提供虚假材料的人员在无须调查取证的情况下采取停职措施，直至公布纪律处理决定。

第144条 公证员职位将在以下情况失效：
1. 辞呈被接受的。
2. 兼任其他公共职务的。然而，若为临时兼任或受委托担任司法部门、公共事务部职务，或担任其他公证处或登记处职务，则无须取消职位。

3. 公证员休年假逾期未归的。

4. 被明令撤职的。
第145条 公证员职位可为职业性质或服务性质，可分为正式岗位、临时岗位或委托岗位。

并行法规：1983年第2148号法令，第65条。
第146条 正式岗位公证员需要满足所有对应级别岗位的法律要求，另外必须通过考核方式选拔。然而，被指派或任命的公证员，若未安排考核或经审核考核通过者名单无合适人选，则可以根据第172条和第174条规定，免去此环节。

realizado y cuando se haya agotado la lista de quienes lo aprobaron, conforme a los artículos 172 y 174.

La designación en propiedad da derecho al titular a no ser suspendido ni destituido sino en los casos y con las formalidades que determina el presente estatuto.

Conc.: Decr.2148 de 1983, art.66.

Art. 147- La estabilidad en el cargo ejercido en propiedad podrá extenderse hasta el retiro forzoso, dentro de las condiciones de la carrera, para quienes pertenezcan a ella, y al término del respectivo período, para quienes sean de servicio.

Art. 148- Habrá lugar a designación en interinidad:

1. Cuando el concurso sea declarado desierto, mientras se hace el nombramiento en propiedad.

2. Cuando la causa que motive el encargo se prolongue más de tres meses; mientras ella subsista o se hace la designación en propiedad.

Conc.: Decr. 2148 de 1983, arts. 66, 67.

Art. 149- Dentro del respectivo período los interinos que reúnan los requisitos legales exigidos para el cargo, tienen derecho de permanencia mientras susbsista la causa de la interinidad y no se provea el cargo en propiedad; los demás podrán ser removidos libremente.

Art. 150- El Notario no podrá separarse del desempeño de sus funciones mientras no se haya hecho cargo de ellas quien deba reemplazarlo

Art. 151- Cuando falte el Notario, la primera autoridad política del lugar podrá designar un encargado de las funciones, mientras se provee el cargo en interinidad o en propiedad según el caso.

Conc.: Decr. 2148 de 1983, arts. 66, 68.

Art. 152- En encargo no podrá durar más de noventa días y recaerá, de ser ello posible, en la persona que el Notario indique, bajo se entera responsabilidad.

Art. 153- Para ser Notario en los círculos de primera categoría se exige, además de los requisitos generales, en forma alternativa:

1. Ser abogado titulado y haber ejercido el cargo de notario o de registrador de instrumentos públicos por un término no menor de cuatro anos, o la judicatura o el profesorado universitario en derecho, siquiera por seis años, o la profesión por diez anos a lo menos.

2. No siendo abogado, haber desempeñado con eficiencia el cargo de Notario o el de Registrador en un Círculo de dicha categoría, por tiempo no menor de ocho

正式任命可保证除发生本章程涉及的情况以外，正式公证员不被停职或撤职。

并行法规：1983 年第 2148 号法令，第 66 条。

第 147 条　对于职业性质的公证员而言，其职位可以保持稳定，直至达到强制退休年龄；对于服务性质的公证员而言，其职位稳定性可保持到相应周期结束。

第 148 条　以下情况可临时指派公证员：

1. 若在进行正式任命时，选拔考核宣布无效；

2. 若委托岗位需求已持续超过 3 个月，并一直存在，或变为长期职位。

并行法规：1983 年第 2148 号法令，第 66 条、第 67 条。

第 149 条　临时任职者在收集任职所需的法律材料期间，若仍然有临时岗位需求且无正式岗位需求，则此人有权留在任上；其他情况可以自由调离岗位。

第 150 条　公证员不得玩忽职守，若未能履行工作职责则应撤职。

第 151 条　若公证员失职，当地最高政府官员可委托其他人员代替行使职能，根据情况决定是临时职位或长期职位。

并行法规：1983 年第 2148 号法令，第 66 条、第 68 条。

第 152 条　委托岗位不得超过 90 日，若发生此情况，公证员指定的委托人承担全部责任。

第 153 条　若要成为一级公证业务网络公证员，除一般要求外还有以下要求：

1. 有执业律师资格的，应至少担任过四年公证员职务或文档登记员职务，或至少担任过 6 年司法职务或大学法学教师职务，或至少 10 年法律专业职务。

2. 没有执业律师资格的，应担任过属于同级别公证业务网络的公证员职务或登记员职务，时间不得少于 8 年，若在低一级别网络任职，则工作经验不得少

anos, o en uno de inferior categoría siquiera por doce anos.

Conc.: Decr. 2148 de 1983, art.62.

Art. 154- Para ser Notario en los Círculos de segunda categoría, además de las exigencias generales, se requiere, en forma alternativa:

1. Ser abogado titulado y haber sido notario durante dos anos, o ejercido la judicatura, o el profesorado universitario en derecho, al menos por tres anos, o la profesión con buen crédito por término no menor de cinco anos, o haber tenido práctica notarial o registral por espacio de cuatro años.

2. No siendo ahogado, haber ejercido el cargo en círculo de igual o superior categoría durante seis anos, o en uno de inferior categoría por un término no menor de nueve años.

Conc.: Decr.2148 de 1983, art.62.

Art. 155- Para ser notario en los círculos de tercera categoría, además de las exigencias generales, se requiere alternativamente:

1. Ser abogado titulado.

2. No siendo abogado, haber sido notario por tiempo no inferior a dos anos, o haber completado la enseñanza secundaria o normalista y tenido práctica judicial, notarial o registral por espacio de tres anos, o tener experiencia judicial, notarial o registral por término no menor de cinco años.

Art. 156- Los notarios no podrán autorizar sus propios actos o contratos ni aquellos en que tengan interés directo o en que figuren como otorgantes su cónyuge 0 sus parientes dentro del cuarto grado de consanguinidad, segundo de afinidad 0 primero civil.

Art. 157- Modificado. Decr. 2163 de 1970, art. 44. Los notarios están obligados a residir en la cabecera de su círculo de notaría, de la cual no podrán ausentarse sino por diligencia en ejercicio de sus funciones o con licencia de la autoridad respectiva.

La Superintendencia de Notariado y Registro determinará la localización de las notarías en los círculos de primera y segunda categoría, de modo que a los usuarios del mismo les sea posible utilizarlo en la forma más fácil y conveniente de acuerdo con la extensión y características especiales de cada ciudad.

Art. 158- Los notarios tendrán las horas de despacho público que sean necesarias para el buen servicio y que señale la vigilancia notarial.

Art. 159- Las oficinas de las notarías estarán ubicadas en sitios de los más públicos del lugar de la sede notarial y

于12年。

并行法规：1983年第2148号法令，第62条。

第154条　若要成为二级公证业务网络公证员，除一般要求外，还有如下要求：

1.有执业律师资格，应至少担任过2年公证员职务，或至少担任过3年司法职务或大学法学教师职务，或至少5年法律专业职务且信誉良好，或曾在公证部门或登记部门有至少4年实习经验。

2.没有执业律师资格的，应在同级别或更高级别公证业务网络任职至少6年，或在更低一级别网络任职至少9年。

并行法规：1983年第2148号法令，第62条。

第155条　若要成为三级公证业务网络公证员，除一般要求外，还有如下要求：

1.有执业律师资格。

2.没有执业律师资格的，则需至少担任过2年公证员职务，或至少完成中等教育或正规学校教育，且在司法、公证或档案部门有3年实习经验，或至少担任过5年司法、公证或档案部门职务。

第156条　公证员不得对自己的法律行为或合同授权公证，不得对与其有直接利益关系的文件进行公证，也不得受理当事人为其配偶、四代以内直系血亲、两代以内旁系血亲和近姻亲的案件。

第157条　已修订。1970年第2163号法令，第44条。公证员必须居住在其所属公证业务网络的主导城市，非因职务需要或得到相关部门批准，不得擅自离开。

国家公证和登记机构监督管理局将根据各城市规模和特性，决定一级和二级公证业务网络内公证处所处的位置，保证同一网络内的用户可以以最简单便捷的方式接受其服务。

第158条　公证员应保证足够的办公时间，以便有效提供服务并实施公证监督。

第159条　公证处应位于公证辖区所在地内最便于公共服务的位置，应具备服务客户的最佳条件并

tendrán las mejores condiciones posibles de presentación y comodidad para los usuarios del servicio.

Art. 160- Las funciones notariales serán ejercidas dentro de las horas y días hábiles, pero en casos de urgencia inaplazable, a requerimiento de personas que se hallen imposibilitadas para concurrir a la oficina, el servicio se prestará en horas extraordinarias o en días festivos. Fuera de estos casos, los notarios no están obligados a prestar su ministerio, pero podrán hacerlo voluntariamente.

CAPITULO III De la provisión, permanencia y período de los Notarios

Art. 161- Subrogado. Decr. 2163 de 1970, art. 5O. Los notarios serán nombrados para periodos de cinco (5) años, así: los de primera categoría por el gobierno nacional; los demás, por los gobernadores, intendentes y comisarios respectivos.

La comprobación de que se reúnen los requisitos exigidos para el cargo se surtirá ante la autoridad que hizo el respectivo nombramiento, la cual lo confirmará una vez acreditados.

Conc.: Decr'. 2148 de 1983, art. 61.

Art. 162- Quienes aspiren a ser designados notarios deberán inscribirse en la oportunidad, lugar y oficina que señale el Consejo Superior de la Administración de Justicia para cl respectivo concurso, y comprobar los factores de calificación que para entonces se fijen.

Conc.: Decr. 2148 de 1983, art. 87.

Art. 163- En toda clase de concursos habrá análisis y evaluación de experiencia, rendimiento en las actividades y capacidad demostrada en ellas con relación al servicio notaria; de los estudios de postgrado o de capacitación y adiestramiento, especialmente los relacionados con el notariado, la judicatura y el foro; del ejercicio de la cátedra, preferentemente la universitaria y en particular en materias relacionadas con el notariado y la administración de justicia de las obras de investigación y de divulgación publicadas y en los mismos sentidos; y se concederá valor propio a la antigüedad y permanencia en el servicio notarial, y a los resultados obtenidos en todos los anteriores concursos en que se haya participado.

Los concursos incluirán, además, entrevistas personales, y según las circunstancias, exámenes orales o escritos o combinados, sobre conocimientos generales de derecho y de técnica notarial, y cursos de capacitación o adiestramiento.

保证客户舒适度。

第160条 公证事务应在工作日和工作时间段内进行，但若有紧急情况，且当事人因无法亲自到访办事处而提出特别申请，公证员可在规定工作时间以外以及节假日工作。若非此类情况，公证员无义务在工作时间以外提供服务，但公证员有权出于自愿，在工作时间以外提供服务。

第三章 公证员的工作规定、任期和周期

第161条 已替换。1970年第2163号法令，第50条。公证员任命工作周期为5年，一级公证员由中央政府任命，其他级别由省长、州长、地区行政长官等地方官员任命。

对其提供所需材料的验证，应在负责任命的相关部门见证下进行，一旦鉴定有效将予以确认。

并行法规：1983年第2148号法令，第61条。

第162条 任何希望担任公证员的候选人，需要在国家司法最高理事会指定的时间、地点和办事处注册参加考核，并验证其相关资质。

并行法规：1983年第2148号法令，第87条。

第163条 在所有类型的考核中均将对候选人在以下方面进行分析和评估：公证业务的经验、效率和能力；对研究生学业或对相关培训成果，特别是与公证、司法和律师行业相关的内容；以及对授课经验，尤其是与公证及调研和信息公示相关的司法管理方面。另外，还将特别参考其在公证服务领域的工作年限和任期，以及在之前参加过的考核取得的成绩。

考核还包含面试环节，根据情况还将对候选人法律和公证业务技能基本知识以及培训或训练课程等方面，以口试和笔试或两种混合的形式进行考察。

Art. 164- La carrera notarial y los concursos serán administrados por el Consejo Superior de la Administración de Justicia, integrado entonces, por cl Ministerio de Justicia, los presidentes de la Corte Suprema de Justicia, el Consejo de Estado y el Tribunal Disciplinario, el Procurador General de la Nación y dos notarios, uno de ellos de primera categoría, con sus respectivos suplentes personales, elegidos para períodos de dos anos por los notarios del país, en la forma que determine el reglamento. Para el primer período la designación se hará por los demás miembros del Consejo.

En el Consejo tendrá voz, entonces, el superintendente de notariado y registro.

Conc.: Decr. 2148 de 1983, arts. 79 a 84.

Art. 165- Con suficiente anticipación el Consejo Superior de la Administración de Justicia fijará las bases de cada concurso, con señalamiento de sus finalidades, requisitos de admisión, calendario, lugares de inscripción y realización, factores que SG tendrán en cuenta, manera de acreditarlos, y sistema de calificaciones, e indicará la divulgación que haya de darse a la convocatoria.

Art. 166- No serán aceptados a concurso quienes no acrediten en tiempo los requisitos para su postulación.

El consejo calificará a los concursantes de conformidad con la norma precedente, el reglamento y las bases que haya sentado para cada ocasión.

Conc.: Decr. 2148 de 1YS3, art 62.

Art. 167- Quien por primera vez pierda un concurso no podrá participar en el siguiente; quien lo pierda por segunda vez no podrá participar en los dos siguientes, y quien por tercera vez lo pierda no podrá volver a concursar.

Art. 168- Los concursos se celebrarán para ingreso al servicio y para ingreso a la carrera y ascenso dentro de ella.

Art. 169- Los concursos para ingreso al servicio para ascenso dentro de la carrera tienen por objeto la selección de candidatos para cargos no desempeñados en propiedad por notarios pertenecientes a ella.

Art. 170- En los concursos para ingreso al servicio y ascenso, el postulante indicará el cargo a que aspira, con precisión de su ubicación territorial, y cuando fueren varios lo vacantes, el orden de su preferencia.

Art. 171 y 172- Derogados. Ley 29 de 1973 j art. 22.

Art. 173- Dentro de los cinco días siguientes al en

第 164 条 公证员职业操守及考核环节将由司法部、最高法院、国务院、纪律法院最高领导以及国家总检察长组成的国家司法最高理事会监督管理。该理事会成员还应包括两名公证员，其中一名应为一级公证员，并可指定代理副手。根据规定，此两名公证员应由全国公证员每两年选举一次。第一届任期由理事会其他成员指定。

在理事会中，公证处及登记处最高领导可发表观点。

并行法规：1983 年第 2148 号法令，第 79 条至第 84 条。

第 165 条 国家司法最高理事会应提前确定每场考核的基本内容，规定考核目的、入选条件、日程安排、注册和考核地点、考察项目、登记方式以及评分体系，并发布启事通知将举办考核。

第 166 条 未按时注册提交材料的人员不得参加考核。

理事会将根据上述规定以及每场考核的具体规定和要求为报名者评定成绩。

并行法规：1983 年第 2148 号法令，第 62 条。

第 167 条 首次考核未通过的人员不得参加下次考核；第二次考核未通过的人员不得参加之后连续两次考核；第三次考核未通过的人员不得再参加考核。

第 168 条 除从事服务性公证业务和职业性公证业务需要考核外，职业型公证员升职也需要考核。

第 169 条 服务型公证员入职考核和职业型公证员升职考核均用于选拔人才担任目前无公务员在岗的正式空缺职位。

第 170 条 入职考核和升职考核中，被考核者应说明希望担任的职务，并准确告知该职务的地点，若有多个职位空缺可供选择，还应按其偏好排列志愿。

第 171 和第 172 条 已废止。1973 年第 29 号法律，第 22 条。

第 173 条 产生正式职位空缺需求后 5 日之内，

que ocurra la necesidad de proveer un cargo en propiedad, el Gobernador, intendente o comisario y el Tribunal avisaran la ocurrencia de la vacante al Consejo, para que este envié actualizada la lista de los candidatos aprobados en concurso.

Nota: El artículo 309 de la Constitución Política de 1991, erigió en departamentos a las antiguas i7ite'7del~cias y comisarías.

Art. 174- Derogado. Ley 29 de 1973, art. 22.

Art. 175- Los presidente de Tribunal y los Gobernadores, intendentes y comisarios comunicarán al Consejo superior ya la vigilancia notarial, las postulaciones y designaciones que hagan, dentro de los cinco días siguientes, a aquel en que las hagan.

Conc.: Decr. 2148 de 1983, arts. 63, 64.

Nota: El artículo 309 de la Constitución Política de I99l, erigió en departamentos a las antiguas intendencias y comisarias.

Art. 176- Para ser admitido a la carrera notarial se exigen los siguientes requisitos de modo concurrente.

1. Estar ejerciendo el cargo con propiedad.

2. Haber ejercido cargo de notario o de registrador, en propiedad o en interinidad, pero con el lleno de los requisitos legales, por tiempo no inferior a cuatro años.

3. Haber aprobado el concurso de ingreso a la carrera.

Art. 177- No será admitido a la carrera notarial:

1. Quien se encuentre en cualquiera de las causales que impiden el ingreso al servicio.

2. Quien haya sido sancionado disciplinariamente con suspensión del cargo durante los dos anos anteriores o con multa en el último ano, o con las mismas sanciones y en iguales tiempos, en el ejercicio de la abogacía o de cargo judicial o del ministerio público, o excluido de lista de auxiliares de la justicia, en cualquier tiempo, por razones de índole ética.

Art. 178- El pertenecer a la carrera notarial implica:

1. Derecho a permanecer en la misma notaría dentro de las condiciones del presente estatuto.

2. Derecho a participar en concurso de ascenso.

3. Preferencia para ocupar. a solicitud propia y dentro de la misma circunscripción político-administrativa, otra notaria de la misma categoría que se encuentre vacante.

4. Prelación en los programas de bienes social general y en los de becas y cursos de capacitación y adiestrami-

省长、州长或地区行政长官应将空缺职位报告给理事会，以便理事会向其发送最新的考核通过者名单。

注：根据1991年《政治宪法》第309条，在过去的州和辖区基础上建立省行政单位。

第174条 已废止。1973年第29号法律，第22条。

第175条 法院院长和省长、州长及专区长应在选拔结束后5日内向最高理事会通报公证监督、公证员任命和指派结果。

并行法规：1983年第2148号法令，第63条、第64条。

注：根据1991年《政治宪法》第309条，在过去的州和辖区基础上建立省行政单位。

第176条 公证员资质若要得到承认需要满足以下要求：

1. 正在实际担任正式公证员职务。

2. 曾担任公证员或登记员职务，无论正式岗位或临时岗位，但必须满足法律规定的要求，担任职务时间不少于4年。

3. 已通过职业型公证员入职考核。

第177条 若发生以下情形，不得承认其公证员资质：

1. 因任何理由无法入职并办理公证业务的。

2. 在过去两年曾因受纪律处分被停职，或在过去一年因纪律处分被罚款，或在同样时限内兼任律师、司法职位或公共部门职位被处罚，或因违反职业道德在任何时间被从司法部门人员名单中除名的。

第178条 就任职业公证员享有下权利：

1. 在本章条件下长期在同一公证处留任的权利。

2. 参加升职考核的权利。

3. 在个人提出申请的情况下，可被优先考虑调任至同政治、行政范围内的其他有职位空缺的公证处。

4. 在一般社会保障项目以及培训和训练项目的奖学金及课程中享有优先权。

ento.

La permanencia en la carrera está subordinada a la continuidad en el servicio, salvo el caso de licencia.

Art. 179- El ingreso a la carrera se hará en el grado correspondiente a la categoría del círculo notarial en que esté clasificada la notaría que se ejerza en propiedad al momento de la admisión, y en la correspondiente sección territorial.

Art. 180- El período de los notarios es de cinco anos, contados a partir del primero de enero de mil novecientos setenta.

Art.181- Los notarios pueden ser reelogidos indefinidamente; los de carrera serán confirmados a la expiración de cada período. Unos y otros deberán retirarse cuando se encuentren en situación de retiro forzoso.

Conc.: Decr. 2148 de 1983, arts. 69 a 74.

Art.182- El notario que llegue a encontrarse en circunstancias de retiro forzoso deberá manifestarlo al funcionario que lo haya designado, tan pronto como ella ocurra.

El retiro se producirá a solicitud del interesado, del ministerio público, o de la vigilancia notarial, o de oficio, dentro del mes siguiente a la ocurrencia de la causal.

Conc.: Decr. 2148 de 1983, art. 75.

Arts. 183 y 184- Derogados. Decr.2163 de 1970, art. 46.

Art. 185- El notario debe retirarse cuando sea declarado en interdicción judicial y cuando 'caiga en ceguera, mudez, sordera o sufra cualquier otro quebranto de salud física o mental permanente que implique notoria disminución del rendimiento en el trabajo, o enfermedad que lo inhabilite por más de ciento ochenta días.

El estado físico o mental deberá ser certificado por entidad pública de previsión o seguridad social del lugar, previo reconocimiento practicado a solicitud del propio notario, de la vigilancia notarial 0 del ministerio público. La renuencia a someterse al examen acarreará la pérdida del cargo, que decretará el funcionario a quien competa la y designación.

Conc.: Decr 2148 de 1983, arts. 76, 104 a 115.

Arts. 186 y 187- Derogados. Decr. 2163 de 1970, art. 46.

CAPITULO IV De las Ucencias y reemplazos

Art. 188- Los notarios tienen derecho a separarse del

若要长期留任，需保证工作连续性，依法休假情况除外。

第179条　职业公证员入职级别应与其获准入职工作的公证网络内公证处对应，且工作辖区也应对应。

第180条　公证员任期为5年，从1970年1月1日起计。

第181条　公证员可无限连任，职业型公证员将在每工作周期结束时进行确认。若达到强制退休年龄，则公证员必须按规定退休。

并行法规：1983年第2148号法令，第69条至第74条。

第182条　到达强制退休年龄的公证员必须向对其提出任命的官员汇报。

公证员达到法定强制退休年龄1个月内，可由本人、公共部门或由公证监督部门、业务监督部门提出退休申请。

并行法规：1983年第2148号法令，第75条。

第183条和第184条　已废止。1970年第2163号法令，第46条。

第185条　若公证员被宣布司法停职；或发生失明、聋哑或其他身体或精神损害，导致其无法履行职能;或因病导致超过180日无法履行职能，则必须离职。

公证员身体或精神状态应在其本人、公证监督或公共部门申请下，由当地公共医疗或社会保护部门提供证明。拒绝接受检测将导致公证员被撤职，相关部门将通过法令指定有能力的人员担任该职位。

并行法规：1983年第2148号法令，第76条、第104条至115条。

第186条和第187条　已废止。1970年第2163号法令，第46条。

第四章　休假及替班

第188条　公证员有权在休年假期间暂离工作

ejercicio de sus cargos mediante licencia hasta por noventa días continuos o discontinuas en cada ano calendario, y a obtener licencia por enfermedad o incapacidad física temporal hasta por ciento ochenta días, en cada caso. Los notarios de carrera, además 20 tendrán derecho a licencia hasta por dos años, pero solo para proseguir cursos de especialización o actividades de docencia o investigación o asesoría científica al Estado, previo concepto favorable del Consejo Superior de la Administración de Justicia.

Conc.: Decr. 2148' de 1983, art* 77, 78

Art. 189- Subrogado. Decr. 2163 de 1970, art. 60. Las licencias de los notarios se solicitarán a la autoridad que haya producido el nombramiento, quien al concederlas encargará, con límite máximo de noventa (90) días, a la persona que el notario indique bajo su responsabilidad. Cuando la licencia no exceda de quince (15) días y el notario no resida en la ciudad capital, el alcalde de su sede podrá concederla y hacer el encargo.

Siempre que por cualquier causa se produzca la separación de un notario de su cargo, y su reemplazo, deberá comunicarse la novedad inmediatamente a la Superintendencia de Notariado y Registro.

Art. 190- Cuando se produzcan faltas absoluta o sanciones de suspensión, el correspondiente gobernador, intendente o comisario encargará a la persona que haya de asumir inmediatamente las funciones y, en el primer evento se procederá a designar el reemplazo para el resto del período, en la forma prevista en el Capítulo 30.

CAPITULO V Del colegio de notaries

Art. 191- Los notarios procurarán su asociación en Colegio de Notarios, con miras a la elevación moral, intelectual y material del notariado colombiano y estimular en sus miembros el cumplimiento de los principios de ética profesional y los deberes del servicio que les está encomendado.

Conc.: Decr. 2148' de 1983, art. 147; Ley 29 del 1973, art. 8° .

Art. 192- Los estatutos y reglamentaciones internas del colegio serán expedidos por este y sometidos a la aprobación del Ministerio de Justicia, a quien informará sobre el nombramiento o cambio de sus directivas y representantes para el permanente registro de los mismos.

Art. 193- El Colegio será cuerpo consultivo de los notarios y de las personas o entidades particulares o del

岗位，每年至多90日年假，可连续休或间断休，除此以外还可因伤病休至多180日假。另外职业型公证员还可请至多两年的特别假期，该假期仅可用于接受继续专业教育或从事教育活动或在国家司法最高理事会许可的情况下为政府担任顾问。

并行法规：1983年第2148号法令，第77条、第78条。

第189条 已替换。1970年第2163号法令，第60条。公证员应向任命单位负责管理此公证员的领导提请休假，单位最多可批准90日假期。若假期不超过15日，且公证员不居住在首都，则由其所在辖区的当地行政长官批准假期，并委托他人替班。

因任何原因，某公证员离岗并由他人替代，均应立即向公证和登记机构监督管理局汇报。

第190条 若发生严重失职或被执行停职处分，相关省长、州长或地方行政长官应委任能够立刻代替其执行任务的人员，并按第三章所示形式，尽快指定该人员为该工作周期剩余期限的负责人员。

第五章 公证员学院

第191条 公证员应在公证员学院加入协会，以便提高哥伦比亚公证业职业道德水平、人才水平和业务水平，并鼓励协会成员严守职业道德并履行这一职务赋予他们的义务。

并行法规：1983年第2148号法令，第147条；1973年第29号法律，第8条。

第192条 学院内部章程及规定应由学院颁布，并送交司法部审批，若管理层及机构注册代表人发生变更应立刻通知司法部。

第193条 学院应作为公证员、个人、特定机构或政府咨询的单位，负责就改善公证体系组织运作

Estado cuando demanden tal servicio. Promoverá estudios e investigaciones sobre organización y funcionamiento de los sistemas notariales, fomentará el estudio de las disciplinas profesionales en forma directa y en colaboración con las universidades y, en general, el mejoramiento del nivel académico, técnico y moral de todos sus miembros.

Art. 194- La vigilancia notarial del Ministerio de Justicia y el Colegio de Notarios estarán en permanente contacto con el fin de mantener información sobre las personas que ejercerán las funciones notariales, la formación de sus hojas de vida y el cumplimiento de los objetivos de la supervigilancia administrativa.

Conc.: Decr. 2148 de 1983, arts. 95 a 103, 146.

TITULO VI
DE LA IRESPONSABILIDAD DE LOS NOTAIRIOS

CAPITULO I De la responsabilidad en el ejercicio de la function

Art. I95- Los notarios son responsables civilmente de los danos y perjuicios que causen los usuarios del servicio por culpa o dolo de la prestación del mismo.

Conc.: Decr. 2148 de 1983, arts. 116 y ss.

Art. 196- Cuando se trate de irregularidades que le sean imputables, el notario responderá de los danos causados siempre que aquellas sean subsanables a su costa por los medios y en los casos previstos en el presente decreto.

Art. 197- La indemnización que tuviere que pagar el notario por causas que aprovechen a otra persona, podrá ser repetida contra ésta hasta concurrencia del monto del provecho que reciba y si éste se hubiere producido con malicia o dolo de ella, el notario será resarcido en todo perjuicio.

CAPITULO II De las faltas

Art. 198- Son conductas del notario, que atentan la majestad, dignidad y eficacia del servicio notarial, y que acarrean sanción disciplinaria:

I. La embriaguez habitual, la práctica de juegos prohibidos, el uso de estupefacientes, el amancebamiento, la concurrencia a lugares indecorosos, el homosexualismo, el abandono del hogar, y en general, un mal comportamiento social.

进行调查研究，与大学合作，直接促进专业纪律教育，从整体上提高成员学术水平、技术水平和道德水平。

第 194 条　司法部公证监督部门与公证员学院应保持长期联系，以随时获取担任公证员职务的人员信息、个人履历，以履行行政监督义务。

并行法规：1983 年第 2148 号法令，第 95 条至第 103 条、第 146 条。

第六篇
对公证员的问责机制

第一章　对公证员执业的问责机制

第 195 条　公证员对客户因其失误或恶意行为造成的损失负有民事责任。

并行法规：1983 年第 2148 号法令，第 116 条及之后诸条。

第 196 条　若为属本法案规定类型的可被控告不端行为，尚能由公证员个人补救，则公证员必须对所造成的损害采取补救措施。

第 197 条　公证员若从他人处攫取利益，应对他人予以补偿，且该补偿行为可不断重复，直至公证员完全归还他人向其支付的费用。他人故意制造事端的，公证员支付的补偿金应全部得到返还。

第二章　失职

第 198 条　公证员失职指其行为影响公证服务的威严、尊严和有效性，应接受纪律处分，具体行为包括：

1. 习惯性酗酒、参与非法赌博、服用毒品、不正当性关系、出入不雅场所、同性恋行为、离家出走以及其他一般不良社会行为。

2 El reiterado incumplimiento de sus obligaciones civiles o comerciales.

3. Solicitar, recibir, ofrecer dádivas, agasajos, préstamos, regalos y cualquier clase de lucros, directa o indirectamente, en razón de su cargo o con ocasión de sus funciones.

4. Solicita o fomentar publicidad, de cualquier clase, respecto de su persona o de sus actuaciones. sin perjuicio del derecho a rectificar o aclarar informaciones o comentarios relativos a ellas.

5. El empleo de propaganda de índole comercial o de incentivos de cualquier orden parta estimular al público a demandar sus servicios.

6. Ejercer directamente o indirectamente actividades incompatibles con e! decoro del cargo o que en alguna forma atenten contra su dignidad.

7. Negarse aprestar su ministerio sin causa justificativa.

8. Omitir el cumplimiento de los requisitos sustanciales en la prestación de sus servicios.

9. Dejar de asistir injustificadamente a la oficina, o cerrarla sin motivo legal, o limitar indebidamente las horas de despacho al público.

10. La afirmación maliciosa de hechos o circunstancias inexactas dentro del ejercicio de sus funciones.

II. El aprovechamiento personal o en favor de terceros de dineros o efectüs negociables que reciba para el pago de impuestos o en depósito.

12. El cobro de derechos mayores o menores que los autorizados en el arancel vigente.

13. La renuncia a cumplir las orientaciones que la vigilancia notarial imparta dentro del ámbito de sus atribuciones, en lo relacionado con la prestación del servicio.

14. Modificado. Ley 29 de 1973, art. 7O. El incumplimiento de sus obligaciones para con la Superintendencia de Notariado y Registro, cl Fondo Nacional del Notariado, el Colegio de Notarios, sus empleados subalternos y las entidades de seguridad o previsión social.

15. La transgresión de las normas sobre prohibiciones, impedimentos e incompatibilidades consagradas en el presente estatuto.

Conc.: Decr. 2148' de 1983, arts. 125 a 129.

CAPITULO III De las sanciones

Art. 199- Independientemente de las sanciones penales a que hubiere lugar, a los notarios que incurran en las

2. 一再违反民事或商业义务的。

3. 以职务之便索取、接受或提供招待、借款、礼品以及其他任何类型的直接或间接得利。

4. 要求或推广对其个人或行为的宣传，但公证员有权对此进行辩解或澄清。

5. 使用商务广告宣传或促销诱使公众使用其服务。

6. 直接或间接从事与其职务不符或从某种程度上影响其形象的活动。

7. 无正当理由拒绝提供服务。

8. 提供服务时严重违反相关要求。

9. 无充分理由不到办事处上班，或无任何法律缘由关闭办事处，或违规限制办事处办公时间。

10. 以职务之便恶意证明不实事实或情况。

11. 使用收取的款项或可转让证券用于个人或第三方缴纳税款或存款。

12. 收取的费用多于或少于现行规定。

13. 不遵守公证监督部门在提供公证服务方面设定的准则。

14. 已修订。1973年第29号法律，第70条。不履行对公证和登记机构监督管理局、国家公证员基金会、公证员学院及其下属职员以及社会保障机构的义务。

15. 本章程中关于禁止、限制或不当行为相关规定的行为。

并行法规：1983年第2148号法令，第125条至第129条。

第三章　处分

第199条　无论公证员应接受何种刑事处罚，只要发生前一章节列举的失职行为，就应根据其违规严

faltas enumeradas en el capítulo precedente, se les aplicará según la gravedad de la infracción, los antecedentes y lo dispuesto expresamente en la ley. una de estas sanciones

1. Multa
2. Suspensión
3. Destitución

Art. 200- Cuando la falta, a juicio de la autoridad competente para el proceso disciplinario no diere lugar a sanción, podrá aquella, de plano y por escrito, amonestar al infractor, previniéndole que una nueva falta le acarrearán sanción.

Art. 201- La multa consiste en la obligación de pagar al Tesoro Nacional una suma no menor de trescientos pesos ni mayor de cinco mil; se impondrá en caso de faltas leves, y se cobrará por coactiva.

Conc.: Decr. 2148 de 198'3, arts. 130. 131.

Art. 202- La suspensión en el cargo hasta por seis meses, podrá imponerse frente a falta grave o reincidencia en las leyes, puede aparejar la exclusión de la carrera en la primera vez, y necesariamente la producirá al repetirse dicha sanción.

Conc.: Decr. 2148 de 1983, arts. 130, 131.

Art. 203- La destitución se aplicará, como primera sanción, en caso de falta muy grave, y como consecuencia de varias faltas de otro orden, según su gravedad y reiteración.

Conc.: Decr. 2148 de 1983, arts. 13O, 131.

Art. 204- Las sanciones disciplinarias se aplicarán teniendo en cuenta la naturaleza de la falta, el grado de participación del notario, y sus antecedentes en el servicio y en materia disciplinaria.

Art. 205- Las pruebas serán apreciadas conforme a las reglas de la sana crítica.

Art. 206- La acción disciplinaria prescribirá en cinco anos contados desde el día en que se cometió el último acto constitutivo de la falta.

La iniciación del proceso interrumpe la prescripción.

La existencia de un proceso penal sobre los mismos hechos no da lugar a suspensión del trámite disciplinario.

Art. 207- La acción disciplinaria y las sanciones procederán aun cuando el notario haya hecho dejación del cargo.

Cuando la suspensión o la destitución no pueda hacerse efectiva por pérdida anterior del cargo se anotarán en

重程度、前科记录以及法律规定执行以下处分：

1. 罚款。
2. 停职。
3. 撤职。

第200条 若纪律检察相关部门认为公证员的失职行为不至受处分，可以书面形式明确发出警告，以防其发生新的失职行为，导致诉诸处分。

第201条 罚款应上缴国库，金额为三百至五千比索不等；罚款为强制性，适用于情节较轻的违规行为。

并行法规：1983年第2148号法令，第130条、第131条。

第202条 停职处分最多持续六个月，适用于严重违法或屡犯不改的情形，可在初次违规时给予撤职警告，若再犯则予以执行。

并行法规：1983年第2148号法令，第130条、第131条。

第203条 撤职处分适用于十分严重的违规行为，首次发生此类违规行为即应予以撤职，另外，若多次发生其他类型的失职，应根据严重程度和累犯程度予以执行。

并行法规：1983年第2148号法令，第130条、第131条。

第204条 实施纪律处分应考虑公证员失职的性质、参与程度以及在服务和纪律方面的前科记录。

第205条 证据应根据合理判断规则进行分析。

第206条 纪律处分的追诉期为5年，从最近一次失职行为发生日期起计。

若立案调查将中断追诉期的计算。
对同一个事实进行刑事立案不会暂停纪律处分流程。

第207条 即使公证员已离职，纪律处分与制裁仍可继续。

若因公证员早已离职，停职或撤职处分无法执行，应将此事记入被处分人履历，以作为限制性惩罚。

la hoja de vida del sancionado, para que surtan sus efectos como impedimento.

Art. 208- El conocimiento de los asuntos disciplinarios corresponde a la vigilancia notarial.

CAPITULO IV De la vigilancia notarial

Art. 209- La vigilancia notarial será ejercida por el Ministerio de Justicia, por medio de la Superintendencia de Notariado y Registro.

Conc.:Decr. 2148de 1983, arts. 132 y ss.

Art. 210- La vigilancia tiene por objeto velar porque el servicio notarial se preste oportuna y eficazmente, y conlleva el examen de la conducta de los notarios y el cuidado del cumplido desempeño de sus deberes con la honestidad, rectitud e imparcialidad correspondientes a la naturaleza de su ministerio.

Art. 211- Quien quiera que tenga conocimiento de irregularidades en el servicio notarial, podrá formular la correspondiente queja ante la Superintendencia de Notariado y Registro, quien la tramitará sin dilación.

Art. 212- La vigilancia notarial se ejercerá principalmente por medio de visitas generales y especiales.

Las generales se practicarán a cada notaria por lo menos una vez al ano, y tiene por finalidad establecer la asistencia de los notarios al despacho, la localización, prestación y estado de las oficinas y sus condiciones de comodidad para el público, la presentación personal del notario y su atención a los usuarios del servicio, y comprobar el orden, actualidad, exactitud y presentación de los libros y archivos.

Las visitas especiales se practicarán cuando así lo disponga la Superintendencia de Notariado y Registro, para comprobar las irregularidades de que por cualquier medio tenga noticia, o para verificar hechos o circunstancias que le interesen dentro de sus funciones legales.

De cada visita de levantará un acta en el respectivo libro con las conclusiones del caso, dejando constancia tanto de las irregularidades, deficiencias y cargos resultantes, como de los aspectos positivos que merezcan ser destacados, según el caso, firmada por quien la practicó y por el notario visitado. Copia del acta se remitirá al Superintendente.

Conc.: Decr. 2148 de 198'3, arts. 132, 133.

Art. 213- Si en el acta aparecieren cargos, se correrá

第208条　纪律相关事务由公证监督部门负责。

第四章　公证监督

第209条　公证监督应由司法部通过公证和登记机构监督管理局执行。

并行法规：1983年第2148号法令，第132条及之后诸条。

第210条　监督的目的在于保障公证处提供的服务恰当有效，并对公证员行为进行检查，确保其诚实、正当、公正地履行义务。

第211条　任何人发现公证服务中存在行为不当现象，均可向公证和登记机构监督管理局投诉，监督局应立刻采取行动。

第212条　公证监督主要通过一般查访和特别查访进行。

监督局每年应对每家公证处进行至少一次查访，以确保公证员按时出勤，办事处位置、服务及状态合理，为前来办事的公众提供舒适条件，公证员亲自正当履行职能且保证客户服务，并验证相关卷宗和文档的顺序、更新情况、准确度等。

特别查访在公证和登记机构监督管理局下令时进行，以确定其从某种渠道得知的不当行为是否属实，或在法律职能范围内验证某些其感兴趣的事项或情况。

任何查访均应在登记簿中生成纪要，包含案情总结，以记录相关不当行为、缺陷及控告，或对公证处的积极方面提出表扬，由监督人和被查访公证员共同签名。纪要副本应移交监督局。

并行法规：1983年第2148号法令，第132条、第133条。

第213条　若在纪要中记录了相关控告，则应将

traslado de ellos al notario afectado, para que dentro del termino de ocho días presente sus descargos y aporte las pruebas del caso, hasta dentro de los ocho días siguientes. Vencido dicho término, la Superintendencia diligenciará las pruebas en quince días, y dentro del mes siguiente dictará resolución, en la que relacionará los cargos que a su juicio no hayan sido desvirtuados, indicará las disposiciones que considere infringidas, expresando la razón de su quebranto, e impondrá la sanción disciplinaria correspondiente, o dará por concluido el trámite, según fuere el caso.

Conc.: Decr. 2148 de 1983, arts. 134, 135; C. C. A., 44, 46y ss.

Art. 214- La resolución se notificará por edicto que se fijará durante cinco días en la secretaría de la Superintendencia y su ejecutoria será de diez días.

Copia de la resolución se remitirá al notario interesado por corroo certificado a más tardar al día siguiente de su expedición.

Conc.: Decr. 2148 de 1983, arts. 136, 137, 141; C. C. A., 4S.

Art. 215- Contra la resolución podrá recurrir el notario interesado en reposición ante el propio Superintendente y en apelación en el efecto suspensivo para ante la Junta de la Superintendencia, en escrito presentado dentro del término de la ejecutoria de aquella, La resolución absolutoria se consultará con la Junta.

Conc.: Decr. 2148 de 1983, art. 141.

Art. 216- En firme la resolución de la Superintendencia, sendas copias de ella se enviarán al Consejo Superior de la Administración de Justicia, al gobernador, intendente o comisario a quien competa la designación' y al Tribunal a quien corresponda la formación de las listas.

En caso de suspensión o de destitución, el gobernador, intendente O comisario respectivo procederá a designar a quien por encargo asuma las funciones notariales durante la suspensión o mientras se hace la provisión en propiedad o en interinidad, según las circunstancias.

Art. 217- La Superintendencia de Notariado y Registro, con el fin de capacitar y especializar a los notarios y a sus empleados, organizará por sí, o con la colaboración de la Escuela Judicial y de Universidades, Escuela o Establecimientos Públicos, cursos de capacitación, técnica y jurídica.

此控告记录转移至当事公证员名下，以便其在8日之内进行答辩，并在之后8日内提交证据。该期限过后，监督局应在15日内对相关证据展开尽职调查，在下个月内公布决议。若其认定相关控告未扭曲事实，应指出当事公证员违反的条例内容，解释其违规原因并执行相关纪律处分，或宣布流程结束。

并行法规：1983年第2148号法令，第134条、第135条；《行政诉讼法》第44条、第46条及以后诸条。

第214条 决议将通过公示进行通告，在监督局秘书处公示5日，判决书将公示10日。

决议副本将在决议公布后一天内以挂号信形式邮寄给相关公证员。

并行法规：1983年第2148号法令，第136条、第137、第141条；《行政诉讼法》第45条。

第215条 公证员可针对决议向监督局提出异议，向监督局理事会提出上诉，上诉应在判决书有效期内以书面形式提交。在作出最终决议时，应征求理事会的意见。

并行法规：1983年第2148号法令，第141条。

第216条 监督局作出决议后，应将决议副本发送给国家司法最高理事会、省长、州长或地方行政长官，由其负责指定；同时还应发往法院，由其制定名单。

若为停职或撤职，省长、州长或专区长应在原公证员停职期间指派并委托他人替代其工作，或准备安排招募正式或临时公证员。

第217条 公证和登记机构监督管理局以培训公证员及其雇员，加强其专业素养为目标，自行或与司法学校、大学、学院或公共机构合作，组织技术和司法培训课程。

TITULO VII
DEL ARANCEL

CAPITULO 1 De los derechos notariales

Art. 218- Las tarifas que señalan los derechos notariales son revisables periódicamente por el gobierno nacional teniendo en consideración los costos del servicio y la conveniencia pública.

Conc.: Decr. 172 de 1992.

Art. 219- Cuando la cuantía de un acto o contrato se determine por el valor de un inmueble y el que estimaren las partes fuere inferior al avalúo catastral, los derechos se liquidarán con base en éste.

Art. 220- Siempre que en una misma escritura se consignen dos o más actos o contratos, se causarán los derechos correspondiente a cada uno de ellos en su totalidad. Sin embargo, no se cobrarán derechos adicionales por la protocolización de los documentos necesarios para el otorgamiento de los actos o contratos que contenga la escritura, ni cuando se trate de garantías accesorias que se pacten entre las mismas parles para asegurar el cumplimiento de las obligaciones surgidas de los actos o contratos otorgados.

Art. 221- Cuando las obligaciones emanadas de lo declarado en una escritura consistan en pensión, renta o cualquier otro tipo de prestación periódica de plazo determinado, los derechos se liquidarán teniendo en cuenta la cuantía total de tales prestaciones. Si el plazo fuere indeterminado, la base de liquidación será el monto de las prestaciones periódicas en cinco anos.

Art. 222- No se causarán derechos especiales señalados en las tantas para remunerar las diligencias que implican la firma de escrituras fuera del despacho del notario, cuando se trate de las visitas que suelen hacer dichos funcionarios a los municipios de su círculo notarial, distintos al que es su cabecera.

CAPITULO II De la obligatoriedad dei pago

Art. 223- En los actos o contratos bilaterales los derechos serán de cargo de las dos partes, por mitades. Los varios integrantes de una parte responderán solidariamente por la cuota de ella.

Conc.: Decr. 2148 de 19S'3, art. 142 inc. 1O.

Art. 224- En los actos o contratos unilaterales el pago de los derechos será de cargo del otorgante que emita la

第七篇
收费标准

第一章 公证费用

第218条 公证费用价目表可由中央政府根据服务成本以及公共便利情况定期重新审核。

并行法规：1992年第172号法令。

第219条 若相关法律行为或合同金额由不动产价值决定，且若认定该金额低于地籍估值，相关权益应按地籍估值为基础计算。

第220条 若同一公证书涉及两份或以上法律行为或合同，相关收费则参考各法律行为或合同金额总和。然而，公证书中所包含的法律行为或合同认证所需的文件归档不需要收取额外费用，各方为保证履行已认可的法律行为或合同义务商定的附属保障行为也不需要收取额外费用。

第221条 若公证书中声明的债务为养老金、租金或任何其他有特定期限的周期性款项，公证费用应根据相关款项总额进行核算。若相关期限未定，则公证费用以该款项在5年周期内的金额为基础核算。

第222条 公证员经常访问其公证业务网络内非主导城市的其他城市，在此情况下，公证员在办事处外签署公证书不产生特殊费用。

第二章 付款义务

第223条 若涉及双边法律行为或合同，应由合同双方平摊应支付给公证员的费用。其中一方若涉及多人，仅需共同担负这一方所需支付的费用即可。

并行法规：1983年第2148号法令，第142条第10款。

第224条 若涉及单边法律行为或合同，应由发布声明的当事人承担费用。

declaración.

Si interviniere representante, este será solidariamente responsable con su representado.

Conc.: Decr. 2148 de 1983, art. 142, inc. 10.

Art. 225- En los contratos de mutuo y en los de garantía los derechos notariales serán de cargo del deudor; igual se dispone respecto de las cancelaciones consecuenciales.

Art. 226- Los contratos de compraventa en que concurra el Instituto de Crédito Territorial para suministrar vivienda a los particulares causarán derechos equivalentes a la mitad de los ordinarios autorizados en las tarifas.

Art. 227- En la liquidación de sociedades conyugales o herencias, en la partición de bienes comunes, en la constitución de sociedades y en los demás actos o contratos en que concurran varios interesados, los derechos notariales serán de cargo de todos ellos, a prorrata de su correspondiente interés, pero frente al notario, todos responderán solidariamente.

Art. 228- Los particulares que contraten con la Nación, los territorios nacionales, los departamentos o lo municipios, responderán ante en notario por los derechos a cargo de aquellas entidades. No causarán derechos los actos exclusivos de las mismas, ni los celebrados entre ellas solas.

Conc.: Decr. 2148 de 1983, art. 142 inc. 2°.

Art. 229- En servicios notariales no comprendidos en las disposiciones precedentes, nos respectivos derechos serán de cargo de quienes los hayan solicitado.

Art. 230- Las reglas del presente capítulo se aplicarán a falta de estipulación diferente de los interesados.

Art. 231- Los notarios podrán abstenerse de autorizar las escrituras o actuaciones en que hayan intervenido, hasta cuando reciban la totalidad de los derechos que les corresponden por la prestación de sus servicios.

Conc.: Decr. 2148 de 1983, art. 143.

TITULO VIII
VIGENCIA DEL ESTATUTO

Art. 232- Derógase el titulo 42 del Libro 4O. del Código Civil, y las disposiciones que lo han adicionado o subrogado, relativas a las materias reguladas por el presente estatuto.

Art. 233- Este ordenamiento rige desde su promulgación. Sin ~ 's7;~ embargo, para la designación de

若存在代理人，则应由代理人与当事人共同负责费用。

并行法规：1983年第2148号法令，第142条第10款。

第225条 若涉及贷款协议和保障协议，公证员酬金将由借贷人负责支付；公证书取消同样如此。

第226条 若涉及国土信贷局向个人提供住房的买卖协议，则公证员酬金为正常情况的一半。

第227条 若涉及清算配偶公司或遗产、共同财产分割，或公司成立协议或其他涉及多方的法律行为和合同，公证员酬金则应由各方共同承担，根据各方对应利益按比例划分，但最终应共同交付给公证员一份费用。

第228条 若涉及个人与中央政府、国家各级行政区划部门、省或市签署协议，应由上述国家机构承担公证员酬金。上述机构特别协议以及机构间协议不产生费用。

并行法规：1983年第2148号法令，第142条第2款。

第229条 上述条款未包含的公证服务应由公证申请人承担费用。

第230条 若当事人无其他约定，则按本章规定执行。

第231条 公证员若未全款收到提供服务的费用，可拒绝对其受理的事项或相关公证书进行授权。

并行法规：1983年第2148号法令，第143条。

第八篇
章程有效期

第232条 《民法典》第40卷第42篇及其附加或代替条款中涉及本章程规定的内容均已废止。

第233条 本章程自颁布当日生效。然而，对于从1970年1月1日开始工作周期相关的公证员指派，

notarios para el período que, comenzó el lo. de enero de 1970, los Tribunales Superiores formarán las listas del modo establecido en el artículo K1, con prescindencia de concurso, pero teniendo en cuenta los requisitos señalados para cada categoría notarial en los artículos 152 a 154, así como lo estatuído sobre impedimentos, prohibiciones e incompatibilidades en los capítulos 2 y 3 del Título V y de conformidad con lo que se dispondrá en decreto extraordinario sobre círculos notariales, comprensión territorial, sede y categoría de ellos y número de notarfas, y los gobernadores, intendentes y comisarios podrán hacer la designación en propiedad, siempre que el candidato reúna los requisitos propios del cargo.

Los Tribunales enviarán las listas al gobernador intendente o comisario respectivo antes del día 9 de julio de 1970, y éstos harán la designación dentro de los cinco días siguientes al recibo de aquellas.

高级法院应采取第 K1 条中规定的模式制作名单，而不采取考核形式。但考虑到第 152 条至第 154 条中对公证级别的要求，以及第五篇第 2 章、第 3 章中关于限制、禁止或不当行为的规定，并参考与公证业务网络、辖区、总部、级别和公证处数量相关的特别法案，只要候选人满足就职要求，省长、州长和专区长即可任命正式岗位公证员。

法院将在 1970 年 7 月 9 日前向省长、州长或地方行政长官发送候选人名单，之后各级行政长官应在收到名单后 5 日内指派公证员。

多米尼克

多米尼克公证人法

CHAPTER 5:71
NOTARIES PUBLIC ACT
An Act to provide for the appointment of notaries public
24th November 1941

第 5：71 章
公证人法
规定公证人的任命的法案
1941 年 11 月 24 日

1. Short title

This Act may be cited as the Notaries Public Act.

2. Appointment of notaries public

It shall be lawful for the Chief Justice, on being satisfied that a person applying to be appointed and enrolled as a notary public to practise within the State is legally and in all other respects qualified and fit therefor, to grant a commission or licence under his or her hand and the seal of the Supreme Court authorising that person to practise within the State and every person, upon the issue to him or her of such commission or licence, shall pay into the Treasury a fee of fifty dollars.

3. Duties of notary public

Every notary public shall discharge the duties assigned to the office by the laws of the United Kingdom and of the State and by the practice of commerce.

4. Notary public may refuse to act

(1) In all cases where the circumstances appear to the notary suspicious and not warranting the protest or other notarial act demanded, he or she shall refuse to act; but any person who considers himself or herself aggrieved by the refusal of the notary to note any protest, or to do any other notarial act demanded, may apply to the High Court for an order calling upon the notary to act in the execution of his or her office, and, before the order is applied for, notice of the application shall be given to the notary, and

1. 简称

本法简称为《公证人法》。

2. 公证人的任命

大法官应判断申请任命或注册成为公证人从而在本州内执业的申请人的合法性，在该人具备其他方面所有的资质后，颁发由大法官签名和最高法院盖章的委任状或执照，授权该人在该州内执业。每一位被授予委任状或执照的人都应向财政部支付 50 美元的费用。

3. 公证人的职责

每一位公证人都应按照英联邦以及该州的法律和商业惯例履行指定的职责。

4. 公证人可拒绝公证的情形

（1）在任何情况下，如公证人存有疑虑，且没有出具拒绝承兑证书或执行其他公证行为的正当理由，公证人可以拒绝执行；但如果该人认为公证人拒绝出具拒绝承兑书或拒绝完成其他要求的公证行为侵犯其合法权利，可以向高等法院申请令状指令该公证人履行职务，并在申请令状之前，将该申请的通知传达给该公证人或递交格林达纳内与该拒绝承兑书有利益关系的人。

to such persons, if any, in Grenada as are interested in the subject of the protest.

(2) When any protest or other notarial act is refused to be noted or done, the notary shall note on the logbook, bill of exchange, or other document, his or her refusal, with his or her signature and the date of refusal.

5. Punishment of notary public for fraud, etc.

Any notary or any other person who—

(a) willfully certifies or propounds any false statement or document; or

(b) fraudulently, with intent to deceive, conceals, withholds, or perverts any fact or document pertinent to the subject of protest or other notarial act,

is liable to imprisonment for two years.

6. Penalty on unqualified person acting as notary public

Any person not appointed under this Act and not sworn as a notary public in manner hereinafter provided who hereafter practise as a notary public or does any notarial act is liable to a fine of three thousand dollars; and if any notary public permit his name to be used for or on account of any person not being a notary public, and complaint thereof is made in a summary way to the High Court, and the Court is satisfied that the notary has so offended, the Court shall order him or her to be struck off from the roll of notaries public, and thereupon he or she shall be struck off and be for ever disabled from practising as a notary public, or doing any notarial act in Grenada.

7. Enrolment of notary and oath to be taken by him or her

Before practising as a notary public or doing any notarial act every person already appointed or hereafter to be appointed a notary public shall cause his or her commission, licence or faculty to be enrolled in the office of the Registrar of the Supreme Court, who is hereby required to enrol it upon the payment of a fee of fifteen dollars, and he shall also, before practising aforesaid, make and subscribe in a book to be kept in the office of the said Registrar the following oath before a judge of The High Court—

"I, A.B., do swear that I will faithfully make contracts or instruments for or between any party or parties requiring the same and I will not add or diminish anything, without the knowledge and consent of such party or parties, that may alter the substance of the fact. I will not make or attest any act, contract, or instrument in which I shall know there is violence or fraud, and in all things I will act uprightly

（2）当公证人拒绝且出具拒绝承兑证书或拒绝完成其他的公证行为时，应当在其工作日志、汇票或其他文件中记录"拒绝"，并附上其签名和拒绝日期。

5. 对公证人欺诈等行为的处罚

任何公证人或其他人：

（a）故意担保或提出任何错误的声明或文件；或者

（b）欺诈、故意欺骗、隐瞒或歪曲与该拒绝承兑事项或其他公证行为相关的事实或文件，

将被处以两年监禁。

6. 对未获得执业资质的人从事公证行为的惩罚

任何未受本法任命或未经宣誓的公证人，如果作为公证人进行执业或作出任何公证行为，将被处以3000美元的罚款；如果任何公证人允许他人使用其名字或由于该人不是公证人而受到指控，由此产生的申诉会通过简易程序到达高等法院，法院确信该公证人确有违法后，将指令将其从公证人名册中除名，除名之后其将永不得再成为一名公证人或在该州内进行任何的公证行为。

7. 公证人的宣誓和注册

在担任公证人或作出公证行为之前，每一位已被任命或将被任命的公证人必须将他的委任状、执照或执业资格证在最高法院司法常务官办公室中进行登记，并支付15美元的费用。前述人员在执业之前，必须将宣誓在司法常务官的办公室的登记簿册中记录并签字，并在高等法院法官面前宣誓：

"我×××，庄严宣誓我将会忠实地为任何一方当事人或要求相同的双方当事人制作合同或文书工作，我不会在不知情或未获一方或双方当事人同意的情况下添加或减少任何可能会改变事实真相的事项。我不会制作或公证任何我认为带有暴力、欺诈的行为、合同或文书，我将会穷尽我的技能和知识，正直而公正地执行公证人的事务。上帝保佑。"

and justly in the business of a notary public, according to the best of my skill and knowledge. SO HELP ME GOD."

And the Registrar shall keep an alphabetical list of all persons so appointed and sworn as notaries public, which shall be called and be the roll of notaries public.

8. Suspension, etc., of notary public to be determined by High Court

No notary public appointed and sworn as aforesaid shall be deprived of his or her commission, licence, or faculty or be suspended from the performance of any act appertaining or belonging to his or her office, unless he or she is guilty of some crime, misdemeanour, gross misconduct, negligence, or unskilfulness, which must be represented to be heard and determined by the High Court in a summary way, and if any notary shall be thereupon condemned, his name shall be struck off the roll by order of the Court, and he or she shall be disabled thenceforth from performing any notarial act whatever, or if the circumstances of the case are such as, in the opinion of the Court, justify a lesser punishment, he shall be suspended from the exercise of his or her office and from the performance of any act appertaining or belonging thereto for such period as to the Court may seem just.

9. District having no notary public, magistrate may be appointed to act

In the event of public inconvenience arising in any district in the State from being no notary public resident therein, it shall be lawful for the Chief Justice to appoint the magistrate of the district to be a notary public, and any magistrate so appointed shall during the President's pleasure have the powers of a notary public, shall be subject to the provisions contained in sections 3, 4 and 5, and shall be entitled to recover the same fees as other notaries.

10. Fees payable to notaries public

The fees in the Schedule shall be payable to and recoverable by notaries public to their own use in respect of the services therein enumerated.

Schedule $ c
Notary's Fees of Office

  1.Noting protest on bill of exchange or promissory note ··5.00

  2.Extending protest on bill or note ··············12.00

  3.Presenting a bill or note ························5.00

  For every additional mile beyond the first mile from

8．由高等法院决定公证人的停职等处理

前述未任命和宣誓的公证人应被剥夺委任状、执照及执业资质，或暂停任何属于职务或与职务相关的行为，除犯有某些罪名、存在轻罪或严重的不当行为、疏忽大意或无法胜任职务外，均将由高等法院派代表出席听审并以简易的方式决定。任何公证人如果受到处罚，高等法院会下令将其从公证人名册中除名，此后他将不得再从事任何的公证行为；但如果根据法院的意见，公证人只被处以较轻的惩罚，则其在听证后的一段时期内将被暂停任何属于职务或与职务相关的公证行为。

9．在没有公证人的地区，该地方法官可被任命为公证人

在州内的某些地区，若由于没有定居的公证人而导致民众不便，首席大法官可依法任命地方法官作为公证人。根据总统的授权，该地方法官享有公证人的权力，并应受本法在第3条、第4条和第5条中相关规定的约束，且有权收取与其他公证人相同的费用。

10. 公证人费用表

表中列举了应向公证人支付的费用以及对公证人为提供服务而支出费用的补偿标准。

附表（单位：美元）
公证行为收费

  1. 汇票和本票的拒绝承兑书················5.00

  2. 延长本票或汇票的拒绝承兑书·············12.00

  3. 提交票据······························5.00

  （在公证处以外办理的公证事务每一英里加收24

the place of business of the notary, an additional sum of twenty-four cents

 4. Minuting or noting ship's protest··············6.00
 5. Extending ship's protest 25 cents per folio of 100 words or a minimum fee of··············15.00
 6. Furnishing copy of extended protest 15 cents per folio of 100 words or a minimum fee of··············9.00
 7. Declaration thereto for the Master, and for each additional declarant··············1.50
 8. Attestation to any document··············15.00
 9. Each attendance··············5.00

Translations

 10. From French, Spanish, Danish, German, or Swedish, per folio of 100 words··············2.50
 11. From Latin, per folio of 100 words··············3.00
 12. From Russian··············5.00
 13. Attestation to translation··············7.5
 14. Translation of common attestation to power for stocks··············8.00

美分）

 4. 登记海事报告··············6.00
 5. 延长海事报告每页100个字25美分或最低不低于··············15.00
 6. 提供延长异议副本每页100个字15美分或最低不低于··············9.00
 7. 声明人以及每一个附加的声明人··············1.50
 8. 对任何文件的认证··············15.00
 9. 每一次出勤··············5.00

翻译

 10. 从法语、西班牙语、丹麦语、德语或瑞典语翻译，每页100个字··············2.5
 11. 从拉丁语翻译，每页100个字··············3.00
 12. 从俄语翻译··············5.00
 13. 对翻译的公证··············7.5
 14. 对股权的普通公证书的翻译··············8.0

多米尼克公证人法修正案

BE IT ENACTED by the Parliment of the Commonwealth of Dominica as follows:

Short title

1 This Act may be cited as the –
NOTARIES PUBLIC (AMENDMENT)ACT 1995

Interpretation

2. In this Act the Notaries Public Act is referred to as "the Act"

Amendment of Section 2 of the Act

3. Section 2 of the Act is amended by replacing—
(a) the word "pratise" with the word "practise"; and
(b) the word "fifty" with the word "one hundred and fifty";

Amendment of Section 7 of the Act

4. Section 7 of the Act is amended by replacing—
(a) the word "fifteen" with the word "fifty"; and
(b) the word "pratising" with the word "practising";
Passed in the House of Assembly this 4th day of January,1995.

本修正案由多米尼克联邦议会制定,如下:

简称
1. 本法简称为《公证人法案 1995 年(修正)版》。

释义
2. 公证人法案在该法中称为"法案"。

该法案第二章节的修正
3. 对法案第二章节作如下修改:
(a)单词"pratise"替换为"practise";以及
(b)单词"fifty"替换为"one hundred and fifty"

该法案第七章节的修正
4. 对法案第七章节作如下修改:
(a)单词"fifteen"替换为"fifty";以及
(b)单词"pratising"替换为"practising";
1995 年 1 月 4 日由议会通过。

圭亚那

圭亚那公证人法

LAWS OF GUYANA Public Notaries L.R.O. 3/1998 CHAPTER 4:02	圭亚那法典 公证人 执照税务署 1998 年 3 月 第 4:02 章

PUBLIC NOTARIES ACT

ARRANGEMENT OF SECTIONS

1. Short title.
2. Appointment of public notary.
3. Oath to be taken by notary.
4. Register to be kept.
5. Fees not to be in excess of those prescribed.
6. Proceedings in case of misconduct of notary.
7. Offences.

1. This Act may be cited as the Public Notaries Act.

2. (1) The President may by warrant under his hand and seal appoint a legal practitioner of not less than ten years' standing to be a public notary, hereinafter referred to as a "notary".

(2) Notaries may be appointed for Guyana or for any of the counties of Demerara, Essequibo or Berbice.

(3) A notary appointed by the President shall perform the same duties and exercise the same functions as a notary in Guyana immediately before the 26th May, 1966.

3. A notary before being admitted to and entering on the duties of his office shall take and subscribe the oath set out in the Schedule before such person as the President shall appoint generally or specially.

4. The Registrar of the Supreme Court shall keep a register in which he shall enter the name of every person who shall be appointed and admitted to the office of notary and the date of his appointment and admission.

公证法

章节安排

1. 简称
2. 公证人的指定
3. 公证人宣誓
4. 注册
5. 不超过规定的费用
6. 公证人不当行为的诉讼
7. 犯罪及处罚

1. 本法应称为《公证人法》。

2.（1）总统可以手令的形式签发授权，指定一名执业不少于 10 年的法律职业人为公证人，以下简称"公证人"。

（2）公证人可以被指定为圭亚那公证人或德梅拉拉、埃塞奎博或伯比斯等地区的公证人。

（3）总统任命的公证人应与在 1966 年 5 月 26 日之前被授予公证人资格的圭亚那公证人履行相同的职责、提供同样的服务。

3. 公证人在被承认并履行其职务之前，应在由总统一般或特别指定的人员面前，根据附表中所载的誓词宣誓。

4. 最高法院司法登记官应备存一份登记册，并在其中记载任何被委任和被承认为公证人之姓名及其任命和录用的日期。

5. A notary shall not charge for the performance of any of the duties of his office any sum in excess of the fee which is prescribed or fixed by rules of court under the High Court Act or under any other Act.

6. (1) If a notary shall be convicted of any offence, or be adjudged guilty of any misconduct whether in his capacity of notary or otherwise, the court before which he is so convicted or by which he is so adjudged shall make a report thereof to the President, the President may revoke his warrant of appointment and direct the Registrar to remove the name of the notary from the register.

(2) If any person shall make a complaint on oath charging a notary with misconduct in his office the President may appoint a fit and proper person to inquire into the facts and report thereon to the President and if the President is of opinion that the notary has been guilty of misconduct he may suspend him from practice for a specified time or revoke his warrant of appointment and direct the Registrar to remove his name from the register.

(3) When a notary has been suspended from practice or the Registrar in pursuance of a direction by the President removes the name of a notary from the register he shall cause notice of the fact to be published in the Gazette.

(4) Every complaint charging a notary with misconduct shall contain a statement of the material facts on which the person complaining relies.

7. If any person who is suspended from practice or whose name is not on the register shall for reward make, do, exercise or perform any act matter or thing appertaining or belonging to the office, function or practice of a notary he shall be liable on summary conviction to a fine of nineteen thousand five hundred dollars and to imprisonment for four months.

SCHEDULE

FORM OF OATH

I, A.B., do swear that I will faithfully exercise the office of a public notary ; I will faithfully make contracts or instruments for or between any party or parties requiring the same, and I will not add or diminish any thing without the knowledge and consent of such party or parties that may alter the substance of the fact ; I will not make or attest any act, contract or instrument in which I shall know there is violence or fraud ; and in all things I will act uprightly and justly in the business of a public notary, according to the best of my skill and ability. So help me God.

5. 公证人履行职务不得在《高等法院法》或其他法律法规的规定外超额征收任何费用。

6. （1）公证人如果以诉讼或其他方式被认定犯有任何罪行或被判定违法，作出有罪判决或违法裁定的法院应当向总统报告。总统可以撤销对该公证人的任用令，并指示登记官从公证人名册中将其除名。

（2）如果任何人通过公证处投诉不法行为的公证人，总统可以委任合适的人调查事实，并将结果向总统报告。如果总统认为公证人已经犯有不当行为，可以责令其暂停执业一段指定的时间或撤销其任用令，并指示登记官将其从公证人名册中除名。

（3）当公证人暂停执业或登记官依照总统的指示，将公证人的姓名从公证人名册中除名时，须将该事实在宪报通报。

（4）每份对不法行为的公证人的投诉书，均应载有对投诉人所指控的重大事实的陈述。

7. 如果任何已暂停执业的公证人或不在公证人名册上的人员以营利为目的，行使或执行任何涉及或属于公证人员的职务或事务，职能或执业的事项，一经简易程序定罪，可对其处以9500元罚款及4个月监禁。

附表

宣誓格式

我×××，发誓，我将忠实地为任何一方或双方或有相同要求的当事人作出合同或文书，如果没有该当事人的知情和同意，我不会增加或减少或在任何方面对该事务作出实质性的改变。我不会作出或证明任何我知道有暴力或欺诈的行为；在所有公证事务上，我会穷尽我的技术和知识，正义公正地行事。上帝保佑。

格林达纳

格林达纳公证人法

CHAPTER 212 NOTARIES PUBLIC ACT

An Act to provide for the appointment and duties of notaries public, and for matters connected therewith.

[Amended by Act No. 26 of 1990, Act No. 52 of 1991.]

[1st May, 1897.]

1. Short title

This Act may be cited as the Notaries Public Act.

2. Appointment of notaries public

It shall be lawful for the Chief Justice, on being satisfied that a person applying to be appointed and enrolled as a notary public to practise within Grenada is legally and in all other respects qualified and fit therefor, to grant a commission or licence under his or her hand and the seal of the Supreme Court authorising that person to practise within Grenada for a period not exceeding five years, and every person, upon the issue to him or her of such commission or licence, shall pay into the Treasury a fee of fifty dollars.

3. Duties of notary public

Every notary public shall discharge the duties assigned to the office by the laws of the United Kingdom and of Grenada and by the practice of commerce.

4. Notary public may refuse to act

(1) In all cases where the circumstances appear to the notary suspicious and not warranting the protest or other notarial act demanded, he or she shall refuse to act:

Provided always that any person who considers himself or herself aggrieved by the refusal of the notary to note any protest, or to do any other notarial act demanded, may apply to the High Court for an order calling upon the notary to act in the execution of his or her office, and,

第212章 公证人法

本法规定公证人的任命及职责,以及有关事宜。

[1990年NO.26法案修订,1991年NO.52法案修订]

[1897年5月1日]

1. 简称

本法简称为《公证人法》。

2. 公证人的任命

大法官应判断申请任命或注册成为公证人从而在本州内执业的申请人的合法性,在该人具备其他方面所有的资质后,颁发由大法官签名和最高法院盖章的委任状或执照,授权该人在该州内执业,但不得超过5年,并且每一个被授予该委任状或执照的人都应向财政部支付50美元的费用。

3. 公证人的职责

每一位公证人都应按照英联邦以及格林达纳的法律和商业惯例去履行指定的职责。

4. 公证人可拒绝执行的情形

(1)在任何情况下,如公证人存有疑虑,且没有出具拒绝承兑证书或执行其他公证行为的正当理由,公证人可以拒绝执行;

如果该人认为公证人拒绝出具拒绝承兑书或拒绝完成其他要求的公证行为侵犯其合法权利,可以向高等法院申请令状指令该公证人履行职务,并在申请令状之前将该申请的通知传达给该公证人或递交格林达纳内与该拒绝承兑书有利益关系的人。

before the order is applied for, notice of the application shall be given to the notary, and to such persons, if any, in Grenada as are interested in the subject of the protest.

(2) When any protest or other notarial act is refused to be noted or done, the notary shall note on the logbook, bill of exchange, or other document, his or her refusal, with his or her signature and the date of refusal.

5. Punishment of notary public for fraud, etc.

If the notary or any other person—

(a) wilfully certifies or propounds any false statement or document; or

(b) fraudulently, with intent to deceive, conceals, withholds, or perverts any fact or document pertinent to the subject of protest or other notarial act,

he shall be guilty of an offence and liable, on summary conviction, to imprisonment for two years.

6. Penalty on unqualified person acting as notary public

Every person not in possession of a valid commission, licence or faculty under the provisions of this Act or according to English law, and sworn as a notary public in manner hereinafter provided, who shall hereafter practise as a notary public, or do any notarial act, shall forfeit and pay for each offence the sum of three thousand dollars, to be sued for and recovered by the Attorney-General in the High Court; and if any notary public shall permit his or her name to be used for or on account of any person not being a notary public, and complaint thereof is made in a summary way to the High Court, and the Court is satisfied that the notary has so offended, the Court shall order him or her to be struck off from the roll of notaries public, and thereupon he or she shall be struck off, and be for ever disabled from practising as a notary public, or doing any notarial act in Grenada.

7. Enrolment of notary and oath to be taken by him or her

Before practising as a notary public or doing any notarial act every person (except the Registrar of the Supreme Court) already appointed or hereafter to be appointed a notary public, shall cause his or her commission, licence, or faculty to be enrolled in the office of the Registrar of the Supreme Court, who is hereby required to enrol it upon the payment of a fee of three dollars, and he or she shall also, before practising as aforesaid, make and subscribe in a book to be kept in the office of the said Registrar the following oath before the Chief Justice—

（2）当公证人拒绝出具拒绝承兑书或拒绝完成其他的公证行为时，应当在其工作日志、汇票或其他文件中记录"拒绝"，并附上其签名和拒绝日期。

5. 对公证人欺诈等行为的处罚

如果公证人或任何其他人：

（a）故意担保或提出任何错误的声明或文件；或者

（b）欺诈、故意欺骗、隐瞒或歪曲与该异议事项或其公证行为相关的事实或文件，

将构成犯罪，并按照简易程序被处以两年监禁。

6. 对未获得执业资格的人从事公证行为的处罚

根据英国公证法案规定，如果该人未持有有效的委任状、执照或资质以及未当场进行宣誓而以公证人自居或从事任何公证行为，将为其每一次的违法行为支付3000美元的罚款，由高等法院的检察长进行起诉和追缴；如果任何公证人允许他人使用其名字或由于该人不是公证人而受到指控，由此产生的申诉会通过简易程序到达高等法院，法院确信该公证人确有违法后，将指令将其从公证人名册中除名，除名之后其将永不得再成为一名公证人或在该州内进行任何的公证行为。

7. 公证人的注册和宣誓

在担任公证人或作出公证行为之前，（除最高法院的司法常务官外）每一位已被任命或将被任命的公证人必须将他的委任状、执照或执业资格证在最高法院司法常务官办公室中进行登记，并支付3美元的费用。前述人员在执业之前，必须将宣誓在司法常务官的办公室的登记簿册中记录并签字，并在首席大法官面前宣誓：

"I, A.B., do swear that I will faithfully make contracts or instruments for or between any party or parties requiring the same and I will not add or diminish anything, without the knowledge and consent of such party or parties, that may alter the substance of the fact. I will not make or attest any act, contract, or instrument in which I shall know there is violence or fraud, and in all things I will act uprightly and justly in the business of a notary public, according to the best of my skill and knowledge. SO HELP ME GOD."

And the Registrar shall keep an alphabetical list of all persons so appointed and sworn as notaries public, which shall be called and be the roll of notaries public.

8. Suspension, etc., of notary public to be determined by High Court

No notary public appointed and sworn as aforesaid shall during the period of validity of his or her commission, licence or faculty be deprived of his or her commission, licence, or faculty, or be suspended from the performance of any act appertaining or belonging to his or her office, unless he or she is guilty of some crime, misdemeanour, gross misconduct, negligence, or unskilfulness, which must be represented to be heard and determined by the High Court in a summary way, and if any notary shall be thereupon condemned, his or her name shall be struck off the roll by order of the Court, and he or she shall be disabled thenceforth from performing any notarial act whatever, or if the circumstances of the case are such as, in the opinion of the Court, justify a lesser punishment, he or she shall be suspended from the exercise of his or her office and from the performance of any act appertaining or belonging thereto for such period as to the Court may seem just.

9. Saving of existing right of Registrar to act as notary public

Nothing herein shall be construed as preventing the Registrar of the Supreme Court from acting as a notary public as provided by section 65 of the West Indies Associated States Supreme Court (Grenada) Act, Chapter 336.

10. In district having no notary public, magistrate may be appointed to act

In the event of public inconvenience arising in any district in Grenada from there being no notary public resident therein, it shall be lawful for the Chief Justice to appoint the magistrate of the district to be a notary public, and any magistrate so appointed shall during the Governor-General's pleasure have the powers of a notary public,

"我×××，庄严宣誓我将会忠实地为任何一方当事人或要求相同的双方当事人制作合同或文书工作，我不会在不知情或未获一方或双方当事人同意的情况下添加或减少任何可能会改变事实真相的事项。我不会制作或公证任何我认为带有暴力、欺诈的行为、合同或文书，我将会穷尽我的技能和知识，正直而公正地执行公证人的事务。上帝保佑。"

司法常务官应当将所有被任命和宣誓成为公证人的人按字母顺序排列进行登记，作为公证人名册。

8. 由高等法院决定公证人的停职等处理

前述未任命和宣誓的公证人应被剥夺委任状、执照及执业资质，或暂停任何属于职务或与职务相关的行为，除犯有某些罪名、存在轻罪或严重的不当行为、疏忽大意或无法胜任职务外，均将由高等法院派代表出席听审并以简易的方式决定。任何公证人如果受到处罚，高等法院会下令将其从公证人名册中除名，此后他将不得再从事任何的公证行为；但如果根据法院的意见，公证人只被处以较轻的惩罚，则其在听证后的一段时期内应被暂停任何属于职务或与职务相关的公证行为。

9. 保留司法常务官作为公证人的既得权利

西部独立州最高法院（格林达纳）法案第65节、336章的规定不可被解释为阻止最高法院的司法常务官作为一名公证人执业。

10. 在没有公证人的地区，该地方法官可被任命为公证人

在格林达纳的某些地区，由于没有居民公证人而导致民众不便，首席大法官可依法任命地方法官作为公证人。根据总督的授权，地方法官拥有公证人的权力，并受法案在第3条、第4条和第5条中相关规定的约束，且有权收取与其他公证人相同的费用。

shall be subject to the provisions contained in sections 3, 4 and 5 hereof, and shall be entitled to recover the same fees as other notaries.

11. Fees payable to notaries public

The fees in the Schedule shall be payable to and recoverable by notaries public to their own use in respect of the services therein enumerated.

Schedule
NOTARIES PUBLIC ACT

Notary's Fees of Office ($ C)

1. Noting protest on bill of exchange or promissory note ···1.25
2. Extending protest on bill or note ····················3.75
3. Presenting a bill or note ·································1.25

For every additional mile beyond the first mile from the place of business of the notary, an additional sum of twenty-five cents

4. Minuting or noting ship's protest ··················2.00
5. Extending ship's protest 25 cents per folio of 100 words or a minimum fee of ······································5.05
6. Furnishing copy of extended protest 15 cents per folio of 100 words or a minimum fee of ·················2.55
7. Declaration thereto for the Master, and for each additional declarant ···0.25
8. Attestation to any document ························4.00
9. Each attendance ··1.50

Translations

10. From French, Spanish, Danish, German, or Swedish, per folio of 100 words ···························0.50
11. From Latin, per folio of 100 words ············0.60
12. From Russian ··2.00
13. Attestation to translation ····························2.30
14. Translation of common attestation to power for stocks ···2.50

11. 公证人费用表

表中列举了公务员的收费以及对公证人为提供服务而支出费用的补偿标准。

附表
公证行为

公证机构费用（单位：美元）

1. 汇票和本票的拒绝承兑书 ······························ 1.25

2. 延长本票或汇票的拒绝承兑书 ····················· 3.75

3. 提交票据 ··· 1.25
（在公证处以外办理的公证事务每一英里加收 24 美分）

4. 登记海事报告 ··· 2.00

5. 延长海事报告每页 100 个字 25 美分或最低不低于 ··· 5.05

6. 提供延长异议副本每页 100 个字 15 美分或最低不低于 ··· 2.55

7. 声明人及每一个附加声明人 ························· 0.25

8. 对任何文件的认证 ······································· 4.00

9. 每一次出勤 ··· 1.5

翻译

10. 从法语、西班牙语、丹麦语、德语或瑞典语，每页 100 个字 ··· 0.5

11. 从拉丁语翻译，每页 100 个字 ················· 0.6

12. 从俄语翻译 ··· 2.00

13. 对翻译的公证 ··· 2.30

14. 对股权的普通公证书的翻译 ······················· 2.50

海地

海地公证人考试规则

ARRÊTÉ

Réglementant les détails de l'examen en Notariat et fixant le mode de versement et d'affectation du cautionnement

DARTIGUENAVE
Président de la République

Vu l'article 75 de la Constitution;
Vu la loi du 24 Février 1919,
Considérant qu'il y a lieu de pouvoir aux détails relatifs à l'examen en notariat, à la fonction du jury et à l'époque où il doit siéger;
Considérant que les notariats et les intéressants doivent être fixés sur le mode de versement et sur l'affectation du cautionnement, en attendant la création de la caisse dépôts et consignations:
Sur le rapport du Secrétaire d'Etat de la Justice,
Et de l'avis du Conseil des Secrétaires d'Etat,
ARRETÉ

Art.1- Deux sessions d'examen auront lieu, chaque année, dans la première quinzaine de juin et de Décembre.
Art.2- L'examen aura lieu sous le contrôle du Commissaire du Gouvernement près le Tribunal de Première Instance et de l'Inspecteur des Écoles en cas d'empêchement de leur part, sous le contrôle d'un substitut et d'un sous-inspecteur spécialement délégués.
Art.3- Le Jury siégera au Parquet ou au local de l'Inspection selon que le Commissaire du Gouvernement le jugera convenable dans l'intérêt des postulants et des examinateurs.
Art.4- Le Jury sera composé de deux notariat

法令

公证员考试细则的规定，确定支付方式以及规定担保金的用途

达蒂格纳夫
共和国总统

基于宪法第 75 条，
基于 1919 年 2 月 24 日法律，
考虑到需要有相关的细则规定公证员考试、考试委员会职责以及特殊时期；

考虑到公证员和当事人需要确定的支付方式以及需要明晰担保金的用途，同时创立提存机构：

根据国家司法部长的报告，
以及国务卿议会的意见，
决定

第1条　每年有两季考试，分别是在六月的前15日和十二月的前15日。
第2条　考试在第一上诉法庭指派的政府特派员和教育署监督员的指导下进行，如果他们不能履行职责，则在一名替代者和一名特别委派的副监督员的指导下进行。

第3条　政府特派员裁定考试委员会符合主考人和应试者的利益时，考试委员会在检察院或地方检察机构中占有席位。

第4条　考试委员会由两名政府特派员指定的公

désignés par le Commissaire du Gouvernement, deux avocats désignés par le Bâtonnier ou le Doyen, un professeur de lettres désigné par l'Inspection.

Le Commissaire du Gouvernement et l'Inspecteur auront voix délibérative et prépondérante en cas de partage

Art.5- En dehors du titre d'avocat ou de licencié en droit seuls les examens subis dans les conditions édictées par la loi du 24 Février 1919 et les présents règlements, sur le nouveau programme, habiliteront à postuler la fonction de notariat.

Art.6- Les examens seront subis en deux jours consécutifs : le premier jour consacré à l'épreuve orale qui durera une heure; le deuxième jour a l'épreuve écrite qui durera deux heures au moins, sans l'aide d'aucun formulaire.

Art.7- Les notes seront données à la majorité des membres du Jury, comme suit: 6-très bien; 5-bien; 4-assez bien; 3-passable; 2-médiocre; 1-mal; 0-nul.

Art.8- L'admission à une épreuve donne à l'étudiant le droit de se présenter dans six mois et le refus pour les deux épreuves impliques l'ajournement à un an.

Art.9- En attendant la première session règlementaire, Le Secrétaire d'Etat de la Justice pourra accorder une session extraordinaire à ceux qui, réunissant les conditions de la loi, désirent subir l'examen.

Art.10- Le postulant qui désire se présenter à une session d'examen en fera la déclaration huit jours d'avance au Parquet du Commissaire du Gouvernement en y déposant:

1°. Son acte de naissance ou toute autre pièce établissement son identité et son âge;

2°. Le certificat de stage de deux ans chez un notariat en sa qualité de clerc;

3°. Son brevet de capacité ou un certificat attestant qu'il a fait ses études classiques au moins jusqu'en quatrième inclusivement dans un Lycée ou dans une institution privée d'enseignement secondaire;

4°. Un certificat de bonnes vies et mœurs signé du Magistrat Communal et du Juge de Paix de sa demeure effective.

Art.11- En attendant la loi sur la création de la caisse de dépôts et consignations, la Banque Nationale de la République d'Haïti recevra en sa maison principale ou dans ses succursales, à titre de dépôt, le cautionnement exigé des notaires. Ce dépôt ne sera levé en tout ou en partie qu'en vertu d'une décision la passée en force de chose jugée.

Art.12- Ce dépôt est affecté à la garantie des con-

证员，两名律师协会会长或院长指定的律师，一名检察院指定的文学教师组成。

如果意见相同，政府特派员和监督员享有表决权（和裁定权）。

第5条 除去持有律师执照或法学学士学位的人，在新的考试大纲下，只有符合1919年2月24日法律中规定的条件并通过现行条例规定的考试才能得到公证员资格授权。

第6条 考试应在连续的两天之内进行：第一天进行口语考试，持续一小时；第二天进行笔试，至少持续两小时，不可以借助任何汇编材料。

第7条 考试分数由考试委员会的绝大多数成员给出，分为以下等级：6—非常好；5—好；4—良好；3—及格；2—不足；1—差；0—无。

第8条 任意一项测试的准考证赋予考生在六个月内参加考试的权利，两项测试的拒考信意味着考生须等到下一年。

第9条 如果符合第一考试季的要求，国家司法部长可以允许那些满足法定条件，希望考试的考生在特殊考试季应考。

第10条 要求参加考试的考生，应当在考试前8日向政府特派机构的检察院提出申请，并提供以下资料：

1. 出生证明或其他所有可以证明其身份和年龄的文件；

2. 跟随公证员，担任书记员两年的实习证明；

3. 最高学历的副本，或能够证实在高中或私立中等教育机构接受过直至四年级以上传统教育的证明；

4. 市镇治安法院和实际住所地治安法官签署的良好行为记录证明。

第11条 在法律设立提存机构的时期内，海地共和国国家银行主要办公机构或分支机构，以保管的名义，接受公证员的强制担保。只有经过司法裁定，担保金才能全部或部分被启用。

第12条 本担保金为公证员在执业过程中必然

damnations que pourront en courir les notaires pour fautes professionnelles commises dans l'exercice ou à l'occasion de l'exercice de leurs fonctions.

Art.13- Le Commissaire du Gouvernement pourra demander à la Banque tout certificat attestant le défaut de dépôt, la diminution ou l'épuisement du cautionnement que le notaire est tenu de compléter ou de rétablir dans les six mois.

Art.14- Le présent arrêté entrera immédiatement en vigueur et sera exécuté à la diligence du Secrétaire d'État de la Justice

Donné au Palais National ce jour 12 Mars 1919 An, 215ème de l'Indépendance.

Par le Président: DARTIGUENAVE

Le Secrétaire d'Etat de la Justice: C. BENOIT

或偶然发生的职业性错误而产生的罚金作担保。

第13条 政府特派员可以要求银行出具缺少担保金的证明书，担保金不足或用尽时公证员需要在六个月内补足或重新缴纳。

第14条 本法令颁布之时立即生效，在国家司法部长的建议下实行。

提交国家机关于1919年3月12日，
第215号独立文件。
由主席：达蒂格纳夫
国家司法部长：C.本努瓦

海地公证人法

LOI	**法律**
Sur le Notariat	**关于公证人团体**
DARTIGUENAVE	达蒂格纳夫
Président de la République	海地共和国总统
Vu l'art 55 de la Constitution	基于宪法第 55 条
Sur la rapport du Secrétaire d'Etat de la Justice	根据国家司法部长的报告
Et de l'avis du Conseil des Secrétaires d'Etat	以及国务卿会议的意见
Et le Conseil d'Etat a voté la loi suivante	以及国家议会投票通过以下法律
A PROPOSÉ	提出

Art.1- Les notaires sont les fonctionnaires publics établis pour recevoir tous les actes et contrats auxquels les parties doivent ou veulent donner le caractère d'authenticité attaché aux actes de l'autorité publique et pour assurer la date, en conserver le dépôt, en délivrer des grosses, expéditions et extraits.

第 1 条 公证员是由公权力设置的公职人员，职责是接收所有当事人需要或者想要得到公权力确认、给予公证性的文件和合同，同时确认日期，提存，发放判决副本、公证书副本和证书副本。

Art.2- Ils sont nommés par le Président d'Haïti, sur la présentation du Secrétaire d'Etat de la Justice dans les formes et conditions de la présente loi.

第 2 条 公证员由国家总统根据国家司法部长依照下列法律规定的形式和条件提名任命。

Ils sont placés sous la surveillant et le contrôle du Commissaire du Gouvernement près le Tribunal de 1ère Instance et justiciables de ce Tribunal. Ils n'ont droit d'exercer qu'à partir du jour de leur prestation de serment.

公证员受到由第一上诉法庭指派的政府特派员的监督和控制，该法院有权对他们进行司法裁判。自宣誓之日起，他们有权接受培训。

Art.3- Chaque Notaire est obligé de résider dans le lieu qui lui a été fixé par le Gouvernement et qui est désigné dans sa commission. En cas de contravention, le notaire est considéré comme démissionnaire, et il est pourvu à son remplacement.

第 3 条 每名公证员必须定居在由政府指定的、在他的委任书中指明的地点。如果违反规定，此名公证员被视作辞职，他的职位将被取代。

Art.4- Il est expressément défendu à un notaire d'instrumenter hors de la Commune pour laquelle il est commissionné, à peine de nullité des actes qu'il aura passés, de destitution, et de tous dommages-intérêts envers les parties lésées, au moins que dans des cas graves et pressants, l'autorisation ne soit donnée par le Doyen du Tribunal de 1ère Instance de la partie, le Ministère public préalablement entendu.

第 4 条 公证员在委任地之外制作证书的行为是被禁止的，违反规定制作的证书是无效的，公证员将被革职，并且应向权利受到侵害的一方当事人赔偿损失，除非在严重或紧急的情况下，得到当地第一上诉法庭庭长的授权，并事先应向检察院报告。

Art.5- En attendant un recensement qui permettra de fixer le nombre des notaires en proportion de la population le nombre des notaire est fixé comme suit:

第 5 条 在此期间，基于人口普查的数据，公证员的人数应当与人口数相称，故公证员人数确定为：

12 Notaires pour	Port-au-Prince	1ère classe
8	Cap-Haïtien, Gonaïves	2ème classe
	Les Cayes, Jacmel	
	Port-de-Paix, Jérémie,	3ème classe
	St-Marc	
5	Anse-à-Veau, Miragoâne,	4ème classe
	Petit-Goâve, Aquin,	
	Fort-Liberté, Borgne,	
	Limbé, Logâne,	
	Gde-Rivière du Nord,	
	Plaisance, Trou	
3	Pour les autres Communes	5ème classe

12 名公证员	在"太子港"	第一级别
8 名公证员	在"海地角"、戈纳伊夫	第二级别
	莱凯、雅克梅勒	
5 名公证员	在"和平港"、热雷米	第三级别
	"圣－马克"	
	昂萨沃、米拉格安	第四级别
	小戈阿夫、阿奎纳	
	自由堡、布尔涅	
	利姆贝、罗卡纳	
	北部大河	
	布莱圣斯、图	
3 名公证员	在"其他市镇"	第五级别

Art.6- Les fonctions de notaires sont incompatibles avec celles de l'Ordre judiciaire, administratif et militaire.

Art7- Pour être admis aux fonctions de notaire, il faut:

1° être Haïtien, avoir la jouissance et l'exercice de tous ses droits civils et politiques;

2° être âgé de 25 accomplis;

3° produire un certificat de bonnes vie et mœurs délivré par le Magistrat Communal de la demeure effective du candidat;

4° être porteur d'une commission d'avocat ou d'un diplôme de licencié en droit et justifier d'un stage d'un an au moins, chez notaire, ou être, muni d'un certificat d'aptitude, délivré par la Commission spéciale d'examen conforme au programme annexé à la présente loi;

Sont exempts de l'examen, les Juges des Tribunaux de 1ère Instance, d'Appel et de Cassation qui ont plus de cinq ans de carrière.

Pour être admis à cet examen, le postulat doit justifier d'un stage de deux ans au moins chez un Notaire, et soumettre son certificat d'études secondaires du 1er degré, à défaut de ce certificat, il doit subir un examen qui roulera sur les matières du programme de la dernière année du premier cycle; en cas de concurrence le candidat, porteur du diplôme de licencié en droit, devra être préféré.

Le Secrétaire d'Etat de la Justice est autorisé à prendre des règlements pour fixer les détails relatifs à l'examen, à la fondation de la Commission et à l'époque où celle-ci doit siéger.

Art.8- Les notaires sont tenus de prêter leur ministère

第6条 公证员不可兼任司法、行政、军事的职务。

第7条 被授权行使公证员职责，需要满足：

1. 具有海地国籍，享有并且能够行使全部的民事权利和公民权利；

2. 年满25周岁；

3. 持有实际居住地的社区行政官员开具的良好生活与品德证明；

4. 持有律师职业资格或法学学士学位，和跟随公证员实习至少一年的证明，或者持有由特殊考试委员会根据之后法律规定的章程颁发的资质证明。

第一上诉法庭法官、上诉法院的法官及执业五年以上的最高法院的法官可以免除考试。

希望参加考试的申请者应当跟随公证员实习至少两年，提供第一程度中等教育的学习证明。如果没有此项证明，他应当接受第一阶段最后一年学习课程的整体测试。相同条件下，持有法学学士学位的候选人会被优先录取。

国家司法部长有权制定条例修正不完善的考试细则，创立考试委员会，及特殊时期的考试规则。

第8条 公证员根据请求行使职责；但是他们不

lorsqu'ils en sont requis; mais ils ne sont pas obligés de recevoir des actes injurieux ou diffamatoires contre des tiers, ni ceux dont les énonciations ont été préparées dans un but frauduleux et illicite.

 Art.9- Ils ne pourront recevoir des actes dans lesquels leurs parents ou alliés en ligne directe à tous les degrés, et en ligne collatérale jusqu'au degré d'oncle ou de neveu inclusivement, seraient parties, ou qui contiendraient quelques dispositions en leur faveur.

 Il leur est également défendu d'instrumenter, pour des individus qu'ils ne connaissent pas personnellement, ou dont deux citoyens qu'ils savent dignes de foi ne leur attestent pas les noms, état et demeure ainsi que pour les personnes qui ne seraient ou qui ne leur paraîtraient pas sains d'esprit, ni jouissant de la plénitude de leur raison sous peine de suspensions ou de destitution en cas de fautes graves relevées à leur charge par autorité de Justice.

 Art.10- Les notaires ne peuvent instrumenter qu'en présence de leurs confrères ou de deux haïtiens majeurs, domiciliés dans la commune, ayant la jouissance de leurs droits civils, sachant lire et écrire, sans déroger à ce que prescrit le Code Civil en matière de testament; ils ne peuvent prendre pour témoins les parents ou alliés aux degrés ci-dessus tant des parties que d'eux-mêmes, leurs clercs ou serviteurs.

 Art.11- Deux notaires, parents ou alliés au degré prohibé, ne peuvent concourir au même acte.

 Art.12- Les notaires ne pourront passer vente d'aucune propriété urbaine ou rurale qu'au préalable cette propriété ait été arpentée. Le contrat de vente devra comporter les désignations contées au procès-verbal d'arpentage et mention d'y celui; le numéro de la quittance communale sera mentionné dans l'acte lorsque l'immeuble est sujet à l'impôt locatif le tout sous peine par le notaire qui a reçu l'acte d'être personnellement rendu responsable de tous les dommages et autres conséquences qui pourront résulter de inobservance des présentes.

 Art.13- Les actes des notaires seront écrits sur papier timbré en un seul et même contexte, lisiblement, sans abréviation, blanc, lacune ou intervalle; ils contiendront, outre les noms et lieu de résidence du notaire qui les reçoit, les noms, qualités et demeures des parties, ainsi que de témoins instrumentaires; individus qui y sont sujet: ils énonceront en toutes lettres les sommes et les dates; les procurations des contractants seront annexées à la minute qui fera mention que lecture de l'acte a été faite aux parties: le tout à peine de Cent Cinquante Gourdes d'amende

必接收辱骂或诽谤第三者的材料，也不接收特别为欺骗、违法为目的而准备的材料。

 第9条 公证员不能接收他们父母或所有亲等关系的直系姻亲，以及三等亲以内旁系亲属作为当事人的材料，也不能接收包含其自身利益的文件。

 禁止为身份不明的人，或者为两个值得信赖的公民不为他们证实姓名、社会身份和住所的人，以及为那些不清楚或没有表现出精神健康情况的人制作文书。没有充分的理由说明并且由司法部门判定造成严重失职的，公证员将被处以停职或免职成分。

 第10条 只有当同事或两名成年的、居住在市镇、享有民事权利、受过教育、没有和民法原则相抵触的海地公民在场时，公证员才可以制作文书；父母及上述近亲属，当事人本人，他们的书记员及辅助人员不能担任见证人。

 第11条 两名公证员，父母和法律禁止的近亲属不能在同一份文件中协同工作。

 第12条 公证员不可以允许销售任何城市或农村事先丈量过的不动产。出售合同应当包含丈量面积时的笔录并且提及所在位置；当面临申请人提出不动产房屋租赁税问题时，公证员应当在文书中记录公社收据的编号，所有的损失和其他可被归结为违反法律规定的后果应当由个人负责。

 第13条 公证员出具的文书应当使用盖章的纸张，行文应当采用唯一且前后一致的语境，语句通顺，没有省略词、空白、缺字或间隔；文书应当包括承办公证员的姓名及住所地，当事人的姓名、身份和住所地，以及制作文书时的见证人；需要注意：用文字陈述总额和日期；当事人阅读原稿之后，缔约人的委托书应当附在原稿之后：违反规定的公证将被处以最高150古德的罚款。

contre le notaire contrevenant.

Art.14- Les actes seront signés par les parties, les témoins et les notaires qui en doivent faire mention à la fin de l'acte;

Quant aux parties qui ne savent ou ne peuvent signer, le notaire instrumentant doit également faire mention à la fin de l'acte de leur déclaration à cet égard.

Art.15- Les renvois et apostillas ne pourront sauf, l'exception ci-après, être écrits qu'en marge; ils seront signés et paraphés, à peine de nullité des renvois et apostillas. Si la longueur du renvoi, exige qu'il soit transporté à la fin de l'acte, il devra être non seulement signé ou paraphé comme les renvois écrits en marge, mais encore expressément approuvés par les parties, à peine de nullité du renvoi.

Art.16- Il n'y aura ni surcharge, ni interligne, ni addition, dans le corps de l'acte, et les mots surchargés, interlignés ou ajoutés seront nuls. Les mots qui doivent être rayés le seront de manière que le nombre puisse en être constaté à la marge le tout à peine d'une amende de Soixante Gourdes contre le notaire, ainsi que de tous dommages-intérêts, même de destitution, en cas de fraude.

Art.17- Tous actes de notaires feront foi en justice et seront exécutoires dans toute l'étendue de la République. Néanmoins en cas de poursuite en faux principal, l'exécution de l'acte argué de faux sera suspendue jusqu'à l'issue du procès; en cas de faux incident civil, les Tribunaux pourront, suivant la gravité des circonstances, suspendre provisoirement l'exécution de l'acte.

Art.18- Les notaires seront tenus de garder minute de tous actes qu'ils recevront. Ils ne sont pas néanmoins compris dans la présente disposition, les certificats de vie, procurations spéciales, quittances d'arrérages, de pensions et rentes, et autres actes simples qui, d'après les lois, peuvent être délivrés en brevet.

Art.19- le droit de délivrer des grosses et des expéditions n'appartiendra qu'au notaire possesseur de la minute; néanmoins il pourra délivrer copie d'un acte qui lui aura été déposé pour minute.

Art.20- Les notaires ne pourront se dessaisir d'aucune minute, si ce n'est dans le cas prévus par les lois, et en vertu d'un jugement.

Avant de s'en dessaisir, ils en dresseront et signeront une copie confonde, qui, après avoir été certifié par le Doyen et le Commissaire du Gouvernement du Tribunal de 1ère Instance de leur résidence, sera substitué à la minute dont elle tiendra lieu jusqu'à sa réintégrations.

第 14 条　公证书应当由当事人、见证人和公证员签字，并在结尾处标明。

对于不会或不能签字的当事人，制作文书的公证员同样应当在公证书结尾记载，就这一点进行声明。

第 15 条　除特殊情况外，引文和旁注只能写在页边空白处；引文与旁注需要签字画押，否则引文和旁注无效。如果引文过长，使得它不得不被放置在公证书结尾处，那么该引文不仅应当参照写在页边空白处签字画押，还要得到当事人的明确同意，否则引文无效。

第 16 条　公证书中不能有涂改、插入或者增添的痕迹，涂改、插入或增添的文字无效。需要修改的文字应当在页边空白处记载修改的数量，违者将被处以 60 古德的罚款，并且赔偿全部损失；如果存在欺诈行为，公证员会被免职。

第 17 条　所有公证文书在司法中具有效力，并且在全国范围内具有执行力。如果因为存在重要错误而提起诉讼，则中止公证书存在错误争议的内容的执行，直到案件审理终结；如果存在附带民事诉讼，法院可以根据案件严重程度，中止公证书的执行。

第 18 条　公证员对收到的文件的原稿具有保管义务。尽管在之后的条文中没有明确规定，人身证明、特殊委托书、欠条、养老金和年金，以及其他根据法律规定可以以公证证书的形式发放的简单文件，应当进行保存。

第 19 条　发放判决书副本及公证书副本的权利只有持有原稿的公证员享有；当公证员需要保存原稿时，可以发放文件的复印件。

第 20 条　如果法律没有规定且不是依据司法判决，公证员不能移交任何原件。

在移交原件之前，他们应当起草并签字确认一份与原件一致的复印件，并且要得到住所地第一上诉法庭庭长和政府特派员的确认。复印件将取代原稿的位置，直到重新取回原件。

Art.21- Les notaires ne pourront également, sans l'ordonnance du Doyen du Tribunal de 1ère classe Instance, délivrer expédition, ni donner connaissance des actes à d'autre qu'aux personnes intéressées en nom direct, héritiers ou ayant-droit, à peine de dommages-intérêts, d'une amende de Cent Cinquante Gourdes, et d'être, en cas de récidive, suspendus de leurs fonctions pendant trois mois sauf néanmoins l'exécution des lois et règlements sur le droit d'enregistrement et des lois relatives aux actes qui doivent être publié dans les Tribunaux.

Art.22- En cas de compulser, le procès-verbal sera dressé par le notaire dépositaire de l'acte, à moins que le Tribunal qui l'ordonne ne commette un de ses membres, ou tout autre juge ou un autre notaire.

Art.23- Les grosses seules seront délivrées en bonne exécutoire: elles seront intitulées et termines dans les même termes que les jugements des Tribunaux.

Art.24- Il doit être fait mention sur la minute de la délivrance d'une première grosse faite à chacune des parties intéressées; il ne peut lui en être délivré d'autre, à peine de destitution sans une ordonnance du Doyen du Tribunal de 1ère Instance, laquelle demeura jointe à la minute.

Art.25- Chaque notaire devra avoir un sceau particulier, aux annexés de la République, portant ses noms qualité et résidence.

Les grosses, extraits et brevets porteront l'empreinte de ce sceau.

Art.26- Quand il doit être fait usage d'un acte notarié hors du ressort du Tribunal de 1ère Instance où se trouve la résidence du notaire qui l'a délivré, la signature de ce notaire a besoin d'être légalisée par le Doyen du Tribunal de 1ère Instance de ce ressort. Si l'acte est destiné à être envoyé à l'étranger, la signature du Doyen sera légalisée par le Secrétaire d'Etat de la Justice.

Art.27- Les notaires sont tenus d'avoir un registre spécial, appelé répertoire, visé cote et paraphe, à chaque feuillet sans frais par le Doyen du Tribunal de 1ère Instance dans le ressort duquel se trouve la Commune pour laquelle il a été commissionné. Sur ce registre, ils inscriront jour par jour et sans blanc, ni surcharge, la nature et l'espèce de l'acte, les noms des parties, et la mention de l'enregistrement, tous les actes en minutes ou en brevet qui seront dans leur étude même les testaments des personnes vivantes.

Art.28- Tous les six mois, les quinze Juillet de chaque année, ils seront tenus de faire viser gratis, leurs

第21条 公证员没有第一上诉法庭庭长的命令不能发放公证书副本，也不能让其他直接利害关系人、继承人或权利所有者知晓公证书的内容，违者应当赔偿损失，受到150古德的罚款。如果屡次重犯，则会被停职三个月，除非是为了执行关于记录权的法律法规或其他涉及文档的法律规定，但这些规定都应当在法院裁判中予以明示。

第22条 出于调卷的需要，询问笔录应当由保管文件的公证员草拟，除非下达命令的法庭委任了其中一名成员或其他法官或者另一名公证员。

第23条 判决书副本应当在具有良好执行力的情形下发放：副本应当与法庭裁判的版本完全一致。

第24条 向每位利害关系当事人发放第一份副本时应当在原件中予以记载；而不应当向其他人发放，否则将被免职，除非有第一上诉法庭庭长的命令，这份命令应当添加在原件中。

第25条 每名公证员都应当有独自的印章，附属于共和国，记载有公证员的姓名、身份及住所地。

判决书副本、证书副本及公证书副本上应当印有该印章。

第26条 当一份公证书使用地超出了在发放该文书的公证员住所地第一上诉法庭的管辖范围时，管辖地第一上诉法庭庭长需要对公证员签字的合法性进行确认。如果公证书需要在外国使用，国家司法部长需要对庭长签字的合法性进行确认。

第27条 公证员保存有一本特殊的登记簿，称之为目录索引，由在市镇所在地管辖范围内的第一上诉法庭庭长基于委托，在每页上免费进行编号和画押。在这本登记簿上，按天记录，不得留有空白且不可修改，登记文书的性质和种类，当事人姓名，并载明记录件，全部公证书的原件或还在处理当中的副本，甚至包括生者的遗嘱。

第28条 每年七月的前15日，市镇登记处的主任将会免费检查全部六个月的登记情况，并由相关当

répertoires par le Directeur de l'Enregistrement de la Commune et doivent se conformer, en ce qui les concerne, aux dispositions de la loi sur l'Enregistrement sous peine d'une amende de Cent Gourdes par chaque quinzaine de retard, conformément à la loi sur l'Enregistrement.

Art.29- Ils devront aussi faire arrêter leurs répertoires, tous les six mois, par le ministère public qui, en cas de prévarication, ou tous autres délits ou cimes, doit les poursuivre d'office par devant les Tribunaux compétences sans préjudice de droit qu'ont les parties de les dénoncer.

Art.30- En cas de destitution, démission, mutation ou décédé d'un notaire, le Juge de Paix du lieu est tenu d'apposer immédiatement les scellés sur ses minutes et répertoire. Le notaire qui sera appelé à le remplacer requerra la levée des scellés et prendra possession, sur inventaire dont un double sera remis au Greffe du Tribunal de 1ère Instance du ressort, des minutes et répertoires trouvés dans l'étude vacante et délivrera lorsqu'il en sera maquis toutes expéditions des dites minutes. Le notaire successeur tiendra compte à son prédécesseur, ou aux héritiers de celui-ci de la moitié du bénéfice, délivrés lors du remplacement.

Durant la suspension d'un notaire, le Secrétaire d'Etat de la Justice désignera celui qui pourra délivrer aux requérants les expéditions des minutes du notaire suspendu, aux mêmes conditions que dessus.

Art.31- Ils sont assujettis pour leurs actes, à la taxe fixée par le tarif annexé, le papier timbré non compris, sans pouvoir s'en écarter, sauf le cas prévu par la présente loi.

Le notaire écrira au bas de la minute et de l'expédition de ses actes le but et les émoluments payés par la partie, sous peine d'une amende de Cinquante Gourdes et en cas de récidive, d'une suspension de trois mois.

Le notaire convaincu d'avoir exigé plus que ce que prévoit le tarif sera destitué.

Art.32- Les inventaires, les actes de pavage, les comptes de gestion et d'administration rendus par un mandataire testamentaire, de bénéfice d'inventaire, de tutelle, cahier des charges et tous actes d'une grande étendue seront payés suivant le tarif, à raison de Quinze Gourdes par chacune des vacations de 3 heures employées à la passation de l'acte.

Les notaires seront tenus décrire eux-mêmes, en toutes lettres, tant sur la minute qu'au bas de l'expédition, le temps qu'ils auront employé et la date de la délivrance de chaque expédition.

Art.33- Lorsque les notaires seront appelés hors de

事人确认。根据登记处的相关法律规定，每延误15日将会被处以100古德的罚款。

第29条 全部六个月的登记工作也应当由检察院审查。如果有渎职行为，或其他违法犯罪行为，检察院应当在不损害当事人检举权的情况下向有管辖权的法院提起公诉。

第30条 当公证人被免职、辞职、调任或死亡时，地区治安法官需要立即在他的原件和登记簿上贴封条。得到任命的下一任公证员请求启封并取得处于无主状态的财产清单（一份复制件需要收入辖区第一上诉法庭的档案馆），及原件和登记簿的所有权，并且当他记录之后分发上述所有原件的副本。继任的公证员应考虑前任公证员，或者前任公证员的继承者们有一半的所有权，在继任的时候分发。

在公证员停职期间，国家司法部长应当指定一名可以为申请者分发被停职的公证员制作的文书副本的人，他也应当遵循上述要求。

第31条 根据价格附录，文书的费用是固定的，其中不包含盖有印章的纸张，不可以分离，法律只有特殊规定除外。

公证员应当在公证书的原件和副本下方注明目的和当事人支付的部分，违者将被处以50古德的罚款，屡次重犯将被停职三个月。

被证实收取超过价格表规定费用的公证员将会被革职。

第32条 制作公证书期间每名公证员或鉴定人员每三小时收取15古德，财产清单，公证书，遗嘱执行人送交的管理和行政账户，材料清单或托管的收益，规章制度和所有大范围的公证书，按照上述价格收费。

公证员应当在原件和副本下方，亲自用文字注明他们工作的时间和分发每份公证书副本的日期。

第33条 当公证员被要求离开办公地点依职权

leur étude pour la confection des actes de leur ministère, il leur sera alloué, si c'est en ville, Deux Gourdes en sus du prix de l'acte fixé au tarif, et s'il y a transport à la campagne jusqu'à deux lieues, il leur sera accordé en sus du coût de l'acte Cinq Gourdes et au delà de deux lieues, une gourdes par chaque lieue, pour tous frais de transport le nombre des lieues sera écrit de leur main comme en l'Art précédent.

Art.34- Tous les cas pour la rédaction desquels les notaires serons appelés de nuit, c'est-à-dire de huit heures du soir à cinq heures du matin, seront payés moitiés en sus du prix porté au tarif, outre les frais de transport.

Art.35- Lorsque deux notaires seront appelés pour passer collectivement un acte, le notaire dépositaire de la minute, aura pour ses honoraires le total ses émoluments alloués par le tarif, le notaire en second n'aura droit d'exiger du requérant que la moitié des dites émoluments.

Art.36- Les notaires ne pourront délivrer expédition des actes restes imparfaits à moins d'être autorisés par le Doyen du Tribunal de 1ère Instance de leur ressort, conformément au Code de procédure Civile, sous peine d'une amende de Six Cent Gourdes pour la première fois, et en cas de récidive, d'interdiction de leurs fonctions pendant un an, sans préjudice des dommages-intérêts envers la partie poursuivante.

Art.37- Toute contravention aux dispositions des Art. 10,11,13,14,16,31,32,33,34 et 35 sera, outre les peines déjà prévues, punie d'une amende de Cent Cinquante Gourdes pour la première fois, en cas de récidive, d'interdiction pour six mois, lesquelles peines seront prononcées sur assignation donnée à la requête du Commissaire du Gouvernement, sauf à la partie intéressée à se pouvoir en réduction de la taxe.

Art.38- Toutes suspension, destitution, condamnation, à l'amende et aux dommages-intérêts seront prononcées contre les notaires par le Tribunal de 1ère Instance de leur ressort sur la poursuite des parties intéressées ou d'office sur celle du Commissaire du Gouvernement.

Les jugements prononçant ces peines, seront sujet à l'appel et exécutoires par provision excepté quant aux condamnations pécuniaires.

Art.39- Les notaires sont tenus, avant d'entrer en fonctions, de déposer au Greffe du Tribunal de 1ère Instance de leur ressort, et sur un registre à ce destomé, la signature et le paraphe dont ils doivent se servir dans l'exercice de leurs fonctions. Ils déposeront également un cautionnement. Le cautionnement est fixé comme suit:

制作公证书时，将会得到津贴。如果是在本城市之内，依照公证书相应的价格之外再补助2古德。如果需要前往乡下两个地方以内，则根据公证书价格之外补助5古德；超过两个地方，每增加一个多补助1古德。所有的交通费用及地点数量参照上一条的规定由公证员自行记录。

第34条　在所有情形下公证员被要求在夜间起草公证书的，即从晚上八点直至凌晨五点，需要额外支付公证书价格的一半费用，不包括交通费用。

第35条　当两名公证员被要求合作完成一份公证书时，保管原件的公证员，以他的名义取得全部价格表中规定的津贴，第二公证人没有权利要求取得上述津贴的一半。

第36条　公证员不可以分发仍处于未完成状态的公证书副本，除非得到管辖地第一上诉法庭庭长的授权，且符合民事诉讼法的规定，违者第一次将被处于600古德的罚款，屡次重犯者在不损害有权起诉者利益的情况下，在一年内禁止行使职权。

第37条　在第10条、第11条、第13条、第14条、第16条、第31条、第32条、第34条和第35条中规定的罚金，除去已经规定的处罚，第一次都处以150古德的罚款，屡次重犯者六个月内禁止行使职权。被处以惩罚的公证员将会受到政府特派员的传讯，除非利害关系当事人同意以减少费用的方式解决。

第38条　对公证员所有的停职、革职、判刑、罚款以及赔偿损失的决定，都应依据利害关系人的起诉或政府特派员提起的公诉，在管辖范围内第一上诉法庭进行宣判。

经过司法判决的处罚，除去涉及财产刑的，上诉和执行的费用由保证金支付。

第39条　在入职之前，公证员需要在管辖地第一上诉法庭的档案馆中存档，在登记簿上应当记录公证员在行使职责时使用的签字和画押。公证员同时需要缴纳担保金。担保金的数额是固定的，规定如下：

Notaire de	1ère classe.	G.1000
Notaire de	2ème classe	G.800
Notaire de	3ème classe	G.600
Notaire de	4ème classe	G.400
Notaire de	5ème classe.	G.200

Ou des effets publics, ou titres de l'Etat au cours de bourse équivalents aux valeurs ci-dessus.

Ce cautionnement doit être versé en espèces à la Banque Nationale de la République d'Haïti, ou à l'une de ses succursales installées dans le ressort du Tribunal de 1ère Instance avant la prestation de serment du notaire.

Les notaires déjà en exercice de leurs fonctions auront quatre mois à partir de la promulgation de la présente loi pour verser le cautionnement applicable à la classe à laquelle ils appartiennent.

Art.40- Ce cautionnement fixé sur les bases ci-dessus sera spécialement affecté à la garantie des condamnations prononcées contre eux par suite de l'exercice de leurs fonctions. Lorsque par l'effet de cette garantie, le montant du cautionnement ait été entièrement rétabli, et faute par lui de rétablir, dans les six mois de la condamnation, l'intégralité du cautionnement il sera considéré démissionnaire et remplacé.

Art.41- Tous notaire suspendu, destitué ou remplacé, devra aussitôt après la notification qui lui aura été faite de sa suspension, de sa destitution, de son remplacement, cesser l'exercice de son état, à peine de tous dommages-intérêts et des autres condamnations prononcées par les lois contre tout fonctionnaire suspendu ou destitué qui continue l'exercice de ses fonctions. Le notaire suspendu ne pourra les reprendre sous les mêmes peines qu'après la cessation du temps de la suspension.

Art.42- En cas d'empêchement d'un notaire pour cause de maladie ou de congé, il est autorisé à se substituer un confrère pour la réception des actes ou la délivrance des expéditions. Les honoraires seront paillages entre le substituant et le substitut et les minutes des actes repus appartiendront de droit au notaire substitué.

Art.43- Les minutes et répertoires d'un notaire destitué, remplacé ou décédé seront remis à son successeur après inventaire dont un exemplaire sera expédié au Commissaire du Gouvernement près le Tribunal de 1ère Instance qui est chargé de veiller à ce que les remises ordonnées soient effectuées.

Le titulaire destitué ou les héritiers du notaire décédé, en retard de faire cette remise, seront condamnés à Cent Gourdes d'amende par chaque mois de retard à compter

第一级别的公证员	1000古德
第二级别的公证员	800古德
第三级别的公证员	600古德
第四级别的公证员	400古德
第五级别的公证员	200古德

或者具有社会影响力，或者正在享有与上述价值相同的国家补贴。

此项担保金应当在公证员宣誓就职之前，以现金的方式缴纳到海地共和国国家银行，或者第一上诉法庭辖区内的国家银行分支机构中。

已经执业的公证员在该法律颁布之日起四个月内向合适的银行缴纳担保金。

第40条 这项担保金将被特别用来为公证员所受的罚金做担保，保证他们可以继续执业。在使用了这笔担保金后，应当补齐担保金的数额；如果在处罚的六个月之后没有补齐，公证员将被视为辞职或可替代。

第41条 所有停职、革职和被取代的公证员应当在收到停职、革职、取代的通知书后立刻停止行使职权，违者需要赔偿全部损失并且根据法律对停职或革职者继续执业的处罚规定处以罚金。被停职的公证员只有在停职期间届满之后才能重新行使职权。

第42条 因公证员生病或请假导致职责履行不能，可以授权一名同事接收文档或分发公证书副本。被授权人承担委托人与被委托人的工作，其收取的文件原件与被替代的公证员收取的享有同等权利。

第43条 被革职、取代或去世的公证员保管的原件和目录索引在盘点后将送回给他的继任者。盘点时的样本需要寄送给管辖前任公证员的第一上诉法庭指派的政府特派员手中，依照特派员的命令送回。

被革职的公证员和已死亡公证员的继承者，如果延误交回上述文件，自催告书通知之日起，每延迟一个月将被处以100古德的罚款。

du jour de la sommation qui leur aura été faite d'effectuer cette remise.

Art.44- Il est défendu au notaire de s'associer, soit avec d'autres notaire, soit avec des tiers pour l'exploitation de leurs offices.

Il leur est également interdit, soit par eux-mêmes, soit par personnes interposées, soit directement, soit indirectement:

1° de se livrer à aucune spéculation de bourse ou opération de commerce, banque, escompte et courtage, de souscrire à quelque titre et sous quelque prétexte que ce soit, des lettres de change en billets à ordre négociables;

2° de s'immiscer dans l'administration d'aucune Société, entreprise ou Compagnie de finances, de commerce ou d'industrie;

3° de faire des spéculations relatives à l'acquisition et à la vente d'immeubles, à la cession des créances, droits successifs, actions industrielles et autres droits incorporels;

4° de s'intéresser dans aucune affaire pour laquelle ils prêtent leur ministère;

5° de placer en leur nom personnel des fonds qu'ils auraient reçus même à la condition d'en servir les intérêts;

6° de se constituer garants ou cautions, à quelque titre que ce soit, des prêts qui auraient été faits par leur intermédiaire, ou qu'ils auraient été chargés de constater par acte public ou privé;

7° de servir de prête-noms en aucune circonstance, même pour des actes autres que ceux désignés ci-dessus.

Les contraventions aux présentes prohibitions sont, ainsi que les autres infractions à la discipline, poursuivies lors même qu'il n'existerait aucune parti plaignante, et punies suivant la gravité des cas de la suspension ou de la destitution. Il n'est en rien dérogé aux dispositions du Code Pénal sur la matière.

Art.45- Le Pouvoir Exécutif pourvoira, par des règlements, à l'établissement des Chambres pour la discipline intérieure des notaires.

En attendant, la discipline des notaires appartient au Commissaire du Gouvernement près le Tribunal de 1ère Instance. Ce dernier prononce contre eux, après les avoir entendus le rappel à l'ordre, la censure simple, la censure avec réprimande, il leur donne tout avertissement qu'il juge nécessaire.

À l'égard des peines plus graves, celles que la suspension le remplacement ou la destination, il les provoque d'office ou sur les réclamations des parties devant le Tribunal de 1ère Instance dont les jugements, dans ces cas,

第 44 条 禁止公证员与其他公证员或第三人结盟利用他们的职权。

下列行为，无论是自己实施，或由中介人实施，或直接，或间接，都是禁止的：

1. 在任何证券交易所、金融交易场所、银行等从事投机、贴现、经纪工作，或假借一定的名目私自兑换汇票；

2. 干预任何公司、企业或金融团体、商业或工业的行政事务；

3. 从事房地产买卖工作，转让债权、继承权、工业行为及其他无形权利；

4. 从事需要提供他们职务的事件；

5. 以他们的名字冠名基金，从中获得收益；

6. 无论出于什么原因，自愿担任保证人或提供担保金，通过中间人出借资金，或出借需要通过公法或私法确认的资金；

7. 无论在任何情形下充当顶替者，包括上述条文中没有规定的行为。

违反上述禁令，以及其他违反规章的行为，即便不存在原告当事人也应该被起诉，并且根据严重程度处以停职或革职的处罚。以上规定不与刑法的相关规定相抵触。

第 45 条 根据规章规定，建立专门法庭执行公证员内部条例。

同时，公证员条例由第一上诉法庭指派的政府特派员执行。在法庭提起对公证员的诉讼中，听取汇报、简易审查和惩戒性的审查后，法庭认为必要时将会给予公证员训斥警告。

关于加重刑罚、停职、取代或革职，由公诉机关提起或由当事人在第一上诉法庭进行抗诉，此时上诉和执行的费用由保证金承担。

seront sujets à l'appel et exécutoires par provisions.

Art.46- La présente loi abroge toutes lois ou dispositions des lois antérieures, tout tarif concernant le notariat et tout programme d'examen précédemment arrêté et sera exécuté à la diligence du Secrétaire d'Etat de la Justice.

Donné au Palais Législatif le 24 Février 1919, An 116ème de l'Indépendance.

Le Président   Les Secrétaires
LEGITIME
V. SAMBOUR, LEO ALEXIS

Au Nom de la République

Le Président de la République ordonne que la loi ci-dessus soit revêtue du Sceau de la République imprimée, publiée et exécutée

Donné au Palais National, à Port-au-Prince, le 11 Mars 1919 An, 116ème de l'Indépendance.

Par le Président: DARTIGUENAVE

Le Secrétaire d'Etat de la Justice
C.BENOIT

第 46 条 自本法施行之日起，先前的法律和规定一律废止，公证所需的费用和前述中止的考试大纲按照国家司法部长的建议实行。

提交立法机关于 1919 年 2 月 24 日
第 116 号独立文件
总统　　　　　　国务卿
合法的
V. 桑布尔，雷欧·阿勒克斯
以共和国之名
共和国总理要求上述法律加盖共和国的印章，由国家印刷、公布和施行

提交国家机关，在太子港，于 1919 年 3 月 11 日，第 116 号独立文件。
由总理：达蒂格纳夫
国家司法部长：
C. 本努瓦

海地公证人法修正案

LOI DU 21 AOUT 1862 SUR LE NOTARIAT	**关于公证人团体的 1862 年 8 月 21 日法律**

Art.1- les notaires sont des fonctionnaires publics pour recevoir tous les actes et contrats auxquels les d'authenticité ou veulent faire donner, le caractère attaché aux actes de l'autorité publique, et pour en assurer le dépôt et en délivrer des grosses, extraits et expéditions.

Art.2- ils sont nommés par le Président d'Haïti, sur la présentation du Secrétaire d'Etat de la justice, dans les attributions duquel ils demeurent; quant à leurs actes ils sont sous la surveillance du Commissaire du Gouvernement et justiciables du tribunal civil de leur ressort, et ils n'ont droit d'exercer qu'à partie du jour où ils sont prêté serment.

Art.3- chaque notaire est obligé de résider dans le lieu qui lui a été fixé par le Gouvernement, et qui est désigné dans sa commission. En cas de contravention, le notaire sera considéré comme démissionnaire, et il est pourvu à son remplacement.

Art.4- il est expressément défendu à tout notaire d'instrumenter hors ressort du tribunal civil où il a prêté sentent sous peine d'être suspendu de ses fonctions pendant 3 mois d'être destitué en cas de récidive, et de supporter tous dommages-intérêts.

Art.5- le nombre des notaires est fixé comme suit:

1- Six pour le Capitale; 2- Quatre pour les chefs-lieux de département; 3- Trois pour les villes dont le port est ouvert au commerce étranger; 4- Deux pour chacun des autres communes.

Art.6- les fonctions de notaire sont incompatibles avec celle de juges, commissaires du Gouvernement près les Tribunaux, leurs substituts, greffiers, huissiers, fonctionnaires de l'Administration judiciaires, commissaires de police et d'ilets et militaires.

Art.7- pour être admis aux fonctions de notaire, il faut :

1- être haïtien ou naturalisé haïtien, et jouir de l'exercice des droits de citoyens;

2- être âgé de 25 ans accomplis;

3- produire un certificat de moralité et de capacité

第 1 条　公证员是由公权力设置的公职人员，职责是接收所有当事人需要或者想要得到公权力确认、给予公证性的文件和合同，同时确认保管物，发放判决副本、证书副本和公证书副本。

第 2 条　公证员由国家总统根据国家司法部长的提名，在他的居住地任命。公证员的行为受到政府特派员的监督，并且由管辖地民事法院进行司法管辖。自宣誓之日起，他们有权行使职责。

第 3 条　每名公证员必须定居在由政府确定的，在委任书中指明的地区。如有违反，公证员将被视作辞职，将由其他人取代他的职位。

第 4 条　明确禁止任何公证员在超出其所在地民事法院管辖范围制作文书，违者将被处以停职三个月的处罚，屡次重犯者将被辞退，并且赔偿全部损失。

第 5 条　公证员的数量规定如下：

1. 首都六名；2. 各省省会城市四名；3. 开放海外贸易的港口城市三名；4. 其他市镇两名。

第 6 条　公证员不可兼任法官，法庭指定的政府特派员、特派员的检察官、书记员、执达员，不能行使司法行政、警察或军队的权力。

第 7 条　担任公证员行使职责，应当满足：

1. 具有海地国籍或入籍取得海地国籍，享有公民权利；

2. 年满 25 周岁以上；

3. 持有道德证明、某公证委员会事先经过考试认

délivré par une commission de notaire désignés à cet effet, après l'examen préalable de l'impétrant qui sera, en outre, tenu de justifier d'un stage d'un an au moins dans l'étude d'un notaire.

L'examen doit porter sur les fonctions et les devoirs des notaires, sur le droit civil, sur la rédaction des actes. Un procès-verbal motivé sera dressé par les examinateurs au Secrétaire d'Etat de la justice, qui statue définitivement en présentant ou refusant de présenter le candidat à la nomination du président d'Haïti.

Art.8- le Gouvernement peut dispenser du stage les individus qui justifient d'une capacité incontestable, jointe à des services judiciaires ou administratifs bien établis et d'une durée notable.

Art.9- les notaires sont tenus de prêter leur ministère lorsqu'ils en sont requis: mais ils ne sont pas obligés de recevoir des actes injurieux et diffamatoires contre des tiers, ni ceux dont les énonciations ont été préparées dans un but frauduleux et illicite.

Art.10- ils ne pourront recevoir des actes dans lesquels leurs parents ou alliés, en ligne directe à tousses degrés, et ne collatérale jusqu'au degré d'oncle ou de neveu inclusivement, seraient parties, ou qui contiendraient quelques dispositions en leur faveur.

Il leur est également défendu d'instrumenter pour des individus qu'ils ne connaissent pas personnellement, ou dont deux citoyens qu'ils savent dignes de foi ne leur attesteront pas les noms, état et demeure, ainsi que pour les personnes qui ne seraient ou qui ne leur apparaitraient pas saines d'esprit, ni jouissant de la plénitude de leur raison.

Art.11- les notaires ne peuvent instrumenter qu'en présence d'un de leurs confrères, ou deux citoyens majeurs, sachant signer, et domiciliés dans l'arrondissement où l'acte est passé, sans déroger à ce que prescrit le code civil en matière de testament: ils ne peuvent prendre pour témoins les parents ou alliés aux degré ci-dessus, tant des parties que d'eux-mêmes, leurs clercs ou serviteurs.

NO.4- LOI DU 8 AOUT 1877 MODIFICATIVE SUR LE NOTARIAT

Art.1- les arts. 32 et 33 de la loi du 21 août 1862, sur le Notariat sont ainsi modifiés

Art.32- les inventaires, les actes de partage, les comptes de gestion, et d'administration rendus par un mandataire testament de bénéfice d'inventaire de tutelle, cahier des charges et tous autres actes d'une grande éten-

定颁发的资质证书，或者在公证员事务所实习至少一年的证明。

考试应当涉及公证员职责及工作，涉及民法，涉及文书的起草。国家司法部的考官应当编制关于应试者动机的询问笔录，在海地总理做出录取或拒绝的最终裁决时作为参考依据。

第8条 政府可以免除被裁定确实具有相关能力的人的实习要求，附上在一定时期内出色从事司法或行政工作的证明。

第9条 公证员在得到请求时行使他们的职责，但是他们可以拒绝接收辱骂或诽谤第三者的材料，也不接收特别为欺骗、违法目的而准备的材料。

第10条 公证员不能接收他们父母或所有亲等关系的直系姻亲，以及三等亲以内旁系亲属作为当事人的材料，也不能接收包含其自身利益的文件。

为身份不明的人，或者为两个值得信赖的公民都不为他们证实姓名、社会身份和住所的人，以及为那些没有表现出精神健康情况，也没有说明理由的人制作文书是禁止的。

第11条 只有当一名同事或两名成年、识字、居住在文书行使效力的区域、没有违背民法关于遗嘱规定的海地公民在场时，公证员才可以制作文书。父母和前文所规定的近亲属，以及当事人本人，他的书记员和辅助人员不可以充当见证人。

第四号 1877年8月8日法律修正案 关于公证人团体

第1条 1862年8月21日关于公证人团体法律第32条、第33条修改如下：

第32条 财产清单、分配方案、管理账户和执行人的行政账户、有财产托管的遗嘱、细则以及其他大范围的文件，签订协议时每小时收取75分，发放协议时的收费为前述的一半（37.5分）。

due, seront payés a raison de soixante-quinze centimes par chacune des heures employées à la passation de l'acte, et de la moitié pour le temps employé à l'expédition.

Art.33- lorsque les notaires seront appelés hors de leur étude pour la confection des actes de leur ministère, il leur sera alloué, si c'est en ville, soixante-quinze centimes en sus du prix de l'acte fixé au tarif et s'il y a transport à la campagne, jusqu'à deux lieues, il leur sera accordé, en sus du coût de l'acte, deux piastres, et au-delà de deux lieues soixante-quinze centimes pour chaque lieu, pour tous frais de transport le nombre des lieues sera écrit de leur main, comme en l'Art. précédent.

Art.2- le tarif des actes notariés annexé à la loi du 21 Août est ainsi modifié:

1- pour toute recherche d'acte dont la date est certaine······1
2- pour toute recherche d'acte dont l'année est certaine ················1.5
3- pour toute recherche d'acte dont l'année est incertaine················4.00
4- mention ou émargement ················0.50
5- procuration en brevet ················2.00
6- tous autres actes en brevet ················1.00
7- contrat divers, donations et tous autres actes ou minutes non désignés par la présente················3.00
8- expédition des mêmes dûment collationnés······1.50
9- note de protêt················1.50
10- extension de protêt················5.00
11- expédition d'extension de protêt················3.00
12- protestation des billets à ordre et lettres de charge ················4.00
13- testament················8.00
14- expédition de testament················4.00
15- contrat de mariage················4.00
16- expédition du contrat de mariage················2.00
17- pour chaque dépôt des pièces················1.00
18- pour vérification des pièces, par heure················0.50
19- droit pour l'argent déposé en l'étude, quelle que soit la durée du dépôt················0.50

**NO.5- LOI DU 6 AVRIL 1889
SUR LES OFFICIERS DE L'ÉTAT CIVIL**
DECRET-LOI DU 20 JUIN 1941 SUR LE NOTAIRE DONT L'ÉTUDE EST DEVENUE VACANTE

ELIE LESCOT
PRESIDÉNT DE LA RÉPUBLIQUE
Vu la loi du 21 Février 1919 sur le notariat:

第33条 当公证员需要离开办公地点依职权制作公证书时,将会得到津贴。如果是在本城市之内,依照公证书确定的价格之外再补助75分。如果需要前往乡下两个地方以内,经过公证员同意,则根据公证书价格之外补助2皮阿斯特;超过两个地方,每增加一个多补助75分。所有的交通费用及地点数量参照上一条的规定由公证员自行记录。

第2条 8月21日法律附录公证书价格表修改如下:

1. 按准确日期查询文档················1
2. 按准确年份查询文档················1.5
3. 按不确定的年份查找文档················4.00
4. 批注或添加旁注················0.50
5. 副本的代理················2.00
6. 其他文档制作副本················1.00
7. 各种合同、赠与证书和其余之后没有提及的文档或原件················3.00
8. 与原件核对无误的副本················1.50
9. 抗议书················1.50
10. 抗议书扩展················5.00
11. 抗议书扩展副本················3.00
12. 期票或汇票抗议书················4.00
13. 遗嘱················8.00
14. 遗嘱副本················4.00
15. 婚前协议················4.00
16. 婚前协议副本················2.00
17. 每项提存物················1.00
18. 检查物品,每小时················0.50
19. 托管在事务所的金钱,无论托管时间······0.50

**第五号 1889年4月6日法律
关于民事登记的官员**
1941年6月20日关于公证员事务所变为无主状态的法律修正案

埃利 莱斯科
共和国总理
基于1919年2月21日关于公证人团体法律:

Considérant qu'il y a lieu d'instituer une procédure prompte et rapide pour assurer, en cas d'urgence, la délivrance des copies, extraits, expéditions, grosses des actes, documents et tous les certificats y relatifs déposés aux Archives d'un Notaire dont l'Étude est devenue vacante, par suite de décès, démission, mutation, interdiction du titulaire.

Art.1- l'Art 30 de la loi du 21 Février 1919 est ainsi modifié:

Art.30- en cas de destitution, démission, interdiction, décès, mutation d'un notaire, le juge de Paix des résidence est tenu d'apposer d'office les scellés sur ses archives aussitôt qu'il aura connaissance d'un des faits plus hauts mentionnés.

Le notaire nommé pour lui succéder, serment préalablement prêté, requerra la levée des scellé, il prendra possession des dites archives, selon inventaire dont un double sera adressé par le Juge de Paix au Commissaire du Gouvernement près le Tribunal Civil de ce ressort.

Le notaire successeur peut, sur réquisition légale, délivrer toutes copies, grosses, expéditions, extraits de tous les actes et documents constituant les archives de l'Étude.

Néanmoins, le notaire successeur, devra compter à son prédécesseur, ou à ses héritiers ou ayant droits, la moitié des émoluments parus sur les expéditions des actes délivrés pour la première fois.

En attendant l'entrée effective du notaire successeur, le Doyen du Tribunal Civil, sur requête du Ministère Publique, désignera un des notaires du ressort, soit de sa résidence ou de la résidence la plus proche, qui sera chargé, en cas d'urgence, de délivrer toutes copies grosse expéditions, extraits, certificat relatifs aux actes et documents formant les archives de l'Étude.

En ce cas le notaire ainsi désigné requerra du Commissaire Gouvernement et du Juge de Paix la levée provisoire des scellés.

Il ne pourra instrumenter que dans le local où sont déposées les archives, en présence du Commissaire du Gouvernement et du Juge de Paix qui viseront tous les actes qu'il aura rédigé.

Aussitôt la rédaction de l'acte qui avait donné lieu à la levée des scellés, ceux-ci seront rétablis par le Commissaire du Gouvernement et le Juge de Paix.

Le notaire remplaçant est soumis aux mêmes obligations que le notaire successeur, vis à vis du notaire prédécesseur, de ses héritiers ou autres ayant droit.

Lorsqu'il s'agira de la suspension d'un notaire le

考虑到需要确定一个程序可以敏捷快速地确定，在紧急情况下，公证员因死亡、辞职、调任或被剥夺职权，事务所变为无主状态时，对分发复印件、公证书、判决书、证书的副本，文档及全部证书进行存档。

第1条　1919年2月21日法律第30条修改如下：

第30条　如果公证员被革职、辞职、被剥夺职权、死亡或调任，居住地的治安法官在得知有极大可能发生上述情形时，应当立即在存档物上贴封条。

被指派继任的公证员，经过宣誓，请求解除封条，根据材料清单取得上述存档的所有权。其中材料清单的复印件需要交给本辖区民事法院指定的政府特派员委任的治安法官。

通过合法的附带请求，继任的公证员可以分发所有复印件、证书副本、公证书副本以及全部在该事务所存档中的文档或材料副本。

然而，继任的公证员应当在第一次分发文档副本时向前任公证员，或他的继承者或权利继承人，索要薪酬的一半。

在继任公证员到岗之前，民事法院的院长，根据检察院的申请，在紧急情况下，可以指定辖区内的一名居住地最近的公证员，分发所有的复印件和副本以及事务所存档中的证书。

这种情况下，被指定的公证员需要向政府特派员和治安法官请求临时解除封条。

他仅可以在存档物保存地，在政府特派员和治安法官在场见证的情况下制作文书。

如果起草文书时需要临时打开封条，应当由政府特派员和治安法官重新进行贴封。

接替的公证员与继任公证员需要同前任公证员、他的继承者或其他权利继承人一样承担债权。

如果有公证员被停职，国家司法部长可以参照前

Secrétaire d'Etat de la Justice désignera celui qui pourra procéder comme il a été dit dans les précédents alinéas.

Art.2- le présent Décret-Loi abroge… etc.
MONITEUR NO. 113, 114
27 NOVEMBRE et 1er DECEMBRE 1969
DECRET-LOI DU 27 NOVEMBRE 1969 HARMONISANT LES DISPOSITIONS DE LA LOI DU 24 FÉVRIER 1919 SUR LE NOTARIAT EN FONCTION DES EXIGENCES NOUVELLES CRÉES PAR LE STATUT ECONOMIQUE ET SOCIAL DU PAYS.

款规定指定接替的公证员。

第 2 条 下列法律修正案废止……
第 113 号、第 114 号通报
1969 年 11 月 27 日和 12 月 1 日
1969 年 11 月 27 日修正案与 1919 年 2 月 24 日的关于"公证员在国家经济和社会形势下行使职权的新要求"法律条文应协调一致。

牙买加

牙买加公证人法

| THE NOTARES PUBLIC ACT | 公证人法 |

ARRANGEMENT OF SECTIONS

1. Short title.
2. Interpretation
3. Appointment of Notaries Public.
4. Oath to be taken.
5. Duty in suspicious cases.
6. Refusal of protest to be noted.
7. Offences.
8. Notaries to be officers of Supreme Court.
9. Commission to be stamped.
10. Adhesive instead of impressed stamp.
11. Fees.

章节安排

1. 简称
2. 定义
3. 公证人的任命
4. 宣誓
5. 可疑案件的责任
6. 拒绝签注拒绝承兑书
7. 违法行为
8. 作为最高法院职员的公证员
9. 盖章的委任书
10 公证印花税
11. 公证费用

THE NOTARIES PUBLIC ACT

1. This Act may be cited as the Notaries Public Act.

2.-In this Act the expression "Corporate Area" has the meaning assigned to it by section 3 of the Kingston and St. Andrew Corporation Act.

3. The Governor-General may, by warrant under his hand and seal, from time to time commission and appoint as many fit and proper persons as he may think fit throughout the Island to be Notaries Public, to discharge the duties assigned to such office by the laws of Great Britain and of this Island, or by the practice of commerce

4. Before entering upon the duties of his office, each notary public shall, under a dedimus to be issued by the Governor-General, be sworn well, truthfully, and faithfully to discharge such duties.

公证法

1. 本法可简称为《公证人法》。

2. 在本法中,"公司区"一词具有金士顿和圣安德鲁公司法第3节赋予它的涵义。

3. 总督有权以自身名义并盖章发布命令,不时委任和指定尽可能多的合适人选,以满足全岛对公证人的需求,以履行根据英国和本岛的法律,或商业惯例分配给公证人的职务。

4. 在公职人员履行职务之前,每个公证人应根据总督发出的委任状,实际、真实、忠实地宣誓履行职责。

5. Before noting any protest, where the circumstances shall appear to the notary to be suspicious, and not warranting the protest demanded, he shall refuse to act, until, by an order of two Justices in Petty Sessions, the person requiring the protest shall have established a right thereto, and, before applying for such order, notice of the application shall be given to the notary refusing the protest, and such persons, if any, in the Island, interested in the subject of protest.

6. When a protest or other notarial act shall be refused, the notary shall mark on the log-book, bill of exchange, or other document, his refusal to the effect, "protest refused", with his signature and the date of refusal subscribed.

7. It shall be a misdemeanour, punishable by fine or imprisonment, with or without hard labour, for a term not exceeding three years, or by both fine and imprisonment as aforesaid, for any notary or other person falsely to certify, or to propound any statement, document, or thing, or fraudulently, with intent to deceive, to conceal, withhold or pervert any fact, document, or thing pertinent to the subject of protest or other notarial act.

8. Notaries Public shall be deemed to be officers of the Supreme Court, and liable to the summary jurisdiction court. thereof; and, on a certificate from the Court of misconduct in office, the Governor-General shall discharge the offending officer from his said office.

9. A stamp duty, according to the understated scale, shall be impressed on each commission of Notary Public to be countersigned by the Registrar of the Supreme Court.

Scale of Stamps on Commissions of Notary Public
For the whole Island·· $30
For any parish outside the Corporate
For the Corporate Area··· $20
Area··· $10

10. Instead of the impressed stamp of forty cents prescribed by the Stamp Duty Act, a fifty Cents adhesive stamp maybe substituted, provided it be duly cancelled as by the said Act prescribed.

11.-(1) The fees payable for notarial acts (which shall be payable in addition to any stamp duty) shall be the fees for the time being prescribed in a tariff of fee framed and approved in accordance with the provisions of this section.

(2) Any two Notaries Public appointed by the Minister for the purposes of this section may frame a tariff of fees payable for notarial acts and may from time to time

5. 如果公证人认为情况可疑，且没有正当理由出具拒绝承兑证书，则应当拒绝公证，直到获得法官小型会议中两名法官的命令，证明要求拒绝承兑的人已经确定了其权利。且在申请此类命令之前，拒绝承兑申请人应向拒绝该拒绝承兑书的公证人以及在岛上与其有利益关系的人（如果有的话）通知该申请。

6. 拒绝出具拒绝承兑书或进行其他公证行为时，公证人应在其登记簿、汇票或其他文件上标注"拒绝承兑书"并注明签名和拒绝日期。

7. 违反上述规定，对公证申请人或者其他人虚假地证明或出具声明、文件等，或故意欺骗、隐瞒、扣留或破坏任何与拒绝承兑或其他公证行为相关的事实、文件或事物，将构成轻罪，被处以罚款或监禁，且可单处或并处不超过三年的强迫劳役。

8. 公证人应当被视为最高法院的职员，并对简易管辖权法院负责。如果法院证明其存在不当职务行为，总督应将违规人员解职。

9. 根据通常的标准，公证人印花税票应在最高法院登记官发布公证人任命时授予公证人。

公证人的印花税收费标准
对于整个岛屿··$30
对于公司外的任何行政区
对于公司区域···$ 20
地区··$ 10

10. 除了《印花税法案》规定的四十美分印花税票之外，五十美分的粘贴税票也可以被替代使用，只要原税票按照上述法案被正式取消。

11.(1) 公证行为（除印花税票外应当收费的服务）应支付的费用为本条规定的费用。

（2）出于本条的立法目的，总理任命的任何两名公证人均可制定公证行为的收费标准，并有权不时进行修改。

amend the same.

(3) Every tariff of fees framed in accordance with the provisions of subsection (2) and every amendment thereof shall be subject to the approval of the Minister who may make such alterations or additions as he may think fit, and shall not have effect unless published in the Cazetee by order made by the Minister.

（3）按照第 2 款的规定构成的每项收费表及其每次修正，均须经总理批准，总理认为更改或增补适当的，将在公报上颁布命令使其生效。

牙买加公证费用法

THE NOTARIES PUBLIC ACT ORDER
(under section ll (3))
THE NOTARIAL FEES (APPROVAL) ORDER, 1983
(Made by the Minister on the 2nd day of August, 1983)

1. This Order may be cited as the Notarial Fees (Approval) Order, 1983.

2. The tariff of fees set out in the Schedule is hereby approved.

SCHEDULE
Item No.　　　Description　　　Fee($)

Affidavits and Declarations

1. Taking oath of each deponent or declarant with or without seal··············5.00 for each quarter hour or part thereof

2. Preparing exhibit note··············1.00

3. Marking each exhibit··············1.00

4. Full notarial certificate to an affidavit or declaration by one deponent or one declarant··············10.00

5. Additional charge for certificate in respect of each additional deponent or declarant after the first attendances ··············5.00

6. In the office or at the telephone··············5.00 for each quarter hour or thereof,

7. Out of the office··············10.00 for each half hour or thereof (exclusive of travelling expenses).

8. Examining papers and date, etc. in office ··············20.00 per hour.

9. At Embassy, Consulate or other office for procuring legality··············10.00 (exclusive of travelling expenses).

10. At Stamp Office or other revenue office··············3.00 (exclusive of any travelling expenses).

Attestations or Certificates and authentication of the execution of Deeds or Instruments under hand and in verifications of signatures, copies, translations, ect.

11. Simple attestation (without certificate)··············5.00

12. For each additional party whose signature is at-

公证人法修订指令
[根据第11（3）条修正]
公证费用（批准）法，1983年
（1983年8月2日由总理发布）

1. 本法案简称为1983年《公证费用（批准）法》。

2. 授权附表所列明的费用安排具有法律效力。

附表
项目编号　　　描述　　　费用（美元）

宣誓书、声明书

1. 宣誓书或声明书，无论是否附有印章··········5.00 每刻钟或每半小时

2. 准备证据记录··············1.00

3. 标记每个证据··············1.00

4. 宣誓人或声明人的宣誓书或声明书的全套公证文书··············10.00

5. 在第一次公证后，每新增加一个宣誓人或声明人的额外费用··············5.00

6. 在办公地点当面交流或电话沟通··············5.00 每刻钟

7. 在办公地点外办理公证··············10.00 每刻钟或每半小时（不包括交通费用）

8. 在办公地点检查文件和日期等··········20.00 每小时

9. 在使馆、领事馆或其他办事处证明合法性··············10.00（不包括交通费用）

10. 在邮政局或其他部门进行公证··············3.00（不包括交通费用）

对现有文书或契约签名、副本、翻译稿等的确认证书或认证

11. 不附证书的简单的证明··············5.00

12. 每增加认证一个当事人的签名··············3.00

tested··3.00

    13. Attestation with notarial certificate and seal ···15.00

    14. For each additional party mentioned in the certificate ···5.00

    15. Ordinary attestation with certificate under notarial seal to execution by a company whether the certificate is already endorsed on the document or is prepared by the notary···20.00

    16. For each additional company executing·········7.50

    17. Ordinary attestation with certificate under notarial seal to execution by a company in liquidation and its liquidator ···20.00

    18. Special attestation with certificate under notarial seal to execution by a company and evidencing that the document is binding on the company according to law ···5.00

    19. Special attestation with certificate under notarial seal to execution by a company in liquidation and its liquidator and evidencing that the document is binding on the Company according to law···············25.00

    20. Authenticating one person's or corporation's execution of instrument in public form·············10.00

    21.For execution by each additional person or corporation···5.00

    22. Attestation to signature or to signature and official seal of a Public Officer················10.00

    23. For signature of the same official to one or more additional documents annexed to the same notarial certificate···5.00

    24. For further notarial certification respecting the jurisdiction of the Court···············20.00

    25. Notarial certificate verifying a copy or translation of one document················10.00

    26. For each document after the first attached to the same certificate and specifically referred to therein ···5.00

    27. For each document not specifically referred to in the certificate················5.00

Commission for Examination of Witnesses

    28. Attendance (exclusive of expenses of clerk and shorthand clerk, if any)···············If an Attorney-at Law to charge in accordance with scale of charges and customs applicable to Attorneys-at-Law in the Supreme Court

    29. Swearing witnesses: each oath or affirmation

13. 附公证证书和公章的证明书··············15.00

14. 每增加一个证书中涉及的当事人···············5.00

15. 对公司进行的一般证明，附盖有公证印章的证书，无论证书上是否有签字或由公证人起草 ···20.00

16. 每额外增加一个公司················7.50

17. 正在清算中的公司和清算人通过用盖有公证印章的证书进行一般证明···············20.00

18. 对公司文件进行附有盖章的公证证书的特殊证明，证明该文件依法对该公司有约束力···············25.00

19. 对清算中的公司进行附有盖章的公证证书的特殊证明，证明该文件依法对该公司约束力··········25.00

20. 以公开形式验证自然人或公司的执行文书 ···10.00

21. 每增加一个执行人或执行公司················5.00

22. 签名或公职人员签名和公章的证明 ···10.00

23. 为同一公职人员签署的一份或多份额外文件附加同一公证文书···············5.00

24. 就法院的管辖权作进一步的公证证明 ···20.00

25. 对文件的副本进行核验或对翻译的公证文书进行核验···············10.00

26. 对已经首次出具公证书的文件和证书中特别提及的文件进行认证···············5.00

27. 对于证书中未特别提及的某个文档进行认证 ···5.00

证据核查程序

28. 出席作证程序（不包括员工和速记员的费用，如果有）···············安装律师根据最高法院适用于律政司的税收和费用标准进行收费

29. 宣誓作证：每个誓约或宣誓书

30. Preparing exhibit note

31. Marking each exhibit

32. Notarial certification under seal (usually covering all depositions)

Copies

Making copies to keep or fair copies(Unattested)

33. in the English language, per folio··············1.00

34. in a foreign language, per folio··············3.00

Making fair copies for notarial vertification

35. in the English language, per folio··············1.00

36. in a foreign language, per folio··············5.00

37. Collating copies in English not prepared by the notary, with the original for notarial certification, per folio ·············· 10.00 plus, 10.00 for every folio after the first four folios.

38. Collating copies in foreign language, not prepared by the notary, with the original for notarial certification per folio……20.00 plus, 20.00 per folio after the first four folios.

Recording in notarial register copy of an Act in the public or authentic form-

39. in the English language, per folio··············1.00

40. in a foreign language, per folio··············3.00

Drawing of Bonds and Debentures for Redemption and Cancellation of Bonds and Debentures

41. Instructions··············20.00 per half hour.

42. Perusing Trust Deed or other Security Document ··············1.00 per folio.

43. Checking tallies for use in the draw, per 100 ··············5.00

Attending the drawing and issuing the Certificate setting out the numbers drawn—

44. for the first 100··············30.00

45. for every subsequent 100··············15.00

46. For incorporating in certificate the names of bondholders or stockholders··············5.00 per one quarter hour or part thereof.

47. Preparing advertisement of results of drawing ··············10.00 plus 5.00 for each folio.

48. Attending arranging for publication··············10.00

49. in office, per hour··············20.00

50. outside office, per hour··············30.00 (exclusive of travelling expenses)

Letters

If an attorney at law to charge in according with scale of charges and customs applicable to attorneys at law in

the supreme court

51. presenting and noting bills and drafts

(a) up to $200.00·······························up to $500 $100(exclusive of travelling expenses)

(b) for each additional $200.00 or part there of ··········· for each additional $100 or part there of $2.50(exclusive of travelling expenses)

52.protesting bills and drafts of all kinds

(a) up to $1000································20.00

(b) exceeding $1000 and not exceeding $1000···········30.00

(c) for each additional $2000 above $10000················1.00(c) for each additional $100 or part thereof $20

53.Act of honour·······························20.00

54.Duplicate protest·····················as for riginal

N.B. the charges under items 52,53 and 54 Are additional to the charges under item51.

Perusals.

55.Perusing in English······················1.00 per folio

56. Perusing in any other languages·······3.00 per folio

Shipping

57. Note of protest·····························30.00

58. Addtional charge for certifying each cop········15.00

59.Extended protest, per folio···················5.00

Note: one folio comprises seventy-two words, any figures being counted as one word.

51. 提出并起草票据及其草稿

（a）面额不超过200.00的······················100.00—500.00（不包括交通费用）

（b）面额超过200.00的，每增加100···············2.5（不包括交通费用）

52. 各种形式的票据拒绝承兑书

（a）面额不超过1000的·····················20.00

（b）面额超过1000但不超过1000的···············30.00

（c）面额在10000美元以上，每超过2,000美元················1.00，再每新增加100美元，20美元

53. 授予荣誉行为·······················20.00

54. 二次拒绝承兑或接受············与第一次一样

注：第52条、第53条和第54条规定的费用是第51条规定的费用的额外费用。

仔细核查

55. 英文文本·····················1.00每页

56. 英语以外的语言文本·················3.00每页

海事

57. 公证海事报告·····················30.00

58. 核验每份额外的副本·················15.00

59. 扩充报告·····················5.00每页

注：每页共有72个字。任何数字都算作一个字

墨西哥

联邦区公证法

PUBLICADO EN LA GACETA OFICIAL DEL DISTRITO FEDERAL EL 28 DE MARZO DE 2000

LEY DEL NOTARIADO PARA EL DISTRITO FEDERAL

(Al margen superior izquierdo un escudo que dice: Ciudad de México. - Jefe de Gobierno del Distrito Federal)

ROSARIO ROBLES BERLANGA. - Jefa de Gobierno del Distrito Federal, a sus habitantes sabed:

Que la Honorable Asamblea Legislativa del Distrito Federal. I Legislatura, se ha servido dirigirme el siguiente

DECRETO

(Al margen superior izquierdo el escudo nacional que dice: (Estados Unidos Mexicanos. - Asamblea Legislativa del Distrito Federal. - I Legislatura)

LA ASAMBLEA LEGISLATIVA DEL DISTRITO FEDERAL, I LEGISLATURA

DECRETA

LEY DEL NOTARIADO PARA EL DISTRITO FEDERAL

TÍTULO PRIMERO
DE LA FUNCIÓN NOTARIAL Y DEL NOTARIADO DEL DISTRITO FEDERAL

CAPÍTULO I EL NOTARIADO COMO GARANTÍA INSTITUCIONAL

SECCIÓN PRIMERA DISPOSICIONES GENERALES

Artículo 1. El objeto de esta Ley es regular, con carácter de orden e interés público y social la función notarial y al notariado en el Distrito Federal.

Artículo 2. Para los efectos de esta Ley se entenderá

于2000年3月28日在《联邦区官方公报》上发布

联邦区公证法

（左上角章：墨西哥城 - 联邦区政府行政长官）

罗萨里奥·罗布莱斯·贝尔兰加 - 联邦区政府行政长官致市民书：

联邦区立法大会，作为立法机关，向我提交了以下

法令

左上角加盖国徽，内容为：墨西哥合众国 - 联邦区立法大会 - 议会

联邦区立法大会 - 议会

批准颁布
联邦区公证法

第一篇
公证职能和联邦区公证人职业

第一章 公证人制度保障

第一节 总则

第1条 本法旨在从公共秩序和社会利益层面上规范联邦区的公证职能和公证人职业。

第2条 在本法中涉及以下概念：

por:

I. "Administración": La Administración Pública del Distrito Federal;

II. "Arancel": El Arancel de notarios para el Distrito Federal;

III. "Archivo": El Archivo General de Notarías, cuyos fines señala esta Ley;

IV. "Archivo Judicial": El Archivo del Tribunal Superior de Justicia del Distrito Federal;

V. "Asamblea Legislativa": La Asamblea Legislativa del Distrito Federal;

VI. "Autoridades competentes": La Consejería Jurídica y de Servicios Legales, por sí, o a través de la Dirección General Jurídica y de Estudios Legislativos y las direcciones y subdirecciones competentes de ésta, salvo que por el contexto de esta ley deba entenderse adicional o exclusivamente otra autoridad;

VII. "Código Civil": El Código Civil vigente para el Distrito Federal;

VIII. "Código de Procedimientos": El Código de Procedimientos Civiles para el Distrito Federal;

IX. "Código Penal". - El Nuevo Código Penal para el Distrito Federal.

X. "Colegio": El Colegio de Notarios del Distrito Federal, A. C.;

XI. "Comisión de Arbitraje, Legalidad y Justicia": La Comisión de Arbitraje, Legalidad y Justicia del Colegio designada por su junta de decanos:

XII. "Comisión de Notariado": Comisión de Notariado de la Asamblea Legislativa del Distrito Federal;

XIII. "Consejo": El Consejo del Colegio de Notarios del Distrito Federal, A. C.;

XIV. "Constitución": La Constitución Política de los Estados Unidos Mexicanos;

XV. "Esta Ley": La Ley del Notariado para el Distrito Federal;

XVI. "Gaceta": La Gaceta Oficial del Gobierno del Distrito Federal;

XVII. "Ley Orgánica": La Ley Orgánica de la Administración Pública del Distrito Federal;

XVIII. "Notariado": El Notariado del Distrito Federal o Notariado de la Ciudad de México bajo el sistema del Notariado Latino;

XIX. "Registro Público": El Registro Público de la propiedad Inmueble; y el Registro Público de las Personas Morales ambos del Distrito Federal.

XX. "Registro Nacional de Testamentos". - A la Di-

（1）行政机关：联邦区公共管理部门。

（2）收费表：联邦区公证人的收费标准。

（3）档案管理局：公证机构档案管理总局，其宗旨目标参见本法的规定。

（4）司法机关档案室：联邦区最高司法法院的档案室。

（5）立法大会：联邦区立法大会。

（6）主管当局：指的是法律咨询与服务理事会本身，或者理事会下辖的法律和立法研究总局以及总局下辖的各分管单位，但在本法中另有明文规定或特指其他机构的情况除外。

（7）民法典：联邦区现行民法典。

（8）诉讼法：联邦区民事诉讼法。

（9）刑法典：新版联邦区刑法典。

（10）学会：联邦区公证人学会。

（11）仲裁、法制与正义委员会：由公证人学会通过公证会长办公会指定的仲裁、法制与正义委员会。

（12）公证事务委员会：联邦区立法大会的公证事务委员会。

（13）理事会：联邦区公证人学会理事会。

（14）宪法：墨西哥合众国政治宪法。

（15）本法：联邦区公证法。

（16）官方公报：《联邦区政府官方公报》。

（17）组织法：联邦区行政机关组织法。

（18）公证人团体：适用于拉丁公证制度的联邦区公证人团体或墨西哥城公证人团体。

（19）公共登记处：联邦区不动产公共登记处和联邦区法人公共登记处。

（20）国家遗嘱登记处：指的是国家遗嘱通知登

rección del Registro Nacional de Avisos de Testamento, dependiente de la Dirección General de Compilación y Consulta del Orden Jurídico Nacional de la Secretaría de Gobernación.

XXI. "Entes Públicos": Los órganos Ejecutivo, Legislativo, Judicial y autónomos del Distrito Federal.

XXII. "Certificado Electrónico": el documento firmado electrónicamente por un prestador de servicios de certificación que vincula los datos de firma de su autor y confirma su identidad.

XXIII. "Firma Electrónica Notarial": "Firma Electrónica Notarial": La firma electrónica en términos de la Ley de la Firma Electrónica del Distrito Federal, asignada a un notario de esta entidad con motivo de sus funciones, con igual valor jurídico que su firma autógrafa y su sello de autorizar, en términos de la normatividad aplicable.

Artículo 3. En el Distrito Federal corresponde al Notariado el ejercicio de la función notarial, de conformidad con el artículo 122 de la Constitución.

El Notariado es una garantía institucional que la Constitución establece para la Ciudad de México, a través de la reserva y determinación de facultades de la Asamblea y es tarea de esta regularla y efectuar sobre ella una supervisión legislativa por medio de su Comisión de Notariado.

El Notariado como garantía institucional consiste en el sistema que, en el marco del notariado latino, esta Ley organiza la función del notario como un tipo de ejercicio profesional del Derecho y establece las condiciones necesarias para su correcto ejercicio imparcial, calificado, colegiado y libre, en términos de Ley.

Su imparcialidad y probidad debe extenderse a todos los actos en los que intervenga de acuerdo con ésta y con otras leyes.

Artículo 4. Corresponde al Jefe de Gobierno la facultad de expedir las patentes de notario y de aspirante a notario, conforme a las disposiciones contenidas en la presente ley.

Artículo 5. Al Jefe de Gobierno y a las Autoridades competentes del Distrito Federal les corresponde aplicar la presente Ley y vigilar su debido cumplimiento.

Las citadas autoridades se auxiliarán de la Unidad de Firma Electrónica de la Contraloría General del Distrito Federal, únicamente tratándose del uso de la firma electrónica notarial en términos del Código Civil, de esta Ley, de la Ley de Firma Electrónica del Distrito Federal y de las demás disposiciones aplicables.

Artículo 6. Esta Ley regula el tipo de ejercicio pro-

记处，隶属于内政部下属的国家法律制度汇编与咨询总局。

（21）公共实体：指的是联邦区的行政、立法、司法机关和自治性机构。

（22）电子证书：指的是由证明人以电子方式签署的文件，其中包含了署名人的签名资料并确认署名人的身份。

（23）公证人的电子签名：指的是根据《联邦区电子签名法》之规定，匹配到联邦区的一名公证人在履行公证人职能时所使用的电子签名。根据适用法规的要求，这一电子签名与公证人的手写签名和授权印鉴具有相同法律效力。

第3条 根据《宪法》第122条之规定，联邦区的公证职能应由当地的公证人行使。

公证人职业的制度保障由《宪法》确立，明确了公证人的职权范围，在墨西哥城议会中设立公证事务委员会，负责对公证人职业予以规范并实施立法监督。

公证人职业作为一种制度保障，其实质是在拉丁公证制度框架内，将公证人的职能视为从事法学领域的专业工作的一种执业形式，并规定了必要的条件来保障公证人依照本法之规定，以公正、适格、共同、自由的方式正确履行公证职责。

公证人根据本法以及其他相关法律之规定介入一切行为时，必须遵循公正和诚实的原则。

第4条 政府首脑应当根据本法之规定，为公证人及候补公证人颁发执业资格证。

第5条 联邦区政府首脑及各主管当局应遵守并监督落实本法。

前面所列的主管当局应当协同联邦区总审计长办公室的电子签名处，根据《民法典》、本法、《联邦区电子签名法》以及其他适用条文之规定，监督公证人正确使用电子签名。

第6条 本法规范了公证人作为法律从业人员的

fesional del derecho como oficio jurídico consistente en que el Notario, en virtud de su asesoría y conformación imparcial de su documentación en lo justo concreto del caso, en el marco de la equidad y el Estado Constitucional de Derecho y de la legalidad derivada del mismo, reciba por fuerza legal del Estado el reconocimiento público y social de sus instrumentos notariales con las finalidades de protección de la seguridad jurídica de los otorgantes y solicitantes de su actividad documentadora.

Artículo 7. Esta Ley establece como principios regulatorios e interpretativos de la función y documentación notarial:

I. El de la conservación jurídica de fondo y forma del instrumento notarial y de su efecto adecuado;

II. El de la conservación del instrumento notarial y de la matricidad en todo tiempo del mismo;

III. El de la concepción del Notariado como Garantía Institucional;

IV. Estar al servicio del bien y la paz jurídicos de la Ciudad y del respeto y cumplimiento del Derecho;

V. El ejercicio de la actividad notarial, en la justa medida en que se requiera por los prestatarios del servicio, obrando con estricto apego a la legalidad aplicable al caso concreto, de manera imparcial, preventiva, voluntaria y auxiliar de la administración de justicia respecto de asuntos en que no haya contienda.

El notario debe prestar su función más allá del interés del solicitante del servicio notarial, lo que implica cumplir sus procedimientos de asesoría notarial y de conformación del instrumento notarial, en estricto apego a la norma y de manera imparcial; debe aconsejar a cada una de las partes o solicitantes del servicio sin descuidar los intereses de la contraparte, en lo justo del caso de que se trate.

VI. El del cuidado del carácter de orden público de la función y su documentación en virtud del otorgamiento de la cualidad para dar fe, por el Jefe de Gobierno, a su actividad como Notario por la expedición de la patente respectiva, previos exámenes que merezcan tal reconocimiento público y social por acreditar el saber prudencial y la practica suficientes para dicha función, con la consecuente pertenencia al colegio y la coadyuvancia de éste a las funciones disciplinarias de vigilancia y sanción por parte de las autoridades, la continuación del archivo del Notario por el Archivo y la calificación y registro de los documentos públicos reconocidos por esta Ley por el Registro Público, tratándose de actos inscribibles.

Artículo 8. - Es obligación de las autoridades com-

执业方式，规范了公证人应当如何针对具体情况，在公平、法治以及由此派生出来的合法性原则框架下，公平公正地履行公证职责，确保公证文书在社会上得到公开承认，具备法律约束力，从而为办理公证的申请人和当事人提供法律保障。

第7条　本法对公证职能和公证资料给出了以下方面的监管和解释原则：

（1）按照法律对公证书内容和格式的要求保存公证书，确保公证文书具有适当效力；

（2）保存公证文书以及在办理公证过程中取得的一切资料；

（3）根据公证的概念，将公证人职业视为一种制度保障；

（4）促进维护本市的法律秩序与和平，尊重并履行法律；

（5）在履行公证职能时，公证人必须按照当事人的要求，严格适用相关法律，对于法律没有明文规定的，应以公正、自愿、有预见性和有助于司法行政管理的方式执行。

公证人在履行公证职能时，不能仅局限于当事人的要求事项，而是要依程序提供公证意见，形成合格的公证文书，严格依法办事；应向办理公证的当事各方提供建议，不得忽视任何一方的利益，做到不偏不倚，公平公正。

（6）由于公证职能具有公共秩序性质，公证人需要取得政府首脑颁发的执业资格证书方具备从业资格。为此，需要事先通过相应的考核，获得社会和公众的认可，证明其具备专业知识技能和充分的实践经验，从而获准加入公证人学会。学会配合主管当局对公证人的执业情况进行监管，对出现任何违法违纪行为的公证人实施制裁。档案管理局对公证人档案管理的连续性进行监督。公共登记处对于应当办理注册登记的事项，以及根据本法完成公证的公共文书进行审查和登记。

第8条　主管当局、公证人学会及公证人有义务

petentes, del Colegio y de los notarios, que la población reciba un servicio notarial pronto, expedito, profesional y eficiente. Si las autoridades competentes observan deficiencias, lo comunicarán al Colegio para que éste instrumente lo necesario para la expedita solución de las mismas y el eficaz cumplimiento de esa obligación.

En el caso de quejas y denuncias, las autoridades solicitarán que sean atendidas con atingencia por el Colegio y se practiquen las medidas preventivas; lo anterior, sin demérito de los procedimientos establecidos y previstos por otras leyes y reglamentos. Para ello y para programas especiales, el Colegio podrá celebrar convenios.

Artículo 9. La Administración instrumentará las medidas necesarias para facilitar la actividad notarial a fin de que la prestación del servicio se lleve a cabo en función de los principios a que se refiere el artículo 7 de esta Ley.

Especial apoyo se ofrecerá, tratándose de programas especiales acordados entre la Administración y el Colegio y de aquellos previstos en los artículos 16 al 19 de esta ley.

El Colegio, los Notarios y el Archivo, otorgaran facilidades y participaran en encuestas, sondeos y demás actividades que relacionadas con el ejercicio de la función notarial, dispongan las autoridades competentes.

Artículo 10. - El Jefe de Gobierno expedirá el decreto de autorización de nuevas notarías, cuando exista la necesidad del crecimiento del servicio, en el que podrá señalar su residencia, siempre y cuando dicha medida no afecte:

I. La preparación que deben tener los solicitantes de los exámenes de Aspirante y oposición y el de sus respectivos aprobados y triunfadores; y

II. La imparcialidad, la calidad profesional, la autonomía, la independencia y el sustrato material y económico de los notarios.

El decreto, fundado y motivado, deberá prever un examen de oposición por cada notaría, tomando en cuenta la población beneficiada y tendencias de su crecimiento, así como las necesidades notariales de ésta, mediando el tiempo conveniente entre cada convocatoria.

El Jefe de Gobierno podrá solicitar la opinión del colegio para los efectos a que se refiere el primer párrafo de este artículo.

Artículo 11. Los notarios son auxiliares en la administración de justicia. La Asamblea, la Administración, el Tribunal y el Colegio coadyuvarán en el desempeño de esta función.

确保居民能够享有快速、便捷、专业和高效的公证服务。主管当局一旦发现问题，应立即通知公证人学会，以便学会采取必要措施尽快加以整改，有效落实此项义务。

出现投诉或举报的，主管当局应当要求学会认真处理，采取必要的预防性措施；同时不妨碍遵照其他法律条例规定程序的执行。为此，学会可通过签署协议来执行专门的方案。

第 9 条　行政机关应出台具体措施，为公证工作提供便利，从而按照本法第 7 条所列的原则开展公证服务。

对于行政机关与公证人学会以及本法第 16 条至第 19 条规定的其他主体之间商定的专门方案，应提供专项支持。

学会、公证人以及档案管理局应为主管当局组织开展的与履行公证职能相关的问卷调查、投票以及其他活动提供便利并积极参与。

第 10 条　随着对公证服务需求的增长，政府首脑有权下令开立新的公证处，在批文中应写明公证处的所在地，但并不影响：

（1）筹备从业人员资格考试和岗位竞聘考试，通过考核选拔出合格的候补公证人和竞聘优胜者；

（2）公证人的公正性、专业素质、自主性、独立性以及物质和经济基础。

在批文中应当写明开立公证处的原因和动机，并写明人员竞聘考试的情况，考试内容应当根据受益群体情况及其增长趋势，以及公证服务的需要确定，并注意人员招聘的时间间隔。

为开展本条第一段所指的竞聘工作，政府首脑应当向公证人学会征求意见。

第 11 条　公证人对司法行政工作负有协助义务。公证人在履行职责时，议会、行政机关、法院和公证人学会均应给予协助。

SECCIÓN SEGUNDA GARANTÍAS SOCIALES DE LA FUNCIÓN NOTARIAL: PRESTACIONES Y SERVICIO

Articulo 12. Toda persona tiene Derecho, en términos de esta ley, al servicio profesional del Notario. El notario está obligado a prestar sus servicios profesionales, cuando para ello fuere requerido por las autoridades, por los particulares o en cumplimiento de resoluciones judiciales, siempre y cuando no exista impedimento legal para realizar el documento notarial solicitado, salvo las causas de excusa a que se refieren los artículos 43 y 44 de esta ley. En los programas especiales previstos por esta ley participarán todos los notarios.

Artículo 13. El notario ejerce su función sin sometimiento al erario y sin sueldo o iguala del Gobierno o de entidades públicas o privadas, ni favoritismo alguno. La fe pública se ejerce en cada caso concreto.

Artículo 14. De conformidad con los postulados del Notariado Latino incorporado al sistema del Notariado local, en cada instrumento y en la asesoría relativa el notario deberá proceder conforme a los principios jurídicos y deontológicos de su oficio profesional; consiguientemente, no podrá tratar a una parte como su cliente y a la otra no, sino la consideración será personal y profesionalmente competente por igual desde la buena fe y la asesoría imparcial a cada parte o persona que solicite su servicio. La violación a este artículo ameritará queja.

Artículo 15. Los notarios tendrán derecho a obtener de los prestatarios de sus servicios el pago de honorarios, de acuerdo con el arancel, y de los gastos suficientes que se causen o hayan de causarse.

El Colegio, presentará a las Autoridades competentes la propuesta de actualización del arancel, a más tardar el último día de noviembre anterior al año en que regirá dicha actualización, a la que anexará las consideraciones que sustenten su propuesta.

Las Autoridades competentes, después de haber recibido las aclaraciones del Colegio a las observaciones que tuviesen, llevarán a cabo las modificaciones fundadas que estimen conducentes; una vez aprobado, éste será publicado en la Gaceta Oficial a más tardar el último día hábil del mes de enero del año siguiente. Llegado el término, y en tanto no se publique la actualización, continuará aplicándose el último arancel publicado.

Artículo 15 BIS. - Los derechos de los prestatarios frente a los notarios serán los siguientes:

第二节 公证职能的社会保障：待遇与服务

第 12 条 人人有权根据本法享有公证人提供的专业服务。应主管当局、个人要求或者根据司法决议的规定，公证人有义务提供专业公证服务，前提是在出具公证文书方面不存在任何法律上的限制规定，但本法第 43 条和第 44 条中规定的情形除外。全体公证人均应参与本法规定的专门方案。

第 13 条 公证人执业不受财政支持，不应接受政府或私人机构给予的工资和酬劳，不应有偏袒倾向，办理每一个具体的公证业务都应当维护社会公信。

第 14 条 根据拉丁公证制度，结合当地公证体系所采用的准则，公证人出具的每一份公证文书以及提供的每一次咨询都必须符合其所属行业的法律原则和道德准则。因此，不得有选择性地对客户区别对待，而是要以专业、诚信的态度提供服务，向所有团体或个人提供公证服务。违反本条规定的，应受到投诉。

第 15 条 公证人有权按照收费表规定的标准，通过提供服务收取报酬，以及由此产生的相关费用。

收费标准调整的，公证人学会应至迟于收费标准调整生效前一年的 11 月最后一天，向主管当局提交调整方案，并一并提交调整方案所依据的理由。

主管当局在接到公证人学会关于说明调整意见的澄清函后，可以做出相应修订并说明理由。一旦收费调整方案获批通过，应当至迟于次年一月份的最后一个工作日在官方公报上发布。逾期没有对调整方案进行公示的，应继续执行之前公布的收费方案。

第 15 条之二 要求办理公证的人员享有以下权利：

I. Ser atendidos personalmente y con profesionalismo;

II. Ser informados por los Notarios de las exenciones, beneficios fiscales y facilidades administrativas aplicables al trámite solicitado;

III. Obtener información por parte del notario en cualquier etapa del procedimiento que realiza ante éste;

IV. Recibir copia de la solicitud de entrada y trámite al Registro Público de la Propiedad y de Comercio o del documento que haga sus veces, así como a ser informado acerca del estado que guarda el trámite registral; y

V. Solicitar y obtener el original o copia certificada de los documentos con los que se acredite el pago de los impuestos y derechos generados por la operación celebrada.

Artículo 16. Las autoridades podrán requerir de los notarios la prestación de sus servicios para atender asuntos de orden público o de interés social. En estos casos las autoridades y el colegio convendrán los honorarios correspondientes.

Artículo 17. Los notarios participarán también, con tarifas reducidas y convenidas por el Colegio con las autoridades correspondientes, en programas de fomento a la vivienda y regularización de la tenencia de la propiedad inmueble.

Artículo 18. - Las Dependencias y Entidades de la Administración Pública del Distrito Federal que realicen actividades relacionadas con la regularización de la propiedad de inmuebles, regularización territorial y el fomento a la vivienda, requerirán los servicios únicamente de los notarios de esta entidad federativa, para el otorgamiento de las escrituras relativas.

Cada una de las Dependencias y Entidades a las que se refiere el párrafo anterior, convendrá con el Colegio el procedimiento para asignar el otorgamiento de las escrituras relativas, mismo que atenderá a los principios de transparencia, equidad y eficacia, el cual deberá ser validado por la Dirección General Jurídica y de Estudios Legislativos y la Dirección General de Legalidad y Responsabilidades.

A partir de la entrada en vigor de esta disposición, cada Notario manifestará por escrito a las Dependencias y Entidades señaladas, su voluntad de participar en la formalización de escrituras relativas a que se refiere este artículo, haciéndolo también del conocimiento de la Dirección General Jurídica y de Estudios Legislativos y del Colegio. Sin el cumplimiento de dicho requisito ningún notario podrá ser considerado en el mecanismo de designación al efecto convenido.

（1）公证人亲自为客户提供专业服务；

（2）公证人向客户告知关于要求办理手续适用何种减免政策、税收优惠和行政便利；

（3）在公证手续办理过程中随时从公证人处获知相关信息；

（4）收到商业和财产公共登记处收录和处理的申请书副本以及相关文件副本，并获悉登记手续的办理进程；以及

（5）申请并取得相关公证手续所产生的税费的付款凭证原件或其经核证副本。

第16条　主管当局有权要求公证人出于社会公益目的或公共事业目的提供公证服务。在此情况下，主管当局和公证人学会应商定相应的服务酬金标准。

第17条　公证人还应按照公证人学会与主管当局商定的收费标准，参与社会性住房福利项目和不动产所有权规范项目。在这种情况下，公证收费应当低于正常收费水平。

第18条　分管不动产所有权、土地所有权事务和住房福利项目的联邦区行政机关各部门和单位，在办理相关公证文书时，仅能委托本辖区内的公证人办理。

上一段所指的每一家行政主管当局或单位，应与公证人学会商定公证文书办理程序，所采用的程序应当遵从透明、公平和高效原则，并经法律和立法研究总局以及合规与问责管理总局论证通过。

自本规定生效之日起，每一名公证人应当书面致函给前面所指的行政主管当局或单位，表示愿意办理本条所指的公证文书，并到法律和立法研究总局以及公证人学会进行备案。任何未完成这一备案程序的公证人均不得被纳入相应的指派机制中。

El Colegio informará mensualmente a las autoridades competentes, dentro de los primeros cinco días hábiles de cada mes, los turnos que hubieren hecho durante el mes anterior.

Los notarios dejarán constancia en el texto de cada instrumento, de las instrucciones recibidas.

Artículo 19. Los Notarios estarán obligados a prestar sus servicios en los casos y en los términos que establezcan los ordenamientos electorales. Las autoridades competentes, con la coadyuvancia del Colegio, a través de su Consejo, y con el auxilio en su caso de la Comisión de Honor y Justicia, estarán muy atentas a cualquier irregularidad a fin de que el servicio notarial en esta materia se preste de la mejor forma posible. En su caso, si así lo pidieren las autoridades o los partidos, los Notarios podrán organizar recorridos para dar fe si es menester, conforme al turno que al efecto establezca el Colegio.

Artículo 20. - Las autoridades competentes del Gobierno deberán concentrar la información de las operaciones y actos notariales y procesarla bajo sistemas estadísticos y cibernéticos que permitan regular y fijar, conforme a esta Ley, las modalidades administrativas que requiere la prestación eficaz del servicio notarial. La recopilación de dicha información será de carácter formal y estadístico cuidando la autoridad se respete siempre el secreto profesional y la intimidad negocial; así como las disposiciones relativas a la transparencia y acceso a la información.

Para la compilación de datos a que se refiere esta disposición, los Notarios deberán proporcionar a las Autoridades competentes, toda información relacionada con las operaciones y actos notariales que realicen.

El Colegio auxiliará a la autoridad competente en la integración de datos y podrá participar de la información generada conforme a los párrafos anteriores.

Artículo 21. La autoridad competente formará expedientes individuales de quienes soliciten examen de aspirante, de los aspirantes y de los notarios, en los que se concentrarán todos los antecedentes relevantes para la prestación del buen servicio; elementos de calificación de actuación y detección de irregularidades; avisos, quejas, procedimientos y demás documentos relacionados; y de todos aquellos que hayan defraudado, declarado falsamente, suplantado o ejercido indebidamente funciones notariales en el Distrito Federal o que en asuntos relacionados con ellos hayan incurrido en prácticas ilícitas.

Los notarios en lo individual y el Colegio, propor-

公证人学会应在每月的前五个工作日内向主管当局通报上一月的轮值情况。

公证人应在每一份公证文书中写明其收到的工作指令。

第19条 公证人有义务按照选举制度规定的情形和要求提供公证服务。主管当局在公证人学会理事会的配合下，应特别关注任何不合规情况，从而确保以最佳方式提供公证服务，必要时还可得到荣誉与正义委员会的协助。如果当局或党派有需要，公证人也可按照公证人学会的排班安排，在必要时到现场办理公证。

第20条 政府主管当局应当汇总关于公证办理和公证文书的信息，并通过在线统计系统进行加工处理，以便根据本法对公证服务的管理模式进行规范，提高公证服务的效率。信息采集工作当采用统计方法，以官方规定的形式实施，注重权威性，始终遵守职业保密和商业保密原则。此外，还要遵守与信息透明和信息访问相关的规定。

为采集本条所指的数据，公证人应当向主管当局提供与其办理的公证业务和公证文书相关的一切信息。

公证人学会应协助主管当局对数据进行整合，并有权访问根据前几段规定生成的信息。

第21条 对于申请参加候补公证人资格考试、申请竞聘公证人岗位和申请办理公证人资格认证的，主管当局应当开立个人档案，在档案中收录与其从业相关的所有资料：关于业绩评定以及不合规情况检查的各项要素；通知、投诉、诉讼以及其他相关文件；以及所有涉嫌弄虚作假、虚假声明、在联邦区执业过程中出现的不当行为或者构成违法的任何相关事项。

无论是公证人个人还是公证人学会，都应及时向

cionarán de manera oportuna a las Autoridades competentes, la información de que dispongan.

Artículo 22. El colegio participará en la conformación y recibirá de parte de las autoridades competentes la información a que se refiere el artículo 20; intercambiará impresiones con dichas autoridades para proveer lo necesario para el mejor servicio notarial. Igualmente el colegio recibirá la información y, en su caso, la documentación a que se refiere el artículo anterior.

Artículo 23. El colegio orientará a los prestatarios del servicio notarial sobre deficiencias de dicho servicio, con especial referencia a grupos sociales vulnerables y a problemas relacionados con el deber de imparcialidad y atención personal del notario.

Si la intervención del Colegio no fue suficiente para la satisfacción de los derechos del prestatario, a solicitud de éste, el Colegio turnará de inmediato los antecedentes a la Autoridad, para el trámite que corresponda, sin que exceda de seis meses el plazo entre la intervención del Colegio y la remisión a las Autoridades competentes.

Las Autoridades competentes darán trámite a la queja hasta que se agote el procedimiento de conciliación que se haya solicitado al Colegio. El término de seis meses se extenderá, a solicitud por escrito del prestatario, si el procedimiento o resolución exigen mayor plazo.

El Colegio informará semestralmente a las Autoridades competentes sobre los asuntos, detallando el nombre del usuario y el notario respectivo.

Los interesados podrán en cualquier momento, acudir en queja ante las autoridades competentes de lo que serán informados por el Colegio. La prescripción se interrumpe durante el tiempo de sustanciación de conciliación ante el Colegio.

Artículo 24. - Los expedientes a que se refieren estos artículos están sometidos al secreto profesional salvo la denuncia o procedimientos correspondientes que conforme a derecho se lleven a cabo para efectos de determinar las responsabilidades a que haya lugar y deberá cumplirse con las disposiciones relativas a la transparencia y acceso a la información.

Artículo 25. Las personas de que se trate tendrán derecho de pedir se dé a conocer si conforme al artículo 22 se ha formado algún expediente relativo y los términos respectivos.

主管当局提供其掌握的相关资料。

第22条 公证人学会应从主管当局接收第20条中所指的资料并参与核实；与主管当局进行意见交流，以便更好地提供公证服务。同样，学会还应接收前一条所指的文件材料（如果有）。

第23条 公证人学会应对公证人在从业中出现的缺陷和不足进行指导，特别要关注社会弱势群体以及与公证人所承担的确保公正性和人道主义关怀义务相关的问题。

学会的干预不足以满足投诉人的权利主张的，经投诉人申请，应立即向主管当局移交资料，以办理相应手续。在学会介入干预与移送主管当局处理之间的时间间隔不得超过六个月。

针对相关投诉，主管当局应进行处理，直至穷尽学会要求采取的调解程序。如果审理程序或得出解决方案需要更长时间，应投诉人书面申请，前面规定的六个月的期限可予以延长。

学会每半年应当向主管当局汇报投诉事项，详细列明投诉方姓名以及被投诉的公证人。

当事人可随时就学会向主管当局的报告事项进行申诉。在学会调解期间，暂停计算时效期。

第24条 前几条中涉及的卷宗属于职业保密范畴，除非出于投诉或诉讼审理，依法准予调阅，以查明相关责任归属的，否则应当按照信息公开透明和信息获取的相关规定执行。

第25条 当事人享有知情权，有权了解自己是否按照第22条的规定被卷入诉讼以及诉讼的相关情况。

CAPITULO II DE LA FUNCIÓN NOTARIAL Y DEL NOTARIADO

SECCIÓN PRIMERA DE LA FUNCIÓN NOTARIAL

Artículo 26. - La función autenticadora es la facultad otorgada por la Ley al Notario para que se reconozca como cierto lo que éste asiente en las actas o escrituras públicas que redacte, salvo prueba en contrario.

La función autenticadora deberá ejercerla de manera personal y en todas sus actuaciones de asesoría, instrumentación y juicio, conducirse conforme a la prudencia jurídica e imparcialmente.

La función notarial es el conjunto de actividades que el notario realiza conforme a las disposiciones de esta Ley, para garantizar el buen desempeño y la seguridad jurídica en el ejercicio de dicha función autenticadora. Posee una naturaleza compleja: es pública en cuanto proviene de los poderes del Estado y de la Ley, que obran en reconocimiento público de la actividad profesional de notario y de la documentación notarial al servicio de la sociedad. De otra parte, es autónoma y libre, para el notario que la ejerce, actuando con fe pública.

Artículo 27. Siendo la función notarial de orden e interés públicos, corresponde a la Ley y a las instituciones que contempla procurar las condiciones que garanticen la profesionalidad, la independencia, la imparcialidad y autonomía del Notario en el ejercicio de la fe pública de que está investido, a fin de que esta última pueda manifestarse libremente, en beneficio de la certeza y seguridad jurídicas que demanda la sociedad y sin más limitaciones ni formalidades que las previstas por la Ley.

En consecuencia, las autoridades administrativas y judiciales proveerán lo conducente para hacer efectiva y expedita la independencia funcional del Notariado auxiliándole de la misma forma, cuando así lo requiera el Notariado, para el eficaz ejercicio de sus funciones.

Artículo 28. Las autoridades del Distrito Federal deberán auxiliar a los Notarios en el ejercicio normal de sus funciones cuando los actos concretos de dación de fe así lo requieran. Particularmente la policía y demás autoridades que tengan a su cargo el uso de la fuerza pública, deberán prestar ayuda a los Notarios cuando sean requeridos por ellos.

Se aplicarán las penas que correspondan al delito de abuso de autoridad al servidor público que obstaculice o impida a un Notario el ejercicio de sus funciones o no le preste el auxilio que requiera para esos fines, debiendo prestarlos.

Artículo 29. Esta Ley reconoce y protege el principio de libertad de elección de notario, en beneficio de la imparcialidad en la relación con las partes y de la ética de la función notarial.

Artículo 30. El ejercicio de la función notarial y la asesoría jurídica que proporcione el Notario debe realizarlos en interés de todas las partes y del orden jurídico justo y equitativo de la ciudad, y por tanto, incompatible con toda relación de sumisión ante favor, poder o dinero, que afecten su independencia formal o materialmente.

El notario no deberá aceptar más asuntos que aquellos que pueda atender personalmente en su función autenticadora.

Artículo 31. El ejercicio de la función notarial es incompatible con toda restricción de la libertad personal, de las facultades de apreciación y de expresión.

Artículo 32. - Igualmente el ejercicio del oficio notarial es incompatible con toda dependencia a empleo, cargo o comisión público, privado o de elección popular, y con el ejercicio de la profesión de abogado en asuntos en que haya contienda. El notario tampoco podrá ser comerciante, ministro de culto o agente económico de cualquier clase en términos de las leyes respectivas.

Artículo 33. El notario sí podrá:

I. Aceptar y desempeñar cargos académicos y docentes, de dirección de carrera o institución académica, de beneficencia pública o privada, de colaboración ciudadana y los que desempeñe gratuitamente a personas morales con fines no lucrativos;

II. Representar a su cónyuge, ascendientes o descendientes, por consanguinidad o afinidad y hermanos;

III. Ser tutor, curador y albacea;

IV. Desempeñar el cargo de miembro del consejo de administración, comisario o secretario de sociedades o asociaciones;

V. Resolver consultas jurídicas objetivamente y ser consultor jurídico extranjero emitiendo dictámenes objetivos;

VI. Ser árbitro o secretario en juicio arbitral;

VII. Ser mediador jurídico;

VIII. Ser mediador o conciliador;

IX. Patrocinar a los interesados en los procedimientos judiciales o administrativos necesarios para obtener el registro de escrituras:

X. Intervenir, patrocinar y representar a los inte-

第29条 本法承认并保护自由挑选公证人的原则，以促进公证职能对当事各方的公正性和弘扬公证职业道德。

第30条 公证人所提供的公证服务和法律咨询服务，应当遵循利于各方、利于城市司法秩序的公平公正的原则。因此，公证人不得兼任可能在形式上或者实质上影响其独立性的任何有利益关系、权力和金钱关系的职务。

公证人除了依职责亲自办理公证外，不得受理其他委托事项。

第31条 公证职能的行使不得构成对人身自由、自由裁量权和自由表达权的任何限制。

第32条 公证职能的行使，同样不得与公共或私营领域的就业、职务或任命或者普选资格有任何依附关系，公证人也不得兼任相应领域的律师职务。根据相关法律要求，公证人不得从商，也不得担任宗教或经济类的代理人。

第33条 公证人有权：

（1）接受并担任学术和教学职务，学科管理职务，学术机构、公共或私人慈善机构、市民合作机构中的管理职务，以及在非盈利性法人实体中免费任职；

（2）作为其配偶、父母或子女、血亲或姻亲以及兄弟姐妹的代表；

（3）充当监护人、财产监护人和遗嘱执行人；

（4）在社团或协会中担任理事会成员、监事或秘书职务；

（5）客观中立地解答法律咨询，担任外国法律顾问，出具客观意见；

（6）在仲裁事项中担任仲裁人或秘书；

（7）担任司法调解员；

（8）担任调解员或调停人；

（9）在司法或行政诉讼中为当事人提供必要的支持，以办理文书的登记；

（10）介入不涉及个人冲突的相关司法程序，以

resados en los procedimientos judiciales en los que no haya contienda entre particulares, así como en trámites y procedimientos administrativos; dichas funciones no inhabilitan al Notario para autorizar, en su caso, cualquier instrumento relacionado; y

XI. Actividades semejantes que no causen conflicto ni dependencia que afecte su dación de fe y asesoría imparcial.

Artículo 34. - Corresponde a los notarios del Distrito Federal el ejercicio de las funciones notariales en el ámbito territorial de la entidad. Los notarios del Distrito Federal no podrán ejercer sus funciones ni establecer oficinas fuera de los límites de éste. Los actos que se celebren ante su fe, podrán referirse a cualquier otro lugar, siempre que se firmen las escrituras o actas correspondientes por las partes dentro del Distrito Federal, y se de cumplimiento a las disposiciones de esta ley.

Se prohíbe a quienes no son notarios usar en anuncios al público, en oficinas de servicios o comercios, que den la idea que quien los usa o a quien beneficia realiza trámites o funciones notariales sin ser notario, tales como "asesoría notarial', "trámites notariales", "servicios notariales","escrituras notariales", "actas notariales", así como otros términos semejantes referidos a la función notarial y que deban comprenderse como propios de ésta.

Artículo 35. - Se aplicarán las penas previstas por el artículo 323 del Código Penal a quien, careciendo de la patente de notario del Distrito Federal expedida en los términos de esta Ley, realizare en el Distrito Federal alguna de las siguientes conductas:

I. Ostentarse, anunciarse como tal o inducir a la creencia de que es Notario para ejercer o simular ejercer funciones notariales, o ejercerlas de hecho.

II. Tener oficina notarial, o lugar donde se realicen actividades notariales o meramente de asesoría notarial o de firmas para instrumentos notariales.

III. Envíe libros de protocolo o folios a firma al Distrito Federal o realice firmas de escrituras o actas en su demarcación.

IV. Produzca instrumentos públicos en los que consten actos jurídicos que para su validez requieran otorgarse en escritura pública ó hagan constar hechos fuera de su ámbito legal de competencia.

Artículo 35 BIS. - Los notarios que en el ejercicio de la función detecten existencia de documentos presumiblemente apócrifos o alterados, deberán dar aviso al Ministerio Público y a las autoridades competentes.

及行政手续和程序中，为当事人提供必要的支持和代办服务；这些职能并不妨碍公证人根据需要出具任何相关文书；以及

（11）与公证人公正地履行其公证和咨询职能不构成冲突或依附关系的其他类似活动。

第34条　联邦区公证人应当在本行政辖区内履行其公证职能。联邦区公证人不得超出其辖区范围行使公证职能或者设立办事机构。公证人出具的公证文书，只要是由当事各方在联邦区内签署相应文书或记录，符合本法规定的，可以涉及其他任何地点。

禁止没有公证人执业资格的人员在其服务处所或从业场所使用混淆性字眼，例如"公证咨询""公证手续""公证服务""公证状""公证记录"，以及其他提及公证职能、致使公众认为其所从事的系公证职业的其他类似文字。使用此类字样将导致公众误认为相关人员有资格办理与公证相关的手续或履行公证职能。

第35条　没有根据本法之规定取得联邦区公证人执业资格却在联邦区擅自开展下列任一行为的，应按《刑法典》第323条之规定进行处罚：

（1）宣称、标榜自己为公证人或诱导他人误认其为公证人，意图行使或者实际行使公证人职能的；

（2）开立公证处，或者拥有从事公证活动或者单纯提供公证咨询或签署公证文书的场所；

（3）开具写有联邦区抬头的公证书簿或者在联邦区签署公证文书；

（4）出具内容中载有需要办理公证方可生效的司法行为的公共文书，或者超出其法定职权范围对相关事项进行证明。

第35条之二　公证人在履行公证职能的过程中发现文书造假或文件篡改的，应当向检察机关和主管当局举报。

Artículo 36. - También se aplicarán las penas previstas por el artículo 323 del Código Penal al que sin ser notario, o siendo notario con patente de otra Entidad distinta del Distrito Federal, introduzca a éste o conserve en su poder, por sí o por interpósita persona, libros de protocolo o de folios de otra entidad, con la finalidad de llevar a cabo actos que únicamente pueden realizar notarios del Distrito Federal.

Artículo 37. - El aspirante a notario, el que haya sido notario del Distrito Federal o el notario suspendido en el ejercicio de su función que realice cualquiera de las conductas previstas en los artículos 35 y 36 de esta ley se hará acreedor al doble de la pena establecida por el artículo 323 del Nuevo Código Penal.

Artículo 38. El Notario que consienta o participe en las conductas descritas por los artículos 35, 35 BIS y 36 de esta Ley, se hará acreedor a la sanción prevista en el artículo anterior.

Artículo 39. Las Autoridades competentes, procederán a la clausura de las oficinas o lugares en donde se realicen las conductas previstas en los artículos 35, 36 y 37 de esta Ley y donde se viole el artículo 40, independientemente de la sanción personal correspondiente.

Artículo 40. El notario, para el ejercicio de su función, únicamente podrá establecer una oficina, sin que pueda hacerlo al interior de un despacho de abogados u otros profesionales, empresas u oficinas públicas.

Artículo 41. La función notarial podrá ejercerse en cualquier día, sea hábil o inhábil y a cualquier hora y lugar. Sin embargo, la notaría podrá cerrarse en días inhábiles y fuera del horario de trabajo señalado.

Cada notario deberá señalar el horario de trabajo de su oficina, anunciarlo al exterior de la misma y lo informará a las autoridades competentes y al colegio, así como los cambios que hiciere al respecto.

SECCIÓN SEGUNDA DEL NOTARIO

Artículo 42. Notario es el profesional del Derecho investido de fe pública por el Estado, y que tiene a su cargo recibir, interpretar, redactar y dar forma legal a la Voluntad de las personas que ante él acuden, y conferir autenticidad y certeza jurídicas a los actos y hechos pasados ante su fe, mediante la consignación de los mismos en instrumentos públicos de su autoría.

El notario conserva los instrumentos en el protocolo a su cargo, los reproduce y da fe de ellos. Actúa también

第 36 条 没有公证人执业资格，或者属于联邦区以外辖区的公证人，亲自或者委托他人在联邦区行使公证职能，擅自办理公证文书，从而越权开展只有联邦区公证人有权开展的行为的，同样应按《刑法典》第 323 条之规定进行处罚。

第 37 条 候补公证人，已经在联邦区正式执业的公证人或者暂停执业的公证人，出现本法第 35 条和第 36 条所载行为的，应按照《刑法典》第 323 条规定的刑罚加倍论处。

第 38 条 默许或者参与本法第 35 条、第 35 条之二和第 36 条所载行为的公证人，应按照上一条之规定论处。

第 39 条 对于出现本法第 35 条、第 36 条和第 37 条所载行为的场所或地点，以及构成违反第 40 条的场所或地点，应由主管当局予以查封，同时不妨碍追究相关责任人的个人责任。

第 40 条 公证人只能开立一处办公场所履行其职责，且不得将办公场所设在律师事务所或其他专业机构、公司或公职机关内部。

第 41 条 公证职能可随时随地行使，无论是否是工作日。但是，公证处在非工作日以及非工作时间段可以停止营业。

每一名公证人必须在其办公处所内部以及室外写明工作时间，并向主管当局和公证人学会申报；如有变更，也必须进行申报。

第二节 公证人职业

第 42 条 公证人系由国家赋予公信力的从事法律工作的专业人士，其职责是听取、接收、理解办理公证的当事人的意愿并依据法律形式予以表达，使之具备相应法律效力，通过出具公证文书对需要公证的文书或事件的真实性和法律确定性进行确认。

公证人应当将公证文书保存在由其负责的公证登记簿中，复制并予以核证。公证人还可配合司法机关

como auxiliar de la administración de justicia, como consejero, árbitro o asesor internacional, en los términos que señalen las disposiciones legales relativas.

Artículo 43. El notario podrá excusarse de actuar en días festivos o en horario que no sea el de su oficina, salvo que el requerimiento sea para el otorgamiento de testamento, siempre y cuando a juicio del propio notario las circunstancias del presunto testador hagan que el otorgamiento sea urgente.

También podrá excusarse de actuar cuando los solicitantes del servicio no le aporten los elementos necesarios o no le anticipen los gastos y honorarios correspondientes.

Artículo 44. El notario también podrá excusarse al momento si circunstancialmente se encuentra atendiendo otro asunto, mas si la persona decide esperarlo se aplicará el principio de obligatoriedad en términos del articulo 12 con las salvedades del artículo anterior, según el orden de atención que le toque.

Artículo 45. Queda prohibido a los notarios:

I. Actuar con parcialidad en el ejercicio de sus funciones y en todas las demás actividades que esta ley le señala;

II. Dar fe de actos que dentro de los procedimientos legales respectivos corresponda en exclusiva hacerlo a algún servidor público; sin embargo, sin tener en principio ese valor procedimental exclusivo, sí podrán cotejar cualquier tipo de documentos, registros y archivos públicos y privados o respecto a ellos u otros acontecimientos certificar hechos, situaciones o abstenciones que guarden personas o cosas relacionadas o concomitantes con averiguaciones, procesos o trámites, lo cual tendrá valor como indicio calificado respecto de los mismos, sujeto a juicio de certeza judicial, y solo será prueba plena con relación a aspectos que no sean parte esencial de dichas facultades públicas, aspectos que deberá precisar en el instrumento indicado, salvo las copias de constancias que obren en expedientes judiciales que le hayan sido turnados por un juez para la elaboración de algún instrumento, que podrá cotejar a solicitud de quien haya intervenido en el procedimiento o haya sido autorizado en él para oír notificaciones.

III. Actuar como notario en instrumentos o asuntos en que tengan interés, disposición a favor, o intervengan por si, representados por o en representación de terceros, el propio notario, su cónyuge o parientes consanguíneos o afines hasta el cuarto y segundo grados, respectivamente, o sus asociados o suplentes y los cónyuges o parientes de ellos en los mismos grados o en asuntos en los cuales ten-

履行职责，或根据相关法律规定充当咨询人、仲裁员或国际顾问。

第43条 公证人有权以节假日或者非工作时间为由拒绝办理公证业务，但遗嘱公证事项除外。经公证人本人判断，立遗嘱人确有需要的，应为其紧急办理遗嘱公证。

公证申请人没有向公证人提供必要的公证要件，或者没有提前缴清相应的公证费用和办理费用的，公证人也有权拒绝办理公证。

第44条 接到公证申请时，公证人正在为其他客户办理公证的，同样有权拒绝办理公证。但是客户愿意排期等候的，应当根据第12条的规定适用强制性原则，按照轮候顺序进行办理，前一条所列情形除外。

第45条 严禁公证人：

（1）在履行公证职责以及本法所载的其他活动时有偏向性。

（2）在办理相应法律程序的过程中指名道姓要求由某个公职人员承办。但是，在不是出于偏向性而专门认定承办人员的前提下，公证人确实有权对任何类型的文件、登记记录、公共和私人文档进行核对，并据此对这些文件材料或其他事项进行查证，以确认相应事件、情况或弃权事项属实；对当事人、拟公证事项按程序进行审查或办理相关手续，确认其证明效力，判断其法律确定性。公证人在拟制公证书时应当明确相关事项，在公证书中附上相关办理材料，但是法官开立的司法档案中的证明材料副本除外。对于司法档案中的证明材料，应当事人要求，或者经授权批准，方可进行核证。

（3）在与公证人有利益关系或者公证人本人、其代理人或者公证人所代表的第三方卷入的事项中作为公证人行事；或者在公证人本人、其配偶、四代以内血亲和两代以内姻亲，或者公证人的合伙人或替补人，以及公证人的合伙人或替补人的配偶、四代以内血亲和两代以内姻亲卷入的事项中作为公证人行事。

ga esta prohibición el o los notarios asociados, o el notario suplente;

IV. Actuar como notario sin rogación de parte, solicitud de interesado o mandamiento judicial, salvo en los casos previstos en esta Ley;

V. Dar fe de actos, hechos o situaciones con respecto a los cuales haya actuado previamente como abogado en asuntos donde haya habido contienda judicial;

VI. Dar fe de actos, hechos o situaciones sin haberse identificado plenamente como notario;

VII. Dar fe de manera no objetiva o parcial;

VIII. Ejercer sus funciones sí el objeto, el motivo -expresado o conocido por el notario; o el fin del acto es contrario a la ley o a las buenas costumbres; asimismo si el objeto del acto es físico o legalmente imposible;

IX. Recibir y conservar en depósito, por sí o por interpósita persona, sumas de dinero, valores o documentos que representen numerario con motivo de los actos o hechos en que intervengan, excepto en los siguientes casos:

a)El dinero o cheques destinados al pago de gastos, impuestos, contribuciones o derechos causados por las actas o escrituras, o relacionados con los objetos de dichos instrumentos;

b)Cheques librados a favor de acreedores en pago de adeudos garantizados con hipoteca u otros actos cuya escritura de extinción vaya a ser autorizada por ellos;

c)Documentos mercantiles y numerario en los que intervengan con motivo de protestos; y

d)En los demás casos en que las leyes así lo permitan.

En los casos señalados en esta fracción, el notario, dará el destino que corresponda a cada cantidad recibida, dentro de los plazos que señalen las disposiciones legales aplicables; en su defecto, tan pronto proceda.

X. Establecer oficinas en una dirección distinta a la registrada por la Autoridad competente, para atender al público en asuntos y trámites relacionados con la notaría a su cargo.

No se considerará violatoria de la presente fracción la atención al público en las sedes o lugares convenidos con las autoridades de los notarios que participen en los programas de regularización de la tenencia de la tierra, de Jornadas Notariales, Sucesiones, de Testamentos, Voluntad Anticipada y cualquier otro programa, o convenio con cualquier autoridad federal o local que tenga como finalidad la accesibilidad y cercanía en los servicios notariales, o de las consultorías gratuitas que implemente el Colegio

（4）未经当事方委托、当事人申请或司法委托而作为公证人行事，但本法另有规定的情形除外。

（5）对公证人事前已经以律师身份在产生法律纠纷的事件中办理的文书、事项或情形，以公证人身份行事。

（6）对没有充分查实的文书、事项或情形进行公证。

（7）在办理公证时没有坚持客观、公正的立场。

（8）经公证人查明或认可，办理公证的对象或动机，或办理公证的目的与法律规定相悖或违反了道德伦理，以及文书目标在现实中或法律上不可能实现时，不得办理公证。

（9）自行或者派代表接收并保存存款、钱款、有价证券或者相应的协议文书，但以下钱款除外：

a）用于支付文书办理或者与此类文书相关事项的税费或者手续费的现金或支票；

b）向债权人开具的用于偿付抵押担保债务或者其他债务的支票；

c）写明拒付理由的商业单据和现金；以及

d）其他法律规定的情形。

在上一目所列情形中，公证人应按照法律规定的权限，将收到的每笔款项按写明用途予以处置；法律没有明文规定权限的，应尽快办理。

（10）在主管当局登记地址以外的地点设立办事处，向公众提供与公证事务相关的服务和手续办理服务。

公证员参与办理土地所有权公证、继承权公证、遗嘱公证相关的方案，或者任何其他与联邦或地方当局订立的方案或协议，以贴近群众、简单便捷的方式，通过公证人学会在联邦区任何地方提供公证服务和免费法律咨询服务。

de Notarios en cualquier lugar del Distrito Federal.

XI. Establecer despachos o negocios, en el interior de las oficinas, cuya dirección tenga registrada ante la autoridad, ajenos a los servicios notariales.

Si el notario designa su oficina notarial para recibir notificaciones de los juicios en los que participe y señale domicilios fiscales de él, de su cónyuge o de sus ascendientes o descendientes o que corresponda a un domicilio fiscal para una persona moral o mercantil, de la que forme parte no se considerará violatorio de la presente fracción.

Artículo 46. El notario que deje de serlo, quedará impedido para intervenir como abogado en los litigios relacionados con la validez o nulidad de los instrumentos otorgados ante su fe o de sus asociados o suplentes que hayan autorizado el instrumento, salvo que se trate de derecho propio para actuar procesalmente.

TITULO SEGUNDO
DEL EJERCICIO DE LA FUNCIÓN NOTARIAL

CAPITULO I DE LA CARRERA NOTARIAL

SECCIÓN PRIMERA DISPOSICIONES GENERALES

Artículo 47. La carrera notarial es el sistema que organiza los estudios e investigación de las diversas disciplinas jurídicas dirigidos al mejor desempeño de la función notarial y para la difusión y puesta en práctica de sus principios y valores ético- jurídicos en beneficio de la ciudad.

Artículo 48. Para la carrera notarial se dispondrán medios para hacer accesible la preparación básica para el examen de aspirante al Notariado a profesionales del Derecho, como condición pública de una mejor competencia profesional para el examen de oposición, de la mejora del nivel jurídico y de la calidad personal y social del servicio notarial, en términos de colaboración entre las autoridades y el colegio, respecto a interesados y a la sociedad en general.

Artículo 49. La preparación notarial y la difusión de la imparcialidad jurídica y de conocimientos en beneficio del medio jurídico está garantizada por esta Ley, y para ello la Carrera Notarial proporciona condiciones de formación teórica y práctica; formación deontológica y personal suficientes para que mediante exámenes públicos por jurados especialmente cualificados, el profesional del Derecho idóneo para la función notarial pueda acceder a la misma en las mejores condiciones de servicio y de igualdad de acceso en bien de la Ciudad y para la evolución

（11）在向当局登记的地址以外的地点，设立隶属于公证处的业务部门或办事处。

如果公证人将其办公地址设定为接收司法通知的联系地址后，将其个人住址、配偶的住址、父母或子女的住址，或者其有出资或参股的法人实体或商业实体的注册地址设定为税务地址的，不视为违反本项之规定。

第46条　公证人不再执业后，不得以律师身份参与到关系其本人、合伙人或者替补公证人出具的公证文书是否有效的诉讼中，但根据程序要求依法有权办理的情况除外。

第二篇
公证执业

第一章　公证学专业

第一节　总则

第47条　公证学指的是组织研究和调查各类法律的一个学科体系，目的是进一步完善公证功能，传播并应用这一领域的道德法律原则和价值观，从而造福社会。

第48条　通过公证学专业的学习，可以获得相应的专业知识储备，从而有希望获得公证从业资格，成为法律专业人士。这是提高专业竞争力，通过竞聘考核的公开条件，也是改善公证行业的法律专业水平、从业人员素质和社会服务水平的必要条件。为此，需要政府与公证人学会大力合作，为学员乃至全社会提供便利。

第49条　本法的一项宗旨就是保障公证从业环境，传播司法公证和法律知识。为此，公证学专业的学习，包括理论学习和实践，以及思想道德教育和个人素质的培养，以通过举办资格考试的方式，吸引符合条件的法学专业人士从事公证工作，在公开、公平的条件下选拔人才，造福社会，并促进公证行业的良性发展。

positiva del Notariado.

Artículo 50. La carrera notarial se regirá por los principios y valores que fundamentan el ejercicio de la fe pública, y especialmente por los principios de excelencia, especialización, legitimación, objetividad, profesionalismo, imparcialidad, sustentabilidad e independencia.

Artículo 51. - Corresponde a la Administración, al colegio y a sus miembros:

I. Desarrollar la carrera notarial, guardar, cumplir y hacer cumplir la realización de sus principios. En dicho desarrollo podrán participar facultades y escuelas de Derecho e instituciones dedicadas e investigación jurídica:

II. Difundir los instrumentos informativos y formativos para el ejercicio imparcial del derecho preventivo y la dictaminación objetiva, en el desarrollo del Estado Constitucional de Derecho.

Artículo 52. - Derogado
Artículo 53. - Derogado

SECCIÓN SEGUNDA DE LOS EXÁMENES

Artículo 54. - Para solicitar el examen de aspirante a notario, el interesado deberá satisfacer los siguientes requisitos:

I. Ser mexicano por nacimiento, tener veinticinco años cumplidos y no más de sesenta al momento de solicitar el examen;

II. Estar en pleno ejercicio de sus derechos y gozar de facultades físicas y mentales que no impidan el uso de sus capacidades intelectuales para el ejercicio de la función notarial. Gozar de buena reputación personal y honorabilidad profesional y no ser ministro de culto;

III. Ser profesional del Derecho, con titulo de abogado o licenciado en Derecho y con cédula profesional;

IV. No estar sujeto a proceso, ni haber sido condenado por sentencia ejecutoriada, por delito intencional;

V. Acreditar cuando menos doce meses de práctica notarial ininterrumpida, bajo la dirección y responsabilidad de algún notario del Distrito Federal, pudiendo mediar un lapso de hasta un año entre la terminación de dicha práctica y la solicitud del examen correspondiente;

VI. Presentar dicha solicitud por escrito a la autoridad competente en el formulario autorizado al efecto por la misma, marcando copia al colegio, requisitando los datos y acompañando los documentos que el mismo formulario señale;

VII. Expresar su sometimiento a lo inapelable del

第 50 条　公证行业受到行业基本原则和价值观的约束，特别奉行卓越、合法、客观、专业、公平、可持续性和独立的原则和精神。

第 51 条　政府、公证人学会及其成员的责任是：

（1）发展公证行业，维护、遵守并监督落实公证从业原则。在这一发展过程中，可以让法学专业院系以及致力于法学研究的机构参与进来。

（2）推行信息和培训工具，确保在公证工作中的公平公正，给出客观的意见，推进法治国家建设。

第 52 条　已废止。
第 53 条　已废止。

第二节　考核

第 54 条　欲参加公证候补人资格考试的，报名人员必须满足下列要求：

（1）因出生具备墨西哥国籍，在申请参加考试时年满 25 周岁且未超过 60 周岁。

（2）具备完全行使权利的资格，满足履行公证职能的身心要求和智力能力。享有良好的个人声誉和职业口碑，不是宗教领袖。

（3）有法学专业背景，持有律师证或者法学专业文凭和职业资格证书。

（4）没有因涉嫌故意犯罪而卷入诉讼或者被定罪判刑。

（5）证明至少已经在具有联邦区执业资格的正式公证人手下连续做满 12 个月的公证实习，自实习期届满之日起至申请考试资格之时的间隔最长为 1 年。

（6）向主管当局提交按要求填写的报名表以及表格中要求提供的材料，公证人学会应对报名材料的全套副本存档。

（7）写明接受评选委员会考核结果的最终效力，

fallo del jurado, y

VIII. No estar impedido temporalmente por reprobación al momento en que se vaya a efectuar el examen.

Una vez presentada la solicitud y acreditados los requisitos que anteceden, la autoridad, dentro de los quince días naturales siguientes, comunicará al interesado el día, hora y lugar en que se realizará el examen. Entre dicha comunicación y la fecha del examen no podrán mediar más de treinta días naturales.

De la comunicación señalada en el párrafo que antecede se marcará copia al colegio.

Artículo 55. - Para acreditar los requisitos a que se refieren las fracciones I y III del artículo anterior, el interesado deberá exhibir con su solicitud de examen, las constancias documentales públicas respectivas. Para acreditar los requisitos a que se refieren las fracciones II y IV del artículo anterior el interesado deberá, con citación del Colegio, realizar opcionalmente ante autoridad judicial la información ad perpetuam prevista en el Código de Procedimientos o con acta notarial que contenga su declaración con la de dos testigos, ante un notario diverso de donde haya realizado su práctica. El requisito señalado por la fracción V del Artículo anterior, se acreditará con los avisos sellados del inicio y terminación de la práctica en cuestión, que el notario respectivo deberá dar en tiempo, a la autoridad competente, marcando copia al colegio, así como con los oficios de contestación de dichos avisos. Tales prácticas podrán ser constatadas por la autoridad competente y por el colegio. Para acreditar la buena salud y el pleno uso de sus facultades físicas e intelectuales, el candidato deberá exhibir certificado médico expedido por médico o institución autorizada; certificados que podrán ser constatados por la autoridad competente y por el colegio.

Artículo 56. - Cuando una o varias notarías estuvieren vacantes o se hubiere resuelto crear una o más, la autoridad competente publicará convocatoria para que los aspirantes al ejercicio del notariado presenten el examen de oposición correspondiente. Esta convocatoria será publicada una sola vez en la Gaceta y por dos veces consecutivas con intervalos de tres días en uno de los periódicos de mayor circulación en el Distrito Federal. Dicha convocatoria deberá contener los siguientes requisitos:

I. Señalar las fechas, horarios y lugar, relativos al inicio y término del periodo de inscripción al examen. En ningún caso el periodo de inscripción excederá de diez días naturales, contados a partir de la última publicación de la convocatoria;

不得申诉。

（8）在参加考试时，不得对临时给出的不合格决议进行申诉。

一旦提交报名表，证明满足上述要求，主管当局应当在15个自然日内向报名人员通知考试日期、时间和地点。通知日期与考试日期之间的时间间隔不得超过30个自然日。

学会应当留存上一段所指通知的副本。

第55条 为证明报名人员满足上一条第1款第1项和第1款第3项的要求，在提交报名表时应一并提交相关证明文件。为证明满足上一条第1款第2项和第4项的要求，报名人员应当根据学会要求，选择按照《民事诉讼法》之规定到司法机关开具证明材料，或者选择在两名证人的见证下宣誓声明，由其实习导师以外的公证人为其出具公证书。上一条第1款第5项所列要求，应当由报名人员的实习导师在规定时间内以密封通知的方式，向当局告知实习起始日期，并将通知内容以及当局针对通知的答复函文的副本提交公证人学会存档。实习情况应由主管当局和学会进行核实。为证明自身健康状况良好以及身体素质和心智情况符合要求，报名人员应当出示由经认可的医师或机构出具的体检证明，主管当局和学会应对证明文书进行核实。

第56条 如果一家或多家公证处出现岗位空缺，或者决定增设一个或多个公证人岗位时，主管当局应当对招聘通知进行公示，以便候补公证人可以报名参加竞聘考核。招聘通知应当在《官方公报》上公示1次，并在联邦区发行量较大的一家报纸上先后公示两次，公示时间间隔为3日。招聘通知中应写明以下要求：

（1）写明考试报名的起始日期、受理时间段和报名地点。在任何情况下报名期限都不得超过10个自然日，自招聘通知的最后一次公示之日起算。

II. Precisar el día, hora y lugar en que se practicarán las pruebas teóricas y prácticas;

III. Indicar el número de las notarías vacantes y de nueva creación, y

IV. Señalar la obligación de pagar previamente, los derechos que determine el Código Financiero del Distrito Federal vigente.

Asimismo, esta convocatoria se publicará en el sitio oficial que el Colegio tiene en la red electrónica de información mundial conocida como Internet o la que haga sus veces.

Artículo 57. - Para obtener la patente de notario, el profesional del Derecho interesado, además de no estar impedido para presentar examen, conforme a la fracción VIII del artículo 60 de esta ley, deberá:

I. Acreditar los requisitos de calidad profesional, práctica y honorabilidad.

Los requisitos a que se refiere esta fracción se presumen acreditados en términos de la información ad perpetuam a que se refiere el articulo 55 de esta Ley, salvo que posteriormente se demuestren hechos concretos que hicieren dudar de dicha cualidad, para lo cual con la opinión del colegio y la determinación de la autoridad competente podrá ser requerida una complementación del procedimiento de información ad perpetuam;

II. Tener patente de aspirante registrada; salvo que la patente no hubiera sido expedida por causas imputables a la autoridad, en cuyo caso bastará acreditar la aprobación del examen con la constancia respectiva que emita el jurado;

III. Solicitar la inscripción al examen de oposición, según la convocatoria expedida por la autoridad y expresar su sometimiento a lo inapelable del fallo del jurado;

IV. Efectuar el pago de los derechos que fije el Código Financiero del Distrito Federal vigente:

V. Obtener el primer lugar en el examen de oposición respectivo, en los términos de los artículos 58 y 60 de esta ley;

VI. Rendir la protesta a que se refiere el artículo 66 de esta ley, lo que implica para quien la realiza la aceptación de la patente respectiva, su habilitación para el ejercicio notarial y su pertenencia al notariado del Distrito Federal.

Artículo 58. - Los exámenes para obtener la patente de aspirante y la de notario, se regirán por las siguientes reglas comunes:

I. El jurado se compondrá por cinco miembros propietarios o sus suplentes respectivos. El suplente actuará a

（2）写明理论考试和实务考试的具体日期、时间和地点。

（3）写明招聘的空缺岗位数量和新增岗位数量。

（4）写明应按照现行《联邦区财政法》之规定事先缴清报名和考试费用。

此外，招聘通知应当在公证人学会的官网上进行公示。

第57条　为顺利竞聘上岗，竞聘人员除应满足考试要求外，还应满足本法第60条第8项中列出的以下规定：

（1）证明满足专业资格、实习资格和诚信要求。

报名人出示本法第55条中规定的司法机关证明材料的，视为满足本项所指的各项要求；但后续有具体证据表明报名人资格存在疑点的，应当征询学会意见，并由主管当局裁定要求进一步进行信息核实。

（2）完成报名资格的注册；但没有获得报名资格的原因应归咎于主管当局的情况除外，在这种情况下，只要凭考评委员会出具的相关凭证证明考试合格即可。

（3）根据主管当局发布的招聘通知申请注册考试资格，并写明接受评选委员会考核结果的最终效力，不得申诉。

（4）按照现行《联邦区财政法》之规定事先缴清报名和考试费用。

（5）按照本法第58条和第60条的规定，在相应的招聘考核中取得第一名。

（6）按照本法第66条之规定宣誓，以证明报名人满足资格要求、具备公证执业能力并加入联邦区公证人团体。

第58条　候补公证人资格考试和正式公证人竞聘考试适用以下通用规则：

（1）考评委员会由五名正式考官或其替补人员组成。正式考官无法履职的，由替补人员递补。

falta del titular:

II. El jurado estará integrado por:

a)Un Presidente nombrado por el Jefe de Gobierno, que será un jurista prestigiado en disciplinas relacionadas con la materia notarial, pudiendo ser notario;

b)Un secretario, designado por el Colegio y que será el notario de menor antigüedad y se encargará de levantar el acta circunstanciada, la que será conservada, foliada en forma progresiva y consecutiva en el Libro de Registro de Exámenes de Aspirante o en su caso en el Libro de Registro de Exámenes de Oposición, y

c)Tres vocales, de los cuales uno será notario designado por el Colegio y los otros dos serán designados libremente por la Consejería Jurídica y de Servicios Legales, dentro de los notarios del Distrito Federal. Los miembros que integren el jurado no podrán ser cónyuges o parientes consanguíneos o afines hasta el cuarto y segundo grados, respectivamente, del sustentante, ni titulares de las Notarías en que éste haya realizado su práctica o prestado servicios, tengan o hubieren tenido relación laboral con el sustentante o sus parientes, en los referidos grados, ni los notarios asociados o suplentes de dichos titulares o los cónyuges o parientes de éstos en los grados indicados. La infracción a lo antes dispuesto por algún miembro del jurado hará acreedor a ese sinodal a la sanción prevista por el artículo 227 de esta Ley.

Los miembros que integren el jurado no podrán ser cónyuges o parientes consanguíneos o afines hasta el cuarto y segundo grados, respectivamente, del sustentante, ni titulares de las Notarías en que éste haya realizado su práctica o prestado servicios, tengan o hubieren tenido relación laboral con el sustentante o sus parientes, en los referidos grados, ni los notarios asociados o suplentes de dichos titulares o los cónyuges o parientes de éstos en los grados indicados. La infracción a lo antes dispuesto por algún miembro del jurado hará acreedor a ese sinodal a la sanción prevista por el artículo 227 de esta Ley.

III. Tanto el examen de aspirante como el de oposición, consistirán en dos pruebas aplicables a cada sustentante, una práctica y otra teórica;

IV. Los exámenes, tanto en su prueba escrita como la teórica, se efectuarán en la sede designada por la autoridad competente;

V. La prueba práctica consistirá en la redacción de uno o varios instrumentos notariales específicos del examen de aspirante o específicos de examen de oposición; su tema será sorteado de entre veinte formulados por el

（2）考评委员会的人员组成如下：

a）主任一名，由政府首脑任命，委员会主任应当是在公证行业中享有盛誉的专家，可以是公证人；

b）秘书一名，由公证人学会任命，可以是从业年限不长的公证人，负责起草相关报告，进行备案并在候补公证人考核登记簿或竞聘考核登记簿（如适用）中进行记录。

c）委员三名，其中一人应当是由公证人学会任命的公证人，另外两人应当由法律咨询和服务委员会从联邦区公证人中自由指定。考评委员会的成员不得是竞聘人员或者竞聘人员实习或者供职过的公证处在任公证人的配偶、四代以内血亲或两代以内姻亲，不得与竞聘人员或其四代以内血亲或两代以内姻亲在当前或一直以来存在工作隶属关系，也不得是上述公证人的合伙人或替补人，或者其配偶或者属于前面列出的血缘或亲缘关系的亲属。违反上述规定的，应按本法第227条之规定予以处罚。

考评委员会的成员不得是竞聘人员或者竞聘人员实习或者供职过的公证处在任公证人的配偶、四代以内血亲或两代以内姻亲，不得与竞聘人员或其四代以内血亲或两代以内姻亲在当前或一直以来存在工作隶属关系，也不得是上述公证人的合伙人或替补人，或者其配偶或者属于前面列出的血缘或亲缘关系的亲属。违反上述规定的，应按本法第227条之规定予以处罚。

（3）无论是候补资格考试还是岗位竞聘考试，都应考核两门科目，即理论和实务。

（4）无论是笔试还是理论考试，都应当在主管当局指定的地点进行。

（5）实务考试的内容就是按照给定题目起草一份或多份公证文书；考试题目应当从公证人学会给定的包含二十个题目的题库中随机抽取，题库由学会拟定并提交主管当局审批。

colegio y serán sometidos por éste, a la aprobación de la autoridad competente.

La prueba práctica, tanto para los aspirantes como para el examen de oposición, serán colocados en sobres cerrados e irán sellados y firmados por el Director General Jurídico y de Estudios Legislativos o por quien éste designe y por el Presidente del Consejo o por un miembro del colegio que aquél designe;

VI. La prueba práctica se desahogará bajo la vigilancia de un representante de la autoridad competente y otro del colegio, quienes no deberán estar en los supuestos a que se refiere el segundo párrafo de la fracción II de este artículo; pudiendo auxiliarse los sustentantes, sí así lo desean de un mecanógrafo que no sea licenciado en Derecho, ni tenga estudios en esta materia; el sustentante únicamente podrá estar provisto de leyes y libros de consulta necesarios. Cada uno de los vigilantes deberá comunicar por separado o conjuntamente al jurado las irregularidades que hubiere percibido durante el desarrollo de esta prueba, con copia a la autoridad competente. Si a juicio del jurado, dichas irregularidades no impiden la continuación del examen, para esos efectos se tendrán por no hechas y no cuestionarán ni afectarán el resultado del mismo:

VII. Para la prueba práctica, los sustentantes dispondrán de seis horas corridas:

VIII. Además de la resolución del caso mediante la redacción del instrumento o instrumentos respectivos, como parte de la misma prueba escrita, en pliego aparte, el sustentante deberá razonar y sustentar la solución que dio, expresará especialmente las alternativas de solución que tuvo y las razones en pro y en contra de dichas alternativas y las que apoyen su respuesta e indicará los apoyos legales, jurisprudenciales y doctrinales que pudiere invocar;

IX. La prueba teórica será pública y consistirá en preguntas relacionadas con el tipo de examen relativo;

X. El jurado calificará la resolución de la prueba práctica y efectuará ordenadamente la prueba teórica mediante turno de réplicas, empezando por el notario de menor antigüedad y continuando en orden progresivo de antigüedad de los demás, para terminar con la réplica del presidente;

XI. Cada sinodal podrá hacer en su turno las interpelaciones que sean suficientes para forjarse un criterio cierto de la idoneidad, preparación del sustentante y la calidad de su resolución, ateniéndose principalmente a la resolución jurídica del caso y al criterio jurídico del sustentante. Para ello considerará, además del pliego de alternativas,

无论是候补资格考试还是岗位竞聘考试的实务考试，题目都应当放入密封信封中，由法律和立法研究总局局长或者局长指定的人选，以及学会理事会会长或会长指定的一名学会成员共同密封并签字确认。

（6）实务考试应当由主管当局和公证人学会各派一名代表监考，监考官不得出现本条第2款第2段规定的情形；如果考生有要求，可以为其配备一名打字员，在这种情况下，打字员不得具备法律专业文凭或者有相关专业背景；考生只能携带工具书应考。每一名监考官应当共同或者单独向考评委员会报告在考试期间发现的违规行为，并将报告材料抄送主管当局。经考评委员会判定，认为违规行为不妨碍考试继续进行的，可继续答题且对考试成绩没有影响。

（7）实务考试的时间为6小时。

（8）除了撰写命题公证文书之外，作为实务考试的一部分，案例解答的附加题应当给出解决方案并说明理由，特别是要说明其他的替代解决方案并给出这些替代方案的支持和反对理由，以及印证其观点的论据，列明为此援引的法律、判例以及理论。

（9）理论考试为开卷考试，考试类型为问答题。

（10）考评委员会负责对实务考试进行评分，然后依次对理论试卷进行评分。打分时按照资历排序，先由从业年限较短的公证人评分，然后依次递增，最后由委员会主任评分。

（11）每一名考官均可向考生提问，对考试的表现、准备情况和答题情况作出判断，主要依据就是考试的案例解答。为此，除了要考察考生的卷面论述情况外，还应考虑考生的解答情况，判断其公证专业知识储备以及审慎性，最后由考评委员会形成评分标准。在任何情况下，考生撰写的公证文书必须有效。

las respuestas del sustentante, tomando en cuenta el conocimiento que tenga del oficio notarial y la prudencia que demuestre, que sirvan al jurado para normar su criterio. En todo caso el o los instrumentos deberán ser válidos;

XII. A continuación, a puerta cerrada, los integrantes del jurado calificarán individualmente cada prueba, atendiendo a lo dispuesto en los artículos 59, respecto de los aspirantes al notariado y 60, tratándose de los exámenes de oposición;

XIII. El Secretario levantará el acta correspondiente que deberá ser firmada por los integrantes del jurado;

XIV. El resultado del examen será inapelable; no obstante, toda irregularidad podrá ser denunciada por los observadores a la autoridad competente y al decanato:

XV. El presidente comunicará el resultado y pedirá al secretario lea el resultado del examen:

XVI. Además, el secretario del jurado comunicará a la autoridad competente y al colegio, en no más de una cuartilla, la calificación razonada otorgada a cada sustentante, la cual será firmada por todos los miembros del jurado, en un plazo no mayor de setenta y dos horas a partir de la terminación del examen. En un lapso igual desde la recepción de la comunicación correspondiente, una y otro podrán hacer las observaciones que juzguen convenientes para el perfeccionamiento permanente de los exámenes, y en su caso llamar la atención sobre algún aspecto en concreto. Estas comunicaciones serán confidenciales entre el jurado y los informados, y no darán lugar a instancia o medio de defensa alguno para el sustentante.

Artículo 59. - Además de regirse por lo anterior, el examen para la obtención de la patente de aspirante al ejercicio del notariado será en un acto continuo. El sustentante elegirá uno de los sobres a que se refiere la fracción V del articulo anterior en presencia de los responsables de vigilar el examen. Inmediatamente después el sustentante abrirá el tema de la prueba práctica y a partir de entonces se cronometrará el tiempo de desarrollo de la prueba escrita. Concluida ésta se iniciará la prueba teórica que será pública y en la que una vez instalado el jurado, el examinado procederá a dar lectura al tema y a su trabajo. Esta prueba consistirá en las preguntas que los miembros del jurado harán al sustentante en términos del artículo anterior, con particular insistencia sobre puntos precisos relacionados con el caso jurídico-notarial a que se refiera el tema sorteado, atendiendo a su validez y efectos.

Los integrantes del jurado calificarán individualmente al sustentante, de lo que resultará una calificación

（12）接下来，考评委员会的考官应当根据第59条"候补公证人"和第60条"竞聘考试"的规定，对每一个科目进行秘密打分。

（13）委员会秘书应当起草相应记录并由委员会考官签字确认。

（14）考试成绩具有最终效力；但是，观察员一旦发现任何违规行为，可向主管当局和公证会长办会举报。

（15）委员会主任应通报成绩并要求秘书宣读考试结果。

（16）此外，自考试结束之时起，考评委员会秘书应当在72小时内向主管当局和公证人学会发送通报函，列明对每一名考生的打分并给出打分理由，篇幅不得超过一页，并由考评委员会所有成员签字确认。自收到通报函之时起，主管当局和公证人学会同样应当在72小时内提出相关意见（如果有），以不断改进考试，并呼吁对某些具体问题予以关注。通报函为保密文件，仅有考评委员会和被通报单位知晓，不得作为考生的申诉或辩护依据。

第59条 除上述规定外，应说明，候补公证人资格考试是一个连续的过程。考生应当在监考官在场的情况下，从上一条第5项所述的题库中抽出1个考题信封。之后考生应立即进入实务答题阶段，笔试时间开始计时。实务考试结束后进入理论考试阶段，该科目应公开进行，一旦考评委员会成员就位，考生开始阅读考试主题及其文章。理论科目的考察形式为考官根据上一条之规定向考生提问，特别是要注意考题所涉及的公证问题考察点，并注重考察考生答题的有效性和针对性。

考评委员会的考官逐一向考生提问，最后形成一个统一的评分，分为通过、一致不通过或多数不通过。

única, aprobatoria, reprobatoria por unanimidad o reprobatoria por mayoría. Si fuere esta última, el sustentante no podrá presentar nueva solicitud para examen sino pasados seis meses, contados a partir del fallo; si es reprobado por unanimidad, el plazo de espera se extenderá a un año.

Con la apertura del sobre que contenga el tema del examen se dará por iniciada la prueba práctica, en consecuencia al sustentante que se desista, se le tendrá por reprobado y no podrá presentar nueva solicitud hasta que transcurra un término de seis meses. Esto último será aplicable en aquellos casos en que el sustentante no se presente puntualmente al lugar en que éste habrá de realizarse.

Artículo 60. - El examen para obtener la patente de notario se regirá por las siguientes reglas:

I. En cada uno podrán concursarse hasta tres notarías, y al examen se hubiesen inscrito al menos tres sustentantes por cada notaria.

Si el aspirante se inscribió y no se presentó a la prueba práctica o habiéndose presentado a esta última no se presenta o desiste de la prueba teórica, sin causa justificada a juicio del jurado, no podrá volverse a presentar para concursar a nueva convocatoria, sino pasados 3 meses a la fecha en la que debió haberse presentado;

II. Para la prueba práctica, se reunirán los aspirantes en el colegio, el día y hora señalados en la convocatoria. En presencia de un representante de la autoridad competente y uno del colegio, alguno de los aspirantes elegirá uno de los sobres que guarden los temas, de entre veinte de ellos, debiendo todos los sustentantes desarrollar el que se haya elegido; asimismo ahí se sorteará el orden de presentación de los sustentantes a la prueba teórica;

III. Al concluirse la prueba práctica, los responsables de la vigilancia de la prueba recogerán los trabajos hechos; los colocarán en sobres que serán cerrados, firmados por ellos y por el correspondiente sustentante, y se depositarán bajo seguro en el colegio;

IV. La prueba teórica será pública; se iniciará en el colegio el día y hora señalados por la convocatoria. Los aspirantes serán examinados sucesivamente de acuerdo al orden de presentación, resultado del sorteo señalado. Los aspirantes que no se presenten oportunamente a la prueba, perderán su turno y tendrán derecho. En su caso, a presentar el examen en una segunda vuelta, respetando el orden establecido;

V. El Aspirante que no se presente a la segunda vuelta se tendrá por desistido;

VI. Reunido el jurado, cada uno de sus miembros

针对多数不通过的情况，自成绩公布之日起，考生必须在6个月后方可再次报名参加考试；如果考官一致判定不通过，则等待期延长至1年。

装有考题的信封开封后，即开始实务考试。因此，一旦考生弃考，即视为考试不通过，必须在6个月后方可再次报名参考。对于考生未按时到考点应考的，同样适用这一规定。

第60条 公证人资格考试应按以下规则执行：

（1）每场考试最多竞聘三个公证人岗位，每个岗位至少有三人竞聘。

如果候补人报名但是没有参加实务考试，或者虽然参加了实务考试，但是没有参加理论考试或者弃考理论科目且没有说明正当理由的，则过三个月后方可重新报名竞聘。

（2）在实务科目中，候补人应按照招聘通知上写明的日期和时间到公证人学会开会。在主管当局和公证人学会各派一名代表在场见证的情况下，由其中一名候补人从二十个考题信封中抽取一个信封，作为本场考试的考题。考生参加理论科目考试的顺序应抽签决定。

（3）实务考试结束后，监考官应收取考卷；将考卷装入信封，封口并与答题考生一同签字确认，之后将考卷安全送至学会保存。

（4）理论考试应按照招聘通知上写明的日期和时间，在学会以公开方式进行。考生应按照抽签顺序依次作答。未按时参加考试的考生的次序顺延。如果需要进行第二轮答题的，应按照规定顺序进行。

（5）第二轮答题时不在场的考生视为弃考。

（6）考评委员会考官就位后，每一名考官通过提

interrogará al sustentante exclusivamente y en profundidad sobre cuestiones de Derecho que sean de aplicación al ejercicio de la función notarial, destacando el sentido de la prudencia jurídica y posteriormente si se considera adecuado se formularán cuestionamientos al caso. Una vez concluida la prueba teórica de cada sustentante, este dará lectura ante el jurado a su trabajo práctico, sin poder hacer aclaración, enmienda o corrección;

VII. Para el desahogo del examen teórico deberán celebrarse cuando menos dos sesiones por semana:

VIII. Concluida la prueba teórica de cada sustentante, los miembros del jurado emitirán separadamente y por escrito, la calificación que cada uno de ellos otorgue a las pruebas, práctica y teórica, en escala numérica del 0 al 100 y promediarán los resultados. La suma de los promedios se dividirá entre cinco para obtener la calificación final, cuyo mínimo para aprobar será el de 70 puntos; los que obtengan calificación inferior a 70, pero no inferior a 65 puntos, podrán presentar nuevo examen tan pronto haya una siguiente oposición, siempre y cuando tuviere satisfechos los requisitos previstos en el artículo 57 de esta ley.

Los aspirantes que obtengan una calificación inferior a 65 puntos, no podrán solicitar nuevo examen de oposición, sino pasado un año a partir de su reprobación.

Quienes desistan antes del tiempo máximo de entrega de la prueba práctica, se entenderá que abandonan el examen y podrán presentar nuevo examen, tan pronto haya una siguiente oposición, siempre y cuando tuviere satisfechos los requisitos previstos en el artículo 57 de esta ley.

Iniciado el sorteo a que se refiere la fracción II de este artículo, si el sustentante no está presente a la hora y en el lugar fijados para el inicio del examen, perderá su derecho a presentar el mismo y se le tendrá por desistido, pudiéndolo presentar nuevamente cuando cumpla los requisitos previstos en el artículo 57 de esta Ley.

IX. Serán triunfadores en la oposición para cubrir la o las notarías respectivas, el o los sustentantes que hayan obtenido las calificaciones aprobatorias más altas.

Las notarías serán asignadas en forma sucesiva, a quien o quienes, conforme a la fracción I de esta disposición, hayan obtenido la mayor calificación aprobatoria.

Artículo 61. - Como labor de supervisión, los Órganos Locales de Gobierno podrán, si lo estiman conveniente, nombrar uno o más observadores del examen, licenciados en Derecho, quienes podrán emitir opinión sobre su perfeccionamiento, sin que esta tenga efecto vinculatorio con el desarrollo y resultado del examen de que se trate.

问深入考察考生对公证执业相关问题的了解，特别注意法律的审慎性；之后，如果认为必要，可以就考题案例提问。每一名考生在理论科目考完后，再向考评委员会宣读其实务答题，但不得作出任何澄清、修订或更正。

（7）理论考试的频率为至少每周两场。

（8）每名考生的理论科目考完后，每一名考官应单独对其实务和理论科目打分，分值在0~100分之间，实务和理论科目得分的平均分即为该名考生的成绩。将平均分总和除以五，得出的就是考生的最终成绩，考试合格的最低分数要求为70分；得分在70分以下但大于等于65分的，只要满足本法第57条中的要求，可以立即参加下一期的竞聘考试。

得分低于65分的，自考试落榜之日起，应间隔1年方可重新参加竞聘考试。

在实务科目交卷时间届满前弃考的考生，视为放弃本次考试，只要满足本法第57条中的要求，可以立即参加下一期的竞聘考试。

本条第2项所述的抽签开始后，如果考生未按时到指定考场就考，则丧失本场考试资格，视为弃考；满足本法第57条中的要求的，可以立即参加下一期的竞聘考试。

（9）考试得分最高的考生即为竞聘优胜者，获得招聘岗位的就任资格。

公证处应按照本条第1项之规定，按照考试合格者的得分高低顺序进行任命。

第61条　地方政府部门负有监督职责，可以在适当时任命一名或多名观察员巡考。观察员应当具有法学专业学历，可以在巡考时发表改进意见，但对考试的进行和考试结果不能产生任何影响。相关意见应当反馈给主管当局和公证人学会，并酌情反馈给公证会长办公会，以便采取必要措施来改进考试办法和流

Dicha opinión la harán del conocimiento de la autoridad competente y del colegio y, en su caso a la junta de decanos, a efecto de que se tomen las medidas necesarias para perfeccionar la práctica y desarrollo de los exámenes. Los observadores designados podrán estar presentes en todas las etapas del examen.

Artículo 62. - Concluidos los exámenes, el Jefe de Gobierno expedirá las patentes de aspirante y de notario, a quien haya resultado aprobado y triunfador en el examen respectivo. En todo caso, de cada patente se expedirán dos ejemplares.

Artículo 63. - El Jefe de Gobierno expedirá las patentes a que se refiere el articulo anterior, y tomará la protesta del fiel desempeño de las funciones del notario, a quien haya resultado triunfador en el examen, en un plazo que no excederá de treinta días hábiles, contados a partir de la fecha de celebración del mismo.

Artículo 64. - Las patentes de aspirante y de notario deberán registrarse ante la autoridad competente, en el Registro Público, en el Archivo y en el colegio, previo pago de los derechos que señale el Código Financiero del Distrito Federal vigente. Una vez registrada una patente, uno de sus ejemplares se entregará a la autoridad competente y el otro lo conservará su titular.

Artículo 65. - Los notarios son inamovibles de su cargo, salvo los casos previstos en esta Ley. Asimismo la patente de los aspirantes es definitiva y permanente.

CAPÍTULO II DE LA ACTUACIÓN NOTARIAL

SECCIÓN PRIMERA DEL INICIO DE LA ACTUACIÓN NOTARIAL

Artículo 66. - Para que la persona que haya obtenido la patente pueda actuar en ejercicio de la función notarial y pertenecer al colegio, deberá rendir protesta ante el Jefe de Gobierno del Distrito Federal, o ante quien éste último delegue dicha atribución, en los siguientes términos:

"Protesto, como notario y como miembro del Colegio de Notarios del Distrito Federal, Asociación Civil, guardar y hacer guardar el Derecho, la Constitución Política de los Estados Unidos Mexicanos, el Estatuto de Gobierno del Distrito Federal y las Leyes que de ellos emanen, en particular la Ley del Notariado; y desempeñar objetiva, imparcial, leal y patrióticamente, el ejercicio de la fe pública que se me ha conferido, guardando en todo momento el estricto respeto al Estado Constitucional de Derecho y a los valores ético jurídicos que el mismo comporta, y si así

程。被任命的观察员应当在考试的各个阶段全程跟进。

第62条 考试结束后，政府首脑应当向考试合格者颁发候补公证人资格证，向竞聘优胜者颁发公证人执业证书。在任何情况下，每一份证书均一式两份。

第63条 政府首脑应在30个工作日的期限内向竞聘考核优胜者颁发前一条所指的证书，自考试之日起算，以便保障其按时到岗，忠实履行公证人职责。

第64条 候补公证人资格证和公证人执业证书应当到登记主管当局、档案管理局和学会办理注册，登记注册费用应当按照现行《联邦区财政法》之规定事先缴清。一旦资格证书完成登记，主管当局应对其中一份证书样本进行存档，另一份由持证人本人保管。

第65条 除本法规定的情形外，不得免除公证人的职务。此外，候补公证人资格证也具备永久效力。

第二章 公证执业行为

第一节 上岗执业

第66条 已经取得候补公证人资格证的人员，为了上岗执业并加入公证人学会，应当向联邦区行政长官或者由行政长官指定的人员宣誓就职，宣誓词内容如下：

我宣誓，作为一名公证人，我已成为联邦区公证人学会这一民间联合会的一员。我将遵守和捍卫国家法制、《墨西哥合众国宪法》、《联邦区政府规约》以及相关法律规定，特别是《公证法》的规定；客观、公平、公正地行使赋予我的公证职权，维护国家利益，坚定不移地尊重国家法治，恪守职业道德，尽心尽力做好本职工作；依法接受公证用户、当局、公证人学会和公证会长办公会的监督。如有违反，将依法接受制裁。

no lo hiciere seré responsable, y pido hoy que en cada caso los particulares a quienes debo servir, las autoridades, el colegio y el decanato, así me lo exijan y demanden, conforme a la ley y sus sanciones".

Artículo 67. - Para que el notario del Distrito Federal pueda actuar, debe:

I. Obtener fianza del Colegio a favor de las Autoridades competentes, por la cantidad que resulte de multiplicar por veinte mil, el importe del salario mínimo general diario en el Distrito Federal, vigente a la fecha de la constitución de la misma. Sólo que el Colegio, por causa justificada, no otorgue la fianza o la retire, el Notario deberá obtenerla de compañía legalmente autorizada por el monto señalado. Dicha fianza deberá mantenerse vigente y actualizarse en el mes de enero de cada año, modificándose en la misma forma en que se haya modificado a esa fecha el salario mínimo de referencia. El Notario deberá presentar anualmente del Colegio o, en su caso, de la compañía legalmente autorizada, el documento que acredite la constitución de la fianza correspondiente ante la Autoridad competente. La omisión en que incurra el Notario a esta disposición será sancionada por la Autoridad administrativa en términos de la presente Ley. El contrato de fianza correspondiente se celebrará en todo caso en el concepto de que el fiador no gozará de los beneficios de orden y excusión;

II. Proveerse a su costa de protocolo y sello, registrar su sello, firma y rúbrica, antefirma o media firma, ante las Autoridades competentes, el Registro Público, el Archivo y el Colegio, previo pago de los derechos que señale el Código Fiscal del Distrito Federal;

III. Establecer una oficina para el desempeño de su función dentro del territorio del Distrito Federal e iniciar el ejercicio de sus funciones en un plazo que no excederá de noventa días naturales contados a partir de la fecha en que rinda su protesta;

IV. Dar aviso de lo anterior a las autoridades competentes y al colegio, señalando con precisión al exterior del inmueble que ocupe, el número de la notaría; su nombre y apellidos; horario de trabajo, días hábiles o si prefiere los inhábiles; teléfonos y otros datos que permitan al público la expedita comunicación con la notaría a su cargo, y

V. Ser miembro del colegio.

VI. Obtener y mantener vigente un certificado de firma electrónica notarial en términos de la Ley de Firma Electrónica del Distrito Federal y las demás disposiciones aplicables.

第 67 条　联邦区公证人在上岗执业前应做好以下准备：

（1）向主管当局出示已经通过公证人学会取得担保书的凭证，担保金数额为联邦区当时现行的最低日工资的两万倍。只有当公证人学会出于正当理由拒绝提供担保书或撤回担保书时，公证人可通过获得合法资质的公司出具担保书，担保金数额同上。担保书应保持有效，担保金数额在每年1月份随着最低基准工资标准的变动进行调整。公证人应当每年向学会或者代理公司提交材料，证明其担保书继续有效。违反这一规定的，应由行政主管当局依照本法之规定予以处罚。在任何情况下，担保协议中都应写明，担保人不享受任何责任豁免。

（2）自费取得公证登记簿和印章，到主管当局、登记机关、档案管理局和学会对其签字、画押和印鉴进行登记。为此，应当按照现行《联邦区财政法》之规定事先缴清相关费用。

（3）自宣誓之日起，在90个自然日内在联邦区辖区内选定经营场所并开业，开始履行公证职责。

（4）将开业事项通知主管当局和公证人学会，在经营场所表明：公证处编号、公证人姓名、营业日期和时间，如果非工作日也对外营业，应清楚写明；联系电话以及其他便于公众快速联系到公证人的联系方式。

（5）加入公证人学会。

（6）根据《联邦区电子签名法》和其他适用法律的规定，取得公证人电子签名证书并保持证书的有效性。

La autoridad competente publicará la iniciación de funciones de los notarios en la Gaceta sin costo para el notario.

Para el caso de que el notario cambie de ubicación la notaría, dará el aviso correspondiente a la autoridad competente, solicitando a su costa la publicación respectiva en la Gaceta.

Artículo 68. - La fianza a que se refiere la fracción I del artículo anterior, garantizará ante la autoridad competente, exclusivamente la responsabilidad profesional por la función notarial y se aplicará de la siguiente manera:

I. Por la cantidad que corresponda y en forma preferente, al pago de multas y otras responsabilidades administrativas cuando, ante la negativa del Notario, se deba hacer el pago forzoso a las autoridades fiscales u otras autoridades;

II. En el orden determinado por la autoridad judicial, cuando se deba cubrir a un particular o al fisco, el monto fijado por sentencia firme condenatoria por responsabilidad civil, penal o fiscal en contra del Notario. Para tal efecto, el interesado deberá exhibir copia certificada de dicha sentencia ante la autoridad competente; y

III. Por la cantidad remanente que se cubrirá a las Autoridades competentes por la responsabilidad administrativa del Notario en los casos de revocación de la patente que hubiere quedado firme.

En los casos previstos en la fracción II de este artículo, la autoridad judicial está obligada a ordenar expresamente a la Tesorería del Gobierno del Distrito Federal, se haga efectiva la fianza a que se refiere el artículo anterior y su aplicación al pago al que hubiere sido condenado el Notario.

Las Autoridades competentes remitirán el documento que acredite la constitución de la fianza a la Tesorería del Gobierno del Distrito Federal, le solicitará se haga efectiva la misma así como la aplicación de las cantidades que correspondan conforme a las fracciones anteriores.

SECCIÓN SEGUNDA DE LOS ELEMENTOS NOTARIALES: SELLO DE AUTORIZAR Y PROTOCOLO.

A. SELLO DE AUTORIZAR

Artículo 69. - El sello del notario es el medio por el cual éste ejerce su facultad fedataria con la impresión del símbolo del Estado en los documentos que autorice. Cada sello será metálico, tendrá forma circular, con un diámetro de cuatro centímetros, reproducirá en el centro el escudo

主管当局应当在官方公报上对新任公证人开始执业的情况进行公示，无须公证人承担任何费用。

公证人变更办公地点的，应当向主管当局报告，并在官方公报上公示相应的情况，费用由公证人自行承担。

第68条　上条第1项所指的担保书，指的是向主管当局提供的履职担保，适用于以下情况：

（1）公证人出现工作过失，需要支付罚金并承担其他行政责任但没有按规定主动执行，由税务机关或其他主管当局强制执行的。

（2）根据司法机关的判决，需要公证人承担民事、刑事或税务责任的，应当按照司法机关指定的顺序向个人或者国库偿付相应金额，对担保金强制执行。为此，当事人应当向主管当局出示判决书的经核证副本。

（3）资格证书确定被吊销的，剩余担保金应由行政主管当局没收。

对于本条第1款第2项所列情形，司法机关有义务明确向联邦区政府财政部门下达指令，按照对公证人的处罚办法执行上一条所指的担保。

主管当局应当出具证明材料，证实已经在联邦区财政部门建立担保、申请执行以及按照前几款之规定执行相应担保。

第二节　公证要素：公证章和公证登记簿

A.　公证章

第69条　公证章是公证人据以行使公证职能的凭证，在公证文书上印上的国家象征标志。公证章为金属材质，圆形，直径为4厘米，在印章中心刻有国徽，围绕国徽刻有"墨西哥联邦区"字样、公证人姓名及其所在公证处的编号。公证处编号应当为数字，

nacional y deberá tener escrito alrededor de éste, la inscripción "Distrito Federal, México" el nombre y apellidos del notario y su número dentro de los de la Entidad. El número de la notaría deberá grabarse con guarismos y el nombre y apellidos del notario podrán abreviarse. El sello podrá incluir un signo.

El sello expresa el poder autentificador del notario y lo público de su función.

Artículo 70. - El sello se imprimirá en el ángulo superior izquierdo del anverso de cada hoja del libro de registro de cotejos y en cada folio que se vaya a utilizar; deberá imprimirse también cada vez que el notario autorice una escritura, acta, testimonio, certificación y en el libro de registro de cotejos.

Artículo 71. - También se imprimirá dicho sello en documentación relacionada a su actuación como notario:

I. En la papelería oficial o de efectos de trámite; en tratándose de los avisos, informes, solicitudes de informes y liquidaciones dirigidos a cualquier autoridad, y

II. En avisos, cédulas de requerimientos y notificaciones; así como en toda clase de constancias dirigidas a particulares.

Artículo 72. - En caso de pérdida o alteración del sello, el notario, so pena de incurrir en responsabilidad por omisión, deberá dar aviso en el primer día hábil siguiente al descubrimiento del hecho a la autoridad competente y con el acuse de dicho aviso, levantará acta circunstanciada ante el Ministerio Público. Dentro del mismo término deberá dar también aviso al Archivo, al Registro y al colegio. Cumplido lo anterior, con los acuses respectivos y la constancia que al efecto le expida el Ministerio Público, tramitará ante la autoridad competente la autorización para la reposición, a su costa del sello, el cual registrará en términos del articulo 67 fracción II de esta ley. El nuevo sello contendrá un signo especial que lo diferencie del anterior. La marca especial deberá estar visible en la impresión del sello.

Artículo 73. - Si apareciere el antiguo sello, no podrá ser usado. El notario entregará personalmente y de inmediato dicho sello al archivo para que ahí en presencia del notario se destruya. De ello se levantará acta por triplicado; un tanto para la autoridad competente, otro para el Archivo y el tercero para el notario.

Artículo 74. - En caso de deterioro o alteración del sello, la autoridad competente autorizará al notario para obtener uno nuevo, sin necesidad de levantar acta ante el Ministerio Público.

公证人姓名可以简写。公证章上可以带有公证人的标识。

公证章表明了公证人权力的真实性和正当性。

第70条 公证章应当盖在公证登记簿中每一页正面的左上角，以及要出具的公证文书的每一页公证纸正面左上角，无论公证人出具任何公证状、记录、正式副本、证明书，还是核对记录册，都必须加盖公证章。

第71条 公证人在履行公证职能的过程中出具的下列材料，也必须加盖公证章：

（1）正式文书或手续材料，包括向任何当局发送的通知、报告、申请书和结算书；

（2）向个人发出的通知、要求书和通知函，以及其他各类材料。

第72条 公证印章丢失的，公证人除应承担过失责任外，还应当在发现印章丢失或损坏后的第一个工作日及时通知主管当局，并凭通知回执到检察机关备案。在同样期限内还应通知档案管理局、登记处和公证人学会。完成上述通知后，凭相应的通知回执以及检察机关开具的证明，到主管当局重新申领印章，费用由公证人自行承担，具体按照本法第67条第2项执行。新印章上应当包含能够与旧印章区分开来的特殊标识。标识应当位于印章的醒目位置。

第73条 旧印章后续被找回的，不得再次使用。公证人应立即亲自将印章送交档案管理局，以便档案管理局在公证人的见证下现场销毁。销毁后，应开具销毁证明，一式三份：一份送交主管当局，一份留在档案管理局存档，一份由公证人留存。

第74条 公证印章损坏的，主管当局应批准公证人重新申领新印章，无须向检察机关报批。

En el supuesto del párrafo anterior, el notario deberá presentar el sello en uso y el nuevo que se le haya autorizado, ante el Archivo, en el que se levantará acta por triplicado, en cuyo inicio se imprimirán los dos sellos y se hará constar que se inutilizó el antiguo, mismo que, con uno de los ejemplares del acta quedará en poder del Archivo, para lo cual éste tomará especiales medidas de seguridad, y con los demás ejemplares el notario procederá a registrar su nuevo sello conforme a lo establecido en el articulo 67 fracción II de la presente Ley. El nuevo sello contendrá un signo especial que lo diferencie del anterior. La marca especial deberá estar visible en la impresión del sello.

Artículo 75. - En todos los casos en los que se deje de utilizar definitivamente un sello, se entregará también al Archivo para que se destruya. De las diligencias de entrega y destrucción se levantará un acta por triplicado. Un tanto de dicha acta quedará depositado en el Archivo, otro en poder del notario, el albacea de su sucesión o el asociado o suplente del Notario fallecido y otro se enviará a la autoridad competente.

B. PROTOCOLO

Artículo 76. Protocolo es el conjunto de libros formados por folios numerados y sellados en los que el notario, observando las formalidades que establece la presente ley, asienta y autoriza las escrituras y actas que se otorguen ante su fe, con sus respectivos apéndices; así como por los libros de registro de cotejos con sus apéndices.

En sentido amplio es la expresión que se refiere a todos los documentos que obran en el haber de cada notaría. El protocolo es abierto, por cuanto lo forman folios encuadernables con número progresivo de instrumentos y de libros. En sentido estricto es tanto el conjunto de instrumentos públicos fuente original o matriz en los que se hace constar las relaciones jurídicas constituidas por los interesados, bajo la fe notarial; como la colección ordenada cronológicamente de escrituras y actas autorizadas por el Notario y aquellas que no pasaron, y de sus respectivos apéndices, conforme a una periodicidad, procedimiento y formalidades reglados en esta Ley; y que adquiridos a costa del Notario respectivo son conservados permanentemente por él o por su sustituto en términos de esta Ley afectos exclusivamente al fin encomendado y, posteriormente, destinados permanentemente al servicio y matricidad notarial del documento en el Archivo como propiedad del Estado, a partir de la entrega de los mismos a dicha oficina, en uno o más libros, observando para su

出现上段所述情形的，公证人应当将在旧印章和新印章都提交档案管理局立档，开具一式三份的证明书，证明格式为加盖新旧印章的印鉴样本，并说明旧章弃用。证明书一份留在档案管理局存档，为此应当采取专门的安全措施，公证人凭其余两份，根据本法第67条第1款第2项之规定办理新印章的启用手续。新印章上应当包含能够与旧印章区分开来的特殊标识。标识应当位于印章的醒目位置。

第75条 在任何情况下，一旦印章弃用，必须提交档案管理局予以销毁，并开具相应的废章上交和销毁证明，一式三份。证明一份留在档案管理局存档，另一份由公证人留存，公证人死亡的，应由其遗嘱执行人、替补人或合伙人保管，其余一份送交主管当局备案。

B. 公证登记簿

第76条 公证登记簿是公证人开具的所有带页码和印鉴的公证文件集成的书册，符合本法规定的格式，其中记录了公证人签发的所有公证文书并带有相应的附录，以及附录核证文本的登记簿。

从广义上说，公证登记簿是指各个公证处开立的所有文档。登记簿为开放性的，由所有顺序编号的文书和卷册组成。从狭义上说，就是当事人为了办理公证而向公证人出示的所有原件的集合；登记簿遵照本法规定的周期、程序和格式，按时间顺序整理并收录经公证人核证的文书及其相应的附录；并由公证人或其接任者按照本法之规定长期保管，费用由公证人承担，专用于法定目的，在后续长效用于公证服务，公证资料应立档归卷，所有权属于国家，并享有本法规定的所有制度保障。

redacción y conformación de actos y hechos las formalidades y solemnidades previstas por esta Ley, todo lo que constituye materia de garantía institucional de origen constitucional regulada por esta Ley.

Los folios que forman el protocolo son aquellas hojas que constituyen la papelería oficial que el notario usa para ejercer la función notarial. Son el sustracto o base material del instrumento público notarial, en términos de esta Ley.

Los instrumentos que integren el protocolo deberán constar además en archivo electrónico, reproducción digitalizada o cualquier otra tecnología, que será agregada como anexo del protocolo, al momento de su entrega al Archivo, en la forma que determinen las Autoridades competentes; tomando las medidas de seguridad y observando en todo momento el secreto profesional que establezcan las leyes.

Artículo 77. - Los instrumentos, libros y apéndices que integren el protocolo deberán ser numerados progresivamente. Los folios deberán utilizarse en forma progresiva por ambas caras y los instrumentos que se asienten en ellos se ordenarán en forma sucesiva y cronológica por el Notario, y se encuadernarán en libros que se integrarán por doscientos folios, excepto cuando el Notario deba asentar un instrumento con el cual rebasaría ese número, en cuyo caso deberá dar por terminado el libro sin asentar dicho instrumento, iniciando con éste el libro siguiente.

Excepcionalmente, un libro de protocolo podrá exceder de doscientos folios, si el instrumento que corresponda asentar rebasare ese número, en cuyo caso, se iniciará la formación del libro siguiente, previa razón de terminación del libro en uso, la que se asentará en hoja común no foliada que se agregará al final del libro que se da por terminado, sin que este contenga doscientos folios. Dicha razón no será necesaria cuando el libro que se de por terminado contuviere mas de ciento ochenta folios usados.

Artículo 78. - El Notario no podrá autorizar acto alguno sin que lo haga constar en los folios que forman el protocolo, salvo los que deban constar en los libros de registro de cotejos. Para lo relativo a la clausura del protocolo se procederá conforme a lo previsto por los artículos 203 y 204 de esta Ley.

Artículo 79. - Todos los folios y los libros que integren el protocolo deberán estar siempre en la notaría, salvo los casos expresamente permitidos por esta Ley, o cuando el Notario recabe firmas fuera de ella, lo cual se hará cuando sea necesario a juicio del Notario. Cuando hubiere

公证登记簿中的文件誊写在公证专用纸上，公证员在履行职责时，应通过公证专用纸来出具公证书。根据本法，这些文件资料是形成公证书的依据或基础。

公证登记簿中的文书还应当通过数字化方式或任何其他技术形成电子文档，按照主管当局规定的形式，作为附录一并提交给档案管理局；采取防伪措施并始终遵守相关法律规定的职业保密要求。

第77条　公证登记簿中的资料、文书和附录，应当按顺序编号。公证纸应按编号顺序双面使用，由公证人将公证文书按照时间先后顺序依次列入，并编订成册。每本公证文书册的篇幅为二百张，但公证人再继续加入下一份文书后篇幅会超过二百张的情况除外。在后一种情况下，当前的文书册视为用完，公证人应当将文书列入下一本文书册。

如果文书过长，超过二百张公证纸的篇幅要求的，应当列入下一本文书册，对于上一本文书册篇幅没有达到页数要求的，可以用普通纸填充。文书册篇幅达到一百八十张以上的，无须再行填充。

第78条　公证人不得对公证登记簿的登记页中没有提到的任何行为进行认可，除非是应当列入核对登记簿中的行为。公证登记簿的封存应当根据本法第203条和第204条规定的程序办理。

第79条　公证登记簿中的所有登记页和登记册，都应当一直在公证处保存，但本法明文允许的情况除外，或者在必要时，公证人在公证处以外签名的情况除外。必须要将登记册或登记页带出登记处的，应当由公证人亲自或者指派他人处理，指派他人办理的，

necesidad de sacar los libros o folios de la notaria, lo hará el propio notario, o bajo su responsabilidad, una persona designada por él.

Artículo 80. - Si una autoridad judicial o administrativa competente ordena la inspección del protocolo o de un instrumento, el acto sólo se podrá efectuar en la misma oficina del Notario y en presencia de éste, su suplente o asociado. En el caso de que un libro del protocolo ya se encuentre en el Archivo, la inspección se llevará a cabo en éste, previa citación del respectivo Notario.

Artículo 81. - El notario es responsable administrativamente de la conservación y resguardo de los folios y libros que integren su protocolo. En caso de pérdida, extravío o robo de los folios y libros del protocolo de un notario, este o el personal subordinado a su cargo, deberán dar aviso de inmediato a las autoridades competentes, y hacerlo del conocimiento del Ministerio Público, levantando en ambos casos acta circunstanciada, de tal manera que la autoridad administrativa proceda a tomar las medidas pertinentes, y la autoridad ministerial inicie la indagatoria que procede.

Artículo 82. - Para integrar el protocolo, el colegio, bajo su responsabilidad, proveerá a cada notario y a costa de éste, de los folios necesarios a que se refiere esta sección, los cuales deberán ir numerados progresivamente. El colegio cuidará que en la fabricación de los folios se tomen las medidas de seguridad más adecuadas. El colegio podrá abstenerse de proveer de folios a un notario, si éste no está al corriente en el pago de las cuotas establecidas por dicho colegio. El colegio informará mensualmente a la autoridad competente de la entrega de folios que efectúe a los notarios, en la forma que para ese efecto determine dicha autoridad.

Artículo 83. - Al iniciar la formación de una decena de libros, el notario hará constar la fecha en que se inician, el número que le corresponda dentro de la serie de los que sucesivamente se hayan abierto en la Notaría a su cargo, y la mención de que los libros de la misma se formarán con los instrumentos autorizados por el notario o por quien legalmente lo substituya en sus funciones, de acuerdo con esta ley. La hoja en la que se asiente la razón a que se refiere este artículo no irá foliada y se encuadernará antes del primer folio del libro con el cual se inicia la decena. El notario asentará su sello y firma y contará con un término de 5 días hábiles para dar el aviso de inicio a la Dirección General Jurídica y de Estudios Legislativos, mencionando el número de folio y el número del instrumento notarial

责任也应由公证人承担。

第80条 如果主管司法或行政部门下令，要求对公证登记簿或公证文书进行检查，检查工作只能在公证人的办公地点，在公证人、其替补人员或合伙人在场的情况下开展。有公证登记册已经交存档案管理局的，应在事先通知公证人到场的情况下，在档案管理局进行检查。

第81条 公证人对其名下公证登记簿中的登记页和登记册的保存和保管负有行政管理责任。出现公证登记簿中的登记页和登记册遗失、丢失或被盗的，公证人或者其下属人员应当立即通知主管当局，向检察机关报告，并出具相应的情况说明，这样行政主管当局就可以采取相应的措施，检察机关则可以立案调查。

第82条 为形成公证登记簿，公证人学会应当根据每一名公证人的需要，向其提供一定数量的带有连续编号的公证纸，费用由公证人承担，学会对此负有管理责任，学会应当注意在公证纸的生产环节中适当采用必要的防伪措施。公证人未按要求缴纳学会规定会费的，学会可以拒绝向其提供公证纸。公证人学会应当每月向主管当局报告向公证人提供公证纸的情况，报告应按主管当局规定的形式执行。

第83条 每当新开立十本公证登记册，公证人应当写明开立日期和公证人所在公证处给定的序列号，并写明被列入登记册的是公证人还是者依照本法之规定合法代替其履行职责的人员所核准的文书。写有以上字样的页面不带编号，应当作为封面附在这十本公证登记册的第一本的第一张公证页之前。公证人应当在五个工作日内登记其印鉴和签名，将新开立登记册的事项通知法律和立法研究总局，在通知中写明这十本公证登记册中第一份公证文书的编号和该文书第一页的编号。

con que dicha decena de libros se inicie.

Artículo 83 BIS. - La pérdida o destrucción total o parcial de algún folio o libro del protocolo deberá ser comunicada inmediatamente por el notario a las Autoridades competentes, la cual autorizará su reposición y la restitución de los instrumentos en ellos contenidos en papel ordinario.

La restitución se hará con el testimonio o las copias certificadas de los testimonios respectivos que se aporten por los interesados para ese fin.

Si no es posible la restitución de alguno de los instrumentos, el notario podrá expedir testimonios ulteriores, los que le sean facilitados por los interesados, haciendo constar al pie de los que expida, de donde fueron tomados y la causa de su expedición.

En caso de pérdida o destrucción parcial o total de un apéndice, se procederá a su reposición obteniendo los documentos que lo integren de sus fuentes de origen o del lugar donde obren.

El procedimiento de reposición se seguirá sin perjuicio de la probable responsabilidad del notario derivada de la pérdida o destrucción de los libros o apéndices.

Las anteriores disposiciones se aplicarán por el Archivo, en lo conducente, cuando el protocolo se encuentre bajo su resguardo, debiendo prestar el notario de cuyo protocolo se trate, todas las facilidades necesarias y proporcionar los elementos con que cuente.

Artículo 84. - Cuando con posterioridad a la iniciación de un libro haya cambio de notario, el que va a actuar asentará a continuación del último instrumento extendido, en una hoja adicional, su nombre y apellidos, su firma y su sello. Se procederá de la misma forma cuando se inicie una asociación o una suplencia, y en el caso de que el notario reanude el ejercicio de sus funciones. En todo caso, cualquiera de los movimientos anteriores se comunicará a la autoridad competente, al Archivo y al colegio.

Artículo 85. - Para asentar las escrituras y actas en los folios, deberán utilizarse procedimientos de escritura o impresión que sean firmes, indelebles y legibles. La parte utilizable del folio deberá aprovecharse al máximo posible, no deberán dejarse espacios en blanco y las líneas que se impriman deberán estar a igual distancia unas de otras, salvo cuando se trate de la reproducción de documentos, la que podrá hacerse ya sea transcribiendo a renglón cerrado o reproduciendo su imagen por cualquier medio firme e indeleble, incluyendo fotografías, planos y en general cualquier documento gráfico.

第83条之二 公证登记簿中的某页或某册出现全部或部分遗失或损毁的，公证人应立即向主管当局报告，经主管当局批准后，使用普通纸补开内容，进行修补和恢复原状。

要恢复原状，应当通过当事人提供的正式副本或者相应副本的经核证副本补开。

如果某些公证文书无法恢复原状，公证人通过当事人提供的材料签发另一份副本，在副本的页脚写明从何处获得以及签发原因。

如果有附录出现全部或部分遗失或损毁，应当从来源处或者开具地点取得相应文件，予以恢复。

恢复原状并不妨碍追究公证人因登记册或附录的遗失或损毁而应承担的责任。

对于档案管理局保管的公证登记簿，同样适用上述规定，为此，相应公证人应提供一切必要便利及其掌握的资料，配合进行补救。

第84条 如果在新开立登记册后出现公证人的变更，接任的公证人应当在上一任公证人出具的最后一份文书后加入一张附页，附上新公证人的姓名、签名和印鉴。在合伙人或替补人代班的情况下，公证人回归岗位后同样要按这一方式执行。在任何情况下，任何人事变动情况都必须向主管当局、档案管理局和公证人学会报告。

第85条 把文书和记录记入公证页，必须使用确凿、不可抹除、字迹清晰的方式进行书写或印刷。必须尽最大可能利用好公证页面上的可书写部分，不得留白，印刷行距必须一致，但复制文件时除外。在后一种情况下可以单纯进行文字转录或者以任何确凿、不可抹除的方式复制图像，包括照片、图纸以及任何一般性的图形文件。

Artículo 86. - La numeración de los instrumentos será progresiva, incluyendo los instrumentos que tengan la mención de "no pasó", los que se encuadernarán junto con los firmados.

Cuando se inutilice un folio, se cruzará con líneas de tinta y se colocará al final del respectivo instrumento.

Artículo 87. - Todo instrumento se iniciará al principio de un folio y si al final del último empleado en el mismo queda espacio, después de las firmas de autorización, éste se empleará para asentar las notas complementarias correspondientes.

Artículo 88. - Si en el último folio donde conste el instrumento no hay espacio para las notas complementarias, se podrán agregar en el folio siguiente al último del instrumento o se pondrá razón de que las notas complementarias se continuarán en hoja por separado, la cual se agregará al apéndice.

Artículo 89. - Toda autorización preventiva o definitiva de los notarios, así como las que efectúe el titular del Archivo en términos del articulo 113 se asentarán sólo en los folios correspondientes del instrumento de que se trate.

Artículo 90. - Dentro de los treinta y cinco días hábiles siguientes a la integración de una decena de libros, el notario deberá asentar en una hoja adicional, que deberá agregarse al final del último libro una razón de cierre en la que se indicará la fecha del asiento, el número de folios utilizados e inutilizados, la cantidad de los instrumentos asentados, y de ellos los autorizados, los pendientes de autorizar y los que no pasaron, y pondrá al calce de la misma su firma y sello.

Artículo 91. - A partir de la fecha en que se asiente la razón a que se refiere el articulo anterior, el notario dispondrá de un plazo máximo de cuatro meses para encuadernar la decena de libros y enviarla al Archivo, el que revisará solamente la exactitud de la razón a que se refiere dicho artículo, debiendo devolver los libros al notario dentro de los cinco días hábiles siguientes a la fecha de entrega, con la certificación de cierre de Protocolo correspondiente, de lo que el Archivo informará al colegio.

Artículo 92. - Por cada libro, el notario llevará una carpeta que se denominará apéndice, en la que se coleccionarán y conservarán los documentos y demás elementos materiales relacionados con la escritura o el acta de que se trate y estos formarán parte integrante del protocolo. Los documentos y demás elementos materiales del apéndice se ordenarán por letras o números en legajos, en cuyas carátulas se pondrá el número del instrumento a que se

第 86 条　文书必须按先后顺序连续编号，包括写有"没有通过"字样的文书，这些文书应当与被认可的文书一起编制成册。

没有内容的公证纸，应当画叉（表明无内容）并列在相应文书的最后。

第 87 条　所有文书都必须从页面顶头书写，如果在最后一页上写完授权签字后仍有空白，可以用来填写相应的补充说明。

第 88 条　如果文书的最后一页上没有空间来书写补充说明，可以在下一页继续书写，或者写明补充说明将单独书写，列入附录。

第 89 条　公证人的所有初步批准或最终批准，以及档案管理局负责人根据第 113 条之规定作出的批准，只能写在对应文书的相应公证页上。

第 90 条　在一套十本登记册全部用完后的 35 个工作日内，公证人应当在最后一册之后加入一张附页，在上面写明这套登记册已经用完，指出记录日期，使用的和没用的公证页的数量，记录的文书数量，其中有哪些已经批准了，哪些尚待批准，哪些没有通过审核，并在下角签字盖章。

第 91 条　自上一条提到的记录日期起，公证人应在 4 个月内将这一套十本登记册装订成集并送至档案管理局。档案管理局仅负责对本条所指的理由是否准确进行审查，并应在一套登记册提交之日后五个工作日内将之返还给公证人，并出具相应的登记簿封存的证明。档案管理局还应将该情况通知公证人学会。

第 92 条　每一本登记册都对应一个名为附录的文件夹，其中收集和保存了与相应的文书或契约有关的文件和其他材料。附录中的文件和其他材料应当以字母或数字编号，在封皮上写明对应的文书日期，并指出补充的内容。

refieran, indicando lo que se agrega.

Artículo 93. - Los expedientes que se protocolicen por mandamiento judicial y los que previamente estén encuadernados, y que se agreguen al apéndice del libro respectivo, se consideran como un solo documento, al igual que los que por su conexidad deban considerarse como tales.

Artículo 94. - El apéndice es accesorio del protocolo y obra en su refuerzo de los juicios y fe documental del Notario relacionado en los instrumentos asentados en los folios. Lo anterior no impide la validez y veracidad de los documentos asentados ni la validez independiente de certificaciones que se hagan con base en ellos. Las carpetas del apéndice deberán quedar encuadernadas en uno o varios volúmenes con indicación del número del libro del protocolo a que corresponden, dentro del plazo a que se refiere el artículo 91 de esta Ley.

Artículo 95. - El notario deberá guardar en la notaría, la decena de libros durante cinco años, contados a partir de la fecha de la certificación de cierre del Archivo a que se refiere el articulo 91 de esta ley. Dentro de los diez días hábiles siguientes a la expiración de este término, los entregará al citado Archivo junto con sus apéndices para su guarda definitiva, de lo que el notario informará al colegio.

Artículo 96. - Los notarios tendrán obligación de elaborar por duplicado y por cada decena de libros, un índice de todos los instrumentos autorizados o con la razón de "no pasó", en el que se expresará respecto de cada instrumento:

I. El número progresivo de cada instrumento;
II. El libro al que pertenece;
III Su fecha de asiento;
IV. Los números de folios en los que consta;
V. El nombre y apellidos de las personas físicas otorgantes y los nombres y apellidos o. en su caso, denominaciones o razones sociales de sus representados;
VI. La naturaleza del acto o hecho que contiene, y
VII. Los datos de los trámites administrativos que el notario juzgue conveniente asentar.

El índice se formará a medida que los instrumentos se vayan asentando en forma progresiva en los folios.

Al entregarse definitivamente la decena de libros al Archivo, se acompañará un ejemplar de dicho índice y el otro lo conservará el notario.

Artículo 97. - El libro de registro de cotejos es el conjunto de los folios encuadernados, con su respectivo apéndice, en el que el notario anota los registros de los

第93条　根据司法命令归卷的文件，以及事先已经装订好并被列入相应登记册附录的文件，与由于相互之间的关联性而被视为单一文件的情况相同，也应被视为单一文件。

第94条　附录是公证登记簿的附件，尽可能收录公证人对写入登记页中的文书的判断和书面公证。这并不妨碍所记录文件的有效性和真实性，也不妨碍根据这些文件出具的证明的独立效力。附录中的文件夹应当在本法第91条规定的期限内装订成一卷或多卷，写明对应的登记簿中的登记册编号。

第95条　公证人应当将一套十册的登记簿在公证处保管5年，自本法第91条中规定的登记簿封存证明日期起算。在5年保管期届满后的10个工作日内，应当将之与相应附录一并交存档案管理局最终保管，公证人还应将情况报告给公证人学会。

第96条　公证人有义务对每十本登记册编制其中批准的所有文书和"没有通过"的文书的目录，一式两份，目录中应写明每份文书的以下信息：

（1）每份文书的顺序号；
（2）所属的登记册；
（3）登记日期；
（4）文书记录所用的公证纸页数；
（5）公证当事人（自然人）的姓名以及其所代表的公司名称或个人姓名（如适用）；
（6）所载行为或事项的性质；
（7）根据公证人判断，认为需要写明的行政手续的资料。

将文书按顺序录入公证纸上后，就应当写入目录。

将一套十本登记册最终交存档案管理局时，应一并提交一份目录，另一份目录由公证人留存。

第97条　核对登记册是指一整套编订成册的公证记录页及其相应的附录，公证人在其中注明收到的文件的核对记录。进行核对的原件不仅可以是公共文

cotejos de los documentos que le presenten para dicho efecto, considerándose como documento original para el cotejo no sólo el documento público o privado que así lo sea, sino también su copia certificada por notario o por autoridad legítimamente autorizada para expedirla y las impresiones hechas vía electrónica o con cualquier otra tecnología.

Cada libro, que constará de doscientos folios, forma parte del protocolo del notario y, en lo no previsto le serán aplicables las normas relativas al protocolo. Se regirá por lo siguiente:

I. El notario hará el cotejo de la copia escrita, fotográfica, fotostática o de cualquier otra clase teniendo a la vista el documento original, sin más formalidades que la anotación en un libro que se denominará Libro de Registro de Cotejos. Si el original se encuentra escrito total o parcialmente en idioma distinto al español no se requerirá traducción a esta lengua. El registro de los cotejos se hará mediante numeración progresiva e ininterrumpida por cada Notaría.

Contendrá un índice que como requisitos mínimos señalará, el año y nombre del solicitante o interesado.

II. En la hoja que en cada libro de registro de cotejos corresponda a lo indicado para los libros de folios en el artículo 83 de esta Ley, el Notario, o en su caso su asociado, asentará una razón de apertura en la que indicará su nombre, el número de la notaría a su cargo, la mención de ser libro de registro de cotejos, con indicación del número que le corresponda dentro de los de su clase, la fecha, su sello y firma. Al terminar cada hoja de este libro asentará su firma y su sello. Inmediatamente después del último asiento que tenga cabida en el libro, el Notario asentará una razón de terminación en la que indicará la fecha en que ésta se efectúe, el número de asientos realizados, con indicación en particular del primero y del último, misma que firmará y sellará;

III. Cada registro de cotejo deberá contener el número progresivo que le corresponda, la fecha en que se efectúe, el nombre del solicitante, el señalamiento de si es por sí o por otro, con mención del nombre o denominación de éste en su caso; el número de documentos exhibidos, el número de copias cotejadas de cada documento con inclusión de la que se agregará al apéndice y un espacio para las observaciones que el notario juzgue oportuno anotar. Entre registro y registro dentro de una misma página se imprimirá una línea de tinta indeleble que abarque todo lo ancho de aquella a fin de distinguir uno del otro y,

件或者私署文件，还可以是公证人出具的公证副本或者当局依法出具的文件，通过电子方式或其他任何技术手段制作的印刷品也可以进行核对。

每一本登记册的张数都是二百张，列入公证人的公证登记簿，具体按照与公证登记簿有关的规定执行。办理程序如下：

（1）公证人将手抄本、影印件、照片或其他任何类型的副本与原件进行核对，然后只要将核对结果标注到核对登记册中即可。如果原件全部或部分不是以西班牙语书写的，不需要翻译成西班牙语。每一个公证处的核对记录都应有连续不间断的顺序编号。

在登记册中应当有目录，目录中至少应写明年份和申请人或利益相关方的姓名／名称。

（2）在每一个核对登记册的符合本法第83条规定的封面页上，公证人或其合伙人（视情况）应当写明开立原因，其中写明公证人名称、所在公证处编号，注明登记册的标题为核对登记册，该登记册所对应的编号、日期、公证人盖章和签名。在登记册每一页的末尾签字并盖章。一旦在登记册中记完最后一条记录，公证人应当写明办结理由，在其中写明办结日期，本册所载记录数量，特别要写明第一条和最后一条，并在此页签字盖章。

（3）每一条核对记录都包含对应的序号，办理日期，申请人姓名，说明申请人是为本人办理还是代办，如果是代办的，写明委托人的姓名或名称；出示的文件数量，每一份文件要核对的副本数量，包括被列入附录中的副本，并留出一定的空间，以便公证人认为必要时填写备注。同一页面上的各条记录之间应当以不可擦除的墨水画上一条长分割线，以便将各条记录区分开来。

IV. El notario certificará con su sello y firma la o las copias cotejadas, haciendo constar en ellas que son fiel reproducción de su original que tuvo a la vista, así como el número y fecha de registro que les corresponda.

Las copias cotejadas deberán contener las medidas de seguridad que señale el Colegio, sin que su omisión sea causa de invalidez de la certificación.

El índice del libro de registro de cotejos deberá constar en archivo electrónico, reproducción digitalizada o cualquier otra tecnología, que será agregada como anexo al Libro de registro de cotejos, al momento de su entrega al Archivo; tomando las medidas de seguridad y observando en todo momento el secreto profesional que establezcan las Leyes.

Artículo 98. - El notario deberá llevar un apéndice de los libros de registro de cotejos, el cual se formará con una copia cotejada de cada uno de los documentos que se ordenarán en forma progresiva de acuerdo a su número de registro. El notario deberá encuadernar el apéndice de los libros de registro de cotejos, procurando que el grosor de cada libro no exceda los siete centímetros.

Artículo 99. - Los libros de registro de cotejos y sus apéndices se remitirán al Archivo para su guarda al año contado a partir de la fecha de su razón de terminación, teniendo como plazo diez días hábiles para cumplir esta obligación, o bien para el caso de que opte por guardar por cuatro años más los libros de registro de cotejos, contará de igual manera con un plazo de veinte días hábiles contados a partir del día hábil siguiente al en que se cumpla el año contado a partir de la fecha de su razón de terminación de cierre para dar aviso al Archivo de que los guardará por cuatro años más.

Si el notario no remite los libros de registro de cotejos o no da aviso de que los conservará en su notaría por cuatro años más, se entenderá que los conservará para su guarda y custodia por dicho plazo.

SECCIÓN TERCERA DE LAS ACTUACIONES Y DOCUMENTOS NOTARIALES

A. ESCRITURAS

Artículo 100. - Escritura es el instrumento original que el notario asienta en los folios, para hacer constar uno o mas actos jurídicos y que firmado por los comparecientes, autoriza con su sello y firma.

Artículo 101. - Las escrituras se asentarán con letra clara y sin abreviaturas, salvo el caso de transcripción o

（4）副本上注明副本是向公证人出示的原件的如实复制，并写明对应的登记编号和登记日期。

经核对副本应当包含公证人学会规定的防伪措施，但是忽略防伪步骤的，并不构成证明书无效的理由。

核对登记册的目录应当有电子版超链接，或者是扫描版，或者采用其他任何技术形成的电子版，在提交到档案管理局时应当作为附件列入核对登记册中；要采取防伪措施并始终遵守法律规定的职业保密要求。

第98条　公证人应当开立核对登记册的附录，附录包含每一份文件的一份经核对副本，按登记号顺序排列。公证人应当将核对登记册的附录编订成册，并确保每本登记册的厚度不超过七厘米。

第99条　核对登记册及其附录记满后应在公证处保管1年，自公证处的保管义务到期之日起，10个工作日内交存至档案管理局保管。如果选择将核对登记册再在公证处多保管4年的，在前面指出的1年保管期届满后，应在20个工作日内将公证处再保管4年的决定通知档案管理局。

如果公证人没有送交核对登记册或者没有通知要将登记册在公证处再保管4年，应理解为在此期间由公证处保管。

第三节　公证程序和文件

A. 公证状

第100条　公证状是公证人眷写在公证纸上的原始文件，用来记录一个或多个法律行为，并由当事人签名，再由公证人签字盖章批准。

第101条　公证状在书写时必须表述明确，不得有缩写，但转录或复制的情况除外。在进行量的表述

reproducción. No se usarán guarismos a menos que la misma cantidad aparezca con letra. Los blancos o huecos, si los hubiere, se cubrirán con líneas antes de que la escritura se firme.

Lo que se haya de testar se cruzará con una línea que lo deje legible, salvo que la ley ordene la ilegibilidad. Puede entrerrenglonarse lo corregido o adicionado. Lo testado o entrerrenglonado se salvará con su inserción textual al final de la escritura, con indicación de que lo primero no vale y lo segundo si vale. Las escrituras se firmarán por los otorgantes y demás comparecientes únicamente al final de lo escrito. Si quedara algún espacio en blanco antes de las firmas, será llenado con líneas. Se prohíben las enmendaduras y raspaduras.

Artículo 102. - El Notario redactará las escrituras en español, sin perjuicio de que pueda asentar palabras en otro idioma, que sean generalmente usadas como términos de ciencia o arte determinados, y observará las reglas siguientes:

I. Expresará en el proemio el número de escritura y de libro a que pertenece, así como el lugar y fecha en que se asienta, su nombre y apellidos, el número de la notaría de que es titular, el acto o actos contenidos y el nombre del o de los otorgantes y el de sus representados y demás comparecientes, en su caso.

II. Indicará la hora en los casos en que la Ley así lo ordene y cuando a su juicio sea pertinente;

III. Consignará los antecedentes y certificará haber tenido a la vista los documentos que se le hubieren presentado para la formación de la escritura;

IV. Si se tratare de inmuebles, examinará el título o los títulos respectivos; relacionará cuando menos el último título de propiedad del bien o del derecho objeto del acto contenido en la escritura y citará los datos de su inscripción en el Registro Público, o señalará, en su caso, que dicha escritura aún no está registrada:

V. Derogada

VI. Los documentos exhibidos al Notario para la satisfacción de requisitos administrativos y fiscales, deberán ser relacionados;

VII. Si no le fuese exhibido el documento que contenga los antecedentes en original, el Notario podrá imponerse, por rogación de parte y bajo su responsabilidad y criterio notarial, de la existencia de documentos o de asientos que obren en archivos y registros públicos o privados y que tutelen a su entender la certidumbre o apariencia jurídica necesarias para hacer la escritura. De ello

时，不得单独使用阿拉伯数字，除非同时附有对应的大写。如果有空白或者没有内容的地方，应当在签署之前画横线填充。

需要删除的内容，应当划单删除线，确保文字仍可辨识，除非法律规定不可辨识。修正或补充的内容应写在行与行之间。删除或者在行间插入的内容，应当在公证书的结尾加注说明改动有效，并指出第一种情况（删除）的内容无效，第二种（插入）的内容有效。公证书应当由公证当事人和其他当事人签名，签名只能放在文末。如果在正文结尾与签名之间仍有空白，应当以横线填充。禁止涂改和刮擦。

第102条 公证人应当以西班牙语撰写公证状，同时也可以在文中穿插使用外语词汇，一般以科学和艺术类专业词汇为主，撰写公证书时应遵循以下规则：

（1）在开头写明公证书编号和被列入的登记册的编号，出具公证书的地点和日期，公证人姓名，公证人所供职的公证处编号，公证书中所载的一个或多个办理事项，公证当事人姓名，其所代表的委托方以及其他在场人员的姓名或名称（如果有）。

（2）法律有规定，或者公证人认为有必要的，还应写明时间。

（3）叙述背景，并证明公证人已经拿到了当事人向其提交的，用来形成公证状的文件。

（4）对于不动产公证，应当检查相应的产权证书；至少要说明公证状中所载事项的标的资产或权利的最新产权证书，并援引其在公共登记处注册登记的相关资料，或者根据情况需要，指出这一契约尚未办理注册登记。

（5）已废止。

（6）为满足行政司法和税务上的办理要求，向公证人出示的相关文件。

（7）如果在背景介绍部分中提到的当事人出示的文件并非原件，公证人应当事人要求，根据公证准则的要求依职责进行核查，确认在公共或私人的档案和记录中确实存在这些文件或记录，确保公证人的了解，这些文件符合确凿性或合法性要求。公证书中应当对此进行说明。

hará mención el instrumento;

VIII. No deberá modificarse en una escritura la descripción de un inmueble, si por una modificación se le agrega un área que no le corresponde conforme a sus antecedentes de propiedad. La adición podrá ser hecha si se funda en una resolución o diligencia judicial, o en una orden o constancia administrativa que provenga de autoridad competente. Por el contrario, cualquier error aritmético material o de transcripción que conste en asientos o instrumentos registrales sí podrá rectificarse mediante escritura, sin los requisitos señalados, teniéndose esto en cuenta para que el Registro haga posteriormente la rectificación correspondiente en términos del Código Civil en el asiento respectivo. En todo caso el Notario asentará expresamente el haber efectuado dicha rectificación por la rogación de parte pudiendo expresar las evidencias que le indujeron a efectuarla;

IX. En las protocolizaciones de actas que se levanten con motivo de reuniones o asambleas, se relacionarán únicamente, sin necesidad de transcribir, o transcribirán los antecedentes que sean necesarios en concepto del Notario para acreditar su legal constitución y existencia, así como la validez y eficacia de los acuerdos respectivos, de conformidad con su régimen legal y estatutos vigentes, según los documentos que se le exhiban al Notario.

En caso de duda judicial esté deberá ser sobre la situación jurídica de fondo de existencia o no de dicha acreditación en el plano de los derechos subjetivos y no por diferencias de criterio formales sobre relación o transcripción. En este caso, sobre dichos antecedentes y dicha acreditación, la carga de la prueba corresponde a quien objeta la validez de los actos contenidos en el documento:

X En caso de urgencia, a juicio del Notario, los interesados podrán liberarlo expresamente en la escritura de tener a la vista alguno de los documentos antecedentes;

XI. Al citar un instrumento pasado ante otro Notario, expresará el nombre de éste y el número de la notaría a la que corresponde el protocolo en que consta, así como el número y fecha del instrumento de que se trate, y en su caso, su inscripción en el Registro Público:

XII. Redactará ordenadamente las declaraciones de los comparecientes, las que en todo caso se considerarán hechas bajo protesta de decir verdad. El Notario les enterará de las penas en que incurren quienes declaren con falsedad;

XIII. Consignará el acto en cláusulas redactadas con claridad, concisión y precisión jurídica y de lenguaje. pref-

（8）公证书中关于不动产介绍的内容，如果对内容的修订会导致不动产面积增加，与背景介绍部分的内容不一致的，不得修订。如果有司法决议或裁定，或者行政主管当局的公文或指令作为依据的，可以添加。反之，在登记文书或记录中出现的任何计算错误或者转录错误，都可以通过公证书进行订正，无须满足上述要求；通过出具公证书进行订正后，登记主管当局后续应当根据《民法典》之规定，对相应的记录进行订正。在任何情况下，公证人应当明确注明，应当事人要求进行了订正，并写明作出订正所依据的证据有哪些。

（9）在将会议记录形成公证文书时，只需要进行陈述即可，无须进行转录。如果公证人认为，根据现行的法律规定和制度条例，出于证明组建合法和事项存续，以及证明相应会议决议的有效性和效力的需要，可以通过向其出示的文件对相关背景介绍进行摘录。

如果在这一点上存在司法质疑，争论点就在于这种证明在主观权利领域能不能得到法律的承认，而不在于陈述或转录的形式差异。在这种情况下，对于背景介绍以及证明事项，对文件中所载行为是否有效的举证责任在于提出质疑的一方。

（10）对于紧急事项，公证人判断可行的，各方当事人可以免于出示公证书中提到的某份背景文件。

（11）在提到其他公证人出具的公证书时，应当写明这名公证人的姓名，其所供职的公证处编号，公证书所在的登记簿，公证书的日期和编号，以及在公共登记处的登记情况（如适用）。

（12）按顺序将当事人的陈述记录成文，在任何情况下都应认为这些陈述是在宣誓声明的前提下陈述的事实。公证人应告知当事人，如果作虚假陈述将会受到何种惩处。

（13）起草公证书时，要逐条逐款列明，表述应当清楚、简洁、准确，行文用语要合乎规定，最好不

erentemente sin palabras ni fórmulas inútiles o anticuadas;

XIV. Designará con precisión las cosas que sean objeto del acto, de tal modo que no puedan confundirse con otras, y si se tratare de bienes inmuebles, determinará su naturaleza, ubicación, colindancias o linderos, y en cuanto fuere posible sus dimensiones y extensión superficial;

XV. Determinará las renuncias de derechos que los otorgantes hagan válidamente conforme a su voluntad manifestada o las consecuencias del acto, y de palabra, subrayando su existencia, explicará a los otorgantes el sentido y efectos jurídicos de las mismas; cuidando proporcionar, en el caso de personas que recientemente hayan cumplido la mayoría de edad, o de cónyuges que por su situación pudieran requerirla, y en general, de grupos sociales vulnerables, una mayor explicitación oral de sus términos y consecuencias, y respondiendo todo cuestionamiento al respecto;

XVI. Dejará acreditada la personalidad de quien comparezca en representación de otro o en ejercicio de un cargo, por cualquiera de los siguientes medios;

a) Relacionando los documentos respectivos, insertándolos en el instrumento o agregándolos en original o en copia total o parcial que en el propio instrumento certifique concuerda con dicho original con el cual lo habrá cotejado, haciendo mención de ello en el instrumento sin anotarlo en el libro de registro de cotejos, o

b) Mediante certificación, en los términos del articulo 155 fracción IV de esta Ley.

En dichos supuestos los representantes deberán declarar en la escritura que sus representados son capaces y que la representación que ostentan y por la que actúan está vigente en sus términos. Aquellos que comparecen en el ejercicio de un cargo protestarán la vigencia del mismo;

XVII. Cuando se presenten documentos redactados en idioma distinto al español, deberán ser traducidos por un perito reconocido como tal por autoridad competente del Distrito Federal, el notario agregará al apéndice el original o copia cotejada del documento con su respectiva traducción;

XVIII. Al agregar al apéndice cualquier documento, expresará la letra o el número que le corresponda en el legajo respectivo;

XIX. Expresará el nombre y apellidos paterno y materno, nacionalidad, fecha y lugar de nacimiento, estado civil, ocupación y domicilio de los otorgantes, y de sus representados, en su caso. Sólo que la mujer casada lo pida, se agregará a su nombre y apellidos, el apellido o

要写无用的套话或陈词滥调。

（14）对需要证明的事项要表述准确，不要产生混淆或歧义，对于不动产，应当确定其性质、方位、界址或边界，并尽可能写清其空间界限和面积。

（15）强调当事人有权利自行阅读公证书，当事人出于自身意愿放弃这方面权利的，经公证人确认后权利放弃生效，之后，由公证人向当事人介绍其行为或表述的后果，向当事人解释公证书的含义和法律效力；对于刚刚成年者，或者有特别需要的夫妻，以及一般的弱势群体，公证人应注意进一步向其口头解释公证书所列事项的条款和后果，并负责对这方面的一切疑问进行解答。

（16）通过以下任何方式来确认以他人名义或者凭职务性质来办理公证的当事人的代理身份资格：

a）列出相关证明文件，将这些文件的（全部或部分）原件或副本列入公证书中。对于副本，应在公证书中证明经核对，副本与原件一致，将这一情况写入公证书，但无须在核对登记册上注明。

b）通过本法第 155 条第 4 款规定的证明书予以证实。

在上述情形中，代表／代理人应当在公证状中声明，其委托人具有法定能力，代表／代理人具有合法代表权限，授权委托书中赋予其的权限仍然有效。当事人系凭职务性质来办理公证的，应证明其仍有效担任这一职务。

（17）提交不是以西班牙语撰写的文件时，应当由联邦区主管当局认可的专家翻译成西班牙语，公证人将文件的原件或经核对的副本与其相应的译文一并列入附录。

（18）在将任何文件列入附录时，都应写明文件在卷宗中的字母或数字编号。

（19）写明公证当事人的姓氏（父姓和母姓）和全名、国籍、出生日期和地点、婚姻状况、职业和住址，如果有委托人的，还应写明委托人的上述信息。如果已婚妇女有要求的，应当在其姓名中再加入其丈夫的父姓。如果是外国人，应该按照移民的相应格式

apellidos paternos del marido. En el caso de extranjeros pondrá sus nombres y apellidos tal como aparecen en la forma migratoria correspondiente. El domicilio se anotará con mención de la población, el número exterior e interior, en su caso, del inmueble, el nombre de la calle o de cualquier otro dato que precise la dirección hasta donde sea posible. Respecto de cualquier otro compareciente, el Notario hará mención también de las mismas generales, y

XX. Hará constar bajo su fe:

a) Su conocimiento, en caso de tenerlo o que se aseguró de la identidad de los otorgantes, y que a su juicio tienen capacidad;

b) Que hizo saber a los otorgantes el derecho que tienen de leer personalmente la escritura y de que su contenido les sea explicado por el Notario;

c) Que les fue leída la escritura a los otorgantes y a los testigos e intérpretes. o que ellos la leyeron, manifestaron todos y cada uno su comprensión plena;

d) Que ilustró a los otorgantes acerca del valor, las consecuencias y alcance legales del contenido de la escritura cuando a su juicio así proceda, o de que fue relevado expresamente por ellos de dar esa ilustración, declaración que asentará;

e) Que quien o quienes otorgaron la escritura, mediante la manifestación de su conformidad, así como mediante su firma, en defecto de ésta, por la impresión de su huella digital al haber manifestado no saber o no poder firmar. En sustitución del otorgante que no firme por los supuestos indicados, firmará a su ruego quien aquél elija;

En los casos que el Notario lo considere conveniente podrá solicitar al usuario, asiente en el instrumento correspondiente, además de su firma, su huella digital.

f) La fecha o fechas en que se firme la escritura por los otorgantes o por la persona o personas elegidas por ellos y por los testigos e intérpretes si los hubiere, y

g) Los hechos que el Notario presencie y que guarden relación con el acto que autorice, como la entrega de dinero o de títulos y otros.

Las enajenaciones de bienes inmuebles y la constitución o transmisión de derechos reales a partir de la cantidad mencionada en el Código Civil al efecto, así como aquellos actos que garanticen un crédito por mayor cantidad que la mencionada en los artículos relativos del Código Civil, deberán de constar en escritura ante Notario, salvo los casos de excepción previstos en el mismo.

Artículo 103. - Cuando ante un Notario se vayan a otorgar diversas escrituras, cuyos actos sean respecto de

填写姓名。住址应当写明城市、街道号和门牌号、大厦名称、街道名称或者其他任何可以帮助准确定位地址的详细信息。对于任何其他当事人，公证人也应介绍其基本信息。

（20）公证人要证明：

a）公证人认识公证当事人或者确认公证当事人的身份属实，且根据公证人的判断，公证当事人具有相应的合法能力。

b）让公证当事人知道，其有权亲自阅读公证状，并由公证人向其解释文中的内容。

c）在公证人向公证当事人、证人和翻译宣读了公证状，或者他们亲自阅读后，每一个人都表示完全理解了公证状内容。

d）向公证当事人说明，根据公证人的判断，公证状内容具有哪些法律效力、后果及其适用范围，或者注明公证当事人明确声明了解这方面的内容。

e）证明是由何人签署的公证状，公证当事人对公证状内容表示认可并签字确认，如果公证当事人表示不会写字或者不会签名的，可以按手印。由于上述情形无法签名的，签名人也可以选择请他人代签。

在公证人认为适当的情况下，可以要求当事人在相应的公证书上签名的同时再按手印。

f）公证当事人在公证状上的签署日期，委托他人签署或者有证人和翻译的，还要写明这些人的签署日期。

g）在交付款项、票据或其他情况下，说明与经公证人见证且授权的行为相关的事件。

对于不动产的转让、物权的建立或转让，达到《民法典》规定的数额要求的，以及提供贷款担保，数额超过《民法典》相关条款规定的，应当由公证人出具公证书，但《民法典》中规定的特殊情况除外。

第 103 条　在公证人的见证下签署若干关于不动产处置的公证状，要出具的多份公证书的所有权情

inmuebles con un mismo antecedente de propiedad, por tratarse de predios resultantes de porciones mayores o de unidades sujetas al régimen de propiedad en condominio, se seguirán las reglas establecidas en el articulo anterior, con las excepciones siguientes:

I. En un primer instrumento, que se llamará de certificación de antecedentes, a solicitud de cualquiera de las partes, el Notario relacionará todos los títulos y demás documentos necesarios para el otorgamiento de dichos actos;

II. En las escrituras en que se contengan éstos, el Notario no relacionará ya los antecedentes que consten en el instrumento indicado en la fracción anterior, sino sólo se haré mención de su otorgamiento y que conforme al mismo quien dispone puede hacerlo legítimamente; describirá sólo el inmueble materia de la operación y citará el antecedente registral en el que haya quedado inscrita la lotificación en los casos de fraccionamiento, o la constitución del régimen de propiedad en condominio, cuando se trate de actos cuyo objeto sean las unidades del inmueble antecedente; así como los relativos a gravámenes o fideicomisos que se extingan;

III. Cuando la escritura de lotificación o constitución del régimen de propiedad en condominio se haya otorgado en el protocolo del mismo Notario ante quien se otorguen los actos sucesivos, dicha escritura hará los efectos del instrumento de certificación de antecedentes. Surtirá también esos efectos la escritura en la que por una operación anterior consten en el mismo protocolo los antecedentes de propiedad de un inmueble, y

IV. Al expedir los testimonios de la escritura donde se contengan los actos sucesivos, el Notario deberá anexarles una certificación que contenga, en lo conducente, la relación de antecedentes que obren en el instrumento de certificación respectivo.

Artículo 104. - El Notario hará constar la identidad de los otorgantes por cualquiera de los medios siguientes:

I. Por la certificación que haga de que los conoce personalmente en términos del articulo 102. fracción XX. inciso a), de esta Ley. Para ello bastará que el Notario los reconozca en el momento de hacer la escritura y sepa su nombre y apellidos, sin necesidad de saber de ellos cualquier otra circunstancia general;

II. Por certificación de identidad en base a algún documento oficial con fotografía, en el que aparezca el nombre y apellidos de la persona de quien se trate o el documento de identidad que llegaren a autorizar las Au-

况相同，不动产面积较大或者属于共有产权的，应按上一条的规定执行，但有下列区别：

（1）在第一份公证书，即应被称为"背景证明"的公证书中，应任何当事方要求，公证人应当列出所有的产权证书和签署此类合同必需的其他文件。

（2）在批准此类合同的公证书中，公证人不会再陈述在上一段提到的公证书中已经介绍过的背景情况，仅仅说明合同的签署并指出据此可以办理产权过户手续；只要介绍一下被处置的不动产并援引其登记记录，对于分隔为多个地块的，要说明相应的划界工作已经完成，对于以前的房产，要说明已经确立了产权共有制度；如果有抵押或信托的，也应当进行说明。

（3）对于地块划界或者共有产权度确立的公证书也是由同一公证人在之前办理的，则该公证书可具备背景证明公证书的效力。在同一公证登记簿中包含的以前出具的公证书，涉及同一标的物的，也可以视为不动产所有权背景的证明文件。

（4）在签发包含了连续行为的公证书原本的证明材料时，公证人应当随附一份证明书，在其中写明在相应的公证书中所载的背景介绍。

第 104 条 公证人应通过下列任何方式对公证当事人的身份进行确认：

（1）以本法第 102 条第 20 项 a 目规定的方式，证明公证当事人系公证人认识之人。为此，公证人只要在起草公证状之时认识公证当事人并知道其姓名即可，不需要知道公证当事人的其他任何基本资料；

（2）根据官方颁发的、写明持证人姓名且带照片的身份证件进行确认，或者将身份证件提交主管当局审查，经主管当局核实后，将身份证件的副本列入附录。

toridades competentes, los cuales examinará y agregará en copia al apéndice; y

III. Mediante la declaración de dos testigos idóneos, mayores de edad, a su vez identificados por el Notario conforme a alguna de las fracciones anteriores, quien deberá expresarlo así en la escritura. Los testigos en cuanto tales están obligados a asegurar la identidad y capacidad de los otorgantes, y de esto serán previamente advertidos por el Notario, deberán saber el nombre y apellidos de éstos, que no han observado en ellos manifestaciones patentes de incapacidad natural y que no tienen conocimiento de que están sujetos a incapacidad civil; para lo anterior el Notario les informará cuáles son las incapacidades naturales y civiles, salvo que el testigo sea perito en Derecho. Igualmente les informará su carácter de testigos instrumentales y las responsabilidades consiguientes. En substitución del testigo que no supiere o no pudiere firmar, lo hará otra persona que al efecto elija el testigo, imprimiendo éste su huella digital. La certificación y consiguiente fe del Notario siempre prevalecerá sobre la de los testigos en caso de duda suscitada posteriormente salvo evidencia debidamente probada que supere toda duda al respecto. En todo caso, el Notario hará constar en la escritura el medio por el que identificó a los otorgantes. Tratándose de testigos, si alguno no supiere o no pudiere firmar, imprimirá su huella digital y firmará a su ruego la persona que aquél elija.

Artículo 105. - Para que el notario haga constar que los otorgantes tienen capacidad bastará con que no observe en ellos manifestaciones de incapacidad natural y que no tenga noticias de que estén sujetos a incapacidad civil.

Artículo 106. - Si alguno de los otorgantes fuere sordo, leerá la escritura por sí mismo; el Notario le indicará por sí o por interprete que tiene todo el tiempo que desee para imponerse del contenido de la escritura y que por esta Ley el Notario está a su disposición para contestar sus dudas, previa explicación que se le dará de la forma descrita arriba; si declarare no saber o no poder leer, designará a una persona que la lea y le dé a conocer su contenido. En caso de que hubiere necesidad de un intérprete, éste deberá firmar la escritura como tal identificándose satisfactoriamente en términos de esta Ley y de ser posible acreditará dicha capacidad con documentos o indicios relativos. En todo caso, el Notario hará constar la forma en que los otorgantes sordos manifestaron su rogación o adherencia, otorgaron su voluntad y consentimiento y se impusieron del contenido de la escritura y de sus consecuencias jurídicas.

Artículo 107. - Los comparecientes que no conozcan

（3）通过两名合格证人的声明进行证实，证人应为成年人，由公证人根据前面任一项的规定核实身份，并将身份核实情况写入公证书。证人有义务确保公证当事人的身份属实并具备能力资格，公证人应当事先将这一义务提醒证人。证人要知道公证当事人的姓名，通过证人的陈述，没有发现公证当事人自然丧失行为能力，且据证人所知，公证当事人没有丧失民事行为能力。为此，公证人应当告知证人，哪些情形属于自然丧失行为能力，哪些情形属于丧失民事行为能力，但证人是法学专家的，无须告知。公证人还应告知证人，其性质为公证证人以及与之相关的责任。对于不会签名或无法签名的证人，可以由证人选定其他人员代为签名，同时由证人按手印。如果公证人给出的身份证明与证人的说法后续出现矛盾，除非有确凿证据证实证人的说法更为可信，否则应当以公证人的证明为准。在任何情况下，公证人应当在公证书中写明通过何种方式核实了公证当事人的身份。证人如果不会签名或无法签名，可以按手印并由证人请他人代签。

第105条　公证人只要没有发现公证当事人自然丧失行为能力，且没有资料表明公证当事人丧失民事行为能力，即可认为公证当事人具备相应能力。

第106条　有公证当事人是聋人的，应当自行阅读公证状；公证人自行或者通过手语翻译告知公证当事人，可随时对公证状中的内容提出质疑，根据本法的规定，公证人应随时解答其疑问，并按照前面规定的方式向其进行解答；如果公证当事人表示其不会读或者无法阅读，应当指定一人为其宣读公证书，使其了解公证书的内容。需要翻译的，翻译人员应当按照本法之规定验明身份资格后作为译员在公证状上签名，如有可能，应当通过文件或相关证据来证明其能力。在任何情况下，公证人应当注明聋人公证当事人采用了何种方式进行意思表达，表明意愿或请求，以及认可公证状中的内容及其法律后果。

第107条　当事人不懂西班牙语或者向公证人

el idioma español o que declararan ante el notario que su conocimiento del mismo no es suficiente para discernir jurídicamente sus obligaciones, se asistirán por un intérprete nombrado por ellos, en este caso los demás comparecientes tendrán el mismo derecho. Los intérpretes deberán rendir ante el notario protesta de cumplir lealmente su cargo.

Artículo 108. - Antes de que la escritura sea firmada por los otorgantes, éstos podrán pedir que se hagan a ella las adiciones o variaciones que estimen convenientes, en cuyo caso el notario asentará los cambios y hará constar que dio lectura y que explicó, de proceder ello a su juicio, las consecuencias legales de dichos cambios. El notario cuidará, en estos supuestos, que entre la firma y la adición o variación, no queden espacios en blanco.

Artículo 109. - Una vez que la escritura haya sido firmada por todos los otorgantes y demás comparecientes, podrá ser autorizada preventivamente por el notario con la razón "ante mí", su firma y sello, o autorizada definitivamente. Cuando la escritura no sea firmada en el mismo acto por todos los comparecientes, siempre que no se daba firmar en un solo acto por su naturaleza o por disposición legal, el notario irá asentando solamente "ante mí", con su firma a medida que sea firmada por las partes y cuando todos la hayan firmado imprimirá además su sello, con todo lo cual quedará autorizada preventivamente.

Artículo 110. - El Notario deberá autorizar definitivamente la escritura cuando se le haya justificado que se ha cumplido con todos los requisitos legales para ello. La autorización definitiva contendrá la fecha, la firma y el sello del Notario.

Artículo 111. - Cuando la escritura haya sido firmada por todos los comparecientes y no exista impedimento para su autorización definitiva, el Notario podrá asentar ésta de inmediato, sin necesidad de autorización preventiva.

Artículo 112. - El Notario asentará la autorización definitiva en el folio correspondiente acto continuo de haber asentado la nota complementaria en la que se indicare haber quedado satisfecho el último requisito para esa autorización del instrumento de que se trate.

Artículo 113. - En caso de que el cumplimiento de todos los requisitos legales a que alude el artículo anterior tuviere lugar cuando el libro de protocolo o los folios donde conste la escritura relativa, estuvieren depositados en el Archivo, o quedara suficientemente acreditado por el cuerpo de la escritura y los documentos del apéndice dicho cumplimiento, aunque haya sido anterior a su depósito en

表明其西班牙语的语言水平有限，无法从充分了解其法律义务的，可以委托翻译人员提供协助，在这种情况下，其他当事人应享有同等权利。翻译人员应当向公证人宣誓声明，表示自己会依法履行其职责。

第108条 公证当事人在公证状上签字确认之前，有权要求在公证状上进行补充或修改。在这种情况下，公证人应当对相应的变更事项进行记录，向公证当事人宣读并视情况需要，对这些变更事项的法律后果做出解释。出现上述情形的，公证人应注意在签名与补充或修改内容之间没有留下空白。

第109条 一旦所有公证当事人都在公证状上签了字，公证人可以初步批准公证状内容，写明"在我面前"，并签字盖章，或最终批准。如果公证状中没有集齐所有当事人的签名，只要不是由于公证行为的性质原因或法律条文规定的特殊情况，公证人应当只写上"在我面前"，并在已经签名的当事人的下面签名。当所有当事人都签名后，再加盖印章，此时方可视为公证状被初步批准。

第110条 公证人查明已经满足所有相关法律要求后，应当最终批准公证状。最终批准书上要有日期和公证人的签名和盖章。

第111条 当公证状上已经有所有当事人的签名，不存在最终批准的障碍的，公证人可以立即最终批准公证书，无须初步批准。

第112条 公证人应当将最终批准标注到补充说明页上，其中指出，已经满足了批准公证书的最后一项要求条件，可以正式出具公证书。

第113条 如果上一条所列的所有法定要求是在记录相关公证状的公证登记册或登记页交存档案管理局期间满足的，或者公证状正文以及附录文件中已经充分证明这些法定要求已经得到满足，时间早于向档案管理局交存时间的，那么应当在文书中注明：所有要求均得到满足，应予最终批准，并注明满足要求的时间是在交存之前还是属于第一种情形。公证人签

el Archivo, su titular pondrá al instrumento relativo razón de haberse cumplido con todos los requisitos, la que se tendrá por autorización definitiva, dejará constancia si el momento del cumplimiento fue anterior a su depósito o en los términos primeramente descritos. Todo testimonio o copia certificada que expida indicará esta circunstancia bajo su certeza y responsabilidad.

Artículo 114. - Las escrituras asentadas en el protocolo por un Notario serán firmadas y autorizadas preventiva o definitivamente por el propio Notario o por sus asociados o suplentes, siempre que se cumplan los requisitos siguientes:

I. Que la escritura haya sido firmada sólo por alguna o algunas de las partes ante el primer Notario, y aparezca puesta por él, la razón "ante mí" con su firma, y

II. Que el Notario asociado o suplente exprese el motivo de su intervención y haga suyas las certificaciones que deba contener el instrumento, con la sola excepción de las relativas a la identidad y capacidad de quienes hayan firmado ante el primer Notario y a la lectura del instrumento a éstos. La autorización definitiva será suscrita por quien actúe en ese momento.

Artículo 115. - Quien supla a un Notario que hubiere autorizado preventivamente una escritura y que dejare de estar en funciones por cualquier causa, podrá autorizarla definitivamente con sujeción a lo dispuesto por los dos artículos anteriores.

Artículo 116. - Si quienes deben firmar una escritura no lo hacen a más tardar dentro de los treinta días naturales siguientes al día en que se extendió ésta en el protocolo, el instrumento quedará sin efecto y el Notario le pondrá al pié la razón de "no pasó" y su firma.

Artículo 117. - Si la escritura contuviere varios actos jurídicos y dentro del término que se establece en el articulo anterior se firmare por los otorgantes de uno o de varios de dichos actos y dejare de firmarse por los otorgantes de otro u otros actos, el notario pondrá la razón "ante mi" en lo concerniente a los actos cuyos otorgantes han firmado, su firma y su sello, e inmediatamente después pondrá la nota "no pasó" sólo respecto del acto no firmado, el cual quedará sin efecto.

Artículo 118. - El Notario que autorice una escritura en la que mencione a otra u otras escrituras anteriores extendidas en su protocolo, que no hayan sido objeto da registro, lo advertirá así al otorgante interesado y cuidará, una vez que haya sido expensado para ello, en su caso, que se haga en aquél la inscripción o inscripciones, así como

发的所有公证书正本或经核证副本，都应写明这一情形，确保这一标注内容的真实性，所述不实的，应追究相应责任。

第114条 公证人列入其公证登记簿的公证状，满足下列要求的，应当由公证人或者其合伙人或替补人签名并初步或最终批准：

（1）有一部分当事人当着正式公证人的面在公证状上签名，且公证状上有公证人标注的"在我面前"字样及公证人的签名。

（2）代班的合伙人或替补人写明其干预原因，并出具公证书中必须包含的证明书，但已经在正式公证人的见证下签署的身份证明文件和办理能力、资格的证明文件，以及关于向当事人阅读公证书的证明内容除外。最终批准书应当由原先的承办公证人签署。

第115条 之前负责批准公证状的公证人由于任何原因不再任职的，其替补人可以最终批准公证状，具体按照前两条之规定执行。

第116条 如果需要在公证状上签名的人员，没有自公证状写入公证登记簿的次日起，在30个自然日内签名，公证书无效，公证人应当在公证书的页脚标注"没有通过"并签名。

第117条 如果公证状中包含了若干法律文书，在上一条规定的期限内公证当事人在其中一个或多个文书上签名，还有一个或多个文书没有签名的，公证人应当在公证当事人已经签名的文书上标注"在我面前"并签字盖章，紧接着在没有签名的文书上标注"没有通过"，标有这一字样的文书无效。

第118条 出具公证状的公证人，如果其出具的公证状中提到了之前在其公证登记簿中已经开立、但没有登记的其他一份或多份公证状，应当向公证当事人进行提醒，在为此付清费用后（如适用），应注意进行登记，并进行相应的标注。对应的登记册已经最终交存档案管理局的，公证人应当将办理情况通知档

la anotación o anotaciones correspondientes. Si el libro de que se trate estuviera depositado definitivamente en el Archivo, el Notario comunicará a dicha dependencia lo procedente para que ésta, sin costo alguno, haga la anotación o anotaciones del caso.

Artículo 119. - Cuando se trate de revocación o renuncia de poderes o de mandatos o ello resulte de documentos que contengan acuerdos de órganos de personas morales o agrupaciones o de renuncias que les afecten a ellas, y que el Notario protocolizare, este procederá como sigue:

I. Si el acto revocado o renunciado consta en el protocolo de la Notaria a su cargo y la escritura está aún bajo su guarda, tomará razón de ello en nota complementaria;

II. Cuando el acto revocado o renunciado conste en protocolo a cargo de otro Notario del Distrito Federal, lo comunicará por escrito a aquél, para que dicho Notario proceda en los términos de la fracción anterior;

III. Si el libro de protocolo de que se trate, sea de la notaría a su cargo o de otra del Distrito Federal, ya estuviere depositado en definitiva en el Archivo, la comunicación de la revocación o renuncia será hecha al titular de esa dependencia para que éste haga la anotación complementaria indicada;

IV. Si el poder o mandato renunciado o revocado constare en protocolo fuera del Distrito Federal, el Notario sólo hará ver al interesado la conveniencia de la anotación indicada y será a cargo de este último procurar dicha anotación; y

V. El Notario advertirá al compareciente la conveniencia de llevar a cabo el aviso o notificación de la revocación del poder, a quien dejó de ser apoderado.

Artículo 119 BIS. - Los Notarios deberán informar a la Autoridad competente sobre el otorgamiento o revocación de los poderes, mandatos, y actos de apoderamiento pasados ante su fe, dentro de los cinco días hábiles siguientes al otorgamiento del instrumento de que se trate.

La Autoridad Competente o en su caso, el notario, ingresará la información a la base de datos del Registro Nacional de Avisos Poderes Notariales, en un término que no excederá de cinco días hábiles contados a partir de su recepción u otorgamiento.

Artículo 120. - Cuando se revoque, rescinda o modifique un acto contenido en una escritura, se deberá extender una nueva escritura y se realizará la anotación o la comunicación que procedan en los términos previstos en el articulo anterior, para que se haga la anotación correspon-

案管理局，以便档案管理局在登记簿上进行标注，这一操作免费。

第119条 要撤销授权、放弃所受权力或职务，或者由于法人机构或团体的决议文件或者向上述机构或团体提交辞呈导致上述结果的，公证人应按以下规定办理公证：

（1）如果撤销授权或辞职在公证处的登记簿中已有记录，公证状仍在公证处保管，在其中标注补充说明即可。

（2）如果撤销或放弃事项是由联邦区的其他公证人进行的公证，应当进行书面通知，以便当时办理的公证人按照上一款之规定办理。

（3）如果对应的公证登记册，无证是此次受理的公证处还是联邦区其他公证处的，已经最终交存档案管理局，应当将撤销或放弃事项通知档案管理局负责人，以便由进行前面提到的补充说明标注工作。

（4）如果撤销或放弃事项记入了联邦区以外的公证登记簿，公证人应向其他公证辖区的经办人员出示相应凭证，然后由该经办人员完成补充说明标注工作。

（5）公证人应当向当事人出示办理凭证，完成撤销事项的通知告知，当事人不再具备受托代理人身份。

第119条之二 对于授权委托书和委任文书的授予或撤销事项，公证人应在出具相应的公证书后5个工作日内向主管当局报告。

主管当局接到报告后，或公证人在出具公证书后（视情况），应在5个工作日内将信息录入国家公证通知登记处的数据库。

第120条 公证状中所载行为被撤销、废除或修改的，应当出具一份新的公证状并进行标注，或者按照上一条之规定进行通知，以便进行相应的标注。

diente.

Artículo 121. - Siempre que ante un notario se otorgue un testamento, éste dará aviso al Archivo, dentro de los cinco días hábiles siguientes, en el que expresará la fecha del otorgamiento, el número de notaría, nombre completo del notario, tipo de testamento, número de escritura, volumen o tomo, el nombre, sus demás generales, en su caso cualquier otro dato que requiera el formato para integrar los avisos de testamento, y recabará la constancia correspondiente. En caso de que el testador manifieste en su testamento los nombres de sus padres, se incluirán éstos en el aviso.

Artículo 122. - El Archivo llevará un registro especialmente destinado a asentar las inscripciones relativas a los testamentos con los datos que se mencionan en el artículo anterior y entregará informes únicamente a notarios y a jueces legitimados para hacerlo. A ninguna otra autoridad, así fuera de jerarquía superior, se entregarán informes sobre dichos actos ni los servidores públicos encargados podrán proporcionar datos relativos a persona alguna fuera del supuesto que señala el artículo anterior.

Artículo 123. - Los jueces y los notarios ante quienes se tramite una sucesión, recabarán los informes de los archivos oficiales correspondientes, acerca de si éstos tienen registrados testamentos otorgados por la persona de cuya sucesión se trate y, en su caso, los datos de otorgamiento de dicho testamento.

Al expedir el informe indicado, los archivos mencionarán en él a qué personas han proporcionado este mismo informe con anterioridad.

Artículo 124. - Cuando en un testamento público abierto se otorguen cláusulas que conforme a las leyes sean irrevocables, el Notario, sin revelar el contenido de dichas cláusulas, hará mención de ello en el aviso a que se refiere el artículo 121, lo cual asentará el Archivo en el registro a que se refiere el artículo 122. El Archivo, al contestar el informe que se solicite, deberá indicar el testamento o testamentos respecto de los cuales tenga asentado que existen dichas cláusulas irrevocables.

Artículo 124 Bis. - Siempre que ante un notario se otorgue la designación de tutor cautelar en los términos del capítulo I Bis, del título noveno, del libro primero del Código Civil, éste dará aviso al Archivo dentro de los cinco días hábiles siguientes, en el que expresará el número de escritura así como la fecha de su otorgamiento, el nombre y demás generales del otorgante, sin indicar la identidad de los designados, y recabará la constancia cor-

第 121 条　在公证人的见证下办理遗嘱公证的，公证人应在办理后 5 个工作日内通知档案管理局，在通知函上应写明签署副本的日期、公证处编号、公证人全名、遗嘱类型、公证状编号、卷号、立遗嘱人姓名和其他基本资料，以及其他任何按规定要求写入遗嘱通知书中的资料，并收集相应凭证。立遗嘱人在其遗嘱中写明父母姓名的，应将其父母的相关资料也写入通知函。

第 122 条　档案处应当有专门用于记录遗嘱登记情况的登记册，登记记录中应当包含前一条所列资料，并只能向具有合法权限需要报告的公证人和法官提供报告。档案管理局不得向任何其他当局，甚至于级别更高的当局提供这方面的报告，负责这方面工作的公职人员也不得将相关资料提供给前款规定人员以外的其他任何人。

第 123 条　负责办理继承的法官和公证人，应当收集相应的官方档案机构的报告，查明档案中是否有继承事项的遗嘱登记，如果有，应取得与遗嘱办理相关的资料。

在出具报告时，档案机构应当在报告中说明之前还曾经给哪些人出具过同样的报告。

第 124 条　当公开遗嘱中包含了依法不得撤销的条款时，公证人在不披露条款内容的前提下，应当将这一情况写入第 121 条提到的通知中，并按照第 122 条的规定记入档案管理局的登记册中。档案管理局在根据申请出具报告时，应当指出遗嘱中是否包含此类不可撤销的条款。

第 124 条之二　只要在公证人的公证下指定了《民法典》第一卷第九篇第一章之二中规定的监护人，公证人应在出证后 5 个工作日内通知档案管理局。在通知书中写明公证书编号、出证日期、公证当事人的姓名和其他基本资料，无须指明监护人的身份，并应收集相应的凭证。

respondiente.

El Archivo llevará un registro especialmente destinado a asentar las inscripciones relativas a las designaciones de tutor cautelar con los datos que se mencionan en el párrafo anterior y entregará informes únicamente a notarios y a jueces competentes para hacerlo. A ninguna otra autoridad, incluyendo las de jerarquía superior, se entregarán informes sobre dichos actos ni los servidores públicos encargados podrán proporcionar datos relativos a persona alguna fuera del supuesto que se señala al principio de este párrafo.

B. ACTAS

Artículo 125. - Acta notarial es el instrumento público original en el que el Notario, a solicitud de parte interesada, relaciona, para hacer constar bajo su fe, uno o varios hechos presenciados por él o que le consten, y que asienta en los folios del protocolo a su cargo con la autorización de su firma y sello.

Artículo 126. - Las disposiciones de esta Ley relativas a las escrituras serán aplicadas a las actas en cuanto sean compatibles con la naturaleza de éstas, o de los hechos materia de las mismas.

Artículo 127. - Cuando se solicite al Notario que dé fe de varios hechos relacionados entre sí, que tengan lugar en diversos sitios o momentos, el Notario los podrá asentar en una sola acta, una vez que todos se hayan realizado, o bien asentarlos en dos o más actas correlacionándolas, en su caso.

Artículo 128. - Entre los hechos por los que el Notario debe asentar un acta, se encuentran los siguientes:

I. Notificaciones, interpelaciones, requerimientos, protestos y entrega de documentos y otras diligencias en las que el Notario intervenga conforme a otras leyes;

II. La existencia, identidad, capacidad legal, reconocimiento y puesta de firmas en documentos de personas identificadas por el Notario;

III. Hechos materiales;

IV. La existencia de planos, fotografías y otros documentos;

V. Protocolización de documentos;

VI. Declaraciones que hagan una o más personas respecto de hechos que les consten, sean propios o de quien solicite la diligencia, y

VII. En general, toda clase de hechos positivos o negativos, estados y situaciones, sean lícitos o no, que guarden las personas y cosas que puedan ser apreciados

档案管理局应当备有专用于记录对监护人指定情况相关信息的登记册，在其中写明上一段提到的资料。档案管理局只能为相关公证人和法官出具报告，不得向任何其他当局，甚至于级别更高的当局提供这方面的报告。负责这方面工作的公职人员也不得将相关资料提供给承办公证人和法官以外的其他任何人。

B. 公证记录

第125条 公证记录指的是公共文书原本，在文书中，公证人应当事人申请，对公证人现场见证的或者当事人向公证人陈述且公证人已经证实的一个或多个事实进行公证，写入其所开立的公证登记簿的带编号的公证页中，并签字盖章予以核准。

第126条 当公证状与公证记录的性质相容，或者其中所载事实的性质相容时，本法对公证状的规定同样适用于公证记录。

第127条 当要求公证人对在不同的时间或地点发生的多个相互关联的事件进行公证时，只要所有的事件都已经发生了，公证人可以只起草一份公证记录，或者根据需要出具两份或多份公证记录并将之关联起来。

第128条 公证员可以将以下事项写入公证记录：

（1）通知，问询，传告，拒付证书，文件交付以及公证人依照其他法律介入的其他事务。

（2）存续情况，身份，法律能力，核实身份以及由被核实身份的人员在文件上的签字。

（3）实质事实。

（4）图纸、照片和其他文件的真实存在。

（5）文件的拟订。

（6）一人或多人就事件作出的表述，无论是主动作出的声明还是根据办理程序的需要被要求作出的声明。

（7）一般意义上可以涵盖各类正面或负面事实，合法或非法状况和形势，只要其中的人和事可以被客观地向公证人进行说明和陈述即可。

objetivamente y relacionados por el Notario.

En todos los casos señalados en las fracciones anteriores, el acta relativa podrá ser levantada por el Notario en las oficinas de la Notaría a su cargo, con posterioridad a que los hechos tuvieron lugar, aún, en su caso, en los dos días siguientes a ello, siempre y cuando con esta dilación no perjudique los derechos de los interesados, o se violen disposiciones legales de orden público.

Artículo 129. - En las actas a que se refiere la fracción I del artículo anterior, se observará lo establecido en el mismo, con las salvedades siguientes:

I. Bastará mencionar el nombre y apellidos que manifieste tener la persona con quien se realice la actuación del Notario fuera de las oficinas de la Notaría a su cargo, sin necesidad de las demás generales de dicha persona; la negativa de ésta a proporcionar su nombre, apellidos o a identificarse no impedirá esa actuación;

II. Una vez que se hubiere realizado cualquiera de dichas actuaciones, la persona que haya sido destinataria del objeto de la diligencia efectuada, podrá concurrir a la oficina del Notario dentro de un plazo que no excederá de cinco días hábiles, a partir del siguiente de la fecha del acta relativa, para conocer el contenido de ésta, conformarse con ella y firmarla, o en su caso, hacer por escrito las observaciones que estime convenientes al acta asentada. Dichas manifestaciones se harán constar en documento por separado firmado por el interesado, que el Notario agregará al apéndice, y una copia del mismo se entregará al concurrente. En caso de que dichas manifestaciones no sean presentadas durante el plazo señalado, no surtirán efecto alguno, y

III. Cuando el Notario expida testimonios o copias certificadas de las actas asentadas con motivo de las actuaciones a que se refiere este articulo, en el transcurso del plazo que tiene el destinatario de las actuaciones para hacer observaciones al acta respectiva, el Notario deberá señalar expresamente esta circunstancia en el propio testimonio o copia certificada de que se trate.

Artículo 130. - Cuando a la primera busca en el domicilio que le fue señalado por el solicitante de la notificación como del destinatario de la misma, el Notario no encuentre a su buscado, pero cerciorado de ser ese efectivamente su domicilio, en el mismo acto podrá practicar la notificación mediante instructivo que entregue a la persona que se encuentre en el lugar o preste sus servicios para el edificio o conjunto del que forme parte el inmueble, en su caso.

在前面各项所列的情形中，相关记录可以在事件发生后，在接下来的两个工作日内由公证人在公证处内出具，只要这一时间差不会损害到各方当事人的权利，或者违反有关法律规定即可。

第 129 条　对于上一条第 1 款第 1 项所指的记录，应符合下列要求：

（1）公证人在公证处以外的场所办理公证的，只需写明陪同办理人员的姓名即可，无须介绍此人的其他基本资料；陪同办理人员拒绝告知姓名或者拒绝验明身份的，不妨碍公证工作的开展。

（2）一旦发生任何此类行为，收件人自记录出具日期的次日起，可以在五个工作日内到公证人的办公室了解记录中的内容，表示同意并签字确认，或者根据情况以书面形式出具对记录的意见。这些意思表示会单独写成一份文件并由当事人签字，公证人将这份文件列入附录，并将文件副本交给当事人。如果这些意思表示没有在规定日期内提交，则不会产生任何效力。

（3）在收件人享有的对记录提出意见的规定期限内，公证人就本条提到的行动形成的记录出具公证文书正本或者经核证副本的，应当在正本或者经核证副本中明确说明这一情况。

第 130 条　如果在第一次按照通知申请人给定的联系地址没有找到收件人本人，但是确认这是收件人的有效联系地址时，可以让当时在场的认识收件人的人员或在大厦供职的人员，或者收件人的室友（视情况）捎口信，这种做法也应视为进行了通知。

Artículo 131. - Si la notificación no puede practicarse en los términos del artículo que precede, pero cerciorado de que a quien busca tiene su domicilio en el lugar señalado, el Notario podrá practicar la notificación mediante la fijación del instructivo correspondiente en la puerta u otro lugar visible del domicilio del buscado, o bien depositando de ser posible el instructivo en el interior del inmueble indicado, por cualquier acceso.

Artículo 132. - Si al ser requerido el Notario para practicar una notificación, el solicitante de la misma le instruye expresamente que la lleve a cabo en el domicilio que al efecto le señala como del notificado, no obstante que al momento de la actuación se le informe al Notario de lo contrario, éste sin su responsabilidad y bajo la del solicitante, practicará el procedimiento formal de notificación que esta Ley regula realizándola en dicho lugar, en los términos de los dos artículos anteriores.

Artículo 133. - En los supuestos a que se refieren los tres artículos anteriores, el Notario hará constar en el acta la forma y términos en que notificó y en todo caso el instructivo contendrá una relación del objeto de la notificación.

Articulo 134. - Las actas que el Notario levante con motivo de los hechos a que se refieren las fracciones II, V y VI del articulo 128, serán firmadas por quien solicite la intervención del Notario y demás comparecientes. En los supuestos previstos en las demás fracciones del mismo artículo, el Notario podrá autorizar el acta levantada sin necesidad de firma alguna.

Si al término del plazo establecido en el artículo 116 de esta Ley, el acta no hubiese sido firmada al menos por quien solicitó la intervención del notario, éste o quien lo supla, le pondrá la razón de "No pasó" y su firma, salvo en los casos a que se refieren las fracciones I, III y VII del artículo 128 en los que si transcurrido ese plazo el acta no hubiese sido firmada por dicho solicitante, el notario podrá autorizarla al término del mismo. Igualmente en los casos a que dichas fracciones se refieren, la autorizará aún cuando no haya transcurrido el plazo mencionado al ser firmada por el solicitante, aún cuando no sea firmada por cualquiera otra persona que haya intervenido en la diligencia como destinatario o participante en la misma.

Artículo 135. - Cuando se trate de reconocimiento o puesta de firmas y de la ratificación de contenido previstos en la fracción II del articulo 128, el Notario hará constar lo sucedido al respecto ante él, así como la identidad de los comparecientes y que éstos tienen capacidad. La firma o su

第131条 如果无法通过上条提到的方式进行通知，但是可以确认要找的人的联系地址无误，公证人可以将通知贴在要找的人的屋门上或者其他醒目位置，或者在可能的情况下通过任何入口将指令放进其房间中，也应视为进行了通知。

第132条 如果公证人在被要求进行通知时，申请人明确告诉公证人一个通知地址，但是在公证人要实际办理的当时，又告诉了另一个地址，那么公证人应当按照本法规定的通知程序到申请人告知的地址进行通知。具体按前两条的规定执行，如有问题，公证人不承担任何责任，所有责任应由申请人承担。

第133条 在前三条提到的情形中，公证人应当在公证记录中写明通知的形式和条件，在任何情况下，通知中应当写明目的。

第134条 公证人针对第128条第1款第2项、第5项和第6项所列事件出具的记录，应当由申请人以及其他当事人签字。在该条其他几款规定的情形中，公证人可以批准其撰写的记录，无须他人签名。

如果本法第116条规定的期限届满后，申请公证人办理通知公证的人员还未在记录上签字，则公证人或者其代班人员应在记录上表明"没有通过"并签字，但第128条第1款第1项、第3项和第7项规定的情况除外。在此类情况下，如果规定期限届满后申请人仍未签字，公证人可以在期满后批准记录。同样在这几款规定的情形中，如果申请人已经签字但被通知人或者其他任何相关人员没有签字的，即使规定期限未过，公证人也可以批准记录。

第135条 对于第128条第1款第2项规定的核实身份或由被核实身份的人员在文件上签字以及批准文书内容，公证人应当证明是在公证人的面前发生的，表明当事人的身份并证明当事人具有相应的能力。签名或签名认证，以及对内容的批准，适用于以

reconocimiento indicados, con su respectiva ratificación de contenido, podrán ser a propósito de cualquier documento redactado en idioma distinto al español, sin necesidad de traducción y sin responsabilidad para el Notario, en el acta respectiva se incluirá la declaración del interesado de que conoce en todos sus términos el contenido del documento y en lo que éste consiste. El Notario deberá abstenerse de intervenir en las actuaciones señaladas en este articulo, cuando el acto que se contenga en el documento exhibido deba constar en escritura por disposición legal o pacto entre las partes; salvo, en este último caso, que todos los sujetos que la hayan acordado o aquellos de los cuales esto dependa jurídicamente estén de acuerdo.

Artículo 136. - Para la protocolización de un documento, el notario lo insertará en la parte relativa del acta que al efecto se asiente mediante su transcripción o la reproducción de su imagen en la forma prevenida por el artículo 85, o lo agregará al apéndice en el legajo marcado con el número de acta y bajo la letra o número que le corresponda.

Artículo 137. - No podrá protocolizarse el documento cuyo contenido sea contrario a las leyes del orden público o a las buenas costumbres. Ni tampoco podrá protocolizarse el documento que contenga algún acto que conforme a las leyes deba constar en escritura o por acuerdo de partes, en término del artículo anterior.

Artículo 138. - Los nombramientos, poderes y facultades, que consten en actas de reuniones legalmente celebradas por órganos de personas morales o comunidades o agrupaciones en general, tendrán efectos aunque no fueren conferidos en escritura por la simple protocolización de dichas actas, siempre que conste la rogación específica de quien haya sido designado delegado para ello en la reunión de que se trate, se cumplan los requisitos específicos para la validez de la asamblea o junta respectiva y el Notario certifique que no tiene indicio alguno de su falsedad. Al instrumento relativo le será aplicable lo establecido en el apartado correspondiente a las escrituras dentro de esta sección.

Artículo 139. - Los instrumentos otorgados en el extranjero, una vez legalizados o apostillados y traducidos, en su caso, por perito, podrán protocolizarse a solicitud de parte interesada sin necesidad de orden judicial.

Artículo 140. - Los poderes otorgados fuera de la República, una vez legalizados o apostillados, y traducidos, en su caso, por perito, deberán protocolizarse para que surtan sus efectos con arreglo a la Ley. Esto no es aplicable

非西班牙语的任何外语书写的文件，无须翻译，公证人也不承担相应的责任，只要在记录上写入当事人声明即可，声明内容是当事人充分了解文件内容以及文件的构成。所出示文件包含法律规定或者经各方协议约定的应当写入公证状中的行为的，公证人应拒绝办理本条所述的业务；但是对于各方协议约定应写入公证状的事项，如果协议所有相关方或者其中涉及这一问题的当事方均表示同意，则可以例外。

第136条　为将文件形成公证书，公证人应当以转录文字或者复制图像的方式，按照第85条规定的形式，在记录的相关部分插入文件，或者将文件列入附录，并在卷宗中标明记录编号，以字母或数字表示。

第137条　内容违反公共秩序方面法律规定或者道德伦理的文件，不得公证。根据法律规定，包含应当按照前款规定写入公证状或者需要各方达成协议的行为的文件，也不得公证。

第138条　在法人组织、社区或一般团体合法召开会议，形成会议纪要的，其中所载的任命、授权和委托事项，即使没有形成公证状，而只是简单地将这些会议记录列入公证登记簿，只要载明在会上被任命或被授权人员的具体要求，符合构成会议合法召开的具体要求，且公证人证明没有任何迹象表明有弄虚作假行为的，也具备法律效力。相关公证书的出具要求，应按本节与公证状相同的规定执行。

第139条　在境外出具的公证书，一旦完成领事认证或海牙认证并由合格译员出具译文，即可经当事人申请列入公证登记簿，无须司法令。

第140条　在墨西哥境外出具的授权委托书，一旦完成领事认证或海牙认证并由合格译员出具译文，即可经当事人申请列入公证登记簿，以便具备相应的法律效力。但在墨西哥领事见证下出具的授权委托书

a los poderes otorgados ante Cónsules Mexicanos.

Artículo 141. - Para la práctica de cualquier diligencia de las previstas en el artículo 128 de esta Ley. Cuando así proceda por la naturaleza de la misma, el Notario deberá identificarse previamente con la persona con quien la entienda y hará saber a ésta el motivo de su presencia en el lugar.

Artículo 142. - Aunque el requirente original deje de tener interés en los hechos para cuya constancia solicitó la intervención del Notario, este deberá permanecer en el lugar, y hacer constar los mismos, si otro interesado presente se lo solicita expresamente, y le cubre o acuerdan previamente el pago de los honorarios correspondientes.

C. TESTIMONIOS, COPIAS CERTIFICADAS, COPIAS CERTIFICADAS ELECTRÓNICAS Y CERTIFICACIONES

Artículo 143. - Testimonio es la copia en la que se transcribe íntegramente una escritura o un acta, y se transcriben, o se incluyen reproducidos, los documentos anexos que obran en el apéndice, con excepción de los que ya se hayan insertado en el instrumento y que por la fe del Notario y la matricidad de su protocolo tiene el valor de instrumento público.

Artículo 144. - Se insertarán en el testimonio los documentos con los que se acredite la satisfacción de requisitos fiscales, aún cuando hubieren sido mencionados en la escritura.

Artículo 145. - Las hojas que integren un testimonio irán numeradas progresivamente y llevarán la rúbrica y el sello del Notario.

Artículo 146. - El notario podrá expedir sin necesidad de autorización judicial, primero, segundo o ulterior testimonio, o copia certificada, al autor del acto o participante en el hecho consignados en el instrumento de que se trate, a cada parte en dicho acto o bien a los beneficiarios en el mismo; también en su caso, a los sucesores o causahabientes de aquéllos.

Artículo 147. - Se podrá expedir testimonio parcial por la supresión del texto de alguno o algunos de los actos consignados, o de alguno o algunos de los documentos que constan en el protocolo, siempre y cuando con ello no se cause perjuicio.

Articulo 148. - Los Notarios al expedir los testimonios deberán tomar las medidas de seguridad que señale el Colegio. Lo mismo harán respecto a aquellas que el Colegio disponga en relación con el protocolo y los folios.

不适用此种情况。

第141条　为落实本法第128条的任何一项规定，根据相应办理事项的性质，公证人应当事先向当事人表明身份，让当事人了解公证人的身份以及公证人现场办理公证的原因。

第142条　公证人到达现场后，即使一开始申请办理公证的人放弃办理，但在场人员中有其他利益相关方明确提出要对同样的事项办理公证，已经支付或同意提前支付相应的办理费用的，公证人应留在现场继续办理公证。

C. 正式副本、经核准副本、电子核证副本或证明书

第143条　正式副本指的是对公证状或记录的完整拷贝，并转录或者复制了附录所载的所有文件，但已经列入公证书且被公证人证明的文件，以及公证记录的原本具有公证书效力的情况除外。

第144条　用于证明满足纳税要求的文件，即使在公证状中没有提及，也应被列入正式副本。

第145条　正式副本的页码应连续编号且带有公证人的签名和印鉴。

第146条　公证人在不需要司法授权的情况下，有权向起草公证书中所载文书的作者或者参与公证书中所载事项的当事人、文书中所涉及的所有利益相关方或者受益人，以及上述人员的继承人或（别人权利的）承受人（如果有）出具第一、第二或后续正式副本。

第147条　如果删除公证书中所载的对一项或多项行为的表述，或者被列入公证卷宗中的一份或多份文件，不会造成任何损害，可以出具省略这些内容的正式副本。

第148条　公证人在签发正式副本时，应按照公证人学会的要求采取防伪措施。这些防伪措施与公证人学会要求对公证案卷和公证纸的防伪要求一致。

Artículo 149. - Al final de cada testimonio se hará constar si es el primero, segundo o ulterior ordinal; el número que le corresponde de los expedidos al solicitante, el nombre de éste y el título por el que se le expide, así como las páginas de que se compone el testimonio. El notario lo autorizará con su firma y sello.

Artículo 150. - El notario tramitará el registro de cualquiera de los testimonios que expida o de una copia certificada electrónica ante el Registro Público, cuando el acto sea inscribible y el Notario hubiere sido requerido y expensado para ello, tomando en cuenta el artículo 16 de esta Ley.

Artículo 151. - Las hojas del testimonio tendrán las mismas dimensiones que las de los folios del protocolo. En la parte superior izquierda del anverso el Notario imprimirá su sello, y las rubricará en el margen derecho de su mismo anverso.

Como medida de seguridad, el Colegio proveerá a los notarios, previo pago de su costo, de los elementos de seguridad que señale el primero para los testimonios, copias certificadas, certificaciones y folios.

Las hojas del testimonio deberán contener las medidas de seguridad que señale el Colegio, sin que la omisión sea causa de su invalidez.

Artículo 152. - Para cualquier expedición, el Notario utilizará un medio indeleble de reproducción o impresión.

Artículo 153. - Expedido un testimonio no podrá testarse ni entrerrenglonarse, aunque se adviertan en él errores de copia o transcripción del instrumento original asentado en el protocolo. En ese caso el solicitante lo presentará al notario quien, una vez constatado el error, hará mención de ello en nota complementaria que consignará en el original y asentará una certificación en el testimonio, haciendo constar la discrepancia y el texto correcto que corresponda en lugar del erróneo.

Artículo 154. - Copia certificada es la reproducción total o parcial de una escritura o acta, así como de sus respectivos documentos del apéndice, o sólo de éstos o de alguno o algunos de estos; que el Notario expedirá sólo para lo siguiente:

I. Para acompañar declaraciones, manifestaciones o avisos de carácter administrativo o fiscal, si las leyes oreglamentos aplicables disponen que con ellos se exhiban copias certificadas o autorizadas; así como para obtener la inscripción de escrituras en los Registros Públicos, o en cualquier otro caso en los que su presentación o expedición sea obligatoria;

第149条 在每份正式副本的末尾应写明这是第一副本、第二副本还是其他后续的副本，向申请人出具副本的序号，申请人姓名或名称以及职务或头衔，以及副本所含页数。公证人应在副本上签字盖章来进行认证。

第150条 公证人出具任何正式副本或者电子核证副本后，其中的事项属于可登记事项，且公证人接到要求并收取办理费用的，应按照本法第16条之规定到公共登记处办理注册登记。

第151条 正式副本所用纸张的尺寸应当与公证登记簿中的公证纸尺寸相同，在公证纸正面的左上角应有公证人的印鉴，并在正面右边缘签字。

作为防伪措施，公证人学会应向公证人提供前面提到的印章，作为出具正式副本、经核准副本证明书和公证纸的防伪措施，制章费用应由公证人提前付清。

正式副本用纸应当包含公证人学会要求的防伪措施，但是不能以没有防伪措施为由判断副本无效。

第152条 出具副本时，公证人应当使用不可抹除的复制或印刷方式。

第153条 出具正式副本，即使发现在复制或转录公证案卷中的原本时出现了错误，也不得删除或在行间书写。发现错误的，申请人应向公证人提出，经公证人确认后，应在公证书原本上添加补充说明，并在正式副本中加入一份证明书，在其中写明原本与副本的差异以及错处所对应的正确文本。

第154条 经核准副本是对一份公证状或公证记录及其附录中文件的全部或部分复制，或者只是对附录中的全部或部分文件的复制。公证人仅出于以下目的签发经核准副本：

（1）相关法律法规或制度条例要求在行政或税务申报、声明或公告中应提供经核准副本或认证副本的；

II. Para acompañar informes solicitados por autoridad legalmente facultada para requerirlos, con relación a alguna escritura o acta;

III. Para remitirlas a las Autoridades competentes, las judiciales, ministeriales o fiscales que ordenen dicha expedición.

IV. Para entregar al otorgante que la solicite, la reproducción de alguno o algunos de los documentos que obren en el apéndice.

ARTÍCULO 154 BIS. - Copia certificada electrónica es la reproducción total o parcial de una escritura o acta, así como de sus respectivos documentos del apéndice, o sólo de éstos o de alguno de estos, que el Notario expide únicamente en soporte electrónico y que autoriza mediante la utilización de su firma electrónica notarial. La copia certificada electrónica que el notario autorice será un documento notarial válido jurídicamente y se considerará con valor equivalente a los testimonios previstos en esta Ley para efectos de inscripción en las instituciones registrales.

ARTÍCULO 154 TER. - Las copias certificadas electrónicas de las escrituras o actas ya autorizadas en el protocolo de un notario podrán remitirse de manera telemática únicamente con la firma electrónica notarial del mismo notario que las autorizó o del que legalmente lo sustituya en los instrumentos originales que constan en el protocolo.

ARTÍCULO 154 QUATER. - El notario expedirá las copias certificadas electrónicas sólo para lo siguiente:

I. Para acompañar declaraciones, manifestaciones o avisos de carácter administrativo o fiscal, si las leyes o reglamentos aplicables lo disponen;

II. - Para obtener la inscripción de escrituras y actas que se otorguen ante su fe con sus respectivos apéndices en el Registro Público o en otros Registros o en cualquier otro caso en los que su presentación sea obligatoria;

III. Para acompañar informes solicitados por autoridad legalmente facultada para requerirlos;

IV. - Para remitir copias auténticas de instrumentos públicos autorizados por el notario y solicitadas u ordenadas por la autoridad judicial;

En los casos a que se refiere la fracción II de este artículo el notario asentará una nota complementaria que contendrá la fecha de expedición, el número de páginas de que conste la copia, así como para quién se expide y a qué título. Las constancias sobre los asientos de inscripción puestas por los Registros Públicos en el acuse electrónico, serán relacionadas por el notario en una nota complementaria del instrumento con rúbrica del notario. En los casos

（2）当局有合法权限要求提供与某份公证状或记录相关的报告的，应随报告一并提交经核准副本；

（3）根据司法行政主管当局、检察机关或税务机关的要求出具经核准副本；

（4）公证当事人要求对附录中的一份或若干份文件进行复制的，应当为其签发经核准副本。

第 154 条之二　电子核证副本是对一份公证状或公证记录及其附录中文件的全部或部分复制，或者只是对附录中的全部或部分文件的复制，公证人仅提供电子格式的副本，通过使用公证人电子签名对副本进行认可。电子核证副本是一种合法有效的公证文书，在向登记主管当局办理注册登记时，电子核证副本与本法所指的正式副本具有同等效力。

第 154 条之三　已经在公证人的公证案卷中认证的公证状或记录，其电子核证副本只有在附有作出认证的公证人，或者合法替代该公证人出具公证书原本的代班公证人的电子签名的情况下，方可通过电子方式发送。

第 154 条之四　公证人仅出于以下目的签发电子核证副本：

（1）相关法律法规或制度条例要求在行政或税务申报、声明或公告中应提供电子核证副本的；

（2）需要到公共登记处或其他登记主管当局对公证人出具的公证状和记录及其相应附录办理注册登记，或者任何其他必须提供电子核证副本的情形的；

（3）当局有合法权限要求提供报告的，应随报告一并提交；

（4）司法当局申请或责令公证人发送由其认证的公共文书的真实副本的；

对于本条第 1 款第 2 项所指的情形，公证人应当写一份补充说明，内容包括电子核证副本的签发日期、副本页数、写明为何人签发及以何名义签发。公证人应当在公证书原本中标注一则补充说明，写明公共登记处办理注册登记的电子回执，并在补充说明上签名。对于本条第三款和第四款所指的情形，公证人应当同时在补充说明和证明书中写明责令签发电子核证副本的当局名称、卷宗编号、相应的公文号和发文日期。

a que se refieren las fracciones III y IV de este artículo, el notario deberá hacer constar, tanto en una nota complementaria como en la razón de certificación respectiva, la autoridad que ordenó la expedición de la copia certificada electrónica, así como el número del expediente en que ella actúa y el número y fecha del oficio correspondiente.

ARTÍCULO 154 QUINQUIES. - Las copias certificadas electrónicas sólo serán válidas para la concreta finalidad para la que fueron expedidas, lo que deberá hacerse constar expresamente en cada copia emitida. Se considera que el notario no viola el secreto profesional al expedir una copia certificada electrónica para alguno de los destinatarios mencionados en esta Ley.

ARTÍCULO 154 SEXIES. - Los Entes Públicos están obligados a aceptar las copias certificadas electrónicas como si se tratase de copias certificadas en soporte papel autorizadas con firma autógrafa y sello de autorizar del notario del Distrito Federal.

ARTÍCULO 154 SEPTIES. - Los notarios no podrán expedir copias simples en soporte electrónico.

ARTÍCULO 154 OCTIES. - La coincidencia de la copia certificada electrónica con el original matriz y los documentos agregados al apéndice, será responsabilidad del notario que la expide electrónicamente.

ARTÍCULO 154 NONIES. - Los registradores del Registro Público y de otros Registros, los servidores públicos, así como los jueces y magistrados de los órganos jurisdiccionales, podrán, bajo su responsabilidad, imprimir en papel las copias certificadas electrónicas que hubiesen recibido, con la única finalidad de incorporarlas a los expedientes o archivos que correspondan por razón de su oficio en el ámbito de su respectiva competencia y harán constar igualmente en una certificación ese hecho.

Artículo 155. - Certificación notarial es la relación que hace el Notario de un acto o hecho que obra en su protocolo, en un documento que él mismo expide o en un documento preexistente, así como la afirmación de que una transcripción o reproducción coincide fielmente con su original, comprendiéndose dentro de dichas certificaciones las siguientes:

I. Las razones que el Notario asienta en copias al efectuar un cotejo conforme a lo previsto en el artículo 97 de esta Ley.

II. La razón que el Notario asienta al expedir las copias a que se refiere el artículo anterior. En estos casos la certificación se asentará al final de la transcripción o reproducción, haciendo constar el número y fecha del instru-

第 154 条之五　电子核证副本仅能用于具体指定目的，在每一份电子核证副本中都应标明其具体用途。公证人为本法提到的某个收件人签发电子核证副本的行为，不构成违反职业保密义务。

第 154 条之六　公共实体有义务接受电子核证副本，其效力等同于联邦区公证人签发的带有其手写签名和印鉴的纸质经核准副本。

第 154 条之七　公证人不得签发电子格式的简单拷贝件。

第 154 条之八　出具电子核证副本的公证人，应确保其以电子方式签发的核证副本与公证书原本及附录所载文件一致。

第 154 条之九　公共登记处和其他登记处的登记员、公务员，以及司法机关的法官和地方行政官，有权依职责将收到的电子核证副本打印成纸质版本，唯一目的就是在其职权范围内，根据工作需要将这些纸质副本纳入其负责的卷宗或档案中，并同样需要为此出具证明书。

第 155 条　公证证明书就是公证人将其公证案卷中，或者公证人自己签发的某份文件，或者在之前已有的文件中记载的某个行为或事实形成文字说明，以及确认转录或复制的内容与原本完全一致。公证证明书包含以下几种情形：

（1）公证人根据本法第 97 条之规定进行文件核对后，在副本上撰写的核对结论证明书。

（2）公证人在签发上一条提到的副本时撰写的证明文字。在此类情况下，证明书应当紧接着转录或复制内容后面撰写，写明对应公证书原本的编号和日期，但在副本开头已经写明这些信息的，不必重复。

mento del protocolo correspondiente, a no ser que estos datos se reproduzcan al principio de la copia. En el caso a que se refiere la fracción I del artículo anterior, bastará señalar para qué efectos se expide, sin que conste petición de parte, ni se tomará razón de su expedición en parte alguna del protocolo.

III. La relación sucinta de un acto o hecho, o de uno de sus elementos o circunstancias que consten en su protocolo, que asiente en un documento que al efecto expida a petición de parte o autoridad facultada para hacerlo, o en un documento preexistente, también a solicitud de parte, lo que hará constar en la propia certificación sin necesidad de tomar razón en nota complementaria.

IV. La razón de existencia de uno o varios documentos que se le exhiban, para acreditar la personalidad de los otorgantes o interesados en una escritura o acta que el Notario asiente en la reproducción total o parcial, lo que será suficiente para dejar acreditada dicha personalidad; bastando para ello relacionar en la escritura o acta respectiva, el número y fecha de la escritura cuyo testimonio o copia se le exhiba, y el nombre y el número del Notario ante quien se haya otorgado, o la autoridad y procedimiento de que se deriven, en caso de ser copias certificadas expedidas respecto de constancias de algún procedimiento judicial. En los casos a que se refieren las fracciones II y III del artículo anterior, se deberá hacer constar, tanto en nota complementaria como en la razón de certificación respectiva, la autoridad que ordenó el informe o expedición de la copia, del expediente en que ella actúa y el número y fecha del oficio correspondiente. Igualmente, podrá hacer constar en nota complementaria y agregar al apéndice la copia de la comunicación mediante la cual haya sido enviada la copia certificada a la autoridad respectiva. Toda certificación será autorizada por el Notario con su firma y sello.

CAPÍTULO III DE LOS EFECTOS, VALOR Y DE LA PROTECCIÓN DE EFECTOS DEL INSTRUMENTO PUBLICO NOTARIAL

Artículo 156. - En tanto no se declare judicialmente la falsedad o nulidad de un instrumento, registro, testimonio, copia certificada, copia certificada electrónica o certificación notariales, estos serán prueba plena de que los otorgantes manifestaron su voluntad de celebrar el acto consignado en el instrumento de que se trate, que hicieron las declaraciones que se narran como suyas, así como de la verdad y realidad de los hechos de los que el Notario dio

对于第 154 条第 1 款的情况，只要指出签发目的为何即可，无须说明是根据何人要求签发的，也无须在公证登记簿中进行任何记录。

（3）在应当事人或者有关部门的要求出具的文件中，对公证登记簿中记录的某一行为或事实，或者其中的某一要素或情形进行简要介绍，或者根据当事人要求，对已有文件中的某一行为或事实，或者其中的某一要素或情形进行简要介绍，相关内容只要在证明书中写明即可，无须在补充说明中标注。

（4）说明一份或若干份向公证人出示的文件确实存在，这些文件适用于证实公证人全部或部分复制的一份契约或记录中的公证当事人或当事人的资格，这些文件的存在足以证实相应的身份或资格。为此，只要在相应的契约或记录中写明向其出示的正式副本或复印件的原本编号和日期，公证书原本的承办公证人姓名和编号；对于为某种司法程序的凭证出具的经核准副本，应说明主管机关的名称和对应的司法程序；对于第 154 条第 2 款和第 3 款所指的情形，应当同时在补充说明和证明书中写明责令签发电子核证副本的当局名称、卷宗编号、相应的公文号和发文日期；还可以在补充说明中写明向主管机关寄送经核证副本的信函并将信函副本列入附录。所有的证明书都应由公证人签名和加盖印章来进行认证。

第三章 公证书的效力、影响以及对公证书效力的保护

第 156 条 司法机关未裁定公证文书、记录、正式副本、经核证副本、电子核证副本或证明书虚假或无效的，应视为此类文书具备充分证明效力，证明当事人确系出于本身意愿缔结协议，其所作的陈述属实，公证人所证明的事项真实有效，且公证的办理符合法定形式要求。

fe tal como los refirió y de que observó las formalidades correspondientes.

Esta presunción admite prueba en contrario, por lo que los casos en que el notario en ejercicio de su función, consigne en un instrumento, registro, testimonio o certificación, hechos que no sean ciertos, de fe de lo que no consta en registro, protocolos o documentos, haga constar hechos falsos, o expida un instrumento, testimonio o certificación de hechos que no sean ciertos, el ejercicio de la acción penal no está sujeto ni condicionado en modo alguno al ejercicio o resolución de la acción civil, ni tampoco el ejercicio de las acciones civiles está sujeto o condicionado al ejercicio de la acción penal ni a su resolución por la autoridad correspondiente.

Artículo 157. - La nulidad de un instrumento o registro notariales sólo podrá hacerse valer por vía de acción y no por vía de excepción, siempre que existan elementos claramente definitorios en contra que ameriten romper, como excepción debidamente comprobada, el principio de prueba plena.

Artículo 158. - Las correcciones no salvadas en las escrituras, actas o asientos de registro, se tendrán por no hechas.

Artículo 159. - Salvo disposición en contrario, la simple protocolización acreditará la existencia del documento objeto de la misma en la fecha de su presentación ante el Notario y la de su conservación posterior. La elevación a escritura pública o la celebración ante Notario como escritura de actos meramente protocolizables tendrán el valor de prueba plena.

Artículo 160. - El cotejo acreditará que la copia que se firma por el notario es fiel reproducción del exhibido como original, sin calificar sobre la autenticidad, validez o licitud del mismo.

La copia cotejada tendrá el mismo valor probatorio que el documento exhibido como original con el cual fue cotejado, salvo que se trate de documento que lleve incorporado su derecho, supuesto en el cual sólo producirá el efecto de acreditar que es copia fiel de su original.

Artículo 161. - Cuando en un instrumento notarial haya diferencia entre las palabras y los guarismos, prevalecerán aquéllas.

Artículo 162. - El instrumento o registro notarial sólo será nulo:

I. Si el Notario no tiene expedito el ejercicio de sus funciones en el momento de su actuación;

II. Si no le está permitido por la Ley intervenir en el

有确凿证据表明公证人在行使职能的过程中，所登记或公证的事项与事实不符，其记录、登记簿或公证书中出现弄虚作假行为，或者为不确定的事项出具了证明书或公证书的，依法追究其民事责任，构成刑事违法的，还应依法追究其刑事责任。同时，依法追究其民事责任的，不妨碍对其刑事责任或行政责任的追究或对该追究构成制约因素。

第157条 有确凿证据表明公证文书或记录与事实不符或违反法律规定的，只能通过诉讼程序判定文书或记录无效，不得通过行政申诉解决。在审理时应充分说明理由，遵循充分举证原则。

第158条 对公证状、公证记录或登记记录的修正，没有加注说明改动有效的，视同未修正。

第159条 除非法律另有明文规定，只要记入公证登记簿，即能证实待公证文件在提交给公证人之日和后续保存期间的存续情况。形成公证书或者在公证人的见证下形成正式文书的，具有充分证明效力。

第160条 核对指的是确认公证人签发的副本，是当事人出示的原件的忠实复印件，但不对原件的真实性、有效性或合法性做出任何判断。

经核对的副本与作为核对参照物的原件具有同等证明效力，但是涉及权利事项的情况除外。在这种情况下，只能证明经核对的副本是对原件的忠实复制。

第161条 当公证书中的数字表述出现大小写（文字和阿拉伯数字）差异时，以大写内容为准。

第162条 出现以下情形的，公证书或公证登记无效：

（1）公证人在办理公证的当时没有取得履职资格的；

（2）出现法律法规禁止的情形的；

acto;

III. Si no le está permitido dar fe del acto o hecho materia de la escritura o del acta por haberlo hecho en contravención de los términos de la fracción II del artículo 45;

IV. Si ha sido redactado en idioma distinto al español;

V Si no está firmado por todos los que deben firmarlo según esta Ley, o no contiene la mención exigida a falta de firma;

VI. Si está autorizado con la firma y sello del Notario cuando debiera tener nota de "no pasó", o cuando el instrumento no esté autorizado con la firma y sello del Notario.

VII. Si el Notario no se aseguró de la identidad de los otorgantes en términos de esta Ley.

En el caso de la fracción II de este artículo, solamente será nulo el instrumento en lo referente al acto o hecho relativos, pero será válido respecto de los otros actos o hechos que contenga y que no estén en el mismo caso. Fuera de los casos determinados en este artículo, el instrumento o asiento será válido. Cuando se demande la nulidad de un acto jurídico no podrá demandarse al Notario la nulidad de la escritura que lo contiene, si no existe alguno de los supuestos a que se refieren las fracciones anteriores. Sin embargo, cuando se dicte la sentencia que declare la nulidad del acto, una vez firme, el juez enviará oficio al Notario o al Archivo según se trate, para que en nota complementaria se tome razón de ello.

Artículo 163. - El testimonio, copias certificadas y certificaciones serán nulos solamente en los siguientes casos:

I. Cuando el original correspondiente lo sea;

II. Si el Notario no se encuentra en ejercicio de sus funciones al expedir la reproducción de que se trate o la expida fuera del Distrito Federal, y

III. Cuando dicha reproducción no tenga la firma o sello del notario.

ARTÍCULO 163 bis. - La copia certificada electrónica será nula en los dos primeros supuestos del artículo 163 o si al momento de expedición el notario no tiene vigente el registro de su firma electrónica notarial en términos del Código Civil para el Distrito Federal, esta Ley y de la Ley de firma electrónica para el Distrito Federal.

Artículo 164. - Cuando se expida un testimonio por Notario, o cuando así corresponda, por el titular del Archivo, se asentará una nota complementaria que contendrá la fecha de expedición, el número de hojas de que conste el testimonio, el número ordinal, que corresponda a éste, según los artículos 146 y 149 de esta Ley, así como para quién se expida y a qué título. Las constancias sobre los

（3）出现违反第45条第2项之规定，依法不得办理公证的；

（4）不使用西班牙语起草文书或进行登记的；

（5）没有依法要求所有的当事人在文书上签字确认的，或者没有说明签字不全的理由的；

（6）虽然公证人在文书上签字盖章，但注明"未通过"字样，或者公证人没有在文书上签字盖章确认的；

（7）公证人没有依法对当事人的身份进行验证的。

出现本条第1款第2项所指情形的，只有被禁止事项对应的部分无效，但文书或记录中包含的其他事项继续有效。不属于本条规定情形的文书或记录均具备合法效力。当主张判定一项法律行为无效时，不符合以上各款规定的任一情形的，不得要求公证人对包含此项法律行为的公证予以作废。但是，如果司法机关判定被起诉的行为无效，一旦形成最终判决，法官应当正式向公证人或档案管理局（如适用）发函，以便公证人或档案管理局在文件上加注。

第163条　出现以下情形的，正式副本、经核证副本和证明书无效：

（1）原件无效；

（2）公证人在签发副本之时不具备合法履职资格或者在联邦区以外签发的；

（3）复制的文本中没有公证人的签字或盖章的。

第163条之二　出现第163条前2项规定情形，或者公证人在出具电子核证副本时，其电子签名没有按照《联邦区民法典》、本法以及《联邦区电子签名法》的相关规定办理登记的，电子核证副本无效。

第164条　公证人或档案管理局负责人出具正式副本时，应当根据本法第146和第149条之规定，在正本上加注，写明副本签发日期、副本页数、编号，为何人以及因何种原因或以何种名义签发的副本。在文件的末尾注明的关于正本在登记主管当局办理登记的说明，应当由公证人在正本上加注，形成超链接或者进行抄录。在任何情况下，加注内容必须由公证人

asientos de inscripción puestas por los registros públicos correspondientes al calce de los testimonios, serán relacionadas o transcritas por el Notario en una nota complementaria del instrumento. En todo caso, las notas complementarias llevarán la rúbrica o media firma del Notario.

Artículo 165. - Se aplicará la pena prevista por el artículo 311 del Nuevo Código Penal al que:

I. Interrogado por notario del Distrito Federal, por el colegio en cumplimiento de las atribuciones establecidas por esta ley, o por el Archivo, falte a la verdad;

II. Hiciere declaraciones falsas ante Notario del Distrito Federal que éste haga constar en un instrumento;

III. Siendo Notario en ejercicio de sus funciones, a sabiendas, haga constar hechos falsos en un instrumento.

La penalidad prevista se duplicará si quien comete el delito es notario.

CAPÍTULO IV DE LA COMPETENCIA PARA REALIZAR FUNCIONES NOTARIALES EN ASUNTOS EXTRAJUDICIALES Y DE LA TRAMITACIÓN SUCESORIA ANTE NOTARIO

SECCIÓN PRIMERA DISPOSICIONES GENERALES

Artículo 166. - En los términos de esta Ley se consideran asuntos susceptibles de conformación por el Notario mediante el ejercicio de su fe pública, en términos de esta Ley:

I. Todos aquellos actos en los que haya o no controversia judicial, los interesados le soliciten haga constar bajo su fe y asesoría los acuerdos, hechos o situaciones de que se trate;

II. Todos aquellos en los que, exista o no controversia judicial, lleguen los interesados voluntariamente a un acuerdo sobre uno o varios puntos del asunto, o sobre su totalidad, y se encuentren conformes en que el notario haga constar bajo su fe y con su asesoría los acuerdos, hechos o situaciones de que se trate, siempre que se haya solicitado su intervención mediante rogación.

III. Todos aquellos asuntos que en términos del Código de Procedimientos Civiles conozcan los jueces en vía de jurisdicción voluntaria en los cuales el notario podrá intervenir en tanto no hubiere menores no emancipados o mayores incapacitados. En forma específica, ejemplificativa y no taxativa, en términos de este capítulo y de esta ley:

a) En las sucesiones en términos del párrafo anterior y de la sección segunda de este capitulo;

b) En la celebración y modificación de capitulaciones

签字画押。

第 165 条　出现以下情形的，应按新《刑法典》第 311 条之规定予以处罚：

（1）联邦区公证人、公证人学会或档案管理局依照本法赋予的职权提出质疑，认为被公证内容不实的；

（2）向联邦区公证人作虚假陈述，由公证人写入公证书的；

（3）公证人在履行法定职责的过程中明知故犯，对不实情况进行公证的。

公证人犯罪的，应加倍处罚。

第四章　在司法外事项中履行公证职能以及办理继承公证

第一节　总则

第 166 条　在本法中，可以由公证人通过公证认定的事项如下：

（1）当事人申请办理公证并就相关协议、事项或情况进行咨询的，无论是否存在法律纠纷；

（2）所有当事人就一个事项的一点或多点，或者全部事项达成协议，要求公证人办理公证并就相关协议、事项或情况进行咨询的，无论是否存在法律纠纷；

（3）根据《民事诉讼法》之规定，通过自愿管辖权由法官受理的所有事项，其中没有涉及不符合法定年龄的未成年人或者失去民事行为能力的成年人的，可由公证人办理公证。具体来说，根据本章以及《民事诉讼法》之规定，包括但不限于以下情形：

a）符合上一段以及本章第二节规定的继承事项；

b）婚姻关系的缔结和变更，婚姻的解体和清算；

matrimoniales, disolución y liquidación de sociedad conyugal,

c)En las informaciones adperpetuam, apeos y deslindes y demás diligencias, excepto las informaciones de dominio.

Las autorizaciones y habilitaciones especiales de sujetos a quienes falte capacidad jurídica se regirán por lo dispuesto en el Código Civil y en las demás normas correspondientes.

SECCIÓN SEGUNDA NORMAS NOTARIALES DE TRAMITACIÓN SUCESORIA

Artículo 167. - Sin perjuicio de lo dispuesto por el artículo 782 del Código de Procedimientos Civiles, las sucesiones en las que no hubiere controversia alguna y cuyos herederos fueren mayores de edad, menores emancipados o personas jurídicas, podrán tramitarse ante Notario. El que se oponga al trámite de una sucesión, o crea tener derechos contra ella, los deducirá conforme lo previene el Código de Procedimientos Civiles. El Juez competente, de estimarlo procedente, lo comunicará al Notario para que, en su caso, a partir de esa comunicación se abstenga de proseguir con la tramitación.

Artículo 168. - Si la sucesión fuere testamentaria, la tramitación notarial podrá llevarse a cabo, independientemente de cual hubiere sido el último domicilio del autor de la sucesión o el lugar de su fallecimiento, siempre y cuando se actualicen las hipótesis previstas en la primera parte del artículo anterior; si hubiere legatarios incapaces podrá tramitarse notarialmente la sucesión en el caso que los legados hayan sido pagados o garantizados su pago total, lo cual deberá hacerse constar en el instrumento.

En este caso, deberán obtenerse previamente los informes del Archivo, así como de la oficina respectiva del último domicilio del autor de la sucesión, en caso de que hubiere sido fuera del Distrito Federal, a fin de acreditar que el testamento presentado al Notario por todos los herederos, es el último otorgado por el testador.

Artículo 169. - La sucesión intestamentaria podrá tramitarse ante notario si el último domicilio del autor de la sucesión fue el Distrito Federal, o si se encuentran ubicados en la entidad uno o la mayor parte de los bienes, lo cual declararán los interesados bajo su responsabilidad, una vez que se hubieren obtenido del Archivo, constancias de no tener depositado testamento o informe de que se haya otorgado alguno, y previa acreditación de los

c）永久真实性认定、地界勘定、划界以及其他事务，但支配权除外。

对于没有法律行为能力的人员的特别许可和授权，应按照《民法典》和其他有关规定执行。

第二节 继承公证的办理规则

第 167 条 除应满足《民事诉讼法》第 782 条的规定外，继承事项不存在任何争议，且继承人为成年人、达到法定年龄要求的未成年人或法人的，可以向公证人办理继承公证。对继承手续有异议，或者认为有权继承的，可以按照《民事诉讼法》之规定提出权利主张。主管法官认定应予受理的，应当通知公证人，公证人自接到通知之时起，应暂停办理公证。

第 168 条 如果是遗嘱继承事项，无论立遗嘱人的最新地址为何或者去世地点为何，只要符合上一条第一部分规定的情形的，即可办理公证；受遗嘱人（遗产承受人）无法律行为能力的，如果遗产已经付清或者可以保证全额付清，即可通过公证人办理继承手续，并在相应的文书中注明。

在这种情况下，应当事前从档案管理局调取资料，管辖地在联邦区以外的，还应到立遗嘱人最新住所地的主管机关调取相关资料，以核实所有继承人提交给公证人的遗嘱确系立遗嘱人的最终遗嘱。

第 169 条 对于无遗嘱继承事项，被继承人的最新住所地在联邦区境内，或者继承标的物中有一部分或大部分在联邦区境内的，可要求联邦区公证人办理公证。为此，公证申请人应当申明，已经到档案管理局开具证明，证实没有任何交存到档案管理局的遗嘱或报告，并通过民事登记处出具的相应证明，事先认定继承人与被继承人之间的关系。办理无遗嘱继承公证的，继承人应当是被继承人的配偶、父母、子女及

herederos de su entroncamiento con el autor de la sucesión mediante las partidas del Registro Civil correspondiente. Podrán tramitar esta sucesión, el o la cónyuge, los ascendientes, descendientes y colaterales hasta el cuarto grado; fuera de estos casos, la sucesión deberá tramitarse por la vía judicial.

Artículo 170. - Si hubiere testamento se exhibirá el testimonio correspondiente y la copia certificada del acta de defunción del autor de la sucesión; el heredero o herederos instituidos y el albacea designado, si lo hubiere, podrán manifestar expresamente y, de común acuerdo ante el notario de su elección:

I. Su conformidad, de llevar la tramitación ante el citado notario;

II. Que reconocen la validez del testamento;

III. Que aceptan la herencia;

IV. Que reconocen por si y entre si sus derechos hereditarios que les sean atribuidos por el testamento, y

V. Su intención de proceder por común acuerdo.

Artículo 171. - El Notario podrá hacer constar también la aceptación o renuncia del cargo de albacea instituido por el autor del testamento, así como las designaciones de albacea que en su caso hagan todos los herederos de común acuerdo, y la aceptación del cargo. También los acuerdos de los herederos para la constitución en su caso de la caución o el relevo de esa obligación. Una vez aceptado el cargo, el albacea procederá a la formación de inventario y avalúo en términos de Ley.

Artículo 172. - También podrá hacer constar el notario, la renuncia o repudio de derechos que haga alguno de los herederos o legatarios.

Los emancipados podrán aceptar o repudiar sus derechos hereditarios.

Artículo 173. - El instrumento de aceptación de herencia podrá otorgarse aún sin la comparecencia de los legatarios instituidos, siempre que los herederos se obliguen al pago de los legados. No se podrá llevar a cabo la adjudicación de bienes sin que se hubiesen pagado o garantizado los legados.

Artículo 174. - Si no hubiere testamento, los herederos, en el orden de derechos previsto por el Código Civil, comparecerán todos ante Notario en compañía de dos testigos idóneos; exhibirán al Notario copias certificadas del acta de defunción del autor de la sucesión y las que acrediten su entroncamiento; declararán bajo protesta de decir verdad sobre el último domicilio del finado, y que no conocen de la existencia de persona alguna diversa de ellos

四代以内血亲；否则，必须通过司法程序办理继承事项。

第 170 条　有遗嘱的，应当出具遗嘱的正式副本以及立遗嘱人死亡证明的经核证副本；继承人或者指定的遗嘱执行人（如果有）可以明确向公证人表达其意愿，对于多人继承的，可以在达成共同意见后向公证人表明其选择：

（1）同意委托公证人办理相应手续；

（2）承认遗嘱的有效性；

（3）接受遗产；

（4）承认并相互承认通过遗嘱赋予自己或其他当事人的继承权；及

（5）已经统一意见，同意依程序办理。

第 171 条　公证人还应证明，立遗嘱人指定的遗嘱执行人是否接受这一委托，所有继承人是否一致同意指定遗嘱执行人全权受理（如适用），以及遗嘱执行人是否接受委托。证明继承人是否根据需要建立了担保或履行了这一义务。一旦接受委托，遗嘱执行人应当依法清点遗产并进行评估。

第 172 条　公证人还可以对继承人或受遗嘱人放弃或拒绝继承权利的情况进行证明。

达到法定年龄要求的未成年人可以接受或拒绝继承权利。

第 173 条　只要继承人有给予遗产的义务，则即使指定的受遗嘱人不到场，遗产继承受领文书也可完成公证。在遗产未给付或建立担保之前，不得判定遗产归属。

第 174 条　没有遗嘱的，所有继承人应当按照《民法典》规定的顺位继承顺序，一起要求公证人办理公证，并需要指定两名合格证人。办理公证时，应向公证人出示被继承人死亡证明的经核证副本和证明继承关系的文书的经核证副本；宣誓声明，所提供的死者的最新地址属实，据在场当事人的了解，没有其他人享有同等的继承权或者更优先的继承权。公证人将分别单独取得两名证人的证言，具体按照《民事诉

con derecho a heredar en el mismo grado o en uno preferente al de ellos mismos. El Notario procederá a tomar la declaración de los testigos por separado, en los términos previstos para las diligencias de información testimonial por el articulo 801 del Código de Procedimientos Civiles. Acto seguido, se procederá en los mismos términos previstos por el articulo anterior, para lo relativo a la aceptación o repudio de los derechos hereditarios, el nombramiento de albacea y la constitución o relevo de la caución correspondiente.

Artículo 175. - El Notario está obligado a dar a conocer las declaraciones de los herederos a que se refieren los artículos anteriores, mediante dos publicaciones que se harán en un diario de circulación nacional, de diez en diez días, con la mención del número de la publicación que corresponda.

Estas publicaciones podrán ser suplidas por otra u otras publicaciones en medios electrónicos u otro medio de comunicación masiva que acuerden el Colegio y las autoridades competentes, salvaguardando siempre la debida publicidad y garantía de audiencia de los posibles interesados.

Artículo 176. - Una vez hechas las publicaciones a que se refiere el artículo anterior, de lo que se dejará constancia en el instrumento, el o los albaceas presentarán al Notario el inventario y avalúos de los bienes que forman el acervo hereditario del autor de la sucesión para que, con la aprobación de todos los coherederos, en su caso, se realice su protocolización.

Artículo 177. - Los herederos y albacea otorgarán las escrituras de parición y adjudicación tal como haya sido ordenado por el autor de la sucesión en su testamento. A falta de éste, conforme a las disposiciones de la Ley de la materia para los intestados, como los propios herederos convengan.

Artículo 178. - Se deroga.

CAPÍTULO V SUPLENCIA, ASOCIACIÓN, SEPARACIÓN, SUSPENSIÓN Y TERMINACIÓN DE FUNCIONES

SECCIÓN PRIMERA PERMUTA DE NOTARÍAS, SUPLENCIAS Y ASOCIACIONES

Artículo 179. - Con la autorización de la autoridad competente, la que recabará opinión del colegio si lo considera conveniente, dos notarios en ejercicio permutarán su respectivo número de notaría y el protocolo en que cada

讼法》第801条关于证人作证程序的规定执行。接下来，应按照本法上一条规定的程序办理，要求当事人对是否接受继承权，是否接受对执行人的指定以及是否建立或取消了相应的担保作出声明。

第175条 公证人应当通过在一份在全国发行的报纸上对前几条中提到的继承人声明进行公示，每隔十日公示一次，共公示两次，并写明相应的刊号。

经公证人学会和主管当局批准，还可以选择在指定的电子报刊或其他媒体上进行公示的方式，只要符合法定的公示程序并确保潜在的利益相关者可以看到即可。

第176条 按上条规定完成公示的，应该写入相应的文书，并由执行人向公证人提交被继承人的遗产盘点清单和估价单，经所有共同继承人一致认可后，形成公证文书。

第177条 继承人和遗嘱执行人应当按照立遗嘱人在遗嘱中的指令交付公证。没有遗嘱的，应按照相关法律法规中关于无遗嘱继承的规定执行。

第178条 已废止。

第五章 候补职位、合伙人职位、离岗、停职和撤职

第一节 公证处的换岗、候补职位和合伙人职位

第179条 主管当局在征求公证人学会意见后，研究认为可行的，可批准两名在职公证人互换公证处编号和公证登记簿，以便自批准之日起，其中一人持另一人的公证处编号和公证登记簿开展工作，

uno actúa, de modo que a partir de la fecha en que se autorice, uno además de ostentar el número del otro actuará en el protocolo en que actuaba éste y viceversa.

Artículo 180. - La autoridad competente, también con la opinión del colegio si lo considera conveniente, podrá autorizar a un notario en ejercicio, el cambio de número de notaría y el protocolo en que actúa por otra notaría que esté vacante, cuando las necesidades del servicio lo permita. En este caso, el notario ostentará el número de la notaría vacante y actuará en el protocolo respectivo, dejando de tener el número de notaría y protocolo que tenía antes de esa autorización.

Artículo 181. - En los supuestos a que se refieren los dos artículos que anteceden la autoridad competente expedirá la o las nuevas patentes en un plazo de treinta días hábiles. Quienes reciban nuevas patentes deberán cambiar su sello y registrarlo en consecuencia, e inutilizar los anteriores en los términos de esta ley.

Artículo 182. - Para suplirse recíprocamente en sus ausencias temporales, en todo tiempo, los notarios celebrarán convenios de suplencia; estos convenios podrán celebrarse hasta por tres de ellos. Mientras subsista un convenio de suplencia, los notarios que lo celebraron podrán suplirse entre si y no podrán suplir a otro notario, salvo la autorización de las autoridades competentes, cuando en los términos del segundo párrafo de este articulo, se trate de suplir a un notario que haya recién obtenido su patente o esté en los supuestos del artículo 197. Los notarios que inicien el ejercicio de sus funciones, gozarán de un plazo de noventa días naturales para celebrar tales convenios. Si un notario no encontrare suplente o no lo presentare a la autoridad en el plazo señalado, ésta le nombrará uno.

Artículo 183. - Cuando un notario tenga más de un suplente, en los convenios respectivos se determinará el orden para el ejercicio de la suplencia.

Artículo 184. - Cuando ejerzan la suplencia, los notarios suplentes tendrán las mismas funciones de los notarios suplidos respecto a cada instrumento.

Artículo 185. - Cada notario estará a cargo de un solo protocolo. Cada notaría será servida por un notario. Quedan a salvo el caso de asociación, las previsiones para la suplencia, las intervenciones en caso de cesación de funciones y la general del archivo, a partir de la entrega de los libros correspondientes en el plazo legal.

Artículo 186. - Podrán asociarse hasta tres notarios por el tiempo que estimen conveniente para actuar indistintamente en el mismo protocolo, que será el del notario de mayor antigüedad, al disolverse los convenios de asociación los notarios actuarán en sus respectivos protocolos.

Artículo 187. - Si la disolución fuere por la cesación en funciones del notario más antiguo, en cuyo protocolo actuaban otros notarios asociados, tal protocolo corresponderá al asociado que continúe en funciones con mayor antigüedad y en él seguirá actuando. Sí subsistiera asociación de ese con otros notarios ellos actuarán en el protocolo del más antiguo.

Artículo 188. - La autoridad competente expedirá la o las nuevas patentes en un plazo de treinta días hábiles; hasta entonces, los asociados actuarán en el protocolo más antiguo con su correspondiente sello.

Quienes reciban nuevas patentes deberán cambiar sus sellos e inutilizar los anteriores en los términos de esta ley. Los notarios que hayan celebrado convenios de asociación, no podrán celebrar convenios de suplencia, mientras aquellos estén en vigor.

Artículo 189. - Las permutas autorizadas, los convenios de suplencia y de asociación, así como sus modificaciones y disolución se inscribirán ante las autoridades a que se refiere el artículo 67, fracción II y ante el colegio, se publicarán por una sola vez en la Gaceta, con cargo a los notarios.

SECCIÓN SEGUNDA SEPARACIÓN DE FUNCIONES

Artículo 190. - Los notarios podrán separarse del ejercicio de sus funciones hasta por treinta días hábiles renunciables, consecutivos o alternados, cada seis meses, previo aviso que por escrito den a las Autoridades competentes y al Colegio.

No será necesario el aviso en los días en que cierren las oficinas públicas y no den servicio al público, por lo que no serán computables en los 30 días hábiles mencionados en el párrafo anterior.

Artículo 191. - Los notarios podrán solicitar de la autoridad competente licencia para separarse del ejercicio de sus funciones hasta por el término de un año renunciable. Para el otorgamiento de la licencia dicha autoridad consultará al colegio.

Artículo 192. - Sin perjuicio de lo de lo dispuesto en el artículo anterior, salvo causa justificada, no se concederá nueva licencia al notario que no hubiere actuado ininterrumpidamente por seis meses a parir del vencimiento de la anterior licencia. Transcurridos los términos de la licencia o aviso a que se refieren los artículos anteriores, el notario deberá reiniciar sus funciones de inmediato.

他公证人各自另开登记簿。

第187条　因资历最老的公证人退休而导致合伙协议解除的，其余公证人可继续使用原登记簿，其中接管人仍是其余公证人中资历最老的公证人。如果退休公证人与其他公证人另有合伙协议的，仍按照资历排序依法执行。

第188条　主管当局应当在30个工作日内颁发新的从业许可；在颁发新证之前，合伙人仍在旧登记簿上进行登记，加盖各自的印章。

收到新从业许可后，应当依照本法之规定更换公章并对旧章进行报废。签署过合伙协议的公证人，在协议有效存续期间，不得签署候补（替班）协议。

第189条　换岗许可、替班协议和合伙协议，以及相应的修订案或协议的解除，均应到本法第67条第2项规定的主管当局和公证人学会登记备案，并在官方公报上登报公示，公示仅一次，相关费用均由相关公证人承担。

第二节　离岗

第190条　公证人经主管当局和公证人学会事先书面许可，每6个月享有30个工作日的离岗假期，可以一次性或分多次休完。

政府部门公休日期无需批假，因此，这些公休假期不计入上一段所指的30个工作日期限内。

第191条　公证人可以向主管当局申请离岗，时间最长为一年。主管当局在向公证人学会征求意见后，认为可行的，可予准假。

第192条　尽管上一条有规定，但除有正当理由外，在前一次休假期满后连续正常工作时间不足6个月的，不得再次离岗。前两条规定的休假或离岗期结束后，公证人应立即回归工作岗位。

Artículo 193. - La autoridad competente concederá licencia, por el tiempo que dure en el ejercicio de su cargo. Al notario que resulte electo para ocupar un puesto de elección popular o designado para la judicatura o para desempeñar algún empleo, cargo o comisión públicos. El notario formulará la solicitud correspondiente, exhibiendo constancia certificada expedida por la autoridad de que se trate, junto con el convenio de suplencia correspondiente. Si no presentare éste último, la autoridad, en un lapso no mayor de siete días hábiles y previa consulta que de estimarla conveniente haga al colegio, procederá a designar al suplente en los términos previstos por el articulo 182 de esta ley.

SECCIÓN TERCERA SUSPENSIÓN Y CESACIÓN DE FUNCIONES

Artículo 194. - Los notarios sólo podrán ser suspendidos en el ejercicio de sus funciones por las siguientes causas:

I. La pérdida de la libertad por dictarse auto de formal prisión u orden de arraigo en su contra, mientras subsista la privación de libertad o el arraigo, hasta en tanto cause ejecutoria la sentencia que en su caso lo absuelva o se le perdone, o termine el arraigo;

II. Por padecer incapacidad física o mental que le impida actuar en cuyo caso la suspensión durará todo el tiempo que subsista el impedimento;

III. Por así ser sancionado por la autoridad competente y dicha sanción cause estado y

IV. Por las demás que procedieran conforme a las leyes.

Artículo 195. - En el supuesto previsto en la fracción II del artículo anterior, la autoridad competente, en cuanto tenga conocimiento del hecho procederá a abrir investigación administrativa, la que integrará con la visita del inspector a la notaría a requerir información sobre el hecho; con el dictamen médico emitido por dos peritos médicos acreditados por las autoridades de salud del Distrito Federal y por otros tantos designados por el interesado o el colegio, en los que se funde y precise la naturaleza del impedimento, la atención médica que requiere el paciente y el diagnóstico procedente sobre su rehabilitación, y con la audiencia al interesado y al Colegio, la referida autoridad hará la declaratoria correspondiente.

Artículo 196. - Cuando se dicte auto de formal prisión o exista sentencia condenatoria privativa de la lib-

第193条 主管当局可向任期内的公证人批假。公证人当选民选职位或者被提名到司法机关或其他政府部门担任公职的，应当提出书面申请，并随附拟任职部门出具的证明材料，还有相应的替班协议。没有提交替班协议的，主管当局应当在事先征求公证人学会意见后，在7个工作日内按照本法第182条之规定确定相应的替班人选。

第三节 临时或永久吊销执业资格

第194条 公证人出现以下情形的，可能被临时取消执业资格：

（1）被判处正式监禁或者被下令逮捕，在被剥夺自由或被逮捕期间应被临时吊销执业资格，直至服刑期满后获释；

（2）因身体或精神原因，暂时无法履行公证职能的，在未完全恢复之前暂停执业；

（3）经主管当局认定，处以相应制裁的；

（4）法律规定的其他情形。

第195条 对于前一条第2项规定的情形，主管当局在得知这一情况后应立即进行调查，并派督察员到公证处查明相关情况。经联邦区卫生主管当局认证的两名医学专家以及由当事人或者公证人学会聘请的医学专家共同出具鉴定报告，在报告中写明病情和当事人无法履行公证职能的理由，对患者的治疗方案以及康复诊断。在听取当事人和学会意见后，主管当局应当作出相应的声明。

第196条 候补公证人或公证人出于主观故意犯罪，罪名成立，被判处正式监禁或被剥夺自由的，

ertad por delito intencional que haya quedado firme, contra un aspirante o Notario, el juez lo comunicará inmediatamente a las Autoridades competentes y al Colegio.

El Ministerio Público y los Jueces, notificarán al colegio la iniciación de cualquier procedimiento contra un notario en el ejercicio de sus funciones. El colegio queda facultado para imponerse de los referidos procedimientos y opinar, en su caso.

Artículo 197. - Son causas de cesación del ejercicio de la función notarial y del cargo de notario:

I. Haber sido condenado por delito intencional, por sentencia ejecutoriada, privativa de la libertad;

II. La revocación de la patente, en los casos previstos por esta ley;

III. La renuncia expresa del notario al ejercicio de sus funciones;

IV. Haberse demostrado ante la autoridad competente, que oirá para ello la opinión del colegio, que tras haber cumplido ochenta años de edad, y por esta circunstancia, el Notario respectivo no pueda seguir desempeñando sus funciones;

V. Sobrevenir incapacidad física o mental permanente que imposibilite el desempeño de la función;

VI. No iniciar o reiniciar sus funciones en los plazos establecidos por esta Ley;

VII. No desempeñar personalmente las funciones que le competen de la manera que esta Ley previene;

VIII. No constituir o no conservar vigente la fianza, y

IX. Las demás que establezcan las leyes.

Artículo 198. - Cuando se promueva juicio de interdicción en contra de un notario, el juez lo comunicará a la autoridad competente y notificará la resolución que dicte, dentro de los cinco días siguientes a su fecha. Al causar ejecutoria la sentencia que decrete la interdicción, cesará el ejercicio de la función notarial.

Artículo 199. - Los Jueces del Registro Civil o los agentes del Ministerio Público que tengan conocimiento del deceso de un notario lo comunicarán inmediatamente a la autoridad competente.

Artículo 200. - En los casos a los que se refieren los artículos 195, 196, 198 y 199, cuando la autoridad competente reciba el aviso o la comunicación respectiva, de inmediato lo comunicará al colegio.

Artículo 201. - En los casos de cesación de la función notarial, junto con la declaratoria que al efecto emita la autoridad competente, se procederá a iniciar el procedimiento de clausura temporal del protocolo correspondiente.

法官应当立即通知主管当局和公证人学会。

检察机关和主管法官应当将执业公证人被起诉的情况通知公证人学会。学会有权介入调查审理程序并根据需要发表意见。

第 197 条　公证人停止执业和不再履行公证职务的原因有：

（1）因主观故意犯罪被定罪判刑，剥夺自由；

（2）根据本法规定的情形被吊销执业资格；

（3）公证人明确声明辞去公证人职务；

（4）年满 80 周岁，因年龄关系无法再胜任公证工作的，应当向主管当局作出声明，由主管当局在听取公证人学会的意见后批准其辞呈；

（5）患有永久性身体或精神残疾，无法胜任公证工作的；

（6）在本法规定期限内未按时到岗或回到工作岗位的；

（7）没有按照本法规定的形式亲自履行公证职能；

（8）没有建立履职担保或维持担保有效；

（9）法律规定的其他情形。

第 198 条　公证人被判定剥夺公民权利的，法官应当在判决下达后 5 日内将决议内容通知主管当局。判处剥夺公证人公民权利的判决一经执行，公证人立即停止履行公证职务。

第 199 条　民事登记处负责人或检察机关工作人员一旦知悉公证人身亡，应立即通知主管当局。

第 200 条　出现第 195 条、第 196 条、第 198 条和第 199 条所指情形的，主管当局一旦接到相应的通知或报告，应立即通知公证人学会。

第 201 条　出现停止履行公证职务的情形的，主管当局应出具声明，启动相应程序，临时封存相应的公证登记簿。为此，主管当局应责令候补公证人或合伙人（视情况）在公证处的醒目位置张贴说明，并在

Para tal efecto, la autoridad ordenará al notario suplente o al asociado, según el caso, la fijación de un aviso visible en la notaria y ordenará una publicación en la Gaceta, con cargo a los notarios señalados.

Artículo 202. - Si el notario que cesare en funciones estuviese asociado o tuviere suplente, al que corresponda de ellos se entregará el protocolo para que concluya los asuntos en trámite, y en caso de asociación, para que continúe su ejercicio en el mismo, en los términos de esta ley. Los asociados o suplentes harán constar en el último folio utilizado por quien cesó en funciones, o en el siguiente, la cesación de funciones, la fecha y pondrán su sello y firma.

Artículo 203. - Al declararse la cesación de funciones de un notario que no esté asociado ni tenga suplente, se procederá a la clausura temporal de su protocolo por el inspector de notarías designado, con la comparecencia del representante que designe el colegio. El inspector de notarías asentará la razón correspondiente en los términos antes prescritos.

Artículo 204. - A la diligencia referida en el artículo anterior comparecerán, en su caso, el notario que haya cesado en sus funciones, su albacea, interventor o sus parientes y un notario designado por el Colegio. Los presentes formarán un inventario de libros de folios, de libros de registro de cotejos, de folios sin utilizar, apéndices, índices y todos los documentos que haya tenido el cesante en su poder para el desempeño de su función, y otro de los diversos bienes que se encuentren en la notaria. Se entregarán los bienes diversos, a quien haya cesado como notario, a su albacea, interventor o parientes, y los libros de folios y demás objetos indispensables para el desarrollo de la función notarial al Archivo. Un tanto de los inventarios y del acta que se levante se entregará a la autoridad competente, otro al Archivo, otro al colegio, uno más al cesante o a su albacea, interventor o familiares.

El suplente que deba actuar por el notario que haya cesado en sus funciones, recibirá todos los elementos necesarios indicados para el ejercicio de la función y los conservará por un plazo de noventa días naturales, para el trámite solamente de los asuntos pendientes. Transcurrido dicho plazo se clausurará temporalmente el protocolo del cesante en los términos de este artículo y se entregará al Archivo, mediante inventario.

Los notarios designados por el Colegio, los inspectores y demás Autoridades deben guardar reserva respecto de los documentos a los que por su función o designación tuvieren acceso y quedan sujetos a las disposiciones del

官方公报上进行公示，费用由公证处承担。

第 202 条　如果停职的公证人有指定的合伙人或候补公证人，可以由其合伙人或候补公证人接管公证登记簿，以完成尚未办完的事项，有合伙人的，应当按照本法之规定由合伙人接管。合伙人或候补公证人应当在停职公证人用过的最后一张公证纸页面或者下一页中写明停职公证人停止任职的情况和停职日期，并签字盖章。

第 203 条　如果停职的公证人没有指定的合伙人或候补公证人，应由指定的公证督察员办理公证登记簿的临时封存手续。在办理封存时应当有公证人学会指派的代表在场见证。公证督察员应当按照前文的规定写明相应的理由。

第 204 条　在办理前一条规定的手续的过程中，停职的公证人以及公证人学会指派的一名公证人应当在场见证。停职的公证人无法到场的，应由其遗嘱执行人、监护人或亲属（视情况）代为到场见证。在场见证人员应当编制一份公证登记簿、核对记录册、尚未使用的公证纸、附录、目录和所有与公证工作相关的文件的盘点清单，以及一份公证人留在公证处的各类杂物的清单。停职公证人的杂物应当交还给其本人、遗嘱执行人、监护人或亲属，相应的工作簿册和其他工作文件应当交存档案管理局。盘点清单和交接凭证应当分别提交给主管当局、档案管理局、公证人学会、停职公证人或者其遗嘱执行人、监护人或亲属（视情况）也要有一份留底。

候补公证人应当接替停职公证人手头的工作，接管一切必要事项，以便顺利开展公证工作，在 90 个自然日内将停职公证人手里现有的待办事项办结。期限届满后，应按照本条规定临时封存公证登记簿并通过盘点提交给档案管理局。

学会指定的公证人、公证督察员以及其他有关部门应当对在工作中接触的文件资料保密，违者将按照《刑法典》关于职业保密的规定予以惩处。

Código Penal sobre el secreto profesional.

Artículo 205. - La autoridad competente cancelará la fianza constituida cuando el notario cesante o sus causahabientes lo soliciten, y hayan transcurrido seis meses, contados a partir de haberse hecho la publicación de tal solicitud en la gaceta, sin que hubiere reclamación de quien demuestre tener interés legitimo y una vez obtenida la opinión del colegio.

Artículo 206. - El notario que vaya a actuar en el protocolo de una notaria que haya quedado vacante, recibirá del Archivo, por inventario, todos los documentos a que se refiere el artículo 204, que por ley no deban permanecer en el Archivo, para continuar su utilización y trámite. De la entrega se levantará y firmará por cuadruplicado un acta y se entregará un respectivo tanto a la autoridad competente, al colegio y al notario que reciba.

TÍTULO TERCERO
DEL RÉGIMEN DE RESPONSABILIDADES, DE LA VIGILANCIA Y DE LAS SANCIONES

CAPÍTULO ÚNICO
DEL RÉGIMEN DE RESPONSABILIDAD

SECCIÓN PRIMERA DE LA VIGILANCIA

Artículo 207. - La autoridad competente vigilará el correcto ejercicio de la función notarial a través de visitas que realizará por medio de inspectores de notarías. Para ser inspector de notarías el interesado, además de satisfacer los requisitos que para el desempeño de un empleo exige el Gobierno del Distrito Federal, deberá reunir aquellos que señalan las fracciones l, ll, lll y IV, del artículo 54 y 55 de esta Ley.

El Colegio coadyuvará con la autoridad competente en la vigilancia del ejercicio de la función notarial, cuando dicha autoridad lo requiera.

Artículo 208. - En todo tiempo, los notarios designados por el Colegio, los inspectores y demás Autoridades deben guardar reserva respecto de los documentos notariales a los que por su función tengan acceso y quedan sujetos a las disposiciones del Código Penal sobre el secreto profesional.

Artículo 209. - Los inspectores de notarías practicarán visitas de inspección y vigilancia a las notarias, previa orden por escrito fundada y motivada, emitida por la autoridad competente, en la que se expresará, el nombre del notario, el tipo de inspección a realizarse, el motivo

第 205 条 停职的公证人或其接替人员提出撤销申请的担保后,自申请事项在官方公报上公示之日起,如果在 6 个月内没有相关当事人提出异议主张,一旦学会表示同意,主管当局即撤销相应的担保。

第 206 条 公证处新聘任的公证人,应当按照盘点清单,从档案管理局接收第 204 条中列出的所有工作文件,以便继续使用和进行后续处理。文件交接应当有书面凭证,一式四份,除档案管理局留底外,主管当局、公证人学会和接任的公证人各执一份。

第三篇
问责制度、监管与惩治

唯一一章
问责制度

第一节 监管

第 207 条 主管当局通过督察员对公证处进行查访,监督公证人正常履行其公证职能。督察员除应满足联邦政府公务员的任职要求外,还应当符合本法第 54 条第 1 款第 1 项至第 4 项和第 55 条的规定。

公证人学会应响应主管当局的要求,配合主管当局对公证人的履职情况进行监督。

第 208 条 公证人学会任命的公证人、督察员以及其他责任单位,应始终对因工作原因接触的公证文件进行保密,并遵守《刑法典》关于职业保密的规定。

第 209 条 督察员应按照主管当局事先下达的理由充分的书面指令,对公证处实施查访和监督。指令中必须写明受检查的公证人姓名,检查类型,查访原因,接受查访的公证处的编号,当局下达指令的日期,并由当局签字盖章。

de la visita, el número de la notaría a visitar, la fecha y la firma de la autoridad que expida dicha orden.

Artículo 210. - La Autoridad competente podrá ordenar visitas de inspección en cualquier tiempo. Ordenará visitas de inspección generales por lo menos una vez al año, y especiales, cuando tenga conocimiento, por queja o vista de cualquier autoridad, de que un notario ha incurrido en una probable contravención a la ley.

Cuando la visita fuere general, se practicará, por lo menos cinco días naturales después de la notificación correspondiente.

Artículo 211. - La notificación previa a la visita, sea ésta general o especial, que practique el inspector autorizado, se hará en días y horas hábiles en el domicilio de la notaría, mediante cédula de notificación que contendrá el nombre y apellidos del notario, el número y domicilio de la notaría, un extracto de la orden de inspección, que expresará el fundamento legal, el motivo de la inspección, fecha, hora, nombre y firma del visitador que la practicará.

El notificador comunicará al colegio la fecha y hora en que habrá de practicar la visita de que se trate, a fin de que éste, si lo estima conveniente, designe un notario que acuda como coadyuvante en la práctica de dicha visita, con el carácter de observador.

Artículo 212. - Al presentarse el inspector que vaya a practicar la visita, se identificará ante el notario. En caso de no estar presente éste, le dejará citatorio en el que se indicará el día y la hora en que se efectuará la visita de inspección; en el supuesto de que el notario no acuda al citatorio, se entenderá la diligencia con su suplente o, en su caso, con su asociado, y en ausencia de éstos, con la persona que esté encargada de la notaría en el momento de la diligencia, a quien se le mostrará la orden escrita que autorice la inspección, con quien el inspector también se identificará.

Artículo 213. - Las visitas especiales se practicarán previa orden de la Autoridad competente y tendrán por objeto verificar los hechos en conocimiento de la autoridad o denunciados por queja de un prestatario, destinatario o puestos en conocimiento por vista de cualquier autoridad, cuando de lo expuesto por éstos se desprenda que el Notario cometió alguna actuación que amerite sanción de carácter administrativo por violaciones a esta Ley y a otras relacionadas directamente con su función.

La notificación de la visita especial se practicará en la forma prevista por el artículo 211 y la inspección se verificará dentro de las setenta y dos horas hábiles después

第 210 条　主管当局有权随时下令进行检查。常规检查至少应每年一次，主管当局接到申诉或者察觉到公证人出现涉嫌违法的行为的，可随时开展专项检查。

对于常规检查，应当至少提前 5 个自然日通知方可进行。

第 211 条　无论是常规检查还是专项检查，都要求负责的督察员提前做出通知，以可靠书面方式在工作日的工作时间段送达到公证人的联系地址。在通知函中写明公证人姓名、编号和联系地址、检查指令内容摘要，其中主要写明实施检查的法律依据、检查原因、检查日期和时间。督察员姓名及其签名。

通知人应当向公证人学会通报检查的日期和时间，学会认为必要的，可委派一名公证人随行，以观察员的身份协助开展检查工作。

第 212 条　督察员到现场查访时，应向公证人证明身份。如果公证人不在场，应当留下传唤口令，写明查访的日期和时间；如果公证人没有按照传唤口令到场，应当由其候补人或者合伙人配合检查，两者均无法在场接受检查的，应当由检查当时的公证处负责人员配合检查。检查时，应当向受检查人员出示主管当局出具的书面指令，同时督察员也必须向受检查人员证明身份。

第 213 条　专项检查应当凭主管当局事先下达的指令执行，目的是核查当局自行了解的或者接到的投诉或举报中陈述的情况，查明公证人是否构成对本法的违反或者出现与其职能直接相关的违法行为，需要接受行政纪律制裁。

专项检查通知应当按照第 211 条规定的形式进行，在公证人和学会接到通知后 72 个小时（工作时间）内实施。公证人学会认为有必要的，可以委派一

de notificar al notario y al Colegio, para que éste último si lo considera conveniente, designe un notario que auxilie al inspector para la práctica de la visita. La orden de autoridad limitará el objeto de la inspección al contenido de la queja.

Artículo 214. - En las visitas de inspección se observarán en lo conducente, las reglas siguientes:

I. Si la visita fuere general, el inspector revisará todo el protocolo, o diversas partes de éste, para cerciorarse del cumplimiento de la función notarial en sus formalidades, sin que pueda constreñirse a un instrumento;

II. Si la visita fuere especial, se inspeccionará aquella parte del protocolo y demás instrumentos notariales, únicamente en lo relativo a los hechos o actos que motivaron a la autoridad para ordenar dicha visita;

III. En una y otra visitas, el inspector se cerciorará si están empastados los correspondientes apéndices que debieran estarlo y así lo hará constar en el acta respectiva; y

IV. De acuerdo a los hechos que motivan la visita, podrán inspeccionarse todos aquellos instrumentos que resulten necesarios al cumplimiento del objeto de la visita.

Artículo 215. - Si la visita tiene por objeto un instrumento determinado, se examinará la redacción, sus cláusulas y declaraciones, así como en su caso su situación registral.

Artículo 216. - Las diligencias de notificación, visitas, actas, audiencias y todo acto administrativo en general que supervise la función de un notario, se realizarán con la debida reserva y discreción. Las constancias y demás documentos del expediente, se pondrán a la vista del interesado, su representante, o las personas autorizadas del colegio, previa autorización de la autoridad competente. El servidor público que contravenga lo anterior será sujeto de responsabilidad administrativa en los términos de la ley de la materia, sin perjuicio de la aplicación de sanciones penales, cuando en el caso procedan.

Artículo 217. - Los notarios estarán obligados a dar las facilidades que requieran los inspectores para que puedan practicar las diligencias que les sean ordenadas. En caso de negativa por parte del notario, el inspector lo hará del inmediato conocimiento de la autoridad competente, quien, previo procedimiento respectivo, impondrá al notario la sanción señalada en el artículo 226 de esta Ley, apercibiéndolo de que en caso de continuar en su negativa se hará acreedor a la sanción contemplada en el articulo 227, según sea la índole de la actitud del notario.

Artículo 218. - El inspector contará con un máximo

名公证人协助督察员开展查访工作。根据主管当局的指令，检查应当限定在举报内容涉及的范围内。

第214条　在查访中，应当遵循以下规则：

（1）对于常规查访，督察员应当全面检查公证登记簿，或者检查公证登记簿的各个部分，而不能局限于单份文书，以确认公证人严格依程序落实了其法定职责；

（2）对于专项检查，应当仅检查公证登记簿中涉及与被调查事项相关的部分以及其他与被调查事项有关的公证文书；

（3）在任何检查中，督察员应核实，相关附录是否完整，是否加盖公证章，并在检查记录中写明；以及

（4）根据被调查的事项，可以检查所有必要的文件，以达成检查目的。

第215条　如果是对一项特定的文书进行检查，检查内容为文书的措辞、条款和声明事项，以及文书的登记情况。

第216条　与对公证认履职情况调查相关的通知、检查、记录、谈话记录以及所有相关行政文书，都应妥善保存并依法保密。被调查的当事人、其授权代表或者公证人学会的授权人员，经主管当局事先批准，可调阅相关证据以及其他审理材料。违反上述规定的公务员，将依法接受相应处罚，构成刑事责任的，还应依法接受刑事制裁。

第217条　公证人必须按督察员的要求积极配合调查。公证人不配合或抗拒调查的，督察员应立即上报主管当局，查明情况属实的，主管当局应按本法第226条之规定对公证人进行处分；接受处分后仍不改正的，应根据公证人的违反程度，处以第227条中规定的制裁。

第218条　督察员自接到检查令之日起，应在

de quince días hábiles, contados a partir de la fecha en que reciba la orden de inspección, para rendir el resultado de la misma. Hará constar en el acta las irregularidades que observe, consignara los puntos, así como las explicaciones, aclaraciones, y fundamentos que el notario exponga en su defensa. Le hará saber al notario que tiene derecho a designar a dos testigos y, en caso de rebeldía, los designará el inspector bajo su responsabilidad. Si el notario no firma el acta ello no invalidará su contenido y el inspector hará constar la negativa, y entregará una copia al notario.

Artículo 219. - Practicadas las diligencias de inspección y levantadas las actas de mérito, el visitador dará cuenta de todo ello a la autoridad administrativa, dentro de los dos días hábiles siguientes a la fecha del cierre del acta de inspección.

Artículo 220. - El notario podrá manifestar lo que a su derecho convenga en el acta de inspección o en un término no mayor de cinco días hábiles, en escrito por separado, con relación a la queja, anomalía o irregularidad asentada en dicha acta y en su caso podrá dentro de dicho plazo ofrecer y desahogar las pruebas que guarden relación con los hechos controvertidos, asimismo, deberá autorizar a una o varias personas para oír y recibir notificaciones que se deriven del procedimiento en cuestión.

Artículo 221. - Cuando se trate de visitas que deban practicarse a notarios asociados o suplentes, se observarán las mismas disposiciones señaladas en esta sección.

SECCION SEGUNDA DE LAS RESPONSABILIDADES Y SANCIONES

Artículo 222. - Los notarios son responsables por los delitos o faltas que cometan en el ejercicio de su función, en los términos que previenen las leyes penales del fuero común y federales. De la responsabilidad civil en que incurran los notarios en el ejercicio de sus funciones conocerán los Tribunales. De la responsabilidad administrativa en que incurran los notarios por violación a los preceptos de esta ley, conocerán las Autoridades competentes. De la responsabilidad colegial conocerá la Junta de Decanos, que estimará si amerita el asunto encausarse a través la Comisión de Arbitraje, Legalidad y Justicia. De la responsabilidad fiscal en que incurra el notario en ejercicio de sus funciones, conocerán las autoridades tributarias locales o federales, según el caso. Salvo los casos expresamente regulados por las leyes, la acción para exigir responsabilidad administrativa a un notario, prescribe en

15个工作日内提交报告，汇报检查结果。在检查报告中说明发现的违规行为，说明要点，并列明公证人给出的解释、澄清和理由。被调查的公证人应被告知，其有权利指定两名证人，如果不能自行指定，可由督察员代为指定。如果公证人不在调查报告上签字，也不会影响报告内容的效力，督察员应对公证人的不配合行为进行记录并向公证人提供一份副本。

第219条 完成检查工作并形成相应报告后，督察员应当在检查报告完成后2个工作日内将调查材料全部提交给行政主管当局。

第220条 公证人有权在检查报告中，或者在5个工作日内单独以书面形式对检查报告中提到的投诉、异常或违规行为作出解释；如有必要，还可在同样期限内进行举证和质证。此外，应当指定一名或多名联系人，负责听取和接收与调查程序相关的通知。

第221条 对于向候补公证人或合伙人进行的调查，同样适用本节所列的规定。

第二节 责任与惩治

第222条 公证人在履职过程中出现犯罪或过失行为的，应根据《普通刑事法》和《联邦刑事法》的相关规定，依法承担相应责任。公证人在履职过程中构成民事责任的，应当由法院审理。公证人因违反本法之规定构成行政违规的，应由主管当局追究其行政纪律责任。违反公证人学会相关规定的，应由公证会长办公会通过仲裁、法制与正义委员会进行审理。公证人在履职过程中出现税务违规的，应当根据情况由地方或联邦税务部门追究其税务责任。除非法律另有明文规定，否则公证人的行政纪律责任的诉讼时效期为8年。

ocho años.

Cuando se promueva algún juicio por responsabilidad en contra de un notario, el juez admitirá como prueba pericial profesional, si así se ofreciere, la opinión del colegio.

Siempre que se inicie una averiguación previa en la que resulte indiciado un notario como resultado del ejercicio de sus funciones, el Ministerio Público solicitará opinión del colegio respecto de la misma, fijándole un término prudente para ello, para lo cual el presidente del colegio o el consejero que éste designe podrá imponerse de las actuaciones del caso.

Artículo 223. - El notario incurrirá en responsabilidad administrativa por violaciones a esta ley o a otras leyes relacionadas con su función pública, y con motivo del ejercicio de la misma, siempre que tales violaciones sean imputables al notario. El notario no tendrá responsabilidad cuando el resultado de sus actuaciones sea por error de opinión jurídica fundada o sea consecuencia de las manifestaciones, declaraciones o instrucciones de los prestatarios, de los concurrentes o partes, o éstos hayan expresado su consentimiento con dicho resultado, sin perjuicio de la legalidad que regula la función notarial.

Artículo 224. - La autoridad competente sancionará a los notarios por las violaciones en que incurran a los preceptos de esta ley, aplicando las siguientes sanciones:

I. Amonestación por escrito;

II. Multas;

III. Suspensión temporal;

IV. Cesación de funciones.

Estas sanciones se notificarán personalmente al notario responsable y se harán del conocimiento del consejo.

Artículo 225. - Las sanciones a que se refiere el artículo anterior serán aplicables de manera gradual, pudiendo ser acumulativas las multas con cualquiera de las previstas en las fracciones I, III y IV del artículo anterior. Para la aplicación de sanciones la autoridad competente, al motivar su resolución, deberá tomar en cuenta las circunstancias y la gravedad del caso, los perjuicios y daños que directamente se hayan ocasionado, si los hubo, el grado de diligencia del notario para la solución del problema, su antigüedad en el cargo, sus antecedentes profesionales y los servicios prestados por el notario al Gobierno, la Sociedad y al Notariado. Las autoridades pedirán la opinión del colegio.

Artículo 226. - Se sancionará al notario con amonestación escrita:

I. Por retraso injustificado imputable al notario en

当对公证人提起诉讼时，法官应当将公证人学会的意见视为专家鉴定报告，具有证据效力。

只要启动预审程序，对公证人的履职情况提起公诉的，检察机关应当要求公证人学会在规定期限内提供专家意见。为此，公证人学会的会长或者由会长指定的理事，应当跟进诉讼程序。

第223条 公证人在履行职责时，因违反本法或其他相关法律，构成行政违规的，应当承担相应的行政纪律责任。公证人的违规是由于其所援引的法律条文不当或者由于公证当事人的表述、陈述或指令不当导致的，或者公证当事人已经表明对公证结果表示认可，公证人没有违反公证程序的合法性的，不承担任何责任。

第224条 违反本法之规定的公证人，将被主管当局实施以下制裁：

（1）书面警告；

（2）罚款；

（3）临时吊销执业资格；

（4）永久撤销执业资格。

制裁措施应当通知肇事公证人本人，并上报理事会。

第225条 上一条规定的制裁措施对应于违规行为的严重程度，第1项、第3项、第4项规定的处罚可与罚金叠加。为执行主管当局的制裁措施，在制裁决议中应当写明违反情形及违反情节的严重程度，由此直接造成的损失和损害（如果有），公证人的从业年限，从业背景以及向政府、社会和公证行业做出的贡献。当局应征求公证人学会的意见。

第226条 公证人出现以下行为的，应受到书面警告：

（1）公证申请人已经按照公证人的要求提供的所

la realización de una actuación o desahogo de un trámite relacionado con un servicio solicitado y expensado por el solicitante, siempre que éste hubiere entregado toda la documentación previa que el notario requiera;

II. Por no dar avisos, no llevar los correspondientes índices de la decena de libros del protocolo, no encuadernar los libros del protocolo y sus apéndices o conservarlos en términos de ley; o no entregar oportunamente los libros del protocolo, libros de registro de cotejos, apéndices e índices al Archivo;

III. Por separarse de sus funciones sin haber dado previo aviso u obtenido licencia, o por no reiniciar funciones oportunamente, en términos de la licencia, o de esta ley y sólo cuando se trate de la primera vez en que incurre en esta falta;

IV. Por negarse a ejercitar sus funciones habiendo sido requerido y expensado en su caso para ello por el prestatario, sin que medie explicación o justificación fundada por parte del notario a dicho solicitante;

V. Por no ejercer sus funciones en actividades de orden público e interés social a solicitud de las autoridades, en los términos previstos por los artículos 16 al 19 de esta ley;

VI. Por no ejercer sus funciones en días y horas hábiles, y excepcionalmente en los inhábiles, en los términos de esta ley;

VII. Por no obtener en tiempo o mantener en vigor la garantía del ejercicio de sus funciones a que se refiere la fracción I del artículo 67 de esta Ley, solo y siempre que se trate de la primera vez que el Notario comete esta falta; y

VIII. Por cualquier otra falta menor que sea subsanable.

Artículo 227. - Se sancionará al notario con multa de uno a doce meses de salario mínimo general vigente en el momento del incumplimiento:

I. Por reincidir, en la comisión de alguna de las faltas a que se refiere el artículo anterior, o por no haber constituido o reconstituido la fianza en el plazo de un mes a partir de la aplicación de la sanción a que se refiere la fracción VII del articulo anterior;

II. Por incurrir en alguna de las hipótesis previstas en el articulo 45, fracciones, I, IV, VI, VIII y IX de esta ley;

III. Por realizar cualquier actividad que sea incompatible con el desempeño de sus funciones de notario, de acuerdo a lo previsto por esta Ley;

IV. Por provocar por culpa o dolo, la nulidad de un instrumento o testimonio, siempre que cause daño o perjuicio directo a los prestatarios o destinatarios;

有相关资料，但公证人无故拖延提供公证服务或办理救济程序的；

（2）未依法进行通知，未按程序归卷立档，未按法定程序保管公证登记簿、相应的办理资料和附录的；未及时向档案管理局提交相应的公证登记簿、归档日志、附录和目录的；

（3）在没有事先通知或获得许可的情况下离岗，或者没有按照执业许可或本法之规定及时重新开展业务，且属于第一次出现此类过失的；

（4）拒绝按照公证申请人的要求行使公证职能，且没有向申请人作出合理解释或说明正当理由的；

（5）未遵照本法第16条至第19条之规定，根据当局的要求履行公证职能，以维护公共秩序和社会利益的；

（6）未按照本法之规定在工作日和工作时间段正常履行职责的，特别是在非工作日或非工作时间的特殊情况；

（7）未按照本法第67条第1款第1项之规定及时取得履职担保金或者维持履职担保金的有效性，且属于第一次出现此类过失的；以及

（8）其他任何可以弥补的轻微过失。

第227条 公证人出现以下行为的，处以相当于一至十二个月现行最低基本工资水平的罚金：

（1）再次犯有上一条所指的某项过失，或者自上一条第7项所指的处罚执行之日起，没有在一个月期限内建立或者重新建立担保金；

（2）出现本法第45条第1款第1项、第4项、第6项、第8项和第9项中所列的任一情形；

（3）出现本法规定的任何不得与公证职能兼容的行为的；

（4）由于过失或主观故意，造成公证文书或经核证副本无效，给公证申请人或当事人造成直接损失或损害的；

V. Por excederse al arancel o a los convenios legalmente celebrados en materia de honorarios legalmente aplicables; y

VI. Por incurrir en los supuestos a que se refieren los artículo 243, 245 y 246 de esta ley.

Artículo 228. - Se sancionará con suspensión del ejercicio de la función notarial de tres días hasta por un año:

I. Por reincidir, en alguno de los supuestos señalados en el artículo anterior o por no haber constituido o reconstituido la fianza a partir de la aplicación de la sanción a que se refiere la fracción I del artículo anterior:

II. Por revelar injustificada y dolosamente datos sobre los cuales deba guardar secreto profesional, cuando por ello se cause directamente daños o perjuicios al ofendido;

III. Por incurrir en alguna de las prohibiciones que señala el artículo 45, fracciones II, III, V y VII;

IV. Por provocar, en una segunda ocasión por culpa o dolo la nulidad de algún instrumento o testimonio;

V. Por no desempeñar personalmente sus funciones de la manera que la presente ley dispone, y

VI. Cuando por dolo o culpa del notario, falte a un testamento otorgado ante su fe, alguna de las formalidades previstas en el Código Civil. En este caso, el testamento quedará sin efecto y el notario será además, responsable de los daños y perjuicios.

Artículo 229. - Se sancionará al notario con la cesación del ejercicio de la función notarial y la consecuente revocación de su patente además de los supuestos señalados en el artículo 197 de esta ley, en los siguientes casos:

I. Por incurrir reiteradamente en alguno de los supuestos señalados en el artículo anterior;

II. Cuando en el ejercicio de su función incurra en reiteradas deficiencias administrativas, y las mismas hayan sido oportunamente advertidas al notario por la autoridad competente, siendo aquél omiso en corregirlas;

III. Por falta grave de probidad, o notorias deficiencias o vicios debidamente comprobados en el ejercicio de sus funciones, y

IV. Por permitir la suplantación de su persona, firma o sello.

La resolución por la que un notario sea cesado en sus funciones, será firmada por el Jefe de Gobierno, quien recibirá, tramitará y resolverá el recurso de inconformidad contra su propia resolución.

（5）收费水平超出了法律规定标准或者相关协议中商定的水平；以及

（6）出现本法第243条、第245条和第246条规定的情形的。

第228条 公证人出现以下行为的，处以三天至一年不等的临时吊销执业资格的制裁：

（1）再次犯有上一条所指的某项过失，或者在上一条第1项所指的处罚生效后，没有建立或者重新建立履职担保的；

（2）没有正当理由或者恶意披露需要保密的信息，给当事人造成直接损失或损害的；

（3）出现本法第45条第2、第3项、第5项和第7项规定的任一禁止情形的；

（4）第二次出于过失或主观故意造成公证文书或经核证副本无效的；

（5）没有按照法定形式亲自履行其法定职能的；以及

（6）公证人出于过失或主观故意，没有完成遗嘱公证事项，触犯《民法典》规定的。在这种情况下，遗嘱无效，由此造成损失和损害的，应追究公证人的责任。

第229条 出现下列情形的，公证人除应接受本法第197条规定的处罚外，还应被永久禁止从事公证工作并撤销其执业资格：

（1）一再出现上一条所列情形的；

（2）在履行职务时一再出现行政管理缺陷，行政主管当局及时作出提醒后公证人仍未改正的；

（3）经查明，在履行公证职责时严重缺乏诚信，或者出现重大过失或缺陷的；以及

（4）允许他人冒用其签名或公章的。

永久撤销公证人执业资格的决议，应当由政府行政长官签署，行政长官还负责受理因不服其决议而提起的申诉并加以解决。

SECCIÓN TERCERA DEL PROCEDIMIENTO DE IMPOSICIÓN DE SANCIONES

Artículo 230. - Para la aplicación de las sanciones previstas en los artículos anteriores, se observará el siguiente procedimiento:

I. Toda persona que acredite fehacientemente su interés jurídico, podrá presentar por escrito ante la autoridad administrativa competente, queja contra el notario al que se le impute la actuación que amerite sanción de carácter administrativo por violaciones a esta ley y a otras relacionadas directamente con su función. El quejoso deberá identificarse asentando nombre o razón social, el de su representante legal, así como el de los autorizados para oír y recibir notificaciones; asimismo deberá asentar sus generales así como una descripción clara y sucinta de los hechos o razones en que apoya su queja; debiendo exhibir las constancias documentales o en su caso señalar los testigos idóneos que acrediten sus manifestaciones, junto con un relato o exposición detallada de los hechos o actos motivo de su queja, a fin de justificarla debidamente. Faltando alguno de los requisitos señalados, la autoridad competente prevendrá al ocursante concediéndole un término de cinco días hábiles para desahogar el requerimiento; vencido dicho término, si el interesado no desahoga la prevención en el tiempo o forma señalados, la autoridad desechará por improcedente la queja presentada.

II. La autoridad recibirá la queja y, de considerarlo necesario, previo a su admisión podrá solicitar al notario en cuestión un informe sobre los hechos que la motivaron, mismo que deberá ser rendido en un término no mayor de siete días hábiles, a efecto de determinar la procedencia de la queja; para el caso que sea procedente o que el notario haga caso omiso al requerimiento, la autoridad acordará su admisión a trámite, procederá a registrar la queja en el libro de Gobierno que al efecto exista; abrirá el expediente respectivo, notificará y correrá traslado del acuerdo de admisión junto con la queja al notario de que se trate, ordenando la visita de inspección especial en los términos de esta ley.

A las partes sólo les será notificado personalmente el acuerdo admisorio de la queja y la resolución que ponga fin al procedimiento. Todas las demás resoluciones de trámite serán notificadas por conducto de las personas autorizadas en las oficinas de la autoridad y mediante los estrados que ésta implemente para tal efecto.

III. Desahogada la visita de inspección especial a

第三节　制裁的实施程序

第 230 条　实施上述几条中规定的制裁，应遵照以下程序：

（1）任何证明其具有正当法定权利的人员，可向行政主管当局提出书面申诉，对公证人出现的违反本法或者其他法律规定的行为进行举报。申诉人必须写明其姓名或公司名称，法定代表人姓名以及负责接收通知的联系人的姓名；写明基本情况，清楚写明其申诉的事实或申诉理由；提交书面凭证，必要时应当提供证人证言，并对投诉的事实和理由进行详细说明，以佐证其申诉的正当性。不满足上述任何要求的，主管当局应当要求申诉人在 5 个工作日内补齐；规定期限届满后，当事人未能按时依照规定方式进行补正的，当局将对申诉予以驳回。

（2）当局接到投诉后，如认为必要，在立案审理之前可要求公证人就被申诉事项进行说明，被投诉的公证人应当在 7 个工作日内做出答辩，以确定是否符合立案要求；如果查明符合立案要求，或者公证人未按要求做出答辩，当局应立案审理，对案件进行排期；立案后，应当将受理决议连同申诉书一并转发被申诉的公证人，遵照本法之规定责令启动专项检查。

只有申诉案件受理决议和审理完结后的处理决议才会通知各方当事人本人。在审理程序中产生的其他决议将通过主管当局授权人员进行通知，或在相应的平台上进行通知。

（3）完成上一项所指的专项检查后，当局将传唤

que se refiere la fracción anterior, la autoridad citará a las partes a una junta de conciliación, la cual solo podrá diferirse una vez, siempre que así lo soliciten las partes; en dicha junta la autoridad exhortará a las partes a conciliar sus intereses. De no haber conciliación la autoridad abrirá el periodo probatorio durante un plazo de diez días hábiles, cuya admisión y valoración estará sujeta a las reglas establecidas en el Código de Procedimientos. No quedando prueba pendiente por desahogar, se procederá en un término de tres días a recibir los alegatos por escrito primero del quejoso, luego del notario; una vez rendidos, la autoridad procederá a solicitar la opinión del colegio sobre los hechos materia de la queja, el cual contará con un plazo de siete días hábiles para emitirla a partir del requerimiento que al efecto se le formule, para lo cual deberá consultar el expediente de queja. Acto seguido, la autoridad citará a las partes para oír la resolución correspondiente, dentro de los siguientes treinta días hábiles.

Las disposiciones anteriores se aplicarán para los casos en que ameriten sanción de carácter administrativo por violaciones a esta Ley y a otras relacionadas directamente con su función, o cuando las Autoridades competentes tomen conocimiento de los hechos por vista de cualquier autoridad o aviso del Colegio.

Será de aplicación supletoria el Código de Procedimientos Civiles para el Distrito Federal, en lo conducente.

Artículo 231. - Contra las resoluciones emitidas respecto de las quejas contra notarios, procederá el recurso de inconformidad, que deberá interponerse por escrito ante el superior jerárquico de la autoridad sancionadora, dentro de los diez días hábiles siguientes a la notificación de la resolución recurrida.

Artículo 232. - El escrito por el que se interponga el recurso de inconformidad, se sujetará a los siguientes requisitos:

I. Expresará el nombre completo y domicilio del promovente, en su caso, el número de la notaría a su cargo y de su patente de notario;

II. Mencionará con precisión la autoridad o funcionario de quien emane la resolución recurrida, indicando con claridad en qué consiste ésta, y citando la fecha y número de los oficios y documentos en que conste la determinación recurrida, así como la fecha en que ésta le hubiere sido notificada;

III. Hará una exposición sucinta de los motivos de inconformidad y fundamentos legales de la misma;

IV. Contendrá una relación con las pruebas que

各方当事人召开调解会，如果当事人有要求，可以顺延一次；在调解会上，当局将促请各方达成和解。无法达成和解的，当局将给予10个工作日的举证期，根据《诉讼法》的规则进行举证和质证。举证质证完成后，首先给予申诉人3日期限提交书面辩护词，再给予公证人3日期限进行书面答辩；期限届满后，当局就被申诉事项征求公证人学会的专家意见，公证人学会接到要求后，应当在7个工作日内给出专业意见，为此，学会有权调阅相关卷宗。之后，当局应在30个工作日内作出审理裁决并传唤各方当事人到庭听取决议。

上述规定适用于因违反本法或者其他法律规定而应接受行政纪律制裁，或者主管当局根据其他部门举报或公证人学会的通报而受理的事项。

如有必要，应按照《联邦区民事诉讼法》之规定执行。

第231条 如不服当局的处理决定，可以在接到处理决定后10个工作日内，向上级主管当局提出行政复议申请。

第232条 行政复议申请应当符合以下要求：

（1）写明复议申请人的姓名全名和联系地址，公证人的工作证号和执业资格证号；

（2）写明下达决议的主管当局名称或官员姓名，清楚说明决议内容、决议日期和编号、以及接到决议的日期；

（3）简要说明不服当局的处理决定的理由和法律依据；

（4）提交证据清单，以证明申诉理由，由上级

pretenda se reciban para justificar los hechos en que se apoye el recurso, cuya admisión, desahogo y valoración serán determinados por la autoridad administrativa correspondiente. Si el escrito de inconformidad fuere oscuro o irregular, la autoridad prevendrá al recurrente para que en un término de tres días lo aclare, corrija o complete, con el apercibimiento de que si no lo cumple dentro del término señalado, el escrito se desechará de plano. Cumplido lo anterior se dará curso al escrito.

A este escrito deberán acompañarse los siguientes documentos:

I. Poder suficiente de quien promueva en representación del recurrente;

II. El que contenga el acto impugnado;

III. La constancia de notificación;

IV. Aquellos en que consten las pruebas ofrecidas, conforme a la fracción IV que antecede. En el caso de pruebas testimoniales y periciales se señalará el nombre y domicilio del testigo y perito, quien será citado para aceptar el encargo, dentro de los cinco días siguientes.

Si los documentos señalados en las fracciones I, II y III que anteceden no se presentan simultáneamente con el escrito por el que se interpone el recurso, se otorgará un plazo de tres días para ello, apercibido el promovente que de no hacerlo se tendrá por no interpuesto el recurso y si se trata de los documentos señalados en la fracción IV que antecede, se tendrán por no presentadas.

Artículo 233. - Concluido el término de recepción y desahogo de pruebas, se dictará la resolución correspondiente en un término que no excederá de diez días hábiles, y se notificará de ella al interesado en un plazo máximo de cinco días contados a partir de su firma, así como al colegio.

Artículo 234. - Los efectos de la resolución del recurso son:

I. Tenerlo por no presentado;

II. Revocar el acto impugnado, y

III. Reconocer la validez del acto impugnado.

TÍTULO CUARTO
DE LAS INSTITUCIONES QUE APOYAN LA FUNCIÓN NOTARIAL

DISPOSICIONES GENERALES

Artículo 235. - El Registro Público, el Archivo, el Colegio, el Decanato y el Registro Nacional de Avisos de Testamento, la Coordinación Especializada en Materia

主管当局接收并评估。如果行政复议申请不明确或不规范，当局应当责令申请人在3日内予以澄清、纠正或补充，并提醒申请人注意，如果没有在规定期限内完成，申请不予受理。满足上述要求的，申请书将被受理。

在提交行政复议申请书时，应一并提交下列文件：

（1）授权委托书，证明行政复议申请人已经指定了全权代表；

（2）被申诉的决议书；

（3）决议通知书；

（4）根据前面第4项之规定提供的证据材料。有证人证言和专家鉴定报告的，应当写明证人和专家的姓名和联系地址。当局应当在5日内联系到证人和专家，向其核实情况。

在提交行政复议申请书时没有同时提交前面第1项、第2项、第3项规定的材料的，可以要求复议申请人在3日内补齐，未按期提交的，视为放弃复议申请；没有提交第4项所列材料的，视同未提交这部分材料。

第233条 举证和论证期结束后，应在10个工作日内作出裁决，并自决议签署之日起，在5日内通知当事人以及公证人学会。

第234条 决议可分为以下几种：

（1）视同未申请复议；

（2）撤销原决议；以后

（3）承认原决议有效。

第四篇
支持公证职能的机构

总则

第235条 公共登记处、档案管理局、公证人学会、公证会长办公会和国家遗嘱通知登记处，以及专门负责协调事前公证事项的部门，都是支持联邦区

de Voluntad Anticipada, son instituciones que apoyan al Notariado del Distrito Federal en beneficio de la seguridad y certeza jurídicas que impone el correcto ejercicio de la fe pública. Los notarios del Distrito Federal podrán comunicarse oficialmente de manera ordinaria con estas instituciones haciendo uso de su firma electrónica notarial en términos de esta ley, la cual tendrá equivalencia a la firma autógrafa y al sello de autorizar del notario. El uso de la firma electrónica notarial podrá extenderse a las dependencias federales y locales en los casos y términos que así lo determinen las leyes correspondientes.

CAPÍTULO I DEL ARCHIVO GENERAL DE NOTARLAS DEL DISTRITO FEDERAL

Articulo 236. - El Archivo General de Notarías depende de la Dirección General Jurídica y de Estudios Legislativos.

Artículo 237. - El Archivo General de Notarías se constituirá:

I. Con los documentos que los notarios del Distrito Federal remitan a éste, según las prevenciones de esta ley;

II. Con los protocolos, que no sean aquellos que los notarios puedan conservar en su poder;

III. Con los sellos de los notarios que deban depositarse o inutilizarse, conforme a las disposiciones de esta ley; y

IV. Con los expedientes manuscritos, libros y demás documentos que conforme a esta ley deba mantener en custodia definitiva.

Artículo 238. - El Consejero Jurídico y de Servicios Legales designará al titular del Archivo, quien ejercerá además de las facultades previstas en otros ordenamientos jurídicos, las siguientes:

I. Celebrar, previo acuerdo del titular de la Dirección General Jurídica y de Estudios Legislativos, convenios para acrecentar, conservar y difundir el acervo documental del archivo;

II. Coadyuvar en todo lo concerniente al ejercicio de la función notarial;

III. Impulsar la investigación para el proceso de codificación de la normatividad notarial;

IV. Estudiar y proponer métodos de conservación y respaldo, de la documentación e información que tenga relación con la función notarial;

V. Expedir y reproducir a solicitud de parte interesada los documentos públicos y privados que obren en los

公证机构的职能部门，以保障司法安全与信誉，确保公证工作的顺利开展。联邦区公证人可以按照本法之规定，在与这些机构的正式沟通中使用公证人电子签名，其效力等同于公证人的手写签名和盖章。根据相关法律的规定，在法律允许的情形和形式下，还可以将公证人电子签名的使用范围扩展到联邦和地方的政府职能部门。

第一章 联邦区公证人档案管理局

第236条 公证人档案管理局隶属于法律和立法研究总局。

第237条 公证人档案管理局的档案包括：

（1）联邦区公证人根据本法之规定向档案管理局交存的文件；

（2）公证人无权自行保管的登记簿；

（3）根据本法之规定，公证人应当交存或者销毁的公章；以及

（4）根据本法之规定，应当妥善保管的手稿、书簿和其他文件。

第238条 法律顾问与服务委员会负责任命档案管理局主任，档案管理局主任除其他法定职权外，还具备以下权限：

（1）经法律和立法研究总局局长事先批准，签署相关协议，以收录、保存和传播档案管理局的档案文件；

（2）开展一切有助于公证工作顺利开展的事宜；

（3）推动公证法规的编纂进程；

（4）研究并制定办法，保存和保管与公证工作相关的文档和资料；

（5）应当事人申请，出具和复制档案管理局保管的公共和私署文书；

acervos en custodia del Archivo e;

VI. Certificar la documentación solicitada por autoridades judiciales, administrativas y legislativas, así como por los particulares que acrediten su interés legítimo, y que esté en custodia del Archivo;

VII. Revisar que los libros cumplan con todos y cada uno de los requisitos previstos en esta ley, para su recepción y custodia definitiva;

VIII. Certificar la razón de cierre con respecto a la revisión previa a la que se refiere la fracción que antecede;

IX. Custodiar en definitiva el protocolo que contenga la razón de cierre y que deba tener una antigüedad de cinco años a partir de la fecha de la razón;

X. Recibir para su inutilización los sellos, que se hayan deteriorado, alterado o aparecido después de su extravío, así como los que no cumplan con los requisitos previstos en esta ley;

XI. Recibir los expedientes, manuscritos, libros, folios y demás documentos que conforme a esta ley deban entregar los notarios y que deban custodiarse en el Archivo;

XII. Devolver a los notarios, en los plazos previstos por esta ley, los expedientes, manuscritos, libros, folios y demás documentos que conforme a la misma, no deban custodiarse en definitiva, después de haber sido dictaminados;

XIII. Regularizar y autorizar en definitiva, los instrumentos que hubieren quedado pendientes de autorización por parte de un notario;

XIV. Recibir de los notarios, los avisos de testamento y de designación de tutor cautelar para su depósito y custodia definitiva en el Archivo;

XV. Recibir, para su deposito y custodia los testamentos ológrafos que presenten los particulares;

XVI. Rendir información a las autoridades judiciales y administrativas competentes, y a los notarios con respecto a los avisos y testamento ológrafos a que se refieren las dos fracciones que anteceden;

XVII. Dictaminar y calificar las solicitudes presentadas por los particulares, para determinar la procedencia de un trámite;

XVIII. Realizar anotaciones marginales de acuerdo a la función notarial, prevista en esta ley;

XIX. Registrar las patentes de aspirante y de notario, así como los convenios de asociación y de suplencia celebrados entre los notarios;

XX. Recibir las inspecciones judiciales, fiscales, ministeriales o de autoridad competente, cuando la Ley así

（6）证明司法、行政和立法机关要求出具的文件以及个人申请出具的证明其合法权益的文件确实在档案管理局保管；

（7）审查交存的簿册是否符合本法规定的所有及每一项要求，以便合法收录档案管理局保管；

（8）证明上一款所指的审查工作已完成；

（9）妥善保管以往年度的公证登记簿，保存期为5年，自登记簿交存之日起算；

（10）接收损坏、缺损或报失后重新找回的印章，以及其他不符合本法所列要求的公证章并予以销毁；

（11）接收公证人根据本法之规定应当交存档案管理局保管的卷宗、手稿、记录簿、公证书以及其他文件；

（12）在本法规定期限内向公证人交还法律规定的经档案管理局审查后应当交还公证人，不应在档案管理局保管的卷宗、手稿、记录簿、公证书以及其他文件；

（13）审查需要公证人签批的文书并承认其最终效力；

（14）接受公证人提交的遗嘱通知书和监护人任命书，以便办理交存并收录档案管理局保管；

（15）接收个人提交的亲笔遗嘱，以便办理交存并收录到档案管理局保管；

（16）按要求向司法、行政主管当局以及经办公证员提供与前两款所指的通知和手写遗嘱相关的资料；

（17）对个人提交的申请进行审查和评估，以确定是否需要办理相关手续；

（18）根据本法之规定在相关公证材料上添加边注；

（19）登记候补公证人和公证人从业资格，以及公证人之前签署的合作协议和替班协议；

（20）根据法律规定，接受司法检查、税务检查以及行政主管当局的检查；

lo permita;

XXI. Colaborar para la integración, alimentación, mantenimiento y actualización del sistema de datos del Registro Nacional de Testamentos y del Registro Nacional de Poderes; y

XXII. Las demás que le confieran otros ordenamientos jurídicos

Artículo 239. - El Archivo es privado tratándose de documentos que no tengan una antigüedad de más de setenta años, de los cuales a solicitud de persona que acredite tener interés jurídico, de autoridades competentes y de notarios, podrán expedirse copias simples o certificadas, previo pago de los derechos que previene el Código Financiero del Distrito Federal.

Artículo 240. - El Archivo es público tratándose de documentos cuya antigüedad sea de más de setenta años:

I. Si a la fecha de la consulta o de la petición de que se trate, la antigüedad del documento tiene más de setenta años y menos de cien, su análisis, consulta y reproducción, serán públicos, previo pago de derechos en los términos del Código Financiero del Distrito Federal;

II. Si a la fecha de la consulta o de la petición de que se trate, la antigüedad del documento tiene más de cien años y menos de ciento cincuenta, los mismos únicamente podrán analizarse y consultarse bajo la supervisión estricta de un historiador designado para tal efecto por el Archivo. Para su reproducción, previo pago de derechos previstos en el Código Financiero del Distrito Federal, se requerirá la autorización del titular del Archivo o del Director General Jurídico y de Estudios Legislativos, la cual se llevará a cabo por un historiador designado por el Archivo, quien deberá cuidar en extremo el uso y manejo del documento de que se trate, y

III. Si a la fecha de la consulta o de la petición de que se trate, la antigüedad del documento tiene más de ciento cincuenta años, los mismos únicamente podrán analizarse y consultarse bajo la supervisión estricta de un historiador designado para tal efecto por el Archivo.

Para su reproducción, se requerirá la autorización del Consejero Jurídico y de Servicios Legales o del Director General Jurídico y de Estudios Legislativos, a través de los acuerdos o convenios respectivos. Esta reproducción sólo se llevará a cabo para fines científicos, docentes y culturales mediante tecnología que garantice el cuidado y la preservación de dichos documentos y a través de instituciones gubernamentales o de Derecho privado, o particulares, peritos en el cuidado extremo de los mismos

（21）配合国家遗嘱登记处和国家授权委托书登记处对相关资料库进行整合、扩容、维护和更新；以及

（22）其他法律法规赋予档案管理局的职能。

第239条 历史年限不超过70年的文件属于档案管理局的非公开资料，经利益相关方、主管当局或公证人申请，在申请人根据《联邦财政法》之规定缴清相关费用后，可为其开具简单复印件或经核证副本。

第240条 历史年限超过70年的文件属于档案管理局的公开资料：

（1）对于在查询时或者申请调阅时，资料的历史年限在70年以上100年以下的，根据《联邦财政法》之规定缴清相关费用后，即可公开对文件进行分析、查询和复制。

（2）对于在查询时或者申请调阅时，资料的历史年限在100年以上150年以下的，仅能在档案管理局指定的历史学家的严格监管下进行分析和查询。要对资料进行复制的，根据《联邦财政法》之规定缴清相关费用后，需要取得档案管理局主任或者法律和立法研究总局局长的批准，方可由档案管理局指定的历史学家代为复制。为此，历史学家必须审慎对待，在使用和处理文档时加倍小心。

（3）对于在查询时或者申请调阅时，资料的历史年限在150年以上的，仅能在档案管理局指定的历史学家的严格监管下进行分析和查询。

要复制此类历史文献，需要通过相应的协议或协定，取得法律顾问与服务委员会成员或法律和立法研究总局局长的批准。此类文件的复制仅能用于科学、教学和文化目的，通过技术手段确保文献的保护和保存，并通过具有这方面的专业知识的政府机构、私营机构或个人实施，并由档案管理局指定的历史学家全程参与和监督；复制文献需要根据《联邦财政法》之规定缴纳相关费用。

y en la aplicación de dicha tecnología, con la participación y supervisión de un historiador designado por el Archivo; para esta reproducción se pagarán los derechos señalados en el Código Financiero del Distrito Federal.

Artículo 241. - El titular y los demás empleados del Archivo tendrán la obligación de guardar secreto de la información y trámites relacionados con la documentación que obre en el mismo. El incumplimiento de dicho secreto será sancionado administrativamente en los términos de la Ley Federal de Responsabilidades de los Servidores Públicos y penalmente conforme lo prevengan las disposiciones penales aplicables.

Articulo 242. - El sello del Archivo será metálico, tendrá forma circular, con un diámetro de cuatro centímetros, reproducirá en el centro el escudo nacional, abajo del mismo dirá "México" y en su circunferencia "Archivo General de Notarías del Distrito Federal". El segundo y ulteriores sellos deberán incluir un signo que los distinga del anterior.

El sello expresa el poder autentificador del Archivo y en los casos previstos por esta ley, lo público de su función.

Artículo 243. - El Archivo General de Notarías para la aplicación de las sanciones que procedan comunicará oportunamente a la Dirección General Jurídica y de Estudios Legislativos, los casos en que los notarios en el ejercicio de sus funciones no cumplan esta ley o sus reglamentos.

Artículo 244. - La expedición y reproducción de documentos públicos y privados se hará según lo previsto en el artículo 240 de esta ley.

La solicitud de trámite, ingresada por Oficialía de Partes, deberá ir acompañada con documentación que acredite el interés y la personalidad jurídica, en su caso, de quien promueva y tendrá la calificación en un término no mayor a cinco días hábiles, en el cual se informará verbalmente al promovente la procedencia de dicha solicitud y la cuantía del pago de derechos respectivos, pagados éstos, se procederá a la expedición o reproducción de que se trate, en un plazo no mayor de ocho días hábiles, contados a parir del día hábil siguiente al del pago; la entrega de la documentación requerida se hará únicamente al promovente. La improcedencia de la solicitud se comunicará al promovente por oficio.

Artículo 245. - La revisión de los libros de protocolo a que se refieren los articulo 91 y 238, fracción VII de esta ley se realizará en un plazo de cinco días hábiles, contados

第 241 条 档案管理局主任和其他员工均有义务对档案文献和与之相关的工作保密。违反保密义务的，将按《联邦公职人员责任法》追究其行政纪律责任，构成刑事犯罪的，将按照相关刑法条文受到刑事制裁。

第 242 条 档案管理局的公章为金属质地，圆形，直径为四厘米，在印章中心刻有国徽，国徽下方为"墨西哥"字样，外围一周为"联邦区公证人档案管理局"字样。旧印章因故弃用的，第二个以及再以后的印章上都应当包含与原印章区分开来的标识。

档案管理局的文件只有加盖印章才具备法定效力，在本法规定的情形下，档案管理局的印章代表了其职能的公共性质。

第 243 条 公证人档案管理局发现公证人在履职过程中出现不符合本法或其规章条例规定的情形的，应当及时通知法律和立法研究总局，以采取相应的处罚措施。

第 244 条 公共或私署文书的签发和复制，应当按照本法第 240 条之规定执行。

当事人依程序提出申请的，必须随申请书一并提交能够证明其合法权益和法人资格的文件材料。档案管理局在接到申请后应当在 5 个工作日内进行评估，并向当事人口头告知评估结果，申请准予受理的，在当事人缴清相关费用后 8 个工作日内按要求出具相应文书或复印件，自缴费后下一个工作日起算；档案管理局签发的文书或复印件只能交付给申请人。申请不符合要求，不予办理的，应当正式通知申请人。

第 245 条 对本法第 91 条和第 238 条第 7 项所指的登记簿进行的审查工作应当自收到登记簿之日起，在 5 个工作日内完成，并在第 6 个工作日交还给

a partir de la recepción de los mismos, disponiendo el notario de ellos, a partir del sexto día. Sí el notario no acudiere a recogerlos a más tardar tres días hábiles después de que están a su disposibilidad se hará del conocimiento de la Dirección General Jurídica y de Estudios Legislativos, para que ésta proceda en los términos del articulo 243 de esta ley.

Artículo 246. - La pérdida, alteración, deterioro, aparición por extravío y la solicitud para inutilización del sello de autorizar, se hará del conocimiento del Archivo conforme a lo dispuesto por los artículos 72, 73, 74 y 238, fracción X, de esta ley.

Si con motivo de las atribuciones que esta ley confiere a la autoridad competente, al momento de que se solicita el registro del sello de autorizar de algún notario, la misma se percata que aquél no reúne las características previstas en el artículo 69 de esta ley, negará el registro a través del levantamiento de un acta circunstanciada y plasmará en una hoja en blanco dicho sello, para comunicarlo de inmediato al Archivo, éste tendrá cuidado de que el sello no registrado no se hubiere utilizado o se utilice en lo futuro por el notario en alguno de sus instrumentos. Si el archivo llegare a detectar esta irregularidad lo informará de inmediato a la autoridad competente para que imponga la sanción a que se refiere el articulo 227, fracción VI de esta ley.

Artículo 247. - Si con motivo del ejercicio de la atribución que esta ley confiere al archivo, al momento de expedir algún testimonio o copia certificada de un instrumento que obre en su poder, el titular del Archivo se percata que el instrumento de referencia carece de:

I. Sello al margen superior izquierdo en alguna de las hojas;

II. Sello en la autorización preventiva, o definitiva de la escritura;

III. Firma en la autorización preventiva o definitiva de la escritura;

IV. Media firma o rúbrica en las notas marginales, en su caso;

V. Leyenda "Ante mi";

VI. Salvadura de lo entrerrenglonado o testado;

En estos casos el titular del Archivo expedirá el testimonio o copia certificada solicitados, con la mención en la certificación de tales omisiones, con el señalamiento de tratarse de una escritura irregular y sin prejuzgar sobre las consecuencias legales de las mismas.

Cuando el documento de que se trate, contenga firma

公证人。如果公证人未在3个工作日内取回接受审查的登记簿，应当通知法律和立法研究总局，以便法律和立法研究总局按照本法第243条之规定处理。

第246条 公证章丢失、损坏、缺损、找回后弃用，以及申请销毁的，应按照本法第72条、第73条、第74条和第238条第10项之规定通知档案管理局。

根据本法赋予主管当局的权力，如果公证人在申请对其公证章办理登记时，主管当局发现印章不符合本法第69条所规定特征的，应当拒绝办理登记，出具情况说明书并在一张空白纸上盖上印章样本，以便立即通知档案管理局。档案管理局应注意，未经登记的印章不曾用在公证人出具的文书中，今后也不得进行使用。如果档案管理局发现公证人违规用章的，应当立即报告主管当局，主管当局将根据本法第227条第6项的规定予以处罚。

第247条 档案管理局主任在行使本法赋予档案管理局的职权，为文书签发正式副本或经核证副本时，如果发现在文书中缺乏下列任何要素：

（1）页面左上角的公证章；

（2）初步认可或者最终认可文书效力的公证章；

（3）初步认可或者最终认可文书效力的签名；

（4）在边注中的签名和画押（如适用）；

（5）"在我面前"字样；
（6）在行间补充的修订内容。

在上述情况下，档案管理局主任在按要求出具正式副本或经核证副本时，应当在证明书中写明上述疏漏，指明原文书并不规范，但不影响文书的合法效力。

如果文书中出现的签名与经办公证人的签名笔迹

ostensiblemente diferente a la del notario que autoriza, se procederá en los mismos términos a que se refiere el párrafo que antecede.

Con independencia de lo anterior, si el interesado consulta al colegio acerca de la posibilidad de regularizar dichas anomalías, éste, bajo su más estricta responsabilidad, coadyuvará con él, ante la instancia competente.

CAPÍTULO II DEL COLEGIO DE NOTARIOS DEL DISTRITO FEDERAL

Artículo 248. - El Colegio de Notarios del Distrito Federal, Asociación Civil, es un medio necesario para el cumplimiento de la garantía institucional del notariado. Por lo anterior, y por desempeñar una función de orden e interés público y social, los notarios del Distrito Federal estarán agrupados en un único Colegio, que es el Colegio de Notarios del Distrito Federal. Asociación Civil, con personalidad jurídica y patrimonio propio, que ejercerá para el notariado y para las autoridades correspondientes, las facultades de representación, organización, gestión, intervención, verificación y opinión que esta ley le otorga.

Artículo 249. - El colegio coadyuvará al ordenado y adecuado ejercicio de la función notarial, para lo cual tendrá las facultades y atribuciones siguientes:

I. Vigilar y organizar el ejercicio de la función notarial por sus agremiados, con sujeción a las normas jurídicas y administrativas emitidas por las autoridades competentes y conforme a sus normas internas, con el fin de optimizar la función notarial;

II. Colaborar con los Órganos de Gobierno del Distrito Federal y con los poderes de la unión, en todo lo relativo a la preservación y vigencia del Estado de Derecho y leyes relacionadas con la función notarial;

III. Colaborar con las autoridades competentes y con la Asamblea Legislativa, actuando como órgano de opinión y de consulta, en todo lo relativo a la función notarial, así como coordinar la intervención de los notarios en todos los instrumentos que se requieran en los programas y planes de la Administración;

IV. Colaborar con las autoridades y organismos de vivienda de la Federación y del Distrito Federal, principalmente en programas de vivienda;

V. Representar y defender al notariado del Distrito Federal y sus intereses profesionales, patrimoniales y morales, así como a cualquiera de sus miembros en particular, cuando éste lo solicite y siempre que ello se funde en lo

不一致，同样应当按照上一段之规定处理。

尽管有上述规定，但如果当事人向公证人学会咨询对上述不规范情况进行补救的，学会应当以高度负责的态度，协助当事人办理相关手续。

第二章 联邦区公证人学会

第248条 联邦区公证人学会是一家民间社会组织，是落实公证领域的体制保障的必要手段。为了维护公共秩序和社会利益，联邦区公证人应当形成一个统一的群体组织，即联邦区公证人学会。学会具有民间社会组织性质，具有独立的法人资格和自有财产，作为公证行业的权威机构，行使本法律赋予其的代表权、组织权、管理权、干预权、核查权以及发表专业意见的权利。

第249条 公证人学会应促进公证工作的有序、顺利开展，学会具有以下职能和权限：

（1）根据主管当局颁布的司法和行政法规以及行业内部规范，监督并组织学会成员履行公证职能，更好地开展公证工作。

（2）配合联邦区政府部门以及合众国各政府机关开展相关工作，监督落实与公证相关的法制工作，将相关规定落到实处。

（3）作为公证领域的咨询顾问机构，配合主管当局和议会开展相关工作，并协调调度公证人参与政府实施的各项方案和计划，按要求办理相关公证文书。

（4）配合国家和联邦区的住房主管当局和组织开展工作，尤其是与住房项目有关的工作。

（5）作为联邦区公证人群体的代表，维护公证人行业以及学会任何成员的合法利益，弘扬公证行业的职业文化和道德操守。奉行社会利益高于公证行业利益，公证行业的集体利益高于公证人个人利

que el colegio considere razonadamente injusto e improcedente. El interés general prevalecerá sobre el del notariado y el de éste, sobre el de un notario en particular;

VI. Promover y difundir una cultura jurídica de asistencia, prevención y actuación notarial, en beneficio de los valores jurídicos tutelados por esta Ley y de la preservación y vigencia de la ética en la función notarial;

VII. Formular y proponer a las autoridades competentes estudios relativos a proyectos de leyes, reglamentos y sus reformas y adiciones;

VIII. Estudiar y resolver las consultas que sobre la interpretación de leyes les formulen autoridades y notarios en asuntos relacionados con la función notarial;

IX. Formar y tener al día informaciones sobre solicitudes de los exámenes de aspirante y de oposición al notariado;

X. Intervenir en los procedimientos para acreditación del cumplimiento de los requisitos para ser aspirante o notario;

XI. Intervenir en la preparación y desarrollo de exámenes de aspirante y de notario para someterlo a la consideración y, en su caso, aprobación de la autoridad competente;

XII. Organizar y llevar a cabo cursos, conferencias y seminarios, así como hacer publicaciones, sostener bibliotecas y proporcionar al público en general y a sus agremiados, medios para el desarrollo de la carrera notarial y para el mejor desempeño de la función notarial;

XIII. Proveer a los notarios de los folios que integren su respectivo protocolo. Para cumplir dicha responsabilidad el colegio elegirá la calidad del papel, medios de seguridad e indelebilidad del mismo, y las condiciones con las cuales reciba los folios encargados de quien los produzca, procurando que sean las más adecuadas para el instrumento notarial, informando de ello a la autoridad competente:

XIV. Tomar las medidas que estime necesarias en el manejo de los protocolos de los notarios, para garantizar su adecuada conservación y la autenticidad de los instrumentos, registros, apéndices y demás elementos que los integren, informando de ello a la autoridad competente;

XV. Colaborar y ser órgano auxiliar con posibilidad de participar en visitas a las instituciones relacionadas con la dación de fe pública;

XVI. Proporcionar capacitación y cursos de formación y especialización a servidores públicos que en el desempeño de sus funciones se relacionen con la función notarial;

益的原则。

（6）弘扬司法公正的文化风气，强调公证工作在司法领域发挥的救助、预防作用和行动力，宣传本法主张的司法价值观，确保贯彻落实公证职业操守。

（7）提议并呼吁主管当局研究制定相关法律、法规草案以及相关的修订案及增编。

（8）研究并解决主管当局和公证人就公证问题的相关司法解释向学会提出的咨询。

（9）发布公证人候补资格考试和公证人竞聘考试的最新信息。

（10）介入候补公证人或公证人资格要求认证程序。

（11）参与公证人候补资格考试和公证人选拔考试的筹备和开展，并根据情况报告主管当局审批。

（12）组织开展培训课程、会议和研讨会，发行出版物，经营图书馆，为公众以及学会成员创造条件了解公证知识，提高学会成员的专业素养，帮助其更好地履行公证职能。

（13）为公证人提供公证登记簿所用素材。为此，公证人学会应当严控纸张质量，确保纸张防伪耐磨，规定公证文书的规格，并向主管当局报告。

（14）针对公证登记簿管理工作采取必要措施，确保登记簿得到妥善保管并对登记簿中的文书、记录、附录和其他要素采取防伪措施，并将相关措施报告主管当局。

（15）与相关部门进行合作，全力提高社会公信力。

（16）推动人才培养和课程培训，提高从事公证工作的公职人员的专业素养。

XVII. Impulsar la investigación y el estudio de la función notarial;

XVIII. Otorgar la fianza que en términos del articulo 67 de esta ley deben ofrecer los Notarios en garantía de la responsabilidad por el ejercicio de su función, para lo cual establecerá y administrará un fondo de garantía;

XIX. Proponer, para la aprobación de la autoridad competente, el arancel de notarios en términos de esta ley y sus actualizaciones;

XX. Determinar las cuotas ordinarias y extraordinarias que deban pagar los notarios para la constitución, mantenimiento e incremento del fondo de garantía que cubre la responsabilidad por el ejercicio de la función notarial, y para cubrir los gastos de administración y funcionamiento del propio colegio;

XXI. Establecer y administrar fondos de previsión, de ayuda y de ahorro entre sus agremiados;

XXII. Coadyuvar con el Archivo, en el control, conservación y custodia de su acervo;

XXIII. Organizar las actividades notariales de guardia, consultoría y las demás tendientes al beneficio de la población de la entidad, en particular a los sectores más vulnerables:

XXIV. Celebrar con las autoridades, convenios para la creación de sistemas y formas para el desempeño de la función notarial en programas especiales;

XXV. Intervenir como mediador y conciliador, sobre la actividad de los agremiados, en caso de conflictos de éstos con terceros y rendir opinión a las autoridades competentes;

XXVI. Actuar como administrador de arbitraje, árbitro, conciliador y mediador para la solución de controversias entre particulares; para tal efecto podrá designar, de entre sus agremiados, a quienes realicen tales funciones;

XXVII. Coadyuvar con las autoridades competentes en la vigilancia del exacto cumplimiento de esta ley;

XXVIII. Vigilar la disciplina de sus asociados en el ejercicio de sus funciones, y aplicar medidas disciplinarias y sanciones a los mismos, de conformidad con su normatividad interna;

XXIX. Adquirir los bienes muebles e inmuebles necesarios o convenientes para el logro de sus fines sociales y profesionales:

XXX. Fomentar el desarrollo del Instituto de Investigaciones Jurídicas del Notariado, como órgano del colegio, con autonomía propia, de su biblioteca y publicaciones, así como los convenios con el Archivo para hacer un fondo

（17）促进对公证工作的调查和研究。

（18）根据本法第67条之规定为公证人提供履职担保金，为此，应建立并管理担保金基金。

（19）经主管当局批准，依照本法规定确定公证人的收费标准并定期更新。

（20）建立、维护并管理公证人履职担保基金，确保基金的一般供款额度和特别供款额度，以承担基金的管理支出以及学会本身的运营费用。

（21）面向学会成员建立并管理养老、救济和储蓄基金。

（22）协助档案管理局管理、保存和保管档案文件。

（23）组织开展公证领域的公益活动，造福当地人民，尤其是弱势群体。

（24）与当局签署协议，明确在专项方案中履行公证职能的制度和形式。

（25）作为调解人和调停人，对学会成员之间以及学会成员与第三方之间的矛盾进行调解，并为主管当局提供专业意见。

（26）作为仲裁人、调解人和调停人，解决个人之间的纠纷；为此，可以指定学会成员执行这方面的工作。

（27）配合主管当局监督落实本法。

（28）在学会成员履行职责时进行纪律监督，并根据行业内部规定采取相应的纪律处分和制裁措施。

（29）根据工作需要取得必要的动产和不动产，以实现其经营宗旨和目标。

（30）促进公证人法律研究会这一学会下属的自治机构的发展，发展学会的图书馆和出版物，推进落实与档案管理局的各项协议，根据本法之规定建立一个法律研究方面的共同基金。

común para la investigación jurídica, en los términos de esta ley;

XXXI. Organizar por riguroso turno las guardias para días festivos;

XXXII. Organizar y vigilar el cumplimiento de los turnos de operaciones que indica esta ley;

XXXIII. Recibir los avisos, realizar internamente los registros y desempeñar las funciones que directamente le atribuya esta ley;

XXXIV. Promover entre sus agremiados el uso de las nuevas tecnologías en materia informática, especialmente, la utilización de la firma electrónica notarial.

Artículo 250. - La Asamblea de notarios será el órgano supremo de decisiones fundamentales del colegio; a ella se le atribuye acordar, ratificar o rectificar lo que corresponda para la marcha y desarrollo del Colegio; en ella todos los notarios tendrán voz y voto, de acuerdo con sus estatutos. Para que se considere legalmente reunida y válidas sus decisiones, tratándose de enajenación de bienes inmuebles, deberá estar presente el sesenta por ciento de sus asociados. Las convocatorias para las asambleas deberán hacerse por acuerdo del consejo, mediante circular dirigida al domicilio de cada notaría, o una sola publicación en un diario de los de mayor circulación en el Distrito Federal; en ella se contendrán el orden del día y el lugar y la hora de su realización.

Los bienes del archivo histórico del Colegio son inalienables.

Artículo 251. - El Consejo del Colegio de Notarios del Distrito Federal será el órgano permanente de administración ordinaria y representación del colegio para ejercer en su nombre las facultades que esta ley otorga al Colegio, salvo las que expresamente reserve a la Asamblea del Colegio; tendrá la firma social por el número par de integrantes que elija la Asamblea, la mitad de ellos en los años nones y la otra en los pares y se regirá por sus estatutos. Los consejeros ejercerán su cargo por dos años y no podrán ser reelectos para el periodo inmediato siguiente.

Artículo 252. - Cada Notario en su ejercicio deberá guardar el secreto profesional respecto de los asuntos que se le encomienden y estará sujeto a las penas que respecto al secreto profesional prevé el Código Penal, pudiendo el juez aumentarlas en una mitad, según sea la gravedad del asunto. La calificación que en su caso se dé por la Comisión de Honor y Justicia o por el arbitraje encomendado por la Junta de Decanos podrá ser un elemento que valore el juez respectivo al efecto.

（31）制定节假日值班安排。

（32）根据本法之规定确定工作轮值安排并监督落实相关安排。

（33）接收通知，进行内部登记，并履行本法规定直接由学会承担的职能。

（34）鼓励学会成员使用信息方面的新技术，特别是推广使用公证人电子签名技术。

第 250 条　公证人大会是学会的最高决策组织。公证人大会有权商讨、批准或修正与学会的发展运作有关的事项；根据大会章程，所有公证人在大会中均享有发言权和表决权。在会议的法定人数要求方面，对于不动产转让事宜，至少有 60% 的成员出席，大会视为合法召开，会上决议方具有合法效力。大会的召集应通过理事会的决议进行，会议召集通知可以送达各公证处，或者仅通过在联邦区发行量较大的一份报纸上进行公示；在会议召集通知中应当写明会议日程以及会议召开的时间和地点。

学会的历史档案是学会不可剥夺的财产。

第 251 条　联邦区公证人学会理事会是学会的常设日常管理机构和代表机构，以学会名义代为行使法律赋予学会的各项职权，但法律明文规定应由公证人大会行使的职权除外。理事会成员由大会任命，成员数量为双数，其中半数成员在奇数年份履行职责，半数成员在偶数年份履行职责，具体按照学会章程规定执行。理事会成员每届任期两年，不得连选连任。

第 252 条　每一名公证人在履行职责时应当按规定保守职业秘密，违者将按照《刑法典》中关于职业保密的规定予以处罚，违反情节严重的，可将处罚力度提高一半。荣誉与正义委员会或者公证会办公会推荐的仲裁员给出的评定，应当在法官判案时作为一项考量因素。

Artículo 253. - En relación con el Colegio y el Notariado, son obligaciones de los Notarios, las siguientes:

I. Desempeñar los cargos y las comisiones que les sean asignadas por los órganos del Colegio de Notarios;

II. Ser parte del jurado o vigilante en exámenes de Aspirante o de Oposición;

III. Asumir el carácter de Notario visitador y coadyuvante de los inspectores de Notarías, cuando fuere designado para ello;

IV. Cumplir con las guardias, la consultoría gratuita y demás actividades notariales tendientes al beneficio de la población del Distrito Federal que organice y convenga el colegio y les asignen sus órganos o sus comisiones;

V. Pagar las siguientes cuotas que fije la Asamblea del Colegio:

a) Las cuotas para constituir, mantener e incrementar el fondo de garantía de la responsabilidad por el ejercicio de la función notarial previsto por esta Ley, salvo que el Colegio no conceda la fianza, en cuyo caso la obligación del Notario cesará en cuanto a este concepto.

b) Las cuotas ordinarias para cubrir los gastos de administración y funcionamiento del propio Colegio.

c) Las cuotas extraordinarias para cubrir los gastos por la realización de actividades gremiales y demás erogaciones previstas en el presupuesto anual de gastos. Las cuotas pagadas por los Notarios no son recuperables.

VI. Asistir personalmente a las asambleas, teniendo en ellas voz y voto;

VII. Desempeñar su función sin práctica ni competencia desleales y con el mayor apego al afán de servicio a quienes le requieran su intervención, y

VIII. La demás que establezcan las leyes y los estatutos internos del Colegio.

Artículo 254. - El fondo de garantía de la responsabilidad por el ejercicio de la función notarial, al que se refieren la fracción I del articulo 67 y el artículo 68 de esta Ley, será permanente, y se constituirá con las cuotas a cargo de cada notario y con los rendimientos de su inversión en valores de renta fija. En ningún caso este fondo tendrá un destino distinto al señalado por esta Ley.

La fianza que el colegio otorgue se regirá en todo lo no previsto por el Código Civil, con la única excepción de que el Colegio no requiere tener bienes raíces para responder de las obligaciones que garantice.

En caso de que con cargo a la fianza a la que se refiere el párrafo anterior, el Colegio tuviere que realizar algún pago por responsabilidad en que hubiere incurrido

第 253 条 公证人学会和公证人团体对公证人具有以下约束力：

（1）公证人应承担公证人学会各部门委派的各项职能和任务。

（2）在公证候补人资格考试或者公证人竞聘考试中担任考官或监考官。

（3）作为陪同人员，配合督察员开展对公证处的检查工作。

（4）根据学会的组织和安排，参加公益活动和提供免费咨询以及其他公证活动，造福联邦区民众。

（5）按照公证人学会大会的规定缴纳以下费用：

a）用于建立、维持和管理本法规定的公证人履职担保基金的会费，但学会不提供担保的情况除外，在这种情况下，公证人的这项义务取消。

b）用于学会自身经营管理支出的会费。

c）用于开展工会活动以及年度支出预算中规定的其他活动的特别会费。此类会费一旦缴纳，公证人无权要求退回。

（6）亲自出席公证人大会，在会上享有发言权和表决权。

（7）按照公证申请人的要求忠实履行公证职责，不得出现任何违规行为或不正当竞争，爱岗敬业。

（8）法律法规以及学会内部章程规定的其他职责。

第 254 条 本法第 67 条第 1 款第 1 项和第 68 条提到的公证人履职担保基金应当是一个常设基金，资金来源为每一名公证人缴纳的会费以及通过投资固定收益证券的理财收入。在任何情况下，该基金不得用于法律规定以外的用途。

本法对于担保金规定的一切未尽事宜，均按《民法典》的相关规定执行，但学会不要求对担保义务提供不动产抵押的情况除外。

担保基金建立后，学会成员出现违规行为，应承担赔偿责任的，学会应当执行担保，以养老、救济和储蓄基金中的相应经费来承担相应的支付义务。

alguno de sus miembros la parte a que éste corresponda en los fondos de previsión, ayuda y ahorro establecidos por el propio Colegio, se destinará para compensar dicho pago.

Artículo 255. - El colegio podrá solicitar a la autoridad competente, ordene la visita a un notario y que la misma se practique por un inspector de notarías, la que deberá practicarse dentro de los quince días hábiles siguientes a la solicitud. Un notario designado por el propio colegio, podrá acompañar al inspector. Pasado dicho plazo, si la autoridad no llevó acabo la visita solicitada, el colegio podrá entrevistar al notario de que se trate en la oficina de éste.

Estas visitas se regirán en lo conducente, por los artículos 207 al 221 de esta ley. Si de las visitas se llegan a detectar irregularidades y conductas que en opinión del Colegio, deban ser sancionadas en los términos de la presente Ley, el Colegio lo hará del conocimiento de las autoridades competentes, las que procederán en términos del articulo 223 de esta Ley. Si en opinión del colegio hubiere elementos suficientes para suponer la posible responsabilidad del notario y la autoridad no inicia el procedimiento correspondiente, cesará la obligación de afianzar del colegio, en cuyo caso el notario deberá caucionar su gestión mediante fianza otorgada por institución afianzadora autorizada por la ley.

CAPÍTULO III DEL DECANATO DEL NOTARIADO DEL DISTRITO FEDERAL

Artículo 256. - El Decanato del Notariado del Distrito Federal se forma por el grupo de expresidentes del Colegio de Notarios, estén o no en funciones.

Artículo 257. - El decanato se podrá reunir en todo tiempo sin necesidad de convocatoria formal previa, bastará que estén reunidos la mayoría de sus miembros para que pueda funcionar válidamente y sus resoluciones se tomarán por la mayoría de votos de los presentes. Para el quórum de reuniones sujetas a convocatoria, es necesaria la mayoría simple.

Artículo 258. - Para el ejercicio de sus funciones la Junta de Decanos podrá designar comisiones de todo tipo, formadas por uno o más de sus miembros o notarios en ejercicio, designados al efecto.

Artículo 259. - Las funciones del Decanato, que se desempeñarán de manera honorífica, serán las siguientes:

I. Asistir cuando sea citado por el consejo a sus sesiones o a las asambleas del Colegio:

II. Solicitar del Colegio intervenir en la instrucción

第 255 条　公证人学会可向主管当局申请对一名公证人进行调查，主管当局接到申请后，应在 15 个工作日内派督察员到公证处检查。学会同样可指派一名公证人陪同督察员一起开展调查工作。规定期限届满后主管当局仍未按要求进行调查的，学会可到公证人的办公地点进行视察。

检查工作应当按照本法第 207 条至第 221 条之规定执行。在检查中一旦发现违规行为或者学会认为应按本法之规定予以惩治的行为，学会应当上报主管当局，按照本法第 223 条之规定执行。学会认为有足够证据证明应当追究公证人责任而主管当局没有启动相应程序的，学会将终止担保义务。在此情况下，公证人必须取得经法律认可的担保机构出具的履职担保方可继续从事公证活动。

第三章　联邦区公证会长办公会

第 256 条　联邦区公证会长办公会是由公证人学会的历任会长组成的，无论当前在任与否。

第 257 条　只要委员会多数成员到会，能确保正常运作且通过与会成员的多数票赞成通过决议的，公证会长办公会无须事先正式召集即可随时召开会议。对于会议召集的法定人数要求，必须达到简单多数。

第 258 条　公证会长办公会为履行其职能，可以成立各类委员会，委员会由一名或多名理事会成员或为此专门任命的在职公证员组成。

第 259 条　公证会长办公会的职务为荣誉头衔，其职能如下：

（1）应理事会或者公证人学会邀请，参加理事会会议或学会会议。

（2）当公证人行为受到质疑，认为其构成违反公

de procedimientos en relación con la actuación de los Notarios que se estime transgreden las obligaciones que la Ley y la reglamentación colegial les imponen o las normas éticas aplicables y emitir opinión.

III. Emitir opiniones respecto de los asuntos de importancia que le sean consultados por el Colegio.

IV. Tener, por iniciativa propia, derecho de opinión ante el Consejo o la Asamblea, en asuntos generales o particulares de transcendencia para el Colegio.

V. Ser árbitro para la solución de quejas o demandas que los solicitantes del servicio presenten en contra de Notarios, cuando ambas partes así lo convengan.

VI. Ser tribunal de arbitraje de ejercicio profesional completo o, en su caso, designar árbitros para ello, los que deberán ser notarios en ejercicio. Los Notarios, en todo tiempo, podrán voluntariamente someter el ejercicio completo de su función al arbitraje del Decanato. En este caso, la notaría sometida al arbitraje del Decanato exhibirá en lugar visible al público la constancia relativa. Las personas que tengan alguna queja o reclamación contra un Notario podrán libremente elegir si optan acudir a los tribunales correspondientes o al arbitraje conforme a este artículo. Tratándose de quejas a las autoridades, podrán también elegir si someten la cuestión a este arbitraje e, inclusive sometiéndose a él, dar parte a las autoridades competentes, si así es su voluntad.

VII. Recibir opinión de los observadores y hacer recomendaciones respecto de los exámenes de aspirante y notario.

VIII. Hacer recomendaciones en caso de denuncias o quejas respecto de un notario.

IX. Formular al Colegio una propuesta de código deontológico de la profesión notarial o, en su caso, una declaración de los principios relativos que deban guiar su ejercicio y un decálogo sobre estas cuestiones. La formulación o aprobación de dicho código no es condición para el ejercicio de las facultades previstas para el Decanato o sus comisiones.

Artículo 260. - El Decanato, para el ejercicio de sus funciones queda facultado para tener acceso a archivos y documentos de toda clase del Colegio y de los notarios que hayan aceptado someterse a sus procedimientos de arbitraje.

Artículo 261. - El Decanato designará y removerá de entre sus integrantes a una Comisión de Arbitraje, Legalidad y Justicia formada por un número impar de sus miembros en ejercicio y designará y removerá al presidente de

证法或公证人学会的制度条例或者道德规范时，经学会申请介入调查审理程序中并发表意见。

（3）就学会咨询的重大事项发表意见。

（4）有权就可能对学会产生深远影响的一般事项或个别事项主动发表意见，行使表达权。

（5）当公证当事人对公证人提供的服务提出投诉或申诉，申诉人与公证人双方有约定的，可由公证会长办公会充当仲裁人，通过仲裁解决。

（6）充当公证执业仲裁庭，或者任命相应的仲裁员，被任命的仲裁员应当是在职公证人。公证人可随时自愿接受公证会长办公会对其履职情况的仲裁。在此情况下，接受公证会长办公室仲裁的公证处应当在其对外办公场所的醒目位置张贴相关说明。对公证人有任何不满或要求投诉的，可以自由选择到主管法院诉诸司法或者按照本条之规定接受仲裁。对当局有投诉的，也可以选择通过仲裁解决，甚至可以根据自身意愿，通过公证会长办公会移交主管当局受理。

（7）接收观察员的意见并就候补公证人或正式公证人考核提出建议。

（8）就针对公证人提起的投诉或申诉提出建议。

（9）向公证人学会提出关于公证行业从业道德规范的提案，或者提出指导公证人从业的相关原则以及关于此类问题的戒律（如适用）。制定或批准上述规范并不是公证会长办公会或其委员会行使其法定职权的先决条件。

第260条 公证会长办公会为履行其职能，有权调阅公证人学会以及同意接受其仲裁的公证人掌握的各类档案和文件。

第261条 仲裁、法制与正义委员会的成员应当由公证会长办公会在其成员中自由任免，委员会成员数量应为单数，委员会主席也由公证会长办公会自由任免。

dicha Comisión.

Artículo 262. - Cuando la Comisión a que se refiere el artículo anterior, en ejercicio de sus funciones constate la existencia de una irregularidad grave fuera del objeto de arbitraje deberá avisar de ello a las autoridades competentes.

Artículo 263. - El notario que se someta a arbitraje si lo cree conveniente podrá exhibir toda clase de pruebas instrumentales o de cualquier naturaleza para justificar su actuación.

Artículo 264. - La Comisión de Honor y Justicia deberá considerar las pruebas y documentos exhibidos y analizarlas en conciencia de equidad. Si considera que le son suficientes para ilustrar su resolución, emitirá esta por mayoría de votos con la decisión que estime conveniente, la cual someterá al Consejo del Colegio y a la autoridad que proceda. Esta resolución será inapelable.

Artículo 265. - La resolución que emita la Comisión de Honor y Justicia no generará responsabilidad civil o penal de ninguna especie a cargo de sus integrantes.

Artículo 266. - El designado al Decanato o a una de sus comisiones estará obligado a aceptar su nombramiento y a desempeñar su encargo con el mayor celo y celeridad posibles.

Artículo 267. - La Junta de Decanos podrá emitir, por mayoría de sus miembros, normas procesales o de otro tipo para efectos del cumplimiento de su encargo previsto en el artículo 259.

TRANSITORIOS

PRIMERO. - Esta ley entrará en vigor a los 60 días naturales siguientes a su publicación en la Gaceta Oficial del Distrito Federal.

SEGUNDO. - Se abroga la Ley del Notariado para el Distrito Federal publicada en el Diario Oficial del Distrito Federal, el 8 de enero de 1980 y sus específicas reformas correspondientes y se derogan las disposiciones que se opongan a esta ley.

TERCERO. - El Decreto de presupuesto de egresos del Distrito Federal para el año 2001 y subsecuentes deberán considerar específicamente una partida anual, a fin de dotar los elementos necesarios para el acervo documental y la adecuada preservación del Archivo.

CUARTO. - Se respetarán los derechos adquiridos y todos los asuntos y trámites iniciados durante la vigencia de la Ley del Notariado que se abroga serán validos hasta

第 262 条　上一条所指的委员会在履行职责时发现存在严重违规现行，需要进行仲裁的，应当通知主管当局。

第 263 条　接受仲裁的公证人，可提交各类文本证据或任何性质的证据，证明其行为的正当性。

第 264 条　荣誉与正义委员会应当对公证人提供的证据和材料进行分析与评估。如果认为理由充分，应当通过投票表决，获得多数票赞成后正式形成决议，并提交学会理事会和主管当局。决议具有最终效力，不可申诉。

第 265 条　荣誉与正义委员会下达的决议不会对委员会成员产生任何民事或刑事责任。

第 266 条　公证会长办公会或其下属委员会的成员接受任命后，应尽职尽责履行职务。

第 267 条　公证会长办公会可通过多数成员的表决同意，颁布程序规则或其他类型的规范，以落实第 259 条中规定的任务。

过渡性条款

第 1 条　本法自在《联邦区官方公报》上发布后第 60 日起生效。

第 2 条　废止在 1980 年 1 月 8 日的《联邦政府公报》上发布的《联邦区公证法》及其相应的修订案，同时废止与本法相悖的任何规定。

第 3 条　在 2001 年度联邦区支出预算办法中应当规定留出专项经费，用于档案管理局开展收录和妥善保管档案资料的工作。

第 4 条　在本法正式生效之前，在原《公证法》有效期间已经取得的权利继续有效，已经开始办理的一切手续和事项继续按原规定处理。本法另有明文规

la etapa procedimental y de gestión en que se encuentren a la entrada en vigor de esta ley, pero si ésta establece gestiones y procedimientos adicionales diversos, se estará a lo que la misma señala y deberán cumplirse en sus términos.

QUINTO. - El colegio tendrá un plazo de tres meses contados a partir de la entrada en vigor de esta ley para adecuar sus estatutos a las disposiciones contenidas en esta ley. Lo anterior sin perjuicio de los efectos que esta ley produce directamente, por su mismo carácter legal.

SEXTO. - Con salvedad de lo dispuesto en el artículo primero transitorio, el inicio del afianzamiento, que por mandato de esta ley corresponde al colegio, se realizará a partir del día siguiente de la publicación de la misma en la Gaceta.

SÉPTIMO. - Con salvedad de lo dispuesto en el artículo primero transitorio de esta ley, el procedimiento de insaculación a que se refiere el articulo 18 de la misma, se llevará a cabo dentro de los tres primeros meses del año 2000.

OCTAVO. - Los folios de Protocolo Especial que preveía la reforma a la Ley del Notariado publicada en el Diario Oficial de 6 de enero de 1994, no utilizados a la fecha de entrada en vigor de la presente Ley en cada Notaría, se deberán utilizar por el Notario respectivo o por el suplente o asociado que le corresponda bajo las siguientes condiciones:

I. El Notario relativo dará aviso al Colegio de cuántos folios sin usar del protocolo especial se encuentran en la Notaría.

II. Al iniciarse la vigencia de la Ley, el Notario utilizará en primer término los mencionados folios del protocolo especial, para lo cual en una hoja no foliada asentará que a partir de esa fecha utilizará los mencionados folios y el número de los que dispone para ello, y

III. Cuando utilice el último de dichos folios, también en una hoja no foliada asentará razón de ello y que a partir de esa fecha inicia o procederá a utilizar los folios del protocolo ordinario, cuya utilización estará suspendida hasta ese momento.

NOVENO. - En tanto no se emitan por la Junta de Decanos las reglas a que se refiere el articulo 260, se aplicarán a las cuestiones de arbitraje las reglas que esta elija de entre las siguientes: las de la Corte Internacional de Arbitraje Comercial de París; las de la Comisión Interamericana de Arbitraje Comercial; las de la Cámara Nacional de Comercio de la Ciudad de México o las reglas de la Comisión de Derecho Mercantil Internacional de las

定的，应当按照新规定办理。

第5条 自本法生效之日起，公证人学会应当在3个月内修订其章程，与本法规定保持一致。同时不妨碍根据本法之规定直接对章程进行修改。

第6条 虽然暂时条例第1条中规定了本法的生效日期，但是其中规定的公证人学会应当设立的担保基金，应当自本法在官方公报上发布后的次日起着手办理。

第7条 虽然暂时条例第1条中规定了本法的生效日期，但是本法第18条中规定的备案程序应当在2000年前三个月内完成。

第8条 在1994年1月6日的官方日报上发布的原《公证法》修订案中规定的公证登记簿专用纸，自本法生效之日起停用，公证人、替补公证人或合伙人满足下列要求的，可继续使用：

（1）公证人向学会提交报告，说明公证处中还有多少专用纸尚未使用。

（2）自本法生效之日起，公证人应当优先使用前面提到的专用活页纸，为此，应当在一张非活页纸上写明自当日起将使用活页纸，以及公证处现有的活页纸库存数量。

（3）在用完最后一张活页纸后，应当在一张非活页纸上写明，由于专用活页纸已用尽，自当日起开始使用普通活页纸。

第9条 在公证会长办公会未出台第260条中提到的规则之前，仲裁事项应当按照下列任一规则处理：国际商会仲裁院（巴黎）仲裁规则、美洲国家商事仲裁委员会仲裁规则、墨西哥城国家商会仲裁规则，或者联合国国际贸易法委员会仲裁规则。

Naciones Unidas.

DÉCIMO. - Para fijar los montos y porcentajes que se apliquen a tos cobros de honorarios por la función notarial en los casos concretos se establecerá, con las siguientes condiciones y procedimiento, un primer arancel que:

I. Deberá ser formulado por el Colegio, el cual hará estudios suficientes y razonables de carácter económico y actuarial para fijar una propuesta de arancel. Dicha propuesta del Colegio deberá ser formulada y entregada a las autoridades dentro de un plazo de dos meses, contados a partir de la entrada en vigor de esta Ley;

II. Tendrá que ser justo y proporcionado para la serie de servicios que se prestan, los solicitantes que los requieren y las funciones que desarrolle el notario, deberá ser suficiente para garantizar la independencia, equilibrio y la adecuada y permanente prestación del servicio;

III. En su regulación se deberán distinguir distintos supuestos, tomando en cuenta en forma especial los de servicio social y de atención a asuntos de orden público así como a grupos sociales vulnerables;

IV. Contendrá previsiones respecto de la prestación organizada por el Colegio a solicitud de las autoridades correspondientes de campañas de regularización de la tenencia de la tierra y testamentos para las clases populares;

V. Tomará en cuenta el servicio de asesoría específica de que se trate, así como la dificultad y riesgo del mismo;

VI. Deberá cubrir los aspectos principales de la función notarial, determinando cuales servicios se encuentran fuera de arancel, esto nunca podrá aplicarse a los casos y supuestos a que se refieren las fracciones III y IV de este artículo.

DÉCIMO PRIMERO. - El Colegio entregará a la Consejería Jurídica la formulación del arancel conjuntamente con los estudios que se hayan efectuado. Las autoridades competentes del Gobierno del Distrito Federal revisarán el arancel respectivo, y el Archivo dará su opinión, pudiendo aprobarlo la Consejería Jurídica, a través de la Dirección General Jurídica y de Estudios Legislativos, si lo considera adecuado. Si en virtud de estudios serios y fundados, suficientes y razonables de carácter económico y actuarial se encontraren supuestos que deban ser corregidos por parte de las autoridades, estas lo harán con citación previa al Colegio para que manifieste su opinión, y presente en su caso alternativas, dentro de un mes de plazo fatal adicional a partir de que se haya dado tal citación. Al

第10条 公证人在具体案件中的收费金额和抽成比例应当按照以下条件和程序确定：

（1）公证人学会在进行充分、合理的经济和精算研究后，提出一个收费标准草案。自本法生效之日起，公证人学会应在2个月内将这一草案提交主管当局审批。

（2）收费标准必须正当合理，与按照公证申请人的要求提供的公证服务相称，收费水平应当足够保障公证服务的独立性、平衡性、适当性和可持续性。

（3）必须根据不同的情形规定不同的收费标准，特别要关注社会性、公益性事项，特别关照弱势群体。

（4）按照有关部门要求，对于面向普通民众开展的土地所有权认证活动和遗嘱公证活动，应当由学会统一组织，执行特别收费标准。

（5）在制定收费标准时应考虑专业咨询活动的难度和风险。

（6）应当涵盖公证工作的主要方面，确定哪些服务不适用统一收费标准，但本条第3项和第4项规定的情形除外。

第11条 公证人学会应向法律咨询理事会提交收费价目表，同时提交这方面的研究结果。联邦区主管当局应当对价目表进行审查并向档案管理局征求意见，论证通过后，应责成法律和立法研究总局予以批准。如果主管当局通过充分、合理的经济和精算研究，认为存在问题需要修正，应事先向学会征询意见，以便学会自接到通知后，在1个月内提出可能的替代方案期。限届满后仍未提出替代方案的，当局视为方案已通过，并将收费标准以及相应的修订案（如果有）进行公示；当局对修订案持保留意见的，可以延后1个月公示。学会制定的收费标准自获批通过后开始生效，联邦区所有公证人都必须按标准执行；如果经研究需要对方案进行修订的，应按修订后的标准执行。

terminar este último plazo, los aspectos sobre los cuales no hubiere hecho correcciones la autoridad se entenderán aprobados, y el arancel será publicado por las autoridades con las modificaciones que haya sufrido, o bien éstas se reservarán por la autoridad, para publicarse posteriormente en un término de un mes. El arancel propuesto por el Colegio comenzará a regir a partir de su aprobación y será de observancia obligatoria para todos los notarios del Distrito Federal; lo mismo se aplicará a las modificaciones que se propongan con base a estudios del tipo descrito.

DÉCIMO SEGUNDO. - Se abroga el "Acuerdo del Ciudadano Jefe del Departamento del Distrito Federal por el que se crea el Consejo Consultivo del Archivo General de Notarías".

DÉCIMO TERCERO. - Los notarios que hayan obtenido la patente antes de la entrada en vigor de esta ley son inamovibles.

Salón de Sesiones de la Asamblea Legislativa del Distrito Federal, a 30 de diciembre de mil novecientos noventa y nueve. - POR LA MESA DIRECTIVA. - DIP. RENE BALDOMERO RODRÍGUEZ RUIZ, PRESIDENTE. - DIP. JOSÉ LUIS BENITEZ GIL, SECRETARIO. - FIRMAS.

En cumplimiento de lo dispuesto por los artículos 122, apartado C, Base Segunda, fracción II, inciso b). de la Constitución Política de los Estados Unidos Mexicanos; 48, 49 y 67. fracción II del Estatuto de Gobierno del Distrito Federal, y para su debida publicación y observancia, expido el presente Decreto Promulgatorio, en la Residencia de la Jefa de Gobierno del Distrito Federal, en la Ciudad de México, a los catorce días del mes de febrero de dos mil. LA JEFA DE GOBIERNO DEL DISTRITO FEDERAL, ROSARIO ROBLES BERLANGA. - FIRMA. - EL SECRETARIO DE GOBIERNO, LEONEL GODOY RANGEL. - FIRMA. - EL SECRETARIO DE FINANZAS. - ARMANDO LÓPEZ FERNÁNDEZ. - FIRMA.

ARTÍCULOS TRANSITORIOS DEL DECRETO QUE REFORMA DIVERSAS DISPOSICIONES DE LA LEY DEL NOTARIADO PARA EL DISTRITO FEDERAL, PUBLICADO EN LA GACETA OFICIAL DEL DISTRITO FEDERAL EL 14 DE SEPTIEMBRE DE 2000.

PRIMERO. - El presente decreto entrará en vigor un día después de su publicación en la gaceta Oficial del Distrito Federal.

SEGUNDO. - La insaculación efectuada por la Dirección General Jurídica rn cumplimiento de lo ordenado

第 12 条 废除《关于成立联邦区公证人档案管理局顾问委员会的协议》。

第 13 条 在本法生效前已经取得从业资格的公证人，其资格继续有效。

1999 年 12 月 30 日在联邦区议会大会堂。圆桌会议。议长：雷内•巴尔多梅罗•罗德里格斯•鲁伊斯（签名）。议会秘书：何塞•路易斯•贝尼特斯•希尔（签名）。

根据《墨西哥合众国宪法》第 122 条 C 款第 2 段第 2 项 b 点及《联邦区政府规约》第 48、第 49 条和第 67 条第 2 款之规定，特于 2000 年 2 月 14 日在墨西哥城联邦区政府行政长官所在地签发本立法令，以便依程序颁布并实施。联邦区行政长官：罗萨里奥•罗布莱斯•贝兰加（签名）。秘书：莱昂内尔•戈多伊•兰赫尔（签名）。财政司司长：阿曼多•洛佩斯•费尔南德斯（签名）。

在 2000 年 9 月 14 日的《联邦区官方公报》上发布的关于修改《联邦区公证法》若干规定的法令的过渡性条款。

第 1 条 本法令自在《联邦区官方公报》上发布后的次日起生效。

第 2 条 本法第 18 条中规定的法律和立法研究总局的备案程序，仍按原规定执行。

por el artículo 18 de esta Ley se mantendrá vigente para todos los efectos previstos por este ordenamiento.

NOTA: LA REPETICIÓN QUE APARECE EN LA FRACCIÓN TERCERA DEL ARTÍCULO 162, FUE COPIADA IDÉNTICAMENTE COMO FUE PUBLICADA EN LA GACETA OFICIAL DEL DISTRITO FEDERAL.

TRANSITORIO DEL DECRETO POR EL QUE SE REFORMA EL ARTICULO 18 DE LA LEY DEL NOTARIADO PARA EL DISTRITO FEDERAL, PUBLICADO EN LA GACETA OFICIAL DEL DISTRITO FEDERAL EL 29 DE ENERO DE 2004

PRIMERO. - Publíquese el presente Decreto en la Gaceta Oficial del Distrito Federal y para su mayor difusión en el Diario Oficial de la Federación.

SEGUNDO. - El presente decreto entrará en vigor al día siguiente de su publicación en la Gaceta Oficial del Distrito Federal.

TERCERO. - En tanto se expidan las disposiciones administrativas que deriven de las presentes adiciones y modificaciones seguirán en vigor aquellas que no las contravengan.

TRANSITORIO DEL DECRETO POR EL QUE SE REFORMA EL ARTÍCULO 18 DE LA LEY DEL NOTARIADO PARA EL DISTRITO FEDERAL, PUBLICADO EN LA GACETA OFICIAL DEL DISTRITO FEDERAL EL 26 DE OCTUBRE DE 2005

PRIMERO. - Remítase al Jefe de Gobierno del Distrito Federal para su promulgación y publicación, en la Gaceta Oficial del Distrito Federal y para su mayor difusión en el Diario Oficial de la Federación.

SEGUNDO. - La presente reforma entrará en vigor al día siguiente de su publicación en la Gaceta Oficial del Distrito Federal.

TERCERO. - Para los efectos de lo dispuesto en el tercer párrafo de este artículo, los notarios contarán con un término de 30 días a partir de su entrada en vigor.

TRANSITORIOS DEL DECRETO QUE REFORMA, ADICIONA Y DEROGA DIVERSAS DISPOSICIONES DE LA LEY DEL NOTARIADO PARA EL DISTRITO FEDERAL, PUBLICADO EN LA GACETA OFICIAL DEL DISTRITO FEDERAL EL 25 DE ENERO DE 2006

PRIMERO. - Remítase al Jefe de Gobierno para su debida promulgación y publicación en la Gaceta Oficial del Distrito Federal y para su mayor difusión en el Diario Oficial de la Federación.

SEGUNDO. - Las presentes reformas entrarán en

注：第162条第3款中的内容，系《联邦区官方公报》上发布内容的真实抄录。

在2004年1月29日的《联邦区官方公报》上发布的关于修改《联邦区公证法》第18条的法令的过渡性条款。

第1条 责令在《联邦区官方公报》上发布本法令并在《联邦政府公报》上进一步传播。

第2条 本法令自在《联邦区官方公报》上发布后的次日起生效。

第3条 在与本法令中所载的若干补充规定和修订条款相关的行政细则颁布后，与新规定不冲突的内容继续有效。

在2005年10月26日的《联邦区官方公报》上发布的关于修改《联邦区公证法》第18条的法令的过渡性条款。

第1条 将法令发送给联邦区政府行政长官，请其下令在《联邦区官方公报》上发布本法令并在《联邦政府公报》上进一步传播。

第2条 本修订案自在《联邦区官方公报》上发布后的次日起生效。

第3条 根据该条第三段之规定，公证人应在该规定生效后30日内予以落实。

在2006年1月25日的《联邦区官方公报》上发布的关于修改、补充和废止《联邦区公证法》若干规定的法令的过渡性条款。

第1条 将法令发送给联邦区政府行政长官，请其下令在《联邦区官方公报》上发布本法令并在《联邦政府公报》上进一步传播。

第2条 本修订案自在《联邦区官方公报》上发

vigor a los treinta días naturales siguientes de su publicación en la Gaceta Oficial del Distrito Federal.

TRANSITORIOS DEL DECRETO POR EL QUE SE REFORMA Y ADICIONA LA LEY ORGÁNICA DE LA ADMINISTRACIÓN PÚBLICA DEL DISTRITO FEDERAL, EL CÓDIGO DE PROCEDIMIENTOS CIVILES PARA EL DISTRITO FEDERAL Y LA LEY DEL NOTARIADO PARA EL DISTRITO FEDERAL, PUBLICADO EN LA GACETA OFICIAL DEL DISTRITO FEDERAL EL 19 DE MAYO DE 2006.

PRIMERO. - Remítase al Jefe de Gobierno del Distrito Federal para su debida promulgación y publicación en la Gaceta Oficial del Distrito Federal y para su mayor difusión en el Diario Oficial de la Federación.

SEGUNDO. - Las presentes reformas entrarán en vigor a los treinta días naturales siguientes de su publicación en la Gaceta Oficial del Distrito Federal.

TRANSITORIO DEL DECRETO POR EL QUE SE REFORMA Y ADICIONA EL CÓDIGO CIVIL PARA EL DISTRITO FEDERAL; SE REFORMA EL CÓDIGO DE PROCEDIMIENTOS CIVILES PARA EL DISTRITO FEDERAL; SE REFORMA Y ADICIONA LA LEY DE NOTARIADO DEL DISTRITO FEDERAL Y SE REFORMA Y ADICIONA EL CÓDIGO FINANCIERO DEL DISTRITO FEDERAL, PUBLICADO EN LA GACETA OFICIAL DEL DISTRITO FEDERAL EL 15 DE MAYO DE 2007.

ÚNICO. El presente Decreto entrará en vigor al día siguiente de su publicación en la Gaceta Oficial del Distrito Federal.

TRANSITORIOS DEL DECRETO POR EL QUE SE REFORMAN DIVERSAS DISPOSICIONES DE LA LEY DEL NOTARIADO PARA EL DISTRITO FEDERAL, PUBLICADO EN LA GACETA OFICIAL DEL DISTRITO FEDERAL EL 31 DE MARZO DE 2011.

PRIMERO. - El presente Decreto entrará en vigor al día siguiente de su publicación en la Gaceta Oficial del Distrito Federal.

SEGUNDO. - Los entes públicos, adoptarán las medidas administrativas necesarias para dar cumplimiento a lo dispuesto en el artículo 154 Sexies y 235 del presente Decreto, conforme a su disponibilidad de recursos humanos, materiales, económicos y tecnológicos.

TERCERO. - Publíquese en la Gaceta Oficial del Distrito Federal y para su mayor difusión en el Diario Oficial de la Federación.

Se reforman los artículos 167, 168, primer párrafo y

布后第 30 个自然日起生效。

在 2006 年 5 月 19 日的《联邦区官方公报》上发布的关于修改和补充《联邦区行政机关组织法》《联邦区民事诉讼法》和《联邦区公证法》若干规定的法令的过渡性条款。

第 1 条 将法令发送给联邦区政府行政长官，请其下令在《联邦区官方公报》上发布本法令并在《联邦政府公报》上进一步传播。

第 2 条 本修订案自在《联邦区官方公报》上发布后第 30 个自然日起生效。

在 2007 年 5 月 15 日的《联邦区官方公报》上发布的关于修改和补充《联邦区民法典》，修改《联邦区民事诉讼法》，修改和补充《联邦区公证法》以及修改和补充《联邦区财政法》若干规定的法令的过渡性条款。

唯一一条 本法令自在《联邦区官方公报》上发布后的次日起生效。

在 2011 年 3 月 31 日的《联邦区官方公报》上发布的关于修改《联邦区公证法》若干规定的法令的过渡性条款。

第 1 条 本法令自在《联邦区官方公报》上发布后的次日起生效。

第 2 条 相关各部门应当根据其人力、物力、技术资源和经济实力，采取必要的行政措施，落实本法令第 154 条之六和第 235 条之规定。

第 3 条 在《联邦区官方公报》上颁布本法令，并在《联邦政府公报》上进一步传播。

修改《联邦区公证法》第 167 条、第 168 条第

169; se adiciona un segundo párrafo al artículo 168, y se deroga el artículo 178 de la Ley de Notariado para el Distrito Federal 23-VII-2012

Primero. - Aquellos testamentos públicos cerrados, públicos simplificados, ológrafos, privados, militares o marítimos que hayan sido otorgados con anterioridad al presente decreto, subsistirán en sus términos y para su apertura y declaración de ser formal testamento se substanciarán de conformidad con las disposiciones vigentes al momento de su otorgamiento.

Segundo. - Las presentes reformas entrarán en vigor al día siguiente de su publicación en la Gaceta Oficial del Distrito Federal.

Tercero. - Publíquese en la Gaceta Oficial del Distrito Federal y para su mayor difusión en el Diario Oficial de la Federación.

一段和第 169 条，在第 168 条中新增第 2 段并废止第 178 条（2012 年 7 月 23 日）

第 1 条　本法令颁布之前已经存在的公开遗嘱、秘密遗嘱、手写遗嘱、私署文书、民事文件或海事文件，应继续按照办理公证时现行有效的规定执行。

第 2 条　本修订案自在《联邦区官方公报》上发布后的次日起生效。

第 3 条　在《联邦区官方公报》上颁布本法令，并在《联邦政府公报》上进一步传播。

巴拿马

关于公证处的组织运作以及其他规定

Asamblea Nacional Secretaría General TRÁMITE LEGISLATIVO 2014-2015	国民大会 秘书处 立法程序 2014-2015

PROYECTO DE LEY: 119

LEY:

GACETA OFICIAL:

TÍTULO: QUE ORGANIZA LAS NOTARIAS PÚBLICAS Y DICTA OTRAS DISPOSICIONES.

FECHA DE PRESENTACIÓN: 20 DE OCTUBRE DE 2014.

PROPONENTE: S.E. MILTON HENRÍQUEZ SASSO., MINISTRO DE GOBIERNO.

COMISIÓN: GOBIERNO, JUSTICIA Y ASUNTOS CONSTITUCIONALES

Apartado 0815-01603 Panamá 4 , Panamá

法案：第 119 号

法律：

官方公报：

标题：关于公证处的组织运作以及其他规定

提案日期：2014 年 10 月 20 日

提案人：政府部部长米尔顿·恩里克斯·萨索

委员会：政府、司法和宪法事务委员会

巴拿马共和国巴拿马城 4 号 0815-01603 号邮箱

GOBIERNO DE LA REPUBLICA DE PANAMA

28 de octubre de 2014.

Nota N.o240-14 CG

巴拿马共和国政府
内阁委员会

2014 年 10 月 28 日

第 240-14 号公告

Honorable Presidente:

Tengo a bien infonnarle que el Consejo de Gabinete, en sesión celebrada el día 28 de octubre de 2014, autorizó al ministro de Gobiemo para que, en ejercicio de la iniciativa

legislativa que otorga el artículo 165 de la Constitución Política de la República, proponga

a la consideración de la Asamblea Nacional el proyecto de Ley:

Que organiza las notarías públicas y dicta otras disposiciones

尊敬的总统：

我很荣幸告知您，在 2014 年 10 月 28 日举行的会议中，内阁委员会授权政府部部长行使共和国宪法第 165 号法令赋予的立法提案权，向国民大会提交本法案以供商讨，法案标题为《关于公证处的组织运作以及其他规定》。

Para los efectos pertinentes, remitimos copia autenticada de la Resolución de Gabinete N.O 168 de 28 de octubre de 2014.

Honorable Diputado ADOLFO
ALVARO ALEMAN H.
Ministro de la Presidencia

Honorable Diputado
ADOLFO VALDERRAMA
Presidente de la Asamblea Nacional
E. S. D.
JC/la

No 27653-8
Gaceta Oficial Digital, miércoles 29 de octubre de 2014

ReI) ública de IJanamá
CONSEJO DE GAlllNETF:
RESOLUCIÓN DE GAIJINETE N.o 168
Oc 28 de octubre de 2014

Que autoriza al ministro de Gobierno para proponer, ante la Asamblea Nacional, el proyecto de Ley Que organiza las notarlas públicas y dicta otras disposiciones

EL CONSEJO DE GABINETE,
en uso de sus facultades constitucionales y legales,

CONSIDERANDO:

Que de acuerdo con el artículo 165 de la Constitución Política de la República, las leyes serán propuestos por los ministros de Estado, en virtud de autorización del Consejo de Gabinete;

Que en la sesión del Consejo de Gabinete del día 28 de octubre de 2014, el ministro de Gobierno presentó el proyecto de Ley Que organiza las notarías públicas y dicta otras disposiciones y solicitó la autorización de este Órgano Colegiado para que el referido proyecto sea propuesto ante la Asamblea Nacional,

RESUELVE:

Articulo I. Autorizar ni ministro de Gobierno para que proponga, ante la Asamblea Nacional, el proyecto de Ley Que organiza las notarías públicas y dicta otras disposiciones.

Artículo 2. Remitir copia autenticada de la presente Resolución de Gabinete al ministro de Gobierno, para que proceda conforme a la autorización concedida.

Artículo 3. Esta Resolución de Gabinete comenzará a regir a partir de su promulgación.

为此，随函附上2014年10月28日第168号内阁决议的认证副本。

顺致崇高敬意。

总统府部长阿尔瓦罗·阿莱曼（签名）
（巴拿马共和国总统府部长办公室印章）

议员
阿道夫·巴尔德莱玛先生
国民大会主席
E.S.D.
JC/la

第27653-B期
2014年10月29日星期三数字版官方公报

巴拿马共和国
内阁委员会
第168号内阁决议
2014年10月28日

兹授权政府部部长向国民大会提出标题为"关于公证处的组织运作以及其他规定"的法案。

内阁委员会
行使立宪与立法权

考虑到：

根据《共和国宪法》第165条，内阁成员经内阁委员会授权，提出各项立法提案；

在2014年10月28日的内阁委员会会议中，政府部部长提出了标题为《关于公证处的组织运作以及其他规定》的法案，并向内阁委员会申请向国民大会提出该法案，

决议如下：

第1条　授权政府部部长向国民大会提出标题为《关于公证处的组织运作以及其他规定》的法案。

第2条　向政府部部长开具本内阁决议的认证副本，部长经授权执行后续程序。

第3条　本内阁决议自颁布之日起生效。

FUNDAMENTO DE DERECHO: Artículo 165 de la Constitución Política de la República.

COMUNIQUESE Y CÚMPLASE.

Dada en la ciudad de Panamá, a los veintiocho (28) dias del mes de octubre del año dos mil catorce (2014) .

La Suscite bubdirectora General de Gaceta Oficial

CERTIFICA
QUE ESTE DOCUMENTO ES FIEL
COPIA DE SU ORIGINAL
LICDA YEXENIA RUIZ
Subdirectora General de Gaceta Oficial
PANAMA 29 DE 10 DE 2014
ETC.

EXPOSICION DE MOTIVOS

En virtud de la iniciativa legislativa conferida por la Constitución Política de la República de Panamá y debidamente facultado por la Resolución de Gabinete N°168 de 28 de octubre de 2014, presentamos a la Asamblea Nacional el proyecto de Ley "QUE ORGANIZA LAS NOTARÍAS PÚBLICAS Y SE DICTAN OTRAS DISPOSICIONES". El proyecto de Ley que se presenta a la consideración de la Honorable Asamblea de Diputados, responde a la impostergable necesidad de establecer pautas transparentes, eficientes y profesionales en el funcionamiento y calidad del sistema notarial y por ende de los servicios notariales que se ofrecen en la República de Panamá.

El Derecho Notarial en nuestro país, mantiene los criterios legislativos vigentes a finales del siglo XIX y principios del siglo XX, por lo que es imperante rescatar nuestro sistema notarial, posicionando a las Notarías en el siglo XXI de manera tal, que garantice al usuario y al Estado, el profesionalismo, la independencia y la imparcialidad del notario en el ejercicio de la certificación de la fe pública de la que está investido, incorporando las herramientas tecnológicas de nuestra época.

El presente proyecto de Ley, propicia una mejor tutela de la fe pública, estableciendo rigurosos parámetros de fiscalización y unificación de los servicios notariales, para que los mismos sean exactamente iguales en toda la República.

En adición con la entrada en vigencia de esta Ley, se inicia un proceso de formación de los futuros notarios, en la que el Estado se compromete a desarrollar la car-

法律依据：《共和国宪法》第 165 条

特此通报并责令执行。

二〇一四年十月二十八日于巴拿马城

签署人，官方公报副主编

兹证明：
本副本与原件完全一致
（签名）
叶赫尼亚·路易斯女士
官方公报副主编
2014 年 10 月 29 日于巴拿马城
（其他签名略）

立法动机说明

根据巴拿马共和国宪法赋予的立法提案权，经 2014 年 10 月 28 日第 168 号内阁决议授权，我们向国民大会提出了标题为《关于公证处的组织运作以及其他规定》的法案。该法案已提交至议会讨论并审议。公证制度的高效运行及巴拿马共和国所提供的公证服务需要建立透明、有效和专业的准则，而该法案的提出与这一需要相吻合。

巴拿马公证法的立法标准从 19 世纪末 20 世纪初一直沿用至今，因此，为保证群众和政府能够得到公证员专业、独立和公平的公证服务以及融入目前的技术手段，改善巴拿马公证制度、建立 21 世纪新型公证处成为一项刻不容缓的任务。

本法案旨在为公证服务建立严格的监督制度和统一的规则，增强公证的可信度，使全国的公证服务得到统一。

此外，在该法律生效后，将着手开展一系列的公证员培训活动。政府承诺与各著名公立、私立高校合作，设立公证专业学科，在未来，公证法的相关培训

rera notarial en conjunto con las universidades públicas y privadas reconocidas, estableciendo hacia el futuro la formación en Derecho Notarial como requisito obligatorio para poder ostentar el cargo público de notario; así mismo se tendrá el período de un año, luego de establecida la carrera en una universidad pública o privada reconocida, para obtener el título y de esta manera, poder seguir ejerciendo como tal.

Actualmente no se mantiene para las Notarías Públicas un sistema de fiscalización real sobre los ingresos que generan, ni sobre los documentos que producen, por lo tanto, a través del presente proyecto de Ley, se crea un sistema de automatización y almacenamiento de todos los instrumentos protocolares, escrituras y archivos públicos y privados, así como la contabilidad de los ingresos y egresos que se generen en las Notarías. Se establece además, de obligatorio cumplimiento, la implementación de estos sistemas para ambos tipos de Notarías previstos en este proyecto de Ley.

Para esto, el Estado contará con la Dirección Nacional de Notarías, entidad adscrita al Ministerio de Gobierno, cuya misión es la fiscalización de la función notarial de acuerdo a las facultades y competencias establecidas en el presente proyecto de Ley y normas reglamentarias. Esta Dirección estará facultada para diseñar el manual de procedimiento para la elaboración de los documentos notariales y presentarlo para su aprobación al ministro de Gobierno, a fin que sea elevado a Decreto Ejecutivo. Este Manual de Procedimiento es necesario para fundamentar prácticas comunes y diarias que los notarios llevan a cabo, sin distanciarse de su misión de otorgar fe pública, para que esta misión se desarrolle con mayor seguridad y el ciudadano pueda confiar plenamente en los servicios notariales; además para formalizar y uniformar los procedimientos de escrituración, reduciendo así, los defectos en los mismos y agilizando los procesos de inscripción en el Registro Público.

Estos nuevos sistemas de fiscalización, aunados al interés del Estado de colaborar en la erradicación del blanqueo de capitales y otros delitos financieros, convertirán a las Notarías en agentes reportadores de operaciones sospechosas, de acuerdo a lo que dispongan las leyes y reglamentos respectivos, y de esta manera coadyuvarían en la misión del Estado de hacerle frente a los nuevos retos internacionales en la prevención del blanqueo de capitales, evasión fiscal, financiamiento de terrorismo, contrabando, entre otros.

经历将成为公证员入职的必备条件。公立或私立高校的公证专业学生将需一年时间取得学位并继续从事该职业。

目前，对于公证处的收入及开具的文书尚未建立实际的监督制度，因此，通过此法案，建立一套自动化和保存系统，内容包括所有协议文书、文件、公共及私人档案、公证处收支状况等。除此之外，还要强制实施本法案中涉及的两类公证制度。

为此，政府将设立国家公证总局。该局为政府部的注册机构，其任务是根据本法案规定的职权及法规对公证工作进行监督。经授权，该局将负责设计公证文件撰写程序手册，并提交政府部部长以被批准为行政令。为使公证员巩固常规的工作、不背离工作宗旨、更加安全地完成工作任务以及公民能够完全信任公证服务，必须制作该程序手册。此外还能统一文书撰写格式，从而减少文书撰写过程中的错误，为在公共登记处登记提供便利。

这些新的监督制度与国家根除洗钱行为及其他金融犯罪的目的相一致，借助法律及相关规定，将会减少公证处的嫌疑操作，帮助国家应对新的国际挑战，预防洗钱、逃税、资助恐怖主义、走私等行为。

Con el fin de poder utilizar en obras sociales y demás proyectos que beneficien a nuestro país a través del Presupuesto General del Estado, las Notarías Públicas, estarán obligadas a pagar el 30% sobre sus ingresos brutos al Tesoro Nacional. Además de esto, los notarios y su personal tributarán mediante su declaración de renta personal en el nivel que les corresponda.

Por otra parte y en virtud del creciente interés de garantizar la seguridad jurídica de los usuarios, para mayor efectividad en la prestación de los servicios notariales en las entidades del sector público, se crean las Notarías Certificadas, pero limitando sus actividades notariales a las escrituras públicas relacionadas con el funcionamiento de la entidad y prohibiéndose terminantemente brindar el servicio notarial a terceros fuera de este parámetro. Todos los ingresos recaudados por este tipo de Notarías entrarán íntegramente al Tesoro Nacional.

En el presente proyecto de Ley se asimila a la categoría de Notarías Certificadas a las Notarías Especiales existentes en entidades públicas, que fueron creadas por leyes anteriores. Así mismo, se incorporarán al régimen de Notarías Públicas, las Notarías Especiales creadas por Ley para el Municipio de San Miguelito y el corregimiento de Cristóbal en Colón. Por razón de la creación de la décima provincia, la Notaría Sexta del Circuito de Panamá, con sede en La Chorrera, pasará a formar parte del Circuito Notarial de la nueva provincia.

Se retoma a la práctica de la utilización del papel notarial exclusivamente impreso por el Estado, el cual contará con numeración corrida e irrepetible, iniciando esta con el número de la provincia en donde se encuentre la Notaría y que contará con las medidas de seguridad establecidas por el Ministerio de Gobierno, mediante Decreto Ejecutivo. Este será exclusivamente vendido a las Notarías, pero se permitirá el cobro de su costo al usuario. Este papel será vendido exclusivamente por el Banco Nacional de Panamá a las Notarías. De igual manera se regulan los sellos notariales estableciendo un único sello notarial que será entregado por el Ministerio de Gobierno y contará con numeración corrida iniciando con el número de provincia donde ejercerá sus funciones el notario y contará con las medidas de seguridad establecidas mediante Decreto Ejecutivo, por el Ministerio de Gobierno.

Ante la falta de uniformidad en el cobro de los servicios notariales, en el presente proyecto de Ley, se establece que será responsabilidad del Ministerio de Gobierno, a través del reglamento que se dicte mediante Decreto

为了能够运用社会工程及其他能够通过国家总预算惠及巴拿马的项目，各公证办事处必须将其毛收入的30%上缴国库。除此之外，公证员及其工作人员将通过申报各自收入的方式进行纳税。

随着保证当事人对保障司法确定性的要求和提高在公共部门实体中公证服务的效率的需求不断增多，成立认证公证处，但将其公证业务限于与实体运作相关的公开文书，并坚决禁止如将公证业务转交给第三方处理等违背此原则的行为。所有此项公证业务产生的收入将全部上缴国库。

在此法案中，公共机构中现有的特别公证处也被纳入认证公证处中，特别公证处是基于前期各项法律而成立的。同样的，基于圣米格里多市和科隆省克里斯托弗市法律而成立的特别公证处将加入公证制度中。由于设立了第十个省，总部位于拉乔雷拉的巴拿马第六公证处将为加入新成立省的公证处中。

要求公证处恢复使用国家专门印刷的公证专用纸的做法，公证专用纸带有连续的、不重复的编号，以公证处所在省份的编号开始，并由政府部通过行政令提供安全措施。公证专用纸应当专供公证处使用，公证处可向当事人收取公证专用纸费用。该公证专用纸仅由巴拿马国家银行（央行）面向公证机构出售。同样规定使用政府部提供的专门公证章，并由政府部通过行政令提供安全措施。

由于公证服务没有统一的收费标准，因此，本法案中规定政府部应通过颁布行政令来出台相应法规，确定公证员的薪资以及收费标准。法案还规定，对于收取规定以外费用的公证员，应予撤职。

Ejecutivo, fijar los honorarios o tarifas que cobren los notarios y se considerará causa de destitución del cargo la aplicación de otras tarifas.

Con base en las consideraciones expuestas, solicitamos a los Honorables Diputados otorgarle el voto favorable a este proyecto de Ley por ser de interés para el desarrollo económico y social de la Nación Panameña.

PROYECTO DE LEY No. _____
QUE ORGANIZA LAS NOTARiAS PÚBLICAS Y DICTA OTRAS DISPOSICIONES

TÍTULO 1
De las Notarías, de las Notarías Públicas, De las Notarías Certificadas, del personal de las, Notarías Públicas

CAPÍTULO 1　De las Notarías

Artículo 1. La fe pública es la garantía otorgada por el Estado, en el sentido de que los hechos que interesan al derecho son verdaderos y auténticos.

Artículo 2. La Notaría es el despacho público en donde se reciben, extienden y autorizan declaraciones, actos y contratos a los cuales las personas naturales o jurídicas deban o quieran dar autenticidad y constancia pública conforme a la Ley.

Artículo 3. Existirán en la República de Panamá dos tipos de Notarías:

1. Notarías Públicas.
2. Notarías Certificadas.

La referencia en la presente Ley al término notario y notarías, sin calificación, comprende a ambas clases de notarios y notarías.

Artículo 4. Se crean las Notarías Públicas, las cuales estarán a cargo de un servidor público denominado notario público sobre quien el Estado delega la potestad de ser garante y depositario de la fe pública y que presta servicios a todos los interesados en su respectivo Circuito Notarial. Este será de libre nombramiento y remoción del Organo Ejecutivo, a través del presidente de la República en conjunto con el ministro de Gobierno. Su período de nombramiento no podrá exceder el período del mandato del presidente que lo nombró.

Artículo 5. Se crean las Notarías Certificadas, las cuales funcionarán dentro de las entidades del sector pú-

鉴于上述情况，我们请求尊敬的各位议员投票赞成此法案，该法案符合巴拿马社会经济发展的利益。

第　号法案
关于公证处的组织运作以及颁布其他规定

第一篇
公证处、普通公证处、认证公证处、公证处人员

第一章　公证处

第1条　公证是国家赋予的保障，是对有法律意义的事实的真实性和可信性予以证明。

第2条　公证处作为公共办事机构，负责对自然人或法人的声明、文书及合同进行收集、记录和核证，以便这些声明、文书及合同的真实性、合法性得到法律认可。

第3条　巴拿马共和国目前有两种公证处：

1. 普通公证处；
2. 认证公证处；

本法中提及的公证员和公证处包括这两个类别，没有区分。

第4条　设立普通公证处后，由被称为普通公证员的公职人员负责，公证员由国家委任，国家授权其在对应的公证辖区内为当事人提供服务。行政机关通过共和国总统和政府部部长对公证员自由任免。公证员的任职期限不得超出对其实施任命的总统的任职期限。

第5条　认证公证处是设立在公共部门实体中的承担公证职能的单位。认证公证处的运作形式为，国

blico. En el caso de las Notarías Certificadas, el Estado delega la potestad de ser garante y depositario de la fe pública, a un miembro de la entidad que ostente un alto nivel directivo para que ejerza en su nombre y representación el cargo de notario certificado, exclusivamente para las escrituras públicas que se tramitan dentro de dicha entidad. Esta autorización podrá ser anulada unilateralmente por el Ministerio de Gobierno cuando este así lo considere.

Artículo 6. La función notarial es de orden e interés público. Corresponde a la Ley establecer las garantías que propicien la profesionalidad, independencia e imparcialidad del notario en el ejercicio de sus funciones.

Artículo 7. El territorio de la República se demarcará en zonas denominadas Circuitos Notariales. En un mismo Circuito Notarial podrá existir más de una Notaría Pública o Certificada y coincidirán con los distritos provinciales y comarcales. Los Circuitos Notariales serán definidos por el Ministerio de Gobierno, mediante Decreto Ejecutivo.

Artículo 8. El número de Notarías para cada Circuito Notarial la determinará el Ministerio de Gobierno, mediante Decreto Ejecutivo, atendiendo la división político-administrativa del país en función de la población, a la extensión geográfica según se determine o a los niveles de actividad notarial. Estos niveles serán definidos por el Ministerio de Gobierno, mediante Decreto Ejecutivo.

Artículo 9. Si en una misma jurisdicción existen dos o más Notarías Públicas o Certificadas, se las distinguirá mediante números ordinales. En el caso de las Notarías Certificadas se les agregará además la palabra "Certificada".

Artículo 10. En un mismo Circuito Notarial no podrán ser nombrados como notario ni como suplente de notario personas emparentadas entre sí dentro del cuarto grado de consanguinidad o segundo de afinidad, ya sea en línea recta ascendente o descendente, colaterales y por adopción; así como los relacionados entre sí por padrinazgo o compadrazgo.

Artículo 11. Los notarios, en el caso de las Notarías Públicas y las Notarías Certificadas, deberán hacer entrega de una fianza al Ministerio de Gobierno, a través de la Dirección Nacional de Notarías, al inicio de su período. El monto de esta fianza será determinado por el Ministerio de Gobierno, mediante Decreto Ejecutivo, de conformidad con los negocios que se tramitan en el Circuito Notarial de la Notaría. En un mismo Circuito Notarial deberá ser la misma cifra para todos los notarios públicos y Notarías Certificadas.

Estas fianzas tendrán vigencia de un año, deben ser

家委任该实体中的一名高级别官员承担公证职能，以其名义代为行使公证职责，专门负责该实体内部处理的公共文书。该公证处的经营许可，可在政府部部长认为情况适当时由其单方面吊销。

第6条 公证职能符合公众要求和利益。依法建立保障机制，确保公证员能够专业、独立、公正地履行公证职能。

第7条 共和国领土划分为若干公证辖区。在同一公证辖区内可能有不止一个普通公证处或认证公证处，负责各自省、县、市或区的公证事务。公证辖区由政府部通过颁布行政令确定。

第8条 每个公证辖区内的公证处数量，应由政府部通过颁布行政令确定，参考每行行政区域的人口数量、面积或公证业务水平而定。公证业务水平由政府部通过颁布行政令确定。

第9条 如果在同一公证辖区内有两个或两个以上普通公证处或认证公证处，将按顺序编号进行区分。如果是认证公证处就在编号上添加"已认证"字样。

第10条 在同一公证辖区内，以下人员不得担任公证员或候补公证员：与现任的公证员或候补公证员有直系、旁系及收养的四代以内血亲或两代以内近亲，以及宗教庇护关系或干亲关系的人员。

第11条 普通公证处和认证公证处的公证员，应当在任期之初通过国家公证总局向政府部缴纳押金。押金金额由政府部通过颁布行政令并根据公证处所辖区域的业务情况而确定。在同一公证辖区内所有公证员和认证公证处缴纳的押金额一致。

此押金有效期为一年，每十二个月续展一次，在

renovadas cada doce meses y cubrirán cualquier perjuicio que, en el ejercicio de sus funciones, causen los notarios durante la vigencia de las mismas así como para las multas disciplinarias que imponga el Ministerio de Gobierno en igual período.

Será causal de destitución inmediata para el notario público o la cancelación de la autorización para operar de la Notaría Certificada la no renovación oportuna de la fianza.

Artículo 12. Plasta tanto entre en funciones la Dirección Nacional de Notarías, corresponderá al Ministerio de Gobierno, en conjunto con las Gobernaciones de cada provincia y comarca de la República de Panamá, la supervisión de las Notarías en todo el territorio de la República de Panamá.

Esta supervisión se llevará a cabo mediante visitas que tendrán como objetivo verificar la localización, presentación y estado de los recintos notariales y sus condiciones de comodidad para el público, la presentación personal del notario y su atención a los usuarios del servicio notarial, el examen de la conducta de los notarios y el cumplimiento de su desempeño y la comprobación del orden, actualización, exactitud y presentación de los libros y archivos notariales.

CAPÍTULO II De las Notarías Públicas

Artículo 13. La Notaría Pública es el despacho público donde se reciben, extienden y autorizan declaraciones, actos y contratos a los cuales las personas naturales o jurídicas deban o quieran dar autenticidad y constancia pública conforme a la Ley.

Artículo 14. La Notaría Pública estará a cargo de un servidor público denominado notario público sobre quien el Estado delega la potestad de ser garante y depositario de la fe pública y que presta servicios a todos los interesados en su respectivo Circuito Notarial. Este será de libre nombramiento y remoción del Órgano Ejecutivo. Su período de nombramiento no podrá exceder el período del mandato del presidente de la República que lo nombró.

Artículo 15. El notario público deberá reunir los mismos requisitos requeridos para ser magistrado del Tribunal Superior de Distrito Judicial. Además de estos requisitos, también deberá cumplir con los establecidos en el Título III Capítulo III de la presente Ley.

Artículo 16. La Notaría Pública atenderá de lunes a viernes dentro de una jornada laboral diaria ininterrumpida

押金有效期内，如果公证员在履职过程中因过失造成任何损失，或者因违纪行为导致政府部实施纪律处罚，将从押金中执行赔偿或者执行罚款。

如不及时续展押金，将会立即撤销公证员职务，或者吊销认证公证处的经营许可。

第12条　在国家公证总局投入运作之前，巴拿马共和国境内各公证处的工作情况，应当由政府部与巴拿马共和国各省、县政府负责监管。

监管工作将通过巡查完成，巡查的目的是核实公证处的位置、工作情况和工作状态、服务条件、公证员个人工作情况及接待和服务当事人的情况，检查公证员行为和履职情况，以及公证文书和档案的归卷立档、更新、准确率和提交的落实情况。

第二章　普通公证处

第13条　普通公证处作为公共办事机构，负责对自然人或法人的声明、文书及合同进行记录和核证，以便这些声明、文书及合同的真实性、合法性得到法律认可。

第14条　普通公证处由被称为普通公证员的公职人员负责，公证员由国家委任，国家授权其在对应的公证辖区内为当事人提供服务。执行机构自由任命和解除普通公证员职务。公证员的任职期限不得超出对其实施任命的总统的任职期限。

第15条　普通公证员应当具备与司法区高等法院法官同等的任职条件。此外，普通公证员也应当遵守本法第三篇第三章中的规定。

第16条　公证处工作时间为周一至周五，每天连续工作七小时。在非工作时段或者非工作日，出现

de siete horas. El notario podrá actuar fuera de la Notaría Pública en jornadas y días no laborables en circunstancias previstas en la reglamentación de la presente Ley.

Cuando un notario público ejerza sus funciones en días y horas no laborables, sus servicios serán tasados, de acuerdo a la tarifa reglamentaria que podrá establecer recargos.

Artículo 17. Es de obligatorio cumplimiento para las Notarías Públicas, la implementación del sistema de automatización y almacenamiento de datos desarrollado y reglamentado por el Ministerio de Gobierno, mediante Decreto Ejecutivo, así como el sistema automatizado para el registro contable de los ingresos y egresos que se generan en la Notaría Pública, balances quincenales y demás informes financieros, que serán reglamentados por el Ministerio de Gobierno, mediante Decreto Ejecutivo.

Estos sistemas serán de obligatorio cumplimiento para el funcionamiento de las Notarías Públicas.

Artículo 18. Las Notarías Públicas deberán llevar los libros requeridos sobre todas las actuaciones que sean autorizadas y expedidas en la Notaría Pública, debidamente foliados y empastados. Estos libros serán determinados y reglamentados por el Ministerio de Gobierno, mediante Decreto Ejecutivo.

Artículo 19. Las Notarías Públicas deberán enviar a los Archivos Nacionales, el Protocolo Notarial debidamente foliado y empastado cada año, de acuerdo al reglamento que establezca el Ministerio de Gobierno, mediante Decreto Ejecutivo.

Artículo 20. Es obligatorio para las Notarías Públicas tributar mensualmente sobre sus ingresos brutos de la siguiente manera:

a. El treinta por ciento (30%) a favor del Tesoro Nacional y,

b. El setenta por ciento (70%) para el Notario Público, del cual deberá sufragar los gastos operacionales y salarios de su personal y los impuestos que se generen de acuerdo a los ingresos recabados, según lo establecido en nuestro Código Fiscal.

CAPÍTULO III De las Notarías Certificadas

Artículo 21. Se crean las Notarías Certificadas, las cuales funcionarán dentro de una persona jurídica del sector público, sobre quien el Estado delega la potestad de ser garante y depositario de la fe pública. Estas solo prestarán el servicio notarial referente a las escrituras públicas y

本法实施条例中规定情形的，公证员也可以办理公证业务。

普通公证员在非工作日或非工作时段行使职权的，其公证服务将根据相关标准收取费用。

第 17 条　普通公证处必须采用数据自动化和存储系统，这些系统是由政府部通过颁布行政令设立并予以规范的；同时，还应采用公证处收支记录、半月账目情况及其他由政府部通过颁布行政令规定的金融报告自动化系统。

普通公证处必须采用这些系统开展日常工作。

第 18 条　公证处应当持有有关被授权在公证处处理的所有业务的必备记录本，并且要保存完好、字迹清晰。这些记录本由政府部通过颁布行政令进行规范。

第 19 条　根据政府部行政令的规定，公证处每年应当向国家档案局提交保存完好、字迹清晰的公证文书。

第 20 条　公证处每月必须以下列方式支配其毛收入：

a）将毛收入的 30% 上缴国家财政；

b）将毛收入的 70% 支付给普通公证员，根据巴拿马税法，普通公证员将负责支付业务支出、工作人员工资及所得税。

第三章　认证公证处

第 21 条　认证公证处是设立在公共部门实体中的承担公证职能的单位，国家授权其作为保证人和公证员负责公共部门内法人的公证业务。认证公证处仅为公开文件及专门对认证公证处所属实体的业务提供服务。

exclusivamente para las actividades de la entidad a la cual está adscrita la Notaría Certificada que así lo requieran.

Artículo 22. La Notaría Certificada estará a cargo de un dignatario que ostente un alto nivel directivo dentro de la persona jurídica del sector público que solicite la autorización para Notaría Certificada, quien se denominará notario certificado.

Artículo 23. El notario certificado deberá cumplir con los mismos requisitos exigidos para ser notario público y con los demás requisitos establecidos por esta Ley, y sus reglamentos, en especial aquellos contenidos en el Título III Capítulo III de la presente Ley.

Queda prohibida, so pena de la pérdida de la condición de Notaría Certificada, la prestación del servicio notarial para casos particulares que no estén relacionados con las actividades de la entidad a la cual está adscrita la Notaría Certificada.

Artículo 24. El número de Notarías Certificadas para cada Circuito Notarial la determinará el Ministerio de Gobierno, mediante Decreto Ejecutivo.

Artículo 25. Las Notarías Certificadas deberán solicitar autorización al Ministerio de Gobierno para su funcionamiento. Esta autorización podrá ser revocada de manera unilateral por parte del Estado. Los requisitos para obtener esta autorización serán definidos por el Ministerio de Gobierno, mediante Decreto Ejecutivo.

Artículo 26. Si en una misma jurisdicción existieran dos o más Notarías Certificadas se les distinguirá mediante números ordinales y agregando la palabra "Certificada".

Artículo 27. Los servicios notariales que presten las Notarías Certificadas se limitarán a la confección de escrituras públicas. No podrán dar fe y certificar otros documentos o actos distintos a los autorizados por la presente Ley.

Queda prohibida la prestación del servicio notarial para casos particulares que no estén relacionados con la entidad a la cual está adscrita la Notaría Certificada. Será nula cualquier actuación de la Notaría Certificada que no guarde relación o esté vinculada con las actuaciones propias de la entidad.

Artículo 28. Los honorarios, tasas y otros gravámenes que se produzcan por la prestación de servicios notariales en las Notarías Certificadas serán cobrados al usuario y depositados íntegramente en la cuenta del Tesoro Nacional. Estos depósitos se realizarán mensualmente, dentro de los primeros diez días hábiles del siguiente mes.

Artículo 29. Las Notarías Certificadas deberán llevar los libros requeridos sobre todas sus actuaciones, debid-

第22条 认证公证处负责处理公共部门中拥有高管的法人实体的公证业务，该高管申请授权进行认证公证并成为认证公证员。

第23条 认证公证员应当具备普通公证员同等条件以及本法规定的其他条件，尤其是本法第三篇第三章的规定。

为避免认证公证处服务条件恶化，禁止为与认证公证处所属实体的活动不相关的特殊案件提供服务。

第24条 每个公证辖区的认证公证处数量由政府部通过颁布行政令确定。

第25条 认证公证处应当向政府部申请授权运作。政府可单方面撤销此授权。取得该授权的条件由政府部通过颁布行政令而定。

第26条 如果在同一辖区内有两个或两个以上认证公证处，将通过按顺序编号和添加"已认证"字样进行区分。

第27条 认证公证处提供的公证服务范围仅限于公开文书的制作。不得为本法授权文书之外的其他文件或证书给予公证和证明。

禁止为与认证公证处所属实体的活动不相关的特殊案件提供服务。与实体自身活动无关联或无联系的认证公证处的任何公证行为均为无效。

第28条 认证公证处提供公证服务所需的酬劳、税款及其他开支都将由当事人承担，且全部存至国家财政账户中。每月存款一次，在下个月前十个自然日内进行。

第29条 认证公证处应当持有所有业务的必备记录本，并且要保存完好、字迹清晰。这些记录本由

amente foliados y empastados. Estos libros serán determinados y reglamentados por el Ministerio de Gobierno, mediante Decreto Ejecutivo.

Artículo 30. Las Notarías Certificadas deberán enviar a los Archivos Nacionales el Protocolo Notarial debidamente foliado y empastado cada año, de acuerdo al reglamento que establezca el Ministerio de Gobierno, mediante Decreto Ejecutivo.

Artículo 31. Es de obligatorio cumplimiento para las Notarías Certificadas la implementación del sistema de automatización y almacenamiento de datos desarrollado y reglamentado por el Ministerio de Gobierno, mediante Decreto Ejecutivo, así como el sistema automatizado para el registro contable de los ingresos y egresos que se generan en la Notaría Certificada, balances quincenales y demás informes financieros.

Estos sistemas serán obligatorios para el funcionamiento de las Notarías Certificadas.

CAPÍTULO IV Del personal de las Notarías Públicas y sus funciones

Articulo 32. El notario público será el responsable jerárquico de la Notaría Pública y del cumplimiento de las obligaciones de sus subalternos. Contará con el siguiente personal dependiendo de la densidad de población que deba atenderse en el Circuito Notarial:

1. un abogado,
2. un secretario,
3. un tesorero con su suplente,
4. un oficial,
5. escribientes cuyo número se determinará según el volumen de documentos que se elaboren, y
6. demás personal subalterno que se estime necesario.

El personal de la Notaría Pública será designado y removido discrecionalmente por el notario público.

El salario del personal de la Notaría Pública será fijado y pagado directamente por el notario público, así como los gastos operacionales en los que se incurra.

Con excepción del notario público, el personal de la Notaría Pública estará regulado bajo las normas laborales establecidas en el Código de Trabajo, por lo que no serán considerados servidores públicos.

Artículo 33. Son funciones del abogado las siguientes:

1. Asistir al notario público en el ejercicio de sus funciones.

政府部通过颁布行政令进行规范。

第30条 根据政府部行政令的规定，认证公证处每年应当向国家档案局提交保存完好、字迹清晰的公证文书。

第31条 认证公证处必须运用数据自动化和存储系统，这些系统是由政府部通过颁布行政令设立并予以规范的；同时，还应运用公证处收支记录、半月账目情况及其他由政府部通过颁布行政令规定的金融报告自动化系统。

认证公证处必须运用这些系统开展日常工作。

第四章 公证处的人事安排及其职能

第32条 普通公证员是公证处的负责人，并对其下属履行的义务负责。根据每个公证辖区接待人口密度配置以下人员：

1. 一名律师；
2. 一名秘书；
3. 一名出纳及其接替者；
4. 一名职员；
5. 抄写员若干，其数量根据文书数量而定；以及
6. 其他必要的职能人员。

公证处的工作人员由普通公证员自由任免。

公证处工作人员薪资固定，由普通公证员直接支付，普通公证员还要支付其他所需的业务费用。

除了普通公证员，公证处工作人员不属于公务员，需遵循劳动法的劳动规定。

第33条 以下是律师的职能：

1. 帮助普通公证员履行职能。

2. Coadyuvar en la revisión de todos los instrumentos públicos que se generen en la Notaría Pública, para garantizar que los mismos contengan la formalidad exigida por la Ley.

3. Asistir al notario público en las reuniones del Colegio de Notarios Públicos.

4. Acompañar al notario público en las diligencias que se realicen en días y horas no laborables o fuera de las oficinas donde tiene su sede la Notaría Pública.

5. Cualquiera otra función establecida en las disposiciones legales aplicables y sus reglamentos o que le encomiende el notario público dentro de su función.

Para ser abogado de una Notaría Pública se debe contar con los mismos requisitos exigidos al notario público y con los demás requisitos establecidos por esta Ley, y sus reglamentos, en especial aquellos contenidos en el Título OI Capítulo III de la presente Ley.

Artículo 34. Serán funciones del secretario las siguientes:

1. Recibir y clasificar la documentación que ingrese a la Notaría Pública, sea de manera física o por los medios tecnológicos aprobados por la presente Ley, así como por las disposiciones legales y reglamentarias aplicables.

2. Distribuir o asignar el trabajo entre el personal de la Notaría Pública.

3. Extender copias y certificaciones que se requieran de la Notaría Pública, previa autorización del notario público.

4. Expedir informes y copias que requieran las autoridades del Órgano Judicial, Ministerio Público, Registro Público y las autoridades públicas competentes, previa autorización del notario público.

5. Llevar los libros requeridos sobre todas las actuaciones que sean autorizadas o expedidas en la Notaría Pública, debidamente foliados y empastados, de acuerdo al reglamento que establezca el Ministerio de Gobierno, mediante Decreto Ejecutivo.

6. Remitir los documentos e instrumentos notariales que deban ser procesados y almacenados de acuerdo al sistema de automatización de documentos ordenado en la presente Ley.

7. Enviar a los Archivos Nacionales el Protocolo Notarial, debidamente foliado y empastado cada año.

8. Llevar el libro de registro de testamentos, actas de protestos y transferencia de bienes muebles registrables.

9. Mantener el orden de los archivos de la Notaría Pública, asegurar la actualización del sistema de automa-

2. 帮助审查所有公证处制作的公共文书，以保证文书符合法律要求的格式。

3. 陪同普通公证员出席的公证员协会的会议。

4. 陪同普通公证员在非工作时间或办公总部以外处理业务。

5. 任何其他适用法律法规规定的职能或任何其他普通公证员在职权范围内委托其执行的工作。

成为公证处的律师需要具备普通公证员同等条件及本法及其实施细则规定的其他条件，尤其是本法第三篇第三章的内容。

第34条　以下是秘书的职能：

1. 接收交给公证处的文件并对其进行分类，使用简单方法或本法及其他适用法律法规许可的高科技手段归类皆可。

2. 为公证处工作人员分配工作任务。

3. 经普通公证员提前授权，开具所需的公证处证明及副本。

4. 经普通公证员提前授权，签发司法部门、公共部、公共登记处及有权限的公共当局需要的报告及副本。

5. 根据政府部行政令的规定，携带在公证处授权处理的所有活动的必备记录本，并且要保存完好、字迹清晰。

6. 提交公证文件和公证书，以便对此进行本法规定的文件自动化处理并储存。

7. 每年向国家档案局提交保存完好、字迹清晰的公证文书。

8. 携带遗嘱、抗议书及登记动产转移记录本。

9. 维持公证处档案顺序，保证依本法设立的数据自动化系统的更新升级并保存数据。

tización de datos ordenado en la presente Ley y custodiar los mismos.

10. Cualquiera otra función establecida en las disposiciones legales aplicables y sus reglamentos o que le encomiende el notario público.

Para ser secretario de una Notaría Pública se debe contar con los mismos requisitos exigidos al notario público y con los demás requisitos establecidos por esta Ley, y sus reglamentos, en especial aquellos dimanantes del Título III Capítulo III de la presente Ley.

Artículo 35. Serán funciones del tesorero:

1. Recibir el pago que se realice en efectivo o a crédito, extender el recibo correspondiente y registrar el mismo de acuerdo a los parámetros establecidos por el sistema de automatización contable, ordenado en la presente Ley y sus reglamentos.

2. Hacer constar al margen del documento cuando se trate de actos exonerados por disposición legal.

3. Llevar al día la contabilidad; hacer el balance general los días quince y último de cada mes, asegurándose que el mismo sea registrado inmediatamente en el sistema de automatización contable, ordenado en la presente Ley y sus reglamentos. El Ministerio de Gobierno podrá acceder presencial o remotamente a la información contable así como a los balances en cualquier momento que así lo estime conveniente.

4. Abrir una cuenta corriente en el Banco Nacional de Panamá, a nombre de la respectiva Notaría Pública, donde deberá depositar diariamente todos los ingresos percibidos.

5. Depositar mensualmente los impuestos generados sobre los ingresos brutos de la Notaría Pública a la cuenta del Tesoro Nacional, de acuerdo a lo establecido en el Título I Capítulo II de la presente Ley.

6. Controlar, liquidar y recaudar los derechos causados por concepto de traslado.

7. Cualquiera otra función establecida en las disposiciones legales aplicables y sus reglamentos o que le encomiende el notario público dentro de sus funciones.

Para ser tesorero de una Notaría Pública se debe ser contador público autorizado.

El tesorero es un funcionario de manejo y, por tanto, deberá cumplir con los requisitos exigibles a los mismos, por las disposiciones legales y reglamentarias aplicables.

Artículo 36. Para ser Oficial de una Notaría Pública se requiere:

1. Ser panameño.

2. Ser idóneo para ejercer la abogacía.

10. 任何其他适用法律法规规定的职能或任何其他普通公证员委托其执行的工作。

成为公证处的秘书需要具备普通公证员同等条件及本法规定的其他条件，尤其是本法第三篇第三章的内容。

第35条 以下是出纳的职能：

1. 收取现金付款或信用卡付款，开具收据，并根据本法及其实施细则所设立的会计自动化系统的规则登记收据。

2. 在文件边缘注明被法令撤销的文件。

3. 每日统计账目，每月中及月末两天盘点总账目，保证账目状况登记在本法规定设立的会计自动化系统中。政府部可根据需要随时在现场或远程获得会计信息及账目情况。

4. 在巴拿马国家银行以相应公证处的名称开设1个活期账户，公证处每日要将当天全部收入存入该账户中。

5. 根据本法第一篇第二章的规定，每月缴纳公证处毛收入的所得税，支付到国家财政的账户中。

6. 管控、清算和收取人员调动产生的费用。

7. 任何其他适用法律法规规定的职能或任何其他普通公证员在职权范围内委托其执行的工作。

成为公证处的出纳必须由被授权的执业会计担任。

出纳为管理人员，因此根据适用法令应当具备管理人员同等条件。

第36条 成为公证处职员所需条件：

1. 巴拿马籍。

2. 具备律师执业资质。

Artículo 37. Serán funciones del oficial las siguientes:

1. Reemplazar a los demás miembros del personal de la Notaría Pública a excepción del notario público y el tesorero en sus faltas temporales, mientras duren las mismas, o faltas absolutas, mientras se hace el nombramiento del titular y hasta la toma de posesión de este.

2. Asistir y sustituir al secretario en diligencias que se practiquen dentro y fuera de la Notaría Pública.

3. Cualquiera otra función establecida en las disposiciones legales aplicables y sus reglamentos o que le encomiende el notario público dentro de sus funciones.

TÍTULO II
Del papel y sellos notariales, de las tasas y tarifas y de los sistemas y procesos

CAPÍTULO I Del papel y sellos notariales

Artículo 38. Las Notarías utilizarán papel notarial que será de su uso exclusivo. Este será impreso por una imprenta estatal designada exclusivamente por el Ministerio de Gobierno.

Artículo 39. El papel notarial contará con las medidas de seguridad establecidas por el Ministerio de Gobierno y será de numeración corrida e irrepetible la cual tendrá como primer dígito el número correspondiente a la provincia en donde se encuentre la Notaría que lo utilice.

Artículo 40. El papel notarial será vendido exclusivamente por el Banco Nacional de Panamá a las Notarías. Este contará con las medidas de seguridad que se establezcan en la reglamentación de esta Ley, y su valor será establecido por el Ministerio de Gobierno, mediante Decreto Ejecutivo.

Artículo 41. Existirá un solo sello por Notaría que será entregado por el Ministerio de Gobierno a cada notario al inicio de su período y al concluirse el mismo será devuelto al Ministerio de Gobierno para su debida destrucción.

Cada sello tendrá una numeración corrida única que iniciará con el número de la provincia donde ejerce su cargo el notario y las medidas de seguridad que establezca el Ministerio de Gobierno, mediante Decreto Ejecutivo.

Artículo 42. Existirán sellos "de cotejo", "fiel copia de su original", "de autenticación" y los demás sellos que sean necesarios para el funcionamiento de la Notaría. Estos sellos serán definidos y reglamentados por el Ministerio de Gobierno, mediante Decreto Ejecutivo y serán

第 37 条　以下是职员的职能：

1. 在公证处除公证员和出纳外的其他工作人员暂时缺勤、长期缺勤或职位空缺以及在被提名为正式员工乃至上任期间顶替其工作。

2. 在公证处内外协助和顶替秘书工作。

3. 任何其他适用法律法规规定的职能或任何其他普通公证员在职权范围内委托其办理的职能。

第二篇
公证专用纸和公证章、收费和价目表、系统与程序

第一章　公证专用纸和公证章

第 38 条　公证处使用公证专用纸。该纸由政府部专门指派的国营印刷厂印刷。

第 39 条　政府部规定安全措施以保证公证专用纸的安全，公证专用纸使用连续、不重复的数字编号，以公证处所在省对应编号起头。

第 40 条　公证专用纸由巴拿马国家银行专售。该银行有本法规定的安全措施，其效力通过政府部颁布行政令来确定。

第 41 条　关于专用公证章的使用，政府部在每位公证员上任之初授予其专用公证章，公证员卸任后将专用公证章交还政府部销毁。

每个公证章都有唯一编号，以公证员任职和实行政府部行政令规定的安全措施的公证处所在省的编号起头。

第 42 条　公证章字样分别有"已核对""与原件一致"和"已验证"，以及其他公证工作中需要的刻章字样。刻章字样由政府部颁布行政令来规定，全国范围内所有公证处的公证章统一。

iguales para todas las Notarías en el territorio nacional.

Artículo 43. En caso de pérdida o alteración del sello, el notario deberá dar aviso en el primer día hábil siguiente al descubrimiento del hecho al Ministerio de Gobierno, mediante la Dirección Nacional de Notarías y, con el acuse de dicho aviso, levantará acta y presentará denuncia ante el Ministerio Público.

Dentro del mismo término deberá dar también aviso a los Archivo Nacionales, al Registro Público y al Colegio de Notarios.

Cumplido lo anterior, con los acuses respectivos tramitará ante la Dirección Nacional de Notarías la autorización para la reposición del sello notarial a su costa. El nuevo sello contendrá un signo especial que lo diferencie del anterior. La marca especial deberá estar visible en la impresión del sello.

Artículo 44. Si apareciere el antiguo sello, no podrá ser usado. El notario entregará personalmente y de inmediato dicho sello al Ministerio de Gobierno, mediante la Dirección Nacional de Notarías, para su destrucción. De ello se levantará acta por duplicado; una para el Ministerio de Gobierno, mediante la Dirección Nacional de Notarías y otra para el notario.

Artículo 45. En caso de deterioro o alteración del sello, el Ministerio de Gobierno, mediante la Dirección Nacional de Notarías, autorizará al notario para obtener uno nuevo.

En el supuesto del párrafo anterior, el notario deberá presentar y entregar el sello en uso. El Ministerio de Gobierno, mediante la Dirección Nacional de Notarías, otorgará el nuevo sello y se levantará acta por duplicado, en cuyo inicio se imprimirán los dos sellos y se hará constar que se inutilizó el antiguo, mismo que será destruido.

El nuevo sello contendrá un signo especial que lo diferencie del anterior y las medidas de seguridad que establezca el Ministerio de Gobierno, mediante Decreto Ejecutivo.

CAPÍTULO II De las tasas y tarifas

Artículo 46. La retribución por los servicios notariales estará a cargo de quienes requieran o soliciten dicho servicio. Los honorarios o tarifas que cobren los notarios serán las que de tiempo en tiempo fije el Ministerio de Gobierno, mediante Decreto Ejecutivo.

Artículo 47. Todos los notarios están obligados a cobrar por sus servicios según las tarifas que apruebe el

第43条 如果公证章丢失或被更改，公证员应当在发现该情况的第二天立即通过国家公证总局通知政府部，得到回复后向公共部提交证明并报案。

同时公证员也应通知国家档案局、公共登记处和注册公证员协会。

综上所述，公证员收到相应的通知后到国家公证总局自费申请挂失公证章。新章带有特殊标识以与旧章进行区分。特殊标识要印在公证章显眼的位置。

第44条 如果旧章被找到将不再被使用，公证员要立即将旧章通过国家公证总局亲自交给政府部予以销毁。需要提交一式两份的证明文件，一份交通过国家公证总局交给政府部，另一份由公证员保留。

第45条 如果公证章损坏或被更改，政府部将通过国家公证总局授予公证员一枚新章。

如遇上述情况，公证员应上交正在使用的公证章。政府部通过国家公证总局授予公证员一枚新章。需要提交一式两份的证明文件，文件开头盖上新旧两章，并注明旧章已经废弃并将被销毁。

新章带有特殊标识及政府部行政令规定的安全措施以与旧章进行区分。

第二章 收费与价目表

第46条 公证费用由要求或申请该服务的人承担。公证员薪资和收费标准由政府部通过颁布行政令灵活确定。

第47条 所有公证员都必须根据政府部通过颁布行政令批准的收费标准收取各辖区内相应的公证费

Ministerio de Gobierno, mediante Decreto Ejecutivo, para cada circunscripción notarial, y se considerará causa de destitución del cargo la aplicación de otras tarifas.

Artículo 48. El Estado, sus instituciones públicas y los municipios, están exentos del pago de derechos notariales. El trámite de las certificaciones para el Estado y los municipios se realizarán en el orden de llegada.

CAPÍTULO III De los sistemas y procesos

Artículo 49. Las Notarías estarán adscritas al Servicio de Verificación de Identidad (SVI), del Tribunal Electoral o al sistema de verificación vigente en su momento, utilizado por esta institución a fin de comprobar la veracidad de las identificaciones de los usuarios de los servicios.

Artículo 50. El Ministerio de Gobierno, en conjunto con la Autoridad para la Innovación Gubernamental o la entidad que en su momento realice sus funciones, creará un sistema de automatización y almacenamiento de todos los instrumentos protocolares, escrituras, archivos y documentos públicos y no públicos generados por la Notaría, de acuerdo a los niveles de acceso y seguridad del sistema.

Así mismo se creará un sistema automatizado para el registro contable de los ingresos y egresos que se generan en la Notaría, balances quincenales y demás informes financieros.

Estos sistemas serán debidamente reglamentados por el Ministerio de Gobierno, mediante Decreto Ejecutivo.

Artículo 51. Apoyados por el sistema de automatización, la tramitación de todos los procedimientos aplicables al manejo de la documentación generada y recibida por la Notaría, será de aplicación uniforme en todas las Notarías de la República de Panamá.

El diseño y aprobación de estos procedimientos se hará por el Ministerio de Gobierno, mediante Decreto Ejecutivo.

TÍTULO III
De los Notarios Públicos, de los Notarios Certificados, de la Can-era Notarial, de la Dirección, Nacional de Notarías y del Colegio de Notarios

CAPÍTULO I De los Notarios Públicos

Artículo 52. Los notarios públicos son servidores públicos de libre nombramiento y remoción por el presidente de la República, en conjunto con el ministro de Gobierno.

用，收取规定以外费用的行为将会导致被撤职。

第48条　中央政府及其公共机构与各市政府无需支付公证费用。中央政府同各市政府按照先来后到的原则办理证明。

第三章　系统与程序

第49条　公证处隶属于选举法院身份验证服务处（简称"SVI"）或者说隶属于目前通用的验证系统，选举法院运用该验证系统来确定服务对象身份的真实性。

第50条　政府部协同政府创新当局或运作实体建立一套储存和自动化系统，根据系统的安全性能和接受水平，适用于所有公证处出具的协议文书、档案和公开及非公开文件。

同样建立公证处收支、半月账目及其他金融报告的自动储存系统。

这些系统通过政府部颁布行政令建立。

第51条　自动化系统支持所有适用于公证处开具和接收文件的管理处理程序，该系统将在巴拿马共和国范围内所有公证处统一使用。

政府部将通过颁布行政令批准这些程序的设计和运用。

第三篇
普通公证处、认证公证处、公证专业、国家公证总局和注册公证员协会

第一章　普通公证处

第52条　普通公证员属于公务员，由共和国总统与政府部长对其自由任免。公证员的任职期限不得超出对其实施任命的总统的任职期限。

Su período de nombramiento no podrá exceder el del mandato presidencial.

Los funcionarios consulares fungirán como notarios públicos en aquellos casos que las Leyes y disposiciones que regulan el Servicio Exterior así lo determinen.

Artículo 53. Cada notario público tendrá un suplente que lo reemplazará en los casos de falta temporal o impedimento.

Si la falta fuere absoluta, el suplente ejercerá las funciones del notario público hasta la posesión del que se nombre en propiedad. El suplente o el reemplazo que se designe, ejercerá por el tiempo restante por el que ftie nombrado el titular del cargo.

En todos los casos se deberá solicitar a la Dirección Nacional de Notarías la autorización para el reemplazo e informe del periodo del mismo.

Artículo 54. Los notarios públicos y sus suplentes deberán reunir los mismos requisitos requeridos para ser magistrados de Tribunal Superior de Distrito Judicial y los contenidos en este capítulo.

Artículo 55. No podrán ser designados como notarios públicos:

1. Quienes se encuentren suspendidos en el ejercicio de la profesión de abogado, o hayan sido suspendidos por faltas graves contra la ética en el ejercicio de dicha profesión.

2. Quienes se hallen en interdicción judicial.

3. Quienes se encuentren bajo detención preventiva, aunque gocen del beneficio de excarcelación, y quienes hayan sido llamados a juicio por infracción penal, mientras se define su responsabilidad por sentencia firme.

4. Quienes hayan sido condenados a penas de prisión por delito doloso.

5. Quienes hayan sido destituidos de cualquier cargo público por faltas graves.

6. Quienes hayan sido sancionados por faltas graves por el Colegio de Notarios.

7. Las personas de las cuales exista la convicción moral de que no observan una vida pública o privada compatible con la dignidad del cargo de notario público.

Artículo 56. El suplente de notario público podrá laborar en la Notaría Pública en el cargo de abogado o de secretario previstos en esta Ley.

Artículo 57. El notario público está autorizado por el Estado para dar fe pública de los actos, contratos y demás documentos avalados por él de conformidad con las solemnidades exigidas por la Ley.

如果外事处法令有规定，使馆官员将担任普通公证员。

第53条　每位普通公证员都应有一位接替者，在其暂时缺勤或出现障碍时接替普通公证员工作。

如果公证员长期缺任，接替者应一直履行普通公证员职务，直到正式公证员上任。被指派的接替者在正式提名后一直履行该职务。

在任何情况下都应当向国家公证总局申请授权接替以及汇报接替期限。

第54条　公证处及其接替者应当具备成为司法区高级法院法官的同等条件及本章规定的其他条件。

第55条　下列人员不得被任命为普通公证员：

1. 在职期间被停职的律师，或在职期间因重大道德错误被停职的律师。

2. 被剥夺公民权利的人。

3. 被预防性拘留的人（即使会被释放）；因触犯刑法被告上法庭等待最终判决的人，同时其责任通过最终判决确定。

4. 因欺诈罪被判处监禁的人。

5. 因重大错误被罢免公共职务的人。

6. 因重大错误被注册公证员协会惩罚的人。

7. 公共生活或私生活中的道德信念与公证员职业不符的人。

第56条　依据本法，普通公证员的接替者可以在公证处担任律师或秘书职务。

第57条　根据法律规定，国家授权普通公证员对文书、合同及其他文件予以公证。

El notario público tiene a su cargo la recepción, extensión y autorización de las declaraciones, actos y contratos solicitados por las personas naturales o jurídicas; conserva los instrumentos en el protocolo a su cargo, los reproduce, da fe de ellos y los archiva conforme al sistema de automatización ordenado en la presente Ley.

Artículo 58. El cargo de notario público es incompatible con cualquiera otro cargo, sea de índole pública o privada, sea judicial, ejercicio de la abogacía o incluso como directivo en organizaciones sin fines de lucro, con excepción de la docencia universitaria y el Colegio de Notarios.

Artículo 59. Los notarios públicos deberán incorporarse a la Notaría Pública donde han sido designados dentro de las veinticuatro horas siguientes a la designación y están en la obligación de afiliarse al Colegio de Notarios dentro del término de treinta días calendario, contados a partir de su nombramiento.

Artículo 60. El notario público tiene las siguientes funciones:

1. Autenticar las firmas que se suscriben en los actos, documentos y contratos públicos y privados.

2. Confeccionar escrituras públicas para la protocolización de instrumentos que así lo requieran, tales como: actas de sociedades anónimas, fundaciones de interés privado, venta de bienes muebles e inmuebles, hipotecas, entre otros.

3. Dar fe pública a los documentos, contratos y demás negocios jurídicos unilaterales, bilaterales y pluri lateral es.

4. Otorgar poderes, sustituciones, renuncias y revocatorias.

5. Expedir protestos de títulos de crédito, de conformidad con lo previsto en el Código de Comercio.

6. Efectuar diligencias notariales fuera de la Notaría Pública, trasladándose al lugar donde requiera dar fe pública de un acto, cuando las circunstancias así lo requieran, incluso en horas y días no laborables.

7. Celebrar matrimonios civiles dentro o fuera de la Notaría Pública.

8. Otorgar los instrumentos relativos a las capitulaciones matrimoniales.

9. Otorgar testamentos cerrados o abiertos con las formalidades exigidas en la Ley.

10. Presentar o entregar testamentos cerrados o abiertos con excepción de las formalidades establecidas en el Código Judicial, cuando así lo requiera el juez de la causa.

普通公证员负责对自然人或法人申请公证的声明、文书及合同进行接收、撰写和证明；应用本法建立的自动化系统，负责保存公证书，出具副本，予以证明并归档。

第 58 条　普通公证员不得兼任除大学教务和注册公证员协会职务外的其他公开、私人或司法性质的职务，如律师甚至非营利性组织管理人员。

第 59 条　普通公证员应当在被任命后的 24 小时内就职，并必须自提名起 30 个自然日内加入注册公证员协会。

第 60 条　以下是普通公证员职能：

1. 对公共文书或私署文书、文件与合同上的签名予以证明。

2. 起草公证书并根据要求列入文书登记簿中，如公司文书、私营基金会文书、动产及不动产售卖文书、抵押文书等。

3. 对文件、合同及其他单边、双边和多边商务文书予以公证。

4. 对授权、职位人选替换、辞职和撤职文书进行公证。

5. 根据《商法典》的规定，出具商业票据的拒付证书。

6. 根据情况需要，在公证处以外的地点开展公证工作，甚至在工作时间段以外或非工作日提供公证服务。

7. 在公证处中或者公证处以外场所对民事婚姻进行见证。

8. 对婚前协议予以公证。

9. 根据法律规定的形式密封或公开遗嘱。

10. 如果主审法官要求，可不根据审判法规定手续提交密封或公开遗嘱。

11. Diligenciar la apertura de testamentos cerrados.

12. Protocolizar los juicios de sucesión que le remitan los juzgados correspondientes.

13. Expedir constancias de cualquier hecho o acto a través de la inspección extrajudicial.

14. Transcribir en acta o por cualquier medio de reproducción o de grabación, el contenido de archivos públicos o de documentos privados, siempre y cuando no esté expresamente prohibido en el primer caso, o lo autorice el dueño o depositario del documento, en el segundo caso.

15. Expedir la constancia de fecha y hora de la celebración de asambleas, reuniones o manifestaciones dejando las constancias personales, gráficas y sonoras del caso.

16. Efectuar la apertura de libros de asambleas de propietarios, actas de juntas de condominios, sociedades y juntas directivas.

17. Autenticar firmas autógrafas, electrónicas, huellas digitales y otros medios de identificación personal de carácter inequívoco.

18. Compulsar o cotejar copias con sus respectivos originales.

19. Realizar otros actos que requieran fe pública.

20. Realizar las demás funciones que le señale el ministro de Gobierno y aquellas que le atribuyan las leyes y disposiciones reglamentarias.

Artículo 61. El notario público realizará cada traslado personalmente, acompañado por personal de la Notaría Pública, quienes presenciarán la diligencia y actuarán como testigos en caso que sea necesario.

Artículo 62. Son obligaciones del notario público:

1. Residir en la cabecera del Circuito Notarial, de la cual no podrá ausentarse en días laborables, sino por diligencia en el ejercicio de sus funciones, dentro del área geográfica de su circunscripción notarial. Cuando la ausencia pueda durar más de veinticuatro horas deberá solicitar la autorización del gobernador de la provincia o comarca.

2. Registrar la firma que utilizará en el ejercicio de la función pública encomendada; la cual deberá coincidir con el Sistema de Verificación de Identidad (SVI), del Tribunal Electoral o sistema de verificación vigente en el momento, ante el Ministerio de Gobierno, mediante la Dirección Nacional de Notarías y el Colegio de Notarios.

3. Recibir el archivo de la Notaría Pública con inventario, el cual será entregado personalmente por su predecesor. El notario público que omite esta solemnidad es responsable del archivo con arreglo al inventario con que lo haya recibido el último de los predecesores, inclusive el

11. 公开密封遗嘱。

12. 登记相关法院发布的继承判决。

13. 通过司法外审查程序，对任何事件或行为进行记录。

14. 通过任何复制或录制手段将公开档案或私人文件的内容誊写在文书上，只要在第一种情况下没有被明确禁止或在第二种情况下文件所有人进行了授权。

15. 记录集会、会议或游行的日期和时间，记录下人员、图像和声音信息并开具证明。

16. 公开业主会议记录，公开物业、企业及董事会文书。

17. 验证亲笔签名、电子签名、指纹及其他明确的个人识别方式。

18. 将副本与其原件进行核对。

19. 完成公证所需的其他活动。

20. 政府部部长规定的其他职能及法律法规赋予的职能。

第 61 条 普通公证员在公证处工作人员的陪同下亲自完成转交，在必要情形下，工作人员作为见证人证明公证员已尽职。

第 62 条 普通公证员的义务如下：

1. 常驻公证辖区首府，工作时间不得离开，在其公证辖区的地域范围内履行职责。缺勤时间超过24小时的，应当向省长或自治区长提出申请。

2. 通过国家公证总局和注册公证员协会向政府部登记履行公职时使用的签名，该签名应与身份识别系统（SVI）、选举法院或现行识别系统的签名一致。

3. 接收公证处附有清单的档案，该档案由前任公证员亲自交付给其继任者。没有经过此程序的普通公证员根据前一任收到的清单负责该档案，包括本应在前一任在任期间以及现任公证员在任时间内增加的档案。根据相应的行政令规定，拒绝交付清单的前任公

aumento que ha debido tener el archivo en tiempo de dicho predecesor y en el notario público de cuya responsabilidad se trate. El predecesor que se niegue a entregar bajo inventario, o cuyo inventario sea defectuoso será multado con base a las sanciones previstas en el respectivo Decreto Ejecutivo.

4. Brindar atención al público no menos de siete horas diarias, de lunes a viernes. Salvo en días festivos previstos por Ley y salvo que solicite a la Dirección Nacional de Notarías del Ministerio de Gobierno, la habilitación de los días sábados para la prestación del servicio

5. Asistir a la Notaría Pública y cumplir con la jornada laboral establecida en la presente Ley.

6. Prestar los servicios notariales autorizados por esta Ley, a las personas que así lo soliciten, sin excepción alguna, con la objetividad, idoneidad, profesionalismo y moralidad e imparcialidad que el cargo exige.

7. Guardar el secreto profesional.

8. Verificar que el secretario remita anualmente y en forma apropiada los libros de protocolo constatando además que no queden renglones con fechas libres o por llenar.

9. Verificar que el tesorero realice el depósito de los impuestos mensuales de la Notaría Pública a la cuenta del Tesoro Nacional, dentro de los primeros diez días hábiles del mes siguiente.

10. Cumplir con las comisiones y responsabilidades que la Dirección Nacional de Notarías le asigne conforme a lo establecido en la presente Ley.

11. Utilizar el Sistema de Verificación de Identidad (SVI), o el sistema de verificación vigente, empleado por el Tribunal Electoral para la correcta identificación de los usuarios, así como los documentos legalmente establecidos para la identificación de extranjeros.

Artículo 63. Está prohibido al notario público:

1. Autorizar instrumentos públicos en los que le concedan derechos y obligaciones, así como a las personas con quienes esté emparentado dentro del cuarto grado de consanguinidad o segundo de afinidad, ya sea en línea recta ascendente o descendente, colaterales y por adopción; o vinculados por padrinazgo o compadrazgo.

2. Autorizar instrumentos públicos de personas jurídicas en las que él o personas vinculadas con él indicados en el inciso anterior, participen en el capital social, fundacional o patrimonio; o tengan la calidad de protectores, administradores, directores, gerentes, apoderados o representación alguna.

证员或清单被损坏的，将被处以罚款。

4. 周一至周五每天面向公众提供公证服务的时间不得低于7小时。除非属于法定节假日或者向政府部国家公证总局另行申请，否则周六也要办公。

5. 在公证处工作并遵守本法规定的工作时间。

6. 客观、适当、专业、公正地为公证申请者提供本法授权的公证服务，恪守职业道德，不设任何例外。

7. 保守职业秘密。

8. 核实秘书是否每年以适当方式提交记录簿，载明记录簿上没有空白日期或待填项。

9. 核实出纳是否在下一个月前十个工作日内向国家财政账户缴纳公证处上一月的应付税费。

10. 根据本法之规定，完成国家公证总局委派的任务和使命。

11. 使用身份识别系统（SVI）或选举法院目前使用的识别系统，正确识别用户身份，以及识别法定文件以验明外国人身份。

第63条 普通公证员不得办理以下公证：

1. 对公证员本人及与之有四代以内血缘关系、两代以内亲缘关系、收养关系、宗教庇护关系或干亲关系的近亲属产生权利或义务的文件进行公证。

2. 为公证员本人或上一款所指的关联人士有股份或出资的法人办理公证；或者为公证员本人或上述关联人士担任监管人、管理者、董事、经理、授权代理人或其他代表身份的法人办理公证。

3. Ser protector, administrador, director, gerente, apoderado o tener representación de personas jurídicas de derecho público o en las que el Estado, Gobiernos Locales o Regionales tengan participación.

4. Autorizar instrumentos públicos contrarios a la Ley, a la moral o a las buenas costumbres.

5. Extender instrumentos cuyos derechos no hayan sido previamente registrados según el tipo de pago, ya sea en efectivo o a crédito ante el tesorero de la Notaría.

6. Ejercer la función fuera de los límites del Circuito Notarial en el cual se desempeña.

7. Delegar parcial o totalmente las funciones propias del cargo a personas no facultadas por esta Ley a recibir dicha delegación.

8. Recibir honorarios o compensaciones que no estén contempladas en esta Ley.

Artículo 64. Son derechos del notario público:

1. Gozar de vacaciones y licencias por enfermedad de acuerdo a las normas aplicables a los servidores públicos.

Si lo tiene a bien, el ministro de Gobierno concederá la licencia respectiva, cuidando que su reemplazo esté debidamente designado.

Los notarios públicos quedan excluidos de la aplicación de las Leyes 39 y 127 de 2013.

Artículo 65. El notario público cesa en sus funciones por las siguientes causas:

1. Muerte.
2. Renuncia, desde que sea aceptada.
3. Destitución.
4. Abandono del cargo.
5. Por haber sido condenado penalmente.
6. Por haber culminado el período presidencial por el cual fue nombrado. En este caso ocupará el cargo de forma interina el notario público saliente hasta la toma de posesión del nuevo notario público.

Artículo 66. En caso de cese de un notario público, el Ministerio de Gobierno, mediante la Dirección Nacional de Notarías, designará al suplente para que se encargue de la Notaría Pública y cierre sus registros sentándose a continuación del último instrumento público de cada registro. El suplente ejercerá las funciones del notario público hasta la toma de posesión del que se nombre en propiedad.

CAPÍTULO II Del Notario Certificado

Artículo 67. El notario certificado es un funcionario o ejecutivo que ostenta un alto nivel directivo dentro de

3. 成为公法人或国家、地方或地方政府有参股的法人的监管人、管理者、董事、经理、代理人或其他代表。

4. 核准违背法律、道德或公序良俗的公共文书。

5. 未按照规定付款方式，无论是现金付款还是信用支付，事先向公证处收费部门付讫办理费用的，不得出具公证书。

6. 在所属公证辖区以外行使其职能。

7. 将职能部分或全部转授权给未被本法授权的人。

8. 接收本法规定以外的酬劳或补贴。

第 64 条　普通公证员享有以下权利：
1. 根据公务员适用规定享有休年假和病假的权利。

在此情况下，政府部部长将根据情况批假，并指派合适的人接替其工作。

2013 年的第 39 号法律和第 127 号法律不适用于普通公证员。

第 65 条　下列情况下普通公证员停止履行职务：

1. 死亡。
2. 辞职，自辞职申请被批准之日生效。
3. 被撤职。
4. 离职。
5. 受到刑事处罚。
6. 对公证员进行任命的总统任期结束。此种情况下，即将离任的公证员将临时担任此职务直到新的普通公证员上任。

第 66 条　如果普通公证员停止履行职务，政府部将通过国家公证总局指派一位接替者负责公证处工作，并在继续完成每份记录簿的最后一份记录工作后不再进行新的记录。接替者将履行普通公证员职务，一直到正式公证员上任。

第二章　认证公证员

第 67 条　认证公证员是在公共部门法人中的获得认证公证处授权的高级别职员。其薪资固定，由其

la persona jurídica del sector público que solicite la autorización para Notaría Certificada. Este devengará un salario que será fijado y pagado por la entidad a la que se encuentra adscrita la Notaría Certificada.

El notario certificado tiene prohibida la prestación del servicio notarial para casos particulares que no estén relacionados con las actividades de la entidad a la cual está adscrita la Notaría Certificada.

Artículo 68. Los notarios certificados deberán reunir los mismos requisitos exigidos para ser magistrados de Tribunal Superior de Distrito Judicial y los establecidos en el Título III Capítulo III de la presente Ley.

Es potestad del Presidente de la República en conjunto con el Ministro de Gobierno, aprobar el nombramiento del notario certificado.

Artículo 69. No podrán ser designados como notarios certificados:

1. Quienes se encuentren suspendidos en el ejercicio de la profesión de abogado, o hayan sido suspendidos por faltas graves contra la ética en el ejercicio de dicha profesión.

2. Quienes se hallen en interdicción judicial.

3. Quienes se encuentren bajo detención preventiva, aunque gocen del beneficio de excarcelación, y quienes hayan sido llamados a juicio por infracción penal, mientras se define su responsabilidad por sentencia firme.

4. Quienes hayan sido condenados a penas de prisión por delito doloso.

5. Quienes hayan sido sancionados por falta grave por el Colegio de Notarios.

6. Las personas de las cuales exista la convicción moral de que no observan una vida pública o privada compatible con la dignidad del cargo de notario público.

7. Quienes mantengan vínculos de parentesco o compadrazgo con el jefe o director de la entidad en la cual funciona la Notaría Certificada.

Artículo 70. Cada notario certificado tendrá dos suplentes, que deberán reunir los mismos requisitos que este, quienes lo reemplazarán en los casos de falta temporal o impedimento.

Si la falta fuere absoluta, el suplente ejercerá las funciones del notario certificado hasta la posesión del que se nombre en propiedad. El suplente o el reemplazo que se designe, ejercerá por el tiempo restante por el que fue nombrado el titular del cargo, por la entidad en donde se autoriza la Notaría Certificada.

En todos los casos se deberá solicitar a la Dirección

所在认证公证处所属实体支付。

认证公证员不得为与认证公证处所属实体活动无关的特殊案件提供公证服务。

第68条 认证公证员应具备司法区高级法院法官同等条件，并符合本法第三篇第三章的规定。

共和国总统有权同政府部部长一同批准对认证公证员的任命。

第69条 下列人员不得被任命为认证公证员：

1. 在职期间被停职的律师，或在职期间因重大道德错误被停职的律师。

2. 被司法机关剥夺公民权利的人员。

3. 被预防性拘留的人（即使会被释放）；因触犯刑法被告上法庭等待最终判决的人，同时其责任通过最终判决确定。

4. 因欺诈罪被判处监禁的人员。

5. 因重大错误被注册公证员协会惩罚的人员。

6. 公共生活或私生活中的道德信念与公证员职业不符的人员。

7. 与认证公证处所属实体领导者或管理者保持宗教庇护关系或干亲关系的人员。

第70条 每位认证公证员配有2位接替者，接替者应符合认证公证员同等条件，在公证员暂时缺勤或因故无法正常履行公证职责时接替其工作。

如果认证公证员长期缺勤，接替者将一直履行认证公证员职务，直到正式公证员上任。被指派的候补人或接替者应当一直顶替至认证公证处对正式公证员任命的剩余任期完成为止。

认证公证处在任何情况下都应当向国家公证总局

Nacional de Notarías la autorización para el reemplazo e informe del periodo del mismo.

Artículo 71. El notario certificado está autorizado por el Estado para dar fe pública de los actos, contratos y demás documentos que se eleven a escritura pública y tengan relación con la entidad a la que están adscritos de acuerdo con las solemnidades exigidas por la Ley.

Artículo 72. El cargo de notario certificado es incompatible con cualquier otro cargo de índole pública o privada, judicial, ejercicio de la abogacía o como directivo en organizaciones sin fines de lucro, con excepción de la entidad en donde ejerza el cargo y de la docencia universitaria.

Artículo 73. El notario certificado está obligado a:

1. Tramitar y archivar los documentos generados conforme al sistema de automatización ordenado en la presente Ley.

2. Verificar que los ingresos de la Notaría Certificada sean depositados íntegramente a la cuenta del Tesoro Nacional. Estos depósitos se deberán realizar dentro de los primeros diez días hábiles del siguiente mes.

Artículo 74. Los notarios certificados están en la obligación de afiliarse al Colegio de Notarios dentro del término de treinta días calendario, contados a partir de su nombramiento, pero no podrán ejercer cargos directivos en este.

CAPÍTULO III De la camera notarial

Artículo 75. La carrera notarial es el sistema que organiza los estudios e investigación de las diversas disciplinas jurídicas dirigidas al mejor desempeño de la función notarial y para la difusión y puesta en práctica de sus principios y valores ético-jurídicos en beneficio de la República.

Artículo 76. Corresponde al Órgano Ejecutivo, a través del Ministerio de Gobierno, desarrollar y reglamentar la Carrera Notarial, así como guardar, cumplir y hacer cumplir la realización de sus principios. En dicho desarrollo podrán participar facultades y escuelas de Derecho públicas y privadas de universidades reconocidas.

Artículo 77. La Carrera Notarial proporcionará condiciones de formación teórica y práctica; formación deontológica y personal suficiente, para que el profesional del Derecho idóneo para la función notarial, pueda acceder a la misma en las mejores condiciones de servicio y de igualdad de acceso, en bien de la República y para la evolución positiva del Notariado.

申请授权接替以及汇报接替期限。

第 71 条 由国家授权，认证公证员依照法律规定的形式对其所属实体有关的行为、合同及其他文件进行认证。

第 72 条 认证公证员不得兼任除所在实体和大学教务相关职务外的其他公开、私人或司法性质职务，如律师甚至非营利性组织管理人员。

第 73 条 认证公证员应履行以下义务：

1. 运用本法要求的自动化系统处理文件并归档。

2. 核实公证处收入是否被全部存入国家财政的账户中。这些款项应在次月的前十个自然日内存入。

第 74 条 认证公证员必须自被任命之日起，在 30 个自然日内加入注册公证员协会，但不得在该协会担任管理职务。

第三章 公证专业

第 75 条 公证专业是一种组织调查研究的专业，研究对象为以更好履行公证职能为目的的各种法律学科，且该专业为保障国家利益，对公证原则和伦理、法律价值观进行传播和实践。

第 76 条 行政机关通过政府部负责公证专业的发展和规范，保持、落实并实现其原则。可以通过报考知名公立和私立大学的法学院、法律系进行公证专业的学习。

第 77 条 公证专业提供理论和实践培训，充分的个人培训和伦理培训，使得适合公证工作的法学专业人才能够在更好条件和平等机会下任职，有利于国家和公证事业的发展。

Artículo 78. La carrera notarial se regirá por los principios y valores que fundamentan el ejercicio de la fe pública, y especialmente por los principios de excelencia, especialización, legitimación, objetividad, profesionalismo e imparcialidad.

Artículo 79. Es obligatorio tener formación en Derecho Notarial para los profesionales del Derecho que ocuparán los cargos de notario público o certificado y sus suplentes.

Artículo 80. La Carrera Notarial será reglamentada por el Ministerio de Gobierno, mediante Decreto Ejecutivo.

CAPÍTULO IV De la Dirección Nacional de Notarías

Artículo 81. Se crea la Dirección Nacional de Notarías, adscrita al Ministerio de Gobierno, cuya misión es la fiscalización de la función notarial de acuerdo a las facultades y competencias establecidas en esta Ley y las normas reglamentarias que se dicten a propósito de la misma.

Artículo 82. Son funciones de la Dirección Nacional de Notarías:

1. Vigilar que los notarios cumplan debidamente sus funciones con arreglo a esta Ley, normas reglamentarias y complementarias.

2. Recomendar o no, al Ministerio de Gobierno, las entidades que apliquen para ser Notarías Certificadas.

3. Realizar visitas de inspección a las Notarías en coordinación con las Gobernaciones.

4. Recibir quejas o denuncias sobre irregularidades en el ejercicio de la función notarial y darles el trámite que corresponda.

5. Llevar un registro actualizado de las Juntas Directivas del Colegio de Notarios.

6. Comunicar las vacantes que deban ser llenadas en las Notarías Públicas.

7. Verificar y aprobar el inventario de los archivos de los notarios salientes los cuales se entregarán personalmente ante la Dirección por el notario anterior.

8. Entregar los sellos a los notarios.

9. Ejercer las demás atribuciones que señale la Ley y normas reglamentarias.

Artículo 83. La Dirección Nacional de Notarías estará a cargo de un director y tendrá la estructura organizacional que sea necesaria para el adecuado desempeño de sus funciones y el logro de sus objetivos y metas, tal y como se establezca en el respectivo reglamento.

Artículo 84. El director será el jefe superior de la Di-

第78条 公证专业受公证原则与价值观规范，尤其是优秀性、专业性、合法性、客观性、职业性和公平性原则。

第79条 普通公证员或认证公证员及其接替者等法律从业者必须具有公证法培训经历。

第80条 公证专业由政府部通过颁布行政令进行规范。

第四章 国家公证总局

第81条 成立国家公证总局，隶属于政府部，其任务是根据本法规定的职权及其他法律法规监督公证职务的履行情况。

第82条 下列是国家公证总局的职能：

1. 监督公证员是否依照法律法规和其他补充规定履行职责。

2. 向政府部推荐可用作认证公证处的实体。

3. 与各地政府协调，对公证处进行巡查。

4. 接受人们对履行公证职务时不规范现象的投诉并履行相应的投诉手续。

5. 实时记录注册公证员协会董事会的情况。

6. 通知公证处职位空缺情况。

7. 核实并批准即将离任公证员的档案清单，该公证员须亲自将档案送至国家公证总局。

8. 授予公证员公证章。

9. 本法和其他法规规定的其他职能。

第83条 国家公证总局由局长负责领导，其组织结构根据职责和工作需要确定，从而更好履行职能，实现各项规定中设立的目标。

第84条 局长是国家公证总局的最高领导，由

rección Nacional de Notarías y será nombrado por el ministro de Gobierno. Estará bajo la dirección e instrucción del ministro de Gobierno o quien este designe.

Artículo 85. Para ocupar el cargo de director se deberán reunir los mismos requisitos requeridos para ser notario público y aquellos establecidos en el Título III Capítulo III de la presente Ley.

Artículo 86. El cargo de director es incompatible con cualquiera otro cargo de índole pública o privada, especialmente en lo judicial, el ejercicio de la abogacía o como directivo en organizaciones sin fines de lucro, con excepción de la docencia universitaria y el Colegio de Notarios.

Artículo 87. El director tendrá las siguientes funciones y facultades:

1. Ejercer la dirección, supervisión y control técnico y administrativo de todas las actividades de la Dirección. .

2. Asesorar al Organo Ejecutivo en todas las materias que guarden relación con el servicio notarial.

3. Ejecutar las políticas que diseñe la Dirección, en coordinación con el ministro de Gobierno, para el mejor cumplimiento de sus objetivos,

4. Proponer la estructura interna de la Dirección, para ser reglamentada por el Ministerio de Gobierno.

5. Proponer las regulaciones internas relativas a los procesos internos de gestión de la Dirección, para que sean reglamentadas por el Ministerio de Gobierno.

6. Ejercer las demás atribuciones que señale la Ley y normas reglamentarias.

Artículo 88. La Dirección Nacional de Notarías, podrá facilitar información documental y contable de las Notarías, cuando esto le sea solicitado por autoridades competentes.

CAPÍTULO V Del Colegio de Notarios

Artículo 89. El Colegio de Notarios está constituido por todos los notarios de la República de Panamá en ejercicio, cuyo funcionamiento se rige por estatuto aprobado por mayoría de votos en Asamblea General y ratificados por el ministro de Gobierno. Los egresados de la Carrera Notarial serán miembros también, pero solo con derecho a voz.

Artículo 90. La Asamblea General es el órgano supremo del Colegio y sus atribuciones se establecen mediante estatuto.

Artículo 91. Deberán enviarse a la Dirección Nacional de Notarías, copias autenticadas de las Actas de Junta

政府部部长任命，受政府部部长或任命人的领导和指挥。

第85条　局长的任职资格要求应当与公证员的任职资格要求相同，并符合本法第三篇第三章的规定。

第86条　局长不得兼任除大学教务和注册公证员协会相关职务外的其他公开或私人尤其是司法性质职务，如律师甚至非营利性组织管理人员。

第87条　下列是局长的职能和权限：

1. 国家公证总局所有活动的指导人、监督人和技术与行政上的控制人。

2. 在与公证服务有关的所有领域协助行政机关。

3. 与政府部部长协调，执行国家公证总局制定的政策，以更好地完成目标。

4. 规划国家公证总局内部结构，使其符合政府部规范。

5. 提出与国家公证总局内部管理程序有关的内部规定，使该规定符合政府部规范。

6. 本法和其他法规规定的其他职能。

第88条　经相关部门申请，国家公证总局可以向其提供公证处文件和会计信息。

第五章　注册公证员协会

第89条　注册公证员协会由巴拿马共和国所有在职公证员组成，其运作遵循国民大会多数票通过、政府部部长批准的规章。公证专业的毕业生也将是协会成员，但只拥有发言权。

第90条　国民大会是协会最高机构，其职权通过规章确定。

第91条　国民大会应当向国家公证总局提交董事会和国民大会记录已核验的副本。

Directiva y de Asamblea General que se celebren.

Artículo 92. Los miembros de la Junta Directiva serán elegidos en Asamblea General, mediante votación secreta, por mayoría absoluta de votos; su mandato es por período de un año.

Artículo 93. El Colegio de Notarios contará con un Tribunal de Ética que solo impondrá sanciones morales que serán establecidas por reglamento. Podrán constituir el Tribunal de Ética tanto miembros plenos como aquellos que solo tienen derecho a voz. Estos últimos tendrán derecho a voto en sus deliberaciones.

TÍTULO IV
Del régimen disciplinario

CAPÍTULO I De la responsabilidad

Artículo 94. El notario es responsable por el incumplimiento de esta Ley, así como de las normas reglamentarias, estatutarias y demás decisiones dictadas por la Dirección Nacional de Notarías.

En el caso de las Notarías Certificadas, el responsable por incumplimiento será el notario certificado de manera solidaria con la persona jurídica a la que se encuentre adscrita la Notaría Certificada.

Artículo 95. El notario es responsable, civil y penalmente, de los daños y perjuicios que, por dolo o culpa, ocasione a las partes o terceros en el ejercicio de sus funciones.

En el caso de las Notarías Certificadas, el responsable civilmente será el notario certificado de manera solidaria con la persona jurídica a la que se encuentre adscrita la Notaría Certificada, penalmente lo será solo el notario certificado.

CAPÍTULO II De la disciplina

Artículo 96. Fuera de los procesos éticos surtidos en el Colegio de Notarios, la disciplina del notariado es competencia privativa del Ministerio de Gobierno como única instancia.

Artículo 97. Las decisiones del ministro de Gobierno para los efectos de esta Ley, solo admitirán el Recurso de Reconsideración, con cuya resolución, queda agotada la vía gubernativa.

Artículo 98. En todo proceso disciplinario se garantizará el derecho de defensa del notario.

第 92 条　董事会成员将通过半数以上的秘密投票当选为国民大会议员，任期为一年。

第 93 条　注册公证员协会设有一个道德法庭，该法庭只进行法律规定的道德惩罚。道德法庭成员包括所有拥有投票权的成员及只拥有发言权的成员。通过商议，只拥有发言权的成员有权进行投票。

第四篇
惩戒制度

第一章　责任

第 94 条　公证员对不遵守本法、其他法律法规、规章制度及国家公证总局其他决定的行为负责。

如果是认证公证处，不遵守规定行为则由认证公证员同该认证公证处所属法人一同负责。

第 95 条　公证员应对因故意或过失对当事人或第三方造成的损害负民事责任或刑事责任。

如果是认证公证处，在民事上则由认证公证员同该认证公证处所属法人一同负责，刑事上则由认证公证员单独负责。

第二章　纪律

第 96 条　在注册公证员协会道德程序以外，公证事务纪律由政府部专门管辖。

第 97 条　政府部部长针对本法效力的决定只承认申诉请求，不承认其他行政救济渠道。

第 98 条　在所有纪律处分环节都应赋予公证员辩护权。

CAPÍTULO III De las faltas

Artículo 99. Los notarios responden por las siguientes faltas:

1. El incumplimiento de los deberes y obligaciones del notario, establecidos en esta Ley, normas reglamentarias, complementarias y los estatutos.

2. El no acatar las prohibiciones contempladas en esta Ley.

3. El incumplimiento del horario laboral establecido en la presente Ley.

4. La conducta no acorde con la dignidad y decoro del cargo.

5. El aceptar o solicitar honorarios extras u otros beneficios fuera de la tarifa reglamentaria, para la realización de actuaciones regulares o irregulares.

6. La embriaguez habitual y el uso de sustancias psicotrópicas.

7. La delegación de sus funciones a terceras personas no autorizadas de acuerdo a la presente Ley.

8. La no implementación de los sistemas y procesos dictados en la presente Ley.

CAPÍTULO IV De las sanciones

Artículo 100. Las sanciones, según la gravedad de la falta y antecedentes del notario, son las siguientes:

1. Amonestación.

2. Suspensión de 1 a 30 días.

3. Destitución.

Artículo 101. La amonestación es una advertencia escrita al notario por la falta cometida, que formula el Ministerio de Gobierno a través de la Dirección Nacional de Notarías.

Artículo 102. La suspensión es la separación temporal del notario del ejercicio de la función, impuesta directamente por el ministro de Gobierno, tiempo durante el cual no podrá actuar, ni percibir ingresos de la Notaría.

Artículo 103. La destitución es la separación definitiva del notario del ejercicio de la función, impuesta por el Organo Ejecutivo, mediante Decreto Ejecutivo.

Artículo 104. El Recurso de Reconsideración será interpuesto ante el ministro de Gobierno dentro del plazo de cinco días hábiles, contados a partir de la notificación de la respectiva resolución.

Artículo 105. El proceso disciplinario se desarrollará en un plazo máximo de sesenta días hábiles, contados a partir de la fecha en que el Ministerio de Gobierno noti-

第三章 过错

第99条　公证员对下列过错负责：

1. 不遵守本法、补充法规、规章规定的公证员职责和义务。

2. 违反本法的禁止性规定。

3. 不遵守本法规定的工作时间。

4. 有违职业尊严和礼仪的行为。

5. 接受或索取薪资以外的酬劳或好处，以从事合规或不合规的活动。

6. 经常醉酒及使用精神药物。

7. 将职权指派给未经本法授权的第三人。

8. 未运用本法规定的系统和程序。

第四章 惩罚

第100条　根据公证员违法情节的严重程度和有无前科，做出以下惩罚：

1. 警告。

2. 停职一至三十日。

3. 撤职。

第101条　警告是指针对公证员所犯错误的书面警告，由政府部通过国家公证总局发出。

第102条　停职是指公证员暂时离开岗位，由政府部部长直接执行，停职期间不能履行职能也不能获得收入。

第103条　撤职是指公证员彻底离开岗位，由行政机关通过行政令执行。

第104条　申诉请求自决议通知起，应在5个自然日内向政府部部长提出。

第105条　纪律处分期最长为60个自然日，从政府部下达处分通知之日起算。

fique la apertura del proceso.

Artículo 106. La acción disciplinaria prescribe al año, contado desde el día en que se tuvo conocimiento de la falta. El inicio del proceso disciplinario y la existencia de un proceso penal interrumpen el término de la prescripción.

Artículo 107. El proceso disciplinario es independiente de los procesos éticos que lleve adelante el Colegio de Notarios.

TÍTULO V
Disposiciones transitorias

Artículo 108. Desde la entrada en vigencia de la presente Ley, y hasta tanto el Ministerio de Gobierno, mediante Decreto Ejecutivo, apruebe una nueva tabla de tarifas, regirán las tarifas existentes a la fecha.

Artículo 109. Las Notarías contarán con un período de transición de seis meses, contados a partir de la promulgación de la presente Ley, para efectuar los cambios y ajustes en su estructura administrativa y técnica, al igual que la reglamentación pertinente establecida por el Ministerio de Gobierno, a través de Decreto Ejecutivo.

Artículo 110. A partir de la entrada en vigencia de la presente Ley, los notarios públicos y certificados, una vez se desarrollen los cursos de Derecho Notarial en las universidades públicas o privadas, tendrán un año para inscribirse, cursar y aprobar los mismos, so pena de ser destituido de no cumplir con este requisito.

Los notarios públicos o certificados podrán solicitar al Ministerio de Gobierno, a través de la Dirección Nacional de Notarías, una extensión de tiempo en caso de que la duración del curso sea superior a un año.

Artículo 111. A partir de la entrada en vigencia de la presente Ley, quedarán asimiladas como Notarías Certificadas, las Notarías Especiales existentes en entidades públicas, creadas por Leyes anteriores a la presente Ley. Así mismo, se incorporarán al régimen de Notarías Públicas, las Notarías Especiales creadas por Ley para el Municipio de San Miguelito y el corregimiento de Cristóbal en Colón.

Por razón de la creación de la décima provincia, la Notaría Sexta del Circuito de Panamá, con sede en La Chorrera, pasará a formar parte del Circuito Notarial del distrito cabecera de la nueva provincia.

第 106 条　纪律处分从获悉犯错事实之日起一年内实施。如果公证员正在接受刑事处分，那么对他的纪律处分就不受前述时间的限制。

第 107 条　纪律处分与注册公证员协会实施的道德处分相互独立。

第五篇
临时规定

第 108 条　自本法生效之日起，在政府部颁布行政令正式出台新收费标准之前，继续使用现行收费标准。

第 109 条　自本法颁布之日起，各公证处应在6个月的过渡期内，完成行政和技术结构的变更和调整，以及符合政府部通过行政令设立的相关规定。

第 110 条　自本法生效之日起，一旦在公立或私立高校开设公证法课程，普通公证员和认证公证员应在一年时间内报名参加这些课程，完成课程的学习并通过考试；不符合这一要求的，将被撤销任职资格。

如果课程时间超过一年，普通公证员或认证公证员可通过国家公证总局向政府部申请延长学习时间。

第 111 条　自本法生效之日起，依据先前法律规定在公共实体中设立的特别公证处被视作认证公证处。此外，依法在圣米格里多市和科隆省克里斯托弗市设立的特别公证处，也应被纳入公证体系中。

由于设立了第十个省，总部位于拉乔雷拉的巴拿马第六公证处将被纳入新设省份的首府所在的公证辖区中。

TÍTULO VI
Disposiciones finales

Artículo 112. Se modifica el artículo 1 de la Ley 83 de 9 de noviembre de 2012, para que quede asi:

"Artículo 1. Ámbito de Aplicación. Esta Ley establece las reglas y principios básicos de obligatoria observancia para la ejecución de trámites gubernamentales en línea, excluyendo las acciones y recursos legales en la vía gubernativa.

Las disposiciones de la presente Ley serán aplicables al Gobierno central, entidades autónomas, semiautónomas, municipales, la Asamblea Nacional, el Organo Judicial, los intermediarios financieros y las sociedades en que el Estado sea propietario del 51% o más del capital accionario o más será establecida de forma gradual para cada una de ellas.

Las Notarías Públicas y Notarías Certificadas deberán aplicar además de su régimen especial la normativa establecida en la presente Ley.

Artículo 113. Esta Ley deroga en todas sus partes el Título XVI Notariado del Libro IV del Código Administrativo de la República de Panamá; la Ley 57 de 5 de octubre de 1976, Ley 3 de 13 de enero de 1998, el Decreto de Gabinete N.°261 de 30 de julio de 1970, así como el Decreto de Gabinete N.°182 de 2 de septiembre de 1971.

Artículo 114. Esta Ley comenzará a regir tres (3) meses contados a partir de su promulgación. COMUNIQUESE Y CÚMPLASE.

Propuesto a la consideración de la Honorable Asamblea Nacional, hoy ____ de ____ de 2014, por S.E. MILTON HENRIQUEZ SASSO, ministro de gobierno en virtud de autorizacion concedida por el Honorable Consejo de Gabinete, mediante la Resolucion de

Gabinete N.o 168 de 28 octubre de 2014.

MILTON HENRIQUEZ
Ministro

第六篇
最终规定

第112条　对2012年11月9日的第83号法律第1条进行修改，修改后的内容如下：

第1条　适用范围。本法确定了在线执行行政手续必须遵守的准则和基本原则，不包括行政救济渠道中的法律行动和补救措施。

本法法令适用于中央政府、自治实体、半自治实体、市政府、国民大会、司法机构、金融中介机构及国家持有51%或以上股本的企业。还有更多企业将逐渐被划入适用范围。

普通公证处和认证公证处还应实施本法规定的特别管理体制。

第113条　本法彻底废除了《巴拿马共和国行政法》第四卷第十六篇关于公证工作的所有条款；并废止1976年10月5日的第57号法律，1998年1月13日的第3号法律，1970年7月30日的第261号内阁令以及1971年9月2日的第182号内阁令。

第114条　本法颁布3个月后生效。

特此通告并责令执行。

经尊敬的内阁委员会通过2014年10月28日第168号内阁决议授权，政府部部长米尔顿·恩里克斯·萨索于2014年10月28日将法案提交至尊敬的国民大会，供其审议并批准。

米尔顿·恩里克斯
政府部部长
（签名）

波多黎各

波多黎各公证人法

LAWS OF PUERTO RICO ANNOTATED

Copyright; 1955-2005 by the Secretary of State of Puerto Rico and LEXISNEXIS of Puerto Rico, Inc.

波多黎各现行法
（国务卿与律商协会注解版）

TITLE 4. JUDICIARY

PART VI. NOTARIAL PRACTICE

CHAPTER 101. 1987 NOTARIAL ACT

SUBCHAPTER I. THE NOTARY AND HIS FUNCTIONS

§2001. Short title

This chapter shall be known as the "Puerto Rico Notarial Act".

§2002. Notary—Concept

The notary is a legal professional who practices a public function, authorized to attest and authenticate pursuant to the laws the juridical business and other acts and extrajudicial events executed before him, without prejudice of what is provided in the special laws. His function is to receive and interpret the will of the parties giving it a legal format, draft the notarial documents and deeds for such purpose and confer authority to them. The notary's public faith is complete with regard to the facts carried out and corroborated by him in the exercise of his functions, and also with regard to the manner, place, date and time of the execution.

§2003. Notary—Autonomy

The notary shall be authorized to practice his office throughout the Commonwealth of Puerto Rico. In that function he shall enjoy full autonomy and independence.

第四编 司法

第六部分 公证执业规则

第101章 1987年公证人法

第一节 公证及其功能

§2001 简称

本章应称为《波多黎各公证人法》。

§2002 公证人的概念

公证人是依法履行公证职能的法定专业人员，其根据法律授权，在不损害特别法规定之前提下，依法对法律事务和法外事宜进行证明和认证。其职能包括在接受和解释双方意愿的基础上赋予该意愿法律格式；以此为目的，起草公证文件实施公证行为并授权。公证人的公信力应与其行使职权时所执行和证实的事实，采用的方式，地点、执行日期和时间相一致。

§2003 公证人的独立性

公证人应被授权在波多黎各联邦执业。在职权范围内，公证人享有充分的自主权和独立性。公证人应依据波多黎各最高法院的行政指示，通过本章规定

He shall exercise it with impartiality and will be under the administrative direction of the Supreme Court of Puerto Rico, through the Office of Notarial Inspection created by this chapter.

§2004. Notary—Public office; incompatibility

In addition to the legal impediments that might exist, the office of notary shall be incompatible with any public office when there is a prohibition of the notarial practice by the public body for which he carries out his functions. The public bodies shall notify the Office of Notarial Inspection of the prohibitions they establish.

§2005. Notary—Prohibitions; ineffectiveness

(a) No notary may authorize documents he is a party to, or which include provisions in his favor. Neither may he authorize them if any one of the executing parties is related to him within the fourth degree of consanguinity or the second degree of affinity, except when he appears in the document as a representative.

(b) The provisions in favor of relatives of the notary who authorized the public document in which they were made within the fourth degree of consanguinity or the second degree of affinity shall have no effect.

§2006. Notary—Deeds; protocols; deposits

The notary shall write original notarial deeds, issue copies and draw up protocols. He shall be the depository of the documents, securities and sums that the parties wish to deposit with the notary to secure their contracts. Admission of these deposits is voluntary and the notary may impose conditions on the depositor which will be consigned in the receipt or collateral agreement issued by the notary.

§2011. Notarial practice—Requirements

Only those presently authorized to practice the notarial profession and those attorneys who in the future are admitted to practice the profession, who are members of the Puerto Rico Bar Association and are thereafter authorized to practice as notaries by the Supreme Court of Puerto Rico, shall practice the notarial profession in the Commonwealth of Puerto Rico.

Every notary shall pledge an oath of fidelity to the Constitution of the United States of America and the Constitution and Laws of the Commonwealth of Puerto Rico before beginning the practice of his office.

No person authorized to practice the profession of notary in Puerto Rico may practice it without having posted and keeping in effect a bond for a sum of not less

的公证处，以公正的方式行事。

§2004 公职机构与公证配伍禁止

除了可能存在的法律障碍外，公证机关在指派人员执行职务时，不得违背任何公职机构发布的关于公证执业的禁令。公职机构应当通知公证机关其所设立的禁令。

§2005 禁止与无效的行为

（a）公证人不得为本人或为对其有利的条款办理公证。公证人也不得为其四代血亲或二代姻亲内的近亲属办理公证，除非其仅作为代表出现在公证文书中。

（b）公证人为其四代血亲或二代姻亲内的近亲属办理的公证无效。

§2006 公证文书、协议和存管

公证人应当签发原始公证书，发放副本并制定协议书。其将作为当事人希望两公证人交存以确保其合同的文件、证券和金额的存放处。接受这些存款须是自愿的，公证人可以对在其签发的收据或抵押协议中注明对存托人施加的条件。

§2011 公证执业规则

目前被授权执业的公证专业人员和将获得执业资格的律师才能作为波多黎各律师协会的成员，并由波多黎各最高法院授权作为执业公证人，在波多黎各联邦进行公证执业。

每名公证人在执业之前必须宣誓忠于美利坚合众国宪法和波多黎各联邦宪法。

授权在波多黎各执业的公证人，执业前必须缴纳不少于15000美元的保证金，保证其适当履行职务以及在履职过程中因作为或不作为所造成的损害进行赔

than fifteen thousand (15,000) dollars to answer for the proper performance of the functions of his office and damages caused by his acts or omissions in the exercise of his duties. This bond's limits do not impair the rights of the Commonwealth of Puerto Rico nor of natural or juridical persons under §5141 of Title 31 or under any other legal or jurisprudential provision. The notary's surety shall be a mortgage bond, or posted by an insurance company authorized to do business in Puerto Rico, or by the Puerto Rico Bar Association, which is hereby authorized to charge the amount it deems reasonable for posting that security as provided in the act.

The surety bond must be renewed annually and approved by the Supreme Court of Puerto Rico which will review its sufficiency with regard to the mortgages, which shall be registered in the corresponding property registry office before its final approval.

The bond shall have preferent liability for the sums that the notary fails to deposit with the Commonwealth of Puerto Rico on account of Internal Revenue, notarial and other legally required stamps, for binding of protocols and any other necessary expense incurred as indicated by the Director of Notarial Inspection in order to carry out the inspection of notaries and their approval. Once the expenses are established, he may proceed against the bond directly to pay the obligations.

If the claimant is adjudicated all or part of the bond in a judicial claim against the notary, he shall not continue to practice until he posts a new bond.

All sums collected by the Bar Association for the posting of this security shall be covered into a fund designated as a "SPECIAL FUND" on account of notarial bond premiums, which shall be administered as it is established by §2141 of this title.

Once the surety bond is approved and the notary takes the oath of office, he must register his signature, sign, seal and flourish at the Department of State pursuant to the provisions of §2012 of this title as well as in a Register kept for that purpose in the office of the Clerk of the Supreme Court of Puerto Rico. That Register shall also include his place of residence and location of the notarial office. The notary is bound to notify the same officer of any change in residence or notarial office within five (5) days after it occurs.

§2012. Notarial practice—Certificate; display

The Secretary of State shall issue a certificate to the notary attesting to his name and residence as well as

偿。关于该保证金的限制不会损害波多黎各联邦的权利，也不损害第31章§5141或任何其他法律或判例条款下的自然人或法人的权利。公证人的担保方式应为抵押债券，或由被授权在波多黎各营业的保险公司或由波多黎各律师协会确定的方式，该律师协会有权对本法中规定的保证金收取其认为合理的费用。

保证金必须每年更新一次，并由波多黎各最高法院审核该保证金的充足性。核准的保证金在最终批准前应在相应的财产登记处登记。

该保证金不能存入公证人在波多黎各联邦内部的收入账户。公证或其他法律要求时，对公证书处长为对公证人进行检查和批准而指示的议定书和产生的其他任何必要费用，有优先偿付的责任。一旦以上费用确定，可以直接以保证金支付。

如果根据司法裁判，索赔人将全部或部分获得保证金，则公证人在缴纳新的保证金前不得继续执业。

由律师协会收取的本保证金款项，将被特定为"特别基金"存入公证保证金账户，具体规定由第2141条确定。

一旦保证金被核准且公证人完成宣誓，必须依照本法第2012条的规定在国务院和波多黎各最高法院书记办公室内备存的登记册上签字、盖章、登记。

该登记内容还应包括公证人的居住地点和公证处的所在地点。上述地点如果发生变更，公证人必须在变更发生后的5日内报告。

§2012 公证执业证书与公示

国务大臣应向公证人出具证明其姓名和居住地的执业证书，证书还应注明最高法院授权其作为公证人

membership number and the date on which the Supreme Court authorized him to practice as a notary, the date on which he registered his signature, sign, flourish and seal as a notary at the Department of State, and the facsimile of his registered signature, sign, seal or flourish, all attested to by the Secretary of State. It shall be the obligation of the notary to display the certificate on one of the walls of his office.

§2013. Notarial practice—Temporary substitutions

The notary may appoint another notary to substitute for him/her when he/she is absent from his/her office for any nonpermanent cause, for a maximum initial period of three (3) months. Said period may be extended after having so requested to the Director of Inspection of Notaries in exceptional cases and when there is a just cause, up to a maximum term of six (6) months.

The notary as well as his substitute shall notify the Office of Notarial Inspection of the substitution in the same document and under their signatures.

The notary shall not authorize original documents in the name of the substituted notary. He shall be responsible for the custody and conservation of the protocols of the notary he is substituting for and, as such, may issue certified copies.

§2021. Duties of the notary—Stamps; exemptions

It shall be the duty of every notary to attach and cancel on each original deed granted and on the certified copies issued thereby, the corresponding internal revenue stamps, and a stamp to be adopted by the Puerto Rico Bar Association and issued at a cost of one dollar, and whose proceeds shall be covered into the funds of said Association. Provided, That the Secretary of the Treasury may adopt and issue notarial tax stamps electronically, per se, or through internal revenue agents. Said stamps will serve the same purpose and shall be used in the same way.

The deed or certified copies of it shall be voidable or ineffective if the corresponding stamps are not attached to it. However, any of the parties to the document may deliver the amount of said fees to the corresponding official without impairing the provisions of the fifth paragraph of §2011 of this title.

The Bar Association of Puerto Rico shall be bound to designate at least one third (1/3) of the total income derived from the notarial stamp to community services programs, such as free legal aid to indigents and continu-

执业的日期，在国务院作为公证人签字、盖章、注册的日期。上述文件的副本均交由国务卿认证。公证人有义务在其办公室公示公证执业证书。

§2013 执业中的暂时替代

公证人以非永久的理由暂离公证处时可以指定另一名公证人接替其公证，但最长不超过3个月。在特殊情况下，在向公证人检查总监说明正当理由后，上述期限可延长至6个月。

公证人及其替补人员应在同一份文件上签字，通过该文件将替代事宜通知公证处。

负责接替的公证人不得以原公证人的名义授权原始文件。临时替代的公证人负责保管和保护其所接替的公证人的公证文书，并且有权发出认证书副本。

§2021 公证印花税及免除

每名公证人应对其附加和取消的每份原始文件和由此发出的认证副本负责，通过相应的印花税票获得收入。该印花税票由波多黎各律师协会通过并以一美元的价格发行，其所得款项将计入该协会的基金。库务局长可以通过电子或内部收入代理人的方式发行公证印花税票，该印花税票将以相同的方式用于相同的目的。

公证文书如果没有附上相应的印花税票，其契约或核证副本将无效或失效。但是，文件的任何一方当事人均可以将该费用自行交给相关官员，而不会损害本编第2011条第5款的规定。

波多黎各律师协会必须将公证印花税所得总收入的至少1/3用于为指定的社区服务计划，例如向贫困者提供免费法律援助，并为律师和公证人提供法律继续教育。协会有义务在每年二月之前，向最高法院提

ing legal education programs for attorneys and the notaries themselves. No later than the month of February, the Association shall be bound to file an annual report before the Supreme Court specifying the income for the previous year from that concept, its use and the remainder.

Notaries from the Puerto Rico Legal Services Corporation, San Juan Legal Services, and any other nonprofit entity or organization certified by the Secretary of Justice whose purposes and functions are similar to those of these corporations shall not be bound to attach and cancel the stamps mentioned in this section when they execute documents for indigent persons following the eligibility criteria established by these bodies, but this circumstance shall be included in the document.

§2022. Duties of the notary—Informative return on segregation, merging or transfer of real estate

In the execution of deeds of segregation, merger or transfer of dominion the transferor or person who segregates or merges will be bound to complement and deposit at the office of the authorizing notary the Informative Return on the Segregation, Merging or Transfer of Real Estate.

That return shall include the following information:

(1) Number, date of the deed and legal business transacted.

(2) Name of those appearing, specifying the nature of their appearance and Social Security number.

(3) Property or cadastre number.

The property cadastre number shall be taken from the latest available tax notice or receipt issued by the Secretary of the Treasury.

It is hereby provided that the District Office of the Bureau of Taxes on Property, Estate and Gifts of the Treasury Department of Puerto Rico shall offer the official records number or code within seven (7) days of its request. If this is not possible, it shall issue a negative certificate stating the reasons for not being able to offer the number requested.

This certificate shall be sent to the Secretary of the Treasury together with the informative return.

(4) The real property registry's data including folio, volume, farm number and town.

(5) Price of transaction.

(6) Type of structure, if applicable.

(7) Type of property, location and address.

The return must be signed by the seller or by the person who segregates or merges, who shall certify the

交年度报告，其中须包括上一年的收入，其使用情况及剩余部分等内容。

来自波多黎各法律服务公司、圣胡安法律服务公司以及任何其他经司法部认证的目的和职能与公证机构相似的非营利实体或组织中的公证人，在按照这些机构确定的资格标准为贫困人员办理公证时，可以不附上或揭下本条所述的印花税票，但这种情况应在文件中注明。

§2022 房地产分割、合并或转让的资料保存

在执行房地产分割、合并或转让行为时，分立人、合并人或转让人应在公证处补充并存放房地产分割、合并或转让的资料。

该资料应记载以下内容：
（1）交易和法定业务办理的数量和日期。

（2）房地产的名称、外观特征和社会保险编号。

（3）财产或地籍编号。
财产地籍编号依库务局长最新提交的税务通知或税收凭证为准。

特此规定，波多黎各财政部下属的财产和礼品税务局民政事务处应在收到出具请求后7日内提供正式记录号或代码。如果无法提供，应出具否定证书，说明无法提供编号的原因。

该证书应与资料一并发送给财政部长。

（4）不动产登记的信息包括对开、数量、农场和城镇住房编号。
（5）交易价格。
（6）如果可行的话，提供结构的类型。
（7）不动产的类型、位置和地址。
交易资料必须由卖方或分离人或合并人签署，签名者对信息的真实性承担证明责任。

veracity of the information given with his signature and responsibility.

The notaries shall be bound to send to the Department of the Treasury during the first ten (10) days of each month the returns corresponding to the deeds executed before them during the previous month.

§2023. Duties of the notary—Monthly indices

The notaries shall send a monthly index of their notarial activities no later than the tenth calendar day of the month following the month reported to the Office of the Director of Notarial Inspection of Puerto Rico that will state, with respect to the original deeds and affidavits authorized by them during the preceding month, the numbers in numerical order, the name of those appearing, date, the subject of the instrument or testimony and the name of the witnesses, if any appeared.

In said report the notary shall certify to having sent the returns to the Treasury Department as required pursuant to §2022 of this title.

If the notary has not had any notarial activity during a particular month, he shall send a negative report for said month to the Inspector of Notaries.

§2031. Public documents—Classes

The original deed is the one that the notary shall write regarding the contract or act submitted for his authorization signed by the grantors, by the attesting witnesses or those having knowledge of the facts of his case, signed, marked, sealed and flourished by the notary himself.

The public documents include public deeds and notarial certificates whether they are originals or certified copies.

§2032. Public documents—Drawing; contents

Notaries shall write the public documents according to the will of the grantors and adapt them to the juridical formalities necessary to their effectiveness.

Whenever the grantors hand over to the notary drafts or certificates concerning the act or contract they have submitted for his authorization, he must state it without impairing his review and editing, with their consent, to the effect that the meaning of the statements of will and agreements comprised therein are clearly and specifically stated.

§2033. Public documents—Formal requirements; cognizance; legal warnings

The expository and dispositive part of the public deed, together with the legal transaction which motivates

公证人必须在每个月的前十日内向财政部发送其上个月在其执业中产生的相对应资料。

§2023 公证人职责：发布每月指数

公证人员应在不迟于向波多黎各公证处处长办公室报告的次月的 10 日内，发布每月公证指数。每个月的公证活动指数包括关于上个月授权的原始行为和誓章，以数字大小顺序排列的数据，出现的名称，日期，文书或证词的主题，如果有证人则还包括证人的姓名。

在该报告中，公证人应证明其已按照第 2022 条的要求向财政部发送了数据报告。

如果公证人在一个月内没有公证活动，则应向公证督察员发送上述月份的负面报告。

§2031 公开文件的分类

原始契约是公证人应就设保人签署的授权签署的合同或行为，由证明证人或知情人证实，并经公证人签字、标记、盖章。

公开文件包括公共文件和公证证书，包括原件及认证副本。

§2032 公共文书的起草和内容

公证人应当按照申请人的意愿书写公共文书，并为其办理保证文件有效性所需的司法手续。

当申请人将公证文件草稿或证明文件交给公证人办理公证时，其必须在不妨碍审查和编辑情况下说明其意图和目的，以确定文件所表明的是其本人的真实意愿。

§2033 公证文件的格式要求、认定和法律警示

公证契约的解释和决定部分，以及促成其法律交易的部分，其前情及公证人目击和受委托查明的事实

its execution, its antecedents and the facts witnessed to and consigned by the notary, shall contain the following:

(a) Its corresponding protocol number written in letters at the beginning thereof.

(b) The classification of the act or contract with its legally recognized name unless it does not have a special one.

(c) The notary's name, his residence, the location of his office, as well as the day, month and year and place of execution which shall be that in which the last of the grantors signs the document if there are no attesting witnesses.

(d) The name and surname or surnames, as the case may be, age or legal age, civil status, profession, and residence of the grantors, their Social Security number, if they have one, name and circumstances of the witnesses, if any, according to their statements.

In the event that any of the grantors is married and the appearance of the spouse is not necessary, the spouse's name and surname shall be stated, even though the spouse does not appear at the execution.

(e) The attestation to [sic] by the notary as to his personal cognizance of the grantors or, in its absence, of having verified their identity by the means established by this chapter that, in his judgment, they have the necessary legal capacity to execute the act or contract concerned, and of having read the deed to them and the witnesses, in their case, or having allowed them the option to read it before signing it, or of a waiver of their right to do so.

(f) Of having orally made the pertinent legal warnings and reservations to the grantors during the act of execution. This notwithstanding, there shall be consigned in the document those warnings that, in the notary's judgment, must be expressly detailed due to their importance.

(g) In a purchase-sale deed in which a juridical transaction of a pro indiviso abstract and undefined portion of land, the notary shall have to advise the grantors of the legal effects of community property, as established by the provisions of the Puerto Rico Civil Code. He/she shall also admonish them that they cannot segregate, subdivide, indicate or otherwise identify their share of said land without the corresponding permit of the Planning Board, the Regulations and Permits Administration or the corresponding agency; that the share acquired by the purchaser is abstract and undefined, and that any arrangement, agreement or pact to segregate, subdivide, indicate, or otherwise identify it would be null and void and could be considered a crime, if no corresponding permit of the regulating agencies ex-

应包含以下内容：

（a）在协议首以字母注明其相应的协议号。

（b）以合法认可的名称对该行为或合同进行分类，除非其没有专门的法定名称。

（c）公证人姓名、居住地、公证处的地点以及执行日期，月份、年份和地点。如果没有经认证的证人，则由最后一位设保人签署该文件。

（d）姓名或姓氏（视情况而定）、申请人的年龄、法定年龄、公民身份、职业和居住地、其社会保障号码（如有）、证人的姓名和概况，以及证人的证词（如有的话）。

如果任何申请人已经结婚，而其配偶的没有必要参与公证事宜，则即使配偶参与公证，也应在公证书中说明申请人配偶的名字和姓氏。

（e）公证人对申请人的认定。该认定源于公证人个人对申请人法律资格的判定，或者在缺席的情况下，通过本章确定的手段验证了他们的身份，认为他们具有执行该行为或合同的必要法律行为能力。还需要注明公证人已向申请人和证人宣读公证文书的情况，并告知其有权在签署之前阅读公证文书，也有权放弃该权利。

（f）在办理公证行为时对申请人口头提出的相关法律警告和保留意见。尽管由口头形式作出，但仍应记载于公证文书的公证人判断部分，并对其重要性进行明确详细的说明。

（g）在购销合同中，如涉及独立抽象和未确权部分土地的司法交易，公证人必须根据《波多黎各民法典》的规定，向申请人告知该财产的法律效力。公证人还应告知申请人，在未取得规划委员会、相关条例和许可证管理局或相关机构的相应许可证前，不得分割、细分、表明或以其他方式标明其在该土地上的份额；由于买方获得的份额是抽象的和未定义的，因此在没有相应的规范许可证之前，任何关于上述土地的安排或协议，以分割、细分、表明或以其他方式标明权利都将是无效的，并可以被认为是犯罪。购销合同中还应注明接受买方作为共同租户收购的情形，上述事宜均应在合同中说明。

ists. It shall also include the acceptance of the purchaser to acquire it as a joint tenant, all of which shall be stated in the text of the deed.

§2034. Public documents—Signatures; initials; flourish and seal

The grantors and witnesses shall sign the deed and shall also affix the initials of their name and surname or surnames to the margin of each one of the pages of the document which shall be flourished and sealed by the notary.

§2035. Public documents—Identification of parties

In the absence of personal cognizance by the notary, the following shall be supplemental means of identification:

(a) An assertion of a person who knows the grantor and is responsible for the identification and is known by the notary, and the notary is responsible for the witness' identity.

(b) The identification of one of the contracting parties by the other, provided that the notary certifies his cognizance of the latter.

(c) Identification by identity document with a photograph and signature issued by competent public authorities of the Commonwealth of Puerto Rico, the United States or a state of the Union, whose purpose is to identify the persons, or by a passport duly issued by a foreign authority.

Witnesses as to identity shall be responsible for the identification of the grantors, as shall the grantor who attests to the identity of other grantors not known by the notary, and the notary shall be responsible for the cognizance of such witnesses.

§2036. Public documents—Representation

The notary shall record the intervention of the grantors by stating whether they do so in their own name or in behalf of another, except when the representation arises from the law, in which case the grantor's investiture shall be accredited, unless it is of general knowledge, in which case the notary may take cognizance of it and record it.

The representative shall sign the document with his own signature without it being necessary to first place the name of the person he represents or use the firm name or name of the entity he represents.

§2037. Public documents—Evidence of representation

Every grantor who appears in representation of another person shall always validate his designation before the notary with authenticating documents, except when

§2034 公证文书的签名、缩写、盖章和密封

申请人和证人应在公证文书上签字，并将其名称、姓名或姓氏在公证文书的每一页边缘签字，公证人须在公证文书的每一页的边缘盖章并密封。

§2035 当事人身份确认

当公证人未能证实个人法律身份时，依照以下补充手段认定：

（a）由公证人可确认的其他人声明了解申请人并对其负责，公证人对证人的身份有证实的义务。

（b）合同一方当事人的身份不明时，公证人查实另一方当事人的身份即可。

（c）个人身份由波多黎各联邦主管公共机构、美国联邦或州签发的附照片的身份证明文件证明，或者由外国当局正式签发的护照证明。

关于个人身份的证人有义务确认申请人的身份，证明公证人无法证实的其他申请人身份的申请人也有义务确认其身份。公证人对上述负责确认他人身份的人有查实认定的义务。

§2036 代理

公证人应当记录申请人对以自己的名义办理或接受他人委托代为办理的声明。只有具备合法形式的授权代理才能被认定；除非依照常识，普遍认为在该种情形下不必完成法律形式上的委托，代理行为已成立。

代理人必须以自己的签名签署公证文书，而不必首先签署被代理人的姓名或被代表的实体或公司的名称。

§2037 代理人身份的证明

除非得到申请人的明确同意，代理人的身份始终应由公证人依据其身份证明文件进行认定。文件的全部效力从属于代理人提交的书面证据。

there is the expressed agreement of the grantors. The full effectiveness of the documents shall be subordinated to the presentation of documentary evidence of the alleged representation.

There shall also be recorded the nature of the intervention of those grantors who appear only to the effect of complementing the capacity or give their authorization or consent to the contract.

Public officials legally authorized to represent the Commonwealth of Puerto Rico, municipalities, instrumentalities or corporations shall not have to validate their powers before the notary.

§2038. Public documents—Attesting witnesses

The intervention of attesting witnesses shall not be necessary in the execution of deeds, except when required by the authorizing notary or any of the parties, or when one of the grantors does not know how to or cannot read or sign. This provision does not apply to wills which shall be governed by what is established by applicable legislation.

Attesting witnesses shall be present at the act of reading, consenting, signing and execution of the public document. Likewise, they may be identifying witnesses who, in turn, may be attestors if they meet the applicable legal requirements.

§2039. Public documents—Executing party who does not know how to or cannot read or sign

When any of the grantors does not know how to, or cannot read, the document in question shall be read out loud twice, once by the notary and another by the witness designated by the grantor, all of which shall be attested to by the notary.

When any of the grantors is deaf or blind who does not know how to read and sign, he must designate a witness who upon his request shall read or sign the public document for him or both. The notary shall record these circumstances.

§2040. Public documents—Witnesses; qualifications

The witnesses, including those as to identity, shall be of legal age, competent and know how to read and write and sign. Employees of the executing notary, his relatives or those of the interested parties within the fourth degree of consanguinity or the second of affinity shall not be attesting witnesses.

§2041. Public documents—Sufficient witnesses

One person shall suffice as attesting witness desig-

公证文书中还应记录只出于补充行为能力或强调授权或同意的目的而参与公证行为的性质。

已经合法授权代表波多黎各联邦，市政当局，机构或公司的公职人员，不必再由公证确认其职权。

§2038 认证证人

签署协议时证明当事人身份的认证证人不必到场，除非公证人或其他当事人要求，或其中有申请人不知道如何或不能阅读或签字。本条不适用于可适用法律规范的遗嘱。

认证证人应参与公证文书的阅读、同意、签署和执行行为。同样的，认证证人如果符合法律的要求，反过来也可能作为证人。

§2039 不知道或不能阅读或签名的签署方

当申请人不知道如何或不能阅读时，有关文件应大声朗读两次，一次由公证人，另一次由申请人指定的证人进行，上述情况均由公证人证明。

当申请人是聋人或盲人，不知道如何阅读和签署文件时，则必须指定一名证人，按照其要求阅读或（并）签署公证文件。对上述情况公证人应予以记录。

§2040 证人的资质

证人，含认证证人，应达到法定年龄，有行为能力，能够阅读、书写和签字。公证人的近亲属或者其四代血亲或二代姻亲关系中有关各方的亲属均不得作为认证证人。

§2041 足够的证人

应申请人或公证人要求，申请人应具备一名申请

nated by the grantors, if they or the notary so require it. However, any of the two may oppose that certain persons act as such.

§2042. Public documents—Unity of action

When the witnesses appear at the execution of the document there shall be unity of action, to which the notary shall attest in the writ.

§2043. Public documents—Executing party who does not know how to or cannot sign

Whenever any of the grantors does not know how to, or cannot sign, the notary shall require that they affix their two (2) thumb prints. If they do not have thumbs, any other fingers, next to the witness' signature who signs at his or their request, and on the margin of the rest of the document's folios, all which the notary shall attest to in the deed. If the grantor or grantors have no fingers, the notary shall state this circumstance and two (2) attesting witnesses shall sign at their request.

§2044. Public documents—Attestation by notary.

It shall not be necessary for the notary to state that he attests to the stipulation included in each clause of the deed, nor of the legal condition or circumstances of the persons or cases to which it refers, it being sufficient that it be consigned once at the end of the document, which will certify its entire contents, so that such statement is understood to apply to all the words, stipulations, statements and conditions, real or personal, contained in the instrument in accordance with the law.

§2045. Public documents—Use of arabic numbers or abbreviations; blanks; possible means of drawing

Numbers shall not be used to express dates and amounts, unless they are also consigned in letters, except those included in direct quotations. Neither may abbreviations be used, nor blank spaces left in the text, and the originals may be handwritten as long as indelible ink, printing or a typewriter with an indelible ribbon are used, or through other mechanical or electronic mechanisms that produce indelible and permanent documents.

§2046. Public documents—Execution

Those persons who sign a public document for any reason shall do so by signing at the end and affixing the initials of their name and surname or surnames in the margin of all the folios, in the manner they usually do so, and the notary shall do so after them, flourishing, signing and sealing it.

人指定的证人。但任何一方当事人都可以对证人提出反对。

§2042 一致行动

当证人参与文件签署时，须由公证人在该令状中证明证人的一致行动。

§2043 不知道如何签名或不能签名的签署方

如果申请人不知道如何签名或不能签名，公证人应要求其用大拇指画押两次，如果其没有拇指，可以用其他任何手指。画押应在文件的边缘、证人应其要求进行签名处的旁边。上述画押均需公证人在契约中证明。如果申请人没有手指，公证人应说明这种情况，两名认证证人应根据要求签字。

§2044 公证人的认证

公证人无须在文件中的每一条款下声明自己的身份符合法律规定，也不需要在涉及的所有个人或个案中声明自己符合法定条件或情形，只需在文件的结尾声明处一次性证明全部内容。该声明将被用于证实依法载于文书中的所有文字、规定、陈述、条件、财产或个人的其他情况。

§2045 阿拉伯数字或缩写的使用、空白和可能的印刷方式

除了直接引用的内容外，数字不得用于表达日期和数量，除非其包含在字母间。文本中不得包含缩写和空白；原件为手写的，只能使用不可擦除的墨水，以印刷方式记载的，需使用不可磨灭色彩的打字机或其他可以产生不可磨灭的永久文件的机械或电子设备。

§2046 公证文书的签署

因任何原因签署公证文书的人都应按照其通常的方式在文件对开的页面边缘签署其姓名、姓氏或名称。公证人应在完成公证之后，在公证文书上签字、盖章并密封。

If there are no witnesses, it shall not be necessary for those appearing to sign the documents together in the notary's presence, since he may personally receive their signatures at any time within the same calendar day of the execution.

§2047. Public documents—Correction of defects

The defects suffered by inter vivos notarial documents may be corrected without damage to third parties by the parties thereto or by their heirs or assigns, by means of a public deed which sets forth the defect, its cause and the correcting statement.

If the notary fails to record any data or circumstance provided by this chapter, or if it concerns an error in the statement as to the facts witnessed by the notary which is his duty to consign, they may be corrected by the executing notary at his own expense, on his own initiative or by petition of any of the parties, through a notarial certificate that shows the error or defect, its cause and the statement that corrects it.

If it is impossible to make the correction in any of the ways indicated above, it may be obtained by any legally-admitted means of proof, through the corresponding judicial procedure before the Court of First Instance.

In any case, the notary shall indicate the fact of the correction in the margin of the original document under his signature and seal, and shall indicate the deed or notarial certificate in which they were made.

§2048. Public documents—Certificates

The notaries, at the request of a party or on their own initiative and under their oath signature, sign, flourish and notarial seal, shall extend and execute certificates which consign facts and circumstances witnessed by them or of which they have personal knowledge and that due to their nature do not constitute a contract or juridical business.

§2049. Public documents—Contents and formalities of certificates

The notarial certificates shall include the corresponding deed number, the date in which they are executed, the declaratory part and the notary's signature. The enjoiner may sign the certificate if he so wishes, or if required by the notary.

§2050. Public documents—Clerical errors; correction

Any additions, annotations, interlineations, erasures and crossouts in the public deeds shall be held as valueless

§2047 瑕疵的更正

公证文件存在的瑕疵，可以由当事人或其接受方以不损害第三方的方式，通过公开的方式，说明瑕疵的原因并作出更正陈述。

如果公证人没有记录本章规定的数据或情况，或应由公证人负责查证的事实陈述中存在错误，公证人应主动或根据任何一方的请求，自费更正上述错误。并通过发布公证书的方式说明错误或缺陷，及其产生的原因和纠正的声明。

如果瑕疵不可能以上述方式进行更正，则可以通过任何法律上允许的证据方式，通过原诉法庭的相应司法程序获得更正。

公证人应在其所作的公证文书或公证证书原始文件边缘的签字盖章下方注明更正的事实。

§2048 公证证书

公证人应当主动或应一方当事人的要求，经宣誓、签署、盖章和密封程序，应当延期并签发申请人委托其证实的事实、情况或由于性质不构成合同或司法业务而由公证人个人知识证实的状况的证书。

§2049 公证证书的内容和形式

公证书应包括相应的文书编码、签署日期、申报内容和公证人的签名。经当事人自愿，或者应公证人要求，可以签署该证书。

§2051 笔误与更正

公证文书上的任何补充、注释、间隔、删除和交叉，除非在最后一行进行再认证，否则必须经过文件

unless they are certified after the last line, with the express approval and signature of those who must sign the document.

However, the mistaken words may be placed within parentheses followed by the words "I say" [I mean] to make it clear that they should not be read.

The blank spaces remaining at the end of a line or when a paragraph begins on the next line shall not be considered as such; but in this case the blank shall be filled with a line or dash.

§2051. Public documents—Acceptance deeds

A party to a juristic act may appear in a public deed and make an offer to be accepted by another party in a different document that may be executed before another notary on another date and place.

In this case the main deed that sets forth the offer shall also include the personal circumstances of the party who will later appear in the deed of assent, as they are informed by the party thereto, as well as the complete text of the juristic act, without leaving any detail to be added by the deed of assent. It shall also fix the term within which the deed of assent will be executed, its requirements and the causes for the revocation or lapse of the offer's, if any.

In the deed of assent, besides complying with the requirements for public documents imposed by this chapter, there shall be a precise and exact statement of the offer, or there shall be attached a certified copy of the deed of offer to which the deed of assent makes reference, and a statement by the person appearing to the effect that he knows, understands and accepts the offer made in said document.

In the event that the notary who executes or officially records the deed of assent is not the notary who executed the original deed, he will send a certified copy of the deed to the latter, under his notarial certification, personally, or by certified mail with acknowledgement of receipt, and he shall also notify the offerer of the acceptance, by certified mail with acknowledgement of receipt. The notary shall record, through a marginal note or at the end of the original deed, the existence of the deed of assent, identifying it by number, date and name of the executing notary. Once this requirement is complied with, it shall be understood that the offerer has knowledge of the acceptance of his offer.

If the offer is accepted outside Puerto Rico, the notary who executes the deed that sets forth the offer shall comply with what is mandated herein upon receipt of the acceptance in an authentic and duly executed document, and shall also comply with the official recording require-

签署人的明确批准和签名。

但是，笔误的词句可以放在括号内，后面加上"我的意思是"补充，以便明确表示笔误的内容是不应该阅读的。

一行尾部留下的空格或下一行开始的空格不得视为笔误；但在这种情况下，空白应填充为横线或破折号。

§2051 接受要约

法律行为的一方在公共契约中提出一个要约，由另一方在另一个日期和地点的另一个公证人之前签署的另一个文件中接受他方的要约。

在这种情况下，提出的要约应包括随后出现在同意契约中的一方的个人情况、该方的通知，以及法律行为的全文，而不能预留任何细节在后一个同意契约中再添加。在要约中应确定同意契约的期限，其要求和要约撤销或失效的原因（如有）。

在同意契约中，除了遵守本章规定的公共文件要求外，还应对原要约进行准确的陈述，或者附上要约契约的核证副本作为参考，且承诺人须发布声明，陈述其对文件中提及的要约表示理解和接受。

如果签署或正式记录同意书的公证人不是签署原始契约的公证人，则其应按公证书的要求亲自或通过认证邮件的方式将契约的证明副本发送给后者，并通过认证邮件通知原公证人接收。公证人应在边注或原始契约结尾处记录同意契约的存在，并对签署公证人的姓名、日期和名称进行确认。同意契约一旦符合这一要求，则应认为受要约人知道并接受了要约。

如果该要约是在波多黎各境外被接受，则执行提出要约的契约的公证人在收到接受书正本和执行书后，执行时应遵守协议的规定以及第2056条的记录要求。

ment of §2056 of this title.

The assent may also be executed by inclusion in the same deed that sets forth the offer, and any other information that facilitates the identification and location of the executing notary.

§2052. Public documents—Null and void
Public instruments shall be null:

(1) That include any provision in favor of the notary who executes it.

(2) Where the witnesses are relatives of the interested parties in the degree prohibited by §2040 of this title, the relatives or employees of the notary himself.

(3) In which the signatures of the parties and witnesses when they should, and the notary's signature, do not appear.

§2053. Public documents—Voidable
Public instruments in which the notary fails to or does not supplement this deficiency in the form be voidable attest to his cognizance of the grantors established by §2035 of this title shall be voidable

§2054. Public documents—Wills and mortis causa conveyances
That which is provided by §§2031-2053 of this title with regard to the form of the instruments and their nullity shall not be applicable to wills and other mortis causa provisions governed by Title 31.

§2055. Public documents—Paper; margins; binding
Public notarial documents shall be written on sheets of paper or folios thirteen (13) inches long by eight-and-a-half (8 1/2) inches wide and on the side by which they are to be bound, they shall have a blank margin of twenty (20) millimeters plus another on the left side of the deed of sixty (60) millimeters and on the right a strip or margin of three (3) millimeters. If the reverse side of the sheet is used, the margins on it shall completely coincide with those on the face of the document.

§2056. Public documents—Executed outside Puerto Rico; protocolization
In order for it to be valid as a public instrument, every notarial document executed outside Puerto Rico must be previously protocolized, with the notary being bound to cancel the same fees as if it had been originally executed in Puerto Rico.

The protocolization of certifications of resolutions adopted by a Board of Directors of a banking entity, cor-

同意书也可以通过提出要约的同一行为以及通过其他便于执行公证人的身份和地点签署。

§2052 公证文书的无效
以下公证事项无效：

（1）涉及办理公证的公证人的任何事项。

（2）证人是利益相关者在第2040条规定的近亲属，或证人是公证人的雇员或近亲属。

（3）当事人、证人或公证人未在应签字处签名。

§2053 可撤销的公证文书
第2035条规定的对申请人的认证在形式上存在缺陷，若公证人不补充或不能补充完整，则公证书无效。

§2054 遗嘱和临终遗赠
本章第2031条至第2053条条关于公证文书形式和无效的认定不适用于遗嘱和临终遗赠的公证，其由第31章专门规定。

§2055 公证文书的纸张、边距和装订
公证文书应用十三英寸长、八幅半英寸宽的纸张或册子书写，在其装订的一侧，预留二十毫米的空白边距。同时，在左侧加上六十毫米的边距，在右侧预留三毫米的边距。如果需在纸张背面书写，则背面纸张的边距应与正面的边距完全一致。

§2056 公证文书的域外签署及效力
为了使域外签署的公证文书有效力，每一份公证文书都必须履行之前规定的标准流程，公证人在办理时需要扣除其如果在境内办理所要收取的费用。

在波多黎各境外的银行业经营者、法人团体或信托办理公证时，其董事会决议不必经过标准流程认

poration or trust, issued outside Puerto Rico shall not be necessary; but they must be duly attested before a notary and the notary's signature authenticated.

§2061. Copies—Certified

A certified copy is the literal, total or partial transcript of a document executed before a notary that is issued by him or the person officially in charge of his protocol, with a certificate regarding the truth of the contents, and the number of folios of the document as well as the signature, sign and flourish, and the seal and flourish of the attesting notary on every page.

§2062. Copies—Partial

At the request of a party the notary may issue partial copies of documents found in his protocol, stating under his responsibility that there is nothing which broadens, restricts modifies or conditions the excerpt in what is issued.

§2063. Copies—Notation of issuance

When issuing a certified copy the notary shall consign in the main deed, by means of a signed annotation, the name of the person to whom it is issued, the date and the number corresponding to the copy according to those already issued. These data shall appear in the copies.

§2064. Copies—Documents incorporated

When another document has been incorporated to the main deed, every page of the copy issued must be sealed and flourished by the notary and the notary shall likewise certify that it is a true and exact copy of the original joined to the main deed.

§2065. Copies—Persons entitled to

In addition to the grantors, their representatives and assigns, any person entitled to some right as a result of the deed, whether directly, or already acquired through a different deed, and who, in the judgment of the notary or the Notarial Registrar concerned, establishes a legitimate interest in the document, except for wills executed prior to the death of the testator, shall be entitled to obtain copies at any time. All persons entitled to obtain copies may conduct said transaction through legal or voluntary representation provided the right for so doing is vouched for by the notary or the Notarial Registrar concerned, and that the latter states in writing under his/her signature, the full name of the person being represented and the basis whereby he/she deems that the person thus represented is entitled, per se, to obtain the copy being requested.

证，但上述机构应当面向公证人妥善证明，并由公证人签字确认。

§2061 公证副本的认证

经核证的副本是指由公证人或正式负责该公证书的人出具的关于公证书内容、文件的数量、签名盖章的全部或部分转录本。在公证书副本的每一页公证人都应签字、盖章。

§2062 部分副本

应当事人的要求，公证人可以出具包含公证文书中部分内容的副本，并有义务声明，其对该副本未做任何扩大、限制或修改负责。

§2063 出具注释

公证人出具核证副本时，还应当在同一文件中出具注明签发人姓名、签发日期、原文件编号的注释。上述数据也应在副本中体现出来。

§2064 文书合并

当另一份公证文书需要与主文件合并时，主文件副本的每一页都需要由公证人盖章，同样的，公证人还应证实该副本是合并后文件的真实准确的复制件。

§2065 有权获得公证文书副本的人

除了在立遗嘱人去世前办理公证的遗嘱，对于其他的公证文书，除申请人、其代理人和权利继受人外，因契约而有权享有某些权利的任何一方，无论该权利是直接的还是通过其他行为获得，或依据公证人或公证处的裁决而确定对该文件享有的合法权益的人，均有权随时获得副本。所有有权获得复印件的人在获得公证人或公证处的授权之后都可以通过法律规定或自愿的方式通过代理进行交易，而代理人需要在签名下方注明被代理人的全名和被代理人有权获得所要求的副本的依据。

§2066. Copies—Refusal to issue

Once a notary has refused to issue a copy one may appear formally or informally before the Director of the Office of Notarial Inspection, who, having heard said notary and the complainant, shall dictate what is in order. If the decision directs that a copy be issued, the notary shall record it on the copy's issuance annotation in the main deed and in its certification annotation. Such a resolution shall be drafted in a brief and concise manner and the notary shall be notified.

The notary's denial, confirmed by the Director of the Office of Inspection of Notarial Offices, may be appealed before the competent part of the Court of First Instance. Said part may order the issuance of the copy or confirm the denial after examining the arguments of the appellant and the resolution of the Director of the Office of Inspection of Notarial Offices. Such resolution may be revised by the Supreme Court through certiorari.

§2067. Copies—Means of production

The notary is hereby empowered to issue certified photographic copies, or copies reproduced by any other electronic means, of original deeds which once they are certified by the notary shall be deemed valid for all legal purposes.

§2068. Copies—Simple

Notaries may issue simple copies of main deeds upon request of the same persons with a right to request certified copies, but without a guaranteed transcription of the document. These copies shall not be signed, sealed or flourished, nor shall a marginal note of its certified copy be placed on the original deed.

The notary shall allow the contents of documents of his protocol to be read by those who, in his judgment, show a legitimate interest as provided in §2065 of this title.

§2071. Protocol—Concept and characteristics

The protocol is the orderly collection of original deeds and acts executed during a calendar year by the notary, as well as the documents included therein.

The protocol shall be secret and shall only be examined according to the provisions of this chapter or by judicial order issued pursuant to the provisions of this chapter.

§2072. Protocol—State property; responsibility for custody

The protocols belong to the State. Notaries shall conserve them in accordance with the provisions of this chap-

§2066 拒绝出具副本的情形及处理

公证人一旦拒绝出具公证书副本，则申请人可以向公证主管机构申诉，主管机构在听取了公证人及申诉人意见的情况下应作出裁决。如果裁决公证人应出具公证书副本，则公证人应将上述情况记录在主文书以及公证证书的副本上。上述决定应以简洁准确的方式作出，并通知公证人。

如果公证主管机构负责人维持了公证人拒绝出具公证书副本的决定，则当事人有权向原诉法院的相关主管部门提出上诉。法院的主管部门有权在审查上诉人的主张和公证主管机构负责人的决议后作出命令公证人出具副本或拒绝出具副本的决议。最高法院可以通过诉讼令状的方式修改以上决议。

§2067 副本的制作方式

公证人有权以包括影印在内的一切电子形式制作公证书副本，且一旦公证书原件经公证人认证，则在其一切法律用途中均被视为有效。

§2068 简单副本

应有权获得认证副本的当事人申请，公证人可以出具主公证文书的简单副本，公证人对该份简单副本的转录不承担责任。对上述简单副本不得签名、盖章，也不得作为认证副本的边注放置在原始公证文书中。

公证人应允许其认为得到本章第 2065 条授权的人阅读公证文书的内容。

§2071 公证总簿的概念和性质

公证总簿是公证人在一个日历年内办理的原始文书和行为的有序收集，以及其中包含的文件。

公证总簿属于机密文件，仅可根据本章的规定或本章提出的司法令状进行查阅。

§2072 公证总簿作为国家财产及保管责任

公证总簿属于国家财产，公证机构应依照本章的规定妥善保管并对其完整性负责。如果公证总簿被损

ter and shall be responsible for their integrity. If they are damaged or lost due to neglect, the notaries shall replace them at their own expense, and the Supreme Court shall also be able to impose the sanctions established in §2102 of this title, at its discretion. If there is reason to suspect the commission of a crime, the competent authority shall be informed, so that the corresponding action is taken.

§2073. Protocol—Foliated pages

All of the protocol's pages, including its attachments, shall be permanently foliated on the upper right hand side with the corresponding numerical order, written in figures.

Each folio shall bear its corresponding number according to the pages of the document.

§2074. Protocol—Opening and closing formalities

The first face of the first document of each document of each protocol shall be labeled in the following manner:

"Protocol of public documents corresponding to the year (X)."

On the last day of each natural year, each protocol shall be closed in the same manner with the notary attesting the following annotation at the end of the last page of the last deed officially recorded:

"Hereby concludes the protocol for the year (X) which contains (so many) public instruments and (so many) folios authorized by me, the undersigned notary, to which I attest."

These notes, at the opening as well as at the protocol's closing, shall be signed, sealed, flourished and dated by the attesting notary.

§2075. Protocol—Additional volumes

If a protocol has more than one volume for any year, each additional volume shall be opened with the following note:

"Hereby commences Volume (X) of my protocol of public deeds corresponding to the year (X)."

By the same token each additional volume that is not the last shall be also closed with the following note:

"Hereby concludes Volume (X) of my protocol of public deeds that contains (so many) instruments and (so many) folios."

§2076. Binding

The protocols of the preceding year together with the corresponding index of the contents of each volume shall be bound by the third month of each year. Said protocols shall be indexed by order of instrument and shall include

坏或丢失，公证人应自费对其进行修正与更换，最高法院有权依据本章第 2102 条的规定对公证人进行制裁。有理由怀疑公证人的行为构成犯罪的，应通知公证人的主管机关以便采取相应的行动。

§2073 叶状页面

公证总簿的所有页面，包括其附件，都应在其右上角按照数字的顺序编写页码进行永久编页。

公证总簿中的每一页都应有单独的文件页码号。

§2074 公证总簿开头和结尾的格式

每本公证总簿的每份文件的第一篇文件的封面应以下列方式进行标记：

"本公证总簿对应（×）年的所有公证文书。"

在每个自然年份的最后一天，每本公证总簿应以相同的方式作结，公证人在最后一次正式记录的最后一页结尾处进行以下官方记录：

"在此，总结（×）年公证总簿，其包含（诸多）公共及授权的文书，文书由本公证人证明，并在下方签名。"

以上注释和公证总簿的开头、结尾均由公证人认证、签名、盖章并注明日期。

§2075 增加的卷

如果某年的公证总簿不止一卷，每增加一卷都应如下开头：

"此处第（×）卷公证文书对应第（×）年的公证总簿。"

同理，每一不构成最后一卷的附卷应由以下方式作结：

"在此，总结本人所作的（×）卷公证簿，其中包含（诸多）文书。"

§2076 装订

前一年的公证总簿以及各卷内容的相应索引，均应在每年第 3 个月完成装订。所述公证总簿应按文书的顺序进行索引，并应包括出现的当事人的全名，代理人的姓名，办理的情况、日期和地点，涉及的司法

the full name of the parties appearing, the name of the person represented, should that be the case, and the date and place of execution, the juridical business transacted and the number of the folios included therein.

The above notwithstanding, notaries may insert other indexes in the protocols as may be convenient to their practice and use as such.

§2077. Protocol—Removal from office prohibited; exceptions

The protocol shall not be removed from the office where it is kept in custody except by judicial decree or by authorization of the Office of Notarial Inspection.

§2078. Protocol—Fire protection

When the notary's office is located in a wooden or mixed construction building, it shall be provided with fireproof steel or iron boxes in which the protocols shall be kept.

§2079. Protocol—Loss or destruction; reconstruction

In the case a protocol is rendered useless or is lost in whole or in part, the notary shall report the fact to the Chief Justice of the Supreme Court, who shall direct the reconstruction of the proper record by summoning the parties. The indexes and books shall be checked and all necessary records data shall be examined in order to restore insofar as practicable, what has been destroyed or rendered useless. The record shall be approved by the Supreme Court upon a recommendation of the Director of the Protocol Inspection Office.

§2091. Testimony or statement of authenticity—Concept; restrictions; extent of notarial responsibility

The document through which a notary, at the request of an interested party, may notarize a non-original document, in addition to the date of the testimony:

(1) Of the legality of the signatures appearing therein, provided it does not deal with acts included in subsections (1) through (6) of §3453 of Title 31;

(2) of having taken a sworn statement;

(3) of it being a true and exact translation of another document, provided he/she has knowledge of both languages and it is thus certified by the statement itself;

(4) of it being a true and exact copy of a document not found in a Notarial Protocol, or

(5) in general, of the identity of any object or thing, be it called testimony or declaration of authority.

The notary shall, at the request of the interested par-

事宜以及其中包含的文件数量。尽管如此，公证人可在协议中插入其他索引，方便他们的实践和使用。

§2077 禁止转移及其例外

除依司法令状或者经公证机关授权外，不得将公证总簿从存放的办公室转移。

§2078 防火保护

当公证处设在木质建筑或木质混合建筑中时，应当配备防火钢制作的保险箱，用于放置公证总簿。

§2079 公证总簿的遗失、损坏和重建

如果公证总簿全部或部分无效或遗失，公证人应向最高法院终审法庭首席法官报告该事实，法院应召集当事方重建适当的公证记录。所有的数据和文件和必要的记录都应被检查，以便在可行的情况下恢复被破坏或无效的内容。以上记录应经最高法院根据公证文书检验局局长的建议核准。

§2091 见证或陈述的真实性——概念；限制；公证责任的范围

除证词的日期之外，应有关方的要求，公证人可以公证非原始的文件：

（1）涉及对签名合法性的认证，前提其不涉及第31章第3453条第1项至第6项所列的行为；

（2）关于宣誓就职的文件；

（3）该文件是另一个文件的真实和精确的翻译，只要当事人能够掌握两种语言，且文件本身证明了这一点；

（4）该文件是在公证总簿中不包含的文件的真实、准确的副本；或者

（5）一般来说，被称作证词或权利声明的任何物体或事物的身份。

公证人根据应有关方面的请求，对原件以外的契

ties, certify in a deed other than the original, the legality of the signatures appearing thereon, provided this does not concern the acts comprised in subsections (1) to (6) of §3453 of Title 31 in effect, which is a translation or a true and exact copy of any deed not in his/her protocol, or in general, of the identity of any object or thing.

Only the notaries shall give testimony of the facts, acts or contracts of mere specific interest without prejudice of the provisions of any of the laws in effect. The statements of authenticity may or may not be part of the oath.

Notaries shall not authenticate testimonies in comprised included in§ 2005 of this title, nor in subsections (1) to (6) of§ 3453 of this title. This prohibition specifically includes sales contracts of real property that expressly or implicitly intend to adjudicate specific portions of real property whose segregation has not been previously approved by the corresponding agencies.

The notary does not assume any responsibility for the contents of the private document whose signature he/she authenticates.

§2092. Testimony or statement of authenticity—Forms; signature

The forms to be used in the affidavits shall be brief and simple and shall include the authenticity of the act, always with the notaries' statement that they personally know the signers or the attesting witness, or certifying to having supplemented his personal knowledge in the manner indicated in §2035 of this title.

In the event that the interested parties do not know how to, or cannot read or sign, the same norms of the public deed shall be applicable.

§2093. Testimony or statement of authenticity—Numbering

The affidavits shall be numbered successively and continuously and shall be headed by their corresponding number which will correlate to that of the inscription in the registry established below.

§2094. Testimony or statement of authenticity—Registry

Notaries shall keep a Registry of Affidavits in concise notes, dated, numbered, sealed and undersigned by them attesting as to the name of the grantors and a brief statement of the authenticated act.

The Registry of Affidavits shall be kept in duly bound books of not more than five hundred (500) sheets with successively numbered pages.

约及附于其上签名的合法性进行认证。该文件是在公证总簿中不包含的文件的真实、精确的副本，或者被称作证词或权利声明的任何物体或事物的身份。前提是上述文件和签名不涉及第31章第3453条1项至第6项中所载的行为。

只有公证人才能证明事实、行为或关于具体利益的合同，但不得损害任何有效法律的规定。真实性的陈述可能是也可能不是宣誓的一部分。

公证人不得对在本章第2005条和本章第3453条第1项至第6项下的事项进行认证。此类禁止具体包括通过明示或暗示意图确定的未经相关部门批准的特定不动产销售合同。

公证人对其认证签名的私人文件的内容不承担任何责任。

§2092 见证或签名的真实性——表格和签名

誓章中使用的表格应简洁明了，并包括对该行为真实性的阐述。表格中还应包括公证人关于其已亲自了解签名者或认证证人或已以本章第2035条所示的方式补充了其对签名人、认证证人的了解的声明。

如果利害关系方不知道或不能阅读或者签字，则应适用关于公共文书签名的规范。

§2093 证词或真实陈述的编号

誓章应连续不断地编号，并以与登记册内的铭文相应的数字为准。

§2094 誓章的整理成册

公证人保存誓章册，其应简明扼要地记载公证文书的日期、编号、密封和签名，以证明申请人的姓名和经认证的行为的简短陈述。

誓章册须用不超过500张连续编号并保存妥善的簿页进行记载。

§2095. Testimony or statement of authenticity—Null and void

Any testimony not included in the index that does not have the executing notary's signature or has not been recorded in the registry of affidavits shall be null.

§2101. Regulations

The Supreme Court may approve regulations for the execution of this chapter, for the regulation of the notarial practice and the admission thereto, and to complement the provisions of this chapter.

§2102. Inspection and examination—Officer in charge

The Chief Justice of the Supreme Court of Puerto Rico shall be in charge of the inspection of notarial offices and the examination of protocols.He shall appoint a Director of the Office of Notarial Inspection and of experienced notaries as inspectors, all of whom shall be covered by the provisions of §§521~525 of this title, known as the "Personnel Act of the Judiciary Branch" and the rules and regulations adopted by virtue thereof. One of the Protocol Inspectors shall reside in the district of San Juan, and another in the district of Ponce. The others shall reside in the location designated by the Chief Justice. The Supreme Court, after giving the notary an opportunity to be heard in his defense, may discipline him through a reprimand, a fine not to exceed five hundred (500) dollars or a temporary or permanent suspension from office in case of any violation of the provisions of this chapter or any other act related to the notarial practice, all subject to the provisions of §2105 of this title. The Supreme Court as well as the Chief Justice may delegate on the Director of Notarial Inspection whatever functions related to the supervision of the notaries and the notarial practice that they deem convenient with the exception of the power to impose disciplinary sanctions.

§2103. Inspection and examination—Disparity of criteria; solution

If, during the course of inspection of the notarial protocol, any difference of criteria arises between the Protocols Inspector and the notary with regard to the form and manner he keeps his protocols and registry of affidavits, with respect to compliance with this chapter, the cancelling of fees, or any other act related to the certification of the documents or instruments, the Inspector shall state it in his report, briefly listing the facts and the grounds of the controversy. This report shall be submitted to the Court of

§2095 无效证词

文件中未经公证人签字或记录的证词无效。

§2101 规范

最高法院为规范公证执业与准入，并补充本章的规定，可以发布实施本章的规范。

§2102 主管人员的检查和考核

波多黎各最高法院首席法官应负责审查议定书和公证机构。首席法官应任命1名公证人员办公室主任和其他经验丰富的公证人作为督查员，上述检查行为由本法第521条至第525条《司法机关人事法》和该法采用的规则和条例规制。公证督查员一位应位于圣胡安区，另一位在庞塞区。其他应安排在由终审法院首席法官指定的地点。最高法院对公证人任何所有违反本章规定或与公证执业有关的违法行为，在给予公证人辩护机会后，都可以对其施以不超过500美元的罚款或临时或永久性停止办理公证业务的惩罚，上述做法均符合第2105条的规定。最高法院和终审法院首席法官可以对公证人员下达任何与公证人监督和公证职务有关的业务的指令，强制执行纪律处分的指令除外。

§2103 检查、考核标准的差异和解决

如果在公证文书的检查过程中，公证督查员和公证人之间对执行公证文书的形式、方式、本章关于誓章的登记的遵守、取消费用或与文件或文书的认证有关的任何其他行为有不同认定标准时，督查员应在其报告中说明，并简要列出事实和争议的理由。本报告须提交原讼法院，不必缴付任何类型的费用或税款，在听取检查专员和公证人的意见后，由法院解决争议。对法院决议不服的，应在接到通知后的30日内向最高法院申请重新审查。上述行为均受本法第2105

First Instance Part, without payment of fees or taxes of any type, so that after hearing the Inspector and the notary it may resolve the controversy. The ensuing resolution may be reviewed by the Supreme Court through certiorari filed within the thirty (30) days after being notified; all of which is subject to the provisions of ' 2105 of this title.

§2104. Death, disability or resignation of notary; surrender of protocol

In case of the death or the permanent mental or physical disability of a notary, or when he voluntarily or compulsorily ceases in the performance of his functions, or in the event that the surety company requests the termination of his bond, or when he accepts permanent appointment to any judicial or executive office which, under the laws of Puerto Rico, is incompatible with the free exercise of the legal or notarial profession, it shall be the duty of the notary, his heirs, successors, or assigns, to surrender within thirty(30) days, his protocols and registries of affidavits, duly bound to the Office of Notarial Inspection for their inspection.

If this surrender is not made voluntarily within said term, the Supreme Court of Puerto Rico may issue the corresponding order to such effects.

Once the protocols surrendered pursuant to this section have been examined and approved they shall be placed under the custody of the custodian of notarial protocols of the corresponding district.

§ 2105. Disciplinary corrections; due process

No notary may be disciplined, separated or suspended from notarial practice except through a process that complies, in all its phases, with all the guarantees of due process of law procedurally as well as substantively.

§ 2106. Delivery of protocol to general custodian; examination; return to the notary

Once the protocols and registries of affidavits have been examined for the reasons established by § 2104 of this title, they shall be delivered to the General Custodian for the corresponding district, thus complying with § 2111(d) of this title with regard to registries of affidavits of less than thirty (30) years. If the result of the examination is that there has been a failure to affix the corresponding Internal Revenue, notarial tax or Legal Assistance stamps, the Attorney General shall proceed to sue for reimbursement of the pending amounts, from the notary, his heirs, successors or assigns or guarantors, in behalf of the Commonwealth, the Bar Association and legal assistance, and

条的规制。

§2104 公证人死亡、残疾或辞职的情形；公证书的上交

当公证人出现了死亡或永久的精神或身体残疾、自愿或被强制停止履行职务、被担保公司要求终止其作为公证人的保证金，或其接受任何司法或行政机构的长期任用而根据波多黎各的法律，其该任职将导致自由行使法律职能和公证职能相违背等情形时，与公证人及其继承人、职务接任者有义务，在30日内将公证人所办理的公证文书、誓章册等，妥善交到公证检验办公室检查。

如果上述文书提交不是在规定时间内出于自愿完成的，则波多黎各最高法院可对其发出相应的令状。

一旦提交的公证文书经过了各种审查和批准，则应按本法的规定将其移交到相应区域的托管人处进行保管。

§2105 惩戒措施的更正、正当程序

除非遵守法定程序，公证人在执行职务的过程中，不得被惩戒、打断或要求暂停，必须保证公证人的执业过程在程序和实质上的正当性。

§2106 公证文书转移给一般托管人；检查和返还给公证人

一旦公证文书或誓章册由于本章第2104条规定的理由被检查，则其应当被送达至相应的一般托管人区域，因而符合本章第2111(d)条下的誓章册将少于30年。如果经检查，发现公证文书一直未能附上相应的内部公证税或法律援助税票的，律政司应代表律师协会和法律援助机构，着手起诉要求公证人及其继承人或继任者或担保人补齐欠缺的款项，上述行动完成后须将处理结果告知法院首席法官。

shall inform the Chief Justice of the outcome of these actions.

When the notary ceases to be disabled or to hold the judicial or executive office to which he was appointed, the General Custodian of the district shall return his protocols to him if he should resume the practice of the notarial profession, and the notary so requests it.

§2107. Notarial districts; general custodians; operation

The territory of the Commonwealth shall be divided into the following comprehensive notarial districts of the demarcation corresponding to the Parts of the Court of First Instance with seats in San Juan, Arecibo, Aguadilla, Mayaguez, Ponce, Guayama, Humacao, Caguas, Bayamon, Aibonito, Utuado, Carolina and Fajardo. The respective General Custodian of notarial protocols shall reside in each of these seats. He shall be a notary appointed by the Chief Justice of the Supreme Court, except as provided below with respect to the Notarial Archives Custodian for San Juan. The Chief Justice of the Supreme Court shall pass upon all matters concerning said notarial archives and the resignations and vacancies of the custodians of protocols and shall take such measures he deems proper in connection with the general archives. The Chief Justice may delegate on the Director of Notarial Inspection whatever relevant powers he deems convenient.

General District Custodians, and, in the case of the San Juan Notarial District, the Director of Notarial Inspection may issue literal, full or partial, handwritten, typewritten, photographic or photostatic copies reproduced by any other electronic means designed to obtain an exact reproduction of an original, of the notarial deeds in his custody through payment of the costs of reproducing said copies plus the scheduled fees prescribed for issuing copies, and payment of the corresponding Internal Revenue stamps required by law. In the San Juan General Archives, the fees shall be paid by receipts issued by the Collector of Internal Revenue, in addition to the Internal Revenue stamps that shall be canceled on the copies of the notarial deeds.

The copies thus issued of any deed duly certified by the General Custodian of the District, or by the Director of the Office Notarial Inspection in the case of the San Juan Notarial District Archives, shall be admissible in evidence.

Present incumbents as General Custodians of notarial protocols shall continue to hold office as long as they observe good conduct, or until they resign or are removed for any reason.

当公证人不再将被禁止任职，或不再在司法或行政办公室任职，得以恢复执行公证职务时，经公证人请求，所在区域的一般托管人应将公证文书交还给公证人。

§2107 公证地区；一般保管人操作

综合公证地区的分界应按照原讼法庭设立时对联邦领土的划分，在圣胡安、阿雷西博、阿瓜迪亚、马亚圭斯、庞塞、瓜亚、乌、卡瓜斯、巴亚蒙、艾沃尼托、乌图阿多、卡罗来纳州和法哈多划分公证地区的边界。公证文书的一般保管人应在上述每一个地区中保留席位。该保管人应是由最高法院首席大法官任命的公证人，除了下文中规定的对圣胡安公证档案保管人。最高法院首席大法官应制定关于公证档案的规则，规定当出现公证档案和文书保管人的辞职、空缺等事项时，应对档案采取的正确措施。终审法院首席法官可以出于便利的考虑而将相关权力转授予公证督察长。

公证督察长可对一般保管人和圣胡安公证区的保管人，发出字面、全部或部分、手写、打印、摄影或任何其他电子手段制作的影印复制品，以获得其保管的公证文书的重新制作的正本。上述复制费用和装订副本的费用由法律规定的相应内部收入印花税支付。在圣胡安一般档案管理处，上述费用由内部收入支付，依法不得在公证书副本使用的内部收入印花税除外。

由一般保管区、公证核验办公室主任或圣胡安公证区发出的任何文件，都应被接纳为证据。

只要一般保管人保持良好的行为，目前在职的公证文书一般保管人应继续任职，直到其辞职或因任何原因被除名。

The Director of Notarial Inspection shall be in charge of the functioning of the Notarial Archives of San Juan as Custodian. All the operating expenses of the San Juan Notarial Archives and the expenses of supervising the other District Notarial Archives shall be included in the annual expense budget of the Supreme Court.

§2108. Notarial Inspection Office; personnel

The officers of the present Notarial Inspection Office shall continue in their office with the same prerogatives as long as they observe good conduct, until they resign, or are removed for any just cause.

§2111. General archives of protocols—Contents and functions

(a) The transfer to the General Archives of Puerto Rico of the notarial protocols that are kept conserved in the Archives of Notarial Protocols of Puerto Rico, which on the effective date of this act have been in existence more than sixty (60) years, is hereby authorized.

The future transfer to the General Archives of Puerto Rico of those protocols that as time goes by reach that limit of antiquity, is also hereby authorized.

(b) The General Archives of Puerto Rico shall be the custodian of the notarial protocols transferred to the General Archives of Puerto Rico pursuant to subsection (a) of this section. It shall be the duty of the General Archives to take the necessary measures to ensure the proper conservation of the protocols placed in its custody, always conserving them in their original form and order.

(c) The protocols referred to in this section shall continue to be secret pursuant to the provisions of this chapter. With regard to bona fide historical investigators, the General Custodian of Puerto Rico shall establish, through regulations to such effect, the norms necessary to establish their condition and to authorize investigations.

(d) The notarial custodian for the District of San Juan is hereby empowered, with the exclusion of any other official, to issue copies of the deeds found in the protocols referred to in this section, pursuant to the provisions of this chapter, including the cases of protocols transferred to the General Archives of Puerto Rico or of those documents in his custody and of those under temporary custody of the Director of Notarial Inspection.

The Director of Notarial Inspection may allow the destruction of all those registries of affidavits whose last entry has been in existence for more than thirty (30) years, and are deposited in each Notarial District's Archives,

公证督察长应作为保管人负责圣胡安作为公证档案管理处的运作。圣胡安公证区和其他公证档案区的所有业务的费用和开支应在最高法院的年度费用预算中列支，并接受监督。

§2108 公证督查机关及其人事任免

只要保持良好行为，目前公证督查机构的人员应继续执业，直到其辞职，或由于任何原因调任。

§2111 一般公证档案——内容和功能

（a）现授权波多黎各普通档案馆向波多黎各公证书档案处转交其保存的公证文书，上述文书在本法案生效之日前已经保存了60年。

此外特此授权未来将存入波多黎各综合档案馆的文书和随着时间的推移达到古代年限的文书的转让。

（b）波多黎各综合档案馆应当作为根据本条(a)款被转移到波多黎各综合档案馆的公证文书的保管人。综合档案馆有义务采取必要措施，确保公证文书一直以原有的形式和秩序被保存。

（c）这一章所提及的文书依本章规定应依然是保密的。波多黎各一般保管人应通过关于善意历史调查的规则，以此对授权调查形成必要的规范。

（d）特此授权圣胡安区的公证管理人而非其他任何官方身份，根据本章的规定发放本条所述的公证文书副本，包括转交给波多黎各综合档案馆保管的文件和公证检查处人员临时监护的文件。

公证督察长有权销毁每个公证区档案馆内已经保存超过30年的誓章册，但须经被指定管理和规范司法部门公共文件的官员事先授权。

subject to prior authorization by the official designated to administer and regulate the Program of Administration of Public Documents in the Judiciary Branch.

The Director of Notarial Inspection shall likewise authorize notaries to destroy any book of affidavits whose last affidavit is dated over thirty (30) years ago. This authorization shall be issued in writing. No registry may be destroyed unless it has been previously examined and approved by an inspector of protocols. Once the destruction of these registries has been authorized, the notary may conserve them in his possession if he wishes, but they shall not be received in any notarial archive, unless so directed by the Supreme Court.

§2112. General archives of protocols—Notarial custodians

Notarial custodians may be disciplined for the same causes and in the same manner as notaries, without impairing the provisions of §§3001 et seq. of Title 33.

§ 2121. Registry of wills—Creation and functions

A registry of wills attached to the Office of Notarial Inspection is hereby created. The functions and faculties of the registry shall be exercised by the Director of Notarial Inspection under the direct supervision of the Chief Justice of the Supreme Court.

§2122. Registry of wills—Regulation

The Supreme Court is hereby empowered to establish, by regulations, everything concerning the operation and functioning of the registry of wills created by this chapter in a manner not incompatible with its provisions.

§2123. Registry of wills—Certified reports

The notaries shall remit to the Director of Notarial Inspection by certified mail with acknowledgment of receipt, or file personally before him, a certification authorized by them bearing their signature and notarial seal, of each original deed granting, modifying, revoking or extending a will, or recording of a holographic or sealed will, stating in said certification the number of the deed or record, the date, place and hour it was executed and the name and surname of the testator and of the witnesses, as the case may be, with their personal circumstances as they appear in the document, and any other information required, within twenty-four (24) hours of its execution, not counting Saturdays and Sundays or legal holidays.

同理，公证督察长有权销毁任何最后一份誓章已保存30年以上的誓章册。以上授权书应以书面形式发出。获得公证文书督察长的检查和批准前，文书注册表不得被销毁。即使上述注册表被授权可以销毁，公证人也可以依其自身的意愿保留它们，不得将其收录任何公证档案，除非由最高法院作出指示。

§2112 公证保管人

在不违反第33编第3001条及其下列条款规定的情形下，公证保管人可能由于与公证人相同而受到纪律惩戒。

§2121 遗嘱注册处——设立和功能

特此设立附属于公证处的遗嘱注册处。该注册处的职能由公证处督察长在最高法院首席法官的直接监督下行使。

§2122 遗嘱注册条例

最高法院有权通过条例，以符合本章规定的方式，制定关于遗嘱注册处的设立和运作的一切规则。

§2123 遗嘱注册的认证报告

公证人应通过附回执的邮件或亲自向公证督察长以签名或盖章的方式确认，每一份原始文书的授予、修改、撤销，或延续遗嘱，或全息或密封遗嘱的记录，在该证明中说明文书中记录的数量、执行日期、地点和时间以及立遗嘱人和证人的姓名、姓氏（视情况而定），与在文件中出现的个人情况和文书中所需的其他任何信息。上述认证应在执行后的24小时内完成，星期六和星期日或法定假日不包含在内。

§2124. Registry of wills—Acknowledgement of certified report; certification thereof

It shall be the duty of the Director of Notarial Inspection to acknowledge receipt of said certification and maintain a register with the name and surname or surnames of the testator and other circumstances which are part of said notarial certification.

These certifications shall be conserved in custody of said official who shall keep them in the order in which they were remitted. He is hereby authorized to certify with his signature and official seal whether the execution of the will sought has been annotated, by written petition of an interested party or his attorney, accompanied by Internal Revenue stamps in the amount of three dollars ($3).

He may also certify, by payment of the same fees, that in the written records in his office there is no evidence that the designated person has executed a will.

§2125. Registry of wills—Negative certification, prerequisite for declaration of heirship

The Court of First Instance shall not admit or process a heirship whatsoever that is not filed with a negative certification of declaration of on from the Office of Notarial Inspection issued pursuant to §2124 of this title.

§2126. Registry of powers of attorney

In the case of granting a power of attorney the notary shall comply with the provisions of the Power of Attorney Registration Act, §§921-927 of this title, and the Regulations of the Supreme Court of Puerto Rico.

§2131. Notarial Fees—Tariff

Notaries are hereby authorized to charge the following fees for their notarial services:

(a) The notary may charge up to the sum of one hundred dollars ($100) for executing notarial documents concerning valuables or where a thing or amount of a determinable value is involved, whose value not exceeds ten thousand dollars ($10,000.00).

(b) The notary shall earn fees equal to one percent (1%) of their value, for executing notarial documents concerning valuables or where a thing or amount of determinable value is involved whose value exceeds ten thousand dollars ($10,000.00), but does not exceed five hundred thousand dollars ($500,000.00).

(c) For executing notarial documents concerning valuable objects or where a thing or amount of a determinable value is involved whose value exceeds five hundred thousand dollars ($500,000.00), the notary shall earn fees

§2124 遗嘱认证报告的承认和确认证书

公证督察长有义务确认收到该认证书,并保存记载了公证人的姓名,立遗嘱人的姓名或姓氏,以及公证书其他情况的记录。

上述认证书应保存在所述公证保管处中,并按照文书的接收顺序保存。特授权公证督察长根据利害关系人或其律师的书面请求,认证签名与公章证明的遗嘱是否已经按照注明的要求执行,并书面提交给有关当事方或其代理人,附加收取面额为3美元的内部印花税票。

公证人也可以收取相同的费用证明在公证处的书面记录中没有证据表明指定人已经履行了遗嘱。

§2125 负面认证,宣誓继承权的先决条件

原讼法院不得承认或处理,任何未依据本法第2124条由公证机关发出负面证明的人的继承权。

§2126 书面授权委托书

给予授权委托书时公证人须遵从本法第921条至第927条和波多黎各最高法院条例的规定。

§2131 公证收费

公证人有权为其提供的公证服务收取以下费用:

(a)公证人为价值或估价不超过10000美元的事务办理公证可收取不超过100美元的费用。

(b)公证人为价值或估价超过10000美元但不超过500000美元的事务办理公证可收取其价值或估价的1%的费用。

(c)公证人为价值或估价超过500000美元的事务办理公证可收取其价值或估价的1%的费用,在此基础上还可加收总价的0.5%。

equivalent to one percent (1%) up to that amount, plus one half percent (0.5%) on the excess of that sum.

(d) For executing nonvaluable notarial documents, including sworn statements, authentication of signatures or affidavits, the fees shall be fixed by agreement between the parties and the notary.

(e) For the issuing certified copies of deeds the charges shall be based on the document's amount, excluding costs, expenses and disbursements, in the following manner:

from 00.00 to $10,000.00 $15.00
from $10,001.00 to 500,000.00 $25.00
from $500,001.00 and over $40

§ 2132. Notarial Fees—Extra tariff

The fees fixed above for executing the documents shall not impair or limit the notary from charging the fees he believes reasonable and prudent in accordance with Canon 24 of Professional Ethics for the fixing of fees, for his prior and preparatory efforts, including the subsequent ones, such as background and titles, studies, consultations, opinions, preparation of certificates and compensated powers of attorney in which the notary renders an additional service as a lawyer.

§2141. Notarial bond; administration

The Notarial Bond Special Fund shall be governed by the Board of Governors of the Bar Association.

The Board of Governors shall have the following obligations:

(1) To establish and maintain a reserve sufficient to answer any legitimate claim against the Special Fund as a result of the notarial bond secured by the Bar Association and to cover expenses needed to administrate, operate and protect the Special Fund.

(2) To take custody of and invest in a prudent manner the balance of the Special Fund once the reserve amount required by the preceding subsection is discounted. The amount corresponding to this balance and its accrued interest may be used or invested for the following purposes:

(a) Conduct studies to modernize the Property Registry system, the Registry of Powers of Attorney and the Registry of Wills and any others assigned to the Office of Notarial Inspection, and collaborate in the achievement of said objectives through the production of forms in electronic format and by enabling the conversion of reports to electronic media and the use of electronic mail for the transmission of reports and other similar measures leading

（d）对无法估量价值的文书办理公证，如誓言、签名的真实性和誓章的公证，公证费用由公证人与当事人协商确定。

（e）对发出公证副本的收费，应在考量副本数量、制作费用、成本和其他支出的基础上，依以下方式收取：

文书标的在10000美元以下（含）的：15美元；
10000至500000美元（含）的：25美元；
250000美元以上的：40美元。

§ 2132 其他费用

上述办理公证文书的费用不得影响或限制公证人根据职业道德准则第24号的规定收取合理审慎的费用，包括为准备工作、善后工作，例如背景、标题、研究、咨询、意见、准备证书以及公证人作为律师提供额外的服务等。

§2141 公证保证金与管理

公证保证金特别基金应由律师协会理事会管理。

该理事会对下列事项负有义务：

(1) 建立和维护储备基金，以应对任何对律师协会公证保证金特别基金提起的合法索赔，以及用于必要的管理费用和保护专项基金所需的费用。

（2）一旦上述基金中的资金减少，应以谨慎的方式保管和对特别基金的余额进行投资。上述金额及其利息可用于或投资于以下目的：

（a）进行关于促进公证文书登记制度现代化的研究，以及关于书记处、遗嘱登记处以及与公证处有关的任何其他人员的研究。可以通过电子表格的形式，并通过使报告转换为电子媒体、使用电子邮件传送报告和其他类似措施来实现所述目标，从而实现系统和注册管理机构程序的现代化。

to the modernization of the systems and procedures of said registries.

(b) To establish and maintain a continuing education program for all of Puerto Rico's attorneys through course, seminars, conferences or any other educational programs the Board deems appropriate.

(c) To establish and maintain the proper coordination with educational institutions to provide a continuing education program for all members of the legal profession and improve teaching in our country's law schools.

(d) To sponsor a scholarship program so that distinguished members of the profession, judges of the General Court of Justice, professors and distinguished graduates of the law schools, may attend advanced studies in order to improve the quality of legal education, the quality of the profession and the quality of justice.

(e) To provide all of the country's lawyers with auxiliary legal investigation services through access to data banks or other means that would enable adequate legal investigation for the proper practice of the profession.

(f) Conduct the pertinent studies to draft a voluntary insurance plan within the term of one year from the date of effectiveness of this act that would cover professional malpractice in the practice of law and the general notarial practice, including the exercise of the competences granted to notaries by the laws in effect or transferred to the latter by special laws. The plan may be offered by the Bar Association or by an insurance company authorized to conduct business in Puerto Rico. Any voluntary insurance plan that the Board of Governors may intend to establish must be organized as an autonomous entity operating under independent accounting and resources systems and limited liability and must be submitted to the Insurance Commissioner for his or her approval.

(g) To carry out the pertinent studies, within a term of one (1) year counted from the effective date of this act, to draft an incremented bonding plan based on the amounts involved in the transactions in the deeds executed by the notaries.

(h) To establish any other program or service that is compatible with the previously mentioned objectives.

Neither the resources of the Special Fund created by this section nor the interest they accrue may be used for purposes other than the ones established above.

（b）建立并维护通过课程、研讨会、会议或任何其他律师协会认为合适的方式对波多黎各的律师开展继续教育项目。

（c）为提供法律职业继续教育和提高全国法律学校教学水平建立和维护适当的配套教育机构。

（d）为杰出的普通法院的法官，教授和优秀的法学院毕业生提供奖学金，使其能够参加高级研究，以提高法律教育的质量、培养专业素养和正义观。

（e）通过数据库或其他为适当履行职务而提供充分法律调查的方法，为全国律师提供辅助法律调查服务。

（f）进行有关研究，在本法案生效之日起一年内起草自愿保险计划，涵盖法律实务和一般公证实践中的职业舞弊行为，包括法律授权公证人行使的职权和依法转移给公证人的职权。该计划可由律师协会或被授权在波多黎各开展业务的保险公司提供。理事会设立任何自愿保险计划，必须组建拥有独立的会计系统、承担有限责任的自主经营实体，且必须提交给保险业务专员以获得批准。

（g）开展相关研究，根据本法案生效起一年之内公证人办理公证活动涉及的金额制定保证金增量计划。

（h）建立与上述目标兼容的任何其他项目或服务。

本条设立的特别基金及其所产生的利息均不能用于上述以外的其他目的。

特立尼达和多巴哥

特立尼达和多巴哥公证人法

Amended by 36 of 1894
CHAPTER 6:51
NOTARIES PUBLIC ACT

根据 1894 年第 36 号法案修订
第 6:51 章
公证人法

ARRANGEMENT OF SECTIONS

SECTION
1. Short title.
2. Interpretation.
3. Appointment of Notaries Public.
4. President to appoint Notary Public for Tobago.
5. Duties of Notary Public.
6. Notaries Public appointed by Master of Faculties in the U.K.
7. Notaries Public to have Notarial Seal.
8. Registrar to keep Roll.
9. Punishment of unauthorised person acting as Notary Public.
10. Notaries not to be suspended except by decision of a Judge.
11. Request to revoke appointment.
12. Notary Public may sometimes refuse to act.
13. Notary Public to mark his refusal on document.
14. Punishment of Notary Public for false certificates.
15. Fees.

SCHEDULE
NOTARIES PUBLIC ACT

An Act relating to Notaries Public.

1. This Act may be cited as the Notaries Public Act.
2. In this Act "Registrar" means the Registrar of the Supreme Court.
3. (1) The President, after consultation with the Chief

章节安排

章节
1. 简称
2. 释义
3. 公证人的任命
4. 总统任命多巴哥公证人
5. 公证人的职责
6. 由大主教特许法院主事官任命的公证人

7. 公证人有公证印章
8. 注册人保留名单
9. 对未经授权而担任公证人的处罚

10. 只有法官才能废黜公证人

11. 请求撤销任命
12. 公证人有时有权拒绝履行职责
13. 公证人在文件上明确表示拒绝
14. 公证人虚假证书的处罚
15. 公证费用

章节
公证人法
与公证人有关的法案。
1. 本法简称为《公证人法》。
2. 在本法中,"登记官"指最高法院登记官。

3.（1）总统与终审法院首席法官磋商后,可签

Justice, may by warrant under his hand and seal appoint any person to be a Notary Public of Trinidad and Tobago.

(2) (a) Before making an appointment under subsection (1) the President shall be satisfied of the fitness of the person to be appointed and that for the due convenience and accommodation of the public the number of Notaries in Trinidad and Tobago is insufficient.

(b) For the purpose of paragraph (a), the President may take into account the views and recommendations of bankers, businessmen and other appropriate groups or bodies resident in Trinidad and Tobago.

(c) Where an application for appointment as a Notary is made to the President, the President may refuse the application without assigning any reasons. A decision to refuse an application shall be final and conclusive and there shall be no appeal or other relief against such a decision.

(3) Subject to section 4, no person shall be appointed a Notary Public unless he is an Attorney-at-law of at least fifteen years standing.

(4) Every person appointed as a Notary Public shall—

(a) on his appointment, pay to the Registrar a fee of one thousand dollars; and

(b) before entering upon the duties of his office, make and subscribe in a book to be kept in the office of the Registrar, the following Oath:

I, AB, do swear or solemnly affirm (as the case may be) that I will truly and honestly conduct myself in the office of Notary Public according to the best of my knowledge and ability—SO HELP ME GOD.

(5) Subsection (3) does not apply—

(a) to the person appointed as Notary Public under section 4;

(b) to a person who is deemed to be appointed as a Notary Public under section 6.

4. The President may appoint the person for the time being discharging the duties of Sub-Registrar of the Supreme Court in Tobago to be a Notary Public for Tobago.

5. Every person appointed to be a Notary Public shall discharge the duties assigned to such office by the laws of the United Kingdom and Trinidad and Tobago and by the practice of commerce.

6. Every person who before the commencement of the Law Revision (Miscellaneous Amendments) Act 1979 (i.e., 31st December, 1979) was entitled to practise as a Notary Public in Trinidad and Tobago shall be deemed to be appointed as a Notary Public under this Act.

发手令，并委任公民作为特立尼达和多巴哥公证人。

（2）（a）在根据第1款作出委任之前，总统应确信对该人被任命是适当的，且出于方便公众的考虑，特立尼达和多巴哥的公证人人数不足。

（b）为了a项的立法目的，总统可以考虑特立尼达和多巴哥的银行家、商人和其他适当团体或机构的意见和建议。

（c）如果向总统提出任命公证人的申请，总统可以在没有任何理由的情况下拒绝申请。拒绝申请的决定是最终决定性的，不得对此类决定提出上诉或其他救济。

（3）除第4条另有规定外，任何人不得被任命为公证人，除非其是从业15年以上的律师。

（4）任何被委任为公证人的人应当：

（a）在任命时，向登记官支付1000美元的费用；以及

（b）在履行其职务之前，作出书面登记并保留在登记官办公室内，作出以下誓言：

我，AB，发誓或庄严声明（视情况而定），我将根据我的知识和能力，尽我所能真诚、诚实地作为公证人工作，上帝保佑。

（5）第3款不适用于：

（a）根据第4条被任命为公证人的人；

（b）根据第6条被视为委任为公证人的人。

4. 总统可以任命正在履行多巴哥最高法院分部登记官职责的登记官，作为多巴哥公证人。

5. 所有被任命为公证人的人均应根据英国和特立尼达和多巴哥的法律和商业惯例履行该职务的职责。

6. 在《1979年法律修订（杂项修订）法》（1979年12月31日）生效之前，有权在特立尼达和多巴哥作为公证人执业的人，应视为本法中的公证人。

7. Every Notary Public entitled to practise under this Act shall provide himself with a seal, to be impressed upon all documents issued by him as a Notary Public.

8. The Registrar shall keep a list of persons entitled to practice as Notaries Public under this Act, which shall be called the Roll of Notaries Public.

9. Any person who discharges the duties of a Notary Public,not being appointed or deemed to be appointed as a Notary Public under this Act, is liable on summary conviction to a fine of two hundred and forty dollars.

10. No Notary Public entitled to practise under this Act shall be suspended from the performance of his duties as a Notary Public, unless he is guilty of some crime, gross misconduct, negligence or unskilfulness which must be represented to be heard and determined by a Judge of the High Court in a summary way, and if any Notary Public is condemned the Court shall order the Registrar to strike off his name from the Roll of Notaries Public, and he shall be disabled thenceforth from performing any notarial act whatever;or if in the opinion of the Court the circumstances of the case are such as to justify a lesser punishment, the Court may suspend him from practising as a Notary Public for such period as the Court thinks fit.

11. Any Notary Public may, by application in writing to the Registrar, request the revocation of his appointment, and the Registrar upon receipt of such application shall remove his name from the Roll of Notaries Public. Nothing in this section shall prohibit any Notary Public whose name has been so removed, from again applying to be appointed as a Notary Public

12. (1) In all cases where the circumstances appear to the Notary Public suspicious and not warranting the protest or other notarial act demanded, the Notary shall refuse to act.

(2) Any person who considers himself aggrieved by the refusal of the Notary to note the protest, or to do any other notarial act demanded, may apply to the High Court or any Judge thereof for an order calling upon the Notary to act in the execution of his office, and before applying for such order, notice of the application shall be given to the Notary refusing to act, and to such persons, if any, in Trinidad and Tobago as are interested in the subject of the protest.

13. When any protest or other notarial act shall be refused to be noted or done, the Notary so refusing shall mark in the logbook, bill of exchange or other document, his refusal with his signature and the date of refusal sub-

7. 根据本法有权执业的所有公证人均应拥有公证公章，用于在其作为公证人印发的所有文件上盖章。

8. 登记官应根据本法将持有公证人资格进行执业的人员列入公证人名单。

9. 任何人不履行根据本法规定被指定任命或为公证人的职务，一经简易程序定罪，将被处以240美元的罚款。

10. 根据本法规定执业的公证人不得被停职，除非其犯有某些犯罪行为、严重不当行为，存在疏忽或能力不够，上述事项必须由高等法院法官指出并以概括的方式确定。如果任何公证人被谴责，法院应责令登记官将其从公证人名单中除名。之后该人将被禁止执行任何公证行为；如果法院认为，案件的情况符合减轻处罚的情形，则法院可以适当予以在一段时间内暂停他公证人职务的惩罚。

11. 任何公证人可以向登记官提出书面申请，要求撤销其任命，书记官长在收到该项申请后，应将其姓名从公证人名单上删除。本条并不禁止任何名称已被删除的公证人再次申请被委任为公证人。

12. （1）如果公证人认为情况可疑，且没有正当理由出具拒绝承兑证书或作出其他公证行为，则公证人应拒绝作出公证行为。

（2）任何人因公证人拒绝签注拒绝承兑证书或拒绝要求作出任何其他公证行为不满的，可向高等法院或其中的任何法官申请指令，要求公证人履行职责。在申请此类指令之前，应通知公证人其将申请此类指令，并通知特立尼达和多巴哥境内的与该拒绝承兑书有利益关系的人员（如果有的话）。

13. 当签注任何拒绝承兑书或做出其他公证行为时，公证人应在记录表、汇票或其他文件中签字并标明拒绝承兑的日期。

scribed thereon.

14. Any Notary Public or other person who wilfully certifies or propounds any false statement or document, or who fraudulently, with intent to deceive, conceals, withholds or perverts any fact or document pertinent to the subject of protest or other notarial act is liable on conviction on indictment to imprisonment for two years.

15. (1) Every Notary Public shall be entitled to demand and to receive in respect of the duties of his office such fees as are prescribed in the Schedule.

(2) If the person performing the duties of Notary Public shall be the Sub-Registrar of the Supreme Court, he shall pay all such fees into the Treasury to the credit of general revenue; if he shall be a person other than the Sub-Registrar of the High Court he shall be entitled to retain all such fees for his own use.

(3) The Minister may from time to time by Order amend the Schedule.

SCHEDULE

$

Presenting and noting protest on Bill of Exchange or promissory note ···25.00
Extending protest on Bill of Exchange or promissory note ··75.00
Attestation of any document ························50.00
Notarial Certificate ······································75.00
Attendances—according to length ········15.00 to 50.00
Minuting or noting ship protest ····················25.00
Extending ship protest according to complication and length ···100.00
Furnishing copy of extended protest per folio of 72 words ···1.00
Declaration to ship protest for the Master and for each additional declarant ····································50.00
Attestation of ships manifest whether in duplicate or more. ···25.00

In all cases where the Notary has to travel to perform his duties under this Act, he may charge a reasonable fee for his travelling expenses.

If any dispute arises as to the reasonableness of the fees charged for travelling expenses, the dispute may be referred to the Registrar whose decision shall be final

委内瑞拉

公共登记和公证法

LEY DE REGISTRO PÚBLICO Y DEL NOTARIADO

República Bolivariana de Venezuela
Ministerio de la Secretaría de la Presidencia
Despacho del Ministro

AVISO OFICIAL

En vista del oficio VP-N° 3118 de fecha 21 de noviembre de 2001, emanado de la Vicepresidencia Ejecutiva de Presidencia de la República, que solicita la reimpresión del Decreto N° 1. 554 de fecha 13 de noviembre de 2001, publicado en la Gaceta Oficial N° 5. 556 Extraordinario, de fecha 13 de noviembre de 2001, correspondiente al DECRETO CON FUERZA DE LEY DE REGISTRO PÚBLICO Y DEL NOTARIADO, toda vez que se incurrió en los siguientes errores materiales:

En el artículo 16:
Donde dice:
"... Los Registradores y Notarios, así como los funcionarios de sus respectivas dependencias ocupan cargos de confianza... . "
Debe decir:
"... Los Registradores y Notarios, así como los funcionarios de sus respectivas dependencias, ocupan cargos de confianza... "

En el artículo 39:
Donde dice:
"... En caso de optar por la vía administrativa esta deberá agotarse... "
Debe decir:
"... En caso de optar por la vía administrativa ésta

公共登记和公证法

委内瑞拉玻利瓦尔共和国
总统府秘书处
部长办公室

官方通知

鉴于共和国副总统于2001年11月21日颁发了第VP-N°3118号函，要求转载刊登在2001年11月13日《官方公报》第5556期特刊上的2001年11月13日的第1554号法令，即《公共登记和公证法》，并对以下内容进行勘误：

在第16条中：
原文为：
"……登记员和公证员，以及在相应的登记机关和公证机关担任重要岗位的人员……"

更正为：
"……登记员和公证员，以及在相应的登记机关和公证机关担任重要岗位的人员……"（在部门-dependencias后面加逗号）

在第39条中：
原文为：
"……选择循行政途径解决的，只有在行政救济手段用竭后，才可以提请司法介入……"

更正为：
"……选择循行政途径解决的，只有在行政救济

deberá agotarse... "

En el artículo 41:
Donde dice:
"... La inscripción no convalida los actos o negocios jurídicos inscritos que sean nulos o anulados conforme a la Ley... "
Debe decir:
"... La inscripción no convalida los actos o negocios jurídicos inscritos que sean nulos o anulados conforme a la ley... "

En el artículo 51 in fine:
Donde dice:
"... con efectos para el caso completo... "
Debe decir:
"... con efectos para el caso concreto... "

En el artículo 53:
Donde dice:
"... así como para solicitar la nulidad de una reunión de socios de las otras sociedades se extinguirá al vencimiento... "
Debe decir:
"... así como para solicitar la nulidad de una reunión de socios de las otras sociedades, se extinguirá al vencimiento... "

En el artículo 66 numeral 7:
Donde dice:
"... Las Fuerza Armada Nacional... "
Debe decir:
"... La Fuerza Armada Nacional... "

En el artículo 84:
Donde dice:
"... Clases de sanciones
Artículo 84
Las sanciones consistirán en suspensión o destitución del cargo... . "
Debe decir:
"... Sanción
Artículo 84
La sanción consistirá en suspensión del cargo... . "

En el artículo 87:
Tanto en la denominación del artículo como en el texto del mismo,

手段用竭后，才可以提请司法介入……"（将 esta 更正为 ésta）

在第 41 条中：
原文为：
"……法律认定为无效或已被取消的行为或者法定交易的登记被视为无效登记……"

更正为：
"……法律认定为无效或已被取消的行为或者法定交易的登记被视为无效登记……"（将 Ley 更正为 ley）

在第 51 条中：
原文为：
"……对全部情况的影响……"
更正为：
"……对具体情况的影响……"（将 completo 更正为 concreto）

在第 53 条中：
原文为：
"……以及对其他企业的合作伙伴会议无效的申请将在到期后生效……"

更正为：
"……以及对其他企业的合作伙伴会议无效的申请，将在到期后生效……"（在 sociedades 后面加逗号）

在第 66 条第 7 款中：
原文为：
"……国家武装力量……"
更正为：
"……国家武装力量（将 Las 更正为 La）……"

在第 84 条中：
原文为：
"... 处罚类型
第 84 条
将受到停职或撤职处罚……"

更正为：
"... 处罚
第 84 条
将受到停职处罚……"

在第 87 条中：
无论是在本条标题中还是在本条文本中所述，

Donde dice:

"... sanciones... "

Debe decir:

"... suspensión... "

En el artículo 95:

Donde dice:

"... Firme la decisión de una suspensión o destitución, se ordenará... "

Debe decir:

"... Firme la decisión de suspensión, se ordenará... "

En la Disposición Transitoria Tercera

Donde dice:

"... modernización de los Registros y Notarías regulados por el presente Decreto Ley esta Comisión será... "

Debe decir:

"... modernización de los Registros y Notarías regulados por el presente Decreto Ley. Esta Comisión será... "

Se procede en consecuencia, de conformidad con lo dispuesto en el artículo 4° de la Ley de Publicaciones Oficiales a una nueva impresión, subsanando los errores antes mencionados.

En Caracas, a los veintitrés del mes de noviembre de dos mil uno. Año 191° de la Independencia y 142° de la Federación.

DIOSDADO CABELLO R.
Ministro de la Secretaría de la Presidencia

Decreto N° 1. 554   13 de noviembre de 2001
HUGO CHÁVEZ FRÍAS Presidente de la República

En ejercicio de la atribución que le confiere el numeral 8 del artículo 236 de la Constitución de la República Bolivariana de Venezuela y de conformidad con lo dispuesto en el literal f, numeral 4, del artículo 1° de la Ley No. 4 que Autoriza al Presidente de la República para Dictar Decretos con Fuerza de Ley en las Materias que se Delegan, publicada en la Gaceta Oficial de la República Bolivariana de Venezuela N° 37. 076, de fecha 13 de noviembre de 2000, en Consejo de Ministros,

DICTA

el siguiente

DECRETO CON FUERZA DE LEY DE REGISTRO PÚBLICO Y DEL NOTARIADO

TÍTULO I
DEL REGISTRO PÚBLICO Y DEL NOTARIADO

Capítulo I Disposiciones Generales

Objeto

Artículo 1

El Objeto de este Decreto Ley es regular la organización, el funcionamiento, la administración y las competencias de los registros y de las notarías.

Finalidad y Medios Electrónicos

Artículo 2

Este Decreto Ley tiene como finalidad garantizar la seguridad jurídica, la libertad contractual y el principio de legalidad de los actos o negocios jurídicos, bienes y derechos reales, mediante la automatización progresiva de sus procesos registrales y notariales.

Para el cumplimiento de las funciones registrales y notariales, de las formalidades y solemnidades de los actos o negocios jurídicos, podrán aplicarse los mecanismos y la utilización de los medios electrónicos consagrados en la ley.

Requisito de Admisión

Artículo 3

Todo documento que se presente ante los Registros y Notarías, deberá ser redactado y tener el visto bueno de abogado debidamente colegiado y autorizado para el libre ejercicio profesional.

Manejo Electrónico

Artículo 4

Todos los soportes físicos del sistema registral y notarial actual se digitalizarán y se transferirán progresivamente a las bases de datos correspondientes.

El proceso registral y notarial podrá ser llevado a cabo íntegramente a partir de un documento electrónico.

Firma Electrónica

Artículo 5

La firma electrónica de los Registradores y Notarios tendrá la misma validez y eficacia probatoria que la ley otorga a la firma autógrafa.

第一篇
公共登记和公证

第一章　总则

目的

第1条

本法令旨在规范登记处和公证处的组织、运营、管理和职权范围。

目的和电子媒介

第2条

本法令旨在通过逐步完善自动登记和公证程序，确保法律保障、契约自由以及法律行为和业务及财产和实际权利的合法性。

为了履行登记和公证的职能，实现法规和法律业务的正当性和严肃性，可以采用法律规定的电子手段机制和功能。

受理要求

第3条

凡提交至登记处和公证处的文件，须经正式登记的专业律师起草和核准。

电子处理

第4条

现已登记和公证的纸质文件将全部实施数字化，并逐步移至相应的数据库。

所有的登记和公证程序均可通过电子文件的方式进行。

电子签名

第5条

登记员和公证员的电子签名与经授权的手稿签名具有同等的法律效力和证明能力。

Formación y Capacitación Continua

Artículo 6

EL Ministerio del Interior y Justicia, en coordinación con el Ministerio de Educación, Cultura y Deportes, promoverá la incorporación de la materia registral notarial en los pensa de estudios de institutos de formación técnica y universitaria, así como la capacitación continua de los Registradores y Notarios en instituciones especializadas.

Capítulo II Principios Registrales

Aplicación

Artículo 7

Con el fin de garantizar el fiel cumplimiento de su función, los Registros deberán observar en sus procedimientos los principios registrales enunciados en el presente Decreto Ley.

Principio de Rogación

Artículo 8

La presentación de un documento dará por iniciado el procedimiento registral, el cual deberá ser impulsado de oficio hasta su conclusión, siempre que haya sido debidamente admitido.

Principio de Prioridad

Artículo 9

Todo documento que ingrese al Registro deberá inscribirse con prelación a cualquier otro título presentado posteriormente.

Principio de Especialidad

Artículo 10

Los bienes y derechos inscritos en el Registro deberán estar definidos y precisados respecto a su titularidad, naturaleza, contenido y limitaciones.

Principio de Consecutividad

Artículo 11

De los asientos existentes en el Registro, relativos a un mismo bien, deberá resultar una perfecta secuencia y encadenamiento de las titularidades del dominio y de los demás derechos registrados, así como la correlación entre las inscripciones y sus modificaciones, cancelaciones y extinciones.

培训和继续教育

第6条

内政和司法部通过与教育、文化和体育部进行协调，将在职业技术学院、大学以及专业机构的登记和公证继续教育中引入登记和公证内容。

第二章 登记原则

适用

第7条

为保证忠实地履行职责，登记机关必须遵守现行法律规定的登记原则。

请求原则

第8条

文档的提交意味着启动了登记程序，文件一经恰当收录，就应根据各部门的职权进行正常推动，直至结束。

优先原则

第9条

提交登记机构的所有文件均比其后提交的文件享有优先权。

专业原则

第10条

在登记机构登记的资产和权利必须根据其所有权、性质、内容和限制进行定义和规定。

连贯性原则

第11条

在登记机构的现有登记条目中，必须就同一产权确定其法律所有权及其与其他登记法律条件之间的连贯性和关联性，以及该财产的登记及其更改、取消和终止之间的相互关联。

Principio de Legalidad

Artículo 12

Sólo se inscribirán en el Registro los títulos que reúnan los requisitos de fondo y forma establecidos por la ley.

Principio de Publicidad

Artículo 13

La fe pública registral protege la verosimilitud y certeza jurídica que muestran sus asientos. La información contenida en los asientos de los Registros es pública y puede ser consultada por cualquier persona.

Capítulo III Dirección Nacional de Registros y del Notariado

Creación y Atribuciones

Artículo 14

Se crea la Dirección Nacional de Registros y del Notariado como servicio autónomo, sin personalidad jurídica, que depende jerárquicamente del Ministro del Interior y Justicia. El titular del servicio autónomo es el Director Nacional de Registros y del Notariado.

El reglamento Orgánico de la Dirección Nacional de Registros y del Notariado desarrollará:

1. La integración y fuentes ordinarias de ingresos.

2. El grado de autonomía presupuestaria, administrativa, financiera y de gestión.

3. Los mecanismos de control a los cuales quedará sometido.

4. El destino que se dará a los ingresos obtenidos en el ejercicio de la actividad y el de los excedentes al final del ejercicio fiscal.

5. La forma de designación del titular que ejercerá la dirección y administración, y el rango de su respectivo cargo.

Fijación de Aranceles

Artículo 15

El Presidente de la República, en Consejo de Ministros, a solicitud del Ministro del Interior y Justicia, fijará los aranceles que cancelarán los usuarios por los servicios registrales y notariales, de conformidad con el estudio de la estructura de costos de producción de cada proceso registral y notarial.

合法性原则

第 12 条

只有在实质上和形式上均符合法律要求的名称才能在登记机构进行登记。

公开性原则

第 13 条

公共登记处保证其登记条目所显示的内容的真实性和法律的确定性，所有的登记条目均对外开放，可供任何人查阅。

第三章 国家登记和公证管理办公室

建立和职权

第 14 条

国家登记和公证管理处办公室是自主性的机构，它适用内政和司法部的级别制度，无法人资格。该服务机构归属于国家登记和公证管理处。

国家登记和公证管理处的法规将制定：

1. 收入的一般来源和整合。

2. 预算、行政、财务和管理的自主化程度。

3. 遵从控制机制。

4. 最终被归入活动收入和财政年度结束时的盈余。

5. 所指定的持有人指导、管理和行使各自职权的范围。

确定收费标准

第 15 条

在部长会议上，一经内政和司法部提出要求，共和国总统应根据对每一个登记和公证程序的成本结构的研究结果，确定向登记和公证服务用户的收费标准。

Las operaciones registrales y notariales y la recaudación de los respectivos aranceles se efectuarán mediante sistemas automatizados.

Régimen Funcionarial

Artículo 16

Los Registradores y Notarios, así como los funcionarios de sus respectivas dependencias ocupan cargos de confianza y por lo tanto son de libre nombramiento y remoción, de conformidad con lo establecido en el presente Decreto Ley y en el reglamento correspondiente.

Capítulo IV Registradores Titulares

Registrador Titular

Artículo 17

Cada Registro estará a cargo de un Registrador Titular, quien será responsable del funcionamiento de su dependencia. La elección de los Registradores Titulares se efectuará mediante concurso de oposición para cada especialidad registral, conforme a lo establecido en el reglamento correspondiente, y su nombramiento estará a cargo del Ministro del Interior y Justicia.

La remuneración de los Registradores será fijada por Resolución del Ministro de Interior y Justicia.

Deberes

Artículo 18

Son deberes de los Registradores Titulares:

1. Admitir o rechazar los documentos que se les presenten para su registro.

2. Dirigir y vigilar el funcionamiento de la dependencia a su cargo.

3. Los demás deberes que la ley les imponga.

Responsabilidad y Fianza

Artículo 19

El Registrador Titular responderá disciplinaria, administrativa, civil y penalmente por sus actos. Para entrar en posesión de su cargo, el Registrador Titular deberá prestar fianza bancaria o de empresa de seguros, a favor de la República y a satisfacción del Servicio Autónomo.

Prohibiciones

Artículo 20

Se prohíbe a los Registradores Titulares:

登记和公证业务办理以及相应的收费清缴工作将通过自动系统进行。

公务员制度

第 16 条

根据本法令及其实施条例的规定，可自由任免登记员和公证员，以及在相应的登记机关和公证机关担任重要岗位的人员。

第四章 主管登记员

主管登记员

第 17 条

主管登记员单独负责每个登记处的运作。主管登记员将根据相关法规，从各专业登记员中竞争选出，并最终由内政部和司法部任命。

主管登记员的薪酬由内政部和司法部确定。

责任和义务

第 18 条

主管登记员的义务是：

1. 同意或者拒绝对提交的文件办理登记。

2. 负责管理和监督登记处的独立运作。

3. 法律赋予的其他义务。

责任和担保

第 19 条

主管登记员应对其行为承担纪律、行政、民事和刑事责任。要上岗就任，主管登记员必须提交银行或者保险公司为其出具的履职担保，该担保以共和国为抬头且必须符合自主经营的要求。

禁止内容

第 20 条

主管登记员不得：

1. Calificar documentos en los cuales sean parte directa o indirectamente, así como aquellos en los que aparezcan su cónyuge, ascendientes, descendientes o parientes hasta el cuarto grado de consanguinidad o segundo de afinidad como interesados, presentantes, representantes o apoderados.

2. Redactar documentos por encargo de particulares.

3. Ejercer cualquier profesión o actividad remunerada, a excepción de los supuestos establecidos en el Reglamento del presente Decreto Ley.

4. Autorizar la inscripción de documentos cuando existan medidas cautelares o de aseguramiento de bienes.

5. Tramitar documentos que no hayan cancelado los tributos correspondientes.

6. Las demás establecidas en la ley.

Suplente

Artículo 21

La Dirección Nacional de Registros y del Notariado designará un Registrador Suplente para que sustituya al Titular en tas ausencias temporales. El Registrador Suplente deberá cumplir los mismos requisitos que se establecen para los Registradores Titulares.

Capítulo V Registradores Auxiliares

Registradores Auxiliares

Artículo 22

Cada Registro podrá tener Registradores Auxiliares para cumplir las funciones que le delegue el Registrador Titular, de conformidad con lo establecido en el Reglamento del presente Decreto Ley.

Los Registradores Auxiliares tendrán las mismas incompatibilidades, prohibiciones, responsabilidades y obligaciones establecidas para los Registradores Titulares.

TÍTULO II
LOS REGISTROS PÚBLICOS

Capítulo I Alcance de los Servicios Registrales

Misión

Artículo 23

La misión de los Registros es garantizar la seguridad jurídica de los actos y . de los derechos inscritos, con respecto a terceros, mediante la publicidad registral.

1. 核证与其有直接或间接利益关系的文件，以及当事人、申请人、代表人或授权代理人为主管登记员的配偶、父母、子女、四代以内直系血亲或二代以内姻亲的文件。

2. 私自撰写登记文件。

3. 从事本法规规定情况之外的任何有偿职业或活动。

4. 在有预防措施或财产保证的情况下授权文件的登记。

5. 处理尚未缴纳相关费用的文件。

6. 法律规定的其他禁止内容。

候补人员

第 21 条

国家登记和公证管理办公室应指定一名候补登记员以临时替代主管登记员。候补登记员应符合与主管登记员相同的要求。

第五章　助理登记员

助理登记员

第 22 条

根据本法规定，每位登记员可以配备助理登记员，以履行主管登记员所授予的职能。

助理登记员应遵守与主管登记员相同的有关不可兼职、禁止行为、责任和义务的规定。

第二篇
公共登记处

第一章　登记服务的范围

任务

第 23 条

登记处的任务是，在尊重第三方的前提下，通过公共登记机构确保登记行为和权利的司法安全。

Publicidad Registral

Artículo 24

La publicidad registral reside en las bases de datos del sistema automatizado de los Registros, en la documentación archivada que de ellas emanen y en las certificaciones que se expidan.

Efectos Jurídicos

Artículo 25

Los asientos e información registrales contenidos y emanados oficialmente del sistema registral surtirán todos los efectos jurídicos que corresponden a los documentos públicos.

Valor Fiscal de los Bienes Inscritos

Artículo 26

Los Registros podrán actualizar de oficio el valor fiscal de los bienes inscritos, cuando a ese efecto el Ministerio correspondiente y las Oficinas de Catastro de los Municipios del país, en su caso, remitan esos datos oficialmente.

Capítulo II Organización de los Registros

Responsabilidad

Artículo 27

La organización de los Registros es responsabilidad del Ejecutivo Nacional, por órgano del Ministerio del Interior y Justicia, a través de la Dirección Nacional de Registros y del Notariado.

Base de Datos Nacional

Artículo 28

En el Distrito Metropolitano de Caracas funcionarán las bases de datos que consolidarán y respaldarán la información de todas las materias registrales correspondientes a los Registros del país, sin perjuicio de los respaldos que se puedan establecer en otras entidades a los fines de salvaguardar la información contenida en la base de datos nacional.

Bases de Datos Regionales

Artículo 29

La Dirección Nacional de Registros y del Notariado determinará las entidades regionales donde se mantendrán

登记的公开性

第 24 条

登记的公开性存在于登记管理处资助系统的数据库及其发布的有关存档文件的颁发和认证中。

法律效力

第 25 条

登记等级条目以及官方发布的登记信息内容具有相应的公共文件所具有的一切法律效力。

登记物业的税值

第 26 条

当相应的管理部门和国家土地登记部门提交相关资料时，登记管理部门可根据其职权更新所登记资产的税值。

第二章 登记组织

责任

第 27 条

登记组织是国家行政部门的责任，由内政部和司法部通过国家登记和公证管理办公室负责。

国家数据库

第 28 条

在加拉加斯大区数据库使用国家登记管理机构所维护和支持的所有资料信息，且在不损坏的前提下，可以创建其他备份文件以保护国家数据库。

登记数据库

第 29 条

国家登记管理机构将确定各地区与登记相关的信息数据库的维护机构。每个登记处将维护一个信息系

las bases de datos que consolidarán y respaldarán la información de todas las materias correspondientes a los Registros. Cada Registro mantendrá un sistema de información donde residirán los datos de su especialidad registral y los demás que señale el Reglamento del presente Decreto Ley.

Digitalización de Imágenes

Artículo 30

Las imágenes de los testimonios notariales y de los documentos judiciales y administrativos que ingresan al Registro serán digitalizadas y relacionadas tecnológicamente por el sistema. Estas imágenes serán incorporadas en la base de datos y podrán ser consultadas de manera simultánea con los asientos registrales relacionados.

Propiedad de los Sistemas Registrales

Artículo 31

Los sistemas, programas, aplicaciones y demás componentes informáticos que sirven de plataforma tecnológica a la operación registral en todo el país, en sus vertientes jurídicas, administrativas, contables y de comunicaciones, son propiedad de la República. Solamente serán permitidos aquellos cambios y usos de otros sistemas de información autorizados por la Dirección Nacional de Registros y del Notariado.

Capítulo III Sistema de Folio Real

Folio Real

Artículo 32

En las zonas urbanas o rurales donde existan levantamientos catastrales, las inscripciones de bienes y de derechos se practicarán de conformidad con el sistema denominado folio real, de manera que los asientos electrónicos registrales tendrán por objeto los bienes y no sus propietarios.

En las zonas urbanas o rurales donde no existan levantamientos catastrales, las inscripciones de bienes y derechos se practicarán conforme al sistema denominado folio personal.

Identificación de Bienes y Derechos

Artículo 33

Las inscripciones de bienes y de derechos se identificarán con un número de matrícula y se practicarán en asientos automatizados que deben mostrar de manera

统用于存放其专有的登记信息，以及本法规定的其他内容。

图像数字化

第 30 条

存入登记管理部门的公证证明文件以及司法和行政文件的图像应进行数字化，并与系统进行技术关联。该图像应录入数据库中，并能与相关的登记条目一起查阅。

登记管理系统的所有权

第 31 条

作为全国登记管理机构技术平台的所有系统、程序、软件以及其他信息组件，在法律、行政、会计以及通信方面，均归共和国所有。仅当国家登记管理部门授权时，公证员或/和登记员才拥有更改权限和使用其他信息系统的权限。

第三章 房产信息系统

房产信息

第 32 条

在开展土地调查的城市或农村，应依照房产信息系统进行不动产和所有权登记，因此，电子登记条目的对象应该是房产而不是业主。

在未开展土地调查的城市或者农村，则应依照个人信息系统进行不动产和所有权登记。

不动产和所有权识别

第 33 条

不动产和所有权的登记均通过登记号进行识别，并进行自动登记，同时显示所有权或者资产的全部识别和描述、所确定的业主以及在其影响下的限制、条

simultánea toda la información vigente que sea relevante para la identificación y descripción del derecho o del bien, la determinación de los propietarios y las limitaciones, condiciones y gravámenes que los afecten.

La Asignación de Matrícula

Artículo 34

Para la identificación de los bienes y de los derechos inscritos, el sistema registral asignará matrículas en orden consecutivo ascendente de manera automatizada, sin que estas matrículas puedan usarse nuevamente hasta tanto el asiento registral de ese bien o derecho se haya extinguido o cancelado. La matrícula podrá ser alfanumérica, según las necesidades de clasificación de los bienes y los derechos que rijan la materia registral.

Procedimientos

Artículo 35

La recepción, identificación y anotación de los documentos, la digitalización de imágenes, la verificación del pago de tributos, la determinación de la clase y cantidad de operaciones, así como la automatización de estos procesos serán desarrolladas en el Reglamento del presente Decreto Ley.

Devolución de los Documentos Inscritos

Artículo 36

Los documentos serán devueltos al interesado una vez que sean debidamente inscritos. El Registrador hará constar los datos relativos a su inscripción.

Certificaciones

Artículo 37

El Registrador expedirá certificaciones sobre todos los actos y derechos inscritos, su descripción, propietarios, gravámenes, cargas legales y demás datos.

Capítulo IV El Sistema Registral

Función Calificadora

Artículo 38

El Registrador Titular está facultado para ejercer la función calificadora en el sistema registral.

件和税收等方面的相关原始信息。

登记地址分配

第 34 条

为了识别所登记的不动产和所有权，登记系统将按照升序自动分配登记号码，并且在取消或者消除该不动产或所有权之前，不得重复使用该登记号。登记号码基于所登记的不动产和所有权的类型，可以是字母或数字。

程序

第 35 条

有关文件的接收、识别和注释，图像的数字化，税收核查，操作类型和数量的确定以及这些程序的自动化操作都将在本法中作出规定。

登记文件的归还

第 36 条

文件一经妥善登记，即应退还给申请人。登记员应该登记所有相关资料内容。

证明文件

第 37 条

登记员应处理有关登记行为和所有权的全部描述、业主、税收、法定费用以及其他资料的证明文件。

第四章 登记系统

鉴定职能

第 38 章

主管登记员有权就登记系统中的内容进行鉴定权利。

Negativa Registral

Artículo 39

En caso de que el Registrador rechace o niegue la inscripción de un documento o acto, el interesado podrá intentar recurso jerárquico ante la Dirección Nacional de Registros y del Notariado, la cual deberá, mediante acto motivado y dentro de un lapso no mayor a diez (10) días hábiles, confirmar la negativa o revocarla y ordenar la inscripción.

Si la Administración no se pronunciare dentro del plazo establecido se entenderá negado el recurso, sin perjuicio de la responsabilidad del funcionario por su omisión injustificada.

El administrado podrá interponer recurso de reconsideración o acudir a la jurisdicción contencioso-administrativa para ejercer los recursos pertinentes. En caso de optar por la vía administrativa esta deberá agotarse íntegramente para poder acudir a la vía jurisdiccional.

Fundamento de la Calificación

Artículo 40

Al momento de calificar los documentos, el Registrador Titular se limitará exclusivamente a lo que se desprenda del título y a la información que conste en el Registro, y sus resoluciones no prejuzgarán sobre la validez de título ni de las obligaciones que contenga.

Efecto Registral

Artículo 41

La inscripción no convalida los actos o negocios jurídicos inscritos que sean nulos o anulables conforme a la Ley. Sin embargo, los asientos registrales en que consten esos actos o negocios jurídicos solamente podrán ser anulados por sentencia definitivamente firme.

Anotaciones Provisionales

Artículo 42

Se anotarán las demandas y medidas cautelares sobre la propiedad de bienes y derechos determinados, y cualesquiera otras sobre la propiedad de derechos reales, o en las que se pida la constitución, declaración, modificación o extinción de cualquier derecho real sobre inmuebles.

拒绝登记

第 39 条

在登记员拒绝或者否决文件或者行为的登记时，申请人可以向国家登记管理机构提出上诉，主管部门应在 10 个工作日之内确认是否存在拒绝的行为，并说明拒绝的原因，或者撤销拒绝，同时下令对其进行登记。

若主管部门在 10 个工作日之内没有做出答复，则默认为拒绝，但不免除公务员固其不合理的疏忽而需承担的责任。

管理人员为进行相关申诉，可以提出复议请求，或者提交行政法庭。选择循行政途径解决的，只有在行政救济手段用竭后，才可以提请司法介入。

鉴定依据

第 40 条

在对文件进行鉴定时，对于出现在登记标题中或包含在内容中的信息，当主管登记员确定不能对标题的有效性或者内容的强制性做出预判的情况下，可限制其登记。

登记影响

第 41 条

登记不对法律行为和交易的登记是否合法有效或已被取消进行验证。对于无效登记条目，仅可通过最终裁定予以取消。

临时注释

第 42 条

应记录所有与以下事务相关的要求或者预防措施：关于业主和所有权，以及其他任何与物权所有者相关的或者关于任何不动产和所有权的建筑、修缮或者取消的申请。

Capítulo V El Registro Inmobiliario

Objeto

Artículo 43

El Registro Inmobiliario tiene por objeto la inscripción y anotación de los actos o negocios jurídicos relativos al dominio y demás derechos reales que afecten los bienes inmuebles.

Además de los actos señalados con anterioridad y aquellos previstos en el Código Civil, en el Código de Comercio y en otras leyes, en el Registro Inmobiliario se inscribirán también los siguientes actos: Los documentos que contengan declaración, transmisión, limitación o gravámenes del la propiedad; todo contrato, declaración, transacción, partición, adjudicación, sentencia ejecutoriada, o cualquier otro acto en el que se declare, reconozca, transmita, ceda o adjudique el dominio o propiedad de bienes o derechos reales o el derecho de enfiteusis o usufructo; la constitución de hogar; los contratos, declaraciones, transacciones, sentencias ejecutoriadas y otros actos que se establezcan sobre inmuebles, derechos de uso, habitación o servidumbre o se constituyan anticresis, hipotecas o se divida, se traslade o reduzca alguno de esos derechos; los documentos que limiten de cualquier manera la libre disposición de inmuebles; las declaraciones, los denuncios, los permisos, los contratos, los títulos, las concesiones y los demás documentos que conforme a las leyes en materia de minas, hidrocarburos y demás minerales combustibles deban registrarse; los contratos de opción para adquirir derechos sobre inmuebles; las donaciones cuando tengan por objeto bienes inmuebles; y la separación de bienes entre cónyuges cuando tenga por objeto bienes inmuebles o derechos reales.

Catastro

Artículo 44

El Catastro Municipal será fuente de información registral inmobiliaria.

Requisitos Mínimos

Artículo 45

Toda inscripción que se haga en el Registro inmobiliario relativa a un inmueble o derecho real deberá contener:

1. Indicación de la naturaleza del negocio jurídico.

2. Identificación completa de las personas naturales o jurídicas y de sus representantes legales.

第五章　不动产登记

目的

第 43 条

不动产登记的目的是登记、注释与不动产所有权及其他与之相关的权利的法定行为和交易。

除上述行为和在《民法典》《商业法》以及其他法律中规定的行为外，必须就以下行为进行不动产登记：不动产申报、变更、限制或者业主的赋税；所有的合同、申报、交易、分割、裁决和强制执行，或者其他对不动产的所有权、物权或使用权任何进行申报、承认、转让、赠与或裁定的行为；住宅建造、合同、申报、交易，强制执行判决和其他与不动产、使用权、房间、土地、建筑、抵押贷款或者拆分、转让或减少等权利相关的行为；以任何方式限制对不动产任意处置的文件；矿山、碳氢化合物和其他可燃物的申报、开矿权申请、许可证、合同、矿主、特许权以及其他符合法律要求的文件；通过期权合约获得不动产；捐赠所含有的不动产；配偶之间的财产分割所包含的不动产或物权。

土地

第 44 条

城市土地部门将作为不动产登记的信息来源。

最低要求

第 45 条

所有在不动产登记部门进行登记的不动产或者物权应包含：

1. 说明法定交易的性质。

2. 充分识别自然人、法人或者其他法定代表人。

3. Descripción del inmueble, con señalamiento de su ubicación física, medidas, linderos y número catastral.

4. Los gravámenes, cargas y limitaciones legales que pesen sobre el derecho que se inscriba o sobre el derecho que se constituya en un nuevo asiento registral.

Modificaciones

Artículo 46

En las siguientes inscripciones relativas al mismo inmueble no se repetirán los datos previstos en el numeral 3 del artículo precedente, pero se hará referencia a las modificaciones que indique el nuevo título y del asiento en que se encuentre la inscripción.

Contenido de la Constancia

Artículo 47

La constancia de recepción de documentos deberá contener:

1. Hora, fecha y número de recepción.

2. Identificación de la persona que lo presenta.

3. Naturaleza del acto jurídico que deba inscribirse.

Capítulo VI Registro Mercantil

Organización

Artículo 48

La organización del Registro Mercantil, que podrá estar integrada por registros mercantiles territoriales y por un Registro Central, será definida en el reglamento correspondiente.

Objeto

Artículo 49

El Registro Mercantil tiene por objeto:

1. La inscripción de los comerciantes individuales y sociales y demás sujetos señalados por la ley, así como la inscripción de los actos y contratos relativos a los mismos de conformidad con la ley.

2. La inscripción de los representantes o agentes comerciales de establecimientos públicos extranjeros o sociedades mercantiles constituidas fuera del país, cuando hagan negocios en la República.

3. La legalización de los libros de los comerciantes.

4. El depósito y publicidad de los estados contables y de los informes periódicos de las firmas mercantiles.

5. La centralización y publicación de la información

---

3. 不动产描述应包含其地理位置、面积、界限以及地籍编号。

4. 所登记的产权或者新建登记条目的产权的法定税、费以及限制。

修改

第 46 条

与同一不动产相关的以下登记将不会重复记录本章第 3 条所要求的信息，但会将新登记条目下的修改内容与已存在的登记相关联的条目重新记录。

证明文件的内容

第 47 条

所接收到的文件必须包含：

1. 接收日期、时间以及编码。

2. 提交人的身份信息。

3. 登记对象的法律性质。

第六章 工商登记机构

组织

第 48 条

工商登记组织可以由地方工商登记机构和中央登记机构组成，将根据相应的法规予以界定。

目的

第 49 条

工商登记机构的目的是：

1. 对贸易个体或贸易企业、法律规定的其他人员以及与他们相关的合法行为和商业合同进行登记。

2. 对在共和国从事商贸活动的外国公共机构或者商业机构的代理人或者代理企业进行登记。

3. 认证贸易手册。

4. 上市公司财务报表的存放、公告以及定期信息报告。

5. 登记信息的集中和发布。

registral.

6. La inscripción de cualquier otro acto señalado en la ley.

Efectos

Artículo 50

La inscripción de un acto en el Registro Mercantil y su posterior publicación, cuando ésta es requerida, crea una presunción iuris et de iure sobre el conocimiento universal del acto inscrito.

Comerciante Individual

Artículo 51

La sola inscripción del comerciante individual en el Registro Mercantil permite presumir la cualidad de comerciante. Esta presunción únicamente podrá ser desvirtuada por los terceros que tengan interés, con efectos para el caso completo.

Boletines Oficiales

Artículo 52

La Dirección Nacional de Registro y del Notariado podrá crear boletines oficiales del Registro Mercantil, en los cuales se podrán publicar los actos que el Código de Comercio ordena publicar en los periódicos. La publicación realizada a través de estos boletines surtirá los mismos efectos legales. Su régimen de publicación, edición, distribución y venta se define en el Reglamento del presente Decreto Ley.

Caducidad de Acciones

Artículo 53

La acción para demandar la nulidad de una asamblea de accionistas de una sociedad anónima o de una sociedad en comandita por acciones, así como para solicitar la nulidad de una reunión de socios de las otras sociedades se extinguirá al vencimiento del lapso de un año, contado a partir de la publicación del acto registrado.

Artículo 54

Corresponde al Registrador Mercantil vigilar el cumplimiento de los requisitos legales establecidos para la constitución y funcionamiento de las compañías anónimas y de las sociedades de responsabilidad limitada, de conformidad con el parágrafo único del artículo 200 del Código de Comercio. A tal efecto, el Registrador Mercantil deberá

6. 登记法律规定的其他任何行为。

影响

第 50 条

一项文书或行为在商业登记处完成注册登记和后续公示（如有必要）后，即可认定为被登记的文书或行为获得普遍承认，合理合法。

贸易个体

第 51 条

凭在商业登记处的个体商户登记记录，可以认定其具有合法经营资格。只有具有利害关系的第三方提出反证时方可使这一认定失效，该推断将影响该个案整体。

官方公告

第 52 章

国家登记管理机构可以就工商登记创立官方公告，并能在该公告上刊登《商业法》中所规定的、必须定期公告的内容。以这种方式发布的官方公告具有同样的法律效力。其出版制度、版权以及销售根据本法规的相关规定进行。

诉讼到期

第 53 条

请求废除有限责任公司或股份公司的股东大会决议，及主张其他社会团体的会议无效的诉讼时效，从登记日起，期满一年后终止。

第 54 条

工商登记机构有义务根据《商业法》第 200 条的唯一章节来监督股份公司以及有限责任公司遵守相关法律法规。因此，工商登记机构需要遵守以下几点：

cumplir, entre otras, las siguientes obligaciones:

1. Rechazar la inscripción de las sociedades con capital insuficiente, aplicando criterios de razonabilidad relacionados con el objeto social.

2. Asegurar que los aportes en especie tengan el valor declarado en el documento de constitución, en los aumentos de capital, en las fusiones o en cualquier otro acto que implique cesión o aporte de bienes o derechos, a cuyo efecto se acompañará un avalúo realizado por un perito independiente y colegiado.

3. Exigir la indicación de la dirección en donde tenga su asiento la sociedad, el cual se considerará su domicilio a todos los efectos legales.

4. Homologar o rechazar el término de duración de la sociedad, respetando la manifestación de voluntad de los socios, a menos que la duración sea estimada excesiva.

5. Registrar la decisión de reactivación de la sociedad después de haber expirado su término.

6. Inscribir los actos de la sociedad disuelta que se encuentre en estado de liquidación.

Folio Personal

Artículo 55

La inscripción en el Registro Mercantil se llevará por el sistema denominado folio personal.

Oponibilidad

Artículo 56

Los actos sujetos a inscripción sólo serán oponibles a terceros de buena fe desde su publicación. La falta de inscripción no podrá ser invocada por quien esté obligado a realizarla.

Legalidad

Artículo 57

Los registradores calificarán la legalidad de las formas extrínsecas de los documentos cuya inscripción se solicite, así como la capacidad y legitimación de los que otorguen o suscriban el documento presentado.

Legitimación

Artículo 58

El contenido del registro se presume exacto y válido, pero la inscripción no convalida los actos y contratos nulos.

1. 根据企业目的有依据地拒绝资本不足的公司。

2. 确保在公司成立文书中正确申报实物投资的价值，资本增加、兼并或其他任何涉及不动产和所有权的转让和投资，需要经由具有相应资格证的独立经营的专业人士对其进行评估。

3. 要求注明企业地址并将其作为法定地址。

4. 在企业的登记有效期被认为过长的情况下，在尊重合作伙伴意愿的前提下，同意或拒绝该期限。

5. 在企业的登记有效期满后，重新对其进行登记。

6. 登记已经完成清算的企业的解散行为。

个人信息

第 55 条

在工商登记机构的登记将通过个人信息系统进行。

反对

第 56 条

登记行为只有在其公布之后，善意第三人才有权反对。
不得以未经登记的公司名义开展经营活动。

认证性

第 57 条

登记员将对登记申请的文件的外在形式的认证以及同意、签署文件人的能力及其合法性进行评估。

合法性

第 58 条

经过登记的内容即被认定为准确有效，但该登记无法证明行为无效和合同无效。

Fé Pública

Artículo 59

La declaración de inexactitud o nulidad de los asientos del Registro Mercantil no perjudicará los derechos de terceros de buena fe adquiridos conforme a derecho.

Publicidad Formal

Artículo 60

El Registro Mercantil es público y cualquier persona puede obtener copia simple o certificada de los asientos y documentos, así como tener acceso material e informático a los datos.

Principios

Artículo 61

En materia registral mercantil se aplicarán los principios del Registro Inmobiliario, en tanto resulten compatibles con la naturaleza y con los fines de la publicidad mercantil.

Capítulo VII Registro Civil

Organización

Artículo 62

La organización del Registro Civil, que podrá estar integrada por registros civiles territoriales y por un Registro Civil Central, será definida en el reglamento correspondiente.

Actos Registrables

Artículo 63

Corresponde al Registro Civil efectuar la inscripción de los actos siguientes:

1. Las partidas de nacimiento, matrimonio y defunción.

2. Las sentencias de divorcio.

3. La separación de cuerpos y bienes.

4. La nulidad de matrimonio.

5. Los reconocimientos de filiación

6. Las adopciones.

7. Las emancipaciones.

8. Las interdicciones e inhabilitaciones civiles.

9. Los actos relativos a la adquisición, modificación o revocatoria de la nacionalidad.

10. La designación de tutores, curadores o consejos

公信

第 59 条

对工商登记条目的不准确或无效申明不得损害善意第三人的合法权益。

正式公告

第 60 条

工商登记对外开放，任何人均能获得简易副本，或是登记条目和文件证明，以及材料和信息的数据库访问权限。

原则

第 61 条

工商登记材料适用不动产登记的原则，须符合自然规律并以公共商业为最终目的。

第七章 民事登记

组织

第 62 条

民事登记机构由地方民事登记机构和中央民事登记机构组成，将根据相应的法规予以界定。

可登记的行为

第 63 条

民事登记机构可登记以下行为：

1. 出生、结婚和死亡证明。

2. 离婚判决。

3. 人身和财产分离。

4. 婚姻无效。

5. 遗嘱的认定。

6. 收养。

7. 脱离监护人。

8. 限制或取消民事资格。

9. 与取得、修改或撤销国籍相关的行为。

10. 确定监护人或监护人委员会。

de tutela.

11. La sentencia que declare la ausencia o presunción de muerte.

12. Los títulos académicos, científicos y eclesiásticos y los despachos militares.

13. Los demás previstos en la ley.

Personas Jurídicas Civiles

Artículo 64

El Registro Civil, a través de una sección registral, inscribirá los actos de constitución, modificación, prórroga y extinción de las sociedades civiles, asociaciones, fundaciones y corporaciones de carácter privado.

Fuente

Artículo 65

El Registro Civil es fuente de información del Registro Civil y Electoral.

Instituciones Auxiliares

Artículo 66

Son responsables en su jurisdicción de informar al Registro Civil los nacimientos, matrimonios, defunciones y todo hecho que afecte el estado civil de las personas:

1. Las Jefaturas Civiles.
2. Las Alcaldías.
3. Los Hospitales, Clínicas y Centros de Salud.
4. Los Consulados venezolanos.
5. Los Procuradores, Tribunales y Consejos del Niño y del Adolescente.
6. Las Instituciones Educativas.
7. Las Fuerza Armada Nacional, en cuanto corresponda a la emisión de Despachos Militares.
8. Los órganos de Seguridad Ciudadana.
9. Las demás que indique la ley.

TÍTULO III
EL NOTARIADO

Capítulo I Disposiciones Generales

Potestad

Artículo 67

Los Notarios son funcionarios de la Dirección Nacional de Registros y del Notariado que tienen la potestad de dar fé pública de los hechos o actos jurídicos ocurridos

11. 判定失踪或者死亡推测。

12. 学术、科学和教会头衔以及军事派遣。

13. 其他法律规定的行为。

民事法人

第 64 条

民事登记机构通过其中某一登记部门，对民间社团、协会、基金会和私营公司的成立、修改、延期以及取消行为进行登记。

来源

第 65 条

民事登记机构是民事登记及选举资料的来源。

辅助机构

第 66 条

以下机构有责任将其管辖范围内的出生、婚姻、死亡以及所有影响到个人婚姻状态的信息告知民事登记机构：

1. 总政办公室。
2. 市长办公室。
3. 医院、诊所和保健中心。
4. 委内瑞拉驻外大使馆。
5. 青少年法庭、检察院和理事会。
6. 教育机构。
7. 国家武装部队，当其负责军事办公室的消息发布时。
8. 公民安全机关。
9. 法律规定的其他机构。

第三篇
公证员

第一章 总则

权力

第 67 条

公证员是国家登记和公证管理机构的公务员，具有为民众亲自或者通过网络做出的事件及法律行为出具证明的权利，在通过网络的情况下，将通过公证书

en su presencia física o a través de medios electrónicos, indicando en este último caso los instrumentos mediante los cuales le otorga presunción de certeza al acto.

Nombramiento y Remuneración

Artículo 68

Cada Notaría estará a cargo de un Notario, quien será responsable del funcionamiento de su dependencia. La elección de los Notarios se efectuará mediante concurso de oposición, conforme a lo establecido en el reglamento correspondiente, y su nombramiento estará a cargo del Ministro del Interior y Justicia.

La remuneración de los Notarios será fijada por Resolución del Ministerio del Interior y Justicia.

Principios de Actuación

Artículo 69

El Notario gozará de autonomía e independencia en el ejercicio de su función. El control disciplinario de los Notarios es competencia de la Dirección Nacional de Registros y del Notariado, conforme a lo establecido en el reglamento correspondiente.

Jurisdicción Voluntaria

Artículo 70

El Notario, como órgano de jurisdicción voluntaria, actuará sólo a solicitud de parte interesada.

Requisitos

Artículo 71

Los requisitos para el ejercicio del cargo de Notario se establecen en el Reglamento del presente Decreto Ley.

Impedimentos

Artículo 72

No podrán ejercer el Notariado:

1. Los militares en servicio activo, los ministros de los cultos, los dirigentes o activistas políticos.

2. Las personas con impedimento físico permanente que los imposibilite para el ejercicio de las funciones del cargo.

3. Las personas en ejercicio privado de cualquier profesión, a excepción de los supuestos establecidos en el Reglamento del presente Decreto Ley.

4. Los abogados en el libre ejercicio de su profesión.

对其行为进行推断和证明。

任命和薪酬

第 68 条

每一个公证处由一位公证员负责，该公证员负责相关操作。公证员的遴选按照相关法律规定，通过竞聘考核遴选并最终由内政和司法部任命。

公证员的薪酬由内政部和司法部的决议确定。

诉讼原则

第 69 条

公证员在履行职务时拥有自主权和独立处理权。其纪律考核由国家登记和公证管理机构依照相关法律规定进行。

自愿管辖权

第 70 条

公证处，作为自愿管辖权机构，根据申请人的申请办理公证事项。

要求

第 71 条

公证员的职位要求参照本法要求。

不得担任

第 72 条

有下列情形之一的，不得担任公证员：

1. 现役军人、宗教部长、政治领导人或政治活动家。

2. 永久残疾，并妨碍其履行职责的人士。

3. 任何私人职业的从业人员，除本法规定的情况以外。

4. 自由从业律师。

5. Las personas declaradas en estado de atraso, quiebra o interdicción, mientras no sean rehabilitadas.

6. Las demás establecidas en la Ley.

Prohibiciones

Artículo 73

Está prohibido a los Notarios:

1. Autorizar actos o negocios jurídicos en los que tengan interés personal, sus respectivos cónyuges y sus parientes dentro del cuarto grado de consanguinidad o segundo de afinidad.

2. Autorizar actos o negocios relativos a personas jurídicas o entidades en las que los parientes por consanguinidad o afinidad mencionados en el numeral anterior, tengan o ejerzan cargos como directores, gerentes, administradores o representantes legales.

3. Autorizar actos o negocios jurídicos en los que tengan interés los intérpretes o testigos instrumentales.

4. Las demás establecidas en la ley.

Capítulo II Función Notarial

Competencia Territorial

Artículo 74

Los Notarios son competentes en el ámbito de su jurisdicción para dar fe pública de todos los actos, hechos y declaraciones que autoricen con tal carácter, particularmente de los siguientes:

1. Documentos, contratos y demás negocios jurídicos, unilaterales, bilaterales y plurilaterales.

2. Poderes, sustituciones, renuncias y revocatorias, con excepción de las sustituciones, renuncias y revocatorias que se efectúen en los expedientes judiciales.

3. Justificaciones para perpetua memoria, con excepción de lo señalado en el artículo 937 del Código de Procedimiento Civil.

4. Protestos de los títulos de crédito, de conformidad con lo previsto en el Código de Comercio.

5. Otorgamiento de testamentos abiertos, de conformidad con los artículos 852 al 856 del Código Civil.

6. Presentación y entrega de testamentos cerrados, con expresión de las formalidades requeridas en los numerales 10, 20 y 30 del artículo 857 del Código Civil.

7. Apertura de testamentos cerrados, de conformidad con lo previsto en los artículos 986 al 989 del Código Civil y 913 al 920 del Código de Procedimiento Civil. El Notar-

5. 被宣布有拖欠，或破产、停职的人员在其恢复正常之前。

6. 法律规定的其他情况。

禁止行为

第 73 条

公证员禁止为以下人员出具公证书：

1. 申请人为其本人、配偶、四代以内直系血亲或二代以内姻亲时，为其行为或法定交易出具公证书。

2. 前文提到的亲属担任董事长、经理、行政人员或法定代表人时，为其法人代表或企业出具公证书。

3. 为翻译人员或见证人出具公证书。

4. 法律规定的其他人员。

第二章 公证员的职能

管辖职能

第 74 章

公证员的职责是在其管辖范围内，为所有具备以下性质的行为、事实以及声明出具证明：

1. 文件、合同以及其他法定交易，单边、双边、多边交易。

2. 授权委托、替换、放弃和撤销，但在司法案件中作出的替换、放弃和撤销除外。

3. 永久记忆证明，但《民事诉讼法》第 937 条规定的内容除外。

4. 按照《商法典》规定拒付信用证。

5.《民法典》第 852 条至第 856 条规定的公开遗嘱。

6.《民法典》第 857 条第 10 款、第 20 款和第 30 款规定的，提交和交付不公开遗嘱。

7. 根据《民法典》第 986 条至第 989 条以及《民事诉讼法》第 913 条至第 920 条的规定，开放不公开遗嘱。公证员有执行上级委派任务的职责。

io tendrá potestades para realizar los actos que se atribuyen al Registrador Subalterno en el Código Civil.

8. Capitulaciones matrimoniales.

9. Autorizaciones de administración separada de comunidad conyugal.

10. Autorizaciones de administración de bienes de menores e incapaces.

11. Otorgamiento de hipotecas mobiliarias y prendas sin desplazamiento de posesión.

12. Otorgamiento de cualquier caución o garantía civil o mercantil.

13. Constancias de cualquier hecho o acto a través de inspección extrajudicial.

14. Transcripciones en acta o por cualquier medio de reproducción o de grabación del contenido de archivos públicos o de documentos privados, siempre y cuando no esté expresamente prohibido en el primer caso o lo autorice el dueño o depositario del documento en el segundo caso.

15. Celebración de asambleas, reuniones o manifestaciones, dejando las constancias personales, gráficas y sonoras del caso.

16. Transacciones que ocurran en medios electrónicos.

17. Apertura de libros de asambleas de propietarios, actas de Juntas de Condominios, sociedades y Juntas Directivas.

18. Autenticar firmas autógrafas, electrónicas y huellas digitales.

19. Las demás que le atribuyan otras leyes.

Otras Atribuciones

Artículo 75

Los Notarios igualmente son competentes para archivar, en los casos en que fuere procedente, los instrumentos privados a que se contrae el artículo 1369 del Código Civil; archivar los documentos relativos a los contratos de venta con reserva de dominio, a los efectos de la fecha cierta de los mismos; extender y autorizar actas notariales, a instancia de parte, que constituyan, modifiquen o extingan un acto o negocio jurídico. Estas actas deben incorporarse cronológicamente en el archivo físico o electrónico notarial.

Copias

Artículo 76

Los Notarios expedirán copias certificadas o simples

8. 婚姻登记。

9. 婚姻财产的分割管理授权。

10. 对未成年人以及无行为能力人的财产管理授权。

11. 不侵占所有权的不动产和服装的抵押贷款。

12. 任何形式的民事或商业担保。

13. 通过法外检查出具的任何事实或行为证明。

14. 在未被明确禁止的情况下，对公共文件或私人文件进行的录音，或经所有者或文件保管者授权，以任何方式进行的复制或转录。

15. 在举行集会、会议或示威游行时留下的事件的人证、视频或音频证据。

16. 电子媒体中出现的录音。

17. 业主、业主委员会、公司或董事会的会议纪要。

18. 验证签名、电子签名和指纹。

19. 法律规定的其他内容。

其他权限

第 75 条

在适当的情况下，公证员也有权为以下行为出具公证书：符合《民法典》第 1369 条规定订立的私人文书；与某一确定日期内的保留所有权的销售合同相关的文件；应一方当事人的要求，延长或更新公证行为，建立、修改或取消某一行为或法定交易。这些行为均要求以纸质文件或者电子文件的形式在公证处存档。

副本

第 76 条

公证员有权签发证明文件副本、文件简易副本或

de los documentos y demás asientos que reposen en su oficina, siempre que las copias se soliciten con indicación de la clase de actos o de sus otorgantes, circunstancias éstas que se harán constar en la correspondiente nota de certificación. También podrán expedir copias de documentos originales por procedimientos electrónicos, fotostáticos u otros semejantes de reproducción.

Publicidad Notarial

Artículo 77

La publicidad notarial reside en las bases de datos del sistema automatizado de las Notarlas, en la documentación archivada que de ellas emanen y en las certificaciones que se expidan.

Deberes

Artículo 78

El Notario deberá:

1. Identificar a las partes y a los demás intervinientes en los actos o negocios jurídicos que autoricen.

2. Informar a las partes del contenido, naturaleza, trascendencia y consecuencias legales de los actos o negocios jurídicos otorgados en su presencia, así como de las renuncias, reservas, gravámenes y cualquier otro elemento que afecten tos bienes o derechos referidos en el acto o negocio jurídico. El Notario dejará constancia en el acto del cumplimiento de esta obligación y su omisión lo hace responsable civil, penal y administrativamente.

3. Actuar de manera imparcial y objetiva en relación con todas las personas que intervengan en los actos o negocios jurídicos otorgados en su presencia.

4. Realizar las diligencias que le encomienden autoridades judiciales o administrativas, de acuerdo con la Ley.

5. Ejercer cualquier otra función que le asigne la ley.

Capítulo III Documentos y Actas Notariales

Documento Notarial

Artículo 79

Documento notarial es él otorgado en presencia del Notario o funcionario consular en el ejercicio de funciones notariales, dentro de los límites de su competencia y con las formalidades de Ley.

其他存在其办公室的文件条目，副本申请需表明行为或授权人的类别，并需记录在证明文件中。公证员同样有权签发原始文件为电子、光碟或其他类似文件的副本。

公证的公开性

第 77 条

公证的公开性体现在公证自动系统数据库、公证处发出的存档文件，及其签发的证明文件中。

义务

第 78 条

公证员必须：

1. 确定参与法律或交易公证行为的各方身份。

2. 告知各方当前法律行为或交易公证的内容、性质、重要性、法律责任以及放弃、保留、赋税以及与当前的法律行为或交易相关的其他部分。公证员在履行该职责时应当予以记录，因疏忽造成遗漏时应承担民事、刑事和行政责任。

3. 以公正客观的态度对待参与该法律或交易行为的所有在场人员。

4. 依法执行司法行政机关委托的程序。

5. 行使法律规定的其他职能。

第三章 公证文件和文书

公证文件

第 79 条

公证文书是公证员或领事官员在在场的情况下，在其管辖范围内依法行使公证职能所出具的证明文件。

Acta Notarial

Artículo 80

Las actas notariales son documentos que tienen por finalidad comprobar, a solicitud de parte interesada, hechos, sucesos o situaciones que le consten u ocurran en su presencia.

Imposibilidad de Firmar

Artículo 81

El otorgante que estuviere impedido para suscribir un documento notarial con su firma, lo hará a ruego o estampará su huella digital al pie del documento y el Notario dejará constancia en el acto.

Archivo y Base de Datos Notarial

Artículo 82

La Dirección Nacional de Registros y del Notariado llevará un Archivo y una Base de Datos Notarial, cuyas funciones y finalidades estarán establecidas en el reglamento del presente Decreto Ley.

TÍTULO IV
RÉGIMEN DISCIPLINARIO

Capítulo I Competencia, Faltas y Sanciones

Competencia

Artículo 83

Corresponde a la Dirección Nacional de Registros y del Notariado ejercer el régimen disciplinario de los Registradores y Notarios, de conformidad con las disposiciones del presente Título. A tal efecto el Director Nacional podrá designar una Comisión Disciplinaria que se encargará de la sustanciación de los expedientes disciplinarios, la imposición de sanciones y la ejecución de las mismas.

Clases de Sanciones

Artículo 84

Las sanciones consistirán en suspensión o destitución del cargo.

Suspensiones Hasta por Un Mes

Artículo 85

Se Impondrá a los Registradores o Notarios, según sea el caso, una suspensión hasta por un mes de acuerdo

公证文书

第 80 条

公证文书是应申请人的要求，对其确定或者其在场时发生的事实、事件或情况，以验证为最终目的而出具的文书。

无法签名

第 81 条

公证申请人无法在公证文件上签名的情况下，应在文件页脚部位留下数字指纹，并由公证人员做出记录。

公证处档案和数据库

第 82 条

国家登记公证管理机构负责公证档案和数据库归档，其职能和目的遵循本法相关规定。

第四篇
纪律处分制度

第一章   权限、违规和惩戒

权限

第 83 条

根据本法规定，国家登记和公证管理机构有责任对其登记员和公证员实施纪律监管。国家管理局可以指定一个纪律监察委员会，负责纪律处分以及处分的执行和强制执行。

处罚类型

第 84 条
将受到停职或撤职处罚。

停职一个月以内

第 85 条

当出现以下情况时，根据违规的程度对登记员或公证员做出停职一个月以内的处分决定：

con la gravedad de la falta, cuando:

 1. Notificados por la Dirección Nacional de Registros y del Notariado actuaren sin estar al día en la garantía exigida por este Decreto Ley.

 2. Actuaren con desapego o falta de interés a los lineamientos, las directrices y las exigencias de la Dirección.

 3. Obstaculicen la exhibición de documentos que tengan carácter de públicos.

 4. Incurran en descuido o negligencia en la guarda y conservación de los documentos o datos informáticos que deben custodiar.

Suspensiones Hasta por Seis Meses

Artículo 86

Se impondrá a los Registradores y Notarios, según sea el caso, suspensión de uno a seis meses, según la gravedad de la falta, cuando:

 1. Atrasen durante más de tres meses y por causa injustificable la tramitación de cualquier documento.

 2. No se ajusten a los aranceles fijados oficialmente para la prestación del servicio.

 3. Autoricen actos o negocios jurídicos ilegales o ineficaces.

 4. Transcriban, reproduzcan o expidan documentos sin ajustarse al contenido del documento transcrito o reproducido.

 5. Incumplan alguna disposición, legal o reglamentaria, que les imponga deberes y obligaciones sobre la forma en que deben ejercer la función notarial.

Sanciones de Seis Meses a Tres Años

Artículo 87

Se impondrá a los Registradores y Notarios, según sea el caso, sanciones desde seis meses y hasta por tres años, cuando:

 1. Cumplido alguno de los supuestos previstos en el artículo anterior, esto produzca daños o perjuicios materiales a terceros.

 2. Cuando continúen ejerciendo funciones estando suspendidos.

Remoción

Artículo 88

Será obligatoria la remoción del Registrador o Notario, según sea el caso, cuando:

 1. Autoricen actos o negocios jurídicos cuyos otor-

 1. 按照国家登记公证管理机构通知，保证金不在本法要求的有效期内。

 2. 不遵守机构的指导方针和管理要求。

 3. 妨碍具备公开性质的文件的展出。

 4. 对需要保存和保管的文件和计算机信息疏忽大意。

停职六个月以内

第 86 章

当出现以下情况时，根据违规的程度对登记员或公证员做出停职一至六个月的处分决定：

 1. 对文件的处理不合理或延迟三个月以上。

 2. 不按官方规定费用提供服务。

 3. 为非法或无效的行为或交易出具公证书。

 4. 转载、复制或发行不符合转载或复制要求的文件。

 5. 不遵守法律法规，或者不履行公证员职责和义务。

停职六个月至三年

第 87 条

当出现以下情况时，根据违规的程度对登记员或公证员做出停职六个月至三年的处分决定：

 1. 符合上述任何一条，并对第三方造成伤害和损失的。

 2. 在停职期间继续行使职能的。

撤职

第 88 条

当出现以下情况下，将免去登记员或公证员的职务：

 1. 为按法律要求必须出席而没有出席的申请人出

gamientos no hayan presenciado y estén obligados a ello por ley.

2. Expidan documentos falsos.

3. Modifiquen o alteren, mediante notas marginales o cualquier otro mecanismo, elementos esenciales del acto o negocio autorizado, con perjuicio para algún otorgante.

Capítulo II Procedimiento Disciplinario

Modos de Proceder

Artículo 89

En materia disciplinaria los procedimientos podrán iniciarse de oficio o mediante denuncia.

Formalidades de la Denuncia

Artículo 90

En el caso de los procedimientos iniciados mediante denuncia, ésta deberá ser presentada ante la Dirección Nacional de Registros y del Notariado, o ante la Comisión designada para actuar como órgano disciplinario. La denuncia deberá indicar los hechos correspondientes y las pruebas que se invocan como fundamento.

Notificación y Comparecencia

Artículo 91

Una vez iniciado el procedimiento mediante el auto respectivo, la Dirección Nacional de Registros y del Notariado, o en su caso la Comisión Disciplinaria designada, notificará al Registrador o Notario sometido a procedimiento disciplinario para que comparezca el quinto día hábil de su notificación, en el lugar y hora indicados, y ser informado por el órgano disciplinario del contenido de la denuncia o de la investigación iniciada de oficio en su contra. En esa oportunidad de comparecencia se le fijará la fecha de la audiencia oral y pública para oír sus descargos y presentar sus pruebas y alegatos de defensa.

La notificación personal del Registrador o Notario se hará mediante boleta, telegrama o fax, de cuya recepción se dejará constancia en el expediente.

Celebración de la Audiencia

Artículo 92

Llegados el día y la hora para la celebración de la audiencia oral y pública, se dará lectura de los hechos imputadas, se oirán los descargos y defensas del funcionado investigado, así como las declaraciones de testigos

具公证书的。

2. 出具虚假公证书的。

3. 通过修改或篡改旁注或其他任何部分，损害公证的基本要素，并且损害到申请人利益的。

第二章　纪律处分程序

处理方式

第 89 条

主管部门依职责发现或者接到投诉的，可启动纪律处分程序。

投诉手续

第 90 条

通过投诉启动纪律处分程序的，应将投诉提交至国家登记和公证管理机构或指定的纪律监察委员会。投诉应以事实为依据，说明真实情况。

通知和出庭

第 91 条

诉讼程序一经启动，国家登记和公证管理机构或指定的纪律监察委将纪律处分程序通知到受处分人，并指令其在接到通知的第 5 个工作日，在指定的时间和地点，由纪律监察委依照投诉内容或职权对其进行调查。在庭审时，将指定公开听证的日期，以听取辩护和收取证据。

登记员或公证员的个人通知将通过挂号信、电报或传真发出，并将回执记录在档案中。

庭审

第 92 条

庭审当日将出示投诉文件，并听取当事人辩护以及证人证言和专家意见。同样，也将收取对登记员或公证员有利或不利的任何形式的证据。

y peritos. Igualmente, se recibirá cualquier tipo de prueba lícita que se produzca a favor o en contra del Registrador o Notario.

Decisión

Artículo 93

La decisión del órgano disciplinario, sea la imposición de una sanción determinada o la absolución, deberá ser tomada el mismo día de la audiencia oral y se le informará al funcionario en ese mismo acto. La decisión motivada será publicada dentro de los tres (3) días hábiles siguientes a la audiencia celebrada.

Recursos

Artículo 94

De las decisiones tomadas conforme al procedimiento disciplinado regulado en el presente Capítulo se podrán ejercer los recursos estableados en la ley que rige los procedimientos administrativos.

Publicación

Artículo 95

Firme la decisión de una suspensión o destitución, se ordenará su publicación en la Gaceta Oficial de la República Bolivariana de Venezuela.

Prescripción

Artículo 96

La acción disciplinaria prescribe en el término de dos (2) años, contados a partir del momento en que el órgano disciplinario tuvo conocimiento del hecho. La prescripción se interrumpe con la notificación al funcionario investigado. Una vez practicado este acto y mientras se tramita el proceso, no correrá lapso de prescripción alguno.

DISPOSICIONES DEROGATORIAS

Primera

Se deroga la Ley de Registro Público de fecha 5 de octubre de 1999, publicada en la Gaceta Oficial Número 5. 391 Extraordinario del 22 de octubre de 1999.

Segunda

El Reglamento de Notarías Públicas dictado el 11 de noviembre de 1998, publicado en la Gaceta Oficial Número 36. 588, de fecha 24 de noviembre de 1998; y el Decreto Ley de Arancel Judicial dictado el 5 de octubre de 1999,

决定

第93条

无论是确定实施制裁惩罚还是宣告无罪，纪律监察委都应在庭审的当天作出决定并通知当事人。决定的原因应在庭审后3个工作日之内进行公示。

上诉

第94条

根据本章对纪律处分程序的相关规定，如不服从判决可按照行政程序依法进行上诉。

公示

第95条

确定实施制裁惩罚或是宣告无罪的决议，应刊登在委内瑞拉玻利瓦尔共和国的官方公报上。

追诉时效期

第96条

纪律处分的追诉期为两年，从纪律监察委员会获悉该事件开始计算，官方调查期间时效中断。一经开始行动并进入程序，便不受追诉时效的限制。

废止的规定

第一

废止1999年10月22日刊登在国家官方公报第5391期特刊上的1999年10月5日版《公共登记法》。

第二

刊登在1998年11月24日的国家官方公报第36588期上、于1998年11月11日发布的《公共公证处条例》和1999年10月22日刊登在国家官方公报第5391期特刊上、于1999年10月5日发布的《司

publicado en la Gaceta Oficial Extraordinaria Número 5. 391, de fecha 22 de octubre de 1999, permanecerán en vigencia y se aplicarán en cuanto no contravengan las disposiciones contenidas en el presente Decreto Ley, hasta tanto el Ejecutivo Nacional dicte las que hayan de reemplazarlos

DISPOSICIONES TRANSITORIAS

Primera

El Ejecutivo Nacional dictará todos los Reglamentos que sean necesarios para desarrollar el presente Decreto Ley, en un lapso de ciento ochenta (180) días continuos, contados a partir de su publicación en la Gaceta Oficial de la República Bolivariana de Venezuela.

Segunda

El Ejecutivo Nacional, por órgano del Ministerio del Interior y Justicia, dentro de un lapso de ciento ochenta (180) días continuos, contados a partir de la publicación del presente Decreto Ley en la Gaceta Oficial de la República Bolivariana de Venezuela, tomará las medidas conducentes para la creación del Servicio Autónomo Dirección Nacional de Registros y del Notariado.

Tercera

El Ministro del Interior y Justicia, en un lapso de treinta (30) días continuos contados a partir de la publicación del presente Decreto Ley en la Gaceta Oficial de la República Bolivariana de Venezuela, designará una Comisión con el fin de coordinar el proceso de reforma y modernización de los Registros y Notarias regulados por el presente Decreto Ley, esta Comisión será el órgano responsable de gestionar el proceso de transición de la actual estructura administrativa al servicio autónomo que este Decreto Ley establece.

Cuarta

El proceso de reforma y modernización de los Registros y Notadas se iniciará desde la fecha en que sea publicada en la Gaceta Oficial de la República Bolivariana de Venezuela, la Resolución mediante la cual se designe la Comisión señalada en la Disposición anterior

Quinta

El Ministerio del Interior y Justicia determinará, mediante Resolución, los tipos de registros que han de ser sometidos al proceso de reforma y modernización, atendiendo al siguiente orden:

法工作收费标准法》，在不违反本法的前提下继续有效，直至国家行政部门出台新规定予以替换为止。

过渡性条款

第一

国家行政机关自本法在委内瑞拉玻利瓦尔共和国官方公报上刊登之日起，应在180个自然日内出台为落实本法所需的所有实施条例。

第二

自本法在委内瑞拉玻利瓦尔共和国官方公报上刊登之日起，在180个自然日内，内政和司法部作为国家行政机关，应采取措施建立自治性机构——国家登记和公证管理局。

第三

自本法在委内瑞拉玻利瓦尔共和国官方公报上刊登之日起，内政和司法部应在30个自然日内，委派委员会协调登记和公证处根据本法进行改革和发展现代化进程，该委员会将负责由现有行政机构向本法规定的自治性机构过渡的操作。

第四

改革和现代化进程自本法在委内瑞拉玻利瓦尔共和国官方公报上刊登日起，由上文提到的委员会决定。

第五

经过决议，内政和司法部决定按照以下顺序推动各类登记处的现代化改革进程：

1° Registro Inmobiliario.
2° Registro Mercantil.
3° Registro Civil.

En ningún caso podrán transcurrir más de dos (2) años entre el inicio de los procesos de reforma y modernización de cada uno de los tipos de registros previstos en esta Disposición. El mismo criterio se aplicará para el llamado a concurso de oposición de las personas que ocuparán los cargos de Registradores, en los Registros sometidos al proceso de reforma y modernización.

El Ministerio del Interior y Justicia podrá ordenar la reforma y modernización simultánea de varios tipos de registros.

Sexta

El Ministro del Interior y Justicia determinará, mediante Resolución, las zonas del país en las cuales se llevará a cabo el proceso de reforma y modernización de las Notadas el cual se realizará en un lapso de dos (2) años contados a partir de la publicación en la Gaceta Oficial de la República Bolivariana de Venezuela de la designación de la Comisión Coordinadora. El mismo criterio se aplicará para el llamado a concurso de oposición de las personas que ocuparán los cargos de Notario, en las Notarías sometidas al proceso de reforma y modernización.

Séptima

Hasta tanto se desarrollen completamente los procesos de reforma y modernización de los Registros y Notarías, los gastos operativos y de inversión que se requieran para el funcionamiento y modernización de la Dirección Nacional de Registros y del Notariado serán incluidos en los presupuestos ordinarios y extraordinarios del Ministerio de Interior y Justicia.

Octava

Hasta tanto se encuentren debidamente levantados las catastros referidos en el presente Decreto Ley, el Ministro del Interior y Justicia determinará, mediante Resolución, las zonas donde sé mantendrá provisionalmente el sistema de folio personal para los correspondientes Registros.

DISPOSICIÓN FINAL

Única

El presente Decreto Ley entrará en vigencia a para de la fecha de su publicación en la Gaceta Oficial de la República Bolivariana de Venezuela.

1. 不动产登记处。
2. 商业登记处。
3. 民事登记处。

在任何情况下，本条款规定的每一类登记处的现代化改革进程不得超过两年。该标准同样适用于在进行现代化改革的登记管理机构的登记员的职位竞争。

内政和司法部可以下令使多种不同类型的登记程序的现代化改革同时进行。

第六

经过决议，内政和司法部决定，共和国哪些地区的公证处将进行现代化改革，并且该改革进程期限自指定协调委员会在委内瑞拉玻利瓦尔共和国官方公报上刊登之日起，不得超过两年。该标准同样适用于在进行现代化改革的公证处的公证员的职位竞争。

第七

在国家登记公证管理机构现代化改革进程取得充分进展之前，国家登记公证管理机构的运行和现代化改革所需的经营和投资费用将被包含在内政和司法部的日常预算和特殊预算中。

第八

在本法提到的条款得到充分落实之前，内政和司法部经过决议决定，将在相应的登记中仍然临时保留个人信息系统记录的地区。

最终规定

第 1 条

本法在委内瑞拉玻利瓦尔共和国官方公报上刊登后生效。

Dado en Caracas, a los trece días del mes de noviembre de dos mil uno. Años 191° de la Independencia y 142° de la Federación.

(L. S.)

HUGO CHÁVEZ FRÍAS

Refrendado

La Vicepresidenta Ejecutiva, ADINA MERCEDES BASTIDAS CASTILLO

El Ministro del Interior y Justicia, LUIS MIQUILENA

El Encargado del Ministerio de Relaciones Exteriores, AREVALO MENDEZ

El Ministro DE FINANZAS, NELSON JOSE MERENTES DÍAZ

El Ministro de la Defensa, JOSE VICENTE RANGEL

El Encargado del Ministerio de la Producción y el Comercio, OMAR OVALLES

El Ministro de Educación, Cultura y Deportes, HECTOR NAVARRO DÍAZ

La Ministra de Salud y Desarrollo Social, MARÍA URBANEJA DURANT

La Ministra del Trabajo, BLANCANIEVES PORTOCARRERO

El Ministro de Infraestructura, ISMAEL ELIEZER HURTADO SOUCRE

El Encargado del Ministerio de Energía y Minas, JOSE LUIS PACHECO

La Ministra del Ambiente y de los Recursos Naturales, ANA ELISA OSORIO GRANADO

El Ministro de Planificación y Desarrollo, JORGE GIORDANI

El Ministro de Ciencia y Tecnología, CARLOS GENATIOS SEQUERA

El Ministro de la Secretaría de la Presidencia, DIOSDADO CABELLO RONDÓN

加拉加斯，2001年11月13日，庆祝独立191周年，联邦建制142周年。

（L.S.）

乌戈·查韦斯·弗里亚斯

会签
副总统：ADINA MERCEDES BASTIDAS CASTILLO

内政和司法部部长：LUIS MIQUILENA

外交部负责人：AREVALO MENDEZ

财政部部长：NELSON JOSE MERENTES DÍAZ

国防部部长：JOSE VICENTE RANGEL

生产贸易部部长：OMAR OVALLES

教育文化体育部部长：HECTOR NAVARRO DÍAZ

社会发展和卫生部部长：MARÍA URBANEJA DURANT

劳工部部长：BLANCANIEVES PORTOCARRERO

基础设施部部长：ISMAEL ELIEZER HURTADO SOUCRE

能源和矿业部部长：JOSE LUIS PACHECO

环境与自然资源部部长：ANA ELISA OSORIO GRANADO

规划与发展部部长：JORGE GIORDANI

科学技术部部长：CARLOS GENATIOS SEQUERA

总统府秘书长：DIOSDADO CABELLO RONDÓN